The Hutchinson History of the World

THE HUTCHINSON
HISTORY
OF THE
WORLD

J. M. Roberts

HUTCHINSON OF LONDON

Hutchinson & Co (Publishers) Ltd
3 Fitzroy Square, London W1

London Melbourne Sydney Auckland
Wellington Johannesburg and agencies
throughout the world

First published 1976
© J. M. Roberts 1976
Maps and diagrams © Hutchinson Publishing Group Ltd 1976

This book has been set in Monotype Ehrhardt and
printed in Great Britain by litho by The Anchor Press Ltd
Tiptree, Essex, and bound by Wm Brendon & Son Ltd
also of Tiptree

ISBN 0 09 126970 9

Contents

Preface

For the last half-century or so, professional historians in this country have left world history well alone. There is no reason to reproach them for this. They were right, in the first place, to study things which interested them more; that is the way that good history gets written, by historians doing what they like doing. Secondly, the reservations some of them felt about history at anything like so general a level are also perfectly proper and respectable. The professional standards of British historians are as high as any in the world and the uneasiness many of my colleagues feel in talking about topics in which they have not at least mastered the secondary scholarship and their awareness of the grave dangers of impressionistic judgement once away from primary evidence are rooted in scruples of which we should be proud. They express a concern for intellectual honesty and integrity which is a noble achievement of our culture. I hope, none the less, that my colleagues will agree with me that it is proper for *someone* to try to write a history of the world for a large lay public, whatever the risks involved. The argument from enjoyment, after all, applies here too. My own interest has always been caught by general themes and this is one reason for the existence of this book, for it would never have been done if I had not enjoyed doing it. Whatever other historians think of the result – and no one can go far without falling into error when he must rely almost entirely on the work of experts whose scholarship he boils down, sometimes to a sentence – I hope they will not deplore the fact that I found my subject-matter as interesting as they found their more specialized studies.

Not that this is the only justification of this book. I also feel that there is a positive value in presenting world history to the general public. Even if we do not know it, the history of the world is part of our mental furniture. As most men and women have some notions, however inadequate, about the way the world came to be what it is, it is all the better if they are made explicit. Keynes' observation that those who say they do not believe in economic theory are usually in thrall to the ideas of an economist long dead can be applied to 'commonsense' views on history, too. Even if the limits of our own historical horizon are not very far away, what we take for granted as the background to our daily lives shows what we think is important in huge areas of the past; striving to make sense of events by getting them 'in perspective', we make judgements about world history all the time. All the better, then, to make them as seriously and as consciously as possible, whatever the shortcomings of our attempts to do so.

One way in which I hope to have made this a little easier is by recalling something too often ignored in the last century or so, the importance of historical inertia and the sheer weight of the inherited past. This is not just a matter of what we can see – ruins and beefeaters are interesting, but of minor importance – but of the mental and institutional history lost to sight in the welter of day-to-day events. It is easy to recall that, say, what was called the 'Cold War' dominated much of the 1950s and 1960s, but we rarely consider its deep background in forces moulding the outlook of Americans, Russians and Chinese centuries before arguments could take place about capitalism and communism. Even our chronology is soaked in history. There is no good reason in this book to set aside the Christian chronology first adopted in the sixth century AD for, say, the Japanese or the Islamic alternatives. But AD 1941 – to take a date important in both Japanese and European history – is just as conventional a way of putting things as is the year 2061, which is the form once favoured by some Japanese nationalists. Calendars are cultural artifacts: our choice of chronologically significant dates around which to construct them is shaped by history.

Nowadays we are unlikely to overlook another fact which shaped the general argument of this book, mankind's unique power to produce change. The acceleration of change, its growth in scale and its wider and wider spread are irresistible evidence of an increase in conscious power to master the world of nature (and one reason why people have underrated the weight of the past). Lately, though, this mastery has been understandably clouded by disaster. The enthusiasm once felt for technical and intellectual achievement has fallen into disfavour in some quarters. The Great Depression, Auschwitz and Hiroshima have been followed by pollution, fear of overpopulation and the threat of war with ever more frightful weapons – to name only a handful of twentieth-century evils. Some people rightly distrust Promethean visions of man which were in the past too easily distorted into an optimism which assumed that inevitable success lay ahead. They think such views dated and shallow; they recall that the cheerfulness with which H. G. Wells contemplated the past in 1920 gave way to despair when he looked at the world at the end of his life a quarter-century or so later.

I can respect such misgivings, but do not share the pessimism which is often drawn from them. I doubt whether a knowledge of historical facts has much to do with most people's optimism or pessimism; such feelings seem to me to be usually a matter of temperament. But even if this impression is wrong, it does not seem to me that many safe predictions can follow from such facts as history provides. We can only make judgements, not necessary inductions. They do not force us to conclude either that we are now facing problems specially recalcitrant, or, on the other hand, that we are not. The resourcefulness and ingenuity so far displayed by mankind in asserting its conscious control of environment is not now invalidated because huge new needs and problems have arisen from human achievement itself. Such problems need not be insoluble in principle, though the cost may be some major discontinuities. The odds seem to me to be that the world organized as we know it certainly cannot last much longer, but that ordered and civilized life will go on in most places where it already exists. We have no reason to suppose that the outcome will be any more intolerable than, say, the results of changes forced on traditional Asia and Africa within the last century by the coming of Western technology. (Many people, of course, may reasonably argue that this would be intolerable enough.)

My ideas on such topics emerged or at least were clarified by writing this book, but they were not my starting-point. At the outset, I was not sure of much except that I wanted, so far as possible, to tell a unified story and not to compile a new collection of accounts of traditionally important themes. My first body of raw material was constituted by miscellaneous reading and thinking over many years and it became a little easier to grapple with the jumble it presented when, a few years ago, an American publisher invited me to write a textbook of world history for American colleges. Such books are specialized tools, meant to do a particular job. I deferred to the views of my publisher's technical advisers in writing it and the outcome was, I hope, good in its way, but not a book which said quite what I wished to say to the general public. Yet by forcing me to a first ordering of my ideas it was a big step towards that goal. When I began to write it, I had already decided that this book, too, would be written, so that work on the two versions could not for some time be distinguished.

They were both shaped by a desire to avoid the encyclopaedic detail which often passes for general history. My aim has been to set out instead the major effective historical processes and their comparative scale and relations, not to provide continuous histories of all major countries or fields of human activity. Those who look for them will not find in this book the names of every American president, nor those of all notable Italian Renaissance painters, nor the dates on which each African state emerged from colonial rule – or *their* names, either, for that matter. The place for such facts is an encyclopaedia. It is also true that I have neglected many areas which interest scholars and some others which possess a certain glamour because of the spectacle of what they have left behind. We still gape in amazement at the ruins of Yucatán and Zimbabwe and wonder over the statues of Easter Island. Yet intrinsically desirable though knowledge of the societies which produced these things is, they remain peripheral to the processes of world history; I have therefore only briefly sketched the early history of black Africa and pre-Columbian America. What Europeans later brought back from and did to such societies is a different matter; that has shaped our lives, even if only in small degree. But nothing in African or American history between very remote times and the coming of the Europeans moulded the great cultural traditions in which the legacies of the Buddha, the Hebrew prophets, Plato, and Confucius were for centuries (and are still today) living and shaping influences.

I hope I have also avoided the seduction which the historian must feel when material is plentiful. What matters is that a topic is important, not that we may be lucky enough to have a lot of information about it. The wars and diplomacy of Louis XIV for instance, though crucial for France and even Europe, seem to me easier to pass over briefly than, say, the Chinese Revolution. In the most recent period of history it is more than ever important to distinguish the wood from the trees and not to mention something simply because it turns up every day in the newspapers or on television.

Finally, though I use the Christian calendar throughout, I have striven not to be trapped by a 'Eurocentric' viewpoint. I have tried to recognize the impulses of my own historical inheritance, which must lie behind the choice of themes, organization and chronological arrangement. I cannot believe (to quote an ideal of historical objectivity set out by Lord Acton three-quarters of a century ago) that 'nothing shall reveal the country, the religion, or the party' to which I belong, nor that I could provide (as he hoped) an account of Waterloo to satisfy French, English, German and Dutch alike (even if there were time or space here to spend on such a theme). But I hope that an awareness of my assumptions and their limitations may nevertheless have made it possible to provide what he termed a history 'which is distinct from the combined history of all countries', and which nevertheless recognizes the variety of the great cultural traditions which give it much of its structure.

Judgement whether this aim has been or has not been achieved rests with the reader. He should blame no one but the author for what he finds inadequate or erroneous, nor, indeed, for anything else in this book. Yet many other people have made important contributions to it which demand my grateful acknowledgement. Those from whose work I have benefited – often long before I considered writing this book – and the teachers, pupils and colleagues from whose conversation and questions I have learned much cannot be acknowledged individually, though I am happy to record the debt I owe to them. Those whose help is more easily identifiable are fortunately not too numerous to be thanked in person.

First among them must come Mrs J. D'Albiac and Mrs N. Sissons, two ladies whose help was given so generously and in so many ways that it is unjust to call them 'research assistants', though I cannot think of a better term. Without their unsparing efforts the book could not have been written in the time I had to give to it and I offer them my warmest thanks. Generous counsel was also given by friends and colleagues who were good enough to read and comment upon versions of parts of it, or to reply patiently to specific questions. My warm thanks for such help are due to the Rev. J. Barton, Mr J. Boardman, Mr T. F. R. G. Braun, Dr Raymond Dawson, Mr Simon Digby, Rear-Admiral D. H. F. Hetherington, Dr J. R. L. Highfield, Dr W. O'Flaherty, Mr Nicholas Richardson, Mr Alan Robson, Mr G. R. Storry, Professor J. M. Wallace-Hadrill, Dr Christopher Watson and Mr David Winfield. I have almost always followed the advice and opinions offered by these ladies and gentlemen but none of them should be thought responsible for what is to be found in these pages. At a later stage Dr Henry Mayr-Harting kindly read portions of the text in proof; for his help, too, I am very grateful.

Academic help and advice is not all that I owe to my friends. To one in particular, Mr Michael Sissons, I am much in debt for his unwavering encouragement and support along what must often have seemed to him a road with no end in sight. Mr Charles Clark of Messrs Hutchinson must also be thanked for the pleasant way in which he has presided over the business of publishing this book and for putting its preparation into the hands of a most helpful and capable editorial group; if I single out from among them for my special thanks by name only Mr Julian Watson, my editor, it is not because I underrate the contributions of his colleagues who copy-edited, illustrated and designed this volume, but only on the principle according to which medals for gallantry (and endurance) are sometimes awarded – that one man's distinction is an acknowledgement of the collective effort of a team. I must also express special gratitude to Miss Barbara Bagnall, who searched for pictures for me with great imagination and care; three-quarters of the book was illustrated as a result of her efforts and only other demands on her time prevented her from assisting me with the whole. Technical assistance of yet another sort was provided also by Miss Clare Bass, who typed most of this book with willingness and despatch; I am most grateful to her for her help.

Finally, there is an acknowledgement to be made which is made so often by authors that it may well be in danger of being regarded as conventional. In the prefaces of two other books I have thanked my wife for her support and now I must do so again, even more emphatically; I should be very sorry if this were thought to diminish the force of what I have said on this score in the past or were to be regarded as mere form. The full extent of what this book owes to her is immeasurable; a moment's reflexion will reveal the implications of such a task for a family's routine, convenience and happiness. My children must share my thanks for respecting the disciplines that flowed from the decision to write this book, but it is to my wife, above all, that recognition is due. Such merits as it may possess could hardly have found expression without her support and in an indispensable sense this book is hers. I am happy to be able to dedicate it to her.

Merton College, Oxford   J.M.R.

Where they are known, dates of birth and death (and, in the case of rulers, regnal dates) for all persons mentioned by name in the text are given in the index.

The Hutchinson History of the World

Book One

Before History – Beginnings

When does history begin? It is tempting to reply 'In the beginning', but like many obvious answers, this soon turns out to be unhelpful. As a great Swiss historian once pointed out in another connexion, history is the one subject where you cannot *begin at the beginning*. If we want to, we can trace the chain of human descent back to the appearance of vertebrates, or even to the photosynthetic cells which lie at the start of life itself. We can go back further still, to almost unimaginable upheavals which formed this planet and even to the origins of the universe. Yet this is not 'history'.

Commonsense helps here : history is the story of mankind, of what it has done, suffered or enjoyed. We all know that dogs and cats do not have histories, while human beings do. Even when historians write about a natural process beyond human control, such as the ups and downs of climate, or the spread of disease, they do so only because it helps us to understand why men and women have lived (and died) in some ways rather than others.

This suggests that all we have to do is to identify the moment at which the first human beings step out from the shadows of the remote past. It is not quite as simple as that, though. We have to know what we are looking for first and most attempts to define humanity on the basis of observable characteristics prove in the end arbitrary and cramping, as long arguments about 'ape-men' and 'missing links' have shown. Physiological tests help us to classify data but do not identify what is or is not human. That is a matter of a definition about which disagreement is possible. Some people have suggested that human uniqueness lies in language, yet other primates possess vocal equipment similar to our own; when noises are made with it which are signals, at what point do they become speech? Another famous definition is that man is a tool-maker, but observation has cast doubt on our uniqueness in this respect, too, long after Dr Johnson scoffed at Boswell for quoting it to him.

What is surely and identifiably unique about the human species is not its possession of certain faculties or physical characteristics, but what it has done with them – its achievement, or history, in fact. Humanity's unique achievement is its remarkably intense level of activity and creativity, its cumulative capacity to create change. All animals have ways of living, some complex enough to be called cultures. Human culture alone is progressive; it has been increasingly built by conscious choice and selection within it as well as by accident and natural pressure, by the accumulation of a capital of experience and knowledge which man has exploited. Human history began when the inheritance of genetics and behaviour which had until then provided the only way of dominating the environment was first broken through by conscious choice. Of course, human beings have always only been able to make their history within limits. These limits are now very wide indeed, but they were once so narrow that it is impossible to identify the first step which took human evolution away from the determination of nature. We have for a long time only a blurred story, obscure both because the evidence is poor and because we cannot be sure exactly what we are looking for.

1 The foundations

The roots of history lie in the prehuman past and it is hard to grasp just how long ago that was. If we think of a century on our calendar as a minute on some great clock recording the passage of time, then white Europeans began to settle in the Americas only about five minutes ago. Slightly less than fifteen minutes before that, Christianity appeared. Rather more than an hour ago a people settled in southern Mesopotamia where they were soon to evolve the oldest civilization known to us. This is already far beyond the furthest margin of written record; people began writing down the past much less than an hour ago, according to our clock. Some six or seven hours further back on our scale and much more remote, we can discern the first recognizable human beings of a modern physiological type already established in western Europe. Behind them, anything from a fortnight to three weeks earlier, are the first traces of creatures with some manlike characteristics

Most primeval landscape must have been almost inconceivably different from what we can now see. Desiccated, three hundred feet deep, strikingly divided into the strata left by millennia of rubbish deposited from nearby volcanoes, the Olduvai Gorge is particularly hard to imagine as the great lake it once was, with early manlike creatures crouched round it. An archaeologist identified it as a prime site for investigation before the First World War but only in 1959 were there discoveries in its oldest layer which opened the way to a transformation of our picture of human origins.

whose contribution to the evolution which followed is still in debate.

How much further back into a growing darkness we need go in order to understand the origins of Man is debatable, but it is worth considering for a moment even larger tracts of time simply because so much happened in them which, even if we cannot say anything very precise about it, shaped what followed.

Both from this past and from the much shorter period of time – two million years or so – in which creatures with at least some claim to human qualities are known to have existed, humanity carried forward into historical times certain possibilities and limitations. Though it is not our direct concern, we need to try to understand what was in the baggage of advantages and disadvantages with which Man alone among the primates emerged from these long millennia as a change-maker. Virtually all the physical and much of the mental formation we still take for granted was by then determined in the sense that some possibilities were excluded and others were not. The crucial process is the evolution of manlike creatures as a distinct branch among the primates, for it is at this fork in the line, as it were, that we begin to look out for the station at which we get off for History. It is here that we can hope to find the first signs of that positive impact upon environment which at an undefinable but early point is already conscious and marks the first stage of human achievement.

The bedrock of the story is the earth itself. Changes recorded in the fossils of flora and fauna, in geographical forms and geological strata, narrate a drama of epic scale lasting hundreds of millions of years. During them the shape of the world changed out of recognition many times. Great rifts opened and closed in its surface, coasts rose and fell; at times huge areas were covered with a long-since vanished vegetation. Many species of plants and animals emerged and proliferated. Most died out. Yet these 'dramatic' events happened with almost unimaginable slowness. Some lasted millions of years; even the most rapid cannot have taken less than centuries. The creatures who lived while they were going on could no more have perceived them than could a twentieth-century butterfly, in its three weeks or so of life, sense the rhythm of the seasons. Yet slowly the earth was taking shape as a collection of habitats permitting different strains to survive. Meanwhile, biological evolution inched forwards with almost inconceivable slowness.

Scholars at present think that for the purpose of studying human origins we need not go further back into the darkness than, say, about two hundred million years. It seems enough to grapple with. The pacemaker of change in prehistoric times was climate, and a great series of climatic spasms at about that time opened a long era of comparatively steady and warm temperature. The age of the great reptiles began; there was nothing remotely resembling a man to be seen on the earth. Then, about sixty million years ago, the earth began to cool. Climate began to operate as an environmental selector in a different way. The reptiles went under as new climatic conditions restricted their habitat, but other animal strains suited to survival in the new conditions prospered. With considerable breaks in sequence and further selection on the way, some of these developed into the ancestors of the mammals we know. The process continued until somewhere about three million years ago. The whole of human evolution known to us has occurred since then.

This period has been labelled the Pleistocene, a name formed from the Greek words meaning 'most recent'. Its characteristic has been that it is marked off from what has gone before by renewed climatic instability. In the last three million years there has taken place the most rapid and violent succession of climatic changes so far known to have occurred. 'Rapid', we should again remind ourselves, is a comparative term; these changes took tens of thousands of years. Still, this was very different from the millions of years of steady conditions which preceded this period.

The most obvious sign of this instability was the onset of four Ice Ages, each lasting between fifty and a hundred and twenty thousand years. They covered much of the northern hemisphere (northern Europe and modern New York, for example) with great ice sheets, sometimes a mile or more thick. We live in a warm period after the end of the last of them some thirteen or fourteen thousand years ago.

The Ice Ages provide the backbone of prehistoric chronology. Dating, it is true, has been much more successfully worked out for Europe than for Asia, and even in Europe very large approximations have to be accepted. None the less, with all its imperfections the chronology based on the great Ice Ages is objective. It enables us to place Man and his forerunners within firm, if broad, limits. We do not have to rely on evolutionary traces for our clues but can relate them to an external scale.

The other interest and importance to us of the Ice Ages is that they are outstanding examples of the operation of climate as a determinant of life and its evolution. The slow onset of the ice was catastrophic for what lay in its path; its retreats, accompanied by huge inundations as the ice sheets melted, were just as decisive, destroying the habitats of creatures which had adapted successfully to the challenge its onset had presented and offering new opportunities to others in a changed environment. After each Ice Age new species spread into the areas slowly uncovered.

Climate can still be very important today, as contemplation of the disasters brought by drought can show. But such effects, even when they affect millions of people, are not so fundamental as the slow transformation of the basic geography of the world and its supplies of food which was what climate did in prehistoric times. Until very recently it determined where and how men lived. It made technique very important (and still does): the possession in early times of a skill such as fishing or fire-making could make new environments available to branches of the human family fortunate enough to possess such skills, or able to discover and learn them. Different food-gathering possibilities in different habitats meant different chances of a varied diet and, eventually, of progressing from gathering to growing. Long before the Ice Ages, though, and even before the appearance of the creatures from which humanity was to evolve, climate was setting the stage for humanity and thus shaping, by selection, the eventual genetic inheritance of humanity itself.

At the beginning of the Pleistocene we are still far from humanity. Speculation about its distant origins only too easily moves away from scanty evidence to pure fantasy, but one more backward glance is useful before plunging into the shallow pool of evidence. Sixty or seventy million years ago, the inheritors of the world of the great reptiles were primitive mammals, of two main sorts. One, rodent-like, remained on the ground; the other took to the trees. In this way the competition of the two families for resources was lessened and strains of each survived to people the world with the creatures we know today. The second group were the prosimians. We are among their descendants, for they were the ancestors of the first primates.

It is best not to be too impressed by talk about 'ancestors' in any but the most general sense, of course. Between the prosimians and ourselves lie millions of generations and many evolutionary blind alleys. It is important none the less that our remotest identifiable ancestors lived in the forests because what survived in the next phase of evolution were genetic strains best suited to the special uncertainties and accidental challenges of the forest environment, one which put a premium on the capacity to learn. Those

survived who had a genetic inheritance responsive and adaptable to the surprising, sudden danger of deep shade, confused visual patterns, treacherous handholds. Strains prone to accident in such conditions were wiped out. Among those who prospered (genetically speaking) were some with long digits which were to develop into fingers and, eventually, the oppositional thumb, and other forerunners of the apes who must have already begun an evolution towards three-dimensional vision and the diminution of the importance of the sense of smell.

The prosimians were little creatures. Tree-shrews still exist which give us some idea of what they were like; they were far from being monkeys, let alone men. Yet for millions of years they carried the traits which made humanity possible. During this time geography probably counted for much in their evolution, by imposing limits on contact between different strains, sometimes effectively isolating them, and thus increasing differentiation. Such changes would not happen quickly. None the less, it seems that fragmentations of the environment caused by geographical disturbance led to the isolation of many zones in which, little by little, the recognizable ancestors of many modern mammals appeared. Among them are the first monkeys and apes. They do not seem to go back more than thirty-five million years or so.

They represent a great evolutionary stride. Physically, the apes were the more obviously advanced, but both families had much greater manipulative dexterity than any predecessor. Within them, species distinct in size or acrobatic quality began to evolve. Physiological and psychological evolution blur in such matters. Like the development of better and stereoscopic vision, the growth of manipulative power seems to imply a growth of consciousness. Perhaps some of these creatures could already distinguish different colours. The brains of the first primates were already much more complex than those of any of their predecessors; they were bigger, too. Somewhere the brain of one or more of these strains became complex enough and its physical powers sufficiently developed for the animal to cross the line at which the world as a mass of undifferentiated sensations becomes at least in part a world of objects. Whenever this happened it was a decisive step towards mastering the world by using it, instead of reacting automatically to it.

Some twenty-five or thirty million years ago, desiccation began to reduce the area of the forests. Competition for the diminishing forest resources became fiercer. A new environmental challenge and opportunity appeared where the trees and the grasslands met. Some of the primates who lived there and were not powerful enough to hold on to their forest homes, but who were able, because of some genetic quality, to penetrate the savannahs in search of food, could meet the challenge and exploit the opportunities. Probably they had a posture and movement marginally more like that of men than, say, that of the gorillas or chimpanzees. An upright stance and the capacity to move easily on two feet makes it possible to carry burdens, among them food. The dangerous open savannah could then be penetrated and its resources withdrawn from it to a safer home base. Most animals consume their food where they find it: man does not. Freedom to use the forelimbs for something other than locomotion or fighting also suggests other possibilities. We do not know what was the first 'tool', but other primates than man have been seen to pick up objects which come to hand and wave them as a deterrent, use them as weapons, or investigate and expose possible sources of food with their aid.

The next step in the argument is enormous, for it takes us to the first evidence of a member of the biological family to which both man and the great apes belong. The evidence is tiny and fragmentary, but suggests that some twenty or fifteen million years ago a very successful species, perhaps capable of an upright stance, was widespread throughout Africa, Europe and Asia. The inference is strong, too, that he was a tool-using creature, like some chimpanzees. Movement on two feet, the upright posture that gave him better observation and the capacity to use tools, would certainly have made him a for-

midable explorer and exploiter of the environment. Unfortunately, the evidence about him is such as to leave him effectively isolated. We have no direct knowledge of his immediate forbears or descendants, but some kind of fork in the road of primate evolution had occurred. While one branch was to lead to the great apes and chimpanzees, the other led to human beings. This line has been named 'hominid'.

The darkness which closes almost at once around the first hominids is not broken for something like another twelve million years. During this time big geological and geographical changes were still going on. New environments must once again have favoured new evolutionary patterns and somewhere in this upheaval there appeared a small African hominid, subsequently named *Australopithecus*. Great uncert-

Many fanciful games have been played with the relics of early hominids. This reconstruction was based on the first skull of Australopithecus *found in the lowest of the Olduvai strata in 1959 and painstakingly reassembled from hundreds of fragments.*

ainty still surrounds him, but for some time there was a tendency to believe that, if the human species has a common ancestor, it came from a species of this genus. He is also especially interesting because of the rapidity with which his impact upon archaeological thinking has been made. Within the last twenty years, something like three million years have had to be added to the period in which the search for human origins goes on because of the discoveries which are associated with *Australopithecus*. It is with this primate and what, for want of a better word, we must call its 'contemporaries' of other species that the difficulties of distinguishing between apes, manlike apes, and other creatures with some human characteristics first present themselves in their full complexity.

Though *Australopithecus* may have appeared as much as two million years earlier still, the first evidence of this species is between two and three million years old. It was found in the Olduvai Gorge in Tanzania and consisted of the fossil relics of about twenty individual creatures and things they had brought to the site. Subsequently, further evidence about early hominids from a site near Lake Rudolf in northern Kenya and later discoveries at Olduvai was added to this. The whole collection comprises bits and pieces of about a hundred individuals; all that was left of about two million years of life could be put on a large table. Yet it made these creatures the best known of all man's possible ancestors.

Big questions nevertheless remain, and in some ways they are becoming more difficult to solve. No simple picture has yet emerged and discoveries are still being made. *Australopithecus*, of whom there is most evidence and of whom anthropologists once spoke with much confidence, is now known to have existed in more than one species. Worse still, it now seems clear that there may have lived beside him creatures even more manlike, to whom the genus name *Homo* has been given. *Homo* was a more upright, bipedal hominid and the latest remains of him (which have been found a little to the south of Olduvai) are said to be dated by

radio-activity to about 3 500 000 BC. An even bigger hominid's remains turned up a few years ago near Lake Rudolf. About five feet tall, with a brain about twice the size of a modern chimpanzee's, he has for the moment the undignified name of '1470 man', that being the number his relics have received in the catalogue of the Kenya National Museum. Still unnamed is yet another member of the genus *Homo* whose fossilized jawbones were found in central Ethiopia in 1974. Claims have been made that these relics, too, are up to four million years old. Finally, Ethiopia has since then also provided more bones, seemingly about three million years old, from which an almost complete hand has been put together by anthropologists. It is more like a human's than an ape's.

Specialists may be expected to argue about such evidence for some time yet and it is not safe for laymen to dogmatize where they disagree. It is clear enough, though, that we can already say much about the extent to which characteristics later associated with humanity were evolved even two or three million years ago. We know most about the australopithecines and physiologically, though smaller than modern human beings, they had hips, legbones and feet which are manlike rather than apelike. They walked upright and could run and carry loads for long distances as apes could not. Their hands showed a flattening at the fingertips characteristic of those of men. These are stages far advanced on the road to human physique even if the actual descent of our species is from some other branch of the hominid tree.

They also left tools behind. Tool-using is not confined to men, but the making of tools has long been thought of as a human characteristic. It is a notable step in achieving control of environment. Tools found in Kenya are the oldest which we have and they consist of stones crudely fashioned by striking flakes off pebbles to give them an edge. The pebbles seem often to have been carried purposefully and perhaps selectively to the site where they were prepared. Conscious creation of implements had begun. Simple pebble choppers of the same type from

Potassium-
Argon
dates
in years

Bed
IV

Wind-blown sand

River deposits

Bed
III

500,000

Lake and wind-blown deposits   Red river deposits

Bed
II

1,100,000

3

Lake deposits   River deposits

1,600,000

Bed
I

Lake deposits   River deposits

1,750,000

2

1

1,900,000

Basalt

Bed IV

Bed III

Bed II

Bed I

later times turn up all over the Old World of prehistory; by about one million BC, for example, they were in use in the Jordan valley. In East Africa, therefore, begins the flow of what was to prove the biggest single body of evidence about prehistoric man and his precursors and the one which has provided most information about their distribution and cultures. It has also been suggested that the Olduvai site has the traces of the first identified building, a wind-break of stones. Finally, the floor of the site provided evidence that its inhabitants were meat-eaters, in the form of bones smashed to enable the marrow and brains to be got at and eaten raw.

Olduvai prompts one tempting suggestion. The bringing of stones and meat to the site combines with other evidence to suggest that the children of early hominids could not easily cling to their mother for long foraging expeditions as do the offspring of other primates. It may be that this is the first trace of the human institution of the home base. Among primates, only humans have them: places where females and children normally stay while the males search for food to bring back to them. Such a base also implies the shady outlines of sexual differentiation in economic roles. It might even register the achievement already of some degree of forethought and planning in that food was not devoured on the spot where it was taken to gratify the immediate appetite (as is the case with most primates), but reserved for family consumption in another place. Whether hunting, as opposed to scavenging, is conceivable is another question, but the meat of large animals was consumed at a very early date at Olduvai.

Ten apparently unremarkable lumps of stone which illustrate the four major divisions of stone technology and of anthropological development which were identified at the Olduvai site. Each 'bed' represents a period of time of a half-million years or so during which silt and dust accumulated to preserve these early artifacts. Homo erectus *was the maker of the hand axes of Bed II.*

Yet such exciting evidence only provides tiny and isolated islands of hard fact. It cannot be presumed that the East African sites were necessarily typical of those which sheltered and made possible the emergence of humanity; we know about them only because they allowed the survival and subsequent discovery of early hominid remains. Some scholars have suggested that a more favourable 'niche' would have been required to ensure the survival of the species. Nor, though the evidence may incline that way, can we be sure that any of these hominids is a direct ancestor of humanity; they may all only be precursors. What can be said is that these creatures show remarkable evolutionary efficiency in the creative manner we associate with human beings, and suggest the uselessness of categories such as ape-men (or men-apes).

Their advantages enabled australopithecines to leave traces of themselves throughout most of the world outside the Americas and Australasia in the next million or so years. Whether this was by spreading from one stock or by the evolution of similar creatures in different places we do not know. Nevertheless, given the climatic violence of the first half of the Pleistocene, the conclusion must be that the survival in so many different places of the hominids showed a superior capacity to grapple with changing conditions; in the end they were the only mammal to settle so widely before *Homo sapiens* (the branch of the human family to which we belong and which was eventually spontaneously to occupy the whole planet, a unique biological achievement). It is again tempting to speculate: a home base would have helped in this by making possible periods of rest and recovery from sickness or accident, thus sidestepping, however slightly, the process of evolution by physical selection.

The next stage in human evolution is nothing less than a revolution in physique. After a divergence between hominoids and more ape-like creatures which may have occurred more than four million years ago, it took rather less than two million years for one successful family of hominids to increase their brain size to about twice that of *Australopithecus*. One of the most important stages of this process and some of the most crucial in the evolution of Man were already reached in a species called *Homo erectus* which was widespread and successful for something like a half-million years before 250000 BC and perhaps even longer. The oldest specimen so far identified (from a fossil skull found near Lake Rudolf) is thought to be about a million and a half years old. This species lasted much longer, that is to say, than the life so far of *Homo sapiens*, the branch of hominids to which we belong. Many signs once more point to an African origin and thence to a spread through Europe and Asia (where *Homo erectus* was first found). Apart from fossils, a special tool helps to plot the distribution of the new species by defining areas into which *Homo erectus* did not spread as well as those into which he did. This is the so-called 'hand-axe' of stone whose use may well have been mainly as a scraper and dresser of other materials (its use as an axe seems unlikely, but the name is established). There can be no doubt of the success of *Homo erectus* as a genetic product.

When we finish with *Homo erectus* there is no precise dividing line (none exists in human prehistory, a fact it is only too easy to overlook or forget), but we are already dealing with a creature who has added to the upright stance of his predecessors a brain of the same order of magnitude as that of modern man. Though we still know little of the way in which the brain is organized, there is a rough correlation between size and intelligence. It is reasonable, therefore, to attribute great importance to the selection of strains with bigger brains and to reckon this a huge advance in the story of the slow accumulation of human characteristics.

Bigger brains meant bigger skulls and other changes, too. An increase in ante-natal size requires changes in the female pelvis to permit the birth of offspring with larger heads, and another consequence was a longer period of growth after birth; physiological evolution in the female was not sufficient to provide ante-natal accommodation to any point approaching physical maturity. Human children need mater-

nal care long after birth. Prolonged infancy and immaturity in their turn imply prolonged dependency: it is a long time before such infants gather their own food. It may be with the offspring of *Homo erectus* that there began that long extension of the period of immaturity whose latest manifestation is the maintenance of young people by society during long periods of higher education.

Biological change also meant that care and nurture came gradually to count for more than

Probable Evolution of Hominids

Pithecanthropus robustus

Neanderthal

Cro-Magnon

Modern man

The Development of the Human Skull

large litters in ensuring the survival of the species. This in turn implied further and sharper differentiation in the rôles of the sexes. Females were being pinned down much more by maternity at a time when food-gathering techniques seem to have become more elaborate and to demand arduous and prolonged cooperative action by males – perhaps because bigger creatures needed more and better food. Psychologically, too, the change may be significant. A new emphasis on the individual is one concomitant of prolonged infancy. This emphasis would be intensified, too, by a social situation in which the importance of learning and memory were becoming more and more important as skills evolved and became more complex.

About this point the mechanics of what is going forward begin to slip from our grasp, if, indeed, they were ever in it. We are somewhere near the area in which the genetic programming of the hominids is infringed by learning. This is the beginning of the great change from the natural physical endowment to tradition and culture – and eventually to conscious control – as evolutionary selectors, though we may never be able to say where precisely this change occurs. One of the most important physiological changes of all, for example, is the loss of oestrus by the female hominid. At this point her sexual rhythm was importantly differentiated from that of other animals. Man is the only animal in which the mechanism of the oestrus (the restriction of the female's sexual attractiveness and receptivity to the limited periods in which she is on heat) has entirely disappeared. It is not hard to envisage the evolutionary connexion between this and the prolongation of infancy: if female hominids had undergone the violent disruption of their ordinary routine which the oestrus imposes, their offspring would have been periodically exposed to a neglect which would have made their survival impossible. The selection of a genetic strain which dispensed with oestrus, therefore, was essential to the survival of the species; such a strain must have been available, though the process in which it emerged may have taken a million or a million and a half

25

LEFT: *The skull of* homo erectus pekinensis – *so called because of discoveries near Pekin of his remains.*

ABOVE: *Hypothetical reconstruction from the evidence of the skull. Fragments of some forty of them were found in a rock cleft where they had lain since about 500 000 BC. They made speculation possible in every particular except one: Pekin man was a cannibal, and to get at the brains which were his dinner he had to smash the base of the skulls. Those fragments of bone do not survive.*

years because it cannot have been effected consciously.

Such a change has radical implications. The increasing attractiveness and receptivity of females to males make individual choice much more significant in mating. The selection of a partner is less shaped by the rhythm of nature; we are at the start of a very long and obscure road which leads to the idea of sexual love. Together with prolonged infant dependency,

the new possibilities of individual selection point ahead also to the stable and enduring family unit of father, mother and offspring, an institution unique to mankind. It has even been suggested that incest taboos (which are in practice well-nigh universal, however much the precise identification of the prohibited relationships may vary) originate in the recognition of the dangers of uncontrolled population growth presented by societies of creatures where socially immature but sexually adult young males are for long periods in close association with females who are always sexually receptive.

In such matters it is best to be cautious. The evidence takes us only a very little way. Yet all such reflexions support the general hypothesis that the changes in hominids observable in *Homo erectus* were especially important in defining the arcs within which humanity was to evolve. He had unprecedented capacity to manipulate his environment, feeble though his handhold on it may seem to us. Besides the hand-axes which make possible the observation of his cultural traditions, *Homo erectus* has left the

27

earliest surviving traces of constructed dwellings (huts, sometimes fifty feet long, built of branches, with stone-slab or skin floors), the earliest worked wood, the first wooden spear and the earliest container, a wooden bowl. Creation on such a scale hints strongly at a new level of mentality, at a conception of the object formed before manufacture is begun, and perhaps an idea of process. Some have argued far more. In the repetition of simple forms, triangles, ellipses and ovals, in huge numbers of examples in stone tools, there has been discerned intense care to produce regular shapes which does not seem proportionate to any small gain in efficiency which may have been achieved. Can there be discerned in this the first tiny budding of the aesthetic sense?

His greatest technical and cultural advance was made when *Homo erectus* learnt to manage fire, the earliest evidence of whose use comes from China, *c.* 600000 BC. It does not seem that he ever learnt how to make it and even his successors did not for a long time possess this skill. That he had the knowledge to use it, on the other hand, is indisputable. The importance of this knowledge is attested by the folklore of many later peoples; in almost all of them a heroic figure or magical beast first seizes fire. A violation of the supernatural order is implied: in the Greek legend Prometheus steals the fire of the gods. This is suggestive, not solid, but perhaps the first fire was taken from outbreaks of natural gas or volcanic activity. It was a revolutionary instrument, though we must again remember that a prehistoric 'revolution' took millennia. It brought the possibility of warmth and light and therefore of a double extension of Man's environment, into the cold and into the dark. In physical terms one obvious expression of this was the occupation of caves. Animals could now be driven out and kept out by fire (and perhaps the seed lies here of the use of fire to drive big game in hunting). Technology could move forward: spears could be hardened in fires and cooking became possible, indigestible substances such as seeds becoming sources of food and distasteful or bitter plants edible. This

must have stimulated attention to the variety and availability of plant life; the science of botany was stirring without anyone knowing it.

Fire must also have influenced mentality directly. It was another factor strengthening the tendency to conscious inhibition and restraint, and therefore their evolutionary importance. The focus of the cooking fire and the source of light and warmth had also the deep psychological power which they still retain. Around the hearths after dark gathered a community almost certainly already aware of itself as a small and meaningful unit against a chaotic and unfriendly background. Language – of whose origins we know nothing – would have been sharpened by a new kind of group intercourse. The group itself would be elaborated, too, in its structure. At some point, fire-bearers and fire specialists appeared, beings of awesome and mysterious importance, for on them depended, it might be, life and death. They carried and guarded the great liberating tool, and the need to guard it must sometimes have made them masters. Yet the deepest tendency of this new power always ran towards the liberation of *Homo erectus*. Fire began to break up the iron rigidity of night and day and even the discipline of the seasons. It thus carried further the breakdown of the great objective natural rhythms which bound *Homo erectus*. His behaviour could be less routine and automatic. There is even a discernible possibility of leisure.

The other great achievement of *Homo erectus* was big-game hunting. Its origins must lie far back in scavenging, the first development in food-gathering which turned vegetarian hominids into meat-eaters. Any meat-eating was a great economy of effort: it provided concentrated protein and so released meat-eaters from the prolonged nibbling of so many vegetarian creatures. It is one of the first signs that the capacity for restraint – conscious inhibition – is at work when food is being carried home to be shared tomorrow rather than consumed on the spot today, and this was a prerequisite for the hunting of big game.

The evidence is difficult to argue against.

There is a parallel growth in the size of the animal remains among the relics of primeval diet and in the size of the cranial capacity of the eaters. At the beginning of the archaeological record, it is true, an elephant and perhaps giraffes and buffaloes were among the beasts whose meat was consumed at Olduvai, but for long after this the bones of smaller animals vastly preponderate in the rubbish. By about 300 000 BC the picture is wholly altered. A revolution has occurred. The remains of large numbers of elephants (at one site about fifty) have been found which were killed and cut up on the spot. Over the same period and down to later times an evolution of the teeth and jaw of hominids away from those of a predominantly vegetable-eating species can also be traced.

This may be where we must seek the opening of the way by which *Australopithecus* and his relatives were replaced by the bigger, more efficient *Homo erectus*. A new food supply permits larger consumption. It also imposes new environments: game has to be followed if meat-eating becomes general and the hominids become more or less parasitic upon certain other species. Increasing exploration of territory follows and new settlements, too, as sites particularly favoured by the mammoth or woolly rhinoceros are identified. Such facts have to be learnt and knowledge of them passed on; knowledge of technique has to be transmitted and guarded, for the skills required to trap, kill and dismember the huge beasts of antiquity were enormous in relation to anything which preceded them. What is more, they were cooperative skills: only large numbers could carry out so complex an operation as the driving – perhaps by fire – of game to a killing-ground favourable because of bogs in which a weighty creature would flounder, or because of a precipice, favourable vantage points or secure platforms for the hunters. Few weapons were available to supplement natural traps and, once dead, the victims presented further problems. With only wood, stone and flint, they had to be cut up and removed to the home base. At one site in Spain the mind of what one scholar called a 'primitive

Archimedes' has been seen at work three hundred thousand years ago, directing the removal and use of the tusks of slaughtered elephants as levers to shift the carcasses for cutting up. Once obtained and carried home, the new supplies of meat mark another step towards the provision of leisure as the consumer is released for a time from the drudgery of ceaselessly rummaging in his environment for small, but continuously available, quantities of nourishment.

This is not man as we know him, but these are beginning to be manlike creatures: the greatest of predators is beginning to stir in his cradle. Something like a true society, too, is dimly discernible, not merely in the complicated cooperative hunting enterprises, but in what this implies in the transmission of knowledge and technique from generation to generation.

It is very difficult not to feel that this is an epoch of crucial significance. Considered against a background of millions of years of evolution, the pace of change is significantly quicker, though still unbelievably slow in terms of later societies. Culture and tradition are slowly taking over from genetic mutation and natural selection as the primary source of change among the hominids. It is the groups with the best 'memories' of effective techniques which will carry forward evolution. The importance of experience was very great, for knowledge of methods which were likely to succeed rested upon it, not (as increasingly in modern society) on experiment and analysis. This fact alone would have given new importance to old men. They knew how things were done and what methods worked and they did so at a time when the home base and big-game hunting made their maintenance by the group easier. They would not have been very old, of course. It is unlikely that many lived more than forty years.

Selection also favours those groups whose members not only have good memory, but the increasing power to reflect upon it given by language. But we know very little about the history of language before recent times. Modern types of language only appeared long after *Homo erectus* disappeared. Yet some sort of language must have been used in big-game hunting and meaningful signals can be seen in all primates. What system of communication early hominids possessed may never be known, but one plausible suggestion is that the first steps were the breaking up of calls akin to those of other animals into particular sounds capable of rearrangement. This would give the possibility of different messages and may be the remote taproot of grammar. Once more, there can be no separation of one process from others: better vision, an increased physical capacity to deal with the world as a set of discrete objects and the multiplication of objects by using tools were all going on simultaneously over the hundreds of thousands of years in which language was evolving. Together they contribute to the growing extension of mental capacity until one

Examples from our best line of evidence for a million years or so of men and manlike creatures – their technology. The scraper is from Libya, the hand axe from Hampshire: thousands of years separate their manufacture. They are both very different and very much the same, speaking for the same prolonged phase of human development, the hundreds of millennia during which different traditions of shaping and working stone are our best guide to the variety of what was going forward.

day conceptualization is possible and abstract thought appears.

It remains true, though, that if nothing very general can be definitely said about the behaviour of hominids before man, still less can anything very precise. We move in a fog, dimly apprehending for a moment creatures now more, now less, manlike and familiar. Their minds, we can be sure, are almost inconceivably unlike our own as instruments for the registration of the outside world. Yet when we look at the range of the attributes of *Homo erectus* it is his human, not pre-human, characteristics which are most striking. Physically, he has a brain of an order of magnitude comparable to our own. He makes tools – and does so within more than one technical tradition – builds shelters, takes over natural shelter by exploiting fire, and sallies out of it to hunt and gather his food. He does this in groups with a discipline which provides the capacity to carry out complicated operations; he therefore has some ability to exchange ideas by speech. The basic biological units of his hunting groups probably prefigure the nuclear family of man, being founded on the institutions of the home base and a sexual differentiation of activity. There may even be some complexity of social organization insofar as fire-bearers and gatherers or old creatures whose memories made them the data banks of their 'societies' could be supported by the labour of others. There has to be some social organization to permit the sharing of cooperatively obtained food, too. There is nothing to be gained by looking for some prehistorical point or dividing line at which such things had come to be, but subsequent human history is unimaginable without them. When, essentially, one or more sub-species of *Homo erectus*, perhaps possessing slightly larger and more complex brains than others, evolved into *Homo sapiens* they did so with an enormous achievement and heritage already secure in their grasp. Whether we choose to call it human or not hardly matters.

2 Homo sapiens

The appearance of *Homo sapiens* is momentous: here, at last, is recognizable humanity, however raw in form. Yet this evolutionary step is another abstraction. It is the beginning of the main drama and the end of the prologue, but we cannot usefully ask precisely when this happens. It is a process, not a point, and it is not a process occurring everywhere at the same rate. All we have to date it are a few physical relics of early men of types recognizably modern or closely related to the modern. Some of them may well overlap by thousands of years the continuing life of earlier hominids. Some may represent false starts and dead ends, for human evolution must have continued to be highly selective, interrupted and diverted as it was by the ebb

Twenty thousand years ago the sculptors of a culture now called Gravettian made what – so far as we now know – were the first representations of what was to be an enduring artistic genre, the female nude. Scattered from Siberia to western France, archaeologists have found grotesque, ugly but powerful figurines and reliefs, the sexual characteristics strongly exaggerated, all notion of individual identity lost in their overwhelming force. This example, known as the Laussel Venus, comes from the Dordogne. Was it a goddess? Were the sculptors seeking somehow to realize a talisman against the extinction of mankind by representing elemental woman, the continuator of the species? We cannot tell. We can only guess that this image was more powerful than any image of man if it was so widely and obsessively reproduced.

and flow of glaciation. Though much faster, too, than in earlier times, this evolution is still very slow: we are dealing with something that took place over perhaps two hundred thousand years in which we do not know when or where our first true 'ancestor' appeared. There would be a large element of fiction and convention even in posing questions about it; the physiological and technical and mental line at which we leave *Homo erectus* behind is a matter of definition.

The few early human fossils have provoked much argument. Two famous European skulls seem to belong to the period between two Ice Ages about 250000 years ago, an age climatically so different from ours that elephants browsed in a semi-tropical Thames valley and the ancestors of lions prowled about in what would one day be Yorkshire. The 'Swanscombe' skull, named after the place where it was found, shows its possessor to have had a big brain (about 1300 cc) but in other ways not much to resemble modern man: if 'Swanscombe man' was *Homo sapiens*, then he represents a very early version. The other skull, that of 'Steinheim man', differs in shape from that of *Homo sapiens* but again held a big brain. Perhaps they are best regarded as the forerunners of early prototypes of *Homo sapiens*, though creatures still living (as their tools show) much like *Homo erectus*.

The next Ice Age then brings down the curtain. When it lifts, somewhat before 100000 BC, in the next warm period, human remains again appear. There has been much argument about what they show but it is indisputable that there has been a great step forward. At this point we

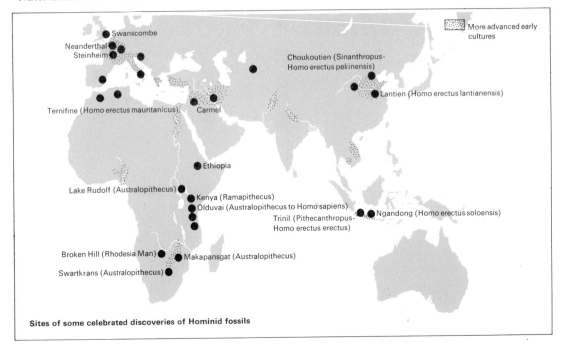

Sites of some celebrated discoveries of Hominid fossils

are entering the age of 'Neanderthal' man and, at last, a period where there is a fairly dense though broken record. Its unravelling can begin in Europe. Creatures we must now call humans lived there from a little before 100 000 BC. There are caves in the Dordogne area which were more or less continuously occupied from *c.* 90 000 to *c.* 40 000 BC. The cultures of these peoples therefore survived a period of huge climatic change; the first traces of them belong to a warm interglacial period and the last run out in the middle of the last Ice Age. This is an impressive continuity to set against what must have been great variation in the animal population and vegetation near these sites; these cultures must have had great adaptability to survive so long.

For all their essential similarity to ourselves, these peoples were physiologically distinguishable from modern Man. The first discovery of their remains was at Neanderthal in Germany (because of this, humans of this type are usually called Neanderthal men) and it was of a skull so curiously shaped that it was for a long time thought to be that of a modern idiot. Scientific

analysis still leaves much about it unexplained. It seems to belong to one of a race with no ancestors and no obvious characteristics linking it specifically to any earlier hominid. It is also unlike later forms in important respects and this has led some people to see in it a sub-species cut off by some accident of glaciation.

Until recently traces of Neanderthal men were limited to western Europe but now they have turned up in Morocco, in the northern Sahara, at Mount Carmel in Palestine and elsewhere in the Near East and Iran. This highly successful species has also been traced in Central Asia and China, where the earliest may go back to something like 200 000 BC. At the beginning of the last Ice Age, about 80 000 BC, the artifacts of Neanderthal man had spread all over the northern hemisphere of the Old World. They show differences of technique and form. The primeval cultural unity seems at last to be fragmenting and distinct cultural traditions are emerging. From the start, there is a kind of provincialism within humanity.

Neanderthal men walked erect and had big brains. Though they were in other ways more primitive than *Homo sapiens* (as the guess about the first skull suggests), they represent none the less a great evolutionary stride and show a new mental sophistication we can still hardly grasp, let alone measure. One striking example is their use of technology to overcome environment: though none have survived we know from the evidence of skin-scrapers used to dress the skins and pelts of Neanderthal man's prey that he wore clothes.* Even this important advance in the manipulation of environment is nothing like so startling as the appearance in Neanderthal culture of formal burial. The act of burial itself is momentous for archaeology; graves are of enormous importance because of the evidence they preserve of ancient society. Yet the Neanderthal graves provide more than this because they contain also the first evidence of ritual or ceremony.

This may mean a great deal and it is very difficult to control conjecture. Perhaps some early totemism explains the ring of horns within which a Neanderthal child was buried near Samarkand. Conjecture is stimulated, too, by a fleeting vision of the primitive community in northern Iraq which went out one day to gather the masses of wild flowers and grasses which eventually lay under and surrounded the dead companion it wished so to honour. Some have suggested that careful burial may reflect a new concern for the individual which was one result of the greater interdependence of the group in the renewed Ice Ages. This could have intensified the sense of loss when a member died and might also point to something more. A skeleton of a Neanderthal man who had lost his right arm years before his death has been found. He must have been very dependent on others, and was sustained by his group in spite of his handicap.

More hazardous still is the suggestion that ritualized burial implies some view of an afterlife. If this were true, it would testify to a huge power of abstraction in the hominids and the origins of one of the greatest and most enduring

*The oldest clothed body yet discovered (dressed in fur trousers and a decorated shirt) has been dated to about 33 000 BC and was found in Russia.

myths, that life is an illusion, that reality lies invisible elsewhere, that things are not what they seem. Without going so far, it is at least possible to agree that a momentous change is under way. Like the hints of rituals involving animals which Neanderthal caves also offer here and there, those of burial may mark a new attempt to dominate the environment. The human brain must already have been capable of discerning questions it wanted to answer and perhaps of providing answers in the shape of rituals. Slightly, tentatively, clumsily – however we describe it and still in the shallows though it may be – the human mind is afloat; the greatest of voyages has begun.

Neanderthal man also provides the first evidence of another great institution, warfare. It may have been practised in connexion with cannibalism, which was directed apparently to the eating of the brains of victims. Analogy with later societies suggests that here again we have the start of some conceptualizing about a soul or spirit; such acts are sometimes directed to acquiring the magical or spiritual power of the vanquished. Whatever the magnitude of the evolutionary step which the Neanderthals represent, however, they failed in the end as a sub-species. After long and widespread success they were not after all to be the inheritors of the earth. Effectively, Neanderthal survivors were genetically 'vanquished' by the strain of *Homo sapiens* which was in the end to be dominant, and about the reasons for this we know nothing. Nor can we know to what extent, if at all, it was mitigated by some genetic transmission through the mingling of stocks.

Neanderthal man's successor was physically distinguished from him by a smaller face, higher forehead, lighter skull and straighter limbs. This was *Homo sapiens sapiens*, the family to which we belong. It spread world-wide in about twenty thousand years but is first traceable to the general area of the Levant, the Near East and south-eastern Europe, about 50 000–40 000 BC. Why he should have first appeared there is unknown, but archaeologists have argued that hominids differed significantly in different areas at earlier periods than this. It has been suggested that warmer climates further from glacial environments allowed hunters to develop their techniques to the utmost while tropical conditions put different sorts of obstacle in the way of those farther south. However this may be, when a shift to drier climates becomes observable some fifty or forty thousand years ago, the coastal corridor between the mountains and the sea in what is today Israel and the Lebanon seems especially significant in the appearance of modern Man.

From this point down to the end of the last Ice Age in about 9000 BC we are at last considering plentiful evidence of men of modern type. This period is normally referred to as the 'Upper' Palaeolithic, a name derived from the Greek for 'old stones'. It corresponds, roughly, to the more familiar term 'Stone Age', but, like other contributions to the chaotic terminology of prehistory, there are difficulties in using such words without careful qualification.

To separate 'Upper' and 'Lower' Palaeolithic is easy; the division represents the physical fact that the topmost layers of geological strata are the most recent and that, therefore, fossils and artifacts found among them are later than those found at lower levels. The Lower Palaeolithic is therefore the designation of an age more ancient than the Upper. Almost all the artifacts which survive from the Palaeolithic are made from stone; none is made from metal, whose appearance makes it possible to follow a terminology used by the Roman poet Lucretius and label what comes after the Stone Age as the Bronze and Iron Ages.

This is, of course, a cultural and technological terminology; its great merit is that it directs attention to the activities of man. At one time tools and weapons are made of stone, then of bronze, then of iron. None the less, it has disadvantages, too. The obvious one is that within the huge tracts of time in which stone artifacts provide the largest significant body of evidence we are dealing for the most with hominids with some human characteristics but not others; many stone tools are therefore not made by men.

Increasingly, too, the fact that this terminology originated in European archaeology created difficulties as more and more evidence accumulated about the rest of the world which did not really fit in. A final disadvantage is that it blurs important distinctions within periods even in Europe. The result has been its further refinement. Within the Stone Age scholars have distinguished (in sequence) the Lower and Upper Palaeolithic and then the Mesolithic and the Neolithic (the last of which blurs the division attributed by the older schemes to the coming of metallurgy).* *Homo sapiens sapiens* appears roughly at the beginning of the Upper Palaeolithic, somewhere about 40000 years ago in Europe, where the most frequent discoveries of his early existence have been made.

For this period in Europe much has been done to classify and group in sequence cultures identified by their implements. The climate was not constant; though usually cold, there were important fluctuations, probably including the sharp onset of the coldest conditions for a million years somewhere about 20000–17000 BC. Such climatic variations still exercised great determinative force on the evolution of society. It was perhaps thirty thousand years ago that they made it possible for human beings for the first time to enter the Americas, crossing from Asia somewhere in the region of what is now the Bering Strait by a link provided by ice or, perhaps, by land left exposed because the ice-caps contained so much of what is now sea-water and sea-level was much lower. They moved southwards for thousands of years as they followed the game which had drawn them to the last uninhabited continent. The Americas were from the first peopled by immigrants. But the ice sheets also retreated and as they did huge transformations occurred to coasts, routes and food supplies. This was all as it had been agelessly, but there was this time a crucial difference. Man was there. A new order of intelligence was avail-

*The period down to the end of the last Ice Age in Europe is also sometimes called the Old Stone Age, another complication, because here we have yet another principle of classification, simply that provided by chronology.

able to use new and growing resources in order to cope with environmental change. The change to history, when conscious human action to control environment will increasingly be effective, is under way.

This may seem a big claim in the light of the resources early men possessed, judging by their tool kits and weaponry. Yet they already represent a huge range of capacities if we compare them with their predecessors'. The basic tools of *Homo sapiens* were stone, but they were made to serve many more precise purposes than earlier tools and were made in a different way, by striking flakes from a carefully prepared core. Their variety and elaboration are another sign of the growing acceleration of human evolution. New materials came into use in the Upper Palaeolithic, too, as bone and antler were added to the wood and flint of earlier workshops and armouries. These provided new possibilities of manufacture; the bone needle was a great step in the elaboration of clothing, softer hammers enabled some skilled workmen to carry the refinement of their flint blades to a point at which it seems non-utilitarian, so delicately thinned have they become. The first man-made

The peak of refinement in the shaping of the stone weapons of the Palaeolithic was attained by what is called the 'Solutrean' culture. Examples of its work are found all over Europe. The characteristic style of working was by applying pressure to produce very fine flakes, rather than by hammering at the flint with another stone.

The acceleration given to a spear-thrower such as this (which effectively lengthened the thrower's arm), was a major step in the technology of hunting and warfare. This one was consciously carved as an image of a creature the primitive hunter must have known well, the grouse. The bird's tailfeathers form the hook which locks the spear into the thrower as it moves through the propelling arc before its release.

37

The spear-thrower, so far as is known, was invented some forty thousand years ago. It is still in use, as this picture of an Australian aborigine shows. The study of peoples still living in elementary hunting and gathering economies has been thought to provide much valuable information about the lives of our remote forbears, risky though inferences are.

material, a mixture of clay with powdered bone, also makes it appearance. Weapons are especially improved. The tendency which can be seen towards the end of the Upper Palaeolithic for small flint implements to appear more frequently and for them to be more regularly geometrical suggests the making of more complex weapon points. In the same era come the invention and spread of the spear-thrower, the bow and arrow, and the barbed harpoon. The last shows an extension of hunting – and therefore of resources – to water. Long before this, in perhaps 600000 BC, hominids had gathered

Barbed spears and/or, in the full development of the idea, the harpoon, are now so familiar as objects that it is difficult to estimate the enormous difference they made to human life. Their appearance marked a huge increase in man's capacity to hunt and therefore to exploit his environment yet further. Harpoons marked a step from the shore into the sea and lake.

molluscs for food in China and doubtless elsewhere. With harpoons and, perhaps, more perishable implements, new and richer aquatic sources of food (some created by the temperature changes of the last Ice Ages) could now be exploited, and this has implications for settlement. The weapon development, too, suggests new achievements in hunting, possibly connected with the growth of forests in post-glacial phases and with a new dependence on and

Manmade beauty is very ancient. On some four inches of reindeer antler used for a spear-thrower someone living forty thousand years ago in the Dordogne etched this bison, its head turned back to lick its flank – apparently because the shape of the antler dictated that pose.

knowledge of the movements of reindeer and wild cattle.

It is tempting to see support of this in the most remarkable and mysterious evidence of all which has survived the men of the Upper Palaeolithic: their art, the first of whose existence we can be sure. Earlier men or even manlike creatures may have scratched patterns in the mud, daubed their bodies, moved rhythmically in the dance or spread flowers in patterns, but of these things we know nothing, because of them, if they ever happened, nothing has survived. Some creature took the trouble to accumulate little hoards of red ochre some forty or sixty thousand years ago, but the purpose of doing so is unknown. It has been suggested that two

indentations on a Neanderthal gravestone are the earliest surviving art, but the first plentiful and assured evidence comes in Europe in about 35 000 BC and swells dramatically until we find

Perhaps one of the first essays in European realism comes from a cave near Lascaux in the Dordogne; the hunter falls back before the bison which charges him, his throwing-stick useless beside him on the ground, the spear having found its mark in the belly of the enraged beast whose entrails drag on the ground.

ourselves in the presence of conscious art. Its great technical achievements, consistency and emotional power, appear, without warning or forerunner, already almost mature. They continue so for thousands of years until they vanish as suddenly as they came. Just as it has no ancestor, this art leaves no descendant, though it seems to have employed almost all the basic processes of the visual arts still in use today.

Its isolation both in space and time must be ground for suspicion that there is more to be discovered. Caves in Africa abound with prehistoric paintings and carvings, but they do not seem to be as old as those of Europe. Yet we do not yet know enough about the dating of cave paintings in other parts of the world, nor about the uniqueness of the conditions which led to the preservation in Europe of objects which may have had parallels elsewhere. Nor do we know what may have disappeared; there is a vast field of possibilities of what may have been produced in gesture, sound or perishable materials which cannot be explored. None the less, the art of western Europe in the Upper Palaeolithic, all qualifications made, has a colossal and solid impressiveness.

Most of it has been found in a relatively small area of south-western France and northern Spain and consists of three main bodies of material: small figures of clay (usually female), decorated objects (often tools and weapons) and the painted walls and roofs of caves. In these caves (and in the decoration of objects) there is an overwhelming preponderance of animal themes. The meaning of these designs, above all in the elaborate sequences of the cave paintings, has intrigued scholars. Obviously, many of the beasts so carefully observed were central to a hunting economy. At least in the French caves, too, it now seems highly probable that a conscious order exists in the sequences in which they are shown. But to go further in the argument is still very hard. Clearly, art in Upper Palaeolithic times has to carry much of a burden later carried by writing, but what its messages mean is still obscure. It seems likely that the paintings were connected with religious or magical practice: the selection of such remote and difficult corners of caves as those in which the paintings have been traced is by itself strongly suggestive that some special rite was carried out when they were painted or gazed upon. (Artificial light, of course, was needed in these dark corners.) The origins of religion have been hinted at in Neanderthal burials and appear even more strongly in those of the Upper Palaeolithic peoples which are often elaborate; here, in their art, is something where inferences are even harder to resist. Perhaps it provides the first surviving relics of organized religion.

The birth, maturity and death of the first artistic achievement of mankind occupies a very long period, perhaps of thirty thousand years. Somewhere about 35000 BC appear decorated and coloured objects, often of bone and ivory. Then, in about 20000 BC, we reach the first figurative art and, soon afterwards, the peak of the prehistoric aesthetic achievement, the great painted and incised cave 'sanctuaries' (as they have been called), with their processions of animals and mysterious repeated symbolic shapes. This high phase lasted about five thousand years, a startlingly long time for the maintenance of so consistent a style and content. So long a period – almost as long as the whole history of civilization on this planet – illustrates the slowness with which tradition changed in ancient times and its imperviousness to outside influence. Perhaps it is an index, too, of the geographical isolation of prehistoric cultures. The last phase of this art which has been discerned takes the story down to about 9000 BC; in it, the stag more and more replaces other animals as subject-matter (no doubt thus reflecting the disappearance of the reindeer and the mammoth as the ice retreated) before a final burst of richly decorated tools and weapons brings mankind's first great artistic achievement to an end. The age which followed produced nothing approaching it in scale or quality; its best surviving relics are a few decorated pebbles. Six thousand years were to pass before the next great art.

For all the splendour of this art, we know little about its collapse. The light is never more than dim in the Upper Palaeolithic and the darkness closes in rapidly – which is to say, of course, over thousands of years. Nevertheless,

Boys discovered this cave at Lascaux in 1940, after it had been lost for thousands of years. Scholars still argue about the meaning of the great cave paintings of the Upper Palaeolithic; whether they are to be interpreted as elements in a magical ritual or as, in some dim sense, the beginnings of something conceivable as 'pure' art, are still debated. What remains unambiguous is the power of the impression such a cave can still produce.

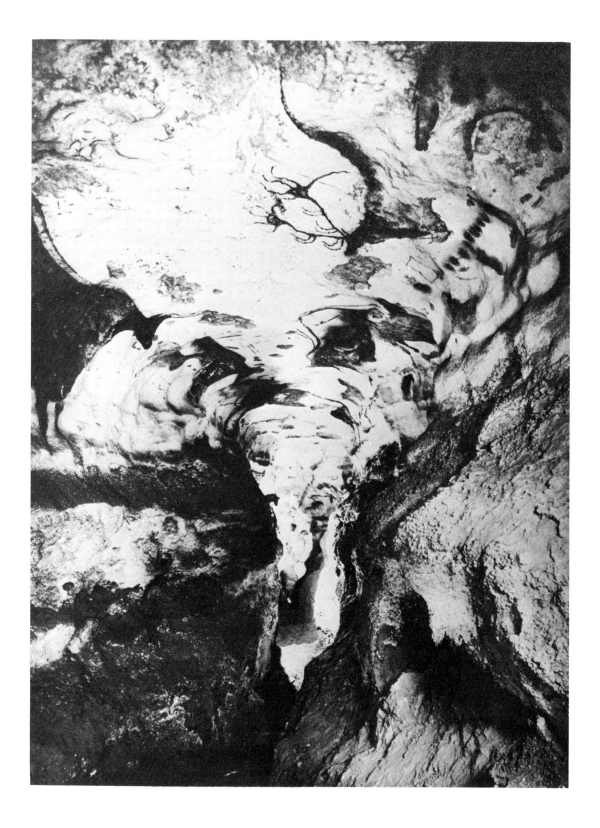

the impression left by the violence of the contrast between what was before and what came after produces a sense of shock. So sudden an extinction is a mystery. We have no precise dates or even precise sequences: nothing ended in one year or another. There was only a gradual closing down of artistic activity over a long time which seems in the end to have been absolute. Some scholars have blamed climate. Perhaps, they argue, the whole phenomenon of cave art was linked to efforts to influence the movements or abundance of the great game herds on which the hunting peoples relied. As the last Ice Age ebbed and each year the reindeer retreated a little, men sought new and magical techniques to manipulate them, but gradually as the ice sheets withdrew more and more, an environment to which they had successfully adapted their lives disappeared. As it did, so did the hope of influencing nature. *Homo sapiens* was not powerless; far from it, he could adapt, and did, to a new challenge. But for a time one cultural impoverishment at least, the abandonment of his first art, was a consequence of adaptation.

It is easy to see much that is fanciful in such speculation, but difficult to restrain excitement over such an astonishing achievement. People have spoken of the great cave sequences as 'cathedrals' of the Palaeolithic world and such metaphors are justified if the level of achievement and the scale of the work undertaken is measured against what evidence we have of the earlier triumphs of man. With the first great art, the hominids are now left far behind and we have unequivocal evidence of the power of the human mind.

Much else that is known of the Upper Palaeolithic confirms the sense that the crucial genetic changes are behind and that evolution is now a mental and social phenomenon. The distribution of races in the world which is to last down to early modern times is already broadly fixed by the end of the Upper Palaeolithic. Geographical and climatic divisions had produced specializations within *Homo sapiens* in skin pigment, hair characteristics, the shape of the skull and the bone structure of the face. In the earliest

Chinese relics of *Homo sapiens* the Mongoloid characteristics are discernible. All the main racial groups are established by 10 000 BC, broadly speaking in the areas they dominated until the great resettlement of the Caucasian stocks which was one aspect of the rise of European civilization to world domination after AD 1500. The world was filling up during the Old Stone Age. Men at last penetrated the virgin continents. Somewhere between 30 000 and 15 000 BC Mongoloid peoples spread over the Americas; the earliest Australian Palaeolithic site has been dated about 17 000 BC, but *Homo sapiens* probably reached that continent much earlier, when it may have been attached to Asia.

Yet the Upper Palaeolithic world was still a very empty place. Calculations suggest that twenty thousand humans lived in France in Neanderthal times, possibly fifty thousand in 20 000 BC. There were then perhaps ten million humans in the whole world. 'A human desert swarming with game' is one scholar's description of it. They lived by hunting and gathering, and this required a lot of land to support a family or a small group.

However doubtful figures may be, if they are of this order of magnitude it is not hard to see that they still mean very slow cultural change. Greatly accelerated though Man's progress in the Old Stone Age may be and much more versatile though he is becoming, he is still taking thousands of years to transmit his learning across the barriers of geography and social division. A man might, after all, live all his life without meeting anyone from another group or tribe, let alone another culture. The divisions which already existed between different groups of *Homo sapiens* open a historical era whose whole tendency was towards the cultural distinction, if not isolation, of one group from another, and this was to increase human variety until reversed by technical and political forces in a very late period of history.

About the groups in which Upper Palaeolithic man lived there is still much unknown. What is clear is that they were both larger in size than in former times and also more settled. The earliest remains of buildings come from the hunters of the Upper Palaeolithic who inhabited what are now Czechoslovakia and southern Russia. In about 10000 BC in parts of France clusters of shelters seem to have contained anything from four to six hundred people, but this must have been unusual. Something like the tribe probably existed, therefore, though about its organization and hierarchies it is virtually impossible to speak. All that is clear is that there was a continuing sexual specialization in the Old Stone Age as hunting grew more elaborate and its skills more demanding, while settlements provided new possibilities of vegetable-gathering by women.

Cloudy though its picture is, none the less, the earth at the end of the Old Stone Age is in important respects one we can recognize. There were still to be geological changes (the English Channel was only to make its latest appearance in about 7000 BC, for example) but we have lived in a period of comparative topographical stability which has preserved the major shapes of the world of about 9000 BC. That world was already firmly Man's world. The descendants of the primates who came out of the trees had, by the acquisition of their tool-making skills, by using natural materials to make shelters and by domesticating fire, by hunting and exploiting other animals, long achieved an important measure of independence of natural rhythms. This has brought them to a high enough level of social organization to undertake important co-operative works. Their needs had provoked economic differentiation between the sexes. Grappling with these and other material problems led to the transmission of ideas by speech, to the invention of ritual practices and the basic notions of religion and, eventually, to a great art. It has even been argued that Upper Palaeolithic man had a lunar calendar. Man is already a conceptualizing creature as he leaves prehistory. He is equipped with intellect, with the power to objectify and abstract. It is very difficult not to believe that it is this new strength which explains Man's capacity to make the last and greatest stride in prehistory, the invention of agriculture.

3 The possibility of civilization

Homo sapiens has lived for something like ten times as long as he has created civilization, perhaps twenty times as long if we count Neanderthal man as part of the family. The waning of the last Ice Age at last permitted the long march to civilization to be completed and is the immediate prelude to history. Within five or six thousand years a series of changes took place which were momentous, and the most important of them was an increase in food supply. Nothing so sharply accelerated human development or had such widespread results until the changes called industrial revolution which have been going on for the last two and a half centuries.

One scholar summed up these changes which mark the end of prehistory with a similar phrase, the 'Neolithic revolution'. Here is another little tangle of misleading terminology, though the last we need consider in prehistory. Archaeologists follow the Palaeolithic era by the Mesolithic and that by the Neolithic (some add a fourth, the Chalcolithic, by which they mean a phase of society in which artifacts of stone and copper are in simultaneous use). The distinction between the first two is really of moment only to the specialist, but these are all terms which describe cultural facts; they identify sequences of artifacts which show growing resources and capacities. Only the term 'Neolithic' need concern us. It means, at its strictest, a culture in which ground or polished stone tools replace chipped ones (though other criteria are sometimes added to this). This may not seem so startling a change as to justify the excitement over the Neolithic which has been shown by some pre-historians, far less talk of a 'Neolithic revolution'. In fact, though the phrase is still sometimes used it is unsatisfactory because it had to cover too many different ideas. None the less, it was an attempt to provide a classification of an important and complex change which can be observed with local variations in many places. It is still worth while, therefore, to try to understand what it was that made the Neolithic so important.

We should begin by noting that even in the narrowest technological sense described above, the Neolithic phase of human development does not begin, flower or end everywhere at the same time. In one place it may last thousands of years longer than in another and its beginnings are separated from what went before not by a clear

A dweller in ancient Jericho. We do not know why the inhabitants of this place took some skulls and reconstructed the features with plaster and cowrie-shell eyes, but to this practice we owe some of our small stock of knowledge of the likely physical appearance of men in the ancient world and one of the first portraits.

line but by a mysterious zone of cultural change. Then, within it, not all societies show themselves to be in possession of the same range of skills and resources; some discover how to make pottery, as well as polished stone tools, others go on to domesticate animals and begin to gather or raise cereal crops. Slow evolution is the rule and not all societies had reached the same level by the time literate civilization appears. Nevertheless, Neolithic culture is the matrix from which civilization appears and provides the preconditions on which it rests, which are by no means limited to the production of the highly finished stone tools which gave the phase its name.

A qualification is also required before using the word 'revolution' when discussing this period. Even though we leave behind the slow evolutions of the Pleistocene and move into an accelerated era of prehistory, it must still be recalled that no clear-cut divisions are implied. They are pretty rare in later history; even when they try to do so, few societies can break cleanly with their past. What we are observing is a slow but radical transformation of human behaviour and organization over more and more of the world, not a sudden new departure. It is made up of the crucial changes which make the last period of prehistory identifiable as a unity, whatever we call it.

At the end of the Upper Palaeolithic, Man existed physically much as we know him. He was, of course, still to change somewhat in height and weight, most obviously in those areas of the world where he gained in stature and life expectancy as nutrition improved. In the Old Stone Age it was still unlikely that a man or a woman would reach an age of forty and if they did then they were likely to live pretty miserable lives, prematurely aged in our eyes, tormented by arthritis, rheumatism and the casual accidents of broken bones or rotting teeth. This would only slowly change for the better. The shape of the human face would go on evolving, too, as diet altered. (It seems to be only after AD 1066 that the edge-to-edge bite gave way among Anglo-Saxons to the overbite which was the ultimate consequence of a shift to more starch and carbohydrate, a development of some importance for the later appearance of the English.)

The physical types of men differed in different continents, but we cannot presume that capacities did. In all parts of the world *Homo sapiens sapiens*, the sub-species to which all men now belong, was showing great versatility in adapting his heritage to the climatic and geographical upheavals of the ebbing phase of the last Ice Age. In the beginnings of settlements of permanence and some size, in the elaboration of technology and in the growth of language and the dawn of characterization in art were some of the rudimentary elements of the compound which was eventually to crystallize as civilization. But much more than these were needed. Above all, there had to be the possibility of some sort of economic surplus to daily requirements.

This was hardly conceivable except in occasional, specially favourable areas of the hunting and gathering economy which sustained all human life and was the only one known to human beings until about ten thousand years ago. What made it possible was the invention of agriculture.

The importance of this was so great that it does seem to justify a strong metaphor and the 'farming revolution' or 'food-gathering revolution' are terms whose meaning is readily clear. They single out the fact which explains why the Neolithic era could provide the circumstances in which civilizations could appear. Even a knowledge of metallurgy, which was spreading in some societies during their Neolithic phases, is not so fundamental. Farming revolutionized the conditions of human existence and it is the main thing to bear in mind when considering the meaning of Neolithic, a meaning concisely summarized by a leading archaeologist as 'not a time phase falling between exact dates, but . . . a period between the end of the hunting way of life and the beginning of a full metal-using economy, when the practice of farming arose and spread through most of Europe, Asia and North Africa like a slow-moving wave'.

The essentials of agriculture are the growing of crops and the practice of animal husbandry. How these came about and at what places and times is more mysterious. Some environments must have helped more than others; while some peoples pursued game across plains uncovered by the retreating ice, others were intensifying the skills needed to exploit the new, prolific river valleys and coastal inlets rich in edible plants and fish. The same must be true of cultivation and herding. Agriculture began in more than one place and in different forms. It seems likely that the earliest agriculture, based on the cultivation of primitive forms of millet and rice, occurred in south-east Asia, somewhere about 10000 BC.

Because of what was to happen later and because of the accidents of historical survival and the direction taken by scholarly effort, much more is known about early agriculture in the Near East than its possible precursors in the Far East. There are good reasons for continuing to regard this as a crucial zone, even if it is not given pride of place in terms of chronology. Both the predisposing conditions and the evidence point to the region later called the 'Fertile Crescent' as especially significant. The Levant coast has already made its appearance in these pages; it forms part of the whole arc of territory running northward from Egypt through Palestine and the Levant, through Anatolia to the hills between Iran and the south Caspian to enclose the river valleys of Mesopotamia. Much of it now looks very different from the same area's lush landscape when the climate was at its best, five thousand or so years ago. Wild barley and a wheatlike cereal then grew in southern Turkey and emmer, a wild wheat, in the Jordan valley. Egypt enjoyed enough rain for the hunting of big game well into historical times, and elephants were still to be found in Syrian forests in 1000 BC. The whole region today is fertile by comparison with the desert which is its boundary, but in prehistoric times was even more favoured. The cereal grasses which are the ancestors of later crops been traced back furthest in these lands. There is evidence

O 2800-4000 B.C.
◑ 4000-5200 B.C.
● 5200 B.C.<
Early Sites of Farming

of the harvesting, though not necessarily of the cultivating, of wild grasses in Asia Minor in about 9500 BC. There, too, the afforestation which followed the end of the last Ice Age seems to have presented a manageable challenge; population pressure could have been a stimulus to deliberate attempts to extend living-space by clearing and planting when hunting-gathering areas became overcrowded. From this region the new foods and the techniques for planting and harvesting them seem to have spread into Europe in about 6000 BC. Within the region, of course, contacts were relatively easier than outside it; a date as early as 8000 BC has been given to discoveries of bladed tools found in southwest Iran made from obsidian which came from Anatolia. But diffusion was not the only process at work. Agriculture was later to appear in the Americas seemingly without any import of techniques from outside.

The jump from gathering wild cereals to planting and harvesting them seems marginally greater than that from driving game for hunting to herding, but the domestication of animals was almost as momentous. The first traces of the keeping of sheep come from northern Iraq, in about 9000 BC. Over such hilly, grassy areas the wild forbears of the Jersey cow and the Sussex White pig roamed untroubled for thousands of years except by occasional contact with their hunters. Pigs, it is true, could be

47

found world-wide but sheep and goats were especially plentiful in Asia Minor and a region running across much of Asia itself. From their systematic exploitation would follow the control of their breeding and other economic and technological innovations. The use of skins and wool opened new possibilities; the taking of milk launched dairying. Riding and the use of animals for traction would come later. So would domestic poultry.

The story of mankind is now far past the point at which the impact of such changes can be easily grasped. Suddenly, with the coming of agriculture, the whole material fabric on which subsequent human history was to be based flashes into view, though not into existence. It was the greatest of man's transformations of the environment. In a hunting-gathering society thousands of acres are needed to support a family, whereas in primitive agricultural society about twenty-five acres is enough. In terms of population growth alone, a huge acceleration became possible.

The supply of an assured or virtually assured food surplus also meant settlements of a new solidity. Bigger populations could live on a smaller area and true villages could appear. Specialists not engaged in food production could be tolerated and fed more easily while they practised their own skills. Before 9000 BC there was a village (and perhaps a shrine) at Jericho. A thousand years later it had grown to some eight to ten acres of mud-brick houses with substantial walls.

It is a long time before we can discern much of the social organization and behaviour of such communities. It seems possible that at this time, as much as at any other, local divisions of mankind were decisive. Physically, men were more uniform than ever, but culturally they were diversifying as they grappled with different problems and appropriated different resources. The adaptability of different branches of *Homo sapiens* in the conditions left behind after the retreat of the last Ice Age is very striking and produced variations in experience unlike those following earlier Ice Ages. They lived for the most part in isolated, settled traditions, in which the importance of routine was overwhelming. This would give new stability to the divisions of culture and race which had appeared so slowly throughout Palaeolithic times. It would take much less time in the historical future which lay ahead for these local peculiarities to crumble under the impact of population growth, speedier communication and the coming of trade – a mere ten thousand years, at most. Within the new farming communities it seems likely that distinctions of rôle multiplied. For some people there must have been more leisure, though it has been pointed out that for others actually engaged in the production of food, leisure may well have diminished. It certainly seems likely that social distinctions became more acute. This may be connected with new possibilities as surpluses became available for barter which led eventually to trade.

The same surpluses may also have encouraged Man's oldest sport after hunting, warfare. New prizes must have made raids and conquest more tempting. Perhaps, too, a conflict, which was to have centuries of vitality before it, finds its origins here – that between nomads and settlers. We may even speculate that the dim roots of the notion of aristocracy are to be sought in the successes (which must have been frequent) of hunter-gatherers, representatives of an older social order, in exploiting the vulnerability of the settlers, tied to their areas of cultivation, by enslaving them. Hunting was long to be the sport of kings and mastery of the animal world was an attribute of the first heroes of whose exploits we have records in sculpture and legend. None the less, though much of the just prehistoric world must have been lawless and violent, it is worth remembering that there was an offsetting factor: the world was still not very full. The replacement of hunter-gatherers by

Thirty feet deep and ten wide, the great defensive ditch at Jericho was cut into rock without metal tools. Within its protection stood the tower whose remains can be seen in the background.

One of the major archaeological sites of Asia Minor is Çatal Hüyük, where graves and shrines have yielded a mass of material throwing light on the Neolithic in Anatolia. This ceremonial dagger – flaked from flint as others had been for hundreds of thousands of years, at the dawn of the age of metal – was found there.

farmers did not have to be a violent process. The ample space and thin populations of Europe on the eve of the introduction of farming, for example, probably explain the lack of archaeological evidence of violent struggle. The increase of population and pressure on the new farming resources increased the likelihood of competition.

In the long run metallurgy changed things as much as did farming, but it was to be a very much longer run. Immediately, it made a less rapid and fundamental difference. This is probably because of the scattered and scarce nature of the deposits of ore first discovered: for a long time there was just not much metal available. The first of whose use we find evidence is copper (which rather weakens the attractiveness of the old term 'Bronze Age' for the beginning of metal-using culture). At some time between 6000 and 7000 BC copper was being hammered into shape without heating at Çatal Hüyük, in modern Turkey. Once the technique of blending it with tin to produce bronze was discovered, a metal was available which was both relatively easy to cast and retained a much better cutting edge. On this much could be built; from it much derived, among other results the quite new importance of ore-bearing areas. In its turn, this was to give a new twist to trade, to markets and to routes. Further complications, of course, followed the coming of iron, which appeared after some cultures had indisputably evolved into civilizations – another reflexion of the way in which the historical and prehistoric eras run so untidily into one another. Its obvious military value springs to the eye, but it had just as much importance when turned into agricultural tools. This is looking a long way ahead, but it made possible a huge extension of living-space and food-producing soil: however hard he burned woodland and scrub, if they covered heavy soils, Neolithic man could only scratch them with an antler or wooden pick. They could only be turned when iron was easily available and the end of this story had not come by the twentieth century, when Indian villagers could still reject the iron plough.

It is already clear how quickly – the term is legitimate against the background of earlier prehistory even if it takes thousands of years in some places – interpenetration and interplay begin to influence the pace and direction of change. Long before these processes have exhausted their effects in some areas, too, the first civilizations are in being. Prehistorians used to argue about the relative importance of the diffusion of innovations from an original single source or their spontaneous appearance independently in different places as general factors in cultural advance, but so complex a background has made this seem a waste of time and energy. There was always implausibility in either of the contesting views, held in its absolute form. To say that in one place, and in one place only, all the conditions for the appearance of new phenomena existed and that these were then simply diffused elsewhere was as implausible as saying that in widely differing circumstances of geography, climate and cultural inheritance exactly the same inventions could be thrown up, as it were, time and time again. What we can observe is a concentration of fac-

tors in the Near East which make it at this crucial moment immeasurably the most concentrated, active and important centre of new developments. It does not mean that similar individual developments may not occur elsewhere: pottery, it seems, was first produced in Japan in about 10 000 BC, and agriculture evolved in America in complete isolation from the Old World perhaps as early as 5000 BC.

This implies a ragged, untidy end to the prologue to human history, but that is what it looks like. At the end of prehistory and on the eve of the first civilizations we discern a world of human societies more differentiated than ever before and more successful than ever in mastering different environments and surviving. Some will continue into history. It is only within the last century or so that the Ainus of northern Japan have disappeared, taking with them a life that is said to have been very similar to one they lived fifteen thousand years ago. Englishmen and Frenchmen who went to North America in the sixteenth century AD found there hunter-gatherers who must have lived much as their own ancestors had done ten thousand years before.

Wall paintings and plaster reliefs of unprecedented elaboration appear in the shrines of Çatal Hüyük, one of which is shown in a reconstructed form here. The three bulls' heads could be remotely connected with later Cretan cults; the rows of moulded women's breasts under them may have played a part in some fertility cult. On the eve of the Bronze Age, though, it is still impossible to say anything precise or certain about religious belief.

Plato and Aristotle were to live and die before prehistory in America gave way to the appearance of the great Mayan civilization of Yucatán, and prehistory lasted for Eskimos and Australian aborigines until the nineteenth century.

No broad front of chronology, therefore, will help in unravelling so interwoven a pattern. What must be emphasized is that the essential basis of civilized life at last existed in one area of the Old World by about 6000–5000 BC. Its deepest roots lay hundreds of thousands of years in the past, in the slow rhythm of genetic and cultural evolution. Through the Upper Palaeolithic eras the pace of change had quickened by a huge factor, but this was as nothing to what was to follow. Civilization brought conscious attempts on a quite new scale to control and organize men and their environment. It builds on a basis of cumulative mental and technological resources and the feedback from its own transformations further accelerates the process of change. Ahead lies acceleration in every field, in the technical control of environment, in the elaboration of mental patterns, in the changing of social organization, in the accumulation of wealth, in the growth of population.

It is important to get our perspective in this matter right. From some modern points of view the centuries of the European Middle Ages look like a long slumber. No medievalist would agree, of course, but the twentieth-century man who is impressed by the rapidity of the change which encompasses him and the relative immobility of medieval society ought to reflect that the art which develops from the Romanesque of Charlemagne's Aachen to the Flamboyant of fifteenth-century France was revolutionized in five or six centuries; in a period about ten times as long, the first known art of Man, that of the Upper Palaeolithic, shows, by comparison, insignificant stylistic change. Further back, the pace is even slower as the long persistence of early tool types shows. Still more fundamental changes are even less easy to comprehend. So far as we know, the last twelve thousand years register nothing new in Man's physiology comparable to the colossal transformations of the early Pleistocene which are registered for us in a handful of relics of a few of nature's experiments, yet those took hundreds of thousands of years.

In part, the contrast in the rate of change is the one with which we began, that between Nature and Man as makers of change. Man increasingly chooses for himself and even in prehistory the story of change is therefore increasingly one of conscious adaptation. So the story will continue into historical times, more intensively still. This is why the most important part of the story of Man is the story of consciousness; it makes all else possible and long ago broke the genetic slow march. Nature and nurture are there from the moment that Man is first identifiable; perhaps they can never be quite disentangled, but man-made culture and tradition are increasingly the determinants of change.

Two reflexions ought, none the less, to be made to balance this indisputable fact. The first is that Man has almost certainly not shown any improvement in innate capacity since the Upper Palaeolithic. His physique has not changed fundamentally in forty thousand years or so and it would be surprising if his mental capacity had done so. So short a time could hardly suffice for genetic changes comparable to those of earlier eras. The rapidity with which humanity has achieved so much since prehistoric times can be accounted for quite simply: there are many more of us upon whose talents humanity can draw and, more important still, human achievements are essentially cumulative. They rest upon a heritage itself accumulating at, as it were, compound interest. Primitive societies had far less inherited advantage in the bank. In them the achievement of the 'primitive Archimedes' whose levers enabled men to butcher the carcasses of elephants was indeed a huge one, perhaps involving a leap of imagination almost inconceivable today, and we should recognize its magnitude.

If this is speculation, the second reflexion need not be: Man's genetic inheritance not only enables him to make conscious change, to undertake an unprecedented kind of evolution, but also controls and limits him. The irrationalities of this century show the limits of Man's capacity for conscious control of his destiny. To this extent, he is still determined, still unfree, still a part of a nature which produced his unique qualities in the first place only by evolutionary selection. It is not easy to separate this part of his inheritance, either, from the emotional shaping he has received from the processes through which he evolved and which still lies deep at the heart of all our aesthetic and affective life. Man must live with an inbuilt dualism. To deal with it has been the aim of most of the great philosophies and religions and the mythologies by which we still live, but they are themselves moulded by it. As we move from prehistory to history it is important not to forget that the determining effect of this was to prove much more resistant to control than those blind prehistoric forces of geography and climate which were to be so quickly overcome. Nevertheless, Man at the edge of history is the creature we know, Man the change-maker.

Book Two

The First Civilizations

Ten thousand years ago, the physical shape of the world was much what it is today. By then the outlines of the continents were broadly those we know and the major natural barriers and channels of communication have remained constant ever since. By comparison with the upheavals of the hundreds of millennia preceding the end of the last Ice Age, climate, too, was from this time stable; from this point the historian need only regard its short-term fluctuations. Ahead there lay the age (in which we still live) in which most change was man-made.

Civilization has been one of the great accelerators of such change. It began at least seven times, says one historian, meaning by that that he can distinguish at least seven occasions on which particular mixes of human skills and natural facts came together to make possible a new order of life based on the exploitation of nature. Though all these beginnings fall within a span of three thousand years or so – barely a moment by comparison with

the vast scale of prehistory – they were neither simultaneous, nor equally successful. They turned out very differently, some of them quickly showing features not shared by others while some underwent epochs of regression. Yet all of them signified an increase in the rate and scale of change dramatic by comparison with anything achieved in earlier times.

Some of these early civilizations are still real foundations of our own world. Some of them, on the other hand, now exercise little or no influence, except perhaps upon our imaginations and emotions when we contemplate the relics which are all that is now left of them. None the less, overall they determined much of the cultural map of the world down to this day because of the power of the traditions which sprang from them. The establishment of the first civilizations took place between about 3500 BC and 500 BC and it provides the first of the major chronological divisions of world history.

1 Early civilized life

For as long as we know there has been at Jericho a never-failing spring feeding what is still a sizable oasis. No doubt it explains why people have lived there on and off for about ten thousand years. Farmers clustered about it in late prehistoric times; its population may then have numbered two or three thousand. Before 6000 BC it had great water tanks which suggest provision for big needs, possibly for irrigation, and there was a massive stone tower which was part of elaborate defences long kept in repair. Clearly its inhabitants thought they had some-

The invention of writing was momentous. This limestone tablet is one of the earliest documents we have of the stages by which it happened. It was found in southern Mesopotamia and has been dated to about 3500 BC. The little pictures are of hands, feet and some kind of sledge (perhaps used for threshing grain); even at so early a date, they mark a big further stride towards letting signs stand for things, a process already foreshadowed in symbols on pottery. Later, the Egyptians clung to such 'pictographic' forms of writing, elaborating them into the 'hieroglyphics' which recorded their life and business for thousands of years. By then, the Mesopotamian tradition had taken another direction, away from picture-writing towards patterns of signs made of identical marks in different arrangements which could be easily formed by a reed-stalk stamp on a soft clay tablet. This process occupied about fifteen hundred years after these tablets were made.

thing worth defending; they had property. Jericho was a considerable place.

For all that, it was not the beginnings of a civilization; too much was still lacking and it is worth considering for a moment at the outset of the era of civilization just what it is we are looking for. It is a little like the problem of pinning down in time the first human beings. There is a shaded area in which we know the change occurs, but we can still disagree about the point at which a line has been crossed. All over the Near East around 5000 BC farming villages provided agricultural surpluses on which civilization could eventually be raised. Some of them have left behind evidence of complex religious practice and elaborate painted pottery, one of the most widespread forms of art in the Neolithic era. Somewhere about 6000 BC brick building was going on in Turkey at Çatal Hüyük, a site only slightly younger than Jericho. But by civilization we usually mean something more than ritual, the presence of a certain technology, or art, and certainly something more than the mere agglomeration of human beings in the same place.

It is a little like speaking of 'an educated man': everyone can recognize one when they see him, but not all educated men are recognized as such by all observers, nor is a formal qualification (a university degree, for example) either a necessary or infallible indicator. Dictionary definitions are of no help in pinning down 'civilization', either. That of the *Oxford English Dictionary* is indisputable but so cautious as to be useless: 'a developed or advanced state of

Without the pottery record, our knowledge of the Neolithic would be immeasurably tinier. Often that record is, in the most literal sense, fragmentary – a matter of bits and pieces. But sometimes there is enough to show what was already capable of being achieved in societies far from 'civilized'. This beaker comes from the high Iranian plateau east of the Zagros mountains and is dated about 4000 BC. It was an area with a long history of painted pottery already; in some other parts of the Near East there was pottery two thousand years before this.

human society'. What we have still to make up our minds about is *how far* developed or advanced and along what lines.

Some have said that a civilized society is different from an uncivilized society because it has a certain attribute – writing, cities, monumental building, are some of those suggested. But agreement is difficult and it seems safer not to rely on any such single test. If, instead, we look at examples of what everyone has agreed to call civilizations and not at the marginal and doubt-

ful cases, then it is obvious that what they have in common is complexity. They have all reached a level of elaboration which allows much more variety of human action and experience than even a well-off primitive community. Civilization is the name we give to the interaction of human beings in a very creative way, when, as it were, a critical mass of cultural potential and a certain surplus of resources has been built up. In civilization this releases human capacities for development at quite a new level and in large measure the development which follows is self-sustaining.

This is somewhat abstract and it is time to turn to examples. Somewhere about 3500 BC is the starting-point of the story of civilizations and it will be helpful to set out a rough overall chronology right at the start. We begin with the first recognizable civilization in Mesopotamia. The next example is in Egypt, where civilization is observable at a slightly later date, perhaps about 3100 BC. Another marker in the Near East is Minoan civilization in Crete, appearing about 2000 BC, and from that time we can disregard

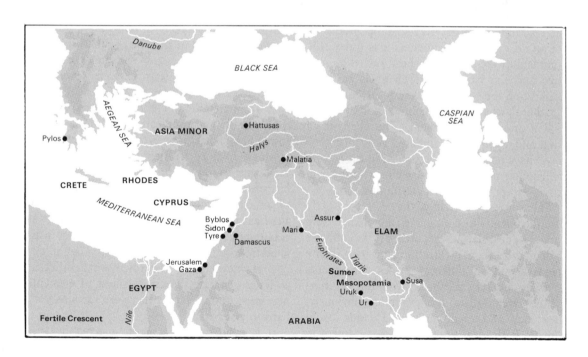

questions of priorities in this part of the world; it is already a complex of civilizations in interplay with one another. Meanwhile, by that time, perhaps about 2500 BC, another civilization has appeared in India and it is at least in a measure literate. China's first civilization starts later, towards the middle of the second millennium BC. Later still come the meso-Americans. Once we are past about 1500 BC, though, only this last example is sufficiently isolated for interaction not to be a big part of explaining what happens. From that time, there are no civilizations to be explained which appear without the stimulus, shock or inheritance provided by others which have appeared earlier. For the moment, then, a preliminary sketch is complete enough at this point.

About these first civilizations (whose appearance and shaping is the subject-matter of the next few chapters) it is very difficult to generalize. Of course they all show a low level of technological achievement, even if it is astonishingly high by comparison with that of their uncivilized predecessors. To this extent their shape and development was still determined to a much larger degree than our own by their setting. Yet they had already begun to overcome the restraints of geography. The topography of the world was already much as it is today; the continents were settled in the forms they now have and the barriers and channels to communication they supplied were to be constants, but there was a growing technological ability to exploit and transcend them. The currents of wind and water which directed early maritime travel have not changed, and even in the second millennium BC men were learning to use them and to escape from their determining force.

This suggests, correctly, that at a very early date the possibilities of human interchange were very considerable and this makes it very unwise to dogmatize about civilization appearing in any standard way in different places. Arguments have been put forward about favourable environments, river valleys for example: obviously, their rich and easily cultivated lands could support fairly dense populations of farmers in

villages which would then grow to form the first cities. In Mesopotamia, Egypt, the Indus valley and China this factor was present. But cities and civilizations have also arisen away from river valleys, in meso-America, Minoan Crete and, later, in Greece. With the last two, there is the strong likelihood of important influence from the outside, but Egypt and the Indus valley, too, were in touch with Mesopotamia at a very early date in their evolution. Evidence of such contact led at one time to the alternative view that we should look for one central source of civilization from which all others came. This is not now very popular. There is not only the difficult case of civilization in the isolated Americas to deal with, but great difficulty in getting the timetable of the supposed diffusion right as more and more knowledge of early chronology is acquired by the techniques of radio-carbon dating.

The most satisfactory answer appears to be that civilization was likely always to result from the coming together of a number of factors predisposing a particular area to throw up something dense enough to be recognized later as civilization, but that different environments, different influences from outside and different cultural inheritances from the past mean that men did not move in all parts of the world at the same pace or even towards the same goals. The idea of a standard pattern of social 'evolution' was discredited even before the idea of 'diffusion' from a common civilizing source. Clearly, a favourable geographical setting was essential; in the first civilizations everything rested on the existence of an agricultural surplus. But another factor just as important was cultural – the capacity of the peoples on the spot to take advantage of an environment or rise to a challenge, and here external contacts may be as important as tradition. China seems at first sight almost insulated from the outside, but there are possibilities of contact even here. The way in which different societies generate the critical mass of elements necessary to civilization therefore remains very hard to visualize.

It is easier to say something generally true

This little picture of a scene at a Sumerian dairy was executed in limestone and shell set into bitumen. It probably decorated the walls of a temple dedicated to a fertility goddess often symbolized by a cow.

about the marks of early civilization than about the way it happened. Again, no absolute and universal statements are plausible. Civilizations have existed without writing, useful as it is for storing and using experience. More mechanical skills have been very unevenly distributed, too: the meso-Americans carried out major building operations with neither draught animals nor the wheel, and the Chinese could cast iron nearly fifteen hundred years before Europeans. Nor have all civilizations followed the same patterns of growth; there are wide disparities between their staying-power, let alone their successes.

None the less, early civilizations, like later ones, seem to have a common positive characteristic in that they change the human scale of things. They bring together the cooperative efforts of larger numbers of men than any earlier societies and usually do this by physically bringing them together in larger agglomerations, too. As the word 'civilization' suggests, it is usually marked by urbanization. Admittedly, it would be a bold man who was willing to draw a precise line at the moment when the balance tipped from a dense pattern of agricultural villages clustered around a religious centre or a market to reveal the first true city. Yet it is perfectly reasonable to say that more than any other institution the city has provided the critical mass which produces civilization and that it has fostered innovation better than any other environment so far. Inside the city the surpluses of wealth produced by agriculture made pos-

sible other things characteristic of civilized life. They provided for the upkeep of a priestly class which elaborated a complex religious structure, leading to the construction of great buildings with more than merely economic functions, and eventually to the writing down of literature. Much bigger resources than in earlier times were thus allocated to something other than immediate consumption and this meant a storing of enterprise and experience in new forms. The accumulated culture gradually became a more and more effective instrument for changing the world.

One change is quickly apparent: in different parts of the world men grew more rapidly more unlike one another. The most obvious fact about early civilizations is that they are startlingly different in style, but because it is so obvious we usually ignore it. The coming of civilization opens an era of ever more rapid differentiation – of dress, architecture, technology, behaviour, social forms and thought. The roots of this obviously lie in prehistory, when there already existed men with different life-styles, different patterns of existence, different mentalities, as well as different physical characteristics. With the emergence of the first civilizations this becomes much more obvious, but is no longer merely the product of the natural endowment as environment, but of the creative power of civilization itself. Only with the rise to dominance of Western technology in the twentieth century has this variety begun to diminish. From the first civilizations to our own day there have always been alternative models of society available even if they knew little of one another.

Much of this variety is very hard to recover. All that we can do in some instances is to be aware that it is there. At the beginning there is still little evidence about the life of the mind except institutions so far as we can recover them, symbols in art and ideas embodied in literature. In them lie presuppositions which are the great coordinates around which a view of the world is built – even when the people holding that view do not know they are there (history is often the recovery of what people did not know about themselves). Many of them are irrecoverable, and even when we can begin to grasp the shapes which defined the world of men living in the old civilizations, a constant effort of imagination must be made to hold in our minds the danger of falling into anachronism which surrounds us on every side. Even literacy does not reveal very much of the minds of creatures so like and yet so unlike ourselves.

It is in the Near East that the stimulating effects of different cultures upon one another first become obvious and no doubt it is much of the story of the appearance of the earliest civilizations there. A turmoil of racial comings and goings for three or four thousand years both enriched and disrupted this area, where our history must begin. The Fertile Crescent was to be for most of historic times a great crucible of cultures, a zone not only of settlement but of transit, through which poured an ebb and flow of people and ideas. In the end this produced a fertile interchange of institutions, language and belief from which stems much of human thought and custom even today.

Why this began to happen cannot exactly be explained, but the overwhelming presumption must be that the root cause was over-population in the lands from which the intruders came. Over-population is at first sight a curious notion to apply to a world whose total population in about 4000 BC has been estimated only at between eighty and ninety millions. In the next four thousand years it grew by about fifty per cent to about one hundred and thirty millions; this implies an annual increase almost imperceptible by comparison with those we take for granted. It shows both the relative slowness with which men added to their power to exploit the natural world and how much and how soon

the new possibilities of civilization had already reinforced Man's propensity to multiply and prosper by comparison with prehistoric times.

Such growth was still slight by later standards because it was always based on a very fragile margin of resources and it is this fragility which justifies talk of over-population. Drought or desiccation could dramatically and suddenly destroy an area's capacity to feed itself and it was to be thousands of years before food could easily be brought from elsewhere. The immediate results must often have been famine, but in the longer run there were others more important. The disturbances which resulted were the prime movers of early history; climatic change was still at work as a determinant, though now in much more local and specific ways. Droughts, catastrophic storms, even a few decades of marginally lower or higher temperatures, could force peoples to get on the move and so help to bring on civilization by throwing together peoples of different tradition. In collision and cooperation they learnt from one another and so increased the total potential of their societies.

The peoples who are the actors of early history in the Near East all belonged to the light-skinned human family (sometimes confusingly termed Caucasian) which is one of the three major ethnic classifications of the species *Homo sapiens* (the others being Negroid and Mongoloid). Linguistic differences make it possible to distinguish them further. All the peoples in the Fertile Crescent of early civilized times can be assigned either to the Hamitic stocks who evolved in Africa north and north-east of the Sahara, to the Semites of the Arabian peninsula, to the Indo-Europeans who, from southern Russia, had spread also by 4000 BC into Europe and Iran, or to the true 'Caucasians' of Georgia. These are the *dramatis personae* of early Near Eastern history. Their historic centres all lay round the zone in which agriculture and civilization appear at an early date. The attractive force for such peripheral peoples of the wealth of this well-settled area is obvious.

By about 4000 BC most of the Fertile Crescent was occupied by Caucasians. Probably Semitic peoples had already begun to penetrate it by then, too; their pressure grew until by the middle of the third millennium BC (well after the appearance of civilization) they would be well established in central Mesopotamia, across the middle sections of the Tigris and Euphrates. The interplay and rivalry of the Semitic peoples with the Caucasians, who were able to hang on to the higher lands which enclosed Mesopotamia from the north-east, is one continuing theme scholars have discerned in the early history of the area. By 2000 BC the peoples whose languages form part of what is called the 'Indo-European' group have also entered on the scene, and from two directions. One of these peoples, the Hittites, pushed into Anatolia from Europe, while their advance was matched from the east by that of the Iranians. Between 2000 BC and 1500 BC branches of these sub-units dispute and mingle with the Semitic and Caucasian peoples in the Crescent itself, while the contacts of the Hamites and Semites lie behind much of the political history of old Egypt. This scenario is, of course, highly impressionistic. Its value is only that it helps to indicate the basic dynamism and rhythms of the history of the ancient Near East. Its detailed operation is highly uncertain (as will appear) and little can be said about what maintained this fluidity. None the less, whatever its cause, this wandering of peoples was the background against which the first civilization appeared and prospered.

2 Ancient Mesopotamia

The best case for the emergence of something which is recognizably civilization has been made for the southern part of Mesopotamia, the seven-hundred-mile-long land formed by the two river valleys of the Tigris and Euphrates. This end of the Fertile Crescent was thickly studded with farming villages in Neolithic times. Some of the oldest settlements of all seem to have been in the extreme south where deposits from centuries of drainage from up-country and annual floodings had built up a soil of great richness. It must always have been much easier to grow crops there than elsewhere

Between four and five thousand years ago, little statues like these were carved by Mesopotamians and placed in shrines where they were to pray and worship on behalf of those they represented. Perhaps they were statues of the sculptors and their families, perhaps those of wealthy men who commissioned them. The second is more likely: stone was scarce and must have been expensive in Sumer (the tallest of these figures is only about thirty inches high). These examples were discovered in what had been a pit under the floor of a temple at Tel Asmar, on a tributary of the Tigris. Besides throwing light on the way the Mesopotamians worshipped, they tell us something of the daily appearance of men and women of early civilization.

provided that the water supply could be made continuously and safely available; this was possible, for though rain was slight and irregular, the river-bed was often above the level of the surrounding plain. A calculation has been made that in about 2500 BC the yield of grain in southern Mesopotamia compared favourably with that of the best Canadian wheatfields. Here, at an early date, was the possibility of growing more than was needed for daily consumption, a possibility therefore of that surplus of production which was indispensable to the appearance of town life. Furthermore, fish could be taken from the nearby sea.

Such a setting was a challenge, as well as an opportunity. The Tigris and Euphrates could suddenly and violently change their beds: the marshy, low-lying land of the delta had to be raised above flood-level by banking and ditching and canals built to take water from them. Thousands of years later, techniques could still be seen in use in Mesopotamia which were probably those first employed to form the platforms of reed and mud on which were built the first homesteads of the area. These patches of cultivation would be grouped where the soil was richest and the drains that drained them and the irrigation channels they all needed could only be managed properly if they were managed collectively. No doubt the social organization of reclamation was another result. However it happened, the seemingly unprecedented achievement of making land from watery marsh must have been the forcing house of a new complexity in the way men lived together.

As the population rose, more land was taken to grow food. Sooner or later men of different villages must have come face to face with others intent on reclaiming marsh which had previously separated them from one another. Differing irrigation needs may even have brought them into contact before this. There was a choice: to fight or to cooperate. Either course meant another stage of collective organization and a new agglomeration of power. Somewhere along this path it made sense for men to band together in bigger units than hitherto for self-protection or management of the environment. One physical result is the town, mud-walled at first to keep out floods and enemies, raised above the waters on a platform. It was logical for the local deity's shrine to be the place chosen: he stood behind the community's authority. It would be exercised by his chief priest, who became the ruler of a little theocracy competing with others.

Something like this explains the differences between southern Mesopotamia in the third and fourth millennia BC and the other zones of Neolithic culture with which by then it had already been long in contact. There is plenty of evidence in the existence of pottery and characteristic shrines of links between Mesopotamia and the Neolithic cultures of Anatolia, Assyria and Iran. They all had much in common. But only in one relatively small area did a pattern of village life common to much of the Near East begin to grow faster and harden into something else. From that background emerges the first true urbanism, that of Sumer, and the first observable civilization.

Sumer is an ancient name for southern Mesopotamia, which then extended about a hundred miles less to the south than it does now. The people who lived there may have been Caucasians, unlike their Semitic neighbours to the south-west and like their northern neighbours the Elamites who lived on the other side of the Tigris. Scholars are still divided about when the Sumerians – that is, those who spoke the language later called Sumerian – arrived in the area: they may have been there since about 4000 BC. But since we know the population of

civilized Sumer to be a mixture of races, perhaps including the earlier inhabitants of the region, with a culture which mixed foreign and local elements, it does not much matter. As one scholar has helpfully observed, 'they may have "always" been in Iraq, and this is all we can say'.

Sumerian civilization had deep roots. The people long shared a way of life not very different from that of their neighbours. They lived in villages and had a few important cult centres which were long and continuously occupied. One of these, at a place called Eridu, probably originated in about 5000 BC. It grew steadily well into historic times and by the middle of the fourth millenium there was a temple there which some have thought to have provided the original model for Mesopotamian monumental architecture, though nothing is now left of it but the platform on which it rested. Such cult centres began by serving those who lived near them. They were not true cities, but places of devotion and pilgrimage. They may have had no considerable resident populations, but they were usually the centres around which cities later crystallized and this helps to explain the close relationship religion and government always had in ancient Mesopotamia. Well before 3000 BC some such sites had very big temples indeed; at Uruk (which is called Erech in the Bible) there was an especially splendid one, with elaborate decoration and impressive pillars of mud brick, eight feet in diameter.

Pottery is among the most important evidence linking pre-civilized Mesopotamia with historic times. It provides one of the first clues that something culturally important is going forward which is qualitatively different from the evolutions of the Neolithic. The so-called Uruk pots (the name is derived from a site where they were found) are often duller, less exciting than earlier ones. They are, in fact, mass-produced, made in standard form on a wheel. The implication of this is strong that when they came to be produced there already existed a population of specialized craftsmen; it must have been maintained by an agriculture sufficiently rich to produce a surplus exchanged for their creations. It is with this change that the story of Sumerian civilization can conveniently be begun.

It lasts about thirteen hundred years (roughly from 3300 to 2000 BC), which is about as much time as separates us from the age of Charlemagne. At the beginning comes the invention of writing, possibly the only invention of comparable importance to the invention of agriculture until we reach the age of steam. Writing had been preceded by the invention of cylinder seals, on which little pictures were incised to be

rolled on to clay; pottery may have degenerated, but these seals were one of the great Mesopotamian artistic achievements. The earliest writings are in the form of pictograms or simplified pictures on clay tablets (a step towards non-representational communication), usually baked after they had been inscribed with a reed stalk. The earliest are in Sumerian and it can be seen that they are memoranda, lists of goods, receipts (their emphasis is economic); they cannot be read as continuous prose. The writing on these early notebooks and ledgers

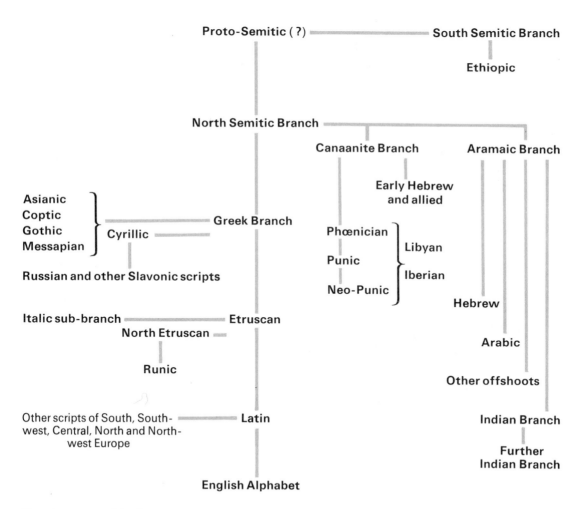

Development of Scripts

evolved slowly towards cuneiform, a way of arranging impressions stamped on clay by the wedge-like section of a chopped-off reed. With this the break with the pictogram form is complete. Signs and groups of signs come at this stage to stand for phonetic and possibly syllabic elements and are all made up of combinations of the same basic wedge shape. It was more flexible as a form of communication by signs than anything used hitherto and Sumer reached it soon after 3000 BC.

A fair amount is known about the Sumerian language. A few of its words have survived to

The impression left by the Gilgamesh seal, a Mesopotamian cylinder seal from the early centuries of the third millennium: the seal was rolled over soft clay to form a continuous pattern like a frieze which could be stopped at any point. They survive in many designs. One of the most frequent themes is the combat of animals with one another, with heroic figures of men, or with mysterious bearded, quasi-human bulls. A recurrent pattern shows a symmetrical group of a hero holding at bay – or helpless – two animals, one on each side of him, an image of mastery over the animal world which crops up again and again in the art of many different traditions and peoples.

this day; one of them is the original form of the word 'alcohol', which is suggestive. But the interest of the language as a social fact lies above all in its appearance in written forms.

Literacy must have been both unsettling and stabilizing. On the one hand it offered new possibilities of communicating knowledge; on the other it stabilized practice because the consultation of record became possible. It made much easier the complex operations of irrigating lands, harvesting and storing crops, which were fundamental to a growing society. Writing was another force making for more efficient exploitation of resources. It also immensely strengthened government and emphasized its links with the priestly castes who at first monopolized literacy. Interestingly, one of the earliest uses of seals appears to be connected with this, since they were used somehow to certify the size of crops at their receipt in the temple. Perhaps they record at first the operations of an economy of centralized redistribution, where men bring their due produce to the temple and receive there the food or materials they themselves need.

Besides such records, the invention of writing opens more of the past to the historian in another way. He can at last begin to deal in hard currency when talking about mentality because writing opens the way to recording literature. The oldest story in the world is the Epic of Gilgamesh. The most complete version of this story, it is true, goes back only to the seventh century BC, but the story itself appears in Sumerian times and is known to have been written down soon after 2000 BC. Gilgamesh was a real person, ruling at Uruk. He became also the first individual and hero in world literature, appearing in other poems, too, and the first person whose name must appear in this book. To a modern reader the most striking part of the Epic is the coming of a great flood which obliterates mankind except for a favoured family who survive by building an ark; from them springs a new race to people the world after the flood has subsided. This was not part of the Epic in its oldest versions, but a separate poem telling a story which turns up in many Near-Eastern forms, though its incorporation is easily understandable. Lower Mesopotamia must always have had much trouble with flooding which would undoubtedly put a heavy strain on the fragile system of irrigation on which its prosperity depended. Floods were the type, perhaps, of general disaster, and must have helped to foster the pessimistic fatalism which some scholars have seen as the key to Sumerian religion.

This sombre mood dominates the Epic. Gilgamesh does great things in his restless search to assert himself against the iron laws of the gods which ensure human failure, but they triumph in the end. Gilgamesh, too, must die.

The heroes, the wise men, like the new moon have their waxing and waning. Men will say, 'Who has ever ruled with might and with power like him?' As in the dark month, the month of shadows, so without him there is no light. O Gilgamesh, this was the meaning of your dream. You were given the kingship, such was your destiny; everlasting life was not your destiny.

Apart from this mood and its revelation of the religious temperament of a civilization, there is much information about the gods of ancient Mesopotamia in the Epic. But it is hard to get at history through it, even more to relate it to the historical Gilgamesh. In particular, attempts to identify a single, cataclysmic flood by archaeological means have not been convincing, though plentiful evidence of recurrent flooding is available. From the water eventually emerges the land: perhaps, then, what we are being given is an account of the creation of the world, of genesis. In the Hebrew Bible earth emerges from the waters at God's will and this account was the one which was to satisfy most educated Europeans for a thousand years. It is fascinating to speculate that we may owe so much of our own intellectual ancestry to a mythical reconstruction by the Sumerians of their own prehistory when farming land had been created out of the morass of the Mesopotamian delta. But it is only speculation; caution suggests we remain satisfied merely to note the undeniable close parallels between the Epic and one of the best of the Bible stories, that of Noah's Ark.

This story hints at the possible importance of the diffusion of Sumerian ideas in the Near East long after the focus of its history had moved away to upper Mesopotamia. Versions and parts of the Epic – to stick to that text alone for a moment – have turned up in the archives and relics of many peoples who dominated parts of this region in the second millennium BC. Though later to be lost to sight until rediscovery in modern times, Gilgamesh was for two thousand years or so a name to which literature in many languages could knowingly refer, somewhat in the way, say, that European authors until recently could take it for granted that an allusion to classical Greece would be understood by their readers. The Sumerian language lived on for centuries in temples and scribal schools, much as Latin lived on for the learned in the muddle of vernacular cultures in Europe after the collapse of the western classical world of Rome. The comparison is suggestive, because literary and linguistic tradition embodies ideas and images which impose and permit ways of seeing the world; they have, that is to say, their own historic weight.

Probably the most important ideas kept alive by Sumerian language were religious. Cities like

Ur and Uruk were the seedbed of ideas which, after transmutation into other religions in the Near East during the first and second millennia BC, were four thousand years later to be influential world wide, albeit in almost unrecognizably different forms. There is, for example, in the Gilgamesh Epic an ideal creature of nature, the man Enkidu; his Fall from his innocence is sexual, a seduction by a harlot, and thereafter, though the outcome for him is civilization, he loses his happy association with nature. Literature makes it possible to observe such hints at the mythologies of other and later societies. In literature, men begin to make explicit meanings earlier hidden in the obscure relics of sacrificial offerings, clay figures and the ground plans of shrines and temples. In earliest Sumer these already reveal an organization of human discourse with the supernatural much more complex and elaborate than anything elsewhere at so early a date. Temples had been the focus of the early cities and they grew bigger and more splendid (in part, because of a tradition of building new ones on mounds enclosing their predecessors). Sacrifices were offered in these temples to ensure good crops. Later their cults elaborated, temples of greater magnificence were built as far north as Assur, three hundred miles away up the Tigris, and we hear of one built with cedars brought from the Lebanon and copper from Anatolia.

No other ancient society at that time gave religion quite so prominent a place or diverted so much of its collective resources to its support.

'Screech owl' was the way the English translators of the Old Testament rendered the name of a Mesopotamian goddess called Lilith (Isaiah, xxxiv, 14): was this terracotta relief an image of her? It dates from the centuries after 2000 BC when the last Sumerian dynasty had been swept away by invaders and old Sumer had settled down into a collection of city-states. Winged and taloned, she stands upon lions resting on a rock plinth which is a conventional Mesopotamian representation of a mountain or high place where a god might dwell.

It has been suggested that this was because no other ancient society left men feeling so utterly dependent on the will of the gods. Lower Mesopotamia in ancient times was a flat, monotonous landscape of mudflats, marsh, water. There were no mountains for the gods to dwell in like men, only the empty heavens above, the remorseless summer sun, the overturning winds against which there was no protection, the irresistible power of flood-water, the blighting attacks of drought. The gods dwelt in these, or in the 'high places' which alone dominated the plains, the brick-built towers and Ziggurats remembered in the biblical Tower of Babel. The Sumerians believed, not surprisingly, that they had been created to work for the gods.

By about 2250 BC a pantheon of gods more or less personifying the elements and natural forces had emerged in Sumer. It was to be the backbone of Mesopotamian religion. This is the beginning of theology. Originally, each city had its particular god. Possibly helped by political changes in the relations of the cities, they were in the end organized into a kind of hierarchy which both reflected and affected men's views of human society. The gods of Mesopotamia in the developed scheme are depicted in human form. To each of them was given a special activity or rôle; there was a god of the air, another of the water, another of the plough. Ishtar (as she was later known under her Semitic name) was the goddess of love and procreation, but also of war. At the top of the hierarchy were three great male gods, whose rôles are not easy to disentangle, Anu, Enlil and Enki. Anu was father of the gods. Enlil was at first the most prominent; he was 'Lord Air', without whom nothing could be done. Enki, god of wisdom and of the sweet waters that literally meant life to Sumer, was a teacher and life-giver, who maintained the order Enlil had shaped.

These gods demanded propitiation and submission in elaborate ritual. In return for this and for living a good life they would grant prosperity and length of days, but not more. In the midst of the uncertainties of Mesopotamian life, some

71

feeling that a possible access to protection existed was essential. Men depended on the gods for reassurance in a capricious universe. The gods – though no Mesopotamian could have put it in these terms – were the conceptualization of an elementary attempt to control environment, to resist the sudden disasters of flood and dust-storm, to assure the continuation of the cycle of the seasons by the repetition of the great spring festival when the gods were again married and the drama of Creation was re-enacted. 'Only then could the king go back to his throne, the shepherd to his flock, the peasant to his field. The Mesopotamian was reassured: the world would exist for another year.'

One of the great demands which men later came to make of religion was that it should help them to deal with the inevitable horror of death. The Sumerians and those who inherited their religious ideas can hardly have derived much comfort from their beliefs, in so far as we can apprehend them; they seem to have seen the world of life after death as a gloomy, sad place. It was 'The house where they sit in darkness, where dust is their food and clay their meat, they are clothed like birds with wings for garments, over bolt and door lie dust and silence.' In it lies the origin of the later notions of Sheol, of Hell. Yet at least one ritual involved virtual suicide, for a Sumerian king and queen of the middle of the third millennium were followed to their tombs by their attendants who were then buried with them, perhaps after taking some soporific drink. This suggests that the dead were going somewhere where a great retinue and gorgeous jewellery would be as important as on earth.

There were important political aspects to Sumerian religion. All land belonged ultimately to the gods; the king, probably a king-priest as much as a warrior-leader in origin, was but their vicar. No human tribunal, of course, existed to call him to account. The vicariate also meant the emergence of a priestly class, specialists whose importance justified economic privilege which could permit the cultivation of special skills and knowledge. In this respect, too,

Some of the most beautiful objects which survive from Sumer were found in what has been called a 'royal cemetery' at Ur, where great personages were buried. Among the treasures found there were harps inlaid with lapis lazuli, jasper and shell set in bitumen and overlaid with gold leaf. This bearded bull was reconstructed from the crushed fragments of one of these instruments, made, perhaps, a century or two after 3000 BC.

Sumer was the origin of a tradition, that of the seers, soothsayers, wise men of the East. They also had charge of the first organized system of education, based on memorizing and copying in the cuneiform script.

One of the by-products of Sumerian religion was the first true likenesses of human beings in art. In particular at one religious centre, Mari, there seems to have been something of a fond-

ness for the portraying of human figures engaged in ritual acts. Sometimes they are grouped
in processions; thus is established one of the
great themes of pictorial art. Two others are also
prominent: war and the animal world. Some
have detected in the early portraiture of the
Sumerians a deeper significance. They have seen
in them the psychological qualities which made
the astonishing achievements of their civilization
possible, a drive for pre-eminence and success.
This, again, is speculative. What we can also see
for the first time in Sumerian art is much of a
daily life in earlier times hidden from us. Given
the widespread contacts of Sumer and its basic
similarity of structure to other, neighbouring
peoples, it is not too much to infer that we can
begin to see something of life much as it was
lived over a large area of the ancient Near East.

Seals, statuary and painting reveal a people
often clad in a kind of furry – goat-skin or

*Little wall-painting survives from ancient
Mesopotamia though we know there was much
of it about. This fragment comes from the king's
palace at Mari, in lower Assyria, sacked by
Hammurabi. It appears to depict some part
of a ceremony, perhaps a sacrificial procession.*

sheep-skin? – skirt, the women sometimes
throwing a fold of it over one shoulder. The
men are often, but not always, clean-shaven.
Soldiers wear the same costume and are only
distinguishable because they carry weapons and
sometimes wear a pointed leather cap. Luxury
seems to have consisted in leisure and possessions other than dress, except for jewellery, of
which quantities have survived. Its purpose
often seems to be the indication of status and it
symptomizes a society of growing complexity.
There survives, too, a picture of a drinking-
party; a group of men sit in armchairs with cups

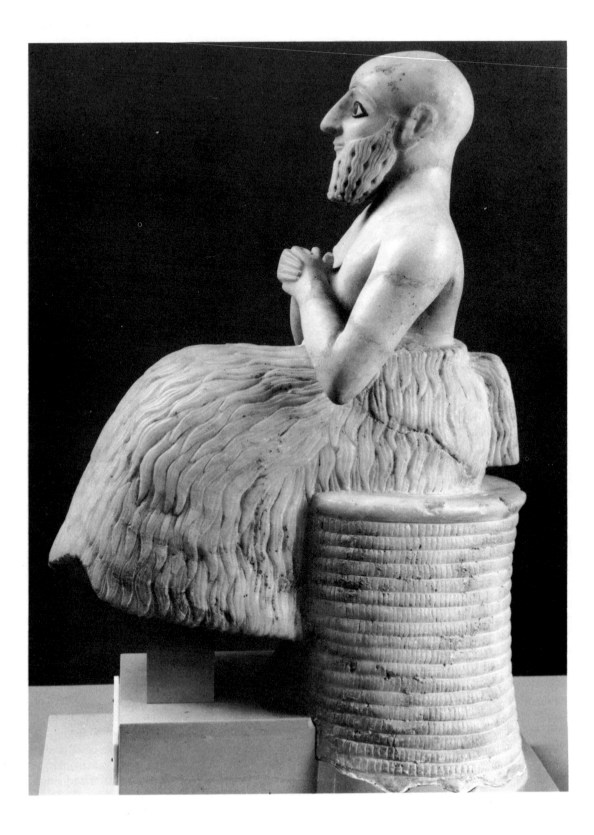

It seems that it was the fashion at Mari and in one or two other cities to shave the head while growing a luxuriant beard, emphasized by deep drilling in this portrait statue from Mari. It comes from the first half of the third millennium BC, when the earlier Sumerian tradition of sculpture was becoming more naturalistic and individual, and we confront individuals in these statues, even knowing the names of some of them. This was Ibihil, a steward.

in their hands while a musician entertains them. At such moments Sumer seems less remote.

Sumerian marriage had much about it which would have been familiar to later societies. The crux of the matter was the consent of the bride's family. Once arranged to their satisfaction, a new monogamous family unit was established by the marriage which was recorded in a sealed contract. Its head was the patriarchal husband, who presided over both his relatives and his slaves. It is a pattern which was until very recently observable in most parts of the world. Yet there are interesting nuances. Legal and literary evidence suggest that even in early times Sumerian women were less downtrodden than their sisters in many later Near-Eastern societies. Semitic and non-Semitic traditions may diverge in this. Sumerian stories of their gods suggest a society very conscious of the

dangerous and even awe-inspiring power of female sexuality; the Sumerians were the first people to write about passion.

It is not easy to relate such things to institutions, but Sumerian law (whose influence can be traced in post-Sumerian times well past 2000 BC) gave women important rights. A woman was not a mere chattel; even the slave mother of a free man's children had rights which could be protected at law. Divorce arrangements provided for women as well as men to seek separations and for the equitable treatment of divorced wives. Though a wife's adultery was punishable by death, while a husband's was not, this difference is to be understood in the light of concern over inheritance and property. It was not until long after Sumerian times that Mesopotamian law begins to emphasize the importance of virginity and to impose the veil on

Among the objects found in the royal graves of Ur was a richly inlaid and decorated object misleadingly known as a 'standard' but more probably the sounding-box of a harp. One side depicts a conquering king leading his army in war; on the other (shown here) he relaxes with the gentlemen of his court, perhaps in celebration of the victory whose booty is recorded in the two lower bands of decoration. It was probably made in about 2700 BC.

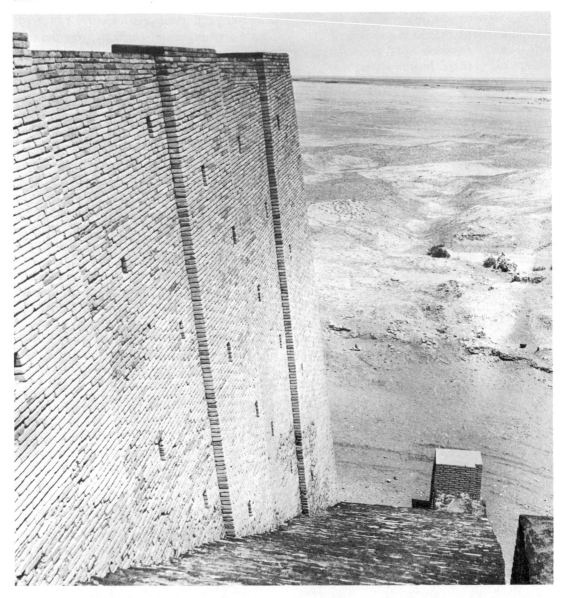

The external facing and one of the stairways of the great Ziggurat at Ur excavated by Sir Leonard Woolley, the greatest of Sumerian archaeologists. It was built by Urnammu, the founder of the last and most successful dynasty of rulers in Ur. It was a colossal achievement in the stoneless Sumerian plain and was venerated and maintained by the biblical Nebuchadnezzar, fifteen hundred years after it was first built.

respectable women. Both were signs of a hardening and more cramping rôle for them.

The Sumerians also demonstrated great technical inventiveness. Other peoples would owe much to them. It was they who laid the foundations of mathematics, establishing the technique of expressing number by position as well as by sign (as we, for example, can reckon the figure 1 as one, one-tenth, ten or several other values, according to its relation to the decimal point), and they arrived at a method of dividing the circle into six equal segments. They knew about the decimal system, too, but did not exploit it.

By the end of their history as an independent civilization they had learnt to live in big groups; one city alone is said to have had thirty-six thousand males. This made big demands on building skill, and even more were made by the large monumental structures. Lacking stone, southern Mesopotamians had first built in reeds plastered with mud, then with bricks made from the mud and dried in the sun. Their brick technology was advanced enough by the end of the Sumerian period to make possible very large buildings with columns and terraces; the greatest of its monuments, the Ziggurat of Ur, had an upper stage over a hundred feet high and a base two hundred feet by a hundred and fifty. The earliest surviving potter's wheel was found at Ur; this was the first way in which man made use of rotary motion and on it rested the large-scale production of pottery which made it a man's trade and not, like earlier pottery, a woman's. Soon, by 3000 BC, the wheel was being used for transport. Another invention of the Sumerians was glass, and specialized craftsmen were casting in bronze early in the third millennium BC.

This example of innovation is another which raises further questions: where did the raw material come from? There is no metal in southern Mesopotamia. Moreover, even in earlier times, during the Neolithic, the region must have obtained from elsewhere the flint and obsidian it needed for the first agricultural implements. Clearly a widespread network of contacts abroad is in the background, above all with the Levant and Syria, huge distances away, but also with Iran and Bahrein, down the Persian Gulf. Before 2000 BC Mesopotamia was obtaining goods – though possibly indirectly – from the Indus valley. Together with the evidence of documentation (which reveals contacts with India before 2000 BC), it makes an impression of a dimly emerging international trading system already creating important patterns of interdependence. When, in the middle of the

third millennium, supplies of tin from the Near East dried up, Mesopotamian bronze weapons had to give way to unalloyed copper ones.

The whole of this was sustained on an agriculture which was from an early date complicated as well as rich. Barley, wheat, millet and sesame were grains grown in quantity; the first may have been the main crop, and no doubt explains the frequent evidence of the importance of alcohol in ancient Mesopotamia. In the easy soil of the flood-beds iron tools were not needed to achieve intensive cultivation; the great contribution of technology here was in the practice of irrigation and the growth of government. Such skills accumulated slowly; the evidence of Sumerian civilization was left to us by fifteen hundred years of history.

So far this huge stretch of time has been discussed almost as if nothing happened during it, as if it were an unchanging whole. Of course it was not. Whatever reservations are made about the slowness of change in the ancient world and though it may now seem to us very static, these were fifteen centuries of great change for the Mesopotamians – history, in the true sense. Scholars have recovered much of the story, but this is not the place to set it out in detail, especially as much of it is still debated, much of it remains obscure and even its dating is for much of the time only approximate. All that is needed here is to relate the first age of Mesopotamian civilization to its successors and to what was going on elsewhere at the same time.

Three broad phases can be marked out in the history of Sumer. The first, lasting from about 3360 BC to 2400 BC has been called its archaic period. Its narrative content is a matter of wars between city-states, their waxings and wanings. Fortified cities and the application of the wheel to military technology in clumsy four-wheeled chariots are some of the evidence of this. Towards the middle of this nine-hundred-year phase, local dynasties begin to establish themselves with some success. Originally, Sumerian society seems to have had some representative, even democratic basis, but a growth of scale led to the emergence of kings whose power was

The new influence of the Semitic peoples of northern Mesopotamia which was manifested in the creation of the empire of Sargon I can be sensed in this bronze head from Nineveh, believed by some scholars to represent him. It suggests kingship's new stature; this ruler's confident grandeur surpasses that of his Sumerian predecessors and presents for the first time an awesomeness which was to pass into the tradition of Near Eastern empires for two and a half millennia.

distinct from that of the first priestly rulers; probably they began as warlords appointed by cities to command their forces who did not give up their power when the emergency which called them forth had passed. From them stemmed dynasties which fought one another. The sudden appearance of a great individual then opens a new phase.

This is Sargon I, a king of the Semitic city of Akkad who conquered the Sumerian cities between 2400 and 2350 BC and inaugurated an Akkadian supremacy. There exists a sculpted head which is probably of him; if it is, it is one of the first royal portraits. He was the first of a long line of empire-builders; he has been thought to have sent his troops as far as Egypt and Ethiopia. His rule was not based on the relative superiority of one city-state to another; he set up a unified empire integrating the cities into a whole. His people were among those which for thousands of years pressed in on the civilizations of the river valleys from outside. They took over from its culture what they wanted but imposed themselves by force and left behind a new style of Sumerian art marked by the theme of royal victory.

Akkadian empire was to prove not to be the end of Sumer but its second main phase. Though itself an interlude, it was important as an expression of a new level of organization. By Sargon's time a true state has appeared. The division between secular and religious authority which had appeared in old Sumer was fundamental. Though the supernatural still interpenetrated daily life at every level, lay and priestly authority had diverged. The evidence is physically apparent in the appearance of palaces beside the temples in the Sumerian cities; the authority of the gods lay behind their occupants, too.

Obscure though the turning of the notables of early cities into kings remains, the evolution of professional soldiery probably played a part in it. Disciplined infantry, moving in a phalanx with overlapping shields and levelled spears, appear on monuments from Ur. In Akkad there is something of a climax to early militarism. Sargon, it was boasted, had 5400 soldiers eating before him in his palace. This, no doubt, was the end of a process which built power on power; conquest provided the resources to maintain such a force. But the beginnings may again have lain originally in the special challenges and needs of Mesopotamia. As population rose, one chief duty of the ruler must have been the conscription of labour for big works of irrigation and flood-control. The power to do this could also provide soldiers and as weapons became more complex and expensive, professionalism

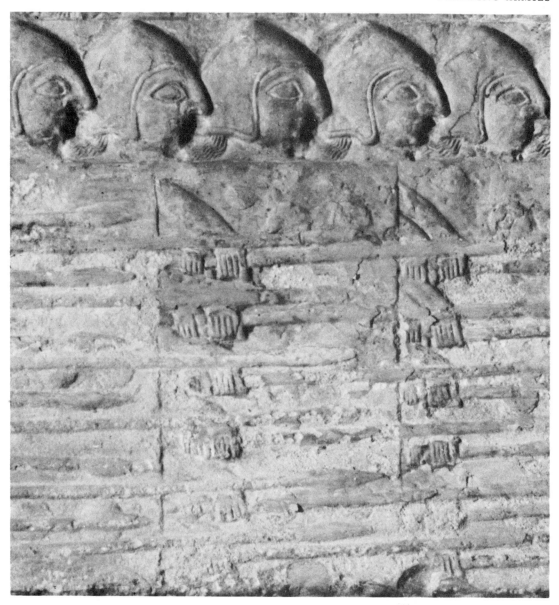

would be more likely. One source of Akkadian success was that they used a new weapon, the composite bow made of strips of wood and horn.

The Akkadian hegemony was relatively short. After two hundred years, under Sargon's great-grandson, it was overthrown, apparently by mountain peoples called Gutians, and the last phase of Sumer, called 'neo-Sumerian' by

Sumerian soldiers in action early in the third millennium BC. This mass of spearmen protected by shield-bearers was carved to commemorate the victory of a king of Lagash over a nearby city-state. Such monuments were no doubt frequent, but only a few fragments survive – perhaps because they were deliberately shattered when the wheel of fortune turned.

scholars, began. For another two hundred years or so, until 2000 BC, hegemony again passed to the native Sumerians. This time its centre was Ur and, though it is hard to see what it meant in practice, the first king of the Third Dynasty of Ur who exercised this ascendancy called himself King of Sumer and Akkad. Sumerian art in this phase showed a new tendency to exalt the power of the prince; the tradition of popular portraiture of the archaic period almost vanished. The temples were built again, bigger and better, and the kings seem to have sought to embody their grandeur in the Ziggurats. Administrative documents show that the Akkadian legacy was strong, too; neo-Sumerian culture shows many Semitic traits and perhaps the aspiration to wider kingship reflects this inheritance. The last successful kings of Ur ruled provinces paying tribute which stretched from Susa, on the frontiers of Elam, to Byblos on the coast of Lebanon.

This was the sunset of the first people to achieve civilization. Of course they did not disappear, but their individuality was about to be merged in the general history of Mesopotamia and the Near East. Their great creative era was behind them and has focussed our attention on a relatively small area; the horizons of history are about to expand. Enemies abounded on the frontiers. In about 2000 BC, the Elamites came and Ur fell to them. Why, we do not know. There had been intermittent hostility between the peoples for a thousand years and some have seen in this the outcome of a struggle to control the routes of Iran which could guarantee access to the highlands where lay minerals the Mesopotamians needed. At all events, it was the end of Ur. With it disappeared the distinctive Sumerian tradition, now merged in the swirling currents of a world of more than one civilization. It would now be only visible from time to time in patterns made by others. For fifteen centuries or so Sumer had built up the subsoil of civilization in Mesopotamia, just as its precivilized forerunners had built up the physical subsoil on which it itself rested. It left behind writing, monumental buildings, an idea

Another royal portrait, this time from the post-Akkadian and neo-Sumerian era. Gudea was ruler in Lagash in about 2100 BC. Mysteriously, the city seems to have escaped submission to the Gutians and to have prospered under Gudea and his son. No doubt this has something to do with the survival of about twenty different statues of this king, all of them showing the complacency and strength which literary sources suggests he drew from his life or prudent and pious service to the gods. The statue is a fine example of a resumed Sumerian tradition, which surpasses earlier examples.

of justice and legalism and the roots of a great religious tradition. It is a considerable record and the seed of much else. The Mesopotamian tradition had a long life ahead of it and every side of it was touched by the Sumerian legacy.

While the Sumerians had been building up their civilization, their influence had contributed to changes elsewhere. All over the Fertile Crescent new kingdoms and peoples had been appearing. They were stimulated or taught by what they saw in the south and by the empire of Ur, as well as by their own needs. The diffusion of civilized techniques was already rapid. This makes it very hard to delineate and categorize the main processes of these centuries in a clear-cut way. Worse still, the Near East was for long periods a great confusion of peoples, moving about for reasons we often do not understand. The Akkadians themselves had been one of them, pushing up originally from the great Semitic reservoir of Arabia to finish in Mesopotamia. The Gutians, a people which took part in the Akkadians' overthrow, were Caucasians. The most successful of all of them were a group called Amorites, Semites who had spread far and wide and joined the Elamites to overthrow the armies of Ur and destroy its supremacy. They had established themselves in Assyria, or upper Mesopotamia, in Damascus, and in Babylon in a series of kingdoms which stretched as far as the coast of Palestine. Southern Mesopotamia, old Sumer, they continued to dispute with the Elamites. In Anatolia their neighbours were the Hittites, an Indo-European people which crossed from the Balkans in the third millennium. At the edges of this huge confusion stood another old civilization, Egypt, and the vigorous Indo-European peoples who had filled up Iran. The picture is a chaos; the area is a maelstrom of races pushing into it from all sides. Patterns grow hard to distinguish.

One convenient landmark is provided by the appearance of a new empire in Mesopotamia, one which has left behind a famous name: Babylon. Another famous name is inseparably linked to it, that of one of its kings, Hammurabi. He would have a secure place in history if we knew nothing of him except his reputation as a law-giver; his code is the oldest statement of the legal principle of an eye for an eye. He was also the first ruler to unify the whole of Mesopotamia, and though the empire was short-lived the city of Babylon was to be from this time the symbolic centre of the Semitic peoples of the south.

It began with the triumph of one Amorite tribe over its rivals in the confused period following the collapse of Ur. Hammurabi may have become ruler in 1792 BC; his successors held things together until sometime after 1600 BC, when the Hittites destroyed Babylon and Mesopotamia was once more divided between rival peoples who flowed into it from all sides.

At its height the first Babylonian empire ran from Sumeria and the Persian Gulf north to Assyria, the upper part of Mesopotamia. Hammurabi ruled the cities of Nineveh and Nimrud on the Tigris, Mari high on the Euphrates, and controlled that river up to the point at which it is nearest to Aleppo. Seven hundred or so miles long and about a hundred miles wide, this was a great state, the greatest, indeed, to appear in the region up to this time, for the empire of Ur had been a looser, tributary affair. It had an elaborate administrative structure, and Hammurabi's code of laws is justly famous, though it owes something of its pre-eminence to chance. As was probably the case with earlier collections of judgments and rules, which have only survived in fragments, Hammurabi's was cut in stone and set up in the courtyard of temples for the public to consult. But it assembled at greater length and in a more ordered way than earlier collections some 282 articles, dealing comprehensively with a wide range of questions: wages, divorce, fees for medical attention and many other matters. This was not legislation, but a declaration of existing law, and to speak of a 'code' may be misleading unless this is remembered. Hammurabi assembled rules already current which would long continue to regulate Mesopotamian society with only occasional modifications; he did not create those laws *de novo*. This body of 'common law' provided one of the major continuities of Mesopotamian history.

The family, land and commerce seem to be the main concerns of this compilation of rules. It gives a picture of a society already far beyond regulation by the ties of kindred, local community and the government of village headmen. By Hammurabi's time the judicial process had

emerged from the temple and non-priestly courts were the rule. In them sat the local town notables and from them appeals lay to Babylon and the king himself. Hammurabi's stele (the stone pillar on which his code was carved) clearly stated that its aim was to assure justice by publishing the law so that all men might read it:

Let the oppressed man who has a cause
Come into the presence of my statue
And read carefully my inscribed stele,

it says. Sadly, perhaps, its penalties seem to have harshened, by comparison with older Sumerian practice, but in other respects, such as the laws affecting women, Sumerian tradition was still intact in Babylon.

The code's provisions in respect of property included laws about slaves. Babylon, like every other ancient civilization and many of modern times, rested on slavery. Very possibly the origin of slavery is conquest; certainly slavery was the fate which probably awaited the loser of any of the wars of early history and his women and children, too. But by the time of the first Babylonian empire, regular slave-markets existed and there was a steadiness of price which indicates a fairly regular trade. Slaves from certain districts were regarded as especially valuable for their reliable qualities. Though the master's hold on the slave was virtually absolute, some Babylonian slaves enjoyed remarkable independence, engaging in business and even owning slaves on their own account. They had legal rights, if narrow ones.

It is hard to assess what slavery meant in practice in a world lacking the assumption which we take for granted that chattel slavery

Hammurabi stands before the Sun God, the law-giver before the source of all justice, conversing with him almost – but not quite – as an equal. This relief forms the tip of a large stone stele, seven feet high and three in circumference at its base, on the rest of which is inscribed in cuneiform Hammurabi's famous code, set up that all men might read.

cannot be justified. Generalities dissolve in the light of evidence about the diversity of things slaves might do; if most lived hard lives, then so, probably, did most men. Yet it is hard to feel anything but pity for the lives of captives being led away to slavery before conquering kings on scores of memorials from the 'golden standard' of Ur in the middle of the third millennium to the stone reliefs of Assyrian conquests fifteen hundred years later. The ancient world rested civilization on a great exploitation of Man by Man; if it was not felt to be very cruel, this is only to say that no other possible way of running things was conceivable.

Babylonian civilization in due time became a legend of magnificence. The survival of one of the great images of city life – the worldly, wicked city of pleasure and consumption – in the name 'Babylon' was a legacy which speaks of the scale and richness of its civilization, though it owes most to a later period. Yet enough remains, too, to see the reality behind this myth, even for the first Babylonian empire. The great palace of Mari is an outstanding example; walls in places forty feet thick surrounded courtyards, three hundred or so rooms forming a complex drained by bitumen-lined pipes running thirty feet deep. It covered an area measuring 150 by over 200 yards and is the finest evidence of the authority the monarch had come to enjoy. In this palace, too, were found great quantities of clay tablets whose writing reveals the business and detail which government embraces by this period.

Many more tablets survive from the first Babylonian empire than from its predecessors or immediate successors. They provide the detail which enables us to know this civilization better, it has been pointed out, than we know some European countries of a thousand years ago. They contribute evidence of the life of the mind in Babylon, too. It was then that the Epic of Gilgamesh took the shape in which we know it. The Babylonians gave cuneiform script a syllabic form, thus enormously increasing its flexibility and usefulness. Their astrology pushed forward the observation of nature and left another myth behind, that of the wisdom of the Chaldeans, a name sometimes misleadingly given to the Babylonians. Hoping to understand their destinies by scanning the stars, the Babylonians built up a science, astronomy, and established an important series of observations which was another major legacy of their culture. It took centuries to accumulate after its beginnings in Ur but by 1000 BC the prediction of lunar eclipses was possible and within another two or three centuries the path of the sun and some of the planets had been plotted with remarkable accuracy against the positions of the apparently fixed stars. This was a scientific tradition reflected in Babylonian mathematics, which has passed on to us the sexagesimal system of Sumer in our circle of 360 degrees and the hour of sixty minutes. The Babylonians also worked out mathematical tables and an algebraic geometry of great practical utility.

Astronomy began in the temple, in the contemplation of celestial movements announcing the advent of festivals of fertility and sowing, and Babylonian religion held close to the Sumerian tradition. Like the old cities, Babylon had a civic god, Marduk; gradually he elbowed his way to the front among his Mesopotamian rivals. This took a long time. Hammurabi said (significantly) that Anu and Enlil, the Sumerian gods, had conferred the headship of the Mesopotamian pantheon upon Marduk, much as they had bidden him to rule over all men for their good. The subsequent vicissitudes of Marduk (sometimes accompanied by the abduction of his statue by invaders) obscured his status, but after the twelfth century BC it was usually unquestioned. Meanwhile, Sumerian tradition remained alive well into the first millennium BC in the use of Sumerian in the Babylonian liturgies, in the names of the gods and the attributions they enjoyed. Babylonian cosmogony began, like that of Sumer, with the creation of the world from watery waste (the name of one God meant 'silt') and the eventual fabrication of Man as the slave of the gods. In one version, gods turned man out like bricks, from clay moulds. It was a world picture suited to absolute mon-

archy, where kings exercised power like that of gods over the men who toiled to build their palaces and sustain a hierarchy of officials and great men which mirrored that of the heavens.

Hammurabi's achievement did not long survive him. Events in northern Mesopotamia indicated the appearance of a new power even before he formed his empire. Hammurabi had overthrown an Amorite kingdom which had established itself in Assyria at the end of the hegemony of Ur. This was a temporary success. There followed nearly a thousand years during which Assyria was to be a battleground and prize, eventually overshadowing a Babylon from which it was separated; the centre of gravity of Mesopotamian history had decisively moved northwards from old Sumer. The Hittites, who were establishing themselves in Anatolia in the last quarter of the third millennium BC, were pushing slowly forwards in the next few centuries; during this time they took up the cuneiform script, which they adapted to their own Indo-European language. By 1700 BC they ruled the lands between Syria and the Black Sea. Then, one of their kings turned southwards against a Babylonia already weakened and shrunken to the old land of Akkad. His successor carried the advance to completion; Babylon was taken and plundered and Hammurabi's dynasty and achievement finally came to an end. But then the Hittites withdrew and other peoples ruled and disputed Mesopotamia for a mysterious four centuries of which we know little except that during them the separation of Assyria and Babylonia which was to be so important in the next millennium was made final.

In 1162 BC the statue of Marduk was taken away from Babylon by Elamite conquerors. This was to be a recurrent symbol; the great god was exiled in defeat and returned in glory in victory. By the time of this conquest, a very confused era has opened and the focus of world history has shifted away from Mesopotamia. The story of the Assyrian empire still lies ahead, but its background is a great new wave of migrations in the thirteenth and twelfth centuries BC which involve other civilizations far more directly and deeply than the successors of the Sumerians. Those successors, their conquerors and displacers, none the less built on the foundations laid in Sumer. Technically, intellectually, legally, theologically, the Near East, which by 1000 BC was sucked into the vortex of world politics – the term is by then not too strong – still bore the stamp of the makers of the first civilization. It would pass their heritage in strangely transmuted forms to others in their turn.

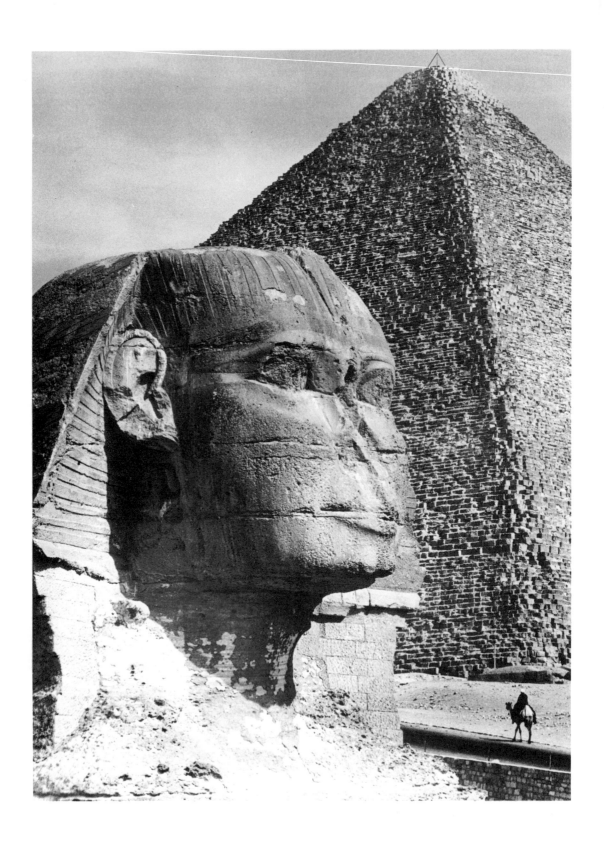

3 Ancient Egypt

Mesopotamia was not the only great river valley to cradle a civilization, but the only early example to rival it in the antiquity and staying-power of what was created was that of Egypt. For thousands of years after it had died, the physical remains of the first civilization in the Nile valley fascinated men's minds and stirred their imaginations; even the Greeks were bemused by the legend of the occult wisdom of a land where gods were half men, half beasts, and people still waste their time trying to discern a supernatural significance in the arrangement of the Pyramids. Ancient Egypt has always been our greatest visible inheritance from antiquity.

The richness of its remains is one reason why we know more about Egyptian than about much of Mesopotamian history. In another way, too, there is an important difference between these civilizations: because Sumerian civilization appeared first, Egypt could benefit from its experience and example. Exactly what this meant has been much debated. Mesopotamian contributions have been seen in the motifs of early Egyptian art, in the presence of cylinder seals at the outset of Egyptian records, in similar techniques of monumental building in brick and in the debt of hieroglyph, the pictorial writing of Egypt, to early Sumerian script. However the

The pyramids at Giza are the greatest of the tomb complexes of ancient Egypt, the supreme achievement of the Old Kingdom and the symbol of a civilization whose fascination has proved as long-lasting as themselves.

balance exactly falls, that there were important and fruitful connexions between early Egypt and Sumer seems incontestable, but how and when the first encounter of the Nile peoples with Sumer came about will probably never be known. It seems at least likely that when it came, Sumerian influence was transmitted by way of the peoples of the delta and lower Nile. In any case, these influences operated in a setting which was always radically to differentiate Egyptian experience from that of any other centre of civilization. This was provided by the Nile itself, the heart of Egypt's prehistory, as of its history.

Egypt was defined by the Nile and the deserts which flanked it; it was the country the river watered, one drawn-out straggling oasis. In prehistoric times it must also have been one great marsh, six hundred miles long, and, except in the delta, never more than a few miles wide. From the start the annual floods of the river were the basic mechanism of the economy and set the rhythm of life on its banks. Farming gradually took root in the beds of mud deposited higher and higher year by year, but the first communities must have been precarious and their environment semi-aquatic; much of their life has been irrecoverably swept away to the delta silt-beds. What remain of the earliest times are things made and used by the peoples who lived on the fringe of the flood areas or on occasional rocky projections within it or at the valley sides. Before 4000 BC they began to feel the impact of an important climatic change. Sand drifted in from the deserts and desiccation set in. Armed

MEDITERRANEAN SEA

Heliopolis
Memphis
Dividing Line of Upper
and Lower Egypt
Saqqara

SINAI

Hermopolis
Tel-el-Amana

Nile

Thebes

RED SEA

Abu Simbel

NUBIA

KUSH

Ancient Egypt

▲ Pyramids
Areas of cultivation

been available as a fertilizing element, it cannot be said that it was decisive; there always existed a potential for civilization in the Nile valley and it may have needed no external stimulus to discharge it. It is at least obvious, when Egyptian civilization finally emerged, that it is unique, in all essentials wholly unlike anything we can find elsewhere.

The deepest roots of this civilization have to be pieced together from archaeology and later tradition. They reveal Hamitic peoples in Upper Egypt (the south, that is, up the Nile) in Neolithic times. From about 5000 BC such peoples were hunting, fishing, gathering crops and finally embarking on purposeful cultivation in the valley. They lived in villages grouped round marketing centres and seem to have belonged to clans which had animals as symbols or totems; these they copied on their pottery. This was the basis of the eventual political organization of Egypt which began with the emergence of clan chiefs controlling the regions inhabited by their followers.

At an early stage these peoples already had several important technological accomplishments to their credit, though they do not seem such advanced farmers as those of other parts of the ancient Near East. They knew how to make papyrus boats, how to work hard materials such as basalt, and how to hammer copper into small

with elementary agricultural techniques, these people could move down to work the rich soils of the flood-plain.

The river was, therefore, from the start the bringer of life to Egypt. It was a benevolent deity whose never-failing bounty was to be thankfully received, rather than the dangerous, menacing source of sudden, ruinous inundations, amid which the men of Sumer struggled to make land out of a watery waste. It was a setting in which agriculture gave a quick and rich return (though it established itself later than in the Levant or Anatolia) and perhaps made possible a population 'explosion' which released its human and natural resources. Although, as signs of contact in the fourth millennium BC show, Sumerian experience may have

The peak of Stone Age technology is exemplified in the fine shaping of the flint blade of this knife and something of the origins of a civilization can be discerned in its finely carved ivory handle. It was made in pre-dynastic times, perhaps in the middle of the fourth millennium BC, and the details of the handle suggest that foreign influences were already then affecting the Nile valley. The hunting scene on one side hints at Mesopotamian themes (there is a hero tackling two lions who is reminiscent of Gilgamesh) and there is also a lion savaging an ibex which some have associated with Libya. The naval battle on the reverse shows boats with prows like those of the traditional vessels of the Tigris, too.

Memphis was the meeting-place of the Two Kingdoms of Upper and Lower Egypt, but some of the kings of the first dynasty continued to be buried far up the Nile at Abydos. One of them, Wadji, the fourth of the first dynasty, was buried in a tomb over which this stele was placed. It is one of the few such monuments to survive from so early a date and suggests the complexity Egyptian architecture had already achieved.

articles for daily use. They were, that is to say, pretty accomplished Chalcolithic peoples well before the dawn of written record, with specialist craftsmen and, to judge by their jewels, well-marked distinctions of class or status. Then, somewhere about the middle of the fourth millennium, there is an intensification of foreign influences, apparent first in the north, the delta. There is a multiplication of signs of trade and contact with other regions, notably Mesopotamia, whose influence is shown in the art of this era. Meanwhile, hunting and occasional farming give way to a more intense cultivation. In art, the bas-relief appears which is to be so important later in the Egyptian tradition; copper goods become more plentiful. Everything seems suddenly to be appearing at once, almost without antecedents, and to this epoch belongs the basic political structure of the future kingdom.

This was to be dual; at some time in the fourth millennium there solidified two kingdoms, one northern, one southern, one of Lower and one of Upper Egypt. This is interestingly different from Sumer; Egypt seems to move straight from pre-civilization to the government of large areas. There was no era of city-states. Egypt's early 'towns' were the market-places of agriculturalists; the agricultural communities and clans coalesced into groups which were the foundation of later provinces. Egypt was to be a united political whole seven hundred years before Mesopotamia, and even later she would have only a restricted experience of city life.

Of the kings of the two Egypts we know little until about 3200 BC, but we may guess that they were the eventual winners in struggles to consolidate power over larger and larger groups of people which had been going on for centuries. It is about the same time that the written record begins and because writing is already there at the beginning of the Egyptian story, a much more historical account of the development of its civilization can be put together than in the case of Sumer. In Egypt writing was used from its first appearance not merely as an administrative and economic convenience but to record events on monuments and relics intended to survive.

In about 3200 BC, the records tell us, a great king in Upper Egypt, Menes, conquered the north. Egypt was thus unified in a huge state six hundred miles long, running up the river as far as Abu Simbel. It was to be even bigger and to extend even further up the great river which was its heart, and it was also to undergo disruption from time to time, but this is effectively the beginning of a civilization which was to survive into the age of classical Greece and Rome. For nearly three thousand years – one and a half times the life of Christianity – Egypt was a historical entity, for much of it a source of wonder and focus of admiration. In so long a period much happened and we by no means know all of it. Yet it is the stability and conservative power of Egyptian civilization which is the most striking thing about it, not its vicissitudes.

Roughly speaking, that civilization's greatest days were over by about 1000 BC. Before that date, Egyptian history can most easily be visualized in five big divisions. Three of these are called respectively the Old, Middle and New Kingdoms; they are separated by two others called the First and Second Intermediate periods. Very roughly, the three 'kingdoms' are periods of success or at least of consolidated government; the two intermediate stages are interludes of weakness and disruption from external and internal causes. The whole scheme can be envisaged as a kind of layer cake, with three tiers of different flavours separated by two of somewhat formless jam.

This is by no means the only way of understanding Egyptian history, nor for all purposes the best. Many scholars use an alternative way of setting out ancient Egyptian chronology in terms of thirty-one dynasties of kings, a system which has the great advantage of being related to objective criteria; it avoids perfectly proper but awkward disagreements about whether (for example) the first dynasties should be put in the 'Old Kingdom' or distinguished as a separate 'archaic' period, or about the line to be drawn

at the beginning or end of the intermediate era. None the less, the five-part scheme is sufficient for our purposes, if we also distinguish an archaic prelude. A dating in one of the most recent presentations, together with the dynastic synchronization, is as follows:[*]

	Dynasties
Protodynastic c. 3200–2665 BC	I–II
Old Kingdom 2664–2155 BC	III–VIII
First Intermediate 2154–2052 BC	IX–XI
Middle Kingdom 2052–1786 BC	XII
Second Intermediate 1785–1554 BC	XIII–XVII
New Kingdom 1554–1075 BC	XVIII–XX

This takes us down to the time at which, as in Mesopotamian history, there is something of a break as Egypt is caught up in a great series of upheavals originating outside its own boundaries to which the overworked word 'crisis' can reasonably be applied. True, it is not until several more centuries have passed that the old Egyptian tradition really comes to an end. Some modern Egyptians insist on a continuing sense of identity among Egyptians since the days of the Pharaohs. None the less, somewhere about the beginning of the first millennium is one of the most convenient places at which to break the story, if only because the greatest achievements of the Egyptians were by then behind them.

These were above all the work of and centred in the monarchical state. The state form itself was the expression of Egyptian civilization. It was focussed first at Memphis whose building was begun during the lifetime of Menes and which was the capital of the Old Kingdom. Later, under the New Kingdom, the capital was at Thebes, though there were also periods of great uncertainty about where it was. Memphis and Thebes were not so much true cities as great religious centres and palace complexes; they did not really progress beyond this to true urbanism. The absence of cities earlier was

*This information is taken from R. A. Parker's table in *The Legacy of Egypt*, 2nd edn, ed. J. R. Harris (Oxford, 1971), pp. 24–5.

An Egyptian king of the fourth dynasty, Mycerinus, accompanied by two goddesses. The group was carved in the middle of the third millennium BC and illustrates the high level of technical proficiency Egyptian stone-carving had already achieved. It is also the first such group in which deities were represented in three dimensions. The goddesses, it may be remarked, have a strong likeness to the king; from this time it was usual to represent deities with the features of reigning kings. The dividing line between god and pharaoh was becoming more and more blurred.

Throughout Egyptian history, kings were to be portrayed in a ritual posture of victory – standing over a defeated enemy clutched by his hair while the king's other hand is raised menacingly to dash out his brains. In this picture, the victor is the founder of united Egypt. He wears the tall crown of the Southern Kingdom on one side of this carved palette, the crown of the North on the reverse. The divine might of the king was an enduring theme of Egyptian art and here it is employed on a palette whose original purpose may have been functional – to hold cosmetics or colours.

politically important, too. Egypt's kings had not emerged like Sumer's as the 'big men' in a city-state community which originally deputed them to act for it. Nor were they simply men who like others were subject to gods who ruled all men, great or small. The tension of palace with temple was missing in Egypt and when Egyptian kingship emerges it is unrivalled. The Pharaohs were to be gods, not servants of gods.

It was only under the New Kingdom that the title 'pharaoh' came to be applied personally to the king. Before that it indicated the king's residence and his court. None the less, at a much earlier stage Egyptian monarchs already had the authority which was so to impress the ancient world. It is expressed in the size with which they are depicted on the earliest monuments.

This they inherited ultimately from prehistoric kings who had a special sanctity because of their power to assure prosperity through successful agriculture. Such powers are enjoyed by some African rainmaker-kings even today; in ancient Egypt they focussed upon the Nile. The Pharaohs were believed to control its annual rise and fall: life itself, no less, to the riparian communities. The first rituals of Egyptian kingship which are known to us are concerned with fertility, irrigation and land reclamation. The earliest representations of Menes show him excavating a canal.

Under the Old Kingdom the idea appears that the king is the absolute lord of the land. Soon he is venerated as a descendant of the gods, the original lords of the land. He becomes a god, Horus, son of Osiris, and takes on the mighty and terrible attributes of the divine maker of order; the bodies of his enemies are depicted hanging in rows like dead game-birds, or kneeling in supplication lest (like less fortunate enemies) their brains be ritually dashed out. Justice is 'what Pharaoh loves', evil 'what Pharaoh hates'; he is divinely omniscient and so needs no code of law to guide him. Later, under the New Kingdom, the Pharaohs were to be depicted with the heroic stature of the great warriors of other contemporary cultures; they are shown in their chariots, mighty men of war, trampling down their enemies and confidently slaughtering beasts of prey. Perhaps a measure of secularization can be inferred in this change, but it does not remove Egyptian kingship from the region of the sacred and awesome. 'He is a god by whose dealings one lives, the father and mother of all men, alone by himself, without an equal', wrote one of the chief civil servants of the Pharaoh as late as about 1500 BC. Until the Middle Kingdom, only he had an after-life to look forward to. Egypt, more than any other Bronze Age state, always stressed the incarnation of the god in the king, even when that idea was increasingly exposed by the realities of life in the New Kingdom and the coming of iron. Then, the disasters which befell Egypt at the hands of foreigners would make it im-possible to continue to believe that Pharaoh was god of all the world.

But long before this the Egyptian state had acquired another institutional embodiment and armature, an elaborate and impressive hierarchy of bureaucrats. At its apex were viziers, provincial governors and senior officials who came mainly from the nobility; a few of the greatest of these were buried with a pomp that rivalled that of the Pharaohs. Less eminent families provided the thousands of scribes needed to staff and service an elaborate government directed by the chief civil servants. The ethos of this bureaucracy can be sensed through the literary texts which list the virtues needed to succeed as a scribe: application to study, self-control, prudence, respect for superiors, scrupulous regard for the sanctity of weights, measures,

The scribe, key-figure of Egyptian administration. More than a mere recorder of the thoughts and decisions of others, he was also civil servant, superintendent of works, commander of troops, estate manager and intellectual. This Old Kingdom portrait was recovered from Saqqara.

landed property and legal forms. The scribes were trained in a special school at Thebes, where not only the traditional history and literature and command of various scripts were taught but, it seems, surveying, architecture and accountancy also.

The bureaucracy directed a country most of whose inhabitants were peasants. They cannot have lived wholly comfortable lives, for they provided both the labour for the great public works of the monarchy and the surplus upon which a noble class, the bureaucracy and a great religious establishment could subsist. Yet the land was rich and was increasingly mastered by irrigation techniques established in the predynastic period; these were probably one of the

The landscape of Egyptian agriculture has been vividly preserved for us in painted scenes on the walls of tombs. This vintage scene is from one at Thebes, for centuries Egypt's cultural and religious cente of gravity.

earliest manifestations of the unsurpassed capacity to mobilize collective effort which was to be one of the hallmarks of Egyptian government. Vegetables, barley, emmer were the main crops of the fields laid out along the irrigation channels; the diet they made possible was supplemented by poultry, fish and game (all of which figure plentifully in Egyptian art). Cattle were in use for traction and ploughing at least as early as the Old Kingdom. With little change this agriculture remained the basis of life in Egypt until modern times; it was sufficient to make her the granary of the Romans.

On the surplus of this agriculture there also rested Egypt's own spectacular form of conspicuous consumption, a range of great public works in stone unsurpassed in antiquity. Houses and farm buildings in ancient Egypt were built in the mud brick already used before dynastic times: they were not meant to outface eternity. The palaces, tombs and memorials of the Pharaohs were a different matter; they were built of the stone abundantly available in some parts of the Nile valley. Though they were carefully dressed with first copper and then bronze tools and often elaborately incised and painted, the technology of utilizing this material was far from complicated. The Egyptians invented the stone column, but their great building achievement was not so much architectural and technical as social and administrative. What they did was based on an unprecedented and almost unsurpassed concentration of human labour. Under the direction of a scribe, thousands of slaves and sometimes regiments of soldiers were deployed to cut and manhandle into position the huge masses of Egyptian building. With only such elementary assistance as was available from levers and sleds – no winches, pulleys, blocks or tackle existed – and by the building of colossal ramps of earth, a succession of still-startling buildings was produced.

They began under the Third Dynasty. The most famous are the pyramids, the tombs of kings, at Saqqara, near Memphis. One of these, the 'Step Pyramid', was the masterpiece of the first architect whose name is recorded, Imhotep, chancellor to the king. His work was so impressive that he was later to be deified – as the god

Conceived as a great staircase to heaven, the step pyramid at Saqqara is in more than one sense a landmark. It was built as a monument for a Third Dynasty king in about 2650 BC by Imhotep, an administrator and engineer of genuis who exploited to the full and for the first time techniques for the handling and shaping of stone just coming to maturity. The enclosure around the two-hundred-foot-high pyramid contains many examples of early Egyptian building style, but for the first time much survived because they were made in stone – to outface death and serve the king in his afterlife – instead of the brick, wood and mud of earlier buildings.

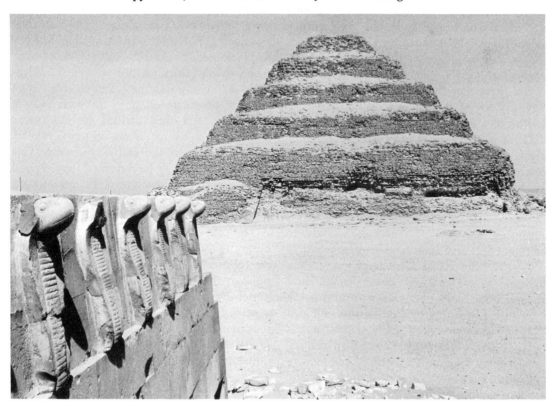

of medicine – as well as being revered as astronomer, priest and sage. The beginning of building in stone was attributed to him and it is easy
to believe that the building of something so unprecedented as the two-hundred-foot-high Pyramid was seen as evidence of godlike power. It
and its companions rose without peer over a
civilization which until then lived only in dwellings of mud. A century or so later, blocks of
stone of fifteen tons apiece were used for the
Pyramid of Cheops, and it was at this time
(during the fourth dynasty) that the greatest
pyramids wre completed at Giza. Cheops'
Pyramid was twenty years in the building; the
legend that 100000 men were employed upon
it is now thought an exaggeration but many
thousands must have been and the huge quantities of stone (between five and six million tons)
were brought from as much as 500 miles away.
This colossal construction is perfectly orientated
and its sides, 9000 inches long, vary by less than
eight inches – only about 0·09 per cent. It is not
surprising that the Pyramids later figured among
the Seven Wonders of the World, nor that they
alone from those Wonders survive. They were
the greatest evidence of the power and self-
confidence of the pharaonic state. Nor, of
course, were they the only great monuments of
Egypt. Each of them was only the dominant
feature of a great complex of buildings which
made up together the residence of the king after
death. At other sites there were great temples,
palaces, the tombs of the Valley of the Kings.

These huge public works were in both the
real and figurative sense the biggest things the
Egyptians left to posterity. They make it less
surprising that the Egyptians were later also to
be reputed to have been great scientists: people
could not believe that these huge monuments
did not rest on the most refined mathematical
and scientific skills. Yet this is invalid as an
inference as well as in fact untrue. Though
Egyptian surveying was highly skilled, it was
not until our own day that a more than elementary mathematical skill became necessary to
engineering; it was certainly not needed for the
erection of the pyramids. What was requisite

was outstanding competence in mensuration and
the manipulation of certain formulae for calculating volumes and weights, and this was as far
as Egyptian mathematics went, whatever later
admirers believed. Modern mathematicians do
not think much of the Egyptians' theoretical
achievement and they certainly did not match
the Babylonians in this art. They worked with
a decimal numeration which at first sight looks
modern, but it may be that their only significant
contribution to later mathematics was the invention of unit fractions.

No doubt a primitive mathematics is a part of
the explanation of the sterility of the Egyptians'
astronomical endeavours – another field in which
posterity, paradoxically, was to credit them
with great things. Their observations were accurate enough to permit the forecasting of the rise
of the Nile and the ritual alignment of buildings,
it is true, but their theoretical astronomy was
valueless. Here again they were left far behind
by the Babylonians. The inscriptions in which
Egyptian astronomical science was recorded
were to command centuries of respect from
astrologers, but their scientific value was low
and their predictive quality relatively short-term.
The one solid work which rested on the Egyptians' astronomy was the calendar. They were
the first people to establish the solar year of
$365\frac{1}{4}$ days and they divided it into twelve
months, each of three 'weeks' of ten days, with
five extra days at the end of the year. This
arrangement, it may be remarked, was revived
in 1793 when the French revolutionaries sought
to replace the Christian calendar by one more
rational.

The calendar, though it owed much to the
observation of stars, must have reflected also in
its remoter origins observation of the great
pulse at the heart of Egyptian life, the flooding of the Nile. This gave the Egyptian farmer
a year of three seasons, each of approximately
four months, one of planting, one of flood, one
of harvest. But the Nile's endless cycle also
influenced Egypt at deeper levels.

The structure and solidity of the religious life
of ancient Egypt greatly struck other peoples.

Herodotus believed that the Greeks had acquired the names of their gods from Egypt; he was wrong, but it is interesting that he should have thought so. Later, the cults of Egyptian gods were seen as a threat by the Roman emperors; they were forbidden, but the Romans had eventually to tolerate them, such was their appeal. Mumbo-jumbo and charlatanry with an Egyptian flavour could still take in cultivated Europeans in the eighteenth century; a more amusing and innocent expression of the fascination of the myth of ancient Egypt can still be seen in the rituals of the Shriners, the secret fraternities of respectable American businessmen who parade about the streets of small towns improbably attired in fezzes and baggy trousers on great occasions. There was, indeed, a continuing vigour in Egyptian religion which, like other sides of Egyptian civilization, long outlived the political forms which had sustained and sheltered it.

Yet it remains something with which it is peculiarly difficult to come to grips. Words like

In the tomb of the Nineteenth Dynasty king Sethos I at Thebes a series of representations has been found which illustrate the constellations identified by Egyptian astronomers. The bull shown in the middle of this section was the Egyptian rendering of the Great Bear. To its right stands the monstrous goddess Heramut, the half-hippopotamus, half-crocodile destroyer of the dead.

'vigour' can be misleading: religion in ancient Egypt was much more a matter of an all-pervasive framework, as much taken for granted as the circulatory system of the human body, than of an independent structure such as what later came to be understood as a church. It was not consciously seen as a growing, lively force: it was, rather, one aspect of reality, a description of an unchanging cosmos. But this, too, may be a misleading way of putting it. An important book about the world outlook of early Mesopotamians and Egyptians has the suggestive title *Before Philosophy*; we have to remember

97

that concepts and distinctions which we take for granted in assessing and even talking about the mentalities of other ages did not exist for the men whose minds we seek to penetrate. The boundary between religion and magic, for example, hardly mattered for the ancient Egyptian, though he might be well aware that each had its proper efficacity. It has been said that

Anubis, the jackal-headed, was the god of the dead, the custodian of their bodies and an embalmer. He is sometimes with the scales that weigh the souls of the dead, sometimes as the guardian of their bodies. Here, in a twentieth dynasty tomb painting from Thebes, he prepares a mummy-case.

magic was always present as a kind of cancer in Egyptian religion; the image is too evaluative, but it is satisfactory in so far as it expresses the intimacy of the link. Another distinction lacking to ancient Egypt was the one most of us make automatically between the name and the thing. For the ancient Egyptian, the name *was* the thing; the real object we separate from its designation was identical with it. So might be other images. The Egyptians lived in symbolism as fishes do in water, taking it for granted, and we have to break through the assumptions of a profoundly unsymbolic age to understand them.

A whole world view is therefore involved in appreciating the meaning and rôle of religion in ancient Egypt. At the outset there is over-

98

whelming evidence of its importance; for almost the whole duration of their civilization, the ancient Egyptians show a remarkably uniform tendency to seek through religion a way of penetrating the variety of the flow of ordinary experience so as to reach a changeless world most easily understood through the life the dead lived there. Perhaps the pulse of the Nile is to be detected here, too; each year it swept away and made new, but its cycle was ever recurring, changeless, the embodiment of a cosmic rhythm. The supreme change threatening men was death, the greatest expression of the decay and flux which was their common experience. Egyptian religion seems from the start obsessed with it: its most familiar embodiments, after all, are the mummy and the grave-goods from funeral chambers preserved in our museums. Under the Middle Kingdom it came to be believed that all men, not just the king, could expect life in another world. Accordingly, through ritual and symbol, through preparation of the case he would have to put to his judges in the afterworld, a man might prepare for the afterlife with a reasonable confidence that he would achieve the changeless well-being it offered in principle. The Egyptian view of the afterlife was, therefore, unlike the gloomy version of the Mesopotamians; men could be happy in it.

The struggle to assure this outcome for so many men across so many centuries gives Egyptian religion a heroic quality. It is the explanation, too, of the obsessively elaborate care shown in preparing tombs and conducting the deceased to his eternal resting-place. Its most celebrated expression is the building of the Pyramids and the practice of mummification. It took seventy days to carry out the funerary rites and mummification of the dead king under the Middle Kingdom.

The Egyptians believed, it appears, that after death a man could expect judgement before Osiris; if the verdict was favourable, he would live in Osiris' kingdom, if not, he was abandoned to a monstrous destroyer, part crocodile, part hippopotamus. This did not mean, though, that in life human beings need do no more than placate Osiris, for the Egyptian pantheon was huge. About two thousand gods existed and there were several important cults. Many of them originated in the prehistoric animal deities. Horus, the falcon god, was also that of the dynasty and probably arrived with the mysterious invaders of the fourth millennium BC. These animals underwent a slow but incomplete humanization; artists stick their animal heads on to human bodies. These totemlike creatures were rearranged in fresh patterns as the Pharaohs sought through the consolidation of their cults to achieve political ends. In this way the cult of Horus was consolidated with that of Amon–Re, the sun-god, of whom the Pharaoh came to be regarded as the incarnation. This was the official cult of the great age of pyramid-building and by no means the end of the story. Horus later underwent another transformation, to appear as the offspring of Osiris, the central figure of a national cult, and his consort Isis. This goddess of creation and love was probably the most ancient of all – her origins, like those of other Egyptian deities – go back to the pre-dynastic era, and she is one development of the ubiquitous mother-goddess of whom evidence survives from all over the Neolithic Near East. She was long to endure, her image, the infant Horus in her arms, surviving into the Christian iconography of the Virgin Mary.

Egyptian religion is an immensely complicated theme. Different places had different cults and there were even occasional variations of a doctrinal and speculative kind. The most famous of these was the attempt of a fourteenth-century pharaoh to establish the cult of Aton, another manifestation of the sun, in which has been discerned the first monotheistic religion. Yet there is a recurring sense of a striving after synthesis, even if it is often the expression of dynastic or political interest. Much of the history of Egyptian religion must be, if we could only decipher it, the story of ebbings and flowings about the major cults: politics, in fact, rather than religion. Not only the pharaohs were interested. The institutions which maintained

Throughout history, most images of kings have been works of propaganda and nowhere more than in ancient Egypt. Akhnaton, promoter of the cult of the Sun God, is often presented as a mediator between him and humanity, the figure through whom personal intercession must be made to the new god who patronizes the new régime. This relief shows Akhnaton with his consort, Nefertiti, and one of their daughters, worshipping Aton, whose beneficent rays pour down on a fortunate land.

these beliefs were in the hands of a hereditary priestly class, initiated into the rituals to whose inner sancta the ordinary worshipper almost never penetrated. The cult statues at the shrine of the temple were rarely seen except by the priests. As time passed, they acquired important vested interests in the popularity and well-being of their cults.

The gods loom large in the subject-matter of ancient Egyptian art, but it contains much more besides. It was based on a fundamental naturalism of representation which, however restrained by conventions of expression and gesture, gives two millennia of classical Egyptian art at first a beautiful simplicity and later, in a more decadent period, an endearing charm and approachability. It permitted a realistic portrayal of scenes of everyday life. The rural themes of farming, fishing and hunting are displayed in them; craftsmen are shown at work on their products and scribes at their duties. Yet neither content nor technique is in the end the most striking characteristic of Egyptian art, which is its enduring style. For some two thousand years, artists were able to work satisfyingly within the same classical tradition. Its origins may owe something to Sumer and it showed itself later able to borrow other foreign influences yet the strength and solidity of the central and native tradition never wavers. It must have been one of the most impressive visual features of Egypt to a visitor in ancient times; what he saw was all of a piece. If we exempt the work of the Upper Palaeolithic, of which we know so very little, it is the longest and strongest continuous tradition in the whole history of art.

It did not prove to be transplantable. Perhaps the Greeks took the column from ancient Egypt, where it had its origins in the mud-plastered bundle of reeds of which a reminiscence survives in fluting. What is clear apart from this is that although the monuments of Egypt continuously fascinated artists and architects of other lands, the result, even when they exploited them successfully for their own purposes, was always superficial and exotic. Egyptian style never took root anywhere else; it pops up from

This picture of a goldsmith at work comes from a Theban tomb built in eighteenth dynasty times for the first minister of a pharaoh. It is a particularly spectacular example of the skill and artistry which the Egyptians lavished on the afterlife of the dead.

writing. Instead of the device of arranging the same basic shape in different ways which had been evolved in Mesopotamia, they deliberately chose lifelike little pictures or near-pictures. It was much more decorative than cuneiform, but also much harder to master. The first hieroglyphs appear before 3000 BC; the last example of which we know was written in AD 394. Nearly 4000 years is an impressively long life for a calligraphy. But the uninitiated could still not read it for another fourteen and a half centuries after its cessation, until a French scholar deciphered the inscription on the 'Rosetta stone' brought back to France after its discovery by scientists accompanying a French army in Egypt. None of the classical writers of antiquity who wrote about Egypt ever learnt to read hieroglyph, it seems, though enormous interest was shown in it. Yet it now seems likely that hieroglyph had importance in world as well as in Egyptian history because it was a model for Semitic scripts of the second millennium BC and thus came to be a remote ancestor of the modern Latin alphabet, which has spread round the world in our own times.

In the ancient world the ability to read hieroglyph was the key to the position of the priestly caste and, accordingly, a closely guarded professional secret. From pre-dynastic times it was used for historical record and as early as the First Dynasty the invention of papyrus – strips of reed-pith, laid criss-cross and pounded together into a homogeneous sheet – provided a convenient medium for its multiplication. Here was a real contribution to the progress of mankind. This invention had much greater importance for the world than hieroglyph; cheaper than skin (from which parchment was made) and more convenient (though more perishable) than clay tablets or slates of stone, it was the most general basis of correspondence and record in the Near East until well into the Christian era, when the invention of paper reached the Mediterranean world from the Far East (and even paper took its name from papyrus). Soon after the appearance of papyrus, writers began to paste sheets of it together into a long roll: thus

time to time down the ages as decoration and embellishment – sphinxes and serpents on furniture, an obelisk here, a cinema there. Only one great integral contribution was made by Egyptian art to the future, the establishment for the purposes of the huge incised and painted figures of the walls of tombs and temples of the classical canons of proportion of the human body which were to pass through the Greeks to western art. Artists were to be still fascinated by them as late as Leonardo, but this contribution was theoretical, not stylistic.

Another great artistic achievement confined to Egypt, though exceptionally important there, was calligraphy. It seems that Egyptians deliberately took the Sumerian invention of representing sounds rather than things, but rejected cuneiform. They invented, instead, hieroglyphic the Egyptians invented the book, as well as the material on which it could first be written and a script which is an ancestor of our own. It may be our greatest debt to the Egyptians, for a huge proportion of what we know of antiquity comes to us directly or indirectly via papyrus.

Undoubtedly, the rumoured prowess of her religious and magical practitioners and the spectacular embodiment of a political achievement in

Some of the finest reliefs from the Old Kingdom are those in the tomb of a city governor, Mereruka, at Saqqara, built in about 2350 BC. They are exceptionally lively, gay pictures of agricultural life, with children playing and dancing and even some of the workers' chatter set out in hieroglyph much as a modern strip-cartoonist might isolate his dialogue in spaces in the corners of his pictures.

art and architecture largely explains Egypt's continuing prestige. Yet if her civilization is looked at comparatively, it seems neither very fertile nor very responsive. Technology is by no means an infallible test – nor one easy to interpret – but it suggests a people slow to adopt new skills, reluctant to innovate once the creative jump to civilization had been made. Stone architecture is the only major innovation for a long time after the coming of literacy. Though papyrus and the wheel were known under the First Dynasty, Egypt had been in contact with Mesopotamia for getting on for two thousand years before she adopted the well-sweep by then long in use to irrigate land in the other river valley. Perhaps the weight of routine was insuperable, given the background of the unchanging reassurance provided by the Nile. Though Egyptian art records workmen organized in teams for the subdivision of manufacturing processes down to a point which faintly suggests the modern factory, many important devices came to Egypt only much later than elsewhere. There is no definite evidence of the presence of the potter's wheel before the Old Kingdom; for all the skill of the goldsmith and coppersmith, bronze-making does not appear until well into the second millennium BC and the lathe has to wait for the Hellenistic age. The bow-drill is almost the only tool for the multiplication and transmission of energy available to the mass of Egyptian craftsmen.

Only in medicine is there indisputable originality and achievement and it can be traced back at least as far as the Old Kingdom. By 1000 BC Egyptian pre-eminence in this art was internationally and justifiably recognized. While Egyptian medicine was never wholly separable from magic (magical prescriptions and amulets survive in great numbers), it had an appreciable content of rationality and pure empirical observation. It extended as far as a knowledge of contraceptive techniques. Its indirect contribution to subsequent history was great, too, whatever its efficiency in its own day; much of our knowledge of drugs and of plants furnishing *materia medica* was first established by the Egyptians and passed from them, eventually, through the Greeks to the scientists of medieval Europe. It is a considerable thing to have initiated the use of a remedy effective as long as has been castor oil. Here Egypt left Mesopotamia far behind.

What can be concluded about the health of the ancient Egyptians is another matter. They do not seem to have been so worried about alcoholic over-indulgence as the Mesopotamians, but it is not easy to infer anything from that. Some scholars have said there was an exceptionally high rate of infant mortality and hard evidence of a negative kind exists for some diseases of adults; whatever the explanation, the many mummified bodies surviving reveal no instance of cancer, rickets, or syphilis. This by itself cannot throw light on the effect of Egyptian medical practice, of course. Such evidence as we have of prescriptions and recommended cures suggests that these were a mixed bag, no better and no worse than most of those deployed in other great centres of civilization at any time before the present. Considerable anatomical and preservative skill was possessed by the practitioners of mummification. Curiously, the products of their art were later themselves regarded as therapeutic value; powdered mummy was for centuries a sovereign cure for many ills in Europe and possessed other properties as well, as is suggested to readers of *Othello*.

Most Egyptians were peasants, a consequence of Egypt long remaining non-urbanized as Mesopotamia did not. The picture of Egyptian life presented by its literature and art reveals a population living in the countryside, using little towns and temples as service centres rather than dwelling places. Egypt was a country of villages, small market towns and a few great cult and administrative centres such as Thebes or Memphis. Life for the poor was hard, but not unremittingly so. The major burden must have been conscript labour services. When these were not exacted by Pharaoh, then the peasant would have considerable leisure at those times when he waited for the flooding Nile to do its work for him. The agricultural base was rich enough, too, to sustain a complex and variegated society with a wide range of craftsmen. About their activities we know more than of those of their Mesopotamian equivalents, thanks to stone-carvings and paintings. The great division of this society was between the educated, who could enter the state service, and the rest. Slavery was important, but, it appears, less fundamental an institution than elsewhere in the ancient Near East.

Tradition in later times remarked upon the seductiveness and accessibility of Egyptian women. With other evidence it helps to give an impression of a society in which women were more independent and enjoyed higher status than elsewhere. Some weight must be given to an art which depicts court ladies clad in the fine and revealing linens which the Egyptians came to weave, exquisitely coiffured and jewelled, wearing the carefully applied cosmetics to whose provision Egyptian commerce gave much attention. We should not lean too strongly on this, but our impression of the way in which women of the Egyptian ruling class were treated is important, and it is one of dignity and independence. The Pharaohs and their consorts – and other noble couples – are sometimes depicted, too, with an intimacy of mood found nowhere else in the art of the ancient Near East before the first millennium BC and suggestive of a real emotional equality; it can hardly be accidental that this is so.

The beautiful and charming women who appear in many of the paintings and sculptures may reflect also a certain political importance for their sex which was lacking elsewhere. The throne theoretically and often in practice descended through the female line. An heiress brought to her husband the right of succession; hence there was much anxiety about the marriage of princesses. Many royal marriages were of brother and sister, without apparently unsatisfactory genetic effects; some Pharaohs married their daughters, but perhaps to prevent anyone else marrying them rather than to ensure the continuity of the divine blood. Such a standing must have made royal ladies influential personages in their own right. Some exercised important power and one even occupied the throne, being willing to appear ritually bearded and in a man's clothes, and taking the title of Pharaoh. It was an innovation, it is true, which seems not to have been wholly approved.

There is also much femininity about the Egyptian pantheon, notably in the cult of Isis, which is suggestive. Literature and art stress a respect for the wife and mother which goes beyond the confines of the circle of the notabilities. Both love stories and scenes of family life reveal what was at least thought to be an ideal standard for society as a whole and it emphasizes a tender eroticism, relaxation and informality, and something of an emotional equality of men and women. Some women were literate and there is even an Egyptian word for a female scribe, but there were, of course, not many occupations open to women except those of

Ladies of ancient Egypt, depicted in a painting from the wall of a tomb. They are the occupant's wife and mother dressed formally; the curious objects on their heads (they also wear wigs) are cones of myrrh.

priestess or prostitute. If they were well-off, however, they could own property and their legal rights seem in most respects to have been akin to those of women in the Sumerian tradition. It is not easy to generalize over so long a period as that of Egyptian civilization but such evidence as we have from ancient Egypt leaves an impression of a society with a potential for personal expression by women not found among many later peoples.

So impressive is the solidity and material richness of Egyptian civilization in retrospect, so apparently unchanging, that it is even more difficult than in the case of Mesopotamia to keep in perspective what were its relations with the world outside or the ebb and flow of authority within the Nile valley. There are huge tracts of time to account for – the Old Kingdom alone, on the shortest reckoning, has a history two and a half times as long as that of the United States – and much happened in them. The difficulty is to be sure exactly what it was that was going on and what was its importance. For nearly a thousand years after Menes, Egypt's history can be considered in virtual isolation. It was to be looked back upon as a time of stability when Pharaohs were impregnable. Yet under the Old Kingdom there has been detected a decentralization of authority; provincial officers show increasing importance and independence. The Pharaoh, too, still had to wear two crowns and was twice buried, once in Upper and once in Lower Egypt; this division was still real. Relations with neighbours were not remarkable, though a series of expeditions was mounted against the peoples of Palestine towards the end of the Old Kingdom. The First Intermediate period which followed saw the position reversed and Egypt becoming the invaded, rather than the invader. No doubt weakness and division helped Asian invaders to establish themselves in the valley of the lower Nile; there is a strange comment that 'the high born are full of lamentation but the poor are jubilant . . . squalor is throughout the land . . . strangers have come into Egypt'. Rival dynasties appeared near modern Cairo; the grasp of Memphis flagged.

The next great period of Egyptian history was the Middle Kingdom, effectively inaugurated by the powerful Amenemhet I who reunified the kingdom from his capital at Thebes. For about a quarter-millennium after 2000 BC, Egypt enjoyed a period of recovery which may have owed much to the impression (which comes to us through the records) of the horrors of the Intermediate period. Under the Middle Kingdom there was a new emphasis on order and social cohesion. The divine status of the Pharaoh subtly changes: not only *is* he God, but it is emphasized that he is descended from gods and will be followed by gods. The eternal order will continue unshaken after bad times had made men doubt. It is certain, too, that there was expansion and material growth. Great reclama-

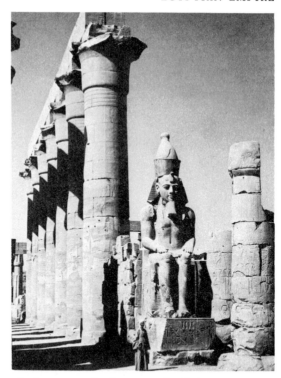

At Luxor stood a huge temple of Amon, to which Ramses II added this court, now called after him.

tion work was achieved in the marshes of the Nile. Nubia, to the south, between the first and third cataracts, was conquered and its goldmines fully exploited. Egyptian settlements were founded even farther south, too, in what was later to be the mysterious kingdom of Kush. Trade leaves more elaborate traces than ever before and the copper mines of the Sinai were now exploited again. Theological change also followed – there was something of a consolidation of cults under the god Amon-Re which reflected political consolidation. Yet the Middle Kingdom ended in political upheaval and dynastic competition.

The Second Intermediate period of roughly two hundred years was marked by another and far more dangerous incursion of foreigners. These were the Hyksos, possibly a Semitic people, who used the military advantage of the

A feast in an Egyptian house of the New Kingdom. The guests are entertained by musicians and dancers; a servant fills the cups.

iron-fitted chariot to establish themselves in the Nile delta as overlords to whom the Theban dynasties paid tribute. Not much is known about them. Seemingly, they took over Egyptian conventions and methods, and even maintained the existing bureaucrats at first, but this did not lead to assimilation. Under the eighteenth dynasty the Egyptians evicted the Hyksos in a war of peoples; this was the start of the New Kingdom, whose first great success was to follow up victory in the years after 1570 BC by pursuing the Hyksos into their strongholds in south Canaan. In the end, the Egyptians occupied much of Syria and Palestine.

The New Kingdom in its prime was internationally so successful and has left such rich physical memorials that it is difficult not to think that the Hyksos domination must have had a cathartic or fertilizing effect. There was under the eighteenth dynasty almost a renaissance of the arts, a transformation of military techniques by the adoption of Asiatic devices such as the chariot, and, above all, a huge consolidation of royal authority. During it a female, Hatshepsut, for the first time occupied the throne in a reign notable for the expansion of Egyptian commerce, or so her mortuary temple seems to show. The next century or so brought further imperial and military glory, her consort and successor, Thotmes III, carrying the limits of Egyptian empire to the Euphrates. Monuments recording the arrival of tribute and slaves or marriages with Asiatic princesses testify to an Egyptian pre-eminence matched at home by a new richness of decoration in the temples and the appearance of a sculpture in the round which produced busts and statues generally regarded as the peak of Egyptian artistic achievement. Foreign influences also touched Egyptian art at this time; they came from Crete.

Towards the end of the New Kingdom, the evidence of multiplied foreign contacts begins to show something else: the context of Egyptian power had already changed importantly. The crucial area was the Levant coast which even Thotmes III had taken seventeen years to subdue. He had to leave unsubdued a huge empire ruled by the Mitanni which continued in eastern Syria and northern Mesopotamia. His successors changed tack. A Mitanni princess married a pharaoh and to protect Egyptian interests in this area the New Kingdom came to rely on the friendship of her people. Egypt was being forced out of the isolation which had long protected her. But the Mitanni were under growing pressure from the Hittites, to the north, one of the most important of the peoples whose ambitions and movements break up the world of the Near East more and more in the second half of the second millennium BC.

We know a lot about the preoccupations of the New Kingdom at an early stage in this process because they are recorded in one of the earliest collections of diplomatic correspondence, for the reigns of Amenhotep III and IV (c. 1400–1362 BC). Under the first of these kings, Egypt reached its peak of prestige and prosperity. It was the greatest era of Thebes. Amenhotep was fittingly buried there in a tomb which was the largest ever prepared for a king, though nothing of it remains but the fragments of the huge statues the Greeks later called the colossi of Memnon (a legendary hero, whom they supposed to be Ethiopian).

Amenhotep IV succeeded his father in 1379 BC. He attempted a religious revolution, the substitution of a monotheistic cult of the sun-god Aton for the ancient religion. To mark his seriousness, he changed his name to Akhnaton and founded a new city at Amarna, 300 miles north of Thebes, where a temple with a roofless sanctuary open to the sun's rays was the centre of the new religion. Although there can be no doubt of Akhnaton's seriousness of purpose and personal piety, his attempt must have been doomed from the start, given the religious conservatism of Egypt, but there may

This carving in a rock temple high up the Nile commemorates the defeat of the Nubians by the great Ramses II, the nineteenth-dynasty Pharaoh who gave Egypt security by campaigns against the Libyans, Ethiopians and Nubians and by concluding an alliance with the Hittites for mutual support against the Assyrians.

have been political motives for his persistence. Perhaps he was trying to recover power usurped by the priests of Amon-Re. Whatever the explanation, the opposition Akhnaton provoked by this religious innovation helped to cripple him on other fronts. Meanwhile, Hittite pressure was producing clear signs of strain in the Egyptian dependencies; Akhnaton could not save the Mitanni who lost all their lands west of the Euphrates to the Hittites in 1372 and dissolved in civil war which foreshadowed their kingdom's disappearance thirty years or so later. The Egyptian sphere was crumbling. There were other motives, perhaps, than religious outrage for the later exclusion of Akhnaton's name from the official lists of kings.

His successor bore a name which is possibly the most famous to descend to us from ancient Egypt and a significant one: Amenhotep IV had changed his to Akhnaton because he wished to erase the reminiscence of the cult of the old god

Amon; his successor and son-in-law changed his name from Tutankhaton to register the restoration of the old cult of Amon and the overthrow of the attempted religious reform. It may have been gratitude for this that led to the magnificent burial in the Valley of the Kings which was given to Tutankhamon after only a short and otherwise unremarkable reign.

When he died, the New Kingdom had two centuries of life ahead, but their atmosphere is

The opening of the tomb of Tutankhamon captured the imagination of the Western world because of the splendour of the treasures it contained. It also provided a bitter confirmation to archaeologists of the extent to which, as they already suspected, other tombs had suffered from the depredations of robbers. The works it contained represented the peak of the delicate and refined style evolved in the isolated court life centered at Amarna, the capital of Akhnaton. Among the tomb's contents were four gilded goddesses, one of whom is shown here. They stood around the shrine containing the jars in which were placed viscera of the embalmed and mummified king.

one of only occasionally interrupted and steadily accelerating decline. Symptomatically, Tutankhamon's widow arranged to marry a Hittite prince (though he was murdered before the ceremony could take place). Later kings made efforts to recover lost ground and sometimes succeeded; the waves of conquest rolled back and forth over Palestine and at one time a pharaoh took a Hittite princess as a bride as his predecessors had taken princesses from other peoples. But there were yet more new enemies appearing; even a Hittite alliance was no longer a safeguard. The Aegean was in uproar, the islands 'poured out their people all together' and 'no land stood before them', say the Egyptian records. These sea peoples were eventually beaten off, but the struggle was hard.

At some time during these turbulent years a small Semitic people, called by the Egyptians 'Hebrews', left the delta and (according to their later tradition) followed their leader Moses out of Egypt into the deserts of Sinai. From about 1150 BC the signs of internal disorganization, too, are plentiful. One king, Ramses III, died as a result of a conspiracy in the harem; he was the last to achieve some measure of success in offsetting the swelling tide of disaster. We hear of strikes and economic troubles under his successors; there is the ominous symptom of sacrilege in a generation of looting of the royal tombs at Thebes. The pharaoh is losing his power to priests and officials and the last of the twentieth dynasty, Ramses XI, was in effect a prisoner in his own palace. The age of Egypt's imperial power was over. So in fact was that of the Hittites, and of other empires of the end of the first millennium. Not only Egypt's unquestioned power, but the world which was the setting of her glories, was passing away.

Undoubtedly, it is in changes affecting the whole ancient world that much of the explanation of the decline of Egypt must be sought, yet it is impossible to resist the feeling that the last centuries of the New Kingdom expose weaknesses present in Egyptian civilization from the beginning. These are not easy to discern at first sight; the spectacular heritage of Egypt's monuments and a history counted not in centuries but in millennia stagger the critical sense and stifle scepticism. Yet the creative quality of Egyptian civilization seems, in the end, strangely to miscarry. Colossal resources of labour are massed under the direction of men who, by the standards of any age, must have been outstanding civil servants, and the end is the creation of the greatest tombstones the world has ever seen. Craftsmanship of exquisite quality is employed, and its masterpieces are grave-goods. A highly literate élite utilizing a complex and subtle language and a material of unsurpassed convenience uses them copiously, but has no philosophical or religious idea comparable to those of Greek or Jew to give to the world. It is difficult not to sense an ultimate sterility, a nothingness at the heart of this glittering *tour de force*.

In the other scale must be placed the sheer staying-power of ancient Egyptian civilization; after all, it worked for a very long time, a spectacular fact. Though it underwent at least two phases of considerable eclipse, it recovered from them, seemingly unchanged. Survival on such a scale is a great material and historical success; what remains obscure is why it should have stopped there. Egypt's military and economic power in the end made little permanent difference to the world. Her civilization was never successfully spread abroad. Perhaps this is because its survival owed much to its setting. If it was a positive success to create so rapidly institutions which with little fundamental change could last so long, this could probably have been done by any ancient civilization enjoying such a degree of immunity from intrusion. China was to show impressive continuity, too.

It is important also to remember once more how slow and imperceptible all social and cultural change was in early times; we are used to it and must find it difficult to sense the huge inertia possessed by any successful social system (one, that is, which enables men to grapple effectively with their physical and mental environment) at almost any age before the most recent. In the ancient world the sources of fundamental change were far fewer and far more occasional than now. The pace of historical change is rapid in ancient Egypt if we think of prehistoric times; it seems glacially slow if we reflect how little an Egyptian's life must have changed between Menes and Thotmes III, a period of more than fifteen hundred years and therefore comparable to that which separates us from the end of Roman Britain. Marked change could only come from sudden and overwhelming natural disaster (and the Nile was a reliable safeguard), or invasion or conquest (and Egypt long stood at the edge of the battleground of peoples in the Near East, affected only occasionally by their comings and goings). Only very slowly could technology or economic forces exert such pressures for change as we assume to be normal. As for intellectual stimuli, these could hardly be strong in a society where the whole apparatus of a cultural tradition was directed to the inculcation of a changeless routine.

In the end, speculation about the nature of Egyptian history tends always to revert to the great natural image of the Nile. It was always present to the Egyptian eyes, so prominent, perhaps, that it could not be seen for the colossal and unique influence it was, for no context broader than its valley needed consideration. While in the background the incomprehensible (but in the end world-making) wars of the Fertile Crescent rage across the centuries, the history of Old Egypt goes on for thousands of years, virtually a function of the remorseless, beneficent flooding and subsidence of the Nile. On its banks a grateful and passive people gather the richness it bestows. From it could be set aside what they thought necessary for the real business of living: the proper preparation for death.

4 Intruders and invaders: The Dark Ages of the ancient Near East

A complicating world

Mesopotamia and Egypt are the foundation-stones of written history. For a long time the first two great centres of civilization dominate chronology and may conveniently be dealt with more or less in isolation. But obviously their story is not the whole story of the ancient Near East, let alone of the ancient world. Soon after 2000 BC the movements of other peoples were already breaking it up into new patterns. A thousand years later, other centres of civilization were in existence elsewhere and we are well into the historical era.

Unfortunately for the historian, there is no simple and obvious sequence to give unity to this story even in the Fertile Crescent, which for a long time continued to show more creativity and dynamism than any other part of the world. Instead there is a muddle of changes whose beginnings lies far back in the second millennium and which go on until the first of a new succession of empires emerges in the ninth century BC. The sweeping political upheavals which stud this confusion are hard even to map in outline, let alone to explain; fortunately, their details do not need to be unravelled here. What is a little easier to discern is their origins in

On the walls of a temple Ramses III celebrated his victory over the 'sea-peoples' at the beginning of the twelfth century BC. This fragment shows Egyptian vessels in action against the invaders, who may have included peoples later termed Philistines and Achaeans.

new sources of change. History was speeding up and civilization was providing men with new opportunities. Before submerging ourselves in the flood of events, it is worth while to try to grasp what some of the change-making forces of the times were.

Great migrations of peoples such as those already touched upon are still the most obvious ones. Their fundamental pattern does not change for a thousand years or so after 2000 BC, nor does the ethnic cast of the drama. The basic dynamic was provided by the pressure of Indo-European peoples on the Fertile Crescent from both east and west. Their variety and numbers grow greater; their names need not be remembered here but some of them bring us to the remote origins of Greece. Meanwhile, Semitic peoples dispute with the Indo-Europeans the Mesopotamian valley; with Egypt and the mysterious 'Peoples of the Sea' they fight over Sinai, Palestine and the Levant. Another great branch of the Indo-European race is established in Iran – and from it will eventually come the greatest of all the empires of the ancient past, that of sixth-century Persia. Still another branch pushes out into India. These movements must explain much of what lies behind a shifting pattern of empires and kingdoms which can only be touched though they went on for centuries. By the standards of modern times some of their creations were quite long-lived; from about 1600 BC a people called Kassites from Caucasia ruled in Babylon for four and a half centuries, which is a duration comparable to that of the entire history of British overseas empire. Yet, by the standards of Egypt such politics are the creatures of a moment, born today and swept away tomorrow.

It would indeed by surprising if they had not proved fragile in the end, for many other new forces were also at work in the first millennium and they multiplied the effect of the wanderings of peoples. One of them which has left deep traces is an improvement in military technique. Fortification and, presumably, siege-craft had already reached a fairly high level in Mesopotamia by 2000 BC. Among the Indo-European peoples who nibbled at the civilization these skills protected were some with recent nomadic origins; perhaps for that reason they were able to revolutionize warfare in the field, though they long remained unskilled in siege-craft. Their introduction of the two-wheeled war chariot and the cavalryman transformed operations in open country. The soldiers of Sumer are depicted trundling about in chariots which are clumsy four-wheeled affairs, drawn by asses; probably they were simply a means of moving generals about or getting a leader into the mêlée, so that spear and axe could be brought to bear. The true chariot is a two-wheeled fighting vehicle, drawn by horses, the usual crew being two, one man driving, the other using it as a platform for missile weapons, especially the composite bow formed of strips of horn. The Kassites were probably the first people to exploit the horse in this way and their rulers seem to have been of Indo-European stock. Access to the high pastures to the north and east of the Fertile Crescent opened to them a reserve of horses in the lands of the nomads. In the river valleys horses were at first rare, the prized possessions of kings or great leaders, and the barbarians therefore enjoyed a great military and psychological superiority. Eventually, though, chariots were used in the armies of all the great kingdoms of the Near East; they were too valuable a weapon to be ignored. When the Egyptians expelled the Hyksos, they did so by, among other things, using this weapon against those who had conquered them with it.

Warfare was changed by riding horses, too. A cavalryman proper not only moves about in the saddle but fights from horseback; it took a long time for this art to be developed, for managing a horse and a bow or a spear at the same time is a complex matter. Cavalry were of military importance in the Near East from about 1000 BC, but riding was widespread well before this and in its homeland, up on the Iranian highlands, had been practised for more than a thousand years; the first centaurs of Greek legend may have been dimly remembered barbarian horsemen. The first millennium brought the armoured horseman, charging home and dominating foot-soldiers by sheer weight and impetus. This was the beginning of a long era in which heavy cavalry were a key weapon, though their full value was only exploited centuries later, when the invention of the stirrup gave the rider real control of his horse.

During the first millennium BC, chariots came to have parts made of iron; soon they had hooped wheels. The military advantages of this metal are obvious and it is not surprising to find its uses spreading rapidly through the Near East and far beyond, in spite of attempts by those who had iron to restrict it. These were initially the Hittites and after their decline iron-working spread rapidly, not only because it was a more effective metal for making arms, but because iron ore was more plentiful than copper or tin. It was a great stimulus to change for it made a great difference to the peoples who possessed it not only militarily but economically. In agriculture, they could use it to till heavy soils which had remained impervious to wood or flint. But there was no rapid and general transfer to the new metal. The date 1000 BC is not a bad rough division between the Bronze and Iron Ages, but it is no more than a helpful prop for the memory. After it, iron implements are much more plentiful, but some parts of even the civilized worlds live long after this still in a Bronze Age culture. Together with the 'Neolithic' elsewhere, the Bronze Age lives on, fading away only slowly like the smile on the face of the Cheshire cat well into the first millennium BC. After all, there was for a long time very little iron to go round.

This may be part of the explanation of another change of these centuries, a new and increasingly complex inter-regional and long-distance trade. This is another of those complicating inter-reactions which seem to give the ancient world a certain unity just before its disruption at the end of the second millennium BC. One symptom of this, for example, is that Spain entered in about 1000 BC upon a rôle in world history she has still not relinquished, as a supplier of minerals (she was also a great centre of metallurgy too, though). Europe as a whole, at the margins of ancient history though she might be, was given growing importance by the demand for metal and metal goods. She had the minerals and had known of them for a long time; mine-shafts in what is now Yugoslavia to get at copper sixty and seventy feet below the surface have been dated before 4000 BC. With such a background, it is not surprising that European peoples seem quickly to have developed a high level of metallurgical skill, notably in the beating of large sheets of bronze and in the handling of iron, a much more difficult problem than bronze until high enough temperatures could be created to cast it.

Much in commerce turns on transport. The carriage of goods was first a matter of using asses and donkeys; the domestication of camels in the middle of the second millennium BC made possible the caravan trade of Asia and the Arabian peninsula which was later to seem to be of ageless antiquity, and opened an environment hitherto almost impenetrable, the waterless desert. Except among nomadic peoples, wheeled transport probably had only local importance, given the poor quality of early roads. Early carts were drawn by oxen or asses; they may have been in service in Mesopotamia before 3000 BC, in Syria around 2250 BC, in Anatolia two or three hundred years later and in mainland Greece about 1500 BC.

For goods in quantity, water transport was already likely to be cheaper and simpler than transport by land; this was to be a constant of economic life until the coming of the steam railway. Long before caravans began to bring up to Mesopotamia and Egypt the gums and resins of the south Arabian coasts, ships were carrying them up the Red Sea and merchants were moving back and forth in trading vessels across the Aegean. Understandably, it was in maritime technology that some of the most important advances in transport were made.

We know that Neolithic peoples could make long journeys by sea in dugout canoes, but by about 2000 BC this stage has been left far behind in the Near East. The Egyptians of the Third Dynasty had already put a sail on a sea-going ship; the central mast and square sail were the beginning of navigation relying on anything but human energy. Improvements of rigging came slowly over the next two millennia. It has been thought that these made some approach to the fore-and-aft rigging which was necessary if ships were to sail closer to the wind, but for the most part the ships of antiquity were square-rigged. Because of this, the direction of prevailing winds was decisive in setting patterns of sea-borne communication. The only other source of energy was human: the invention of the oar is an early one and it provided the motive power for long sea crossings as well as for close handling. It seems likely, though, that oars were used more frequently in warships, and sail in what it is at a very early date possible to call merchantmen. By 1000 BC these were already being fitted with watertight decks.

Even in recent times goods have been exchanged or bartered and no doubt this was what trade meant for most of antiquity. Yet a great step was taken when money was invented. This seems to have happened in Mesopotamia, where values of account were being given in measures of grain or silver before 2000 BC. The first officially sealed means of exchange which survives comes from Cappadocia in the form of ingots of silver of the same era and this was a true metal currency. Yet though money is an important invention and one which was to spread, we have to wait until the seventh century BC for the first coins. Refined monetary devices (and Mesopotamia had a credit system and bills of exchange in early times) may help to promote trade, but they are not indispensable. Peoples in the ancient world could get along without them. The Phoenicians, a trading people of legendary skill and acumen, did not have a currency until the sixth century BC; Egypt, a centrally controlled economy and of legendary wealth, did not adopt a coinage until two centuries after that, and Celtic Europe, for all its trade in metal goods, did not coin money until two centuries later still.

Meanwhile, men exchanged goods without money, though there is a difficulty in understanding quite what this means. Although there was an important rise in the volume of goods moved about the world, by 1000 BC or so, it is very hard to say whether all of this represented what would now be termed 'trade'. Economic organization in ancient times is for a long time very obscure. Any specialized function – pottery-making, for example – implies a machinery which on the one hand distributes its products and, on the other, ensures subsistence to the specialist by redistributing to him and his fellows the food they need to survive, and perhaps other goods. But this does not require 'trade', even in the form of barter. Many peoples in historic times have been observed operating such distribution through their chiefs: these men presided over a common store, 'owning', in a sense, everything the community possessed, and doling out such shares from it as were required to keep society working smoothly. This may be the basic mechanism of exchange whose echo can be detected in the centralization of goods and supplies in Sumerian temples; it would also explain the importance of the recording and sealing of consignments deposited there and hence the early association of writing with accounting.

As for economic exchange between communities, confident generalization about its earliest stages is even more hazardous. Once into the time of historical record, we can see a large range of activities going on which involve the transfer of commodities besides those involving monetary gain as does commerce in our sense. Payment of tribute, symbolic or diplomatic gifts, votive offerings, were some of the forms it took. We should not rush to be over-definite; right down to the nineteenth century AD the Chinese empire conceived its foreign trade in terms of tribute from the outside world and the pharaohs had a way of translating trade with the Aegean into similar notions, to judge by tomb paintings. In the ancient world, such transactions might include the transfer of standard objects such as tripods or vessels of a certain weight or rings of uniform size which therefore present at an early date some of the characteristics of currency. Sometimes such things were useful; sometimes they were merely tokens. All that is wholly certain is that the movement of commodities increased and that much of this increase in the end took the form of the profitable exchanges we now think of as commerce.

The appearance of new towns must have helped. They sprang up all over the old Near East no doubt in part because of population growth. They register the successful exploitation of agricultural possibilities but also a growing parasitism. The literary tradition of the alienation of countrymen from the city is already there in the Old Testament. Yet city life also offers a new intensity of cultural creativity, a new acceleration of civilization.

One index is the spreading of literacy. In about 2000 BC, literacy was still largely confined to the river-valley civilizations and the areas they influenced. Cuneiform had spread throughout Mesopotamia and two or three languages were written in it; in Egypt the monumental inscriptions were hieroglyphic and day-to-day writing was done on papyrus in a simplified form of it called hieratic. A thousand years or so later, the picture had changed. Literate peoples could by then be found over the Near East, and in Crete and Greece, too. Cuneiform had been adapted to yet more languages with great success; even the Egyptian government adopted it for its diplomacy. But other scripts were being invented. One, in Crete, takes us to the edge of modernity, for it reveals a people in about 1500 BC whose language was Greek. With the adoption of a Semitic alphabet, the Phoenician, the medium of the first western literature was in existence by about 800 BC, and so, perhaps, was its first expression, in what were later called the works of Homer.

Such themes make nonsense of chronology; they register changes lost to sight if history is pinned too closely to specific countries. Yet individual countries and their peoples, though subject to general forces and in more and more frequent contact, also become increasingly distinct. Literacy pins down tradition; in its turn, tradition accentuates communal self-consciousness. Presumably tribes and peoples have always felt their identity; such awareness is much strengthened when states take on more continuing and institutionalized forms. The dissolution of empires into more viable units is a familiar story from Sumer to modern times, but some areas emerge time and time again as enduring nuclei of tradition. Even in the second millennium BC, states are getting more solid and show greater staying-power. They were still far from achieving that extensive and continuing control of their peoples whose possibilities have only fully been revealed in modern times. Yet even in the most ancient records there seems to be an unchecked trend towards a great regularity in government and greater institutionalizing of power. Kings surround themselves with bureaucracies and tax-collectors find the resources for larger and larger enterprises. Law becomes a widely accepted idea; wherever it penetrates, there is a limitation, even at first only implicit, of the power of the individual and an increase of that of the lawgiver. Above all, the state expresses itself in military power; the problem of maintaining standing, professional armies is solved by 1000 BC.

When such things happen, the story of governmental and social institutions begins to escape from the general categories of early civilization. In spite of a new cosmopolitanism made possible by easier intercourse and cross-fertilizing, societies take very diverse paths. The same is true of the life of the mind; its most conspicuous expression is religion. While

This damaged but reconstructed fresco from Knossos appears to show different stages of the acrobatic bull-leaping practised there. Its ritual content remains unknown, but the bull played a central part in Minoan mythology. It may have been as a representation of the elemental force of earthquakes – not uncommon in the Aegean – that the bull fascinated the Cretans. More than a thousand years later, Greeks at Ephesus still celebrated a feast at which Poseidon, the 'earth-shaker' and god of the sea, was addressed as a bull and had black bulls sacrified to him.

some have discerned in the pre-classical era a tendency towards simpler, monotheistic systems, the most obvious fact is a huge and varied pantheon of local and specialized deities, mostly coexisting tolerantly, with only an occasional indication that one god is jealous of his distinction.

There is a new scope for differentiation in new activity, too. Before civilization began art had already established itself as an autonomous activity not necessarily linked to religion or magic (often so linked though it continues to be). The first literature has already been mentioned and of other sides of the mind we also begin to see something. There is the possibility of play; gaming-boards appear in Mesopotamia, Egypt, Crete. Perhaps men were already gambling. Kings and noblemen hunted with passion, and in their palaces were entertained by musicians and dancers. Among sports, boxing seems to go back into Bronze Age Crete, an island where a unique and probably ritualistic sport of bull-leaping was also practised.

In such matters it is more obvious than anywhere else that we need not pay much heed to chronology, far less to particular dates, even when we can be sure of them. The notion of an individual civilization is less and less helpful over the era with which we have so far been concerned, too. There is too much interplay for it to bear the weight it can do in Egypt and Sumer. Somewhere between about 1500 and 800 BC big changes took place which ought not to be allowed to slip through the mesh of a net woven to catch the history of the first two great civilizations. In the confused, turbulent Near East and eastern Mediterranean of the centuries around 1000 BC a new world different from that of Sumer and the Old Kingdom was in the making.

Early civilized life in the Aegean

A new interplay of cultures brought many changes to peoples on the fringe of the Near East but the neolithic provided the foundations for civilization to emerge in the Aegean islands as it had done elsewhere. The first metal object found in Greece – a copper bead – has been dated to about 4700 BC, and European as well as Asian stimuli may have been at work. Crete is the largest of the Greek islands and several centuries before 2000 BC towns with a regular layout were being built on the island by an advanced people which had been there through neolithic times. They may have had contacts with Anatolia which spurred them to exceptional achievements, but the evidence is indecisive. They could well have arrived at civilization for themselves. At any rate, for about a thousand years they built the houses and tombs by which their culture is distinguished and these did not change much in style. By about 2500 BC there were important towns and villages on the coasts, built of stone and brick; their inhabitants practised metal-working and made attractive seals and jewels. At this stage, that is to say, the Cretans shared much of the culture of mainland Greece and Asia Minor. They exchanged goods with other Aegean communities. There then came a change. About five hundred years later they began to build the series of great palaces which are the monuments of what we call Minoan civilization; the greatest of them, Knossos, was first built about 1900 BC. Nothing quite as impressive appears anywhere else among the islands.

Minoan is a curious name; it is taken from the name of a King Minos who, although celebrated in legend, may never have existed. Much later, the Greeks believed – or said – that he was a great king in Crete who lived at Knossos, parleyed with the gods, and married Pasiphaë, the daughter of the sun. Her monstrous offspring, the Minotaur, devoured sacrificial youths and maids sent as tribute from Greece at the heart of a labyrinth eventually penetrated successfully by the hero Theseus, who slew him. This is a rich and suggestive theme and has excited scholars who believe it can throw light on Cretan civilization, but there is no proof that King Minos ever existed. It may be that, as legend suggests, there was more than one of that name, or that his name was a titular identification of several Cretan rulers. He is one of those fascinating figures who, like King Arthur, always remains just beyond the borders of history and inside those of mythology.

Minoan, then, simply means the civilization of people who lived in Bronze Age Crete; it has no other connotation. This civilization lasted some six hundred years, but only the outlines of a history can be put together. They reveal a people living in towns linked in some dependence on a monarchy at Knossos. For three or four centuries they prosper, exchanging goods with Egypt and the Greek mainland, and subsisting on a native agriculture. It may have been this which explains Minoan civilization's leap forward. Crete seems then, as today, to have been better for the production of olives and vines than both the other islands and mainland Greece. It seems likely, too, that she raised large numbers of sheep and exported wool. Whatever its precise forms, Crete experienced an important agricultural advance in late neolithic times which led not only to better cereal-growing but, above all, to the cultivation of the other two great staples of Mediterranean agriculture,

The Greeks always looked back on prehistoric Crete as a mysterious land of legend. This vase of about 500 BC shows the hero Theseus, about to ward off a boulder hurled at him by the Minotaur, the monster at the heart of the labyrinth of King Minos.

the olive and vine. They could be grown where grains could not and their discovery changed the possibilities of Mediterranean life. Immediately they permitted a larger population. On this much else could then be built because new human resources were available, but it also made new demands, for organization and government, for the regulation of a more complex agriculture and the handling of its produce.

Whether or not this explains the appearance of Minoan civilization, its peak came about 1600 BC. A century or so later, the Minoan palaces were destroyed. The mystery of this end is tantalizing. At about the same time other major towns of the Aegean islands were destroyed by fire, too. There had been earthquakes in the past; perhaps this was another of them.

117

Recent scholarship identifies a great eruption in the island of Thera at a suitable time; it could have been accompanied by tidal waves and earthquakes in Crete, seventy miles away and followed by the descent of clouds of ash which blighted Cretan fields. Some people have preferred to think of a rising against the rulers who lived in the palaces. Some have discerned signs of a new invasion, or postulated some great raid from the sea which carried off booty and prisoners, destroying a political power for ever by the damage it inflicted, but leaving no new settlers behind. None of these can be conclusively established. It is only possible to guess about what happened and the view which does least violence to the lack of evidence is that there was a natural cataclysm originating in Thera which broke the back of Minoan civilization.

Whatever the cause, this great disaster did not end early civilization in Crete, for Knossos was

On the Aegean island of Thera, at the southern edge of the Cyclades about seventy miles from Crete, a fresco has been discovered which provides one of the best surviving impressions of Minoan shipping. It depicts a magnificent fleet accompanied by leaping dolphins, making its way to harbour. All of its ships, except one, are rowed by oarsmen facing the bow, paddling rather than rowing, propelling their vessels as do the crews of small boats still today in some parts of the Mediterranean.

occupied for another century or so by people from the mainland. Nevertheless, though there were still some fairly prosperous times to come, this was in effect the end of the indigenous civilization, which never recovered to achieve so much again, though seemingly Knossos still prospered. Then, early in the fourteenth century BC it, too, was destroyed by fire. It had happened before, but this time it was not rebuilt and the story of early Cretan civilization ends.

Fortunately the salient characteristics of Minoan civilization are easier to understand than the detail of its history. The most obvious is its close relationship with the sea. More than a thousand years later, Greek tradition said that Minoan Crete was a great naval power exercising political hegemony in the Aegean through her fleet. This idea has been much blown upon by modern scholars anxious to reduce what they believe to be an anachronistic conception to more plausible proportions and it certainly seems misleading to see behind this tradition the sort of political power later exercised through their navies by such states as fifth-century Athens or nineteenth-century Great Britain. The Minoans may have had a lot of ships, but they were unlikely to be specialized at this early date and there is no hope in the Bronze Age of drawing a line between trade, piracy and counter-piracy in their employment. Probably there was no permanent Cretan 'navy' in a public sense at all. Nevertheless, the Minoans felt sufficiently sure of the protection the sea gave them – and this must have implied some confidence in their ability to dominate the approaches to the natural harbours, most of which are on the north coast – to live in towns without fortifications, built near to the shore on only slightly elevated ground. We do not have to look for a Cretan Nelson among their defenders; that would be silly. But we can envisage a Cretan Hawkins or Drake, combining trade, freebooting and protection of the home base.

The Minoans thus exploited the sea as other peoples exploited their natural environments. The result was an interchange of products and ideas providing another example of the way civilization can accelerate where there is the possibility of cross-fertilization. Minoans had close connexions with Syria before 1550 BC and traded as far west as Sicily, perhaps further. Someone took their goods up the Adriatic coasts. Even more important was their penetration of Greece. By such routes they may well have been the most important single conduit through which the products and ideas of the first civilizations reached Bronze Age Europe. Certain products begin to turn up in Egypt in the second millennium BC and this was a major outlet; the art of the New Kingdom shows Cretan influence. There was even, some scholars think, an Egyptian resident for some time at Knossos, presumably to watch over well-established interests, and it has been argued that Minoans fought with the Egyptians against the Hyksos. Cretan vases and metal goods have been found at several places in Asia Minor: these are the things which survive, but it has been argued that a wide range of other products – timber, grapes, oil, wood and even opium – were supplied by the Minoans to the mainland. In return, they took metal.

Trade and agriculture made possible a civilization of considerable solidity. One evidence of its health is its power of recovering from natural disaster, as the repeated rebuilding of the palace at Knossos seems to show. The palaces are the finest relics of Minoan civilization, but the towns were well built too, and had elaborate

For this almost spherical flask of about 1500 BC, ten inches or so in diameter, a Cretan arist found a decorative motif in the fronds of seaweed and octopus so plentiful on the shores of the Aegean Islands. It is an outstanding example of the relating of a naturalistic design to the form of the artwork, but Cretan art was for a long time rich in observation, particularly of marine subjects.

piped drains and sewers. This was technical achievement of a high order; early in the sequence of palaces at Knossos the bathing and lavatory provision is on a scale unsurpassed before Roman times. Other cultural achievement was less practical, though artistic rather than intellectual; Minoans seem to have taken their mathematics from Egypt and left it at that. Their religion went under with them, apparently leaving nothing to the future, but the Minoans had an important contribution to make to the style of another civilization on the Greek mainland. Art embodied Minoan civiliza-

tion at its highest and remains its most spectacular legacy. Its genius was pictorial and
reached a climax in palace frescoes of startling
liveliness and movement. Here is a really original
style, influential across the seas, in Egypt and in
Greece. Through other palatial arts, too, notably
the working of gems and precious metals, it was
to shape fashion elsewhere.

Minoan art provides a little evidence about
the Cretans' style of life because it is often
representational. They seem to have dressed
scantily, the women often being depicted
bare-breasted; the men are beardless. There
is an abundance of flowers and plants to suggest
a people deeply and readily appreciative of
nature's gifts; this does not give the impression that the Minoans found the world an unfriendly place. Their relative wealth – given the
standards of ancient times – is attested by the
rows of huge and beautiful oil-jars found in
their palaces. Their concern for comfort and
what cannot but be termed elegance comes
clearly through the dolphins and lilies which
decorate the apartments of a Minoan queen.

Archaeology has also provided evidence of a
singularly unterrifying religious world, though
this does not, perhaps, take us very far since we
have no texts. Though we have representations
of the Cretans' gods and goddesses, it is not
easy to be sure who they are. Nor can we
penetrate their rituals, beyond registering the
frequency of sacrificial altars, double-headed
axes, and the apparent centring of Minoan cults
in a female figure. She is perhaps, a neolithic
fertility figure such as was to appear again and
again as the embodiment of female sexuality: the
later Astarte and Aphrodite. In Crete she
appears elegantly skirted, bare-breasted, standing between lions and holding snakes. Whether
there was a male god, too, is less clear. But the
appearance of bulls' horns in many places and
of frescoes of these noble beasts is suggestive if
it is linked to legend (Minos' mother, Europa,
had been seduced by Zeus in the shape of a
bull; his wife Pasiphaë enjoyed a monstrous
coition with a bull from which was born the
half-bull, half-man Minotaur), and to the ob-

*Cretan religion has attracted much speculation;
what goddess can have represented by this
little faience statuette from Knossos? More
can perhaps be inferred from it about Cretan
dress than about Cretan mentality: other
archaeological finds suggest that she wears
much the same costume as that of court ladies
in Minoan times.*

scure but obviously important rites of bull-
leaping. It is striking that whatever it was,
Cretan religion does not seem gloomy; pictures
of sports and dancing or delicate frescoes and
pottery do not suggest an unhappy people.

The political arrangements of this society are
obscure. The palace was not only a royal residence, but in some sense an economic centre – a
great store – which may perhaps best be understood as the apex of an advanced form of exchange based on redistribution by the ruler. The

palace was also a temple, but not a fortress. In its maturity it was the centre of a highly organized structure whose inspiration may have been Asian; knowledge of the literate empires of Egypt and Mesopotamia was available to a trading people. One source of our knowledge of what Minoan government was trying to do is a huge collection of thousands of tablets which are its administrative records. They indicate rigid hierarchy and systematized administration, but not how this worked in practice. However effective government was, the only thing the records certainly show is what it aspired to, a supervision far closer and more elaborate than anything conceivable by the later Greek world. If there are any analogies, they are again with the Asian empires and Egypt.

At present, the tablets tell us only of the last phase of Minoan civilization because many of them cannot be read. The weight of scholarly opinion now inclines to the view put forward a few years ago that the script of a great mass of them found at Knossos is used to write Greek and that they date from about 1450 to 1375 BC. This confirms the archaeological evidence of the arrival of successful invaders from the mainland at about this time and of their supersession of the native rulers. The tablets are their documents, and the script in which they are written has been termed 'Linear B'. The earlier written records are found at first in hieroglyph, with some symbols borrowed from Egypt, and then in another script (not yet deciphered) termed 'Linear A' and used from perhaps as early as 1700 BC. Almost certainly it was wholly non-Greek. It seems likely that the incoming Greeks took over pre-existing Minoan administrative practice and put down records, such as were already kept, in their own tongue. The earlier tablets probably contain, therefore, information very like the later, but it is about Crete before the coming of the Greek-speaking invaders who presided over the last phase and mysterious end of Minoan civilization.

Successful invasion from the mainland was itself a sign that the conditions which had made this civilization possible were crumbling away in the troubled times of the closing Bronze Age. Crete for a long time had no rival to threaten her coasts. Perhaps the Egyptians had been too busy; in the north there had long been no possible threat. Gradually, the second of these conditions had ceased to hold. Stirring on the mainland were the same Indo-European peoples who have already cropped up in so many places in this story. Some of them penetrated Crete again after the final collapse of Knossos; they were apparently successful colonists who exploited the lowlands and drove away the Minoans with the fragments of their culture to lonely little towns of refuge where they disappear from the stage of world history.

Ironically, only two or three centuries before this, Cretan culture had exercised something like hegemony in Greece, and Crete was always to hang about mysteriously at the back of the Greek mind, a lost and golden land. A direct transfusion of Minoan culture to the mainland had taken place through the first Achaean peoples (the name usually given to these early Greek-speakers) who came down into Attica and the Peloponnese and established towns and cities there in the seventeenth and eighteenth centuries BC. They entered a land long in contact with Asia, whose inhabitants had already contributed to the future one enduring symbol of Greek life, the fortification of the high place of the town, or *acropolis*. The new arrivals were by no means culturally more advanced than those they conquered, though they brought with them the horse and war-chariot. They were barbarians by comparison with the Cretans, with no art of their own. More aware of the rôle of violence and war in society than were the islanders (no doubt because they did not enjoy the protection of the sea and had a sense of continuing pressure from the homelands from which they had come), they fortified their cities heavily and built castles. Their civilization had a military style. Sometimes they picked sites which were to be the later centres of Greek city-states; Athens and Pylos were among them. They were not very large, the biggest containing at most not more than a few thousand people. One of the most important was at Mycenae, which gave its name to the civilization that finally spread over Bronze Age Greece in the middle of the second millennium.

It left some splendid relics, for it was very rich in gold; strongly influenced by Minoan art, it was also a true synthesis of Greek and indigenous cultures on the mainland. Its institutional basis seems to have been rooted in the patriarchal ideas found among many of the Indo-European peoples, but there is more to it than this. The bureaucratic aspiration revealed by the Knossos tablets and by others from Pylos of about 1200 BC suggests currents of change flowing back from conquered Crete towards the mainland. Each considerable city had a king. The one at Mycenae, presiding over a society of warrior landowners whose tenants and slaves were the aboriginal peoples, may have been at an early date the head of some sort of federation of kings. There is suggestive evidence in Hittite diplomatic records which points to some political unity in Mycenaean Greece. Below the kings, the Pylos tablets show a close supervision and control of community life and also important distinctions between officials and, more fundamentally, between slave and free. What cannot be known is just what such differences meant in practice. Nor can we see much of the economic life which lay at the root of Mycenaean culture, beyond its centralization in the royal household, as in Crete.

Whatever its material basis, the culture represented most spectacularly at Mycenae had by 1400 BC spread all over mainland Greece and to many of the islands. It was a whole, though well-established differences of Greek dialect persisted and distinguished one people from another down to historic times. Mycenae replaced the Minoan trading supremacy in the Mediterranean with its own. It had trading-posts in the Levant and was treated as a power by Hittite kings. Sometimes exported Mycenaean pottery replaced Minoan, and there are even examples of Minoan settlements being followed by Mycenaean.

The Mycenaean empire, if the term is permissible, was at its height in the fifteenth and fourteenth centuries BC. For a while, the weakness of Egypt and the crumbling of the Hittite power favoured them; for a time a small people enriched by trade had disproportionate importance while great powers waned. Mycenaean colonies were established on the shores of Asia Minor; trade with other Asian towns, notably Troy, prospered. But there are signs of a flagging from about 1300 BC. War seems to have been one answer; Achaeans took important parts in attacks on Egypt at the end of the century and it now seems that a great raid by them which was immortalized as the Siege of Troy took place about 1200 BC. The troubled background to these events was a series of dynastic upheavals in the Mycenaean cities themselves.

What can be called the Dark Ages of the Aegean were about to close in and they are as obscure as what was happening in the Near Eastern upheavals of about the same time. When Troy fell, new barbarian invasions of mainland Greece had already begun. In the second half of the twelfth century the great Mycenaean centres were destroyed and the first Greece broke up into disconnected centres. As an entity Mycenaean civilization collapsed, but the evidence provided by archaeology is varied; not all the Mycenaean centres were abandoned, though where life continued in them it did so at a lower level of achievement. The kingly treasures disappear, the palaces are not rebuilt. In some places the established resident peoples hung on successfully for centuries; elsewhere they were ruled as serfs or driven out by their new conquerors, Indo-Europeans from the north who had been on the move from about a century before the fall of Troy. These new peoples destroyed much and brought little. It does not seem likely that they always or even usually settled the lands they ravaged, but they swept away the existing political structures and the future would be built on their kinships, not on the Mycenaean institutions. There is a picture of confusion as the Aegean Dark Age deepens; only just before 1000 BC are there a few signs that a new pattern – the ground-plan of classical Greece – is emerging.

Legendary accounts of this attribute much to one particular group among the newcomers, the Dorians. Vigorous and bold, they were to be remembered as the descendants of Heracles. Though it is very dangerous to argue back from the presence of later Greek dialects to identifiable and compact groups of early invaders, tradition makes them the speakers of a tongue, Doric, which lived on into the classical age as a dialect setting them apart. In this case, tradition has been thought by scholars to be justified. In Sparta and Argos, Dorian communities which would be future city-states established themselves. But other peoples also helped to crystallize a new civilization in this obscure period. The most successful were those later identified as speakers of 'Ionic' Greek, the Ionians of the Dark Age. Setting out from Attica (where Athens had either survived or assimilated the invaders who followed Mycenae), they took root in much of the Cyclades and Ionia, the present Turkish coast of the Aegean. Here, emulating the Dorians as migrants and pirates, they seized or founded towns, if not on islands, almost always on or near the coast, which were the future city-states of a seafaring race. Often the sites they chose had already been occupied by the Mycenaeans. Sometimes – at Smyrna, for example – they displaced earlier Greek settlers.

This a confusing picture at best and for much of it there is only fragmentary evidence. Yet from this turmoil there would slowly re-emerge the unity of civilization enjoyed by the Bronze Age Aegean. At first, though, there were centuries of disruption and particularism, a new period of provincialism in a once cosmopolitan world. Trade flagged and ties with Asia languished. What replaced them was the physical transference of people, sometimes taking centuries to establish new settled patterns, but in the end setting out the ground-plan of a future Greek world.

Immediately, there was a colossal setback in civilized life which should remind us how fragile it could be in ancient times. Its most obvious sign was a depopulation between 1100 and 1000 BC, so widespread and violent that some scholars have sought explanations in a sudden cataclysm – plague, perhaps, or a climatic change such as might have suddenly and terribly reduced the small cultivable area of the Balkan and Aegean hillsides. Whatever the cause, the effects are to be seen also in a disappearance of all elegance and skill; the carving of hard gems, the painting of frescoes and the making of fine pottery all come to a stop. Such cultural continuity as the age permitted must have been largely mental, a matter of songs, myths and religious ideas.

Of this troubled time a very little is dimly and remotely reflected in the bardic epics later set down in writing in the *Iliad* and the *Odyssey*. They include material transmitted for generations by recitation, whose origins lie in tradition near-contemporary with the events they purport to describe, though later attributed to one poet, Homer. Exactly what is reflected, though, is much harder to agree about; the consensus has recently been that it is hardly anything for Mycenaean times, and little more for what immediately followed them. The central episode of the *Iliad*, the attack on Troy, is not what matters here, though the account probably reflects a real preponderance of Achaean initiative in the settlement of Asia Minor. What survives is a little social and conceptual information carried incidentally by the poems. Though Homer gives an impression of some special pre-eminence attributed to the Mycenaean king this is information about the post-Mycenaean Aegean of the eighth century, when recovery from the Dark Ages begins. It reveals a society whose assumptions are those of barbarian warlords rather than those of kings commanding regular armies or supervising bureaucracies like those of Asia. Homer's kings are the greatest of great nobles, the heads of great households, their acknowledged authority tempered by the real power of truculent near-equals and measured by their power to impose themselves; their lives are troubled and exacting. The atmosphere is individualistic and anarchic: they are more like a band of Viking leaders than the kings whose rule is commemorated by the Mycenaean tablets. Whatever reminiscences of detail may survive from earlier times (and these have sometimes been confirmed in their accuracy by excavation) and however many reflections of later society they eventually contained, the poems only fitfully illuminate a primitive society, still in confusion, settling down perhaps, but neither so advanced as Mycenae had been, nor even dimly foreshadowing what Greece was to become.

The new civilization which was at last to emerge from the centuries of confusion owed much to the resumption of intercourse with the East. It was very important that the Hellenes (the name by which the invaders of Greece came to be distinguished from their predecessors) had spread out into the islands and on to the Asian mainland; they provided many points of contact between two cultural worlds. But they were not the only links between Asia and Europe. Seeds of civilization were always carried about by the go-betweens of world history, the great trading peoples.

One of them, another seafaring race, had a long and troubled history, though not so long as its legends said; the Phoenicians claimed that they had arrived in Tyre in about 2700 BC. This may be treated on a level with stories about the descent of the Dorian kings from Heracles. None the less, they were already settled on the coast of the modern Lebanon in the second millennium BC when the Egyptians got their supplies of cedar-wood from them. The Phoenicians were a Semitic people. Like the Arabs of the Red Sea, they became sea-farers because geography urged them to look outwards rather than inland. They lived in the narrow coastal strip which was the historic channel of communication between Africa and Asia. Behind them was a shallow hinterland, poor in agricultural resources, cut up by hills running down from the mountains to the sea so that the coastal settlements found it difficult to unite. There were parallels with the experience of later Greek states tempted to the sea in similar

circumstances and in each case the result was not only trade but colonization.

Weak at home – they came under the sway of Jew, Egyptian and Hittite in turn – it cannot be entirely coincidental that the Phoenicians emerge from the historical shadows only after the great days of Egypt, Mycenae and the Hittite empire. They, too, prospered in others' decline. It was after 1000 BC, when the great era of Minoan trade was long past, that the Phoenician cities of Byblos, Tyre and Sidon had their brief golden age. Their importance then is attested by the biblical account of their part in the building of Solomon's Temple; 'thou knowest', says Solomon, 'that there is not among us any that can skill to hew timber like unto the Sidonians', and he paid up appropriately (I Kings, V, 6). This is perhaps evidence of a uniquely large and spectacular public works contract in ancient times, and there is copious later material to show the continuing importance of Phoenician enterprise up and down the Mediterranean. Ancient writers often stressed their reputation as traders and colonizers. They even exchanged goods with the savages of Cornwall, and must have been navigators of some skill to get so far. Phoenician dyes were long famous and much sought after down to classical times. No doubt commercial need stimulated their inventiveness; it was at Byblos (from which the Greeks were to take their name for a book) that the alphabet later adopted by the Greeks was invented. This was a great step, making a more widespread literacy possible, but no remarkable Phoenician literature survives. The Phoenicians seem practical and materialist and their art usually reflects the rôle of the middleman, borrowing and copying from Asian and Egyptian models, perhaps as the customer demanded.

Trade was their great occupation and did not at first require settlement overseas. Yet the Phoenicians came to base themselves more and more on their Mediterranean colonies or trading stations, sometimes where Mycenaeans had traded before them. There were some twenty-five of these, none clearly established before the eighth century BC, though some may have followed earlier Phoenician activity on the spot. This may reflect the time of troubles which overtook the Phoenician cities after a brief phase of independence at the beginning of the first millennium. In the seventh century Sidon was razed to the ground and the daughters of the king of Tyre were carried off to the harem of the Assyrian Ashurbanipal. Phoenicia was then reduced to its colonies elsewhere in the Mediterranean and little else. Yet their foundation may also have reflected anxiety at a wave of Greek colonization in the west which threatened the supply of metal, especially of British tin and Spanish silver. This could explain the foundation of Carthage a century earlier; it was to become the seat of a power more formidable by far than Tyre and Sidon had ever been and went on to establish its own chain of colonies.

Cyprus, the place of origin of this silver bowl, was the site of important Phoenician settlements. Its closeness to the home cities of Phoenicia gave it an art much like that of the older centres. This example, decorated with sphinxes and other Egyptian figures as well as with Assyrian warriors, shows the diversity of the motifs it drew on.

Further west, beyond the Straits of Gibraltar, Cadiz was already known to Phoenicians who called there while looking for an Atlantic trade further north.

The Phoenicians were among the most important traffickers in civilization but so, willy-nilly, had been others, the Mycenaeans by their diffusion of a culture and the Hellenes by their stirring up of the ethnic world in the Aegean. The Minoans had been something more, for

Sir Henry Layard (1817–94), politician, diplomat and art-collector was also one of the founders of modern archaeology. His great work was the excavation of Nineveh and this drawing by him is of a relief from Sennacherib's palace which shows the flight of a Phoenician king before the Assyrians in 701 BC. Somewhat mysteriously, two fleets seem to be passing one another. They contain two different kinds of vessels; some are cargo-carriers and others war-vessels, equipped with rams.

they were true originators, who not only took from the great established centres of culture, but who remade what they took before diffusing it again. The rise and fall of these peoples help to explain the imposition of new shapes on the world. One important side-effect, of which little has yet been said, is the stimulation of continental Europe, though the Minoans were quickly followed by Greeks on the Mediterranean shores. The search for minerals would take explorers and prospectors further and further into that barbarian unknown. Already in the second millennium there are the first signs of a complicated future; beads found at Mycenae turned out to be manufactured in Britain from amber found in Denmark. Trade was always slowly at work, eating away isolation, changing peoples' relations with one another, imposing new shapes on the world. But it is hard to relate this story to the stirring of the ethnic pot in the Aegean, let alone to the troubled history of the Asian mainland from the second millennium BC.

The Near East in the ages of confusion

'Confusion' is a matter of perspective. For about eight hundred years, from, say, the end of Knossos, the history of the Near East is indeed very confused if our standpoint is that of world history. It is hard to find any continuing thread. Invaders came and went rapidly, some of them leaving new communities behind them, some setting up new states to replace those they overthrew. This could hardly have been grasped by many people at the time to whom these events would only have come home occasionally and suddenly, when (for instance) their homes were burned, their wives raped, their sons carried off to slavery – or, less dramatically, when they discovered their taxes would be going up again. This would be confusing enough – if a stronger word is not required. On the other hand, millions of people must also in those times have lived out their lives unaware of any change more dramatic than the arrival one day in their village of the first iron sword or sickle; hundreds of communities lived within a pattern of ideas and institutions which did not change in many generations. This is an important reservation and it must not be forgotten when we stress the dynamic and violent nature of the Near East's history during the transition from the Bronze to Iron Ages, the era already considered from the standpoint of the peoples of the Aegean.

On the mainland, the wandering peoples moved about in a zone where there were powerful and long-lasting political structures, well-established centres of government and population, numerous hierarchies of specialists in administration, religion and learning. These partly explain why the coming of new peoples obliterated less of what had already been achieved than in the Aegean. Another conservative force was the long contact many of the barbarians had already had with civilization in this region. It left them wanting not to destroy it but to enjoy its fruits themselves. These two forces helped in the long run to diffuse civilization further and to produce the increasing cosmopolitanism of a large and confused, but civilized and interconnected, Near East.

The story begins very early, somewhere back towards the beginning of the second millennium BC, with the arrival in Asia Minor of the Hittites. Perhaps they belonged to the same group of people as the Minoans; at any rate they were established in Anatolia at about the same time that Minoan civilization was rising to its greatest triumphs. They were far from being primitive barbarians. They had a legal system of their own and absorbed much of what Babylon could teach. They long enjoyed a virtual monopoly of iron in Asia; this not only had great agricultural importance but, together with the chariot, gave the Hittites a military superiority which was felt both by Egypt and by the states of the Mesopotamian valleys. The raid which cut down Babylon in about 1590 BC was something like the high-water mark of the first Hittite 'empire'. A period of eclipse and obscurity followed. Then, in the first half of the fourteenth century, came a renaissance of power. This second and even more splendid era saw a Hittite hegemony which stretched at one brief moment from the shores of the Mediterranean to the Persian Gulf. It dominated all of the Fertile Crescent except Egypt and successfully challenged even that great military power. But like other empires it crumbled after a century or so, the end coming in about 1200 BC.

The culmination and collapse of this great organizing effort at the beginning of 'dark ages' for Greece and the Aegean has two in-

A Hittite chariot carved on basalt in about 900 BC. This shows a very advanced form of the weapon, the wheels having six spokes for greater strength and the axle having been moved to the rear of the platform so that most of the weight is borne by the yoke.

teresting features. The first is that the Hittites by this time no longer enjoyed a monopoly of iron; by about 1000 BC it is to be found in use all over the Near East and its diffusion must surely be a part of the story of the swing of power against the Hittites. The other interesting feature is a coincidence with the rhythm of migrations, for it seems that the great diffusers of iron technology were the Indo-European peoples who from about 1200 were throwing everything into turmoil. The disappearance of Troy, which never recovered from the Achaean destruction, has been thought of great strategic importance in this respect; the city seems to have played until this time a leading rôle in an alliance of powers of Asia Minor who had held

the line against the barbarians from the north. After its overthrow, no other focus for resistance appeared. There is a closeness of timing which some have thought too pronounced to be merely coincidental between the collapse of the last Hittite power and the attacks of 'sea peoples' recorded in the Egyptian records. The particular conquerors of the Hittites were a people from Thrace called the Phrygians.

Meanwhile, Egypt was under grave strain. One of the attacks of the sea peoples was repelled by Ramses III about 1190 and they fell back to what was later to be called Palestine. We know that the Philistines (who were to give their name to their new home) arrived in Canaan from the sea in about 1175 BC. They may have come from Crete; they were certainly a part of the same great folk movements and they had iron and the advantages it brings. The Egyptians, of course, were their main victims. Like Vikings in the Northern Seas nearly two thousand years later, the sea-invaders plunged down on them again and again and at one time wrested from the monarchy control of the delta itself. In the early eleventh century Egypt broke apart and was disputed between two kingdoms. The great surge of barbarian peoples was wearing away the old structures of the Near East just as it had worn away Mycenaean Greece, and they were no longer Egypt's only enemies. At one point, a Libyan fleet appears to have raided the delta, though it was drawn off. In the south, the Nubian frontier did not yet present a problem, but around about 1000 BC an independent kingdom emerged in the Sudan which would later be troublesome.

This is far enough into the welter of events to make it clear that we have entered an age both too complex and too obscure for straightforward narration. Mercifully, there soon appear two threads through the turmoil. One is an old theme renewed, that of the continuing Mesopotamian tradition about to enter its last phase. The other is quite new. It begins with an event we cannot date and know only through tradition recorded centuries later, but which probably occurred during the testing time imposed on Egypt by the sea peoples. Whenever and however it happened, a turning-point has been reached in world history when there went out of Egypt people the Egyptians called Hebrews and the world later called Jews.

For many people during many centuries, mankind's history before the coming of Christianity was the history of the Jews and what they recounted of the history of others. Both were written down in the books called the Old Testament, the sacred writings of the Jewish people, subsequently diffused world-wide in many languages by the Christian missionary impulse and the invention of printing. They were to be the first people to arrive at an abstract notion of God and to forbid his representation by images. No people has produced a greater historical impact from such comparatively insignificant origins and resources, origins so insignificant indeed that it is still difficult to be sure of very much about them in spite of the huge efforts and attention directed to their uncovering.

These origins lie among the Semitic, nomadic peoples of Arabia, whose pre-historic and historic tendency was to press into the richer lands of the Fertile Crescent nearest to their original homes. The first stage of their story of which history must take notice is the age of the patriarchs, whose traditions are embodied in the biblical accounts of Abraham, Isaac and Jacob. There do not seem to be good grounds for denying that men who were the origins of these gigantic and legendary figures actually existed. If they did, they lived in about 1800 BC and their story is a part of the confusion following the end of Ur. The Bible states that Abraham came from Ur to Canaan; this is quite plausible and would not conflict with what we know of the dispersal of Amorite and other tribes in the next four hundred years. Those among them who were to be remembered as the descendants of Abraham became known in the end as 'Hebrews', a word meaning 'wanderer' which does not appear before Egyptian writings and inscriptions of the fourteenth or thirteenth centuries BC, long after their first settlement in

Canaan. Though this word is not wholly satisfactory, it is probably the best name to give the tribes with which we are concerned at this time. It is a better term to identify this group than 'Jews', and for all the traditional associations gathered round that word by centuries of popular usage it is best to reserve it (as scholars usually do) for a much later era than that of the patriarchs.

It is in Canaan that Abraham's people are first distinguishable in the Bible. They are depicted as pastoralists, organized tribally, quarrelling with neighbours and kinsmen over wells and grazing, still liable to be pushed about the Near East by the pressures of drought and hunger. One group among them went down into Egypt, we are told, perhaps in the early seventeenth century BC; it was to appear in the Bible as the family of Jacob. As the story unfolds in the Old Testament, we learn of Joseph, the great son of Jacob, rising high in Pharaoh's service. At this point we might hope for help from Egyptian records. It has been suggested that this happened during the Hyksos ascendancy, since only a period of large-scale disturbance could explain the improbable pre-eminence of a foreigner in the Egyptian bureaucracy. It may be so, but there is no evidence to confirm or disprove it. There is only tradition, as there is only tradition for all Hebrew history until about 1200 BC. This tradition is what is embodied in the Old Testament; its texts did not take the form they now have until the seventh century BC, perhaps eight hundred years after the story of Joseph, though older elements can be and have been distinguished in them. As evidence, it stands in something like the relation to Jewish origins in which Homer stands to those of Greece.

None of this would matter very much, and certainly would not interest anyone except professional scholars, were it not for events which occurred from one to three thousand years later. Then, the destinies of the whole world were swayed by the Christian and Islamic civilizations whose roots lay in the religious tradition of a tiny, not very easily identifiable Semitic people for centuries hardly distinguishable from many similar wanderers by the rulers of the great empires of Mesopotamia and Egypt. This was because the Hebrews somehow arrived at a unique religious vision.

Throughout the world of the ancient Near East it is possible to see at work forces which were likely to make monotheistic religious views more appealing. The power of local deities was likely to be questioned by contemplation of the great upheavals and disasters which time and time again swept across Mesopotamia after the first Babylonian empire. The religious innovations of Akhnaton and the growing assertiveness of the cult of Marduk have both been seen as responses to such a challenge. Yet only the Hebrews and those who came to share their beliefs were able to push the process home, transcending polytheism and localism to arrive at a coherent and uncompromising monotheism.

The timing of this process is very difficult to establish but its essential steps were not complete before the eighth century BC. In the earliest times at which Hebrew religion could be distinguished it was probably polytheistic, but also monolatrous – that is to say, that like other Semitic peoples the tribes who were the forerunners of the Jews believed that there were many gods, but worshipped only one, their own. The first stage of refinement was the idea that the people of Israel (as the descendants of Jacob came to be called) owed exclusive allegiance to Yahweh, the tribal deity, a jealous God, who had made a covenant with his people to bring them again to the promised land, the Canaan to which Yahweh had already brought Abraham out of Ur, and which remains a focus of racial passion right down to the present. The covenant was a master idea. Israel was assured that *if* it *did* something, then something desirable *would* follow. This is very unlike the religious atmosphere of Mesopotamia or Egypt.

The exclusive demands of Yahweh opened the way to monotheism, for when the time came for this the Israelites felt no respect for other gods which might be an obstacle for such an evolution. Nor was this all. At an early date Yahweh's nature was already different from that of other tribal gods. That no graven image was to be made of him was the most distinctive feature of his cult. At times, he appears as other gods, in an immanent dwelling place, such as a temple made with hands, or even in manifestations of nature, but, as the Israelite religion developed, he could be seen as transcendent deity: 'the LORD is in his holy temple, the LORD's throne is in heaven', says a hymn.* He had created everything, but existed independently of his creation, a universal being. 'Whither shall I go from thy spirit? or whither shall I flee from thy presence?' asked the Psalmist.†

The creative power of Yahweh was something else differentiating the Jewish from the Mesopotamian tradition. Both saw Man's origins in a watery chaos; 'the earth was without form, and void; and darkness was upon the face of the deep', says the book of Genesis. For the Mesopotamian, no pure creation was involved; somehow, matter of some sort had always been there and the gods only arranged it. It was different for the Hebrew; Yahweh had already created the chaos itself. He was for Israel what was later described in the Christian creed, 'maker of all things, by whom all things are made'. Moreover, he made Man in his own image, as a companion, not as a slave; Man was the culmination and supreme revelation of His creative power, a creature able to know good from evil, as did Yahweh Himself. Finally, Man moved in a moral world set by Yahweh's own nature. Only He was just; man-made laws might or might not reflect His will, but He was the only author of right and justice.

The implications of such ideas were to take centuries to clarify and millennia to show their full weight. At first, they were well wrapped up in the assumptions of a tribal society looking for a god's favour in war. Much in them reflected the special experience of a desert-dwelling people. Later Jewish tradition placed great emphasis on its origins in the exodus from Egypt, a story dominated by the gigantic and

*Psalm xi, 4.   †Psalm cxxxix, 7.

mysterious figure of Moses. Clearly, when the Hebrews came to Canaan, they were already consciously a people, grouped round the cult of Yahweh. The biblical account of the wanderings in Sinai probably reports the crucial time when this national consciousness was forged. But the biblical tradition is again all that there is to depend upon and it was only recorded much later. It is certainly credible that the Hebrews should at last have fled from harsh oppression in a foreign land – an oppression which could, for example, reflect burdens imposed by huge building operations. Moses is an Egyptian name and it is likely that there existed an historical original of the great leader who dominates the biblical story by managing the exodus and holding the Hebrews together in the wilderness. In the traditional account, he founded the Law by bringing down the Ten Commandments from his encounter with Yahweh. This was the occasion of the renewal of the Covenant by Yahweh and his people at Mount Sinai, and it

may be seen as a formal return to its traditions by a nomadic people whose cult had been eroded by long sojourn in the Nile delta. Unfortunately, the exact rôle of the great religious reformer and national leader remains impossible to define and the Commandments themselves cannot be convincingly dated until much later than the time when he lived.

Yet though the biblical account cannot be accepted as it stands, it should be treated with respect as our only evidence for much of Jewish history. It contains much that can be

The making of bricks in Egypt, shown on a wall-painting from a Theban tomb. Some of these workers have features unlike the Egyptians shown in such records; we know that many of such labourers were foreigners and prisoners of war conscripted for such heavy work. They were called by the Egyptians apiru *– a word scholars have connected with the later appearance of the name Hebrew.*

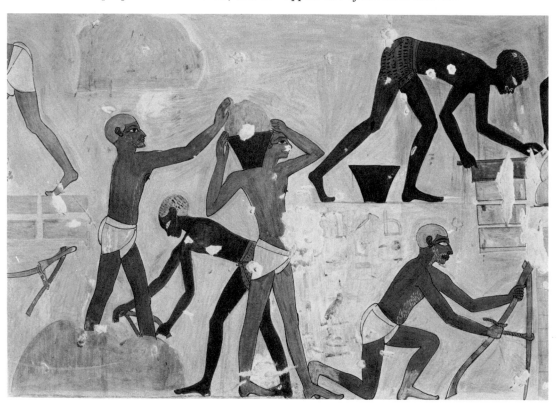

related to what is known or inferred from other sources. Archaeology comes to the historians' help only with the arrival of the Hebrews in Canaan. The story of conquest told in the book of Joshua fits evidence of destruction in the Canaanite cities in the thirteenth century BC. What we know of Canaanite culture and religion also fits the Bible's account of Hebrew struggles against local cult practice and a pervasive polytheism. Palestine was disputed between two religious traditions and two peoples throughout the twelfth century and this, of course, again illustrates the collapse of Egyptian power, since this crucial area could not have been left to be the prey of minor Semitic peoples had the monarchy's power still been effective. It now seems likely that the Hebrews attracted to their support other nomadic tribes, the touchstone of alliance being adherence to Yahweh. After settlement, although the tribes quarrelled with one another, they continued to worship Yahweh and this was for some time the only uniting force among them, for tribal divisions formed the only political institution of Israel.

The Hebrews took as well as destroyed. They were clearly in many ways less advanced culturally than the Canaanites and they took over their script. They borrowed their building practice, too, though without always achieving the same level of town life as their predecessors. Jerusalem was for a long time a little place of filth and confusion, not within striking-distance of the level reached by the town life of the Minoans long before. Yet in Israel lay the seeds of much of the future history of the human race.

Settlement in Palestine had been essentially a military operation and military necessity provoked the next stage in the consolidation of a nation. It seems to have been the challenge from the Philistines (who were obviously more formidable opponents than the Canaanites) which stimulated the emergence of the Hebrew kingship at some time about 1000 BC. With it appears another institution, that of the special distinction of the prophets, for it was the prophet Samuel who anointed (and thus, in effect, designated) Saul, the first king, and his successor, David. When Saul reigned, the Bible tells us, Israel had no iron weapons, for the Philistines took care not to endanger their supremacy by permitting them. None the less, the Jews learnt the management of iron from their enemies; the Hebrew words for 'knife' and 'helmet' both have Philistine roots. Ploughshares did not exist, but had they existed they could have been beaten into swords.

Saul won victories, but died at last by his own hand and his work was completed by David. Of all Old Testament individuals, David is outstandingly credible both for his strengths and weaknesses. Although there is no archaeological evidence that he existed, he lives still as one of the great figures of world literature and was a model for kings for two thousand years. The literary account, confused though it is, is irresistibly convincing. It tells of a noble-hearted but flawed and all-too-human hero who ended the Philistine peril and reunited the kingdom which had split at Saul's death. Jerusalem became Israel's capital and David then imposed himself upon the neighbouring peoples. Among them were the Phoenicians who had helped him against the Philistines, and this was the end of Tyre as an important independent state.

Yet it was David's son and successor, Solomon who was the first king of Israel to achieve major international standing. He gave his army a chariot arm, launched expeditions to the south against the Edomites, allied with Phoenicia and built a navy. Conquest and prosperity followed. 'And Solomon reigned over all kingdoms from the river [Euphrates] unto the land of the Philistines, and unto the border of Egypt . . . and Judah and Israel dwelt safely, every man under his vine and under his fig tree, from Dan even to Beersheba, all the days of Solomon.'* Again, this sounds like the exploitation of possibilities available to the weak when the great are in decline; the success of Israel under Solomon is further evidence of the eclipse of the older

*I Kings iv, 21, 25.

empires and it was matched by the successes of other now-forgotten peoples of Syria and the Levant who constituted the political world depicted in the obscure struggles recorded in the Old Testament. Most of them were descendants of the old Amorite expansion. Solomon was a king of great energy and drive and the economic and technical advances of the period were also very great. He was an entrepreneur ruler of the first rank. The legendary 'King Solomon's Mines' have been said to reflect the activity of the first copper refinery of which there is evidence in the Near East, though this is disputed. Certainly the building of the Temple (after Phoenician models) was only one of many public works, though perhaps the most important. David had given Israel a capital, thus increasing the tendency to political centralization. He had planned a temple and when Solomon built it the worship of Yahweh was given a more splendid form than ever before and an enduring focus.

A tribal religion had successfully resisted the early dangers of contamination by the fertility rites and polytheism of the agriculturalists among whom the Hebrews had settled in Canaan. But there was always a threat of backsliding which would compromise the covenant. With success came other dangers, too. A kingdom meant a court, foreign contacts and – in Solomon's day – foreign wives who cherished the cults of their own gods. Denunciation of the evils of departing from the law by going a-whoring after the fertility gods of the Philistines had been the first rôle of the Prophets; a new luxury gave them a social theme as well.

The prophets brought to its height the Israelite idea of God. They were not soothsayers such as the Near East already knew (though this is probably the tradition which formed the first two great prophets, Samuel and Elijah), but preachers, poets, political and moral critics. Their status depended essentially on the conviction they could generate in themselves and others, that God spoke through them. Few preachers have had such success. In the end Israel would be remembered not for the great

deeds of her kings but for the ethical standards announced by her prophets. They shaped the connexions of religion with morality which were to dominate not only Judaism but Christianity and Islam.

The prophets evolved the cult of Yahweh into the worship of a universal God, just and merciful, stern to punish sin but ready to welcome the sinner who repented. This was the climax of religious culture in the Near East, a point after which religion could be separated from locality and tribe. The prophets also bitterly attacked social injustice. Amos, Isaiah and Jeremiah went behind the privileged priestly caste to do so, denouncing religious officialdom directly to the people. They announced that all men were equal in the sight of God, that kings might not simply do what they would; they proclaimed a moral code which was a given fact, independent of human authority. Thus the preaching of adherence to a moral law which Israel believed was god-given became also a basis for a criticism of political power. Since the law was not made by man it did not ostensibly emerge from that power; the prophets could always appeal to it as well as to their divine inspiration against king or priest. It is not too much to say that, if the heart of political liberalism is the belief that power must be used within a moral framework independent of it, then its tap-root is the teaching of the prophets.

Most of the prophets after Samuel spoke against a troubled background, which they called in evidence as signs of backsliding and corruption. Israel had prospered in the eclipse of paramount powers, when kingdoms came and went with great rapidity. After Solomon's death in 935 BC Jewish history had ups as well as downs, but broadly took a turn for the worse. There had already been revolts; soon the kingdom split. Israel became a northern kingdom, built on ten tribes gathered together around a capital at Samaria; in the south the tribes of Benjamin and Judah still held Jerusalem, capital of the kingdom of Judah. The Assyrians obliterated Israel in 722 BC and the ten tribes disappeared from history in mass deportations.

A Jewish king makes obeisance to the
Assyrian ruler Shalmaneser III in 841 BC.
Jehu, the king shown here, may be the first
Jew of whom a picture survives. Above the
figures is an inscription in cuneiform.

Judah lasted longer. It was more compact and somewhat less in the path of great states; it survived until 587 BC, when Jerusalem's walls and Temple were razed by a Babylonian army. The Judaeans, too, then suffered deportations, many of them being carried away to Babylon, to the great experience of the Exile, a period so important and formative that after it we may properly speak of 'the Jews', the inheritors and transmitters of a tradition still alive and easily traced. Once more great empires had established their grip in Mesopotamia and gave its civilization its last flowering. The circumstances which had favoured the appearance of a Jewish state had disappeared. Fortunately, the religion of Judah now ensured that this did not mean that the national identity of the Jewish people was doomed too.

Since the days of Hammurabi, the peoples of the Mesopotamian valley were long squeezed in a vice of migratory peoples. For a long time its opposing jaws had been the Hittites and the Mitanni, but from time to time others had ruled in Assur and Babylon. When, in due course, the Hittites also crumbled, ancient Mesopotamia was the seat of no great military power until the ninth century BC, though such a sentence conceals much. One Assyrian king briefly conquered Syria and Babylon early in the eleventh century; he was soon swept away by a cluster of pushful Semitic tribes whom scholars call Aramaeans, followers of the old tradition of expansion into the fertile lands from the desert. Together with a new line of Kassite kings in Babylon they were the awkward and touchy neighbours of the reduced kings of Assyria for two hundred years or so – for about as long as the United States has existed. Though one of these Semitic peoples was called the Chaldees and therefore subsequently gave its name somewhat misleadingly to Babylonia, there is not much to be remarked in this story except further evidence of the fragility of the political constructions of the ancient world.

Shape only begins to reappear in the turmoil

of events in the ninth century BC when Meso-potamia recovered. Then, the Old Testament tells us, Assyrian armies were once more on the move against the Syrian and Jewish kingdoms. After some successful resistance the Assyrians came back again and again, and they con-quered. This was the beginning of a new, impor-tant and unpleasant phase of Near Eastern history. A new Assyrian empire was in the making. In the eighth century it was moving to its apogee, and Nineveh, the capital high up the Tigris, which had replaced the ancient centre of Assur, became the focus of Mesopotamian history as Babylon had once been. Assyrian empire was a unity in a way that other great empires were not; it did not rely on the vassali-zation of kings and the creation of tributaries. Instead, it swept native rulers away and in-stalled Assyrian governors. Often, too, it swept away peoples. One of its characteristic tech-niques was mass deportation, of which perhaps the most famous example was that of the Ten Tribes of Israel.

Assyrian expansion was carried forward by repeated and crushing victory. Its greatest successes followed 729 BC, when Babylon was seized. Soon after, Assyrian armies des-troyed Israel, Egypt was invaded, its kings were confined to Upper Egypt and the delta was annexed. By then Cyprus had submitted, Cilicia and Syria had been conquered. Finally, in 646 BC, Assyria made its last important conquest, part of the land of Elam, whose kings dragged the Assyrian conqueror's chariot through the streets of Nineveh. The consequences were of great importance for the whole Near East. A standardized system of government and law spanned the whole area. Conscript soldiers and deported populations were moved about within it, sapping its provincialism. Aramaic spread widely as a common language. A new cosmo-politanism was possible after the Assyrian age.

This great formative power is commemorated in monuments of undeniable impressiveness. Sargon II (721–705 BC) built a great palace at Khorsabad, near Nineveh, which covered half a square mile of land and was embellished with more than a mile of sculpted reliefs. The profits of conquest financed a rich and splendid court. Ashurbanipal (668–626 BC) also left his monu-ments (including obelisks carried off to Nineveh from Thebes), but he was a man with a taste for learning and antiquities and his finest relic is what survives of the great collection of tablets he made for his library. In it he accumulated copies of all that he could discover of the records and literature of ancient Mesopotamia. It is to these copies that we owe much of our know-ledge of Mesopotamian literature, among them the Epic of Gilgamesh in its fullest edition, a translation made from Sumerian. The ideas that moved this civilization are thus fairly accessible from literature as well as from other sources. The frequent representation of Assy-rian kings as hunters may be a part of the image of the warrior-king, but may also form part of a conscious identification of the king with legendary conquerors of nature who had been the heroes of a remote Sumerian past.

The stone reliefs which commemorate the great deeds of Assyrian kings also repeat, mono-tonously, another tale, that of sacking, enslave-ment, impalement, torture, and the Final Solution of mass deportation. Assyrian empire had a brutal foundation of conquest and intimi-dation. It was made possible by the creation of the best army seen until that time. Fed by con-scription of all males and armed with iron weapons, it also had siege artillery able to breach walls until this time impregnable, and even some mailed cavalry. It was a coordinated force of all arms. Perhaps, too, it had a special religious fervour. The god Assur is shown hovering over the armies as they go to battle and to him kings reported their victories over unbelievers.

Whatever the fundamental explanation of Assyrian success, it quickly waned. Possibly, empire put too great a strain on Assyrian numbers. The year after Ashurbanipal died, the empire began to crumble, the first sign being a revolt in Babylon. The rebels were supported by the Chaldeans and also by a great new neigh-bour, the kingdom of the Medes, now the leading Iranian people. Their entrance as a

The Assyrian war-machine in action. This relief comes from Nimrud, in the reign of Tiglathpileser III (745–727 BC), the ruler ruler who, more than any other, created the second Assyrian empire. In an attack on a walled city, archers operate from behind wickerwork screens while a protected battering-ram is trundled up a specially-built ramp. Meanwhile, infantry assault the walls with scaling-ladders and the defenders are intimidated with a preview of their likely fate – the impaled prisoners in the background.

major power on the stage of history marks an important change; for a long time the Medes had been distracted by having to deal with yet another wave of barbarian invaders from the north, the Scythians, who poured down into Iran from the Caucasus (and at the same time down the Black Sea coast towards Europe). They were light cavalrymen, fighting with the bow from horseback, and it took time to come to terms with them in the seventh century. This was, in fact, the first major eruption into western Asia of a new force in world history, nomadic peoples straight from Central Asia. Like all other great invasions, too, the Scythian advance pushed other peoples before them (the kingdom of Phrygia was overrun by one of these). Meanwhile, the last of the political units of the Near East based on the original Caucasian inhabitants was gobbled up by Scyths, Medes or Assyrians. All this took a century and more, but amounted to a great clearing of the stage. The instability and fragmentation of the periphery of the Fertile Crescent had long favoured Assyria; it ceased to do so when Scyths and Medes joined forces. This pushed Assyria over the edge and gave the Babylonians independence again; Assyria passes from history with the sack of Nineveh by the Medes in 612 BC.

This thunderbolt was not quite the end of the Mesopotamian tradition. Assyria's collapse left the Fertile Crescent open to new masters. The north was seized by the Medes, who pushed across Anatolia until halted at the borders of Lydia and at last drove the Scyths back into Russia. An Egyptian pharaoh made a grab at the south and the Levant, but was defeated by a Babylonian king, Nebuchadnezzar, who gave Mesopotamian civilization an Indian summer of grandeur and a last Babylonian empire which more than any other captured the imagination of posterity. It ran from Suez, the Red Sea and Syria across the border of Mesopotamia and the old kingdom of Elam (by then ruled by a minor Iranian dynasty called the Achaemenids). If for nothing else, Nebuchadnezzar would be remembered as a great conqueror. He destroyed Jerusalem in 587 BC after a Jewish revolt and carried off the tribes of Judah into captivity, using them as he used other captives, to carry out the embellishment of his capital, whose 'hanging gardens' or terraces were to be remembered as one of the Seven Wonders of the World. He was the greatest king of his time, perhaps of any time until his own.

The glory of the empire came to a focus in the cult of Marduk, which was now at its zenith. At a great New Year festival held each year all the Mesopotamian gods – the idols and statues of provincial shrines – came down the rivers and canals to take counsel with Marduk at his temple and acknowledge his supremacy. Borne down a processional way three-quarters of a mile long (which was, we are told, probably the most magnificent street of antiquity) or landed from the Euphrates nearer to the temple, they were taken into the presence of a statue of the god which, Herodotus reported two centuries later, was made of two and a quarter tons of gold. No doubt he exaggerated, but it was indisputably magnificent. The destinies of the whole world, whose centre was this temple, were then debated by the gods and determined

for another year. Thus theology reflected political reality. The re-enacting of the drama of creation was the endorsement of Marduk's eternal authority, and this was an endorsement of the absolute monarchy of Babylon. The king had responsibility for assuring the order of the world and therefore the authority to do so.

It was the last flowering of the Mesopotamian tradition and was soon to end. More and more provinces were lost under Nebuchadnezzar's successors. Then came an invasion in 539 BC by new conquerors from the east, the Persians, led by the Achaemenids. The passage from worldly pomp and splendour to destruction had been swift. The book of Daniel telescopes it in a magnificent closing scene, Belshazzar's feast. 'In that night', we read, 'was Belshazzar the king of the Chaldeans slain. And Darius the Median took the kingdom.' Unfortunately, this account was only written three hundred years later and it was not quite like that. Belshazzar was neither Nebuchadnezzar's son, nor his successor, as the book of Daniel says, and the king who took Babylon was called Cyrus. None the less, the emphasis of the Jewish tradition has a dramatic and psychological truth. In so far as the story of antiquity has a turning-point, this is it. An independent Mesopotamian tradition going back to Sumer is over. We are at the edge of a new world. A Jewish poet summed it up exultantly in the book of Isaiah, where Cyrus appears as a deliverer to the Jews, 'Sit thou silent, and get thee into darkness, O daughter of the Chaldeans: for thou shalt no more be called, The lady of kingdoms.'*

*Daniel v, 30–31, Isaiah xlvii, 5, xlv, 1–2.

5 The beginnings of civilization in eastern Asia

Ancient India

From the beginnings to the most recent times the centre of gravity of world history has usually swung about between the Atlantic and Iran. Yet, also until the most recent times, what went on there had little direct impact elsewhere. Much of the life of other parts of the world long remained virtually impervious to the influence of its civilizations and two areas were especially resistant: India and China. By 1000 BC civilizations appeared in these countries which were in spite of peripheral contacts, quite independent of the Near East. They were the foundations of major and enduring cultural traditions which would long outlive those of Meso-

Over a thousand seals were found at Mohenjo-Daro, a striking index of the commercial and civic vitality of that city. Unlike the Mesopotamian cylinder seals they were not rolled to make an impression, but used as stamps. Cut with tiny chisels and drills on steatite which was subsequently slightly fired, most of them are hardly more than an inch square. They depict a rich survey of the animal life of the ancient Indus plain. Some of them, like this zebu, are magnificent works of art, evocations of huge power in a tiny compass. The pictographs which accompany this beast cannot yet be read; they might reveal whether the bull was the object of a fertility cult as he was in ancient Mesopotamia. The emotional and mythical power of this noble beast was later to re-emerge in Hinduism, in the form of Nandi, a symbol of Shiva.

potamia and Egypt and they would each enjoy a huge sphere of influence.

Even now, ancient India is still visible and accessible to us in a very direct sense. At the beginning of this century, some Indian communities still lived as all our primeval ancestors must once have lived, by hunting and gathering. The bullock-cart and the potter's wheel of many villages today are, as far as can be seen, identical with those used four thousand years ago. A caste-system whose main lines were set by about 1000 BC still regulates the social assumptions even of some Indian Christians and Moslems. Gods and goddesses whose cults can be traced to the Stone Age are still worshipped at village shrines.

In some ways, then, ancient India is with us still as is no other ancient civilization. Yet though such examples of the conservatism of Indian life are commonplace, the country that contains them contains many other things too. The hunter-gatherers of the early twentieth century were the contemporaries of other Indians used to travelling in railway trains. The diversity of Indian life is enormous, but wholly comprehensible given the size and variety of its setting. The sub-continent is, after all, about the size of Europe and is divided into regions clearly distinguished by climate, terrain and crops. There are two great river valleys, the Indus and Ganges systems, in the north; between them lie desert and arid plains, and to the south the highlands of the Deccan, largely forested. When written history begins, India's racial complexity, too, is already very great:

The solid-wheeled, single-shafted carts of many country districts in modern India still closely resemble models in terracotta and bronze found in the Indus cities. They were probably toys, though some may have been votive objects. The descendants of the humped oxen which draw them still provide the better-off Indian peasant with his draught-power today.

scholars identify six main ethnic groups. Many others were later to arrive and make themselves at home in the Indian sub-continent and society, too. All this makes it hard to find a focus.

Yet Indian history has a unity in the fact of its enormous power to absorb and transform forces playing on it from the outside. This provides a thread to guide us through the patchy and uncertain illumination of its early stages which is provided by archaeology and texts long transmitted only by word of mouth. Its basis is to be found in another fact, India's large measure of insulation from the outside world by geography, in spite of its size and variety. Until the oceans began to be opened up in the sixteenth and seventeenth centuries India had only to grapple with occasional, though often irresistible, incursions by alien peoples. To the north and northwest she was protected by some of the highest mountains in the world; to the east lay belts of jungle. On the other two sides of the sub-continent's great triangle lay the huge expanses of the Indian ocean. This natural definition not only channelled and restricted communication

with the outside world; it also gave India a distinctive climate. Much of India does not lie in the tropics, but none the less that climate is tropical. The mountains keep away the icy winds of Central Asia; the long coasts open themselves to the rain-laden clouds which roll in from the oceans and cannot go beyond the northern ranges. The climatic clock is the annual monsoon, bringing the rain during the hottest months of the year. It is still the central prop of an agricultural economy.

Protected in some measure from external forces though she has always been before modern times, India's north-western frontier is more open than her others to the outside world. Baluchistan and the frontier passes were the most important zones of contact between India and other peoples right down to the seventeenth century AD; in civilized times even India's contacts with China were first made by this roundabout route (though it is not quite as roundabout as Mercator's familiar projection makes it appear). At times, this north-western region has fallen directly under foreign sway, which is suggestive when we consider the first Indian civilizations; we do not know much about the way in which they arose but we know that Sumer and Egypt antedated them. Mesopotamian records of Sargon I of Akkad report contacts with a 'Meluhha' which scholars have believed to be the Indus valley, the alluvial plains forming the first natural region encountered by the traveller once he has entered India. It was there, in rich, heavily forested countryside, that the first Indian civilizations appeared at the time when, farther west, the great movements of Indo-European peoples were beginning to act as the levers of history. There may have been more than one stimulus at work.

The evidence also shows that agriculture came later to India than to the Near East. It, too, can first be traced in the sub-continent in its north-west corner. There is archaeological evidence of domestication of animals in Baluchistan as far back as 3700 BC. By 3000 BC there are signs of settled life on the alluvial plains and parallels with other river-valley cultures begin to appear. Wheel-thrown pottery and copper implements begin to be found here. All the signs are of a gradual build-up in intensity of agricultural settlements until true civilization appears as it did in Egypt and Sumer. But there is the possibility of direct Mesopotamian influence in the background and, finally, there is at least a reasonable inference that already India's future was being shaped by the coming of new peoples from the north. At a very early date the complex racial composition of India's population suggests this, though it would be rash to be assertive about it.

When at last indisputable evidence of civilized life is available, the change is startling. One scholar speaks of a cultural 'explosion'.

Few pieces of sculpture have attracted so much speculation as this soapstone figure of a priest or deity from Mohenjo-Daro. The ornamentation of the cloak perhaps reflects a theme to be found in Mesopotamia and Persia, the arrangement of the same garment anticipates the later style in which robes were worn by Buddhist monks, the modelling of the head and features suggests faint reminiscences of Sumerian style. Nothing about the relationship of sculpture from Mohenjo-Daro – of which this is one of only a few fragmentary examples – to the sculpture of other times and places can safely be deduced from it. Too little survives of this form of art from the Indus valley cities to place much weight on it.

There may have been one crucial technological step, the invention of burnt brick (as opposed to the sun-baked mud brick of Mesopotamia) which made flood control possible in a flat plain lacking natural stone. Whatever the process, the outcome was a remarkable civilization which stretched over a half-million square miles of the Indus valley, an area greater than either the Sumerian or Egyptian.

This civilization has been given the name 'Harappan', because one of its great sites is the city of Harappa on a tributary of the Indus. There is another such site at Mohenjo-Daro; others are being discovered. Together they reveal a society highly organized and capable of carefully regulated collective works on a scale equalling those of Egypt and Mesopotamia. The creation of large granaries in the cities, together

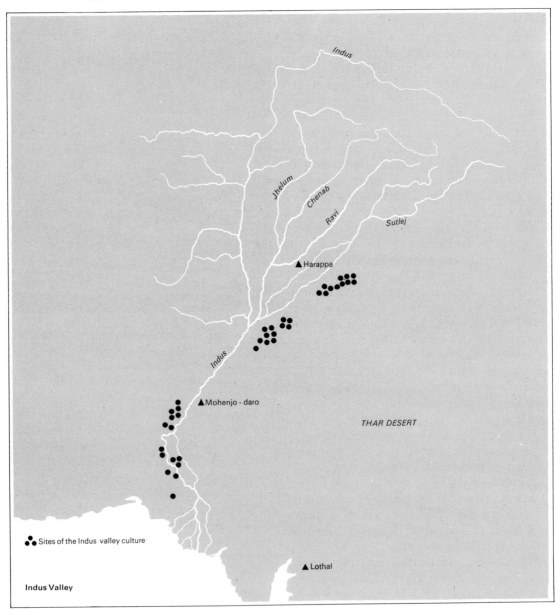

Sites of the Indus valley culture

Indus Valley

with the uniformity of weights and measures and the existence of similar schemes of building over so wide an area suggest that there may have been some real political unity, perhaps a Harappan state – some have spoken of a Harappan 'empire' –, but because Harappan writing is still undeciphered this remains speculative. It is clear that Harappan culture was established by 2250 BC and lasted for something like four hundred years with very little change.

The two cities which are its greatest monu-

The main streets of Mohenjo-Daro, thirty to forty feet wide, ran north and south, probably because of the direction of the prevailing winds. The city was ordered and planned to a degree superior to the earlier Mesopotamian cities or later Indian ones. Even the carefully laid-out drains running along these streets were provided with inspection holes. It was a rich, well-ordered place, apparently investing its wealth in its comfort and material well-being, rather than in temples and palaces.

*Four hundred miles south-east of Mohenjo-Daro
and the Indus, a city in the same style was
built at Lothal on the coast. This huge dock
some seven hundred feet long has been found
there. Seals and pottery indisputably link it to
the Indus cities, yet it appears to have outlasted
their destruction, continuing to flourish down
to perhaps as late as 1000 BC. As time passed,
its tradition waned and archaeology shows the
the growing influence of central and southern
Indian cultures upon its inhabitants.*

ments may have contained more than thirty
thousand people each. This says much for the
agriculture which sustained them; the region
was then far from being the arid zone it later
became. Mohenjo-Daro and Harappa were
between two and two and a half miles in
circumference and the uniformity and complexity of their building speaks for a very
high degree of administrative and organizational
skill. They each had a citadel and a residential
area; streets of houses were laid out on rec-
tangular grid plans and made of bricks of
standardized sizes. Both the elaborate and effective drainage systems and the internal layout of
the houses show a strong concern for bathing
and cleanliness; in some streets of Harappa
nearly every house has a bathroom. Perhaps it is
not fanciful to see in this some of the first manifestations of what has become an enduring
feature of Indian religion, the bathing and
ritual ablutions which are still as important to
Hindus.

Before 2000 BC these cities were trading far
afield and living an economic life of some complexity. A great dockyard, connected by a mile-
long canal to the sea at Lothal, four hundred
miles south of Mohenjo-Daro, suggests the importance of an external trade which reached,
through the Persian Gulf, as far north as
Mesopotamia. In the Harappan cities themselves

evidence survives of specialized craftsmen drawing their materials from all over the 'empire' and subsequently sending out again across its length and breadth the products of their skills. This civilization had cotton cloth (the first of which we have evidence) which was plentiful enough to wrap bales of goods for export whose cordage was sealed with seals found at Lothal. These seals are part of our evidence for Harappan literacy.

Inference, again, takes us a long way: the standardization – and enforcement – of weights and measures seems an inseparable concomitant of an economy covering so large an area. The seals are probably related to this. About 2500 survive. They cannot yet be read but they provide the information that the Harappans wrote from right to left in pictographic forms. Animals often appear on them. It is not evidence strong enough to postulate literacy in the full sense of a habitual use of written symbols to communicate ideas, but it is strikingly analogous in its bearing to the first appearances of literacy elsewhere: it appears to have originated in an administrative and accounting device.

This civilization diffused ideas and techniques throughout Sind and the Punjab, and down the west coast of Gujarat. The process took centuries and the picture revealed by archaeology is too confused for a consistent pattern to emerge. Where its influence did not reach, in the Ganges valley, the other great silt-rich area where large populations could live, and the south-east, different cultural processes were at work, but they have left nothing so spectacular behind them. Some of India's culture must derive from other sources; there are traces elsewhere of Chinese influence. But it is hard to be positive. Rice, for example, began to be grown in India in the Ganges valley; we simply do not know where it came from, but one possibility is China or South-East Asia, on whose coasts it was grown from about 3000 BC. Two thousand years later, this crucial item in Indian diet was used over most of the north.

Nor do we know why the first Indian civilizations began to decline, though their passing can be roughly dated. It has been suggested that the river is the explanation. Floods and uncontrollable alterations of its course may have wrecked the delicate balance of the agriculture on its banks. The forests may have been destroyed by tree-felling to provide fuel for the brick-kilns on which Harappan building depended. But there may be other agencies at work. Skeletons, perhaps those of men killed where they fell, were found in the streets of Mohenjo-Daro. Harappan civilization seems to end in the Indus valley about 1750 BC and this coincides strikingly with the irruption into Indian history of one of its great creative forces, the invading Aryans.

Strictly speaking, 'Aryan' is a linguistic term, like 'Indo-European'. None the less, it has customarily and conveniently been used to identify one group of those Indo-European peoples whose movements make up so much of the dynamic of ancient history in other parts of the Old World after 2000 BC. At about the time when other Indo-Europeans were flowing into Iran, somewhere about 1750 BC, a great influx of Aryans began to enter India from the Hindu Kush. This was the beginning of centuries during which waves of these migrants washed deeper and deeper into the Indus valley and the Punjab and eventually to the upper Ganges valley. They did not obliterate the native peoples, though the Indus valley civilization crumbled. No doubt much violence marked their coming, for the Aryans were warriors and nomads, armed with bronze weapons, bringing horses and chariots, but they settled and there are plenty of signs that the native populations lived on with them, keeping their own beliefs and practices alive. There is much archaeological evidence of the fusion of Harappan with later ways. However qualified, this was an early example of the assimilation of cultures which was always to characterize Indian society and was eventually to blossom in classical Hinduism's remarkable digestive power.

It seems clear that the Aryans brought to India no culture so advanced as that of the Harappans. It is a little like the story of the coming of Indo-Europeans in the Aegean. Writing, for example, disappears and does not emerge again until the middle of the first millennium BC; cities, too, have to be re-invented and when they are again to be found they lack the elaboration and order of their Indus valley predecessors. Instead, the Aryans appear to have slowly given up their pastoral habits and settled into agricultural life, spreading east and south from their original settlement areas in a sprawl of villages. This took centuries and not until the coming of iron was it complete and the Ganges valley colonized; iron implements made cultivation easier. Meanwhile, together with this physical opening up of the northern plains, Aryan culture had made two decisive contributions to Indian history, in its religious and in its social institutions.

The Aryans laid the foundations of the religion which has been the heart of Indian civilization. Theirs centred on sacrificial concepts; through sacrifice the process of creation which the gods achieved at the beginning of time was to be endlessly repeated. Agni, the god of fire, was very important, because it was through his sacrificial flames that men could reach the gods. Great importance and standing came to accrue to the brahmans, the priests who presided over these ceremonies. There was a pantheon of gods of whom two of the most important were Varuna, god of the heavens, controller of natural order and the embodiment of justice, and Indra, the warrior god who, year after year, slew a dragon and thus released again the heavenly waters which came with the breaking of the monsoon. We learn about them from the *Rig-Veda*, a collection of more than a thousand hymns performed during sacrifice, collected for the first time in about 1000 BC but certainly accumulated over centuries. It is one of our most important sources not only for the history of Indian religion but of Aryan society.

The *Rig-Veda* seems to reflect an Aryan culture as it had been shaped by settlement in India and not Aryan culture as it had existed at earlier times. It is, like Homer, the eventual written form of a body of oral tradition, but quite different in being much less difficult to use as a historical source, since its status is much more certain. Its sanctity made its memorization in exact form essential, and though the *Rig-Veda* was not to be written down until after AD 1300, it was then still almost certainly largely uncorrupted from its original form. Together with later Vedic hymns and prose works, it is our best source for Aryan India, whose archaeology is cramped for a long time because building materials less durable than the brick of the Indus valley cities were used in its towns and temples.

There is a suggestion again of the world of Homer in the world revealed by the *Rig-Veda*, which is one of Bronze Age barbarians. Some archaeologists now believe they can identify in the hymns references to the destruction of the Harappan cities. Iron is not mentioned and appears only to have come to India after 1000 BC (there is argument about how late and from what source). The setting of the hymns is a land which stretches from the western banks of the Indus to the Ganges, inhabited by Aryan peoples and dark-skinned native inhabitants. These formed societies whose fundamental units were families and tribes, but the legacies of these were less enduring than the pattern of Aryan social organization which eventually emerges and which we call caste.

About the early history of this vast and complicated subject and its implications it is impossible to speak with assurance. Once the rules of caste were written down, they appeared as a hard and solid structure, incapable of variation. Yet this did not happen until caste had been in existence for hundreds of years, during which it was still flexible and evolving. Its root appears to be a recognition of the fundamental class-divisions of a settled agricultural society, a warrior-aristocracy (*kshatriyas*), priestly *brahmans* and the ordinary peasant-farmers (*vaishyas*). These are the earliest divisions of Aryan society which can be observed and seem not to have been exclusive; movement between them was possible. The only unleapable barrier in early times seems to have been that between non-Aryans and Aryans; one of the words used to denote the aboriginal inhabitants of India by Aryans was *dasa*, which came eventually to denote 'slave'. To the occupational categories was soon added a fourth category for non-Aryans. Clearly it rested on a wish to preserve a degree of racial integrity. These were the *shudras*, or 'unclean', who might not study or hear the Vedic hymns.

This structure has been elaborated almost ever since. Further divisions and subdivisions appeared as society became more complex and movements within the original threefold structure took place. In this, the brahmans, the highest class, played a crucial rôle. Landowners and merchants came to be distinguished from farmers; the first were called *vaishyas*, and *shudras* became cultivators. Marriage and eating taboos were codified. This process gradually led to the appearance of the caste system as we know it. A vast number of castes and sub-castes slowly inserted themselves into the system. Their obligations and demands eventually became a primary regulator of Indian society, perhaps the only significant one in many Indians' lives. By modern times there were thousands of castes with members restricted to marrying within them, eating only food cooked by fellow-members, and obeying their regulations. Usually, too, a caste limited those who belonged to it to the practice of one craft or profession. For this reason (as well as because of the traditional ties of tribe, family and locality and the distribution of wealth) the structure of power in Indian society right down to the present day has been only in minor part a matter of formal political institutions and central authority.

In early times Aryan tribal society threw up kings, who emerged, no doubt, because of military skill. Gradually, some of them acquired something like divine sanction, though this must always have depended on a nice balance of relations with the brahman caste. But this was not the only political pattern. Not all Aryans accepted this evolution. By about 600 BC, when some of the detail of early Indian political history at last begins to be dimly discernible

through a mass of legend and myth, two sorts of political communities can be discerned, one non-monarchical, tending to survive in the hilly north, and one monarchical, established in the Ganges valley. This reflected centuries of steady pressure by the Aryans towards the east and south during which peaceful settlement and intermarriage seem to have played as big a part as conquest. Gradually, during this era, the centre of gravity of Aryan India had shifted from the Punjab to the Ganges valley as Aryan culture was adopted by the peoples already there.

As we emerge from the twilight zone of the Vedic kingdoms, it is clear that they established something like a cultural unity in northern India. The Ganges valley was by the seventh century BC the great centre of Indian population (and it may be that the cultivation of rice made this possible). A second age of Indian cities began there, the first of them market-places and centres of manufacture, to judge by the way they brought together specialized craftsmen. The great plains, together with the development of armies on a larger and better-equipped scale (we hear of the use of elephants), favoured the consolidation of larger political units. At the end of the seventh century BC, northern India was organized in sixteen kingdoms, though how this happened and how they were related to one another is still hard to disentangle from their mythology. None the less, the existence of coinage and the beginnings of writing make it likely that they provided governments of growing solidity and regularity.

The processes in which they emerged are touched on in some of the earliest literary sources for Indian history, the *Brahmanas*, texts composed during the period when Aryan culture came to dominate the Ganges valley (*c.* 800–600 BC). But more of them and the great names involved can be found in later documents, above all in two great Indian epics, the *Ramayana* and the *Mahabharata*. The present texts are the result of constant revision from about 400 BC to AD 400, when they were written down as we know them for the first time, so their interpretation is not easy. In consequence, it remains hard to get at the political and administrative reality behind, say, the kingdom of Magadha, based on southern Bihar, which emerged eventually as the preponderant power and was to be the core of the first historical empires of India. On the other hand (and possibly more importantly), the evidence is clear that the Ganges valley was already what it was to remain, the seat of empire, its cultural domination assured as the centre of Indian civilization, the future Hindustan.

The availability of later Vedic texts and the general richness of the Aryan literary record makes it all too easy to forget half the sub-continent. It tends to confine Indian history down to this point (and even after) to the history of the north. The state of archaeological and historical scholarship also reflects and further explains the concentration of attention on northern India. There is just much more known about it in ancient times than about the south. But there are also better and less accidental justifications for such an emphasis. The archaeological evidence shows, for example, a clear and continuing cultural lag in this early period between the area of the Indus system and the rest of India, to which, it may be remarked, the river was to give its name.

Enlightenment (if it may be so expressed) came from the north. In the south, near modern Mysore, settlements roughly contemporaneous with Harappa show no trace of metal, though there is evidence of the domestication of cattle and goats. Bronze and copper only begin to appear at some time after the Aryan arrival in the north. Once outside the Indus system, too, there are no contemporary metal sculptures, no seals and fewer terracotta figures. In Kashmir and eastern Bengal there are strong evidences of Stone Age cultures with affinities with those of south China, but it is at least clear that, whatever the local characteristics of the Indian cultures with which they were in contact and within the limits imposed by geography, first Harappan and then Aryan civilizations were dominant. They gradually asserted themselves

States of the Ganges Valley c500 BC

towards Bengal and the Ganges valley, down the west coast towards Gujarat, and into the central highlands of the sub-continent. This is the pattern of the Dark Age, and when we reach that of history, there is not much additional light. The survival of Dravidian languages in the south shows the region's persistent isolation.

Topography explains much of it. The Deccan has always been cut off from the north by jungle-clad mountains, the Vindhya. Internally, too, the south is broken and hilly, and this did not favour the building of large states as did the open plains of the north. Instead, south India remained fragmented, some of its regions persisting, thanks to their inaccessibility, in the hunting and gathering cultures of a tribal age. Others, by a different accident of geography, turned to the seas and provide another contrast with the predominantly agrarian empires of the north.

Millions of people must have been affected by the changes so far described. Estimates of ancient populations are notoriously unreliable. India's has been thought to have been over a hundred million in about 400 BC; as this would probably mean it then contained over half the people in the world, it seems unlikely. The importance of India's early history in any case lies less in the difference it then made to very large numbers of people than in the way it laid down patterns still shaping the lives of even larger numbers today. This is above all true of religion. Classical Hinduism crystallized in the first millenium BC and a great world religion, Buddhism, was launched then in India; it was eventually to dominate wide areas of Asia. What men do is shaped by what they believe they can do; it is the making of a culture that is the pulse of Indian history, not the making of a nation or

Over a thousand seals have been found at Mohenjo-Daro. Three have particularly interested scholars because they show a seated figure which provide us with the earliest surviving representation of a god in human form in Indian art. In this one, the horns suggest Mesopotamian influence but the seated posture and surrounding beasts have led to interpretation of it as an early version of the later Hindu Shiva, lord of the beasts.

an economy, and to this culture religion was central.

The deepest roots of the Indian religious and philosophical synthesis go very deep indeed. One of the great popular cult figures of the Hindu pantheon today is Shiva, in whose worship many early fertility cults have been brought together. A seal from Mohenjo-Daro already shows a figure who looks like an early Shiva, and stones like the *lingam* found in modern temples, the phallic cult-object which is his emblem, have been found as far back as the Harappan cities. There is some presumptive evidence therefore for the view that worship of Shiva may be the oldest surviving religious cult in the world. Though he has assimilated many important Aryan characteristics, he is pre-Aryan and survives in all his multi-faceted power, still an object of veneration in the twentieth century. Nor is Shiva the only possible survival from the remote past of Indus civilization. Other Harappan seals seem to suggest a religious world centred about a mother-goddess and a bull. The bull survives to this day, the Nandi of countless village shrines all over Hindu India (and newly vigorous in his latest incarnation, as the electoral symbol of the Congress Party).

Vishnu, another focus of modern popular Hindu devotion, is much more an Aryan. Vishnu joined hundreds of local gods and goddesses still worshipped today to form the Hindu pantheon. Yet his cult is far from being either the only or the best evidence of the Aryan contribution to Hinduism. Whatever survived from the Harappan (or even pre-Harappan) past, the major philosophical and speculative traditions of Hinduism stem from Vedic religion. These are the Aryan legacy. To this day, Sanskrit is the language of religious learning; it transcends ethnic divisions, being used in the Dravidian-speaking south as much as in the north by the brahman. It was a great cultural adhesive and so was the religion it carried. The Vedic hymns provided the nucleus for a system of religious thought more abstract and philosophical than primitive animism. Out of Aryan notions of hell and paradise, the House of Clay

and the World of the Fathers, there gradually evolved the belief that action in life determined human destiny. An immense, all-embracing structure of thought slowly emerged, a world view in which all things are linked in a huge web of being. Souls might pass through different forms in this immense whole; they might move up or down the scale of being, between castes, for example, or even between the human and animal worlds. The idea of transmigration from life to life, its forms determined by proper behaviour, was linked to the idea of purgation and renewal, to the trust in liberation from the transitory, accidental and apparent and to belief in the eventual identity of soul and absolute being in *Brahma*, the creative principle. The duty of the believer was the observation of *Dharma* – a virtually untranslatable concept, but one which embodies something of the western ideas of a natural law of justice and something of the idea that men owed respect and obedience to the duties of their station.

These developments took a long time. The steps by which the original Vedic tradition began its transformation into classical Hinduism are obscure and complicated. At the centre of the early evolution had been the brahmans who long controlled religious thought because of their key rôle in the sacrificial rites of Vedic religion. The brahmanical class appears to have used its religious authority to emphasize its seclusion and privilege. To kill a brahman soon became the gravest of crimes; even kings could not contend with their powers. Yet they seem to have come to terms with the gods of an older world in early times; it has been suggested that it may have been the infiltration of the brahmanical class by priests of the non-Aryan cults which ensured the survival and later popularity of the cult of Shiva.

The sacred *Upanishads*, texts dating from about 700 BC, mark the next important evolution towards a more philosophical religion. They are a mixed bag of about two hundred and fifty devotional utterances, hymns, aphorisms and reflexions of holy men pointing to the inner meaning of the traditional religious truths. They give much less emphasis to personal gods and goddesses than earlier texts and also include some of the earliest ascetic teachings which were to be so visible and striking a feature of Indian religion, even if only practised by a small minority. The *Upanishads* met the need felt by some men to look outside the traditional structure for religious satisfaction. Doubt appears to have been long felt about the sacrificial principle. New patterns of thought had begun to appear at the beginning of the historical period and uncertainty about traditional beliefs had already been expressed in the later hymns of the *Rig-Veda*. It is convenient to mention such developments here because they cannot be understood apart from the Aryan and pre-Aryan past. Classical Hinduism was to embody a synthesis of the kind of ideas to be found in the *Upanishads* (pointing to a monistic conception of the universe) with the more polytheistic popular tradition represented by the brahmans.

Abstract speculation and asceticism were often favoured by the existence of monasticism, a stepping-aside from material concerns to practise devotion and contemplation. The practice appeared in Vedic times. Some monks threw themselves into ascetic experiment, others pressed speculation very far and we have records of intellectual systems which rested on outright determinism and materialism. One very successful cult which did not require belief in gods and expressed a reaction against the formalism of the brahmanical religion was Jainism, a creation of a sixth-century teacher who, among other things, enjoined a respect for animal life which made agriculture or animal husbandry impossible. Jains therefore tended to become merchants, with the result that in modern times the Jain community is one of the wealthiest in India. But much the most important of the innovating systems was the teaching of the Buddha, the 'enlightened one' or 'aware one' as his name may be translated.

It has been thought significant that the Buddha like some other religious innovators, was born in one of the states to the northern edge of the Ganges plain where the orthodox,

Gandhara, in the extreme north-west, was the first great centre of Buddhist art. The peak of its achievements in sculpture came in the Christian era and often reflected the influence of Greek and Roman models; it is from that period that the most familiar images of the Buddha come (no contemporary representation of him exists). This statue, which comes from Gandhara, may be from as late as the fourth century AD. It shows the prince Siddhartha fasting before he had achieved enlightenment.

monarchical pattern emerging elsewhere was not acceptable. This was early in the sixth century BC. Siddhartha Gautama was not a brahman, but a prince of the warrior class. After being given a comfortable and gentlemanly upbringing he found it unsatisfying and left home. His first recourse was asceticism. Seven years of this proved to him that he was on the wrong road. He began instead to preach and teach. His reflexions led him to propound an austere and ethical doctrine, whose aim was liberation from suffering by achieving higher states of consciousness. This was not without parallels in the teaching of the *Upanishads*.

An important part in this was to be played by *yoga*, which was to become one of what were termed the 'Six Systems' of Hindu philosophy. The word has many meanings but in this context is roughly translatable as 'method' or 'tech-

The stupa, *or relic-mound, at Sanchi is one of the greatest monuments of early Buddhist art in India. This detail comes from one of four magnificent carved gateways to it and shows a* yakshi, *or tree-sprite, an embodiment both of the popular superstition with which Buddhist art came to terms and of the continuing and charming eroticism of Indian religious imagery.*

nique'. It sought to achieve truth through meditation after a complete and perfect control of the body had been attained. Such control was supposed to reveal the illusion of personality which, like all else in the created world, is mere flux, the passage of events, not identity. This system, too, had already been sketched in the *Upanishads* and was to become one of the aspects of Indian religion which struck visitors from Europe most forcibly. The Buddha taught his disciples so to discipline and shed the demands of the flesh that no obstacle should prevent the soul from attaining the blessed state of *Nirvana* or self-annihilation, freedom from the endless cycle of rebirth and transmigration, a doctrine urging men not to do something, but to be something – in order not to be anything. The way to achieve this was to follow an Eightfold path of moral and spiritual improvement. All this amounts to a great ethical and humanitarian revolution.

The Buddha apparently had great practical

and organizing ability which, together with his unquestionable personal quality, quickly made him a popular and successful teacher. He side-stepped, rather than opposed, the brahmanical religion and this must have smoothed his path. The appearance of communities of Buddhist monks gave his work an institutional setting which would outlive him. He also offered a rôle to those not satisfied by traditional practice, in particular to women and to low-caste followers, for caste was irrelevant in his eyes. Finally, Buddhism was non-ritualistic, simple and atheistic. It soon underwent elaboration, and, some would say, speculative contamination, and like all great religions it assimilated much pre-existing belief and practice, but by doing so it retained great popularity.

Yet Buddhism did not supplant brahmanical religion and for two centuries or so was confined to a relatively small part of the Ganges valley. In the end, too – though not until well into the Christian era – Hinduism was to be the victor and Buddhism would dwindle to a minority belief in India. But it was to become the most widespread religion in Asia and a potent force in world history. It is the first world religion to spread beyond the society in which it was born, for the older tradition of Israel had to wait for the Christian era before it could assume a world rôle. In its native India, Buddhism was to be important until the coming of Islam. The teaching of the Buddha marks, therefore, a recognizable epoch in Indian history; it justifies a break in its exposition. By his day, an Indian civilization still living today and still capable of enormous assimilative feats stood complete in its essentials. This was a huge fact; it would separate India from the rest of the world.

Much of the achievement of early civilization in India remains intangible. There is a famous figure of a beautiful dancing-girl from Mohenjo-Daro, but ancient India before the Buddha's time did not produce great art on the scale of Mesopotamia, Egypt or Minoan Crete, far less their great monuments. Marginal in her technology, she came late – though how much later than other civilizations cannot be exactly said –

A famous statuette of a dancing girl found at Mohenjo-Daro. Her features may represent a Dravidian, an Indian of the physical type later dominated in the north by the Aryans. Naked except for the numerous bangles she wears, the subject's easy, relaxed stance already foreshadows the success with which Indian sculptors in later centuries were time and time again to capture the plasticity and suppleness of the human form.

to literacy, too. Yet the uncertainties of much of India's early history cannot obscure the fact that her social system and her religions have lasted longer than any other great creations of the mind. Even to guess at what influence they exercised through the attitudes they encouraged, diffused through centuries in pure or impure forms, is rash. Only a negative dogmaticism is safe; so comprehending a set of world views, institutions so careless of the individual, philosophy so assertive of the relentless cycles of being, so lacking in any easy ascription of responsibility for good and evil, cannot but have made a history very different from that of men reared in the great Semitic traditions. And these attitudes were formed and settled for the most part a thousand years before Christ.

Ancient China

The most striking fact of China's history is that it has gone on for so long. For about two and a half thousand years there has been a Chinese nation using a Chinese language. Its government as a single empire has long been taken to be normal, in spite of intervals of division and con-

Pataling, a section of the Great Wall near Peking.

fusion. China has had a continuing experience of civilization rivalled in duration only by that of ancient Egypt and this experience is the key to Chinese historical identity; it is as much cultural as political. The example of India shows how much more important culture can be than government, and China makes the same point in a different way; in China, culture made unified government easier. Somehow at a very early date she crystallized certain institutions and attitudes which were to endure because they suited her circumstances. Some of them seem even to transcend the revolution of the twentieth century.

We must begin with the land itself, for at first sight it does not suggest much that makes for unity. The physical theatre of Chinese history is vast. China is bigger than the United States and now contains three to four times as many people. The Great Wall which guarded the northern frontier is 1400 miles long. From Peking to Hong Kong, more or less due south, is another 1200 miles as the crow flies. This

MONGOLIA

MANCHURIA

GOBI DESERT

Hsi Liao

● Mukden

● Peking

● Tientsin

Fen

Yellow

SINKIANG

Wei

● Sian

HONAN

● Nanking

● Shanghai

Yangtse-Kiang

Chungking ●

● Hangchow

● Wenchow

TIBET

Hsi

● Amoy

● Canton

Hong Kong
Macao

N

9843 ft

Physical China

huge expanse contains many climates and many regions. One great distinction stands out among them, that between northern and southern China. In summer the north is scorching and arid while the south is humid and used to floods; the north looks bare and dustblown in the winter, while the south is always green. This is not all that this distinction implies. One of the major themes of early Chinese history is of the spread of civilization, sometimes by migration, sometimes by diffusion, from north to south, of the tendency of conquest and political unification to take the same broad direction, and of the continual stimulation and irritation of northern civilization by currents from the outside, from Mongolia and Central Asia.

China's major internal divisions are set by mountains and rivers. There are three great river valleys, from north to south the Hwang-Ho, or Yellow River, the Yangtze and the Hsi. It is surprising that a country so vast and thus divided should form a unity at all. Yet China is isolated, too. One scholar thinks the country a world by itself since the start of the Pleiocene. Much of China is mountainous and except in the extreme south and north-east her frontiers still sprawl across and along great ranges and plateaux. The headwaters of the Yangtze, like those of the Mekong, lie in the high Kunlun, north of Tibet. These highland frontiers are great insulators. The arc they form is broken only where the Yellow River flows south into China from inner Mongolia and it is on the banks of this river that the story of civilization in China begins.

Skirting the Ordos desert, itself separated by another mountain range from the desolate wastes of the Gobi, the Yellow River opens a sort of funnel into north China. Through it have flowed people and soil; the *loess* beds of the river valley, easily worked and fertile, laid down by wind from the north, are the basis of the first Chinese agriculture. Once this region was richly forested and well watered but it became colder and more desiccated in one of those climatic transformations which are behind so much primeval social change. To Chinese pre-history overall, of course, there is a bigger setting than one river valley. 'Peking man' turns up as a fire-user somewhere about 600 000 BC, and there are Neanderthal traces in all three of the great river basins. The trail from these forerunners to the dimly discernible cultures which are their successors in early Neolithic times leads us to a China already divided into two cultural zones, with a meeting place and mixing area on the Yellow River. It is impossible to separate the great maze of cultural interconnexions already detectable by that time. But there was no even progress towards a uniform or united culture; even in early historical times, we are told, 'the whole of China . . . was teeming with Neolithic survivals'. Against this varied background emerged settled agriculture; nomads and settlers were to coexist in China until our own day. Rhinoceri and elephants were still hunted in the north not long before 1000 BC.

As in other parts of the world, the coming of agriculture meant a revolution. It has been argued that peoples who lived in the semitropical coastal areas of South-East Asia and south China were clearing forests to make fields as far back as 10 000 BC. Certainly they exploited vegetation to provide themselves with fibres and food. But this is still a topic about which much more needs to be known. A much better record exists in northern China where ground just above the flood level of the Yellow River begins to yield evidence of agriculture from about 5000 BC. Somewhat like that of early Egypt, it seems to have been exhaustive or semi-exhaustive. The land was cleared, used for a few years, and then left to revert to nature while the cultivators turned attention elsewhere. From this area agriculture can be seen later to spread both north to Manchuria and to the south. It has been called the 'nuclear area of North China'. Within it there soon appeared complex cultures which combined with agriculture the use of jade and wood for carving, the domestication of silkworms, the making of ceremonial vessels in forms which were to become traditional and perhaps even the use of chopsticks. In other words, this was in neolithic times already the site of much that is characteristic of the Chinese tradition of historic times.

Ancient writers recognized the importance of this revolutionary social change and legends identified a specific inventor of agriculture, yet very little can be inferred confidently or clearly about social organization at this stage. Perhaps because of this there has been a persistent tendency among Chinese to idealize it. Long after private property had become widespread it was assumed that 'under heaven every spot is the sovereign's ground' and this may reflect early ideas that all land belonged to the community as a whole. The Chinese Marxists have maintained this tradition, discerning in the archaeological evidence a golden age of primitive Communism preceding a descent into slave and

One of the earliest prehistoric clay images of a human face – from Honan in pre-Shang times. It may represent a shaman or magician wearing some kind of professional costume (the ruff suggests something special), but this is speculation. It is at least as probable that the form was determined by the shape of the pot for which this was the lid. Other such pots to which human faces form lids have been found.

feudal society. Argument is unlikely to convince those interested in the question one way or the other. Ground seems to be firmer in attributing to these times the appearance of a clan structure and totems, with prohibitions on marriage within the clan. Kinship in this form is almost the first institution which can be seen to have survived to be important in historical times. The evidence of the pottery, too, suggests some new complexity in social rôles. Already things were being made which cannot have been intended for the rough and tumble of everyday use; a stratified society seems to be emerging before we reach the historical era.

The material basis of a future China is foreshadowed at this stage in the pervasiveness of millet, a grain well adapted to the sometimes arid farming of the north. It was the basic staple of Chinese diet until about a thousand years ago and sustained a society which in due course arrived at literacy, at a great art of bronze-casting based on a difficult and advanced technology, at the means of making exquisite

Huge graves, some of them seven metres square at even their deepest levels were found near Anyang in Honan, an ancient capital of the Shang. Pictures taken during excavation show how the bodies of human funeral victims and attendants were placed on ledges around the central grave, horses being buried in the long ramps – sometimes twenty metres in length – which led down to the central grave.

pottery far finer than anything made anywhere else in the world, and, above all, at an ordered political and social system which identifies the first major age of Chinese history. But it must be remembered once more that the agriculture which made this possible was for a long time confined to north China and that many parts of this huge country only took up farming when historical times had already begun.

The narrative of early times is very hard to recover, but can be outlined with some confidence. It has been agreed that the story of civilization in China begins under rulers from a people called the Shang, the first name with independent evidence to support it in the traditional list of dynasties which was for a long time the basis of Chinese chronology. From the late eighth century BC we have better dates, but we still have no chronology for early Chinese history as well founded as, say, that of Egypt. It is more certain that somewhere about 1700 BC (and a century each way is an acceptable margin of approximation) a tribe called the Shang, which enjoyed the military advantage of the chariot, imposed itself on its neighbours over a sizable stretch of the Yellow River valley. Eventually, the Shang domain was a matter of about 40000 square miles in northern Honan; this made it somewhat smaller than England, though its cultural influences reached far beyond its periphery, as evidence from as far away as south China, Chinese Turkestan and the northeastern coast shows.

Shang kings lived and died in some state; slaves and human sacrificial victims were buried with them in deep and lavish tombs. Their courts had archivists and scribes, for this was the first truly literate culture east of Mesopotamia. This is one reason for distinguishing between Shang civilization and Shang dynastic paramountcy; this people showed a cultural influence which certainly extended far beyond any area they could have dominated politically. The political arrangements of the Shang domains themselves seem to have depended on the uniting of landholding with obligations to a king; the warrior landlords who were the key

Much of our knowledge of early China is derived from royal burials. Both Shang and Chou graves were deposits of many precious and useful objects – this one is a bronze ceremonial axe, from about the thirteenth century BC. It had a utilitarian as well as an artistic significance, and a somewhat gruesome one; it was used to behead the human sacrifices placed with the body of the king.

figures were the leading members of aristocratic lineages with semi-mythical origins. Shang government could also utilize writing and a standardized currency and its effectiveness is shown in its ability to mobilize large amounts of labour for the building of fortifications and cities.

Shang China succumbed in the end to another tribe from the west of the valley, the Chou. A probable date is 1027 BC. Under the Chou,

From both Shang and Chou tombs there survive the remains of chariots buried with their horses (and, in the case of the Shang tombs, with their drivers). In some cases the decay of the wood and wicker of the chariot is so complete that removal is impossible and the excavators have had to proceed to a painstaking removal of the surrounding earth to recover a mould of the chariot's shape, guided solely by changes of colour and texture in the earth. These chariots had to be light vehicles, for they relied upon collars on the horses' necks which tended to choke them when heavy pulling was required. Nonetheless, the chariot was a decisive military weapon in Chou times.

many of the already elaborate governmental and social structures inherited from the Shang were preserved and further refined. Burial rites, bronze-working techniques and decorative art also survived in hardly altered forms. The great work of the Chou period was the consolidation and diffusion of this heritage. In it can be discerned the hardening of the institutions of a future Imperial China which would last two thousand years.

The Chou thought of themselves as surrounded by barbarian peoples waiting for the benevolent effects of Chou tranquillization (an idea, it may be remarked, which still underlay the persistent refusal of Chinese officials two thousand years later to regard diplomatic missions from Europe as anything but respectful bearers of tribute). Chou supremacy in fact rested on war, but from it flowed great cultural consequences. As under the Shang, there was no truly unitary state and Chou government represented a change of degree rather than kind. It was usually a matter of a group of notables and vassals, some more dependent on the dynasty than others, offering in good times at least a formal acknowledgement of its supremacy and all increasingly sharing in a common culture. Political China (if it is reasonable to use such a term) rested upon big estates which had sufficient cohesion to have powers of long survival and in this process their original lords turned into rulers who could be called kings, served by elementary bureaucracies.

This system collapsed from about 700 BC, when a barbarian incursion drove the Chou from their ancestral centre to a new home farther east, in Honan. The dynasty did not end until

FACING PAGE: *On bronze vases of late Chou and Warring State times, scenes of hunting and combat often appear, sometimes repeated several times as a pattern on the same pot from a mould. It has been suggested that these reflect animal themes from the north-west and the Ordos, from the barbarian regions which so often stimulated and irrigated Chinese culture.*

256 BC, but the next distinguishable epoch dates from 403 to 221 BC and is significantly known as the Period of the Warring States. In it, a process of historical selection by conflict reached a new level of intensity. Big fish ate little fish until one only was left and all the lands of the Chinese were for the first time ruled by one great empire, the Ch'in, from which the country was to get its name. This is matter for discussion elsewhere; here it is only apropos in that it registers an epoch in Chinese history.

Reading about these events in the traditional Chinese historical accounts produces a slight feeling of beating the air, and historians who are not experts in Chinese studies may perhaps be forgiven if they cannot trace over this period of some fifteen hundred years or so any helpful narrative thread in the dimly discernible struggles of kings and over-mighty subjects. They should be; after all, scholars have not yet provided one. Nevertheless, two basic processes were going on for most of this time which were very important for the future and which give the period some unity, though their detail is elusive.

The first of these was a continuing diffusion of culture outwards from the Yellow River basin.

To begin with, Chinese civilization is a matter of tiny islands in a sea of barbarism. Yet by 500 BC it was the common possession of scores, perhaps hundreds, of 'states' scattered across the north, and it had also been carried into the Yangtze valley. This had long been a swampy, heavily forested region very different from the north and inhabited by far more primitive peoples. Chou influence – in part thanks to military expansion – irradiated this area, and helped to produce the first major culture and state of the Yangtze valley, the Ch'u civilization. Although owing much to the Chou, it had many distinctive linguistic, calligraphic, artistic and religious traits of its own. By the end of the Period of Warring States we have reached the point at which the stage of Chinese history is about to be much enlarged.

The second of these fundamental and continuing processes under both Shang and Chou was the establishment of landmarks in institutions which were to survive until modern times. Among them was a fundamental division of Chinese society into a landowning nobility and the common people. Most of these were peasants, making up the vast majority of the population and paying for all that China produced in the way of civilization and state power. What little we know of their countless lives can be quickly said; even less can be discovered than about the anonymous masses of toilers at the

Still crude as representation, but immensely appealing, this little bronze figure less than five inches high comes from late Chou times. The serving-man who is its subject has been posed so as to hold a ring which, together with the one below it, provided support for the stem of a lamp. Several similar figures have been found, but whether they were made especially for the tombs in which they were discovered or for use by the living is not known. Through them, nonetheless, we begin to sense just a little of the appearance of the ordinary Chinese of early historic times.

base of every other ancient civilization. There is one good physical reason for this: the life of the Chinese peasant was an alternation between his mud hovel in the winter and an encampment where he lived during the summer months to guard and tend his growing crops. Neither has left much trace. For the rest, he appears sunk in the anonymity of his community (he does not belong to a clan), tied to the soil, occasionally taken from it to carry out other duties and to serve his lord in war or hunting. His depressed state is expressed by the classification of modern Chinese communist historiography which lumps Shang and Chou together as 'Slavery Society' preceding the 'Feudal Society' which comes next.

Though Chinese society was to grow much more complex by the end of the Warring States period, this distinction of common people from the nobly born remained intrinsic to it. Other social distinctions were adapted to reflect it. There were important practical consequences: the nobility, for example, were not subject to punishments – such as mutilation – inflicted on the commoner; it was a survival of this in later times that the gentry were exempt from the beatings which might be visited on the commoner (though, of course, they might suffer appropriate and even dire punishment for more serious crimes). The nobility long enjoyed a virtual monopoly of wealth, too, which outlasted its earlier monopoly of metal weapons. None the less, these were not the crucial distinctions of status, which lay elsewhere, in the nobleman's special religious standing. The nobility had a monopoly of certain ritual practices because only its members could share in the cults of ancestor-worship which were the heart of the Chinese notion of kinship. Only the nobleman belonged to a family – which meant that he had ancestors. Ancestor-worship had existed before the Shang, though it does not seem that in early times many ancestors were thought likely to survive into the spirit world. Possibly the only ones lucky enough to do so would be the spirits of particularly important persons; the most likely, of course, were the rulers themselves,

Some of the bronze vessels of Shang times have marks on their inner surfaces thought to be clan signs; in this example they take the form of a stylized human figure and a bat.

whose ultimate origin, it was claimed, was itself godly.

The family emerged as a legal refinement and subdivision of the clan, and the Chou period was the most important one in its clarification. There were about a hundred clans, within each of which marriage was forbidden. Each was supposed to be founded by a hero or a god. The patriarchal heads of the clan's families and houses exercised special authority over its members and were all qualified to carry out the rituals of ancestor-worship and thus influence spirits to act as intermediaries with the powers which controlled the universe on the clan's behalf. These practices came to identify persons entitled to possess land or hold office. The clan offered a sort of democracy of opportunity at this level: any of its members could be appointed to the highest place in it, for they were all qualified by the essential virtue of a descent whose origins were godlike. In this sense, a king was only *primus inter pares*, a patrician outstanding among all patricians.

Ancestor-worship absorbed enormous quanties of religious feeling and psychic energy; its rituals were exacting and time-consuming. The common people, not sharing in this, found a religious outlet in maintaining the worship of nature gods. These always got some attention from the élite, too, the worship of mountains and rivers and the propitiating of their spirits being an important imperial duty from early times, but they were to influence the central developments of Chinese thought less than similar notions in other religions.

Religion had considerable repercussions on political forms. The heart of the ruling house's claim to obedience was its religious superiority. Through the maintenance of ritual, it had access to the goodwill of unseen powers, whose intentions might be known from the oracles. When these had been interpreted, the ordering of the agricultural life of the community was possible, for they regulated such matters as the time of sowing or harvesting. Much turned, therefore, on the religious standing of the king; it was of the first importance to the state. This was reflected in the fact that the Chou displacement of the Shang was religious as well as military. The idea was introduced that there existed a god superior to the ancestral god of the dynasty and that from him derived a mandate to rule. Now, it was claimed, he had decreed that the mandate should pass to other hands. This was the introduction of another idea fundamental to the Chinese conception of government and it was to be closely linked to the notion of a cyclic history, marked by the repeated rise and fall of dynasties. Inevitably, it provoked speculation about what might be the signs by which the recipient of the new mandate should be recognized. Filial piety was one, and to this extent, a conservative principle was implicit. But the Chou writers also introduced an idea rendered not very comfortably into English by the word 'virtue'. Clearly, its content

remained fluid; disagreement and discussion were therefore possible.

In its earliest forms the Chinese 'state' – and one must think over long periods of more than one coexisting – seems little more than an abstraction from the idea of the ruler's estate and the necessity to maintain the rituals and sacrifices. The records do not leave an impression of a very busy monarchy. Apart from the extraordinary decisions of peace or war, the king seems to have had little to do except fulfil his religious duties, hunt, and initiate building projects in the palace complexes which appear as early as Shang times. Yet there are indications of Chou kings also undertaking (with the labour of prisoners) extensive agricultural colonization. This helps to explain the relatively long time during which the early Chinese did without any very considerable bureaucracy. Gradually a hierarchy of ministers emerged who regulated court life, but the king was a landowner who needed only bailiffs, overseers and a few scribes. No doubt much of his life was spent on the move about his lands. The only other aspect of his activity which needed expert support was the supernatural. Out of this much was to grow, not least the intimate connexion between rule in China and the determination of time and the calendar, both very important in agricultural societies. These were based on astronomy, and though this came to have a respectable basis in observation and calculation, its origins were magical and religious.

Archaeologists have now recovered more than a hundred thousand fragments of the oracles of Shang times. They have provided examples of some five thousand of the first Chinese characters (about a third of them have been interpreted). This is an especially fine and complete example of an oracle on a tortoise shell which has survived almost intact. After cracks had been observed in answer to the questions previously engraved on the shell or bone, these answers were then themselves also inscribed; thus a permanent record was available for consultation.

In the earliest days all the great decisions of state, and many lesser ones, were taken by consulting oracles. This was done by engraving turtle shells or the shoulder-blades of certain animals with written characters and then applying to them a heated bronze pin so as to produce cracks on the reverse side. The direction and length of these cracks in relation to the characters would then be considered and the oracle read accordingly. This was an enormously important practice from the point of view of historians, for such oracles were kept, presumably as records. They also provide us with evidence for the foundation of Chinese language, for the characters on the oracle bones (and some early bronzes) are basically those of classical Chinese. The Shang had about 5000 such characters, though not all can be read. Nevertheless, the principles of this writing show a unique consistency; while other civilizations gave up pictographic characterization in favour of phonetic systems, the Chinese language grew and evolved, but remained essentially within the pictographic framework. Already under the Shang, moreover, the structure of the language was that of modern Chinese – monosyllabic and depending on word order, not the inflection of words, to convey meaning. The Shang, in fact, already used a form of Chinese.

Writing was to remain high on the scale of Chinese arts and has always retained some trace of the religious respect given to the first characters. Examples of Mao Tse-tung's calligraphy are widely reproduced today and enhance his prestige. This reflects the centuries during which writing remained the jealously guarded privilege of the élite. The readers of the oracles, the so-called *shih*, were the primitive form of the later scholar-gentry class; they were indispensable experts, the possessors of hieratic and arcane skills. Their monopoly was to pass to the much larger class of the scholar-gentry in later times. The language thus remained the form of communication of a relatively small élite which not only found its privileges rooted in its possession but also had an interest in preserving it against corruption or variation. It was of enormous importance as a unifying and stabilizing force because written Chinese became a language of government and culture transcending divisions of dialect, religion and region. Its use by the élite tied the country together.

Several great determinants of future Chinese history had thus been settled in outline by the end of the Chou period. That end came after increasing signs of social changes which were affecting the operation of the major institutions. This is not surprising; China long remained basically agricultural, but this did not prevent change, which was often initiated by the pressure of population upon resources. Such a change followed, for example, the introduction of iron, probably in use about 500 BC. It made possible a sharp rise in agricultural production (and therefore in population) as iron tools were brought into action on soils which stone implements could only tackle with difficulty. The first tools which have been found come from the fifth century BC; iron weapons came later. At an early date, too, tools were made by casting, for iron moulds for sickle blades have been found dating from the fourth or fifth centuries. Chinese technique in handling the new metal was thus advanced in very early times. Whether by development from bronze casting or by experiments with pottery furnaces which could produce high temperatures, China somehow arrived at the casting of iron at about the same time as knowledge of how to forge it. Exact precedence is unimportant; what is noteworthy is that sufficiently high temperatures for casting were not available elsewhere for another nineteen centuries or so.

Another important change under the later Chou was a great growth of cities. They tended to be sited on plains near rivers, but the first of them had probably taken their shape and location from the use of landowners' temples as centres of administration for their estates. This drew to them other temples, those of the popular nature gods, as communities collected about them. Then, under the Shang, a new scale of government begins to make itself felt; we find stamped-earth ramparts, specialized aristocratic and court quarters and the remains of large buildings. At Anyang, a Shang capital in about 1300 BC, there were metal foundries and potters' kilns as well as palaces and a royal graveyard. By late Chou times, the capital Wang Ch'eng is surrounded by a rectangle of earth walls each nearly three kilometres long.

There were scores of cities by 500 BC and their prevalence implies an increasingly varied society. Many of them had three well-defined areas: a small enclosure where the aristocracy lived, a larger one inhabited by specialized craftsmen and merchants, and the fields outside the walls which fed the city. A merchant class was another important development. It may not have been much regarded by the landowners but well before 1000 BC a cowry shell currency was used which shows a new complexity of economic life and the presence of specialists in trade. Their quarters and those of the craftsmen were distinguished from those of the nobility by walls and ramparts round the latter, but they, too, fell within the walls of the city – a sign of a growing need for defence. In the commercial streets of cities of the Warring States Period could be found shops selling jewellery, curios, food and clothing, as well as taverns, gambling houses and brothels.

The heart of Chinese society, none the less, still beat to the slow rhythms of the countryside. The privileged class which presided over the land system showed unmistakable signs of a growing independence of its kings as the Chou period came to an end. Landowners originally had the responsibility of providing soldiers to the king and development in the art of war helped to increase their independence. The nobleman had always had a monopoly of arms; this was already significant when, in Shang times, Chinese weaponry was limited for the most part to the bow and the bronze halberd. As time passed only noblemen could afford the more expensive weapons, armour and horses which increasingly came into use. The warrior using a chariot as a platform for archery before descending to fight the last stage of the battle on foot with bronze

The classical Chinese sword was a heavy, two-edged weapon of bronze, its hilt flanged so that it was easier to bind it with cord (as was the case with the remarkably preserved example, found in its lacquered scabbard, shown here). The coming of iron led to the gradual displacement of these weapons by a longer sword, though bronze was long used for ceremonial weapons.

167

weapons evolved in the last centuries of the pre-Christian era into a member of a team of two or three armoured warriors, moving with a company of sixty or seventy attendants and supporters, accompanied by a battle-wagon carrying the heavy armour and new weapons like the cross-bow and long iron sword which were needed at the scene of action. The nobleman remained the key figure under this system as in earlier times.

As historical records become clearer, it can be seen that economic supremacy was rooted in customary tenure which was very potent and far-reaching. Ownership of estates – theoretically all granted by the king – extended not only to land but to carts, livestock, implements and, above all, people. Labourers could be sold, exchanged, or left by will. This was another basis of a growing independence for the nobility, but it also gave fresh importance to distinctions within the landowning class. In principle, estates were held by them in concentric circles about the king's own demesne, according to their closeness to the royal line and, therefore, according to the degree of closeness of their relations with the spirit world. By about 600 BC, it seems clear that this had effectively reduced the king to dependence on the greatest princes. There appear a succession of protectors of the royal house; kings could only resist the encroachments of these oriental Bolingbrokes and Warwicks in so far as the success of any one of them inevitably provoked the jealousy of others, and because of the kingly religious prestige which still counted for much with the lesser nobility. The whole late Chou period was marked by grave disorder and growing scepticism, though, about the criteria by which the right to rule was recognizable. The price of survival for the princes who disputed China was the elaboration of more effective governments and armed forces, and often they welcomed innovators prepared to set aside tradition.

In the profound and prolonged social and political crisis of the last, decaying centuries of the Chou and the Period of Warring States (433–221 BC), it is not surprising that there should have been a burst of writing and thinking about the foundations of government and ethics. The era was to remain famous as the time of the 'Hundred Schools', when wandering scholars moved about from patron to patron, expounding their teachings. One sign of this new development was the appearance of a school of writers known as the 'Legalists'. They urged that law-making power should replace ritual observance as the principle of organization of the state; there should be one law for all, ordained and vigorously applied by one ruler. The aim of this was the creation of a wealthy and powerful state. This seemed to many of their opponents to be little more than a cynical doctrine of power, but the Legalists were to have important successes in the next few centuries because kings, at least, liked their ideas. The debate went on for a long time. In this debate the main opponents of the Legalists were the followers of the teacher whose name is the best known of all Chinese thinkers, Confucius. He was born in the middle of the sixth century BC and was to be more profoundly respected in China than any other philosopher. What he said – or was said to have said – shaped his countrymen's thinking for two thousand years and is nowadays paid the compliment of bitter attack by the first post-Confucian Chinese state.

Confucius came from a *shih* family. He was a member of the lesser nobility who had spent some time as a minister of state and an overseer of granaries. When he could not find a ruler to put into practice his recommendations for just government he turned to meditation and teaching; his aim was to present a purified and more abstract version of the doctrine he believed to lie at the heart of the traditional practices and thus to revive personal integrity and disinterested service in the governing class. He was a reforming conservative, seeking to teach his pupils the essential truths of a system materialized and obscured by routine. Somewhere in the past, he thought, lay a mythical age when each man knew his place and did his duty; to return to that was Confucius' ethical goal. He advocated the principle of order – the attribution to everything of its correct place in the great whole of experience. The practical expression of this was the strong Confucian predisposition to support the institutions likely to ensure order – the family, hierarchy, seniority – and due reverence for the many nicely graded obligations between men.

This was a teaching likely to produce men who would respect the traditional culture, emphasize the value of good form and regular behaviour, and seek to realize their moral obligations in the scrupulous discharge of duties. It was immediately successful in that many of Confucius' pupils won fame and worldly success (though his teaching deplored the conscious pursuit of such goals, urging, rather, a gentlemanly self-effacement). But it was also successful in a much more fundamental sense, since generations of Chinese civil servants were later to be drilled in the precepts of behaviour and government which he laid down. 'Documents, conduct, loyalty and faithfulness', four precepts attributed to him as his guidance on government, made reliable, disinterested and humane civil servants for hundreds of years, even if not always with uniform success.

Confucian texts were later to be treated with something like religious awe. His name gave great prestige to anything with which it was associated. He was said to have compiled some of the texts later known as the Thirteen Classics, a collection which only took its final form in the thirteenth century AD. Rather like the Old Testament, they were a somewhat miscellaneous collection of old poems, chronicles, early state documents, moral sayings and an early cosmogony called the Book of Changes, but they were used for centuries in a unified and creative way to mould generations of Chinese civil servants and rulers in the precepts which were believed to be those approved by Confucius (the parallel with the use of the Bible, at least in Protestant countries, is striking here, too). The stamp of authority was set upon this collection by the tradition that Confucius had selected it and that it must therefore contain doctrine which digested his teaching. Almost incidentally it also

reinforced still more the use of the Chinese in which these texts were written as the common language of Chinese intellectuals; the collection was another tie pulling a huge and varied country together in a common culture.

It is striking that Confucius had so little to say about the supernatural. In the ordinary sense of the word he was not a 'religious' teacher (which probably explains why other teachers had greater success with the masses). He was essentially concerned with practical duties, an emphasis he shared with several other Chinese teachers of the fourth and fifth centuries BC. Possibly because the stamp was then so firmly taken, Chinese thought seems less troubled by agonized uncertainties over the reality of the actual or the possibility of personal salvation than other, more tormented, traditions. The lessons of the past, the wisdom of former times and the maintenance of good order came to have more importance in it than pondering theological enigmas or seeking reassurance in the arms of the dark gods.

For all his great influence, Confucius was not the only maker of Chinese intellectual tradition. In part, the tone of Chinese intellectual culture is perhaps not attributable to any individual's teaching, but shares something with other oriental philosophies in its emphasis upon the meditative and reflective mode rather than the methodical and interrogatory which is more familiar to us. The mapping of knowledge by systematic interrogation of the mind about the nature and extent of its own powers is not characteristic of Chinese intellectual culture. This does not imply other-worldliness and fantasy, for Confucianism was emphatically practical. Unlike the ethical sages of Judaism, Christianity and Islam, those of China tended always to turn to the here and now.

This can also be said of systems rivalling Confucianism which were evolved to satisfy Chinese needs. One was the teaching of Mo-Tzu, a fifth-century thinker, who preached an active creed of universal altruism: men were to love strangers like their own kinsmen. Some of his followers stressed this side of his teaching, others a religious fervour which encouraged the worship of spirits and had greater popular appeal. Lao-Tse, another great teacher (though one whose vast fame conceals the fact that we know virtually nothing about him), was supposed to be the author of the text which is the key document of the philosophical system later called Taoism. This was much more obviously competitive with Confucianism, for it advocated the positive neglect of much that Confucianism upheld; respect for the established order, decorum and scrupulous observance of tradition and ceremonial, for example. Taoism urged submission to a conception already available in Chinese thought and familiar to Confucius, that of the *Tao* or 'way', the cosmic principle which runs through and sustains the harmoniously ordered universe. The practical results of this were likely to be political quietism and non-attachment; one ideal held up to its practitioners was that a village should know that other villages existed because it would hear cockerels crowing in the mornings, but should have no further interest in them, no commerce with them and no political order binding them together. Such an idealization of simplicity and poverty was the very opposite of the empire and prosperity Confucianism upheld.

Still another and later sage, the fourth-century Mencius, taught men to seek the welfare of mankind. The following of a moral code based on this principle would assure that Man's fundamentally beneficent nature would be able to operate; this was more a development of Confucian teaching than a departure from it. But all schools of Chinese philosphy had to take account of Confucian teaching, so great was its prestige and influence. Eventually, with Buddhism (which had not reached China by the end of the Warring States Period) and Taoism, Confucianism was habitually referred to as one of the 'three teachings' which were the basis of Chinese culture.

The total effect of such views is imponderable, but enormous. It is hard to say how many people were directly affected by such doctrines and, in the case of Confucianism, its great period of influence lay still in the remote future at the time of Confucius' death. Yet Confucianism's importance for the directing élites of China was to be immense. It set standards and ideals to China's leaders and rulers whose eradication was to prove impossible until our own day. Moreover, some of its precepts – filial piety, for example – filtered down to popular culture through stories and the traditional motifs of art.

Confucianism thus further solidified a civilization many of whose most striking features were well entrenched by the third century BC. One example which may be significant is evidence which has led some scholars to conclude that after the fifth century BC a tradition of astronomical observation which had already permitted the prediction of lunar eclipses fell into decline. If this is so, it suggests a conservatism resistant to true science; Confucianism may have been part of the explanation of this. Certainly its teachings accentuated the preoccupation with the past among China's rulers which was already implicit in ancestor-worship and was to give its characteristic bias to Chinese historiography.

China's great schools of ethics are one striking example of the way in which all the categories of her civilization differ from those of our own tradition and, indeed, from those of any other civilization of which we have knowledge. Its uniqueness is not only a sign of its comparative isolation, but also of its vigour. Both are displayed in its art, which is what now remains of ancient China that is most immediately appealing and accessible. Of the architecture of the Shang and Chou, not much survives; their building was often in wood, and the tombs do not reveal very much. Excavation of cities, on the other hand, reveals a capacity for massive

A Shang vase of a unique white stoneware found at Anyang. The design may have been an imitation of work in bronze.

ABOVE LEFT: *The purpose of the great bronze vessels of Shang times which are its major works of art was a ritual one. They held the wine and food which was offered in sacrifice to the gods. At a very early date the tripod form was established in bronze, but it had been employed first in pottery and it was to be exploited in many variations.*

ABOVE RIGHT: *The carving of jade in China goes back even beyond Shang times. It has left behind a rich heritage of objects which map the development of this art. Under the Shang jade was used for amulets, often carved to represent animals and birds, and for larger ceremonial objects. The pi, large discs with a hole in the centre such as this one, were already being made in about 2000 BC and later were used by the emperors themselves in Chou times for sacrifices and they still continued to be made in some numbers during the fourth century BC, when there was a revival of jade carving. Some believe the craft to have reached its height at that time.*

LEFT: *A rare Chinese gold dagger-handle of interlacing dragon motifs for ceremonial or ornamental purposes.*

construction; the wall of one Chou capital was made of pounded earth thirty feet high and forty thick.

Smaller objects survive much more plentifully and they reveal a civilization which even in Shang times is capable of exquisite work, above all in its ceramics, unsurpassed in the ancient world, with a tradition going back to neolithic times behind them. Pride of place must be given none the less to the great series of bronzes which begin in early Shang times and continue thereafter uninterruptedly. The skill of casting sacrificial containers, pots, wine-jars, weapons, tripods was already at its peak so far as casting in moulds is concerned as early as 1600 BC. And it is argued by some scholars that the lost-wax method, which made new triumphs possible, was also known in the Shang era. Bronze casting appears so suddenly and at such a high level of achievement that people long sought to explain it by transmission of the technique from outside. But there is no evidence for this and the most likely origin of Chinese metallurgy is from locally evolved techniques in several centres in the late Neolithic.

None of the bronzes reached the outside world in early times, or at least there has been no discovery of them elsewhere which can be dated before the middle of the first millennium BC. Nor are there many discoveries outside China at earlier dates of the other things to which Chinese artists turned their attention, to the carving of stone or the appallingly hard jade, for example, into beautiful and intricate designs. Apart from what she absorbed from her barbaric nomadic neighbours China not only had little to learn from the outside until well into the historical era, it seems, but had no reason to think that the outside world – if she knew of it – wanted to learn much from her.

6 The other worlds of the ancient past

So far in this account huge areas of the world have hardly been mentioned. Though Africa has priority in the story of the evolution and spread of humanity and though the entry of men to the Americas and Australasia calls for remark, once those remote events have been touched upon, the beginnings of history focus attention elsewhere. The homes of the creative cultures which have dominated the story of civilization were the Near East and the Aegean, India and China. In all these areas some meaningful break in rhythm can be seen somewhere in the first millennium BC; there are no neat divisions, but there is a certain rough synchrony which makes it reasonable to divide their histories in this era. But for the great areas of which nothing has so far been said, such a chronology would be wholly unrevealing.

This is, in the main, because none of them had achieved levels of civilization comparable to those already reached in the Mediterranean and Asia by 1000 BC. Remarkable things had been done by then in western Europe and the Americas, but when they are given due weight there still remains a qualitative gap between the complexity and resources of the societies which produced them and those of the ancient civiliza-

Still the most evocative of all the great European Megalithic centres, Stonehenge continues to draw visitors who seek to penetrate the mysteries of its alignment and design. The site was already in use much earlier, but the stones of the surviving arrangement have been dated to about 1660 BC.

tions which were to found durable traditions. The interest in the ancient history of these areas lies rather in the way they illustrate that varied roads might lead towards civilization and that different responses might be demanded by different environmental challenges than in what they left as their heritage. In one or two instances they may allow us to reopen arguments about what constitutes 'civilization', but for the period of which we have so far spoken the story of Africa, of the Pacific peoples, of the Americas and western Europe is not history but still prehistory. There is little or no correspondence between its rhythms and what was going on in the Near East or Asia, even when there were (as in the case of Africa and Europe though not of the Americas) contacts with them.

Africa is a good place to begin, because that is where the human story first began. Historians of Africa, sensitive to any slighting or imagined slighting of their subject, like to dwell upon Africa's importance in prehistory. As things earlier in this book have shown, they are quite right to do so; the bulk of the evidence for the life of the earliest hominids is African. With the Upper Palaeolithic and the Neolithic the focus moves elsewhere. Much continues to happen in Africa but the period of its greatest creative influence on the rest of the world is over.

Why this happened we cannot say, but there is a strong possibility that the primary force may have been a change of climate. Even recently, say in about 3000 BC, the Sahara supported animals such as elephants and hippopotami which have long since disappeared there; more

Thousands of rock-paintings and engravings from the ancient societies of the Tassili, on the southern edge of the Sahara desert. They present big problems of interpretation; here, for example, a hunting scene which shows an astonishing power of observing and recording animal movement has been superimposed on a much cruder, but still appealing, giraffe, between whose legs a human family seems to move. This is the art of cultures of which we still know little, though some have thought that at times between 6000 and 2000 BC the southern Sahara may have been more densely populated than any other part of the world – a striking testimony to the comparative suddenness of the change which replaced a green land with the rocky desert of those regions today.

remarkably, it was the home of pastoral peoples herding cattle, sheep and goats. In those days, what is now desert and arid canyon was fertile savannah intersected and drained by rivers running down to the Niger and by another system seven hundred and fifty miles long, running into Lake Tchad. The peoples who lived in the hills where these rivers rose have left a record of their life in rock painting and engraving very different from the earlier cave art of Europe which depicted little but animal life and only an occasional human. This record also suggests that the Sahara was then a meeting place of Negroid and what some have called 'Europoid' peoples, those who were, perhaps, the ancestors of later Berbers and Tuaregs. One of these peoples seems to have made its way down from Tripoli with horses and chariots and perhaps to have conquered the pastoralists. Whether they did so or not, their presence and that of the Negroid peoples of the Sahara show that Africa's vegetation was once very different from that of later times: horses need grazing. Yet when we reach historical times the Sahara is already desiccated, the sites of a once prosperous people are abandoned, the animals have gone.

Perhaps, therefore, it is climate which drives us back upon Egypt as the beginning of African history. Yet Egypt exercised little creative influence beyond the limits of the Nile valley. Though there were contacts with other cultures, it is not easy to penetrate them. Presumably the Libyans of Egyptian records were the sort of people who are shown with their chariots in the Sahara cave-paintings, but we do not certainly know. When the Greek historian Herodotus came to write about Africa in the fifth century BC, he reflected the domination of African history by Egypt by still finding little to say about the rest. His Africa was a land defined by the Nile, which he took to run south roughly parallel to the Red Sea and then to swing west along the borders of Libya. South of the Nile there lay for him in the east the Ethiopians, in the west a land of deserts, without inhabitants. He could obtain no information about it, though a travellers' tale spoke of a dwarfish people who were sorcerers. Given his sources, this was topographically by no means an unintelligent construction, but Herodotus had grasped only a third or a quarter of the ethnic truth. The Ethiopians, like the old inhabitants of upper Egypt, were members of the Hamitic peoples who make up one of three racial groups in Africa at the end of the Stone Age later distinguished by anthropologists. The other two were the ancestors of the modern Bushmen, inhabiting, roughly, the open areas running from the Sahara south to the Cape, and the Negroid group, eventually dominant in the central forests and West Africa. (Opinion is divided about the origin and distinctiveness of a fourth group, the Pygmies.) To judge by the stone tools, cultures associated with Hamitic or proto-Hamitic peoples seem to have been the most advanced in Africa before the coming of farming. This was, except in Egypt, a slow evolution and in Africa the hunting and gathering cultures of

prehistory have coexisted with agriculture right down to modern times.

The same growth which occurred elsewhere when food began to be produced in quantity soon changed African population patterns, first by permitting the dense settlements of the Nile valley which were the preliminary to Egyptian civilization, then by building up the Negroid population south of the Sahara, along the grasslands separating desert and equatorial forest in the second and first millennia BC. This seems to reflect a spread of agriculture southwards from the north. It also reflects the discovery of nutritious crops better suited to tropical conditions and other soils than the wheat and barley which flourished in the Nile valley. These were the millets and rice of the savannahs. The forest areas could not be exploited until the coming of other plants suitable to them from South-East Asia and eventually America. None of this happened before the birth of Christ. Thus was established one of the major characteristics of

Mediterranean region in North Africa today

MEDITERRANEAN SEA

Mediterranean flora during the Saharan pluvial

Present northern limit of tropical influences on the Sahara

TASSILI

Northern limit of the tropical African region

● Principal places where Mediterranean pollens have been found.

Climatic changes in the Sahara

Lake Chad

African history, a divergence of cultural trends within the continent. The growth of Bantu Africa at the pace of Negroid has been a matter of the last two thousand years, beginning somewhere about the start of the Christian era.

By that time, iron had come to Africa and it had already produced the first exploitation of African ores. This occurred in the first independent African state other than Egypt of which we have information, the kingdom of Kush, high up the Nile, in the region of Khartoum. This had originally been the extreme frontier zone of Egyptian activity. After Nubia had been absorbed, the Sudanese principality which existed to its south was garrisoned by the Egyptians, but in about 1000 BC it emerged as an independent kingdom, showing itself deeply marked by Egyptian civilization. Probably its inhabitants were Hamitic people and its capital was at Napata, just below the Fourth Cataract. By 730 BC Kush was strong enough to conquer Egypt and five of its kings ruled as the pharaohs known to history as the Twenty-Fifth or 'Ethiopian' dynasty. None the less, they could not arrest the Egyptian decline. When the Assyrians fell on Egypt, the Kushite dynasty ended. Though Egyptian civilization continued in the kingdom of Kush, a pharaoh of the next dynasty invaded it in the early sixth century BC. After this, the Kushites, too, began to push their frontiers further to the south and in so doing their kingdom underwent two important changes. It became more Negroid, its language and literature reflecting a weakening of Egyptian trends, and it extended its territory over new territories which contained both iron ore and the fuel needed to smelt it. The technique of smelting had been learnt from the Assyrians. The new Kushite capital at Meroe became the metallurgical centre of Africa. Iron weapons gave the Kushites the advantages over their neighbours which northern peoples had enjoyed in the past over Egypt, and iron tools extended the area which could be cultivated. On this basis was to rest some three hundred years of prosperity and civilization in the Sudan, though later than the age we are now considering.

It has already become clear that the history of man in the Americas is much shorter than that in Africa or, indeed, in any other part of the world except Australasia. Something like thirty thousand years ago, Mongoloid peoples crossed into North America from Asia. Over the next few thousand years they filtered slowly southwards. Cave-dwellers have been traced in the Peruvian Andes as early as 18 000 BC. The Americas contain very varied climates and environments; it is scarcely surprising, therefore, that archaeological evidence shows there were almost equally varied patterns of life, based on different opportunities for hunting, food-gathering and fishing. What they learnt from one another is probably undiscoverable. What is indisputable is that some of these cultures arrived independently of the Old World at the invention of agriculture.

Disagreement is still possible about when precisely this happened because, paradoxically, a great deal is known about the early cultivation of plants at a time when the scale on which this took place cannot reasonably be called agriculture. It is, nevertheless, a change which comes later than in the Fertile Crescent. Maize began to be cultivated in Mexico in about 5000 BC, but had been improved by 2000 BC in Meso-america into something like the plant we know today. This is the sort of change which made possible the establishment of large settled communities. Farther south, potatoes and manioc (another starchy root vegetable) also begin to appear at about this time and a little later there are signs that maize has spread southwards from Mexico. Everywhere, though, change is gradual; to talk of an 'agricultural revolution' is even less appropriate in the Americas than in the Near East.

Farming, villages, weaving and pottery all appear in Central America in the second millennium BC and towards the end of it come the first stirrings of the culture which produced the first recognized American civilization, that of the Olmecs of the eastern Mexican coast. It was focussed, it seems, on important ceremonial sites with large earth pyramids. At these sites

Olmec civilization mysteriously appears and disappears. At one time it may have been dominant over the whole of Mexico and influential as far south as Peru. Of its monuments, the most impressive are colossal basalt heads (such as this one from the state of Tabasco), some of them eight feet high and weighing many tons. Enormous labour must have been needed to move these monsters and the blocks from which they were cut, but virtually nothing can be said about the religion or culture which provided the necessary psychological drive for such an expenditure of effort.

have been found colossal monumental sculpture and fine carvings of figures in jade. The style of this work is highly individual. It concentrates on human and jaguar-like images, sometimes fusing them. From soon after 800 BC it seems to have prevailed right across Central America as far south as El Salvador for several centuries. But it retains its mystery, appearing without antecedents or warning in a swampy, forested region which makes it hard to explain in economic terms. We do not know why civilization which elsewhere required the relative plenty of the great river valleys should in America spring from such unpromising soil.

Olmec civilization transmitted something to the future, for the gods of the later Aztecs were to be descendants of those of the Olmecs. It may also be that the early hieroglyphic systems of Central America originate in Olmec times, though the first survivals of the characters of these systems follow only a century or so after the disappearance of Olmec culture in about 400 BC. Again, we do not know why or how this

The date of this Olmec stone figure is unknown, but it is thought to represent either a wrestler or a player in a ball game. Such a game may have been the ancestor of games later played in courts of temple complexes in other temple cultures.

179

The art of the people of the mysterious Chavín culture of Peru left to the future certain stylistic motifs – the dislocation of the face of a god such as this one into a series of disconnected conventional signs, for example – and probably some skill in the working of metal; this plaque is one of the earliest gold objects to survive from the Americas and was hammered to shape.
The inhabitants of Peru may have been metal-workers two thousand years before the Mexicans emerged from the Stone Age. The peak of their civilization came in the last one or two centuries BC.

happened. Much further south, in Peru, a culture called Chavín (after a great ceremonial site) also appeared and survived a little later than Olmec civilization to the north. It, too, had a high level of skill in working stone and spread vigorously only to dry up mysteriously.

What should be thought of these early lunges in the direction of civilization is very hard to see. Whatever their significance for the future, they are millennia behind the appearance of civilization elsewhere, whatever the cause of that may be. When the Spanish landed in the New World nearly two thousand years after the disappearance of Olmec culture they would still find most of its inhabitants working with stone tools. They

would also find complicated societies (and the relics of others) which had achieved prodigies of building and organization far out-running, for example, anything Africa could offer after the decline of ancient Egypt. It is clear only that there are no unbreakable sequences in these matters.

The only other area where a startlingly high level of achievement in stone-working was reached was western Europe and this has led to enthusiastic advocacy of the claim that it should be regarded as another seat of early 'civilization', almost as if its inhabitants were some sort of depressed class needing historical rehabilitation. Europe has already been touched upon as a supplier of metals to the ancient Near East. Yet, though much that we now find interesting was happening there at earlier dates, this does not provide a very impressive or striking story for the prehistory of the peninsula which was one day to be the heart of modern history. Prehistoric Europe is insignificant to world history except for its illustrative value. While great civilizations rose and fell in the river valleys of the Near East, Europe was largely an irrelevance to them. It sometimes received the impress of the outside world and contributed only marginally and fitfully to the process of historic change. A parallel might be Africa at a later date, another region interesting for its own sake, but not for its positive contribution to world history. It was to be a very long time before men would even be able to think of it as an entity, to conceive that there existed a geographical, let alone a cultural, unity corresponding to the later idea of Europe. To the ancient world, the northern lands where the barbarians came from before they appeared in Thrace were irrelevant (and most of them probably came from further east anyway). The north-western hinterland was only important because it occasionally disgorged commodities wanted in Asia and the Aegean.

There is not much to say, therefore, about prehistoric Europe, but in order to get a correct perspective, one more point should be made. Two Europes must be separated. One is that of the Mediterranean coasts and their peoples. Its rough boundary is the line which delimits the cultivation of the olive. South of this line, literate, urban civilization comes fairly quickly once we are into the Iron Age, and apparently comes by direct contact with more advanced areas. By 800 BC the coasts of the western Mediterranean were already beginning to experience fairly continuous contact with the East. The Europe north and west of this line is a different matter. In this area literacy was never achieved; it was only imposed much later by conquerors. It long resisted cultural influences from the south and east – or at least did not offer a favourable reception to them – and it is for two thousand years important not for its own sake but because

The superb electrum torc from Snettisham in Norfolk may resemble the one an ancient historian describes the legendary Boadicea as wearing when she rode into battle; whether or not this is so, it is a fine example of the skill of the Celtic jewellers as its peak, combining as it does different techniques – moulding and the plaiting of wire. It was probably made within the half-century or so before Julius Caesar landed in England.

of its relationship to other areas. Its rôle was not entirely passive: the movements of its peoples, its natural resources and skills all at times impinged marginally on events elsewhere. But in 1000 BC – to take an arbitrary date – or even at the beginning of the Christian era, Europe has little of its own to offer the world except its minerals, and nothing which represents cultural achievement on the scale reached by the Near East, India or China. Europe's age was still to come; hers would be the last great civilization to appear.

This was not because the continent's natural endowment was unfavourable. It contains a disproportionately large area of the world's land naturally suitable for cultivation. It would be surprising if this had not favoured an early development of agriculture and this the archaeological evidence shows. The relative ease of simple agriculture in Europe may have had a negative effect on social evolution; in the great river valleys men *had* to work collectively to control irrigation and exploit the soil if they were to survive, while in much of Europe an individual family could scratch a living on its own. There is no need to fall into extravagant speculation about the origins of western individualism in order to recognize that here is something very distinctive and potentially very important.

Recently, much earlier dates have been given to the evolution of prehistoric European farming – and metallurgy – than was once thought probable. Before 4000 BC there were farming settlements in France and the British Isles. Perhaps a thousand years before this copper was being worked in the Balkans – some two thousand years before the appearance of recognizable civilization in Sumer. This early dating is not just of interest to scholars. It weakens the case, once generally accepted, that Europe acquired its major cultural advances in prehistoric times by diffusion from the Aegean and Near East. The dates are now hard to fit. It seems certain that agriculture and copper-working were arrived at independently in Europe; this emphasizes once again the relative isolation of the area in ancient times, though important transfers to it from the outside could take place. While agriculture appeared there unaided from outside, for example, the major cereals were brought in thousands of years later from the Near East.

Most of the north-western and western parts of Europe were occupied in about 3000 BC by peoples sometimes termed western Mediterranean, who were gradually squeezed during the third millennium by Indo-Europeans from the east. By about 1800 BC the resulting cultures seem to have fragmented sufficiently distinctly for us to identify among them the ancestors of the Celts, the most important of prehistoric European peoples, a society of warriors rather than traders or prospectors. They had wheeled transport. One group among them was enterprising enough to spread as far as the British Isles and have some claim to being the first north-European sea-travellers. There is much disagreement about how far Celtic influence is to be traced, but it will not much disfigure the truth if we think of Europe divided in about 1800 BC into three groups of peoples. The ancestors of the Celts then occupied most of modern France, Germany, the Low Countries and upper Austria. To their eastward were the

The 'Hallstatt' culture was named after a place in upper Austria where a great cemetery of an iron-using Celtic people was found. In the middle of the first millennium BC, in the seventh and six centuries, these people were in touch with Mediterranean civilization, probably by way of what was later Marseilles and the Rhône valley. They may have traded salt from their mines with the Mediterranean peoples. This bronze cauldron not only shows the metallurgical skill of the Iron Age peoples of Europe, but employs decorations and forms derived from the Aegean. In this example they are interestingly combined with the very un-Mediterranean device of riveting to the bottom of the cauldron a cow and a her calf to serve as a handle.

future Slavs, to the north (in Scandinavia) the future Teutonic tribes. Outside Europe, in northern Scandinavia and northern Russia, are the Finns, a non-Indo-European race.

Except in the Balkans and Thrace, the movements of these peoples affected the older centres of civilization only in so far as they affected access to the resources of the areas into which they moved. This was above all a matter of minerals and skills. As the demands of the Near East civilizations grew, so did the importance of access to Europe. The first centre of metallurgy to develop there had been in the Balkans, where before 4000 BC metalwork was being done

A remarkable series of prehistoric tombs approached through passages lined with slabs of stone, sometimes decorated like this one, can be found in Spain, western France and Ireland. They date from the second millennium BC and similarities of design have suggested to some that they must be expressions of a common culture or technological source. This example is from Brittany.

which was superior to anything then possible in the Near East. Developments in southern Spain, Greece and the Aegean and central Italy followed by 2000 BC. In the later Bronze Age, metal-working was advanced to high levels even in places where no local ores were available. We have here one of the earliest examples of the emergence of crucial economic areas. Copper and tin shaped the penetration of Europe and also its coastal and river navigation because these commodities were needed and were only available in the Near East in small quantities. Europe was the major primary producer of the ancient metallurgical world, and also a major manufacturer. Metal-working was

carried to a high level and produced beautiful objects long before the metal-workers of the Aegean, but it is possibly an argument against exaggerated awe about material factors in history that this skill, even when combined with a bigger supply of metals after the collapse of Mycenaean demand, did not release European culture for the achievement of a full and complex civilization.

Ancient Europe had, of course, one other art form which remains impressive. It is preserved in the great megalithic monuments to be found stretching in a broad arc from Malta, Sardinia and Corsica, round through Spain and Brittany to the British Isles and Scandinavia. 'Megalith' is a word derived from the Greek for 'large stone' and many of the stones used are of very large size indeed. Some of these monuments are tombs, roofed and lined with slabs of stone, some are stones standing singly, or in groups. Some of them are laid out in patterns which run for miles across country; others enclose small areas like groves of trees. The most complete and striking megalithic site is Stonehenge, in southern England. What such places originally looked like is hard to guess or imagine. Their modern austerity and weathered grandeur may well be misleading; great places of human resort are not like that when in use and it is more likely that the great stones were daubed in ochres and blood, hung with skins and fetishes. They are more likely to have produced the emotional impact of totem-poles than to have been the solemn, brooding shapes we see today. Except for the tombs, it is not easy to say what they were for, though it has been argued that some were giant clocks or huge solar observatories, for they are often carefully aligned to the rising and setting of sun, moon, and stars at the major turning-points of the astronomical year. Careful observation underlay such work, even if it falls far short in detail and precision of what could be done by astronomers in Babylon and Egypt.

These relics represent huge concentrations of labour and argue for well-developed social organization. Stonehenge contains several blocks

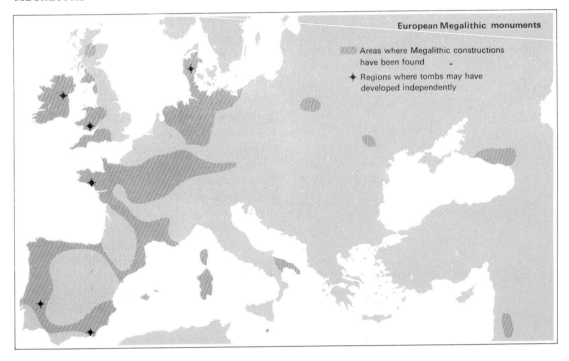

European Megalithic monuments

///// Areas where Megalithic constructions have been found

✦ Regions where tombs may have developed independently

weighing about fifty tons apiece and they had to be brought eighteen or so miles to the site before being erected. There are some eighty pieces of stone there weighing about five tons which came 150 miles or so from the mountains of Wales. The peoples who put up Stonehenge, like those who built the carefully lined tombs of Ireland, the lines of standing stones of Brittany or the dolmens of Denmark were capable of work on a scale approaching that of ancient Egypt, therefore, though without its fineness or any means of recording their purposes and intentions except these great constructions themselves. Such skill, coupled with the fact of the monuments' distribution in a long chain along a possible sea route, has suggested that their explanation might lie in ancient Europe learning such skills from some wandering stone-masons from the East, perhaps from Crete, Mycenae, or the Cyclades, where the technique of dressing and handling such masses was understood. But once again recent advances in dating

have removed a plausible hypothesis; Stone-henge was probably complete before Mycenaean times, Megalithic tombs in Spain and Brittany antedate the pyramids, and Malta's mysterious temples with their huge carved blocks of building stone were there before 3000 BC. Nor do the monuments have to form part of any one process of distribution, even in the north-west. They may all have been achieved more or less in isolation by four or five cultures made up of relatively small and simple agricultural societies in touch with one another, and the motives and occasions of their building may have been very different. Like prehistoric Europe's agriculture and metallurgy, its engineering and architecture arose independently of the outside world.

In spite of these considerable achievements, the Europeans of ancient times seem strangely passive and unresisting when they finally appear in regular contact with advanced civilization. Perhaps their hesitations and uncertainties resembled those of other primitive peoples

*The Villanovans may have come originally
from across the Alaps, already bringing with them
the elements of their later metallurgical
prowess, but once established in Italy their
culture rapidly shows the influence of models
and styles from the Aegean and the Eastern
Mediterranean. Among the objects which have
survived there are splendid crested helmets
(sometimes used as lids for the funeral urns
in which they placed the ashes of their
cremated dead) and highly ornamented
body-armour.*

meeting advanced societies at later dates –
eighteenth-century Africans for example. But
regular contact only begins at a late date,
shortly before the Christian era. Before then,
the European peoples seem to have exhausted
their energies in grappling with an environment
which, though easily worked to satisfy modest
needs, required the coming of iron to make it
fully exploitable. Though far more advanced
than their American or African contemporaries
south of the Nile valley, they never reached the
stage of urbanization. Their greatest cultural
achievements were decorative and mechanical.
Their importance in history was essentially to
be that they would provide the stocks which
would receive the impress of civilization later.
At best, in their metallurgy, the ancient Europeans serviced other civilizations' needs.

Only in one place did western barbarian
Europe have a more positive contribution to
make to the future and that was south of the
olive-line. An Iron Age people of central Italy,
given the name Villanovan, after one of the
sites of their culture, had already during the
eighth century BC trading contacts with Greeks
established further south in Italy and with
Phoenicia. In the next two hundred years they
adopted Greek characters for writing their language. By then they were organized in city-
states, producing art of high quality. These were
the Etruscans. One of their city-states would
one day be known as Rome.

7 The end of the Old World

Of what was going on in India and China and its importance for the future the rulers of the Mediterranean and Near Eastern peoples knew hardly anything. Some of them, listening to traders, may have had a dim perception of what life was like in barbarian Europe. Of what happened beyond the Sahara and of the existence of the Americas they knew nothing. Yet their world was to expand rapidly in the first millennium BC. Possibly more obvious, none the less, was its integration, as its internal communications grew more complex and efficient. A world in which a few highly distinctive civilizations stood out almost independently of one another was giving way to one where larger and larger areas shared in the same achievements of civilization – literacy, government, technology, organized religion, city life – and, under their influence, changed more and more rapidly as the interplay of different traditions increased. It is important not to think of this in terms too abstract or grandiose. It is not only registered

The stately figure of a Persian king still looks out over what is left of the great palace at Persepolis begun in the reign of Darius I and continued by Xerxes and Artaxerxes I, his two successors. Completed in about 460 BC, its ruins are still one of the greatest monuments of antiquity. In its complete splendour it must have been an unparalleled embodiment of royal grandeur, standing on a terrace measuring 500 yards by 300 and enclosing, among its state apartments, a great hall, 250 feet square, in which 10 000 people could assemble.

by art and speculative thought, but also by much that is more down-to-earth. Small things show it as well as great. On the legs of the huge statues at Abu Simbel, seven hundred miles up the Nile, sixth-century Greek mercenaries in the Egyptian army cut inscriptions which recorded their pride in coming that far, just as two thousand five hundred years later English county regiments would leave their badges and names cut into the rocks of the Khyber Pass.

There is no clear chronological line to be drawn in this increasingly complicated world. If one exists it has already been several times crossed before we reach the eve of the classical age of the West. The military and economic drive of the Mesopotamians and their successors, the movements of the Indo-Europeans, the coming of iron and the spread of literacy have all thoroughly mixed up the once-clear patterns of the Near East well before the appearance of a Mediterranean civilization which is the matrix of our own. Nevertheless, there is a sense in which it becomes manifest that an important boundary was crossed somewhere early in the first millennium BC. The greatest upheavals of the *Völkerwanderung* in the ancient Near East were then over. The patterns set there in the late Bronze Age would still be modified locally by colonization and conquest, but not again by the major comings and goings of peoples for another thousand years. The political structures left behind from antiquity would be levers of the next era of world history in a zone which stretched from Gibraltar to the Indus. Civilization

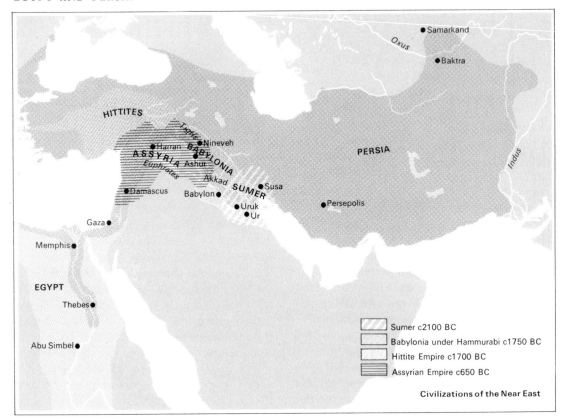

Sumer c2100 BC
Babylonia under Hammurabi c1750 BC
Hittite Empire c1700 BC
Assyrian Empire c650 BC

Civilizations of the Near East

within this area would more and more be a matter of interplay, borrowing and cosmopolitanism. The framework for this was provided by the great political change of the middle of the first millennium BC, the rise of a new power, Persia, and the final collapse of the Egyptian and Babylonian–Assyrian traditions.

The story of Egypt is the easiest to summarize, for it records little except decline. She has been called a 'Bronze Age anachronism in a world that steadily moved away from her' and an explanation of her fate seems to be an inability to change or adapt. She survived the first attacks of the iron-using peoples and had beaten off the Peoples of the Sea at the beginning of the age of turmoil. But this was the last considerable achievement of the New Kingdom: thereafter the symptoms are unmistakably those of a machine running down. At home kings and priests disputed power while Egypt's suzerainty beyond her borders declined to a shadow. A

period of rival dynasties was briefly followed by a reunification which again took an Egyptian army to Palestine, but by the end of the eighth century a dynasty of Kushite invaders had established itself; in 671 BC it was ejected from Lower Egypt by the Assyrians. Ashurbanipal sacked Thebes. As Assyrian power ebbed, there was again an illusory period of Egyptian 'independence'. By this time, evidence of a new world towards which Egypt had to make concessions not merely political can be seen in the establishment of a school for Greek interpreters and of a Greek trading enclave with special privileges at Naucratis in the delta. Then again, in the sixth century, Egypt went down to defeat first at the hands of the forces of Nebuchadnezzar (588 BC) and sixty years later, before the Persians (525 BC), to become a province of an empire which was to set the boundaries of a new synthesis and to dispute for centuries world supremacy with new powers appearing in the

Mediterranean. This was not quite the end of Egyptian independence, but from the fourth century BC to the twentieth AD, she was to be ruled by foreigners or immigrant dynasties and passes from view as an independent nation. The last bursts of Egyptian recovery show little innate vitality. They express, rather, temporary relaxations of the pressures upon her which always, in the end, were followed by their resumption. One of these, at the end, was fatal: the Persian threat.

Once again, the starting-point is a migration. On the high plateau which is the heart of modern Iran there were settlements in 5000 BC, but the word 'Iran' (which does not appear until about AD 600) in its oldest form means 'land of the Aryans' and it is somewhere around 1000 BC, with an irruption of Aryan tribes from the north, that the history of the Persian empire begins. In Iran, as in India, the impact of the Aryans was to prove ineffaceable and founded a long-enduring tradition. Among their tribes two, especially vigorous and powerful, have been remembered by their biblical names as the Medes and Persians. The Medes moved west and north-west to Media; their great age came at the beginning of the sixth century, after they had overthrown Assyria, their neighbour. The Persians went south towards the Gulf, establishing themselves in Khuzistan (on the edge of the Tigris valley and in the old kingdom of Elam) and Fars, the Persia of the ancients.

Oral tradition preserves a history of legendary kings which is more important for the light it throws on later Persian attitudes to kingship than as an historical account. It was none the less from the Persian dynasty of the Achaemenids that there descended the first king of a united Persia – anachronistic though this term is. This was Cyrus, the conqueror of Babylon. In 549 BC he humbled the last independent king of the Medes and thenceforth the boundaries of conquest rolled outwards, swallowing Babylon and advancing through Asia Minor to the sea, dropping down into Syria and Palestine. Only in the east (where he was eventually killed fighting the Scythians) did Cyrus find it difficult

to stabilize his frontiers, though he crossed the Hindu Kush and set up some sort of supremacy over the region of Gandhara, north of the Jhelum.

This was the largest empire the world had seen until that time. Its style was different from its predecessors; the savagery of the Assyrians seems muted and, instead, Cyrus was careful to respect the institutions and ways of his new subjects. The result was a diverse empire, but a powerful one, commanding loyalties of a kind lacking to its predecessors. There are some notable religious symptoms; the protection of Marduk was solicited for Cyrus's assumption of the Babylonian kingship and at Jerusalem he launched the rebuilding of the Temple. A Jewish prophet saw in his victories God's hand, named him the Lord's anointed and gloated over the fate of the old enemy, Babylon. 'Let now the astrologers, the stargazers, the monthly prognosticators, stand up, and save thee from these things that shall come upon thee.'*

Cyrus's success owed much to the material resources of his kingdom. It was rich in minerals, above all in iron, and in the high pastures of the valleys lay a great reserve of horses and cavalrymen. Yet it is impossible to resist the conclusion that sheer personal ability also counted for much; Cyrus lives as a world-historical figure and he was recognized as such by other would-be conquerors who were to strive in the next few centuries to emulate him. He based his government upon provincial governors who were the forbears of the later Persian satraps, and required from his subject provinces little beyond tribute – usually in gold, which replenished the treasuries of Persia – and obedience.

Thus began the empire which, though with setbacks in plenty, provided for nearly two centuries a framework for the Near East, sheltering a great cultural tradition which grew to nourish itself both from Asia and Europe. Large areas knew longer periods of peace than for centuries under it and it was in many ways

*Isaiah xlv, 1, xlvii, 1–13.

189

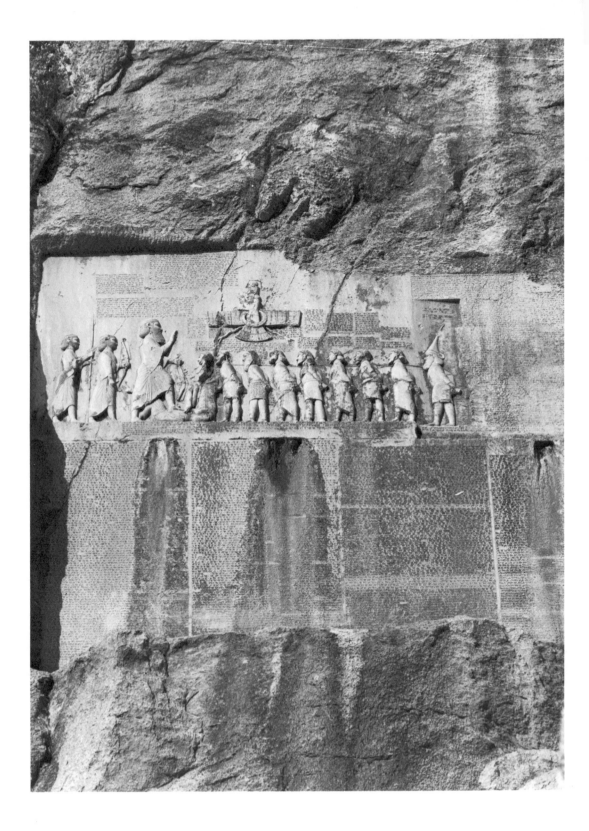

a beautiful and gentle civilization. Greeks were told already by Herodotus that the Persians loved flowers and there are many things we could do without more easily than the tulip, which we owe to them. Cyrus' son added Egypt to the empire; yet he died before he could deal with a pretender to the throne whose attempts encouraged Medes and Babylonians to seek to recover their independence. The restorer of Cyrus' heritage was a young man who claimed Achaemenid descent, Darius.

Darius (who reigned 522–486) did not achieve all he wished. His work, none the less, was at the level of that of Cyrus. His own inscription on the monument recording his victories over rebels may be thought to be justified by what followed under his reign: 'I am Darius the Great King, King of Kings, King in Persia'. It was a recitation of an ancient title whose braggadocio was now justified. In the east the boundaries of the empire were carried further into the Indus valley. In the west they advanced to Macedonia, though they were checked there, and in the north Darius failed, as Cyrus before him, to make much headway against the Scythians. Inside the empire a remarkable work of consolidation was undertaken. The decentralization of Cyrus was institutionalized with the division of the empire into twenty provinces, each under a satrap who was a royal prince or great nobleman. Royal inspectors surveyed their work and their control of the machine was made

On a cliff three hundred feet high above the road from Teheran to Hamadan, the ancient capital of the Medes, Darius I placed this relief commemorating the submission of twelve kings. Such monuments had been traditional since Assyrian times, but this one also had great linguistic importance for it was set out in three languages, Babylonian, Persian and Elamite, each written in a different form of cuneiform. Their recording in the 1840s – by the English archaeologist Rawlinson, who wrote them down while suspended dizzily in a rope saddle from the top of the cliff – made possible at last the decipherment of cuneiform.

easier by the institution of a royal secretariat to conduct correspondence with the provinces, and Aramaic, the old *lingua franca* of Assyrian empire, became the administrative language. It was well adapted to the conduct of affairs because not written in cuneiform but in the Phoenician alphabet. The bureaucracy rested on better communications than any yet seen, for much of the provincial tribute was invested in road-building. At their best these roads could convey messages at two hundred miles a day.

A monument to this imperial achievement was to have been a great new capital whose building was begun at Persepolis. Here Darius himself was buried in a rock tomb cut into the cliff face. Intended as a colossal glorification of the king, it remains impressive even when it seems pompous. It was in the end a collective creation of Darius and the later kings who added their palaces to it, fittingly embodying the diversity and cosmopolitanism of the empire which produced it. Assyrian colossi, man-headed bulls and lions guarded its gates as they had done those of Nineveh. Up its staircases marched stone warriors bearing tribute; they are a little less mechanical than the regimented Assyrians of earlier sculpture, but only a little. The decorative columns recall Egypt, but it is an Egyptian device transmitted through Ionian stone-cutters and sculptors. Greek details are to be found also in the reliefs and decoration and a similar mixture of reminiscences is to be found in the royal tombs not far away. They recall the Valley of the Kings in their conception while their cruciform entrances speak of something else. Cyrus's own tomb, at Pasargadae, had also been marked by Greek design. A new world is coming to birth.

These monuments fittingly express the continuing diversity and tolerance of Persian culture. It was one always open to influence from abroad and would continue to be. Persia took up not only the language of those she conquered, but also sometimes their ideas. She also contributed. Vedic and Persian religion mingled in Gandhara, where stood the Indian city the Greeks called Taxila, but both, of course, were

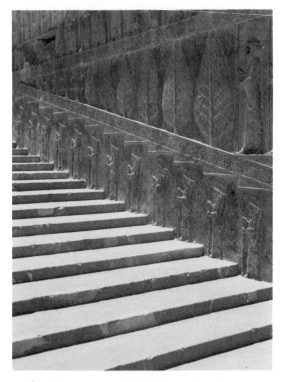

It is now difficult to imagine the visual impact of the great repetitive friezes and processions of Achaemenid architectural sculpture. These guards at the side of the staircase leading to the Audience Hall at Persepolis would have been brightly coloured, their metal accoutrements and weapons probably gilded. Unlike the reliefs of Egypt and Assyria, which were set out to tell a story, Achaemenid sculpture was purely ornamental and decorative; this puts another difficulty in the way of appreciating it, for the buildings to whose composition these reliefs contributed are now only fragments and their overall effect is almost impossible to imagine.

Aryan. The core of Persian religion was sacrifice and centred on fire. By the age of Darius the most refined of its cults had evolved into what has been called Zoroastrianism, a dualist religion accounting for the problem of evil in terms of the struggle of a good with an evil god. Of its prophet, Zoroaster, we know little, but it seems that he taught his disciples to uphold the cause of the god of light with ritual and moral behaviour; ahead lay a messianic deliverance, the resurrection of the dead and life everlasting after judgement. This creed spread rapidly through western Asia with Persian rule, even though it was probably never more than the cult of a minority. It would influence Judaism and the oriental cults which were to be part of the setting of Christianity; the angels of Christian tradition and the notion of the hellfire which awaited the wicked both came from Zoroaster.

At Susa, the ancient capital of Elam, where Darius I built another palace, his inscription tells us that 'a splendid task was ordered; very splendidly did it turn out'. It was, the inscription also reveals, the work of men of many nations and is an interesting expression of the cosompolitanism of the Achaemenid empire. These guards were portrayed in glazed and coloured bricks, made in moulds in the old Mesopotamian style: 'the men who brought the baked brick, those were Babylonians' reads one entry in the list of materials and workmen.

It is too early to speak of the interplay of Asia and Europe, but there are few more striking examples of the interplay of reciprocal influences which marks the end of the ancient world. We can mark an epoch. Right across the Old World Persia suddenly pulled peoples into a common experience. Indians, Medes, Babylonians, Lydians, Greeks, Jews, Phoenicians, Egyptians were for the first time all administered by one empire whose eclecticism showed how far civilization had already come. The era of civilization embodied in distinct units of history in the Near East was over. Too much had been shared, too much diffused for the direct successors of the first civilizations to be any longer intelligible independent units of study. Indian mercenaries fought in the Persian armies; Greeks in those of Egypt. City-dwelling and literacy were widespread through the Near East. Men lived in cities round much of the Mediterranean, too. Agricultural and metallurgical techniques stretched even beyond that area and were to be spread further as the Achaemenids transmitted the irrigation skill of Babylon to Central Asia and brought rice from India to be planted in the Near East. When Asian Greeks came to adopt a currency it would be based on the sexagesimal numeration of Babylon. The base of a future world civilization was in the making.

Book Three

The Classical Mediterranean

Simply in terms of chronology, more than half the story of civilization was already over by about 500 BC. We are still nearer to that date than were the men who lived then to their first civilized predecessors. In the three thousand or so years between them, humanity had come a long way; however imperceptibly slow the changes of daily life in them had been, there is an enormous qualitative gap between Sumer and Achaemenid Persia. A great period of foundation and acceleration already lay behind in the sixth century. From the western Mediterranean to the coasts of China a variety of cultural traditions had established themselves. Distinct civilizations were already rooted in them, some firmly and deeply enough to survive into our own era. Some of them lasted, moreover, with little but superficial and temporary

change for hundreds of years. Virtually isolated, they contributed little to mankind's shared life outside their own areas. For the most part, even the greatest centres of civilization were indifferent to what lay outside their spheres for at least two thousand years after the fall of Babylon except when troubled by an occasional invasion. Only one of the civilizations already discernible by the sixth century BC in fact showed much potential for expanding beyond its cradle, that of the eastern Mediterranean. It was the youngest of them but was to be very successful, lasting for over a thousand years without a break in its tradition, but even this is less remarkable than what it left behind, for it was the seedbed of almost all that played a dynamic part in shaping the world we still inhabit.

1 The roots of one world

The appearance of a new civilization in the eastern Mediterranean owed much to older Near Eastern and Aegean traditions. From the start we confront an amalgam of Greek speech, a Semitic alphabet, ideas whose roots lie in Egypt and Mesopotamia, reminiscences of Mycenae. Even when this civilization matured it still showed the diversity of its origins. It was never to be a simple, monolithic whole and in the end was very complex indeed. For all that integrated it and gave it unity, it was always hard to delimit, a cluster of similar cultures around the Mediterranean and Aegean, their frontier zones blurring far outwards into Asia, Africa, barbarian Europe and southern Russia. Even when its boundaries with them were clear, other traditions always played upon Mediterranean civilization and received much from it.

This civilization also varied in time. It showed greater powers of evolution than any of its pre-decessors. Even when they had undergone important political changes their institutions remained fundamentally intact, while Mediterranean civilization displays a huge variety of transient political forms and experiments. In religion and ideology, whereas other traditions tended to develop without violent changes or breaks, so that civilization and religion were virtually coterminous, the one living and dying with the other, Mediterranean civilization begins in a native paganism and ends by succumbing to an exotic import, Christianity; it was a revolutionized Judaism which produced the first world religion. This was a huge change, which in fact transformed this civilization's possibilities of influencing the future.

Of all the forces making for its crystallization, the most fundamental was the setting itself, the Mediterranean basin. It was both a collecting area and a source; currents flowed easily into it from the lands of the old civilizations and from this central reservoir they also flowed back to where they came from and northwards into the barbarian lands. Though it is large and contains a variety of peoples, this basin has well-defined general characteristics. Most of its coasts are narrow plains behind which quickly rise fairly steep and enclosing mountain ranges, broken by few important river valleys. Those who lived on the coasts always tended to look along them and outward across the sea, rather than behind them to their hinterland. This, combined with a climate they all shared, made the spreading of ideas and techniques within the Mediterranean natural for enterprising peoples.

Early in the sixth century BC *an anonymous sculptor carved this herdsman, one of the earliest Attic statues to be found on the Athenian Acropolis. An inscription tells us that the subject may have been Rhombos, who to judge by his dress was probably a wealthy man. Yet he has been caught in a pose which is simple and even consciously so, one evocative of the pastoral and rural background of classical civilization. Similar figures, carrying lambs or even rams on their shoulders, have been found as far away as Crete and were dated a century or so earlier than this one.*

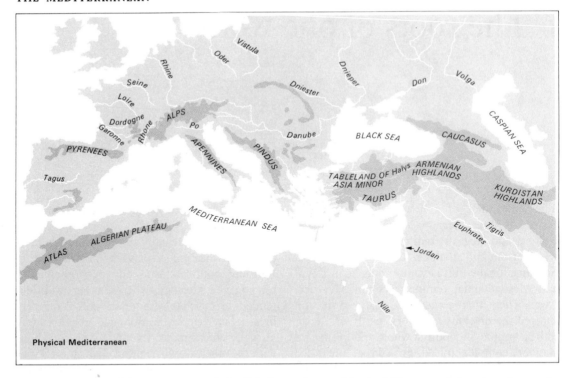

Physical Mediterranean

The Romans, with reason, named the Mediterranean *Mare Magnum*, the Great Sea. It was the outstanding geographical fact of their world, the centre of classical maps. Its surface was a great uniting force for those who knew how to use it, and by 500 BC maritime technology was advanced enough to make this possible except in winter. Prevailing winds and currents determined the exact routes of ships whose only power was provided by sails or oars, but no region of the Mediterranean was inaccessible by water from any other. The upshot was a littoral civilization, with a few languages spoken widely within it. It had specialized trading centres, for exchanges of materials were easy by sea, but the economy rested firmly on the growing of wheat and barley, olives and vines, mainly for local consumption. The metals increasingly needed by this economy could be brought in from outside. In ancient days the southern Mediterranean coasts were not as they are today, being more heavily wooded, better watered, more fertile. The deserts to the south were held at bay further from the coast and for perhaps thousands of years North Africa was richer than it now is. The same sort of civilization therefore tended to appear all round the Mediterranean and such a difference between Africa and Europe as we take for granted did not exist for over a thousand years after 500 BC.

The outward-looking littoral peoples of this civilization created a new world. The great valley civilizations had not colonized, they had conquered. Their peoples looked inward to the satisfaction of limited aims under local despots.

Individual artists begin to emerge from the anonymous flow of early art in the sixth century. One master of potting and the painting of pots was Exekias of Athens whose cup decorated with the ship of Dionysus bears his signature. The god of wine lies back in his ship holding a drinking-vessel, perhaps contemplating the vine which decorates its mast and breaks out into bunches of grapes over his head, or perhaps amused by the leaping dolphins into which (legend said) he had transformed a gang of pirates he had encountered on his voyage.

Many later societies, even within the classical world, were to do the same, but there is a discernible change of tempo and potential from the start, and eventually Greeks and Romans grew corn in Russia, worked tin from Cornwall, built roads into the Balkans and enjoyed spices from India and silk from China.

About this world we know a great deal. In part, this is because of the huge archaeological and monumental legacy which has survived from it. Much more important, though, is the new richness of its records. With them, we enter the era of full literacy. Among other things, they include the first true works of history; important as were to be the great folk records of the Jews, the narrations of a cosmic drama built about the pilgrimage of one people through time, they are not critical history. In any case, they, too, reach us through the classical Mediterranean world. Without Christianity, their influence would have been limited to Israel; through it, the myths they presented and the possibilities of meaning they offered were to be injected into a world with four hundred years of what we can recognize as critical writing of history already behind it. Yet the work of ancient historians, important as it is, is only a tiny part of the record. Soon after 500 BC, we are in the presence of the first complete great literature, ranging from drama to epic, lyric hymn, history and epigram, though what is left of it is only a small part – seven out of more than a hundred plays by its greatest tragedian, for example. Nevertheless, it enables us to enter the mind of a civilization as we can enter that of no earlier one.

Even for Greece, of course, the source of this literature, and *a fortiori* for other and more remote parts of the classical world, the written record is not enough on its own. The archaeology is indispensable, but it is all the more informative because literary sources are so much fuller than anything from the early past. The record they offer us is for the most part in Greek or Latin, the two languages which provided the intellectual currency of Mediterranean civilization. The persistence in English, the most widely used of languages today, of so many words drawn from them is by itself almost enough evidence to show this civilization's importance to its successors. All seven nouns in the last sentence but one, for example, are based on Latin words. It was through writings in these languages that later men approached this civilization and in them they detected the qualities which made them speak of what they found simply as '*the* classical world'.

This is a perfectly proper usage, provided we remember that the men who coined it were heirs to the traditions they saw in it and stood, perhaps trapped, within its assumptions. Other traditions and civilizations, too, have had their 'classical' phases. What it means is simply that men see in some part of the past an age setting standards for later times. Many later Europeans were to be hypnotized by the power and glamour of classical Mediterranean civilization. Some men who lived in it, too, thought that they, their culture and times were exceptional, though not always for reasons we should now find convincing. Yet it *was* exceptional; vigorous and restless, it provided standards and ideals, as well as technology and institutions, on which huge futures were to be built. In essence, the unity later discerned by those who admired the Mediterranean heritage was a mental one.

Inevitably, there was to be much anachronistic falsification in some of the later efforts to study and utilize the classical ideal, and much romanticization of a lost age, too. Yet even when this is discounted, and when the classical past has undergone the sceptical scrutiny of recent scholars, there remains a big indissoluble residue of mental achievement which somehow places it on our side of a mental boundary, on the other side of which lie the great empires of Asia. With whatever difficulty and possibility of misconstruction, the mind of the classical age is recognizable and comprehensible in a way perhaps nothing earlier can be. 'This', it has been well said, 'is a world whose air we can breathe.'

The rôle of the Greeks was pre-eminent in making this world and with them, therefore, its story must begin. They contributed more than any other single people to its dynamism and to its mythical and inspirational legacy. The Greek search for excellence defined for later men what excellence was and their achievement remains difficult to exaggerate. It is the core of the process of making classical Mediterranean civilization.

2 The Greeks

In the second half of the eighth century BC, the clouds which have hidden the Aegean since the end of the Bronze Age begin to part a little. Processes and sometimes events become somewhat more discernible. There is even a date or two, one of which is important in the history of a civilization's self-consciousness: in 776 BC, according to later Greek historians, the first Olympian games were held. After a few centuries the Greek would count from this year as we count from the birth of Christ.

The people who gathered for that and later festivals of the same sort recognized by doing so that they shared a culture. Its basis was a common language; Dorians, Ionians, Aeolians all spoke Greek. What is more they had done so for a long time; the language was now to acquire the definition which comes from being

Athens is still the city which dominates our vision of ancient Greece. Its most sacred shrine was that of Pallas Athene, whose magnificent image was to be found in the Parthenon. The statue of the goddess shown here is a different one and was discovered less than twenty years ago; it comes from the fourth century BC, when it was cast in bronze – a material in which few works of art survive from ancient Greece, because of the standing temptation to melt them down. This specimen may have avoided destruction through the chance of war; it had been looted from its usual place and then been put in a warehouse awaiting transport to Italy when a fire destroyed the building and buried it in the ruins.

written down, an enormously important development, making possible, for example, the recording of the traditional oral poetry which was said to be the work of Homer. Our first surviving inscription in Greek characters is on a jug of about 750 BC. It shows how much the renewal of Aegean civilization owed to Asia. The inscription is written in an adaptation of Phoenician script; Greeks were illiterate until their traders brought home this alphabet. It seems to have been used first in the Peloponnese, Crete and Rhodes; possibly these were the first areas to benefit from the renewal of intercourse with Asia after the Dark Ages. The process is mysterious and can probably never be recovered, but somehow the catalyst which precipitated Greek civilization was contact with the East.

Who were the Greek-speakers who attended the first Olympiad? Though it is the name by which they and their descendants are still known, they were not called Greeks; that name was only given them centuries later by the Romans. The word they would have used was the one we render in English as 'Hellenes'. First used to distinguish invaders of the Greek peninsula from the earlier inhabitants, it became the name of all the Greek-speaking peoples of the Aegean. This was the new conception and the new name emerging from the Dark Ages and there is more than a verbal significance to it. It expressed a consciousness of a new entity, one still emerging and one whose exact meaning would always remain uncertain. Some of the Greek-speakers had in the eighth

*Like other weapons, the chariot found a place
in organized sport at an early date, though
exactly when is not known. But chariot-racing
was established – presumably as a pastime of the
rich, for horses and chariots were expensive
playthings – at least by the sixth century* BC.
This specimen is harnessed four-in-hand.

century already long been settled and their roots
were lost in the turmoil of the Bronze Age
invasions. Some were much more recent arrivals.
None came as Greeks; they became Greeks by
being there, all round the Aegean. Language
identified them and wove new ties between
them. Together with a shared heritage of religion and myth, it was the most important constituent of being Greek, always and supremely
a matter of common culture.

Yet such ties were never politically effective.
They were unlikely to make for unity because

of the size and shape of the theatre of Greek
history, which was not what we now call Greece,
but was, rather, the whole Aegean. The wide
spread of Minoan and Mycenaean influences in
earlier civilized times had foreshadowed this,
for between the scores of its islands and the
shores which closed about them it was easy to
voyage during much of the year. The explanation of the appearance of Greek civilization at
all may well be largely a matter of this geography. The past certainly counted for something, too, but Minoan Crete and Mycenae
probably left less to Greece than Anglo-Saxon
England left to a later Great Britain. The setting
was a much more important factor than history.
It offered a specially dense distribution of
economically viable communities using the same
language and easily accessible not only to one
another but to older centres of civilization in the
Near East. Like the old river valleys – but for
different reasons – the Aegean was a propitious
place for civilization to appear.

Much of the Aegean was settled by Greeks as
a consequence of limitations and opportunities
which they found on the mainland. Only in very
small patches did its land and climate combine
to offer the chance of agricultural plenty. For
the most part, cultivation was confined to narrow
strips of alluvial plain which had to be dry-
farmed. They lay in valleys, usually with rocky
or wooded sides; minerals were rare, there was
no tin, copper or iron. Such valleys usually ran
direct to the sea and communication between
them was difficult. All this inclined the inhabitants of Attica and the Peloponnese to look outward to the sea. None of them, after all, lived
more than forty miles from it.

This predisposition was intensified as early
as the tenth century by a growth of population
which brought greater pressure on available
land. Ultimately this led to a great age of colonization; by the end of it, in the sixth century,
the Greek world stretched far beyond the
Aegean, from the Black Sea in the east to the
Balearics, France and Sicily in the west and
Libya in the south. But this was the result of
centuries during which other forces than popu-

Greek world of the Aegean

- Major cities
- Important shrines and oracles

lation pressure had also been at work. While Thrace was colonized by agriculturalists looking for land, other Greeks settled in the Levant or south Italy in order to trade, whether for the wealth it would bring or for the access it offered to the metals they needed and could not find in Greece. Some Black Sea Greek cities seem to be where they are because of trade, some because of their farming potential. Nor were traders and farmers the only agents diffusing Greek ways and teaching Greece about the outside world. The historical records of other countries show us a flow of Greek mercenaries from the seventh century (when they fought for the Egyptians against the Assyrians) onwards. All these facts were to have important social and political reper-

cussions on the homeland, but before considering them there is much to be said about what kind of civilization it was which was being diffused in this way and was absorbing, by way of return, what others had to give.

Quarrel violently among themselves though they did, and cherish the traditional and emotional distinctions of Boeotian, or Dorian, or Ionian though they might, the Greeks were always very conscious that they were different from other peoples. It could be practically important; prisoners of war, for example, were in theory not to be enslaved, unlike 'barbarians'. This word expressed self-conscious Hellenism in its essence but is both more inclusive and less dismissive than it is in modern speech; the bar-

To the Greeks the expedition to Troy and the great deeds of the heroes who fought there were history, and their own history, too. The combat between Hector and Achilles was one of the great episodes of the story, and it is depicted on this early fifth-century vase. The other figures shown are divinities – Apollo, the patron of Hector, the Trojan hero, and Athene, protector of Achilles.

barians were the rest of the world, those who did not speak an intelligible Greek (dialect though it might be) but who made a sort of 'bar-bar' noise which no Greek could understand. The great religious festivals of the Greek year, when people from many cities came together, were occasions to which only the Greek-speaker was admitted.

Religion was the other foundation of Greek identity. The Greek pantheon is enormously complex, the amalgam of a mass of myths created by many communities over a wide area at different times, often incoherent or even self-contradictory until ordered by later, rationaliz-

ing minds. Some were imports, like the Asian myth of golden, silver, bronze and iron ages. Local superstition and belief in such legends was the bedrock of the Greek religious experience. Yet it was a religious experience very different from that of other peoples in its ultimately humanizing tendency. Greek gods and goddesses, for all their supernatural standing and power, are remarkably human. They express the man-centred quality of later Greek civilization. Much as it owed to Egypt and the East, Greek mythology and art usually presents its gods as better, or worse, men and women, a world away from the monsters of Assyria and Babylonia, or from Shiva the many-armed. Whoever is responsible, this was a religious revolution; its converse was the implication that men could be godlike. This is already apparent in Homer; perhaps he did as much as anyone to order the Greek supernatural in this way and he does not give much space to popular cults. He presents the gods taking sides in the Trojan war in postures all too human. They compete with one another; while Poseidon harries the hero of the *Odyssey*, Athena takes his part. A later Greek critic grumbled that Homer 'attributed to the gods everything that is disgraceful and blameworthy among men: theft, adultery and deceit'. It was a world which operated much like the actual world.

The *Iliad* and *Odyssey* have already been touched upon because of the light they throw on prehistory; they were also shapers of the future. They are at first sight curious objects for a people's reverence. The *Iliad* gives an account of a short episode from a legendary long-past war; the *Odyssey* is more like a novel, narrating the wandering of one of the greatest of all literary characters, Odysseus, on his way home from the same struggle. That, on the face of it, is all. But they came to be held to be something like sacred books. If, as seems reasonable, the survival rate of early copies is thought to give a true reflexion of relative popularity, they were copied more frequently than any other text of Greek literature. Much time and ink have been spent on argument about how they were composed. It now seems most likely that they took their present shape in Ionia slightly before 700 BC. The Greeks referred to their author without qualification as 'the poet' (a sufficient sign of his standing in their eyes) but some have found arguments for thinking the two poems are the work of different men. For our purpose, it is unimportant whether he was one author or not; the essential point is that someone took material presented by four centuries of bardic transmission and wove it into a form which acquired stability and in this sense these works are the culmination of the era of Greek heroic poetry. Though they were probably written down in the seventh century, no standard version of these poems was accepted until the sixth; by then they were already regarded as the authoritative account of early Greek history, a source of morals and models, and the staple of literary education. Thus they became not only the first documents of Greek self-consciousness, but the embodiment of the fundamental values of classical civilization. Later they were to be even more than this: together with the Bible, they are the source of western literature.

Human though Homer's gods might be, the Greek world had also a deep respect for the occult and mysterious. It was recognized in such embodiments as omens and oracles. The shrines of the oracles of Apollo at Delphi or at Didyma in Asia Minor were places of pilgrimage and the sources of respected if enigmatic advice. There were ritual cults which practised 'mysteries' which re-enacted the great natural processes of germination and growth at the passage of the seasons. Popular religion does not loom large in the literary sources, but it was never wholly separated from 'respectable' religion. It is important to remember all this irrational subsoil, given that the achievements of the Greek élite during the later classical era are so impressive and rest so importantly on rationality and logic; the irrational was always there and in the earlier, formative period with which this chapter is concerned, it loomed large. This was the period in which the foundations of the drama were laid, but there is no lack of evidence later for the Greek respect for the darker and elemental forces of the cosmos with which they saw man contending.

The literary record and accepted tradition also reveal something, if nothing very precise, of the social and, if the word is appropriate, political institutions of early Greece. Homer shows us a society of kings and aristocrats, but by his day this was already anachronistic. The title of king sometimes lived on, and in one place, Sparta, where there were always two kings at once, it had a shadowy reality which sometimes was effective, but by historical times power had passed from monarchs to aristocracies in almost all the Greek cities. The council of the Areopagus at Athens is an example of the sort of restricted body which usurped the kingly power in many places. Such ruling élites rested fundamentally on land; their members were the outright owners of the estates which provided not only their livelihood but the surplus for the expensive arms and horses which made leaders in war. Homer depicts such aristocrats behaving with a remarkable degree of independence of his kings: this probably reflects the reality of his own day. They were the only people who counted; other social distinctions have little importance in these poems. Thersites is properly chastised for infringing the crucial line between Gentlemen and the Rest.

A military aristocracy's preoccupation with courage may also explain a continuing self-assertiveness and independence in Greek public life; Achilles, as Homer presents him, was as prickly and touchy a fellow as any medieval baron. To this day a man's standing in his peers' eyes is what is cared about by many Greeks more than anything else and their politics have often reflected this. It was to prove true during the classical age when time and time again individualism wrecked the chances of cooperative action. The Greeks were never to produce an enduring empire, for it could only have rested on some measure of subordination of the lesser to the greater good, or some willingness to accept the discipline of routine service. This may have been no bad thing, but meant that for all their Hellenic self-consciousness the Greeks could not unite even their homeland into one state.

Below the aristocrats of the early cities were the rest of the ranks of a still not very complex society. Freemen worked their own land or sometimes for others. Wealth did not change hands rapidly or easily until money made it available in a form more easily transferred than land. The idea that trade and menial tasks were degrading was essentially aristocratic and accounts for the fact that in Athens (and perhaps elsewhere) commerce was long in the hands of metics, foreign residents who enjoyed no civic privilege, but who provided the services Greek citizens would not provide for themselves.

Slavery, of course, was taken for granted, though much uncertainty surrounds the institution. It was clearly capable of many different interpretations. In archaic times, if that is what Homer reflects, most slaves were women, the prizes of victory, but the slaughter of male prisoners later gave way to enslavement. Large-scale plantation slavery such as Rome and the European colonies of modern times later

permitted was unusual. Many Greeks of the fifth century who were freemen owned one or two slaves and one estimate is that about one in four of the population was a slave when Athens was most prosperous. They could be freed; one fourth-century slave became a considerable banker. They were also, clearly, often well treated and loved. One has become famous: Aesop. But they were not free and the Greeks thought that absolute dependence on another's will was intolerable for a free man though they hardly ever developed this notion into positive criticism of slavery. It would be anachronistic to be surprised at this. The whole world outside Greece, too, was organized on the assumption that slavery would go on. It was the prevailing social institution almost everywhere well into Christian times and it still survives. It is hardly cause for comment, therefore, that Greeks took it for granted. There was no task that slavery did not sustain for them, from agricultural labour to teaching (our word 'pedagogue' originally meant a slave who accompanied a well-born boy to school). A famous Greek philosopher later tried to justify this state of affairs by arguing that there were some human beings who were truly intended to be slaves by nature, since they had been given only such faculties as fitted them to serve the purposes of more enlightened men. To modern ears this does not seem a very impressive argument, but in the context of the way Greeks thought about nature and man there was more to it than simple rationalization of prejudice.

Slaves may and foreign residents must have been among the many channels by which the Greeks continued to be influenced by the Near East long after civilization had re-emerged in the Aegean. Homer had already mentioned the *demiourgoi*, foreign craftsmen who must have brought with them to the cities of the Hellenes not only technical skill but the motifs and styles of other lands. In later times we hear of Greek craftsmen settled in Babylon and there were many examples of Greek soldiers serving as mercenaries to foreign kings. When the Persians took Egypt in 525 BC, Greeks fought on each

Greek themes and styles flowed into Asian art, but the traffic was not only one-way. At an early date creatures from Asian mythology made their way into Greek decoration. A vase-painter known to us as 'the Gorgon painter' decorated an amphora with the legendary griffin from Eastern sources, somewhere soon after 600 BC.

*Early in the fifth century an Athenian vase-painter depicted Croesus, king of Lydia, on the funeral pyre from which (legend said) he had been rescued by supernatural agencies.
Herodotus, on the other hand, said that Cyrus, who overran Croesus' kingdom in 547 BC, had relented of his decision to burn Croesus.
Whatever the truth of the matter, it is clear that within sixty years or so of an important event, Greek oral tradition was quite capable of turning it into a myth.*

side. Some of these men must have returned to the Aegean, bringing with them new ideas and impressions. Meanwhile, there was all the time a continuing commercial and diplomatic intercourse between the Greek cities in Asia and their neighbours.

The multiplicity of day-to-day exchanges resulting from the enterprise of the Greeks makes it very hard to distinguish native and foreign contributions to the culture of archaic Greece. One tempting area is art; here, just as Mycenae had reflected Asian models, so the animal motifs which decorate Greek bronze work, or the postures of goddesses such as Aphrodite,

recall the art of the Near East. Later, the monumental architecture and statuary of Greece was to imitate Egypt's, and Egyptian antiquities shaped the styles of the things made by Greek craftsmen at Naucratis. Although the final product, the mature art of classical Greece, was unique, its roots lie far back in the renewal of ties with Asia in the eighth century. What is not possible to delineate quickly is the slow subsequent irradiation of a process of cultural inter-

209

play which was by the sixth century working both ways, for Greece was by then both pupil and teacher. Lydia, for example, the kingdom of the legendary Croesus, richest man in the world, was Hellenized by its tributary Greek cities; it

Not much pottery survives from Sparta – for her citizens were debarred from manual labour and looked down on craftsmen. What has survived is for the most part from the sixth century; some was exported and includes pieces of high quality. This example has a certain commercial interest, for it represents the king of Cyrene in North Africa supervising the weighing and storing of bales of a medicinal plant which was one of his kingdom's most important exports. As he watches, workmen call out the weights of the bales and his pets play round his chair.

took its art from them and, probably more important, the alphabet, indirectly acquired via Phrygia. Thus Asia received again what Asia had given.

Well before 500 BC, this civilization is so complex that it is easy to lose touch with the exact state of affairs at any one time. By the standards of its contemporaries, early Greece was a rapidly changing society, and some aspects of its evolution are more observable than others. One important development seems to have occurred towards the end of the seventh century and it is marked in many of the city-states. Its mainspring seems to have been a second and more important wave of colonization, often from the eastern Greek cities. There followed an upsurge of commerce: new economic relationships appearing as trade with the non-Greek world became easier. Part of the evidence is an increased circulation of silver. A true coinage makes its appearance and is soon used in both foreign and internal trade; only Sparta resisted its introduction. Specialization became a possible answer to land shortage at home; Athens assured the grain imports she needed by specializing in the produce of great quantities of pottery and oil; Chios exporting oil and wine. Some Greek cities became notably more dependent on foreign corn, Egyptian in particular.

Commercial expansion meant not only that land was no longer the only important source of wealth, but also that more men could buy the land which was so important in status. This began a revolution both military and political. The old Greek ideal of warfare had been single combat, a form of fighting natural to a society whose warriors were aristocrats, riding or driving to the field of battle to meet their equals while less well-armed inferiors brawled about them. The new groups of wealthy men could afford the armour and arms which provided a better military instrument, the regiment of 'hoplites', the heavy-armed infantry who were to be for two centuries the backbone of Greek armies and give them superiority. They would prevail by disciplined cohesion, rather than by individual derring-do.

The hoplite wore helmet and body-armour and carried a shield. His main weapon was the spear, which he did not throw, but with which he thrust and stabbed in the mêlée which followed a charge by an ordered formation of spearmen whose weight gave it its effect. It could only be deployed on relatively level ground, but it was such ground that was usually being contested in Greek wars, for the agriculture on which a Greek city depended could be devastated by seizure of the little plains of the valley floor where most of its crops were grown. On such terrain, the hoplites would charge as a cohesive mass, with the aim of sweeping away defenders by their impact. They depended completely on their power to act as a disciplined unit. This both maximized the effect of the charge and enabled them to prevail in the hand-to-hand fighting which followed, because each

hoplite had to rely for protection on his right-hand side by the shield of his neighbour. To keep an ordered line was therefore crucial. The Spartans were in particular admired for their expertise in performing the preliminary evolutions which preceded such an encounter and for retaining cohesion as a group once the scrimmage had begun.

The ability to act collectively was the heart of the new warfare. Though bigger numbers now took part in battles numbers were no longer all that counted, as three centuries of Greek success against Asian armies were to prove. Discipline and tactical cohesion began to matter more and they implied some sort of regular training, as well as a social widening of the warrior group. More men thus came to share in the power which comes from a near-monopoly of the means of exercising force.

This was not the only crucial innovation of these years. It was then, too, that the Greeks invented politics; the notion of running collective concerns by discussion of possible choices in a public setting is theirs. The magnitude of what they did lives on in the language we still use, for 'politics' and 'political' are terms derived from the Greek word for a city, *polis*. This was the framework of Greek life. It was much more than a mere agglomeration of people living in the same place for economic reasons. That it was more is shown by another Greek turn of speech: they did not speak of Athens doing this, or Thebes doing that, but of the Athenians and the Thebans. Bitterly divided though it might often be, the *polis* – or, as for convenience it can be called, the city-state – was a community, a body of men conscious of shared interests and common goals.

Such collective agreement was the essence of the city-state; those who did not like the institutions of the one they lived in could look for alternatives elsewhere. This helped to produce a high degree of cohesiveness, but also a narrowness; the Greeks never long transcended the passion for local autonomy (another Greek word) and the city-state characteristically looked outwards defensively and distrustfully. Gradually, it acquired its protecting gods, its festivals and its liturgical drama which connected living men with the past and educated them in its traditions and laws. Thus it came to be an organism living in time, spanning generations. But at its root lay the hoplite ideal of disciplined, cooperative action in which men stood shoulder to shoulder with their neighbours, relying on them to support them in the common cause. In early days the citizen body – those, that is to say, who constituted the politically effective community – was confined to the hoplites, those who could afford to take their place in the ranks on which the defence of the city-state depended. It is not surprising that in later times Greek reformers who were worried about the results of political extremism would often turn hopefully to the hoplite class when looking for a stable, settled foundation for the *polis*.

At the roots of city-states lay also other facts: geography, economics, kinship. Many of them grew up on very ancient sites, settled in Mycenaean times; others were newer, but almost always the territory of a city-state was one of the narrow valleys which could provide just enough for its maintenance. A few were luckier: Sparta sat in a broad valley. A few were specially handicapped: the soil of Attica was poor and Athens would have to feed its citizens on imported grain in consequence. Dialect intensified the sense of independence latent in the mountains separating a city from its neighbours. In it was preserved a sense of common tribal origin which lived on in the great public cults.

By the beginning of historical times these forces had already generated intense feelings of community and individuality which made it virtually impossible for Greeks to transcend the city-state: a few shadowy leagues and confederations did not count for much. Within the city the involvement of citizens in its life was close; we might find it excessive. Yet because of its scale the city-state could do without elaborate bureaucracies; the citizen body, always much smaller than the whole population, could always assemble at one meeting place. There was no likelihood that a city-state could or

would aspire to a minute bureaucratic regulation of affairs; anything like this would probably have been beyond the capacity of its institutions. If we judge by the evidence of Athens, the state of which we know most because it recorded so much in stone, the distinction between administration, judgement and law-making was not as we know it; as in the Europe of the Middle Ages, an executive act might be clothed as a decision of a court interpreting established law. Law-courts were, formally speaking, only sections of the assembly of the citizens.

The size and qualification of the membership of this body determined the constitutional character of the state. Upon it depended, more or less, the authorities of day-to-day government, whether magistrates or courts. There was nothing like the modern permanent civil service, though it is still risky to generalize about such matters. There were over a hundred and fifty city-states and about many of them we know nothing; of most of the rest we know only a little. Obviously there were important differences between the ways in which they ran their affairs; in the fourth century BC, Aristotle made a great collection of their constitutions and there would not have been much point in a political scientist doing this unless they were significantly different from one another. But the detail of what went on is hard to discern, even in the few cases where we have good information.

As for the history of political forms, the origins are usually buried in legends as informative as the story of Hengist and Horsa to the historian of England. Even Homer is unhelpful about the city-state; he hardly mentions it because his subject is warrior bands. Yet when the historical age dawns the city-state is there, ruled by aristocracies. The forces which determined the broad lines of its later evolution have already been touched upon. New wealth meant new men, and the new men battered away at the existing élites to get admission to citizenship. The aristocracies which had supplanted the kings themselves became objects of rivalry and attack. The new men sought to replace them by a government less respectful of traditional interests; the result was an age of rulers the Greeks called tyrants. They were often moneyed but their justification was their popularity; they were strong men who set aside the aristocracies. The later sinister connotations of the term did not then exist; many tyrants must have seemed benevolent despots. They brought peace after social struggles which seem to have been intensified by a new crisis arising from pressure on land. This must have accelerated economic growth as did the usually good relations the tyrants enjoyed with one another. Yet the institution did not long survive. Few tyrannies lasted two generations. The seventh century was the tyrants' golden age and in the sixth the current was set almost everywhere towards collective government; oligarchies, constitutional governments and incipient democracies spread everywhere.

Athens was an outstanding example. For a long time it seems that though it was poor Attica had sufficient land for Athens to escape the social pressures which in other states led to the colonization movement. In other ways, too, her economy early reflected a special vigour; even in the eighth century her pottery suggests that Athens was something of a commercial and artistic leader. This may have made it easier later for Athens to come to terms with a growing population by specializing her agriculture and manufactures. Oil from olives which would grow on land unfruitful for cereals, pottery and silver from the mines at Laurium paid for the grain imports which she needed. Like Corinth, she became a great city feeding a bigger population than her own land could support, and by the beginning of the sixth century Athens fully reflected the anti-aristocratic movement.

From economic crisis at the beginning of the century emerged the almost legendary reforms of the law-giver Solon, who secured the admission of Athens' new wealthy to the old landed class. There followed an age of tyrants, which came to a close with the expulsion of the last in 510 BC. Then there was set up a complex series

The first major style of Athenian pottery is called 'geometric'; the formal, repetitive, concentrated design of this eighth-century example makes it clear why. Painted in brownish black on a yellow-brown clay ground, it is a relatively small specimen; some amphorae are four or five feet high, while this one is less than two.

of institutions which were eventually to give Athens the most democratic government in Greece. All political decisions were taken in principle by majority vote of the *ecclesia*, or general assembly of all citizens, which also elected the important magistrates and military commanders. Ingenious arrangements provided for the organization of the citizens in units which would prevent the emergence of sectional factions representing city-dwellers as against farmers or merchants. This was the beginning of a great age, which was also one of prosperity, when Athens would consciously foster festivals and cults which looked beyond the city and offered something to all Greeks. This was something of a bid for leadership, and historians have always enjoyed drawing attention to the contrast between Athens and her great rival, Sparta.

The contrast admirably illustrates the variety of Greek political experience. Unlike Athens, Sparta had met the pressures upon her not by modifying her institutions but by resisting change. She embodied the most conservative approach to the problem, solving it for a long time by rigid social discipline at home and by conquest among her neighbours which allowed her to meet the demand for land at others' expense. A very early consequence was a fossilizing of the social structure. So tradition-bound was she that it was alleged that her legendary law-giver, Lycurgus, had even forbidden her to write down her laws; they were driven home in the minds of the Spartiates by a rigorous training all underwent in youth, boys and girls alike.

Sparta had no tyrants. Her effective government appears to have been shared between a council of old men and five magistrates called 'ephors', while the two hereditary kings had special military powers. These oligarchs were in the last resort answerable to the assembly of the Spartiates (of whom, according to Herodotus, there were early in the fifth century about five thousand). Sparta was, therefore, a large aristocracy whose origins, ancient writers agreed, was the hoplite class. Society remained agricultural; no commercial class was allowed to appear and when the rest of Greece took up the use of money, around 600 BC, Sparta stood out and permitted only an iron currency for internal use. Spartans were not supposed to own silver or gold until the fourth century. Sparta even stood aside from the colonizing movement; she launched only one enterprise of this sort.

This produced a sort of militarized egalitarianism often admired by later puritans, and an atmosphere strongly suggestive, for good and ill, of the aspirations of the more old-fashioned English public school. Though the passing of time and the position of kings slightly softened their practice, Spartiates knew no great distinctions of wealth or comfort existed. Until well into classical times they avoided dressing differently and ate at communal messes. Their contions of life were, in a word, 'spartan', reflecting the idealization of military virtues and strict discipline. The details are often strikingly unpleasant as well as curious. Marriage, for example, was a ceremony for which the bride's hair was cropped and she was dressed as a boy. It was followed by a simulated rape, after which the couple did not live together, the man continuing to live with his companions in a male dormitory and eating in messes with them. It is interesting that Sparta exported nursemaids to other Greek states (later parallels will again occur to the reader). She had no artistic or cultural achievement to speak of and her internal politics remain mysterious.

Possibly Spartan politics were simplified or muted by Sparta's gravest problem, the division between the citizen commune and the rest. The bulk of the inhabitants of the Spartan state were not citizens. Some were freemen, but most were helots, serf-like workers bound to the land who shared with the free peasants the task of producing the food consumed at the Spartiates' communal meals. Originally the helot population may have been the native population enslaved by the Dorian invasions, but they were like later serfs in being tied to land rather than being the chattels of individual owners. Certainly their number was later swollen by conquest, above all by the annexation in the eighth century of the plain of Messenia, which disappeared from Greek history as an independent state for more than three hundred years. As a result, a cloud hung over the Spartan achievement, the fear of a helot revolt, and it was remarked by other Greeks. It hobbled the Spartans in their relations with other states. Increasingly they feared to have their army abroad lest its absence should tempt revolt at home. Sparta was always on sentry-go and the feared enemy was at home.

Sparta and Athens were to quarrel fatally in the fifth century and this has led them to be seen as always the poles of the political world of ancient Greece. They were not, of course, the only models available, and herein lies one of the secrets of the Greek achievement. It would draw upon a richness of political experience and data far greater than anything seen in the world until this time. This experience would provide the first systematic reflexions upon the great problems of law, duty, and obligation which have exercised men's minds ever since, and have done so largely in terms set by the classical Greeks. In pre-classical times, speculation on such themes is almost nonexistent. The weight of custom and the limitations of local experience sufficiently explain this.

The city-state was the shared inheritance and experience of the Greeks, but they knew of other types of political organization through contacts made in the course of trade and because of the exposed nature of many of their own settlements. The Greek world had frontier regions where conflict was likely. In the west they once seemed to be pushing ahead in an almost limitless expansion, but two centuries of striking advance came to an end round about 550 BC, when Carthaginian and Etruscan power prescribed a limit. The first settlements – once again, at sites sometimes used centuries earlier by Minoans and Mycenaeans – show that trade mattered as much as agriculture in their foundation. Their main strength lay in Sicily and in southern Italy, an area significantly to be called *Magna Graecia* in later classical times. The richest of these colonies was Syracuse, founded by Corinthians in 733 BC and eventually the dominating Greek state in the west. It had the best harbour in Sicily. Beyond this colonial area, settlements were made in Corsica, Sardinia, and southern France (at Massilia, the later Marseilles) while some Greeks went to live among the Etruscans and Latins of central Italy. Greek products have turned up even as far afield as Sweden and Greek influence has been seen in sixth-century fortification in Bavaria. More impalpable influence is hard to pin down, but a Roman historian believed that Greek example first civilized the barbarians of what was later to be France and set them not only to tilling their fields, but to cultivating the vine. If so, posterity owes Greek commerce a debt indeed.

This vigorous expansion seems to have provoked Phoenician envy and imitation. It led the Phoenicians to found Carthage and the Carthaginians to seize footholds in western Sicily. Eventually they were able to close down Greek trade in Spain and Sardinia. They were not, however, able to evict the Greeks from Sicily any more than the Etruscans could drive them from Italy. Coincidentally, the decisive battle in which the Syracusans routed a Carthaginian force was in 480 BC.

This was a date of even greater significance for Greek relations with Asia, where the Greek cities of Asia Minor had often been at loggerheads with their neighbours. They had suffered much from the Lydians until they came to terms with the Lydian king, Croesus of legendary wealth, and paid him tribute. Before this, Greece already influenced Lydian fashions; one of Croesus' predecessors had sent offerings to the shrine at Delphi. Now the Hellenization of Lydia went even more quickly ahead. Nonetheless, a much more formidable opponent was now looming up even further east: Persia.

The Greek struggle with Persia is the climax of the early history of Greece and the inauguration of the classical age. Because the Greeks made so much of their long conflict with the Persians it is easy to lose sight of the many ties that linked their cultures. The Persian fleets – and, to a lesser extent, Persian armies – launched against the Peloponnese had thousands of Greeks, mainly from Ionia, serving in them. Cyrus had employed Greek stone-cutters and sculptors and Darius had a Greek physician. Probably the war did as much to create as to feed the antagonism, however deep the emotional revulsion proclaimed by the Greeks for a country which treated its kings like gods.

The origins of the war lay in the great expansion of Persia under the Achaemenids. In about 540 BC, the Persians overthrew Lydia (and that

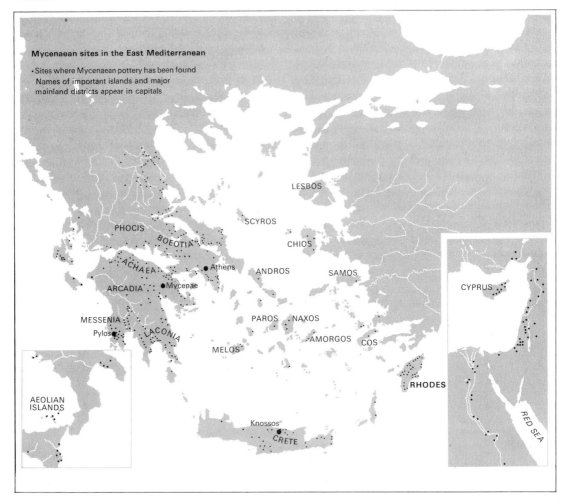

Mycenaean sites in the East Mediterranean

• Sites where Mycenaean pottery has been found
Names of important islands and major
mainland districts appear in capitals

LESBOS

SCYROS

PHOCIS

BOEOTIA

CHIOS

ACHAEA

Athens

ANDROS

SAMOS

ARCADIA

Mycenae

CYPRUS

MESSENIA

PAROS   NAXOS

Pylos

LACONIA

AMORGOS   COS

MELOS

RHODES

AEOLIAN
ISLANDS

Knossos

RED SEA

CRETE

was the end of Croesus, who was supposed to have provoked the assault by an incautious interpretation of an utterance of the Delphic oracle, which said that if he went to war with Persia, a great empire would be overthrown – but not which one). This brought Greeks and Persians face to face; elsewhere, the tide of Persian conquest rolled on. When the Persians took Egypt they damaged Greek traders' interests there. Next, the Persians crossed to Europe and occupied the cities of the coast as far west as Macedon; they failed to cross the Danube and move north into Scythia. At this point there was something of a pause. Then, in the first decade of the fifth century, the Asian Greek cities revolted against Persian suzerainty, encouraged, perhaps, by Darius' failure against

the Scythians. The mainland cities, or some of them, decided to help. Athens and Eretria sent a fleet to Ionia. In the subsequent operations the Greeks burnt Sardis, the former capital of Lydia and the seat of the western satrapy of the Persian empire. But the revolt failed in the end and left the mainland cities facing an enraged opponent.

Things did not usually happen very quickly in the ancient world, and large-scale expeditions still take a long time to prepare, but almost as soon as the Ionian revolt was crushed the Persians sent a fleet against the Greeks; it was wrecked off Mount Athos. A second attempt, in 490 BC, sacked Eretria but then came to grief at the hands of the Athenians in a battle whose name has become legendary: Marathon.

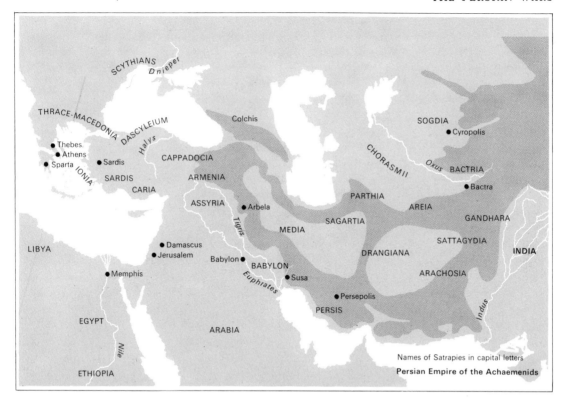

SCYTHIANS
Dnieper
THRACE-MACEDONIA
DASCYLEIUM
Colchis
SOGDIA
● Cyropolis
Thebes
Athens
● Sardis
CHORASMII
Oxus
BACTRIA
Sparta
IONIA
Halys
CAPPADOCIA
● Bactra
SARDIS
ARMENIA
PARTHIA
CARIA
ASSYRIA
● Arbela
AREIA
GANDHARA
SAGARTIA
Tigris
MEDIA
SATTAGYDIA
LIBYA
● Damascus
DRANGIANA
INDIA
● Jerusalem
Babylon ●
BABYLON
ARACHOSIA
● Memphis
Euphrates
● Susa
● Persepolis
PERSIS
Indus
EGYPT
ARABIA
Nile
Names of Satrapies in capital letters
Persian Empire of the Achaemenids
ETHIOPIA

Though this was an Athenian victory, the leader in the next phase of the struggle with Persia was Sparta, the strongest of the city-states on land. Out of the Peloponnesian League, an alliance whose origins had been domestic in that its aim had been to assure Sparta's future by protecting her from the need to send her army abroad, there devolved upon Sparta something like national leadership. When the Persians came again, ten years later, almost all the Greek states accepted this – even Athens, whose strengthening of her fleet had made her the preponderant power of the League at sea.

The Greeks said, and no doubt believed, that the Persians came again (in 480 BC, through Thrace) in millions; if, as now seems more likely, there were in fact well under a hundred thousand of them, this was still an overwhelming enough disproportion for the defenders of Greece. The Persian army moved slowly along the coast and down towards the Peloponnese, accompanied by a huge fleet which hung on its flanks. Yet the Greeks had important

advantages in their better-armed and trained heavy infantry, a terrain which nullified the Persian cavalry superiority, and morale.

This time the crucial battle was at sea. It followed another legendary episode, the overwhelming of Leonidas the Spartan king and his three hundred at the pass of Thermopylae, after which Attica had to be abandoned to the Persians. The Greeks retired to the isthmus of Corinth, their fleet massed in the bay of Salamis near Athens. Time was on their side. It was autumn; a winter which would catch the Persians unprepared would soon be coming and Greek winters are severe. The Persian king threw his numerical advantage away by deciding to engage the Greek fleet in the narrow waters of Salamis. His fleet was shattered and he began a long retreat to the Hellespont. The next year the army he had left behind was defeated at Plataea and the Greeks won another great sea fight, at Mycale on the other side of the Aegean, on the same day. This was the end of the Persian War.

217

Neutral states

Persian Empire

Anti-Persian states

------- The Route of Persian Fleet 490 BC

═══ Xerxes' land and sea route 481-480 BC

Persian Wars

It was a great moment in Greek history, perhaps the greatest, and Sparta and Athens had covered themselves with glory. The liberation of Asiatic Greece followed. It opened an age of huge self-confidence for the Greeks. Their outward drive was to continue until its culmination in a Macedonian empire a century and a half later. The sense of Greek identity was at its height, and men looking back at these heroic days were to wonder later if some great chance to unite Greece as a nation had not then been missed for ever. Perhaps, too, it was something more, for in the repulse of Asia by Greece lay the beginnings of a distinction between Europe and Asia whose reality would not appear for centuries but which would eventually lead men to look back anachronistically at Marathon and Salamis as the first time that Europe was saved.

*A small bronze carving of the figure of a
Spartan warrior.*

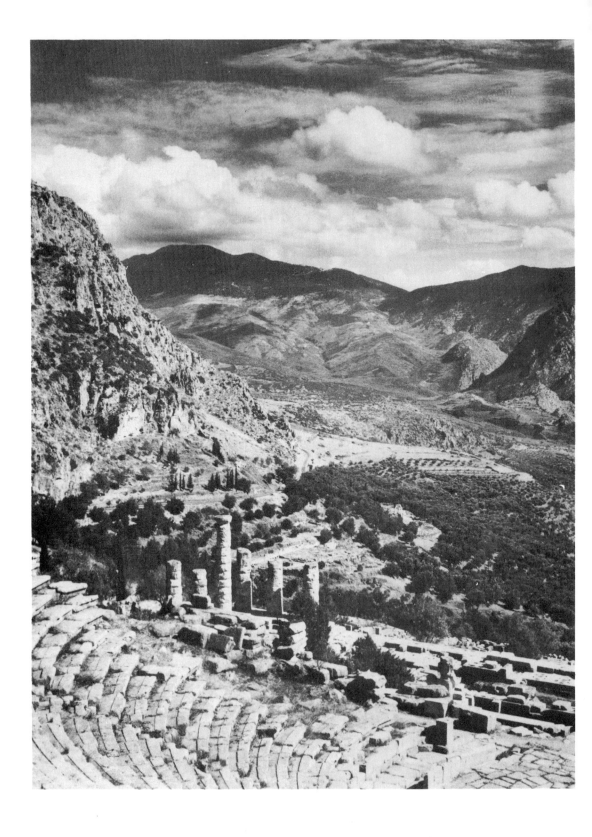

3 Greek civilization

Victory over the Persians opened the greatest age of Greek history. Some have spoken of a 'Greek miracle', so high do the achievements of classical civilization appear. Yet those achievements had as their background a political history so embittered and poisoned that it ended in the extinction of the institution which sheltered Greek civilization, the city-state. Complicated though it is in detail, the story can easily be summarized.

For thirty years after Plataea and Mycale the war with Persia dragged on, but as a background to a more important theme, a sharpening rivalry between Athens and Sparta. Survival assured, the Spartans had gone home with relief, anxious about their helots. This left Athens undisputed leader of those states which wanted to press ahead with the liberation of other cities from the Persians. A confederation

A modern visitor who stands today in the theatre at Delphi will be moved by the antiquity of what he sees as well as by the magnificence of the natural setting. The theatre itself dates from the second century BC. Beyond it are columns which are the remains of a fourth-century temple to Apollo and in the distance lies the plain of Crisa, renowned in ancient times for its olive groves. Yet the site is far more ancient in its associations than even these monuments. Delphi was one of the greatest of all the religious centres of the Greeks, the shrine of Apollo, the seat of the most famous of their oracles, a place hallowed by religion, superstition and myth.

called the Delian League was formed which was to support a common fleet to fight the Persians and command of it was given to an Athenian. As time passed, the members contributed not ships but money. Some did not wish to pay up as the Persian danger declined. Athenian intervention to make sure that they did not default increased and grew harsher. Naxos, for example, which tried to leave the alliance, was besieged back into it. The League was turning gradually into an Athenian empire and the signs were the removal of its headquarters from Delos to Athens, the use of the tribute money for Athenian purposes, the imposition of resident Athenian magistrates and the transfer of important legal cases to Athenian courts. When peace was made with Persia in AD 449 and the Athenian service of protection seemed less justifiable, the League continued, though its excuse had gone. At its peak, over one hundred and fifty states were paying tribute to Athens.

Sparta had welcomed the first stages of this process, happy to see others take up commitments outside her own borders. Like other states, Sparta only became aware gradually of a changing situation. When it happened this had much to do with the fact that Athenian hegemony increasingly affected the internal politics of the Greek states. They were often divided about the League, the richer, tax-paying citizens resenting the tribute, while the poorer did not object to it; they did not have to find the money to pay it. When Athenian interventions occurred they were sometimes followed by internal revolution, the result of which was a more

Note: References to "Victory", and "Defeat" are from the Athenian point of view

Sparta and allies

Athens and allies

Peloponnesian War

democratic pro-Athenian régime. Athens was herself living through struggles which steadily drove her in the direction of democracy. By 460 BC, the issue at home was really settled, so that irritation over her diplomatic behaviour soon came to have an ideological flavour. Other things, too, may have added to an irritation with Athens. She was a great trading state and another big trading city, Corinth, felt herself threatened. The Boeotians were directly the subjects of Athenian aggression, too. The materials thus accumulated for a coalition against Athens, and Sparta eventually took the lead in it by joining in war against Athens begun in 460. Fifteen years of not very determined fighting followed and then a doubtful peace. It was only

after almost another fifteen years, in 431 BC, that there began the great struggle which was to break the back of classical Greece, the Peloponnesian War.

It lasted, with interruptions, twenty-seven years, until 404 BC. Essentially it was a struggle of land against sea. On one side was the Spartan league, with Boeotia, Macedon (an unreliable ally) and Corinth as its most important members; they held the Peloponnese and a belt of land separating Athens from the rest of Greece. Athens' allies were scattered round the Aegean shore, in the Ionian cities and the islands, the area she had dominated since the days of the Delian League. Strategy was dictated by the means available. Sparta's army, clearly, was best used to occupy Athenian territory and then exact submission. The Athenians could not match their enemies on land. But they had the better navy. This was in large measure the creation of a great Athenian statesman and patriot and bitter enemy of Sparta, the demagogue Pericles. On the fleet he based a strategy of abandoning the Athenian countryside to annual invasion by the Spartans – it was in any case never capable of feeding the population – and withdrawing the inhabitants to the city and its port, the Piraeus, to which it was linked by two walls some five miles long, two hundred yards apart. There the Athenians could sit out the war, untroubled by bombardment or assault, which were beyond the capacities of Greek armies. Their fleet, still controlling the sea, would assure they were fed in war as in peace, by imported corn, so that blockade would not be effective.

Things did not work as well as this, because of plague within the city and the absence of leadership after Pericles' death in 429 BC, but the basic sterility of the first ten years of the war rests on this strategical deadlock. It brought peace for a time in 421 BC, but not a lasting one. Athenian frustrations found an outlet in the end in a scheme to carry the war further afield.

In Sicily lay the rich city of Syracuse, the most important colony of Corinth, herself the greatest of Athens' commercial rivals. To seize Syracuse would deeply wound an enemy, finish off a major grain-supplier of the Peloponnese, and provide immense booty. With this wealth Athens could hope to build and man a yet bigger fleet and thus achieve a final and unquestioned supremacy in the Greek world – perhaps the mastery of the Phoenician city of Carthage and a western Mediterranean hegemony, too. The result was the disastrous Sicilian Expedition of 415–413 BC. It was decisive, but as a death-blow to the ambitions of Athens. Half her army and all her fleet were lost; a period of political upheaval and disunion began at home. Finally, the defeat crystallized once more the alliance of Athens' enemies.

This time, the Spartans sought and obtained

In the middle of the fifth century a portrait head was carved of Pericles, the great statesman of the Athenian democracy. We know it only through this, possibly Roman, copy which is almost certainly an idealized likeness. That was the Greek way in portraiture in the classical age; until well into the fourth century the sculptor sought to catch the ethos of his subject, rather than its appearance. The approach partly accounts for the impression of almost super-human qualities which has sometimes stood between later historians and an understanding of what Greek society was really like.

Persian help in return for a secret undertaking that the Greek cities of mainland Asia should again become vassals of Persia (as they had been before the Persian War). This enabled them to raise the fleet which could help the Athenian subject cities who wanted to shake off her imperial control. Military and naval defeat undermined morale in Athens. In 411 BC an un-

223

successful revolution replaced the democratic régime briefly with an oligarchy. Then there were more disasters, the surrender of the Athenian fleet, and, finally, blockade. This time starvation was effective. In 404 BC Athens made peace and her fortifications were razed.

This could be the end of the story, for what followed was implicit in the damage both material and psychological the leading states of Greece had done to one another in these bitter years. There followed a brief Spartan hegemony during which she attempted to prevent the Persians cashing the IOU on the Greek Asian cities, but this had to be conceded after a war which brought a revival of Athenian naval power and the rebuilding of the Long Walls. In the end, Sparta and Persia had a common interest in preventing a renaissance of Athenian power and made peace in 387 BC. The settlement included a joint guarantee of all the other Greek cities except those of Asia. Ironically, the Spartans soon became as hated as the Athenians had been. Thebes took the leadership of their enemies. At Leuctra, in 317 BC, to the astonishment of Greece, the Spartan army was defeated. It marked a psychological and military epoch in something of the same way as the battle of Jena in Prussian history over two thousand years later. The practical consequences made this clear, too; a new confederation was set up in the Peloponnese as a counterweight to Sparta on her very doorstep and the foundation of a revived Messenia in 369 BC was another blow. The new confederation was a fresh sign that the day of the city-state was passing. The next half-century would see it all but disappear, but 369 BC is far enough to take the story for the moment.

Such events would be tragic in the history of any country. The passage from the glorious days of the struggle against Persia to the almost effortless recouping of the Persians' losses, thanks to Greek divisions, is a rounded drama which must always grip the imagination. Another reason why such intense interest has been given to it is that it was the subject-matter of an immortal book, Thucydides' *History of the Peloponnesian War*, the first work of contemporary as well as of scientific history. But the fundamental explanation why these few years should fascinate us when greater struggles do not is because we feel that at the heart of the jumble of battles, intrigues, disasters and glory still lies an intriguing and insoluble puzzle: was there a squandering of real opportunities after Mycale, or was this long anticlimax simply a dissipation of an illusion, circumstances having for a moment seemed to promise more than in fact was possible?

The war years have another startling aspect, too. During them there came to fruition the greatest achievement in civilization the world had ever seen. Political and military events then shaped that achievement in certain directions and in the end limited it and determined what should continue to the future. This is why the century or so of this small country's history whose central decades are those of the war is worth as much attention as the millennial empires of antiquity.

At the outset we should recall how small a plinth supported Greek civilization. There were many Greek states, certainly, and they were scattered over a large expanse of the Aegean, but even if Macedonia and Crete were included, the land-surface of Greece would fit comfortably into England without Wales or Scotland – and of it only about one-fifth could be cultivated. Of the states, most were tiny, containing 20000 souls at most; the biggest might have had 300000, thus just surpassing (but not by much) the size of, say, Bournemouth. Within them only a small élite took part in civic life and the enjoyment of what we now think of as Greek civilization.

The other thing to be clear about at the outset is that civilization's essence. The Greeks were far from underrating comfort and the pleasures of the senses. The physical heritage they left behind set the canons of beauty in many of the arts for two thousand years. Yet in the end the Greeks are remembered as poets and philosophers; it is an achievement of the mind that constitutes their claim on our attention.

The Acropolis was the site of the most sacred place in Athens, the home of the divine guardians of the city. Under Pericles' leadership there began to be built upon it (from money subscribed by the allies of Athens to resist Persia) the astonishing range of buildings which have made it also the greatest shrine of Greek classical architecture. The most celebrated of its buildings is the Parthenon, first a temple to Athene, later an Orthodox church, a Catholic cathedral, an Islamic mosque and finally a gunpowder magazine until it blew up in 1687. Then began the era of ruin and spoliation which lasted until very recent times.

This has been recognized implicitly in the idea of classical Greece, a creation of later ages rather than of the Greeks themselves. Certainly some Greeks of the fifth and fourth centuries BC saw themselves as the bearers of a culture which was superior to any other available, but the force of the classical ideal lies in its being a view from a later age, one which looked back to Greece and found there standards by which to assess itself. Later generations saw these standards above all in the fifth century, in the years following victory over the Persians, but there is a certain distortion in this. There is also an Athenian bias in such a view, for the fifth century was the apogee of Athenian cultural success. Nevertheless, to distinguish classical Greece from what went before – usually named 'archaic' or 'pre-classical' – makes sense. The fifth century has an objective unity because it saw a special heightening and intensification of Greek civilization, even if that civilization was ineradicably tied to the past, ran on into the future and spilled out over all the Greek world.

That civilization was rooted still in relatively simple economic patterns; essentially, they were those of the preceding age. No great revolution had changed it since the introduction of money and for three centuries or so there were only

The title of 'The Foundry Painter' has been given by scholars to the Athenian vase painter of the early fifth century whose work included this remarkably detailed representation of work in a bronze foundry. At the left the furnace is being stoked (a boy working bellows can be seen behind it) while another boy watches the workman. At the right, a second craftsman is finishing off a statue of Achilles.

gradual or specific changes in the direction or materials of Greek trade. Some markets opened, some closed, but that was all; the technical arrangements grew slightly more elaborate as the years went by. And trade between countries and cities was the most advanced economic sector. Below this level, the Greek economy was still nothing like as complicated as would be now taken for granted. Barter, for example, persisted for everyday purposes well into the era of coinage. It also speaks for relatively simple markets, with only limited demands made on them by the consumer. The scale of manufacture, too, was small. It has been suggested that at the height of the craze for the best Athenian pottery not more than 150 craftsmen were at work making and painting it. We are not dealing with a world of factories; most craftsmen and traders probably worked as individuals with a few employees and slaves. Even great building projects, such as the embellishment of Athens, reveal subcontracting to small groups of workers. The only exception seems to have been in mining, where the silver mines of Laurium in Attica seem to have been worked by thousands of slaves, though the arrangements under which this was done – the mines belonged to the state and were in some way sublet – remain obscure. The heart of the economy almost everywhere was subsistence agriculture. In spite of the specialized demand and production of an Athens or a Miletus (which had something of a name as a producer of woollens) the typical community depended on the production by

Spinning and weaving were traditionally at the core of women's occupations in Greek homes. Though workshops specializing in these crafts increased in number in the fifth century in order to meet more sophisticated tastes, textile working did not become a predominantly male activity as it was later to do in Western Europe. This illustration of domestic work comes from an Athenian vase of about 460 BC.

small farmers of the grain, olives, vines and timber needed by the home market.

Such men were the typical Greeks. Some were rich, most of them were probably poor by modern standards, but even now the Mediterranean climate makes a relatively low income more tolerable than it would be elsewhere. Commerce on any scale, and other kinds of entrepreneurial activity, were likely to be in the hands mainly of metics. They might have considerable social standing and were often rich men, but (for example) they could not in Athens

acquire land without special permission, though they were liable for military service (which gives us a little information about their numbers, for at the beginning of the Peloponnesian War there were some 3000 who could afford the arms and armour needed to serve as hoplite infantry). The other male inhabitants of the city-state who were not citizens were divided between freemen and slaves.

Women, too, were excluded from citizenship, though it is hazardous to generalize any further about their legal rights. In Athens, for example, they could neither inherit nor own property, though both were possible in Sparta. Nor could they in Athens undertake a business transaction if more than the value of a bushel of grain was involved. Divorce at the suit of the wife was, it is true, available to Athenian women, but it seems to have been rare and was probably practically harder to obtain than it was for men, who seem to have been able to get rid of wives fairly easily. Literary evidence suggests that the life of

227

most wives except those of rich men was the life of a drudge. The social assumptions that governed all women's behaviour were very restrictive; even women of the upper classes stayed at home in seclusion for most of the time. If they ventured out, they had to be accompanied; to be seen at a banquet put their respectability in question. Entertainers and courtesans were the only women who could normally expect a public life; they could enjoy a certain celebrity, but a respectable woman could not. Significantly, in classical Greece girls were thought unworthy of education. Such attitudes suggest the primitive atmosphere of the society out of which they grew, one very different from, say, Minoan Crete among its predecessors, or later Rome.

So far as sexuality is revealed by literature, Greek marriage and parenthood could produce deep feeling and as high a mutual regard between individual men and women as in our own societies. One element in it which is nowadays hard to weigh up exactly was a tolerated and even romanticized male homosexuality. Convention regulated this; it was an acceptable form of behaviour for young upper-class males in many Greek states, and was not thought to disqualify them for subsequent heterosexual marriage. Something must be allowed for fashion in this, but all societies can provide examples of homosexual relationships which suit many men at one stage of their lives; those of the ancient Greeks have attracted undue attention, perhaps because of the absence of inhibitions and controls which made the expression of homosexual affection improper in other societies and because the general prestige of their civilization has rubbed off on even its minor embodiments. At root, it may only have been a function of the restrictions which segregated and circumscribed the lives of free women.

In this as in everything else we know much more about the behaviour of an élite than about that of most Greeks. Citizenship, which must often have spanned very different social levels in practice, is a category too big to permit generalizations about the lives of citizens. Even

The huntsman shown on this flask appears to have been given an especially spruce and dapper appearance by the artist, an Athenian vase painter of the early fifth century. A vase of this sort, called a lekythos, was used to hold perfumed oil. In other paintings such vases appear usually to be handled by women. Greek pottery developed many such specialized forms.

in democratic Athens the kind of man who rose in public life and of whom, therefore, we read in the records, was usually a landowner; he was not likely to be a businessman, far less a craftsman. A craftsman might be important as a member of his group in the assembly, but he could hardly make his way to leadership. Businessmen may have been handicapped by the long-engrained conviction of upper-class Greeks that trade and industry were no proper occupations for a gentleman, who should ideally live a life of cultivated leisure based on the revenues of his own lands. This was a view which was to pass into European tradition with important effect.

Social history therefore blurs into politics. The Greek preoccupation with political life – the life of the *polis* – and the fact that classical Greece is neatly delimited by two distinct political epochs (that of the Persian Wars and that of a new, Macedonian, empire), makes it easy to appreciate the importance of Greek political history to civilization. Yet to reconstruct it in any complete sense is impossible. Many, perhaps most, English parishes have records richer than those we can recover for most of the city-states of Greece. What can be discovered from the evidence is much of the history of Athens, quite a lot of that of a few other states, almost nothing of many, and a fairly full narrative of their relations with one another. Together, these facts provide us with a pretty clear picture of the political context of classical Greek civilization, but uncertainty about many of its details.

Athens dangerously dominates this picture. There are big risks in arguing too readily from Athens to what was typical. What we know most about we often tend to think most important and because some of the greatest of fifth-century Greeks were Athenians and Athens is one pole of the great story of the Peloponnesian War, scholars have given its history enormous attention. Yet we also know that Athens was – to take only two points – both big and a commercial centre; it must, therefore, have been very untypical in important ways.

The temptation to over-value Athens' cultural importance is less dangerous. Such a primacy was, after all, recognized at the time. Though many of the greatest Greeks were not Athenians, and many Greeks rejected the Athenians' claims to superiority, the Athenians felt themselves the leaders of Greece. They did not scruple to use the tribute of the Delian League for embellishing its leading city. Thus were built the buildings whose ruins still crown the Acropolis, the Parthenon and Propylaea, but, of course, the money spent on them was available just because so many Greek states recognized Athens' paramountcy. This reality is what the tribute lists record. When on the eve of the Peloponnesian War Pericles told his countrymen that their state was a model for the rest of Greece there was an element of propaganda in what he said, but there was also conviction.

Solid grounds for the importance traditionally given to Athens ought, indeed, to be suggested *a priori* by the basic facts of geography. Her position recalls the tradition that she played an ill-defined but seemingly important rôle in the Ionian plantation of the Aegean and Asia Minor. Easy access to this region, together with poor agricultural resources, made her a trading and maritime power early in the sixth century. Thanks to this she was the richest of the Greek cities; at the end of it the discovery of the silver deposits of Laurium gave her the windfall with which to build the fleet of Salamis. From the fleet came her undisputed pre-eminence in the Aegean and thence, eventually, the tribute which refreshed her treasury in the fifth century. The peak of her power and wealth was reached just before the Peloponnesian War, in the years when creative activity and patriotic inspiration reached their height. Pride in the extension of empire was then linked to a cultural achievement which was truly enjoyed by the people.

Commerce, the navy, ideological confidence and democracy are themes as inseparably and traditionally interwoven in the history of fifth-century Athens as of late nineteenth-century England, though in very different ways. It was widely recognized at the time that a fleet of ships whose movement depended ultimately upon about two hundred paid oarsmen apiece was both the instrument of imperial power and the preserve of the democracy. Hoplites were less important in a naval state than elsewhere, and no expensive armour was needed to be an oarsman, who would be paid by the tribute of the League or the proceeds of successful warfare – as it was hoped, for example, the Sicilian Expedition would prove. Imperialism was genuinely popular among Athenians who would expect to share its profits, even if only indirectly and collectively, and not to have to bear its burdens. This was an aspect of Athenian democracy which was given exaggerated attention by its critics, though understandably.

The attacks on Athenian democracy began in early times and have continued ever since. They have embodied as much historical misrepresentation as have over-zealous and idealizing defences of the same institutions. The misgivings of frightened conservatives who had never seen anything like it before are understandable, for democracy emerged at Athens unexpectedly and at first almost unobserved. Its roots lay in sixth-century constitutional changes which replaced the organizing principle of kinship with that of locality; in theory and law, at least, local attachment came to be more important than the family you belonged to. This was a development which appears to have been general in Greece and it put democracy on an institutional basis which it has usually had ever since. Other changes followed from this. By the middle of the fifth century all adult males were entitled to take part in the assembly and through it, therefore, in the election of major administrative officers. The powers of the Areopagus were steadily reduced; after 462 BC it was only a law-court with jurisdiction over certain offences. The other courts were at the same time rendered more susceptible to democratic influence by the institution of payment for jury-service. As they also conducted much administrative business, this meant a fair amount of popular participation in the daily running of the city. Just after the Pelo-

ponnesian War, when times were hard, pay was also offered for attendance at the assembly itself. Finally, there was the Athenian belief in selecting by lot; its use for the choice of magistrates told against hereditary prestige and power.

At the root of this constitution lay distrust of expertise and entrenched authority and confidence in collective common sense. From this derived, no doubt, the relative lack of interest Athenians showed in rigorous jurisprudence – argument in an Athenian court was occupied much more with questions of motive, standing and substance, than with questions of law – and the importance they gave to the skills of oratory. The effective political leaders of Athens were those who could sway their fellow-citizens by their words. Whether we call them demagogues or orators does not matter; they were the first politicians seeking power by persuasion.

Towards the end of the century, though even then by no means usually, some such men came to be drawn from families outside the traditional ruling class. The continuing importance of old political families was nevertheless an important qualification of the democratic system. Themistocles at the beginning of the century and Pericles when the war began were members of old families, their birth making it proper for them even in the eyes of conservatives to take the lead in affairs; the old ruling classes found it easier to accept democracy because of this practical qualification of it. There is a rough parallel in the grudging acceptance of Whig reform by nineteenth-century English aristocrats; government in Athens as in Victorian England remained for a long time in the hands of men whose forefathers might have expected to rule the state in more aristocratic days. Another tempering qualification was provided by the demands of politics on time and money. Though jurors and members of the assembly might be paid, the fee for attendance was small; it seems to have been prompted, too, by the need to make sure of a quorum, which does not suggest that the assembly found it easy to get the mass of the citizens to attend. Many of them must have lived too far away and it has been calculated that not more than about one in eight of them were present at the average meeting. These facts tend to be lost to sight both in the denunciation and the idealization of Athenian democracy and they go some way to explaining its apparent mildness. Taxation was light and there was little discriminatory legislation against the rich such as we would now associate with democratic rule and such as Aristotle said would be the inevitable result of the rule of the poor.

Even in its emergent period Athenian democracy was identified with adventure and enterprise in foreign policy. Popular demand lay behind support for the Greek cities of Asia in their revolt against Persia. Later, for understandable reasons, it gave foreign policy an anti-Spartan bias. The struggle against the Areopagus was led by Themistocles, the builder of the Athenian fleet of Salamis, who had sensed a potential danger from Sparta from the moment the Persian War was over. Thus the responsibility for the Peloponnesian War and for its exacerbation of the factions and divisions of all the other cities of Greece came to be laid at the door of democracy. It not only brought disaster upon Athens itself, its critics pointed out, but exported to or at least awoke in all the Greek cities the bitterness of faction and social conflict. Oligarchy was twice restored in Athens – not that it helped matters – and by the end of the century faith in Athenian democracy was grievously weakened. Thucydides could take his history only down to 411 BC but it closes in misgiving and disillusion over his native city – which had exiled him – and Plato was to imprint for ever upon the Athenian democrats the stigma of the execution of Socrates in 399 BC.

If Athenian democracy's exclusion of women, metics and slaves is also placed in the scale, the balance against it seems heavy; it was to modern eyes both narrow and materially disastrous. Yet it should not disqualify Athens for the place she later won in the regard of men. Anachronistic and invalid comparisons are too easy; Athens is not to be compared with ideals still imperfectly

realized after two thousand years, but with her contemporaries. For all the survival of the influence of the leading families and the practical impossibility that even a majority of its members would turn up to any particular meeting of the assembly, more Athenians were engaged in self-government than was the case in any other state. Athenian democracy more than any other institution brought about the liberation of men from the political ties of kin which is one of the great Greek achievements. Many who could not have contemplated office elsewhere could undergo the political education of taking responsible decisions which is the heart of political culture. Men of modest means could help to run the institutions which nurtured and protected Athens' great civilized achievement. They listened to arguments of an elevation and thoughtfulness which makes it impossible to dismiss them as mere rhetoric; they must surely have weighed them seriously *sometimes*. Just as the physical divisions between the old Greek communities fostered a variety of experience which led in the end to a break with the world of god-given rulers and a grasp of the idea that political arrangements could be consciously chosen, so the stimulus of participation in affairs worked on unprecedentedly large numbers of men in classical Athens, not only in the assembly, but in the obligatory meetings of subordinate divisions of the citizen body. Even without the eligibility of all citizens to office, Athenian democracy would still have been the greatest instrument of political education contrived down to that time.

It is against that background that the errors, vanities and misjudgements of Athenian politics must be seen. We do not cease to treasure the great achievements of British political culture because of the shallowness and corruptness of many of the appeals to its twentieth-century democracy. Athens may be judged, like any political system, by its working at its best; under the leadership of Pericles it was outstanding. It left behind the myth of the individual's responsibility for his own political fate. We need myths in politics and have yet to find a better.

Bound safely to his mast and with the ears of his crew stopped with wax, Odysseus hears the song of the sirens who had lured so many sailors to their deaths. This Athenian jar of about 480 BC shows one of the most famous episodes in the Odyssey.

The Athenians, in any case, would have been uninterested in many modern criticisms of their democracy. Its later defenders and attackers have both often fallen into another sort of anachronism, that of misinterpreting the goals Greeks thought worth achieving. Greek democracy, for example, was far from being dominated, as is ours, by the mythology of cooperativeness, and cheerfully paid a larger price in destructiveness than would be welcomed today. There was a blatant competitiveness in Greek life apparent from the Homeric poems onwards.

Greeks admired men who won and thought men should strive to win. The consequent release of human power was colossal, but also dangerous. The ideal expressed in the much-used word which we inadequately translate as 'virtue' illustrates this. When Greeks used it, they meant that people were able, strong, quick-witted, just as much as just, principled, or virtuous in a modern sense. Homer's hero, Odysseus, frequently behaved like a rogue, but he is brave and clever and he succeeds; he is therefore admirable. To show this quality was good; it did not matter that the social cost might sometimes be high. The Greek was concerned with 'face': his culture taught him to avoid shame rather than guilt and the fear of shame was never far from the fear of public evidence of guilt. Some of the explanation of the bitterness of faction in Greek politics lies here; it was a price

Phidias' great statue of Athene was of gold and ivory; probably for that very reason it has perished. Quite a lot is known none the less about its appearance. A detail from one of the scenes on her shield is shown here; it was a copy made in marble probably for shipment to Rome, but was sunk in a shipwreck off the Piraeus, where it remained for more than two thousand years.

willingly paid.

When all is said, Athenian democracy must be respected above all for what it cradled, a series of cultural triumphs which are peaks even in the history of Greek civilization. These were public facts. The art of Athens was applauded and sustained by many men; the tragedies were tested not by the takings of a box-office but by judges interpreting a public taste vigorously expressed. The sculptor Phidias worked to beautify the city and not for an individual patron. And as democracy degenerated, so it seems, there was a waning of artistic nerve. This was the loss to the whole of Greece.

The achievement which made Greece teacher of Europe (and through her of the world) is too rich and varied to generalize about even in long and close study; it is impossible to summarize in a page or so. But there is a salient theme which emerges in it: a growing confidence in rational, conscious enquiry. The Greeks invented the philosophical question as part and parcel of one of the great intuitions of all time, that a coherent and logical explanation of things could be found, that the world did not ultimately rest upon the meaningless and arbitrary fiat of gods or demons. Put like that, of course, it is not an attitude which could be or was grasped by all, or even most, Greeks. It was an attitude which had to make its way in a world permeated with irrationality and superstition. Nevertheless, it was a revolutionary and beneficial idea. It looked forward to the possibility of a society where such an attitude would be generalized; even Plato, who thought it impossible that most men could share it, gave to the rulers of his ideal state the task of rational reflexion as the justification both of their privileges and of the discipline laid upon them. If civilization is advance towards the control of mentality and environment by reason, then the Greeks did more for it than any of their predecessors. Their challenge to the weight of irrationality in social and intellectual activity tempered its force as it had never been tempered before. For all the subsequent exaggeration and myth-making about it, the liberating effect of this emphasis was felt again and again for thousands of years. It was the greatest single Greek achievement.

This was so big a revolution in modes of thought in the Aegean that it now obscures its own scale. So remarkable are the works of the Greek intellectuals and so large have they loomed that it requires effort to penetrate through them to the values of the world from which they emerged. It is made a little easier because no such revolution is ever complete. A look at the other side of the coin reveals that most Greeks continued to live in cocoons of traditional irrationality and superstition; even those who were in a position to understand something of the speculations which were opening new mental worlds rarely accepted the implications. A continuing respect was shown to the old public orthodoxies. It was impiety in late fifth-century Athens, for example, to deny belief in the gods. One philosopher believed that the sun was a red-hot disc; it did not protect him that he had been the friend of Pericles when he said so, and he was banished. It was at Athens, too, that public opinion was convulsed, on the eve of the Sicilian Expedition, by the mysterious and ominous mutilation of certain public statues, the 'Hermae', or busts of Hermes. The disasters which followed were attributed by some to this sacrilege. Socrates the Athenian philosopher who became, thanks to his pupil Plato, the archetypal figure of the man of intellect, and left as a maxim the view that 'the unexamined life is not worth living', offended the pieties of his state and was condemned to die for it by his fellow-citizens; he was also condemned for questioning received astronomy. It does not seem that similar trials took place elsewhere, but they imply a background of popular superstition which must have been more typical of the Greek community than the presence of a Socrates.

In spite of such important historical residues, Greek thought, more than that of any earlier civilization, reflected changes of emphasis and fashion which arose from its own dynamism and these did not always lead to a greater ability to grapple with nature and society, rather than surrender to them, but sometimes to dead ends and blind alleys, to exotic and extravagant fantasies. Greek thought is not monolithic; we should think not of a bloc with a unity pervading all its parts, but of a historical continuum extending across three or four centuries, in which different elements are prominent at different times and one which is hard to assess.

One reason for this is that Greek categories of thought – the way, so to speak, in which they laid out the intellectual map before beginning to think about its individual components in detail at all – are not our own, though often deceptively like them. Some of those we use did not exist for the Greeks and their knowledge led them to draw different boundaries between fields of enquiry from those which we take for granted. Sometimes this is obvious and presents no difficulties; when a philosopher, for example, locates the management of the household and its estate (economics) as a part of a study of what we should call politics, we are not likely to misunderstand him. In more abstract topics it can cause trouble.

One example is to be found in Greek science. For us, science seems to be an appropriate way of approaching the understanding of the physical universe, and its techniques are those of

Thales, Socrates, Plato; these portraits are all Roman copies of Greek originals. There are several such replicas, so that it is possible to guess at the fidelity of individual examples to the original without seeing it. Thales lived before the age of classical portraiture and his appearance must remain conjectural, but Socrates' features are among the best known of his age, and it seems highly likely that we have here a good impression of him and of his pupil, Plato.

empirical experiment and observation. Greek thinkers found the nature of the physical universe just as approachable through abstract thought, through metaphysics, logic and mathematics. It has been said that Greek rationality actually came in the end to stand in the way of scientific progress, because enquiry followed logic and abstract deduction, rather than the observation of nature. Among the great Greek philosophers, only Aristotle gave prominence to collecting and classifying data, and he did this for the most part only in his social and biological studies. This is one reason for not separating the history of Greek science and philosophy too violently. They are a whole, the product of scores of cities and developing across four centuries or so in time.

Their beginnings constitute a revolution in human thought and it has already taken place when there appear the earliest Greek thinkers of whom we have information. They lived in the Ionian city of Miletus in the seventh and sixth centuries BC. Important intellectual activity went on there and in other Ionian cities right down to the remarkable age of Athenian speculation which begins with Socrates. No doubt the stimulus of an Asian background was important here as in so many other ways in getting things started; it may also have been significant that Miletus was a rich place; early thinkers seem to have been rich men who could afford the time to think. None the less, the early emphasis on Ionia gives way before long to a spectrum of intellectual activity going on all over the Greek world. The western settlements of *Magna Graecia* and Sicily were crucial in many sixth- and fifth-century developments and primacy in the later Hellenistic age was to go to Alexandria. The whole Greek world was involved in the success of the Greek mind and even the great age of Athenian questioning should not be given exaggerated standing within it.

In the sixth century BC, Thales and Anaximander launched at Miletus the conscious speculation about the nature of the universe which shows that the crucial boundary between myth and science has been crossed. Egyptians had set about the practical manipulation of nature and had learned much inductively in the process, while Babylonians had made important measurements. The Miletan school made good use of this information, and possibly took more fundamental cosmological notions from the old civilizations, too; Thales is said to have held that the earth had its origin in water. Yet the Ionian philosophers soon went beyond their inheritance. They set out a general view of the nature of the universe which replaced myth with impersonal explanation. This is more impressive than the fact that the specific answers

they put forward were in the end to prove unfruitful. The Greek analysis of the nature of matter is an example. Although an atomic theory was adumbrated which was over two thousand years before its time, this was by the fourth century rejected in favour of a view, based on that of the early Ionian thinkers, that all matter was composed of four 'elements' – air, water, earth, fire – which combined in different proportions in different substances. This theory subsequently dominated western science down to the Renaissance. It was of enormous historical importance because of the boundaries it set and the possibilities it opened. It was also, of course, erroneous.

This should be firmly kept in place as a secondary consideration at this point. What mattered about the Ionians and the school they founded was what has rightly been called their 'astonishing' novelty. They pushed aside gods and demons from the understanding of nature. Time was to overwhelm some of their achievement in part. In Athens in the late fifth century more than a temporary alarm in the face of defeat and danger has been seen in the condemnation as blasphemous of views far less daring than those of Ionian thinkers two centuries before. One of them had said 'If the ox could paint a picture, his god would look like an ox'; a few centuries later, classical Mediterranean civilization has lost much of such perceptiveness. Its early appearance is the most striking sign of the vigour of Greek civilization.

Not only popular superstition swamped such ideas. Other philosophical tendencies also played a part. One coexisted with the Ionian tradition for a long time and was to have much longer life and influence. Its crux was the view that reality was immaterial, that, as Plato later put it in one of its most persuasive expressions, in life we experience only the images of pure Form and Ideas, the heavenly embodiments of true reality, which can only be apprehended by thought, a matter not only of systematic speculation, but of intuition, too. For all its immateriality, this kind of thinking also had its roots in Greek science, though not in the speculations of the Ionians about matter but in the activities of mathematicians.

Some of their greatest advances were not to be made until long after Plato's death, when they would round off what is the biggest single triumph of Greek thought, its establishment of most of the arithmetic and geometry which served western civilization down to the seventeenth century. Every schoolboy used to know the name of Pythagoras, who lived at Crotone in southern Italy in the middle of the sixth century and may be said to have founded the deductive proof. Fortunately or unfortunately, he did more than this. He discovered the mathematical basis of harmonics by studying a vibrating string and he became especially interested in the relationship of numbers and geometry. His approach to them was semi-mystical; Pythagoras, like many mathematicians, was a religiously minded man who is said to have celebrated the satisfactory conclusion of his famous proof by sacrificing an ox. His school – there was a secret Pythagorean 'Brotherhood' – later came to hold that the ultimate nature of the universe was mathematical and numerical. 'They fancied that the principles of mathematics were the principles of all things', reported Aristotle, somewhat disapprovingly, yet his own teacher, Plato, had been greatly influenced by this belief, and by the scepticism of Parmenides, an early fifth-century Pythagorean, about the world known to the senses. Numbers seemed more attractive than the physical world; they possessed both the defined perfection and the abstraction of the Idea which embodied reality.

Pythagorean influence on Greek thought is an immense subject; fortunately, it need not be summarized. What matters here is its ultimate repercussions in a view of the universe which, because it was constructed on mathematical and deductive principles, rather than from observation, fixed astronomy on the wrong lines for nearly two thousand years. From it came the vision of a universe built up of successively enclosing spheres on which moved sun, moon and planets in a fixed and circular pattern about the earth. The Greeks noticed that this did not seem to be the way the heavens moved in practice. But – to summarize crudely – appearances were saved by introducing more and more refinements into the basic scheme while refusing to scrutinize the principles from which it was deduced. The final elaborations were not achieved until work in the second century AD by a famous Alexandrian, Ptolemy. These efforts were remarkably successful, and only a few dissentients demurred (which shows that other intellectual results were possible in Greek science). For all the inadequacies of Ptolemy's system, predictions of planetary movement could be made which would still serve as adequate guides for oceanic navigation in the age of Columbus, even if they rested on misconceptions which sterilized cosmological thinking until his day.

Both the theory of the four elements and the development of Greek astronomy illustrate the deductive bias of Greek thought and its characteristic weakness, its urge to set out a plausible theory to account for the widest possible range of experience without submitting it to the test of experiment. It affected most fields of thought which we now think to be covered by science and philosophy. Its fruits were on the one hand argument of unprecedented rigour and acuteness and on the other an ultimate scepticism about sense-data. Only the Greek doctors, led by the fifth-century Hippocrates, made much of empiricism.

In the case of Plato – and, for good or ill, philosophical discussion has been shaped more by him and his pupil Aristotle than by any other two men – this bias may have been reinforced by his low opinion of what he observed. By birth an aristocratic Athenian, he turned away from the world of practical affairs in which he had hoped to take part, disillusioned with the politics of the Athenian democracy, and, in particular, with its treatment of Socrates, whom it had condemned to death. From Socrates, Plato had learnt not only his Pythagoreanism, but an idealist approach to ethical questions, and a technique of philosophical enquiry. The Good, he thought, was discoverable by enquiry and intuition; it was reality. It was the greatest of a series of 'ideas' – Truth, Beauty, Justice were others – which were not ideas in the sense that at any moment they had shape in anyone's mind (as one might say 'I have an idea about that'), but real entities, enjoying a real existence in a world fixed and eternal, of which such ideas were the elements. This world of changeless reality, thought Plato, was hidden from us by the senses, which deceived us and misled us. But it was accessible to the soul, which could understand it by the use of reason.

Such ideas had a significance going far beyond technical philosophy. In such ideas (like those of Pythagoras) can be found, for example, traces of a familiar later idea, that of puritanism, that man is irreconcilably divided between the soul, of divine origin, and the body which imprisons it. Not reconciliation, but the victory of one or another, must be the outcome. It was an idea which would pass into Christianity with enormous effect. Immediately, too, Plato had an intensely practical concern since he believed that knowledge of the Ideal world of universals and reality could be helped or hindered by the arrangements under which men lived. He set out his views in a series of dialogues between Socrates and people who came to argue with him. They were the first textbooks of philosophical thinking and the one we call the *Republic* was the first book in which anyone had ever set out a scheme for a society directed and planned to achieve an ethical goal. It describes an authoritarian state (reminiscent of Sparta) in which marriages would be regulated to produce the best genetic results, families and private property would not exist, culture and the arts would be censored and education carefully supervised. The few who ruled this state would be those of sufficient intellectual and moral stature to fit them for the studies which would enable them to realize the just society in practice by apprehending the Ideal world. Like Socrates, Plato held that wisdom was the understanding of reality and he assumed that to see truth was to make it impossible not to act in accordance with it. Unlike his teacher, he held that for most

people education and the laws should impose exactly that unexamined life which Socrates had thought not worth living.

The *Republic* and its arguments were to provoke centuries of discussion and imitation, but this was true of almost all Plato's work. As a twentieth-century English philosopher put it, practically all subsequent philosophy in the West was a series of footnotes to Plato. In spite of Plato's distaste for what he saw about him and the prejudice it engendered in him, he anticipated almost all the great questions of philosophy, whether they concerned morals, aesthetics, the basis of knowledge, or the nature of mathematics, and he set out his ideas in great works of literature, which have always been read with pleasure.

The Academy which Plato founded has some claim to be the first university. From it emerged his pupil Aristotle, a thinker more comprehensive and balanced, less sceptical of the possibilities of the actual, and less adventurous than he. Aristotle never altogether rejected his master's teaching but he departed from it in fundamental ways. He was a great classifier and collector of data (with a special interest in biology) and did not reject sense experience as did Plato. Indeed, he sought both firm knowledge and happiness in the world of experience, rejecting the notion of universal ideas and arguing inductively from facts to general laws. Aristotle was so rich a thinker and interested in so many sides of experience that his historical influence is as hard to delimit as that of Plato. What he wrote provided a framework for the discussion of biology, physics, mathematics, logic, literary criticism, aesthetics, psychology, ethics and politics for two thousand years. He provided ways of thinking about these subjects and approaches to them which were elastic and capacious enough eventually to contain Christian philosophy. He also founded a science of deductive logic which was not displaced until the end of the nineteenth century. It is a vast achievement, different in kind but not less important than that of Plato.

Aristotle's political thinking was in one sense

in agreement with Plato's: the city-state was the best conceivable social form, but required reform and purification to work properly, he thought. But beyond this point he diverged greatly from his master. Aristotle saw the proper working of the *polis* as being that which would give each of its parts the rôle appropriate to it and that was essentially for him a matter of understanding what led in most existing states to happiness. In formulating an answer, he made use of a Greek idea to which his teaching was to give long life, that of the Mean, the idea that excellence lay in a balance between extremes. The empirical facts seemed to confirm this and Aristotle assembled greater quantities of such evidence in a systematic form than any predecessor, it seems; but in stressing the importance of facts about society, he had been anticipated by another Greek invention, that of history.

This was another major achievement. In most countries, chronicles or annals precede history. In Greece, this was not so, and historical writing in Greek at once reached its highest level in its first embodiments, two books by masters which were never equalled by their successors. The first of them, Herodotus, has reasonably been termed 'the father of history'. The word – *historie* – existed before him; it meant enquiry. Herodotus gave it an added meaning, that of enquiry about events in time, and in putting down the results wrote the first prose work of art in a European language which survives. He accumulated information about the Persian Wars and their antecedents by reading a huge mass of the available literature and by interrogating people on his travels and assiduously recording what he was told and read. For the first time, these things are the subject of more than a chronicle. The result is his *Histories*, a remarkable account of the Persian empire, with, built into it, much information abut early Greek history and a sort of world survey, followed by an account of the Persian Wars down to Mycale. He spent much of his life travelling, having been born (it was traditionally said) in the Dorian town of Halicarnassus in south-west Asia Minor in 484 BC. At one point he came to Athens where he remained for a few years, living as a metic, and while there he may have been rewarded for public recitations of his work. He went later to a new colony in south Italy; there he completed his work and died, a little after 430 BC. He therefore knew something by experience of the whole spread of the Greek world and travelled in Egypt and elsewhere as well. Thus wide experience lay behind his great book, an account scrupulously based on witnesses, even if Herodotus sometimes treated them somewhat credulously.

It is usually conceded that one of the superiorities of Thucydides, Herodotus' greater successor, was his more rigorous approach to reports of fact and his attempts to control them in a critical way. The result is a more impressive intellectual achievement, though its austerity throws into even stronger relief the charm of Herodotus' work. Thucydides' subject was contemporary, the history of the Peloponnesian War. The choice reflected deep personal involvement and a new conception. Thucydides was a member of a leading Athenian family (he served as a general until disgraced for an alleged failure in command) and he wanted to discover the causes which had brought his city and Greece into their dreadful plight. He shared with Herodotus a practical motive, for he thought (as most Greek historians were to do after him) that what he found out would have practical value, but he sought not merely to describe, but to explain. The result is one of the most striking pieces of historical analysis ever written and the first ever to seek to penetrate through different levels of explanation. In the process he provided a model to future historians of disinterested judgement, for his Athenian loyalties rarely obtrude. The book was not completed – it takes the story only to 411 BC – but the overall judgement is concise and striking: 'the growth of Athens' power and Sparta's fear was, in my view, the cause which compelled them to go to war'.

The invention of history is itself evidence of the new intellectual range of the literature created by the Greeks. It is the first complete one known to man. The Jewish is almost as comprehensive, but contains neither drama nor critical history, let alone the lighter *genres*. But Greek literature shares with the Bible a primacy shaping the whole of subsequent western writing. Besides its positive content, it imposed the major forms of literature and the first themes of a criticism by which to judge them.

From the beginning, as Homer shows, it was closely linked to religious belief and moral teaching. Hesiod, a poet who probably lived in the late eighth century and is usually considered to be the first Greek poet of the post-epic age, consciously addressed himself to the problem of justice and the nature of the gods, thus confirming the tradition that literature was for more than enjoyment and setting out one of the great themes of Greek literature for the next four centuries. For the Greeks, poets were always likely to be seen as teachers, their work suffused with mystical overtones, inspiration. Yet there were to be many poets, many styles of poetry in Greek. The first which can be distinguished is writing in a personal vein which was to the taste of aristocratic society. But as private patronage became concentrated during the era of the tyrants, so it passed slowly into the collective and civic area. The tyrants deliberately fostered the public festivals which were to be vehicles of the greatest specimens of Greek literary art, the tragedies. The drama's origins lie everywhere in religion and its elements must have been present in every civilization. The ritual of worship is the first theatre. Yet there, too, the Greek achievement was to press this towards conscious reflexion on what was going forward; more was to be expected of the audience than passive resignation or orgiastic possession. The didactic impulse emerges in it.

The first form of the Greek drama was the dithyramb, the choral song recited at the festivals of Dionysus, together with dance and mime. In 535 BC, we are told, this was the subject of a crucial innovation, when Thespis added to it an individual actor whose speech was some kind of antiphone to the chorus. Further innovation and more actors followed and within a

hundred years we have reached the full, mature theatre of Aeschylus, Sophocles and Euripides. Of their work, thirty-three plays survive (including one complete trilogy), but we know that more than three hundred different tragedies were performed in the fifth century. In this drama the religious undertone is still there, though not so much in the words as in the occasions at which they would have been performed. The great tragedies were performed in trilogies as 'liturgies', civic festivals attended by citizens who were already familiar with the basic story (often mythological) they had come to see. This, too, suggests the educational effect. Probably most Greeks never saw a play by Aeschylus; certainly an infinitesimally small number by comparison with the number of modern Englishmen who have seen a play of Shakespeare. None the less, those who were not too busy on their farms, or too far away, provided a large audience.

More men than in any other ancient society were able to scrutinize and reflect upon the content of their own moral and social world. What

Dionysus, depicted in about 500 BC, holds in his hands the vine-staff and the empty cup which symbolize his rôle as god of wine. To the Greeks he was also much more – the focus of a major religious cult. Probably Dionysus was in origin a nature god but his cult evolved into an interesting and psychologically fruitful complement to that of Apollo, the embodiment above all of the qualities of harmony, rationality, equity. The cult of Dionysus gave expression to another side of human nature and an important one, for it stressed abandon, frenzy, even violence. It was celebrated in the winter months when Apollo was supposed to be absent from his shrine at Delphi; then troops of young women, Maenads as they were called, would follow the priests of Dionysus to remote places in the mountains for the secret rites of the cult, dancing in ecstasy, impervious to cold and exposure, destroying animals which fell in their way and, perhaps, human intruders too.

This panel from an Attic jar of about 540 BC shows a flute player facing a chorus of performers dressed as horses and their riders. It may be a scene from a traditional dance or comic chorus later to be recalled by poets when in the following century comedy was first presented in the theatre.

they expected was a revealing emphasis in familiar rites, a new selection from their meaning, and this is what the great dramatists mostly gave them, even if some plays went beyond this and some, even, at a favourable moment satirized the social pieties. It was not, of course, a naturalistic picture that was presented, but the operation of the laws of a heroic, traditional world and their agonizing impact on individuals caught in their working. In the second half of the fifth century Euripides had even begun to use the conventional tragic form as a vehicle for questioning conventional assumptions; thus he inaugurated a technique to be exploited in the western theatre by authors as late and as different as Gogol and Ibsen. The framework provided by plot, though, was familiar, and at its heart lay a recognition of the weight of inexorable law and *nemesis*. The acceptance of this setting may be thought, in the last resort, to be testimony to the irrational rather than the rational side of the Greek mind. Yet it was a long way from the state of mind in which the congregation of an eastern temple fearfully or hopefully witnessed the round of unchanging ritual and sacrifice.

In the fifth century the scope of the theatre was also broadening in other ways. This was when Attic comedy developed as a form in its own right, and found in Aristophanes its first

Beside the Parthenon on the Acropolis at Athens stands a small temple called the Erechtheum, or house of Erechtheus, one of the legendary kings of Athens. It contained a small wooden image of the goddess Athene supposed to have been placed there by the gods, and was a shrine as sacred as the Parthenon itself – from some points of view it was even more sacred. The south porch of the Erechtheum is supported by what are probably the finest examples of the female figures called Caryatids and used by the Greeks (as they had been earlier used in the Near East) as a variant on the usual columns for the support of architectural loads. How they came to be named is not exactly known, but it may have been as the result of a joke comparing them to to the (allegedly) robust ladies of Caryae, a district of Sparta.

great manipulator of men and events for others' amusement. His material was often political, almost always highly topical, and frequently scurrilous. His survival and success is the most striking evidence we possess of the tolerance and freedom of Athenian society. A hundred years later, we have almost reached the modern world in a fashion for plays about the intrigues of slaves and unhappy love-affairs. It has not the impact of Sophocles, but it can still amuse; it remains a near-miracle, for nothing like it had been there two hundred years before. The rapidity with which Greek literature grew after the age of epic poetry and its enduring power is evidence of Greek powers of innovation and mental development which is easy to appreciate even when we cannot explain it.

Literature at the end of the classical age still had a long and important life ahead when the

243

city-states disappeared. It had a growing audience, for Greek was to become both *lingua franca* and an official language over all the Near East and much of the Mediterranean. It was not to reach again the heights of Athenian tragedy, but it was still to show us masterpieces. The sense of decline in the visual arts is more apparent. Here, above all in monumental architecture and the nude, Greece had again set standards for the future. From the first borrowings from Asia a wholly original architecture was evolved, the classical style whose elements are still consciously evoked even by the austerities of twentieth-century builders. Within a few hundred years it spread over much of the world from Sicily to India; in this art, too, the Greeks were cultural exporters.

They were in one respect favoured by geology, for Greece contained much high-quality stone. Its durability is attested by the magnificence of the relics we look at today. Yet there is an illusion in this. The purity and austerity with which fifth-century Athens speaks to us in the Parthenon conceals its image in Greek eyes. We have lost the garish statues of gods and goddesses, the paint and ochre and the clutter of monuments, shrines and *stelae* that must have encumbered the Acropolis and obscured the simplicity of its temples. The reality of many great Greek centres may have been more like, say, modern Lourdes; a jumble of untidy little shrines cluttered by traders, booths, and the rubbish of superstition is the impression gained when approaching the Temple of Apollo at Delphi (though we must make allowances for the contribution made by the archaeologist to this impression).

None the less, this qualification made, the erosion of time has allowed a beauty of form which is almost unequalled to emerge from the superficial experience. There is no possibility here of discounting the interplay of judgement of the object with standards of judgement which derive ultimately from the object itself. It remains simply true that to have originated an art that has spoken so deeply and powerfully to men's minds across such ages is itself not easily

interpreted except as evidence of an unsurpassed artistic greatness and an astonishing skill in giving it expression.

This quality is also present in Greek sculpture. Here, too, the presence of good stone was an advantage, and the original influence of oriental, often Egyptian, models important. Like pottery, the eastern models once absorbed, sculpture evolved in the direction of greater

The inspiration of Greek sculpture came first from Asia, then from Egypt. The basic posture of the statues known as kouroi – *youths – reflects this. The four-square stance is meant to be seen from the front; one leg is in advance of the other, as if in a walking position. The rigidity of the posture, the clenched fists and set smile, all characterized this type of statue from its first appearance in the Greek islands (this example is from Melos) until it gave way to a more relaxed, naturalistic manner at the beginning of the fifth century. Such statues stood over graves or as dedications to gods; they were not portraits, but figures only one degree removed in their nature from the anonymous cult figures of shrines.*

naturalism. The supreme subject of the Greek sculptors was the human form, portrayed no longer as a memorial or cult object, but for its own sake. Again it is not always possible to be sure of the finished statue the Greeks saw; these figures were often gilded, painted or decorated with ivory and precious stones. Some bronzes have undergone looting or melting down, so that the preponderance of stone may itself be misleading. Their evidence, though, records a clear evolution. We begin with statues of gods and of young men and women whose identity is often unknown, simply and symmetrically presented in poses not too far removed from those of the orient. In the classical figures of the fifth century, naturalism begins to tell in an uneven distribution of weight and the abandonment of the simple frontal stance and evolve steadily towards the mature, human style of Praxiteles and the fourth century in which the body – and for the first time the female nude – is treated.

A great culture is more than a mere museum and no civilization can be reduced to a catalogue. For all its élite quality, the achievement and importance of Greece comprehended all sides of life; the politics of the city-state, a tragedy of Sophocles and a statue by Phidias are all part of it. Later ages grasped this intuitively, happily ignorant of the conscientious discrimination which historical scholarship made possible between periods and places. This was a fruitful error, because in the end what Greece was to be thought to be was as important to the future as what she was.

What Greece was, in spite of all the ways in which her civilization fell short of later idealization and for all the strength of its ties with the past, was quite simply the most important extension of Man's grasp of his own destiny down to that time. Within four centuries, Greece invented philosophy, politics, most of arithmetic and geometry, and the categories of western art. It would be enough, even if her errors, too, had not been so fruitful. Europe has drawn interest on the capital Greece laid down ever since, and through Europe the rest of the world has traded on the same account.

This early fifth-century statue comes from the Acropolis of Athens and though it still shows its subject in a standing, frontal pose, the evolution of Greek style away from the monumental formality it inherited from Egypt is very marked. The kouroi *are being replaced by figures in more relaxed postures; the conventional positioning is being set aside in favour of one which demands a subtler representation of the response of the body in its modelling. The evolution from this degree of innovation to a still more complete naturalism was to be very rapid.*

245

4 The Hellenistic world

The history of Greece rapidly becomes less interesting after the fifth century. It is also less important. What remains important is the history of Greek civilization and the shape of this, paradoxically, was determined by a kingdom in northern Greece which some said was not Greek at all: Macedon. In the second half of the fourth century it created an empire bigger than any yet seen, the legatee of both Persia and the city-states. It organized the world we call Hellenistic because of the preponderance and uniting force within it of a culture, Greek in inspiration and

For more than two thousand years the glamour of Alexander the great conqueror fascinated men who dreamed they might carry out exploits as astonishing. No doubt it added to the glamour of his legend that Alexander's physical image had to be evoked from representations of him of doubtful authenticity. This one is at least second-hand – a copy in mosaic by a Roman artist of a Hellenistic painting long since perished. The original may have been near-contemporary (and was perhaps even commissioned by Cassander, the king of Macedon, murderer of Alexander's mother, wife and heir); by the time it was embodied in this version it is more an idealization of a soldier, pictured in the vigour of his onslaught on the Persians than a portrait. The huge mosaic at Pompeii (sixteen feet by eight) from which this detail is taken was no doubt a copy of one painting in a series which represented the whole cycle of Alexander's almost immediately legendary life.

language. Yet Macedon was a barbarous place, perhaps centuries behind Athens in the quality of its life and culture.

The story begins with the decline of Persian power. Persian recovery in alliance with Sparta had masked important internal weaknesses. One of them is commemorated by a famous book, the *Anabasis* of Xenophon, the story of the long march of an army of Greek mercenaries back up the Tigris and across the mountains to the Black Sea after an unsuccessful attempt on the Persian throne by a brother of the king. This was only a minor and subsidiary episode in the important story of Persian decline, an offshoot of one particular crisis of internal division. Throughout the fourth century that empire's troubles continued, province after province (among them Egypt which won its independence as early as 404 and held it for sixty years) slipping out of control. A major revolt by the western satraps took a long time to master and though in the end imperial rule was restored the cost had been great. When at last reimposed, Persian rule was often weak.

One ruler tempted by the possibilities of this decline was Philip II of Macedon, a not very highly regarded northern state whose power rested on a warrior aristocracy; it was a rough, tough society, its rulers still somewhat like the warlords of Homeric times, their power resting more on personal ascendancy than institutions. Whether this was a state which was a part of the world of the Hellenes was disputed; some Greeks thought Macedonians barbarians, though their kings claimed descent from Greek houses

247

(one going back to Heracles) and their claim was generally recognized. Philip himself sought status; he wanted Macedon to be thought of as Greek. When he became regent of Macedon in 359 BC he began a steady acquisition of territory at the expense of other Greek states. His ultimate argument was an army which became by the end of his reign the best-trained and organized in Greece. The Macedonian military tradition had emphasized heavy, armoured cavalry, and this continued to be a major arm. Philip added to this tradition the benefit of lessons he had drawn about infantry while a hostage at Thebes in his youth. From hoplite tactics he evolved a new weapon, the ten-deep phalanx of pikemen. The men in its ranks carried pikes twice as long as a hoplite spear and they operated in a more open formation, pike shafts from the second and third ranks running between men in the front to present a much denser array of weapons for the charge. Another advantage of the Macedonians was a grasp of siege-warfare techniques not shown by other Greek armies; they had catapults which made it possible to force a besieged town's defenders to take cover while battering-rams, mobile towers and mounds of earth were brought into play. Such things had previously been seen only in the armies of Assyria and their Asian successors. Finally, Philip ruled a fairly wealthy state, its riches much increased once he had acquired the gold-mines of Mount Pangaeum, though he spent so much that he left huge debts.

He used his power first to ensure the effective unification of Macedon itself. Within a few years the infant king for whom he was regent was deposed and Philip was elected king. Then he began to look to the south and north-east. In these areas expansion sooner or later meant encroachment upon the interests and position of Athens. Her allies in Rhodes, Cos, Chios and Byzantium placed themselves under Macedonian patronage. Another, Phocis, went down in a war in which Athens had egged her on but failed to give effective support. Although Demosthenes, the last great agitator of Athenian democracy, made himself a place in history,

which is recalled by the word 'philippic', by warning his countrymen of the dangers they faced, he could not save them. When a war with Macedon (355–346 BC) at last ended, Philip had won not only Thessaly, but had established himself in central Greece and controlled the pass of Thermopylae.

His situation favoured designs on Thrace and this implied a return of Greek interests towards Persia. One Athenian writer advocated a Hellenic crusade to exploit Persia's weakness (in opposition to Demosthenes who continued to denounce the Macedonian 'barbarian'), and once more plans were made to liberate the Asian cities, a notion attractive enough to bear fruit in a reluctant League of Corinth formed by the major Greek states other than Sparta in 337 BC. Philip was its president and general and it was somewhat reminiscent of the Delian League; the apparent independence of its members was a sham, for they were Macedonian satellites. Though the culmination of Philip's work and reign (he was assassinated the following year), it had only come into being after Macedon had defeated a last attempt to rally the Greeks against her. Athenian and Theban armies were defeated in 339 and 338 BC. The terms of peace then imposed by Philip were not harsh, but the League of Corinth had to agree to go to war with Persia under Macedonian leadership. There was one more kick of Greek independence after Philip's death, but his son and successor Alexander crushed the Greek rebels as he did others in other parts of his kingdom. Thebes was then razed to the ground and its population enslaved (335 BC).

This was the real end of four centuries of Greek history. During them civilization had been created and sheltered by the city-state, one of the most successful political forms the world has ever known. The immediate future for Greece was Macedonian governors and garrisons. Not for the first time nor the last, the future seemed to belong to the bigger battalions, the bigger organizations. Mainland Greece was from this time a political backwater. Like his father, Alexander sought to conciliate the

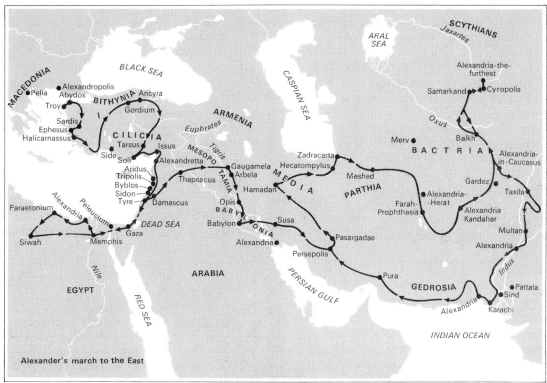

Alexander's march to the East

Greeks by giving them a large measure of internal self-government in return for adherence to his foreign policy. This was always to leave some Greeks, notably the Athenian democrats, unreconciled. When Alexander died, Athens once more tried to organize an anti-Macedonian coalition. The results were disastrous. A part of the price of defeat was the replacement of democracy by oligarchy at Athens (322 BC); Demosthenes fled to an island off the coast, seeking sanctuary in the temple of Poseidon there, but poisoned himself when the Macedonians came for him. A Macedonian governor henceforth ruled the Peloponnese.

Alexander's reign had thus begun with difficulties, but once they were surmounted, he could turn his attention to Persia. In 334 BC he crossed to Asia at the head of an army of which a quarter was drawn from Greece. There was more than idealism in this; aggressive war might also be prudent, for the fine army left by Philip had to be paid if it was not to present a threat to a new king, and conquest would provide the money. He was twenty-two years old and before him lay a short career of conquest so brilliant that it would leave his name a myth for the ages and provide a setting for the widest expansion of Greek culture. He drew the city-states into a still wider world.

The story is simple to summarize. Legend says that after crossing to Asia Minor he cut the Gordian knot. He then defeated the Persians at the battle of Issus. This was followed by a campaign which swept south through Syria, destroying Tyre on the way, and eventually to Egypt, where Alexander founded the city still bearing his name. In every battle he was his own best soldier and he was wounded several times in the mêlée. He pushed into the desert, interrogated the oracle at Siwah and then went back into Persia to inflict a second and decisive defeat on Darius III in 331 BC. Persepolis was sacked and burnt and Alexander proclaimed successor to the Persian throne; Darius died the next year. On went Alexander, pursuing the Iranians of the north-east into Afghanistan (where Kandahar, like many cities elsewhere, commemorates his name) and penetrating as far as the Punjab and a hundred miles or so beyond the Indus. Then he turned back because his army would go no further. It was tired and having defeated an army with 200 elephants may have been disinclined to face a further 5000 reported to be waiting for it in the Ganges valley. Alexander returned to Babylon. There he died in 323 BC, thirty-two years old just ten years after he had left Macedon.

Both his conquests and their organization in empire bear the stamp of individual genius; the word is not too strong, for achievement on this scale is more than the fruit of good fortune, favourable historical circumstance or blind determinism. Alexander was a creative mind, but self-absorbed, obsessed with his pursuit of glory, and something of a visionary. With great intelligence he combined almost reckless courage; he believed his mother's ancestor to be Homer's Achilles and strove to emulate the hero. He was ambitious as much to prove himself in men's eyes – or perhaps those of his forceful and repellent mother – as to win new lands. The idea of the Hellenic crusade against Persia undoubtedly had reality for him, but he was

also, for all his admiration of the Greek culture of which he had learnt from his tutor Aristotle, too egocentric to be a missionary, and his cosmopolitanism was grounded in an appreciation of realities. His empire had to be run by Persians as well as Macedonians. Alexander himself married first a Bactrian and then a Persian princess, and accepted – unfittingly, thought some of his companions – the homage which the East rendered to rulers it thought to be godlike. He was also at times rash and impulsive; it was his soldiers who finally made him turn back at the Indus, and the ruler of Macedon had no business to plunge into battle with no attention for what would happen to the monarchy if he should die without a successor. Worse still, he killed a friend in a drunken brawl and he may have arranged his father's murder.

Alexander lived too short a time either to ensure the unity of his empire in the future or to prove to posterity that even he could not have held it together for long. What he did in this time is indubitably impressive. The foundation of twenty-five 'cities' is by itself a considerable matter, even if some of them were only spruced-up strongpoints; they were keys to the Asian land routes. The integration of east and west in their government was still more difficult, but Alexander took it a long way in ten years. Of course, he had little choice; there were not enough Greeks and Macedonians to conquer and govern the huge empire. From the first he ruled through Persian officials in the conquered areas and after coming back from India he began the reorganization of the army in mixed regiments of Macedonians and Persians. His adoption of Persian dress and his attempt to exact prostration – an obligatory kow-tow like that which so many Europeans found degrading

This piece of harness, depicting an armed war-elephant such as those whose routing is described in the records of Alexander's Indus campaign, comes from the remote Grecian kingdom of Bactria, established in the course of Alexander's conquests. The ankus held by the driver is formed like those still used twenty-four centuries later by the mahouts of India.

when it was asked for by Chinese rulers – from his compatriots as well as from Persians, also antagonized his followers, for they revealed his taste for oriental manners. There were plots and mutinies; they were not successful, and his relatively mild reprisals do not suggest that the situation was ever very dangerous for Alexander. The crisis was followed by his most spectacular gesture of cultural integration when, himself taking Darius' daughter as a wife (in addition to his Bactrian princess, Roxana), he then officiated at the mass wedding of 9000 of his soldiers to eastern women. This was the famous 'marriage of East and West', an act of state rather than of idealism, for the new empire had to be cemented together if it was to survive.

What the empire really meant in cultural interplay is more difficult to assess. There was certainly a wider physical dispersal of Greeks. But the results of this were only to appear after Alexander's death, when the formal framework of empire collapsed and yet the cultural fact of a Hellenistic world emerged from it. We do not in fact know very much about life in Alexander's empire and it must be unlikely, given its brief duration, the limitations of ancient government and a lack of will to embark upon fundamental change, that most of its inhabitants found things very different in 323 BC from what they had been ten years before.

Alexander's impact was made in the east. He did not reign long enough to affect the interplay of the western Greeks with Carthage which was the main preoccupation of the later fourth century in the west. In Greece itself things stayed quiet until his death. It was in Asia that he ruled lands no Greeks had ruled before. In Persia he had proclaimed himself heir to the Great King and rulers in the northern satrapies of Bithynia, Cappadocia and Armenia did him homage.

Weak as the cement of the Alexandrine empire must have been, it was submitted to intolerable strain when he died without a competent heir. His generals fell to fighting for what they could get and keep, and the empire was dissolving even before the birth of his posthumous son by Roxana. She had already murdered his second wife, so when she and her son died in the troubles any hope of direct descent vanished. In forty-odd years of fighting it was settled that there would be no reconstitution of Alexander's empire. There emerged instead in the end a group of big states, each of them a hereditary monarchy. They were founded by successful soldiers, the *diadochi*, or 'Successors'.

Ptolemy Soter, one of Alexander's best generals, had at once seized power in Egypt at his master's death and to it he subsequently conveyed the valuable prize of Alexander's body. Ptolemy's descendants were to rule the province for nearly three hundred years until the death of Cleopatra in 30 BC. Ptolemaic Egypt was the longest-lived and richest of the successor states. Of the Asian empire, the Indian territories and some of Afghanistan passed out of Greek hands altogether, being ceded to an Indian ruler in return for military help. The rest of it was by 300 BC a huge kingdom of one and a half million square miles and perhaps thirty million subjects, stretching from Afghanistan to Syria, the site of its capital, Antioch. This vast domain was ruled by the descendants of Seleucus, another Macedonian general. Attacks by migrating Celts from northern Europe (who had already invaded Macedonia itself) led to its partial disruption early in the third century BC and part of it thenceforth formed the kingdom of Pergamon, ruled by a dynasty called the Attalids, who pushed the Celts further into Asia Minor. The Seleucids kept the rest, though they were to lose Bactria in 225 BC, where descendants of Alexander's soldiers set up a remarkable Indo-Greek kingdom. Macedon, under another dynasty, the Antigonids, strove to retain a control of the Greek states contested in the Aegean by the Ptolemaic fleet and in Asia Minor by the Seleucids. Once again, about 265 BC, Athens made a bid for independence but failed.

These events are complicated, but not very important for our purpose. What mattered more was that for about sixty years after 280 BC the Hellenistic kingdoms lived in a rough balance of

The Celtic peoples broke into the history of the Hellenistic world in the second half of the fourth century BC. *In Asia Minor they were finally turned back by the Attalid kings of Pergamon. A great monument commemorated this deliverance and we have this Roman copy of an original bronze statue forming part of it. It depicted a Gaul killing his wife and then himself rather than face capture after defeat. Possibly some of these barbarians did indeed do this, but they may not have much resembled these heroic, idealized figures, who seem to belong wholly to the world of Greek tradition which formed the artist who designed them.*

power, preoccupied with events in the eastern Mediterranean and Asia and, except for the Greeks and Macedonians, paying little attention to events further west. This provided a peaceful setting for the greatest extension of Greek culture and this is why these states are important. It is their contribution to the diffusion and growth of a civilization that constitute their claim on our attention, not the obscure politics and unrewarding struggles of the *diadochi*.

Greek was now the official language of the whole Near East; even more important, it was the language of the cities, the foci of the new world. Under the Seleucids the union of Hellenistic and oriental civilization to which Alexander may have aspired began to be a reality. They urgently sought Greek immigrants and founded new cities wherever they could as a means of providing some solid framework for their empire and of Hellenizing the local population. The cities were the substance of Seleucid power, for beyond them stretched a heterogeneous hinterland of tribes, Persian satrapies, vassal princes. Seleucid administration was still based fundamentally upon the satrapies; the theory of absolutism was inherited by the Seleucid kings from the Achaemenids just as was their system of taxation. Yet it is not certain what this could mean in practice and the east seems to have been less closely governed than Mesopotamia and Asia Minor, where Hellenistic influence was strongest and the capital lay. The size of the Hellenistic cities here far surpassed those of the older Greek emigrations; Alexandria, Antioch and the new capital city, Seleucia, near Babylon, quickly achieved populations of between one and two hundred thousand.

This reflected economic growth as well as conscious policy. The wars of Alexander and his successors released an enormous booty, much of it in bullion, accumulated by the Persian empire. It stimulated economic life all over the Near East, but also brought the evils of inflation and instability. Nevertheless, the overall trend was towards greater wealth. There were no great innovations, either in manufacture or in the tapping of new natural resources. The

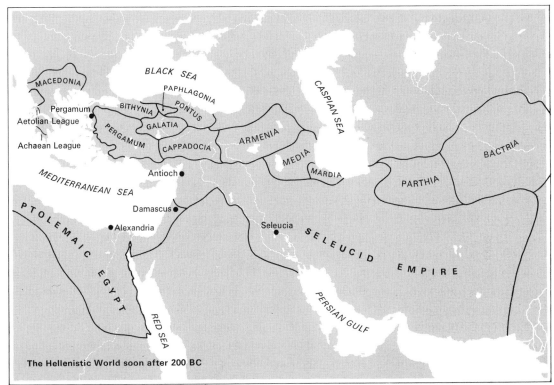

The Hellenistic World soon after 200 BC

Mediterranean economy remained much what it had always been except in scale, but Hellenistic civilization was richer than its predecessors and population growth was one sign of this.

Its wealth sustained governments of some magnificence, raising large revenues and spending them in spectacular and sometimes commendable ways. The ruins of the Hellenistic cities show expenditure on the appurtenances of Greek urban life; theatres and gymnasia abound, games and festivals were held in all of them. This probably did not much affect the native populations of the countryside who paid the taxes and some of them resented what would now be called 'westernization'. None the less, it was a solid achievement. Through the cities the east was Hellenized in a way which lasted until the coming of Islam. Soon they produced their own Greek literature.

Yet though this was a civilization of Greek cities, it was in spirit unlike that of the past, as some Greeks noted sourly. The Macedonians had never known the life of the city-state and

their creations in Ionia lacked its vigour; the Seleucids founded scores of cities but maintained the old autocratic and centralized administration of the satrapies above that level. Bureaucracy was highly developed and self-government languished. Ironically, besides having to bear the burden of disaster in the past, the cities of Greece itself, where a flickering tradition of independence lived on, were the one part of the Hellenistic world which actually underwent economic and demographic decline.

Though the political nerve had gone, city culture still served as a great transmission system for Greek ideas. Large endowments provided at Alexandria and Pergamum the two greatest libraries of the ancient world. Ptolemy I also founded the Museum, a kind of institute of advanced study. In Pergamum a king endowed schoolmasterships and it was there that people began to use parchment (*pergamene*) when the Ptolemies cut off supplies of papyrus. In Athens the Academy and the Lyceum survived and from such sources the tradition of Greek intel-

Alexandria, the most famous of the many cities bearing that name, enjoyed great prosperity as an entrepôt in the surge of commercial activity which was released by an influx of bullion from the Eastern conquests. The city was depicted as mistress of the seas in the Hellenistic picture from which this later mosaic was copied.

Possibly the most celebrated work of sculpture of the classical world and certainly the best-known of the Hellenistic age is this statue of Aphrodite found on the island of Melos.

lectual activity was everywhere refreshed. Much of this activity was academic in the narrow sense that it was in essence commentary on past achievement, but much of it was also of high quality and now seems lacking in weight only because of the gigantic achievements of the fifth and fourth centuries. It was a tradition solid enough to endure right through the

Christian era, though much of its content has been irretrievably lost. Eventually, the world of Islam would receive the teaching of Plato and Aristotle through what had been passed on by Hellenistic scholars.

Hellenistic civilization preserved the Greek tradition nowhere more successfully than in science, and here Alexandria, the greatest of all Hellenistic cities, was pre-eminent. Euclid was the greatest systematizer of geometry, defining it until the nineteenth century, and Archimedes, who is famous for his practical achievements in the construction of war-machines in Sicily, was probably Euclid's pupil. Another Alexandrian, Eratosthenes, was the first man to measure the size of the earth, and yet another, Hero, is said to have invented a steam engine and certainly used steam to transmit energy. It is inconceivable that the state of contemporary metallurgy could ever have made the widespread application of this discovery practicable, which probably explains why we hear no more of it. The point is of general relevance; the intellectual achievements of the ancient world (and of the subsequent European medieval civilization) often pushed up to the limits of existing technical skills. They could not be expected to go further until better instrumentation became available. One Hellenistic Greek, Aristarchus of Samos, even said that the earth moved round the sun, though his views were set aside by contemporaries and posterity because they could not be squared with Aristotelian physics which stated the contrary, the truth or falsity of either view remaining untested experimentally. In hydrostatics, it is true, Archimedes made great strides (and invented the windlass, too) but the central achievement of the Greek tradition was always mathematical, not practical, and in Hellenistic times it reached its apogee with the theory of conic sections and ellipses and the founding of trigonometry.

These were important steps and great additions to humanity's toolkit. Yet they were less distinct from what went before than was Hellenistic moral and political philosophy. It is tempting here to find the reason in the political change from the city-state to larger units. It was still in Athens that the philosophy of the age found its greatest centre and Aristotle had hoped to reinvigorate the city-state; in the right hands, he thought, it could still provide the framework for the good life. The unhappy last age of the city-state after the Peloponnesian War and the size and impersonality of the new monarchies must have soon sapped such confidence. In them, the old patriotic impulse of the city-states had dried up. Efforts were made to find other ways of harnessing loyalty and emotion to the new states. Perhaps because of the need to impress non-Greeks, perhaps because they felt the positive attraction of the world beyond Greek culture, the new monarchs buttressed themselves more and more with oriental cults attached to the person of the ruler whose origins went back into the Mesopotamian and Egyptian past. Extravagant titles were employed but perhaps much of this was flattery: 'Soter', as Ptolemy I was called, meant 'Saviour'. The Seleucids allowed themselves to be worshipped, but the Ptolemies outdid them; they took over the divine status and prestige of the Pharaohs (and practice, too, to the extent of marrying their sisters). Meanwhile, the real basis of the Hellenistic states was bureaucracy unchecked by traditions of civic independence – since the Seleucids had founded or refounded most of the Greek cities in Asia, what they had given they could take back – and armies of Greek and Macedonian mercenaries which relieved them of dependence on native troops. Powerful and awe-inspiring though they might be, there was little in such structures to capture their very mixed subjects' loyalty and emotions.

Twenty feet high, this huge statue found near Luxor evokes in its style and stance the images of the Egyptian kings. Yet its face is curiously un-Egyptian. Made in Ptolemaic times, it is now thought to represent Alexander the Great.

Probably the erosion of those emotions had gone too far even before Alexander. The triumph of Greek culture was deceptive. Language went on being used, but with a different meaning. Greek religion, for example, a great force for unity among Hellenes, rested not on ecclesiastical institutions but on respect for the Homeric gods and goddesses and the behaviour they exemplified. Beyond this, there were the city cults and official mysteries. This had already begun to change, possibly as early as the fifth century, when, under the impact of the prolonged war, the Olympian gods began to lose the respect paid to them. There was more than one cause of this. The rationalism of much Greek fourth-century philosophy is as much a part of the story as the rise of new fears. With the Hellenistic age another influence is felt, that of a pervasive irrationality, of the pressure of fortune and fate. Men sought reassurance in new creeds and faiths. The popularity of astrology was one symptom. All this only came to its climax as late as the first century BC, 'the period', says one scholar, 'when the tide of rationalism, which for the past hundred years had flowed ever more sluggishly, has finally expended its force and begins to retreat'. This is perhaps further ahead than we need look at this point in the story, but one thing about this reversal is striking at an early date. Swamped as the Hellenistic world was with mysteries and crazes of all kinds, from the revival of Pythagorean mysticism to the raising of altars to dead philosophers, traditional Greek religion was not a beneficiary. Its decay had already gone too far. The decline of Delphi, remarked from the third century, was not arrested.

This collapse of a traditional religious framework of values was the background to philosophical change. The study of philosophy was still vigorous in Greece itself and even there its Hellenistic development suggests that men were falling back upon personal concerns, contracting out of societies they could not influence, seeking shelter from the buffets of fate and the strain of daily life. It seems somewhat familiar. One example was Epicurus, who sought the good in an essentially private experience of pleasure. Contrary to later misinterpretations, he meant by this something far from self-indulgence. For Epicurus, pleasure was psychological contentment and the absence of pain – a view of pleasure rather too austere to modern eyes. But symptomatically its importance is considerable because it reveals a shift in men's preoccupations towards the private and personal. Another form of this philosophic reaction advocated the ideals of renunciation and non-attachment. The school known as the Cynics expressed contempt for convention and sought release from dependence on the material world. One of them, who lived at Athens, was a Cypriot, Zeno, who himself began to teach a doctrine of his own in a public place, the *stoa Poikile*. The place gave its name to those he taught, the Stoics. They were to be among the most influential of philosophers because their teaching was readily applicable to daily life. Essentially the Stoics taught that life should be lived to fit the rational order they discerned running through the universe. Man could not control what happened to him, they said, but he could accept what was sent by fate, the decree of the divine will in which they believed. Virtuous acts, accordingly, should not be performed for their likely consequences, which might well be unfortunate or thwarted, but for their own sake, because of their intrinsic value.

In stoicism, which was to have great success in the Hellenistic world, lay doctrine which gave the individual a new ground for ethical confidence at a time when neither *polis* nor traditional Greek religion retained their authority. Stoicism also had the potential for a long life, because it applied to all men, whom, it taught, were all alike: this was the seed of an ethical universalism which gradually transcended the old distinction between Greek and barbarian, as it would any other distinction between reasonable men. It spoke to a common humanity and actually produced a condemnation of slavery, an amazing step in a world built by forced labour. It was to be an immensely fecund source for thinkers for two thousand years. Soon its ethic of disciplined common sense was to have great success at Rome.

Philosophy thus showed the symptoms of the eclecticism and cosmopolitanism which strikes the eye in almost every other aspect of Hellenistic culture. Perhaps their most obvious expression was the adaptation of Greek sculpture to the monumental statuary of the East which produced such monsters as the hundred-foot-high Colossus of Rhodes, but they are everywhere. In the end, they appeared in the aspirations of the Stoics just as in the exotic oriental cults which displaced the Greek gods. It was the scientist Eratosthenes who said that he saw all good men as fellow-countrymen and the remark expresses the new spirit which was Hellenism at its best.

The political framework of this world was bound in the end to change, because sources of change grew up beyond its circumference. One early omen was the appearance of a new threat in the east, the kingdom of Parthia. By the middle of the third century BC the weakness imposed by the Seleucid kingdom's concentration of population and wealth in its western half was leading to over-preoccupation with relations with the other Hellenistic states. The north-east was threatened – as always – by nomads from the steppes, but government was distracted from this danger by the need to supply money and resources for quarrels with Ptolemaic Egypt. The temptation to a remote satrap to strike out on his own as a warlord was often irresistible. Scholars contest the details, but one of the satrapies in which this happened was Parthia, an important area to the south-east of the Caspian. It was to become more important still as the centuries passed for it lay across the caravan route to Central Asia by which the western classical world and China came to be remotely in touch, the Silk Road.

Who were the Parthians? They were originally the Parni, one of those Indo-European nomadic peoples who emerged from Central Asia to create and re-create a political unity in the highlands of Iran and Mesopotamia. They became a byword for a military skill then peculiar to them: the discharging of arrows by mounted horsemen. They did not build nearly five hundred years of political continuity only on this, though. They also inherited an administrative structure which the Seleucids were left by Alexander, who had taken it from the Persians. Indeed, in most things the Parthians seemed inheritors, not originators; their great dynasty used Greek for its official documents, and they seem to have had no law of their own but to have readily accepted existing practice, whether Babylonian, Persian or Hellenistic.

Much about their early history remains obscure. There was a kingdom, whose centre remains undiscovered, in Parthia in the third century BC, but the Seleucids do not seem to have reacted strongly to it. In the second century, when the Seleucid monarchy was much more disastrously engaged in the west, two brothers, the younger of whom was Mithridates I, established a Parthian empire which at his death stretched from Bactria (another fragment of the Seleucid inheritance which had been finally separated from it at about the same time as Parthia) in the east to Babylonia in the west. Consciously reminiscent of those who had gone before, Mithridates described himself on his coins as the 'great king'. There were setbacks after his death but his namesake Mithridates II recovered lost ground and went even further. The Seleucids were now confined to Syria. In Mesopotamia the frontier of his empire was the Euphrates and the Chinese opened diplomatic relations with him. The coins of the second Mithridates bore the proud Achaemenid title, 'King of Kings', and the inference is reasonable that the Arsacid dynasty to which Mithridates belonged was now being consciously related to the great Persian line. Yet the Parthian state seems a much looser thing than the Persian. It is more reminiscent of a feudal grouping of nobles about a warlord than a bureaucratized state.

On the Euphrates, Parthia was eventually to meet a new power from the West. Less remote from it than Parthia and therefore with less excuse, even the Hellenistic kingdoms had been

The Parthian rulers Mithridates I and II, depicted on their coins.

This more than life-size statue of a Parthian prince of the second century BC was one of a store of objects found in a temple at Shami in south-west Iran. The excavation revealed the impressive artistic achievements of Parthian style and its synthesizing of elements drawn from Greek and Persian tradition.

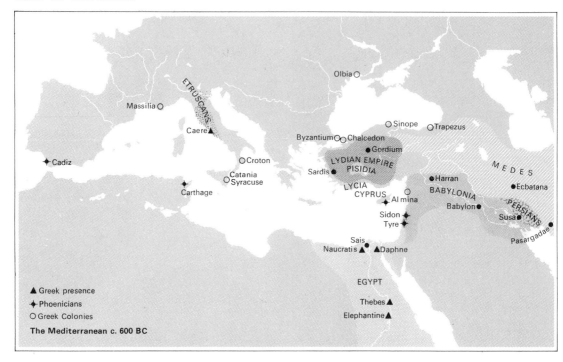

Olbia○

ETRUSCANS

Massilia○

Caere▲

○Sinope   ○Trapezus

Byzantium○○Chalcedon

●Gordium

LYDIAN EMPIRE

Sardis● PISIDIA

LYCIA

CYPRUS ○

Al mina ✦

M E D E S

●Harran

BABYLONIA   ●Ecbatana

PERSIANS

Babylon●

Susa● ●

Pasargadae●

✦Cadiz

○Croton

Catania

Syracuse

○

Carthage

✦

Sidon ✦

Tyre ✦

Sais

Naucratis▲● ▲Daphne

▲ Greek presence

✦ Phoenicians

○ Greek Colonies

The Mediterranean c. 600 BC

EGYPT

Thebes ▲

Elephantine▲

almost oblivious of the rise of Rome, this new star of the political firmament, and went their way almost without regard for what was happening in the West. The western Greeks, of course, knew more about it, but they long remained preoccupied with the first great threat they had faced, Carthage, a mysterious state which almost may be said to have derived its being from hostility to the Greeks. Founded by Phoenicians somewhere about 800 BC, perhaps even then to offset Greek commercial competition on the metal routes, Carthage had grown to surpass Tyre and Sidon in wealth and power. But she long remained a city-state, using alliance and protection rather than conquests and garrisons, her citizens preferring trade and agriculture to fighting. Unfortunately, the native documentation of Carthage was to perish when, finally, the city was razed to the ground and we know little of its own history.

Yet it was clearly a formidable commercial competitor for the western Greeks. By 480 BC these had been confined commercially to little more than the Rhône valley, Italy and, above

all, Sicily. The last, and one city in the island, Syracuse, was the key to the Greek west. Syracuse for the first time protected Sicily from the Carthaginians when she fought and beat them in the year of Salamis. For most of the fifth century Carthage troubled the western Greeks no more and the Syracusans were able to turn to supporting the Greek cities of Italy against the Etruscans. Then Syracuse was the target of the ill-fated Sicilian Expedition from Athens (415–413 BC) because she was the greatest of the western Greek states. The Carthaginians came back after this, but Syracuse survived defeat to enjoy soon afterwards her greatest period of power, exercised not only in the island, but in southern Italy and the Adriatic. During most of it she was at war with Carthage. There was plenty of vigour in Syracuse; at one moment she all but captured Carthage, and another expedition added Corcyra (Corfu) to her Adriatic possessions. But soon after 300 BC it was clear that Carthaginian power was growing while Syracuse had also to face a Roman threat in mainland Italy. The Sicilians fell out with a man who might have saved them, Pyrrhus of Epirus, and by mid-century the Romans were masters of the mainland.

There were now three major actors in the arena of the West, yet the Hellenistic east seemed strangely uninterested in what was going forward (though Pyrrhus was aware of it). This was perhaps short-sighted, but at this time the Romans did not see themselves as world conquerors. They were as much moved by fear of Carthage as by greed in entering on the Punic Wars, from which they would emerge victors. Then they would turn east. Some Hellenistic Greeks were beginning to be aware by the end of the century of what might be coming. A 'cloud in the west' was one description of the struggle between Carthage and Rome viewed from the Hellenized east. Whatever its outcome, this struggle was bound to have great repercussions for the whole Mediterranean. None the less, the east was to prove in the event that it had its own strengths and powers of resistance. As one Roman later put it, Greece would take her captors captive, she would Hellenize yet more barbarians.

5 Rome

All round the western Mediterranean shores and across wide tracts of western Europe, the Balkans and Asia Minor, relics can still be seen of a great achievement, the empire of Rome. In some places – Rome itself, above all – they are very plentiful. The explanation why they are there is a thousand years of history. If we no longer look back on the Roman achievement – as our ancestors sometimes did – feeling dwarfed by it, we still feel puzzled and even amazed that men could do so much. Of course, the closer the scrutiny historians give to those mighty remains and the more scrupulous their sifting of the documents which explain Roman ideals and Roman practice, the more we realize that Romans were not, after all, superhuman. The grandeur that was Rome sometimes looks more like tinsel and the virtues its publicists proclaimed sound as much like cant as do political slogans of today, of left and right alike. Yet when all is said and done, there remains an astonishing and solid core of creativity. In the end, Rome remade the setting of Greek civilization and thus determined the shape of the first civilization embracing all the West. This was a self-conscious achievement. Romans who looked back on it as it crumbled about them still felt themselves to be Romans like those who had built it up. They were, but only in the sense that they believed it,

The best-known of all the symbols of Rome and the expression of one of her oldest legends: the she-wolf which suckled Romulus and Remus, the twin boys cast into the Tiber by a wicked uncle but who survived to found the city.

yet that was the most important sense. For all its material impressiveness and occasional grossness, the core of the explanation of the Roman achievement was the idea of Rome itself, the values it embodied and imposed, the notion of what was one day to be called *Romanitas*.

It was believed to have deep roots. Romans said their city was founded by one Romulus in 753 BC. We need not take this very seriously, but the legend of the foster-mother wolf which suckled both Romulus and his twin, Remus, is worth a moment's pause; it is a good symbol of early Rome's debt to a past that was dominated by the people called Etruscans, among whose cults has been traced a special reverence for the wolf.

In spite of a rich archaeological record with many inscriptions and much scholarly effort to make sense of it the Etruscans remain a mysterious people. All that has been delineated with some certainty is the general nature of Etruscan culture, not its history or chronology. Different arguments have been put forward to say that Etruscan civilization came into existence at a wide range of different times, stretching from the tenth to the seventh century BC. Nor have scholars been able to agree about where the Etruscans came from; one hypothesis points to immigrants from Asia just after the end of the Hittite empire, but several other possibilities have their supporters. All that is obvious is that they were not the first Italians. Whenever they came to the peninsula and wherever from, Italy was then already a confusion of peoples.

There were probably still at that time some aboriginal natives among them whose ancestors had been joined by Indo-European invaders in the second millennium BC. In the next thousand years some of these Italians developed advanced cultures. Iron-working was going on in about 1000 BC. The Etruscans probably adopted the skill from the peoples there before them, possibly from a culture which has been called Villanovan (after an archaeological site near modern Bologna). They brought metallurgy to a high level and vigorously exploited the iron deposits of Elba, off the coast of Etruria. With iron weapons, they appear to have established an Etruscan hegemony which at its greatest extent covered the whole central peninsula, from the valley of the Po down to Campania. Its organization remains obscure, but Etruria was probably a loose league of cities governed by kings. The Etruscans were literate, using an alphabet derived from Greek which may have been acquired from the cities of *Magna Graecia* (though hardly anything of their writing can be understood), and they were relatively rich. In the sixth century BC their domains included an important bridgehead on the south bank of the river Tiber. This was the site of Rome, one of a number of small cities of the Latins, an old-established people of the Campania. Through this city something of the Etruscan legacy was to survive to flow into and eventually be lost in the European tradition.

Near the end of the sixth century BC the Romans broke away from Etruscan dominion and led a revolt of the Latin cities against their masters. Until then, Rome had been ruled by kings, the last of whom, tradition later said, was expelled in 509 BC. Whatever the exact date, this was certainly about the time at which Etruscan power, over-strained by struggle with the western Greeks, was successfully challenged by the Latin peoples, who thereafter went their own ways. Rome was to retain much from her Etruscan past. Through it she had first had access to the Greek civilization with which she continued to live in contact both by land and sea. Rome was high enough up the Tiber for her to

Southern Italy 509–272 BC

bridge it, but not so high that she could not be reached by sea-going vessels and was thus a focus of important sea and land routes. Fertilization by Greek influence was perhaps the most important inheritance from her past, but Rome carried forward also many Etruscan institutions. One was the way she organized her people in 'centuries' for military purposes; more superficial but striking instances were her gladiatorial games, civic triumphs and reading of auguries – a consultation of the entrails of sacrifices in order to discern the shape of the future.

The Republic was to last for more than four hundred and fifty years and even after that its institutions survived in name. Romans always harped on the continuity of their institutions and their loyal adherence (or reprehensible non-adherence) to the good old ways of the early republic. There was some reality in such claims, much as there is, for example, in the claims made for the continuity of parliamentary

These figures of a man and his wife reclining on a couch have something of the feel of archaic Greek art about them. They come, in fact, from Cerveteri in Italy: they form the lid of an Etruscan sarcophagus made in about 500 BC.

Even in recent times, the backbone of the population of Italy has been provided by the peasantry. These farmers were depicted on a bronze vessel used for the ashes of the cremated dead in a cemetery of the fifth century BC near Bologna.

Probably an Etruscan gentleman but said to represent the legendary Brutus who drove out the kings in the sixth century and whose sister was the unfortunate Lucretia, the ravished victim of Tarquin. The head shows the expressiveness and skill already available which went into the making of the long-lived Roman tradition of excellence in this art form.

government in Great Britain or for the wisdom of the founding fathers of the United States in agreeing a constitution which still operates successfully. Yet, of course, great changes took place as the centuries passed. They eroded the institutional and ideological continuities and historians still argue about how to interpret them. Yet the importance of Rome's institutions was that for all these changes they made possible a Roman Mediterranean and a Roman empire stretching far beyond it which was to be the cradle of Europe and Christianity. Thus Rome, like Greece (which often reached later men through Rome), shaped much of the modern world. It is not just in a physical sense that men still live among her ruins.

Broadly speaking, the changes of republican

times were symptoms and results of two main processes. One was of decay; gradually the republic's institutions ceased to provide a workable framework for political and social realities and, in the end, this destroyed them, even when their names survived. The other was the extension of Roman rule first beyond the city and then beyond Italy. For about two centuries both things were happening rather slowly.

Internal politics were rooted in arrangements originally meant to make impossible the return of monarchy. Constitutional theory was concisely expressed in the motto carried by the monuments and standards of Rome until well into imperial times: *SPQR*, the abbreviation of the Latin words for 'the Roman Senate and People'. Theoretically, ultimate sovereignty always rested with the people, which acted through a complicated set of assemblies attended by all citizens in person (of course, not all inhabitants of Rome were citizens). This was similar to what went on in many Greek citystates. The general conduct of business was the concern of the Senate; it made laws and regulated the work of elected magistrates. It was in the form of tensions between the poles of Senate and people that the most important political issues of Roman history were usually expressed.

Somewhat surprisingly, the internal struggles of the early republic seem to have been comparatively bloodless. Their sequence is complicated and sometimes mysterious, but their general result was that they gave the citizen body as a whole a greater say in the affairs of the republic. The Senate, which concentrated political leadership, had come by 300 BC or so to represent a ruling class which was an amalgamation of the old patricians of pre-Republican days with the wealthier members of the *plebs*, as the rest of the citizens were termed. The Senate's members constituted an oligarchy, self-renewing though some were usually excluded in each census (which took place once every five years). Its core was a group of noble families whose origins might be plebeian, but among whose ancestors were men who had held the office of consul, the highest of the magistracies.

The two consuls, appointed for a year, ruled the state through the Senate and were the most important magistrates. They were bound to be men of experience and weight, for they had to have passed through at least two subordinate levels of elected office, as *quaestors* and *praetors*, before they were eligible. The quaestors (of whom there were twenty elected each year) also automatically became members of the Senate. These arrangements gave the Roman ruling élite great cohesiveness and competence; for progress to the highest office was a matter of selection from a field of candidates who had been well tested and trained in office. That this constitution worked well for a long time is indisputable. Rome was never short of able men. What it masked was the natural tendency of oligarchy to decay into faction, for whatever victories were won by the plebs, the working of the system ensured that it was the rich who ruled and the rich who disputed the right to office among themselves. Even in the electoral college which was supposed to represent the whole people, the *comitia centuriata*, organization gave an undue proportion of influence to the wealthy.

Plebs, in any case, is a misleadingly simple term. The word stood for different social realities at different times. Conquest and enfranchisement slowly extended the boundaries of citizenship and even in early times they ran well beyond the city and its environs as other cities were incorporated in the republic. At that time, the typical citizen was a countryman. The basis of Roman society was always agricultural and rural. It is significant that the Latin word for money, *pecunia*, is derived from the word for a flock of sheep or herd of cattle and that the Roman measure of land was the *iugerum*, the extent that could be ploughed in a day by two oxen. Land and the society it supported were related in changing ways during the republic, but always the rural population was its base. The later preponderance in men's minds of the image of imperial Rome, the great parasitic city, obscures this.

The free citizens who made up the bulk of the population of the early republic were therefore peasants, some much poorer than others. They were legally grouped in complicated arrangements whose roots were sunk in the Etruscan past. Such distinctions were economically insignificant though they had constitutional importance for electoral purposes but tell us less about the social realities of republican Rome than those made by the Roman census between those able to equip themselves with the arms and armour needed to serve as soldiers, those whose only contribution to the state was to breed children (the *proletarii*) and those who were simply counted as heads, because they neither owned property nor had families. Below them all, of course, were the slaves.

There was a persistent tendency, accelerating rapidly in the third and second centuries BC, for many of the plebs who in earlier days had preserved some independence through possession of their own land to sink into poverty. Meanwhile, the new aristocracy increased its relative share of land as conquest brought it new wealth. This was a long-drawn-out process, and while it went on, new subdivisions of social interest and political weight appeared. Furthermore, to add one more complicating factor, there grew up the practice of granting citizenship to Rome's allies. The republic in fact saw a gradual enlargement of the citizen class but a real diminution of its power to affect events.

This was not only because wealth came to count for so much in Roman politics. It was also because everything had to be done at Rome, though there were no representative arrangements which could effectively reflect the wishes of even those Roman citizens who lived in the swollen city, let alone those scattered all over Italy. What tended to happen instead was that threats to refuse military service or to withdraw altogether from Rome and found a city elsewhere enabled the plebs to restrict somewhat the powers of Senate and magistrates. After 366 BC, too, one of the two consuls had to be a plebeian and in 287 BC the decisions of the plebeian assembly were given overriding force of law. But the main restriction on the tradi-

A peasant drives his cow to market along a road lined with shrines – this must have been very common under the early Republic.

tional rulers lay in the ten elected Tribunes of the People, officers chosen by popular vote, who could initiate legislation or veto it (one veto was enough) and were available night and day to citizens who felt themselves unjustly treated by a magistrate. The tribunes had most weight when there was great social feeling or personal division in the Senate, for then they had to be courted by the politicians. In the earlier republic and often thereafter, the tribunes, who were members of the ruling class and might be nobles, worked for the most part easily enough with the consuls and the rest of the Senate. The administrative talent and experience of this body and the enhancement of its prestige because of its leadership in war and emergency could hardly be undermined until

there were social changes grave enough to threaten the downfall of the republic itself.

The constitutional arrangements of the early republic were thus very complicated, but effective. They prevented violent revolution and permitted gradual change. Yet they would be no more important to us than those of Thebes or Syracuse, had they not made possible and presided over the first phase of victorious expansion of Roman power. The story of the republic's institutions is important for even later periods, too, because of what the republic itself became. Almost the whole of the fifth century was taken up in mastering Rome's neighbours and her territory was doubled in the process. The other cities of the Latin League were next subordinated; when some of them revolted in the middle of the fourth century they were forced back into it on harsher terms. It was a little like a land version of the Athenian empire a hundred years before; Roman policy was to leave her 'allies' (*socii*) to govern themselves, but they had to subscribe to Roman foreign policy and supply contingents to the Roman army. In return, their citizens were admitted to rights of citizenship if they migrated to Rome. Etruscan hegemony in central Italy was thus replaced by Roman.

Roman military power grew as did the number of subjected states. It rested fundamentally on conscription. Every male citizen who owned property was obliged to serve if called and the obligation was heavy, sixteen years for an infantryman and ten for cavalry. The army was organized in legions of 5000 which fought at first in solid phalanxes with long pike-like spears. It not only subdued Rome's neighbours, but also beat off a series of fourth-century incursions by Gauls from the north, though on one occasion they sacked Rome itself (390 BC). The last struggles of this formative period came at the end of the fourth century when the Romans conquered the Samnite peoples of the Abruzzi.

Rome was now at last face to face with the western Greek cities. Syracuse was by far the most important of them. Early in the third century the Greeks asked the assistance of a great military leader of mainland Greece, Pyrrhus, King of Epirus who campaigned for ten years against the Romans (282–272 BC), achieving only the costly and crippling victories to whose type he gave his name. He could not destroy the Roman threat to the western Greeks. Within a few years they were caught up willy-nilly in a struggle between Rome and Carthage in which the whole western Mediterranean was at stake – the Punic Wars.

They form a duel of more than a century. Their name comes from the Roman rendering of the word Phoenician and, unfortunately, we have only the Roman version of what happened. There were three bursts of fighting, but the first two settled the question of preponderance. In the first (264–241 BC) the Romans began naval warfare on a large scale for the first time. With their new fleet they took Sicily. Syracuse abandoned an earlier alliance with Carthage and western Sicily became the first

A Samnite lady of the fifth century BC prepares herself for an important occasion – perhaps a funeral, since the painting comes from a tomb.

Roman province, a momentous step, in 227 BC. After the peace, Rome also established herself in the islands of Sardinia and Corsica.

This was only round one. As the end of the third century approached, the final outcome was still not discernible and there is still argument about which side, in this touchy situation, was responsible for the outbreak of the second Punic War (218–201 BC). It was the greatest of the three and was fought in a greatly extended theatre, for when it began the Carthaginians were established in Spain. Some of the Greek cities there had been promised Roman protection. When one of them was attacked and sacked by a Carthaginian general, Hannibal, the war began. Its course was famous for Hannibal's great march to Italy and passage of the Alps with an army including elephants and for its culmination in the crushing Carthaginian victories of Lake Trasimene and Cannae (217 and 216 BC), where a Roman army twice the size of Hannibal's was destroyed. At this point Rome's grasp on Italy was badly shaken; some of her allies and subordinates began to look at Carthaginian power with a new respect. Virtually all the south changed sides, though central Italy

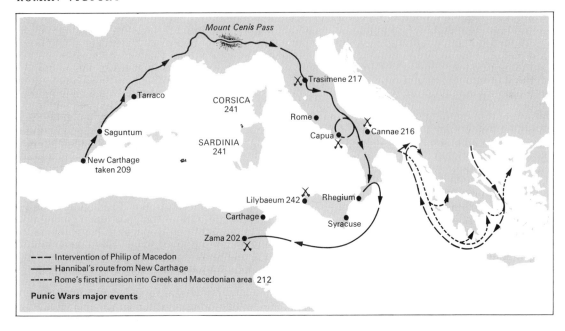

Mount Cenis Pass

Trasimene 217

Tarraco

CORSICA
241

Rome

Saguntum

Capua

Cannae 216

SARDINIA
241

New Carthage
taken 209

Lilybaeum 242

Rhegium

Carthage

Syracuse

Zama 202

- - - Intervention of Philip of Macedon
—— Hannibal's route from New Carthage
- - - - Rome's first incursion into Greek and Macedonian area 212

Punic Wars major events

remained loyal. With no resources save her own exertions and the great advantage that Hannibal lacked the numbers needed to besiege Rome, Rome hung on and saved herself. Hannibal campaigned in an increasingly denuded countryside far from his base. The Romans mercilessly destroyed Capua, a rebellious ally, without Hannibal coming to help it and then boldly embarked upon a strategy of striking at Carthage in her own possessions, especially in Spain. In 209 BC 'New Carthage' (Cartagena) was taken by the Romans. When an attempt by Hannibal's younger brother to reinforce him was beaten off in 207 BC the Romans transferred their offensives to Africa itself. There, at last, Hannibal had to follow them, to meet his defeat at Zama in 202 BC, the end of the war.

This battle settled more than a war; the fate of the whole western Mediterranean was decided. The peace imposed on Carthage was humiliating and crippling. Roman vengeance pursued Hannibal himself and drove him to exile at the Seleucid court. Because Syracuse had once more allied with Carthage during the war, her presumption was punished by the loss of her independence; she was the last Greek state in the island so that all Sicily was now Roman. So was

southern Spain, where another province was set up.

Nor was this all. These events opened the way to the east. At the end of the second Punic War it is tempting to imagine Rome at a parting of the ways. On the one hand lay the alternative of moderation and the maintenance of security in the west, on the other of expansion and imperialism in the east. Yet this over-simplifies reality. Eastern and western issues were already too entangled to sustain so simple an antithesis. As early as 228 BC the Romans had been admitted to the Greek Isthmian games; it was a recognition, even if only formal, that for some Greeks they were already a civilized power and part of the Hellenistic world. Through Macedon, that world had already been involved directly in the wars of Italy, for Macedon had allied with Carthage; Rome had therefore taken the side of Greek cities opposed to Macedon and thus began to dabble in Greek politics. When a direct appeal for help against Macedon and the Seleucids came from Athens, Rhodes and a king of Pergamum in 200 BC, the Romans were already psychologically ready to commit themselves to eastern enterprise. It is unlikely, though, that any of them saw that this could be the beginning

Acquisitions before 100 B.C.

Acquisitions down to 31 BC.

Roman Expansion

of a series of adventures from which would emerge a Hellenistic world dominated by the republic.

Another change in Roman attitudes was not yet complete, but was beginning to be effective. Most upper-class Romans probably saw the struggle against Carthage as essentially defensive at the outset and for long after. Some went on fearing even the crippled enemy left after Zama. The call of Cato in the middle of the next century – 'Carthage must be destroyed' – was to be famous as an expression of an implacable hostility arising from fear. None the less, the provinces won by war had begun to awake men's minds to other possibilities and therefore to supply other motives for its continuation. Slaves and gold from Sardinia, Spain and Sicily were soon opening the eyes of Romans to what the rewards of empire might be. A tradition grew up under the

republic, too, of generals distributing some of the spoils of victory to their troops.

The twists and turns are complicated, but the main stages of Roman expansion in the east in the second century BC are obvious enough. The conquest and reduction to a province of Macedon was accomplished in a series of wars ending in 148 BC; the phalanxes were not what they had been, nor Macedonian generalship. On the way the cities of Greece had also been reduced to vassalage and forced to send hostages to Rome. An intervention by a Syrian king led to the first passage of Roman forces to Asia Minor; next came the disappearance of the kingdom of Pergamum, Roman hegemony in the Aegean and the establishment of the new province of Asia in 133 BC. Elsewhere, the conquest of the remainder of Spain except the north-west, the organization of a tributary confederacy in Illyria, and the provincial organ-

271

ization of southern France in 121 BC, meant that the coasts from Gibraltar to Thessaly were all under Roman rule. Finally, the chance long sought by the enemies of Carthage came in 149 BC with the start of the third and last Punic War. Three years later the city *was* destroyed, ploughs were run over its site and a new Roman province, Africa, existed in its stead.

Thus the empire was made by the republic. Like all empires, but perhaps more obviously than any earlier one, its appearance owed as much to chance as to design. Fear, idealism and eventually cupidity were the mingled impulses which sent the legions further and further afield. Military power was the ultimate basis of Roman empire, but this was inseparably linked to administrative and political skill. Numbers were decisive in overcoming Carthaginian experience and tenacity and the Roman army was large. It could draw upon an expanding pool of first-class manpower available because Roman preponderance reassured her allies and satellites, and republican rule brought order and regular government to new subjects. The basic units of the empire were its provinces, each ruled by a governor with proconsular powers whose posting was formally for one year. Beside him stood a taxing officer.

Empire inevitably had political consequences at home. In the first place it made it even more difficult to ensure popular participation – that is, the participation of poor citizens – in government. Prolonged warfare reinforced the day-to-day power and the moral authority of the Senate, and it must be said that its record was a remarkable one. Yet the expansion of territory carried even further shortcomings already apparent in the extension of Roman rule over Italy. Serious and novel problems arose. One was posed by the opportunity presented by warfare and imperial rule to generals and provincial governors. The fortunes to be made, and made quickly, were immense; not until the days of the Spanish *conquistadores* or the British East India Company were such prizes so easily available to those in the right place at the right time.

Much of this was legal; some was simply looting and theft. Significantly, in 149 BC a special court was created to deal with illegal extortion by officials. Whatever its nature, access to this wealth could only be obtained through participation in politics, for it was from the Senate that governors were chosen for the new provinces and it was the Senate which appointed the tax-gatherers who accompanied them from among the wealthy but non-noble class of *equites*, or 'knights'.

Another constitutional weakness arose because the principle of annual election of magistrates had more and more frequently to be set aside in practice. War and rebellion in the provinces provided emergencies which consuls elected for their political skill might well find beyond them. Inevitably, proconsular power fell into the hands of those who could deal with emergencies effectively, usually proven generals. It is a mistake to think of the Republic's commanders as professional soldiers in the modern sense; they were members of the ruling class who might expect in a successful career to be civil servants, judges, barristers, politicans and even priests. One key to the administrative proficiency of Rome was its acceptance of the principle of non-specialization in its rulers. None the less, a general who stayed years with his army became a different sort of political animal from the proconsuls of the early republic who commanded an army for one campaign and then returned to Rome and politics. Paradoxically, it was a weakness that the provincial governorships were themselves annual. In that lay a temptation to make hay while the sun shone. If this was one way by which irresponsibility crept into the administrative structure, there was a corresponding tendency for successful generals long in the field to draw to themselves the loyalty which soldiers owed to the republic. Finally, there was even a kind of socialized corruption, for all Roman citizens benefited from an empire which made possible their exemption from any direct taxation; the provinces were to pay for the homeland. Awareness of such evils lies behind much moralizing con-

Trade between Asia and Rome

demnation and talk of decline which arose in the first century BC, when their impact became fatal.

Another change brought by empire was a further spread of Hellenization. Here there are difficulties of definition. In some measure, Roman culture was already Hellenized before conquest went beyond Italy. The republic's conscious espousal of the cause of the Greek cities' independence of Macedon was a symptom. On the other hand, whatever Rome already possessed, there was much that could be hers only after more direct contact with the Hellenized world. In the last resort, to many Greeks Rome looked like another barbarian power, almost as bad as Carthage. There is symbolism in the legend of the death of Archimedes, struck down while pondering geometrical problems in the sand, by the sword of a Roman soldier who did not know who he was.

With empire the contact became direct and the flow of Hellenistic influence manifold and frequent. Later ages were to wonder at the Roman passion for baths; the habit was one they had learnt from the Hellenized East. The first Roman literature was translated Greek drama and the first Latin comedies were imitations of Greek models. Art began to flow to Rome through pilfering and looting, but Greek style – above all its architecture – was already familiar from the western cities. There was a movement of people, too. One of the thousand hostages sent to Rome from the Greek cities in the middle of the second century BC was Polybius, who provided Rome with its first scientific history in the tradition of Thucydides. His history of the years 220–146 BC was a conscious exploration of a phenomenon which he felt to mark a new epoch, Rome's success in overthrowing Carthage and conquering the Hel-

273

lenistic world. He first among historians recognized a complement to the earlier civilizing work of Alexander in the new unity given to the Mediterranean by Rome. He also admired the disinterested air Romans appeared to bring to imperial government – a reminder to be set against the Romans' own denunciation of their wickednesses under the late Republic.

Rome's greatest triumph rested on the bringing of peace and it was a second great Hellenistic age in which men could travel from one end to another of the Mediterranean without hindrance. The essential qualities of the structure which sustained it were already there under the republic, above all in the cosmopolitanism encouraged by Roman administration, which sought not to impose a uniform pattern of life but only to collect taxes, keep the peace and regulate the quarrels of men by a common law. The great achievements of Roman jurisprudence lay still far ahead, but the early Republic launched Roman law on its history of definition by the consolidation of the Twelve Tables which little Roman boys lucky enough to go to school had still to get by heart hundreds of years later. On them was eventually built a framework within which many cultures might survive to contribute to a common civilization.

It is convenient to finish the story of the spread of the rule of the republic to its limits before considering how such success in the end proved fatal. Transalpine Gaul (southern France) was a province in 121 BC but (like north Italy) it remained troubled from time to time by the incursions of Celtic tribes. The Po valley was given provincial status as Cisapline Gaul in 89 BC and nearly forty years later (51 BC) the rest of Gaul – roughly northern France and Belgium – was conquered and with that the Celtic danger effectively came to an end. Meanwhile there had been further conquests in the east. The last king of Pergamum had bequeathed his kingdom to Rome in 133 BC. There followed the acquisition of Cilicia in the early first century BC, and then a series of wars with Mithridates, King of Pontus, a state on the Black Sea. The outcome was the reorganization of the Near East, Rome being left with possession of a coast running from

Egypt to the Black Sea, all of which was divided between client kingdoms or provinces. Finally, Cyprus was annexed in 58 BC.

Ironically, the counterpoint of this continuing and apparently irresistible success abroad was growing strife at home. The crux of the matter was the restriction of access to office to members of the ruling class. Electoral institutions and political conventions had come to work differently because of two grave long-term problems. The first was the gradual impoverishment of the Italian peasant who had been the typical figure of the early republic. It had several causes, but the root of the matter was the terrible cost of the second Punic War. Not only had conscripted soldiers been absent for long years of almost continual campaigns, but the physical damage to southern Italy was enormous. Meanwhile, those who were lucky enough to amass wealth in imperial enterprise laid it out in the only good investment available, land. The effect in the long run was to concentrate property in large estates usually worked by slaves made cheaper by the wars; there was no place on them for the smallholder, who now had to make his way to the city and fend for himself as best he could, a Roman citizen in name, but a proletarian in the making. Yet as a citizen he still had a vote. To those with wealth and political ambition he became someone to buy or to intimidate. Since the road to lucrative office lay through popular elections, the politics of the republic could hardly fail increasingly to reflect the power of money. This, too, had repercussions far and wide in Italy. Once votes had a price, the citizen proletariat of Rome was unlikely to welcome their continual devaluation by extending civic rights to other Italians, even though Rome's allies had to put up with conscription.

The second problem was a change in the army. The legions had more than four hundred years' history under the republic and their evolution can hardly be condensed in a simple formula, but if one is to be sought, it is perhaps best to say that the army became increasingly professional. The burden of conscription had always been heavy and became unpopular. When campaigns carried men further and further

Mithridates VI, King of Pontus, reconquered the province of Asia from the Romans and then installed himself at Pergamon. Many Greeks saw him as a liberator; clearly admiration of some sort – or flattery? – lies behind this first-century BC *representation of him as Heracles, liberator of Prometheus.*

afield for year after year, and as garrisons had sometimes to remain for decades in conquered provinces, even the Roman pool of manpower showed signs of drying up. In 107 BC a formal change registered what was happening: the property qualification for service was abolished. This was the work of a consul called Marius, who thus solved the problem of recruitment, for after this there were usually enough poor volunteers for conscription to be unnecessary. Military service still continued to be restricted to citizens, but there were many of these; in the end, though, service itself was to confer citizenship. Another innovation of Marius was to give the legions their 'eagles', the standards so important to their *esprit de corps*, something between an idol and a modern regimental badge.

Such changes gradually turned the army into a new kind of political force, available to a man like Marius who was an able general and much called upon for service in the provinces. He actually exacted a personal oath of allegiance from one army under his own command.

The widening gap of rich and poor and the new possibilities open to political soldiers proved fatal to the republic in the end. Attempts such as those of the Gracchi brothers, Tribunes of the People, to do something about the social problem in the only way open to an agrarian economy, by land reform, reduction of senatorial power and a bigger rôle for the equites in government, only ended in their deaths. This itself marked the raising of the stakes of politics; in the last century of the republic factional bitterness reached its peak because politicians knew their lives might be forfeit. It also saw the beginning of what has been called the Roman revolution, for the conventions of Roman politics were set aside when Tiberius Gracchus (the elder brother), then consul, persuaded the plebs to unseat the tribune who had vetoed his land-bill and thus announced that he would not accept the traditional circumvention of the popular will by the prerogative of a tribune to use his veto.

The final plunge of the republic into confusion was precipitated by a new war. A north African king massacred a great number of Roman businessmen in 112 BC and not long afterwards a wave of barbarian invaders in the north threatened Roman rule in Gaul. The emergency brought forward the consul Marius, who dealt successfully with the enemies of the republic, but at the cost of further constitutional innovation, for he was elected to the consulship for five years in succession. He was, in fact, the first of a series of warlords who were to dominate the last century of the republic, for other wars rapidly followed. Gaius Gracchus had suggested that one needed reform was the extension of Roman citizenship to the other Latin and Italian states. This was not done and in 90 BC these allies (*socii*) revolted (in what is somewhat misleadingly called the 'Social War'). They were defeated, but only pacified with concessions on a scale which made nonsense of the notion that the Roman popular assemblies were the ultimate sovereign. Citizenship was extended to most of Italy. Then came new Asian wars – from which emerged another general with political ambitions, Sulla. There was civil war, Marius died after once more being consul, and Sulla returned to Rome in 82 BC to launch a dictatorship (voted by the Senate) with a ruthless 'proscription' of his opponents (a posting of their names which signified that anyone who could do so was entitled to kill them), an assault on the popular powers of the constitution and an attempted restoration of those of the Senate.

One former supporter and protégé of Sulla was a young man whose name has passed into English as Pompey. Sulla had advanced his career by giving him posts normally held only by consuls. In 70 BC he was elected consul. He left for the east three years later to eliminate piracy from the Mediterranean and went on to conquer huge Asian territories in the wars against Pontus. Pompey's youth, success and outstanding ability began to make him feared as a potential dictator. But the interplay of Roman politics was complicated. As the years passed, disorder increased in the streets of Rome and corruption in ruling circles. Fears of dictatorship were intensified, but the fears were those of one oligarchic faction among several and it was less and less clear where the danger lay. Moreover one danger went long disregarded before people awoke to it.

In 59 BC another aristocrat, the nephew of Marius' wife, had been elected consul. This was the young Julius Caesar. For a time he had cooperated with Pompey. The consulship led him to the command of the army of Gaul and a succession of brilliant campaigns in the next seven years ending in its complete conquest. Though he watched politics closely, these years kept Caesar away from Rome where gangsterism, corruption and murder disfigured public life and discredited the Senate. After them he was enormously rich and had a loyal, superbly experienced and confident army looking to him for the leadership which would give

them pay, promotion and victory in the future. He was also a cool, patient and ruthless man. There is a story of him joking and playing at dice with some pirates who captured him. One of his jokes was that he would crucify them when he was freed. The pirates laughed, but crucify them he did.

Some senators suddenly became alarmed when this formidable man wished to remain in Gaul in command of his army and the province, although its conquest was complete, retaining command until the consular election. His opponents strove to get him recalled to face charges about illegalities during his consulship. Caesar then took the step which, though neither he nor anyone else knew it, was the beginning of the end of the republic. He crossed the Rubicon, the boundary of his province, beginning a march which brought him in the end to Rome. This was in January 49 BC. It was an act of treason, though he claimed to be defending the Republic against its enemies.

In its extremity the Senate called Pompey to defend the republic. Without forces in Italy, Pompey withdrew across the Adriatic to raise an army and the consuls and most of the Senate went with him. Civil war was now inevitable. Caesar marched quickly to Spain to defeat seven legions there which were loyal to Pompey; they were then mildly treated in order to win over as many as possible of the soldiers. Ruthless and even cruel though he could be, mildness to his political opponents was politic and prudent; he did not propose to imitate Sulla, said Caesar. Then he went after Pompey, chasing him to Egypt, where he was murdered. Caesar stayed long enough to dabble in an Egyptian civil war and become, almost incidentally, the lover of the legendary Cleopatra. Then he went back to Rome, to embark almost at once for Africa and defeat a Roman army there which opposed him. Finally, he returned again to Spain and destroyed a force raised by Pompey's sons. This was in 45 BC, four years after the crossing of the Rubicon.

Brilliance like this was not just a matter of winning battles. Brief though Caesar's recent visits to Rome had been, he had organized his political support carefully and packed the Senate with his men. The victories brought him great honours and real power. He was voted dictator for life and became in effect a monarch in all but name. His power he used without much regard for the susceptibilities of politicians and without showing an imaginativeness which suggests his rule would have been successful in the long term, though he imposed order in the Roman streets, and undertook steps to end the power of the money-lenders in politics. To one reform in particular the future of Europe was to owe much – the introduction of the Julian calendar. Like much else we think of as Roman, it came from Hellenistic Alexandria, where an astronomer suggested to Caesar that the year of 365 days, with an extra day each fourth year, would make it possible to emerge from the complexities of the traditional Roman calendar. The new calendar began on 1 January 45 BC.

Fifteen months later Caesar was dead, struck down by assassins at the height of his success. Their motives were complex. The timing was undoubtedly affected by the knowledge that he planned a great eastern campaign against the Parthians. Were he to join his army, it might be to return again in triumph, more unassailable than ever. There had been talk of a kingship; a Hellenistic despotism was envisaged by some. The complicated motives of his enemies were given respectability by the distaste some felt for the flagrant affront to republican tradition in the *de facto* despotism of one man. Minor acts of disrespect for the constitution antagonized others and in the end his assassins were a mixed bag of disappointed soldiers, interested oligarchs and offended conservatives. On 15 March 44 BC he was murdered in the Senate.

His murderers had no answer to the problems which Caesar had not had the time and their predecessors had so conspicuously failed to solve. Nor could they protect themselves for long. The Republic was pronounced restored, but Caesar's acts were confirmed. There was a revulsion of feeling against the conspirators who soon had to flee the city. Within two years they

There survive many likenesses of Julius Caesar, several made soon after his death. Almost alone among the portraits of him, this one is believed to date from his lifetime.

The leader among Caesar's assassins (and reputedly a descendant of the Brutus who founded the Republic) was Brutus; like other politicians and rulers of the ancient world, he used coins as vehicles for propaganda. This one commemorates the day of Caesar's death as a day of liberation – a cap of liberty stands between two daggers – and may be the beginning of a tradition of idolizing republican tyrannicide which runs down to modern times.

were dead and Julius Caesar was proclaimed a god. The republic was in fact moribund. Damaged fatally long before the crossing of the Rubicon, the heart had gone out of its constitution whatever attempts were made to restore it. Only its ideology and forms lived on. Romans could not bring themselves to turn their backs on the institutional heritage and admit that they had done with it. When eventually they did, they had already ceased in all but name to resemble the Romans of the republic.

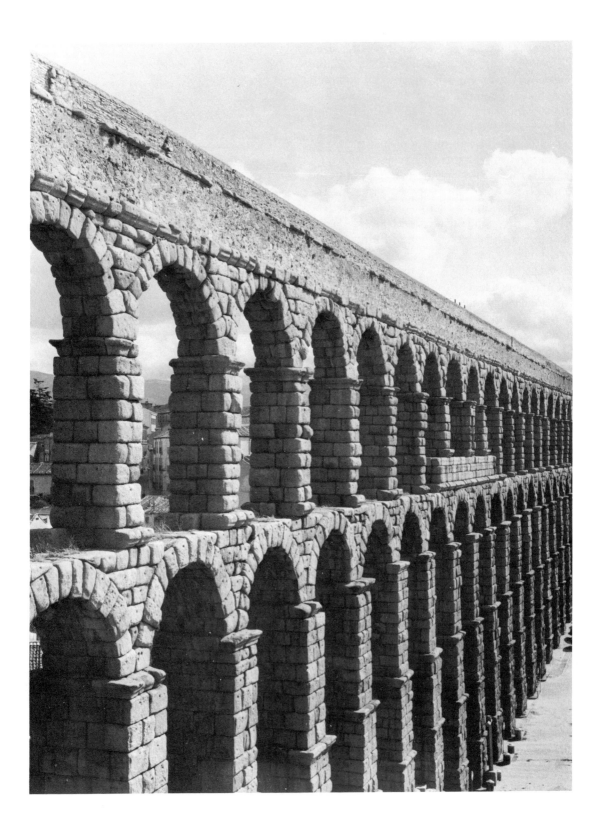

6 The Roman achievement

If the Greek contribution to civilization was essentially mental and spiritual, that of Rome was structural and practical; its essence was the empire itself. Though no man is an empire, not even the great Alexander, its nature and government were to an astonishing degree the creation of one man of outstanding ability, Julius Caesar's great-nephew Octavian. Later he was celebrated as Caesar Augustus and an age has been named after him; his name gave an adjective to posterity. Sometimes one has the feeling that he invented almost everything that characterized imperial Rome, from the new Praetorian Guard, which was the first regular military force stationed permanently in the capital, to the taxation of bachelors. One reason for this feeling (though only one) is that he was a master of public relations; significantly, more representations of him than of any other Roman emperor have come down to us.

Though a Caesar, Octavian came of a junior branch. He was adopted as heir by his great-uncle Julius and thus inherited aristocratic con-

After almost nineteen centuries, the water-supply of the Spanish city of Segovia is still carried to it by this Roman aqueduct, borne by 128 arches which raise the water-channel to a hundred feet above ground at its highest point. Such monuments understandably made barbarians gape as at the works of gods. The Romans were the greatest engineers yet to set about extending the human exploitation of the material world and it was to take centuries before works of comparable scale and utility again became possible.

nexions and military support. For a time he co-operated with one of Caesar's henchmen, Mark Antony, in a ferocious series of proscriptions to destroy the party which had murdered the great dictator. Mark Antony's departure to win victories in the east, failure to do so and injudicious marriage to Cleopatra, Julius Caesar's sometime mistress, gave Octavian further opportunities. He fought in the name of the Republic against a threat that Antony might make a proconsular return bringing oriental monarchy in his baggage-train. The victory of Actium (31 BC) was followed by the legendary suicides of Antony and Cleopatra; the kingdom of the Ptolemies came to an end and Egypt too was annexed a province of Rome.

This was the end of civil war. Octavian returned to become consul. He had every card in his hand and judiciously refrained from playing them, leaving it to his opponents to recognize his strength. In 27 BC he carried out what he called a republican restoration with the support of a Senate whose republican aristocracy, purged and weakened by civil war and proscription, he reconciled to his real primacy by his careful preservation of forms. He carefully re-established the reality of his great-uncle's power behind a façade of republican piety. He was *imperator* only by virtue of his command of the troops of the frontier provinces – but that was where the bulk of the legions were. As old soldiers of his and his great-uncle's armies returned to retirement, they were duly settled on small-holdings and were appropriately grateful. His consulship was prolonged from

Roman warships fought by ramming and boarding; hence they carried a complement of marine infantry. It has been suggested that the crocodile on this ship of the first century BC may denote service against Egypt (of which the crocodile was the emblem), perhaps at Actium against Cleopatra's navy.

year to year and in 27 BC he was given the honorific title of Augustus, the name by which he was to be remembered. At Rome, though, he was formally and usually called by his family name, or was identified as *princeps*, first citizen. As the years passed Augustus' power still grew. The Senate accorded him a right of interference in those provinces which it formally ruled (that is, those where there was no need to keep a garrison army). He was voted the tribunician power. His special status was enhanced and formalized by a new recognition of his state or *dignitas*, as the Romans called it; he sat between the two consuls after his resignation from that office in 23 BC and his business was given precedence in the agenda of the Senate. Finally, in 12 BC he became *Pontifex maximus*, the head of the official cult, as his great-uncle had been. The forms of the Republic with their popular elections and senatorial elections were maintained, but Augustus said who should be elected.

The political reality marked by this supremacy was the rise to domination within the ruling class of men who owed their position to the Caesars. But the new élites were not to be allowed to behave like the old. The Augustan benevolent despotism regularized the provincial administration and army by putting them into obedient and salaried hands. The conscious resuscitation of republican tradition and festivals had a part to play in this, too. Augustan government was heavily tinged with concern for moral revival; the virtues of ancient Rome

In about AD 10, this gem was carved from onyx. It expresses much of the imperial mythology then still in the making. Augustus, accompanied by the goddess Roma, is shown sitting in state, presumably contemplating the glory of his position while another figure places on his head a crown representing the civilized world. At the side, Tiberius steps from his chariot after his victory over the warlike Pannonians, while soldiers erect a trophy below. This remarkable work has been attributed to Augustus' official engraver and so no doubt expresses themes the emperor approved.

seemed to some to live again. Ovid a poet of pleasure and love was packed off to exile in the Black Sea when a sexual scandal at the edge of the imperial family provided an excuse. When to this official austerity is added the peace which marked most of the reign and the great visible monuments of the Roman architects and engineers, the reputation of the Augustan age is hardly surprising. After his death in AD 14 Augustus was deified as Julius Caesar had been.

Augustus intended to be succeeded by a member of his own family. Although he respected republican forms (and they were to endure with remarkable tenacity) Rome was now really a monarchy and this was demonstrated by the succession of five Caesars. Augustus' only child was a daughter; his immediate successor was his adopted stepson, Tiberius, one of his daughter's three husbands. The last of his descendants to reign was Nero, who died in AD 68.

The rulers of the classical world did not

281

usually live easy lives. Some Roman emperors had great mirrors installed at the corners of the corridors of their palaces so that would-be assassins could not lurk around them. None of Tiberius' four successors as emperor died a natural death, and Tiberius himself may have not. The fact is significant of the weaknesses inherent in Augustus' legacy. There was still scope for pinpricks from a Senate which formally continued to appoint the first magistrate and always room for intrigue and cabal about the court and imperial household. Yet the Senate could never hope to recover power for the ultimate basis of power was always military. If there was confusion and indecision at the centre, then the soldiers would decide. This was what happened in the first great burst of civil war to shake the empire, in the year of the Four Emperors, AD 69, from which there emerged Vespasian, the grandson of a centurion, and far from an aristocrat. The first magistracy had passed out of the hands of the great Roman families.

When Vespasian's younger son was murdered in AD 96 this upstart house came to an end. Its successor was an elderly senator, Nerva, who solved the problem of succession by breaking with attempts to ensure natural dynastic continuity. Instead, he institutionalized the adoption to which Augustus had perforce been driven. The result was a succession of four emperors, Trajan, Hadrian, Antoninus Pius and Marcus Aurelius, who gave the empire a century of good government; it has been named (after the third of them) the age of the Antonines. Three of these men were Spaniards, one was a Greek, an evidence of the degree to which the empire was a cosmopolitan reality, the framework of the post-Hellenistic world of the West, and not merely the property of Italians or Romans. Adoption made it easier to find candidates upon whom army, provinces and Senate could agree and it is noteworthy that this golden age came to an end when there was a reversion to the hereditary principle, the succession of Commodus, son of Marcus Aurelius. A new AD 69 followed, in AD 192, when he was murdered, and in the following year there were four emperors, each acclaimed by his own army. The Illyrian army prevailed in the end, imposing Septimius Severus, an African married to a Syrian. Later emperors were to be the nominees of soldiers; bad times lay ahead.

By this time, the emperors ruled a far larger area than had Augustus. In the north Julius Caesar had carried out reconnaissances into Britain and Germany, but had left Gaul with the Channel and the Rhine as its frontiers. Augustus pressed into Germany, and also up to the Danube from the south. The Danube eventually became the frontier of the empire, but incursions beyond the Rhine were less successful and the frontier was not stabilized on the Elbe as Augustus had hoped. Instead, a grave shock was given to Roman confidence in AD 9 when the teutonic tribes led by Arminius (in whom later Germans were to see a national hero) destroyed three legions. The ground was never recovered, nor the legions, for their numbers were thought so ill-omened that they never again appear in the army lists. Eight remained stationed along the Rhine, the most strongly

Hadrian's Wall was begun in about AD 121 and this defence for Britannia from northern barbarians was not finally abandoned until almost the end of the fourth century. At first, part of it was built of turf, but eventually almost the whole length from Tyne to Solway was rebuilt in stone. Hadrian was a great builder of works with more peaceful purposes, too: the present castle of Sant'Angelo at Rome was his mausoleum.

For the empire as for the republic, the final argument remained the same: the Roman army. Its exploits were the subject of much of the narrative relief work in stone which looms so large in our vision of Roman art. This instance is taken from what is perhaps the supreme example of the form, the huge column set up in the Forum at Rome by the Emperor Trajan in AD 113 to commemorate his campaigns in Dacia. Around the column winds the unrolling story, a strip-cartoon in stone 215 yards long. In this episode barbarian soldiers attack a Roman camp.

held part of the frontier because of the dangers which lay beyond it.

After this, empire unrolled elsewhere. In AD 43 Claudius began the conquest of Britain, which was carried to its furthest enduring limit when Hadrian's wall was built across the north as an effective boundary forty or so years later. Also in the first century Mauretania became a province. In the east Trajan conquered Dacia, the later Romania, in AD 105, but this was more than a century and a half after a quarrel which was to be long enduring had opened in Asia.

Rome had first faced Parthia on the Euphrates when Sulla's army campaigned there in 92 BC. Nothing of importance followed until thirty years later when Roman armies began to advance against Armenia. Two spheres of influence were overlapping and Pompey at one moment arbitrated between the Armenian and Parthian kings in a boundary dispute. Then, in 54 BC, the Roman politician Crassus launched an invasion of Parthia across the Euphrates. Within a few weeks he was dead and a Roman army of forty thousand destroyed. It was one of the worst military disasters of Roman history. Evidently there was a new great power in Asia. The Parthian army had more than good mounted archers to it by this time. It also had heavy cavalry of unrivalled quality, the cataphracts, mail-clad horsemen with their mounts mailed, too, charging home with a heavy lance. The fame of their great horses even awoke the envy of the distant Chinese.

After this, the eastern frontier on the Euphrates was to remain undisturbed for a century, but the Parthians did not endear themselves to Rome. They dabbled in the politics of the civil war, harassing Syria and encouraging unrest among the Palestinian Jews. Mark Antony had to retreat in disgrace and distress to Armenia after losing thirty-five thousand men in a disastrous campaign against them. But Parthia suffered from internal divisions, too, and in 20 BC Augustus was able to obtain the return of the Roman standards taken from Crassus and thankfully set aside any need to attack Parthia for reasons of honour. Yet the likelihood of

conflict persisted, both because of the sensitivity with which each power regarded Armenia and because of the instability of Parthia's dynastic politics. One emperor, Trajan, conquered the Parthian capital of Ctesiphon and fought his way down to the Persian Gulf, but his successor Hadrian wisely conciliated the Parthians by handing back much of his conquest.

It was the Roman boast that their new subjects all benefited from the extension to them of the *Pax Romana*, the imperial peace which removed the threats of barbarian incursion or international strife. The claim has to be qualified by recognition of the violence with which many subject peoples resisted Roman rule, and the bloodshed this cost, but there is something in it. Within the frontiers there was order and peace as never before. In some places this permanently changed the patterns of settlement as new cities were founded in the east or descendants of Caesar's soldiers were settled in new military colonies in Gaul. Sometimes there were even more far-reaching results. The adoption of the Rhine frontier permanently affected the history of Europe by its division of the Germanic peoples. Meanwhile, everywhere, as things settled down, a gradual romanization of the local notables occurred. They shared a common civilization whose spread was made easier by the new swiftness of communication along the roads whose main purpose was the movement of the legions. Napoleon could not move couriers faster from Paris to Rome than could the emperors of the first century AD.

The empire was a huge area and required the solution of problems of government which had not been faced by Greeks or solved by Persians. A complex bureaucracy appeared, with remarkable scope. To cite one small example, the records of all officers of centurion rank and above (company commanders upwards, as it were) were centralized at Rome. The corps of provincial civil servants was the administrative armature, sustained by a practical reliance for many purposes in many places upon the army, which did much more than merely fight. Bureaucracy was controlled by the adoption of fairly limited

Major roads, cities and garrisons of the Empire in the Age of Antonines

Roads

Hadrian's Wall

Eburacum
Lindum
Camulodunum
Deva
Isca
Londinium
Alauna
Portus Itus
Brigantium
Asturica
Olisipo
Emerita
Toletum
Caesaraugusta
Corduba
Malaca
Gades
Tingi
Ad Mercurium
Volubilis
Valentia
Carthago Nova
Rusaddir
Cartenna
Castellum Oppidum
Tingitanum Novum
Pomaria
Caesarea
Saldae
Rapidum
Tamallenia
Capsa
Turris
Zarai
Thamugadi
Thagaste
Tacapae
Sabrata
Oea
Tubactis
Leptis Magna
Carthago
Utica
Hippo Regius
Cirta
Narbo
Tarraco
Tolosa
Burdigala
Nemausus
Avaricum
Augustodunum
Vienna
Lugdunum
Forum Iulii
Genua
Placentia
Mediolanum
Bononia
Verona
Ariminum
Roma
Capua
Tarentum
Rhegium
Messana
Syracusae
Agrigentum
Salonae
Narona
Apollonia
Nicopolis
Brundisium
Patrae
Corinthus
Athenae
Cyrene
Alexandria
Memphis
Aelana
Petra
Philadelphia
Damascus
Caesarea
Tyrus
Sidon
Salinus
Attalia
Rhodus
Ephesus
Smyrna
Sardes
Pergamum
Laodicea
Thessalonica
Amphipolis
Byzantium
Nicomedia
Apollonia
Phillippopolis
Oescus
Novae
Ratiaria
Odessus
Istropolis
Sinope
Tyana
Tarsus
Antiochia
Caesarea
Laodicea
Samosata
Melitene
Sebastea
Vminacium
Naissus
Singidunum
Sirmium
Siscia
Poetovio
Aquincum
Brigetio
Carnuntum
Vindobona
Vesontio
Basilia
Vindonissa
Turicum
Aventicum
Divodurum
Augusta Treviroum
Mogontiacum
Bonna
Col. Agrippina
Vetera
Noviomagus
Novaesium
Ulpia
Augusta Vindelicorum
Launiacum
Virunum
Porolissum
Poroлissum
Ad Mercurium

The loser: a bronze head of a Gallic chief of the first century AD.

aims. These were above all fiscal; if the taxes came in, then Roman rule did not want to interfere in other ways with the operation of local custom. Rome was tolerant. It would provide the setting within which the example of its civilization would wean barbarians from their native ways. The reform of the administrators had begun under Augustus. The Senate still appointed to many posts on an annual basis, but the emperor's *legati* who acted for him in the frontier provinces held office at his pleasure. All the evidence is that whatever the means were by which it was achieved, the administration underwent a notable improvement under the empire by comparison with the corruption of the last century of the Republic. It was much more centralized and integrated than the satrapy system of Persia.

The cooperation of the subject peoples was tempted with a bait. First the Republic and then the empire had been extended by granting citizenship to wider and wider numbers of

Rome's subjects. It was an important privilege; among other things, as the Acts of the Apostles remind us, it carried with it rights of appeal from local courts to the emperor at Rome. On the granting of citizenship could be based the winning of the loyalties of local notables; more and more non-Romans make their appearance in the Senate and at Rome as the centuries pass. Finally, in AD 212 citizenship was granted to all free subjects of the empire.

This was an outstanding instance of Roman digestive power. The empire and the civilization it carried were unashamedly cosmopolitan. The administrative framework contained an astonishing variety of contrasts and diversities. They were held together not by an impartial despotism exercised by a Roman élite, but by a constitutional system which took local élites and romanized them. From the first century AD the senators themselves included only a dwindling number of men of Italian descent. Roman tolerance in this was diffused among other peoples. The empire was never a racial unity whose hierarchies were closed to non-Italians. Only one of its peoples, the Jews, felt strongly about the retention of their distinction within it and it rested on religion.

Already Hellenistic civilization had achieved a remarkable mixing of East and West; now Rome continued the process over an even wider area. The element in the new cosmopolitanism which was most obvious was, indeed, the Greek, for the Romans themselves made much of their inheritance from the Greeks, though it was the Greeks of the Hellenistic era with whom they were most at home. All educated Romans were bilingual and this illustrates the tradition upon which they drew. Latin was the official language and always remained the language of the army; it was spoken widely in the West and to judge by the military records, literacy in it was high. Greek was the *lingua franca* in the eastern provinces, understood by all civil servants and merchants, and used in the courts if the litigants wished. Educated Romans grew up to read the Greek classics and drew from them their standards; the creation of a literature which could stand on an equal footing with the older was the laudable ambition of most Roman writers. In the first century AD they got nearest to this and the coincidence of a cultural and an imperial achievement is striking in Virgil, the conscious renewer of the epic tradition who was also the poet of imperial mission.

It may be that in this lies one clue to explain the peculiar feel of Roman culture. Perhaps it is the obviousness and pervasiveness of the Greek background which does much to deprive it of the air of novelty. Its weight was accentuated by the static, conservative concern of Roman thinkers. Between them, their attention was absorbed almost exclusively by the two foci provided by the Greek inheritance and the moral and political traditions of the republic. Both lived on curiously and somewhat artificially in a material setting which more and more ceased to fit them. Formal education changed little in practice and content from century to century, for example. Livy, the great Roman historian, sought again to quicken republican virtues in his history, but not to criticize and reinterpret them. When Roman civilization was irreversibly urban the (almost extinct) virtues of the independent peasant continued to be celebrated and rich Romans longed (they said) to get away from it all to the simple life of the countryside. In art Roman sculpture only provided again what Greeks had already done better. The philosophies of Rome were Greek, too. Epicureanism and Stoicism held the centre of the stage, neo-Platonism was innovatory, but came from the East, as did the mystery religions which were eventually to provide Roman men and women with something their culture could not give them.

Only in two practical fields were the Romans to be great creators, law and engineering. The achievements of the lawyers were relatively late; it was in the second and early third centuries AD that the jurisconsults began the accumulation of commentary which would be so valuable a legacy to the future when codification passed their work to medieval Europe. In engineering – and Romans did not distinguish it from archi-tecture – the quality of their achievement is more immediately impressive. It was a source of pride to the Romans and one of the few things in which they were sure they outstripped the Greeks. A large contribution to it was made by the availability of cheap labour: at Rome it was slaves and in the provinces often the un-employed legions on garrison duty in peaceful times who carried out the great works of hydraulic engineering, bridging and road-building. But more was involved than material factors. The Romans founded town-planning as an art and administrative skill west of the Indus, and their inventions of concrete and the vaulted dome revolutionized the shapes of buildings. For the first time the interiors of buildings became more than a series of surfaces for decor-ation. Volumes and lighting became part of the subject-matter of architecture and the later Christian basilicas were to be the first great expressions of a new concern with the spaces inside buildings.

The visible relics of Roman technical accom-plishment were diffused over an area running from the Black Sea to Hadrian's Wall in the north and the Atlas mountains in the south. The capital, of course, contained some of the most spectacular. It was there, too, that the wealth of empire expressed itself in a richness of finish and decoration not so concentrated elsewhere. When their marble facings were intact, and the paint and stucco moulding there to relieve the sheer mass of stone, Rome must have had some of the appeal to the imagination earlier possessed by Babylon. There was an ostentation about it which spoke of a certain vulgarity, too, and in this again it is not hard to sense a difference of quality between Rome and Greece; Roman civil-ization has a grossness and materiality ines-capable in even its greatest monuments.

In part this was the simple expression of the social realities on which the empire rested; Rome, like all the ancient world, was built on a sharp division of rich and poor, but in the capital itself this division was an abyss not concealed but consciously expressed. The contrasts of wealth were flagrant in the difference between the

The eruption of the volcano Vesuvius in AD *79 destroyed Pompeii and Herculaneum, two flourishing towns, but also preserved much of the setting of their daily life for us. This mosaic is from a villa at Herculaneum.*

sumptuousness of the houses of the new rich, drawing to themselves the profits of empire and calling on the services of perhaps scores of slaves on the spot and hundreds on the estates which maintained them, and the swarming tenements in which the Roman proletariat lived. Romans found no difficulty in accepting such divisions as part of the natural order; for that matter, few civilizations have ever much worried about them before our own, though few displayed them so flagrantly as imperial Rome. Unfortunately, though easy to recognize, the realities of wealth in Rome still remain curiously opaque to the historian. The finances of only one senator, the younger Pliny, are known to us in any detail.

The Roman pattern was reflected in all the other great cities of the empire. It was central to the civilization which Rome sustained everywhere in the provincial cities which stood like islands of Graeco-Roman culture in the aboriginal countrysides of the subject-peoples. Due allowance made for climate, they everywhere reflected a pattern of life of remarkable uniformity. Almost everywhere a Roman contribution was permanently absorbed unless violent disruption followed barbarian conquest. The cities displayed Roman priorities. Each had a forum, temples, a theatre, baths. These things were added to old cities, built as part of the basic plan of the many new or refounded old ones. Regular grid-patterns were adopted as ground plans. The government of the cities was in the hands of local bigwigs, the *curiales* or city-fathers who at least until Trajan's time enjoyed

The last sight seen by many a Roman prisoner must have been the beast which was to tear him to pieces in the arena. This mosaic of about AD 200 shows a Libyan prisoner, tied to a stake in the chariot from which he attacked the Romans, about to be finished off by a panther.

a very large measure of independence in the conduct of municipial affairs, though later a tighter supervision was to be imposed on them. Some of these cities, such as Alexandria or Antioch, or Carthage (which the Romans refounded), grew to a very large size. The greatest of all cities was Rome itself, eventually containing more than a million people.

In this civilization the omnipresence of the amphitheatre is a standing reminder of the brutality and coarseness of which it was also capable. It is important not to get this out of perspective, just as it is important not to infer too much about 'decadence' from the much-quoted works of would-be moral reformers. One disadvantage under which the repute of Roman civilization has laboured is that it is one of the few before modern times in which we have very much insight into the popular mind through its entertainments, for the gladiatorial games and the wild-beast shows were emphatically mass entertainment in a way in which the Greek theatre was not. Popular relaxation is in any era hardly likely to be an edifying spectacle and the Romans institutionalized its least attractive aspects by building great centres for their shows, and by permitting the mass-entertainment industry to be used as a political device; the provision of spectacular games as one of the

ways in which a rich man could bring to bear his wealth to secure political advancement. Nevertheless, when all allowances are made for the fact that we cannot know how, say, the ancient masses of Egypt or Assyria amused themselves, we are left with the uniqueness of the gladiatorial spectacle; it was an exploitation of cruelty as entertainment on a bigger scale than ever before and not to be rivalled until the twentieth-century cinema. In this respect, of course, it was made possible by the urbanization of Roman culture, which could deliver mass audiences on a larger scale than ever. The ultimate roots of the 'games' were Etruscan, but their development owed most to a new scale of urbanism and the exigencies of Roman politics.

Another aspect of the brutality at the heart of Roman society was, of course, far from unique to it; this was the omnipresence of slavery. As in Greek society, it was so varied in its expression that it cannot be summarized in a generalization. Many slaves earned wages, some bought their freedom and the Roman slave had rights at law. The growth of large plantation estates, it is true, provided examples of a new intensification of it in the first century or so, but it would be hard to say Roman slavery was worse than that of other ancient societies. A few questioners of the institution were very untypical: stoics reconciled themselves to slave-owning as easily as later Christians.

The main access to popular mentality which is possible before modern times is by means of religion. Roman religion was a very obvious part of Roman life, but that may be misleading if we think in modern terms. It had nothing to do with individual salvation and not much with individual behaviour; it was above all a public matter. It was a part of the *res publica*, a series of rituals whose maintenance was good for the state, whose neglect would bring retribution. There was no priestly caste set apart from other men (if we exclude one or two antiquarian survivals in the temples of a few special cults) and priestly duties were the task of the magistrates who found priesthood a useful social and political lever. Nor was there creed or dogma. What was required of Romans was only that the ordained services and rituals should be carried out in the accustomed way; for the proletarian this meant little except that he should not work on a holiday. The civic authorities were everywhere responsible for the rites, as they were responsible for the maintenance of the temples. The proper observances had a powerfully practical purpose: Livy reports a consul saying the gods 'look kindly on the scrupulous observance of religious rites which has brought our country to its peak'. Men genuinely felt that the peace of Augustus was the *pax deorum*, a divine reward for a proper respect for the gods which Augustus had reasserted. Somewhat more cynically, Cicero had remarked that the gods were needed to prevent chaos in society. This, if different, was also an expression of the Roman's practical approach to religion. It was not insincere or disbelieving; the recourse to diviners for the interpretation of omens and the acceptance of the decisions of the augurs about important acts of policy would alone establish that. But it was unmysterious and down-to-earth in its understanding of the official cults.

The content of these was a mixture of Greek mythology and festivals and rites derived from primitive Roman practice and therefore heavily marked by agricultural preoccupations. One which lived to deck itself out in the symbols of another religion was the December Saturnalia, which is with us still as Christmas. But the religion practised by Romans stretched far beyond official rites. The most striking feature of the Roman approach to religion was its eclecticism and cosmopolitanism. There was

room in the empire for all manner of belief, provided it did not contravene public order or inhibit adherence to the official observances. For the most part, the peasants everywhere pursued the timeless superstitions of their local nature cults, and townsmen took up new crazes from time to time, while the educated professed some acceptance of the classical pantheon of Greek gods and led the people in the official observances. Each clan and household, finally, sacrificed to its own god with appropriate special rituals at the great moments of human life: childbirth, marriage, sickness and death. Each household had its shrine, each street-corner its idol.

Under Augustus there was a deliberate attempt to reinvigorate old belief, which had been somewhat eroded by closer acquaintance with the Hellenistic East and about which a few sceptics had shown cynicism even in the second century BC. After Augustus, emperors always held the office of chief priest (*pontifex maximus*) and political and religious primacy were thus combined in the same person. This began the increasing importance and definition of the imperial cult itself. It fitted well the Roman's innate conservatism, his respect for the ways and customs of his ancestors. The imperial cult linked respect for traditional patrons, the placating or invoking of familiar deities and the commemoration of great men and events to the ideas of divine kingship which came from the East, from Asia. It was there that altars were first raised to Rome or the Senate, and there that they were soon reattributed to the emperor. The cult spread through the whole empire, though it was not until the third century AD that the practice was wholly respectable at Rome itself, so strong was republican sentiment. But even there the strains of empire had already favoured a revival of official piety which benefited the imperial cult.

This was not all that came from the East. By the second century, the distinction of a pure Roman religious tradition from others within the empire is virtually impossible. The Roman pantheon, like the Greek, was absorbed almost indistinguishably into a mass of beliefs and cults, their boundaries blurred and fluid, merging imperceptibly over a scale of experience running from sheer magic to the philosophical monotheism popularized by the stoics. The intellectual and religious world of the empire was omnivorous, credulous and deeply irrational. It is important here not to be over-impressed by the visible practicality of the Roman mind; practical men are often superstitious. Nor was the Greek heritage understood in an altogether rational way; its philosophers were seen by the first century BC as men inspired, holy men whose mystical teaching was the most eagerly studied part of their works, and even Greek civilization had always rested on a broad basis of popular superstition and local cult practice. Tribal gods swarmed throughout the Roman world.

All this boils down to a large measure of practical criticism of the ancient Roman ways. Obviously, they were no longer enough for an urban civilization, however numerically preponderant the peasants on which it rested. Many of the traditional festivals were pastoral or agricultural in origin, but occasionally even the god they invoked was forgotten. City-dwellers gradually came to need more than piety in a more and more puzzling world. Men grasped desperately at anything which could give meaning to the world and some degree of control over it. Old superstitions and new crazes benefited. The evidence can be seen in the appeal of the Egyptian gods, whose cults flooded through the empire as its security made travel and intercourse easier (they were even patronized by an emperor, Septimius Severus). A civilized world of greater complexity and unity than any earlier was also one of greater and greater religiosity and a curiousness almost boundless. One of the last great teachers of pagan antiquity, Apollonius of Tyana, lived and studied with the Brahmans of India. Men were looking about for new saviours long before one was found in the first century AD.

Another symptom of eastern influence was the popularization of mysteries, cults which rested upon the communication of special virtues and powers to the initiated by secret rites. The sacrificial cult of Mithras, a minor Zoroastrian deity especially favoured by soldiers, was one of the most famous. Almost all the mysteries register impatience with the constraints of the material world, an ultimate pessimism about it and a preoccupation with (and perhaps a promise of survival after) death. In this lay their power to provide a psychological satisfaction lost by the old gods and never really possessed by the official cult. They drew individuals to them; they had the appeal that was later to draw men to Christianity, which in its earliest days was often seen, significantly, as another mystery.

That Roman rule did not satisfy all Roman subjects all the time was even true in Italy itself, where as late as 73 BC a great slave revolt required three years of military campaigning and was punished with the crucifixion of 6000 slaves along the roads from Rome to the south. In the provinces revolt was endemic, always likely to be provoked by a particular burst of harsh or bad government. Such was the famous rebellion of Boadicea in Britain, or the earlier Pannonian revolt under Augustus. Sometimes such troubles could look back to local traditions of independence, as was the case at Alexandria where they were frequent. In one particular instance, that of the Jews, they touched chords not unlike those of later nationalism. The spectacular Jewish record of disobedience and resistance goes back beyond Roman rule to 170 BC, when they bitterly resisted the 'westernizing' practices of the Hellenistic kingdoms which first adumbrated policies later to be taken up by Rome. The imperial cult made matters worse. Even Jews who did not mind Roman tax-gatherers and thought that Caesar should have rendered unto him what was Caesar's were bound to draw the line at the blasphemy of sacrifice at his altar. In AD 66 came a great revolt; there were others under Trajan and Hadrian. Jewish communities were powder-barrels. Their sensitivity makes somewhat more understandable the unwillingness of a Procurator of Judaea to press too hard for strict

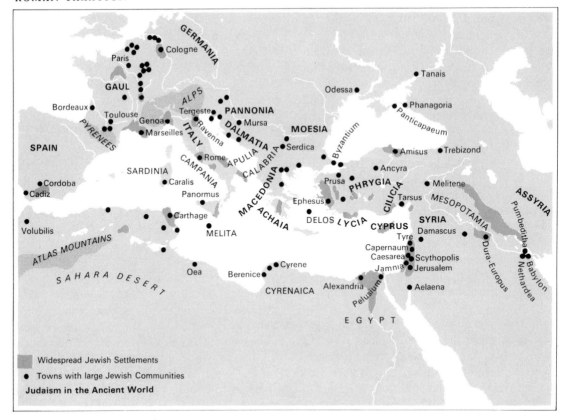

Widespread Jewish Settlements

● Towns with large Jewish Communities

Judaism in the Ancient World

adherence to the rights of an accused man before the law when Jewish leaders demanded his death at a time of tension somewhere about AD 30.

Taxes sustained the empire. They were not heavy in normal times, when they paid for administration and police quite comfortably. For a long time, they drew on a prosperous and growing economy. This was not only a matter of such lucky imperial acquisitions as the gold-mines of Dacia. The growth in the circulation of trade and the stimulus provided by the new markets of the great frontier encampments also favoured the appearance of new industry and suppliers. Yet the economic base of empire was always agriculture. This was not rich by modern standards, for its techniques were primitive; no Roman farmer ever saw a windmill and water-mills were still rare when the empire ended in the West. For all its idealization, rural life was a harsh and laborious thing. To it too, therefore,

the *pax Romana* was essential: it meant that taxes could be found from the small surplus produced and that lands would not be ravaged.

In the last resort almost everything seems to come back to the army, on which the Roman peace depended, yet it was an instrument which changed over six centuries as much as did the Roman state itself. From the time of Augustus it was a regular long-service force, no longer relying even formally upon the obligation of all citizens to serve. The ordinary legionary served for twenty years, four in reserve, and he more and more came from the provinces as the empire grew older. Surprising as it may seem, given the repute of Roman discipline, volunteers seem to have been plentiful enough for letters of recom-mendation and the use of patrons to be resorted to by would-be recruits. The twenty-eight legions which were the normal establishment after the defeat in Germany were distributed along the frontiers, about 160000 men in all.

They were the core of the army, which contained about as many men again in the cavalry, auxiliaries and other arms. The legions continued to be commanded by senators (except in Egypt) and the central issue of politics at the capital itself was still access to opportunities such as this. For, as had become clearer and clearer as the centuries passed, it was in the camps of the legions that the heart of the empire lay, though the Praetorian Guard at Rome sometimes contested their right to choose an emperor.

For bulk transport, rivers and coastal shipping were even more important to the Roman empire than its famed roads. Here, a small barge carrying wine barrels is being hauled upstream somewhere in Gaul.

7 Jewry and the coming of Christianity

Few readers of this book are likely to be familiar with the name of Abgar, or even with that of his east Syrian kingdom, Osrhoene; both were unknown to the writer until he was well embarked upon this book. Yet this little-known and obscure monarch is a landmark: he was long believed to be the first Christian king. In fact, the story of his conversion is a legend; it was under his descendant, Abgar VIII (or IX, so vague is our information) that Osrhoene became Christian at the end of the second century AD and the conversion may not even have included the king himself, but this did not matter for early hagiographers. For them Abgar stood at the head of a long and great tradition; in the end it

Thirteen hundred feet above the Dead Sea, the rock of Masada was chosen by Herod the Great as a site for a fortress containing palaces, arsenals, barracks and great water tanks. It was virtually a personal refuge for him and his family. This was in about 30 BC and a century later, in AD 73, this fortress was the scene of the a siege endured by Jewish rebels whose revolt against the Romans had by then been crushed everywhere else. In the end, faced with defeat, the entire garrison and their families destroyed themselves, only two women and five children whom they had hidden surviving, reports Josephus. Excavated in the 1960s, the scene of this heroic struggle is now a shrine of Jewish patriotism.

was to incorporate virtually the whole history of monarchy in Europe. From there, in turn, it was to spread to influence rulers in other parts of the world.

All these monarchs would behave differently because they saw themselves as Christian, yet, important though it was, this is only a tiny part of the difference Christianity has made to history. Until the coming of industrial society, in fact, it is the only historical phenomenon we have to consider whose implications, creative power and impact are comparable with the great determinants of prehistory in shaping the world we live in. Christianity grew up within the classical world of the Roman empire, fusing itself in the end with its institutions and spreading through its social and mental structures to become our most important legacy from that civilization. Often disguised or muted, its influence runs through all the great creative processes of the last fifteen hundred years; almost incidentally, it defined Europe. We are what we are today because a handful of Jews saw their teacher and leader crucified and believed he rose again from the dead.

The Jewishness of Christianity is fundamental and was probably its salvation (to speak in purely human terms), for the odds against the historical survival, let alone world-wide success, of a small sect centred upon a holy man in the Roman eastern empire were enormous. Judaism was a matrix and protecting environment for a long time as well as the source of the most fundamental Christian ideas. In return, Jewish ideas and myths were to be generalized through

Christianity to become world forces. At the heart of these was the Jewish view that history was a meaningful story, providentially ordained, a cosmic drama of the unfolding design of the one, omnipotent God for His chosen people. Through His covenant with that people could be found guidance for right action, and it lay in adherence to His law. The breaking of that law had always brought punishment; it had come to a whole people in the deserts of Sinai and by the waters of Babylon. This great drama was the inspiration of Jewish historical writing, in which the Jews of the Roman empire still discerned the pattern which made their lives meaningful.

The original sense was deeply rooted in Jewish historical experience, which, after the great days of Solomon, had been bitter, fostering an enduring distrust of the foreigner and an iron will to survive. Few things are in fact more remarkable in the life of this remarkable people than the simple fact of its continued existence. The Exile which began in 587 BC when Babylonian conquerors took many of the Jews away after the destruction of the Temple was the last crucial experience in the moulding of their national identity before modern times. It finally crystallized the Jewish vision of history. The exiles heard prophets like Ezekiel promise a renewed covenant; Judah had been punished for her sins by exile and the Temple's destruction, now God would turn His face again to her, she would return again to Jerusalem, delivered out of Babylon as Israel had been delivered out of Ur, out of Egypt. The Temple would be rebuilt. Perhaps only a minority of the Jews of the Exile heeded this, but it was a large one and it included Judah's religious and administrative élite, if we are to judge by the quality of those – again, probably a minority – who, when they could do so, returned to Jerusalem, a saving Remnant, according to prophecy.

Before then, the experience of the Exile had transformed Jewish life as well as confirming the Jewish vision. Scholars are divided as to whether the more important developments occurred among the exiles or among the Jews who were left in Judah to lament what had occurred. In one way or another, though, Jewish religious life was deeply stirred. The most important change was the implanting of the reading of the scriptures as the central act of Jewish religion. While the Old Testament was not to assume its final form for another three or four centuries, the first five books, or 'Pentateuch', traditionally ascribed to Moses, were substantially complete soon after the return from the Exile. Without the focus of cult practice at the Temple the Jews seem to have turned to weekly meetings to hear these sacred texts read and expounded. They contained the promise of a future and guidance to its achievement through maintenance of the Law, now given a new detail and coherence. This was one of the slow effects of the work of the interpreters and scribes who had to reconcile and explain the sacred books. In the end there was to grow out of these weekly meetings both the institution of the synagogue and a new liberation of religion from locality and ritual, however much and long Jews continued to pine for the restoration of the Temple. The Jewish religion could eventually be practised wherever Jews could come together to read the scriptures; they were to be the first of the peoples of a Book, and Christians and Moslems were to follow them. It made possible greater abstraction and universalizing of the vision of God.

There were narrowings, too. Although Jewish religion might be separated from the Temple cult, some prophets had seen the redemption and purification which must lie ahead as only to be approached through an even more rigid enforcement of what was now believed to be Mosaic law. Ezra brought back its precepts from Babylon and observances which had been in origin those of nomads were now imposed rigorously on an increasingly urbanized people. The self-segregation of Jews became much more important and obvious in towns; it was seen as a part of the purification which was needed that every Jew married to a gentile wife (and there must have been many) should divorce her.

This was after the Persian overthrow of Babylon. In 538 BC some of the Jews took the

Dura Europos on the Euphrates was an early centre of Christianity, but earlier still the home of an important Jewish community. Seleucids, Parthians and Romans had fought for it and it has proved a rich source of archaeological discoveries. Among the buildings was a synagogue which contained frescoes; this one (painted about AD 200–30) depicts Ezekiel's vision in the valley of dry bones (Ezekiel xxxvii). Ezekiel appears both in Parthian and in Greek dress and the work also shows the influence of the Greek idea of man as both body and soul.

opportunity offered to them and came back to Jerusalem. The Temple was rebuilt and Judah became under Persian overlordship a sort of theocratic satrapy, effective administrative power being in the hands of the priestly aristocracy, which provided the political articulation of Jewish nationhood until Roman times.

With the ending of Persian rule, the age of Alexander's heirs brought new problems. After being ruled by the Ptolemies, the Jews eventually passed to the Seleucids. The social behaviour and thinking of the upper classes underwent the influence of Hellenization; this sharpened divisions by exaggerating contrasts of wealth and differences between townsmen and countrymen. It also separated the priestly families from the people, who remained firmly in the tradition of the Law and the Prophets, as expounded in the synagogues. It was against a king of Hellenistic

Syria, Antiochus, and cultural 'westernization' approved by the priests, but resented as have been such processes in modern times by the masses, that the great Maccabaean revolt broke out (168–164 BC). Antiochus had tried to go too fast; not content with the steady erosion of Jewish insularity by Hellenistic civilization and the friction of example, he had interfered with Jewish rites and profaned the Temple. After the revolt had been repressed with difficulty (and guerrilla war went on long after), a more conciliatory policy was resumed by the Seleucid kings. It did not satisfy many Jews, who in 142 BC were able to take advantage of a favourable set of circumstances to win an independence which was to last for nearly eighty years until 63 BC. Pompey then imposed Roman rule and there disappeared the last independent Jewish state in the Near East for nearly two thousand years.

Independence had not been a happy period. A succession of kings drawn from the priestly families had thrown the country into disorder by innovation and high-handedness. They and the priests who acquiesced in their policies excited opposition. They were challenged in their authority by a new school of interpreters, who clung to the Law, rather than the cult, as the heart of Judaism and gave it new and searchingly rigorous interpretation. These were the Pharisees, the representatives of a puritan strain which was time and time again to express itself

The menorah or seven-branched candlestick symbolizes for Jews the seven days of creation. This carving of one (from a sarcophagus at Rome in about AD 300) is combined with classical figures and shows how assimilated members of the large Roman Jewish community could become. Conventional 'victories' support the menorah; the cupid-like figure represents winter, the other three seasons, once part of the design, having been lost.

in Jewry in protest against the danger of creeping Hellenization. They also accepted proselytism among non-Jews, teaching a belief in the resurrection of the dead and a divine Last Judgement; there was a mixture in their stance of national and universal aspiration and they were drawing out further the implications of Jewish monotheism.

Most of these changes took place in Judaea, the tiny rump of the once great kingdom of David; fewer Jews lived there in the time of Augustus than in the rest of the empire. From the seventh century onwards they had spread over the civilized world. The armies of Egypt, Alexander and the Seleucids all had Jewish regiments. Others had settled abroad in the course of trade. One of the greatest Jewish colonies was at Alexandria, where they had gathered from about 300 BC. The Alexandrian Jews were Greek-speakers; there the Old Testament was first translated into Greek and when Jesus was born there were probably more Jews there than in Jerusalem. At Rome there were probably 50 000 or so. Such agglomerations increased the opportunities to proselytize and therefore the danger of friction between communities.

Jewry offered much to a world where traditional cults had waned. Circumcision and dietary restraints were obstacles, but were far outweighed for many a proselyte by the attractions of a code of behaviour of great minuteness, a form of religion not dependent on temples, shrines or priesthood for its exercise, and, above all, the assurance of salvation. A prophet whose message was ascribed by the Old Testament compilers to Isaiah, but who is almost certainly of the Exile, had already announced a message to bring light to the gentiles, and many of them had responded to that light long before the Christians, who interpreted this message in a special sense. The proselytes could identify themselves with the Chosen People in the great story which inspired Jewish historical writing, the only achievement in this field worthy of comparison with the Greek invention of scientific history, because it gave meaning to the tragedies of the world. In their history the Jews discerned an unfolding pattern by which they were being refined in the fire for the Day of Judgement. A fundamental contribution of Jewry to Christianity would be its sense of the people apart, its eyes set on things not of this world; Christians were to go on to the idea of the leaven in the lump, working to redeem the world. Both myths were deeply rooted in Jewish historical experience and in the remarkable though simple fact of this people's survival at all.

The big communities of Jews and Jewish proselytes were important social facts to Roman governors, standing out not only because of their size but because of their tenacious separateness. Archaeological evidence of synagogues as distinct and separate buildings does not appear until well into the Christian era, but Jewish quarters in cities were distinct, clustering about their own synagogues and courts of law. While proselytizing was widespread and even some Romans were attracted by Jewish belief, there were also early signs of popular dislike of Jews at Rome itself. Rioting was frequent in Alexandria and easily spread to other towns of the Near East. This led to distrust on the part of authorities and (at least at Rome) to the dispersal of Jewish communities when things became difficult.

Judaea itself was regarded as a particularly ticklish and dangerous area and to this the religious ferment of the last century and a half BC had greatly contributed. In 37 BC the Senate appointed a Jew, Herod the Great, King of Judaea. He was an unpopular monarch. No doubt this was in part a matter of national distaste for a Roman nominee and a ruler anxious – with reason – to preserve the friendship of Rome, but it was exacerbated by the Hellenistic style of life at his court (though he was careful to display his loyalty to the Jewish religion) and by the heavy taxes which he raised, some of

them for grandiose building. Even if it were not for the legendary Massacre of the Innocents and his place in Christian demonology, Herod would not have had a good historical press. At his death, in 4 BC, his kingdom was divided between his three sons, an unsatisfactory arrangement which was superseded in AD 6, when Judaea became part of the Roman province of Syria governed from Caesarea. In AD 26 Pontius Pilate became governor and was to hold the uncomfortable and exacting post for ten years.

It was a bad moment in the history of a turbulent province. Something of a climax to the

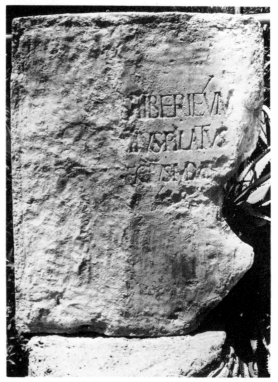

From the whole New Testament, no non-Jew is better remembered than Pontius Pilate, Roman governor of Judaea from AD 26 to 36. His historical existence has long been attested not only by the Gospels but by other literary sources; only in 1961, though, did this fragment of inscribed stone come to light and provide evidence of his existence in the form of a dedication by him of a building to the emperor.

Of all the Dead Sea scrolls the best preserved contains almost the whole book of Isaiah. It is also the longest scroll; in all it stretches 24 feet. It is likely that it was part of a monastic library belonging to the apocalyptic and strict sect which established itself in Qumran sometime after the Roman occupation of Palestine in 63 BC. Its adherents were not dispersed or destroyed until after the rising of AD 66.

excitements of nearly two centuries was being reached. The Jews were at loggerheads with their Samaritan neighbours and resented an influx of Greek-Syrians noticeable in the coastal towns. They detested Rome as the latest of a long line of conquerors and also because of its demands for taxes; tax-gatherers – the 'publicans' of the New Testament – were unpopular not just because of what they took but because they took it for the foreigner. But worse still, the Jews were also bitterly divided between themselves. The great religious festivals were often stained by bloodshed and rioting. Pharisees were divided from Sadducees while other sects rejected them both. One of the most interesting of them has become known to us only in recent

years, through the discovery and reading of the Dead Sea Scrolls, in which it can be seen to have promised its adherents much that was also the promise of early Christianity. It looked forward to a last deliverance which would follow Judaea's apostasy and would be announced by the coming of a Messiah. Jews attracted by such teaching searched the writings of the Prophets for the prefigurings of these things. Others sought a more direct way. The Zealots looked to the nationalist resistance movement as the way ahead.

Into this electric atmosphere Jesus was born in about 6 BC, into a world in which thousands of his countrymen awaited the coming of a Messiah, a leader who would lead them to military or symbolic victory and inaugurate the last and greatest days of Jerusalem. The evidence for the facts of his life is contained in the records written down after his death in the Gospels, the assertions and traditions which the early Church based on the testimony of those who had actually known Jesus. The Gospels are not by themselves satisfactory evidence but their inadequacies can be exaggerated. They were no doubt written to demonstrate the supernatural authority of Jesus and the confirmation

provided by the events of his life for the prophecies which had long announced the coming
of Messiah. This interested and hagiographical
origin does not demand scepticism about all the
facts asserted; many have inherent plausibility
in that they are what might be expected of a
Jewish religious leader of the period. They need
not be rejected; much more inadequate evidence about far more intractable subjects has
often to be employed. There is no reason to be
more austere or rigorous in our canons of
acceptability for early Christian records than
for, say, the evidence in Homer which illumi-
nates Mycenae. Nevertheless, it is very hard to
find corroborative evidence of the facts stated in
the Gospels in other records.

The picture of Jesus presented in them is of
a man of modest though not destitute family,
with a claim to royal lineage. Such a claim would
no doubt at once have been denied by his opponents if there had not been something in it.
Galilee, where Jesus grew up, was something
of a frontier area for Judaism, where it was most
exposed to the contact with Syrian-Greeks
which often irritated religious sensibilities.
There preached in the neighbourhood a man
called John, a prophet to whom crowds had
flocked in the days before his arrest and execution. Scholars now believe John to have been
connected with the Qumran community which
left behind the Dead Sea Scrolls. One evangelist
tells us that he was the cousin of Jesus; this is
possibly true, but less important than the agreement of all the Gospels that John baptized
Jesus as he baptized countless others who came
to him fearing the approach of the Last Day.
He is also said to have recognized in Jesus a
teacher like himself and perhaps something
more: 'Art thou He that cometh, or look we for
another?' Jesus knew himself to be a holy man;
his teaching and the evidence of his sanctity
which was seen in miracles soon convinced the
excited multitude of Jerusalem. His triumphal
entry to the city was based on their spontaneous
feeling. They followed him as they followed
other great teachers in the hope of the Messiah
that was to come. The end was a charge of

blasphemy before the Jewish court and the
relaxation of the letter of Roman law by a
Roman governor in order to avoid further
trouble in a riotous city. Jesus was not a Roman
citizen and for such men the extreme penalty
was crucifixion after scourging. The inscription
on the cross on which he was nailed said: 'Jesus
of Nazareth, King of the Jews'; it made clear
that a political act was envisaged and that the
significance of it should not go unmissed was
ensured by posting the inscription in Latin,
Greek and Hebrew. This was probably in
AD 33, though AD 29 and AD 30 have also been
put forward as dates. Shortly after his death,
Jesus' disciples believed that he had risen from
the dead, that they had seen him and his
ascension into heaven, and that they had
received a divine gift of power from him at
Pentecost which should sustain them and their
adherents until the Last Day. That would
soon come, they also believed, and would bring
back Jesus as the judge sitting at the right hand
of God. All this the Gospels tell us.

If this was what the first Christians saw in
Christ (as he came to be called, by the Greek
word meaning 'the anointed one') there were
also in his teaching other elements susceptible
of far wider application. The reported devotional ideas of Jesus do not go beyond the
Jewish observances; service in the Temple,
together with private prayer, were all that he
indicated. The moral teaching was a greater
advance from Jewish piety, for it focussed upon
repentance and deliverance from sin, and upon
a deliverance available to all, and not just to
Jews. Retribution plays little part in Jesus'
teaching. Fulfilment of the Law was essential,
but not enough; beyond observance lay the
duties of repentance and restitution in the case
of wrong done, even self-sacrifice. The law of
love was the proper guide to action. Emphatically, Jesus rejected the rôle of the political
leader and a political quietism was one of the
meanings later discerned in a dictum which was
to prove to be of terrible ambiguity: 'My kingdom is not of this world.'

Yet a Messiah who would be a political leader

was expected by many. Others sought a leader against the Jewish religious establishment and therefore were potentially a danger to order even if they aimed only at religious purification and reform. Inevitably, Jesus, of the house of David, became a dangerous man in the eyes of the authorities. One of his disciples was Simon the Zealot, an alarming associate because he was a member of an extremist sect. Many of Jesus' teachings encouraged feeling against the dominant Sadducees and Pharisees, and they in their turn strove to draw out any anti-Roman implication which could be discerned in what he said.

Such facts provide the background to Jesus' destruction and the disappointment of the people; they do not explain the survival of his teaching. He had appealed not only to the politically dissatisfied but to Jews who felt that the Law was no longer guide enough and to non-Jews who, though they might win second-class citizenship of Israel as proselytes, wanted something more to assure them of acceptance at the Last Day. Jesus had also attracted the poor and outcast; they were many in a society which offered enormous contrasts of wealth and no mercy to those who fell by the wayside. These were some of the appeals and ideas which were to yield in the end an astonishing harvest. Yet though they were effective in his own lifetime, they seemed to die with him. At his death his followers were only one tiny Jewish sect among many. But they believed that a unique thing had happened. They believed that Christ had risen from the dead, that they had seen him, and that he offered to them and those that were saved by his baptism the same overcoming of death and personal life after God's judgement. The generalization of this message and its presentation to the civilized world was achieved within a half-century of Jesus' death.

The conviction of the disciples led them to remain at Jerusalem, an important centre of pilgrimage for Jews from all over the Near East, and therefore a seminal centre for a new doctrine. Two of Jesus' disciples, Peter and Jesus' brother, James, were the leaders of the tiny group who awaited the imminent return of the Messiah, striving to prepare for it by penitence and the service of God in the Temple. They stood emphatically within the Jewish fold; only the rite of baptism, probably, distinguished them. Yet other Jews saw in them a danger; their contacts with Greek-speaking Jews from outside Judaea led to questioning of the authority of the priests. The first martyr, Stephen, one of this group, was lynched by a Jewish crowd. One of those who witnessed this was a Pharisee of the tribe of Benjamin from Tarsus, Paul. It may have been that as a Hellenized Jew of the dispersion he was especially conscious of the need for orthodoxy. He was proud of his own. Yet he is the greatest influence in the making of Christianity after Jesus himself.

Somehow, Paul underwent a change of heart. From being a persecutor of the followers of Christ, he became one himself: it seems to have followed a sojourn of meditation and reflexion in the deserts of east Palestine. Then, in AD 47 (or perhaps earlier; dating Paul's life and travels is a very uncertain business), he began a series of missionary travels which took him all over the eastern Mediterranean. In AD 49 an apostolic council at Jerusalem took the momentous decision that there should be a mission by him to gentiles, who would not be required to undergo the circumcision which was the most important act of submission to the Jewish faith; it is not clear whether he, the council, or both in agreement were responsible. There were already little communities of Jews following the new teaching in Asia Minor, where it had been carried by pilgrims. Now these were given a great consolidation by Paul's efforts. His especial targets were Jewish proselytes, gentiles to whom he could preach in Greek and who were now offered full membership of Israel through the new covenant. The doctrine that Paul taught was new in another way, for he strove to reconcile the essentially Jewish ideas at the heart of Jesus' teaching with the conceptual world of the Greek language. He continued to emphasize the imminence of the coming end of things, but offered all nations, through Christ, the chance of understanding the mysteries of

Paul's Missions

----- Paul's first journey
——— Paul's second journey

creation and, above all, of the relationship of things seen and things invisible, of the spirit and the flesh, and of the overcoming of the second by the first. In the process, Jesus himself became more than a human deliverer who had overcome death, and was God Himself – and this was to shatter the mould of Jewish thought within which the faith had been born. There was no lasting place for such an idea within Jewry, and Christianity was now forced out of the Temple, into the intellectual world of Greece. A colossal theoretical structure was to be built on this change.

The Acts of the Apostles give plentiful evidence of the uproar which such teaching could cause and also of the intellectually tolerant attitude of the Roman administration when public order was not involved. But it often was. In AD 59, Paul had to be rescued from the Jews at Jerusalem by the Romans. When put on trial in the following year, he appealed to the emperor and to Rome he went, apparently with success. From that time he is lost to history; he may

have perished in a persecution by Nero in AD 67.

The first age of Christian missions permeated the civilized world by sinking roots everywhere in the first place in the Jewish communities. The 'Churches' which emerged were administratively wholly independent of one another, though the community at Jerusalem was recognized to have an understandable primacy. There were to be found those who had seen the risen Christ and their successors. The only links of the Churches other than their faith was the institutional one of baptism, the sign of acceptance in the new Israel, and the ritual practice of the eucharist, the re-enactment of the rites performed by Jesus at his last supper with his disciples, the evening before his arrest. It has remained the central sacrament of the Christian Churches to this day.

The local leaders of the Churches exercised independent authority in practice, therefore, but this did not cover much. There was nothing except the conduct of the affairs of the local Christian community to be decided upon, after

303

A man carrying an animal slung across his shoulders was one of the oldest themes of Greek art. It passed through the classical tradition into Christian art as a manifestation of Christ the Saviour, the Good Shepherd seeking and finding the one lost sheep among the hundred – 'and when he hath found it, he layeth it on his shoulders, rejoicing' (Luke xv, 4–7). This was the central figure of early Christian iconography, though this example comes from a Roman catacomb painting of the third century.

all. Meanwhile, Christians waited for the Second Coming. Such influence as Jerusalem had flagged after AD 70, when a Roman sack of the city dispersed many of the Christians there; after this time Christianity had less vigour within Judaea. By the beginning of the second century the communities outside Palestine were clearly more numerous and more important and had already evolved a hierarchy of officers to regulate their affairs. These identified the three later orders of the Church: bishops, presbyters and deacons. Their sacerdotal functions were at this stage minimal, and it was their administrative and governmental rôle which mattered.

The response of the Roman authorities to the rise of a new sect was largely predictable; its governing principle was that unless specific cause for interference existed, new cults were tolerated provided they implied no disrespect or disobedience to the empire. There was a danger at first that the Christians might be confounded with other Jews by a vigorous Roman reaction to Jewish nationalist movements which culminated in a number of bloody encounters, but this was avoided by their own political quietism and the announced hostility of other Jews. Galilee itself had been in rebellion in AD 6 (perhaps a memory of it influenced Pilate's handling of the case of a Galilean among whose disciples was a Zealot) but a real distinction from Jewish nationalism came with the great Jewish rising of AD 66. This was the most important in the whole history of Jewry under the empire, when the extremists gained the upper hand in Judaea and took over Jerusalem. The Jewish historian Josephus has recorded the atrocious struggle which followed, the final storming of the Temple, the headquarters of resistance, and its burning after the Roman victory. Before this, the unhappy inhabitants had been reduced to cannibalism in their struggle to survive. Archaeology has recently revealed at Masada, a little way from the city, what was probably the site of the last stand of the Jews before it, too, fell to the Romans in AD 73.

This was not the end of Jewish turbulence, but it was a turning-point. The extremists never

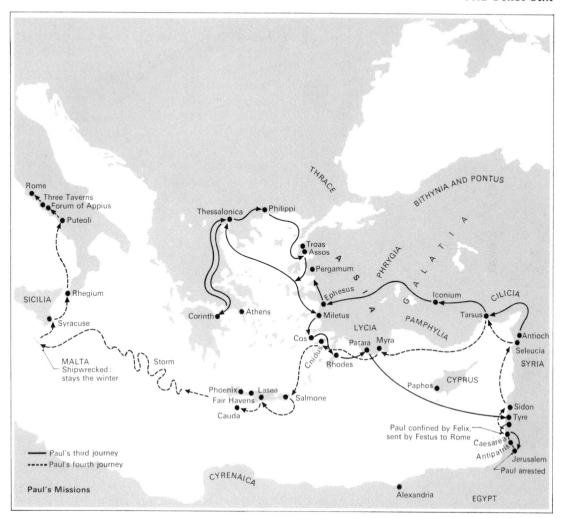

Rome
Three Taverns
Forum of Appius
Puteoli

THRACE

BITHYNIA AND PONTUS

Thessalonica
Philippi

Troas
Assos
Pergamum

MYSIA

PHRYGIA

GALATIA

Ephesus
Iconium

CILICIA

SICILIA
Rhegium

Syracuse

Corinth
Athens
Miletus
Tarsus

LYCIA
PAMPHYLIA

Antioch
Seleucia
SYRIA

MALTA
Shipwrecked:
stays the winter

Storm

Cos
Cnidus
Patara
Myra
Rhodes

Paphos
CYPRUS

Phoenix
Fair Havens
Lasea
Salmone
Cauda

Sidon
Tyre

Paul confined by Felix,
sent by Festus to Rome

Caesarea
Antipatris
Jerusalem
Paul arrested

———— Paul's third journey
- - - - Paul's fourth journey

Paul's Missions

CYRENAICA

Alexandria
EGYPT

enjoyed such support again and must have been discredited. The Law was now more than ever a focus of Jewishness, for Jewish scholars and teachers (after this time, they are more and more designated as 'rabbis') had continued to unfold its meaning in centres other than Jerusalem while the revolt was in progress. Their good conduct may have saved these Jews of the dispersion. Later disturbances were never so important as had been the great revolt, though in AD 117 Jewish riots in Cyrenaica developed into full-scale fighting, and in 132 the last 'Messiah', Simon Bar Kochba, launched another revolt in Judaea. But the Jews emerged with their special status at law still intact. Jerusalem had been

taken from them (Hadrian made it an Italian colony, which Jews might enter only once a year), but their religion was granted the privilege of having a special officer, a patriarch, with sovereignty over it and they were allowed exemption from the obligations of Roman law which might conflict with their religious duties. This was the end of a volume of Jewish history. For the next eighteen hundred years Jewish history was to be the story of the communities of the *diaspora* (dispersion), until a national state was again established in Palestine among the debris of the Turkish empire.

The nationalists of Judaea apart, Jews were for a long time thereafter safe enough in the

The crushing of the Jewish Revolt in AD 66 was commemorated as a great triumph of Roman arms. On the Arch of Titus in Rome were placed reliefs, this one recording the bringing to Rome from the Temple of the Menorah, the table of the shewbread and the sacred trumpets, all of them spoils of war.

empire during the troubled years. Christians did less well, though their religion was not much distinguished from Judaism by the authorities; it was, after all, only a variant of Jewish monotheism with, presumably, the same claims to make. It first attracted the hostility not of Romans but of Jews, as the Crucifixion itself, the martyrdom of Stephen and the adventures of Paul had shown. It was a Jewish king, Herod Agrippa, who, according to the author of the Acts of the Apostles, first persecuted the community at Jerusalem. It has even appeared plausible to some scholars that Nero, seeking a scapegoat for a great fire at Rome in AD 64, should have had the Christians pointed out to him by hostile Jews. Whatever the source of this persecution, in which, according to popular Christian tradition, St Peter and St Paul both perished, and which was accompanied by horrific and bloody scenes in the arena, it seems to have been the end of any official attention by

Rome to the Christians for a long time. The Christians did not take up arms against the Romans in the Jewish revolts, and this must have soothed official susceptibilities with regard to them.

When they emerge in the administrative records as worth notice by government it is in the early second century AD. This is because of the overt disrespect which Christians showed in refusing to sacrifice to the emperor and the Roman deities. This was their distinction. Jews had a right to refuse; they had possessed a historic cult which the Romans respected – as they always respected such cults – when they took Judah under their rule. The Christians were now clearly seen as distinct from other Jews and were a recent creation. Yet the Roman attitude was that although Christianity was not legal it should not be the subject of general persecution. If, on the other hand, breaches of the law were alleged – and the refusal to sacrifice might be one – then the authorities should punish when the allegations were specific and shown in court to be well founded. This led to many acts of martyrdom, as Christians refused the well-intentioned attempts of Roman civil servants to persuade them to sacrifice or abjure their god, but it was not anything like a systematic attempt to eradicate the sect.

Indeed, the authorities' hostility was much less dangerous than that of the Christians' fellow-subjects. As the second century passed, there is more evidence of pogroms and popular attacks on Christians, who were not protected by the authorities since they followed an illegal religion. They may sometimes have been acceptable scapegoats for the administration or lightning-conductors diverting dangerous currents. It was easy for the popular mind of a superstitious age to attribute to Christians the offences of the gods which led to famine, flood, plague and other natural disasters. Other equally convincing explanations of these things were lacking in a world with no other technique of explaining natural disaster. Christians were alleged to practice black magic, incest, even cannibalism (an idea no doubt explicable in terms of misleading accounts of the eucharist). They met secretly at night. More specifically and acutely, though we cannot be sure of the scale of this, the Christians threatened by their control of their members the whole customary structure which regulated and defined the proper relations of parents and children, husbands and wives, masters and slaves. They proclaimed that in Christ there was neither bond nor free and that he had come to bring not peace but a sundering sword to families and friends. It is not hard, therefore, to understand the violent outbursts in the big provincial towns, such as that at Smyrna in AD 165, or Lyons in AD 177. They were the popular aspect of an intensification of opposition to Christianity which had an intellectual counterpart in the first attacks on the new cult by pagan writers.

Persecution was not the only danger facing the early Church. Possibly it was the least grave. A much more serious one was that it might develop into just another cult of the kind of which many examples could be seen in the Roman empire and, in the end, be engulfed like them in the magical morass of ancient religion. All over the Near East could be found examples of the 'mystery religions', whose core was the initiation of the believer into the occult knowledge of a devotion centred on a particular god (the Egyptian Isis was a popular one, the Persian Mithras another). Almost always the believer was offered the chance to identify himself with the divine being in a ceremony which involved a simulated death and resurrection and thus overcame mortality. Such cults offered, through their impressive rituals, the peace and liberation from the temporal which many craved. They were very popular.

That there was a real danger that Christianity might develop in this way is shown by the importance in the second century of the Gnostics. Their name derives from the Greek word *gnosis*, meaning 'knowledge': the knowledge the Christian Gnostics claimed was a secret, esoteric tradition, not revealed to all Christians but only to a few (one version said only to the Apostles and the sect to which it had subsequently descended). Some of their ideas came from Zoroastrian, Hindu and Buddhist sources which stressed the conflict of matter and spirit in a way which distorted the Judaeo-Christian tradition; some came from astrology and even magic. There was always a temptation in such a dualism, the attribution of evil and good to opposing principles and entities and the denial of the goodness of the material creation. The Gnostics were haters of this world and in some of their systems this led to the pessimism typical of the mystery cults; salvation was only possible by the acquisition of arcane knowledge, secrets of an initiated elect. A few Gnostics even saw Christ not as the saviour who confirmed and renewed a covenant but as one who delivered men from Yahweh's error. It was a dangerous creed in whatever form it came, for it cut at the roots of hopefulness which was the heart of the Christian revelation. It turned its back on the redemption of the here and now of which Christians could never wholly despair, since they accepted the Judaic tradition that God made the world and that it was good.

In the second century, with its communities scattered throughout the *diaspora* and their organizational foundations fairly firmly settled, Christianity thus seems to stand at a parting of ways, either of which could prove fatal to it.

Had it turned its back on the implications of Paul's work and remained merely a Jewish heresy, it would at best have eventually been reabsorbed into the Judaic tradition; on the other hand, a flight from a Jewry which rejected it might have driven Christians into the Hellenistic world of the mystery cults or the despair of the Gnostics. Thanks to a handful of men, it escaped both.

The achievement of the Fathers of the Church who navigated these perils was, for all its moral and pietistic content, above all intellectual. They were stimulated by their danger. Irenaeus who succeeded the martyred Bishop of Lyons in AD 177, provided the first great outline of Christian doctrine, a creed and a definition of the scriptural canon. All of these set off Christianity from Judaism. But he wrote also against the background of the challenge of Gnostic and other heretical beliefs. In AD 172 the first Council met to reject Gnostic doctrines. Christian doctrine was squeezed into intellectual respectability by the need to resist the pressures of competitors. Heresy and orthodoxy were born twins. One of the pilots who steered an emerging Christian theology through this period was the prodigiously learned Clement of Alexandria, a Christian Platonist (perhaps born in Athens), through whom Christians were brought to an understanding of what the Hellenistic tradition might mean apart from the mysteries. In particular, he directed Christians to the thought of Plato. To his even greater pupil, Origen, he transmitted the thought that God's truth was a reasonable truth, a belief which could attract men educated in the stoic view of reality.

The intellectual drive of the early Fathers and the inherent social appeal of Christianity made it possible for it to utilize the huge possibilities of diffusion and expansion inherent in the structure of the classical and later Roman world. Its teachers could move freely and talk and write to one another in Greek. It had the great advantage of emerging in a religious age; the sheer credulousness of the second century is a monstrosity which cloaks deep longings. There is a sense in them that the classical world is already run-

A fragment of a mosaic in a third-century Roman tomb, showing the assimilation of the Christ-figure to the pagan sun-god, riding his chariot across the sky.

ning out of vigour; the Greek capital needed replenishment and one outcome was a search for new ways in religion. Philosophy had become a religious quest and rationalism or scepticism appealed only to an infinitesimally small minority. Yet this promising setting was also a challenge to the Church; early Christianity has to be seen always in the context of thriving competitors. To be born in a religious age was a threat as well as an advantage. How successfully Christianity survived the threat and seized its opportunity was only to be seen in the crisis of the third century, when the classical world all but collapsed and survived only by colossal, and in the end mortal, concession.

*Among the oriental cults which spread widely
throughout the empire, one of the most successful
was that of the ancient Egyptian goddess Isis.
A Coptic fresco of the third century here depicts
her with her son Harpocrates, god of silence
(hence his finger before his mouth). There is an
obvious similarity to Christian iconography
of the Virgin and Child. Such parallels could go
deeper, too: the myth of Osiris, consort of Isis,
centred upon his death and resurrection.*

8 The waning of the classical West

After 200 there are many signs that Romans were beginning to look back on the past in a new way. Men had always talked of golden ages in the past, indulging in a conventional, literary nostalgia. But the third century brought something new, a sense of conscious decline.

Historians have spoken of a 'crisis' during it. Its most obvious expressions were in fact surmounted and the changes Romans carried out or accepted by 300 gave a new lease of life to much of classical Mediterranean civilization. They may even have been decisive in ensuring that it would in the end transmit so much of itself to the future. Yet the changes themselves took a toll, for some of them were essentially destructive of the spirit of that civilization. Somewhere about the beginning of the fourth century we can sense that the balance has tipped against the Mediterranean heritage. It is easier to feel it than to see what was the crucial moment. The signs are a sudden multiplication of ominous innovations – the administrative structure of the empire is rebuilt on new principles, its ideology is transformed, the religion of a once-obscure Jewish sect becomes established orthodoxy, and, physically, large tracts of terri-

The circus became under the late empire the centre and focus of factional rivalries which awoke the sort of loyalties today imaginable only in terms of the devotion given to well-known football teams or shown by the enthusiasts of a major political party. This fourth-century mosaic shows a consul officiating from his chariot at the circus, perhaps by starting the races.

tory are given up to settlers from outside, alien immigrants. In another hundred years the consequence of these changes is apparent in political and cultural disintegration.

The ups and downs of imperial authority mattered a lot in this process. Classical civilization had come by 200 to be coterminous with the empire and was dominated by the conception of *romanitas*, the Roman way of doing things. Because of this, the weaknesses of the structure of government were fundamental to what was going wrong. The imperial office had long since ceased to be held, as Augustus had carefully pretended, by the agent of the Senate and people; the reality was a despotic monarch, his rule tempered only by such practical considerations as the placating of the Praetorian Guard on which he depended. A round of civil wars which followed the accession of the last, inadequate, Antonine emperor in 180 opened a terrible era. This wretched man, Commodus, was strangled by a wrestler at the bidding of his concubine and chamberlain in 192, but this solved nothing. From the struggles of four 'emperors' in the months following his death there finally emerged an African, Septimius Severus, who strove to base the empire again on heredity, attempting to link his own family with the Antonine succession and thus to deal with one fundamental constitutional weakness.

This was really to deny the fact of his own success. Severus, like his rivals, had been the candidate of a provincial army. Soldiers were the real makers of emperors throughout the third century and their power lay at the root of the empire's tendency to fragment. Yet the soldiers could not be dispensed with; indeed, because of the barbarian threat, now present on several frontiers simultaneously, the army had to be enlarged and pampered. Here was a dilemma to face emperors for the next century. Severus' son Caracalla, who prudently began his reign by bribing the soldiers heavily, was none the less murdered by them in the end.

In theory the Senate still appointed the emperor. In fact it had little effective power except in so far as it could commit its prestige to one of a number of contending candidates. This was not much of an asset but still had some importance so long as the moral effect of maintaining the old forms was still significant. It was inevitable, though, that the arrangements should intensify the latent antagonism of Senate and emperor. Severus gave more power to officers drawn from the equestrian class; Caracalla inferred that a purge of the Senate would help and took this further step towards autocratic rule. More military emperors followed him and soon there was for the first time one who did not come from the senatorial ranks, though he was from the equites. Worse was to follow. In 235 Maximinus, a huge ex-ranker from the Rhine legions, contested the prize with an octogenarian from Africa who had the backing of the African army and, eventually, of the Senate. Many emperors were murdered by their troops; one died fighting his own commander-in-chief in battle (his conqueror subsequently being slain by the Goths after his betrayal to them by one of his other officers). It was a dreadful century; altogether, twenty-two emperors came and went during it and that number does not include mere pretenders (or such semi-emperors as Postumus, who for a while maintained himself in Gaul, thus pre-figuring a later division of the empire).

Though Severus' reforms had for a time improved matters, the fragility of his successors' position accelerated a decline in administration. Caracalla was the last emperor to try to broaden the basis of taxation by making all free inhabitants of the empire Roman citizens and thus liable to inheritance taxes, but no fundamental fiscal reform was attempted. Perhaps decline was inevitable, given the emergencies to be faced. With irregularity and extemporization went growing rapacity and corruption as those with power or office used it to protect themselves. This reflected another problem, the economic weakness which the empire was showing in the third century.

Few generalizations are safe about what this meant to the consumer and supplier. For all its elaboration and organization around a network of cities, the economic life of the empire was overwhelmingly agrarian. Its bedrock was the estate of the countryside, the *villa*, large or small, which was both the basic unit of production and also, in many places, of society. Such estates were the source of subsistence for all those who lived on them (and they were, effectively, nearly all the rural population). Probably, therefore, most people in the countryside were less affected by the long-term swings of the economy than by requisitioning and heavier taxation which resulted from the empire ceasing to expand; the armies had to be supported from a narrower base. Sometimes, too, the land was devastated by fighting. But peasants lived at subsistence level, had always been poor, and continued to be so, whether bond or free. As times got worse, some sought to bind themselves as serfs, which suggests an economy in which money was in retreat before payment in goods and services. It also probably reflects another impact of troubled times such as drove peasants to the towns or to banditry; men everywhere sought protection.

Requisitioning and higher taxation may in some places have helped to produce depopulation – though the fourth century provides more evidence of this than the third – and to this extent were self-defeating. In any case, they were likely to be inequitable, for many of the rich were exempt from taxation and the owners of the estates cannot have suffered much in inflationary times unless they were imprudent. The continuity of many of the great estate-owning families in antiquity is impressive and does not suggest that the troubles of the third century bit deeply into their resources.

The administration and the army felt most of the effects of economic troubles, and particularly the major ill of the century, inflation. Its sources and extent are complex and still disputed. In part it derived from an official debasement of the coinage which was aggravated by the need to pay tribute in bullion to barbarians who from time to time were best placated by this means. But barbarian incursions themselves often helped to disrupt supply, and this again told against the cities, where prices rose. Because the soldiers' pay was fixed it fell in real value (this made them, of course, more susceptible to generals who offered lavish bribes). Although the overall impact is hard to assess, it has been suggested that money may have fallen during the century to about one-fiftieth of its value at the beginning.

The damage done by this is obvious both in the towns and in imperial fiscal practice. From the third century onwards many towns shrank in size and prosperity; their early medieval successors were only pale reflexions of the important places they once had been. One cause was the increasing demands of the imperial tax-collectors. From the beginning of the fourth century the depreciation of coin led imperial officials to levy taxes in kind – they could often be used directly to supply local garrisons but were also the means of payment to civil servants – and this not only made the government more unpopular, but also the curiales or municipal office-holders who had the task of raising these impositions. By 300 they often had to be forced to take office, a sure sign that a once-sought-after dignity had become a strenuous obligation. Some towns suffered from actual physical damage, too, especially those in the frontier regions. As the third century wore on, towns well within the frontier significantly began to rebuild (or build for the first time) walls for their protection. Rome began again to fortify itself soon after 270.

Meanwhile, the army steadily grew bigger. If

Stilicho, the last general of the western empire, was himself the son of a Vandal, but he twice saved Italy from barbarian invasion with the aid of armies composed of Visigoths, Alans and even Huns. When in the end he turned against the eastern empire, the emperor Honorius, his godson and former pupil, permitted Stilicho's murder. Three months later, Alaric sacked Rome.

313

the barbarians were to be kept out it had to be paid, fed and equipped. If the barbarians were not kept out there would be tribute to pay to them instead. And there was not only the barbarian to contend with. Only in Africa was the imperial frontier reasonably secure against Rome's neighbours (because, effectively, there were no neighbours there). In Asia things were much grimmer. Ever since the days of Sulla a cold war had gone on with Parthia which sometimes flared up into full-scale campaigning. Two things prevented the Romans and Parthians from ever really settling down peacefully. One was the overlapping of their spheres of interest. This was most obvious in Armenia, a kingdom which was alternately a buffer and a shuttlecock between them for a century and a half, but the Parthians also dabbled in the disturbed waters of Jewish unrest, another sensitive matter for Rome. The other factor making for disturbance was the temptation presented to Rome time and time again by Parthia's own internal dynastic troubles.

Such facts had led in the second century AD to intense fighting over Armenia, its details often obscure. Severus eventually penetrated Mesopotamia but had to withdraw; the Mesopotamian valleys were too far away. The Romans were trying to do too much and faced the classic problem of over-extended imperialism. But their opponents were tiring and at low ebb, too. Parthian written records are fragmentary, but the tale of exhaustion and growing incompetence emerges from a coinage declining into unintelligibility and blurred derivations from earlier Hellenized designs.

In the third century Parthia disappeared, but the threat to Rome from the East did not. A turning-point was reached in the history of the old area of Persian civilization. In about 225 a king called Ardashir (later known in the West as Artaxerxes) killed the last king of Parthia and was crowned in Ctesiphon. He was to re-create the Achaemenid empire of Persia under a new dynasty, the Sassanids; it would be Rome's greatest antagonist for more than four hundred years. There was much continuity here; the

Sassanid empire was Zoroastrian, as Parthia had been, and evoked the Achaemenid tradition as Parthia had done.

Within a few years the Persians had invaded Syria and opened three centuries of struggle with the empire. In the third century there was not a decade without war. The Persians conquered Armenia and took one emperor (Valerian) prisoner. Then they were driven from Armenia and Mesopotamia in 297. This gave the Romans a frontier on the Tigris, but it was not one they could keep for ever. Neither could the Persians keep their conquests. The outcome was a long-drawn-out and ding-dong contest. A sort of equilibrium grew up in the fourth and fifth centuries and only in the sixth did it begin to break down. Meanwhile, commercial ties appeared. Though trade at the frontier was officially limited to three designated towns, important colonies of Persian merchants came to live in the great cities of the empire. Persia, moreover, lay across trade routes to India and China which were as important to Roman exporters as to those who wanted oriental silk, cotton and spices. Yet these ties did not offset other forces. When not at war, the two empires tended to co-exist with cold hostility; their relations were complicated by communities and peoples settled on both sides of the frontier, and there was always the danger of the strategic balance being upset by a change in one of the buffer kingdoms – Armenia, for instance. The final round of open struggle was long put off, but came at last in the sixth century.

This is to jump too far ahead for the present; by then huge changes had taken place in the Roman empire which have still to be explained. The conscious dynamism of the Sassanid monarchy was only one of the pressures encouraging them. Another came from the barbarians along the Danube and Rhine frontiers. The origins of the folk-movements which propelled them forward in the third century and thereafter must be sought in a long development and are less important than the outcome. These peoples grew more insistent, acted in larger groupings and had, in the end, to be allowed to settle inside Roman

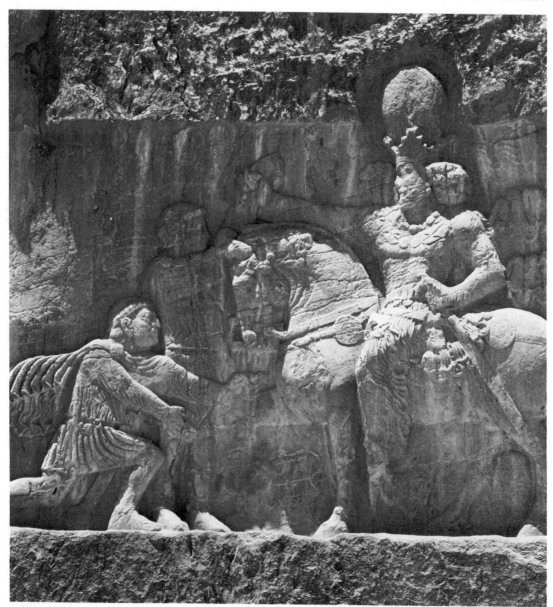

territory. Here they were first engaged as soldiers to protect the empire against other barbarians and then, gradually, began to take part in running the empire themselves.

In 200 this still lay in the future; all that was clear then was that a new intensity of pressure was building up. The most important barbarian peoples involved were the Franks and Alamanni on the Rhine and the Goths on the

The triumph of a Sassanid emperor. Sapor I looks down from his charger on the Roman prisoner – the emperor Philip the Arab – kneeling in supplication. Valerian stands at his side bound by the wrists. Sapor was one of the most successful emperors of his line, who mastered the Kushans of the North-East frontier as well as pursuing a victorious campaign in the West.

315

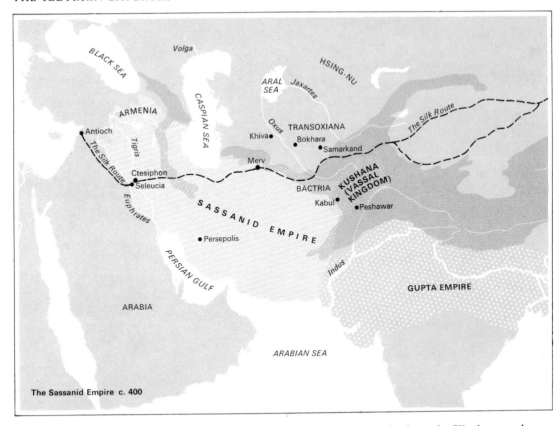

The Sassanid Empire c. 400

lower Danube. From about 230 the empire was trying to hold them off and the cost of over-extension was soon apparent when preoccupation with Persia led one emperor to make concessions to the Alamanni. When his immediate successors added to their Persian burdens their own quarrels the Goths took advantage of a promising situation and invaded Moesia, the province immediately south of the Danube, killing an emperor there *en passant* in 251. Five years later, the Franks crossed the Rhine. The Alamanni followed and got as far as Milan. Gothic armies invaded Greece and raided Asia and the Aegean from the sea. Within a few years the European dams seemed to give way everywhere at once.

The scale of these incursions is not easy to establish. Perhaps the barbarians could never field an army of more than twenty or thirty thousand. But this was too much at any one place for the imperial army. Its backbone was provided by recruits from the Illyrian provinces; appropriately, it was a succession of emperors of Illyrian stock who turned the tide. Much of what they did was simple good soldiering and intelligent extemporization. They recognized priorities; the main dangers lay in Europe and had to be dealt with first. Alliance with Palmyra helped to buy time against Persia. Losses were cut; trans-Danubian Dacia was abandoned in 270. The army was reorganized to provide effective mobile reserves in each of the main danger areas. This was all the work of Aurelian, whom the Senate significantly called 'Restorer of the Roman empire'. But the cost was heavy. A more fundamental reconstruction was implicit if the work of the Illyrian emperors was to survive and this was the aim of Diocletian. A soldier of proven bravery, he sought to restore the Augustan tradition but brought about a revolutionary transformation of the empire instead.

He had in fact an administrator's genius rather than a soldier's. Without being especially imaginative, he had an excellent grasp of organization and principles, a love of order and great skill in picking and trusting men to whom he could delegate. He was also energetic. Diocletian's capital was wherever the imperial retinue found itself; it moved about the empire, passing a year here, a couple of months there, and sometimes only a day or two in the same place. The heart of the reforms which emerged from this court was the division of the empire so that it could be delivered at once from the dangers of internal quarrels between pretenders in remote provinces and from the over-extension of its administrative and military resources. This he sought by appointing a co-emperor, Maximian, in 285 with responsibility for the empire west of a line running from the Danube to Dalmatia. The two *augusti* were subsequently each given a *caesar* as co-adjutor; these were to be both their assistants and successors, thus making possible an orderly transfer of power. In fact, the machine of succession only once operated as Diocletian intended, at his own abdication and that of his colleague, but the practical separation of administration in two imperial structures was not reversed. After this time emperors had to accept a large measure of delegation even when there was nominally still only one for the whole empire.

There also now emerged explicitly a new conception of the imperial office. No longer was the title *princeps* employed; the emperors were the creation of the army, not the Senate, and were deferred to in terms recalling the semi-divine kingship of oriental courts. Practically, they acted through pyramidal bureaucracies. 'Dioceses' responsible directly to the emperors through their 'vicars' grouped provinces much smaller and about twice as numerous as the old ones had been. The senatorial monopoly of governmental power had long since gone; senatorial rank now meant in effect merely a social distinction (membership of the wealthy land-owning class) or occupation of one of the important bureaucratic posts. Equestrian rank dis-

The lands between Dacia and Thrace, now divided between Bulgaria and Romania, were known to the Romans as the province of Moesia. This funerary stele comes from this region and shows how the primitive traditions of barbarian art could survive within the frontiers of the empire.

317

Palmyra, an oasis city of the Syrian desert, was a wealthy centre of trade brought by caravans of camels such as the one shown in this relief. Its golden age came in the middle of the third century AD when one of its kings was recognized as an emperor of Rome. But in 273 a Roman army sacked the city and it never recovered its former prosperity.

appeared.

The military establishment of the Tetrarchy, as it was called, was much larger (and, therefore, more expensive) than that laid down originally by Augustus. The theoretical mobility of the legions, deeply dug into long-occupied garrisons, was abandoned and the army of the frontiers was broken up into smaller units which remained permanently in the same places and provided some contingents for new mobile forces, grouped in smaller units than the old legions. Conscription was reintroduced. Something like a half-million men were under arms.

Their direction was wholly separated from the civilian government of the provinces with which it had once been fused.

The results of this system do not seem to have been exactly what Diocletian envisaged. None the less, they included a considerable measure of military recovery and stabilization, but its cost was enormous. An army which doubled in size in a century had to be paid for by a population which had probably grown smaller. Heavy taxation not only compromised the loyalty of the empire's subjects and encouraged corruption; it also required a close control of social arrangements so that the tax base should not be eroded. There was great administrative pressure against social mobility; the peasant, for example, was obliged to stay where he was recorded at the census. Another celebrated, though so far as can be seen totally unsuccessful, example was the attempt to regulate wages and prices throughout the empire by a freeze. Such efforts, like those to raise more taxation, meant a bigger civil service, and as the number of administrators increased so, of course, did the overheads of government.

In the end Diocletian probably achieved most by facilitating the expression of changed attitudes to the imperial office itself. The new religious aura which it acquired was a response to a real problem. Somehow under the strain of continued usurpation and failure the empire had ceased to be unquestioningly accepted. This was not merely dislike of high taxation or fear of its growing numbers of secret police. Its ideological basis had been eroded and it could not focus men's loyalties. A crisis of civilization was going on as well as a crisis of government. The spiritual matrix of the classical world was breaking up, neither state nor civilization was any longer to be taken for granted and they needed a new ethos before they could be.

A new emphasis on the unique status of the emperor and his sacral rôle was one early response to this need. Consciously, Diocletian acted as a saviour, a Jupiter-like figure holding back chaos. Something in this spoke of affinities with those thinkers of the late classical world who saw life as a perpetual struggle of good and evil. Yet this was a vision not Greek or Roman at all, but oriental. The acceptance of a new vision of the emperor's relation to the gods, and therefore of a new conception of the official cult, did not bode well for the traditional practical tolerance of the Greek world. Decisions about worship might now decide the fate of the empire.

These possibilities shaped the history of the Christian Churches for both good and ill. In the end Christianity was to be the legatee of Rome. Many religious sects have risen from the position of persecuted minorities to become establishments in their own right. What sets the Christian Church apart is that this took place within the uniquely comprehensive structure of the late Roman empire, so that it both attached itself to and strengthened the lifeline of classical civilization, with enormous consequences not only for itself but for Europe and ultimately the world.

At the beginning of the third century mis-

sionaries had already carried the faith to the non-Jewish peoples of Asia Minor and North Africa. Particularly in North Africa, Christianity had its first mass successes in the towns and it long remained a predominantly urban phenomenon. But it was still a matter of minorities. Throughout the empire, the old gods and the local deities had the allegiance of the peasant. It has been suggested that by the end of the century Christians may have made up only about a tenth of the population of the empire. More striking were some signs of official favour and even concession. One emperor was nominally a Christian and another had included Jesus Christ among the gods honoured privately in his household. Such contacts with the court illustrate an interplay of Jewish and classical culture which is an important part of the story of the process by which Christianity took root in the empire. Perhaps St Paul, the Jew who could talk to Athenians in terms they understood, had launched this. Later, early in the second century, Justin Martyr, a Palestinian Greek, had striven to show that Christianity had a debt to Greek philosophy. This had a political point; cultural identification with the classical tradition helped to rebut the charge of disloyalty to the empire. If a Christian could stand in the ideological heritage of the Hellenistic world he could also be a good citizen, and Justin's rational Christianity (for which, however, he was martyred in about 165) envisaged a revelation of the Divine Reason in which all the great philosophers and prophets had partaken, Plato among them, but which was only complete in Christ. Others were to follow similar lines, notably the learned Clement of Alexandria, who strove consciously to integrate pagan scholarship with Christianity, and another Alexandrian, Origen, whose exact teaching is still debated because of the disappearance of many of his writings. The North African Christian, Tertullian, had contemptuously asked what the Academy had to do with the Church; he was answered by the Fathers who deliberately employed the conceptual armoury of Greek philosophy to provide a statement of the Faith which

Two reliefs, a century or so apart, show the gradual blurring of classical and Christian ideas. The first is from the sarcophagus of a philosopher, the second, from an ivory casket of the fourth century, shows Christ teaching the Apostles. The latter is clearly modelled on the first.

anchored Christianity to rationality as St Paul had not done.

When coupled to its promise of salvation after death and the fact that the Christian life could be lived in a purposeful and optimistic way, such developments might lead us to suppose that Christians were by the third century confident about the future. In fact, favourable portents were much less striking than the persecutions so prominent in the history of the early Church. There were two great outbreaks. That of the middle of the century expressed the spiritual crisis of the establishment. It was not only economic strain and military defeat that were troubling the empire, but a dialectic inherent in Roman success itself: the cosmopolitanism which had been so much the mark of the empire was, inevitably, a solvent of the *romanitas* which was less and less a reality and more and more a slogan. The emperor Decius seems to have been convinced that the old recipe of a return to traditional Roman virtue and values could still work; it implied the revival of service to the gods whose benevolence would then be once more deployed in favour of the empire. The Christians, like others, must sacrifice to the Roman tradition, said Decius, and many did, to judge by the certificates issued to save them from persecution; some did not, and died. A few years later, Valerian renewed persecution on the same grounds, though his proconsuls addressed themselves rather to the directing personnel and the property of the Church – its buildings and books – than to the mass of believers. Thereafter, persecution ebbed, and the Church resumed its shadowy, tolerated existence just below the horizon of official attention.

A scribe (shown at the top) and a woman depicted in an attitude of prayer are the subjects of this example of an early Christian mosaic from North Africa. Made in the fourth or fifth century it decorated a double tomb (whose occupants were presumably the two persons shown) in a martyr's chapel at Tabarka.

Persecution had shown, nevertheless, that it would require great efforts and prolonged determination to eradicate the new sect; it may even have been already beyond the capacities of Roman government to carry out such an eradication. The exclusiveness and isolation of early Christianity had waned. Christians were increasingly prominent in local affairs in the Asian and African provinces. Bishops were often public figures with whom officials expected to do business; the development of distinct traditions within the Faith (those of the churches of Rome, Alexandria and Carthage being the most important) spoke for the degree to which it was rooted in local society and could express local needs.

Outside the empire, too, there had been signs that favourable conjunctures for the new religion might lie ahead. The local rulers of the client states under the shadow of Persia could not afford to neglect any source of local support. Respect for widely held religious views was at least prudent. In Syria, Cilicia and Cappadocia Christianity had been very successful in its missionary work and in some towns Christians formed a social élite. Simple superstition was another factor in convincing kings; the Christian god might prove powerful and it could hardly be damaging to insure against his ill-will. Thus Christianity's political and civic prospects improved.

Christians noted with some satisfaction that their persecutors did not prosper; the Goths slew Decius, and Valerian was said to have been skinned alive by the Persians (and stuffed). But Diocletian did not appear to draw any conclusions from this and in 303 launched the last great Roman persecution. It was not at first harsh. The main targets were Christian officials, clergy and the books and buildings of the Church. The books were to be handed over for burning but for some time there was no death penalty for failing to sacrifice. (Many Christians none the less did sacrifice, the bishop at Rome among them.) Constantius, the Caesar of the West, did not enforce the persecution after 305 when Diocletian abdicated, though his eastern colleague (Diocletian's successor Galerius) felt strongly about it, ordering a general sacrifice on pain of death. This meant that persecution was worst in Egypt and Asia where it was kept up a few years longer. But before this it had been cut across by the complicated politics which led to the emergence of the emperor Constantine the Great.

This was the son of Constantius, who died in Britain in 306, a year after his accession as *Augustus*. Constantine was there at the time and although he had not been his father's Caesar he was hailed as emperor by the army at York. A troubled period of nearly two decades followed. Its intricate struggles demonstrated the failure of Diocletian's arrangements for the peaceful transmission of the empire and only ended in 324 when Constantine reunited the empire under one ruler.

By this time he had already addressed himself vigorously and effectively to its problems though with more success as a soldier than as an administrator. Often with barbarian recruits, he built up a powerful field army distinct from the frontier guards; it was stationed in cities within the empire. This was a strategically sound decision which proved itself in the fighting power the empire showed in the East for the next two centuries. Constantine also disbanded the Praetorian Guard and created a new, German, bodyguard. He restored a stable gold currency and paved the way to the abolition of payments of taxes in kind and the restoration of a money economy. His fiscal reforms had more mixed results but attempted some readjustment of the weight of taxation so that more should be borne by the rich. None of these things, though, so struck contemporaries as his attitude to Christianity.

A huge seated statue of Constantine, more than 30 feet tall, dominated his basilica in Rome. It represented a new kind of imperial iconography setting the emperor far above other men and foreshadowing the later exaltation of the emperor's image under the Christian empire of Byzantium.

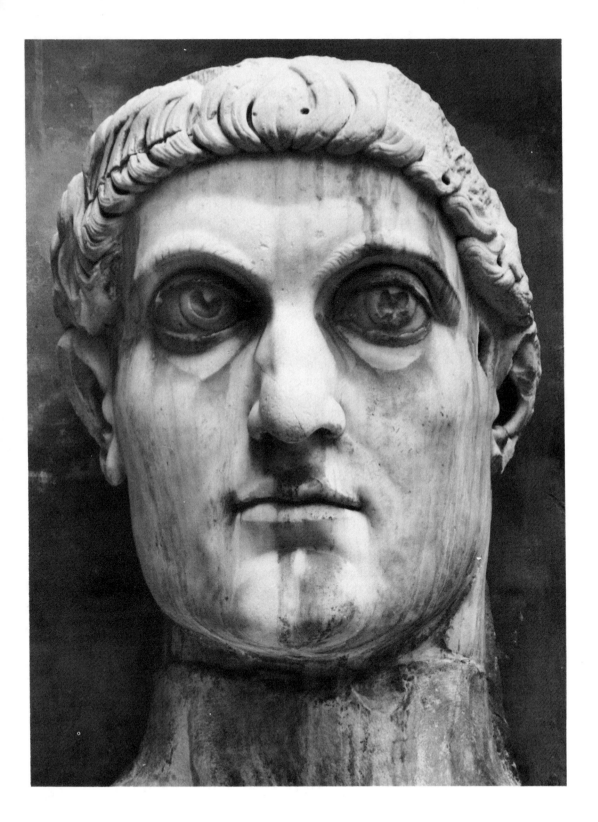

Constantine was the emperor who gave the Church official houseroom. He thus played a more important part in shaping its future than any other Christian layman and was to be called the 'thirteenth Apostle'. Yet his personal relationship to Christianity was complicated. He grew up intellectually with the monotheistic predisposition of many late classical men and was in the end undoubtedly a convinced believer (it was not then unusual for Christians to do as he did and postpone baptism until their deathbed). But he believed from fear and hope, for the god he worshipped was a god of power. His first adherence was to the sun-god whose sign he bore and whose cult was already officially associated with that of the emperor. Then, in 312, on the eve of battle and as a result of what he believed to be a vision he ordered his soldiers to put on their shields a Christian monogram. This showed a willingness to show suitable respect to whatever gods there might be. He won the battle and thenceforth, though continuing publicly to acknowledge the cult of the sun, he began to show important favours to the Christians and their god.

One manifestation of this was an edict the following year which was issued by another of the contenders for the empire, after agreement with Constantine at Milan. It restored to Christians their property, and granted them the toleration that other religions enjoyed. The justification may reveal Constantine's own thinking as well as his wish to arrive at a satisfactory compromise formula with his colleague, for it explained its provisions by the hope 'that whatever divinity dwells in the heavenly seat may be appeased and be propitious towards us and to all who are placed under our authority'. Constantine went on to make considerable gifts of property to the churches, favouring, in particular, that of Rome. Besides providing important tax concessions to the clergy, an unlimited right to receive bequests was conferred on the Church. Yet for years his coins continued to honour pagan gods, notably the 'Unconquered Sun'.

Constantine gradually came to see himself as having a quasi-sacerdotal rôle, and this was of the first importance in the further evolution of the imperial office. He saw himself as responsible to God for the well-being of the Church to which he more and more publicly and unequivocally adhered. After 320 the sun no longer appeared on his coins and his soldiers had to attend church parades. But he was always cautious of the susceptibilities of his pagan subjects. Though he later despoiled temples of their gold while building splendid Christian churches and encouraging converts by preferment, he did not cease to tolerate the old cults.

In some of Constantine's work (like that of Diocletian) there was the development of things latent and implicit in the past, an extension of earlier precedents. This was true of his interventions in the internal affairs of the Church. As early as 272, the Christians of Antioch had appealed to the emperor to remove a bishop and Constantine himself in 316 tried to settle a controversy in North Africa by installing a bishop of Carthage against the will of a local sectarian group known as Donatists. Constantine came to believe that the emperor owed to God more than a grant of freedom to the Church or even an endowment. His conception of his rôle evolved towards that of the guarantor and, if need be, the imposer of the unity which God required as the price of His continuing favour. When he turned on the Donatists it was this view of his duty which gave them the unhappy distinction of being the first schismatics to be persecuted by a Christian government. Constantine was the creator of Caesaropapism, the belief that the secular ruler has divine authority to settle religious belief, and of the notion of established religion in Europe for the next thousand years.

Constantine's greatest act in the ordering of religion came just after he had formally declared himself a Christian in 324 (a declaration preceded by another victory over an imperial rival who had, interestingly, been persecuting Christians). This was the calling of the first ecumenical council, the Council of Nicaea. It met for the first time in 325, nearly 300 bishops being present, and Constantine presided over it. Its task was to settle the response of the Church to a new heresy, Arianism. Its founder, Arius, taught that the Son did not share the divinity of the Father; though technical and theological, the nice issues to which this gave rise prompted enormous controversy. Grave scandal was alleged by Arius' opponents. Constantine sought to heal the division and the Council laid down a Creed which decided against the Arians, but went on in a second reunion to readmit Arius to communion after suitable declarations. That this did not satisfy all the bishops (and that there were few from the West at Nicaea) was less important than that Constantine had presided at this crucial juncture; this proclaimed the emperor's enjoyment of special authority and responsibility. The Church was clothed in the imperial purple.

There were other great implications, too. Behind the hair-splitting of the theologians lay a great question both of practice and principle: in the new ideological unity given to the empire by the official establishment of Christianity, what was to be the place of diverging Christian traditions which were social and political, as well as liturgical and theological, realities? The churches of Syria and Egypt, for example, were strongly tinctured by their inheritance of thought and custom both from the Hellenistic culture and the popular religion of those regions. The importance of such considerations helps to explain why the practical outcome of Constantine's ecclesiastical policy was less than he had hoped. The Council did not produce an emollient formula to make easier a general reconciliation in a spirit of compromise. Constantine's own attitude to the Arians soon relaxed (in the end, it was to be an Arian bishop who baptized him as he lay dying) but the opponents of Arius, led by the formidable Athanasius, bishop of Alexandria, were relentless. The quarrel remained unsettled when Arius died, and Constantine's own death followed not long after though Arianism was not to prosper in the East. Its last successes, instead, were won

by Arian missionaries to the Germanic tribes of south-east Russia; borne by these barbarian nations, Arianism was to survive until the seventh century in the West – but this is to anticipate.

How much of the Church's rise was in the end inevitable it is not profitable to consider. Certainly – in spite of a North African Christian tradition which saw the state as an irrelevancy – something so positively important as Christianity could hardly have remained for ever unrecognized by the civil power. Yet someone had to begin and Constantine was the man who took the crucial steps which linked Church and

Who is depicted in this ivory, one of the finest surviving from antiquity, is not certainly known; it may be Justinian, it may be another emperor. It is a triumphal piece; Scythians and Indians bring tribute to the emperor, a general stands by with a classical statuette of victory and Christ (at this time still usually portrayed without a beard) raises his hand in blessing.

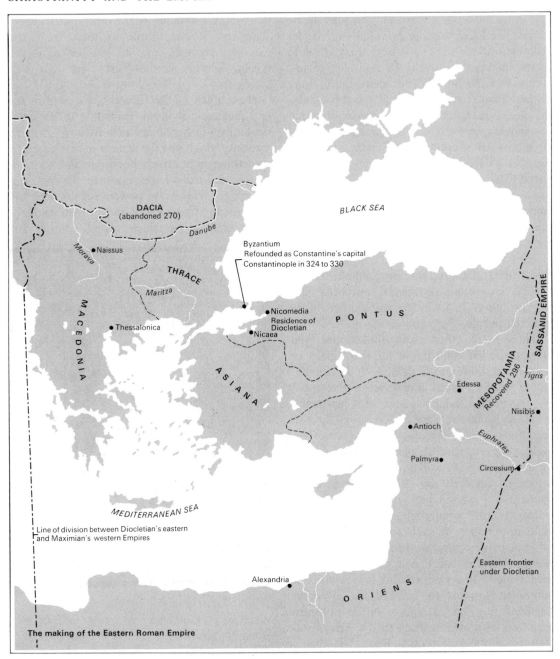

DACIA
(abandoned 270)

Danube

BLACK SEA

Morava

●Naissus

Byzantium
Refounded as Constantine's capital
Constantinople in 324 to 330

THRACE

Maritza

MACEDONIA

●Nicomedia
Residence of
Diocletian

●Nicaea

P O N T U S

●Thessalonica

SASSANID EMPIRE

A S I A N A

MESOPOTAMIA
Recovered 296

Edessa●

Tigris

Nisibis●

●Antioch

Euphrates

Palmyra●

Circesium●

MEDITERRANEAN SEA

Line of division between Diocletian's eastern
and Maximian's western Empires

Eastern frontier
under Diocletian

Alexandria●

O R I E N S

The making of the Eastern Roman Empire

empire for so long as the empire should last. His choices were historically decisive. The Church gained most, for it acquired the charisma of Rome. The empire seemed less changed. Yet Constantine's sons were brought up as Christians and even if the fragility of much in the new establishment was to appear soon after his death in 337, he had registered a decisive break with the tradition of classical Rome. Ultimately, and unwittingly, he was founding Christian Europe and, therefore, the modern world.

One of his decisions only slightly less enduring in its effects was his foundation, 'on the command of God', he said, of a city to rival Rome on the site of the old Greek colony of Byzantium. There, at the entrance to the Black Sea, it was dedicated in 330 as Constantinople. Though his own court remained at Nicomedia and no emperor was to reside there permanently until another fifty years were past, Constantine was again shaping the future. For a thousand years Constantinople would be a Christian capital, unsullied by pagan rites. After that, for five hundred years more, it would be a pagan capital and the constant ambition of would-be successors to its traditions.

Once again, though, this is anticipating too much. We must return to the empire as Constantine left it, still coterminous with civilization itself in Roman eyes. Its frontiers ran for the most part along natural features which recognized, more or less, the demarcations of distinct geographical or historical regions. Hadrian's wall in Britannia was their northern limit; in continental Europe they followed the lines of the Rhine and Danube. The Black Sea coasts north of the mouths of the Danube had been lost to barbarians by 305 BC, but Asia Minor remained in the empire; it stretched as far east as the shifting boundary with Persia. Further south, the Levant coast and Palestine were within a frontier which ran to the Red Sea. The lower Nile valley was still held by the empire and so was the North African coast; the African frontiers were the Atlas and the desert.

This unity was, for all Constantine's great work, in large measure an illusion. As the first experiments with co-emperors had shown, the world of Roman civilization had grown too big for a unified political structure, however desirable the preservation of the myth of unity might be. Growing cultural differentiation between a Greek-speaking East and a Latin-speaking West, the new importance of Asia Minor, Syria and Egypt (in all of which there were large Christian communities) after the establishment of Christianity and the continuing stimulus of direct contact with Asia in the East all drove the point home. After 364 the two parts of the old empire were only once more and then only briefly ruled by the same man. Their institutions diverged further and further. In the East the emperor was a theological as well as a juridical figure; the identity of Empire and Christendom and the emperor's standing as the expression of divine intention were unambiguous. The West, on the other hand, had by 400 already seen adumbrated the distinction of the rôles of Church and State which was to father one of the most creative arguments of European politics. There was an economic contrast, too: the East was populous and could still raise great revenues, while the West was by 300 already unable to feed itself without Africa and the Mediterranean islands. It now seems obvious that two distinct civilizations were to emerge, but it was a long time before any of the participants could see that.

Instead, they saw something much more appalling: the western empire simply disappeared. By 500, when the boundaries of the eastern empire were still much what they had been under Constantine, and his successors were still holding their own against the Persians, the last western emperor had been deposed and his *insignia* sent to Constantinople by a barbarian king who claimed to rule as the eastern emperor's representative in the West.

This is striking: what, actually had collapsed? What had declined or fallen? Fifth-century writers bewailed it so much that it is easy to have the impression, heightened by such dramatic episodes as two sackings of Rome itself, that the whole of society fell apart. This was not so. It was the state apparatus which collapsed, some of its functions ceasing to be carried out, and some passing into other hands. This was quite enough to explain the alarm which was felt. Institutions with a thousand years of history behind them gave way within a half-century. It is hardly surprising that people have asked why ever since.

One explanation is cumulative: the state apparatus in the West gradually seized up after the recovery of the fourth century. The whole concern became too big for the demographic, fiscal and economic base which carried it. The main purpose of raising revenue was to pay for the military machine, but it became more and more difficult to raise enough. There were no more conquests after Dacia to bring in new tribute. Soon the measures adopted to squeeze more taxes out of them drove rich and poor alike to devices for avoiding them. The effect was to make agricultural estates rely more and more upon meeting their own needs and becoming self-supporting, rather than producing for the market. Parallel with this went a crumbling of urban government as trade languished and the rich withdrew to the countryside.

The military result was an army recruited from inferior material, because better could not be paid for. Even the reform of dividing it into mobile and garrison forces had its defects, for the first lost their fighting spirit by being stationed at the imperial residence and becoming used to the pampering and privileges that went with city postings, while the second turned into settled colonists, unwilling to take risks which would jeopardize their homesteads. Another descent in the unending spiral of decline logically followed. A weaker army drove the empire to rely still more on the very barbarians the army was supposed to keep at bay. As they had to be recruited as mercenaries, soothing and conciliatory policies were needed to keep them sweet. This led the Romans to concede more to the barbarians just when the pressure of the Germanic folk-movements was reaching a new climax. Migration and the attractive prospect of paid service with the empire probably counted for much more in the barbarian contribution to imperial collapse than the simple desire for loot. The prospect of booty might animate a raiding-party but could hardly bring down an empire.

At the beginning of the fourth century Germanic peoples were stretched along the whole length of the frontier from the Rhine to the Black Sea, but it was in the south that the most

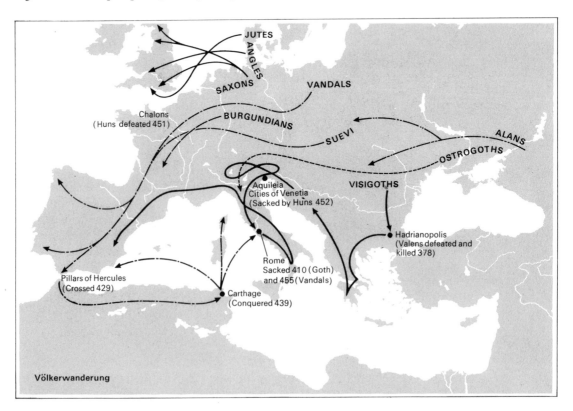

Völkerwanderung

formidable concentration was at that moment assembled. These were the Gothic peoples, Ostrogoth and Visigoth, who waited beyond the Danube. Some of them were already Christian, though in the Arian form. Together with Vandals, Burgundians and Lombards, they made up an east Germanic group. To the north were the west Germans: Franks, Alamanni, Saxons, Frisians and Thuringians. They would move into action in the second phase of the *Völkerwanderung* of the fourth and fifth centuries.

The crisis began in the last quarter of the fourth century. The pressure on the Huns, a formidable nomadic people from central Asia, was mounting after 370. They overran the Ostrogothic territory, defeated the Alans and then turned on the Visigoths near the Dniester. Unable to hold them, the Visigoths fled for refuge to the empire and in 376 were allowed to cross the Danube to settle within the frontier. The Emperor Valens intended to disarm them; it was not done and instead there was fighting. At the battle of Adrianople in 378 the emperor was killed and a Roman army defeated by the Visigoth cavalry. The Visigoths ravaged Thrace.

This was in more than one way a turning-point. Germans had already been employed as soldiers and had risen high in the Roman army; now whole tribes were enrolled as confederates – *foederati*, a word first used in 406 – and entered Roman territory to serve against other barbarians under their own chiefs. A temporary settlement with the Visigoths could not be maintained and the eastern empire was helpless to protect its European territories outside Constantinople, but when the Visigothic armies moved north towards Italy early in the fifth century, they were checked for a while by a Vandal general. By now the imperial position in Italy, the old heart of the empire, was entirely dependent on barbarian auxiliaries and soon even this was not enough; Constantinople might be held, but in 410 Alaric the Goth sacked Rome. After an abortive move to the south, with a view to seizing Africa, the Visigoths again turned north, crossed the Alps into

Gaul and eventually settled as the new kingdom of Toulouse in 419, a Gothic state within the empire, where a Gothic aristocracy shared its overlordship with the old Gallo-Roman landlords.

These are confused events, difficult to follow, but there is still one other major movement of peoples which has to be noticed in order to explain the fifth-century re-making of the European racial and cultural map. In return for their settlement in Aquitania, the western emperor had succeeded in getting the Visigoths to promise that they would help him to clear Spain of other barbarians. Of these the most important were the Vandals. In 406 the Rhine frontier, denuded of soldiers sent to defend Italy against the Visigoths, had given way too and the Vandals and Alans had broken into Gaul, from which they made their way southward, sacking and looting as they went. In 409 they crossed the Pyrenees to establish a Vandal state in Spain. From there they were tempted to Africa twenty years later by a dissident Roman governor who wanted their help. Visigothic attacks encouraged the removal. By 439 they had taken Carthage and the Vandal kingdom of Africa had a naval base. They were to stay there for nearly a century and in 455 they, too, crossed to sack Rome and leave their name to history as a synonym for mindless destructiveness. Terrible as this was, though, it was less important than the seizure of Africa. The western empire had lost much of its economic base. Thus disasters unrolled and trouble accumulated. Though great efforts could and would still be made in the West by eastern emperors, the empire there was on its last legs. The dependence on one barbarian against another was a fatal handicap. The cumulative impact of fresh pressure made recovery impossible. The protection of Italy meant abandoning Gaul and Spain to the Vandals; their invasion of Africa meant the loss of Rome's grain-growing provinces.

The collapse was completed in Europe in the third quarter of the century. It followed the greatest of the Hun assaults. These nomads had followed the Germanic tribes into the Balkans and central Europe after a preliminary diversion to ravage Anatolia and Syria. By 440 the Huns were led by Attila, under whom their power was at its height. From Hungary, where the great steppe corridor of Asia peters out, he drove west for the last time with a huge army of allies, but was defeated near Troyes in 451 by a 'Roman' army of Visigoths under a commander of barbarian origin. This was the end of the Hun threat; Attila died two years later, apparently scheming to marry the western emperor's sister and perhaps become emperor himself. A great revolt the following year by the Huns' subjects in Hungary finally broke them and they are thenceforth almost lost to sight. In Asia, their home, new confederations of nomads were forming to play a similar part in the future, but their story can wait.

The Huns had all but delivered the *coup de grâce* in the West; one emperor had sent the pope to intercede with Attila. The last western emperor was deposed by a Germanic warlord, Odoacer, in 476 and formal sovereignty passed to the eastern emperors. It was a real end, not a formal one, for though Italy, like the rest of the former western provinces, was henceforth a barbarian kingdom, independent in all but name, Italians regarded their sovereign as now resident in Constantinople.

The structure which had finally given way under these blows has in its last decades something of the Cheshire cat about it. It was fading away all the time; it is not particularly meaningful to pick one date rather than another as its end. The barbarian kingdoms were only a logical development of the reliance upon barbarian troops for the field army and their settlement as *foederati* within the frontiers. The barbarians themselves usually wanted no more, unless it was simple loot. Certainly they did not plan to replace imperial authority with their own. It is a Goth, Alaric's successor, who is reported saying, 'I hope to go down to posterity as the restorer of Rome, since it is not possible that I should be its supplanter.' Other dangers were greater and more fundamental than barbarian swagger.

Socially and economically, the tale of the third century had been resumed in the fifth as cities decayed and population fell. The civil service fell deeper into disorder as officials sought to protect themselves against inflation by taking payment for carrying out their duties. Though revenue declined as provinces were lost, the sale of offices somehow kept up the lavish expenditure of the court. But independence of action was gone. From being emperors whose power rested on their armies, the last emperors of the West declined through the stage of being the equals in negotiation of barbarian warlords whom they had to placate, to being their puppets, cooped up in the last imperial capital, Ravenna. Contemporaries had been right in this sense to see the sack of Rome in 410 as the end of an age, for then it was revealed that the empire could no longer preserve the very heart of *romanitas*.

One of the great minds of the later classical world specifically bent itself to the task of explaining the significance of that event to a stunned world. The result was a masterpiece, the book called *The City of God*. The first striking thing about St Augustine's book is its explicit intention: if so tremendous an event was to be understood, he argued, it was to be understood by the Christian religion and interpreted by the guardians of its traditions. Such a claim (and the absence of challenge to it) showed how far the Church had come since Constantine had established Christianity as the official cult. Almost a quarter of a century after his death the last emperor of his house, Julian, began a brief reign (361–3) during which he tried to restore the pagan cults: he earned himself historical fame (or, in Christian eyes, infamy) and the title 'the Apostate', but he was not successful. He believed that a restoration of the old sacrifices would ensure the return of prosperity, but he had too little time to test the proposition. What is now perhaps more striking is the unquestioned assumption that religion and public life were inseparably intertwined, on which his policy was based and which commanded general agreement; it was

A silver dish from Spain shows the emperor Theodosius I investing a high dignitary with his office in the presence of his two sons and Germanic guardsmen.

an assumption whose origins were Roman, not Christian. In any case, Julian did not threaten Constantine's work for he reigned too briefly to do so and Theodosius, the last ruler of a united empire, at last forbade the worship of the ancient gods.

What this meant in practice is hard to say. In Egypt it seems to have been the final landmark in the process of overcoming the ancient civilisation which had been going on for eight centuries or so. The victory of Greek ideas first won by the philosophers of Alexandria was now confirmed by the clergy. The priests of the ancient cults were now to be harried as pagans. Roman paganism found outspoken defenders still in the fifth century and only at the end of it were pagan teachers expelled from the universities at Athens and Constantinople. None the less a great turning-point had been reached; in principle the closed Christian society of the Middle Ages was now in existence.

Christian emperors soon set about developing it in a particular direction which became only too familiar by depriving Jews, the most easily identifiable of groups alien to the closed society, of their juridical equality with other citizens. Here was another turning-point. Judaism had long been the only monotheistic representative in the pluralistic religious world of Rome and now it was ousted by its derivative, Christianity. A prohibition on proselytising was the first blow and others soon followed. In 425 the patriarchate under which Jews had enjoyed administrative autonomy was abolished. When pogroms occurred, Jews began to withdraw to Persian territory. Their growing alienation from the empire was to be of great importance, for they could soon call for help upon Rome's enemies and there were Jewish Arab states, as well, which lay along trade-routes to Asia through the Red Sea, able to inflict damage on Roman interests in support of their co-religionists. Ideological rigour bore a high price.

Theodosius' reign is also notable in Christian history because of his quarrel with St Ambrose, Bishop of Milan. In 390, after an insurrection at Thessalonica, Theodosius pitilessly massacred thousands of its inhabitants. To the amazement of contemporaries, the emperor was soon seen standing in penance for the deed in a Milan church. Ambrose had refused him communion. The superstition of the age had won the first round of one of the great battles of humanity and enlightenment. Other men of might were to be tamed by excommunication or its threat, but this was the first time the spiritual arm had been so exercised and it is significant that it happened in the western Church. Ambrose had alleged a higher duty for his office than that owed to the emperor. It is the inauguration of a great theme of western European history, the tension of spiritual and secular claims which was time and time again to pull it back into a progressive channel, the conflict of Church and State.

By then, a glorious century for Christianity was almost over. It had been a great age of evangelization, in which missionaries had penetrated as far afield as Ethiopia, a brilliant age of theology and, above all, the age of establishment.

AMBROSIVS

Though it is dated nearly seventy-five years after his death, this mosaic in the basilica of Sant'Ambrogio at Milan may well be a true likeness of St Ambrose.

Yet the Christianity of the age has about it much which now seems repellent and bilious. Establishment gave Christians power they did not hesitate to use. 'We look on the same stars, the same heavens are above us all,' pleaded one pagan to St Ambrose, 'the same universe surrounds us. What matters it by what method each of us arrives at the truth?' But Symmachus asked in vain. East and West, the temper of the Christian Churches was intransigent and enthusiastic; if there was a distinction between the two, it lay between the Greeks' conviction of the almost limitless authority of a Christianized empire, blending spiritual and secular power, and the defensive, suspicious hostility to the whole secular world, state included, of a Latin tradition which taught Christians to see them-

selves as a saving remnant, tossed on the seas of sin and paganism in the Noah's Ark of the Church. Yet to be fair to the Fathers, or to understand their anxieties and fears, a modern observer has to recognize the forces of superstition and mystery which hung over the whole late classical world. Christianity shared and expressed much of this. The demons among whom Christians walked their earthly ways were real to them and to pagans alike, and a fifth-century pope consulted the augurs in order to find out what to do about the Goths.

This is part of the explanation of the bitter pursuit of heresy and schism. Arianism had not been finished off at Nicaea; far from it, it flourished among the Gothic peoples. Arian Christianity was therefore the dominant religion over much of Italy, Gaul and Spain. The Catholic Church was not persecuted in the Arian barbarian kingdoms, but it was neglected there and when everything depended on the patronage of rulers and the great, neglect could be dangerous. Another threat was the Donatist schism in Africa, which had taken on a social content and broke out in violent conflicts of town and country. In Africa, too, the old threat of Gnosticism lived again in Manichaeism which came to the West from Persia; another heresy, Pelagianism, showed the readiness of some Christians in Latinized Europe to welcome a version of Christianity reminiscent of stoic teaching, in which mystery and sacramentalism were subordinated to the moral aim of living a good life.

Few men were better fitted by temperament or education to discern, analyse and combat such dangers than was St Augustine. He was the greatest of the Fathers. It was important that he came from Africa – that is to say, the Roman province of that name, which corresponded roughly to Tunisia and eastern Algeria – where he was born in 354. African Christianity had more than a century's life behind it by then but was still a minority affair. The African Church had a special temper of its own since the days of Tertullian, its great founding figure. Its roots were not those of the Hellenized cities of the

East, but in soil laid down by the religions of Carthage and Numidia which lingered on amid the Berber peasantry. The humanized deities of Olympus had never been at home in Africa. The local traditions were of remote gods dwelling in mountains and high places, worshipped in savage and ecstatic rituals (the Carthaginians are supposed to have practised child sacrifice).

The intransigent, violent temper of the African Christianity which grew up against this background was reflected to the full in Augustine's own personality. He responded to the same psychological stimuli and felt the need to confront the fact of an evil lurking in himself. One answer was available and popular. The stark dualism of Manichaeism had a very wide appeal in Africa; Augustine became a Manichee for nearly ten years. Characteristically, he then reacted against his errors with great violence.

Before adulthood and Manichaeism, Augustine's education had orientated him towards a public career in the western empire. That education was overwhelmingly Latin (Augustine probably spoke only that language and certainly found Greek difficult) and very selective. Its skills were those of rhetoric and it was in them that Augustine first won prizes, but as for ideas, it was barren. Augustine taught himself by reading; his first great step forward was the discovery of the philosophical works of Cicero, probably his first contact, though at second-hand, with the classical Athenian tradition.

Augustine's lay career ended in Milan (where he had gone to teach rhetoric) with his baptism as a Catholic by St Ambrose himself in 387. At that time Ambrose exercised an authority which rivalled that of the empire itself in one of its most important cities and Augustine's observation of the relation of religion and secular power confirmed him in views very different from those of Greek churchmen, who welcomed the conflation of lay and religious authority in the emperor which followed establishment. Augustine then returned to Africa, first to live as a monk at Hippo and then, reluctantly, to become its bishop. There he remained until his death in

Much use was made of ivory throughout antiquity. In the fifth and sixth centuries it was especially employed in diptych pairs of covers for important documents. This is an example belonging to a well-known conservative and anti-Christian family, the Symmachi, and it shows a pagan subject, a priestess sacrificing.

430, building up Catholicism's position against the Donatists and almost by the way, thanks to vast correspondence and a huge literary output, becoming a dominant personality of the western Church.

In his lifetime Augustine was best known for his attacks on the Donatists and the Pelagians. The first was really a political question: which of two rival Churches was to dominate Roman Africa? The second raised wider issues. They

The earliest known representation of St Augustine, in a fresco of about 600 in the Lateran, Rome. His personal contribution through his great book to the idea of the primacy of Rome was greater than that of any of the other Latin Fathers of the Church.

must seem abstruse to a non-theologically minded age but on them turned much future European history. Essentially, the Pelagians preached a kind of stoicism; they were part of the classical world and tradition, dressed up in Christian theological language though it might be. The danger this presented – if it was a danger – was that the distinctiveness of Christianity would be lost and the Church simply become the vehicle of one strain in classical Mediterranean civilization, with the strengths and weaknesses which that implied. Augustine was uncompromisingly other-worldly and theological; for him the only possibility of redemption for mankind lay in the Grace which God conferred and no man could command by his works. In the history of the human spirit

Augustine deserves a place for having laid out more comprehensively than any predecessor the lines of the great debate between predestination and free will, Grace and Works, belief and motive which was to run for so long through European history. Almost incidentally, he established Latin Christianity firmly on the rock of the Church's unique power of access to the source of Grace through the sacraments.

This is now largely forgotten except by specialists. St Augustine now enjoys instead some notoriety as one of the most forceful and insistent exponents of a distrust of the flesh which was long especially to mark Christian sexual attitudes and thereby the whole of western culture. He stands in strange company – with Plato, for example – as a Founding Father of puritanism. But his intellectual legacy was far richer than this suggests. In his writings can also be found the foundations of much medieval political thought in so far as they are not Aristotelian or legalistic, and a view of history which would long dominate Christian society in the West and would affect it as importantly as the words of Christ himself.

The book now called *The City of God* contains the writing of Augustine which had most future impact. It is not so much a matter of specific ideas or doctrines – there is difficulty in locating his precise influence on medieval political thinkers, perhaps because there is much ambiguity about what he says – as of an attitude. He laid out in this book a way of looking at history and the government of men which became inseparable from Christian thinking for a thousand years and more. The subtitle of the book is *Against the Pagans*. This makes explicit his aim: to refute the reactionary and pagan charge that the troubles crowding in on the empire were to be blamed on Christianity. He was inspired to write by Alaric's sack of Rome; his overriding aim was to demonstrate that the understanding of even such an appalling event was possible for a Christian, but his book swoops far and wide over the past, from the importance of chastity to the philosophy of Thales of Miletus, and expounds the civil wars of Marius and Sulla as carefully as the meaning of God's promises to David. It is impossible to summarize this huge work: 'It may be too much for some, too little for others', said Augustine wryly in his last paragraph. It is a Christian interpretation of a whole civilization and what went to its making. Its most remarkable feature is its central judgement: that the whole earthly tissue of things is dispensable, and culture and institutions – even the great empire itself – of no final value, if God so wills.

That God did so will was suggested by Augustine's central image of two cities. One was earthly, founded in men's lower nature, imperfect and made with sinful hands, however glorious its appearance and however important the part it might from time to time have to play in the divine scheme. Sometimes its sinful aspect predominates and it is clear that men must flee the earthly city – but Babylon, too, had had its part in the divine plan. The other city was the heavenly city of God, the community founded on the assurance of God's promise of salvation, a goal towards which mankind might make a fearful pilgrimage from the earthly city, led and inspired by the Church. In the Church was to be found both the symbol of the City of God and the means of reaching it. History had changed with the appearance of the Church: from that moment the struggle of good and evil was clear in the world and human salvation rested upon its defence. Such arguments would be heard long into modern times.

The two cities sometimes make other appearances in St Augustine's argument, too. They are sometimes two groups of men, those who are condemned to punishment in the next world and those who are making the pilgrimage to glory. At this level the cities are divisions of the actual human race, here and now, as well as of all those since Adam who have already passed to judgement. But Augustine did not think that membership of the Church explicitly defines one group, the rest of humanity being the other. Perhaps the power of Augustine's vision was all the greater because of its ambiguities, dangling threads of argument and suggestion. The state was not *merely* earthly and wicked; it had its rôle in the divine scheme and government, in its nature, was divinely given. Much would be heard about that; the state would be asked to serve the Church by preserving it from its carnal enemies and by using its own power to enforce the purity of the Faith. Yet the Mandate of Heaven (as another civilization might put it) could be withdrawn and, when it was, even an event like the sack of Rome was only a landmark in the working of judgement on sin. In the end the City of God would prevail.

St Augustine escapes simple definition in his greatest book, but perhaps he escapes it in every sense. Much remains to be said about him for which there is no room here. He was, for example, a careful and conscientious bishop, the loving pastor of his flock; he was also a persecutor with the dubious distinction of having persuaded the imperial government to use force against the Donatists. He wrote a fascinating spiritual study which, though profoundly misleading on the facts of his early life, virtually founded the literary genre of romantic and introspective autobiography. He could be an artist with words – Latin ones, not Greek (he had to ask St Jerome for help with Greek translation) – and a prize-winning scholar, but his artistry was born of passion rather than of craftsmanship and his Latin is often poor. Yet he was soaked in the classical Roman past and it was from the high ground of his mastery of this tradition that he looked out with the eyes of Christian faith to a cloudy, uncertain and, to other men, frightening future. He embodied two cultures more completely, perhaps, than any other man of those divided times and perhaps this is why, fifteen hundred years later, he still seems to dominate them.

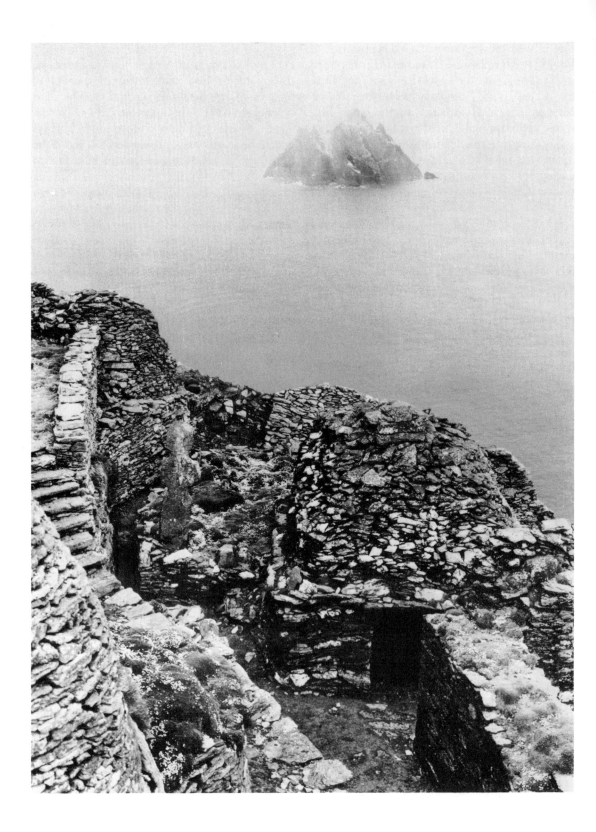

9 The elements of a future

From the Germanic invasions grew in the end the first nations of modern Europe, but when the western empire disappeared the barbarian peoples did not occupy areas looking much like later states. They fall clearly into four major and distinctive groups. The northernmost, the Saxons, Angles and Jutes, were moving into the old Roman province of Britain from the fourth century onwards, well before the island was abandoned to its inhabitants when the last emperor to be proclaimed there by his soldiers crossed with his army to Gaul in 407. Britain was then contested between successive waves of invaders and the Romano-British inhabitants until there emerged from it at the beginning of the seventh century a group of seven Anglo-Saxon kingdoms fringed by a Celtic world consisting of Ireland, Wales and Scotland.

Though the first British still lived on in communities which seem to have survived sometimes to the tenth century, and perhaps longer, Romano-British civilization disappeared more completely than its equivalents anywhere else in the western empire. Even the language was to

Eight miles off the west coast of Ireland lies the seven-hundred-foot-high rock of Skellig Michael. Some beehive cells for monks and a tiny church are the remains of an old Celtic monastery established there at an unknown but early date. From such precarious footholds at the edge of the civilized world came the Irish monks who were the first Christians to evangelize the former Roman province of Britain and the Celtic peoples of Scotland.

go; a Germanic tongue almost completely replaced it. We may have a fleeting glimpse of the last spasms of Romano-British resistance in the legend of King Arthur and his knights, who could be a reminiscence of the cavalry-fighting skills of the late imperial army, but that is all. Of administrative or spiritual continuity between this imperial province and the barbarian kingdoms there is virtually no trace. The imperial heritage of the future England was purely physical. It lay in the ruins of towns and villas, occasional Christian crosses, or the great constructions like the wall which were to puzzle newcomers until they came at last to believe that they were the work of giants of superhuman power. Some of these relics, like the complex of baths built upon the thermal springs at Bath, disappeared physically from sight for hundreds of years until rediscovered by the antiquaries of the eighteenth and nineteenth centuries. The roads remained, sometimes serving for centuries as trade-routes even when their engineering had succumbed to time, weather and pillage. Finally, there were the natural immigrants who had come with the Romans and stayed: animals like the ferrets which often give an English country boy his first taste of the excitement of the hunt, or plants like the mustard which was to spice the roast beef that became a minor national mythology over a thousand years later. But of the things of the mind left by the Romans we have no trace. Romano-British Christianity, whatever it may have been, disappeared and the keepers of the faith retired for a time to the misty fastnesses where there brooded the monks of

The greatest hoard of Roman silver found in England, that discovered at Mildenhall, near Cambridge, included this magnificent engraved dish.

The Frankish warrior. Taken from a Saxon funeral stele of about 700, this is one of the earliest naturalistic renderings of a barbarian which survives.

the Celtic Church. It was another Rome which was to convert the English nation, not the empire. Before that, Germanic tradition would be the preponderant formative influence as nowhere else within the old imperial territory.

Across the Channel, things were very different. Much survived. After its devastation by the Vandals, Gaul continued to lie in the shadow of the Visigoths of Aquitaine. Their share in repelling the Huns gave them greater importance than ever. To the north-east of Gaul, nevertheless, lay German tribes which were to displace them from this superiority, the Franks. Unlike the Visigoths, they were not Arian and in part because of this the future was to belong to them. They were to have a bigger impact than any other barbarian people on the shaping of Europe.

The graves of the first Franks reveal a warrior society, divided into a hierarchy of ranks. More willing to settle than some other barbarians, they were established in the fourth century in modern Belgium, between the Scheldt and the Meuse, where they became Roman *foederati*. Some of them moved on into Gaul. One group, settled at Tournai, threw up a ruling family subsequently called Merovingians; the third king (if this is the correct word) of this line was Clovis. This prince's is the first great name in the history of the country which was one day to inherit its own from the land of his peoples which Clovis put together, Francia.

Clovis was a king of the western Franks. Though formally the subject of the emperor, he soon turned on the last Roman rulers of Gaul and conquered lands far to the west and down to the Loire. Meanwhile the eastern Franks defeated the Alamanni and when Clovis had been elected their king, too, a united Frankish kingdom straddled the lower Rhine valley and northern France. This was the heartland of the Frankish state which was the heir to Roman supremacy in north Europe. Clovis married a princess from another Germanic confederation, the Burgundians who had settled in the Rhône valley and the area running south-east to modern Geneva and Besançon. She was a Catholic,

The Merovingians were skilled workers with jewels and precious metals. One of the earliest examples of their work for the Church is this chalice and paten (or possibly portable altar) from the reign of Clovis. It shows a blending of barbarian and classical styles: the chalice is in the shape of a Roman vase.

though her people were Arians, and at some time after his marriage (traditionally in 496) and after a battlefield conversion which is reminiscent of Constantine's, Clovis himself embraced Catholicism. This gave him the support of the Roman Church, the most important power still surviving from the empire in the barbarian lands, in what it now chose to regard as a religious war against the other Germanic peoples of Gaul. Catholicism was also the way to friendship with the Romano-Gaulish population. No doubt the conversion was political; it was also momentous. A new Rome was to rule in Gaul.

The Burgundians were Clovis' first victims, though they were not subjugated completely until after his death, when they were given Merovingian princes but kept an independent state structure. The Visigoths were tackled next; they kept only the south-eastern territories they held north of the Pyrenees (the later Languedoc and Roussillon) and Provence. Clovis was now the successor of the Romans in all Gaul; the emperor recognized it by naming him a consul.

The Frankish capital was moved to Paris by Clovis and he was buried in the church he had built there, the first Frankish king not to be buried as a barbarian. But this was not the start of the continuous history of Paris as a capital. A Germanic kingdom was not what later times would think of as a state nor what a Roman

Cut gems were used by the Romans to portray the features of emperors. Here, an amethyst is carved with the face of Theodoric, king of Goths and Romans, conscious copier of the great ways of the imperial past. As a letter in his name to the emperor at Constantinople put it, 'our royalty is an imitation of yours'.

would recognize. It was a heritage composed partly of lands, partly of kinship groups. Clovis' heritage was divided among his sons. The Frankish kingdom was not reunited until 558. A couple of years later it broke up again. Gradually, it settled down in three bits. There was an eastern kingdom, Austrasia, whose capital was Metz and which had its centre of gravity east of the Rhine; Neustria was the western equivalent and had its capital at Soissons; under the same ruler, but distinct, was the kingdom of Burgundy. Their rulers tended to quarrel over the lands where these regions touched.

In this structure there begins to appear a Frankish nation no longer a collection of barbarian warbands, but peoples belonging to a recognizable state, speaking a Latin vernacular, and with an emerging class of landowning nobles. Significantly, from it there also comes a Christian interpretation of the barbarian rôle in history, the *History of the Franks*, by Gregory,

Bishop of Tours, himself from the Romano-Gaulish aristocracy. Other barbarian peoples would produce similar works (the greatest, perhaps, is that written for England by Bede) which sought to reconcile traditions in which paganism was still strong to Christianity and the civilized heritage. It must be said that Gregory presented a picture of the Franks after the death of his hero Clovis which was pessimistic; he thought the Frankish rulers had behaved so badly that their kingdom was doomed.

The Merovingians kept other barbarians out of Gaul; the Ostrogoths lost their lands north of the Alps to Clovis' sons. Their greatest king was Theodoric whose right to rule in Italy, where he fought off other Germans, was recognized by the emperor in 497. His entry to the peninsula to protect it had been sanctioned by the emperor, too. He was utterly convinced of Rome's authority; he had an emperor as godfather and had been brought up at Constantinople until he was eighteen. Theodoric was the only Ostrogoth who was a Roman citizen, his authority accepted by the Senate; his countrymen were technically the mercenary soldiers of the empire. Only Romans held civil appointments. He seems to have been a judicious ruler, maintaining good relations with other barbarian peoples (he married Clovis' sister) and enjoying some sort of primacy among them. He did not share his own people's Arian faith. But the religious division told against Ostrogothic power in the long run. Unlike the Franks they were not to ally with the Roman past and after Theodoric, the Ostrogoths were expelled from Italy and history by the generals from the eastern empire. They left a ruined Italy, soon to be invaded by yet another barbarian people, the Lombards.

In the west Clovis had left the Visigoths virtually confined to Spain, from which they had driven the Vandals. Other Germanic peoples were already settled there. Its terrain presented quite special problems – as it has continued to do to all invaders and governments – and the Visigothic kingdom of Spain was not able to resist much more romanization than its founders

The Ostrogothic Kingdom declined after Theodoric. One of its rulers was his daughter Amalauntha; this Byzantine ivory may represent her, though that is not certain.

had undergone in Gaul, where they had fused much less with existing society than had the Franks. The Visigoths – and there were not so very many of them, less than 100000 at most – clustered about their leaders who spread out from Old Castile through the provinces; they then quarrelled so much that imperial rule was able to re-establish itself for more than a half-century in the south. Finally, the Visigothic kings turned to Catholicism and thus enlisted the authority of the Spanish bishops. In 587 begins the long tradition of Catholic monarchy in Spain.

What this adds up to is hard to say. Enough is known about the civilization of the barbarian kingdoms to make generalization hazardous. Their duration alone almost explains this; the Visigoths underwent three centuries of evolution between the creation of the kingdom of Toulouse and their monarchy's ending in Spain. Much changed in so long a time. Though economic life and technology hardly altered, mental and institutional forms were undergoing radical, if slow, transformations in all the barbarian kingdoms. Soon it is not quite right to think of them still as merely such (except, perhaps, the Lombards). The Germanic tribesmen were a minority, often isolated in alien settings, dependent on routines long established by the particular environment for their living and forced into some sort of understanding with the conquered. The passage of their invasions must sometimes have seemed at close quarters like a flood tide, but when it had passed there were often left only tiny, isolated pools of invaders, here and there replacing the Roman masters, but often living alongside them. In Frankish Gaul they intermarried with them and took up their language, mixing with its Frankish words. By the seventh century, western European society has already a very different atmosphere from that of the turbulent fifth.

None the less, a barbarian past left its imprint on all western Europe. In almost all the barbarian kingdoms society was long and irreversibly shaped by Germanic custom. This sanctioned a hierarchy reflected in the characteristic

MAXIMIANVS

Germanic device for securing public order, the blood feud. Men – and women, and cattle, and property of all sorts – had in the most literal sense their price; wrongs done were settled by interesting a whole clan or family in the outcome if customary compensation were not forthcoming. Kings more and more wrote down and thus in a sense 'published' what such customs were. Literacy was so rare that there can have been no point in imagining devices such as the stele of Babylon or the white boards on which the decrees of Greek city-states were set out. Recording by a scribe on parchment for future consultation was all that could be envisaged. None the less, in this Germanic world lie the origins of a jurisprudence one day to be carried across oceans to new cultures of European stock. The first institution to open the way to this was the acceptance of kingly or collective power to declare what was to be recorded. All the Germanic kingdoms moved towards the writing down and codification of their law.

After Justinian's re-conquest of Italy much was done to beautify Ravenna, the last Imperial capital there. These mosaics in the church of San Vitale date from this period and show the Emperor and Empress approaching the altar with offerings, attended by their suites. Theodora was in fact a tiny woman, but in accordance with Byzantine convention she, like the Emperor, is shown taller than the attendants.

Where the early forms of public action are not religious or supernatural they are usually judicial, and it is hardly surprising that, for example, the Visigothic court of Toulouse should have sought the skills of Roman legal experts. But this was only one form of a respect which almost every barbarian aristocracy showed for Roman tradition and forms. Theodoric saw himself as the representative of the emperor; his problem did not lie in identifying his own rôle, but in the need to avoid irritating his followers who would be provoked by any excess of Romanization. Perhaps similar consideration weighed with Clovis before his conversion, which was an act of identification with Empire as well as with Church. At the level just below such heroic figures, both Frankish and Visigothic noblemen seem to have taken pleasure in showing themselves the heirs of Rome by writing to one another in Latin and patronizing light literature. There was a tie of interest with the Romans, too; Visigothic warriors sometimes found employment in putting down the revolts of peasants who menaced the Romano-Gaulish landowner as well as the invaders. Yet so long as Arianism stood in the way, there was a limit to the identification with *romanitas* possible for the barbarians. The Church, after all, was the supreme relic of empire west of Constantinople.

The eastern emperors had not seen these changes with indifference. But troubles in their own domains hamstrung them and in the fifth century their barbarian generals dominated them too. They watched with apprehension the last years of the puppet emperors of Ravenna but recognized Odoacer, the deposer of the last of them. They maintained a formal claim to rule over a single empire, east and west, without actually questioning Odoacer's independence in Italy until an effective replacement was available in Theodoric, to whom the title of patrician was given. Meanwhile, Persian wars and the new pressure of Slavs in the Balkans were more than enough to deal with. It was not until the accession of the Emperor Justinian in 527 that reality seemed likely to be restored to imperial government.

Justinian in retrospect seems something of a failure. Yet he behaved as people thought an emperor should; he did what most people still expected that a strong emperor would one day do. He boasted that Latin was his native tongue; for all the wide sweep of the empire's foreign

343

relations, he could still think plausibly of re-uniting and restoring the old empire, centred on Constantinople though it now had to be. We labour under the handicap of knowing what happened, but he reigned a long time and his contemporaries were more struck by his temporary successes. They expected them to herald a real restoration. After all, no one could really conceive a world without the empire. The barbarian kings of the West gladly deferred to Constantinople and accepted titles from it; they did not grasp at the purple themselves. Justinian sought autocratic power, and his contemporaries found the goal both comprehensible and realistic. There is a certain grandeur about his conception of his rôle; it is aesthetically a pity that he should have been so unattractive a man.

Justinian was almost always at war and often victoriously. Even the costly Persian campaigns (and payments to the Persian king) were successful in the limited sense that they did not lose the empire much ground. Yet they were a grave strategic handicap; the liberation of his resources for a policy of recovery in the West which had been Justinian's aim in his first peace with the Persians always eluded him. Nevertheless, his greatest general, Belisarius, destroyed Vandal Africa and recovered that country for the empire (though it took ten years to reduce it to order). He went on to invade Italy and begin the struggle which ended in 554 with the final eviction of the Ostrogoths from Rome and the unification once more of all Italy under imperial rule, albeit an Italy devastated by the imperial armies as it had never been by the barbarians. These were great achievements, though badly followed up. More were to follow in southern Spain, where the imperial armies exploited rivalry between Visigoths and again set up imperial government in Córdoba. Throughout the western Mediterranean, too, the imperial fleets were supreme; for a century after Justinian's death, Byzantine ships moved about unmolested.

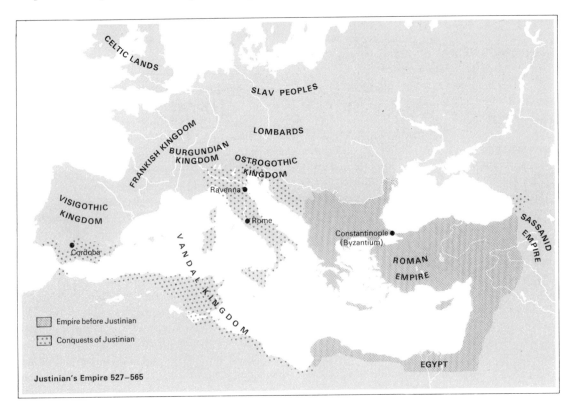

Justinian's Empire 527–565

Empire before Justinian

Conquests of Justinian

It did not last. By the end of the century most of Italy was gone again, this time to the Lombards, the final extinguishers of imperial power in the peninsula. In eastern Europe, too, in spite of a vigorous diplomacy of bribery and missionary ideology, Justinian had never been successful in dealing with the barbarians. Perhaps enduring success there was impossible. The pressure from behind on these migrant peoples was too great and, besides, they could see great prizes ahead; 'the barbarians,' wrote one historian of the reign, 'having once tasted Roman wealth, never forgot the road that led to it'. By Justinian's death, in spite of his expensive fortress-building, the ancestors of the later Bulgars were settled in Thrace and a wedge of barbarian peoples separated west and east Rome.

Justinian's conquests, great as they were, could not be maintained by his successors in the face of the continuing threat from Persia, the rise of Slav pressure in the Balkans and, in the seventh century, a new rival, Islam. A terrible time lay ahead. Yet even then Justinian's legacy would be operative through the diplomatic tradition he founded, the building of a network of influences among the barbarian peoples beyond the frontier, playing off one against another, bribing one prince with tribute or a title, standing godparent to the baptized children of a second. If it had not been for the client princedoms of the Caucasus who were converted to Christianity in Justinian's day, or an alliance with the Crimean Goths which was to last seven centuries, the survival of the eastern empire would have been almost impossible. In this sense, too, the reign sets out the groundplan of a future Byzantine sphere.

Within the empire, Justinian left an indelible imprint. At his accession the monarchy was handicapped by the persistence of party rivalries which could draw upon popular support, but in 532 this led to a great insurrection which made it possible to strike at the factions and though much of the city was burned, this was the end of domestic threats to Justinian's autocracy. It showed itself henceforth more and more consistently and nakedly.

Its material monuments were lavish; the greatest is the basilica of St Sophia itself (AD 532–7), but all over the empire public buildings, churches, baths and new towns mark the reign and speak for the inherent wealth of the eastern empire. The richest and most civilized provinces were in Asia and Egypt; Alexandria, Antioch and Beirut were their great cities. A non-material, institutional, monument of the reign was Justinian's codification of Roman law. In four collections a thousand years of Roman jurisprudence was put together in a form which gave it deep influence across the centuries and crucially affected the shaping of the modern state. Justinian's efforts to win administrative and organizational reform were far less successful. It was not difficult to diagnose ills known to be dangerous as long before as the third century. But given the expense and responsibilities of Empire, permanent remedies were hard to find. The sale of offices, for example, was known to be an evil and Justinian abolished it, but then had to tolerate it when it crept back.

The main institutional response to the empire's problem was a progressive regimentation of its citizens. In part, this was in the tradition of regulating the economy which he had inherited. Just as peasants were tied to the soil, craftsmen were now attached to their hereditary corporations and guilds; even the bureaucracy tended to become hereditary. This rigidifying of structures was unlikely to make imperial problems easier to solve.

It was unfortunate, too, that a quite exceptionally disastrous series of natural calamities fell on the empire at the beginning of the sixth century: they go far to explain why it was hard for Justinian to leave the empire in better fettle than he found it. Earthquake, famine, plague devastated the cities and even the capital itself, where men saw phantoms in the streets. The ancient world was a credulous place, but tales of the emperor's capacity to take off and then put on again his head, or to disappear from sight at will, already suggest that under these strains the mental world of the eastern empire was detaching itself rapidly from its moorings in classical civilization. Justinian was to make the separation easier by his religious outlook and policies, another paradoxical outcome, for it was far from what he intended. After it had survived for eight hundred years, he abolished the academy of Athens; he was to be a Christian emperor, not a ruler of unbelievers and decreed the destruction of all pagan statues in the capital. Worse still, he accelerated the demotion of the Jews in civic status and the reduction of their freedom to exercise their religion. Things had already gone a long way. Pogroms had long been connived at and synagogues destroyed, but Justinian went on to alter the Jewish calendar and interfere with the Jewish order of worship. He even encouraged barbarian rulers to persecute Jews. Long before the cities of western Europe, Constantinople had a ghetto.

Justinian was all the more confident of the rightness of asserting imperial authority in ecclesiastical affairs because (like the later James I of England) he had a real taste for theological disputation. Sometimes the consequences were unfortunate; such an attitude did nothing to renew the loyalty to the empire of the Nestorians and Monophysites, heretics who had refused to accept the definitions of the precise relationship of God the Father to God the Son laid down in 451 at a council at Chalcedon. Their theology mattered less than the fact that such symbolic tenets were increasingly identified with important linguistic and cultural groups. The empire began to create its own Ulsters. Harrying heretics only intensified separatist feeling in parts of Egypt and Syria. In the former, the Coptic Church went its own way in opposition to Orthodoxy in the later fifth century and the Syrian monophysites followed, setting up a 'Jacobite' church. Both were encouraged and sustained by the numerous and enthusiastic monks of those countries. Some of these sects and communities, too, had important connexions outside the empire, so that foreign policy was involved. The Nestorians found refuge in Persia and, though not heretics, the Jews were especially influential beyond the

frontiers; Jews in Iraq supported Persian attacks on the empire and Jewish Arab states in the Red Sea interfered with the trade routes to India when hostile measures were taken against Jews in the empire.

Justinian's hopes of reuniting the western and eastern Churches were to be thwarted in spite of his zeal. A potential division between them had always existed because of the different cultural matrices in which each had been formed. The western Church had never accepted the union of religious and secular authority which was the heart of the political theory of the eastern empire; the empire would pass away as others had done (and the Bible told) and it would be the Church which would prevail against the gates of hell. Now such doctrinal divergences became more important, and separation had been made more likely by the breakdown in the West. A Roman pope visited Justinian and the emperor spoke of Rome as the 'source of priesthood', but in the end two Christian communions were first to go their own ways and then violently to quarrel. Justinian's own view, that the emperor was supreme, even on matters of doctrine, fell victim to clerical intransigence on both sides.

This seems to imply (as do so many others of his acts) that Justinian's real achievement was not that which he sought and temporarily achieved, the re-establishment of the imperial unity, but a quite different one, the easing of the path towards the development of a new, Byzantine civilization. After him, Byzantium was a reality, even if not yet recognized. It was evolving away from the classical world towards a style clearly related to it, but independent of it. This was made easier by contemporary developments in both eastern and western culture, by now overwhelmingly a matter of new tendencies in the Church.

As often in later history, the Church and its leaders had not at first recognized or welcomed an opportunity in disaster. They identified themselves with what was collapsing and understandably so. The collapse of Empire was the collapse of civilization; the Church in the West was, except for municipal authority in the impoverished towns, often the sole institutional survivor of *romanitas*. Her bishops were men with experience of administration, at least as likely as other local notables to be intellectually equipped to grapple with new problems. A semi-pagan population looked to them with superstitious awe and attributed to them near-magical power. In many areas they were the last embodiment of authority left when imperial armies went away and imperial administration crumbled and they were lettered men among a new unlettered ruling class which craved the assurance of sharing the classical heritage. Socially, they were often drawn from the leading provincial families; they were sometimes great aristocrats and proprietors with material resources to support their spiritual rôle. Naturally, new tasks were thrust upon them.

This was not all. The end of the classical world also saw two new institutions emerge in the western Church which were to be lifelines in the dangerous rapids between a civilization which had collapsed and one yet to be born. The first was Christian monasticism, a phenomenon first appearing in the East. It was in about 270 that a Copt, St Anthony, retired to a hermit's life in the Egyptian desert. His example was followed by others who watched, prayed and strove alone with demons or mortified the flesh by fasting and more dubious disciplines. In the next century this new form of spirituality established itself in a communal form in the Levant and Syria. From there, the idea spread to the West, to the Mediterranean coast of France. In a crumbling society such as fifth-century Gaul the monastic ideal of undistracted worship and service to God in prayer, within the discipline of an ascetic rule, was attractive to many men and women of intellect and character. Through it they could assure personal salvation. The communities attracted many from among the well-born who sought a refuge from a changing world. Unfriendly critics who hankered after the old Roman ideal of service to the state condemned them for shirking their proper responsibilities to society by withdrawing from

it. Yet many of the greatest churchmen of the age were monks and the institution prospered. Landowners founded communities or endowed existing ones with lands. There were some scandals and no doubt many compromises of principle in grappling with patrons and men of power.

One Italian monk, of whom we know little except his achievement and that he was believed to work miracles, found the state of monasticism shocking. This was St Benedict, one of the most influential men in the Church's history. He founded a monastery at Monte Cassino in southern Italy, giving it a new rule which he had compiled by sifting and selecting among others available. It is a seminal document of western Christianity and therefore of western civilization. It directed the attention of the monk to the community, whose abbot was to have complete authority. The community's purpose was not merely to provide a hotbed for the cultivation of the salvation of individual souls but was to worship and live as a whole. The individual monk was to contribute to its task in the framework of an ordered routine of worship, prayer and labour. From the individualism of traditional monasticism a new human instrument was forged; it was to be one of the main weapons in the armoury of the Church.

St Benedict did not set his sights too high and this was one secret of his success; the Rule was within the powers of ordinary men who loved God and his monks did not need to mutilate either body or spirit. Its success in estimating their need was demonstrated by its rapid spread. Very quickly Benedictine monasteries appeared everywhere in the West. They became the key sources of missionaries and teaching for the conversion of pagan England and Germany. Only the Celtic Church at the edge of the western world clung to the older, eremitical model of the monkish life.

The Church's other new great support was the Papacy. The prestige of St Peter's see and the legendary guardianship of the Apostle's bones always gave Rome a special place among the bishoprics of Christendom. It was the only

347

one in the West to claim descent from one of the Apostles. But in principle she had little else to offer; the western Church was a junior branch and it was in the Churches of Asia that the closest links with the Apostolic age could be asserted. Something more was required for the Papacy to begin its rise to the splendid pre-eminence which was taken for granted by the medieval world.

To begin with there was the city. Rome had been for centuries the capital of the world. Its bishops were the business colleagues of Senate and Emperor and the departure of the imperial court only left their eminence more obvious. The arrival in Italy from the eastern empire of alien civil servants whom the Italians disliked as much as they did the barbarians directed new attention to the Papacy as the focus of Italian loyalties. It was, too, a wealthy see, with an apparatus of government commensurate with its possessions. It generated administrative skill superior to anything to be found outside the imperial administration itself. This distinction, too, stood out all the more clearly in times of trouble, when the barbarians lacked these skills. The see of Rome had the finest records of any; already in the fifth century papal apologists were exploiting them. The characteristically conservative papal stance, the argument that no new departures are being made but that old positions are being defended, is already present and was wholly sincere; popes did not see themselves as conquerors of new ideological and legal ground, but as men desperately trying to keep the small foothold the Church had already won.

This was the setting of the Papacy's emergence as a great historical force. The fifth-century Leo the Great was the first pope under whom the new power of the bishop of Rome was clearly visible. An emperor declared papal decisions to have the force of law and Leo vigorously asserted the doctrine that the popes spoke in the name of St Peter. He assumed the title *pontifex maximus* discarded by the emperors. It was believed that his intervention by visiting Attila had staved off the Hun attack on Italy; bishops in the West who had hitherto resisted claims for Rome's primacy became more willing to accept them in a world turned upside-down by barbarians. Still, though, Rome was a part of the state church of an empire whose religion Justinian saw as above all the emperor's concern.

The pope in whom the future medieval Papacy is most clearly revealed was also the first pope who had been a monk. In Gregory the Great, who reigned from 590 to 604, there thus came together the two great institutional innovations of the early Church. He was a statesman of great insight. A Roman aristocrat, loyal to the empire and respectful of the emperor, he was nevertheless the first pope who fully accepted the barbarian Europe in which he reigned; his pontificate at last reveals a complete break with the classical world. He saw as his duty the first great missionary campaign, one of whose targets was pagan England, to which he sent Augustine of Canterbury in 596. He struggled against the Arian heresy and was delighted by the conversion of the Visigoths to Catholicism. He was as much concerned with the Germanic kings as with the emperor in whose name he claimed to act, but was also the doughtiest opponent of the Lombards for help against whom he turned both to the emperor and, more significantly, the Franks. Yet the Lombards also made the pope, of necessity, a political power. Not only did they cut him off from the imperial representative at Ravenna, but he had to negotiate with them when they stood before the walls of Rome. Like other bishops in the West who found themselves the surviving civilian authority, he had to feed his

The tenth-century Rhenish artist who made this ivory chose for his subject St Gregory, writing under the influence of the Holy Spirit, here shown as a dove on his shoulder. Below him are the scribes of a monastic copying-school, one holding the inkhorn for the others. Gregory left a large number of writings which were to influence the future developments of the church after his death as much as he had done through the great decisions of his pontificate.

city and govern it. Slowly, Italians came to see the pope as successor to Rome as well as to St Peter.

In Gregory the classical-Roman heritage and the Christian are subsumed; he represented something new though he can hardly have seen it like that. Christianity had been a part of the classical heritage, yet it was now turning away from much of it and was distinct from it. Significantly, Gregory did not speak Greek; nor did he feel he needed to. There had already been signs of transformation in the Church's relations with the barbarians. With Gregory, one focus of this story has come at last to be Europe, not the Mediterranean basin. There were already sown in it the seeds of the future, though not of the near future; for most of the world's people the existence of Europe for the next thousand years or so is almost irrelevant. But a Europe is at last discernible, unimaginably different though it may be from what was to come.

It was also decisively different from the past. The ordered, literate, unhurried life of the Roman provinces had given way to a fragmented society with, encamped in it, a warrior aristocracy and their tribesmen, sometimes integrated with the earlier inhabitants, sometimes not. Their chiefs were called kings and were certainly no longer merely chiefs, any more than their followers, after nearly two centuries of involvement with what Rome had left behind, were mere barbarians. It was in 550 that a barbarian king – a Goth – for the first time represented himself on his coins decked in the imperial insignia. Through the impression wrought on their imaginations by the relics of a higher culture, through the efficacy of the idea of Rome itself and through the conscious and unconscious work of the Church, above all, these peoples were on their way to civilization and their art remains to prove it.

Of formal culture, they brought nothing with them to compare with antiquity. There was no barbarian contribution to the civilized intellect. Yet the cultural traffic was not all in one direction at less formal levels. The extent to which Christianity, or at least the Church, was still an elastic form must not be underestimated. Everywhere Christianity had to flow in the channels available and these were defined by layers of paganism, Germanic upon Roman upon Celtic. The conversion of a king like Clovis did not mean that his people made at once even a formal adherence to Christianity; some were still pagan after generations had passed, as their graves showed. But this conservatism presented opportunities as well as obstacles. The Church could utilize the belief in folk magic, or the presence of a holy site which could associate a saint with respect for age-old deities of countryside and forest. Miracles, knowledge of which was assiduously propagated in the saints' lives read aloud to pilgrims to their shrines, were the persuasive arguments of the age. Men were used to the magical interventions of the old Celtic deities or manifestations of Woden's power. For most men then, as for most of human history, the rôle of religion was not the provision of moral guidance or spiritual insight, but the propitiation of the unseen. Only over blood-sacrifice did Christianity draw the line between itself and the pagan past unambiguously; much other pagan practice and reminiscence it simply christened.

The process by which this came about has often been seen as one of decline and there are certainly reasonable arguments to be made to that effect. In material terms, barbarian Europe was an economically poorer place than the empire of the Antonines; all over Europe tourists gape still at the monuments of Rome's builders as our barbarian predecessors must have done. Yet out of this confusion something quite new and immeasurably more creative than Rome would emerge in due course. It was perhaps impossible for contemporaries to view what was happening in anything but apocalyptic terms. But some may have seen just a little beyond this, as the concerns of Gregory suggest.

This eighth-century font from Tuscany shows the durability of pre-Christian imagery and forms, some of which in this example have been thought to have Celtic origins.

Book Four

The Age of Diverging Traditions

The 'Romans' of Justinian's day knew they were very different from other men and were proud of it. They belonged to a particular civilization; some of them, at least, thought it was the best conceivable. They were not unique in this. The same was true of men in other parts of the globe. Long before the birth of Christ, civilization was at work in every continent except Australasia, deepening and quickening the divisions opened in human behaviour in prehistoric times. Mankind's cultural variety even in the earliest historical times already escapes all but the finest net and when the classical Mediterranean world had at last cracked irreparably – 500 will do as a rough marker – the world was full of contrasting cultures.

Most of the globe's surface was then still without civilization, but what was civilized fell into a relatively few zones in each of which powerful, distinctive, often self-conscious and largely independent traditions were at work. Their differences were to go on deepening for another thousand years or so, until by about 1500 mankind was probably more diversified than ever before or since. There was no single dominant cultural tradition.

One result was that Chinese, Indian, western European and Islamic civilizations all lived independently long enough to leave ineradicable traces in the ground-plan of our world. They coexisted and part of the explanation, paradoxically, is that in one respect all these civilizations were much alike. Broadly speaking, they were all based on subsistence agriculture and all had to find their main sources of energy in wind, running water, and animal or human muscles.

They could not bring to bear overwhelming power to change one another. Everywhere, too, the weight of tradition was enormous; the unquestioned, if different, routines under which all mankind then lived would seem intolerable today. Of course, variety in cultural development could affect technology. It was to be a long time before Europeans could again undertake engineering on the Roman scale, yet the Chinese had already long before that discovered how to print with movable characters and knew about gunpowder. Nevertheless, the impact of such advantages or disadvantages was only marginal, largely because intercourse between traditions was difficult except in a few favoured areas. Yet the insulation of civilizations from one another was never absolute; there was always some physical and mental interaction going on. The barriers between them resembled permeable membranes rather than impenetrable walls, though for the most part men in these times lived contentedly in traditional patterns, ignoring others following other ways a few hundred – or even a few score – miles from them.

This great era of cultural diversity spans a very long time. In some traditions we must go back to the third century BC to resume the story, and the breaches in the defences which separated them from others only became irreparable well after 1500. Before then, most civilizations lived largely to rhythms of their own, only occasionally showing the effect of major disturbance from outside. One such disturbance which affected men from Spain to Indonesia, and from the river Niger to China, originated in the Near East, the zone of the oldest civilized traditions and the logical place to begin to examine this diverse world.

1 Islam and the re-making of the Near East

With relatively brief interruptions, great empires based in Iran hammered away at the West for a thousand years before 500. Wars can sometimes bring civilizations closer, and in the Near East two cultural traditions had so influenced one another that their histories, though distinct, are inseperable. Through Alexander and his successors, the Achaemenids had passed to Rome the ideas and style of a divine kingship whose roots lay in ancient Mesopotamia; from Rome they went on to flower in the Byzantine Christian empire which fought the Sassanids. Persia and Rome fascinated and, in the end, helped to destroy one another; their antagonism was a fatal commitment to both of them when their attention and resources were urgently needed elsewhere. In the end both succumbed.

The first Sassanid, Ardashir, or Artaxerxes,

In about 1620 the emperor Jahangir, ruler of a great Moslem empire in India, dreamed of a visit from the Persian Shah Abbas, in which this neighbour and frequent enemy embraced him in friendship. So struck by his dream was Jahangir, that he ordered a painting to be made of this striking reconciliation – never completed in reality, though in the picture the lion lies down with the lamb – of two of the three great Islamic states of the age (Turkey was the seat of another). Europe was not much in the thoughts of these rulers, nor very clearly delineated in their minds if the map in this picture is anything to go by. Yet the cherubs are a European artistic convention and the sun-nimbus which surrounds the two emperors is derived from the old pagan deification of the emperors of Rome.

had a strong sense of continuing Persian tradition. He deliberately evoked memories of the Parthians and the Great King, and his successors followed him in cultivating them by sculpture and inscription. Ardashir claimed all the lands once ruled by Darius and went on himself to conquer the oases of Merv and Khiva, and invade the Punjab; the conquest of Armenia took another hundred and fifty years to confirm but most of it was in the end brought under Persian hegemony. This was the last reconstitution of the ancient Iranian empire which in the sixth century even dominated the Yemen.

Geographical and climatic variety always threatened this huge sprawl of territory with disintegration, but for a long time the Sassanids solved the problems of governing it. There was a bureaucratic tradition running back to Assyria to build on and a royal claim to divine authority. The tension between these centralizing forces and the interests of great families was what the political history of the Sassanid state was about. The result and pattern was of alternating periods of kings encumbered or unsuccessful in upholding their claims. There were two good tests of this. One was their ability to appoint their own men to the major offices of state and resist the claims on them of the nobility. The other was their retention of control over the succession. Some kings were deposed and though the kingship itself formally passed by nomination by the ruler, this gave way at times to a semi-electoral system in which the leading officers of state, soldiers and priests made a choice from the royal family.

The dignitaries who contested the royal power and often ruled in the satrapies came from a small number of great families which claimed descent from the Parthian Arsacids, the paramount chiefs of that people. They enjoyed large fiefs for their maintenance but their dangerous weight was balanced by two other forces. One was the mercenary army, largely officered by members of the lesser nobility, who were thus given some foothold against the greater. Its *corps d'élite*, the heavy-armed household cavalry, was directly dependent on the king. The other force was the priesthood.

Sassanid Persia was a religious as well as a political unity. Zoroastrianism had been formally restored by Ardashir, who gave important privileges to its priests, the *magi*. They led in due course to political power as well. Priests confirmed the divine nature of the kingship, had important judicial duties, and came, too, to supervise the collection of the land-tax which was the basis of Persian finance. The doctrines they taught seem to have varied considerably from the strict monotheism attributed to Zoroaster but focussed on a creator, Ahura Mazda, whose viceroy on earth was the king. The Sassanids' promotion of the state religion was closely connected with the assertion of their own authority.

The ideological basis of the Persian state became even more important when the Roman empire became Christian. Religious differences began to matter much more; religious disaffection came to be seen as political. The wars with Rome made Christianity treasonable. Though Christians in Persia had at first been tolerated, their persecution become logical and continued well into the fifth century. Nor was it only Christians who were tormented. In 276 a Persian religious teacher called Mani was executed – by the particularly agonizing method of being flayed alive. He was to become known in the West under the Latin form of his name, Manichaeus, and the teaching attributed to him had a great future as a Christian heresy. Manichaeism brought together Judaeo–Christian beliefs and Persian mysticism and saw the whole cosmos as a great drama in which the forces of Light and Darkness struggled for salvation. Those who apprehended this truth sought to participate in the struggle by practising austerities which would open to them the way to perfection and to harmony with the cosmic drama of salvation. Manichaeism sharply differentiated good and evil, nature and God; its fierce dualism appealed to some Christians who saw in it a doctrine coherent with what Paul had taught. St Augustine was a Manichee in his youth and Manichaean traces have been detected much later in the heresies of medieval Europe. Perhaps an uncompromising dualism has always a strong appeal to a certain cast of mind. However that may be, the distinction of being persecuted both by a Zoroastrian and a Christian monarchy preceded the spread of Manichaean ideas far and wide. Their adherents found refuge in central Asia and China, where Manichaeism appears to have flourished as late as the thirteenth century.

As for orthodox Christians in Persia, although a fifth-century peace stipulated that they should enjoy toleration, the danger that they might turn disloyal in the continual wars with Rome made this a dead letter. Only at the end of the century did a Persian king issue an edict of toleration and this was merely to conciliate the Armenians. It did not end the problem; Christians were soon irritated by the vigorous proselytizing of Zoroastrian enthusiasts. Further later assurances by Persian kings that Christianity was to be tolerated do not suggest that they were very successful or vigorous in seeing that it was. Perhaps it was impossible against the political background: the exception which proves the rule is provided by the Nestorians, who *were* tolerated by the Sassanids, but this was just because they were persecuted by the Romans. They were, therefore, thought likely to be politically reliable.

Though religion and the fact that Sassanid power and civilization reached their peak under Chosroes I in the sixth century both help to give the rivalry of the empires something of the dimensions of a contest between civilizations, the renewed wars of that century are not very interesting. They are for the most part a dull,

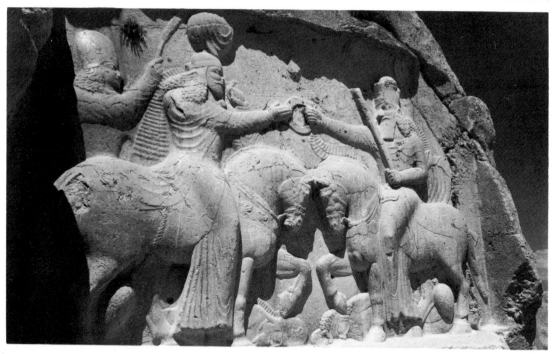

King meets god: Ardashir I, founder of the Sassanid line, receives his diadem from Ahura Mazda, the god of fire, after his overthrow of the last Parthian king. This forms one of the huge sculptured reliefs cut in a rock-face at Naqsh-i Rustam, a few miles from Persepolis; the tombs of Achaemenid kings were already to be found there and this relief was an implicit claim that the Sassanids, after expelling interlopers, were the true successors of the Achaemenids.

ding-dong story, though they were the last round but one of the struggle of East and West begun by the Greeks and Persians a thousand years earlier. The climax to this struggle came at the beginning of the seventh century in the last world war of antiquity. Its devastations may well have been the fatal blow to the Hellenistic urban civilization of Asia Minor.

Chosroes II, the last great Sassanid, then ruled Persia. His opportunity seemed to have come when a weakened Byzantium – Italy was already gone and the Slavs and Avars were pouring into the Balkans – lost a good emperor, murdered by mutineers. Chosroes owed a debt

of gratitude to the dead Maurice, for he had been restored to the Persian throne with his aid. He seized on the crime as an excuse and said he would avenge it. His armies poured into the Levant, ravaging the cities of Syria. In 615 they sacked Jerusalem, bearing away the relic of the True Cross which was its most famous treasure. The Jews, it may be remarked, often welcomed the Persians and seized the chance to carry out pogroms of Christians no doubt all the more delectable because the boot had for so long been on the other foot. The next year Persian armies went on to invade Egypt; a year later still, their advance-guards paused only a mile from Constantinople. They even put to sea, raided Cyprus and seized Rhodes from the empire. The empire of Darius seemed to be restored almost at the moment when, at the other end of the Mediterranean, the Roman empire was losing its last possessions in Spain.

This was the blackest moment for Rome in her long struggle with Persia, but a saviour was at hand. In 610 the imperial viceroy of Carthage, Heraclius, had revolted against Maurice's successor and ended that tyrant's bloody reign by killing him. In his turn he received the imperial

Among the major achievements of Sassanian art was its silverware, some of it engraved with scenes from palace life – such as this dancing-girl at a feast. It was made in the sixth or seventh century and the appearance of the nude in Sassanid art probably derives from foreign influences, perhaps from India.

358

crown from the Patriarch. The disasters in Asia could not at once be stemmed but Heraclius was to prove one of the greatest of the soldier emperors. Only sea-power saved Constantinople in 626, when the Persian army could not be transported to support an attack on the city by their Avar allies. Next year Heraclius broke into Assyria and Mesopotamia, the old disputed heartland of Near Eastern strategy. The Persian army mutinied, Chosroes was murdered and his successor made peace. The great days of Sassanid power were over. The relic of the True Cross – or what was said to be such – was restored to Jerusalem. The long duel of Persia and Rome was at an end and the focus of world history was to shift at last to another conflict.

The Sassanids went under in the end because they had too many enemies. The year 610 had brought a bad omen: for the first time an Arab force defeated a Persian army. But for centuries Persian kings had been much more preoccupied with enemies on their northern frontiers than with those of the south. They had to contend with the nomads of central Asia who have already made their mark on this narrative, but whose history it is hard to see either as a whole or in detail. None the less, one salient fact is clear – for nearly fifteen centuries these peoples provided an impetus in world history which was felt spasmodically and confusedly and had results ranging from the Germanic invasions of the West to the revitalizing of Chinese government in east Asia.

The best starting-point is geography. The place from which they came, 'central Asia', is not very well named. The term is imprecise. 'Land-locked Asia' might be better, for it is its remoteness from oceanic contact which distin-

The Sassanid king Chosroes I, the most famous of his line, contemplates the chastisement of an African people – perhaps Abyssinians – by his armies. This tapestry was probably copied from a Persian original, though in fact woven in about 600 AD by Egyptians who gave the scene a late Hellenistic flavour.

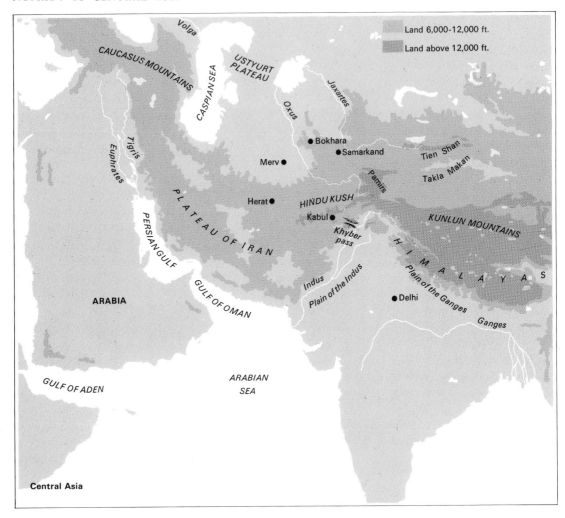

Land 6,000–12,000 ft.

Land above 12,000 ft.

Central Asia

guishes the crucial area. In the first place, this remoteness produced a distinctive and arid climate; secondly, it ensured until modern times an almost complete seclusion from external political pressure, though Buddhism, Christianity and Islam all showed that it was open to external cultural influence.

One way to envisage the area is in a combination of human and topographic terms. It is that part of Asia which is suitable for nomads and it runs like a huge corridor from east to west for four thousand miles or so. Its northern wall is the Siberian forest mass; the southern is provided by deserts, great mountain ranges, and the plateaux of Tibet and Iran. For the most part it is grassy steppe, though the boundary with the

desert fluctuates and it extends into it to important oases which have always been a distinctive part of its economy. They sheltered a settled population whose way of life both aroused the antagonism and envy of the nomads and also complemented it. The oases were most frequent and richest in the area of the two great rivers known to the Greeks as the Oxus and the Jaxartes. Cities rose there which were famous for their wealth and skills – Bokhara, Samarkand, Merv – and the trade-routes which bound distant China to the West passed through them.

No one knows the ultimate origins of the peoples of central Asia. They seem distinctive at the moment they enter history, but more for their culture than for their genetic stock. By the first millennium BC they were specialists in the difficult art of living on the move, following pasture with their flocks and herds and mastering the special skills this demanded. It is almost completely true that until modern times they remained illiterate and they lived in a mental world of demons and magic except when converted to the higher religions. They were skilled horsemen and especially adept at the use of the composite bow, the weapon of the mounted archer, which took extra power from its construction not from a single piece of wood but from strips of wood and horn. They could carry out elaborate weaving, carving and decoration, but, of course, did not build, for they lived in their tents.

Much still remains to be discovered about the Scythians, first mentioned in historical narrative by Herodotus and in the twentieth century acclaimed by Russian enthusiasts as the original stock on which their national tradition was founded, but archaeology has already made it clear that contact with the Greek communities of the Black Sea zone stimulated them to a high level of artistry in precious metals. Much of our knowledge of this gifted people comes from objects laid in their tombs, such as the vessels on which these reliefs appear.

The first to be named among these peoples were the Scythians, though it is not easy to say very precisely who they were. Scythians have

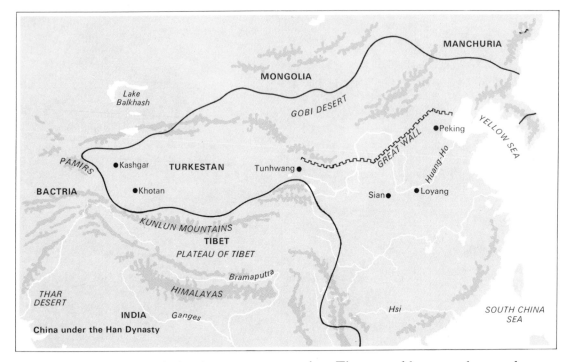

China under the Han Dynasty

been identified by archaeologists in many parts of Asia and Russia, and as far into Europe as Hungary. They seem to have had a long history of involvement in the affairs of the Near East. Some of them are reported harrying the Assyrian borders in the eighth century BC. Later they attracted the attention of Herodotus, who had much to say about a people who fascinated the Greeks. Possibly they were never really one people, but a group of related tribes. Some of them seem to have settled in south Russia long enough to build up regular relations with the Greeks as farmers, exchanging grain for the beautiful gold objects made by the Greeks of the Black Sea coasts which have been found in Scythian graves. But they also always first impressed the Greeks as warriors, fighting in the way which was to be characteristic of the Asian nomads, using bow and arrow from horseback, falling back when faced with a superior force. They harassed the Achaemenids and their successors for centuries and shortly before 100 BC overran Parthia.

The Scythians can serve as an example of the way in which such peoples are set in motion, for they were responding to very distant im-

pulses. They moved because other peoples were moving them. The balance of life in central Asia was always a nice one; even a small displacement of power or resources could deprive a people of its living-space and force it to long treks in search of a new livelihood. Nomads could not travel fast with flocks and herds, but seen from a background of long immunity their irruptions into settled land could seem dramatically sudden. It is through its periodic upheavals on a large scale rather than the more or less continuous frontier raiding and pillaging that central Asia has made its impact on world history.

In the third century BC another nomadic people was at the height of its power in Mongolia, the Hsing-Nu, in whom some recognize the first appearance on the historical stage of those more familiar as Huns. For centuries they were a byword; all sources agree at least that they were most unpleasant opponents, ferocious, cruel and, unfortunately, skilled warriors. It was against them that the Chinese emperors built the Great Wall, a fourteen-hundred-mile-long insurance policy. Later Chinese governments none the less found it inadequate protection and suffered at the Huns' hands until they embarked on a forward policy, penetrating Asia so as to outflank the Hsing-Nu. This led to a Chinese occupation of the Tarim basin up to the foothills of the Pamirs and the building on its north side of a remarkable series of frontier works. It was an early example of the generation of imperialism by suction; great powers can be drawn into areas of no concern to them except as sources of trouble. Whether or not this Chinese advance was the primary cause, the Hsing-Nu now turned on their fellow nomads and began to push west. This drove before them another people, the Yueh-chih, who in turn pushed out of their way more Scyths. At the end of the line stood the post-Seleucid Greek state of Bactria; it disappeared towards 140 BC and the Scyths then went on to invade Parthia.

They also pushed into south Russia, and into India, but that part of the story may be set aside for a moment. The history of the central Asian peoples quickly takes the non-specialist out of his depth; experts are in much disagreement, but it is clear that there was no comparable major upheaval such as that of the third century BC for another four hundred years or so. Then about AD 350 came the re-emergence of the Hsing-Nu in history when Huns began to invade the Sassanid empire (where they were known as Chionites). In the north, Huns had been moving westwards from Lake Baikal for centuries, driven before more successful rivals as others had been driven before them. Some were to appear west of the Volga in the next century; we have already met them near Troyes in 451. Those who turned south were a new handicap to Persia in its struggle with Rome.

Only one more major people from Asia remains to be introduced, the Turks. Again, the first impact on the outside world was indirect. The eventual successors of the Hsing-Nu in Mongolia had been a tribe called the Juan-Juan. In the sixth century its survivors were as far west as Hungary, where they were known as Avars; they are noteworthy for introducing a revolution in cavalry warfare to Europe by making known the stirrup, which had given them an important

advantage. But they were only in Europe because in about 550 they had been displaced in Mongolia by the Turks, a clan of iron-workers who had been their slaves. Among them were several tribes some of which – Khazars, Pechenegs, Cumans – played important parts in the later history of the Near East and Russia. The Khazars were Byzantium's allies against Persia, when the Avars were allies of the Sassanids. What is called the first Turkish empire seems to have been a loose dynastic connexion of such tribes running from the Tamir river to the Oxus. A Turkish khan sent emissaries to Byzantium in 568, roughly nine centuries before other Turks were to enter Constantinople in triumph. In the seventh century the Turks accepted the nominal suzerainty of the Chinese emperors, but by then a new element had entered Near Eastern history, for in 637 Arab armies overran Mesopotamia.

This follow-up to the blows of Heraclius announced the end of an era in Persian history. In 620 Sassanid rule stretched from Cyrenaica to Afghanistan and beyond; thirty years later it no longer existed. The Sassanid empire was gone, its last king murdered by his subjects in 651. More than a dynasty passed away, for the Zoroastrian state went down before a new religion as well as Arab armies and it was one in whose name the Arabs would go on to yet greater triumphs.

Islam has shown greater expansive and adaptive power than any other religion except Christianity. It has appealed to peoples as different and as distant from one another as Nigerians and Indonesians; even in its heartland, the lands of Arabic civilization between the Nile and the Hindu Kush, it encompasses huge differences of culture and climate. Yet none of the other great shaping factors of world history was based on fewer initial resources, except perhaps the Jewish religion. Perhaps significantly, the Jews' own nomadic origins lay in the same sort of tribal society, barbaric, raw and backward, which supplied the first armies of Islam. The comparison inevitably suggests itself for another reason, for Judaism, Christianity and Islam are the great monotheistic religions. None of them,

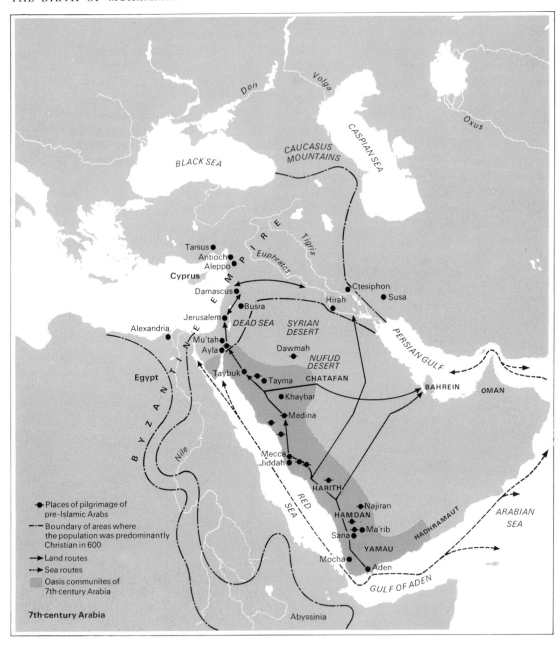

Places of pilgrimage of pre-Islamic Arabs
Boundary of areas where the population was predominantly Christian in 600
Land routes
Sea routes
Oasis communites of 7th-century Arabia

7th-century Arabia

in their earliest stages, could have been predicted to be world-historical forces, except by their most obsessed and fanatical adherents.

The history of Islam begins with Muhammad, but not with his birth, for its date is one of many things which are not known about him. His earliest Arabic biographer did not write until a century or so after he died and even his

account survives only indirectly. What is known is that around about 570 Muhammad was born in the Hejaz of poor parents, and was soon an orphan. He emerges as an individual in young manhood preaching the message that there is one God, that He is just and will judge all men, who may assure their salvation by following His will in their religious observance and their personal and social behaviour. This God had been preached before, for he was the God of Abraham and the Jewish prophets, of whom the last had been Jesus of Nazareth.

Muhammad belonged to a minor clan of an important Bedouin tribe, the Qurayshi. It was one of many in the huge Arabian peninsula, an area six hundred miles wide and over a thousand long. Those who lived there were subjected to very testing physical conditions; scorched in its hot season, most of Arabia was desert or rocky mountain. In much of it even survival was an achievement. But round its fringes there were little ports, the homes of Arabs who were sea-farers already in the second millennium BC. Their enterprise linked the Indus valley to Mesopotamia and brought the spices and gums of east Africa up the Red Sea to Egypt. The origins of these peoples and those who lived inland is disputed, but both language and the traditional genealogies which go back to Old Testament patriarchs suggest ties with other early Semitic pastoralists who were also ances-tors of the Jews, however disagreeable such a conclusion may be to Arabs today.

Arabia had not always been so uninviting. Just before and during the first centuries of the Christian era it contained a group of prosperous kingdoms. They survived until, possibly, the fifth century AD; both Islamic tradition and modern scholarship link their disappearance with the collapse of the irrigation arrangements of south Arabia. This produced migration from south to north, which created the Arabia of Muhammad's day. None of the great empires had penetrated more than briefly into the penin-sula, and Arabia had undergone little sophisti-cating fertilization from higher civilizations. It declined swiftly into a tribal society based on nomadic pastoralism. To regulate its affairs, patriarchal and kinship arrangements were enough so long as the Bedouin remained in the desert.

At the end of the sixth century new changes can be detected. At some oases, population was growing. There was no outlet for it and this was straining traditional social practice. Mecca, where the young Muhammad lived, was such a place. It was important both as an oasis and as a pilgrim centre, for people came to it from all over Arabia to venerate a black meteoric stone, the Kaaba, which had for centuries been impor-tant in Arab religion. But Mecca was also an important junction of caravan routes between the Yemen and Mediterranean ports. Along them came foreigners and strangers. The Arabs were polytheists, believing in nature gods, demons and spirits, but as intercourse with the outside world increased, Jewish and Christian communities appeared in the area; there were Christian Arabs before there were Moslems.

At Mecca some of the Qurayshi began to go in for commerce (another of the new early bio-graphical facts we know about Muhammad is that in his twenties he was married to a wealthy Qurayshi widow who had money in the caravan business). But such developments brought fur-ther social strains as the unquestioned loyalties of tribal structure were compromised by com-mercial values. The social relationships of a pastoral society assumed noble blood and age to be the accepted concomitants of wealth and this was no longer always the case. Here were some of the formative psychological pressures work-ing on the tormented young Muhammad. He began to ponder the ways of God to man. In the end he articulated a system which helpfully resolved many of the conflicts arising in his disturbed society.

The roots of his achievement lay in the obser-vation of the contrast between the Jews and Christians who worshipped the God familiar also to his own people as Allah, and the Arabs; Christians and Jews had a scripture for re-assurance and guidance, and Muhammad's people had none. One day while he contem-plated in a cave outside Mecca a voice came to him revealing his task:

Recite, in the name of the Lord, who created,
Created man from a clot of blood.

For twenty-two years Muhammad was to recite and the result is one of the great formative books of mankind, the Koran. Its narrowest significance is still enormous and, like that of Luther's Bible or the Authorized Version, it is

Kufa, a town on the southern border of Mesopotamia, was the seat of one of the first major Islamic garrisons and the source of a particularly beautiful and stylized form of Arabic script which was to be widely used in decoration and carving. It became known as Kufic script and is here employed for the most sacred of purposes, the transcription of part of the Koran.

linguistic; the Koran crystallized a language. It was the crucial document of Arabic culture not only because of its content but because it was to propagate the Arabic language. But it is much more; it is a visionary's book, passionate in its conviction of divine inspiration, vividly conveying Muhammad's spiritual genius and vigour. Though not collected in his lifetime, it was taken down by his entourage as delivered by him in a series of revelations; Muhammad saw himself as a passive instrument, a mouthpiece of God. The word *Islam* means submission or surrender. Muhammad believed he was to convey God's message to the Arabs as other messengers had earlier brought His word to other peoples. But Muhammad was sure that his position was special; though there had been prophets before him, their revelations heard (but falsified) by Jew and Christian, he was the final Prophet. Through him, Moslems were to believe, God spoke his last message to mankind.

The message demanded exclusive service for Allah. Tradition says that Muhammad on one occasion entered the Kaaba's shrine and struck with his staff all the images of the other deities which his followers were to wash out, sparing only that of the Virgin and Child. His teaching began with the uncompromising preaching of monotheism in a polytheistic religious centre. He went on to define a series of observances necessary to salvation and a social and personal code which often conflicted with current ideas, for example in its attention to the status of the individual believer, whether man, woman or child. It can readily be understood that such teaching was not always welcome. It seemed yet another disruptive and revolutionary influence – as it was – setting its converts against those of their tribe who worshipped the old gods and would certainly go to hell for it. It might damage the pilgrim business, too (though in the upshot it improved it, for Muhammad insisted strictly on the value of pilgrimage to so holy a place). Finally, as a social tie it placed blood second to belief; it was the brotherhood of believers which was the source of community, not the kinship group.

It is not surprising that the leaders of his tribe turned on Muhammad. Some of his followers emigrated to Ethiopia, a monotheistic country already penetrated by Christianity. Economic boycott was employed against the recalcitrant who stayed. Muhammad heard that the atmosphere might be more receptive at another oasis about two hundred and fifty miles further north, Yathrib. Preceded by some two hundred followers, he left Mecca and went there in 622. This *Hegira*, or emigration, was to be the beginning of the Moslem calendar and Yathrib was to change its name, becoming the 'city of the prophet', Medina.

It, too, was an area unsettled by economic and social change. Unlike Mecca, though, Medina was not dominated by one powerful tribe, but was a focus of competition for two; moreover, there were other Arabs there who adhered to Judaism. Such divisions favoured Muhammad's leadership. Converted families gave hospitality to the immigrants. The two groups were to form the future élite of Islam, the 'Companions of the Prophet'. Muhammad's writings for them show a new direction in his concerns, that of organizing a community. From the spiritual emphasis of his Mecca revelations he turned to practical, detailed statements about food, drink, marriage, war. The characteristic flavour of Islam, a religion which was also a civilization and a community, was now being formed.

Medina was the base for subduing first Mecca and then the remaining tribes of Arabia. A unifying principle was available in Muhammad's idea of the *umma*, the brotherhood of believers. It integrated Arabs (and, at first, Jews) in a society which maintained much of the traditional tribal framework, stressing the patriarchal structure in so far as it did not conflict with the new brotherhood of Islam, even retaining the traditional primacy of Mecca as a place of pilgrimage. Beyond this it is not clear how far Muhammad wished to go. He had made approaches to Jewish tribesmen at Medina, but they had refused to accept his claims; they were therefore driven out, and a Moslem community alone remained, but this need not have implied any enduring conflict with either Judaism or its continuator, Christianity. Doctrinal ties existed in their monotheism and their scriptures even if Christians were believed to fall into polytheism with the idea of the Trinity. Nevertheless, Muhammad enjoined the conversion of the infidel and for those who wished there was a justification here for proselytizing.

Muhammad died in 632. At that moment the community he had created was in grave danger of division and disintegration. Yet on it two Arab empires were to be built, dominating successive historical periods and focussed on two different centres of gravity. In each the key institution was the caliphate, the inheritance of Muhammad's authority as the head of a community. The first 'patriarchal' caliphs were all Qurayshi, most of them related to the Prophet by blood or marriage. Soon, they were criticized for their wealth and status and alleged to act as tyrants and exploiters. The last of them was deposed and killed in 661 after a series of wars in which conservatives contested what they saw as the deterioration of the caliphate from a religious office to a secular one. The year 661 saw the beginning of the Ummayad caliphate, the first of the two major chronological divisions of Arab empire. It did not bring struggle within the Arab world to an end for in 750 the Abbassid caliphate displaced it. The new caliphate lasted longer, surviving nearly two centuries (until

The early spread of Islam

946) as a real power and even longer as a puppet régime. Between them the two dynasties gave the Arab peoples three centuries of ascendancy in the Near East.

The first and most obvious expression of this was a great series of conquests in the first century of Islam which remade the world map from Gibraltar to the Indus. They had in fact begun immediately after the Prophet's death with the assertion of the first caliph's authority. Abu-Bakr set about conquering the unreconciled tribes of southern and eastern Arabia for Islam. But this led to fighting which spread to Syria and Iraq. Something analogous to the processes by which barbarian disturbances in central Asia rolled outward in their effects was at work in the over-populated Arabian peninsula; this time there was a creed to give it direction as well as a simple love of plunder.

Once beyond the peninsula, the first victim of Islam was Sassanid Persia. The challenge came just as she was under strain at the hands of the Heraclian emperors who were likewise to suffer from this new scourge. In 633 Arab armies invaded Syria and Iraq. Three years later the Byzantine forces were driven from Syria and in 638 Jerusalem fell to Islam. Mesopotamia was wrested from the Sassanids in the next couple of years, and at about the same time Egypt was taken from the empire. An Arab fleet was now created and the absorption of North Africa began. Cyprus was raided in the 630s and 640s; later in the century it was divided between the Arabs and the empire. At the end of the century the Arabs took Carthage, too. Meanwhile, after the Sassanids' disappearance the Arabs had conquered Khurasan in 655, Kabul in 664; at the beginning of the eighth century they crossed the Hindu Kush to invade Sind, which they occupied between 708 and 711. In the latter year an Arab army with Berber allies crossed the Straits of Gibraltar (the Arab commander, Tariq, is commemorated in its name which means *Jebel Tariq,* or mount of Tariq) and advanced into Europe, shattering at last the Visigothic kingdom. Finally, in 732, a hundred years after the death of the Prophet, the Arabs' army, deep in France, puzzled by over-extended communications and the approach of winter, turned back near Poitiers. The Franks who faced them and killed their commander claimed a victory; at any rate, it was the high water-mark of Arab conquest, though in the next few years Arab expeditions raided into France as far as the upper Rhône. Whatever brought it to an end (and possibly it was just because the Arabs were not much interested in European conquest, once away from the warm lands of the Mediterranean littoral), the Islamic onslaught in the West remains an astonishing achievement, even if Gibbon's vision of an Oxford teaching the Koran was never remotely near realization.

The Arab armies were at last stopped in the East, too, although at a cost of two sieges of Constantinople and the confining of the empire to the Balkans and Anatolia. From eastern Asia there is a report that an Arab force reached China in the early years of the eighth century; even if questionable, such a story is evidence of the conquerors' prestige. What is certain is that the frontier of Islam settled down along the Caucasus mountains and the Oxus after a great Arab defeat at the hands of the Khazars in Azerbaijan, and in 751 a victory over a Chinese army commanded by a Korean general at Talas, in the high Pamirs. On all fronts, in western Europe, central Asia, Anatolia and in the Caucasus, the tide of Arab conquest at last came to an end in the middle of the eighth century.

That tide had not flowed without interruption. There had been something of a lull in Arab aggressiveness during the intestine quarrelling just before the establishment of the Ummayad caliphate and there had been bitter fighting of Moslem against Moslem in the last two decades of the seventh century. But there were long-term factors working in favour of the Arabs' continuing success. Their first great enemies, Byzantium and Persia, had both had heavy commitments on other fronts and had been for centuries one another's fiercest antagonists. After Persia went under, Byzantium still had to contend with enemies in the west and to the north, fending them off with one hand while grappling with the Arabs with the other. Nowhere did the Arabs face an opponent comparable to the Byzantine empire nearer than China. Because of this, they pressed their conquests to the limit of geographical possibility or attractiveness, and sometimes their defeat showed they had overstretched themselves.

Even when they met formidable opponents, though, the Arabs still had great military advantages. Their armies were recruited from hungry fighters to whom the Arabian desert had left small alternative; the spur of over-population was behind them. Their assurance in the Prophet's teaching that death on the battlefield against the infidel would be followed by certain removal to paradise was a huge moral advantage. They fought their way, too, into lands whose peoples were often already disaffected with their rulers; in Egypt, for example, Byzantine religious orthodoxy had created dissident and alienated minorities. Yet when such influences have all been weighed, the Arab effort remains amazing. The fundamental explanation must lie in the movement of large numbers of men by a religious ideal. The Arabs thought they were doing God's will and creating a new brotherhood in the process; they generated an excitement in themselves like that of later revolutionaries. And conquest was only the beginning of the story of the impact of Islam on the world, which can only be compared to that of Judaism or Christianity. At one time it looked as if Islam might be irresistible everywhere. That was not to be, but one of the great traditions of civilization was to be built on its conquests and conversions and it is time to turn to that story.

2 The Arab empires

In 661 the Arab governor of Syria, Mu-Awiyah, murdered the last caliph related by blood or marriage to the Prophet. By taking the title himself he ended a period of anarchy and division and in the eyes of many pious Moslems this excused what he did. Though the history of Islam is the history of a faith and not that of a state – or even of a series of states – it will be convenient to follow for a little while the thread of political narrative of which this is the beginning. Mu-Awiyah's act was the foundation of the Ummayad caliphate.

This insurpation gave political ascendancy among the Arab peoples to the aristocrats of the Qurayshi, the very people who had opposed Muhammad at Mecca. Mu-Awiyah set up his capital at Damascus and later named his son crown prince, an innovation which introduced the dynastic principle. This usurpation was also the beginning of a schism within Islam, for a dissident group, the Shiites, henceforth

The great mosque of Córdoba remains one of the most remarkable buildings of the Arab world but is almost all that is left of the splendour of a once-great Arab city which had no rival west of Constantinople. It was built as a forest of short columns, probably because the architect had many short Roman pillars at his disposal, but none tall enough for a high ceiling. Later the Spanish built a church in the middle of it. In spite of this and though it is now difficult to imagine it in its glory as the spiritual centre of western Islam, the mosque still remains a building of surpassing beauty and mystery.

claimed that the right of interpreting the Koran was confined to Muhammad's descendants. The murdered caliph, they said, had been divinely designated as *imam* to transmit his office to his descendants and was immune from sin and error. The Ummayad caliphs, correspondingly, had their own party of supporters, called Sunnites, who believed that doctrinal authority changed hands with the caliphate. Together with the creation of a regular army and a system of supporting it by taxation of the unbelievers, a decisive movement was thus made away from tribal Arabism. The site of the Ummayad capital, too, was important in changing the style of Islamic culture, as were the personal tastes of the first caliph. Syria was a Mediterranean state, but Damascus was roughly on the border between the cultivated land of the Fertile Crescent and the barren expanses of the desert; its life was fed by two worlds. To the desert-dwelling Arabs, the former must have been the more striking. Syria had a long Hellenistic past and both the caliph's wife and his doctor were Christians.

The first Ummayad speedily reconquered the East from dissidents who resisted the new régime and the Shiite movement was driven underground. There followed a glorious century whose peak came under the sixth and seventh caliphs between 685 and 705. Unfortunately we know little about the detailed and institutional history of Ummayad times. Archaeology sometimes throws light on general trends and reveals something of the Arabs' impact on their neighbours. Foreign records and Arab chroniclers also logged important events. Nevertheless, the early centuries of Arab history produce virtually no archive material apart from an occasional document quoted by an Arab author. Nor did Islamic religion have a bureaucratic centre of ecclesiastical government. Islam had nothing remotely approaching in scope the records of the papacy, for example, though the analogy between it and the caliphate might in this respect arouse similar expectations. Instead of administrative records throwing light on continuities the historian of pre-Mongol Islam has only occasional collections preserved almost by chance, such as a mass of papyri from Egypt, special accumulations of documents by minority communities such as the Jews, and coins and inscriptions. The huge body of Arabic literature in print or manuscript provides further details, but it is much more difficult to make general statements about the government of the caliphates with confidence than, say, similar statements about Byzantium.

It seems, none the less, that the early arrangements of the caliphates, inherited from the orthodox caliphs, were loose and simple – perhaps too loose, as the Ummayad's own defection showed. Their basis was conquest for tribute, not for assimilation, and the result was a series of compromises with existing structures. Administratively and politically, the early caliphs took over the structures of earlier rulers. Byzantine and Sassanid arrangements continued to operate; Greek was the language of government in Damascus, Persian in Ctesiphon, the old Sassanid capital, until the early eighth century. Institutionally, the Arabs left the societies they took over by and large undisturbed except by taxation. Of course, this does not mean that institutions always went on working in the same way. In north-western Persia, for example, Arab conquest seems to have been followed by a decline in commerce and a drop in population, and it is hard not to associate this with the collapse of a complex drainage and irrigation system successfully maintained in Sassanid times. In other places, Arab conquest had less drastic effects. The conquered were not antag-

onized by having to accept Islam, but took their places in a hierarchy presided over by the Arab Moslems. Below them came the converted neo-Moslems of the tributary peoples, then the *dhimmi*, or 'protected persons' as the Jewish and Christian monotheists were called. Lowest down the scale came unconverted pagans or adherents of no revealed religion. In the early days the Arabs were segregated from the local population and lived as a military caste in special towns paid by the taxes raised in the areas, forbidden to enter commerce or own land.

This could not be kept up. Like the Bedouin customs brought from the desert, segregation was eroded by garrison life. Gradually the Arabs became landowners and cultivators, and so their camps changed into new, cosmopolitan cities such as Kufa or Basra, the great *entrepôt* of the trade with India. More and more Arabs mixed with the local inhabitants in a two-way relationship, as the indigenous élites underwent an administrative and linguistic arabization. The caliphs appointed more and more of the officials of the provinces and by the mid-eighth century Arabic was almost everywhere the language of administration. Together with the standard coinage bearing Arabic inscriptions it is the major evidence of Ummayad success in laying the foundations of a new, eclectic civilization. Such changes went fastest in Iraq, where they were favoured by prosperity as trade revived under the Arab peace.

The assertion of their authority by the Ummayad caliphs was one source of their troubles. Local bigwigs, especially in the eastern half of the empire, resented interference with their practical independence. Whereas many of the aristocracy of the former Byzantine territories emigrated to Constantinople, the élites of Persia could not; they had nowhere to go and had to remain, irritated by their subordination to the Arabs who left them much of their local authority. Nor did it help that the later Ummayad caliphs were men of poor quality, who did not command the respect won by the great men of the dynasty. Civilization softened them. When they sought to relieve the tedium of life in the towns they governed, they moved out into the desert, not to live again the life of the Bedouin, but to enjoy their new towns and palaces, some of them remote and luxurious, equipped as they were with hot baths and great hunting enclosures and supplied from irrigated plantations and gardens.

There were opportunities here for the disaffected among whom the *Shi'a*, the party of the Shiites, were especially notable. Besides their original political and religious appeal, they increasingly drew on social grievances among the non-Arab converts to Islam, particularly in Iraq. From the start, the Ummayad régime had distinguished sharply between those Moslems who were and those who were not by birth members of an Arab tribe. The numbers of the latter class grew rapidly, the Arabs had not sought to convert (and sometimes even tried to deter from conversion in early times) but the attractiveness of the conquering creed was powerfully reinforced by the fact that adherence to it might bring tax relief. Around the Arab garrisons, Islam had spread rapidly among the non-Arab populations which grew up to service their needs. It was also very successful among the local élites who maintained the day-to-day administration. Many of these neo-Moslems, the *mawali*, as they were called, eventually became soldiers, too. Yet they increasingly felt alienated and excluded from the aristocratic society of the pure Arabs. The puritanism and orthodoxy of the Shiites, equally alienated from the same society for political and religions reasons, made a great appeal to them.

Increasing trouble in the east heralded the breakdown of Ummayad authority. In 749 a new caliph, Abu-al-Abbas, was hailed publicly in the mosque at Kufa in Iraq. This was the beginning of the end for the Ummayads. The pretender, a descendant of an uncle of the Prophet, announced his intention of restoring the caliphate to orthodox ways; he appealed to a wide spectrum of opposition including the Shiites. His full name was promising: it meant 'Shedder of Blood'. In 750 he defeated and executed the last Ummayad caliph. A dinner-

party was held for the males of the defeated house; the guests were murdered before the first course, which was then served to their hosts. With this clearing of the decks began nearly two centuries during which the 'Abassid caliphate ruled the Arab world, the first of them the most glorious.

The support the Abassids enjoyed in the eastern Arab dominions was reflected by the shift of the capital to Iraq, to Baghdad, until then a Christian village on the Tigris. The change had many implications. It gave a new weight to Persian influence which was both politically and culturally to be very important. There was a change in the ruling caste, too, and one sufficiently important to lead some historians to call it a social revolution. They were from this time Arabs only in the sense of being Arabic-speaking; they were no longer Arabian. Within the matrix provided by a single religion and a single language the élites which governed the Abassid empire came from many peoples right across the Middle East. They were almost always Moslem but they were often converts or children of convert families. The cosmopolitanism of Baghdad reflected the new cultural atmosphere. A huge city, rivalling Constantinople, with perhaps a half-million inhabitants, it was a complete antithesis of the ways of life brought from the desert by the first Arab conquerors. A great empire had come again to the whole Middle East. It did not break with the past ideologically, though, for after dallying with other possibilities the Abassid caliphs confirmed the Sunnite orthodoxy of their predecessors. This was soon reflected in the disappointment and irritation of the Shiites who had helped to bring them to power.

The Abassids were a violent lot and did not take risks with their success. They soon carried out a ruthless extirpation of opposition and even of former allies who might turn sour. Loyalty to the dynasty, rather than the brotherhood of Islam, was increasingly the basis of the empire and this reflected the old Persian tradition. Much was made of religion as a buttress to the dynasty and the Abassids persecuted religious

373

dissidents. The machinery of government became more elaborate. Here one of the major developments was that of the office of vizier (monopolized by one family until the legendary caliph Haroun-al-Raschid wiped them out). The whole structure became somewhat more bureaucratized, the land taxes raising a big revenue to maintain a magnificent monarchy. Nevertheless, provincial distinctions remained very real. Governorships tended to become hereditary, and, because of this, central authority was eventually forced on to the defensive. The governors exercised a greater and greater power in appointments and the handling of taxation. It is not easy to say what was the caliphate's real power, for it regulated a loose collection of provinces whose actual dependence was related very much to the circumstances of the moment. But of Abassid wealth and prosperity at its height there can be no doubt. They rested not only on its great reserves of manpower and the large areas where agriculture was untroubled during the Arab peace, but also upon the revival of commerce along the caravan routes which passed through the Arab lands from east to west. The riches of Haroun-al-Raschid's Baghdad reflected the prosperity they brought.

Islamic civilization in the Arab lands reached its peak under the Abassids. Paradoxically, one reason was the movement of its centre of gravity away from Arabia and the Levant. Islam provided a political organization which, by holding together a huge area, cradled a culture which was essentially synthetic, mingling, before it was done, Hellenistic, Christian, Jewish, Zoroastrian and Hindu ideas. Arabic culture under the Abassids had closer access to the Persian tradition and closer contact with India which brought to it renewed vigour and new creative elements.

One aspect of Abassid civilization was a great age of translation into Arabic, the new *lingua franca* of the Middle East. Christian and Jewish scholars made available to Arab readers the works of Plato and Aristotle, Euclid and Galen, thus importing the categories of Greek thought into Arab culture. The tolerance of Islam for its tributaries made this possible in principle from the moment when Syria and Egypt were conquered, but it was under the early Abassids that the most important translations were made. So much it is possible to chart fairly confidently. To say what this meant, of course, is more difficult, for though the texts of Plato might be available, it was the Plato of late Hellenistic culture, transmitted through interpretations by Christian monks and Sassanid academics.

The culture these sources influenced was predominantly literary; Arabic Islam produced beautiful buildings, lovely carpets, exquisite ceramics, but its great medium was the word, spoken and written. Even the great Arab scientific works are often huge prose compendia. The accumulated bulk of this literature is immense and, to put it at its simplest, much of it remains unread by western scholars and large numbers of manuscripts have never been

At Samarra, on the banks of the Tigris, only ruins now record the presence in the ninth century of a city which was for fifty years the capital of the Caliphs and ran for miles along its banks. One of the caliphs built a magnificent palace there; this reconstruction gives an impression of the decoration of the walls of the harem, where its remains were found.

374

examined at all. The prospect is promising; the absence of archive material for early Islam is balanced by a huge corpus of literature of all varieties and forms except the drama. How deeply it penetrated Islamic society remains obscure, though it is clear that educated people expected to be able to write verses and could enjoy critically the performances of singers and bards. Schools were widespread; the Islamic world was probably highly literate by comparison, for example, with medieval Europe. Higher learning, more closely religious in so far as it was institutionalized in the mosques or special schools of religious teachers, is more difficult to assess. How much, therefore, the potentially divisive and stimulating effect of ideas drawn from other cultures was felt below the level of the leading Islamic thinkers and scientists is hard to say, but potentially the elements for a questioning and self-critical culture were there from the eighth century onwards.

Judged by its greatest men, Arabic culture reached its apogee in the East in the ninth and tenth centuries and in Spain in the eleventh and twelfth. Although Arab history and geography are both very impressive, its greatest triumphs were scientific and mathematical; we still employ the 'arabic' numerals which made possible calculations with far greater simplicity than did Roman numeration and which were set out by an Arab arithmetician (although in origin they were Indian). This transmission function of Arabic culture was always important and characteristic but must not obscure its originality. The name of the greatest of Islamic astronomers, Al-Khwarizmi, indicates Persian Zoroastrian origins; it expresses the way in which Arabic culture was a confluence of sources. His astronomical tables, none the less, were an Arabic achievement, an expression of the synthesis made possible by Arab empire.

The translation of Arabic works into Latin in the later Middle Ages, and the huge repute enjoyed by Arab thinkers in Europe, testify to the quality of this culture. Of the works of Al-Kindi, one of the greatest of Arab philosophers, more survive in Latin than in Arabic,

Islamic mechanics built upon Hellenistic texts which transmitted the skills of such men as Archimedes and Hero of Alexandria. This elaborate machine, depicted in a fourteenth-century miniature (probably from Syria), is a clock. It indicated the passage of time by an elaborate series of movements by the little figures making it up and finally by the depositing of a little ball inside the elephant to mark each half-hour.

while Dante paid Ibn-Sina (Avicenna in Europe) and Averroës the compliment of placing them in limbo (together with Saladin, the Arab hero of the crusading epoch) when he allocated great men to their fate after death in his great poem, and they were the only men of the Christian era whom he treated thus. The Persian practitioners who dominated Arabic medical studies wrote works which remained for centuries the standard textbooks of western training. European languages are still marked by Arabic words which indicate the special importance of Arabic study in certain areas: 'zero', 'cipher', 'almanac', 'algebra' and 'alchemy' are among them. The survival of a

This picture of the constellation Sagittarius is one of the earliest examples of Islamic book illustration, showing both Abassid and Persian influence. It comes from Shiraz where it was drawn (or possibly traced from a celestial globe) in the early eleventh century for a book of constellations based on Ptolemy.

technical vocabulary of commerce, too – tariff, *douane*, magazine – is a reminder of the superiority of Arab commercial technique; the Arab merchants taught Christians how to keep accounts. Strikingly, this cultural transmission to Europe was almost entirely one way. Only one Latin text, it appears, was ever translated into Arabic during the Middle Ages, at a time when Arabic scholars were passionately interested in the cultural legacies of Greece, Persia and India. A single fragment of paper bearing a few German words with their Arabic equivalents is the only evidence from eight hundred years of Islamic Spain of any interest in western languages outside the peninsula. The Arabs regarded the civilization of the cold lands of the north as a meagre, unsophisticated affair, as no doubt it was. But Byzantium impressed them.

An Arabic tradition in visual art founded under the Ummayads also flourished under the Abassids, but it was narrower in its scope than Islamic science. Islam came to forbid the making of likenesses of the human form or face; this was not scrupulously enforced, but it long inhibited the appearance of naturalistic painting or sculpture. Of course, it did not restrict architects. Their art developed very far within a style whose essentials had appeared at the end of the seventh century; it was at once in debt to the past and unique to Islam. The impression produced upon the Arabs by Christian building in Syria was the catalyst; from it they learnt, but they sought to surpass it, for believers should, they were sure, have places of worship better and more beautiful than the Christians' churches. Moreover, a distinctive architectural style could visibly serve as a separating force in the non-Moslem world which surrounded the first Arab conquerors of Egypt and Syria.

The Arabs borrowed Roman technique and Hellenistic ideas of internal space, but what resulted was distinctive. The oldest architectural monument of Islam was the Dome of the Rock built at Jerusalem in 691. Stylistically, it is a landmark in architectural history, the first Islamic building with a dome. It appears to have been built as a monument to victory over

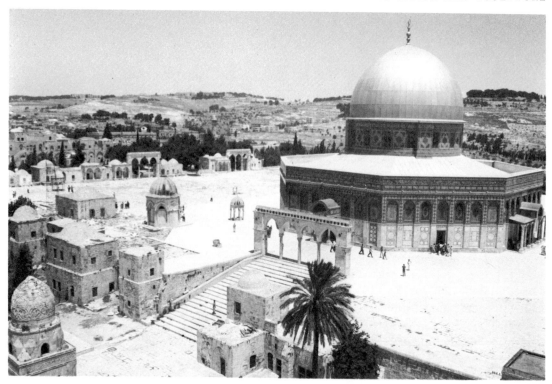

The Dome of the Rock at Jerusalem was in part built in the 690s to offset the appeal of Mecca as a place of pilgrimage. On the summit of Mount Moriah, a site sacred in the Old Testament as well as to Moslems, it is the oldest place of worship built by an Islamic ruler to survive intact.

Jewish and Christian belief, but unlike the congregational mosques which were to be the great buildings of the next three centuries, the Dome of the Rock was a great shrine glorifying and sheltering one of the most sacred places of Jew and Moslem alike; men believed that on the hill-top it covered Abraham had offered up his son Isaac in sacrifice and that from it Muhammad was taken up into heaven.

Soon afterwards came the Ummayad mosque at Damascus, the greatest of the classical mosques of a new tradition. As so often in this new Arab world, it embodied much of the past; a Christian basilica (which had itself replaced a temple of Jupiter) formerly stood on its site, and it was itself decorated with Byzantine mosaics. Its novelty was that it established a design derived from the pattern of worship initiated by the Prophet in his house at Medina; its essential was the *mihrab*, or alcove in the wall of the place of worship, which indicated the direction of Mecca.

Architecture and sculpture, like literature, continued to flourish and to draw upon elements culled from traditions all over the Near East and Asia. Potters strove to achieve the style and finish of the Chinese porcelain which came to them down the Silk Road. The performing arts were less cultivated and seem to have drawn little on other traditions, whether Mediterranean or Indian. There was no Arab theatre, though the storyteller, the poet, the singer and the dancer were esteemed. Arabic musical art is commemorated in European languages, which have retained the names of lute, guitar, and rebec; its achievements, too, have been seen as among the greatest of Arabic culture, though they remain less accessible to western sensibility than those of the plastic and visual arts.

Many of the greatest names of this civilization were writing and teaching when its political framework was already in decay, even visibly collapsing. In part this was a matter of the gradual displacement of Arabs within the caliphate's élites, but the Abassids in their turn lost control of their empire, first of the peripheral provinces and of then Iraq itself. As an international force they peaked early; in 782 an Arab army appeared for the last time before Constantinople. They were never to get so far again. Haroun-al-Raschid might be treated with respect by Charlemagne but the first signs of an eventually irresistible tendency to fragmentation were already there in his day.

In Spain, in 756, an Ummayad prince who had not accepted the fate of his house had proclaimed himself *emir*, or governor, of Córdoba. So El-Andalus passed out of the effective control of the caliphate. It acquired its own caliph only in the tenth century (until then its rulers remained emirs) but long before that was independent *de facto*. This did not mean that Ummayad Spain was untroubled. Islam had never conquered the whole peninsula and the Franks recovered the north-east by the tenth century. There were by then Christian kingdoms in northern Iberia and they were always willing to help stir the pot of dissidence within Arab Spain where a fairly tolerant policy towards Christians did not end the danger of revolt.

Yet El-Andalus prospered. The Ummayads developed their sea-power and contemplated imperial expansion not towards the north, at the expense of the Christians, but into Africa, at the expense of Moslem powers, even negotiating for alliance with Byzantium in the process. Meanwhile, in Spain Islamic civilization reached its greatest beauty and maturity in a golden age of creativity in the eleventh and twelfth centuries which rivalled that of Abassid Baghdad. This left great monuments behind as well as producing great learning and philosophy. The

The fifteenth-century Islamic potters of Spain produced tableware which was highly prized in both Christian Europe and the Middle East. Some combined themes from Europe and the Islamic world such as this Portuguese ship set among arabic lettering.

378

Alfonso the Wise, King of Castile, added Murcia to his kingdom and took Cadiz from the Arabs, but it is less for this that he is remembered as a great king, than for his patronage of scholars and artists, and for the splendour and eclecticism of Spanish culture during his reign. Something of its spirit is expressed by this illumination from a book on chess by the king which shows an Arab nobleman and a Christian knight, his guest, peacefully at play. Christian culture in Spain was for centuries refreshed by currents from the Islamic world; the intransigence of the Christian crusaders of the Reconquest was to obscure much of this from later Spaniards.

seven hundred mosques of tenth-century Córdoba numbered among them one which can still be thought the most beautiful building in the world. Arab Spain was of enormous importance to Europe, a door to the learning and science of the East, but one through which were also to pass more material goods as well: through it Christendom received knowledge of agricultural and irrigation techniques, oranges and lemons, sugar. As for Spain itself, the Arab stamp went very deep, as many students of the later, Christian, Spain have pointed out, and can still be observed in language, manners and art.

Another important breakaway within the Arab world came when the Fatimids set up their own caliph and moved their capital to Cairo in 973. The Fatimids were Shiites and maintained their government of Egypt until a new Arab invasion destroyed it in the twelfth century. Less conspicuous examples could be found elsewhere in the Abassid dominions as local governors began to term themselves emir and sultan. The power base of the caliphs narrowed more and more rapidly; they were unable to reverse the trend. Civil wars among the sons of Haroun led to a loss of the support by the religious teachers and the devout. Bureaucratic corruption and embezzlement alienated the subject populations. Recourse to tax-farming as a way round these ills only created new examples of oppression. The army was increasingly recruited from foreign mercenaries and slaves; even by the death of Haroun's successor it was virtually Turkish. Thus, barbarians were incorporated within the structure of the caliphates as had been the western barbarians within the Roman empire. As time went by they took on a praetorian look and increasingly dominated the caliphs. And all the time popular opposition was exploited by the Shiites and other mystical sects.

Abassid rule effectively ended in 946 when a Persian general and his men deposed a caliph and installed a new one. Theoretically, the line of Abassids continued, but in fact the change was revolutionary; the new Buwayhid dynasty lived henceforth in Persia. Arab Islam had fragmented; the unity of the Near East was once more at an end. No empire remained to resist the centuries of invasion which followed, although it was not until 1258 that the last Abassid was slaughtered by the Mongols. Before that, Islamic unity had a last revival in response to the Crusades, but the great days of Islamic empire were over.

The peculiar nature of Islam meant that religious authority could not long be separated from political supremacy; the caliphate was eventually to pass to the Ottoman Turks, therefore, when they became the top dogs of Near-Eastern history and they would carry the frontier of Islam still farther afield. But their Arab predecessors' work was awe-inspiringly vast for all its ultimate collapse. They had destroyed both the old imperial Near East and Sassanid Persia, hemming Byzantium in to Anatolia; in the end this was to call western Europeans back into the Levant. The Arabs had also implanted a new tradition ineradicably from Morocco to Afghanistan. Its coming was in many ways revolutionary. It kept women, for example, in an inferior position, but gave them legal rights over property not available to women in many European countries until the nineteenth century. Even the slave had rights and inside the community of the believers there were no castes nor inherited status. This revolution was rooted in a religion which – like that of the Jews – was not distinct from other sides of life, but embraced them all; no words exist in Islam to express the distinctions of sacred and profane, spiritual and temporal, which our own tradition takes for granted. Religion *is* society for the Moslems, and the unity this has provided has outlasted centuries of political division. It was a unity both of law and of a certain attitude; Islam is not a religion of miracles, but of practice and intellectual belief.

Besides having a great intellectual impact on Christendom, Islam also spread far beyond the world of Arab hegemony, to central Asia in the tenth century, India between the eighth and eleventh and in the eleventh beyond the Sudan and to the Niger. Between the twelfth and sixteenth centuries still more of Africa would

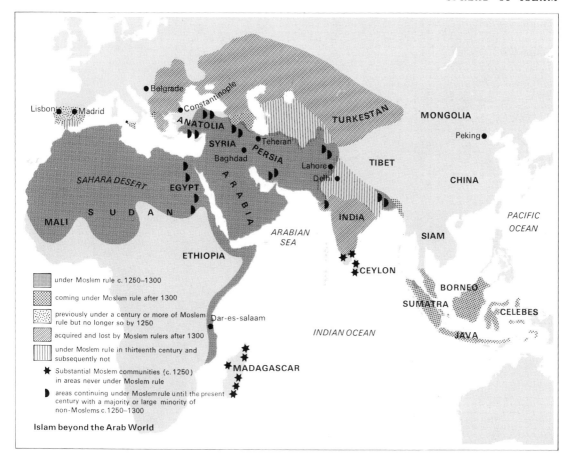

under Moslem rule c. 1250–1300

coming under Moslem rule after 1300

previously under a century or more of Moslem rule but no longer so by 1250

acquired and lost by Moslem rulers after 1300

under Moslem rule in thirteenth century and subsequently not

Substantial Moslem communities (c. 1250) in areas never under Moslem rule

areas continuing under Moslem rule until the present century with a majority or large minority of non-Moslems c. 1250–1300

Islam beyond the Arab World

become Moslem; Islam remains today the fastest-growing faith of that continent. Thanks to the conversion of Mongols in the thirteenth century, Islam would also reach China. In the fifteenth and sixteenth centuries it spread across the Indian ocean to Malaya and Indonesia. Missionaries, migrants and merchants carried it; among them, the Arabs were still important, whether they moved in caravans into Africa or took their dhows from the Persian Gulf and Red Sea to the bay of Bengal. There would even be

a last, final, extension of the faith into southeast Europe in the sixteenth and seventeenth centuries. It was a remarkable achievement for an idea at whose service there had been in the beginning no resources except those of a handful of Semitic tribes. But in spite of its majestic record no Arab state was ever again to provide unity for Islam after the tenth century. Even Arab unity was to remain only a dream, though one cherished still today.

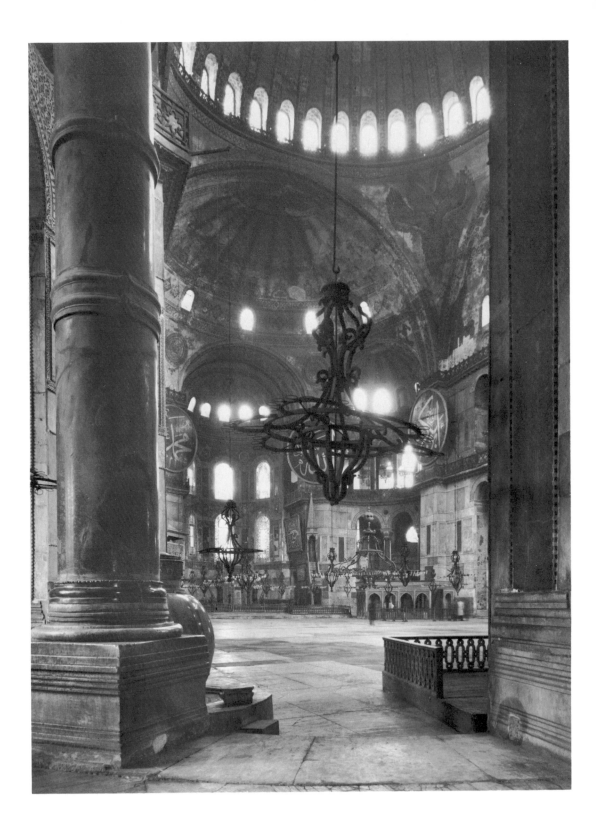

3 Byzantium and its sphere

In 1453, nine hundred years after Justinian, Constantinople fell to an infidel army. 'There has never been and there never will be a more dreadful happening', wrote one Greek scribe. It was indeed a great event. No one in the West was prepared; the whole Christian world was shocked. More than a state, Rome itself was at an end. The direct descent from the classical Mediterranean civilization had been snapped at last; even if few saw this in quite so deep a

Hagia Sophia, the church of the Holy Wisdom, better known as Saint Sophia, was for centuries the greatest of Christendom's temples. It was Justinian's architectural masterpiece. The dome is an extraordinary feat of engineering (though it collapsed on one occasion) and its three aisles a huge theatre for the religious ritual of the court and the hierarchy of the Church. It was not a place of worship for the commonalty; as one scholar has put it, 'the audience was God'. Its original appearance, bedecked with hangings of silk and gold and blazing with the colour of its mosaics and marbles is hard now to recapture, for what the modern visitor sees is a building first 'purged' by iconoclasts, then redecorated and embellished again over the centuries until the Ottoman conquest which turned it into a mosque, adding minarets to the outside and Koranic inscriptions, pulpit, chandeliers and railings to the interior. Nowadays a museum, it became also in its last phase a model for Moslem architects and the inspiration of one of their finest works, the great Blue mosque which stands about three-quarters of a mile away.

perspective as the literary enthusiasts who detected in it retribution for the Greek sack of Troy, it was still the end of two thousand years' tradition. And if the pagan world of Hellenistic culture and ancient Greece were set aside, a thousand years of Christian empire at Byzantium itself was impressive enough for its passing to seem an earthquake.

This is one of those subjects where it helps to know the end of the story before beginning it. Even in their decline Byzantine prestige and traditions had amazed strangers who felt through them the weight of an imperial past. To the end its emperors were *augusti* and its citizens called themselves 'Romans'. For centuries, St Sophia had been the greatest of Christian churches, the Orthodox religion it enshrined needing to make even fewer concessions to religious pluralism as previously troublesome provinces were swallowed by the Moslems. Though in retrospect it is easy to see the inevitability of decline and fall, therefore, this was not how the men who lived under it saw the eastern empire. They knew, consciously or unconsciously, that it had great powers of evolution. It was a great conservative *tour de force* which had survived many extremities and its archaic style was almost to the end able to cloak important changes.

None the less, a thousand years brought great upheavals in both east and west; history played upon Byzantium, modifying some elements in its heritage, stressing others, obliterating others, so that the empire was in the end very different from Justinian's while never becoming wholly distinct from it. There is no clear dividing line between antiquity and Byzantium. The centre of gravity of the empire had begun to shift eastward before Constantine and when his city became the seat of world empire it was the inheritor of the pretensions of Rome. The office of the emperors showed particularly sharply how evolution and conservatism could combine. Until 800 there was no formal challenge to the theory that the emperor was the secular ruler of all mankind. With the coronation of a western emperor in that year, whatever might be said of the exact relationship of his power to that of the East, the uniqueness of the imperial purple had gone. Yet Byzantium continued to cherish the fantasy of universal empire; there would be emperors right to the end and their office was one of awe-inspiring grandeur. Still theoretically chosen by Senate, army and people, they had none the less an absolute authority. While the realities of his accession might determine for any particular emperor the actual extent of his power – and sometimes the dynastic succession broke under the strains – he was *autocrat* as a western emperor never was. Respect for legal principle and the vested interests of bureaucracy might muffle the emperor's will in action, but it was always supreme in theory. The heads of all the great departments of state were responsible to no one but him. This authority explains the intensity with which Byzantine politics focussed at the imperial court, for it was there, and not through corporate and representative institutions such as evolved slowly in the West, that authority could be influenced.

This autocratic power had its harsh side. The *curiosi* or secret police informers who swarmed through the empire were not there for nothing. But the nature of the imperial office also laid obligations on the emperor. Crowned by the Patriarch of Constantinople, the emperor had the enormous authority, but also the responsibilities, of God's representative upon earth. The line between lay and ecclesiastical was always more blurred in the East than in the West. Though this meant that there was in the East nothing like the western opposition of Church

and State there was a continuing pressure upon God's vice-regent to act appropriately, to show *philanthropia*, a love of mankind, in his acts. The purpose of the autocratic power was the preservation of mankind and of the conduits by which it drew the water of life – orthodoxy and the Church. Appropriately most of the early Christian emperors were canonized – just as pagan emperors had been deified. Other traditions than the Christian also affected the office, as this suggested. Byzantine emperors were to receive the ritual prostrations of oriental tradition and the images of them which look down from their mosaics show their heads surrounded by the nimbus in which the last pre-Christian emperors were depicted, for it was part of the cult of the sun god. Some representations of Sassanid rulers have it, too. It was, none the less, above all as a Christian ruler that the emperor justified his authority.

The imperial office itself thus embodied much of the Christian heritage of Byzantium. That heritage also marked the eastern empire off sharply from the West at many other levels. There were, in the first place, the ecclesiastical peculiarities of what came to be called the Orthodox Church. Islam, for example, was sometimes seen by the eastern clergy less as a pagan religion than a heresy. Other differences lay in the Orthodox view of the relationship of clergy to society; the coalescence of spiritual and lay was important at many levels below the throne. One symbol of it was the retention of a married clergy; the Orthodox priest, for all his reputed holiness, was never to be quite the man apart his western Catholic colleague became. This suggests the great rôle of the Orthodox Church as a cementing force in society down to modern times. Above all, no sacerdotal authority as great as that of the papacy would emerge. The focus of authority was the emperor, whose office and responsibility towered above the equally ranked bishops. Of course, so far as social regulation went, this did not mean that Orthodoxy was more tolerant than the Church of the medieval West. Bad times were always liable to be interpreted as evidence that the emperor had not been doing his Christian duty – which included the harrying of such familiar scapegoats as Jews, heretics and homosexuals.

Distinction from the West was in part a product of political history, of the gradual loosening of contact after the division of the empires, in part a matter of an original distinction of style. The Catholic and Orthodox traditions were on divergent courses from early times, even if at first the divergence was only slight. At an early date Latin Christianity was somewhat estranged by the concessions the Greeks had to make to Syrian and Egyptian practice. Yet such concessions had also kept alive a certain polycentrism within Christendom. When Jerusalem, Antioch and Alexandria, the other three great patriarchates of the East, fell into Arab hands, the polarization of Rome and Constantinople was accentuated. Gradually, the Christian world was ceasing to be bilingual; a Latin west came to face a Greek east. It was at the beginning of the seventh century that Latin finally ceased to be the official language of the army and of justice, the two departments where it had longest resisted Greek. That the bureaucracy was Greek-speaking was to be very important. When the eastern Church failed among Moslems, it opened a new missionary field and won much ground among the pagans to the north. Eventually, south-eastern Europe and Russia owed their evangelizing to Constantinople. The outcome – among many other things – was that the Slav peoples would owe to their teachers not only the creation of a literature and written language based on Greek, but many of their most fundamental political ideas. And because the West was Catholic, its relations with the Slav world were sometimes hostile, so that the Slav peoples came to view the western half of Christendom with deep reservations. This lay far in the future and takes us further afield than we need go for the present.

The distinctiveness of the eastern Christian tradition could be illustrated in many ways. Monasticism, for example, remained closer to its original forms in the East and the importance of the Holy Man has always been greater there

than in the more hierarchically aware Roman Church. The Greeks, too, seem to have been more disputatious than Latins; the Hellenistic background of the early Church had always favoured speculation and the eastern Churches were open to oriental trends, always susceptible to the pressures of many traditional influences. Yet this did not prevent the imposition of dogmatic solutions to religious quarrels.

Some of these were about issues which now seem trivial or even meaningless. Inevitably, a secular age such as our own finds even the greatest of them difficult to fathom simply because we lack a sense of the mental world lying behind them. It requires an effort to recall that behind the exquisite definitions and logic-chopping of the Fathers lay a concern of appalling importance, nothing less than that mankind should be saved from damnation. A further obstacle to understanding arises for the diametrically opposed reason that theological differences in eastern Christianity often provided symbols and debating forms for questions about politics and society, about the relationship of national and cultural groups to authority, much as hair-splitting about the secular theology of Marxist-Leninism masks differences of a different order in the Communist world of today. There is, therefore, more to these questions than appears at first sight and much of it affected world history just as powerfully as the movements of armies or even peoples. The slow divergence of the two main Christian traditions is of enormous importance; it may not have originated in any sense in theological division, but theological disputes propelled divergent traditions yet further apart. They created circumstances which make it more and more difficult to envisage an alternative course of events.

One episode provides an outstanding example, the debate on Monophysitism, a doctrine which divided Christian theologians from about the middle of the fifth century. The significance of the theological issue is at first sight far from clear to a layman. It originated in an assertion that Christ's nature while on earth was single;

A twelfth-century emperor, John II Comnenus, and his empress, Irene, are depicted in this mosaic from St Sophia. John ascended the imperial throne in 1118 and did much to arrest the decline of Byzantium in the twelfth century; during their reigns, too, the great church of St Sophia was kept in good repair and was further embellished. His empress was the daughter of a Hungarian king who was himself to be beatified; none the less, her son threw the empire into huge efforts to conquer his mother's homeland, fighting ten wars with that object.

it was wholly divine, instead of dual (that is, both divine and human), as had generally been taught in the early Church. The delicious subtleties of the long debates which this view provoked must, perhaps regrettably, be bypassed here. It is sufficient only to notice the non-theological setting of the uproar of Aphtharto-docetists, Corrupticolists and Theopaschitists (to name a few of the contesting schools). One element in it was the slow crystallization of three Monophysite Churches separated from eastern Orthodoxy and Roman Catholicism. These

were the Coptic Church of Egypt and Ethiopia, the Syrian Jacobite and the Armenian Churches; they became, in a sense, national Churches in their countries. It was in an endeavour to reconcile such important groups and consolidate the unity of the empire in the face of first the Persian and then the Arab threat that the emperors were drawn into theological issues; there was more to it, that is to say, than the special responsibility of the office first revealed by Constantine's presiding at the Council of Nicaea. The emperor Heraclius, for example, did his best in the early seventh century to produce a compromise formula to reconcile the disputants over Monophysitism. It was a theological definition soon called Monothelitism, and on it, for a time, agreement seemed likely, though Monothelitism was in the end condemned as Monophysitism under a new name.

Meanwhile, the issue had pushed East and West still further apart, though, ironically, the final theological outcome was agreement between the two in 681. But Monophysitism had produced a forty-year schism between Latins and Greeks as early as the end of the fifth century. This was healed, but then came the further trouble under Heraclius. The empire had to leave Italy to its own devices when threatened by the Arab onslaught but both pope and emperor were anxious to show a common front. This partly explains the pope's endorsement of Monothelitism (on which Heraclius had asked his view so as to quieten the theological misgivings of the Patriarch of Jerusalem). Pope Honorius, successor of Gregory the Great, supported Heraclius and so enraged the anti-Monophysites that almost half a century later he achieved the distinction of being condemned by an ecumenical council at which the western

A Coptic icon from Egypt shows Christ with a local holy man, possibly the abbot of a monastery, St Menas. This is an example of the earlier form of the icon, when it did not yet represent a historical scene or a wholly heavenly one, but focussed attention on particular saints.

representatives at the council joined in the decision. At a crucial moment of danger Honorius had done much damage. The sympathies of many eastern churchmen in the early seventh century had been alienated still further from Rome by his imprudent action.

The Byzantine inheritance was not only imperial and Christian. It also owed debts to Asia. These were not merely a matter of the direct contacts with alien civilizations symbolized by the arrival of Chinese merchandise along the Silk Road, but also of the complex cultural inheritance of the Hellenistic East. Naturally, Byzantium preserved the prejudice which confused the idea of 'barbarians' with that of peoples who did not speak Greek, and many of its intellectual leaders felt they stood in the tradition of Hellas. Yet the Hellas of which they spoke was one from which the world had long been cut off except through the channels of the Hellenistic East. When we look at that area it is hard to be sure how deep Greek roots went there and how much nourishment they owed to Asiatic sources. The Greek language, for example, seems in Asia Minor to have been used mainly by the few who were city-dwellers. Another sign comes from the imperial bureaucracy and leading families, which reveal more and more Asian names as the centuries go by. Asia was bound to count far more after the losses of territory the empire suffered in the fifth and sixth centuries, for these pinned it increasingly into the strip of mainland Europe behind the capital. Then the Arabs hemmed it in to Asia Minor, bounded in the north by the Caucasus and in the south by the Taurus. On the edges of this, too, ran a border always permeable to Moslem culture. The people who lived on it naturally lived in a sort of marcher world, but sometimes there are indications of deeper external influence than this upon Byzantium. The greatest of all the Byzantine ecclesiastical disputes, that over Iconoclasm, had its parallels almost contemporaneously within Islam.

The most characteristic features of a complicated inheritance were set in the seventh and eighth centuries: an autocratic tradition of government, the Roman myth, the guardianship of eastern Christianity and practical confinement to the East. There had by then begun to emerge from the late Roman empire the medieval state which was sketched under Justinian. Yet of these crucial centuries we know little. Some say that no adequate history of Byzantium in that era can be written, so poor are the sources and so skimpy the present state of archaeological knowledge. At the start of this disturbed period the empire's assets are clear enough. It had at its disposal a great accumulation of diplomatic and bureaucratic skills, a military tradition and enormous prestige. Once its commitments could be reduced in proportion, its potential tax resources were considerable and so were its reserves of manpower. Asia Minor was a recruiting ground which relieved the eastern empire of the need to rely upon Germanic barbarians as had been necessary in the West. It had a notable war-making technology; the 'Greek fire' which was its secret weapon was used powerfully against ships which might attack the capital. The situation of Constantinople, too, was a military asset. Its great walls, built in the fifth century, made it hard to attack by land without heavy weapons unlikely to be available to barbarians; at sea the fleet could prevent a landing.

What was less secure in the long run was the social basis of the empire. It was always to be difficult to maintain the smallholding peasantry and prevent powerful provincial landlords from encroaching on their properties. The law courts would not always protect the small man. He was, too, under economic pressure from the steady expansion of church estates. These forces could not easily be offset by the imperial practice of making grants to smallholders on condition that they supplied military service. But this was a problem whose dimensions were only to be revealed with the passage of centuries; the short-term prospects gave the emperors of the seventh and eighth centuries quite enough to think about.

They were over-extended. In 600 the empire still included the North African coast, Egypt, the Levant, Syria, Asia Minor, the far coast of the Black Sea beyond Trebizond, the Crimean coast and that from Byzantium up to the mouths of the Danube. In Europe there were Thessaly, Macedonia and the Adriatic coast, a belt of territory across central Italy, enclaves in the toe and heel of the peninsula, and finally the islands of Sicily, Corsica and Sardinia. Given the empire's potential enemies and the location of its resources, this was a strategist's nightmare. The story of the next two centuries was to be of the return again and again of repeated waves of invaders. Persians, Avars, Arabs, Bulgars and Slavs were to harry the main body of the empire, while in the West the territories won back by the generals of Justinian were almost all soon taken away again by Arabs and Lombards. Eventually, the West, too, was to reveal itself as a predator; that the eastern empire for centuries absorbed much of the punishment which might otherwise have fallen on the West, would not save her. The result of this was that the eastern empire faced continual warfare. In Europe it meant fighting up to the very walls of Constantinople; in Asia it meant wearisome campaigning to dispute the marches of Asia Minor.

This challenge was offered to a state which, even at the beginning of the seventh century, already had only a very loose control over its domain and depended for much of its power on a penumbra of influence, diplomacy, Christianity and military prestige. Its relations to its neighbours might be seen in more than one way; what looks to a later eye like blackmail paid by every emperor from Justinian to Basil II to menacing barbarians was in the Roman tradition bounty to subject allies and *foedorati*. Its diversity of peoples and religions was masked by official ideology. Its Hellenization was often superficial. The reality was expressed in the willingness with which many of the Christian communities of Syria welcomed the Arab, as, later, many of those in Anatolia were to welcome the Turk. Here, religious persecution came home to roost. Moreover, Byzantium numbered no great power among her allies. In the troubled seventh and eighth centuries the most important friendly power was the Khanate of Khazaria, a huge, but loose, state founded by nomads who by 600 dominated the other peoples of the Don and Volga valleys. This established them across the Caucasus, the strategic land bridge which

Three medieval capital cities compared. Constantinople in 1200, Paris in 1400, and London in 1400.

they thus barred to Persians and Arabs for two centuries. At its widest the Khazar state ran round the Black Sea coast to the Dniester and northwards to include the Upper Volga and Don. Byzantium made great efforts to keep the goodwill of the Khazars and seems to have tried, but failed, to convert them to Christianity. What exactly happened is a mystery, but the Khazar leaders, while tolerating Christianity and several other cults, were apparently converted to Judaism in about 740, possibly as a result of Jewish immigration from Persia after the Arab conquest and probably as a conscious act of diplomacy. As Jews they were not likely to be sucked either into the spiritual and political orbit of the Christian empire, or into that of the Caliphs. Instead they enjoyed diplomatic relations and trade with both.

The first great hero of the Byzantine struggle for survival was Heraclius, who strove to balance the threats in Europe with alliances and concessions so that he could campaign vigorously against the Persians. Successful though he eventually was, the Persians had by then done appalling damage to the empire in the Levant and Asia Minor before finally being expelled. They have been believed by some scholars to be the

Above: It is still not clear how 'Greek fire' could be projected over considerable distances, but this illustration from a fourteenth-century manuscript shows its use against enemy ships. Time and again this weapon proved decisive in actions against Arabs, Bulgars and Rus.

Above right: From an eleventh-century illustration to a gospel story (Matthew xx, 1–16) something can be grasped of the appearance and life of the farm labourer of the eastern empire.

real destroyers of the Hellenistic world of great cities; the archaeology is mysterious still, but after Heraclius' victory there are signs that once great cities lay in ruins, that some were reduced to little more than the Acropolis which was their core and that population fell sharply. It was, then, on a structure much of which was already badly shaken that the Arab onslaughts fell – and they were to continue for two centuries. Before Heraclius died in 641 virtually all his military achievements had been overturned. Some of the emperors of his line were men of ability, but they could do little more than fight doggedly against a tide flowing strongly against them. In 643 Alexandria fell to the Arabs and that was the end of Greek rule in Egypt. Within a few

ό θ θαμμος ου πομηρος ό τημ· ό τι ήρα θραδος έμ· ου
ροσου ταοι ελατοι ουχαι πρω τοι εαι οι πρω τοι ου χα
τοι· πολλοι γαρ ζοι εελ ετοι· ο μεγοι δε ελε ζοκ τοι·

ο οι κο

The Byzantine Empire c. 1265

SERBIAN KINGDOM

BULGARIA

BLACK SEA

Sophia

Philippopolis

Adrianopolis

B Y Z A N T I N E   E M P I R E

Constantinople

Thessalonica

Gallipoli

Corinth

Ephesus

MONGOL EMPIRE

CRETE

c. 1354

SERBIAN KINGDOM

BULGARIA

BLACK SEA

Sophia

Philippopolis

Adrianopolis

BYZANTINE EMPIRE

Constantinople

Thessalonica

Gallipoli

OTTOMAN EMPIRE

Corinth

Ephesus

CRETE

years they had lost North Africa and Cyprus. Armenia, that old battleground, went in the next decade and finally the high-water mark of Arab success came with the five years of attacks on Constantinople (673–8); it may have been Greek fire that saved the capital from the Arab fleet. Before this, in spite of a personal visit by the emperor to Italy, no progress had been made in recovering the Italian and Sicilian territories taken by Arabs and Lombards. And so the century went on, with yet another menace appearing in its last quarter as Slavs pressed down into Macedonia and Thrace and another race, the Bulgars, themselves one day to be Slavicized, crossed the Danube.

The century ended with a revolt in the army and the replacement of one emperor by another. All the symptoms suggested that the eastern empire would undergo the fate of the West, the imperial office becoming the prize of the soldiers. A succession of beastly or incompetent emperors at the beginning of the eighth century let the Bulgars come to the gates of Constantinople and finally brought about a second siege of the capital by the Arabs in 717. But this was a true turning-point, though it was not to be the last Arab appearance in the Bosporus. In 717 there had already come to the throne one of the greatest Byzantine emperors, Leo III. He was an Anatolian, a provincial official who had successfully resisted Arab attacks on his territory and who had come to the capital to defend it and force the emperor's abdication. His own elevation to the purple followed and was both popular and warmly welcomed by the clergy. This was the foundation of the Isaurian dynasty, so-called from their place of origin; it was an indication of the way in which the élites of the eastern empire were gradually transformed into those of Byzantium, an oriental monarchy.

The eighth century brought the beginning of a period of recovery, though with setbacks. Leo himself cleared Anatolia of the Arabs and his son pushed back the frontiers to those of Syria, Mesopotamia and Armenia. From this time, the frontiers with the caliphate had rather more stability than hitherto, although each campaign-

The most powerful of the early rulers of the Bulgars, Krum, shares with his followers a feast to celebrate their victory over the Byzantines in 811. In this picture, his cup-bearer is about to serve him with a goblet made from the skull of the emperor Nicephorus, the unfortunate loser.

ing season brought border raids and skirmishes. From this achievement – in part attributable, of course, to the relative decline in Arab power – opened out a new period of progress and expansion which lasted until the early eleventh century. In the West little could be done. Ravenna was lost and only a few toeholds remained in Italy and Sicily. But in the East the empire expanded again from the base of Thrace and Asia Minor which was its heart. A chain of 'themes', or administrative districts, was established along the fringe of the Balkan peninsula; apart from them, the empire had no foothold

The other side of the long Byzantine struggle with the Bulgarians; the emperor Basil II, 'slayer of Bulgars'. At his feet grovel Bulgarian princes; Michael, standard-bearer of the heavenly host, steadies his spear and Gabriel places a crown upon his head. Above them all, the figure of Christ is seen, extending a heavenly crown to his champion. The psalter from which the painting is taken was made in Constantinople in the early eleventh century.

there for two centuries. In the tenth century Cyprus, Crete and Antioch were all recovered. Byzantine forces at one time crossed the Euphrates and the struggle for north Syria and the Taurus continued. The position in Georgia and Armenia was improved.

In eastern Europe the Bulgar threat was finally contained after reaching its peak at the beginning of the tenth century, when the Bul-

gars had already been converted to Christianity. Basil II, who has gone down in history as *Bulgarocthonos*, the 'slayer of Bulgars', finally destroyed their power at a great battle in 1014 which he followed up by blinding 15000 of his prisoners and sending them home to encourage their countrymen. The Bulgar ruler is said to have died of shock. Within a few years Bulgaria was a Byzantine province, though it was never to be successfully absorbed. Shortly afterwards the last conquests of Byzantium were made when Armenia passed under its rule.

The overall story of these centuries is therefore one of advance and recovery. It was also one of the great periods of Byzantine culture. Politically there was an improvement in domestic affairs in that, by and large, the dynastic principle was observed between 820 and 1025. The Isaurian dynasty had ended badly in an empress who was followed by another series of short reigns and irregular successions until Michael II the founder of the Phrygian dynasty, succeeded a murdered emperor in 820. His house was replaced in 867 by the Macedonian dynasty, under whom Byzantium reached its summit of success. Where there were minorities the device of a co-emperor was adopted to preserve the dynastic principle.

One major source of division and difficulty for the empire in the earlier part of this period was, as so often before, religion. This plagued the empire and held back its recovery because it was so often tangled with political and local issues. The outstanding example was a controversy which embittered feelings for over a century, the campaign of the iconoclasts.

The depicting of the saints, the Blessed Virgin and God Himself had come to be one of the great devices of Orthodox Christianity for focussing devotion and teaching. In late antiquity such images, or icons, had a place in the West, too, but to this day they occupy a special place in Orthodox churches where they are displayed in shrines and on special screens to be venerated and contemplated by the believer. They are much more than mere decoration, for their arrangement conveys the teachings of the

Church and (as one authority has said) provides 'a point of meeting between heaven and earth', for the faithful surrounded by the icons can feel himself surrounded by the whole invisible Church, the departed, the saints and angels, and Christ and His mother themselves. It is hardly surprising that something concentrating religious emotion so intensely should have led in paint or mosaic to some of the highest achievements of Byzantine (and, later, Slav) art.

Icons had become prominent in eastern churches by the sixth century. There followed two centuries of respect for them and in many places growing popular devotion to them, but then their use came to be questioned. Interestingly, this happened just after the caliphate had mounted a campaign against the use of images in Islam, but it cannot be inferred that the iconoclasts took their ideas from Moslems. The critics of the icons claimed that they were idols, perverting the worship due to God to the creations of men. They demanded their destruction or expunging and set to work with a will with whitewash, brush and hammer.

Leo III favoured such men. There is still much that is mysterious about the reason why imperial authority was thrown behind the iconoclasts, but he acted on the advice of bishops, and Arab invasions and volcanic eruptions were no doubt held to indicate God's disfavour. In 730, therefore, an edict forbade the use of images in public worship. A persecution of those who resisted followed; enforcement was always more marked at Constantinople than in the provinces. The movement reached its peak under Constantine V and was ratified by a council of bishops in 754. Persecution became fiercer, and there were martyrs, particularly among monks, who usually defended icons more vigorously than did the secular clergy. But iconoclasm was always dependent on imperial support and there were ebbings and flowings in the next century. Under Leo IV and Irene, his widow, persecution was relaxed and the 'iconophiles' (lovers of icons) recovered ground, though this was followed by renewed persecution. Only in 843, on the first Sunday of Lent, a day still celebrated

as a feast of Orthodoxy in the eastern Church, were the icons finally restored.

What was the meaning of this strange episode? There was a practical justification, in that the conversion of Jews and Moslems was said to be made more difficult by Christian respect for images, but this does not take us very far. Once again, a religious dispute cannot be separated from factors external to religion, but the ultimate explanation probably lies in a sense of religious precaution, and given the passion often shown in theological controversy in the eastern empire, it is easy to understand how the debate became embittered. No question of art or artistic merit arose: Byzantium was not like that. What was at stake was the feeling of reformers that the Greeks were falling into idolatry in the extremity of their (relatively recent) devotion to icons and that the Arab disasters were the first rumblings of God's thunder; a pious king, as in the Israel of the Old Testament, could yet save the people from the consequences of sin by breaking the idols. This was easier in that the process suited the mentalities of a faith which felt itself at bay. It was notable that iconoclasm was particularly strong in the army. Another fact which is suggestive is that icons had often represented local saints and holy men; they were replaced by the uniting, simplifying symbols of eucharist and cross, and this says something about a new, monolithic quality in Byzantine religion and society from the eighth century onwards. Finally, iconoclasm was also in part an angry response to a tide which had long flowed in favour of the monks who gave such prominence to icons in their teaching. As well as a prudent step towards placating an angry God, therefore, iconoclasm represented a reaction of centralized authority, that of emperor and bishops, against local pieties, the independence of cities and monasteries, and the cults of holy men.

Iconoclasm offended many in the western Church but it showed more clearly than anything yet how far Orthodoxy now was from Latin Christianity. The western Church had been moving, too; as Latin culture was taken over by the Germanic peoples, it drifted away

The iconoclasts at work. A ninth-century illustration in the margin of a manuscript showing the application of whitewash to an image of Christ.

in spirit from the churches of the Greek east. The iconoclast synod of bishops had been an affront to the papacy, which had already condemned Leo's supporters. Rome viewed with alarm the emperor's pretensions to act in spiritual matters. Thus iconoclasm drove deeper the division between the two halves of Christendom. Cultural differentiation had now gone very far – not surprisingly when it could take two months by sea to go from Byzantium to Italy and by land a wedge of Slav peoples soon stood between two languages.

Contact between East and West could not be altogether extinguished at the official level. But here, too, history created new divisions. The appearance of an empire in the West, where a Frankish king was crowned 'emperor' by the Pope of Rome in 800, was a challenge to the Byzantine claim to be the legatee of Rome. Distinctions within the western world did not much matter in Constantinople; the Byzantine officials identified a challenger in the Frankish realm and thereafter indiscriminately called all westerners 'Franks', a usage which was to spread as far as China. The two states failed to cooperate against the Arab and offended one another's susceptibilities. The Roman coronation was in part a response to the assumption of the title of

395

This carved façade of the Armenian church of the Holy Cross at Aght'amer survived Byzantine, Arab and Turkish rule. Built by Gagik, king of Vaspirakan between 915 and 921; shown here offering his church to the Saviour, who is portrayed on the other side of the central arch.

emperor at Constantinople by a woman, Irene, an unattractive mother who had blinded her own son. But the Frankish title was only briefly recognized in Byzantium; later emperors in the West were regarded only as kings. Italy divided the two Christian empires, too, for the remaining Byzantine lands there came to be threatened by Frank and Saxon as much as they had ever been by Lombards. In the tenth century the manipulation of the papacy by Saxon emperors made matters worse.

Of course the two Christian worlds could not altogether lose touch. One German emperor of the tenth century had a Byzantine bride and German art of the tenth century was much influenced by Byzantine themes and techniques. But it was just the difference of two cultural worlds that made such contacts fruitful, and as the centuries went by, the difference became more and more palpable. The old aristocratic

families of Byzantium were replaced gradually by others drawn from Anatolian and Armenian stocks. Above all, there was the unique splendour and complication of the life of the imperial city itself, where religious and secular worlds seemed completely to interpenetrate one another. The calendar of the Christian year was inseparable from that of the court; together they set the rhythms of an immense theatrical spectacle in which the rituals of both Church and State displayed to the people the majesty of the empire. There was some secular art, but the art constantly before men's eyes was overwhelmingly religious. Even in the worst times it had a continuing vigour, expressing the greatness and omnipresence of God, whose vice-regent was the emperor. Ritualism sustained the rigid etiquette of the court about which there proliferated the characteristic evils of intrigue and conspiracy. The public appearance of even the Christian emperor could be like that of the deity in a mystery cult, preceded by the raising of several curtains from behind which he dramatically emerged. This was the apex of an astonishing civilization which showed half the world for perhaps half a millennium what true empire was. When a mission of pagan Russians came to Byzantium in the tenth century to examine its form of the Christian religion as they had examined others, they could only report that what they had seen in Hagia Sophia had amazed them. 'There God dwells among men,' they said.

What was happening at the base of the empire, on the other hand, is not easy to say. There are strong indications that population fell in the seventh and eighth centuries; this may be connected both with the disruptions of war and with plague. At the same time there was little new building in the provincial cities and the circulation of the coinage diminished. All these things suggest a flagging economy, as does more and more interference with it by the state. Imperial officials sought to ensure that its primary needs would be met by arranging for direct levies of produce, setting up special organs to feed the cities and by organizing artisans and tradesmen bureaucratically in guilds and corporations. Only one city of the empire retained its economic importance throughout, and that was the capital itself, where the spectacle of Byzantium was played out at its height. Trade never dried up altogether in the empire and right down to the twelfth century there was still an important transit commerce in luxury goods from Asia to the West; its position alone guaranteed Byzantium a great commercial rôle and stimulation for the artisan industries which provided other luxuries to the West. Finally, there is evidence across the whole period of the continuing growth in power and wealth of the great landowners. The peasants were more and more tied to their estates and the later years of the empire see something like the appearance of important local economic units based on the big landholdings.

This economy was able to support both the magnificence of Byzantine civilization at its height and the military effort of recovery under the ninth-century emperors. Two centuries later an unfavourable conjuncture once more overtaxed the empire's strength and opened a long era of decline. It began with a fresh burst of internal and personal troubles. Two empresses and a number of short-lived emperors of poor quality weakened control at the centre. The rivalries of two important groups within the Byzantine ruling class got out of hand; an aristocratic party at court whose roots lay in the provinces was entangled in struggles with the permanent officials, the higher bureaucracy. In part this reflected also a struggle of a military with an intellectual élite. Unfortunately, the result was that the army and navy were starved of the funds they needed by the civil servants and were rendered incapable of dealing with new problems.

At one end of the empire these were provided by the last barbarian migrants of the West, the Christian Normans, now moving into south Italy and Sicily. In Asia Minor they arose from Turkish pressure. Already in the eleventh century a Turkish sultanate of Rum was established inside imperial territory (hence its name,

The magnificence of this reliquary lid provides an outstanding example of the richness and beauty of Byzantine ecclesiastical art. Relics lay literally at the root of Byzantine civilization, where religion and state were identified from the start. When the city was dedicated in 330 there were buried on its site not only relics of saints, but (it was alleged) crumbs from the bread with which Christ fed the five thousand, the crosses of the thieves who died with him, the adze with which Noah built the Ark and even the palladium which Aeneas took from Troy to Italy to found Rome!

for 'Rum' signified 'Rome'), where Abassid control had slipped into the hands of local chieftains. After a shattering defeat by the Turks at Manzikert in 1071 Asia Minor was virtually lost, and this was a terrible blow to Byzantine fiscal and manpower resources. The caliphates with which the emperors had learnt to live were giving way to fiercer enemies. Within the empire there was a succession of

Bulgarian revolts in the eleventh and twelfth centuries and there spread widely in that province the most powerful of the dissenting movements of medieval Orthodoxy, the Bogomil heresy, a popular movement drawing upon hatred of the Greek higher clergy and their Byzantinizing ways.

A new dynasty, the Comneni, once again rallied the empire and managed to hold the line for another century (1081–1185). They pushed back the Normans from Greece and they fought off a new nomadic threat from south Russia, the Pechenegs, but could not crack the Bulgars or win back Asia Minor and had to make important concessions to do what they did. Some concessions were to their own magnates; some were to allies who would in turn prove dangerous.

To one of these, the Republic of Venice, once a satellite of Byzantium, concessions were especially ominous, for her whole *raison d'être* had come to be aggrandizement in the eastern Mediterranean. She was the major beneficiary of Europe's trade with the East and at an early time had developed a specially favoured position. In return for help against the Normans in the eleventh century, the Venetians were given the right to trade freely throughout the empire; they were to be treated as subjects of the emperor, not as foreigners. Venetian naval

power grew rapidly and, as the Byzantine fleet fell into decline, it was more and more dominant. In 1123 the Venetians destroyed the Egyptian fleet and thereafter were uncontrollable by their former suzerain. One war was fought with Byzantium, but Venice did better from supporting the empire against the Normans and from the pickings of the Crusades. Upon these successes followed commercial concessions and territorial gains and the former mattered most; Venice, it may be said, was built on the decline of the empire, which was an economic host of huge potential for the Adriatic parasite – in the middle of the twelfth century there were said to be 10000 Venetians living at Constantinople, so important was their trade there. By 1204 the Cyclades, many of the other Aegean islands, and much of the Black Sea coasts belonged to them: hundreds of communities were to be added to those and Venetianized in the next three centuries. The first commercial and maritime empire since ancient Athens had been created.

The appearance of the Venetian challenge and the persistence of old ones would have been embarrassing enough for the Byzantine emperors had they not also faced new trouble at home. In the twelfth century revolt became more common. This was doubly dangerous

Growth of Venice as a Mediterranean Power

■ Acquisitions held and lost before 1500
■ Acquisitions held c.1500

1 Zara 1202-1358
2 Spalato 1327-1358
3 Prevesa 1499-1530
4 Lepanto 1407-99
5 Patras 1408-13, 1417-19
6 Vostitsa 1470
7 Argos 1388-1463
8 Nauplia 1388-1540
9 Aegina 1451-1537
10 Monemvasia 1464-1540 (Malvasia)
11 Naxos 1437-1500
12 Amorgos 1370-1446
13 Mylonos 1390-1537
14 Tinos 1390-1715
15 Andros 1437-40
16 Sporades 1453-1538
17 Lemnos 1464-79
18 Imbros 1466-79
19 Thasos 1464-79
20 Samothrace 1464-79

when the West was entering upon enterprise in the East in the great and complex movement which is famous as the Crusades. The western view of the Crusades need not detain us here; from Byzantium these irruptions from the West looked more and more like new barbarian invasions. In the twelfth century they left behind four crusading states in the former Byzantine Levant as a reminder that there was now another rival in the field in the Near East. When the Moslem forces rallied under Saladin, and there was a resurgence of Bulgarian independence at the end of the twelfth century, the great days of Byzantium were finally over.

The fatal blow came in 1204, when Constantinople was at last taken and sacked, but by

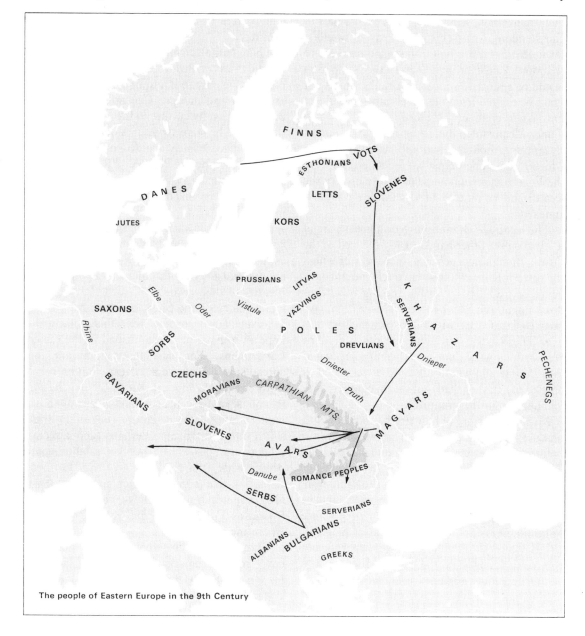

The people of Eastern Europe in the 9th Century

Christians, not the pagans who had threatened it so often. The Fourth Crusade was turned against the empire by the Venetians and the crusading army terrorized the city and ensconced prostitutes on the altar of St Sophia. The division of East and West could not have been more sharply established; the act was to live in Orthodox memory as one of infamy. The crusaders did not see Byzantium as a part of their civilization, nor, perhaps, as even a part of Christendom, for a schism had existed in effect for a century and a half. Though they were to abandon Constantinople and the emperors would be restored in 1261 the Franks would not again be cleared from the old Byzantine heritage until a new conqueror came along, the Ottoman Turk. Meanwhile, the heart had gone out of Byzantium, though it had still two centuries in which to die. The immediate beneficiaries were the Venetians and Genoese to whose history the wealth and commerce of Byzantium was now annexed.

The legacy of Byzantium – or a great part of it – was on the other hand already secured to the future, though not, perhaps, in a form in which the eastern Roman would have felt much confidence or pride. It lay in the rooting of Orthodoxy among the Slav peoples. This was to have huge consequences, with many of which we still live. The Russian state and the other modern Slav nations would not have been incorporated into Europe and would not now be reckoned as part of it, if they had not been converted to Christianity in the first place.

Much of the story of how this happened is still obscure, and what is known about the Slavs before Christian times is even more debatable. Though the ground-plan of the Slav peoples of today was established at roughly the same time as that of western Europe, its geography makes for confusion. Slav Europe covers a zone where nomadic invasions and the nearness of Asia still left things very fluid long after barbarian society had settled down in the west. Much of the central and south-eastern European landmass is mountainous. There, river valleys channelled the distribution of stocks. Most of modern Poland and European Russia, on the other hand, is a vast plain. Though for a long time covered in forests, it provided neither obvious natural lodgements nor insuperable barriers to settlements. In its huge spaces, rights were disputed for many centuries. By the end of the process, at the beginning of the thirteenth century, there had emerged in the East a number of Slav peoples who would have independent historical futures. The pattern thus set has persisted down to our own day.

There had also come into existence a characteristic Slav civilization, though not all Slavs belonged wholly to it and in the end the peoples of Poland and modern Czechoslovakia were to be closely tied by culture to the West rather than the East. The state structures of the Slav world came and went fairly rapidly, but two of them, those evolved by the Polish and Russian nations, proved particularly tenacious and capable of survival in organized form. They would have much to survive, for the Slav world was at times – notably in the thirteenth and twentieth centuries – under pressure as much from the West as from the East. Western aggressiveness is another reason why the Slavs retained a strong identity of their own.

The story of the Slavs has been traced back at least as far as 2000 BC when this ethnic group appears to have been established in the eastern Carpathians. For two thousand years they spread slowly both west and east, but especially to the east, into modern Russia. From the fifth to the seventh century Slavs from both the western and eastern groups began to move south into the Balkans. Perhaps their direction reflects the power of the Avars, the Asiatic people who, after the ebbing of the Hun invasions, lay like a great barrier across the Don, Dnieper and Dniester valleys, controlling south Russia as far as the Danube and courted by Byzantine diplomacy.

Throughout their whole history the Slavs have shown remarkable powers of survival. Harried in Russia by Scythians and Goths, in Poland by Avars and Huns, they none the less stuck to their lands and expanded them; they must have been tenacious agriculturists. Their early art shows a willingness to absorb the culture and techniques of others; they learnt from masters whom they outlasted. It was important, therefore, that in the seventh century there stood between them and the dynamic power of Islam a barrier of two peoples, the Khazars and the Bulgars. These strong peoples also helped to channel the gradual movement of Slavs into the Balkans and down to the Aegean. Later it was to run up the Adriatic coast and was to reach Moravia and central Europe, Croatia, Slovenia and Serbia. By the tenth century they must have been numerically dominant throughout the Balkans.

In this process the first Slav state to emerge was Bulgaria, though the Bulgars were not Slavs, but stemmed from tribes left behind by the Huns. Some of them gradually became Slavicized by intermarriage and contact with Slavs; these were the western Bulgars, who were established in the seventh century on the Danube. They cooperated with the Slav peoples in a series of great raids on Byzantium; in 559 they had penetrated the defences of Constantinople and camped in the suburbs. Like their allies, they were pagans. Byzantium exploited differences between Bulgar tribes and a ruler from one of them was baptized in Constantinople, the Emperor Heraclius standing godfather. He used the Byzantine alliance to drive out the Avars from what was to be Bulgaria. Gradually, the Bulgars were diluted by Slav blood and influence. When a Bulgar state finally appears at the end of the century we can regard it as Slav. In 716 Byzantium recognized its independence; now an alien body existed on territory long taken for granted as part of the empire. Though there were alliances, this was a thorn in the side of Byzantium which helped to cripple her attempts at recovery in the West. At the beginning of the ninth century the Bulgars killed an emperor in battle (and made a cup for their king from his skull); no emperor had fallen in battle against the barbarians since 378.

A turning-point – though not the end of conflict – was reached when the Bulgars were converted to Christianity. After a brief period during which, significantly, he dallied with Rome and the possibility of playing her off against Constantinople, a Bulgarian prince accepted baptism in 865. There was opposition among his people, but from this time Bulgaria was Christian. It was a momentous step in a great process, the christianizing of the Slav peoples. It was also an indication of how this would happen, from the top downwards, by the conversion of their rulers.

What was at stake was a great prize, the nature of the future Slav civilization. Two great names dominate the beginning of its shaping, those of St Cyril and St Methodius, two Byzantine priests still held in honour in the Orthodox communion. Methodius had earlier been on a mission to Khazaria and their work must be set in the overall context of the ideological diplomacy of Byzantium; Orthodox missionaries cannot neatly be distinguished from Byzantine diplomatic envoys, and these churchmen would have been hard put to it to recognize such a distinction in what they did. But they did much more than convert a dangerous neighbour. Cyril's name is commemorated still in the name of the alphabet which he devised for the Slavs, Cyrillic. It was rapidly diffused through the Slav peoples, soon reaching Russia, and it made possible not only the radiation of Christianity but the crystallization of Slav culture. That culture was potentially open to other influences, for Byzantium was not its only neighbour, but eastern Orthodoxy was in the end the deepest single influence upon it.

From the Byzantine point of view a still more important conversion was to follow, though not for more than a century. In 860 an expedition with 200 ships raided Byzantium. The citizens were terrified. They listened tremblingly in St Sophia to the prayers of the patriach: 'a people has crept down from the north . . . the people is fierce and has no mercy, its voice is as the roaring sea . . . a fierce and savage tribe . . . destroying everything, sparing nothing'. It might have been the voice of a western monk invoking divine protection from the sinister longships of the Vikings, and understandably so, for Vikings in essence these raiders were. But they were known to the Byzantines as Rus (or Rhos) and the raid marks the tiny beginnings of Russia's military power.

As yet, there was hardly anything that could be called a state behind it. Russia was still in the making. Its origins lay in an amalgam to which the Slav contribution was basic. The east Slavs had over the centuries dispersed over much of the upper reaches of the river valleys which flow down to the Black Sea. This was probably because of their agricultural practice, a primitive matter of cutting and burning, exhausting the soil in two or three years and then moving on. By the eighth century there were enough of them for there to be signs of relatively dense inhabitation, perhaps of something that could be called town life, on the hills near Kiev. They lived in tribes whose economic and social arrangements remain obscure, but this was the basis of future Russia. We do not know who their native rulers were, but they seem to have lived in the defended stockades which were the first towns, exacting tribute from the surrounding countryside.

On to these Slav tribes fell the impact of Norsemen who became their overlords or sold them as slaves in the south. These Scandinavians combined trade, piracy and colonization, stimulated by land-hunger. They brought with them important commercial techniques, great skill in navigation and the management of their longships, formidable fighting power and, it seems, no women. As in the Humber and the Seine, they used the Russian rivers, much longer and deeper, to penetrate the country which was their prey. Some went right on; by 846 we hear of the 'Varangians', as they were called, at Baghdad. One of their many sallies in the Black Sea was that to Constantinople in 860. They had to contend with the Khazars to the east and may have first established themselves in Kiev, one of the Khazar tributary districts, but Russian traditional history begins with their establishment in Novgorod, the Holmgardr of Nordic saga. Here, it was said,

a prince called Rurik had established himself with his brothers in about 860. By the end of the century another Varangian prince had taken Kiev and transferred the capital of a new state to that town.

The appearance of a new power caused consternation but provoked action in Byzantium. Characteristically, its reponse to a new diplomatic problem was cast in ideological terms; there seems to have been an attempt to convert some Rus to Christianity and one ruler may have succumbed. But the Varangians retained their northern paganism – their gods were Thor and Woden – while their Slav subjects, with whom they were increasingly mingled, had their own gods, possibly of very ancient Indo-European origins; in any case, these deities tended to merge as time passed. Soon there were renewed hostilities with Byzantium. Oleg, a prince of the early tenth century, again attacked Constantinople while the fleet was away. He is said to have adopted the device of putting his fleet on wheels to outflank the blocked entrance to the Golden Horn. However he did it, he was successful in extracting a highly favourable treaty from Byzantium in 911. It gave the Russians exceptionally favourable trading privileges and made clear the enormous importance of trade in the life of the new principality. Half a century or so after the legendary Rurik, it was a reality, a sort of river-federation centred on Kiev and linking the Baltic to the Black Sea. It was pagan, but when civilization and Christianity came to it, it would be because of the easy access to Byzantium which water gave to the young principality, which was first designated as Rus in 945. Its unity was still very loose. An incoherent structure was made even less rigid by the Vikings' adoption of a Slav principle which divided an inheritance. Rus princes tended to move around as rulers among the centres of which Kiev and Novgorod were the main ones. Nevertheless, the family of Kiev became the most important.

During the first half of the tenth century the relation between Byzantium and Kiev Rus was slowly ripening. Below the level of politics and trade a more fundamental re-orientation was taking place as Kiev relaxed its links with Scandinavia and looked more and more to the south. Varangian pressure seems to have been diminishing, and this may have had something to do with the success of Norsemen in the West, where one of their rulers, Rollo, had been granted in 911 land later to be known as the duchy of Normandy. Yet it was a long time before there were closer ties between Kiev and Byzantium. One obstacle was the caution of Byzantine diplomacy, still quite as concerned in the early tenth century to fish in troubled waters by negotiating with the wild tribes of the Pechenegs as to placate the Rus whose territories they harried. The Pechenegs had already driven to the west the

Kiev Rus

Magyar tribes which had previously formed a buffer between the Rus and the Khazars and more trouble could be expected there. Nor did Varangian raids come to an end, though there was something of a turning-point when the Rus fleet was driven off by Greek fire in 941. A treaty followed which significantly reduced the trading privileges granted thirty years earlier. But the reciprocity of interests was emerging more clearly as Khazaria declined and the Byzantines realized that Kiev might be a valuable ally against Bulgaria. Signs of contact multiplied; Varangians appeared in the royal guard at Constantinople and Rus merchants came there more frequently. Some are believed to have been baptized.

Christianity, though long despising the merchant, has often followed the trader's wares. There was already a church in Kiev in 882, and it may have been there for foreign merchants. But nothing seems to have followed from this. There is little evidence of Russian Christianity until the middle of the next century. Then, in 945, the widow of a Kievan prince assumed the regency on behalf of his successor, her son. This was Olga. Her son was Sviatoslav, he was the first prince of Kiev to bear a Slavonic and not a Scandinavian name. Later, Olga made a state visit to Constantinople. She may have been secretly baptized a Christian before this, but she was publicly and officially converted on this visit in 957, the emperor himself attending the ceremonies in St Sophia. Because of its diplomatic overtones it is difficult to be sure exactly how to understand this event. Olga had, after all, also sent to the West for a bishop, to see what Rome had to offer. Furthermore, there was no immediate practical sequel. Sviatoslav, who reigned from 962 to 972, turned out to be a militant pagan, like other Viking military aristocrats of his time. He clung to the gods of the north and was doubtless confirmed in his belief by his success in raiding Khazar lands. He did less well against the Bulgars, though, and was finally killed by the Pechenegs.

This was a crucial moment. Russia existed but was still Viking, poised between eastern and western Christianity. Islam had been held back at the crucial period by Khazaria, but Russia might have turned to the Latin West. Already the Slavs of Poland had been converted to Rome and German bishoprics had been pushed forward to the east in the Baltic coastlands and Bohemia. The separation, even hostility, of the two great Christian Churches was already a fact, and Russia was a great prize waiting for one of them.

In 980 a series of dynastic struggles ended with the victorious emergence of the prince who made Russia Christian, Vladimir. It seems possible that he had been brought up as a Christian, but at first he showed the ostentatious paganism which became a Viking warlord. Then he began to enquire of other religions. Legend says that he had their different merits debated before him; Russians treasure the story that Islam was rejected by him because it forbade alcoholic drink. A commission was sent to visit the Christian Churches. The Bulgarians, they reported, smelt. The Germans had nothing to offer. But Constantinople had won their hearts. There, they said in words often to be quoted,

This twelfth-century Byzantine icon, the 'Virgin of Vladimir', is perhaps the most treasured of all Russian works of religious art. It is prized not only for its beauty but for its place in the national life, for it came to be regarded as the guardian of Russia and was moved to successive capital cities as if reflecting the movement of power. The icon also had a huge impact upon the native Russian tradition of icon-painting, for it became the inspiration of hundreds of attempts to portray the Virgin and Child with a comparable rendering of the tenderness with which the unknown painter at Constantinople endowed this subject. It was commissioned by a prince of Kiev as a gift for a church he was building and it arrived there soon after 1132. In 1167 it was moved to Vladimir, and it kept the name of that city though removed in the late fourteenth century to Moscow, where it can now be found.

'we knew not whether we were in heaven or earth, for on earth there is no such vision nor beauty, and we do not know how to describe it; we know only that there God dwells among men'. The choice was accordingly made. Around about 986–8 Vladimir accepted Orthodox Christianity for himself and his people.

It was a turning-point in Russian history and culture, as Orthodox churchmen have recognized ever since. 'Then the darkness of idolatry began to leave us, and the dawn of orthodoxy arose,' said one, eulogizing Vladimir a half-century or so later. Yet for all the zeal Vladimir showed in imposing baptism on his subjects (by physical force if necessary), it was not only enthusiasm which influenced him. There were diplomatic dimensions to the choice, too. Vladimir had been giving military help to the emperor and now he was promised a Byzantine princess as a bride. This was an unprecedented acknowledgement of the standing of a prince of Kiev. The emperor's sister was available because Byzantium needed the Rus alliance against the Bulgars. When things did not go smoothly, Vladimir put on the pressure by occupying Byzantine possessions in the Crimea. The marriage then soon took place. Kiev was worth a nuptial mass to Byzantium, though Vladimir's choice was decisive of much more than diplomacy. Two hundred years later his countrymen acknowledged this: Vladimir was canonized. He had made the single decision which, more than any other, determined Russia's future.

Probably Kiev Rus had in many ways in the tenth century a richer culture than most of the West could offer. Its towns were great trading centres, channelling goods into the Near East, where Russian furs and beeswax were prized. This commercial emphasis reflects another difference from the West, where the self-contained, subsistence economy of the manor emerged as the institution bearing the strain of the collapse of the classical economic world. Without the western manor Russia would also be without the western feudal nobleman. A territorial aristocracy would take longer to emerge in Russia than in the West and the first Russian nobles were for a long time very much the companions and followers of a war-leader. Some of them opposed Christianity and paganism hung on in the north for decades. As in Bulgaria, the adoption of Christianity was a political act with internal as well as external dimensions and though the capital of a Christian principality, Kiev was not yet the centre of a Christian nation. The monarchy had to assert itself against a conservative alliance of aristocracy and paganism. Lower down the social scale, in the towns, the new faith gradually took root, at first thanks to Bulgarian priests, who brought with them the liturgy of the south Slav Church and the Cyrillic alphabet which created Russian as a literary language. Ecclesiastically, the influence of Byzantium was strong and the Metropolitan of Kiev was usually appointed by the Patriarch of Constantinople.

Kiev became famous for the magnificence of its churches; it was a great time of building in a style showing Greek influence. Unhappily, being of wood, few of them survive. But the repute of this artistic primacy reflects Kiev's wealth. Its apogee came under Jaroslav 'the Wise', when one western visitor thought she rivalled Constantinople. Russia was then culturally as open to the outside world as it was ever to be for centuries. In part this reflected Jaroslav's military and diplomatic standing. He exchanged diplomatic missions with Rome while Novgorod received the merchants of the German Hanse. Having himself married a Swedish princess, he found husbands for the womenfolk of his family in kings of Poland, France and Norway. A harried Anglo-Saxon royal family took refuge at his court. Links with the West were never to be so close again. Culturally, too, the first fruits of the Byzantine implantation on Slav culture were being gathered. Educational foundation and legal creation reflected this. From this reign comes also one of the first great Russian works of literature, *The Primary Chronicle*, an interpretation of Russian history with a political purpose, like much other early Christian history, that of pro-

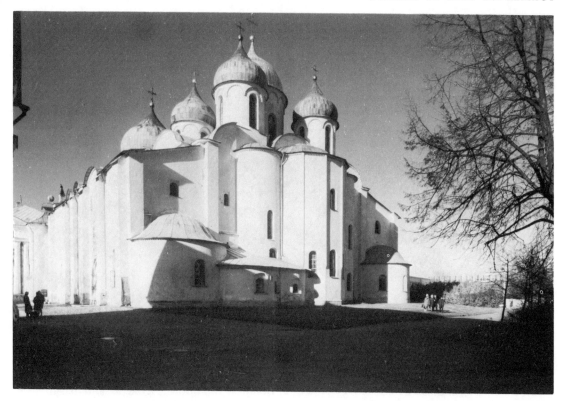

Novgorod: the early Russian city that developed furthest its links with western Europe. The building of the plain, austere cathedral of St Sophia (1045–52) suggests the appearance of an artistic style showing its independence of Byzantium.

viding a Christian and historical argument for the unification of Russia under the Kiev princes. It stressed the Slav heritage and offered an account of Russian history in Christian terms.

The weaknesses of Kiev Rus lay in the persistence of a rule of succession which almost guaranteed division and dispute at the death of the major prince. After Jaroslav, though one other eleventh-century prince managed to assert his authority and hold foreign enemies at bay, the Kiev supremacy waned. The northern princedoms showed greater autonomy; Moscow and Novgorod were, eventually, the two most important among them, though another 'grand' princedom to match Kiev's was established at

Vladimir in the second half of the thirteenth century. In part this shift of the centre of gravity of Russia's history reflects a new threat to the south in the pressure of the Pechenegs, now reaching its peak.

This was a momentous change. In these northern states, the beginnings of future trends in Russian government and society can be discerned. Slowly, grants from the princes were transforming the old followers and booncompanions of the warlord kings into a territorial nobility. Even settled peasants began to acquire rights of ownership and inheritance. Many of those who worked the land were slaves, but there was no such pyramid of obligations as constituted the territorial society of the medieval West. Yet these changes unrolled within a culture whose major direction had been settled by the Kiev period of Russian history.

Another enduring national entity which began to crystallize at about the same time as Russia was Poland. Its origins lay in a group of Slav

407

*This Romanesque tympanum from the
Benedictine abbey in Olbin shows Christ in
Majesty receiving gifts from Boleslav IV, his
wife and sons. The headless figure carrying
the model of the church with the inscription
'Bitom', presumably the building in question, is
Boleslav, known sometimes as 'the Curly'.*

tribes who appear at the outset, in the tenth
century, struggling against pressure from the
Germans in the west. It may well have been
politics, therefore, that dictated the choice of
Christianity as a religion by Poland's first historically recorded ruler, Mieszko I. The choice
was not, as in Russia's case, the eastern Orthodox Church. Mieszko plumped for Rome.
Poland, therefore, would be linked throughout
her history to the West as would be Russia to
the East. This conversion, in 966, opened a half-
century, struggling against pressure from the
A vigorous successor began the creation of an
administrative system and extended his lands to
the Baltic in the north and through Silesia,
Moravia and Cracow in the west. One German
emperor recognized his sovereignty in 1000 and

in 1025 he was crowned King of Poland as
Boleslav I. Political setbacks and pagan reactions dissipated much of what he had done and
there were grim times to come, but Poland was
henceforth a historical reality. Moreover, three
of the dominating themes of her history had
also made their appearance: the struggle against
German encroachment from the west, the identification with the interests of the Roman
Church, and the factiousness and independence
of the nobles towards the Crown. The first two
of these do much to account for Poland's unhappy history, for they tugged her in different
directions. As Slavs, Poles guarded the glacis
of the Slav world; they formed a breakwater of
the tides of Teutonic immigration. As Catholics,
they were the outposts of western culture in its
confrontation with the Orthodox East.

During these confused centuries other
branches of the Slav peoples had been pushing
on up the Adriatic and into central Europe.
From them emerged other nations with important futures. The Slavs of Bohemia and
Moravia had in the ninth century been converted by Cyril and Methodius, but then were

reconverted by Germans to Latin Christianity. The conflict of faiths was important, too, in Croatia and Serbia, where another branch settled and established states separated from the eastern Slav stocks first by Avars, and then by Germans and Magyars, whose invasions from the ninth century were especially important in cutting off central European Orthodoxy from Byzantine support.

A Slav Europe therefore existed at the beginning of the twelfth century. It was divided, it is true, by religion and into distinct areas of settlement. One of the peoples settled in it, the Magyars, who had crossed the Carpathians from south Russia, were not Slav at all. The whole of the area was under growing pressure from the West, where politics, crusading zeal and land-hunger all made a drive to the East irresistibly attractive to Germans. The greatest Slav power, Kievan Russia, developed less than its full potential; it was handicapped by political fragmentation after the eleventh century and harried in the next by the Cumans. By 1200 it had lost its control of the Black Sea river route; Russia had retreated to the north and was becoming Muscovy. Bad times for the Slavs lay ahead. A hurricane of disasters was about to fall upon Slav Europe, and for that matter on Byzantium. It was in 1204 that the crusaders sacked Constantinople and the world power which had sustained Orthodoxy was eclipsed. Worse still was to come. Thirty-six years later the Christian city of Kiev fell to a terrible nomadic people. These were the Mongols.

South Eastern Europe about 1400

X 14th century Ottoman victories

Genoese possessions

Venetian possessions

4 The disputed legacies of the Near East

Byzantium was not alone in attracting the attention of the predators prowling about the Near East; indeed, she survived their attentions longer than her old enemy the Abassid caliphate. The Arab empire slipped into decline and disintegration and from the tenth century we enter an age of confusion which makes any brief summary of what happened a despairing exercise. Fortunately, very little need be said about it. The most important fact of the age of Arab decline is negative; for all the comings and goings of rulers and raiders, nothing disturbed the foundations of Islamic society. The whole area from the Levant to the Hindu Kush was pervaded for the first time in history by a single culture and it was to endure. The Christian inheritance of Rome hung on within it only until the eleventh century, bottled up beyond the Taurus in Asia Minor. After that, Christianity was everywhere in this zone only a matter of the communities tolerated by Islam.

The stability and deep-rootedness of Islamic social and cultural institutions were enormously important. They far transcended the weaknesses – which were mainly political and administrative – of the semi-autonomous states which emerged to exercise power under the formal supremacy of the caliphate in its deca-

Genghis Khan – or 'universal khan', in the language of his own people – as a sixteenth-century Persian artist pictured this greatest of the Mongol rulers.

dent period, and about them little need be said. Interesting to Arabists though they are, they need be noted here rather as convenient landmarks than for their own sake. The most important and strongest of them was ruled by the Fatimid dynasty which controlled Egypt, most of Syria and the Levant, and the Red Sea coast. This territory included the great shrines of Mecca and Medina and therefore the profitable and important pilgrim trade. On the borders of Anatolia and northern Syria another dynasty, the Hamdanid, stood between the Fatimids and the Byzantine empire, while the heartland of the caliphate, Iraq and western Iran, together with Azerbaijan, was ruled by the Buwayhid. Finally, the north-eastern provinces of Khurasan, Sijistan and Transoxiana had passed to the Samanids. Listing these four groupings of power far from exhausts the complications of the unsettled Arab world of the tenth century, but it provides all the background now needed to narrate the unrolling of the process by which two new empires appeared within Islam, one based on Anatolia and one on Persia.

The thread is provided by a central Asian people already introduced into this story, the Turks. Some of them had been granted a home by the Sassanids in their last years in return for help. In those days the Turkish 'empire', if that is the right word for their tribal confederation, ran right across Asia; it was their first great era. Like that of other nomadic peoples, this ascendancy soon proved to be transient. The Turks faced at the same time inter-tribal divisions and a resurgence of Chinese power and it was on a

411

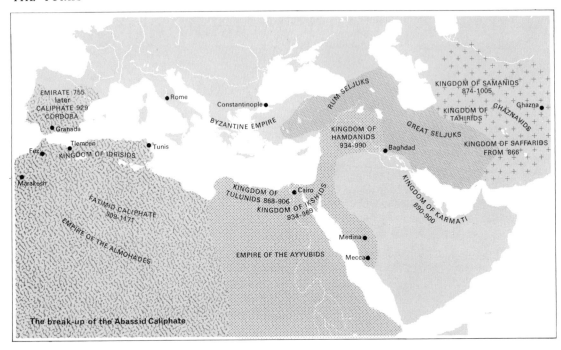

The break-up of the Abassid Caliphate

divided and disheartened people that there had fallen the great Arab onslaught. In 667 the Arabs invaded Transoxiana and in the next century they finally shattered the remains of the Turkish empire in western Asia. They were only stopped at last in the eighth century by the Khazars, another Turkish people. Before this the eastern Turkish confederation had broken up.

In spite of this collapse what had happened was very important. For the first time a nomadic polity of sorts had spanned Asia and had lasted for more than a century. All four of the great contemporary civilizations, China, India, Byzantium, and Persia, had felt bound to undertake relations with the Turkish khans, who had learned much from these contacts. Among other things, they acquired the art of writing; the first surviving Turkish inscription dates from the early eighth century. Yet in spite of this, for long stretches of Turkish history we must rely upon other people's accounts and records, for no Turkish authority seems to go back beyond the fifteenth century and the archaeological record is sporadic.

This, combined with the fragmentation of the Turkish tribes, makes for obscurity until the tenth century. Then came the collapse of the T'ang dynasty in China, a great event which offered important opportunities to the eastern and Sinicized Turks, just at the moment when signs of weakness were multiplying in the Islamic world. One was the emergence of the Abassid successor states. Turkish slaves or 'Mamelukes' had long served in the caliphates' armies; now they were employed as mercenaries by the dynasties which tried to fill their vacuum of power. But the Turkish peoples themselves were again on the move by the tenth century. In the middle of it a new dynasty reestablished Chinese power and unity; perhaps it was this which provided the decisive impetus for another of the long shunting operations by which central Asian peoples jostled one another forward to other lands. Whatever the cause, a people called the Oghuz Turks were in the van of those who pressed into the northeastern lands of the old caliphate and set up their own new states there. One clan among them were the Seljuks and they were notable because they were already Moslem. In 960 they had been

A thirteenth-century ship engaged in the Indian ocean trade. The details of the oriental shipping of the era can be seen easily in this Arabic manuscript.

converted by the assiduous missionary efforts of the Samanids, when still in Transoxiana.

Many of the leaders of the new Turkish régimes were former slave soldiers of the Arab-Persians; one such group were the Ghaznavids, a dynasty who briefly built a huge dominion which stretched into India (this was also the first post-Abassid régime to choose its generals as *sultans*, or heads of state). But they were in their turn pushed aside as new nomadic invaders arrived. The Oghuz came in sufficient numbers to produce a major change in the ethnic composition of Iran and also in its economy. In another way, too, their arrival means a deeper change than any preceding one and opened a new phase of Islamic history. Because of what the Samanids had done, some of the Oghuz Turks were already Moslem and respected what they found. There now began the translation into Turkish of the major works of Arabic and Persian scholarship which was to give the Turk-

ish peoples access to Arab civilization as never before.

Early in the eleventh century the Seljuks crossed the Oxus, too. This was to lead to the creation of a second Turkish empire, which lasted until 1194, and, in Anatolia, to 1243. After evicting the Ghaznavids from eastern Iran, the Seljuks turned on the Buwayhids and seized Iraq, thus becoming the first central Asian invaders of historical times to penetrate further than the Iranian plateau. Perhaps because they were Sunnites they seem to have been readily welcomed by many of the former subjects of the Shiite Buwayhid. They went on, though, to much greater deeds than this. After

413

occupying Syria and Palestine they invaded Asia Minor, where they inflicted on the Byzantines one of the most shattering defeats of their history at Manzikert in 1071. Significantly, the Seljuks called the sultanate they set up there the Sultanate of Rum, for they saw themselves henceforth as the inheritors of the old Roman territories. That Islam should have a foothold inside the old Roman empire touched off crusading zeal in the West; it also opened Asia Minor to the settlement of Turks.

In many ways, then, the Seljuks played an outstanding historic rôle. Not only did they begin the conversion of Asia Minor from Christianity to Islam, but they provoked the crusades and long bore the brunt of resisting them, too. This cost them heavily on other fronts. By the mid-twelfth century Seljuk power was already dwindling in the Iranian lands. Nevertheless, the Seljuk empire lasted long enough to make possible a final crystallization over the whole Islamic heartlands of a common culture and institutions which this time included Turkish peoples.

This was less because Seljuk government innovated than because it recognized social (and in Islam that meant religious) realities. The essence of the Seljuk structure was tribute rather than administrative activity. It was something of a confederation of tribes and localities and was no more capable of standing up to long-term stress than its predecessors. The central apparatus of the empire was its armies and what was necessary to maintain them; locally, the notables of the *ulema*, the teachers and religious leaders of Islam, ruled. They provided a consolidation of authority and social custom which would survive the caliphates and become the cement of Islamic society all over the Middle East. They would run things until the coming of nationalism in the twentieth century. Although there were divisions of schools within the *ulema*, it provided at local levels a common cultural and social system which ensured that the loyalty of the masses would be available to new régimes which replaced one another at the top and might have alien origins.

It provided political spokesmen who could assure satisfaction at the local level and legitimize new régimes by their support.

This produced one of the most striking differences between Islamic and Christian society. Religious élites were the key factor in the *ulema*; they organized the locally, religiously based community, so that bureaucracy, in the western sense, was not needed. Within the political divisions of the Islamic world in the age of the caliphates' decadence these élites provided its social unity. The Seljuk pattern spread over the Arabic world, and was maintained under the successor empires. Another basic institution was the use of slaves, a few as administrators, but many in the armies. Though the Seljuks granted some great fiefs in return for military service, it was the slaves – often Turkish – who provided the real force on which the régime rested, its armies. Finally, it relied also on the maintenance, where possible, of the local grandee, Persian or Arab.

The declining years of the Seljuk régime exposed the weaknesses in this structure. It depended heavily for its direction upon the availability of able individuals supported by tribal loyalties. But the Turks were thin on the ground and could not keep their subjects' loyalties if they did not suceed. When the first wave of Moslem settlement in Anatolia was spent, that area was still only superficially Turkish, and Moslem towns stood in the middle of a countryside linguistically distinct; local language was not arabized as it was further south and the submergence of the Greek culture of the area was only very slowly achieved. Further east, the first Moslem lands to be lost were lost to pagans in the twelfth century; a nomad ruler (widely supposed in the West to be a Christian king, Prester John, on his way from central

An Arabic manuscript, probably from Syria, shows a spellbound audience in the mosque at Samarkand, a city which had been devastated by the pagan Mongols long before this scene was drawn.

Asia to help the crusaders) took Transoxiana from the Seljuks.

The crusading movement was in part a response to the establishment of Seljuk power. The Turks, perhaps because of their late conversion to Islam, were less tolerant than the Arabs and began to trouble the access of Christian pilgrims to the holy places. The other causes which promoted the crusades belong rather to European than to Islamic history and can be dealt with elsewhere, but by 1100 the Islamic world felt itself on the defensive even though the Frankish threat was not yet grave. Still, the reconquest of Spain had begun, and the Arabs had already lost Sicily. The first crusade (1096–9) was favoured by Moslem divisions which enabled the invaders to establish four Latin states in the Levant: the kingdom of Jerusalem, and its three fiefs, the county of Edessa, the principality of Antioch and the county of Tripoli. They were not to have much of a future, but in the early twelfth century their presence seemed ominous to Islam. The crusaders' success provoked Moslem reaction and a Seljuk general seized Mosul as a centre from which he built up a new state in northern Mesopotamia and Syria. He recaptured Edessa (1144); his son saw the possibilities of exploiting the Christians' alienation of the local Moslem population by bad treatment. It was a nephew of this prince, Saladin, who seized power in Egypt in 1171, declaring the Fatimid caliphate at an end.

Saladin was to be the hero of the Moslem reconquest of the Levant and he remains a captivating figure even after strenuous efforts by unromantic and sceptical scholars to cut through the image of the *beau idéal* of Saracenic chivalry. The fascination he exercised over the minds of his Christian contemporaries was rooted in paradoxes which must have had real educational force. He was indisputably a pagan, yet he was good, a man of his word and just in his dealings; he was chivalrous, yet of a world that did not know the knightly ideal. (This puzzled some Frenchmen so much that they were forced to believe he had in fact been knighted by a Christian captive and that he baptized himself on his deathbed.) On a more mundane level, Saladin's first great triumph was the recapture of Jerusalem (1187), which provoked a new, and third, crusade (1189–92). This could achieve little against him, though it further intensified the irritation of Moslems who now began to show a quite new and unprecedented bitterness and ideological hostility towards Christianity. Persecution of Christians followed and with it began the slow but irreversible decline of the formerly large Christian populations of the Moslem lands.

Saladin founded a dynasty, the Abbuyid sultans, which ruled the Levant (outside the crusader enclaves), Egypt and the Red Sea coast. It lasted until it was replaced by rulers drawn from its own palace guards, the Turkish Mamelukes. It was these last who were the destroyers of the remaining crusader conquests in Palestine. The revival of the caliphate which followed at Cairo (it was given to a member of the Abassid house) is of small significance in comparison with this. It registered, nevertheless, that so far as Islam still had a preponderant power and a cultural focus, both were now to be found in Egypt. Baghdad was never to recover.

The Mamelukes had another great achievement to their credit by this time. It was they who finally halted the tide of a conquest far more threatening than that of the Franks when it had been rising for more than half a century. This was the onslaught of the Mongols. Their history makes nonsense of chronological and territorial divisions. In an astonishingly short time this nomadic people drew into their orbit China, India, the Near East and Europe and left ineffaceable marks behind them. Yet there is no physical focus for their history except the felt tents of their ruler's encampment; they blew up like a hurricane to terrify half a dozen civilizations, slaughtered and destroyed on a scale the twentieth century alone has emulated, and then disappeared almost as suddenly as they came. They demand to be considered alone as the last and most terrible of the nomadic conquerors.

Twelfth-century Mongolia is as far back as a search for their origins need go. A group of peoples speaking the languages of the family called Mongol then lived there who had long demanded the attention of Chinese governments. Generally, China played off one of them against another in the interests of its own security. They were barbarians, not much different in their cultural level from others who have already crossed these pages. Two tribes among them, the Tatars and that which became known as the Mongols, competed and on the whole the Tatars had the best of it. They drove one young Mongol to extremes of bitterness and self-assertion. The date of his birth is uncertain, but in the 1190s he became khan to his people. A few years later he was supreme among the Mongol tribes and was acknowledged as such by being given the title of Chinghis Khan. By an Arabic corruption of this name he was to become known in Europe as Genghis Khan. He extended his power over other peoples in central Asia and in 1215 he was strong enough to seize northern China. This was only the beginning. By the time of his death, in 1227, he had become the greatest conqueror the world has ever known.

He seems unlike all earlier nomad warlords. Chinghis genuinely believed he had a mission to conquer the world. Conquest, not booty or settlement, was his aim and what he conquered he often set about organizing in a systematic way. This led to a structure which deserves the name 'empire' more than do most of the nomadic polities. He was superstitious, tolerant of religions other than his own paganism, and, said a Persian historian, 'used to hold in esteem beloved and respected sages and hermits of every tribe, considering this a procedure to please God'. Indeed, he seems to have held that he was himself the recipient of a divine mission. This religious eclecticism was of the first importance, as was the fact that he and his followers (except for some Turks who joined them) were not Moslem, as the Seljuks had been when they arrived in the Near East. Not only was this a matter of moment to Christians and Buddhists

– there were both Nestorians and Buddhists among the Mongols – but it meant that the Mongols were not identified with the religion of the majority in the Near East.

In 1218 Chinghis Khan turned to the west and the era of Mongol invasions opened in Transoxiana and northern Iran. He never acted carelessly, capriciously, or without premeditation, but it may well be that the attack was provoked by the folly of a Moslem prince who killed his envoys. From there Chinghis went on to a devastating raid into Persia followed by a swing northward through the Caucasus into south Russia, and returned, having made a complete circuit of the Caspian to the east to deal with the Chinese.

All this was accomplished by 1223. Bokhara and Samarkand were sacked with massacres of the townspeople which were meant to terrify others who contemplated resistance. (Surrender was always the safest course with the Mongols and several minor peoples were to survive with nothing worse than the payment of tribute and the arrival of a Mongol governor.) Transoxiana never recovered its place in the life of Islamic Iran after this. Christian civilization was given a taste of Mongol prowess by the defeat of the Georgians in 1221 and of the southern Russian princes two years later. Even these alarming events were only the overture to what was to follow.

Chinghis died in the East in 1227, but his son and successor returned to the West. In 1236 his armies poured into Russia. They took Kiev and settled on the lower Volga, from which they organized a tributary system for the Russian principalities they had not occupied. Meanwhile they raided western Europe. The Teutonic knights, the Poles and the Hungarians all went down before them. Cracow was burnt and Moravia devastated. A Mongol patrol crossed into Austria while the pursuers of the king of Hungary chased him through Croatia and finally reached Albania before they were recalled.

The Mongols left Europe because of dissensions of their leaders and the arrival of the news

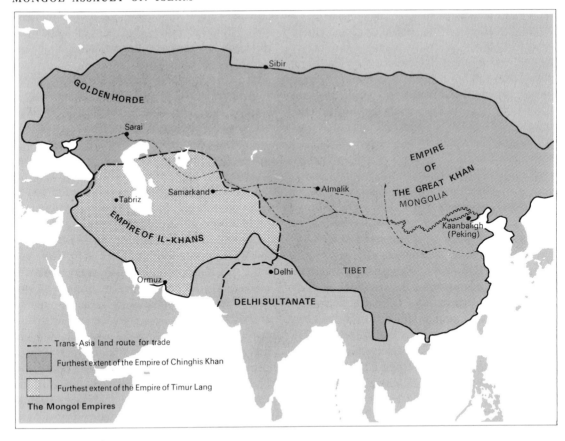

The Mongol Empires

- - - - Trans-Asia land route for trade

☐ Furthest extent of the Empire of Chinghis Khan

☐ Furthest extent of the Empire of Timur Lang

of the death of the khan. A new one was not chosen until 1246. A Franciscan friar attended the ceremony (he was there as an emissary of the pope); so did a Russian grand duke, a Seljuk sultan, the brother of the Abbuyid sultan of Egypt, an envoy from the Abbasid caliph, a representative of the king of Armenia, and two claimants to the Christian throne of Georgia. The election did not solve the problems posed by dissension among the Mongols and it was not until another Great Khan was chosen (after his predecessor's death had ended a short reign) that the stage was set for another Mongol attack.

This time it fell almost entirely upon Islam, and provoked unwarranted optimism among Christians who noted also the rise of Nestorian influence at the Mongol court. The area nominally still subject to the caliphate had been in a state of disorder since Chinghis Khan's cam-

paign. The Seljuks of Rum had been defeated in 1243 and were not capable of asserting authority. In this vacuum, the local Mongol forces could be relatively small and the Mongol empire relied mainly upon vassals among numerous local rulers.

The campaign was entrusted to the younger brother of the Great Khan and began with the crossing of the Oxus on New Year's Day 1256. After destroying the notorious sect of the Assassins *en route*, he moved on Baghdad, summoning the caliph to surrender. The city was stormed and sacked and the last Abassid caliph murdered – because there were superstitions about shedding his blood he is supposed to have been rolled up in a carpet and trampled to death by horses. It was a black moment in the history of Islam as, everywhere, Christians took heart and anticipated the overthrow of their Moslem overlords. When, the following year, the Mongol

In about 1300 one Arab vizier serving Mongol rulers wrote a world history, abundantly illustrated with pictures of which this is one. Its interest lies less in the information it provides about Mongol siegecraft (it is not even clear whether the main business of the artist is to emphasize the attack or the defence), but in its artistic style, which shows the influence of Chinese art, in contrast to works produced by and for Mongols under the influence of Seljuk and Near Eastern contacts. It is possible, some have hazarded, that the event depicted is actually the Mongol attack upon Baghdad.

offensive was launched against Syria, Moslems were forced to bow to the cross in the streets of a surrendered Damascus and a mosque was turned into a Christian church. The Mamelukes

of Egypt were next on the list for conquest when the Great Khan died. The Mongol commander in the West favoured the succession of his younger brother, Kubilai, far away in China. But he was distracted and withdrew many of his men to Azerbaijan to wait on events. It was on a weakened army that the Mamelukes fell at the Goliath Spring near Nazareth on 3 September 1260. The Mongol general was killed, the legend of Mongol invincibility was shattered and a turning-point in world history was reached. For the Mongols the age of conquest was over and that of consolidation had begun.

The unity of Chinghis Khan's empire was at an end. After civil war the legacy was divided among the princes of his house, under the nominal supremacy of his grandson Kubilai, Khan of China, who was to be the last of the Great Khans. The Russian khanate was divided into three: the khanate of the Golden Horde ran from the Danube to the Caucasus and to the east of it lay the 'Cheibanid' khanate in the north (it was named after its first khan) and that of the White Horde in the south. The khanate of Persia included much of Asia Minor, and stretched across Iraq and Iran to the Oxus. Beyond that lay the khanate of Turkestan. The quarrels of these states left the Mamelukes free to mop up the crusader enclaves and revenge themselves upon the Christians who had compromised themselves by collaboration with the Mongols.

In retrospect it is still far from easy to understand why the Mongols were so successful for so long. In the west they had the advantage that there was no single great power such as Persia or the eastern Roman empire had been, to stand up to them, but in the east they defeated China, undeniably a great imperial state. It was undoubtedly an advantage, too, that they faced divided enemies; Christian rulers toyed with the hope of using Mongol power against the Moslem and even against one another, while any combination of the civilizations of the west with China against the Mongols was inconceivable given Mongol control of communication between the two. Their tolerance of religious

A fifteenth-century Persian painting on silk of a Mongol warrior, plaiting the tail of his mount.

diversity, except during the period of implacable hatred of Islam, also favoured the Mongols; those who submitted peacefully had little to fear. Would-be resisters could contemplate the ruins of Bokhara or Kiev, or the pyramids of skulls where there had been Persian cities; much of the Mongol success must have been a result of the sheer terror they inspired which defeated many of their enemies before they ever came to battle. In the last resort, though, simple military skill explained their victories. The Mongol soldier was tough, well trained and led by generals who exploited all the advantages which a fast-moving cavalry arm could give them. The rapidity of their movement was all the faster because of the care with which reconnaissance and intelligence work was carried out in preparation for a campaign. The discipline of the Mongol cavalry and their mastery of the techniques of siege warfare (which, none the less, they preferred to avoid) made them much more formidable than a horde of nomadic freebooters. As conquests continued, too, the Mongol army was recruited by specialists among its captives; by the middle of the thirteenth century there were many Turks in its ranks.

Though the Mongol army's needs were simple, the empire of Chinghis Khan and, in somewhat less degree, of his successors was an administrative reality over the vast territories it ruled. One of the first innovations of Chinghis was the reduction of Mongol language to writing, using the Turkish script. This was done by a captive. It was always a striking feature of Mongol rule that it drew willingly upon the skills made available to it by its conquests. Chinese civil servants organized the conquered territories for revenue purposes; it was the Chinese device of paper money which, when introduced by the Mongols into the Persian economy in the thirteenth century, brought about a disastrous collapse of trade, but the failure does not make the example of the use of alien techniques by these conquerors less striking.

In so great an empire, communications were the key to power. A network of post-houses was set up along the main roads, by means of which messengers and agents could be maintained during a rapid journey. The roads helped trade, too, and for all their ruthlessness to the cities which resisted them, the Mongols usually encouraged rebuilding and the renaissance of commerce, from the taxation of which they sought revenue. Asia knew a sort of *Pax Mongolica*. Caravans were protected against nomadic bandits by the policing of the Mongols, poachers turned gamekeepers. The most successful nomads of all, they were not going to let other nomads spoil their game. Land trade was as easy between China and Europe during the Mongol era as at any time; Marco Polo is the most famous of Europe's travellers to the Far East in the thirteenth century and by the time he went there the Mongols had conquered China, but before he was born his father and uncle had begun travels in Asia which were to last years. They were both Venetian merchants and were sufficiently successful to set off again almost as soon as they got back, taking the young Marco with them. By sea, too, China's trade was linked with Europe, through the port of Ormuz on the Persian Gulf, but it was the land-routes to the Crimea and Trebizond which carried most of the silks and spices westward and provided the bulk of Byzantine trade in its last centuries. The land-routes depended on the khans, and, significantly, the merchants were always strong supporters of the Mongol régime.

In its relations with the rest of the world, the Mongol empire came to show the influence of China in its fundamental presuppositions. The khans were the representatives on earth of the one sky god, Tengri; his supremacy had to be acknowledged, though this did not mean that the practice of other religions would not be tolerated. But it did mean that diplomacy in the western sense was inconceivable. Like the Chinese emperors whom they were to replace, the khans saw themselves as the upholders of a universal monarchy; those who came to it had to come as suppliants. Ambassadors were the bearers of tribute, not the representatives of powers of equal standing. When in 1246 emissaries from Rome conveyed papal protests against the Mongol treatment of Christian Europe and a recommendation that he should be baptized, the new Great Khan's reply was blunt: 'If you do not observe God's command, and if you ignore my command, I shall know you as my enemy. Likewise I shall make you understand.' As for baptism, the pope was told to come in person to serve the khan. It was not an isolated message, for another pope had the same reply from the Mongol governor of Persia

The Mongols never lost their aboriginal and legendary skills as horsemen and in China annual displays of horsemanship were held; this comes from a scroll probably of the late thirteenth or early fourteenth century.

a year later: 'If you wish to keep your land, you must come to us in person and thence go on to him who is master of the earth. If you do not, we know not what will happen: only God knows.'

The cultural influences playing upon the Mongol rulers and their circle were not only Chinese. There is much evidence of the importance of Nestorian Christianity at the Mongol court and it encouraged European hopes of a rapprochement with the khans. One of the most remarkable western visitors to the khan, the Franciscan William of Roebruck, was told just after New Year 1254, by an Armenian monk, that the Great Khan would be baptized a few days later, but nothing came of it. William went on, however, to win a debate before him, defending the Christian faith against Moslem and Buddhist representatives and coming off best. This was, in fact, just the moment at which Mongol strength was being gathered for the double assault on world power, against Sung China and the Moslems which was finally checked in Syria by the Mamelukes in 1260.

Not that this was the end of attempts by

Mongols to conquer the Levant. None was successful, though; the Mongols' quarrels among themselves had given the Mamelukes a clear field for too long. Logically, Christians regretted the death of Hulugu, the last khan to pose a real threat to the Near East for decades. After him a succession of Il-khans, or subordinate khans, ruled in Persia, preoccupied with their quarrels with the Golden and White Hordes. There was a clear sign of a change in the relative position of Mongol and European when the Il-khans began to suggest to the pope that they should join in an alliance against the Mamelukes. Gradually Persia recovered under them from the invasions it had suffered earlier in the century. As in the East, the Mongols ruled through locally recruited administrators and were tolerant of Christians and Buddhists, though not, at first, of Moslems.

When Kubilai Khan died in China in 1294 one of the few remaining links that held together the Mongol empire had gone; he was the last Great Khan. In the following year an Il-khan called Ghazan made a momentous break with the Mongol tradition; he became a Moslem. Since then the rulers of Persia have always been Moslem. But this did not do all that might have been hoped and the Il-khan died young, with many problems unsolved. Ghazan's embracing of Islam had been a bold stroke, but it was not enough. It had offended many Mongols and in the last resort the khans depended upon their captains. Nevertheless, the contest with the Mamelukes was not yet abandoned under him. Though in the end unsuccessful, Ghazan's armies took Aleppo in 1299; he was prayed for in the Ummayad mosque at Damascus the next year. He was the last khan to attempt to realize the plan of Mongol conquest of the Near East set out a half-century before, but was frustrated in the end when the Mamelukes defeated the last Mongol invasion of Syria in 1303. The Il-khan died the following year.

As in China, it soon appeared in Persia that Mongol rule had enjoyed only a brief Indian summer of consolidation before it began to crumble. Ghazan was the last Il-khan of stature.

At Samarkand stands the Gur-i-Mir. There Timur Lang is buried. Commissioned by him as the tomb of a favourite nephew, it became his own and a part of a complex of buildings which grew to be a family mausoleum. Craftsmen were brought from Isfahan to work upon this masterpiece of Timurid art, covered with coloured tiles and surmounted by a dome of unusual magnificence.

Outside their own lands, his successors could exercise little influence; the Mamelukes terrorized the old allies of the Mongols, the Christian Armenians, and Anatolia was disputed between different Turkish princes. There was little to hope for from Europe, where the illusion of the crusading dream had been dissipated. As Mongol states crumbled, one last flash of the old terror in the West came with a conqueror who rivalled even Chinghis.

In 1369 Timur Lang, or Timur the lame, became ruler of Samarkand. For thirty years the history of the Il-khans had been one of civil strife and succession disputes; Persia was conquered by Timur in 1379. Timur (who has passed into English literature, thanks to Marlowe, as Tamberlane) aspired to rival Chinghis. In the extent of his conquests and the ferocity of his behaviour he did; he may even have been as great a leader of men. None the less he lacked the statesmanship of his predecessors. Of creative art he was barren. Though he ravaged India and sacked Delhi (he was as hard on his fellow-Moslems as on Christians), thrashed the Khans of the Golden Horde, defeated Mameluke and Turk alike and incorporated Mesopotamia as well as Persia in his own domains, he left little behind. His historic rôle was, except in two respects, almost insignificant. One negative achievement was the almost complete extinction of Asiatic Christianity in its Nestorian and Jacobite form. This was hardly in the Mongol tradition, but Timur was as much a Turk by blood as a Mongol and knew nothing of the nomadic life of central Asia from which Chinghis came, with its willingness to indulge Christian clergy. His sole positive achievement was unintentional and temporary: briefly, he prolonged the life of Byzantium. By a great defeat of an Anatolian Turkish people, the Ottomans, in 1402, he prevented them for a while from going in to the kill against the eastern empire.

This was the direction in which Near Eastern history had been moving ever since the Mongols had been unable to keep their grip on Seljuk Anatolia. The spectacular stretch of Mongol campaigning – from Albania to Java – makes it hard to sense this until Timur's death, but then it was obvious. Before that, the Mongols had already been overthrown in China. Timur's own legacy crumbled, Mesopotamia eventually becoming the emirate of the attractively named Black Sheep Turks, while his successors for a while still hung on to Persia and Transoxiana. By the middle of the fifteenth century, the Golden Horde was well advanced in its break-up. Though it could still terrorize Russia, the Mongol threat to Europe was long over.

By then, Byzantium was at its last gasp. For more than two centuries she fought a losing battle for survival, and not merely with powerful Islamic neighbours. It was the West which had first reduced Byzantium to a tiny patch of territory and had sacked her capital. After 1204 Byzantium was only a small Balkan state. A Bulgarian king had seized the opportunity of that year to assure his country's independence and this was one of several ephemeral successor states which made their appearance. Furthermore, on the ruins of Byzantine rule there was established a new western European maritime empire, that of Venice, the cuckoo in the nest which had been in the first place bribed to enter it. This former client, though having to sustain a bitter commercial and political rivalry with another Italian city-state, Genoa, had by the middle of the fourteenth century taken for herself from the Byzantine heritage the whole Aegean complex of islands, with Rhodes, Crete, Corfu and Chios.

In 1261 the Byzantines had regained possession of their own capital. They did so with the help of a Turkish power in Anatolia, the Osmanlis. Two factors might still benefit the empire; the crucial phase of Mongol aggression was past (though this could hardly have been known and Mongol attacks continued to fall on peoples who cushioned her from them), and in Russia there existed a great Orthodox power which was a source of help and money. But there were also new threats and these outweighed the positive factors. Byzantine recovery in Europe in the later thirteenth century was soon faced by a new threat, a Serbian prince with aspirations to empire. He died before he could take Constantinople, but he left the empire with little but the hinterland of the capital and a fragment of Thrace. Against the Serbs, the empire once more called on Osmanli help. The Turks were now firmly established on the Asian shores of the Bosphorus; in 1333 they took a toehold in Europe at Gallipoli.

The best that the last eleven emperors, the Palaeologi, could manage in these circumstances was a rearguard action. They lost Asia Minor to the Osmanlis in 1326 and it was in this quarter that the fatal danger lay. In the eastern Black

Sea they had an ally in the Greek empire of Trebizond, a great trading state which was just to outlive Byzantium itself, but in Europe they could hope for little. The ambitions of the Venetians and Genoese, and the King of Naples, gave Byzantium little respite. One emperor desperately accepted papal primacy and reunion with the Roman Church; this did little except antagonize his own clergy and was abandoned by his successor.

Religion still divided Christendom. As the fourteenth century wore on, the Byzantines had a deepening sense of isolation. They felt abandoned to the infidel. An attempt to draw upon western mercenaries from Catalonia only led to their attacking Constantinople and setting up yet another breakaway state, the Catalan duchy of Athens, in 1311. Occasional victories when an island or a province was retaken did not offset the general tendency of these events, nor the debilitating effect of occasional civil war within the empire. True to their traditions, the Greeks managed even in this extremity to invest some of these struggles with a theological dimension.

At the beginning of the fifteenth century the Byzantine empire was reduced to Constantinople, Salonica and the Morea. The Turks surrounded the capital on all sides, and had already carried out their first attack on it. There was a second in 1422. John VIII made a last attempt to overcome the deepest barrier to cooperation with the West. He went in 1439 to an ecumenical council which was sitting in Florence and there accepted papal primacy and union with Rome. Western Christendom rejoiced; the bells were rung in all the parish churches of England. But the Orthodox East scowled. The council's formula ran headlong against its tradition; too much stood in the way – papal authority, the equality of bishops, ritual and doctrine. The most influential of the Greek clergy refused to attend the council; the large number who did all signed the formula of union except one (who, significantly, was later canonized) but many of them recanted when they went home. 'Better,' said one Byzantine dignitary, 'to see in the city the power of the Turkish turban than that of the Latin tiara.' Submission to the pope was for most Greeks a renegade act; they were denying the true Church, whose tradition Orthodoxy had conserved. In Constantinople itself the offices of priests known to accept the council were shunned; the emperors were loyal to the agreement but thirteen years passed before they dared to proclaim the union publicly at Constantinople. Only a formal and diplomatic benefit could be drawn from the submission; the pope urged support for a last crusade, which ended in disaster in 1444. In the end the West and East made no common cause against the infidel, who was, as yet, battering only at the West's outermost defences. France and Germany were absorbed in their own affairs and Venice and Genoa saw their interest might lie as much in conciliation of the Turk as in opposition to him. Even the Russians, harried by Tatars, could do little to help in the death agonies of Byzantium, cut off as they were from direct contact with it. The imperial city, and little else, was left alone and divided within itself to face the Ottomans' final effort.

Who were the Osmanlis, or, as they became known in Europe, the Ottomans? They were one of the Turkish peoples who had survived as a political unit in the collapse of the sultanate of Rum. When the Seljuks arrived they found on the borderlands between the dissolved Abassid caliphate and the Byzantine empire a number of Moslem marcher lords, petty princes called *ghazis*, sometimes Turkish by race, lawless, independent and the inevitable beneficiaries of the ebbing of paramount power. Their existence was precarious, and the Byzantine empire had absorbed some of them in its tenth-century recovery, but terrain and commitments elsewhere made it difficult to eliminate them. Many survived the Seljuk era and benefited from the Mongol destruction of the Seljuks at a time when Constantinople was in the hands of the Latins. One of these *ghazis* was Osman, a Turk who may have been an Oghuz. But his appeal lay in his leadership and enterprise and men gathered to him. His quality is shown by the transformation of the word *ghazi*: it came to

mean 'warrior of the faith'. Fanatical frontiers-
men, his followers seem to have been distinguished by a certain spiritual *élan*. Some of
them were influenced by a particular mystical
tradition within Islam. They also rapidly
showed themselves to be more than just a formerly nomad ascendancy lording it over an alien
population, for they developed highly characteristic institutions of their own. They had a
military organization somewhat like that of
merchant guilds or religious orders in medieval
Europe and it has even been suggested that the
West learnt in these matters from the Ottomans.
Their situation on a curious borderland of cultures, half-Christian, half-Islamic, must also
have been provoking. Whatever its ultimate
source their staggering record of conquest rivals
that of Arab and Mongol. They were in the end
to reassemble the territory of the old eastern
Roman empire and more.

The first Ottoman ruler to take the title of
Sultan did so in the early fourteenth century.
This was Orkhan, Osman's son. Under him
began the settlement of conquered lands which
was eventually to be the basis of Ottoman military power. Like his foundation of the 'Janis-
saries', the 'New Army' of infantry which he
needed to fight in Europe, the change marked
an important stage in the evolution of Ottoman
empire away from institutions which were still
those of a nomadic people of natural cavalrymen
even after prolonged settlement in Anatolia.
Another sign that things were settling down was
Orkhan's issue of the first Ottoman coinage. By
his death his dominions were the strongest of
the post-Seljuk states of Asia Minor and already
had European lands. Orkhan was important
enough to be three times called upon by the
Byzantine emperor for help and he married one
of the emperor's daughters.

His two successors steadily ate up the Balkans,
conquering Serbia and Bulgaria. They defeated
another 'crusade' against them in 1396 and
went on to take Greece. In 1391 they began
their first siege of Constantinople, which they
maintained successfully for six years. Meanwhile, Anatolia was absorbed by war and dip-

*In 1480 a Venetian artist Gentile Bellini painted
this portrait of Mehmet II, the great Ottoman
conqueror – an interpretation of a ruler and man
of action as a pensive, introspective spirit, perhaps
even with something wistful about his expression.*

lomacy. There was only one bad setback, the
defeat by Timur which brought on a succession
crisis and almost dissolved the Ottoman empire.
The advance was then resumed and the Venetian
empire now began to suffer, too. But for
Byzantine and Turk alike, the struggle was
essentially a religious one and its heart was the
possession of the thousand-year-old Christian
capital, Constantinople.

It was under Mehmet II, named the Conquer-
or, that in 1453 Constantinople fell to the Turks
and the western world shuddered. It was a great
feat of arms, depleted though the resources of
Byzantium were, and supremely Mehmet's
achievement, for he had persisted against all
obstacles. The age of gunpowder was now well
under way and he had a Hungarian engineer
build him a gigantic cannon whose operation
was so cumbersome that it could only be moved
by a hundred oxen and fired only seven times a
day (the Hungarian's assistance had been turned
down by the Christians though the fee he asked
was a quarter of what Mehmet gave him). It was

425

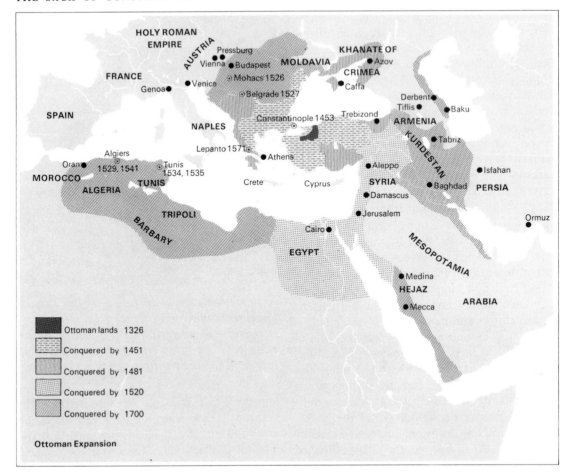

Ottoman Expansion

- Ottoman lands 1326
- Conquered by 1451
- Conquered by 1481
- Conquered by 1520
- Conquered by 1700

a failure. Mehmet did better with orthodox methods, driving his soldiers forward ruthlessly, cutting them down if they flinched from the assault. Finally, he carried seventy ships overland to get them behind the imperial squadron guarding the Horn.

The last attack began early in April 1453. After nearly two months, on 29 May, Roman Catholics and Orthodox alike gathered for a service in St Sophia and the fiction of the religious reunion was given its last parade. The Emperor Constantine XI, eightieth in succession since his namesake, the first great Constantine, took communion and then went out to die worthily, fighting. Soon afterwards, it was all over. Mehmet entered the city, went straight to St Sophia and there set up a triumphant throne. The church which had been the heart of Ortho-

doxy was made a mosque.

This was only a step, great as it was; the banner of Ottoman success was to be raised yet higher. The invasion of Serbia in 1459 was almost at once followed by the conquest of Trebizond. Unpleasant though this may have been for the inhabitants, it would merit only a footnote to the roll of Turkish conquest were it not also the end of Hellenism. At this remote spot on the south-eastern coast of the Black

In 1526 the sultan Suleiman the Magnificent inflicted a shattering defeat on the Christian Hungarian army at Mohacs, south of Budapest. This Turkish painting reveals much of the appearance of an Ottoman army; Hungarian knights flee while the heads of others litter the field.

Sea in 1461 the world of Greek cities made possible by the conquest of Alexander the Great gave its last gasp. It marked an epoch as decisively as the fall of Constantinople, which a humanist pope bewailed as 'the second death of Homer and Plato'. From Trebizond, Turkish conquest rolled on. In the same year the Turks occupied the Peloponnese. Two years later they took Bosnia and Herzegovina. Albania and the Ionian islands followed in the next twenty years. In 1480 they captured the Italian port of Otranto and held it for nearly a year. In 1517 Syria and Egypt were conquered. They took longer to pick up the remainder of the Venetian empire, but at the beginning of the sixteenth century Turkish cavalry were near Vicenza. In 1526 at Mohacs they wiped out the army of the Hungarian king in a defeat which is remembered still as the black day of Hungarian history. Three years later they besieged Vienna for the first time. In 1571 Cyprus fell to them and nearly a century later Crete. By this time they were deep into Europe. They again besieged Vienna in the seventeenth century; their second failure to take it was the high-water mark of Turkish conquest. But they were still conquering new territory in the Mediterranean as late as 1715. Meanwhile, they had taken Kurdistan from Persia, with whom they had hardly ceased to quarrel since the appearance of a new dynasty there in 1501, and had sent an army as far south as Aden.

The Ottoman empire was of unique importance to Europe. It is one of the factors which have marked off decisively the history of its eastern from that of its western half. It was crucial that the Church survived and was tolerated in the Ottoman empire. That preserved the heritage of Byzantium for its Slav subjects (and, indeed, ended any threat to the supremacy of the patriarch at Constantinople either from the Catholics or from national Orthodox churches in the Balkans). Outside the former empire, only one important focus of Orthodoxy remained; it was crucial that the Orthodox Church was now the heritage of Russia. The establishment of the Ottoman empire for a time

sealed off Europe from the Near East and the Black Sea and, therefore, in large measure from the land routes to Asia. The Europeans had really only themselves to blame; they had never been (and were never to be) able to unite effectively against the Turks. Byzantium had been left to her fate. 'Who will make the English love the French? Who will unite Genoese and Aragonese?' asked a fifteenth-century pope despairingly; not long after, one of his successors was sounding out the possibilities of Turkish help against France. Yet the challenge had awoken another sort of response, for even before the fall of Constantinople Portuguese ships were picking their way southwards down the African coast to look for a new route to the spices of the East and, possibly, an African ally to take the Turk in the flank from the south. People had mused over finding a way round the Islamic barrier since the thirteenth century, but the means had long been inadequate. By one of history's ironies they were just about to become available as Ottoman power reached its menacing peak.

Behind the Ottoman frontiers a new multi-racial polity was organized. Mehmet was a man of wide, if volatile, sympathies and later Turks found it hard to understand his forbearance to the infidel. He was a man who could slaughter a boy, the godson of the emperor, because his sexual advances were refused, but he allowed a band of Cretans who would not surrender to sail away after the fall of Constantinople because he admired their courage. He seems to have wanted a multi-religious society. He brought back Greeks to Constantinople from Trebizond and appointed a new patriarch under whom the Greeks were eventually given a kind of self-government. The Turkish record towards Jew and Christian was better than that of Spanish Christians towards Jew and Moslem.

Thus the Ottomans reconstructed a great power in the eastern Mediterranean. While they rebuilt something like the Byzantine empire, another power was emerging in Persia which was also reminiscent of the past, this time of the empire of the Sassanids.

This Persian picture of a painter at work shows a man in Turkish dress; it may be a copy of a painting by Gentile Bellini.

Between 1501 and 1736 the Safavid dynasty ruled Persia. Like their predecessors, the Safavids were not themselves Persian. Since the days of the Sassanids, conquerors had come and gone. The continuities of Persian history were meanwhile provided by culture and religion.

Persia was defined by geography, by its language and by Islam, not by the maintenance of national dynasties. The Safavids were originally Turk, *ghazis* like the Osmanlis and succeeded, like them, in distancing possible rivals. The first ruler they gave to Persia was Ismail, a descendant of the fourteenth-century tribal ruler who had given his name to the line.

At first, Ismail was only the most successful leader of a group of warring Turkish tribes

429

The helmet of Shah Abbas, an outstanding specimen of the armourer's art. Its steel is inlaid with gold and round its rim are inscribed verses in praise of the great Shah. Plumes would have been worn with the helmet, fixed into sockets on the front.

rather like those further west, exploiting similar opportunities. The Timurid inheritance had been in dissolution since the middle of the fifteenth century. In 1501 Ismail defeated the White Sheep Turks, entered Tabriz and proclaimed himself shah. Within twenty years he had carved out an enduring state and had also embarked upon a long rivalry with the Ottomans.

This rivalry had a religious dimension, for the Safavids were Shiites. When in the early sixteenth century the caliphate passed to the Ottomans they became the leaders of Sunnite Moslems who saw the caliphs as the proper interpreters and governors of the faith. The Shiites were therefore automatically anti-Ottoman. Ismail's establishment of the sect in Persia thus gave a new distinctiveness to Persia's civilization and this was to prove of great importance in preserving it.

His immediate successors had to fight off the Turks several times before a peace was made in 1555 which left Persia intact and opened Mecca and Medina to Persian pilgrims. There were domestic troubles, too, and fighting for the throne, but in 1587 there came to it one of the most able of Persian rulers, Shah Abbas the Great. Under his rule the Safavid dynasty was at its zenith. Politically and militarily he was very successful, defeating the Uzbeks and the Turks and taming the old tribal loyalties which had weakened his predecessors. He had important advantages: the Ottomans were distracted in the West, the potential of Russia was sterilized by internal troubles and Moghul India was past its peak. He was clever enough to see that Europe could be enrolled against the Turk. Yet a favourable conjuncture of international forces did not lead to schemes of world conquest. The Safavids did not follow the Sassanid example. They never took the offensive against Turkey except to recover earlier loss and they did not push north through the Caucasus to Russia, or beyond Transoxania.

Persian culture enjoyed a spectacular flowering under Shah Abbas, who built a new capital at Isfahan. Its beauty and luxury astounded European visitors. Literature flourished. The only ominous note was religious. The shah insisted on abandoning the religious toleration which had until now characterized Safavid rule and imposed conversion to Shiite views. This did not at once mean the imposition of an intolerant system; that would only come later. But it did mean that Safavid Persia had taken a significant step towards decline and towards the devolution of power into the hands of religious officials.

After Shah Abbas' death in 1629 events rapidly took a turn for the worse. His unworthy successor did little about this, preferring to withdraw to the seclusion of the harem and its

Oh, my beloved, fill the Cup that clears
Today of past regrets and future fears . . .
A Persian lady drinks a cup of wine, in a
miniature from seventeenth-century Isfahan,
from which the works of art most evocative of the
hedonistic civilization of Persia have reached us.

pleasures, while the traditional splendour of the Safavid inheritance cloaked its actual collapse. The Turks took Baghdad again in 1638. In 1664 came the first portents of a new threat: Cossack raids began to harry the Caucasus and the first Russian mission arrived in Isfahan. Western Europeans had already long been familiar with Persia. In 1507 the Portuguese had established themselves in the port of Ormuz where Ismail levied tribute on them. In 1561 an English merchant reached Persia overland from Russia and opened up a first period of Anglo-Persian trade. In the early seventeenth century this connexion was well established and by then

Shah Abbas had Englishmen in his service. This was the result of Shah Abbas' encouragement of relations with the West, where he hoped to find support against the Turk.

The growing English presence was not well received by the Portuguese. When the East India Company opened operations the Portuguese attacked them unsuccessfully. A little later the English and Persians joined forces to eject the Portuguese from Ormuz. By this time other European countries were becoming interested, too. In the second half of the seventeenth century the French, Dutch and Spanish all tried to penetrate the Persian trade. The shahs did not rise to the opportunity of playing off one set of foreigners against another.

At the beginning of the eighteenth century Persia was suddenly exposed to a double onslaught. The Afghans revolted and established an independent Sunnite state; religious antagonism had done much to feed their sedition. From 1719 to 1722 the Afghans were at war with the last Safavid shah. He abdicated in that year and an Afghan, Mahmud, took the throne, thus ending Shiite Persia. The story must none the less be taken a little further forward, for the Russians had been watching with interest the progress of Safavid decline. The Russian ruler had sent embassies to Isfahan in 1708 and 1718. Then, in 1723, on the pretext of intervention in the succession, the Russians seized Derbent and Baku and obtained from the defeated Shiites promises of much more. The Turks decided not to be left out and, having seized Tiflis, agreed in 1724 with the Russians upon a dismemberment of Persia. That once great state seemed to be ending in nightmare. In Isfahan a massacre of possible Safavid sympathizers was carried out by orders of a shah who had now gone mad. There was, before long, to be a last Persian recovery by the last great Asiatic conqueror, Nadir Kali. But though he might restore a Persian empire of great size, the days when the Iranian plateau was the seat of a power which could shape events far beyond its borders were over until the twentieth century and then it would not be armies which gave Iran its leverage.

5 The Making of Europe

In comparison with Byzantium or the caliphate, Europe west of the Elbe was for centuries after the Roman collapse an almost insignificant backwater. Its boundaries were soon far narrower than had been those of western Christianity. Its inhabitants felt themselves a beleaguered remnant and in a sense so they were. Islam cut them off from Africa and the Near East and Arab raids tormented their southern coasts. From the eighth century the seemingly inexplicable violence of the Norse peoples we call Vikings fell like a flail time and time again on the northern coasts, river valleys and islands. In the ninth century the eastern front was harried by the pagan Magyars. Europe was formed in a hostile, heathen world.

The foundations of a new civilization had to be laid in barbarism and backwardness, which only a handful of men was available to tame and cultivate. No city in the West could approach in magnificence Constantinople, Córdoba, Baghdad or Peking. Europe would long be a cultural importer. It took centuries before its architecture could compare with that of the classical past

Under Moslem rule, Spanish Christians produced what was later called Mozarabic or 'arabized' art. One of its most astonishing productions is a collection of illuminated manuscripts of a popular work of devotion and scholarship, a commentary on the Apocalypse by an eighth-century monk, Beatus of Liebana. About twenty copies survive and this illustration of the text 'Behold, he cometh with clouds; and every eye shall see him' is from an eleventh-century version.

or the contemporary East and when it emerged it did so by borrowing the style of Byzantine Italy and the pointed arch of the Arabs. For just as long, no science, no school in the West could match those of Arab Spain or Asia. Nor could the West produce an effective political unity or theoretical justification of power such as the eastern empire and the caliphates; for centuries even the greatest European kings were only a stage removed from the barbarian warlords to whom men clung for protection and in fear of something worse. Had it come from Islam, that something might well have been better. At times, it must have seemed a possibility, for the Arabs established themselves not only in Spain but in Sicily, Corsica, Sardinia and the Balearics; men long feared they might go further. They had more to offer than the Scandinavian barbarians, yet the northerners made more of a mark in the end on the kingdoms established by earlier migrants. In the East lay Slavic Christendom and Byzantium, both culturally sundered from the West and able to contribute little to it. Yet they were a cushion which just saved Europe from the full impact of eastern nomads and of Islam. A Moslem Russia would have meant a very different history for the West.

Roughly speaking, western Christendom before the beginning of the eleventh century meant half the Iberian peninsula, all modern France and Germany west of the Elbe, Bohemia, Austria, the Italian peninsula and England. At the fringes of this area lay barbaric, but Christian, Ireland and Scotland, and, just at the end of these centuries, the Scandinavian kingdoms. To this area the word 'Europe' began to be applied in the tenth century; a Spanish chronicle even spoke of the victors of 732 as 'European'. The area they occupied was all but landlocked; though the Atlantic was wide open, there was almost nowhere to go in that direction once Iceland was settled by the Norwegians, while the western Mediterranean, the highway to other civilizations and their trade, was an Arab lake. Only a thin channel of seaborne communication with an increasingly alien Byzantium brought Europe some relief from its introverted, narrow existence. Men grew used to privation rather than opportunity. They huddled together under the rule of a warrior class which they needed for their protection.

In fact, the worst was over in the tenth century. The Magyars were checked, the Arabs were beginning to be challenged at sea, and the northern barbarians were on the road to Christianity. Though, as the portentous date 1000 approached, men thought that the end of the world might be at hand, that year can serve, very approximately, as the marker of an epoch. Not only had the pressures upon Europe begun to relax, but the lineaments of a later, expanding Europe were already hardening. Her basic political and social structure was set and her Christian culture had already much of its peculiar flavour. The eleventh century was to begin an era of revolution and adventure, for which the centuries sometimes called the Dark Ages had provided raw materials. As a way to understand how this happened, a good starting-point is the map.

Down to the eleventh century, three great changes began the making of the European map we know. One was a cultural and psychological shift away from the Mediterranean, the focus of classical civilization. The centre of European life, in so far as there was one, moved between the fifth and eighth centuries to the valley of the Rhine and its tributaries. By preying on the sea-lanes to Italy and by its distraction of Byzantium in the seventh and eighth centuries, Islam, too, helped to throw back the West upon this heartland of a future Europe. The second change

was more positive, a gradual advance of Christianity and settlement in the East. Though far from complete by 1000, the elements of Christian civilization had by then long been pushed out beyond the old Roman frontier. The third change was the slackening of barbarian pressure. The Magyars were checked in the tenth century; the Norsemen who were eventually to provide rulers in England, northern France, Sicily and some of the Aegean came from the last wave of Scandinavian expansion, which was in its last phase in the early eleventh century. Europe was no longer to be just a prey to others – though as late as the thirteenth century, when the Mongols menaced her, it must have been difficult to feel this. None the less, even by 1000 she was ceasing to be wholly plastic.

Western Christendom can be considered in three big divisions. In the central area built round the Rhine valley the future France and the future Germany were to emerge. Then there was a west Mediterranean littoral civilization, embracing at first Catalonia, the Languedoc and Provence. With time and the recovery of Italy from the barbarian centuries, this extended itself further to the east and south. A third Europe was the somewhat varied periphery in the west, north-west and north where there were to be found the first Christian states of northern Spain, which emerged from the Visigothic period, England, with its appended but independent Celtic and semi-barbarous satellites, Ireland, Wales and Scotland, and the Scandinavian states. We must not be rigid about such a picture. There were areas one might allocate to one or the other of these three regions, such as Aquitaine, Gascony and sometimes Burgundy. Nevertheless, when all qualifications are made, these distinctions are real enough to be useful. Historical experience, as well as climate and race, made these regions significantly different, yet of course most men living in these areas would not have known in which one they lived; they would certainly have been more interested in differences between them and their neighbours in the next village than of those between their region and its neighbour.

Dimly aware that they were a part of Christendom, very few of them would have had even an approximate conception of what lay in the awful shadows beyond that comforting idea.

The origin of the heartland of the medieval West was the Frankish heritage. It had fewer towns than the south and they mattered little; a settlement like Paris was less troubled by the collapse of commerce than, say, Milan. Life centred on the soil, and aristocrats were successful warriors turned landowners. From this base, the Franks began the colonization of Germany, protected the Church and hardened and passed on a tradition of kingship whose origins lay somewhere in the magical powers of Merovingian rulers. But for centuries, state structures were fragile things, dependent on strong kings, for ruling was a personal activity.

Frankish ways and institutions did not help. After Clovis, though there was dynastic continuity, a succession of impoverished and therefore feeble kings led to more independence for landed aristocrats, who warred with one another; they had the wealth which could buy power. One family from Austrasia came to overshadow the Merovingian royal line. It produced Charles Martel, the soldier who turned the Arabs back at Tours in 732 and the supporter of St Boniface, the evangelizer of Germany. This is a considerable double mark to have left on European history (St Boniface said he could not have succeeded without Charles' support) and it confirmed the alliance of Martel's house with the Church. His second son, Pepin the Short, was chosen king by the Frankish nobles in 751. Three years later, the pope came to France and anointed him king as Samuel had anointed Saul and David.

The papacy needed a powerful friend. The pretensions of the emperor in Constantinople were a fiction and in Roman eyes he had fallen into heresy, in any case, through taking up iconoclasm. To confer the title of Patrician on Pepin, as Pope Stephen did, was really a usurpation of imperial authority, but the Lombards were terrorizing Rome. The papacy drew the dividend on its investment almost at once, for Pepin

defeated the Lombards and in 756 established the Papal States of the future by granting Ravenna 'to St Peter'. This was the beginning of eleven hundred years of the Temporal Power, the secular authority enjoyed by the pope over his own dominions as a ruler like any other ruler. A Romano-Frankish axis was created. From it stemmed the reform of the Frankish Church, further colonization and missionary conversion in Germany (where wars were waged against the pagan Saxons), the throwing back of the Arabs across the Pyrenees and the conquest of Septimania and Aquitaine. These were big gains for the Church. Nor did the new magic of anointing benefit only kings. Though it could replace or blur mysteriously with the old Merovingian thaumaturgy and raise kings above common men in more than their power, the pope gained the subtle implication of authority latent in the bestowing of the sacral oil.

Pepin, like all Frankish kings, divided his land at his death but the whole Frankish heritage was united again in 771 in his elder son. This was Charlemagne, crowned emperor in 800 and the greatest of the Carolingians, as the line came to be called. He was soon to be a legend. This increases the difficulties, always great in medieval history, of penetrating a man's biography. Charlemagne's actions speak for certain continuing prepossessions. He was obviously still a traditional Frankish warrior-king; he conquered and his business was war. What was more novel was the seriousness with which he took the Christian sanctification of this rôle. He took his duties seriously, too, in patronizing learning and art; he wanted to magnify the grandeur and prestige of his court by filling it with evidence of Christian learning.

Territorially, Charlemagne was a great builder, overthrowing the Lombards in Italy and becoming their king; their lands, too, passed into the Frankish heritage. For thirty years he hammered away in campaigns on the Saxon March and achieved the conversion of the Saxon pagans by force. Fighting against the Avars, Wends and Slavs brought him Carinthia and Bohemia and, perhaps as important, the opening

DANISH MARCH

SAXONY
●Magdeburg

SLAVS

FLANDERS
Aachen
AUSTRASIA
●Fulda

BOHEMIA

BRITTANY
Rouen●
Paris●
Mainz●

WENDS

MORAVIA

Tours●

ALLEMANNIA BAVARIA

CARINTHIA

AVARS

AQUITAINE
●Bordeaux
GASCONY

BURGUNDY

Milan●

FRIULI

Pamplona●
●Roncesvalles
SEPTIMANIA

PATRIMONY OF
ST PETER
●Ravenna

UMMAYAD EMIRATE
OF CORDOBA

SPANISH
MARCH
●Barcelona
Tortosa●

Marseilles●

Corsica

Rome●

Sardinia

BYZANTINE EMPIRE

▨ Frankish tributaries
▨ Frankish Kingdoms at 768
▨ Areas conquered by Charlemagne

Charlemagne's Europe

of a route down the Danube to Byzantium. To master the Danes, the Dane Mark (March) was set up across the Elbe. Charlemagne pushed into Spain early in the ninth century and instituted the Spanish March across the Pyrenees down to the Ebro and the Catalonian coast. But he did not put to sea; the Visigoths had been the last western European sea-power.

Thus he put together a realm bigger than anything in the West since Rome. Historians have been arguing almost ever since about what

its reality was and about what the assumption of the title of emperor and Charlemagne's coronation by the pope on Christmas Day, 800, actually meant. The problem was that there already was an emperor whom everybody acknowledged to be such: he lived in Constantinople. Did a second ruler with the title mean that there were two emperors of a divided Christendom, as in later Roman times? Clearly, it was a claim to authority over many peoples; by this title, Charlemagne said he was more than

436

just a ruler of Franks. Perhaps Italy mattered most in explaining it, for among the Italians a link with the imperial past might be a cementing factor as nowhere else. An element of papal gratitude – or expediency – was involved, too; Leo III had just been restored to his capital by Charlemagne's soldiers. Yet Charlemagne is reported to have said that he would not have entered St Peter's had he known what the pope intended to do. He may have disliked the pope's implied arrogation of authority and foreseen the irritation the coronation would cause at Constantinople. He must have known that to his own people, the Franks, and to many of his northern subjects he was more comprehensible as a traditional Germanic warrior-king than as the successor of Roman emperors.

In fact, Charlemagne's relations with Byzantium were troubled, though his title was a few years later recognized as valid in the West in return for a concession to Byzantium of sovereignty over Venice, Istria and Dalmatia. With another great state, the Abassid caliphate, Charlemagne had somewhat formal but not unfriendly relations; Haroun-al-Raschid is said to have given him a cup bearing a portrait of Chosroes I, the king under whom Sassanid power and civilization was at its height (perhaps it is significant that it is from Frankish sources that we learn of these contacts; they do not seem to have struck the Arab chroniclers as important enough to mention). The Ummayads of Spain were different; they were marked down as the enemies of a Christian ruler because near enough to be a threat. To protect the faith from pagans was a part of Christian kingship but in government this kingship had other expressions. For all his support and protection, the Church was firmly subordinate to Charlemagne's authority. He presided over the Frankish synods, pronouncing upon dogmatic questions as authoritatively as had Justinian, and seems to have hoped for an integrated reform of the Frankish Church and the Roman, imposing upon them both the Rule of St Benedict. In such a scheme there is the essence of the later European idea that a

Many representations of Charlemagne exist; none is of unquestionable authenticity. This one comes from a Swiss church in the Grisons and may well date from his lifetime.

Christian king is responsible not only for the protection of the Church but for the quality of the religious life within his dominions. Charlemagne also used the Church as an instrument of government, ruling through bishops.

Further evidence of religion's special importance to Charlemagne lies in the tone of the life of his court at Aachen. He strove to beautify its physical setting with architecture and decorative treasures. There was, of course, much to be done. The ebbing of economic life and of literacy meant that a Carolingian court was a primitive thing by comparison with Byzantium – and possibly even in comparison with those of some of the early barbarian kingdoms which were sometimes open to influence from a more cultivated world, as the appearance of Coptic themes in early barbarian art attests. When Charlemagne's men brought materials to beau-

437

tify Aachen from Ravenna, Byzantine art, too, moved more freely into the north European tradition. But it was its scholars and scribes which made Charlemagne's court most spectacular. It was an intellectual centre. From it radiated the impulse to copy texts in a new refined and reformed hand called Carolingian minuscule which was to be one of the great instruments of culture in the West. The standardization which this made possible was first evident in the copying of the Bible; the purpose was more than religious, for the scriptural story was to be interpreted as a justification of Carolingian rule. The Jewish history of the Old Testament was full of examples of pious and anointed warrior-kings. The Bible was the major text in the monastic libraries which now began to be assembled throughout the Frankish lands.

Copying and the diffusion of texts went on for a century after the original impulse had been given at Aachen and were the core of what modern scholars have called 'the Carolingian Renaissance'. It had none of the pagan connotations of that word as it was used of a later revival of learning which focussed attention on the classical past, for it was emphatically Christian. Its whole purpose was the training of clergy to raise the level of the Frankish Church and carry the faith further to the east. The lead-

ing men in the beginnings of this transmission of sacred knowledge were not Franks. There were several Irishmen and Anglo-Saxons in the palace school at Aachen and among them the outstanding figure was Alcuin, a cleric from York, a great centre of English learning. His most famous pupil was Charlemagne himself, but he had several others and managed the palace library. Besides writing books of his own he set up a school at Tours, where he became abbot, and began to expound Boethius and Augustine to the men who would govern the Frankish church in the next generation.

Alcuin's pre-eminence is as striking a piece of evidence as any of the shift in the centre of cultural gravity in Europe, away from the classical world and to the north. But others than his countrymen were involved in teaching, copying and founding the new monasteries which spread outwards into east and west Francia; there were Franks, Visigoths, Lombards and Italians among them, too. One of these, a layman called Einhard, wrote a life of the emperor from which we learn such fascinating human details as the fact that he could be garrulous, that he was a keen hunter and that he passionately loved swimming and bathing in the thermal springs which explain his choice of Aachen as a residence. Charlemagne comes to life in Einhard's pages as an intellectual, too, speaking Latin as well, we are told, as Frankish, and understanding Greek. This is made more credible because we hear also of his attempts to write, keeping notebooks under his pillow so that he could do so in bed, 'but', Einhard says, 'although he tried very hard, he had begun too late in life'.

From this account and from his work a remarkably vivid picture can be formed of a dignified, majestic figure, striving to make the transition from warlord to ruler of a great Christian empire, and having remarkable success in his own lifetime in so doing. Clearly his physical presence was impressive, but men saw in him the image of a kingly soul, gay, just and magnanimous, as well as that of the heroic paladin of whom poets and minstrels would be singing for centuries. His power was a more majestic spectacle than anything seen to that time in barbarian lands. But it was also very personal. This may be inferred from the efforts he made to prevent his noblemen from replacing tribal rulers by settling down into a hereditary position of their own, or from the repeated issuing of his 'capitularies' or instructions to his servants (a sign that such regulation was ineffective). In the last resort, even a Charlemagne could only rely on personal rule, and that meant a monarchy based on his own domain and its produce and on the big men close enough to him for supervision. These vassals were bound to him by especially solemn oaths, but even they began to give trouble as he grew older.

Charlemagne thought in traditional Frankish terms of his territorial legacy. He made plans to divide it and only the accident of sons dying before him ensured that the empire passed undivided to the youngest, Louis the Pious, in 814. With it came the imperial title (which Charle-

Originally, the cathedral at Aachen was the chapel of Charlemagne's palace. An octagonal central space gave the building its special character which can be sensed in this picture (though the chandelier was a twelfth-century innovation).

St Matthew, depicted as a scribe, inkhorn in hand, in a Gospel book commissioned by an archbishop early in the ninth century. The presence of Byzantine artists at Charlemagne's court is now thought to have been the channel through which such Hellenistic influence as can be detected in such pictures reached the north.

magne gave to his son) and the alliance of monarchy and papacy; two years after his succession the pope crowned him at a second coronation. Partition was only delayed by this. Charlemagne's successors had neither his authority nor his experience, nor perhaps an interest in controlling fissiparous forces. Regional loyalties were forming around individuals and a series of partitions finally culminated in one between three of Charlemagne's grandsons, the Treaty of Verdun of 843 which had great consequences. It gave a core kingdom of Frankish lands centred on the western side of the Rhine valley and containing Charlemagne's capital, Aachen, to Lothair, the reigning emperor (thus it was called Lotharingia) and added to this the kingdom of Italy. North of the Alps, this united Provence, Burgundy, Lorraine and the lands

439

A psalter copied at a French abbey in about 825 provides an example of the new, easily-read style in which Carolingian copyists worked.

between Scheldt, Meuse, Saône and Rhône. To the east lay a second block of lands of Teutonic speech between the Rhine and the German Marches; it went to Louis the German. Finally, in the west, a tract of territory including Gascony, Septimania and Aquitaine, and roughly the equal of the rest of modern France, went to a half-brother of these two, Charles the Bald.

This settlement was not long untroubled, but it was decisive in a broad and important way; it

effectively founded the political distinction of France and Germany, whose roots lay in west and east Francia. Between them it set up a third unit with much less linguistic, ethnic, geographical and economic unity. Lotharingia was there in part because three sons had to be provided

Duke Tassilo of Bavaria was a great German magnate. Charlemagne was determined to bring him to heel and condemned him to death (though his sentence was commuted to life imprisonment). Earlier, the duke had tried to insure his position by winning the support of important ecclesiastical bodies. One way of doing so was by making lavish gifts to them. In about 780 this chalice of copper gilt, in whose decoration Lombard and perhaps Northumbrian motifs can be detected, was given by him to an abbey he had founded at Kremsmünster.

An early essay in pictorial journalism: this may be the first representation of a contemporary event in Christian Europe's art. The Bible carried by the group of monks on the left of this picture is in fact the one in which this picture appears. Copied and illuminated in their monastery at Tours, it was presented by the lay abbot of the house to the Carolingian king, Charles the Bald, probably when he visited Tours in 851. The king resembles other representations of King David in Carolingian painting; his guards are like Roman soldiers.

for, and much Franco-German history in the future was going to be about the form in which it was eventually to be divided between neighbours bound to covet it and therefore likely to grow apart from one another in rivalry. One way of seeing the Common Market, as some of its supporters sometimes enthusiastically point out, is as an attempt to reconstitute Charlemagne's empire.

Gradually, and like their predecessors, the Carolingians declined in power. No royal house could guarantee a continuous flow of able kings, nor could they for ever buy loyalty from their supporters by giving away lands. The signs of break-up multiplied, an independent kingdom of Burgundy appeared and people began to dwell on the great days of Charlemagne, a significant symptom of decay and dissatisfaction. The histories of west and east Franks diverged more and more.

441

In west Francia the Carolingians lasted just over a century after Charles the Bald. By the end of his reign Brittany, Flanders, and Aquitaine were to all intents and purposes independent. The west Frankish monarchy thus started the tenth century in a weak position and it had the attacks of Vikings to deal with as well. In 911 Charles III, unable to expel the Norsemen, conceded lands in what was later Normandy to their leader, Rollo. Baptized the following year, Rollo set to work to build the duchy for which he did homage to the Carolingians; his Scandinavian countrymen continued to arrive and settle there until the end of the tenth century, yet somehow they soon became French in speech and law. After this, the unity of the west Franks fell even more rapidly apart. From confusion over the succession there emerged a son of a count of Paris who steadily built up his family's power around a domain in the Ile de France. This was to be the core of France. When the last Carolingian ruler of the west Franks died in 987, this man's son, Hugh Capet, was elected king. His family was to rule France for nearly four hundred years. For the rest, the west Franks were divided into a dozen or so territorial units ruled by magnates of varying standing and independence.

Among the supporters of Hugh's election was the ruler of the east Franks. Across the Rhine, the repeated division of their heritage had quickly proved fatal to the Carolingians. When the last Carolingian king died in 911 there emerged a political fragmentation which was to characterize Germany down to the nineteenth century. The assertiveness of local magnates combined with stronger tribal loyalties than in the west to produce a half-dozen powerful dukedoms. The ruler of one of these, Conrad of Franconia, was chosen as king by the other dukes, somewhat surprisingly. They wanted a strong leader against the Magyars. The change of dynasty made it advisable to confer some special standing on the new ruler; the bishops therefore anointed Conrad at his coronation. He was the first ruler of the east Franks so to be treated. But Conrad was not successful against the Magyars; he lost and could not win back Lotharingia and he strove, with the support of the Church, to exalt his own house and office. Almost automatically, the dukes gathered their peoples about them to safeguard their own independence. The four whose distinction mattered most were the Saxons, the Bavarians, the Swabians and the Franconians (as the east Franks became known). Regional differences, blood and the natural pretensions of great nobles stamped on Germany in Conrad's reign the pattern of its history for a thousand years: a tug-of-war between central authority and local power not to be resolved in the long run in favour of the centre as elsewhere, though in the tenth century it looked otherwise for a while. Conrad faced ducal rebellion but nominated one of the rebels his successor and the dukes agreed. In 919, Henry 'the Fowler' (as he was called), Duke of Saxony, became king. He and his descendants, the 'Saxon emperors', or Ottonians, ruled the eastern Franks until 1024.

Henry the Fowler avoided the ecclesiastical coronation. He had great family properties and the tribal loyalties of the Saxons on his side and brought the magnates into line by proving himself a good soldier. He won back Lotharingia from the west Franks, created new Marches on the Elbe after victorious campaigns against the Wends, made Denmark a tributary kingdom and began its conversion, and, finally, he defeated the Magyars. His son, Otto I, thus had a goodly inheritance and made good use of it. In disciplining the dukes, he continued his father's work. In 955 he inflicted on the Magyars a defeat which ended for good the danger they had presented. Austria, Charlemagne's east March, was recolonized. Though he faced some opposition, Otto made a loyal instrument out of the German church; it was an advantage of the Saxon emperors that in Germany, unlike west Francia, churchmen tended to look with favour to the monarchy for protection against predatory laymen. A new archiepiscopal province, Magdeburg, was organized to direct the bishoprics established among the Slavs. With Otto ends, it has been said, the period of mere anarchy in central Europe; certainly, under him, we have the first sense of something we might call Germany. But Otto's ambition did not stop there.

In 936 Otto had been crowned at Aachen, Charlemagne's old capital. Not only did he accept the ecclesiastical service and anointing his father had avoided, but he afterwards held a coronation banquet at which the German dukes served him as his vassals. This was in the old Carolingian style. Fifteen years later he invaded Italy, married the widow of a claimant to the crown of Italy, and assumed it himself. Yet the pope refused him an imperial coronation. Ten years later, in 962, Otto was back in Italy again in response to an appeal by the pope for help, and this time he got his papal coronation.

Thus was revived the Roman and the Carolingian ideal of empire. The German and Italian crowns were united again in what would one day be known as the Holy Roman Empire and would last nearly a thousand years. Yet it was not so wide an empire as Charlemagne's, nor did Otto dominate the Church as Charlemagne had done. For all his strength (and he deposed two popes and nominated two others) Otto was the Church's protector who thought he knew what

The emperor Otto III receives the homage of the four parts of the empire, Sclavonia, Germania, Gallia and Roma. Like the leading personage in a Byzantine painting, he is drawn larger than the accompanying figures.

was best for it, but he was not its governor. Nor was the structure of the empire very solid; it rested on the political manipulation of local magnates rather than on administration.

Nevertheless, the Ottonian empire was a remarkable achievement. Otto's son, the future Otto II, married a Byzantine princess. Both he and Otto III had reigns troubled by revolt, but successfully maintained the tradition established by Otto the Great of exercising power south of the Alps. Otto III made a cousin pope (the first German to sit in the chair of St Peter) and followed him by appointing the first French pope. Rome seemed to captivate him. Otto settled down there. Like both his immediate predecessors, he called himself *augustus* but in addition his seals bore the legend 'Renewal of the Roman empire' – which he equated with the Christian empire. Half Byzantine by birth, he saw himself as a new Constantine. A diptych of a gospel-book painted nearly at the end of the

443

tenth century shows him in state, crowned and orb in hand, receiving the homage of four crowned women: they are Sclavonia (Slavic Europe), Germany, Gaul and Rome. His notion of a Europe organized as a hierarchy of kings serving under the emperor was eastern. In this there was megalomania as well as genuine religious conviction; the real basis of Otto's power was his German kingship, not the Italy which obsessed and detained him. Nevertheless, after his death in 1002, he was taken to Aachen, as he had ordered, to be buried beside Charlemagne.

He left no heir, but the direct Saxon line was not exhausted; Henry II, who was elected after a struggle, was a great-grandson of Henry the Fowler. But his coronation at Rome masked the reality; he was a German ruler, not emperor of the West, at heart. His seal's inscription read 'Renewal of the kingdom of the Franks' and his attention was focussed on pacification and conversion in east Germany. Though he made three expeditions to Italy, Henry relied there not on government but on politics, the playing off of factions against one another. With him the Byzantine style of the Ottonian empire began to wane.

Thus the eleventh century opened with the idea of western empire still capable of beguiling monarchs, but with the Carolingian inheritance long since crumbled into fragments which set out the lines of European history for ages to come. The idea of Germany barely existed but the country was a political reality, even if still inchoate. The curious federal structure which was to emerge from German medieval history was to be the last refuge of the imperial idea in the West, the Holy Roman Empire. Meanwhile, in France, too, the main line of the future was settled, though it could not have been discerned at the time. West Francia had dissolved into a dozen or so major units over which the suzerainty of the Capetians was for a long time feeble. But they had on their side a centrally placed royal domain, including Paris and the important diocese of Orleans, and the friendship of the Church. These were advantages in the hands of able kings, and able kings would be forthcoming in the next three centuries.

The other major component of the Carolingian heritage had been Italy. It had gradually become more and more distinct from the territories north of the Alps; since the seventh century it had been evolving away from the possibility of integration with northern Europe and back towards re-emergence as a part of Mediterranean Europe. By the middle of the eighth century, much of Italy had been subjugated by the Lombards. This barbarian people had settled down in the peninsula and had adopted an Italianate speech, but they remained an aggressive minority, whose social tensions demanded release in frequent wars of conquest and they had shaped the Catholicism they had adopted to their own needs and institutions. In spite of the theoretical survival of the legal claims of the eastern emperors, the only possible balancing power to them in Italy until the eighth century was the pope. When the Lombard principalities began to consolidate under a vigorous monarchy, this was no longer enough; hence the evolution of papal diplomacy towards alliance with the Carolingians. Once the Lombard kingdom had been destroyed by Charlemagne, there was no rival in the peninsula to the Papal States, though after the waning of the Carolingians' power the popes were faced with the rising power of the Italian magnates and their own Roman aristocracy. The western Church was at its lowest ebb of cohesion and unity and the Ottonians' treatment of the papacy showed how little power it had. An anarchic Italian map was another result of this situation. The north was a scatter of feudal statelets. Only Venice was very successful; for two hundred years she had been pushing forward in the Adriatic and her ruler had just assumed the title of duke. She is perhaps better regarded as a Levantine and Adriatic rather than a Mediterranean power. City-states which were republics existed in the south, at Gaeta, Amalfi, Naples. Across the middle of the peninsula ran the Papal States. Over the whole fell the shadow of Islamic raids taking place as far north as Pisa, while emirates

The empire under the Hohenstaufen Emperor c. 1250

PRUSSIA

POMERANIA

POLAND

FRISIA

Lübeck

Bremen

SAXONY

Brandenburg

Bruges
Ghent

LOWER
LORRAINE

Aachen
Cologne

THURINGIA

FRANCONIA

Mainz
Worms

Prague

BOHEMIA

MORAVIA

Trier

UPPER
LORRAINE

Toul

Augsburg

Passau

AUSTRIA

Vienna

Freiburg

SWABIA

BAVARIA

Salzburg

Besançon

Citeax

KINGDOM OF
BURGUNDY–ARLES

HUNGARY

LOMBARDY

Milan

Pavia

Venice

Avignon

Genoa

Canossa

Bologna

Arles

PROVENCE

Pisa

Florence

Marseilles

Assisi

Sutri

Rome

Gaeta

Naples

Amalfi
Salerno

Holy Roman Empire c. 1200

Holy Roman Empire gains after 1200

Limit of Holy Roman Empire at 950

Limit at 1100

Limit at 1300

appeared at Taranto and Bari in the ninth century. These were not to last, but the Arabs completed the conquest of Sicily in 902 and were to rule it for a century and a half with profound effects.

The Arabs shaped the destiny of the other west Mediterranean coasts of Europe, too. Not only were they established in Spain, but even in Provence they had more or less permanent bases (one of them being St Tropez). The inhabitants of the European coasts of the Mediterranean had, perforce, a complex relationship with the Arabs, who appeared to them both as freebooters and as traders; the mixture was not unlike that observable in the Viking descents except that the Arabs showed little tendency to settle. Southern Provence and Catalonia were areas in which Frankish had followed Gothic conquest, but many factors differentiated them from the Frankish north. The physical reminiscences of the Roman past were plentiful in these areas and so was a Mediterranean agriculture. Another distinctive characteristic was the appearance of a family of Romance languages in the south, of which Catalan and Provençal were the most enduring.

The peripheral Europe of the north barely included Scandinavia in 1000, if Christianity is the test of inclusion. Missionaries had been at work for a long time but the first Christian monarchs only appear there in the tenth century and not until the next were all Scandinavian kings Christian. Long before that, pagan Norsemen had changed the history of the British Isles and the northern fringe of Christendom.

For reasons which, as in the case of many other folk-movements, are by no means clear, but are possibly rooted in over-population, the Scandinavians began to move outwards from the eighth century onwards. Equipped with two fine technical instruments, a longboat which oars and sails could take across seas and up shallow rivers and a tubby cargo-carrier which could shelter large families, their goods and animals for six or seven days at sea, they thrust out across the water for four centuries, and left behind a civilization which in the end stretched from Greenland to Kiev. Not all sought the same things. The Norwegians who struck out to Iceland, the Faroes, Orkney and the far west wanted to colonize. The Swedes who penetrated Russia and survive in the records as Varangians were much busier in trade. The Danes did most of the plundering and piracy the Vikings are remembered for. But all these themes of the Scandinavian migrations wove in and out of one another. No branch of these peoples had a monopoly of any one of them.

The Viking colonization of remote islands was their most spectacular achievement. They wholly replaced the Picts in the Orkneys and the Shetlands and from them extended their rule to the Faroes (previously uninhabited except for a few Irish monks and their sheep) and the Isle of Man. Offshore, the Viking lodgement was more lasting and profound than on the mainland of Scotland and Ireland, where settlement began in the ninth century. Yet the Irish language records their importance by its adoption of Norse words in commerce, and the Irish map marks it by the situation of Dublin, founded by the Vikings and soon turned into an important trading-post. The most successful colony of all was Iceland. Irish hermits had anticipated Vikings there, too, and it was not until the end of the ninth century that they came in large numbers. By 930 there may have been 10000 Norse Icelanders, living by farming and fishing, in part for their own subsistence, in part to produce commodities such as salt fish which they might trade. In that year the Icelandic state was founded and the *Thing* (which romantic antiquarians later saw as the first European 'parliament') met for the first time. It was more like a council of the big men of the community than a modern representative body and it followed earlier Norwegian practice, but Iceland's continuous historical record is in this respect a remarkable one.

Colonies in Greenland followed in the tenth century; there were to be Norsemen there for five hundred years. Then they disappeared, probably because the settlers were wiped out by Eskimoes pushed south by an advance of the

The Viking ship was one of the most beautiful machines of its age. The Oseberg ship, shown here, was buried as the bier of a prince, but was probably originally a king's ship, for it is exceptionally finely carved and decorated.

ice. Of discovery and settlement further west we can say much less. The Sagas, the heroic poems of medieval Iceland, tell us of the exploration of 'Vinland', the land where Norsemen found the wild vine growing, and of the birth of a child there (whose mother subsequently returned to Iceland and went abroad again as far as Rome as a pilgrim before settling into a highly sanctified retirement in her native

land). There are reasonably good grounds to believe that a settlement found in Newfoundland is Norse. But we cannot at present go much further than this in uncovering the traces of the predecessors of Columbus.

In western European tradition, the colonial and mercantile activities of the Vikings were from the start obscured by their horrific impact as marauders. Certainly, they had some very nasty habits, spread-eagling among them, but so did most barbarians. Some exaggeration must therefore be allowed for, especially because our main evidence comes from the pens of churchmen doubly appalled, both as Christians and as victims, by attacks on churches and monasteries; as pagans, of course, Vikings saw no special

447

A pagan memorial to an eighth-century Viking warrior, shown in battle, at sea – or in what is perhaps a pit of snakes – and in either defending or attacking a homestead. From Gotland, Sweden.

sanctity in the concentrations of precious metals and food so conveniently provided by such places, and found them especially attractive targets. Nor were the Vikings the first people to burn monasteries in Ireland.

None the less, however such considerations are weighed, it is indisputable that the Viking impact on northern and western Christendom was very great and very terrifying. They first attacked England in 793, the monastery of Lindisfarne being their victim; the attack shook the ecclesiastical world (yet the monastery lived on another eighty years). Ireland they raided two years later. In the first half of the ninth century the Danes began a harrying of Frisia which went on regularly year after year, the same towns being plundered again and again. The French coast was then attacked; in 842 Nantes was sacked with a great massacre. Within a few years a Frankish chronicler bewailed that 'the endless flood of Vikings never ceases to grow bigger'. Towns as far inland as Paris, Limoges, Orleans, Tours and Angoulême were attacked. The Vikings had become professional pirates. Soon Spain suffered. The Arabs, too, were harassed; in 844 the Vikings stormed Seville. In 859 they even raided Nîmes and plundered Pisa, though they suffered heavily at the hands of an Arab fleet on their way home.

Not all the efforts to meet the Viking threat were failures. Charlemagne and Louis the Pious – who, admittedly, did not have to face attacks as heavy and persistent as they later became – managed to defend the vulnerable ports and river-mouths with some effectiveness. The Vikings, too, could be (and were) defeated if drawn into full-scale field engagements and though there were dramatic exceptions, the main centres of the Christian West were on the whole successfully defended. What could not be prevented was repeated small-scale raids on the coasts and Vikings increasingly made attacks of this sort as the ninth century went on. As they had learnt to avoid pitched battles, the only way to deal with them was to buy them off and Charles the Bald began paying them tribute so that his subjects should be left in peace.

This was the beginning of what the English called Danegeld. Their island had soon become a major target, to which Vikings began to come to settle as well as to raid. A small group of kingdoms had emerged there from the Germanic invasions; by the seventh century many Romano-British were living alongside the communities of the new settlers while others had been driven back to the hills of Wales and Scotland. Christianity continued to be diffused by Irish missionaries and from a Roman mission which had established Canterbury and competed with the older Celtic Church. At different times some of these kingdoms held sway over others. Only one of them successfully resisted a wave of Danish attacks from 851 onwards which in the end led to the occupation of two-thirds of the country. This was Wessex and it gave England its first national hero who is also a historical figure, Alfred the Great.

GREENLAND
c. 982

VINLAND
c. 1000

ICELAND
FROM 860

FAROE ISLANDS
c. 800

SHETLAND ISLANDS
c. 700

ORKNEY
ISLANDS
c. 800

IONA 795

LINDISFARNE

Dublin
839

York

Danelaw

Wessex

Dorestad

Louvain

Normandy
896/991

Great Army
879-882

Mainz

Noirmoutier
843-882

GERMAN

EMPIRE

Santiago
de Compostela

Oviedo

FRANCE

Lyons

Toulouse

ITALY

Aquileia

MAGYARS

Barcelona

Luna

Lisbon

EMIRATE OF
CORDOBA

Valencia

Rome

Seville

Trondheim

NORWEGIANS

Uppsala

Birka

SWEDES

Ripen

DANES

Hamburg

Jomsburg

Grobin

Wiskiuten

GARDARIKE

Trusa

Old Ladoga

Novgorod

Rostov

Bulgar

Chernigov

Kiev

Itil

KHAZARS

Constantinople

B Y Z A N T I N E   E M P I R E

ISLAMIC STATES

Campaigns

Norseman Homeland

Conquests

Campaigns along rivers

Bases

Viking Onslaughts

*One of the most attractive of the few surviving
Anglo-Saxon churches which were the product of
the first great age of English church architecture,
St Lawrence, Bradford-on-Avon. Some
of the work in it is of the seventh century.*

As a child of four, Alfred had been taken to
Rome by his father and was given consular
honours by the pope. The monarchy of Wessex
was indissolubly linked with Christianity. It
defended the faith against paganism as much as
England against an alien people. In 871 Alfred
inflicted the first decisive defeat on a Danish
army in England. Significantly, a few years later
the Danish king agreed not only to withdraw
from Wessex but to accept conversion as a
Christian. This registered that the Danes were
in England to stay (they had settled in the
north) but also that they might be divided from
one another. Soon Alfred was leader of all the
surviving English kings; eventually, none was
left but he. He recovered London and when he
died in 899 the worst period of Danish raids was
over and his descendants were to rule a united
country. Even the settlers of the Danelaw, the
area marked to this day by Scandinavian place-
names and fashions of speech as that of Danish
colonization defined by Alfred, accepted their
rule. Nor was this all. Alfred had also founded

a series of strongholds as a part of a new system
of national defence by local levies. They not
only gave his successors bases for the further
reduction of the Danelaw but set much of the
pattern of early medieval urbanization in England and on them were built towns whose sites
are still inhabited today. Finally, with tiny resources, Alfred deliberately undertook the
cultural and intellectual regeneration of his
people. The scholars of his court, like those of
Charlemagne, proceeded by way of copying and
translation; the Anglo-Saxon nobleman and
cleric were intended to learn of Bede and
Boethius in their own tongue.

This was the beginning of a great age for
England. The shire structure took shape and
boundaries were established which lasted until
1974. The English Church was soon to experience a remarkable surge of monasticism, the
Danes were held in a united kingdom through
a half-century's turbulence. It was only when
ability failed in Alfred's line that the Anglo-
Saxon monarchy came to grief and a new
Viking offensive took place. Colossal sums of
Danegeld were paid until a Danish king (this
time a Christian) overthrew the English king
and then died, leaving a young son to rule his
conquest. This was the celebrated Canute, under
whom England was briefly part of a great
Danish empire (1006–35). There was a last
great Norwegian invasion of England in 1066,
but it was shattered at the battle of Stamford
Bridge. By that time, all the Scandinavian
monarchies were Christian and Viking culture
was being absorbed into Christian forms. It
left many evidences of its individuality and
strength in both Celtic and continental art. Its
institutions survive in Iceland and other islands.
The Scandinavian legacy is strongly marked for
centuries in English language and social patterns,
in the emergence of the duchy of Normandy,
and, above all, in the literature of the Sagas.
Yet where they entered settled lands, the Norsemen gradually merged with the rest of the
population. When the descendants of Rollo and
his followers turned to the conquest of England
in the eleventh century they were really French-

rten wam tranum vhanao mœtte hœthét wôr heœnne e. shuu t o

A medieval king should rule with counsel from his great men, according to Germanic tradition. In England the witenagemot *joins the king in judgement of a criminal.*

men and the war-song they sang at Hastings was about Charlemagne the Frankish paladin. They conquered an England where the men of the Danelaw were by then English. Similarly, the Vikings lost their distinctiveness as an ethnic group in Kiev Rus and Muscovy.

The only other western peoples of the early eleventh century who call for remark because of the future that lay before them were those of the Christian states of northern Spain. Geography, climate and Moslem division had all helped Christianity's survival in the peninsula and in part defined its extent. In the Asturias and Navarre there were Christian princes or chieftains early in the eighth century. Aided by the establishment of the Spanish March by Charlemagne and its subsequent growth under the new Counts of Barcelona, they nibbled away successfully at Islamic Spain while it was distracted by civil war and religious schism. A kingdom of León emerged in the Asturias to take its place beside a kingdom of Navarre. In the tenth century, however, it was the Christians who fell

The massive earth fortifications built round the Wessex town of Wareham to hold the Danes at bay in the tenth century still virtually enclose it on three sides as this photograph shows.

451

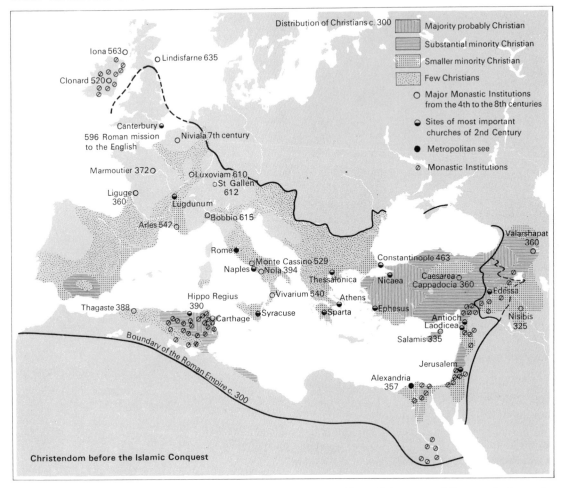

Distribution of Christians c. 300

Majority probably Christian
Substantial minority Christian
Smaller minority Christian
Few Christians

○ Major Monastic Institutions from the 4th to the 8th centuries
◑ Sites of most important churches of 2nd Century
● Metropolitan see
⊘ Monastic Institutions

Iona 563○
Clonard 520○
○ Lindisfarne 635
Canterbury ●
596 Roman mission to the English
○ Niviala 7th century
Marmoutier 372○
○ Luxoviam 610
Liguge ○ 360
○ St Gallen 612
Lugdunum
○ Bobbio 615
Arles 542 ○
Rome ●
○ Monte Cassino 529
Naples ● ○ Nola 394
Thessalonica
Constantinople 463
Nicaea
Caesarea ○ Cappadocia 360
Valarshapat 360
○ Vivarium 540
Athens
◑ Edessa
Hippo Regius 390
Thagaste 388 ○
Carthage
○ Syracuse
◑ Sparta
◑ Ephesus
Antioch
Laodicea
Nisibis 325
Salamis 335
Jerusalem
Alexandria 357 ●

Boundary of the Roman Empire c. 300

Christendom before the Islamic Conquest

out with one another and the Arabs who again made headway against them. The blackest moment came at the very end of the century when a great Arab conqueror, Al-Mansur, took Barcelona, León, and in 998 the shrine of Santiago de Compostela itself at which St James the Apostle was supposed to be buried. The triumph was not long-lived, for here, too, what had been done to found Christian Europe proved ineradicable. Within a few decades Christian Spain had rallied. In the Iberian peninsula as elsewhere, the age of expansion which this inaugurated belongs to another historical era, but it was based on long centuries of confrontation with another civilization. For Spain, above all, Christianity was the crucible of nationhood.

The Iberian example suggests just how much of the making of the map of Europe is the making of the map of the Church, but an emphasis on successful missions and the ties with powerful monarchs is misleading on its own. There was much more to early Christian Europe and the Christian life than this. The western Church provides one of the great success stories of history, yet its leaders between the end of the ancient world and the eleventh or twelfth century long felt isolated and embattled in a pagan or semi-pagan world. Increasingly at odds with, and finally almost cut off from, eastern Orthodoxy, it is hardly surprising that western Christianity developed an aggressive intransigence almost as a defensive reflex. It was another sign of its insecurity. Nor was it merely threatened by enemies without. Inside western

Christendom in the 11th century

Christendom, too, the Church felt at bay and beleaguered. It strove in the middle of still semi-pagan populations to keep its teaching and practice intact while christening what it could of a culture with which it had to live, judging nicely the concession which could be made to local practice or tradition and distinguishing it from a fatal compromise of principle. All this it had to do with a body of clergy of whom many, perhaps most, were men of no learning, not much discipline and dubious spirituality. Perhaps it is not surprising that the leaders of the Church sometimes overlooked the enormous asset they enjoyed in being faced by no spiritual rival in western Europe after Islam was turned back by Charles Martel; they had to contend only with vestigial paganism and superstition,

and these the Church knew how to use. Meanwhile, the great men of this world surrounded it, sometimes helpfully, sometimes hopefully, always a potential and often a real threat to the Church's independence of the society it had to strive to save.

Inevitably, much of the history which resulted is the history of the papacy. It is the central and best-documented institution of Christianity. Its documentation is part of the reason why so much attention has been given to it, a fact that should provoke reflexion about what can be known about religion in these centuries. Though papal power had alarming ups and downs, the division of the old empire meant that if there was anywhere in the West a defender of the interests of religion, it was Rome, for it

453

*In the second half of the tenth century a school
of copying and illumination flowered at
Winchester under the influence of currents
from continental Europe. The newly founded
Benedictine abbey – the New Minster – received
a charter which is the oldest manuscript made
for the house and contains this miniature
showing King Edgar offering to Christ the
charter he has granted to the monks.*

had no ecclesiastical rival. After Gregory the
Great it was obviously implausible to maintain
the theory of one Christian Church in one
empire, even if the imperial exarch did stay at
Ravenna. The last emperor who came to Rome
did so in 663 and the last pope to go to Constantinople went there in 710. Then came iconoclasm, which inflicted grievous ideological
damage. When Ravenna fell to the renewed
advance of the Lombards, Pope Stephen set out
for Pepin's court, not that of Byzantium. There

was no desire to break with the eastern empire,
but Frankish armies could offer protection no
longer available from the east. Protection was
needed, too, for the Arabs menaced Italy from
the beginning of the eighth century, and, increasingly, the native Italian magnates became
obstreperous in the ebbing of Lombard hegemony.

There were some very bad moments in the
two and a half centuries after Pepin's coronation.
Rome seemed to have very few cards in its
hands and at times only to have exchanged one
master for another. Its claim to primacy was a
matter of the respect due to the guardianship of
St Peter's bones and the fact that the see was
indisputably the only apostolic one in the West:
a matter of history rather than practicality. For
a long time the popes could hardly govern
effectively even within the temporal domains,
for they had neither adequate armed forces nor
a civil administration. As great Italian property-
owners, they were exposed to predators and
blackmail. Charlemagne was only the first, and
perhaps he was the most high-minded, of
several emperors who made clear to the papacy
their views of the respective standing of pope
and emperor as guardians of the Church. The
Ottonians were great makers and unmakers of
popes. The successors of St Peter could not
welcome confrontations, for they had too much
to lose.

Yet there was another side to the balance
sheet, even if it was slow to reveal its full implications. Pepin's grant of territory to the papacy
would in time form the nucleus of a powerful Italian territorial state. In the pope's coronation of
emperors there rested veiled claims, perhaps to
the identification of rightful emperors; significantly, as time passed, popes withdrew from
the imperial coronation ceremony (as from that
of English and French kings) the use of the
chrism, the specially sacred mixture of oil and
balsam for the ordination of priests and the
coronation of bishops, substituting simple oil.
Thus was expressed a reality long concealed but
easily comprehensible to an age used to symbols: the pope conferred the crown and the

A tenth-century history of the councils of Spain, the 'Codex Vigilanus' (or codex of Vigila) described the history of Spain, as the chroniclers of other former barbarian peoples described theirs, as a story of Christian monarchy. The Codex ends with a page showing five kings, three Visigothic, two kings of Leon, with the wife of the one who commissioned the Codex. The bottom row depicts some of the very few individual artists who emerge from the anonymity of early medieval art, the scribe Vigila himself (in the centre) with an assistant and a pupil.

stamp of God's recognition of the emperor. Perhaps, therefore, he could do so conditionally. Leo's coronation of Charlemagne, like Stephen's of Pepin, may have been expedient, but it contained a potent seed. When, as often happened, personal weaknesses and succession disputes disrupted the Frankish kingdoms, Rome might gain ground.

More immediately and practically, the sup-

port of powerful kings was needed for the reform of local Churches and the support of missionary enterprise in the East. For all the jealousy of local clergy, the Frankish Church changed greatly; in the tenth century what the pope said mattered a great deal north of the Alps. From the *entente* of the eighth century there emerged gradually the idea that it was for the pope to say what the Church's policy should be and that the individual bishops of the local Churches should not pervert it. A great instrument of standardization was being forged. It was there in principle when Pepin used his power as a Frankish king to reform his countrymen's Church and did so on lines which brought it into step with Rome on questions of ritual and discipline, and further away from Celtic influences.

The balance of advantage and disadvantage long tipped to and fro, the boundaries of the effective powers of the popes ebbing and flowing. Significantly, it was after a further subdivision of the Carolingian heritage so that the crown of Italy was separated from Lotharingia that Nicholas I pressed most successfully the papal claims. A century before, a famous forgery, the 'Donation of Constantine', purported to show that Constantine had given to the Bishop of Rome the former dominion exercised by the empire in Italy; Nicholas addressed kings and emperors as if this theory ran everywhere in the West. He wrote to them, it was said, 'as though he were lord of the world', reminding them that he could appoint and depose. He used the doctrine of papal primacy against the emperor of the East, too, in support of the Patriarch of Constantinople. This was a peak of pretension which the papacy could not long sustain in practice, for it was soon clear that force at Rome would decide who should enjoy the imperial power the pope claimed to confer. Nicholas's successor, revealingly, was the first pope to be murdered. None the less, the ninth century laid down precedents, even if they could not yet be consistently followed.

Especially in the collapse of papal authority in the tenth century, when the throne became

455

the prey of Italian factions whose struggles were occasionally cut across by the interventions of the Ottonians, the day-to-day work of safeguarding Christian interests could only be in the hands of the bishops of the local Churches. They had to respect the powers that were. Seeking the cooperation and help of the secular rulers, they often moved into positions in which they were all but indistinguishable from royal servants. They were under the thumbs of their secular rulers just as, often, the parish priest was under the thumb of the local lord – and had to share his ecclesiastical proceeds in consequence. This humiliating dependency was later to lead to some of the sharpest papal interventions in the local Churches.

The bishops did much good, too. In particular, missionary work came to owe much to them. This also had a political side to it. In the eighth century the Rule of St Benedict won a position of great strength in England. A great Anglo-Saxon missionary movement, whose outstanding figures were St Willibrord in Frisia and St Boniface in Germany, followed and it redounded much to the credit of the Holy See. Largely independent of the east Frankish bishops, the Anglo-Saxons asserted the supremacy of Rome; their converts tended therefore to look directly for religious authority to the throne of St Peter. Many made pilgrimages to Rome. This papal emphasis died away in the later phases of evangelizing the East, or, rather, became less conspicuous because of the direct work of the German emperors and their bishops. Missions were combined with conquest and new bishoprics were organized as governmental devices.

Another great creative movement, that of reform in the tenth century, owed something to the episcopate but nothing to the papacy. It was a monastic movement which enjoyed the support of some rulers. Its essence was the renewal of monastic ideals; a few noblemen founded new houses which were intended to recall a degenerate monasticism to its origins. Most of them were in the old central Carolingian lands, running down from Belgium to Switzerland, west into Burgundy and east into Franconia, the area from which the reform impulse radiated outwards. At the end of the tenth century it began to enlist the support of princes and emperors. Their patronage in the end led to fear of lay dabbling in the affairs of the Church but it made possible the recovery of the papacy from a narrowly Italian and dynastic nullity.

The most celebrated of these foundations was the Burgundian abbey of Cluny, founded in 910. For nearly two and a half centuries it was the heart of ecclesiastical reform. Its monks followed a revision of the Benedictine rule and evolved something quite new, a religious order resting not simply on a uniform way of life, but on a centrally disciplined organization. The Benedictine monasteries had all been independent communities, but the new Cluniac houses were all subordinate to the abbot of Cluny itself; he was the general of an army of eventually thousands of monks who only entered their own monasteries after a period of training at the mother house. At the height of its power, in the middle of the twelfth century, more than three hundred monasteries throughout the West – and even some in Palestine – looked for direction to Cluny, whose abbey contained the greatest church in western Christendom after St Peter's at Rome.

This is to look too far ahead for the present. Even in its early days, though, Cluniac monasticism was an outstanding instrument for the dissemination of new practices and ideas throughout the Church. This takes us beyond questions of ecclesiastical structure and law, though it is not easy to speak with certainty of all other aspects of the Christian life in the early Middle Ages. Religious history is always liable to be especially falsified by records which sometimes make it very difficult to see dimensions beyond the workings of bureaucracy. They make it clear, though, that the Church was unchallenged in its uniqueness and that it pervaded the whole fabric of society. It had, for example, something like a monopoly of culture. The classical heritage had been terribly damaged and narrowed by the barbarian invasions and the

Winfrith, the Wessex-born monk later famous as St Boniface, was probably the greatest missionary England ever produced. After his death at eighty-two (he was killed by the pagan Frisians in 754) his relics were removed to the monastery of Fulda, one of the homes he had himself founded. It was at Fulda that the tenth-century illuminated manuscript was written from which this picture of his martyrdom is taken.

intransigent other-worldliness of early Christianity: 'What has Athens to do with Jerusalem?' Tertullian had asked. This intransigence had subsided. By the tenth century what had been preserved of the classical past had been preserved by churchmen, above all by the Benedictines and the copiers of the palace schools who transmitted not only the Bible but Latin compilations of Greek learning. Through their version of Pliny and Boethius a slender line connected early medieval Europe to Aristotle and Euclid.

Literacy was virtually coterminous with the clergy. The Romans had been able to post their laws on boards in public places, confident that enough literate people existed to read them; far into the Middle Ages, even kings were normally illiterate. The clergy controlled virtually all access to such writing as there was. In a world without universities, only a court or church school offered the chance of letters beyond what might be offered, exceptionally, by an individual cleric-tutor. The effects of this on all the arts and intellectual activity was profound; culture was not just related to religion but took its rise only in the setting of overriding religious assumptions. The slogan 'art for art's sake' could never

457

One of the oldest pieces of monumental sculpture in the Christian West is the life-sized crucified Christ placed in Cologne cathedral in the late tenth century – probably by the archbishop himself.

have made less sense than in the early Middle Ages. History, philosophy, theology, illumination, all played their part in sustaining a sacramental culture, but, however narrowed it might be, the legacy they transmitted, in so far as it was not Jewish, was Classical.

In danger of dizziness on such cultural peaks, it is salutary to remember that we can know very little directly about what must be regarded both theologically and statistically much more important than this and, indeed, as the most important of all the activities of the Church. This is the day-to-day business of exhorting, teaching, marrying, baptizing, shriving and praying, the whole religious life of the secular clergy and laity which centred about the provision of the major sacraments. The Church was in these centuries deploying powers which often cannot have been distinguished clearly by the faithful from those of magic. It used them to drill a barbaric world into civilization. It was enormously successful and yet we have almost no direct information about the process except at its most dramatic moments, when a spectacular conversion or baptism reveals by the very fact of being recorded that we are in the presence of the untypical.

Of the social and economic reality of the Church we have much more information. The clergy and their dependents made up a great number of people and the Church controlled much of society's wealth. The Church was a great landowner. The revenues which supported its work came from its land and a great monastery or chapter of canons might have very large estates. The roots of the Church were firmly sunk in the economy of the day and to begin with that implied something very primitive indeed.

Difficult though it is to measure exactly, there are many symptoms of economic regression in the West at the end of antiquity. Not everyone felt the setback equally. The most developed economic sectors went under most completely. Barter replaced money and a money economy emerged again only slowly. The Merovingians began to coin silver, but for a long time there was not much coin – particularly coin of small denominations – in circulation. Spices disappeared from ordinary diet; wine became a costly luxury; most people ate and drank bread and porridge, beer and water. Scribes turned to parchment, which could be obtained locally, rather than papyrus, now hard to get; this turned out to be an advantage, for minuscule was possible on parchment, and had not been on papyrus, which required large, uneconomical strokes, but none the less reflects difficulties within the old Mediterranean economy. Though recession can hardly have bothered the self-sufficient estate, it ruined the towns. The universe of trade also disintegrated from time to time because of war. Contact was maintained with Byzantium and further Asia, but the western Mediterranean's commercial activity dwindled during the seventh and eighth centuries as the Arabs seized the North African coast. Later, thanks again to the Arabs, it was partly revived (one sign was a brisk trade in slaves, many of whom came from eastern Europe, from the Slav peoples who thus gave their name to a whole category of forced labour). In the north, too, there was a certain amount of exchange with the Scandinavians, who were great traders. But this did not matter to most Europeans, for whom life rested on agriculture.

Subsistence was for a long time to be almost all that they could hope for. That it was the main concern of the early medieval economy is one of the few safe generalizations about it. Animal manure or the breaking of new and more fertile ground were the only ways to improving a return on seed and labour which was by modern standards derisory. Only centuries of laborious husbandry could change this. The animals who lived with the stunted and scurvy-ridden human tenants of a poverty-stricken landscape were themselves undernourished and undersized, yet for fat, the luckier peasant depended upon the pig, or, in the south, on oil. Only with the introduction of plants yielding food of higher protein content, in the tenth century, did the energy return from the soil begin to improve. There were some technological innovations, notably the diffusion of mills and the adoption of a better plough, but when production rose it did so for the most part because new land was brought into cultivation. And there was much to exploit. Most of France and Germany and England were still covered with forest and waste.

The economic relapse at the end of antiquity left behind few areas where towns thrived. The main exception was Italy, where some com-

The oldest surviving free-standing statue of the Virgin is this little 'golden Madonna' now at Essen. It was made in about 1000. Mary holds out an apple to the Christ-child; she thus signifies her role as a 'second Eve', offering the means of redemption where her predecessor had tempted Man to disobedience.

mercial relations with the outside world always persisted. Elsewhere, towns did not begin much to expand again until after 1100; even then, it would be a long time before western Europe contained a city comparable with the great centres of the classical Islamic and Asian civilizations. Almost universally in the West the self-sufficient agricultural estate was for centuries the rule. It fed and maintained a population probably smaller than that of the ancient world in the same area, though even approximate figures are almost impossible to establish. At any rate, there is no evidence of more than a very slow growth of population until the eleventh century. The population of western Europe may then have stood at about forty million – fewer than live in the United Kingdom today.

In this world, possession of land or access to it was the supreme determinant of the social order. Somehow, slowly, but logically, the great men of western society, while continuing to be the warriors they had always been in barbarian societies, became landowners too. With the dignitaries of the Church and their kings, they were the ruling class. From the possession of land came not only revenue by rent and taxation, but jurisdiction and labour service, too. Landowners were the lords, and gradually their hereditary status was to loom larger and their practical prowess and skill as warriors was to be less emphasized (though in theory it long persisted) as the thing that made them noble.

The lands of some of these men were granted to them by a king or great prince. In return they were expected to repay the favour by turning out when required to do him military service. Moreover, administration had to be decentralized after imperial times; barbarian kings did not have the bureaucratic and literate resources to rule directly over great areas. Thus the grant of exploitable economic goods in return for specific obligations of service was very common, and this idea was what lay at the heart of what later historians, looking back at the European Middle Ages, called feudalism.

Many tributaries flowed into this stream. Both Roman and Germanic custom favoured the elaboration of such an idea. It helped, too, that in the later days of the empire, or in the troubled times of Merovingian Gaul, it had become common for men to 'commend' themselves to a great lord for protection; in return for his protection they offered him a special loyalty and service. This was a usage easily assimilated to the practices of Germanic society. Under the

Carolingians, the practice began of 'vassals' of the king doing him homage; that is to say, they acknowledged with distinctive ceremonies, often public, their special responsibilities of service to him. He was their lord; they were his men. The old loyalties of the blood-brotherhood of the warrior-companions of the barbarian chief began to blend with notions of commendation in a new moral ideal of loyalty, faithfulness and reciprocal obligation. Vassals then bred vassals and one lord's man was another man's lord. A chain of obligation and personal service might stretch in theory from the king down through his great men and their retainers to the lowest of the free. And, of course, it might produce complicating and conflicting demands. A king could be another king's vassal in respect of some of his lands. Below the free were the slaves, more numerous perhaps in southern Europe than in the north and everywhere showing a tendency to evolve marginally upwards in status to that of the serf – the unfree man, born tied to the soil of his manor, but nevertheless, not quite without rights of any kind.

Some people later spoke as if the relationship of lord and man could explain the whole of medieval society. This was never so. Though much of the land of Europe was divided into fiefs – the *feuda* from which 'feudalism' takes its name – which were holdings bearing obligation to a lord, there were always important areas, especially in southern Europe, where the 'mix' of Germanic overlay and Roman background did not work out in the same way. Much of Italy, Spain and southern France was not 'feudal' in this sense. There were also always some freeholders even in more 'feudal' lands, an important class of men, more numerous in some countries than others, who owed no service for their lands but owned it outright.

For the most part, nevertheless, contractual obligations based on land set the tone of medieval civilization. Corporations, like men, might be lords or vassals; a tenant might do homage to the abbot of a monastery (or the abbess of a nunnery) for the manor he held of its estates, and a king might have a cathedral chapter or a community of monks as one of his vassals. There was much room for complexity and ambiguity in the feudal order. But the central fact of an exchange of obligations between superior and inferior ran through the whole structure and does more than anything else to make it intelligible to modern eyes. Lord and man were bound to one another reciprocally: 'Serfs, obey your temporal lords with fear and trembling; lords, treat your serfs according to justice and equity' was a French cleric's injunction which concisely summarized a principle in a specific case. On this rationalization rested a society of growing complexity which it long proved able to interpret and sustain.

It also justified the extraction from the peasant of the wherewithal to maintain the warrior and build his castle. From this grew the aristocracies of Europe. The military function of the system which supported them long remained paramount. Even when personal service in the field was not required, that of the vassal's fighting-men (and later of his money to pay fighting-men) would be. Of the military skills, that which was most esteemed (because it was the most effective) was that of fighting in armour on horseback. At some point in the seventh or eighth century the stirrup was adopted; from that time the armoured horsemen had it for the most part his own way on the battlefield until the coming of weapons which could master him. From this technical superiority emerged the knightly class of professional cavalrymen, maintained by the lord either directly or by a grant of a manor to feed them and their horses. They were the source of the warrior aristocracy of the Middle Ages and of European values for centuries to come. Yet for a long time, the boundaries of this class were ill-defined and movement in (and out) of it was common.

Political realities often militated against theory. In the intricate web of vassalage, a king might have less control over his own vassals than they over theirs. The great lord, whether lay magnate or local bishop, must always have loomed larger and more important in the life of the ordinary man than the remote and probably never-seen king or prince. In the tenth and eleventh centuries there are everywhere examples of kings obviously under pressure from great men. The country where this seemed to present the least trouble was Anglo-Saxon England, whose monarchical tradition was the strongest of any. But pressure was not always effective against even a weak king if he were shrewd. He had, after all, other vassals, and if wise he would not antagonize all of them at once. Furthermore, his office was unique. The anointing of the Church confirmed its sacred, charismatic authority. Kings were set apart in the eyes of most men by the special pomp and ceremony which surrounded them and which played as important a part in medieval government as does bureaucratic paper in ours. If in addition a king had the advantage of large domains of his own, then he stood an excellent chance of having his way.

Not always in the technical and legal sense, but in common sense, kings and great magnates were the only men who enjoyed much freedom in early medieval society. Yet even they led lives cramped and confined by the absence of much that we take for granted. There was nothing much to do, after all, except pray, fight, hunt and run your estate; there were no professions for men to enter, except that of the Church, small possibility of innovation in the style or content of daily life. For women, the possibilities were even more restricted, and so they were for men as one went further down the social scale. Only with the gradual revival of trade and urban life, with the expansion of the economy was this to change. Obviously, dividing lines are of almost no value in such matters, but it is not really until after 1100 that important economic expansion begins, and only then that we have the sense of moving out of a society still semi-barbarous, whose pretensions to civilization are sometimes negligible.

6 India

Though accompanied and advised by scholars and savants, Alexander the Great had only hazy ideas of what he would find in India; he seems to have thought the Indus part of the Nile and that beyond it lay more of Ethiopia. A fair amount had long been known by the Greeks about the Indian north-west, the seat of the Persian satrapy of Gandhara. But beyond that all was darkness. So far as political geography is concerned, the obscurity has remained; the relations between and, for that matter, the nature of the states of the Ganges valley at the time of Alexander's invasion are still hard to get at. A kingdom of Magadha, based on the lower river and exercising some sort of hegemony over the rest of the valley, had been the most important political unit in the subcontinent for two centuries or more, but not much is known about its institutions or history. Indian sources say nothing of Alexander's arrival in India and as the great conqueror never penetrated beyond the Punjab we can learn from Greek accounts of his day only of his disruption of the petty kingdoms of the north-west, not about the heartland of Indian power.

Under the Seleucids more reliable information became available in the West about what lay beyond the Punjab. This new knowledge roughly coincides with the rise of a new Indian power, the Maurya empire, with which the

The most famous of all Indian buildings and the supreme achievement of Islamic architecture in the sub-continent: the Taj Mahal, erected by Shah Jahan as a mausoleum for his favourite wife.

India of historical record really begins. One of our informants is a Greek ambassador, Megasthenes, sent to India by the Seleucid king in about 300 BC. Fragments of his account of what he saw were preserved long enough for later writers to quote him at length. As he travelled as far as Bengal and Orissa and was respected both as a diplomat and as a scholar, he met and interrogated many Indians. Some later writers found him a credulous and unreliable reporter; they dwelt upon his tales of men who subsisted on odours instead of food and drink, of others who were cyclopean or whose feet were so large that they used them to shelter from the sun, of pygmies and men without mouths. Such tales were, of course, nonsense. But they were not necessarily without foundation. They probably represent only the highly developed awareness shown by Aryan Indians of the physical differences which marked them off from neighbours or remote acquaintances from central Asia or the jungles of Burma. Some of these must have looked very strange indeed, and some of their behaviour was, no doubt, also very strange in Indian eyes. Others among these tales may dimly reflect the curious ascetic practices of Indian religion; they have never ceased to impress outsiders and usually improve in the telling. Such tales need not discredit the teller, therefore – they may even have a positive value if they suggest something of the way in which Megasthenes' Indian informants saw the outside world. Whether this is so or not, such stories certainly do not mean that other things he reports must be wholly untrue.

463

He describes the India of a great ruler, Chandragupta, founder of the Maurya line. Something is known about him from other sources. The ancients believed that he had been inspired to conquest by having as a youth seen Alexander the Great during his invasion of India. However this may be, Chandragupta usurped the Magadha throne in 321 BC and on the ruins of that kingdom built a state which encompassed not only the two great valleys of the Indus and Ganges, but most of Afghanistan (taken from the Seleucids) and Baluchistan. His capital was at Patna, where Chandragupta inhabited a magnificent palace. It was made of wood; archaeology still cannot help us much at this stage of Indian history. From Megasthenes' account it might be inferred that Chandragupta exercised a sort of monarchical presidency but Indian sources seem to reveal a centralized, bureaucratic state, or at least something that aspired to be one. What it was like in practice is hard to see. It had been built from political units formed in earlier times, many of which had been republican or popular in organization, and many of these were connected to the emperor through great men who were his officers; some of these, nominally subjects, must often have been very independent in practice.

About the empire's inhabitants, too, Megasthenes is informative. Besides providing a long list of different peoples, he distinguished two religious traditions, one the Brahmanical and the other apparently Buddhist, mentioned the rice-eating habits of Indians and their abstention from wine except for ritual purposes, said much about the domestication of elephants, and remarked on the fact (surprising to Greek eyes) that in India there were no slaves. He was wrong, but excusably so. Though Indians were not bought and sold in absolute servitude, there were those bound to labour for their masters and legally incapable of removal. Megasthenes also reported that the king diverted himself by hunting, which was done from raised platforms, or from the backs of elephants – much as tigers still are shot today.

Chandragupta is said to have spent his last days in retirement with Jains, ritually starving himself to death in a retreat near Mysore. His son and successor turned the expansive course of empire already shown by his father to the south. Maurya power began to penetrate the dense rain-forests east of Patna, and to push down the eastern coast. Finally, under the third Maurya, the conquest of Orissa gave the empire control of the land and sea routes to the south and the subcontinent acquired a political unity not matched in extent for over two thousand years. The conqueror who achieved this was Asoka, the ruler under whom a documented history of India at last begins to be possible.

From Asoka's era survive many inscriptions bearing decrees and injunctions to his subjects. The use of this means of propagating official messages and the individual style of the inscriptions both suggest Persian and Hellenistic influence and India under the Mauryas was certainly more continually in touch with the civilizations to the West than ever before. At Kandahar, Asoka left inscriptions in both Greek and Aramaic.

Such evidence reveals a state capable of much more than that sketched by Megasthenes. A royal council ruled over a society based on caste. There was a royal army and a bureaucracy; as elsewhere, the coming of literacy was an epoch in government as well as in culture. There seems also to have been a large secret police, or internal intelligence service. Besides raising taxes and maintaining essential services of communication and irrigation, this machine, under Asoka, undertook the promotion of an official ideology. Asoka had himself been converted to Buddhism early in his reign. Unlike Constantine's conversion, this did not precede but followed a battle whose cost in suffering appalled Asoka. Be that as it may, the result of his conversion was the abandonment by Asoka of the pattern of conquest which had marked his career until then. Perhaps this is why he felt no temptation to campaign outside the subcontinent – a limitation which, however, he shared with most Indian rulers, who never aspired to rule over barbarians

Once thought to belong to the era of Asoka, but now believed earlier, this capital from Rampurva uses the traditional bull figure which recurs so often in Indian decorative imagery. Besides being the symbol of Shiva it was also a motif of Buddhist art.

the less striking. He enjoined respect for the dignity of all men, and above all, religious toleration and non-violence. His precepts were general rather than precise and they were not laws. But their central themes are unmistakable and they were intended to provide principles of action. While Asoka's own bent and thinking undoubtedly made such ideas agreeable to him, they suggest less a wish to advance the ideas of Buddhism (this was something Asoka did in other ways) than a wish to allay differences; they were probably in the main a device of government for a huge, heterogeneous and religiously divided empire. Asoka was seeking to establish some focus for a political and social unity spanning all India, which would be based on men's interests as well as upon force and spying. 'All men', said one of his inscriptions, 'are my children.'

This may also explain his pride in what might be called his 'social services', which sometimes took forms appropriate to the climate: 'on the roads I have had banyan trees planted', he proclaimed, 'which will give shade to beasts and men'. The value of this apparently simple device would have been readily apparent to those who toiled and travelled in the great Indian plains. Almost incidentally, improvements also smoothed the path of trade, but like the wells he dug and the rest-houses he set up at nine-mile intervals, the banyan trees were an expression of *Dhamma*. Yet *Dhamma* does not appear to have succeeded, for we hear of sectarian struggles and the resentment of priests.

Asoka did better in promoting simple Buddhist evangelization. His reign brought the first great expansion of Buddhism, which had prospered, but had remained hitherto confined to north-eastern India. Now Asoka sent missionaries to Burma who did well; in Ceylon others did better still, and from his day the island was predominantly Buddhist. Those sent, more optimistically, to Macedonia and Egypt were less successful though Buddhist teaching left its mark on some of the philosophies of the Hellenistic world and some Greeks were converted.

and one which, of course, was only evident when he had completed the conquest of India.

The most remarkable consequence of Asoka's Buddhism has usually been thought to be expressed in the recommendations he made to his subjects in the rock-inscriptions and pillars dating from this part of his reign (roughly after 260 BC). They really amounted to a complete new social philosophy. Asoka's precepts have the overall name of *Dhamma*, a variant of a Sanskrit word meaning 'Universal Law', and their novelty has led to much admiration of Asoka's modernity by Indian politicians of this century. This is anachronistic, but Asoka's ideas are none

The vitality of Buddhism under Asoka may in part explain signs of reaction in the Brahmanical religion. It has been suggested that a new popularization of certain cults which dates from about this time may have been a conscious reaction of challenge by the brahmans. Notably, the third and second centuries BC brought a new prominence to the cults of two of the most popular avatars of Vishnu. One is the proteiform Krishna, whose legend offers vast possibilities of psychological identification to the worshipper, and the other Rama, the embodiment of the benevolent king, good husband and son, a family god. It was in the second century, too, that the two great Indian epics, the *Mahabharata* and the *Ramayana*, began to take their final form. The first of these was extended by a long passage which is now the most famous work of Indian literature and its greatest poem, the *Bhagavad Gita*, or 'Song of the lord'. It was to become the central testament of Hinduism, weaving around the figure of Vishnu/Krishna the ethical doctrine of duty in the performance of the obligations laid upon one by membership of one's class (*dharma*) and the recommendation that works of devotion, however meritorious, might be less efficacious than love of Krishna as a means to release into eternal happiness.

These were important developments for the future of Hinduism, but were to develop fully only over a period which ran on far past the crumbling of the Mauryan empire, and this began soon after Asoka's death. Such a disappearance is so dramatically impressive – and the Mauryan empire had been so remarkable a thing – that, unlike other empires, we are tempted to look for some special explanation.

Perhaps there is only a cumulative one. In all ancient empires except the Chinese, the demands made on government eventually outgrew the technical resources available to meet them: when this happened, they broke up. The Mauryas had done great things. They conscripted labour to exploit large areas of wasteland, thereby both feeding a growing population and increasing the tax base of the empire. They undertook great irrigation works which survived them for centuries. Trade prospered under Maurya rule, if we may judge from the distribution of northern pottery throughout India in the third century BC. They kept up a huge army and a diplomacy which ranged as far afield as Epirus. The cost, however, was great. The bureaucracy was huge, and, like the army, parasitical upon an agricultural economy which could not be limitlessly expanded. There was a limit to what it could pay for. Nor, though bureaucracy was highly centralized in principle, was it flawless. Without a system of control and recruitment to render it independent of society, it fell at one end into the control of the favourites of the monarch on whom all else depended and at the other into the gift of local élites who knew how to seize and retain power.

Another weakness may have been rooted deep in pre-Maurya times. Indian society had already sunk its anchors in the family and in the institutions of caste. Here, in social institutions rather than in a dynasty or an abstract notion of a continuing state or nation was the focus of Indian loyalties. When an Indian empire began to crumble under economic, external or technical pressures, it could fall back on no unthinking popular support. Evidently, this is a striking indication of the lack of success of Asoka's attempts to provide ideological integument for his empire.

The assassination of the last Maurya was followed by a Ganges dynasty of Brahmanical origin and thereafter the story of India for five hundred years is once more one of political disunity. References in Chinese sources become available from the end of the second century BC, but it cannot be said that they have made agreement between scholars about what was happening in India any easier; even the chronology is still largely conjectural. Only the general processes stand out.

The most important of these is a new succession of invasions of India from the historic north-western routes. First came Bactrians, descendants of the Greeks left behind by Alexander's empire on the upper Oxus, where they formed an independent kingdom by 239 BC standing between India and Seleucid Persia. Our knowledge of this mysterious realm is largely drawn from its coins and has grave gaps in it, but it is known that a hundred years later the Bactrians were pushing into the Indus valley. They were the foremost in a current which was to flow for four centuries. A complex series of movements was in train whose origins lay deep in the nomadic societies of Asia. Parthians and Scythians were among those who followed the Indo-Greeks of Bactria and established themselves at different times in the Punjab. One Scythian king, according to legend, received the apostle St Thomas at his court.

One important people came all the way from the borders of China and left behind them the memory of another big Indian empire, stretching from Benares beyond the mountains to the caravan routes of the steppes. These were the Kushanas. Historians still argue about how they are related to other nomadic peoples, but two things about them seem clear enough. The first is that they (or their rulers) were both enthusiastically Buddhist and also patronized some Hindu sects. The second was that their political interests were focussed in central Asia, where their greatest king died fighting.

The Kushana period brought strong foreign influences once more into Indian culture, often from the West, as the Hellenistic flavour of sculpture, particularly of the Buddha, shows. It marks an epoch in another way, for the depicting of the Buddha was something of an innovation in Kushan times. The Kushanas carried it very far and the Greek models gradually gave way to the forms of Buddha familiar today. This was one expression of a great complicating and developing of Buddhist religion: new influences were playing on it as never before. One aspect of what was happening was that Buddhism was being popularized and materialized; Buddha was turning into a god. But this was only one among many developments. Millenarianism, more emotional expressions of religion and more sophisticated philosophical systems were all interplaying with one another. To distinguish

The operation in the sub-continent of Hellenistic influence appears clearest of all in the art of Gandhara, in north-west India. This head of the Buddha, perhaps of the first or second century AD, has reminiscences of conventional representations of Apollo, while the projection on top of the head which was one of the Buddha's auspicious marks is disguised by a treatment of the hair like that on representations of the Greek sun god.

Hindu or Buddhist 'orthodoxy' in this is somewhat artificial.

In the end the Kushanas succumbed to a greater power. Bactria and the Kabul valley were taken by Artaxerxes early in the third century AD. Soon after another Sassanid king took the Kushana capital of Peshawar – and such statements make it easy to feel impatient with such a narrative. Contemplating them, the reader may well feel with Voltaire: 'What is it to me if one king replaces another on the banks of the Oxus and Jakartes?' It is like the fratricidal struggles of Frankish kings, or of Anglo-Saxon states of the Heptarchy, on a slightly larger scale. It is indeed difficult to see much significance in this ebb and flow beyond its recording of two great constants of Indian history, the importance of the north-western frontier as a cultural conduit and the digestive power of Hindu civilization. None of these peoples could in the end resist the assimilative power India always showed. New rulers were before long ruling Hindu kingdoms (whose roots went back possibly beyond Maurya times to political units of the fourth and fifth centuries BC) and they adopted Indian ways.

Invaders never penetrated far to the south. After the Maurya break-up, the Deccan long remained separate and under its own Dravidian rulers. Its cultural distinction persists even today. Though Aryan influence was stronger there after the Maurya era and Hinduism and Buddhism were never to disappear, the south was not again truly integrated politically with the north until the coming of the British Raj.

Not all India's contacts with outsiders were violent during this confusing period. Trade with Roman merchants grew so visibly that Pliny blamed it (wrongly) for draining gold out of the empire. We have little hard information, it is true, except about the arrival of embassies from India to negotiate over trade but the remark suggests that one feature of India's trade with the West was already established; what Mediterranean markets sought were luxuries which only India could supply and there was little they could offer in return except bullion. This pattern held until the nineteenth century. There are also other signs of intercontinental contacts arising from trade which are interesting. The sea is a uniter of the cultures of trading communities and Tamil words for commodities turn up in Greek; Indians from the south had traded with Egypt since Hellenistic times. Later, Roman merchants lived in southern ports where Tamil kings kept Roman bodyguards. Finally, it seems likely that whatever the truth may be about the holy apostle Thomas, Christianity appeared in India first in the western trading ports, possibly as early as the first century AD.

Political unity did not appear again even in the north until hundreds of years passed. A new Ganges valley state, the Gupta empire, was then the legatee of five centuries of confusion. Its centre was at Patna, where a dynasty of Gupta emperors established itself. The first of these, another Chandra Gupta, began to reign in 320, and within a hundred years north India was once more united and relieved of external pressure and incursion. It was not so big an empire as Asoka's, but the Guptas preserved theirs longer. For some two centuries north India enjoyed under them a sort of Antonine age, later to be imagined with nostalgia, India's classical period.

The Gupta age brought the first great consolidation of an Indian art. From the earlier times little has survived until the perfection of stone-carving under the Mauryas. The columns which are its major monuments were the culmination of a native tradition of stonework. For a long time stone-carving and building still bore the stamp of wooden models, but techniques were well advanced before the arrival of Greek influence, once thought to be the origin of Indian stone sculpture. What the Greeks brought were new artistic motifs and techniques from the West. If we are to judge by what survives, the major deployment of these influences was found in Buddhist sculpture until well into the Christian era. But before the Gupta era, a rich and indigenous tradition of Hindu sculpture, too, had been established and from this time India's artistic life is mature and self-sustaining. In Gupta times there began to be built the great numbers of stone temples (as distinct from excavated and embellished caves) which are the great glories both of Indian art and architecture before the Moslem era.

Gupta civilization was also remarkable for its literary achievement. Again, the roots are deep. The standardization and systematization of Sanskrit grammar just before Maurya times opened the path to a literature which could be shared by the élite of the whole subcontinent. Sanskrit was a tie uniting north and south in spite of their cultural differences. The great epics were given their classical form in Sanskrit (though they were also available in translations into local languages) and in it wrote the greatest of Indian poets, Kalidasa. He was also a dramatist, and in the Gupta era there emerges from the shadowy past the Indian theatre whose traditions have been maintained and carried into the popular Indian film of the twentieth century.

Intellectually, too, the Gupta era was a great one. It was in the fifth century that Indian arithmeticians invented the decimal system. A layman can perhaps glimpse the importance of this

At Mamallapuram is a collection of shrines and temples from the seventh and eighth centuries. Beside them stands a gigantic piece of sculpture, carved from a single huge boulder and depicting the Descent of the Ganges from the Himalayas. It incorporates the finest evocations of animal forms to be found anywhere in the Eastern world in one colossal celebration of thankfulness for Shiva's gift of water.

469

more readily than he can that of the Indian philosophical resurgence of the same period. This was not confined to religious thought but what can be gathered from it about general attitudes or the direction of culture seems highly debatable. In a literary text such as the *Kama Sutra* a western observer may be most struck by the prominence given in it to the acquisition of techniques whose use, however stimulating for the individual, can at most have absorbed only a small fraction of the interest and time of a tiny élite. A negative point is perhaps safest: neither the emphasis on *dharma* of the Brahmanical tradition, nor the ascetic severities of some Indian teachers, nor the frank acceptance of sensual pleasure suggested by many texts besides the *Kama Sutra* have anything in common with the striving, militant puritanism so strong in both the Christian and Islamic traditions. Indian civilization moved to very different rhythms from those further west; here, perhaps, lay its deepest strength and the explanation of its powers of resistance to alien cultures.

This was the era when Indian civilization came to its mature, classical form. Chronology derived from politics is a hindrance here; important developments flow across the boundaries of any arbitrary period. Nevertheless, in Gupta culture we can sense the presence of the fully evolved Hindu society. Its outstanding expression was a caste system which by then had come to overlay and complicate the original four-class division of Vedic society. Within castes which locked them into well-defined groups for marriage and, usually, to their occupations, most Indians lived a life close to the land. The cities were for the most part great markets or great centres of pilgrimage. Most Indians were, as they are now, peasants, and even in the twentieth century their lives must often be little different from that of their ancestors under the Guptas. These lives were lived within the assumptions of a religious culture whose fundamentals had been established in pre-Maurya times. Some of its later developments have been mentioned already; others run on past the Gupta

A twelfth-century bronze statue of the most appealing of the Hindu deities: Ganesh, the god of wisdom and learning, son of Shiva and Parvati. The elephant's wisdom is proverbial in India and this no doubt explains the god's head; he is usually shown with his trunk dipping into a pot of spices.

period and will have to be discussed elsewhere. Of their vigour and power there can be no doubt; with centuries of further elaboration ahead, they were already expressed in Gupta times in a huge development of carving and sculpture which manifest the power of popular religion and take their place alongside the stupas and Buddhas of pre-Gupta times as an enduring feature of the Indian landscape. Paradoxically, India, largely because of its religious art, is a country where we have perhaps more evidence about the mind of the men of the past than we have about their material life. We may know little about the way in which Gupta taxation actually weighed on the peasant (though we can guess), but in the contemplation of the endless dance of the gods and demons, the forming and dissolving patterns of animals and symbols, we can touch a world still alive and to be found in the village shrines and juggernauts of our own day. In India as nowhere else, there is some chance of access to the life of the uncounted millions whose history should be recounted in such books as this, but which usually escapes us.

In the climax of Hindu civilization between Gupta times and the coming of Islam, the fertility of Indian religion, the soil of Indian culture, was hardly troubled by political events. One symptom was the appearance by 600 or thereabouts of an important new cult which quickly took a place it was never to lose in the Hindu worship, that of the mother-goddess Devi. Some have seen in her an expression of a new sexual emphasis which marked both Hinduism and Buddhism. Her cult was part of a general effervescence of religious life, lasting a couple of centuries or more, for a new popular emotionalism is associated with the cults of Shiva and Vishnu at about the same time. Dates are not very helpful here; we have to think of continual change during the whole of the centuries corresponding to those of the early Christian era whose result was the final evolution of the old Brahmanical religion into Hinduism.

From this evolution emerged a spectrum of practice and belief offering something for all needs. It ran from the philosophic system of *Vedanta*, an abstract creed stressing the unreality of the actual and material and the desirability of winning disengagement from it in true knowledge of reality – *brahma* – to the crudities of the village shrines at which local deities were worshipped which had been easily assimilated to the cults of Shiva or Vishnu by the belief that these two leading deities might appear in more than one incarnation. Religious effervescence thus found expression antithetically in the simultaneous growth of image worship and the rise of a new austerity. Animal sacrifice had

To a western eye, the artistic traditions of Jainism seem very similar to those of Buddhism, and the two religions have much in common. Both cults were founded by sages dissatisfied with orthodox brahmanical religion and Jain sculptors seem deliberately to have copied Buddhist forms. The adherents of Jainism worship a number of Jina, or patriarchs, all of whom achieved perfection by asceticism and austerity. The imitation of Buddhist style can be seen clearly in this tenth-century statue of one of the Jina, from Khajurao in central India.

never stopped. It was one of the things now endorsed by a new strictness of conservative religious practice. So was a new rigidity of attitudes towards women and their intensified subordination. The religious expression of this was an upsurge of child marriage and the practice called *suttee*, or self-immolation of widows on their husband's funeral pyres.

Yet the richness of Indian culture is such that this coarsening of religion was accompanied also by the development to their highest pitch of the philosophical tradition of the Vedanta, the culmination of Vedic tradition, and the new development of Mahayana Buddhism, which asserted the divinity of the Buddha. The roots of the latter went back to early deviations from the Buddha's teaching on contemplation, purity and non-attachment. These deviations had favoured a more ritualistic and popular religious approach and also stressed a new interpretation of the Buddha's rôle. Instead of merely being understood as a teacher and an example, Buddha was now seen as the greatest of *bodhisattvas*, saviours who, entitled to the bliss of self-annihilation themselves, nevertheless rejected it to remain in the world and teach men the way to salvation.

To become a *bodhisattva* gradually became the aim of many Buddhists. In part, the efforts of a Buddhist council summoned by the Kushan ruler Kanishka had been directed towards re-integrating two tendencies in Buddhism which were increasingly divergent. This had not been successful. *Mahayana* Buddhism (the word means 'great vehicle') focussed upon a Buddha who was effectively a divine saviour who might be worshipped and followed in faith, one manifestation of a great, single heavenly Buddha who begins to look somewhat like the undifferentiated soul behind all things found in Hinduism. The disciplines of austerity and contemplation Gautama had taught were now increasingly confined to a minority of orthodox Buddhists, the followers of *Mahayana* winning conversions among the masses. One sign of this was the proliferation in the first and second centuries AD of statues and representations of the Buddha, a practice hitherto restrained by the Buddha's prohibition of idol-worship. *Mahayana* Buddhism eventually replaced earlier forms in India, and spread also along the central Asian trade routes through Nepal and Tibet to China and Japan. The more orthodox tradition did better in south-eastern Asia and Indonesia.

Hinduism and Buddhism were thus both marked by changes which broadened their appeal. The Hindu religion prospered better, though there is a regional factor at work here; since Kushan times, the centre of Indian Buddhism had been the north-west, the region most exposed to the devastations of the Hun raiders. Hinduism prospered most in the south. Both the north-west and the south, of course, were zones where cultural currents intermingled most easily with those from the classical Mediterranean world, in the one across land and in the other by sea.

These changes provoke a sense of culmination and climax. They matured only shortly before Islam arrived in the subcontinent, but early enough for a philosophical outlook to have solidified which has marked India ever since and has shown astonishing invulnerability to competing views. At its heart was a vision of endless cycles of creation and reabsorption into the divine, a picture of the cosmos which predicated a cyclic and not a linear history. What difference this made to the way Indians have actually behaved – right down to the present day – is a huge subject, but almost impossible to grasp. It might be expected to lead to passivity and scepticism about the value of practical action yet this is very debatable. Few Christians live lives logically deducible from their beliefs and there is no reason to expect Hindus to be more consistent. The practical activity of sacrifice and propitiation in Indian temples survives still. Yet the direction of a whole culture may none the less be determined by the emphasis of its distinctive modes of thought and it is difficult not to feel that much of India's history has been determined by a world outlook which stressed the limits rather than the potential of human action.

For the background to Islam in India we have to return to 500 or so. From about that time, northern India was once again divided in obedience both to the centrifugal tendencies which afflicted early empires and to the appearance of a mysterious invasion of 'Hunas'. Were they really Huns? Certainly they behaved like them, devastating much of the north-west,

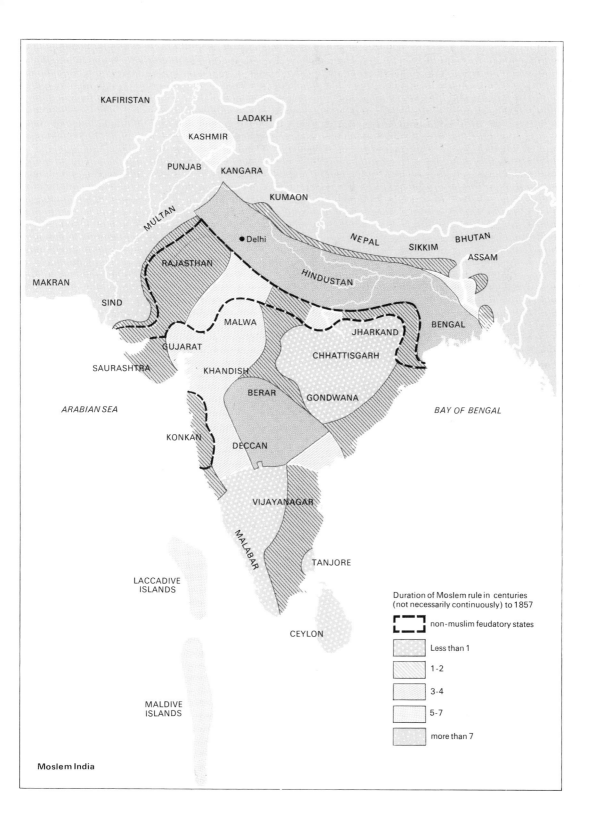

KAFIRISTAN

LADAKH

KASHMIR

PUNJAB   KANGARA

MULTAN   KUMAON

●Delhi

NEPAL   SIKKIM   BHUTAN

RAJASTHAN   ASSAM

MAKRAN   HINDUSTAN

SIND

MALWA   JHARKAND   BENGAL

GUJARAT   CHHATTISGARH

SAURASHTRA   KHANDISH

BERAR   GONDWANA

ARABIAN SEA   BAY OF BENGAL

KONKAN

DECCAN

VIJAYANAGAR

MALABAR   TANJORE

LACCADIVE
ISLANDS

CEYLON

MALDIVE
ISLANDS

Duration of Moslem rule in centuries
(not necessarily continuously) to 1857

▢ non-muslim feudatory states

Less than 1

1-2

3-4

5-7

more than 7

Moslem India

sweeping away many of the established ruling families. Across the mountains, in Afghanistan, they mortally wounded Buddhism, which had been strongly established there. In the subcontinent itself, this anarchic period did less fundamental damage. Though the northern plains had broken up into warring kingdoms, Indian cities do not seem to have been much disturbed and peasant life recovers quickly from all but the worst blows. Indian warfare appears rapidly to have acquired important and effective conventional limits on its potential for destructiveness. The state of affairs which obtained seems in some ways rather like the more anarchic periods of the European Middle Ages, when feudal relationships more or less kept the peace between potentially competitive grandees but could not contain completely outbreaks of violence which were essentially about different forms of tribute.

Then, in the eighth century, the Arabs conquered Sind. They got no further, gradually settled down and ceased to trouble the Indian peoples. A period of calm followed which lasted until a Ghaznavid ruler broke deep into India early in the eleventh century with raids which were destructive, but again did not produce radical change. Indian religious life for another two centuries moved still to its own rhythms, the most striking changes being the decline of Buddhism and the rise of Tantrism, a semi-magical and superstitious growth of practices promising access to holiness by charms and ritual. Cults centred on popular festivals at temples also prospered, no doubt in the absence of a strong political focus in post-Gupta times. Then came a new invasion of central Asians.

These invaders were Moslems and were drawn from the complex of Turkish peoples. Theirs was a different sort of Islamic onslaught from earlier ones, for they came to stay, not just to raid. They first established themselves in the Punjab in the eleventh century and then launched a second wave of invasions at the end of the twelfth century which led within a few decades to the establishment of Turkish sultans at Delhi who ruled the whole of the Ganges

valley. Their empire was not a united state. Hindu kingdoms survived within it on a tributary basis, as Christian kingdoms survived to be tributaries of Mongols in the West. The Moslem rulers, perhaps careful of their material interests, did not always support their co-religionists of the *Ulema* who sought to proselytize and were willing to persecute. The destruction of Hindu temples shows their determination.

The heartland of the first Moslem empire in India was the Ganges valley. The invaders rapidly overran Bengal and later established themselves on the west coast of India and the tableland of the Deccan. Further south they did not penetrate and Hindu society survived there largely unchanged. In any case, their rule was not to last long even in the north. In 1398 Timur Lang's army sacked Delhi after a devastating approach march which was made all the speedier, said one chronicler, because of the Mongols' desire to escape from the stench of decay arising from the piles of corpses they left in their wake. In the troubled waters after this disaster, generals and local potentates struck out for themselves and Islamic India fragmented again. None the less, Islam was by now established in the subcontinent, the greatest challenge yet seen to India's assimilative powers, for its active, prophetic, revelatory style was wholly antithetical both to Hinduism and to Buddhism (though Islam, too, was to be subtly changed by them).

New Sultans emerged at Delhi but long showed no power to restore the former Islamic empire. Only in the sixteenth century was it revived by a prince from outside, Babur of Kabul. On his father's side he descended from Timur and on his mother's from Chinghis, formidable advantages and a source of inspiration to a young man schooled in adversity. He quickly discovered he had to fight for his inheritance and there can have been few monarchs who, like Babur, conquered a city of the importance of Samarkand at the age of fourteen (albeit to lose it again almost at once). Even when legend and anecdote are separated, he remains, in spite of cruelty and duplicity, one of the most attractive figures among great rulers, munificent, hardy, courageous, intelligent and sensitive. He left a remarkable autobiography, written from notes made throughout his life, which was to be treasured by his descendants as a source of inspiration and guidance. It displays a ruler who did not think of himself as Mongol in culture, but Turkish in the tradition of those peoples long settled in the former eastern provinces of the Abassid caliphate. His taste and culture were formed by the inheritance of the Timurid princes of Persia; his love of gardening and poetry came from that country and fitted easily into the setting of an Islamic India whose court cultures were already much influenced by Persian models. Babur was a bibliophile, another Timurid trait; it is reported that when he took Lahore he went at once to his defeated adversary's library to choose texts from it to send as gifts to his sons. He himself wrote, among other things, a forty-page account of his conquests in Hindustan, noting its customs and caste structure and, even more minutely, its wildlife and flowers.

This young prince was called in to India by Afghan chiefs, but had his own claims to make to the inheritance of the Timurid line in Hindustan. This was to prove the beginning of Moghul India; Moghul was the Persian word for Mongol, though it was not a word Babur applied to himself. Originally, those whose discontent and intrigue called him forward had only aroused in him the ambition of conquering the Punjab, but he was soon drawn further. In 1526 he took Delhi after the Sultan had fallen in battle. Soon Babur was subduing those who had invited him to come to India while at the same time conquering the infidel Hindu princes who had seized an opportunity to renew their own indepedence. The result was an empire which in 1530, the year of his death, stretched from Kabul to the borders of Bihar. Babur's body, significantly, was taken as he directed to Kabul, where it was buried, in his favourite garden with no roof over his tomb, in the place he had always thought of as home.

The reign of Babur's son, troubled by his own

Moghul India

Empire under Babur 1526

Expansion under Akbar to 1605

Expansion under Shah Jahan and Aurungzebe to 1707

instability and inadequacy and by the presence of half-brothers anxious to exploit the Timurid tradition which, like the Frankish, prescribed the division of a royal inheritance, showed that the security and consolidation of Babur's realm could not be taken for granted. For five years of his reign, he was driven from Delhi, though he returned there to die in 1555. His heir, Akbar, born during his father's distressed wanderings, but enjoying the advantages of a very auspicious horoscope and the absence of rival brothers, thus came to the throne as a boy. He inherited at first only a small part of his grandfather's domains, but was to build from them an empire recalling that of Asoka, winning the awed respect of Europeans, who called him 'the Great Moghul'.

Akbar had many kingly qualities. He was brave to the point of folly – his most obvious weakness was that he was headstrong – enjoying as a boy riding his own fighting elephants and preferring hunting and hawking to lessons (one

475

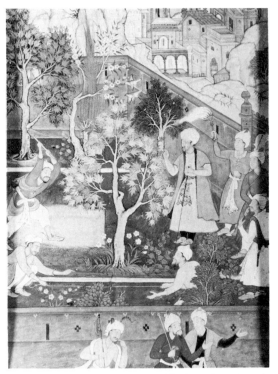

A sixteenth-century picture of Babur, founder of the Moghul empire, indulging his taste for gardening by supervising the laying out of flowerbeds.

consequence was that, uniquely in Babur's line, he was almost illiterate). He once killed a tiger with his sword in single combat and was proud of his marksmanship with a gun (Babur had introduced firearms to the Moghul army). Yet he was also, like his predecessors, an admirer of learning and all things beautiful. He collected books and in his reign Moghul architecture and painting came to their peak, a department of court painters being maintained at his expense. Above all, he was statesmanlike in his handling of the problems posed by religious difference among his subjects.

He reigned for almost half a century, until 1605, thus just overlapping at each end the reign of his contemporary, Queen Elizabeth I of England. Among his first acts on reaching maturity was to marry a Rajput princess who was, of course, a Hindu. Marriage always played an important part in Akbar's diplomacy

and strategy, and this lady (the mother of the next emperor) was the daughter of the greatest of the Rajput kings and therefore an important catch. None the less, something more than policy may be seen in the marriage. Akbar had already permitted the Hindu ladies of his harem to practise the rites of their own religion within it, an unprecedented act for a Moslem ruler. Before long, he abolished the poll-tax on non-Moslems; he was going to be the emperor of all religions, not a Moslem fanatic. Akbar even went on to listen to Christian teachers; he invited the Portuguese who had appeared on the west coast to send missionaries learned in their faith to his court and three Jesuits duly arrived there in 1580, to dispute vigorously with Moslem divines before the emperor and receive many marks of his favour, though they were disappointed in their long-indulged hope of his conversion. He seems, in fact, to have been a man of genuine religious feeling and eclectic mind; he went so far as to try to institute a new religion of his own, a sort of mish-mash of Zoroastrianism, Islam and Hinduism. It had little success except among prudent courtiers and offended some.

However this is interpreted, it is evident that the appeasement of non-Moslems would ease the problems of government in India. Babur's advice in his memoirs to conciliate defeated enemies pointed in this direction too, for Akbar launched himself on a career of conquest and added many new Hindu territories to his empire. He rebuilt the unity of northern India from Gujarat to Bengal and began the conquest of the Deccan. The empire was governed by a system of administration much of which lasted well into the era of the British Raj, though Akbar was less an innovator in government than the confirmer and establisher of institutions he inherited. Officials ruled in the emperor's name and at his pleasure; they had the primary function of providing soldiers as needed and raising the land tax, now reassessed on a national and flexible system devised by a Hindu finance minister which seems to have had an almost unmatched success in that it actually led to increases in production which raised the standard of living in Hindustan. Among other reforms which were notable in intention if not in effect was the discouragement of *suttee*.

Above all, Akbar stabilized the régime. He was disappointed in his sons and quarrelled with them, yet the dynasty was solidly based when he died, not least because good administration had provided an alternative financial resource to further conquest in greater prosperity. There were revolts nevertheless. Some of them seem to have been encouraged by Moslem anger at Akbar's apparent falling-away from the faith. Even in the 'Turkish' era the sharpness of the religious distinction between Moslem and non-Moslem had somewhat softened as invaders settled down in their new country and took up Indian ways. One earlier sign of assimilation was the appearance of a new language, Urdu, the tongue of the camp. It was the *lingua franca* of rulers and ruled, with a Hindi structure and a Persian and Turkish vocabulary. Soon there were signs that the omnivorous power of Hinduism would perhaps even incorporate Islam; a new devotionalism in the fourteenth and fifteenth centuries had spread through popular hymns an abstract, almost monotheistic, cult, of a God whose name might be Rama or Allah, but who offered love, justice and mercy to all men. Correspondingly, some Moslems even before Akbar's reign had shown interest in and respect for Hindu ideas. There was some absorption of Hindu ritual practice. Soon it was noticeable that converts to Islam tended to revere the tombs of holy men: these became places of resort and pilgrimage which satisfied the scheme of a subordinate focus of devotion in a monotheistic religion and thus carried out the functions of the minor and local deities who had always found a place in Hinduism.

Another important development before the end of Akbar's reign was the consolidation of India's first direct relations with Atlantic Europe. Links with Mediterranean Europe may already have been made slightly easier by the coming of Islam; from the Levant to Delhi a common religion provided continuous, if distant, contact. European travellers had turned up from time to time in India and its rulers had been able to attract the occasional technical expert to their service, though they were few after the Ottoman conquests. But what was now about to happen was to go much further and would change India for ever. The Europeans who now arrived would be followed by others in increasing numbers and they would not go away.

The process had begun when a Portuguese admiral reached Malabar at the end of the fifteenth century. Within a few years his countrymen had installed themselves as traders – and behaved sometimes as pirates – at Bombay and on the coast of Gujarat. Attempts to dislodge them failed in the troubled years following Babur's death and in the second half of the century the Portuguese moved round to found new posts in the Bay of Bengal. They made the running for Europeans in India for a long time. They were liable, none the less, to attract the hostility of good Moslems because they brought with them pictures and images of Christ, His mother and the saints, which smacked of idolatry. Protestants were to prove less irritating to religious feeling, when they arrived. The British age in India was still a long way off, but with rare historical neatness, the first British East India Company was founded on 31 December 1600, the last day of the sixteenth century. Three years later the Company's first emissary arrived at Akbar's court at Agra and by then Elizabeth I, who had given the merchants their charter of incorporation, was dead. Thus at the end of the reigns of two great rulers, came the first contact between two countries whose historical destinies were to be entwined so long and with such enormous effect for them both and for the world. At that moment no hint of the future could have been sensed. The English then regarded trade in India as less interesting than that with other parts of Asia. The contrast between the two realms, too, is fascinating: Akbar's empire was one of the most powerful in the world, his court one of the most sumptuous and he and his successors ruled over a civilization more glorious and spectacular than anything India had known since the Guptas, while Queen Elizabeth's kingdom, barely a great power, even in European terms, was crippled by debt and contained fewer people than modern Calcutta. Akbar's successor was contemptuous of the presents sent to him by James I a few years later. Yet the future of India lay with the subjects of the queen.

The Moghul emperors continued in Babur's line in direct descent though not without interruption, until the middle of the nineteenth century. After Akbar, so great was the prestige of the dynasty that it became fashionable in India to claim Mongol descent. Only the three rulers who followed Akbar matter here, for it was under Jahangir and Shah Jahan that the empire grew to its greatest extent in the first half of the seventeenth century and under Aurungzebe that it began to decay in the second. The reign of Jahangir was not so glorious as his father's, but the empire survived his cruelty and alcoholism, a considerable test of its administrative structure. The religious toleration established by Akbar also survived intact. For all his faults, too, Jahangir was a notable promoter of the arts, above all of painting. During his reign there becomes visible for the first time the impact of European culture in Asia, through artistic motifs drawn from imported pictures and prints. One of these motifs was the halo or nimbus given to Christian saints and, in Byzantium, to emperors. After Jahangir, all Moghul emperors were painted with it.

Shah Jahan began the piecemeal acquisition of the Deccan sultanates though he had little success in campaigns in the north-west and failed to drive the Persians from Kandahar. In domestic administration there was a weakening of the principle of religious toleration, though not sufficiently to place Hindus at a disadvantage in government service; administration remained multi-religious. Although the emperor decreed that all newly built Hindu temples should be pulled down, he patronized Hindu poets and musicians. At Agra,

Shah Jahan maintained a lavish and exquisite court life. It was there, too, that he built the most celebrated and the best-known of all Islamic buildings, the Taj Mahal, a tomb for his favourite wife; it is the only possible rival to the mosque of Córdoba for the title of the most beautiful building in the world. She had died soon after Shah Jahan's accession and for over twenty years his builders were at work. It is the culmination of the work with arch and dome which is one of the most conspicuous Islamic legacies to Indian art and the greatest monument of Islam in India. The waning of Indian representational sculpture after the Islamic invasions had its compensations. Shah Jahan's court brought also to its culmination a great tradition of miniature painting.

Below the level of the court, the picture of Moghul India is far less attractive. Local officials had to raise more and more money to support both the household expenses and the campaigns of Shah Jahan. The flight of peasants from the land and rise of rural banditry is a telling symptom of the suffering and resistance this provoked. Yet Shah Jahan's demands probably did the empire less damage than the religious enthusiasm of his third son, Aurungzebe, who set aside three brothers and imprisoned his father to become emperor in 1658. He combined, disastrously, absolute power, distrust of his subordinates and a narrow religiosity. To have succeeded in reducing the expenses of his court is not much of an offsetting item in the account. New conquests were balanced by popular revolts against Moghul rule which were said to owe much to Aurungzebe's attempt to prohibit the Hindu religion and destroy its temples and his restoration of the poll-tax on non-Moslems. The Hindu's advancement in the service of the state was less and less likely; conversion became necessary for success. A century of religious toleration was cancelled

Madras was long to be associated in Europe with its cottons. This painted hanging of the seventeenth century provides an early example of the Indians' vision of the European.

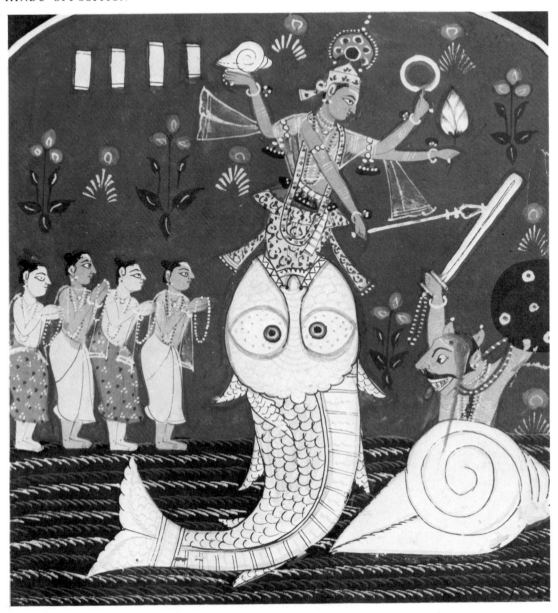

Miniature painting reached its peak in India in the Islamic courts, but flourished also in the Hindu kingdoms. This seventeenth-century example comes from Malwa in central India and shows Vishnu, who has taken the form of a fish, destroying a sea-demon.

and one result was the alienation of many subjects' loyalties.

Among other results, this helped to make it impossible finally to conquer the Deccan which has been called an ulcer which ruined the Moghul empire. The Mahrattas, the hillmen who were the core of Hindu opposition, constituted themselves under an independent ruler in 1674 and allied with the remains of the Moslem armies of the Deccan sultans to resist the Moghul armies in a struggle which threw up a heroic figure who has become something of a paladin in the eyes of modern India – that is, Hindu nationalists. This was Shivagi, who built from fragments a Mahratta political identity. Aurungzebe was continuously campaigning against the Mahrattas down to his death in 1707. There then lay ahead a grave crisis for the régime, for his three sons disputed the succession. The empire almost at once began to break up and a much more formidable legatee than the Hindu or local prince was waiting in the wings – the European.

Perhaps the negative responsibility for the eventual success of the Europeans in India is Akbar's for he did not scotch the serpent in the egg. Shah Jahan, on the other hand, destroyed the Portuguese station on the Hooghly, though later Christians were again tolerated at Agra. Strikingly, Moghul policy never seems to have envisaged the building of a navy, a weapon used formidably against the Mediterranean Europeans by the Ottomans. One consequence was already felt under Aurungzebe, when coastal shipping and even the pilgrim trade to Mecca were in danger from the Europeans. On land, the Europeans had been allowed to establish their toeholds and bridgeheads. After beating a Portuguese squadron, the English won their first west-coast trading concession early in the seventeenth century. In 1639, with the permission of the local ruler, they founded at Madras Fort St George, the settlement which was the first territory of British India; the headstones over their graves in its little cemetery still commemorate the first English who lived and died in India. Thousands more would do the same in the next three centuries.

The English later fell foul of Aurungzebe, but got further stations at Bombay and Calcutta before the end of the century. English naval force maintained the paramountcy in trade it won from the Portuguese, but a new European rival was also in sight by 1700. A French East India Company had been founded in 1664. It soon established its own first Indian settlements.

A century of conflict lay ahead, and not only between Europeans. Europeans were already having to make nice political choices because of the uncertainties aroused by a Moghul power no longer as strong as it once had been. Relations had to be undertaken with his opponents as well as with the emperor, as the English in Bombay discovered, looking on helplessly while a Mahratta squadron occupied one island in Bombay harbour and a Moghul admiral the one next to it. In 1677 an official sent back a significant warning to his employers in London: 'the times now require you to manage your general commerce with your sword in your hands'. By 1700 the English were well aware that much was at stake.

With that date we are into the era in which India is increasingly caught up in events not of her own making, the era of world history, in fact. Little things show it as well as great; with them in the sixteenth century the Portuguese brought chili, potatoes and tobacco from America. Soon maize, paw-paws and pineapple were to follow. The story of Indian civilizations and rulers can be broken once this new connexion with the larger world is achieved even though this was not the end of independence for the subcontinent, except briefly. It was not, however, the coming of the European which ended the great period of Moghul empire; that was merely coincidental, though important because the newcomers were there to reap the advantages. No Indian empire was ever able to maintain itself for more than a few centuries; perhaps the diversity of the subcontinent and the irrelevance of political institutions to so much of its life are the explanations at the root of this. In the very long run the European tide, too, would recede. Unlike early conquerors, though Europeans were to stay a long time, they were not to become part of India. The British would not be overcome by India's assimilative power as had their predecessors. They would go away defeated, but would not be swallowed. And when they went they would leave as deep an imprint as any of their predecessors.

7 The Chinese sphere

China

One explanation of the striking continuity and independence of Chinese civilization is obvious: China was even more remote, more inaccessible to disturbance from the outside, more powerful in its capacity to assimilate and tame alien influences than India, which was crucially nearer to sources of disturbance further west. Empires came and went in both countries, but Islamic rule made more difference to India than any empire's rise or fall made to China. This was mainly because the tradition of civilization rested on different foundations in each country. In India the great stabilizers were provided by religion and a caste system inseparable from it. In China it rested on the culture of an administrative élite which survived dynasties and empires and kept China on the same course.

One thing we owe to this élite is the maintenance of written records from very early times. Thanks to them, we know more of the detail of early Chinese history than we do of India's. Chinese historical accounts provide an incomparable documentation, crammed with often reliable facts, though the selection of them was dominated by the assumptions of a minority, whose preoccupations they reflect, and they

This celebrated bronze horse buried at Kansu in north-west China in the second century AD may have been meant to be a magical creature; it seems to be galloping through the air, momentarily startling the swallow brushed by its foot. Similar models were often made of real horses and were buried with their owners.

still leave us uninformed about many things. The Confucian élite who kept up the historical records had a utilitarian and didactic aim: they wanted to provide a body of examples and data which would make easier the maintenance of traditional ways and values. Their histories emphasize continuity and the smooth flow of events. Given the needs of administration in so huge a country this is perfectly understandable; uniformity and regularity were clearly to be desired. Yet such a record leaves much out. It remains very difficult even in historical times – and much more difficult than in the classical Mediterranean world – to recover the concerns and life of the vast majority of Chinese. Moreover, official history may well give a false impression both of the unchanging nature of Chinese administration and of the permeation of society by Confucian values. For a long time, the assumptions behind the Chinese administrative machine can only have been those of a minority, even if they came in the end to be shared by many Chinese and accepted, unthinkingly and even unknowingly, by most.

The official culture was extraordinarily self-sufficient. Few outside influences played upon it with any effect and this remains impressive. The fundamental explanation, again, is China's isolation. China was much further removed from the classical West than India. She had little intercourse with it even indirectly, although until the beginning of the seventh century Persia, Byzantium and the Mediterranean depended upon her for silk and they always valued her porcelain. Always, too, China had complicated and close relations with the people of central Asia, though, once unified, she had no great states on her borders with whom relations had to be carried on. This isolation was, if anything, to increase as the centre of gravity of western civilization moved west and north and as the Mediterranean was more and more cut off from Asia first by the inheritors of the Hellenistic legacy in the East (the last and most important of which was Sassanid Persia), and then by Islam.

China's history between the end of the period of Warring States, and the beginning of the T'ang in 618, is one of internal consolidation. For a narrative, there is a backbone of sorts in the waxing and waning of dynasties. Dates can be attached to these, but there is an element of the fictitious or at least a danger of being over-emphatic in using them. It could take decades for a dynasty to make its power a reality over the whole empire and even longer to lose it. With this reservation, the dynastic reckoning can still be useful. It gives us major divisions of Chinese history down to this century which are called after the dynasties which reached their peaks during them. The first three which concern us fall in the period 221 BC–AD 618; they are the Ch'in, the Han, and the Later Han.

The first of these ended the disunity of the period of Warring States. The Ch'in came from a western state still looked upon by some as a barbarous place as late as the fourth century BC. Nevertheless, the Ch'in prospered, perhaps in part because of a radical reorganization carried out by a legalist-minded minister in about 356 BC; perhaps also because of their soldiers' use of a new long iron sword. After swallowing Szechwan, the Ch'in claimed the status of a kingdom in 325 BC. The climax of Ch'in success was the defeat of their last opponent in 221 BC and the unification of China for the first time in one empire under the dynasty which gives the country its name.

This was a great achievement and China from this time may be considered the seat of a single, self-conscious civilization. There had been earlier signs that such an outcome was likely. Given the potential of their own Neolithic cultures and the stimuli of cultural diffusion and some migration from the north, many parts of China had seen cultures evolving into civilization before the middle of the first millennium BC. By the end of the Warring States period some of them showed marked similarities which offset the differences between them. In a way, political unity achieved by the Ch'in through conquest extending over a century was the logical corollary of a cultural unification which had already gone far. Even a sense of Chinese nationality has been said to have been apparent before 221 BC; if so, it must have made conquest itself somewhat easier.

Fundamental administrative innovations were also made by the Ch'in which were to survive the dynasty's displacement after less than twenty years by the Han, who ruled for two hundred years (206 BC–AD 9). A brief interlude was followed by the almost equally successful Later Han dynasty (AD 25–220). Though they had their ups and downs, the Han emperors showed unprecedented strength and generated a unity extending over almost the whole of modern China, including southern Manchuria and the south-eastern province of Yueh. The Later Han went on to create an empire as big as that of their Roman contemporaries. They faced an old threat from Mongolia and a great opportunity towards the south. They handled both with skill aided by the tactical superiority given their armies by the new crossbow. This weapon was probably invented soon after 200 BC and was both more powerful and more accurate than the bows of the barbarians, who did not for a long time have the skill in casting to make the bronze locks required. It was the last major achievement of Chinese military technology before the coming of gunpowder.

In Mongolia at the beginning of Han times lived the Hsing-Nu, whom we have already met as the forerunners of the Huns. The Han emperors drove them north of the Gobi desert and then seized control of the caravan routes of central Asia, sending armies far west into Kashgaria in the first century BC. To the south,

Principal Chinese Dynasties

SHANG ?1523-?1027

CHOU ?1027-256

CH'IN 221-206
(having annihilated CHOU in 256 and other rival states afterwards)

FORMER HAN 206 BC-AD 9

HSIN AD 9-23

LATER HAN 25-220

WEI 220-265   SHU 221-263   WU 222-280

WESTERN CHIN 265-316

SIXTEEN KINGDOMS 304-439   EASTERN CHIN 317-420

LIU SUNG 420-479

NORTHERN WEI 386-581   SOUTHERN CH'I 479-502

WESTERN WEI 535-557   EASTERN WEI 534-550   LIANG 502-557

NORTHERN CHOU 557-581   NORTHERN CH'I 550-577   CH'EN 557-589

SUI 581-618

T'ANG 618-907

FIVE DYNASTIES 906-960   TEN KINGDOMS 907-979

NORTHERN HAN 951-979
(reckoned as one of the Ten Kingdoms)   SUNG 960-1126

(the extreme north of China being ruled by the LIAO 947-1125)

CHIN 1126-1234   SOUTHERN SUNG 1127-1279

YUAN 1279-1368
(having succeeded the CHIN in North China in 1234)

MING 1368-1644

CH'ING 1644-1912

they occupied the coasts as far as the Gulf of Tonkin; Annam accepted their suzerainty and Indo-China has been regarded by Chinese statesmen as part of their proper sphere ever since. To the north-east they penetrated Korea. All this was the work of the later, or 'eastern', Han whose capital was at Loyang. From there they continued to press forward in Turkestan and raised tribute from the oases of central Asia. One general in AD 97 got as far as the Persian Gulf.

This expansion gave China much more contact with the rest of the world. Before the nineteenth century this was almost solely by land and besides the silk trade which linked her regularly with the Near East (caravans were leaving for the West with silk from about 100 BC), China also developed more elaborate exchanges with her nomadic neighbours. Sometimes this was within the framework of tribute and a fictional acknowledgement of it by goods in return, sometimes within official monopolies which were

the foundation of great merchant families. Nomadic contacts may explain one of the most astonishing works of Chinese art, the great series of bronze horses found in tombs at Wu-Wei. These were only one among many fine works of Han bronze-workers; they evidently broke more readily with tradition than the Han potters, who showed more antiquarian respect for past forms. At a different level, though, Han pottery provides some of the very few exploitations in art of the subject-matter of the daily life of most Chinese in the form of collections of tiny figures of peasant families and their livestock.

This was a brilliant culture, centred on a court with huge, rich palaces built in the main of timber – unhappily, for the result is that they have disappeared, like the bulk of the huge Han collections of paintings on silk. Much of this cultural capital was dissipated or destroyed during the fourth and fifth centuries, when the barbarians returned to the frontiers. After failing at last to guarantee China's defence from

485

her own manpower, the Han emperors fell back on a policy tried elsewhere, that of bringing within the Wall some of the tribes who pressed on it from outside and deploying them in its defence. This raised problems of relations between the newcomers and the native Chinese. The Han emperors could not prolong for ever their empire, and after four hundred years China once more dissolved into a congeries of kingdoms.

Some of these had barbarian dynasties, but in this crisis there is observable for the first time the striking powers of China's cultural digestion. Gradually the barbarians were swallowed by Chinese society, losing their own national identity and becoming only another kind of Chinese. One Tatar ruler actually imposed Chinese customs and dress on his people by decree in 500. The central Asian threat was not over; far from it, there appeared in Mongolia in the fifth century the first Mongol empire. None the less, when the T'ang, a northern dynasty, came to receive the mandate of heaven in 618 China's essential unity was in no greater danger than it had been at any time in the preceding two or three centuries.

Political disunity and barbarian invasion had not damaged the foundations of Chinese civilization, which entered its classical phase under the T'ang. Among those foundations, the deepest continued to lie in kinship. Throughout historical times the clan retained its importance because it was the mobilized power of many linked families, enjoying common institutions of a religious and sometimes of an economic kind. The diffusion and ramification of family influence was all the easier because China did not have primogeniture; the paternal inheritance was usually divided at death. Over a social ocean in which families were the most significant fish presided one authority, that of the state. To it and the family the Confucians looked for authority, their acceptance of it untroubled by the existence of church and communes which confused questions of right and government so fruitfully in Europe.

The state's essential institutions, too, were

Early Chinese architecture, of which little has survived, is somewhat known to us through Han pottery models such as this one. They were made to be placed in the tombs of the rich along with other replicas of the goods, animals and servants they had enjoyed in life.

there by T'ang times. They also lasted until this century and the attitudes they built up linger on still. In their making, the consolidating work of the Han had been especially important, but the office of the emperor, holder of the mandate of heaven, could be taken for granted even in Ch'in times. The comings and goings of dynasties did not compromise the standing of the office since they could always be ascribed to the withdrawal of the heavenly mandate. The emperor's liturgical importance was, if anything, enhanced by the inauguration under the Han of a sacrifice only he could make. Yet his position also changed in a positive sense. Gradually, a ruler who was essentially a great feudal magnate, his power an extension of that

486

of the family or the manor, was replaced by one who presided over a centralized and bureaucratic state.

This had begun a long way back. Already in Chou times a big effort was made to build canals for transport. Great competence in organization and large human resources were required for this and only a potent state could have deployed them. A few centuries later the Ch'in dynasty was strong enough to standardize weights and measures and impose a degree of disarmament on its subjects while itself putting in the field perhaps a million soldiers. The Han were able to impose a monopoly of coining and standardized the currency. Under the Han, too, entry to the civil service by competitive examination began, though it was to fade out again, not to be resumed until T'ang times.

This was very important. The bureaucracy was to survive centuries of disunion (a proof of its vigour) and remained to the end one of the most striking and characteristic institutions of imperial China. It was probably the key to China's successful emergence from the era when collapsing dynasties were succeeded by competing petty and local states which broke up the unity already achieved. It linked China together by an ideology as well as by administration. The civil servants were trained and examined in the Confucian classics; under the Han, legalism finally lost its grip after a lively ideological struggle. Literacy and political culture were thus wedded in China as nowhere else.

The scholars had been deeply offended by the Ch'in. Though a few of them had been favoured and gave the dynasty advice, there had been a nasty crisis in 213 BC when the emperor turned on scholars who had criticized the despotic and militaristic character of the régime. Books were burned and only 'useful' works on divination, medicine or agriculture were spared; more than four hundred scholars perished. What was really at stake is not clear; some historians have seen this attack as an offensive aimed at 'feudal' tendencies opposed to Ch'in centralization. If so, it was far from the end of the confusion of cul-

An eighteenth-century album contains this painting of an examination, a traditional procedure long unchanged in China. Magistrates are here shown at their re-examination in the Confucian classics. The emperor himself (a T'ang monarch of the eighth century) assesses the results, on which promotion or dismissal was based.

tural and political struggle with which China continues to mystify observers today. Whatever the sources of this policy, the Han took a different tack and sought to conciliate the intellectuals.

This led first to the formalization of Confucian doctrine into what soon became an orthodoxy. The canonical texts were established soon after 200 BC. True, Han Confucianism was a syncretic matter; it had absorbed much of legalism. But the important fact was that Confucianism had been the absorbing force. Its ethical precepts remained dominant in the philosophy which formed China's future rulers. In AD 58 sacrifices to Confucius were ordered

487

in all government schools. Eventually, under the T'ang, came the reservation of administrative posts to those trained in this orthodoxy. For over a thousand years it provided China's governors with a set of moral principles and a literary culture painfully acquired by rote-learning. The examinations they underwent were designed to show which candidates had the best grasp of the moral tradition discernible in the classical texts as well as to test mechanical abilities and the capacity to excel under pressure. It made them one of the most effective and ideologically homogeneous bureaucracies the world has ever seen and also offered great rewards to those who successfully made the values of Confucian orthodoxy their own.

The official class was in principle distinguished only by educational qualification (the possession of a degree, as it were) from the rest of society. Most civil servants came from the landowning gentry, but they were set apart from them. Their office achieved by success in the test of examination, they enjoyed the highest status below the imperial family, and great material and social privileges besides. Official duties were general rather than specific, but they had two crucial annual tasks, the compilation of the census returns and the land registers on which Chinese taxation rested. Their other main work was judicial and supervisory, for local affairs were very much left to local gentlemen acting under the oversight of about two thousand or so district magistrates from the official class. Each of these lived in an official compound, the *yamen*, with his clerks, runners and minor staff about him.

The gentry undertook a great range of quasi-governmental and public service activities which were both an obligation of the privileged class and also an insurance of much of its income. Local justice, education, public works were all part of this. The gentry also often organized military forces to meet local emergencies and even collected the taxes, from which it might recoup its own expenses. Over the whole of these arrangements and the official class itself, there watched a state apparatus of control, checking and reporting on a bureaucracy bigger by far than that of the Roman empire and at its greatest extent ruling a much larger area.

This structure had huge conservative power. Crisis only threatened legal authority, never the social order. The permeation of governmental practice by the agreed ideals of Confucian society was rendered almost complete by the examination system. Moreover, though it was very hard for anyone not assured of some wealth to support himself during the long studies necessary for the examination – writing in the traditional literary forms itself took years to master – the principle of competition ensured that a continuing search for talent was not quite confined to the wealthier and established gentry families; China was a meritocracy in which learning always provided some degree of social mobility. From time to time there were corruption and examples of the buying of places, but such signs of decline usually appear towards the end of a dynastic period. For the most part, the imperial officials showed remarkable independence of their background. They were not supposed to act on such assumptions of obligation to family and connexion as characterized the public servants drawn from the eighteenth-century English gentry. The civil servants were the emperor's men; they were not allowed to own land in the province where they served, serve in their own provinces, or have relatives in the same branch of government. They were not the representatives of a class, but a selection from it, an independently recruited élite, renewed and promoted by competition.

Imperial China was thus not an aristocratic state; political power did not pass by descent within a group of noble families, though noble birth was socially important. Only in the small closed circle of the court was hereditary access to office possible, and there it was a matter of prestige, titles and standing, rather than of power. To the imperial counsellors who had risen through the official hierarchy to its highest levels and had become more than officials, the only rivals of importance were the court eunuchs. These creatures were often trusted with great authority by the emperors and were thus the only political force escaping the restraints of the official world.

Yet in the Chinese state there was little sense of the European distinction between government and society. Official, scholar and gentleman were usually the same man, combining many rôles which in Europe were increasingly divided between governmental specialists and the informal authorities of society. He combined them, too, within the framework of an ideology which was much more obviously central to society than elsewhere. The preservation of Confucian values was not a light matter, nor satisfiable by lip-service. The bureaucracy maintained those values by exercising a moral supremacy somewhat like that long exercised by the clergy in the West – and in China there was no Church to rival the state. The ideas which inspired it were profoundly conservative; the predominant administrative task was seen to be the maintenance of the established order; the aim of Chinese government was to oversee, conserve and consolidate, rarely to innovate. Its aim was regularity and the maintenance of common standards in a huge and diverse empire, where many district magistrates would be divided from the people in their charge even by language. In the achievement of its conservative aims, the bureaucracy was spectacularly successful and its ethos survived intact across all the crises of the dynasties.

Below the Confucian orthodoxy of the officials and gentry, it is true, other creeds were important. Even some who were high in the social scale turned to Taoism or Buddhism. The latter was to be very successful after the Han collapse when disunity gave it an opportunity to penetrate China. In its Mahayana variety it postulated more of a threat to China than any other ideological force before Christianity, for, unlike Confucianism, it posited the rejection of worldly values. It was never to be eradicated altogether, in spite of persecution under the T'ang; attacks on it were, in any case, probably mounted for financial rather than ideological reasons. Unlike

The influence of Buddhist style (deriving ultimately from India) is strong in this carved wooden effigy of an unidentified Taoist deity from Sung times, an era when Chinese art reached unsurpassed levels of sophistication in other forms, notably painting and ceramics.

the persecuting Roman empire, the Chinese state was more interested in property than in the correction of individual religious eccentricity. Under the fiercest of the persecuting emperors (who is said to have been a Taoist) over four thousand monasteries were dissolved, and over a quarter of a million monks and nuns dispersed from them. Nevertheless, in spite of such material damage to Buddhism, Confucianism had to come to terms with it. No other foreign religion was so successful with China's rulers until Marxism in the twentieth century; even some emperors were Buddhists.

Well before this, Taoism had developed into a

489

mystical cult (borrowing something from Buddhism in the process) appealing both to those who sought personal immortality and to those who felt the appeal of a quietistic movement as an outlet from the growing complexity of Chinese life. As such it would have enduring significance. Its recognition of the subjectivity of human thought gives it an appearance of humility which some people in different cultures with more self-confident intellectual traditions find attractive today. Such religious and philosophical traditions, important as they were, touched the life of the peasant directly only a little more than Confucianism, except in debased forms. A prey to the insecurities of war and famine, his outlet lay in magic or superstition. What little can be discerned of his life suggests that it was often intolerable, sometimes terrible. A significant symptom is the appearance under the Han of what became one of the major themes of Chinese history, punctuating it almost as rhythmically as the passing of dynasties, peasant rebellion. Oppressed by officials acting either on behalf of an imperial government seeking taxes for its campaigns abroad or in their own interest as grain speculators, the peasants turned to secret societies, another recurrent Chinese phenomenon. Their revolts often took religious forms, too. There is a recurrent millenarian, manichaean theme in Chinese revolution which burst out in many guises, but always posited a world dualistically divided into good and evil, the righteous and the demons. Sometimes this threatened the social fabric, but the peasants were rarely successful for long.

Chinese society in this period therefore changed very slowly. In spite of some important cultural and administrative innovations, the lives of most Chinese were for centuries little altered in style or appearance. The comings and goings of the dynasties were accounted for by the notion of the mandate of heaven and although great intellectual achievements were possible, China's civilization already seemed self-contained, self-sufficient, stable to the point of immobility. No innovation compromised the fundamentals of a society more closely woven into a particular governmental structure than anything in the West. This structure proved quite competent to contain such changes as did take place and to regulate them so as not to disturb the traditional forms.

One visibly important change was the continuing growth of commerce and towns which made it easier to replace labour service by taxation. Such new resources could be tapped by government to rule larger areas effectively and to provide a series of great material monuments of what the dynasties might realize. The Ch'in completed the line of the Great Wall to keep out the central Asians and protect a settled, agricultural society; later dynasties extended and sometimes rebuilt portions of it. It still astonishes the observer and far outranks the walls of Hadrian and Antoninus. Just before the inauguration of the T'ang, too, at the other end of this historical epoch, a great system of canals was completed which linked the Yangtze valley with the Yellow River valley to the north, and Hangchow to the south. Millions of labourers were employed on this and on great irrigation schemes. Such works are comparable with the Pyramids. They imposed equally heavy social costs, too, and there were revolts against conscription for building and guard duties. None the less, it was a state with potential and a civilization with impressive achievements already to its credit which entered its phase in 618.

For the next thousand years, as for the previous eight hundred, China's formal development can be linked to the comings and goings of five dynasties which provide a chronological structure (T'ang, 618–907; Sung, 960–1126; Mongol ascendancy, 1264–1368; Ming, 1368–1644; Manchu or Ch'ing, 1644–1912); some historical themes overrun their divisions. One is provided by demography. There was an important shift of the demographic centre of gravity towards the south during the T'ang period; henceforth most Chinese were to live in the Yangtze valley rather than the old Yellow River plain. The exploitation of new lands fed them, but new crops became available, too. Together they made possible an overall growth of population which accelerated under the Mongols and the Ming. Estimates have been made that a population of perhaps sixty-five million in the fourteenth century more than doubled in the next two hundred years, so that in 1600 there were about 150 million Chinese. This was a huge number, given contemporary populations elsewhere, but there was still greater increase to come.

The weight of this fact is great. Apart from the enormous importance it gives to China in world population history it puts in perspective the great manifestations of Chinese culture and imperial power, which rested on the huge mass of desperately poor peasants utterly unconcerned with such things. For the most part their lives were confined to their villages; only a few could hope to escape from this, or can have envisaged doing so. Most could have dreamed only of obtaining the precarious, but best, security available to them; the possession of a little land. Yet this became more and more difficult as numbers grew and, gradually, all available cultivatable land was occupied. It was farmed more and more intensively in smaller and smaller plots. The one way out of the trap of famine was rebellion. At a certain level of intensity and success this could usually win support from the gentry and officials whether from motives of prudence or sympathy. When that happened, the end of a dynasty was probably approaching, for Confucian principles taught that, although rebellion was wrong if a true king reigned, a government which provoked rebellion and could not control it ought to be replaced for it was *ipso facto* illegitimate. At the *very* end of this long road lay the success of a Chinese revolution based upon the peasants in the twentieth century.

For many centuries, population pressure, a major fact of modern China's history, was evident to the authorities only in indirect and ambiguous ways. A much more pressing and familiar threat came from the outside. Essentially the problem was rather like that of Rome, a long frontier beyond which lay barbarians. T'ang influence over them was weakened when

central Asia succumbed to Islam. Like their Roman predecessors, too, the T'ang emperors found that military measures led to a reliance on soldiers which could be dangerous. There were hundreds of military rebellions by local warlords under the T'ang and any rebellion's success, even if short-lived, had a multiplier effect, tending to disrupt administration and damage the irrigation arrangements on which food (and therefore internal peace) depended. An empire which had sent armies to fight the Arabs and received ambassadors from Haroun-al-Raschid and which had been thought of as a possible ally by Byzantium was a great world power, but in the end the huge task of survival was too much for it. Unable effectively to police their frontier, the T'ang went under in the tenth century, China collapsing again into political chaos. The Sung who emerged from it had to face an even graver external threat, that of the Mongols, and were swallowed after the barbarian dynasty which had evicted them from north China had itself been engulfed by the warriors of Chinghis Khan.

During the whole of this time, the continuity and recuperative power of the bureaucracy and the fundamental institutions of society kept China going. After each dynastic change, the inheritors of power, even if they came from outside, turned to the relatively small number of officials (an estimate for the eighteenth century gives less than 30000 civil and military officers actually in post). They thus drew into the service of each new government the unchanging values of the Confucian system, which were strengthened, if narrowed, by disaster. Only a small number of especially crucial matters were ever expected to be the reserved province of the imperial government. Confucian teaching supported this distinction of spheres of action and made it easy for the dynasty to change without compromising the fundamental values and structure of society. A new dynasty would have to turn to the officials for its administration and to the gentry for most of its officials who, in their turn, could get some things done only on the gentry's terms.

Recurrent disunity did not prevent China's

Chinese artists always found horses endlessly fascinating as subjects. This is a highly naturalistic moulding in the green and yellow glazed pottery of T'ang times.

rulers, sages and craftsmen from bringing Chinese civilization to its peak in the thousand years after the T'ang inauguration. Some have placed the classical age as early as the seventh and eighth centuries, under the T'ang themselves, while others discern it under the Sung. This depends partly on the art-form considered, but Sung achievement was in any case a culmination of development begun under the T'ang, between whom and the Han much more of a break in style is apparent. It was in fact the last important break in the continuity of Chinese art until this century.

T'ang culture reflects the stimulus of contacts with the outside world, but especially with cen- tral Asia, which China enjoyed to an unprecedented degree under this dynasty. The capital was then at Ch'ang-an, in Shensi, a western province. Its name means 'long-lasting peace' and to this city at the end of the Silk Road came Persians, Arabs and central Asians who made it one of the most cosmopolitan cities in the world. It was an especially tolerant era and the city contained Nestorian churches, Zoroastrian temples, Moslem mosques. Ch'ang-an was probably the most splendid and luxurious capital of its day, as the objects which remain to us show. Many of them reflect Chinese recognition of styles other than their own – the imitation of Iranian silverware, for example – while the flavour of a trading entrepôt is preserved in the pottery figures of horsemen and loaded camels which reveal the life of central Asia swirling in the streets of Ch'ang-an. These figures were often finished with the new polychromatic glazes achieved by

T'ang potters; their style was imitated as far away as Japan and Mesopotamia. The presence of the court was as important a stimulus to such craftsmanship as the visits of merchants from abroad and from tomb-paintings something of the life of the court aristocracy can be seen. The men relax in hunting, attended by central Asian retainers; the women, vacuous in expression, are luxuriously dressed and, if servants, elaborately equipped with fans, cosmetic boxes, back-scratchers and other paraphernalia of the boudoir. Great ladies, too, favour central Asian fashions borrowed from their domestic staff.

The culture of Ch'ang-an never recovered from its disruption by rebellion in 756, only two years after the foundation of an Imperial Academy of Letters (about nine hundred years before any similar academy in Europe). After this the dynasty was in decline. The Sung ascendancy produced more great pottery; the earlier, northern phase of Sung history was marked by work still in the coloured, patterned tradition, while southern Sung craftsmen came to favour monochromatic, simple products. Significantly, they attached themselves to another tradition; that of the forms evolved by the great bronze-casters of earlier China. For all the beauty of its ceramics, though, Sung culture is more notable for some of the highest achievements of Chinese painting, their subject-matter being, above all, landscape.

Other Chinas are obscured by the bias of the documentation towards the official culture and the dazzling achievements of Chinese art. One is that of women. We hear little of them, except in sad little poems and love-stories. Yet they must have made up about half of the population, or perhaps slightly less, for girl babies rather than boys were exposed by poor families in hard times to die. That fact, perhaps, characterizes women's place in China until very recent times even better than the more familiar and superficially striking practice of foot-binding, which produced grotesque deformations and could render a high-born lady almost incapable of walking. Another China still all but excluded from the historical evidence by the

nature of the established tradition was that of most male Chinese, the peasants. They become visible only as numbers in the census returns and as eruptions of revolt; after the Han pottery figures, there is little in Chinese painting or literature to reveal them, and certainly nothing to match the uninterrupted recording of the life of the common man in the fields which runs from medieval European illumination, through the vernacular literature to the Romantics, and into the peasant subjects of the Impressionists.

Official culture also excluded the tenth or so of the Chinese population who lived in the cities, some of which grew as time passed to become the biggest in the world. Ch'ang-an, when the T'ang capital, is said to have had two million inhabitants. No eighteenth-century European city was as big as Canton or Peking, which may have then had as many as two million inhabitants. These and other cities housed societies of growing complexity. Their development fostered a new commercial world; the first Chinese paper money was issued in 650. Prosperity created new demands, among other things for a literature which did not confine itself to the classical models and in a colloquial style far less demanding than the elaborate classical Chinese. City life thus gradually secreted a literate alternative to the official culture, and because it was literate, it is the first part of unofficial China to which we have some access. Such popular demand could be satisfied because of two enormously important inventions, that of paper in the second century AD, and of printing in the tenth. This derived from the taking of rubbed impressions from stone under the Han. Printing from wood blocks was taking place under the T'ang and movable type appeared in the eleventh century AD. Large numbers of books were soon published in China and this was long before they appeared anywhere else. In the cities, too, flourished popular poetry and music which abandoned the classical tradition.

It is very striking that this did not add up to conditions such as those which in Europe produced a dynamic, progressive society. In spite

493

Wall-paintings in rich tombs of the eastern Han period often show the cortège of a high official making a progress through his jurisdiction. This example from the second century AD was found at An-p'ing, Hopei.

of printing, the great mass of Chinese remained illiterate down to the present century. China's great cities, for all their growth and commercial vitality, produced neither the freedom and immunities which sheltered men and ideas in Europe, nor the cultural and intellectual life which in the end revolutionized European civilization, nor effective questioning of the established order. In technology there is a similar strange gap between fertility and revolutionary change. The Chinese had a far more efficient wheelbarrow than other civilizations, but agricultural innovation in technology after Chou times was slight. The most important improvements were in irrigation techniques, which favoured the production of rice. Increased production of other foods arose from the introduction of new varieties and crops which could be grown on marginal land rather than from new tools.

Other examples of a low rate of innovation are even more striking. Chinese sailors already had the magnetic compass in Sung times, but though a naval expedition was sent to the Persian Gulf, Aden and East Africa in the fifteenth century, its aim was to impress those places with the power of the Ming, not to accumulate information and experience for further voyages of exploration and discovery. Masterpieces had been cast in bronze in the second millennium BC and the Chinese knew how to cast iron fifteen hundred years before Europeans, yet the engineering potential of this metallurgical tradition was unexplored. What he called 'a sort of black stone' was burnt in China when Marco Polo was there; it was coal, but there was to be no Chinese anticipation of the revolutionary use made of it elsewhere.

This list could be much lengthened. Perhaps the explanation lies in the very success of Chinese civilization in pursuit of a different goal, the assurance of continuity and the preven-

The opening of the roll of the Diamond Sutra, *virtually the world's first printed page. It was printed from a woodblock in 868. The scroll contains part of the Buddhist scriptures and the picture shows the Buddha preaching to an audience of monks, idols and Bodhisattvas.*

tion of fundamental change. Neither officialdom nor the social system favoured the innovator. Moreover, pride in the Confucian tradition and the confidence generated by great wealth and remoteness made it difficult to learn from the outside. This was not because the Chinese were intolerant. Jews, Nestorian Christians, Zoroastrian Persians, and Arab Moslems long practised their own religion freely, and the last even made some converts, creating an enduring Islamic minority. Contacts with the West multiplied, too, in Mongol times. But already by then, what has been called a 'neo-Confucian' movement was manifesting tendencies of defensive hostility, and formal tolerance had never meant that there was much receptivity in Chinese culture.

Invasion by the Mongols showed China's continuing seductive power over its conquerors. By the end of the thirteenth century, all China had been overrun by them, but the centre of gravity of the Mongol empire had moved from the steppes to Peking, Kubilai's capital. This grandson of Chinghis was the last of the Great Khans and after his time Mongol China can be considered Chinese, not Mongol. It changed the Mongols more than the Mongols changed China, and the result was the magnificence reported by the amazed Marco Polo. Kubilai made a break with the old conservatism of the steppes, the distrust of civilization and its works. The Mongols in China slowly succumbed to Chinese culture in spite of their initial distrust of the scholar officials. They were, after all, a tiny minority of rulers in a sea of Chinese subjects; they needed cooperation to survive. Kubilai spent nearly all his life in China, though his knowledge of Chinese was poor.

But the relationship of Mongol to Chinese was long ambiguous. Like the British in nineteenth-century India who set up social conven-

'Bamboo in Wind' was painted by Ku An during the Yuan Dynasty. The theme is common to painters of the period and was intended to symbolize Chinese courage in the face of Mongol oppression.

tions to prevent their assimilation by their subjects, so the Mongols sought by positive prohibition to keep themselves apart. Chinese were forbidden to learn the Mongol language, carry arms or marry Mongols. Foreigners, rather than Chinese, were employed in administration where possible, a device paralleled in the western khanates of the Mongol empire: Marco Polo was for three years an official of the Great Khan; a Nestorian presided over the imperial bureau of astronomy; Moslems from Transoxiana administered Yunan. For some years, too, the traditional examination system was suspended. Some of the persistence of Chinese hostility to the Mongols may be explained by such facts, especially in the south. When Mongol rule in China collapsed, seventy years after Kubilai's death, there appeared an,

if possible, even more exaggerated respect for tradition and a renewed distrust of foreigners among the Chinese ruling class.

The short-run achievement of the Mongols, none the less, was very impressive. It was most obvious in the re-establishment of China's unity and the realization of its potential as a great military and diplomatic power. The conquest of the Sung south was not easy, but once it was achieved (in 1279) Kubilai's resources were more than doubled (they included an important fleet inherited from the Sung) and he began to rebuild the Chinese sphere of influence in Asia. Only in Japan was he totally unsuccessful.

In the south, Vietnam was invaded (Hanoi was three times captured) and Thailand submitted a few years later. After Kubilai's death Burma was conquered in 1294. These conquests were not, it is true, to prove long-lasting and they resulted in tribute rather than prolonged occupation. In Java, too, success was qualified; a landing was made there and the capital of the island taken in 1292, but it proved impossible to hold it. Another legacy of Mongol times which was more long-lived was the further development of maritime trade with India, Arabia and the Persian Gulf which had been begun under the Sung.

Since, obviously, it failed to survive, the Mongol régime cannot be considered successful, but this does not take us far. Much that was positive was done in just over a century. Foreign trade flourished as never before. Marco Polo reports that the poor of Peking were fed by the largesse of the Great Khan, and it was a big city. A modern eye finds something attractive, too, about the Mongols' religious tolerance. Only Moslems were hindered in the preaching of their doctrine; Taoism and Buddhism were positively encouraged, for example, by relieving Buddhist monasteries of taxes (this, of course, meant heavier impositions on others, as any state endorsement of religion must; the peasants paid for religious enlightenment).

In the fourteenth century, natural disasters combined with Mongol exactions to produce a

A Taoist fresco of the Mongol period showing deities and the constellations of stars of which they form part.

wave of rural rebellions, the telling symptom of a dynasty in decline. They may have been made worse by Mongol concessions to the Chinese gentry. To give landlords new rights over their peasants would hardly bring the régime popular support. Secret societies began to appear again and one of them, the 'Red Turbans', attracted support from gentry and officials. One of its leaders, Chu Yüan-chang, a monk, seized Nanking in 1356. Twelve years later he drove the Mongols from Peking and the Ming era began.

Like many other Chinese revolutionary leaders Chu Yüan-chang gradually became an upholder of the traditional order. The dynasty he founded, though it presided over a great cultural flowering and managed to maintain the political unity of China which lasted from Mongol times to the twentieth century, confirmed China's conservatism and isolation. Naval ventures to Indonesia and across the Indian ocean were soon given up. An imperial decree forbade Chinese ships to sail beyond coastal waters or individuals to travel abroad. The merchants who had prospered under the Mongols were harassed.

In the end the Ming dynasty ran to seed. A succession of emperors was virtually confined to their palaces while favourites and imperial princes disputed around them the enjoyment of the imperial estates. Except in Korea, where the

Japanese were beaten off at the end of the sixteenth century, the Ming could not maintain the peripheral zones of Chinese empire. Indo-China fell away from the Chinese sphere, Tibet went more or less out of Chinese control and in 1544 the Mongols burnt the suburbs of Peking.

Under the Ming, too, came the first Europeans to seek more than a voyage of trade or discovery. In 1557 Portuguese established themselves at Macao. They had little to offer which China wanted, except silver; but missionaries followed and the official tolerance of Confucian tradition gave them opportunities they successfully exploited. They became very influential at the Ming court and in the early seventeenth century Chinese officials began to feel alarmed and ordered them back to Macao. Besides the mechanical toys and clocks which the missionaries added to the imperial collections and the scientific and cosmographical learning with which they interested Chinese intellectuals, they had other valuable skills. The correction of the Chinese calendar, which one Jesuit carried out, was of great importance, for the authenticity of the emperor's sacrifices depended on accurate dating. From the Jesuits the Chinese learnt also to cast heavy cannon, another useful art.

Early in the seventeenth century, the Ming needed any military advantages they could procure. They were threatened from the north by a people who were established in Manchuria, a province to which they later gave its name, but who were not known as Manchu until after their conquest of China. The way was opened to

497

them in the 1640s by peasant revolt and an attempted usurpation of the Chinese throne. An imperial general asked the Manchu to help him and they came through the Wall, but only to place their own dynasty, the Ch'ing, on the throne in 1644 (and incidentally wipe out the general's own clan). Like other barbarians and semi-barbarians, the Manchu had long been fascinated by the civilization they threatened and were already somewhat sinicized before their arrival. They were familiar with the Chinese administrative system, which they had imitated at their own capital at Mukden and found it possible to cooperate with the Confucian gentry as they extended their grip on China. The attachment of Manchu inspectors stimulated the bureaucracy who needed to change little in their ways except to conform to the Manchu practice of wearing pigtails (thus was introduced what struck Europeans of the nineteenth century as one of the oddest features of Chinese life).

The Manchu period opened with a great revival of Chinese power whose climax came under the Emperor K'ang-hsi. He reigned from 1662 to 1722, a period roughly corresponding to the reign of Louis XIV of France, whose own exercises in magnificence and aggrandizement were taking place in different forms but with curious parallels on the other side of the world. K'ang-hsi was capable of a personal violence which the Sun King would never have permitted himself (he once attacked two of his sons with a dagger) but for all the difference in the historical backgrounds which formed them, there is a similarity in their style of rule. Jesuit observers speak of K'ang-hsi's 'nobility of soul' and the description seems to have been prompted by more than the desire to flatter, and justified by more than his patronage. He was hard-working, scrutinizing with a close eye the details of business (and its manner, for he would painstakingly correct defective calligraphy in the memorials placed before him), and he refreshed himself by indulging his passion for hunting.

Characteristically, though K'ang-hsi was unusual among the Chinese emperors in admiring European skill (he patronized the Jesuits for their scientific knowledge), the merits of his reign were set firmly within accepted tradition; he identified himself with the enduring China. He rebuilt Peking, destroyed in the fighting of the Manchu invasion, carefully restoring the work of the Ming architects and sculptors. It was as if Versailles had been built in the Gothic style or London rebuilt in Perpendicular after the Great Fire. K'ang-hsi's principles were Confucian and he had classical works translated into Manchu. He sought to respect ancient tradition and assured his Chinese subjects their usual rights; they continued to rise to high office in the civil service in spite of its opening to Manchus, and K'ang-hsi appointed Chinese generals and viceroys. In the style of his personal life the emperor was, if not austere, at least moderate. He enjoyed the bracing life of the army and on campaigns lived simply and un-luxuriously; in Peking the pleasures of the palace were deliberately reduced and the emperor relaxed from the burdens of state with a harem of a mere three hundred girls.

K'ang-hsi restored Chinese control of Formosa, occupied Tibet, mastered the Mongols and made them quiescent vassals. This was something of a turning-point, as final as anything can be in history, for in central Asia the nomadic peoples from this time at last begin gradually to recede before the settler. On the other hand, further north, in the Amur valley, another chapter of the future opened when, in 1685, a Chinese army attacked a Russian post at Albazin. Negotiations led to the withdrawal of the Russians and the razing of their fort. This was far from being the final settlement of accounts between China and the only European power with which she shared a land frontier but it quietened things for a time. Later, in the eighteenth century, the Chinese again invaded Tibet and reimposed vassal status on Korea, Indo-China and Burma. These were major feats of arms.

On these foundations were based the domestic peace and prosperity which outstandingly marked the last years of Manchu success. It was a silver age of the Chinese classical civilization

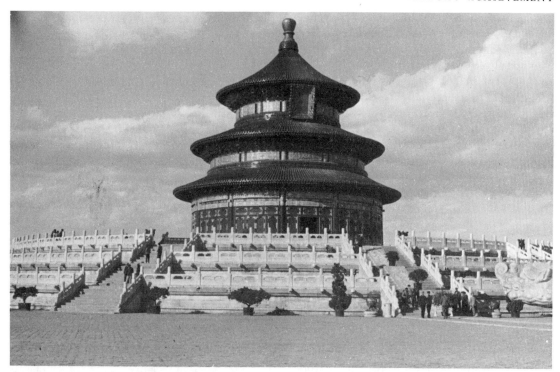

On the site of an ancient shrine, the wooden Temple of Heaven of Peking as it now appears is largely the creation of an eighteenth-century repair programme. Its basic design, though, goes back to pre-Han times, an example of the conservatism of Chinese architecture exemplified in the ground plan of the 'forbidden city' of Peking itself which followed the gridiron street-plan prescribed by the ancient books of architecture. Properly speaking, the 'forbidden city' was the Palace compound only; the Temple of Heaven lay outside this central area.

which some scholars believe to have reached its peak under the later Ming. If it did, it was still to produce much beauty and scholarship under the Manchu. Great efforts of compilation and criticism, initiated and inspired by K'ang-hsi himself, opened a hundred years of transcription and publication which not only spawned such monsters as a five-thousand-volume encyclopedia, but also large collections of classical editions now given canonical form.

In K'ang-hsi's reign, too, the imperial kilns began a century of technical advance in enamelling which produced exquisite glazes. However the level of the Manchu achievement is judged, though, and however the emphasis is distributed between its various expressions in different arts, Manchu China's civilization was still, like that of its predecessors, the civilization of an élite. Although there was at the same time a popular culture of great vigour, Chinese civilization was as much the property of the Chinese ruling class as it always had been, a fusion of artistic, scholarly and official activity. Its connexion with government still gave Chinese civilization its distinctive tone and colour. It was profoundly conservative, not only in social and political matters but also in its aesthetic. The art it esteemed was based on a distrust of innovation and originality; it strove to imitate and emulate the best, but the best was always past. The traditional masterpieces pointed the way. Nor was art seen as the autonomous expression of aesthetic activity. Moral criteria were brought to the judgement of artistic work and these criteria were, of course, the embodiments of

Confucian values. Restraint, discipline, refinement, and respect for the great masters were the qualities admired by the scholar–civil servant who was also artist and patron.

This is, of course, to say no more than that whatever appearances might suggest at first sight, Chinese art was as little directed to escape from conventional life, and the values that governed it, as that of any other culture before the European nineteenth century. This was also paradoxically apparent in another of its traditional characteristics, the exaltation of the amateur and the disapprobation shown towards professionals. The man most esteemed was the official or landowner who was able to execute with sureness and apparent lack of effort works in the major fields of painting, calligraphy or literature. Brilliant amateurs were greatly admired and in their activities, Chinese art escapes from its anonymity; we often know such artists' names. Its beautiful ceramics and textiles, on the other hand, are the products of tradesmen whose names are lost, often working in the imperial kilns whose directors were civil servants. Artisans were not esteemed for originality; the craftsman was not encouraged to develop his skill to the point of innovation but towards technical perfection. Central direction of large bodies of craftsmen within the precincts of the imperial palace only imposed upon these arts a firmer stamp of traditional style. Even a brilliant explosion of new technical masteries at the imperial kilns during the reign of K'ang-hsi still expressed itself within the traditional canons of restraint and simplicity.

The final paradox is the most obvious and by the eighteenth century it seems starkly apparent. China had long made great technological advances yet never arrived at a mastery of nature which enabled her to resist western intervention. Gunpowder is the most famous example; the Chinese had it before anyone else, but could not make guns as good as those of Europe, nor even employ effectively those made for them by European craftsmen. Chinese sailors had long had the use of the mariner's compass and the use of a cartographical heritage which produced the first grid map, but they were not exploring navigators. They neither made great voyages across the Pacific like the more primitive Melanesians, nor did they map it, as did later the Europeans. For six hundred years or so before Europe had them, the Chinese made mechanical clocks fitted with the escapement which is the key to successful time-keeping by machines, yet the Jesuits brought with them an horological technology far superior to the Chinese when they arrived in the sixteenth century. The list of unexploited intellectual triumphs could be continued, by important

For six centuries China produced blue and white pottery and porcelain; it was widely exported and highly esteemed in Europe and the Middle East. Examples such as this vase, from the reign of Chia-ching, have been especially admired for the brilliance of their blue glazes and are also unusual in their frequent use of Taoist symbolism in their decorative motifs: Chia-ching was especially and even intolerantly Taoist.

OPPOSITE *A Sung scroll contains this picture of scholars writing – the most esteemed of the arts in China.*

Chinese innovations in hydraulics, for example, but there is no purpose in this. The main point is clear. Somehow, inventiveness went neglected by Confucian officialdom. A lack of interest was rooted in a social system which, unlike that of Europe, did not regard as respectable any association between the gentleman and technician.

Pride in a great cultural tradition long continued to make it very hard for China's rulers to learn from outside; to do so would have been to recognize an inadequacy in that tradition, an intolerably painful admission. To make things worse, Chinese morality prescribed contempt for the soldier and for military skills. In a period when external threats would multiply, China was, therefore, dangerously cramped in her possibilities of response. Even under K'ang-hsi there were signs of new challenges ahead. In his old age he had to restore Manchu power in Tibet, where Mongol tribes had usurped it. The Russians were by the beginning of the eighteenth century installed in Kamchatka, were expanding their trade on the caravan routes and were soon to press down into the Trans-Caspian region. Even peace and prosperity had a price, for they brought faster population growth. Here, insoluble, was another problem to upset the stability of the order authorized by the Mandate of Heaven. By 1800 the population of China was 300 million, perhaps even 400. There were then already signs all too clear of what such an increase might portend.

Japan

There was once something of a vogue in England for seeing Japan as the Great Britain of the Pacific. The parallel was developed at many levels; some were less plausible than others, but there was an indisputable hard nugget of reality in the facts of geography. Both are island kingdoms whose people's destinies have been shaped deeply by the sea. Both, too, are by no means far from neighbouring land masses whose influence on them was bound to be profound. The Straits of Tsushima which separate Korea from Japan are about five times as wide as the Straits of Dover, it is true, and Japan was able sometimes to maintain an isolation from the Asian *terra firma* far more complete than any England could hope for from Europe. Nevertheless, the parallel can be pressed a good way and its validity is shown by the excitement which the Japanese have always shown about the establishment of a strong power in Korea; it rivals that shown by the British over the danger from the northern French coast and the Low Countries.

Even before Japan emerges in her own historical records, in the eighth century AD, she had for a time held territory in the Korean peninsula. At that time, Japan was a country divided up among a number of clans, presided over by an emperor with an ill-defined supremacy and an ancestry traced back to the Sun Goddess. They did not take up the whole of the territory of modern Japan, but were centred on the southern and central islands. Here were the mildest climate and the best agricultural prospects. In prehistoric times, the introduction of rice-growing and the fishing potential of Japanese waters had already made it possible for this mountainous land to feed a disproportionately large population, but pressure on land was to be a recurrent theme of Japanese history.

In 645 a political crisis in the dominant clan brought about its downfall and the rise of a new one which was to preside over a great age of Japanese civilization by controlling the emperors. This was the Fujiwara. There was more than political significance in the change. What was involved was a conscious effort to redirect Japanese life along paths of renewal and reform. The direction could only be sought from the guidance offered by the highest example of civilization and power of which Japanese were aware, and possibly the finest in the world at that time, that of imperial China. It was also an example of an expanding, menacing power.

A continuing and often changing relationship with China is another continuing theme of Japanese history. Both peoples were of Mongoloid stock, though some Caucasoids whose presence it is difficult to account for also form a part of the Japanese ethnic heritage (these were, at the beginning of the historical era, mainly to be found in the north-east; they were Ainus). In prehistoric times Japan appears to have followed in the wake of the civilization of the mainland; bronze artifacts, for example, appear in the islands only in the first century or so BC. Such innovations in the last millennium BC may owe something to immigrants displaced by the Chinese as they moved southwards on the mainland. But the first references to Japan in the Chinese records (in the third century AD) still depict a country not much affected by Asian events and Chinese influence was not very specifically marked until the centuries following the Han collapse. Then a vigorous Japanese intervention in Korea seems to have opened the way to closer contact. It was subsequently fostered by the movement of Buddhist students. Confucianism, Buddhism, and iron technology were all brought from China to Japan. There were movements towards the carrying out of administrative changes on Chinese lines. Above all, Chinese writing had been brought to Japan and adopted for the transcription of the native language. Yet this cultural dependence had not been purchased at a cost of political submission.

The Japanese central administration was already quite considerable in scope and scale at the beginning of the period of centralization and great efforts of reform were made in the seventh and eighth centuries. Yet, in the end, Japan evolved not in the direction of a centralized monarchy but of what might be termed, in a western analogy, feudal anarchy. For almost nine hundred years it is impossible to find a political thread to Japanese history. Its social continuity, on the other hand, is much more obvious. From the beginnings of the historical era, even down to the present day, the keys to the continuity and toughness of Japanese society have been the family and the traditional religion. The clan was an enlarged family, and the nation a national family, the largest of all. Patriarchally, the emperor presided over the national family as did a clan leader over his clan or, even, the small farmer over his family. The focus of the family or clan was participation in the tradi-

From very ancient times, female images in clay were involved in Japanese devotion. With the coming of Buddhism both the practice of carving them in wood and also a new composure and tranquility began to characterize such objects. This is a ninth-century carving of Nakatasuhime, one of the supposed progenitors of the Japanese people.

tional rites, the religion known as Shinto, whose essence was the worship at the proper times of certain local or personal deities. When Buddhism came to Japan it was easily conjoined with this traditional way.

The institutional coherence of old Japan was less marked than its social unity. The emperor was its focus, but from the beginning of the eighth century, the emperor's power was more and more eclipsed and it remained so, in spite of the efforts of an occasional vigorous emperor, until the nineteenth century. This eclipse arose in part from the activities of the reform party of the seventh century itself, for one of its members was the founder of the great Fujiwara clan which, within a hundred years or so, tied itself by marriage closely to the imperial household. As children were frequently brought up in the household of their mother's family, the clan could exercise a crucial influence upon future emperors while they were children. In the ninth century the chief of the Fujiwara was made regent for the emperor – who was an adult – and for most of what is called the 'Heian' period (794–1185), that clan effectively controlled the central government in the emperor's name, through marriage alliances and court office. The power of the Fujiwara did something to disguise the decline of the royal authority, but, in fact, the imperial clan was tending to become simply one among several which existed in the shade of the Fujiwara, each of them governing its own estates more or less independently of the imperial régime.

The displacement of the emperor became much more obvious after the passing of the power of the Fujiwara. During the Heian era the focus of government had still been at the court, situated at the town of that name (the modern Kyoto). The 'Kamakura' period (1185–1333) was so called because power passed to a clan whose estates were in that area and 'the by-passing of the imperial court was much more obvious. It was early in the Kamakura period that there appeared the first of a series of military dictators who bore the title of *shogun*. These ruled in the name of the emperor, but in fact with a large independence. The emperor himself became in effect only one more clan leader living on the revenues of his own estates, even if the most eminent. So long as he acquiesced in the shogun's intentions he would have military power behind him; when he did not, he would be overruled.

This eclipse of the imperial power was so different from what had occurred in China, the model of the seventh-century reformers, that the explanation is not easy to see. Clearly, it was a complex one. There was a steady progression through the centuries from the exercise of a usurped central authority in the emperor's name to the virtual disappearance of any central authority at all. No doubt there was a funda-mental bias in the traditional clan loyalties of

Minamoto Yoritomo, the unscrupulous, brave and resourceful warrior who established in Kamakura a power which was the base of the first bakufu, *and who was the first of the Shoguns. This is a contemporary portrait; we have no such likenesses of the lords of early medieval Europe, some of whom must have been not dissimilar in their ambitions for their families – however inferior in their successes.*

Japanese society and the topography of Japan which would have told against any central power; remote valleys provided lodgements for great magnates. But other countries have met these problems successfully: the Hanoverian governments tamed the Scottish highlands with punitive expeditions and military roads. A more specific explanation can be seen in the way in which the land reforms of the seventh century, which were the key to political change, were in practice whittled away by the clans who exer-cised influence at court. Some of these were always important enough to exact privileges and exemptions, as were some religious institu-tions which held land. The commonest example of the abuses which resulted from this was the granting of tax-free manors to noblemen, who were imperial court officials, by way of payment for carrying out their duties. The Fujiwara themselves were unwilling to check this practice. At a lower level, smaller proprietors would then seek to commend themselves and their land to a powerful clan in order to get assured tenure in return for rent and an obligation to provide service. The double result of such developments was to create a solid base for the power of local magnates while starving the central administrative structure of support from taxation. Taxes (in the form of a share of the crops) went not to the imperial administration but to the person to whom a manor had been granted.

Such a civil service as there was, unlike the Chinese, was firmly reserved to the aristocracy. Not being recruited by competition, it would not provide a foothold for a group whose interests would be opposed to the hereditary aristocracy. In the provinces, indeed, the posts just below the highest level tended to go to the local notables, only the most senior appointments being reserved to civil servants proper.

No one planned that this should happen. Nor did anyone plan a gradual transition to military rule, whose origins lay in the need to make some of the families of the frontier districts responsible for defence against the still unsubdued Ainu peoples. Slowly the prestige of the military clans drew to their leaders the loyalties of men seeking security in troubled times. And, indeed, there was a need of such security. Provincial dissidence began to express itself in outbreaks of the tenth century. In the eleventh there was clearly discernible the emergence of a class of manorial officers of the great estates who enjoyed the reality of ownership of the lands of their formal masters and felt loyalties to the warrior clans in an elementary tie of service and loyalty. This was the situation in which the Minamoto clan rose to a dominance which recreated central government in the early Kamakura period.

In one way these struggles were a luxury. The Japanese could indulge them because they lived in an island-state where no foreign intruder was ever more than occasionally threatening.

Amongst other things, this meant that there was no need for a national army which might have mastered the clans. For the whole of her history Japan has never been successfully invaded, a fact which has done much to shape her peculiar national psychology. The consolidation of the national territory was for the most part achieved in the ninth century when the peoples of the north were mastered. After this, Japan rarely faced any serious external threat to her national integrity, though her relations with other states underwent many changes.

In the seventh century the Japanese had been ousted from Korea and this was the last time for many centuries that they were physically installed there. It was the beginning of a phase of cultural subservience to China which was matched by an inability to resist her on the mainland. Japanese policy in these years was to send embassies to China in the interests of trade, good relations and cultural contact. The last one went in the first half of the ninth century. Then, in 894, another envoy was appointed. His refusal to serve marks something of an epoch, for he gave it as his reason that China was too much disturbed and distracted by internal problems and that she had, in any case, nothing to teach the Japanese. Official relations were not resumed until the Kamakura period.

There were exploratory gestures in the thirteenth century. They did not prevent the expansion of irregular and private trade with the mainland in forms some of which looked much like freebooting and piracy. It may have been this which did much to provoke the two attempted Mongol invasions of 1274 and 1281. Both retired baffled, the second after grievous losses by storm – the *Kamikaze*, or 'divine wind', which came to be seen in much the same light as the English saw the storms which shattered the Armada – and this was of the greatest moment in strengthening the belief which Japanese came to hold in their own invincibility and national greatness. Officially, the Mongols' motive had been the Japanese refusal to recognize their claim to inherit the Chinese pretensions to empire and to receive

505

On her balcony, in the moonlight, the Lady Murasaki composes another chapter of the Tale of Genji, *the greatest work of Japanese literature and an unsurpassed exploration of the human heart and the life of love. The painting is of the seventeenth century.*

tribute from them. In fact, this conflict once more killed off the recently revived relations with China; they were not taken up again until the coming of Ming rule. By then the Japanese reputation as pirates was well established. They ranged far and wide through the Asian seas. They had the support of many of the feudal lords of the south and it was almost impossible for the shoguns to control them even when they wished (as they often did) to do

so for the sake of good relations with the Chinese.

The collapse of the Kamakura shogunate in 1333 brought a brief and ineffective attempt to restore real power to the emperor, which ended when confronted with the realities of the military power of the clans. In the ensuing period neither shogun nor emperor often had real power. Until the end of the sixteenth century civil warfare was almost continuous.

Yet these troubles did nothing to check the consolidation of a Japanese cultural achievement which remains across the centuries a brilliant and moving spectacle and still shapes Japanese life and attitudes even in an era of industrialism. It is an achievement notable for its power to borrow and adopt from other cultures without sacrificing its own integrity or nature.

Even at the beginning of the historical era, when the prestige of T'ang art makes the derivative nature of what is done in Japan very obvious, there was no merely passive acceptance of a foreign style. Soon, in the first of the great periods of high Japanese culture, in the eighth century, this is apparent in Japanese painting and poetry already written in Japanese, though men for centuries still wrote in Chinese when they were consciously producing works of art or learning (it had something of the status long held by Latin in Europe). At this time, and still more during the climax of the Fujiwara ascendancy, Japanese art other than religious architecture was essentially a court art, shaped by the court setting and the work and enjoyment of a relatively few. It was hermetically sealed from the world of ordinary Japan by its materials, subject-matter and standards. The great majority of Japanese would never even see what can now be discerned as the first great peak of Japanese culture. The peasant wove hemp and cotton; his womenfolk would no more be likely to touch the fine silks whose careful gradations of colour established the taste displayed by a great court lady's twelve concentric sleeves than would he be to explore the psychological complexities of the subtle novel of the Lady Murasaki, a study as compelling as Proust and

Kyoto: the palace of Ieyasu, founder of the Tokugawa shogunate, who persecuted the Christians and excluded the foreigner from Japan.

and even a cultural arrogance confirmed by the defeat of the Mongol invasions. A new element, too, was added to this culture during the centuries of war, and this was a military ideal, in part originating in criticism of the apparently effete tradition of the court circles, but then to blend with it. It was fed by the feudal ideal of loyalty and self-sacrificing service, by the warrior ideals of discipline and austerity, and by an aesthetic arising out of them. One of its characteristic expressions was an offshoot of Buddhism, Zen. Gradually there emerged a fusion of the style of the high nobility with the austere virtues of the *samurai* warrior which was to run through Japanese life down to the present day. Buddhism itself left a visible mark on the Japanese landscape in its temples and the great statues of the Buddha himself. Overall, the anarchy was the most creative of all periods of Japanese culture for in it there appeared the greatest landscape painting, the culmination of the skill of landscape gardening and the arts of flower arrangement, and the *No* drama.

In particular areas, civil war and lawlessness during these centuries often inflicted grave social and economic damage. As was long to be the case, most Japanese were peasants:

almost as long. Such art had the characteristics to be expected of the art of an élite insulated from society by living in the compound of the imperial palace. It was beautiful, refined, subtle, and sometimes brittle, insubstantial and frivolous. But it already found a place for an emphasis which was to become traditional in Japan, that on simplicity, discipline, good taste and a love of nature.

The culture of the Heian court attracted criticism in a broad sense from those provincial clan leaders who saw in it an effete and corrupting influence, sapping both the independence of the court nobles and their loyalty to their own clans. From the Kamakura period, a new subject-matter – the warrior – appears in both literature and painting. Yet, as the centuries passed, a hostile attitude to traditional arts changed into one of respect and during the troubled centuries the warring magnates showed by their own support for them that the central ideals of Japanese culture were holding fast. It was protected more and more by an insularity

Swordsmanship was highly esteemed in Japan in the age of the great fencing-masters, and the beautiful weapons of the Japanese smiths have remained treasured and revered possessions.

507

they might suffer terribly from an oppressive lord, from banditry, or the passage of such an army of retainers from a rival fief. Yet such damage was nationally insignificant, it seems. In the sixteenth century a great burst of castle-building testifies to the availability of substantial resources, there was a prolonged expansion of the circulation of copper coinage, and Japanese exports – particularly the exquisite examples of the work of the swordsmiths – began to appear in the markets of China and south-eastern Asia.

Sooner or later the Europeans were bound to come to find out more about this source of beautiful things. The first were the Portuguese who stepped ashore from Chinese ships in 1543. Others followed in the next few years and in their own ships. It was a promising situation. Japan was virtually without a central government to undertake the regulation of intercourse with foreigners and many of the southern magnates were themselves highly interested in competing for foreign trade. Nagasaki, then a little village, was opened to foreign trade by one of them in 1570. This nobleman was a zealous Christian and had already built a church there; in 1549 the first Christian missionary had arrived, St Francis Xavier. Nearly forty years later Portuguese missionaries were forbidden, so much had the situation changed, though the ban was not at once enforced.

Among the things brought by the Portuguese to Japan were muskets. The Japanese soon learnt to make them. This new weapon played an important part in assuring that the baronial wars of 'feudal' Japan came to an end, as did those of medieval Europe, with the emergence of a preponderant power, the revived shogunate. Its assumption by the Tokugawa family in the late sixteenth century inaugurated a period of Japanese history known as the 'great peace', which lasted until a revolutionary change in 1868.

During this time, for two and a half centuries, the emperor passed even further into the wings of Japanese politics and was firmly kept there. Court gave way to camp; the shogunate rested on a military overlordship. The shoguns themselves changed from being outstandingly im-portant feudal lords to being in the first place hereditary princes and in the second the heads of a stratified and centralized social system over which they exercised viceregal powers in the name of the emperor and on his behalf. This régime was called the *bakufu*. The *quid pro quo* provided by Ieyasu, the first Tokugawa shogun, was order and the assurance of financial support from the emperor.

The key to the structure was the power of the Tokugawa family itself. Ieyasu's origins had been pretty humble, but by the middle of the seventeenth century the clan is said to have controlled about one-quarter of Japan's rice-growing land. The feudal lords became in effect vassals of the Tokugawa house and many were related to it by ties of family and patronage. The term 'centralized feudalism' has been coined to label this system. Not all the lords, or *daimyo*, were linked in the same way to the shogun. Some were directly dependent, being vassals with a hereditary family attachment to the Tokugawa family. Others were related to it by marriage, patronage or business. Others, less reliable, formed an outer category of those families which had only at length submitted. But all were carefully watched. The lords lived alternately at the capital or on their estates; when they were on their estates, their families lived as potential hostages of the shogun at Yedo, the modern Tokyo.

Below the lords was a society strictly and legally separated into hereditary classes. The noble *samurai* were the lords and their retainers, the warrior rulers who dominated society and gave it its tone as did the gentry bureaucrats of China. They followed a spartan, military ideal symbolized by the two swords they carried – and were allowed to use on commoners guilty of disrespect. *Bushido*, their creed, stressed above all the loyalty owed by a man to his lord. The original links of the retainers with the land were virtually gone by the seventeenth century and they lived in the castle towns of their lords. The other classes were the peasants, the artisans, and the merchants, the lowest in the social hierarchy because of their non-productive character; the self-assertive ethos of the merchant which emerged in Europe was unthinkable in Japan, in spite of the vigour of Japanese trade. As the aim of the whole system was stability, attention to the duties of one's station and confinement to them was determinedly enforced. Japan wanted stability and her society accordingly came to emphasize the things that could ensure it: discipline, regularity, scrupulous workmanship, stoical endurance. At its best it remains one of the most impressive of man's social achievements.

The difficulty of this system was one it shared with the Chinese; it presumed effective insulation from the sources of change. It was for a long time threatened by the danger of a relapse into internal anarchy; there were plenty of discontented *daimyo* and restless swordsmen about in seventeenth-century Japan. At this time, one obvious external danger came from Europeans. They had already brought to Japan both guns, whose powerfully disruptive effect went beyond that which they achieved on their targets, and Christianity. This faith had at first been tolerated and even welcomed as something tempting traders from outside, and in the early seventeenth century the percentage of Japanese Christians in the population was higher than it has ever been since, but this happy state of affairs did not last. Christianity has always had great subversive potential. Once this was grasped by Japan's rulers, a savage persecution began. It not only cost the lives of thousands of Japanese martyrs, but brought trade with Europe almost to an end. The English left and the Spanish were excluded in the 1620s. After the Portuguese had undergone a similar expulsion they rashly sent an embassy in 1640 to argue the toss; almost all of its members were killed. Only the Dutch, who promised not to proselytize and were willing to trample on the cross, kept up Japan's henceforth tiny contact with Europe from an island on which they were allowed a trading station in Nagasaki harbour.

After this, there was no real danger of foreign trade linking up with internal discontent. But there were other difficulties besides the foreigners. In the new settled conditions of the 'great peace' of the Tokugawa shogunate, military skill declined. The retainers sat about in the castle towns of their lords, their leisure broken by little except the ceremonial parade in outdated armour which accompanied a lord's progress to Yedo. When the Europeans came back in the nineteenth century with up-to-date weapons, Japan's military forces would be technically unable to match them.

This could, perhaps, hardly have been foreseen. Nor could a paradoxical result of the general peace in which internal trade prospered. The Japanese economy became more dependent on money. Old relationships were weakened by this. Payment in cash forced lords to sell most of the tax rice which was their subsistence to pay for their visits to the capital. At the same time, the economy became a national one. Merchants did well: some of them soon had money to lend their rulers. Gradually the warriors became dependent on the bankers. Besides feeling a shortage of cash, those rulers also found themselves sometimes embarrassed by their inability to deal with economic change and its social repercussions. If retainers were to be paid in coin, they might more easily transfer loyalty to another paymaster. Towns were growing, too, and this meant other changes would follow. Price fluctuations in the rice market of the towns sharpened hostility towards the wealthy dealers. There were also good results, of course. The new prosperity of the towns created a clientele for printed books and the coloured wood-block prints, which were later to excite European artists' admiration, as well as audiences for the *kabuki* theatre. Yet successful in some ways though it was, it is not clear that the Tokugawa system could have survived even without the coming of a new threat from the West in the nineteenth century. Towards the end of the Tokugawa period there were signs of uneasiness as Japanese intellectuals began to sense that somehow their isolation had preserved them from Europe but also had cut them off from Asia. Japan had already made for herself a unique historical destiny which would mean that she faced the West in a way very different from the subjects of Manchu or Moghul.

8 Worlds apart

The movement of Africa and the Americas towards civilization was governed by rhythms very different from those operating elsewhere. Of course, this was not quite so true of Africa as of the Americas, which were cut off by the ocean from all but the most fleeting contacts with the rest of the world. The Africans, by contrast, not only lived in a continent much of which was eventually Islamized, but also in one which long had peripheral encounters of growing importance with first Arab and then European traders. Yet they never sucked Africa completely into the mainstream of world history until the late nineteenth century. This isolation combines with an almost complete dependence for much of the story on archaeological evidence to make African and American history an obscure business. Written records give only limited help in understanding these continents.

For early Africa, such evidence is in any case and for a very long time limited to references in Egyptian records and travellers' tales. African history before the coming of European trade and exploration is largely a matter of an internal dynamic we can barely discern, but we may presume folk-movements to have played a large part in it. African history is full of legends of migration and always they speak of movement

8000 feet up in the Andes, the Inca city of Machu Picchu was never reached by the Spaniards and its ruins were well preserved until their discovery in 1911. No written records survive to explain its history, but it seems to have been a religious centre, built in the fifteenth century AD.

from the north to the south and west. In each case, scholars have to evaluate the legend in its context, but the general tendency is striking. It seems to register a general trend, the enrichment and elaboration of African culture in the north first and its appearance in the south only much later.

The kingdom of Kush whose connexions with Egypt have been noted is there at the beginning of the story. Though by the fifth century BC the Kushites had lost control of Egypt and retreated once more to Meroe, their capital in the south, they had centuries of flourishing culture still ahead of them. From Egypt, perhaps, they had brought a hieroglyph which cannot yet be read (though claims are now being made to have penetrated it). Certainly they diffused their knowledge to the south and west in the Sudan, where notable metallurgical skills were later to flourish among the Nubians and Sudanese. In the last few centuries BC iron-working appears south of the Sahara, in central Nigeria. Its importance was recognized by its remaining the closely guarded secret of kings, but so valuable a skill slowly travelled southwards. By about the twelfth century AD it had penetrated the south-east and then the pygmies and the bushmen of the south were the only Africans still living in the Stone Age.

Probably the greatest importance of this spread of iron-working was the difference it made to agriculture. It made possible a new penetration of the forests, new tilling of the soil (which may be connected with the arrival of new food-crops from Asia in the early Christian era), and led therefore to new folk-movements and more population growth. Hunting and gathering areas were broken up by the coming of herdsmen and farmers who can be discerned already by about 500 in much of East and south-east Africa, in modern Rhodesia and the Transvaal. Yet Africans did not acquire the plough. Possibly the reason lies in the lack in most parts of the continent south of Egypt of an animal resistant enough to African diseases to draw one. One area which did have the plough was Ethiopia and there animals could be bred successfully, as the early use of the horse there indicates. Horses were also bred for riding in the southern Sahara.

This suggests once again the important limiting factor of the African environment. Most of the continent's history is the story of response to influences from the outside – iron-working and new crops from the Near East, Asia, Indonesia and the Americas; steam engines and medicine from nineteenth-century Europe – which made it possible gradually to grapple with African nature. Without these, Africa south of the Sahara seems almost inert in the face of the huge pressures exercised upon it by geography, climate and disease. It remained (with some exceptions) for the most part tied to a shifting agriculture, not achieving an intensive one; this was an adequate response but could not sustain more than a slow population growth. Nor did black Africa arrive at the wheel and thus it lagged behind in transport, milling and pottery.

The story was different north of the Equator. Much Kushite history waits, in the most literal sense, to be uncovered, for few of the major cities have yet been excavated. It is known that in about 300 Kush was overthrown by the Ethiopians. They were not then the unique people they were to become, whose kings would claim descent from Solomon and who would be for centuries the only Christian people in Africa outside Egypt. They were only converted to Christianity by Copts later in the fourth century; at that time they were still in touch with the classical Mediterranean world. But the

Egyptian civilization flowed into black Africa through the Sudanese kingdom of Meroe. This lion-headed god inscribed on a votive tablet in Meriotic is a relic of it.

Islamic invasions of Egypt placed between them and it a barrier which was not breached for centuries, during which the Ethiopians battled for survival against pagan and Moslem, virtually isolated from Rome or Byzantium. An Amharic-speaking people, they were the only literate non-Islamic African nation.

The only other place in Africa where Christianity established itself was in the Roman north. Here it had been a vigorous, if minority, cult. The violence of its dissensions and the pursuit of the Donatists as heretics probably explain its weakness when the Arab invasions brought it face to face with Islam. Except in Egypt, Christianity was extinguished in the Africa of the Arab states. Islam, on the other hand, was and has remained enormously successful in Africa. Borne by Arab invasion it spread in the eleventh century right across to the Niger and western Africa. Arab sources therefore provide our main information about the non-literate African societies which stretched across the Sudan and Sahara after the passing of Kush. They were often trading communities and may reasonably be thought of as city-states; the most famous was Timbuctoo, impoverished by the time Europeans finally got there, but in the fifteenth century important enough to be the site of an Islamic university. Politics and economics are still as closely intertwined in Africa as in any part of the world, and it is not surprising that the early kingdoms of black Africa should have appeared and prospered at the end of important trade routes where there was wealth to tap and merchants who appreciated stability.

Another African state, the earliest recorded by the Arabs, had a name later to be given to a modern nation: Ghana. Its origins are obscure, but may well have lain in the assertion of its supremacy by a people in the late pre-Christian era who had the advantage of iron weapons and horses. However this may be, the Ghana recorded by Arab chroniclers and geographers is already an important kingdom when it appears in the records in the eighth century AD. It collapsed in the twelfth and thirteenth centuries. At its greatest extent, Ghana spanned an area about five hundred miles across in the region framed to the south by the upper reaches of the Niger and Senegal and protected to the north by the Sahara. The Arabs spoke of it as 'the land of gold'; the gold came from the upper Senegal and the Ashanti, and was passed by Arab traders up to the Mediterranean by trans-Saharan routes or through Egypt. The most important other commodities traded across the Sahara were salt and slaves.

Ghana's collapse was followed by the pre-eminence of Mali, a kingdom whose ruler's wealth caused a sensation when in 1307 he made a pilgrimage to Mecca. This was a much bigger affair, taking in the whole Senegal basin and running about a thousand miles inland from the coast at the beginning of the fourteenth century. The Mali ruler is said to have had ten thousand horses in his stables. This empire broke up in the sixteenth century after defeat by the Moroccans. Other states were to follow. But although in some cases the Arab records speak of African courts attended by men of letters there is no native documentation which enables us to reach these peoples. Clearly they remained pagan

while their rulers belonged to the Islamic world. It may be that the dissolution of Ghana owed something to dissent caused by conversions to Islam. Arab reports make it obvious that the Islamic cult was associated with the ruler in the Sudanese and Saharan states but had also still to accommodate traditional practice from the pagan past – rather as early Christianity in Europe accepted a similar legacy. Nor did social custom always adapt itself to Islam: Arabic writers expressed shocked disapproval at the public nakedness of Mali girls.

Africa further south of the Sahara is even harder to get at. At the roots of the history which determined its structure on the eve of its absorption into world events was a folk-migration of the negroid peoples who speak languages of the group called Bantu. This is a term somewhat like 'Indo-European', referring to identifiable linguistic characteristics, not genetic qualities. The detailed course of this movement is, of course, still highly obscure but its beginnings lie in eastern Nigeria, where there existed early Bantu-speakers. From there they took their language and agriculture south, first into the Congo basin. There followed a rapid spread, round about the beginning of the Christian era, over most of southern Africa. This set the ethnic pattern of modern Africa.

Some peoples, speaking the language the Arabs called 'Swahili' (from the Arabic word meaning 'of the coast') established towns on the east African coasts which were linked to mysterious kingdoms in the interior. This was before the eighth century AD, when the Arabs began to settle in these towns and turn them into ports. The Arabs called the region the land of the Zanz (from which was later to come the name of Zanzibar) and said that its peoples prized iron above gold. It is probable that these polities had some kind of trading relations with Asia even before Arab times; who the intermediaries were it is not possible to say, but they may have been Indonesians such as those who colonized Madagascar. The Africans had gold and iron to offer for luxuries.

Even an approximate notion of the working

of these states is hard to arrive at. Monarchy was by no means the rule in them and a sense of the importance of ties of kin seems to have been the only widespread characteristic of black African polities. Organization must have reflected the needs of particular environments and the possibilities presented by particular resources. Yet kingship was widely diffused. Again, the earliest signs are northern, in Nigeria and Benin. By the fifteenth century there are kingdoms in the region of the great eastern lakes and we hear of the kingdom of the Kongo, on the lower Congo River. There are not many signs of organization on this scale and African states were for a long time not to produce bureaucratized administration or standing armies. The powers of kings must have been limited, not only by custom and respect for tradition, but by the lack of resources to command men's allegiance beyond the ties imposed by kinship and respect. No doubt this accounts for the transitory and fleeting nature of many of these 'states'. Ethiopia was an untypical African country.

Yet some remarkable traces were left by these dim and shadowy kingdoms. A high level of culture in the east African interior in about the twelfth century is demonstrated by the remains of mine-workings, roads, rock paintings, canals and wells; these were the product of a technology which archaeologists have called 'Azanian'. It was the achievement of an advanced Iron Age culture. Agriculture had been practised in the region since about the beginning of the Christian era. On the basis it provided, it was possible to exploit the gold which was for a long time easily accessible in what is now Rhodesia. Only simple techniques were needed at first; large quantities could be obtained by little more than scratching the surface. This drew traders to the area – Arabs first, and later Portuguese – but also other Africans as migrants. The search for gold had in the end to be taken underground as the most easily available supplies ran out.

None the less there was a rich enough supply to support a state lasting four centuries and the only significant stone building in southern

The Oba, or supreme ruler, of Benin. The leopards he holds are the symbols of the authority of this king-like figure. Such plaques were made to commemorate the Obas; this one was made in about 1600.

Africa. There are relics of it in hundreds of places in south-east Rhodesia, but the most famous is at Zimbabwe (whose name means only 'stone houses'). From about 1400 this was a royal capital, the burial place of kings and a sacred site for worship. So it remained for about four centuries, until it was sacked in about 1830 by another African people. The Portuguese of the sixteenth century had reported a great fortress built of dry-stone masonry but only in the nineteenth century have we records by Europeans of what we know to be this site. They were amazed to find massive walls and towers in carefully shaped stone, laid in courses without mortar but with great accuracy. There was dis-

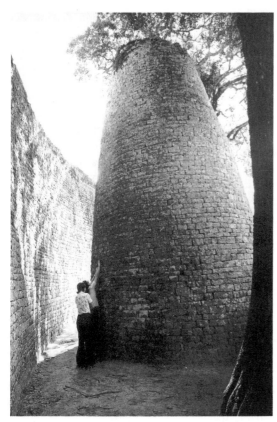

In the Zimbabwe ruins a massive tower stands in the middle of what has been called the 'Temple'. Built of shaped and fitted dry-stone masonry, it is fifty-eight feet round at its base. Its purpose is not known.

inclination to believe that Africans could have produced anything so impressive; some suggested the Phoenicians should have the credit and a few romantics toyed with the idea that Zimbabwe had been put there by the builders of the Queen of Sheba. Today, remembering the world of other Iron Age peoples in Europe and the civilizations of America, such hypotheses do not seem necessary. The Zimbabwe ruins may reasonably be attributed to the Africans of the fifteenth century.

Advanced as East Africa was, its peoples still failed to arrive at literacy for themselves; like Europeans, they were to acquire it from other civilizations. Perhaps the absence of a need for

careful records of land, or of crops which could be stored, is a part of the explanation. Whatever the reason, the absence of literacy was a handicap in acquiring and diffusing information and in consolidating government. It was also a cultural impoverishment; Africa would not have a native tradition of learned men from whom would come scientific and philosophic skill. On the other hand, the artistic capacity of black Africa was far from negligible, as the achievement of Zimbabwe, or the bronzes of Benin which captivated later Europeans, show.

Islam had been at work in Africa for nearly eight hundred years (and before that there had been the influence of Egypt) by the time the Europeans arrived in America. They found there civilizations which had achieved much more than those of Africa and appeared to have done so without the stimuli available to African cultures from the outside. This has seemed so improbable to some people that much time has been spent investigating and discussing the possibility that the elements of civilization were implanted in the Americas by trans-Pacific voyagers a very long time ago. It is generally considered that the evidence is inconclusive. Undoubtedly, if there was such contact in remote times, it had long since ceased. There is no unequivocal trace of connexion between the Americas and any other continent from the time when the first Americans crossed the Bering Straits to the landings of Vikings. There is then none thereafter until the Spanish arrived at the end of the fifteenth century. To an even greater degree than Africa, and for a longer time, we must assume the Americas to have been cut off from the rest of the world.

Their isolation accounts for the fact that even in the nineteenth century pre-agricultural peoples still survived in North America. On the eastern plains of the modern United States there were Indians practising agriculture before the arrival of Europeans, but further west other communities were then still hunting and gathering. They were to continue to do so, though not without important changes of techniques as first the horse and metal, brought by Europeans, and

A bronze head made by Iyoba craftsmen in Benin, possibly in the sixteenth century. It is one of the finest examples of the skill of West African smiths.

then firearms were added to their technical equipment. Further west still, there were peoples on the west coast who fished or collected their subsistence on the seashore, again in ways fixed since time immemorial. Far to the north, a *tour de force* of specialization has enabled the Eskimos to live with great efficiency in an all but intolerable environment; this pattern survives in its essentials even today. Yet although the Indian cultures of North America are respectable achievements in their overcoming of environmental challenge, they are not civilization. For the American achievement in indigenous civilization it is necessary to go south of the Rio Grande. Here were to be found a series

of civilizations linked by common dependence on the cultivation of maize and by possessing pantheons of nature gods, but strikingly different in other ways.

In Meso-america the Olmec foundation proved very important. The calendars, hieroglyphics and the practice of building large ceremonial sites which mark so much of the region in later times may all be ultimately derived from it; the gods of Meso-america were already known in Olmec times, too. Between the beginning and the fourth centuries of the Christian era the successors of the Olmecs built the first great American city, Teotihuacán, which for two or three centuries was a major trading centre and probably of outstanding religious importance, for it contained a huge complex of pyramids and great public buildings. Mysteriously, it was destroyed in about the seventh century, possibly by one of a series of waves of invaders moving southwards into the valley of central Mexico. These movements produced several regional societies of some brilliance but with them began an age of migration and warfare which was to last until the coming of the Spaniards.

The most remarkable of these was the Maya society of Yucatán, Guatemala and Honduras. Even its setting was extraordinary. Virtually all the great Mayan sites lie in tropical rain-forest, a setting which when cleared is briefly immensely fertile, but demands big efforts under heavy attacks from animals, insects, climate and disease. Yet in such a setting the Mayans not only maintained themselves for many centuries with a primitive agricultural technique (they lacked ploughs and metal tools and after burning and clearing land could only use it for a couple of seasons before moving on to another site), but also raised stone buildings comparable to those of ancient Egypt.

Many Maya sites may remain undiscovered in the jungle, but enough have now been found to reconstruct an outline of Maya history and society. Maya culture begins to appear from about 100, blossoming into a great period between 600 and 900, when its finest buildings,

A Mayan clay beaker from Guatemala showing a dignitary seated in state, receiving offerings or homage.

have knowledge; they calculated an antiquity of hundreds of thousands of years. They may even have arrived at the idea that time has no beginning.

Stone hieroglyph and three surviving books tell us something about this calendar and also help to provide a chronology; the Maya of the classical era used to put up dated monuments every twenty years to record the passage of time. The last of them is dated to 928. By then, Mayan civilization had reached its peak. For all the skill of its builders and craftsmen in jade and obsidian, it had considerable limitations. The makers of the great temples never achieved the arch, they could not employ carts in their operations for the Mayans never discovered the wheel, while the religious world in whose shadow they lived was peopled by two-headed dragons, jaguars and grinning skulls.

Maya civilization was, that is to say, a very specialized achievement, requiring huge investments of labour in economically unproductive building. The Egyptians had done the same, but also much more. Remarkable though this was – for it arose out of a formidably difficult context – it may be the fundamental reason for a decline which begins to be apparent after the tenth century; perhaps Mayan civilization was overloaded at an early date. Soon after its beginning a people from the valley of Mexico, probably Toltec, seized Chichen Itza, the capital, and from this time the jungle centres of the south began to be abandoned. The invaders brought metal with them and also the Mexican practice of sacrificing prisoners of war. Their gods begin to appear in sculpture at the Mayan sites. Seemingly, there was also a shift of power from priests to secular rulers among the Mayans and a cultural recession marked by cruder pottery and sculpture; hieroglyph declined, too. Chichen Itza was abandoned in the thirteenth century after being sacked and the Mayan capital removed to a site defended by five miles of wall; the earlier sites had been usually undefended. This capital, too, was sacked, apparently by a rising among the Maya peasantry in about 1460, and with this Maya civilization may be con-

sculpture and pottery were produced. The Maya did not build cities, but great ceremonial complexes, combinations of temples, pyramids, tombs and ritual courts, usually uninhabited except by priests and their attendants. This in part explains their impressiveness; like the ziggurats and pyramids the great Maya towers were meant to impress the beholder with a sense of the remoteness of the gods and the importance of those who climbed the long flights of steps to commune with them. Whatever their social organization, the Maya at this stage appear to have been governed theocratically. Religious practice consisted of the performance of regular acts of intercession and worship in a cycle calculated from a calendar derived from astronomical observation. Many scholars have found this the only Mayan achievement worthy of comparison with the buildings and it was indeed a great feat of mathematics. Through the calendar, enough of Mayan thinking can be grasped to make it evident that this people's religious leaders had an idea of time much vaster than that of any other civilization of which we

A Mayan relief once forming part of the decoration of the lintel of a house shows a form of ritual self-torture. Before a priest-like figure kneels a suppliant who draws through his or her tongue a cord studded with thorns.

sidered at an end. In the sixteenth century Yucatán passed into the hands of the Spanish, though only in 1699 did the last Maya stronghold fall to them.

The Spaniards were only in the most formal sense the destroyers of Mayan civilization. It had already collapsed from within by the time they arrived. Explanation is not easy, given our information, and it is tempting to fall back on metaphor: Mayan civilization was the answer to a huge challenge, could meet it for a time, but only at the cost of burdens colossal in relation to resources and a narrow specialization. The result, as in the case of other American civilizations, was a virtually complete extinction; for not quite the same reasons as elsewhere, but equally decisively, Mayan tradition came to an end, leaving behind no technology, no living style, no literature, no institutions except at the most elementary level. What it left, instead, was a series of ruins which would bemuse and fascinate those who had later to try to explain them.

While Maya society was in its final decay, one of the last peoples to arrive in the valley of Mexico set up an empire there which amazed the Spanish more than anything they found in Yucatán. These were the Aztecs, who had entered the valley in about AD 1350, overthrowing the Toltecs who then exercised supremacy there. They settled in two villages on marshy land at the edge of Lake Texcoco; one of these was called Tenochtitlan and it was to be the capital of an Aztec empire which expanded in less than two centuries to cover the whole of central Mexico. Aztec expeditions went far south into what was later the republic of Panama but showed no diligence in settlement. The Aztecs were warriors and preferred an empire of tribute: their army gave them the obedience of some thirty or so minor tribes or states which they left more or less alone, provided the agreed tribute was forthcoming. The gods of these peoples were given the compliment of inclusion in the Aztec pantheon, but they preserved their own cults.

The centre of Aztec civilization was Tenochtitlan, the capital they had built up from the village. It stood in Lake Texcoco on a group of islands connected to the lake shores by causeways, one of which was five miles long and took eight horsemen abreast. The Spanish left excited descriptions of this city; its magnificence, said one, exceeded that of Rome or Constantinople. It probably contained about 100 000 inhabitants at the beginning of the sixteenth century and to its maintenance went what was received from the subject peoples. By comparison with European cities, it was an astonishing place, filled with temples and dominated by huge artificial pyramids, yet its magnificence seems to have been derivative, for the Aztecs exploited the skills of their subjects. Not a single important invention or innovation of Mexican culture can confidently be assigned to the post-Toltec period. The Aztecs controlled, developed and exploited the civilization that they found.

When the Spanish arrived, the Aztec empire was still expanding. Not all of its subject peoples were completely subdued, but Aztec rule ran from coast to coast. At its head was a semi-divine but elected ruler, chosen from a royal family. He directed a highly ordered and centralized society, making heavy demands on its members for compulsory labour and military service, but also providing them with an annual subsistence. It was a civilization pictographically literate, highly skilled in agriculture and the handling of gold, but knowing nothing of iron-working or the wheel. Its central rituals – which greatly shocked the Spaniards – included human sacrifice; no less than twenty thousand victims were killed at the dedication of the great pyramid of Tenochtitlan. Such holocausts re-enacted a cosmic drama which was the heart of Aztec mythology; it taught that the gods had been obliged to sacrifice themselves to give the sun the blood it needed as food.

This religion struck Europeans by its revolting details – the tearing out of victims' hearts, the flayings and ceremonial decapitations – but its bizarre and horrific accompaniments were

A figure of a kind often showing Toltec presence at a particular site before a pyramid at Chichén-Itzá, in Yucatán.

Fifteen-foot-high Toltec columns carved as the figures of warriors once supported the roof of a temple at Tula in Mexico.

The Mixtec Indians of Mexico were conquered by the Aztecs. This is a surviving Mixtec manuscript sent by Cortés to the emperor Charles V.

less significant than its profound political and social effects. The importance of sacrifice meant that a continual flow of victims was needed. As these were usually supplied by prisoners of war – and because death in battle was also a route to the paradise of the sun for thè warrior – a state of peace in the Aztec empire would have been disastrous from a religious point of view. Hence, the Aztecs did not really mind that their dependencies were only loosely controlled and that revolts were frequent. Subject tribes were allowed to keep their own rulers and governments so that punitive raids could be made upon them at the slightest excuse. This ensured that the empire could not win the loyalty of the subject peoples; they were bound to welcome the Aztec collapse when it came. Religion was also to affect in other ways the capacity to respond to the threat from Europeans, notably in the Aztecs' desire to take prisoners in battle, for sacrifice (rather than to kill) and in their belief that one day their great god, Quetzalcoatl, white-skinned and bearded, would return from the east, where he had gone after instructing his people in the arts.

Altogether, for all its aesthetic impressiveness and formidable social efficiency, the feel of Aztec civilization is harsh, brutal and unattractive. Few civilizations of which there is good

knowledge have pressed so far their demands on their members. It lived always in a state of tension, a pessimistic civilization, its members uneasily aware that collapse was more than a possibility.

To the south of Mexico and Yucatán lay several other cultures distinct enough in their degree of civilization but none of them was so remarkable as that furthest away, the Andean civilization of Peru. The Mexican peoples still lived for the most part in the Stone Age; the Andeans had got much further than this. They had created a true state. If the Maya excelled among the American cultures in the mathematics of their calendar, the Andeans were far ahead of their neighbours in the complexity of their government. The imagination of the Spaniards was captured by Peru even more than by Mexico, and the reason was not simply its immense and obvious wealth in precious metals, but its apparently just, efficient and highly complex social system. Some have always found accounts of it attractive, for it required an almost total subordination of the individual to the collective.

This was the society ruled by the Incas. In the twelfth century a people began to extend its control over earlier centres of civilization in Peru from their centre at Cuzco. Like the Aztec, they began as neighbours of old sites of civilization; they were barbarians who soon took over the skills and fruits of higher cultures. At the end of the fifteenth century the Incas ruled a realm extending from Ecuador to central Chile, their conquest of the coastal areas being the most recent. This was an astonishing feat of government, for it had to contend with the natural obstacles provided by the Andes. The Inca state was held together by about ten thousand miles of roads passable in all weathers by chains of runners who bore oral messages or others recorded in *quipu*, a code of knots in coloured cords. With this device elaborate records were kept. Though preliterate, the Andean empire was formidably totalitarian in the organization of its subjects' lives. The Incas became the ruling caste of the empire, its head

The wealth of gold found in the Americas obsessed the conquistadores; *this figure forms a handle for a ceremonial knife from Peru.*

becoming *Sapa Inca* – the 'only Inca'. His rule was a despotism based on the control of labour. The population was organized in units of which the smallest was that of ten heads of families. From these units, labour service and produce were exacted. Careful and tight control kept population where it was needed; removal or marriage outside the local community was not allowed. All produce was state property; in this way agriculturists fed herdsmen and craftsmen and received textiles in exchange (the llama was the all-purpose beast of Andean culture, providing wool as well as transport, milk and meat). There was no commerce. Mining for precious metals and copper resulted in an exquisite adornment of Cuzco which amazed the Spaniards when they came to it. Tensions inside this system were not dealt with merely by force, but by the resettlement of loyal populations in a disaffected area and a strict control of the educational system in order to inculcate the notables of conquered peoples with the proper attitudes.

Like the Aztecs, the Incas organized and exploited the achievements of culture which they found already to hand, though less brutally. Their aim was integration rather than obliteration and they tolerated the cults of conquered peoples. Their own god was the sun. The absence of literacy makes it hard to penetrate the mind of this civilization, but it is noticeable that though in a different way the Peruvians seem to have shared the Aztecs' preoccupation with death. Accidents of climate, as in Egypt, favoured its expression in rites of mummification; the dry air of the high Andes was as good a preservative as the sand of the desert. Beyond this it is not easy to say what divisions among the conquered peoples persisted and were expressed in the survival of tribal cults. When a challenge appeared from Europe it became apparent that Inca rule had not eliminated discontent among its subjects, for all its remarkable success.

All the American civilizations were in important and obvious ways very different from those of Asia or Europe. A complete literacy escaped them, though the Incas had record-keeping processes satisfactory enough for the maintenance of complex governmental structures. Their technologies, though they had certain skills at a high level, were not so developed as those of other centres of civilization at earlier dates. Though these civilizations provided satisfactory settings and institutions for cultures of intense (but limited) power, therefore the contribution of the indigenous Americans to the future was not to be made through them, but through the obscure, unrecorded discoveries of primitive cultivators who had first discovered how to exploit the ancestors of maize, potatoes and squash. In so doing they had unwittingly made a huge addition to the resources of mankind. The glittering civilizations built on this in the Americas, though, were not in the end to be more than beautiful curiosities in the margin of world history, ultimately without progeny.

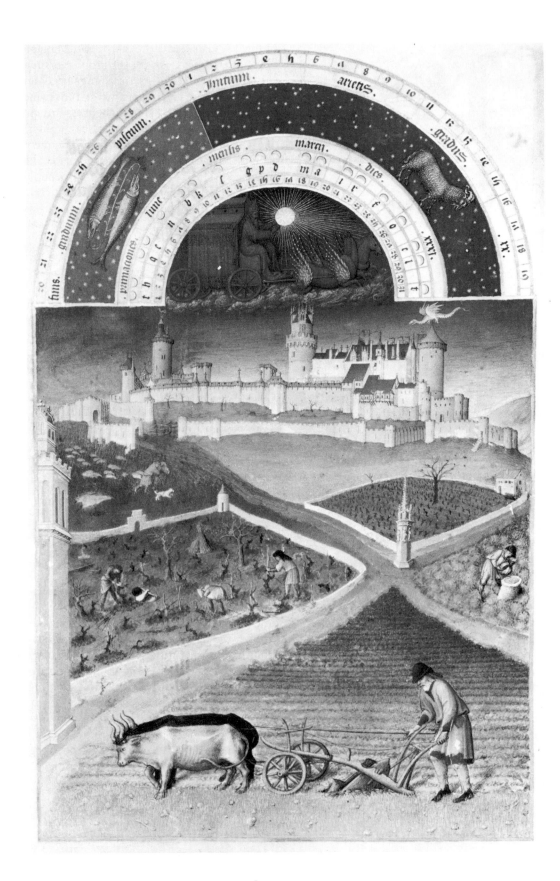

9 Europe: the first revolution

Few terms have such misleading connotations as 'the Middle Ages'. A wholly Eurocentric usage, meaning nothing in the history of other traditions, the phrase embodies the negative idea that no interest attaches to certain centuries except their position in time. They were first singled out and labelled by men in the fifteenth and sixteenth centuries who felt they were recapturing something of a classical antiquity long cut off from them. In that remote past, they thought, men had done and made great things; a sense of rebirth and quickening of civilization upon them, they could believe that in their own day great things were being done once more. But in between two periods of creativity they saw only a void – *Medio Evo, Media Aetas*, the Middle Ages – defined just by

Vine-trimming and ploughing, the farm-work which opened the medieval agricultural year in spring. The neat, tidied-up picture tells little of the back-breaking toil of the ordinary peasant, but shows much that would have been a familiar sight in western Europe in the fifteenth century – the castle dominating the landscape, or the oxen pulling a plough. The painting comes from a book of devotions belonging to a great patron of the arts, the Duc de Berry. Even in a magnificent collection of works of art which included many beautiful manuscripts, the Très riches heures *was acknowledged to be one of the finest possessions of the duke. It was executed for him by three brothers from Nimwegen (today in the Netherlands), the de Limbourgs.*

falling in between, and in itself dull, uninteresting, barbaric.

It was not long before people did better than this. One way in which they gained perspective on the past was by searching it for the origins of what they knew; seventeenth-century Englishmen talked about a 'Norman Yoke' supposedly laid on their ancestors and eighteenth-century Frenchmen idealized their nobility by attributing its origins to Frankish Conquest. Such reflexions, none the less, were very selective; in so far as the Middle Ages were thought of as a whole they were still, even two hundred years ago, usually thought of with contempt. Then, quite suddenly, came a great change. Men started to idealize those lost centuries as vigorously as their forbears had ignored them. Europeans began to fill out their picture of the past with historical novels about chivalry and their countryside with mock baronial castles inhabited by cotton-spinners and stockbrokers. More important, a huge effort of scholarship was then brought to bear on the records of these times. This was an improvement, but still left impediments to understanding, some of which are still with us. Men came to idealize the unity of medieval Christian civilization and the seeming stability of its life, but in so doing blurred the huge variety within it.

Consequently, it is still very hard to be sure we understand the European Middle Ages, though one crude distinction in this great tract of time nevertheless seems obvious enough. The centuries from the end of antiquity to the eleventh century can best be regarded as an age of foundation, when certain great markers laid out the pattern of the future, but within which change was slow, limited, and its achievement uncertain. From the eleventh century, though, a change of pace implies a change of quality which expressed itself in the end in the creation of a civilization of world significance. It is an age of adventure and revolution, beginning in Europe and ending when European currents begin to mingle with those of world history.

This makes it hard to say when the Middle Ages 'end'. In many parts of Europe, much of medieval social and economic life was still intact at the end of the eighteenth century, the moment at which an independent European offshoot, the United States of America, came into existence across the Atlantic. A supernatural view of life and a religious outlook then still kept a hold on millions of Europeans on both sides of the Atlantic just as effectively as traditional belief satisfies millions of Indians today. Yet by then even the 'Middle Ages' were long over in any institutional sense in some countries, the unquestioned tradition of authority had gone in others, and something we can recognize as modern life was certainly going on here and there. What needs to be considered now is the age when this became first possible, then likely and perhaps unavoidable, for it is Europe's second formative phase, visibly irreversible by about 1500. By then Europe had undergone the first of its revolutionary eras, and it was one which opened the way to modern history for the rest of the world.

The Church

The Church is a good place to begin, for by 'the Church' on earth Christians mean the whole body of the faithful, lay and cleric alike. In this sense the Church came to be the same thing as European society during the Middle Ages. By 1500 only a few Jews, visitors and slaves stood apart from the huge body of people who (at least formally) shared Christian beliefs. Europe was Christian. Explicit paganism had disappeared from the map between the Atlantic coasts of Spain and the eastern boundaries of Poland.

This was a great qualitative as well as a quantitative change. The religious beliefs of Christians were the deepest spring of a whole civilization which had matured for hundreds of years and was not yet threatened seriously by division or at all by alternative mythologies. Christianity had come to define Europe's purpose and to give its life a transcendent goal.

Nowadays, non-Christians are likely to think of something else as 'the Church'. People use the word to describe ecclesiastical institutions, the formal structures and organizations which maintain the life of worship and discipline of the believer. In this sense, too, the Church had come a long way by 1500. Whatever qualifications and ambiguities hung about its successes, those successes were huge; its failures might be great, too, but within the Church there were plenty of men who confidently insisted on the Church's power (and duty) to put them right. The Roman Church which had been a backwater of ecclesiastical life in late antiquity was, long before the fall of Constantinople, the possessor and focus of unprecedented power and influence. It had not only acquired new institutional and political importance after the eleventh century, but also gave a new temper to the Christian life. Christianity became both more disciplined and more aggressive. It also became more rigid: many doctrinal and liturgical practices dominant until this century are no older than the Middle Ages.

These changes constituted a revolution and took roughly from 1000 to 1250, but their beginnings lie in the Cluniac movement. Four of the first eight abbots of Cluny were later canonized: seven of them were outstanding men. They advised popes, acted as their legates, served emperors as ambassadors. They were men of culture and often of great birth, sprung from the highest nobility of Burgundy and the west Franks (which helped to widen Cluny's influence) and they threw their weight behind the moral and spiritual reform of the Church. Leo IX, the pope with whom papal reform really begins, eagerly promoted Cluniac ideas. He spent barely six months of his five years' pontificate at

European Universities founded before 1500

Rome, moving about, instead, from synod to synod in France and Germany, correcting local practice, checking interference with the Church by lay magnates, punishing clerical impropriety, imposing a new pattern of ecclesiastical discipline. Greater standardization of practice within the Church was one of the first results of reform. It begins to look more homogeneous.

Another result was the founding of a second great monastic order, the Cistercians (so named after the place of their first house, at Cîteaux) by monks dissatisfied with Cluny and anxious to return to the original strictness of the Benedictine rule, in particular by resuming the practical and manual labour Cluny had abandoned. It was a Cistercian monk, St Bernard, who was to be the greatest leader and preacher of both Christian reform and crusade in the twelfth century, and his Order had widespread influence both on monastic discipline and upon ecclesiastical architecture. It, too, was in this way a standardizing influence.

The success of reform was also shown in the fervour and moral exaltation of the crusading movement, a genuinely popular manifestation of religion. But new ways also aroused opposition, some of it among churchmen themselves. Bishops did not always like papal interference in their affairs and parochial clergy did not always see a need to change inherited practices which their flock accepted – clerical marriage, for example. The most spectacular opposition to ecclesiastical reform was at the top, from kings and emperors. Its apex was the great quarrel which has gone down in history as the Investiture Contest.

The order of this world: against the background of the Church stand pope and emperor, God's vicars, flanked in due order by ecclesiastical and lay magnates and officers, guarding Christ's sheep, at their feet. Also guarding the flock are black and white dogs protecting it from the wolf of heresy; a pun was intended, for these 'dogs of the Lord' (Domini canes in Latin) are the Dominicans, in whose honour the fresco was painted in 1355 in Santa Maria Novella at Florence.

The attention given to it has been perhaps slightly disproportionate; it dominates many accounts of the Middle Ages. The central episodes lasted only a half-century or so and the issue was by no means clear-cut as one of Church versus State – indeed, the very distinction of them in anything like the modern sense was still unthinkable to medieval man. The specific administrative and legal practices at issue were by and large quite soon the subject of agreement and many clergy felt more loyalty to their lay rulers than to the Roman pope. In the background moreover, loomed very material questions about conflicts over power and wealth within the ruling classes who supplied the personnel of both royal and ecclesiastical government in individual countries. Yet the theoretical importance of the controversy can never quite be argued away, because there was indeed a great issue of principle at stake. Different countries faced the issue at different times, the French in the late eleventh century, the English in the early twelfth, but the most spectacular battle was between the German emperors and Rome, and

Hardly anything is now left of the great abbey church at Cluny except a fragment of one of the transepts, dating from about 1100.

A Cistercian at work, perhaps clearing woodland, helped by a layman. The little drawing comes from a commentary on Job by St Gregory.

it was fought fiercely just after the election of Pope Gregory VII in 1073.

Hildebrand (his name before his election: hence the adjective 'Hildebrandine' sometimes used of his policies and times) was far from attractive as a person, but a pope of great personal and moral courage. He had been one of Leo IX's advisers and fought all his life for the independence and dominance of the Papacy within western Christendom. He was an Italian, but not a Roman, and this, perhaps, made it understandable for him to have played a prominent part before he was himself pope in the transfer of papal election to the college of cardinals, and the exclusion from it of the Roman lay nobility. When reform became a matter of politics and law rather than morals and manners (as it did during his twelve years' pontificate)

Hildebrand was likely to provoke rather than avoid conflict. He was a lover of decisive action without too nice a regard for possible consequences.

Perhaps strife was already inevitable. At the core of reform lay the ideal of an independent Church. It could only perform its task, thought Leo and his followers, if free from lay interference. The Church should stand apart from the state and the clergy should live lives different from laymen's lives: they should be a distinct society within Christendom. From this ideal came the attacks on simony (the buying of preferment), the campaign against the marriage of priests and a long struggle over the exercise of hitherto uncontested lay interference in appointment and promotion. This last was the essence of the long quarrel over lay 'investiture':

who rightfully appointed to a vacant bishopric, the temporal ruler or the Church? The right was symbolized in the act of giving his ring and staff to the new bishop.

Further potential for trouble lay in more mundane issues. Perhaps the emperors were bound to find themselves in conflict with the Papacy sooner or later, once it ceased to be in need of them against other enemies, for they inherited big, if shadowy claims of authority from the past which they could hardly abandon without a struggle. In Germany the Carolingian tradition of subordinating the Church to a royal protection which easily blurred into direction was very much alive. Furthermore, within the Italian peninsula the empire had allies, clients and interests to defend. Since the tenth century, both the control of the Papacy by the empire and the formal authority of the emperor had declined. One expression of this was the new way of electing popes; it left the emperor with a theoretical veto and no more. The working relationship, too, had deteriorated in that some popes had already begun to seek support among the emperor's vassals by dabbling in the troubled waters of their opposition to him.

The temperament of Gregory VII was no emollient in this delicate situation. Once elected, he took his throne without imperial assent, simply informing the emperor of the fact. Two years later he issued a decree on lay investiture. Curiously, what it actually said has not survived, but its general content is known: Gregory forbade the emperor or any other layman to invest a cleric with a bishopric or other ecclesiastical office and excommunicated some of the emperor's councillors on the grounds that they had been guilty of simony in purchasing their preferment. To cap matters, Gregory summoned Henry IV to Rome to appear before him and defend himself against charges of misconduct.

Henry responded at first through the Church itself; he got a German synod to declare Gregory deposed. This earned him excommunication, which would have mattered less had he not faced powerful enemies in Germany who now had the support of the pope. The result was that Henry had to give way. He came in humiliation to Canossa, where he waited in the snow barefoot until Gregory would receive his penance in one of the most dramatic of all confrontations of lay and spiritual authority. But Gregory had not really won. His position was too extreme; he went beyond canon law to assert a revolutionary doctrine, that kings were but officers who could be removed when the pope judged them unfit or unworthy. This was almost unthinkably subversive to men whose moral horizons were dominated by the idea of the sacredness of oaths of fealty; it foreshadowed later claims to papal monarchy but was bound to be unacceptable to any king.

Investiture in fact ran on as an issue in a confrontation of authorities for the next fifty years. Gregory lost the sympathy he had won from Henry's bullying and it was not until 1122 that another emperor agreed to a concordat which was seen as a papal victory, though one diplomatically disguised. Yet Gregory had been a true pioneer; he had made claims for the distinction and superiority of papal power of which much more was to be heard in the next two centuries. Though his immediate successors acted less dramatically than he, they steadily pressed papal claims to papal advantage. One of them used the first crusade to become the diplomatic leader of Europe's lay monarchs; they looked to Rome, not the empire. This was Urban II, who also built up the Church's administrative machine. Under him emerged the *curia*, a Roman bureaucracy which corresponded to the household administrations of the English and French kings from which national civil services were to grow. Through it the papal grip on the Church itself was strengthened. In 1123, a historic date, the first ecumenical council was held in the West and its decrees were promul-

Of all the Romanesque churches, St Etienne at Nevers is one of the most magnificent and unaltered in France. It was built between 1063 and 1097, as the chapel of a Cluniac priory.

The death of Becket, the Canterbury martyr whose shrine became the major resort of English pilgrims – one episode in the struggles of churchmen and kings in the middle ages.

gated in the pope's own name. And all the time, papal jurisprudence and jurisdiction ground away; more and more legal disputes found their way from the local church courts to papal judges, whether resident at Rome, or sitting locally.

Prestige, dogma, political skill, administrative pressure, judicial practice and the control of more and more benefices all buttressed the new ascendancy of the papacy in the Church. By 1100 the groundwork was done for the emergence of a true papal monarchy. As the investiture contest receded, secular princes were on the whole well-disposed to Rome and it appeared that no essential ground had been lost on this issue. There was indeed a spectacular quarrel in England over the question of clerical privilege and immunity from the law of the land

which would be an issue of the future; immediately, it led to the murder (and then the canonization) of an archbishop. But on the whole, the large legal immunity of clergy was not much diminished.

Under Innocent III papal pretensions to monarchical authority reached a new theoretical height. True, Innocent did not go quite so far as Gregory. He did not claim an absolute plenitude of temporal power everwhere in western Christendom, but he said that the papacy had by its authority transferred the empire from the Greeks to the Franks. Within the Church his power was limited by little but the inadequacies of the bureaucratic machine through which he had to operate. Yet papal power was still often deployed in support of the reforming ideas – which shows that much remained to be done. Clerical celibacy became much more widespread. Among other new practices which were pressed on the Church in the thirteenth century was frequent individual confession. It was a powerful instrument of control in a religiously-minded and superstitious society and long served the Church well as a disciplinary instrument. Among doctrinal innovations, the theory of transubstantiation, that by a mystical process the body and blood of Christ was actually present in the bread and wine used in the communion service, was imposed from the thirteenth century onwards.

The final christening of Europe in the central Middle Ages was a great spectacle. Monastic reform and papal autocracy were wedded to intellectual effort and the deployment of new wealth in architecture to make this the next peak of Christian history after the age of the Fathers. It was an achievement whose most fundamental work lay, perhaps, in intellectual developments which culminated in scholasticism, or the spirituality of new orders of clergy, but its most visible expression was in stone. What we think of as 'Gothic' architecture was the creation of this period, and there now appeared the European landscape which, until the coming of the railway, was dominated or punctuated by a church tower or spire rising above a little town. Until the twelfth century the major buildings

Typical of the medieval parish churches with which Somerset is so richly endowed is Weston Zoyland, where, in 1685, the King's prisoners were temporarily detained after the Battle of Sedgemoor.

Eve, the mother of all men, was carved in the twelfth century for the cathedral at Autun, in Burgundy, by one of the greatest of medieval sculptors, Gislebertus. It is one of the masterpieces of Romanesque art.

of the Church were usually monastic; then began the building of the astonishing series of cathedrals, especially in northern France and England, which remains one of the great glories of European art and, together with castles, constitutes the major architecture of the Middle Ages. There was great popular enthusiasm, it seems, for these huge investments; they make the Maya pyramids a shade more comprehensible, though it is difficult to penetrate the heart of the mental attitudes involved. Analogies might be sought in the feeling of some Americans and Russians today about space exploration, but this omits the supernatural dimension of these great buildings. They were both offerings to God and an essential part of the instrumentation of evangelism and education on

earth. About their huge naves and aisles moved the processions of relics and the crowds of pilgrims who had come to see them. Their windows were filled with the images of the biblical story which was the core of European culture; their façades were covered with the didactic representations of the fate awaiting just and unjust. Christianity achieved in them a new publicity and collectiveness. Nor is it possible to assess the full impact of these great churches on the imagination of medieval Europeans without recalling consciously how much greater was the contrast their splendour presented to the reality of everyday life than any imaginable today.

The power and penetration of organized Christianity had further reinforcement from new religious orders. Two of them were out-

531

*St Francis steps forward to save the Church –
represented here by the Lateran basilica – from
falling. Giotto's fresco of the legendary dream of
Innocent III was painted in the thirteenth
century for the church where Francis lies buried
in Assisi. The allegory is appropriate, for the
saint renewed the dangerously weakened ties
between the poor and a rich and worldly
ecclesiastical society by his example and the
foundation of his order.*

standing, the mendicant Franciscans and Dominicans, who in England came to be called respectively the Grey and Black Friars, from the
colours of their habits. The Franciscans were
true revolutionaries: their founder, St Francis
of Assisi, left his family to lead a life of poverty
among the sick, the needy and the leprous. The
followers who soon gathered about him eagerly
took up a life directed towards the imitation of
Christ's poverty and humility. There was at
first no formal organization and Francis was
never a priest, but Innocent III, shrewdly
seizing the opportunity of patronizing the
Franciscans instead of letting this potentially
divisive movement escape from control, bade

them elect a superior. Through him the new
fraternity owed and maintained rigorous obedience to the Holy See. They could provide a
counterweight to local episcopal authority,
because they could preach without the licence
of the bishop of the diocese. The older monastic
orders recognized a danger and opposed the
Franciscans, but they prospered, though becoming divided by a dispute about their organization. In the end they acquired a considerable
administrative structure, but they always remained peculiarly the evangelists of the poor
and the mission field.

The Dominicans were founded to further a
narrower end and made a primarily intellectual
impact. Their founder was a Castilian priest
who went to preach in the Languedoc to heretics,
the Albigensians. From his companions grew
a new preaching order and when Dominic
died in 1221 his seventeen followers had become over five hundred friars. Like the Franciscans, they were vowed to poverty and were
mendicants, and like them, too, they threw
themselves into missionary work. They also
became a great force in a new institution of great
importance, just taking shape, the first western
universities. Thus it came about that there was
diffused throughout western Christendom and
far beyond its borders an evangelical effort
which operated directly under the influence of
the assertive, reforming Papacy.

Dominicans came to provide many of the
personnel of the Inquisition, an organization to
combat heresy which gradually took shape in the
early thirteenth century. From the fourth century onwards, churchmen had urged the persecution of heretics. Nevertheless, it was only
under Innocent III that persecution came to be
the duty of Catholic kings. The Albigensians
were certainly not Catholic, but there is some
doubt whether they should really be regarded
even as Christian heretics. Their beliefs reflect
Manichaean doctrines in that they were dualists;
some of them rejected all material creation as
evil. Like those of many later heretics, heterodox
religious views were taken to imply aberration
or at least nonconformity in social and moral

Thirteenth-century French heretics are burned in the presence of their king; the manuscript from which this picture was taken was written nearly two centuries after the event.

practices. Innocent III seems to have decided upon their persecution after the murder of a papal legate in the Languedoc and in 1209 an Albigensian crusade began. Though it attracted many laymen (especially from northern France) because of the chance it offered for a quick grab at the lands and homes of the Albigensians, its importance in the broadest perspective of Christian history lies rather in its marking a great innovation: the joining of state and Church in western Christendom to prevent by force dissent which might place either in danger. It was for a long time an effective device, though never a complete one.

In judging the theory and practice of medieval intolerance it must be remembered that the danger in which society was felt to stand in from heresy was appalling: its members might face eternal torment. Yet persecution did not prevent the appearance of new heresies again and again in the next three centuries, because they expressed real needs. Heresy was, in one sense, an exposure of a hollow core to the success which the Church had so spectacularly achieved. Heretics were living evidence of dissatisfaction with the results of a long and often heroic battle. Other critics would also make themselves heard in due course and different ways. Papal monarchical theory provoked counter-doctrine; thinkers would argue that the Church had a defined sphere of activity which did not extend to meddling in secular affairs. As men became more conscious of national communities and respectful of their claims, this would seem more and more appealing. The rise of mystical religion, too, was another phenomenon always tending to slip outside the

533

ecclesiastical structure. In movements like the Brethren of the Common Life, following the teachings of the mystic Thomas à Kempis, laymen created religious practices and devotional forms which often escaped from the control of the clergy.

These movements expressed the paradox of the Church's success in the Middle Ages. The Church had risen to a pinnacle of power and wealth. It deployed lands, tithes, papal taxation in the service of a magnificent hierarchy whose worldly greatness reflected the glory of God and whose lavish cathedrals and great monastic churches and libraries embodied the devotion and sacrifices of the faithful. Yet this great concentration of power and grandeur was only there to preach a faith at whose heart lay the glorification of poverty and humility.

The worldliness of the Church drew increasing criticism. It was not just that a few ecclesiastical magnates lolled back upon the cushion of privilege and endowment to gratify their appetites and neglect their flocks. There was also a more subtle corruption inherent in power. The identification of the defence of the faith with the triumph of an institution had given the Church an increasingly bureaucratic and legalistic face. The point had arisen as early as the days of St Bernard; even then, too many lawyers were needed. By the mid-thirteenth century it was blatant and the papacy itself was soon criticized. The idea appeared that a higher authority than that of the pope might lie in an ecumenial council. At the death of Innocent III the Church of comfort and of the sacraments was already obscured behind the granite face of papal centralization. The claims of religion were confused with the assertiveness of an ecclesiastical monarchy demanding freedom from constraint of any sort. It was already difficult to keep the government of the Church in the hands of men of spiritual stature; Martha was pushing aside Mary, because administrative and legal gifts were needed to run a machine which more and more generated its own purposes.

There came a dramatic illustration of this in

Boniface VIII, the most arrogant, autocratic and ambitious of the medieval popes – and one who may have done more to damage the office he held than almost any other. A contemporary statue in copper by a Sienese artist.

1294. A pope was elected who had been a hermit of renowned piety. Any hopes this roused were quickly dashed. Celestine V was forced to resign within a few weeks, seemingly unable to impose his reforming wishes on the curia. His successor was Boniface VIII, a man who has been called the last medieval pope because he embodied all the pretensions of the papacy at its most political and its most arrogant. He was by training a lawyer and by temperament far from a man of spirituality. He quarrelled violently with the kings of England and France and in the Jubilee of 1300 had two swords carried before him to symbolize his possession of temporal as well as spiritual power. Two years later he asserted that a belief in the sovereignty of the pope over every human being was necessary to salvation.

Under him a long battle with kings came to a head. Nearly a hundred years before, the kingdom of England had been laid under interdict by the pope; this was a terrifying sentence, for it forbade the administration of any of the sacraments while the king remained unrepentant and unreconciled. It proved one of the most successful assertions of papal authority and John had been forced to yield. A century later, things had changed. Bishops and their clergy were often estranged from Rome, which had undermined their authority, too. They expressed one side of a stirring national sense of opposition to the papacy whose pretensions reached a peak under Boniface. When the kings of France and England rejected his authority they found churchmen to support them. They also had resentful Italian noblemen to fight for them and in 1303 some of them in French pay pursued the old pope to his native city and there seized him with, it was said, appalling physical indignity. His fellow-townsmen released Boniface. He was not, like Celestine whom he had put in prison, to die in confinement, but die he did, no doubt of shock, a few weeks later.

This was only the beginning of a particularly bad time for the Papacy. For more than four centuries it was to face recurrent and mounting waves of hostility which, though often bravely met, ended by calling Christianity itself in question. By the end of Boniface's reign, the legal claims he had made were almost beside the point; no one stirred to avenge him. It was the spiritual failure which increasingly drew fire; henceforth the Papacy was to be condemned rather for standing in the way of reform than because it claimed too much of kings. For a long time, though, the assumptions of religion contained criticism within certain limits. The notion of autonomous, self-justified criticism was unthinkable in the Middle Ages: it was for failures in their traditional religious task that churchmen were criticized.

Immediately, a period of closer association with the French weakened the Papacy's prestige and narrowed the pope's freedom of manoeuvre. Some saw in what followed a confirmation of this: a French pope and the transfer in 1309 of the Papacy to Avignon, a town belonging to the king of Naples but overshadowed by the power of the French kings whose lands overlooked it.

The friars were often unpopular with beneficed clergy, who saw them as interlopers and disturbers of settled ways. A manuscript on the subject of poverty (a virtue said to be abused by the friars) by an Irish bishop contains this drawing of a Dominican and a Franciscan with a couple of demons egging them on.

There was to be a preponderance of French cardinals, too, during the papal residence at Avignon (which lasted until 1377). The English and Germans soon believed the popes had become the tool of the French kings and took steps against the independence of the Church in their own territories. The imperial electors declared that their vote required no approval or confirmation by the pope and that the imperial power came from God alone.

At Avignon the popes lived in a huge palace, whose erection was a symbol of their decision to stay away from Rome, and whose luxury was a symbol of growing worldliness. The papal court was of unexampled magnificence, attended by a splendid train of servitors and administrators paid for by ecclesiastical taxation and misappropriation. Unfortunately the fourteenth century was a time of economic disaster; a much reduced population was being asked to pay more for a more extravagant Papacy. Centralization continued to breed corruption – the abuse of the papal rights to provide to benefices was an obvious instance – and accusations of simony and pluralism had more and more plausibility. The personal conduct of the higher clergy was more and more obviously at variance with apostolic ideals. A crisis arose among the Franciscans themselves, some of the brothers, the 'spirituals', insisting that they take seriously their founder's rule of poverty, while their more relaxed colleagues refused to give up the wealth which had come to their order. Theological issues became entangled with this dispute. Soon there were Franciscans preaching that Avignon was Babylon, the scarlet whore of the Apocalypse, and that the Papacy's overthrow was at hand, while a pope condemned the ideal of apostolic poverty, asserted that Christ Himself had respected property, and unleashed the Inquisition against the spirituals. They were burned for their preaching, but not before they had won audiences.

Thus the Avignon exile fed a popular anticlericalism and anti-papalism different from that of kings exasperated against priests who would not accept their jurisdiction. Many of the clergy themselves felt that rich abbeys and worldly bishops were only the most deplorable expressions of a Church that had become to an alarming degree, and without realizing it, secularized. This was the irony that tainted the triumph of Gregory VII. Criticism eventually rose to the point at which the Papacy returned to Rome in 1377, only to face the greatest scandal in the history of the Church, a 'Great Schism'. Secular monarchs determined to set up quasi-national churches in their own realms, and the college of twenty or so cardinals, manipulating the Papacy so as to maintain their own revenues and position, together brought about the election of two popes, the second by the French cardinals alone. Thus began thirty years in which popes at Rome and Avignon simultaneously claimed the headship of the Church. In eight further years there was a third contender as well. As the schism wore on, the criticism

directed against the Papacy became more and more virulent. 'Antichrist' was a favourite term of abuse for the claimant to the patrimony of St Peter. It was complicated by the involvement of secular rivalries, too. For the Avignon pope, broadly, there stood as allies France, Scotland, Aragon and Milan; for the Roman, there was support from England, the German emperors, Naples and Flanders.

Yet the schism at one moment seemed to promise a genuine renovation and reformation. The instrument through which reformers sought deliverance was an ecumenical or general council of the Church; they wanted to return to the days of the apostles and the Fathers for a means to put the papal house in order and to many Catholics this sounded good sense. Unfortunately, it did not turn out well. Four councils were held. The first, at Pisa (1409), struck out boldly by proclaiming the deposition of both popes and choosing another. As the two claimants did not recognize it this meant there were now three pretenders to the chair of St Peter; moreover, when the new one died after a few months, another was elected whose choice was said to be tainted by simony. This was the first John XXIII (now no longer recognized as a pope and the victim of one of Gibbon's most searing judgements). The next council (Constance, 1414–18) removed John (though he had summoned it), obtained the abdication of one of his competitors and then deposed the third pretender. At last there could be a fresh start; the schism was healed. In 1417 a new pope was elected, Martin V. This was a success, but some people had hoped for more from the council; they had sought reform. From this, though, the council had been diverted; instead it devoted its time to heresy, and support for reform dwindled once the unity of the Papacy was restored. After another council (Siena) had been dissolved by Pope Martin V for urging reform ('that the Supreme Pontiff should be called to account was perilous' he declared), the last met at Basle (1431–49) but was ineffective long before its dissolution. The conciliar movement did not achieve the desired reform and papal power was restored. From this time, the conciliar principle that there existed an alternative source of authority inside the Church was always regarded with suspicion at Rome. Within a few years it was declared heresy to appeal from pope to General Council.

The conciliar failure meant that the Church had not risen to the level of the crisis now upon it. The Papacy had maintained its superiority, but its victory was only partial; secular rulers had reaped the benefits of anti-papal feeling in new freedoms for the national Churches. As for the moral authority of the Rome, that had clearly not been restored and the result would be a more damaging movement for reform a century later. The Papacy now began to look more and more Italian, and so it has remained. There were some dismal popes to come in the next two centuries, but this was less damaging to the Church than the evolution of their See towards becoming just one more Italian state.

Heresy, always smouldering, had burst out in a blaze of reforming zeal during the conciliar period. Two outstanding men, Wyclif and Hus, focussed the discontents to which schism had given rise. They were first and foremost reformers, though Wyclif was a teacher at Oxford, a thinker rather than a man of action. Hus, a Bohemian, became the leader of a movement which involved national issues as well as ecclesiastical ones and exercised huge influence as a preacher in Prague. He had been condemned by the council of Constance for heretical views on predestination and property and was burned in 1415. The great impulse given by Wyclif and Hus flagged as their criticisms were muffled, but, apart from their attention to ecclesiastical and doctrinal error, they too had tapped the nerve of national anti-papalism which was to prove so destructive of the unity of the western Church. Catholics and Hussites were still disputing Bohemia in bitter civil wars twenty years after Hus's death. Meanwhile, the Papacy itself made concessions to nationalism in its diplomacy with the lay monarchies of the fifteenth century.

There was plenty of religious zeal in the fif-

Changing images of Christ and his mother reflect the spiritual and cultural preoccupations of different ages. These figures in painted wood come from early-fourteenth-century Germany. They show a shift in the focus of devotional attention towards the events succeeding Christ's death, the Descent from the Cross, the Entombment and the personality of the suffering Virgin. Originating in German mystical movements, such concerns spread to Italy, where they shaped the idiom of the pietà so popular with Italian sculptors and painters for the next two centuries or so.

teenth century, but it more and more bypassed the central apparatus of the Church. Fervour manifested itself in a continuing flow of mystical writing and in new fashions in popular religion: a new absorption in the agony of the passion was reflected in art, new devotions to saints, the craze for flagellation, the outbreaks of dancing frenzy all seem to show a heightened excitability. Popular preaching acquired new audiences and by the end of the century produced the outstanding example of its appeal and power in Savonarola, a monk who was for a time moral dictator of Florence. But most of this escaped the formal and ecclesiastical structures. In the fourteenth and fifteenth centuries the emphasis of popular religion was individual and devotional. Another impression of the inadequacy of both vision and machinery within the hierarchies is to be found, too, in a collapse of missionary work outside Europe.

All in all, the fifteenth century leaves a sense of withdrawal, an ebbing after a big effort which had lasted nearly two centuries. Yet to leave the medieval Church with that impression uppermost in our minds would be to risk a grave misunderstanding of the place of religion in a society which is made more different from our own by that than by any other factor. To begin with, Europe was still Christendom and was so even more consciously after 1453. Within its boundaries, almost the whole of men's lives was defined by religion. The Church was for most men and women the only recorder and authenticator of the great moments of their existence – their marriages, their children's births and baptisms, their deaths. Many of them gave themselves up totally to it; a much greater proportion of the whole population became monks and nuns than is the case today, but though they might think of withdrawal to the cloister from a hostile everyday, they could not conceive a secular world such as ours, wholly distinct from and indifferent to the Church. Learning, charity, administration, justice and huge stretches of economic life all fell within the ambit and regulation of a pervasive religion. Even when men attacked churchmen, they did so in the name of the standards the Church had itself taught them and with appeals to the knowledge of God's purpose it gave them. Religious myth was not only the deepest spring of a civilization, it was still the life of all men. It defined human purpose and did so in terms of a transcendent good. Outside the Church, the community of all believers, lay only paganism. The devil – conceived in a most material form –

Baptism, the first of many sacraments for the Christian. The godparents look on complacently while the priest prepares to immerse the child. This scene is taken from a tapestry presented to a church at Tournai in 1475 by one of the town's master-weavers.

lay in wait for those who strayed from the path of grace. If some bishops and popes were among them, so much the worse for them. Human frailty could not compromise the religious view of life. God's justice would be shown and He would divide sheep from goats in the Day of Wrath when all things would end.

Principalities and powers

Most people in the world today are familiar, at least in a rough and ready way, with the idea of the state. They accept that the world's surface is divided by impersonal organizations working through officials marked out in special ways, and that such organizations provide the final public authority for any given area. Often, they might also think that the state – if they used that word – in some way represented a people or a nation. But whether they did so or not, states would be the building blocks from which most of us would construct a political account of the modern world.

Hardly any of this would have been intelligible to a European in 1000; five hundred years later much of it would have been. The process by which the modern state emerged, though far from complete by 1500 is one of the markers which delimit the modern era of history. The realities had come first, before principles and ideas. From the thirteenth century onwards many rulers, usually kings, were able for a variety of reasons to increase their power over those they ruled. This was often because they could keep up large armies and arm them with the most effective weapons. Especially after the coming of gunpowder (and in the fourteenth century the use of cannon became common), great men could no longer brave the challenges of their rulers from behind the walls of their castles. Many rulers were by 1500 well on the way to exercising a monopoly of the use of armed force within their realms. These realms, too, had increasingly well-defined frontiers and this expressed more than just an improvement in surveying. It marked a change in emphasis within government from a claim to control persons who had a particular relationship to the ruler to one to control people who lived in a certain area. Territorial dependence was replacing personal dependence.

Over such territorial agglomerations, royal power was by 1500 coming to be exercised directly through officials. Like cannon, they had to be paid for. A kingship which worked through vassals known to the king who did much of his work for him in return for his favours and who supported him in the field when his needs went beyond what his own estates could supply, gave way to one in which royal government was carried out by its own employees, paid for by the taxation (more and more in cash, not kind), the raising of which was one of their most important tasks. The parchment of charters and rolls began by the sixteenth century to give way to the first

trickles and rivulets of what was to become the flood of modern bureaucratic paper.

Such a sketch hopelessly blurs this immensely important and complicated change, as it was linked to every side of life, to religion and the sanctions and authority it embodied, to the economy, the resources it offered and the social possibilities it opened or closed, to ideas and the pressure they exerted on still plastic institutions. But the upshot is not in doubt. Somehow, Europe was beginning by 1500 to organize itself in a way unlike the Europe of Carolingians and Ottonians. Though personal and local ties remained overwhelmingly the most important ones for most Europeans – and were to be for centuries – society was institutionalized in a different way from the eleventh century when even tribal survivals still counted. The relationship of lord and vassal which, with the vague claims of pope and emperor in the background, so long seemed to exhaust political thought, gave way to an idea of princely power over all the inhabitants of a domain. In its extreme assertions, such as that of Henry VIII of England, that a prince knew no external superior save God, it was really quite new.

Necessarily, the change to such a state of affairs neither took place everywhere in the same way nor at the same pace. By 1800 France and England had been for centuries unified in a way that Germany and Italy were still not. But wherever it happened, the centre of the process was usually the steady aggrandizement of royal families. Kings had great advantages. If they ran their affairs carefully they had a more solid base for their power than their nobles in their own, usually large, domains. Their office had a mysterious aura about it, reflected in the solemn circumstances of their coronations and anointings. Their courts and laws seemed to promise a more independent, less expensive justice than could be got from the local feudal lord. They could therefore appeal not only to the resources of the feudal structure at whose head – or somewhere near it – they stood, but also to forces outside. One of these which was slowly revealed as of growing importance was only

VBI hAROLD:SACRAMENTVM:FECIT: hIC hAROLD:DVX:
VVILLELMO DVCI:

appearing in the Middle Ages. This was the sense of nationhood.

This is another idea which modern man takes for granted, but we must be careful not to ante-date the moment at which men began to think of themselves as Englishmen and Frenchmen. No medieval state was national in our sense. Nevertheless, by 1500 the subjects of the kings of England and France could often think of themselves as different from aliens who were not their fellow-subjects, even if they might also regard people who lived in the next village as virtually foreigners. Even two hundred years earlier this sort of distinction between those born within and those born outside the realm was being made and the sense of community of the native-born was steadily enhanced. One symptom was the appearance of belief in national patron saints; in the fourteenth century St George's red cross on a white background became a kind of uniform for English soldiers and he was recognized as official protector of England, though churches had been dedicated to him under the Anglo-Saxon kings. (His exploit in killing the dragon was only attributed to him in the twelfth century and may be the result of mixing him up with a legendary Greek hero, Perseus.) Another was

The Bayeux 'tapestry', worked in wools on linen, is a huge strip cartoon, a narrative over two hundred feet long of the downfall of a hero, Harold, who broke faith with the man to whom he had sworn loyalty, William of Normandy. It was hung almost yearly for centuries in Bayeux cathedral and a public who could not read could none the less learn from it the story of the Norman conquest of the Anglo-Saxon kingdom and appreciate the way in which it followed from a breach of the code of medieval fealty. In this scene, the climax of the early part of the story, Harold makes his oath of allegiance before William in the most solemn manner possible, his hands resting on caskets containing sacred relics, one probably holding those of two British martyrs which were kept at Bayeux.

the writing of national histories (already fore-shadowed by the Dark Age histories of the Germanic peoples) and the discovery of national heroes. In the twelfth century a Welshman more or less invented the mythological figure of Arthur, while an Irish chronicler of the same period built up an unhistorical myth of the High King Brian Boru and his defence of Christian Ireland against the Vikings. Above all, there was more vernacular literature. First

A fourteenth-century bust of Charlemagne from Aachen, made to contain relics.

Spanish and Italian, then French and English began to break through the barrier set by Latin about literary creativity. The ancestors of these tongues are recognizable in twelfth-century romances such as the Song of Roland which transformed a defeat of Charlemagne by Pyrenean mountaineers into the glorious stand of his rearguard against the Arabs, or the Poem of the Cid, the Spanish national hero. With the fourteenth century came Dante, Langland and Chaucer, each of them writing in a language modern men can read with little difficulty.

We must not exaggerate the immediate impact of such developments. For centuries yet, family, local community, religion or trade were still to be the only focus of most men's loyalties. Such national institutions as they could have seen growing among them would have done little to break into this conservatism; in few places was it more than a matter of the king's justices and the king's tax-gatherers – and even in England, in some ways the most national of medieval states, many people might never have seen either. The rural parishes and little towns of the Middle Ages, on the other hand, were real communities, and in ordinary times they exhausted any man's need to go further in thinking about social responsibilities. We really need another word than 'nationalism' to suggest the occasional and fleeting glimpses of a community of the realm which might once in a while touch a medieval man, or even the irritation which might suddenly burst out in a riot against the presence of foreigners, whether workmen or merchants. (Medieval anti-Semitism, of course, had different roots.) Yet such hints of national feeling occasionally reveal the slow consolidation of support for new states in western Europe.

The first of them to cover anything like the areas of their modern successors were England and France. The Normans, a few thousand of whom came over from France to establish themselves after the invasion of 1066 as a new ruling class, were England's last successful invaders. Their leader, William the Conqueror, gave them lands, but retained more for himself (the royal estates were larger than those of his Anglo-Saxon predecessors) and asserted an ultimate lordship over the rest: he was to be lord of the lands and all men held what they held either directly or indirectly of him. He inherited the prestige of the old English monarchy, too, and this was important, for it raised him decisively above his fellow-Norman warriors. Below him, the greatest of them became William's earls and barons, the lesser ones among them knights, ruling England at first from the wooden and earth castles which they spread over the length of the land. They had conquered one of the most civilized societies in Europe, which went on under the Anglo-Norman kings to show unusual vigour. A few years after the Conquest, English government carried out one of the most remarkable administrative acts of the Middle

Ages, the compilation of Domesday Book, a huge survey of rural England for royal purposes. The evidence was taken from juries in every shire and hundred and its minuteness deeply impressed the Anglo-Saxon chronicler who bitterly noted ('it is shameful to record, but did not seem shameful for him to do') that not an ox, cow or pig escaped the notice of William's men. In the next century there was rapid, even spectacular, development in the judicial strength of the Crown. Though minorities and weak kings from time to time brought about royal concessions to the magnates, the essential integrity of the monarchy was not compromised. The constitutional history of England is for five hundred years the story of the authority of the Crown. This owed much to the fact that England was separated from possible enemies, except to the north, by water; it was hard for foreigners to interfere in her domestic politics.

For a long time, though, the Anglo-Norman kings thought of themselves as something more than kings of an island state. They were heirs of a complex inheritance of possessions and feudal dependencies which at its furthest stretched far into south-western France, and like their followers they spoke Norman-French. The loss of most of this 'Angevin' inheritance at the beginning of the twelfth century was decisive for France as well as for England. A sense of nationhood was nurtured in each of them by their quarrels with one another.

The Capetians had hung on grimly and with increasing success to the French crown. From the tenth century to the fourteenth their kings succeeded one another in unbroken hereditary succession. They kept and then began to add to the domain lands which were the basis of royal power. The Capetians' lands were rich, too. They fell in the heartland of modern France, the cereal-growing area round Paris called the Ile de France, which was for a long time the only part of the country bearing the old name of Francia, thus commemorating the fact that it was a fragment of the old kingdom of the Franks. The domains of the first Capetians were so distinguished from the other west Carolingian territories, such as Burgundy; by 1300 their

Only one French king has been canonized, Louis IX, a ruler celebrated in his own day for his love of justice and his passion for the Faith (he campaigned, unsuccessfully, in the Holy Land, where he was captured by the Saracens, and he died on an expedition to Tunis). His moral stature gave him a pre-eminence recognized by the willingness of other kings to accept his arbitration. Here, in a manuscript of the fourteenth century, some of his good deeds are recorded for the edification of the faithful: St Louis is shown serving a meal to a pious monk, washing a beggar's feet, collecting the bones of martyrs and undergoing a scourging.

vigorous successors had expanded 'Francia' to include Bourges, Tours, Gisors and Amiens. By then the French kings had also acquired Normandy and other feudal dependencies from the English kings.

This is a reminder that in the fourteenth

Longbow and crossbow gave way only slowly to what Shakespeare called 'villainous saltpetre', but the coming of the first guns heralded the end of a long era of warfare during which men could rely only on the extra power given to missile weapons by the tension of cord, wood or steel, or the acceleration of sling or throwing-stick. Early guns, like the mortar shown in this fifteenth-century manuscript, were crude, unreliable and inaccurate, but they rapidly improved and by 1500 were essential elements in any royal armoury.

century (and later) there were still great fiefs and feudal principalities in what is now France which make it improper to think of the Capetian kingdom as a monolithic unity. Yet it was a unity of sorts, though much rested on the personal tie. During the fourteenth century that unity was greatly enhanced by a long struggle with England remembered by the misleading name of the Hundred Years' War. In fact, English and French were only sporadically at war from 1337 to 1453, fighting being far from continuous. Yet it was always easy to make it flare up again in a new campaign because the opportunities it offered to English noblemen for booty and ransom money made war seem a plausible investment to many of them. On the other hand, sustained warfare was difficult to keep up; it was too expensive. Formally, what was at stake was the maintenance by the kings of England of territorial and feudal claims on the French side of the Channel; in 1350 Edward III had quartered his arms with those of France.

For England, the long-run loser, the most important immediate results of these quarrels were new additions to the infant mythology of nationhood (largely because of the great victories won at Crécy and Agincourt) and the creation of a long-lived distrust of the French. Dislike was heartily reciprocated; after all, the campaigning took place in France. The Hundred Years' War was also indirectly important to the French monarchy because it did something to check feudal fragmentation and moved Frenchmen about, breaking down in some degree the barriers between Picard and Gascon, Norman and French. In France, too, the national mythology benefited; its greatest acquisition was the story and example of Joan of Arc whose astonishing career accompanied the turning of the balance of the long struggle against the English, though possibly only a few Frenchmen at the time knew she existed. But two long-term results of the war mattered most. One was that Crécy soon led to the English conquest of Calais and its retention for two hundred years. This opened Flanders, where a cluster of manufacturing towns was ready to absorb English wool and later cloth exports, to English trade. The other important result was England's defeat in the longer run; her territorial connexion with France was virtually at an end by 1500 (though in the eighteenth century George III was still entitled 'King of France'). England became almost an island again. After 1453 French kings could push forward with the consolidation of their state undisturbed by the obscure claims of England's rulers from which the wars had sprung. They could settle down to establish their sovereignty over their rebellious magnates at their leisure. In each country, war in the long run strengthened the state.

Such a clear outcome to the process of national consolidation was only observable in one other western European kingdom, Spain. She, too, achieved at the end of the sixteenth century a cohesion and power which would make her a great monarchy for the next three centuries. It had been made easier by the Reconquest, the long struggle against Islam, which from the start gave Spanish nationhood a quite special flavour because of its intimate connexion with Christian faith and fervour; the Reconquest was a crusade. Toledo was a Christian capital again in the mid-twelfth century, and Portugal a Christian kingdom. A hundred years later, Seville belonged to the kingdom of Castile and the crown of Aragon ruled the great Arab city of Valencia. In 1340, when the last great Arab offensive was defeated, success brought the threat of anarchy as the turbulent nobles of Castile strove to assert themselves. The monarchy took the burghers of the towns into alliance. The establishment of strong rule followed the union of the crowns of Aragon and Castile by the marriage of *Los Reyes Católicos*, 'the Catholic Monarchs', Ferdinand of Aragon and Isabella of Castile in 1479. This made easier both the final expulsion of the Moors and the eventual creation of one nation though the two kingdoms long remained formally and legally separate while

pursuing common policies. Only Portugal in the peninsula remained outside the new Spain, clinging to an independence often threatened by her powerful neighbour.

Little sign of the ground-plans of future nations was to be found in Italy and Germany. Potentially, the claims of the Holy Roman Emperors were an important and broad base for political power. Yet after 1300 they had lost virtually all the special respect due to their title. A long thirteenth-century dispute between rival emperors was part of the explanation of this. Another was the incapacity of the emperors to consolidate monarchical authority in any part of their dominions.

In Germany, the domains of successive imperial families were usually scattered and ill-consolidated; later emperors were poorer than their great predecessors. Their position rested upon their election by the great magnates. They had no obvious capital to provide a centre for a nascent German nation. Political circumstances led them more and more to devolve such power as they possessed. Important cities began to exercise imperial powers within their territories and in 1356, by a document which is a landmark in German constitutional history, the Golden Bull, the seven electoral princes acquired the exercise of almost all the imperial rights in their own lands. Their jurisdiction, for example, was henceforth absolute: no appeals lay from their courts to the emperor. What persisted in this situation of attenuated imperial power was a reminiscence of the mythology which would prove a temptation to vigorous princes.

An Austrian family, the house of Habsburg, eventually succeeded in establishing itself on the imperial throne. Theirs was to be a great name; Habsburgs were to hold almost unbroken imperial authority from the accession of Maximilian I, who became emperor in 1493 and opened his house's greatest era, to the end of the empire in 1806. And even then they were to survive another century as the rulers of a great state. They began with an important advantage in that as German princes went they were rich. But their most important resources only became available after a marriage which in the end brought them the inheritance of the duchy of Burgundy, the most affluent of all fifteenth-century European states. From this, the Habsburgs obtained much of the Netherlands. Other inheritances and marriages would bring them Hungary and Bohemia. For the first time since the thirteenth century, it seemed possible that an effective political unity might be imposed on Germany and central Europe; Habsburg family interest in uniting the scattered dynastic territories now had an instrument in the imperial dignity.

By that time the imperial supremacy in Italy had vanished. The struggle to preserve it long provided the main organization of Italian politics: the contestants in feuds which tormented Italian cities called themselves Guelph and Ghibelline long after those names ceased to mean, as they once did, allegiance respectively to pope or emperor. After the fourteenth century there was no imperial domain in Italy and the emperors hardly went there except to be crowned with the Lombard crown. Imperial authority was delegated to 'vicars' who made of their vicariates units almost as independent as the electorates of Germany. Titles were given to these rulers and from their vicariates there emerged some of the states which were to be the political units of Italian history until the nineteenth century; the duchy of Milan was one of the first. But others had different origins. Besides the Norman south, there were the republics, of which Venice and Genoa were the greatest.

The city republics represented the outcome of two great trends in early Italian history, the communal movement and the rise of commercial wealth. They were connected in some towns, though not in Venice. In the tenth and eleventh centuries, in much of north Italy, general assemblies of the citizens emerged as the effective governments of many towns. They described themselves sometimes as *parlamenta*, or, as we might say, town meetings, and represented municipal oligarchies who profited from a revival of trade beginning to be felt from 1100

onwards. In the twelfth century the Lombard cities took the field against the emperor and beat him. Thereafter they ran their own internal affairs.

The greatest beneficiary of the revival of trade after 1100 was Venice and she, too, contributed much to it. Formally a dependency of Byzantium, she was long favoured by the detachment from the troubles of the European mainland which her position on a handful of islands in a shallow lagoon gave her. Men fled there from the Lombards. Geography not only offered security, but imposed a destiny: Venice, as its citizens loved later to remember, was wedded to the sea, and a great festival of the Republic long commemorated it by the symbolic act of throwing a ring into the waters of the Adriatic. Venetian citizens were forbidden to acquire estates on the mainland and instead turned their energies to commercial empire overseas. Venice was the first west European city to live by trade. She was also the most successful of the pillagers of the eastern empire and fought and won a long struggle with Genoa for commercial supremacy in the East. Yet there was enough to go round: Genoa, Pisa and the Catalan ports all prospered with the revival of Mediterranean trade with the East.

Much of the political ground-plan of modern Europe was, therefore, in being by 1500. Portugal, Spain, France and England were recognizable in their modern form, though in Italy and Germany, where vernacular language defined nationhood, there was no correspondence between the nation and the state. This structure, of course, was still far from enjoying the firmness it later acquired. The kings of France were still not kings of Normandy: in that province they were local rulers, dukes. Many other examples complicated survivals and constitutional relics still cluttered up everywhere the idea of monarchical sovereignty. Nor was the power of kings assured or absolute. There would still be feudal rebellions in England and one explanation of the success of Henry VII, the first of the Tudors, was that by judicious marriages he drew much of the remaining poison from the bitter struggle of great families which had bedevilled the English Crown in the fifteenth-century Wars of the Roses.

In one respect, too, a limitation on monarchical power had appeared which has a distinctly modern look. In the fourteenth and fifteenth centuries can be found the first examples of the representative, parliamentary bodies which are so characteristic a feature of the modern state. The most famous of them all, the English Parliament, was the most mature by 1500. Their origins are complex and have been much debated. One root is Germanic tradition, which imposed on a ruler the obligation of taking counsel from his great men and acting on it. The Church, too, was an early exponent of the representative idea, using it, among other things, to obtain taxation for the Papacy. It was a device which united towns with monarchs, too: in the twelfth century representatives from Italian cities were summoned to the Diet of the empire. By the end of the thirteenth century most countries had seen examples of representatives with full powers being summoned to attend assemblies which princes had called to find new ways of raising taxation.

This was the nub of the matter. New resources had to be tapped by the new (and more expensive) state. Once summoned, princes found representative bodies had other advantages. They enabled other voices to be heard than those of the magnates. They provided local information. They had a propaganda value. On their side, the early parliaments (as we may loosely call them) of Europe were discovering that the device had advantages for them, too. In some of them the thought arose that taxation needed consent and that someone other than the nobility had an interest and therefore ought to have a voice in the running of the realm.

Working and living

From about the year 1000 another fundamental change was under way in Europe: it began to get richer. As a result, more men slowly acquired a freedom of choice almost unknown in earlier times; society became more varied and complicated. Slow though it was, this was a revolution; wealth at last began to grow faster than population. It was by no means obvious everywhere in the same degree and it did not end the overwhelming predominance of agriculture. It was also punctuated by a bad setback in the fourteenth century. Yet it was decisive and launched Europe on a career of economic growth lasting to our own day.

One crude but by no means misleading index is the growth of population. Only approximate estimates can be made but they are based on better evidence than is available for any earlier period. The errors they contain are unlikely to qualify much the overall trend. They suggest a Europe of about forty million in 1000 rose to sixty million or so in the next two centuries. Growth then seems to have further accelerated to reach a peak of about seventy-three million around 1300, after which there is indisputable evidence of decline. The total population is said to have gone down to about fifty million by 1460 and only to have begun to rise in the fifteenth century. Then it began to go up again, and overall growth has been uninterrupted ever since.

Of course, the rate of increase varied even from village to village. The Mediterranean and Balkan lands did not succeed in doubling their population in five centuries and by 1450 had relapsed to only a little above their levels in 1000. The same appears to be true of Russia, Poland and Hungary. Yet France, England, Germany and Scandinavia trebled their populations before 1300 and after bad setbacks in the next hundred years still had twice the population of the year 1000. Contrasts within countries could be made, too, sometimes between areas very close to one another, but the general effect is indisputable: population grew overall as never before, but unevenly, the north and west gaining more than the Mediterranean, Balkan and eastern Europe.

The explanation of this lay in food supply, and therefore in agriculture. It was for a long time

*December was the month for killing pigs, whose
salted or smoked meat was the best that could
be had during the long winter months, and
whose blood and offal could be turned into
sausages and stored.*

*In the margin of this fifteenth-century picture
can be seen a little of a lighter side of medieval
life - little boys playing some kind of tug-of-war
on their sledges.*

the only possible source of new wealth. More
food was obtained by bringing more land under
cultivation and by increasing its productivity.
This began an expansion of food production
which has gone on ever since. Europe had great
natural advantages (which she has retained) in
her moderate temperatures and good rainfall
and these, combined with a physical relief
whose predominant characteristic is a broad
northern plain, have always given her a large
area of potentially productive and agricultural

land. Huge areas of it still wild and forested in
1000 were brought into cultivation in the next
few centuries.

Land was not short in medieval Europe, then,
and a growing population provided the labour
to clear and till it. The landscape changed. The
huge forests were cut into gradually as villages
pushed out their fields. In some places, new
colonies were deliberately established by landlords and rulers. The building of a monastery in
a remote spot – as many were built – was often
the beginning of a new nucleus of cultivation or
stock-raising in an almost empty desert of scrub
and trees. Some new land was reclaimed from
sea or marsh. In the east, much was won in the
colonization of the first German *Drang nach
Osten*. Propaganda for settlement there was
circulated just as it was to be when promoters
sought settlers for the New World in Elizabethan times.

The breaking in of fresh land slowed down by
about 1300. There were even signs of over-
population. The first big increase in the cultivated and grazed area was over and there was a
long pause. But an indispensable increase in
productivity had occurred, too. Some say it
roughly doubled output on some land. In part
it was the slow result of more cultivation, the
effect of regular fallows and cropping, of the
slow enrichment of the soil, but new crops had
been introduced, too. Although grain-growing

547

went on being the main business of the cultivator, the appearance of beans and peas of various sorts in larger quantities from the tenth century onwards meant that more nitrogen was being returned to the soil. Cause and effect are difficult to disentangle in economic history; other suggestive signs of change go along with them. It was in this phase of expansion that the first manuals of agricultural practice appear and the first agricultural book-keeping, a monastic innovation. More specialized cultivation brought a tendency to employ wage labourers instead of serfs carrying out obligatory work. By 1300 it is likely that most household servants in England were recruited and paid as free labour and probably a third or so of the peasants as well. The bonds of servitude were relaxing and a money economy was spreading slowly into the countryside.

Some peasants benefited, but increased wealth usually went in the main to the landlord who took most of the profits provided by the rising demand. Most men lived poor and cramped lives. The peasant lived on coarse bread and various grain-based porridges, seasoned with vegetables and only occasionally fish or meat. Calculations suggest he consumed about two thousand calories daily, and this sustained him for very laborious work. If he grew wheat he did not eat its flour, but sold it to the better-off, keeping barley or rye for his own food. He had little elbow-room to better himself. Even when his lord's legal grip through bond labour became less firm, the lord still had practical monopolies – of mills and carts, which the peasants needed to work the land. 'Customs', or taxes for protection, were levied without regard to distinctions between freeholders and tenants and could hardly be resisted.

More cash crops for growing markets gradually changed the self-sufficient manor into a unit producing for sale. The new markets were to be found in towns which grew steadily between 1100 and 1300; urban population increased faster than rural. This is a complicated phenomenon. The new town life was in part a revival going hand in hand with the revival of trade, in part a reflexion of growing population. It is a chicken-and-egg business to decide which comes first. A few new towns grew up because there was a castle or a monastery to serve. Sometimes this led to the establishment of a market. In other places, a focus in a great establishment was lacking but a village grew because it was well placed in relation to rising commercial activity. Many new towns, especially in Germany, were deliberately settled as colonies. On the whole long-established towns grew bigger – Paris may have had about 80000 inhabitants in 1340 and Venice, Florence and Genoa were probably comparable – but few towns were big by our standards. Fourteenth-century Germany had only fifteen towns of more than 10000, and London, with about 35000 people at that time, was by far the biggest English city. Of the great medieval towns, only those in the south had been important Roman centres (though many in the north, of course, had Roman nuclei, as had London). New cities tended to be linked distinctively to economic possibilities. They were markets, or lay on great trade routes such as the Meuse and Rhine, or were grouped in an area of specialized production as was Flanders, where already in the late twelfth century Ypres, Arras and Ghent were famous as textile towns. Wine was one of the first agricultural commodities to loom large in international trade and this underpinned the early growth of Bordeaux. Ports often became the metropolitan centres of maritime regions, as did Genoa and Bruges.

The area where the revival of trade was most conspicuous was Italy, where European trade with the outside world was first resumed on an important scale. The agents were the cities, above all Venice. It was in that great commercial centre that banking for the first time separated itself from the changing of money. By the middle of the twelfth century Italian merchants were at work in central Asia and China. They sold slaves from Germany and central Europe to the Arabs of Africa and the Levant. They bought Flemish and English cloth and took it to Constantinople and the Black Sea. In the thirteenth century the first voyage was made from Italy to Bruges; before this the Rhine, Rhône and overland routes had been used. Roads were built across Alpine passes. Trade fed on trade and the northern European fairs drew other merchants from the north-east. The German towns of the Hansa, the league which controlled the Baltic, provided a new outlet for the textiles of the West and the spices of the East.

European economic geography was revolutionized in the process. In Flanders and the Low Countries economic revival soon began to generate a population density which would stimulate agricultural innovation. Everywhere, towns which could escape from the cramping monopolies of the earliest manufacturing centres enjoyed the most rapid new prosperity. One visible result was a great wave of building. It was not only a matter of the houses and guildhalls of newly prosperous cities; it left a glorious legacy in Europe's churches, not only the great cathedrals, but the scores of magnificent parish churches of little English towns.

Building was one of the major achievements of medieval technology, whose development is another sign of economic growth. The architecture of a cathedral, for example, posed complex engineering problems; slowly, from the medieval craftsmen, the engineer was to emerge. Medieval technology was in no sense science-based, but it achieved much by the accumulation of experience and reflexion on it. Possibly its most important service was the harnessing of new forms of energy to do the work of muscles and, therefore, to deploy muscle-power effectively and productively. This was most obvious in agriculture, where metal tools had been becoming more common since the tenth century. The iron plough had made available the heavier soils of valley lands; since it required oxen to pull it the evolution of a more efficient yoke followed and with it more efficient traction. The whippletree and the shoulder collar for the horse also made possible bigger loads. There were not many such innovations, but they were sufficient to effect a considerable increase in the cultivators' control of the land. They also imposed

Medieval industry: the whole operation of glass-making, from a fifteenth-century manuscript. Improvements in technique during the Middle Ages made possible the production of lenses, something never achieved by the ancients, and the beginnings of the work which led to huge strides in the science of optics in the sixteenth and seventeenth centuries.

new demands. Using horses meant that more grain had to be grown to feed them, and this imposed new crop rotations. Another innovation was the spread of milling; both windmills and watermills, first known in Asia, were widely spread in Europe even by 1000. In the centuries to come they were put to more and more use, both industrially and agriculturally.

In milling foodstuffs, wind often replaced muscle-power as it had already done in the evolution of better ships; water usually provided the power for industrial operations. It drove hammers for fulling and for forging (here the invention of the crank was of the greatest

549

importance). Forging was essential to the great expansion of Europe's metallurgical industry in the fifteenth century, an expansion closely connected with the demand for a technological innovation of the previous century, artillery. Water-driven hammers were also used in paper-making. Because of printing, this industry soon had an importance which perhaps even surpassed that of the new metal-working industry of Germany and Flanders. Print and paper had their own revolutionary potential because books made the diffusion of techniques faster and easier in the growing pool of craftsmen and artificers able to use such knowledge.

Some technical devices simplified mental processes as well as physical ones. Medieval Italians invented much of modern accountancy as well as new credit devices for the financing of international trade. The bill of exchange appears in the thirteenth century and with it and the appearance of the first true bankers we are at the edge of capitalism. Limited liability appears at Florence in 1408, a year after the first modern bank at Genoa. Yet though the change from the past was colossal, it is easy to get it out of proportion if we do not recall its scale. For all the magnificence of its palaces, the goods shipped by medieval Venice in a year could all have fitted comfortably into one large modern bulk-carrying ship.

The change was also precarious. The economy was never far from the edge of collapse. Medieval agriculture, in spite of such progress as had been made, was appallingly inefficient. It abused the land and exhausted it. Little was put back into it except manure. As land got short, family holdings got smaller; probably most European households farmed less than eight acres in 1300. Only in a few places (the Po valley was one of them) was there a big investment in collective irrigation or improvement. Above all, agriculture was vulnerable to weather; two successive bad harvests in the early fourteenth century reduced the population of Ypres by a tenth. Local famine could rarely be offset by imports. Roads had broken down since Roman times, carts were crude and for the most part goods had to be carried by packhorse or mule. Water transport was cheaper and swifter, but could rarely meet the need. As for commerce, the Ottoman onslaught brought a gradual recession in eastern trade. Demand was small enough for a very little change to determine the fate of cities: cloth production at Florence and Ypres fell by two-thirds in the fourteenth century.

It is very difficult to generalize but about one thing there is no doubt: a great and cumulative setback occurred in the fourteenth century. There was a sudden rise in mortality, not occurring everywhere at the same time, but notable in many places after a series of bad harvests around about 1320. This started a slow decline of population which suddenly became a disaster with the onset of attacks of epidemic disease which are often called by the name of one of them, the 'Black Death' of 1348–50. This was the worst single attack. It was of bubonic plague, but no doubt it masked many other killing diseases which swept Europe with it and in its wake. Europeans died of typhus, influenza and smallpox, too, and all of them contributed to a great demographic disaster. In some areas a half or a third of the population may have died; over Europe as a whole the total loss has been calculated as a quarter. A papal enquiry put the figure at more than forty million. Toulouse was a city of 30 000 in 1335 and a century later only 8000 lived there; once 1400 died in three days at Avignon.

There was no universal pattern of disaster, but everywhere Europeans shuddered under these blows. In the most extreme cases a kind of collective madness seized men. Pogroms of Jews were a common expression of a search for scapegoats or those guilty of spreading the plague; the burning of witches and heretics was another. The European psyche bore a scar for the rest of the Middle Ages, which were haunted by the imagery of death and damnation in painting, carving and literature. The fragility of settled order illustrated the precariousness of the balance of food and population. When disease killed enough people, agricultural production would collapse; then the inhabitants of the towns would die of famine if they were not already dying of plague. Probably a plateau of productivity had already been reached by about 1300. Both available techniques and easily accessible new land for cultivation had reached a limit and some have seen signs of population pressure treading close upon resources even by that date. From this flowed the huge setback of the fourteenth century and then the next century's slow recovery.

It is scarcely surprising that an age of such colossal dislocations and disasters should have been marked by violent conflicts between rulers and ruled. It was most marked in the countryside. Everywhere in Europe the fourteenth and fifteenth centuries were times of peasant troubles. The French *jacquerie* of 1358 which led to over thirty thousand deaths and the English Peasants' Revolt of 1381 which for a time captured London were especially notable. The roots of rebellion lay in the ways in which landlords had increased their demands under the spur of necessity and in the new demands of royal tax collectors. Combined with famine, plague and war they made an always miserable existence intolerable. 'We are made men in the likeness of Christ, but you treat us like savage beasts' was the complaint of English peasants who rebelled in 1381. Significantly, they appealed to the Christian standards of their civilization; the demands of medieval peasants were often well formulated and effective but it is anachronistic to see in them a nascent socialism.

Demographic disaster on such a scale in the long run made things better for many poor men. One obvious and immediate result was a severe shortage of labour; the pool of permanently under-employed had been brutally dried up. A rise in wages followed. It is even possible that once the immediate impact of the fourteenth-century disasters had been absorbed the standard of living of the poor may actually have risen slightly. The tendency for the economy, even in the countryside, to move on to a money basis was now accelerated by the labour shortage. By the sixteenth century, serf labour and servile

The later Middle Ages were even more preoccupied with the transitory nature of this world, with the awareness of death, than their forbears. This French ivory of the fifteenth century reflects the theme in an obvious allegory.

status had both receded a long way in western Europe, particularly in England. This weakened the manorial structure and the feudal relationships clustered about it. Landlords were also suddenly confronted with a grave setback to their rent incomes. In the previous two centuries the habits of consumption of the better-off had become more expensive. Now people suddenly ceased to grow more prosperous. On the other hand, some landlords could adapt by switching from cultivation which required much labour to sheep-running which required little. In Spain there were even still possibilities of taking in more land; Moorish estates were the reward of the soldiers of the Reconquest. War

551

itself suited some noblemen, who could do well out of its ransoms and booty.

The results are very hard to pin down, but they were bound to stimulate further and faster social change. Medieval society changed dramatically, and sometimes in oddly assorted ways, between the tenth century and the sixteenth. Even at the end of that age, though, it seems still almost unimaginably remote. Its obsession with status and hierarchy is one index of this. Medieval European man was defined by his legal status. Instead of being an individual social atom, so to speak, he was the point at which a number of coordinates interacted. Some of them were set by birth and the most obvious expression of this was the idea of nobility. The noble society which was to remain a reality until the twentieth century was already completely present in its essentials in the thirteenth. Gradually, warriors had turned into noble landowners. Descent then became important. One of the things which showed this was the rise of the sciences of heraldry and genealogy, which were to have a profitable life right down to our own day. New titles appeared as distinctions within the nobility ripened. The first English duke was created in 1337, an expression of the tendency to find ways of singling out the greater magnates from among their peers. Symbolic questions of precedence became of intense interest; rank was at stake. From this rose the dread of disparagement, the loss of status which might follow for a woman from an unequal marriage or for a man from contamination by a lowly occupation. For centuries it was to be assumed that only arms, the Church or the management of his own estates were fit occupations for a nobleman in northern Europe. Trade, above all, was closed to him except through agents and even when, centuries later, this barrier gave way, hostility to retail trade was the last thing to be abandoned by those who cared about these things. When a sixteenth-century French king called his Portuguese colleague 'the grocer king' he was being rude as well as witty and no doubt his courtiers appreciated the sneer.

The values of the nobility were, at bottom, military. Through their gradual refinement there emerged slowly the notions of honour, loyalty, disinterested self-sacrifice which were to be held up as models for centuries to well-born boys and girls. The ideal of chivalry articulated these values and did much to soften the harshness of a military code. It was blessed by the Church, which provided religious ceremonies to accompany the bestowal of knighthood and the knights' acceptance of Christian duties. The heroic figure who came supremely to embody the notion was the mythological English King Arthur, whose cult spread to many lands. It was to live on in the ideal of the gentleman and gentlemanly conduct.

Of course, it never worked as, ideally, it should have done. But few great creative myths do; neither did the feudal theory of dependence, nor does democracy. The pressures of war and, more fundamentally, economics, were always at work to fragment and confuse the obligations of lord and man. The increasing unreality of feudal obligations was one factor favouring the growth of kingly power. The coming of a money economy made further nonsense of them; service had increasingly to be paid for and that meant that rents became more important than the services that had gone with them. Some of the sources of feudal income remained fixed in terms made worthless by changes in real prices. Lawyers evolved devices which enabled new aims to be realized within a 'feudal' structure more and more unreal and worm-eaten.

Medieval nobility had been for a long time very open to new entrants, but usually this became less and less true as time passed. In some places attempts were actually made to close for ever the noble caste. Yet European society was all the time generating new concentrations of wealth and even of power which did not always find a place in the old hierarchies and challenged them. The most obvious example was the emergence in most western countries of rich merchants for whom there was no appropriate niche in the status system of feudal society. In Italy these sometimes themselves became the

Art emerged slowly from the religious sphere into the secular, and it is not clear whether such a picture as this sixteenth-century representation of a banker and his wife by Quentin Matsys, a great Antwerp artist, is meant to illustrate a moral or is simply a realistic image of life in one of the little money-changers' shops of that prosperous city.

nobility of trading and manufacturing cities. Merchants who were successful in trade often bought land; it was not only the supreme economic investment in a world where there were few, but it might open the way to a change of status for which landownership was either a legal or social necessity.

The rise of the merchant class was intimately linked with the growth of towns and trade; that is to say that they were linked with the most dynamic element in medieval European civilization and one hostile to its feudal setting. It was an element which not only produced new wealth but new institutions. Feudal institutions did not work easily in a society of tradesmen and craftsmen for which they had no adequate theoretical place. Yet feudal lords sought the support of towns against kings and kings sought the support of townsmen and their wealth against over-mighty subjects. They gave towns charters and

An early fifteenth-century Flemish painting of a carpenter at work; the work was commissioned as a picture of St Joseph, the earthly father of Jesus, but shows us incidentally the tools and a bench of a workman of the painter's own day.

privileges. The walls which surrounded the medieval city were often the symbol and guarantee of its immunity. The landlords' writ did not run in them and sometimes their anti-feudal implication was even more explicit: in some of them villeins, for example, could acquire their freedom if they lived in a town for a year and a day. 'The air of the town makes you free' said a German proverb. The communes and within them the guilds were associations of free men for a long time isolated in a world unfree. The burgher – the *bourgeois*, the dweller in *bourg* or borough – was a man who stood up for himself in a universe of dependence.

In this blossoming of urban life lies buried much which shaped European history and made it different from that of other continents. In other civilizations, both in the classical world and in Asia, city life never developed the political and social power which characterized it in Europe. Somehow, the countryside there kept its dominance and the ownership of land was often the only route to political power or mark of status. The merchant, the craftsman, the lawyer and the doctor remained in other cultures appendages of the landowning class, and social differentiation was not continuous and progressive. Even when rich, the townsmen of other cultures acquiesced in their own social inferiority. Though this was long true in Europe, it never closed society in quite the same way or so completely. The medieval European city stood apart from the countryside in which it was rooted, legally, socially and economically distinct though organically linked to it. Townsmen were equal and free, even if some were freer and more equal than others.

The history behind this remains obscure because it is for the most part the history of obscure men. The wealthy merchants who became the typically dominant figures of the new town life and fought for their corporate privileges are visible enough, but their humbler predecessors are usually not. In earlier times a merchant can have been little but the pedlar of the few exotica and luxuries which the medieval European estate could not provide for itself.

Ordinary commercial exchange for a long time hardly needed a middleman: craftsmen sold their own goods and cultivators their own crops. Yet somehow there emerged in the towns men who dealt between them and the countryside and their successors were to be men using capital to order in advance the whole business of production for the market. There is a constant accretion of complexity as one part of the economy plays upon another. The new towns both favoured and were favoured by the appearance of new social groups. They offered a focus of opportunities of new kinds and guarded these opportunities jealously. Unwittingly, they held within their walls much of the future history of Europe, though their independence varied greatly in law and practice. There were parallels in some other countries to the Italian communal movement, and, by and large, towns in the German east were especially independent. This helps to explain the existence there of the powerful Hanseatic League of more than a hundred and fifty free towns. The Flemish towns also tended to enjoy a fair degree of freedom; French and English towns usually had less.

Freedom was a matter of men, except in so far as the distinction of free and unfree status survived at the bottom of society. Women, like men, could be either of noble or common blood, but in any rank of society they suffered, by comparison with their menfolk, from important legal and social disabilities. Their rights of inheritance were often restricted; broadly speaking they could inherit a fief, for example, but not enjoy personal lordship, having to appoint men to carry out their obligations. In all classes below the highest there was much drudgery to be done by women; until this century European peasant women worked on the land as they do in Africa and Asia today.

There were theoretical elements in the subjection of women and it is not possible to avoid the conclusion that a large contribution was made to them by the Church. In part this was a matter of its hostile stance towards sexuality. Women being seen as the origin of Man's Fall

A great German nobleman, the Margrave of Meissen, and his wife look down from the walls of Naumberg cathedral. As the title – literally 'count of the march' – shows, the margrave was the ruler of a frontier zone, his office one of great powers and independence. The statues were carved in the thirteenth-century; that of the lady provides one of the few portraits of a noblewoman of this epoch to survive.

and a standing temptation to concupiscence, the Church threw its weight behind a male-dominated society. Yet this is not all there is to be said. Other societies have done more to seclude women than Christendom and the Church at least offered women the only respectable alternative to domesticity; the history of the female religious is studded with outstanding women of learning, spirituality and administrative gifts. In one other way, too, the position of at least a minority of well-born women was

marginally bettered by the idealization of women in the chivalric codes of behaviour of the thirteenth and fourteenth centuries. There lay in this a notion of romantic love and an entitlement to service and it was a stage towards a higher civilization.

Yet it can have affected very few women. Among themselves, they were more equal before death than would be rich and poor in Asia today, but, then, so were men. Women lived less long than men, it seems, and frequent confinements and a high mortality rate no doubt explain this. Medieval obstetrics remained, as did other branches of medicine, rooted in Aristotle and Galen: there was nothing better available. But men died young, too. Aquinas lived only to forty-seven and philosophy is not nowadays thought to be physically unduly exacting. This was about the age to which a man of twenty in a medieval town in good conditions might expect to survive: he was lucky to have got as far already and to have escaped the ferocious toll of infant mortality which imposed an average life of about thirty-three years and a death-rate about twice that of modern industrial countries. Judged by the standards of antiquity, so far as they can be grasped, this was by no means bad.

This reminds us of one last novelty of this huge variety of the Middle Ages: it left behind the means for us to measure just a little more of the dimensions of human life. From these centuries come the first collections of facts upon which reasoned estimates can be made. The year 1087 is a memorable date because it was the year in which William the Conqueror's officers rode out into England to record its structure and wealth in Domesday Book, an amazing achievement. Other collections, usually for tax purposes, followed in the next few centuries. Some have survived. So have many accounting documents which reduce farming and business to quantities. Thanks to them historians can talk with a little more confidence about society and economy than at any earlier time.

10 New limits, new horizons

Europe looks outward

In the Near East until very recently Europeans were habitually called 'Franks'. The word had caught on after the Byzantine government used it for all western Christians. A thousand years later it was still used in various distortions and mispronunciations from the Persian Gulf to China. This is more than just a historical curiosity; it is a helpful reminder across centuries of strife between Europeans that their neighbours were struck from the start by the unity, not the diversity, of the western peoples and long thought of them as one.

The roots of this idea can be seen even in the remote beginnings of Europe's long and victorious assault on the world, when a relaxation of pressure on her at last began to be felt on her eastern land frontier and on northern coasts. First the barbarians were checked; then they began to be Christianized, too. Within a short space of time Christian kings appeared in Poland, Hungary, Denmark and Norway. The

With Time clutching a relentless hour-glass as his companion, and the Devil, cloven-hooved and eager behind him, a knight rides out – to war? in quest of the Holy Grail? – as the Middle Ages die about him. Perhaps he has something of Don Quixote about him, too. This engraving is one of the most enigmatic left by the master of the new medium provided by print, Albrecht Dürer. Superbly skilled in drawing, painting and engraving, he remains the outstanding figure of the German Renaissance.

Mongol onslaught still lay ahead, but was unthinkable in AD 1000. By then the Islamic world also posed less of a danger because of the decline into which the Abassid caliphate had fallen in the eighth and ninth centuries. The rolling back of Islam had already begun and was to continue vigorously until the fifteenth century.

The struggle with the Arabs was given unity and fervour by religion, the deepest source of European self-consciousness. It provided a licence for the predatory appetites of the military class which dominated lay society. The Normans were in the vanguard, taking south Italy and Sicily from the Arabs, a task effectively complete by 1100. Almost incidentally in the process they swallowed the last Byzantine possessions in the West as well. The other great struggle in Europe against Islam was one of the most glorious epics of Spanish history, the Reconquest, whose climax came in 1492, when Granada, the last Moslem capital of Spain, fell to the armies of the 'Catholic Monarchs'.

The Spaniards had always seen the Reconquest as a crusade, and as such it had drawn warriors from all over Europe since its opening in the eleventh century. The background to its early history was the same religious revival and quickening of vigour in the West which also expressed itself in a succession of great enterprises in Palestine and Syria which began with the first crusade preached by Urban II in 1095. The expeditions which followed, though unsuccessful in their aim of delivering the Holy Land from Islamic rule, left profound marks not only on the Levant, but also on European

557

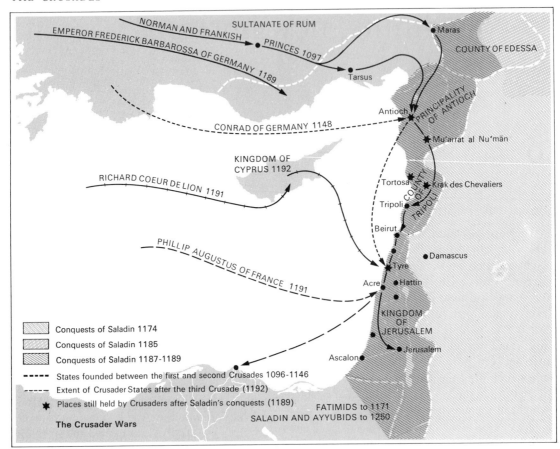

The Crusader Wars

Conquests of Saladin 1174
Conquests of Saladin 1185
Conquests of Saladin 1187-1189
----- States founded between the first and second Crusades 1096-1146
----- Extent of Crusader States after the third Crusade (1192)
★ Places still held by Crusaders after Saladin's conquests (1189)

FATIMIDS to 1171
SALADIN AND AYYUBIDS to 1250

society and psychology. There were four important crusades. The first and most successful was launched in 1096 and in three years recaptured Jerusalem, where the crusaders celebrated the triumphs of the Gospel of Peace by an appalling massacre of their prisoners, their women and children. The second crusade (1147–49) began with a massacre of Jews in the Rhineland, but thereafter, though an emperor and a king of France gave it greater importance than its predecessor, it was a disaster. It failed to recover Edessa, the city whose loss had largely provoked it and did much to discredit St Bernard, its most fervent advocate. (There was, however, a by-product of some importance when an English fleet took Lisbon from the Arabs and it passed into the hands of the King of Portugal.) Then in 1187 Saladin recaptured Jerusalem for Islam. The third crusade which followed (1189–92)

was socially the most spectacular of all. A German emperor (drowned in the course of it) and the kings of England and France all took part. They quarrelled and the crusaders failed to recover Jerusalem. No great monarch answered Innocent III's appeal to go on the next crusade, though many land-hungry magnates did and the Venetians financed the expedition, which left in 1202. It was at once diverted by interferences in the dynastic troubles of Byzantium, which suited the Venetians, who helped to recapture Constantinople for a deposed emperor. There followed the terrible sack of the city in 1204 and that was the end of the fourth crusade, whose monument was the establishment of a 'Latin Empire' at Constantinople which survived there only for a half-century.

Several more crusades set out in the thirteenth

558

Krak des Chevaliers, the greatest of the fortresses built by Crusaders in the Levant, an affirmation of staggering confidence by a few men far from home in a strange land.

The Reconquest: the Moors go down before James I of Aragon in 1235. By the fifteenth century, when this altar-piece was painted, such episodes were part of the continuing drama of Spanish history, the expulsion of Islam.

century, but though they helped to divert a little longer the dangers which faced Byzantium, crusading to the holy land was dead as an independent force. Its religious impulse could still prove an ancillary aid and rationalization for other motives, but the first four crusades had shown the unpleasant face of greed and cupidity. They were the first examples of European overseas imperialism, both in their characteristic mixture of noble and ignoble aims and in their abortive colonialism. In Syria and Palestine, Europeans were not simply pushing forward their frontier in a movement of settlement as in Spain or on the pagan marches of Germany. They were attempting to transplant western institutions to a remote and exotic setting, to seize lands and goods no longer easily available in the West, and they could do all this with clear consciences because their opponents were infidels who had by conquest installed themselves in Chris-

tianity's most sacred shrines. 'Christians are right, pagans are wrong', said the *Song of Roland* and that probably sums up fairly enough the average crusader's response to any qualms about what he was doing.

The brief successes of the first crusade had owed much to a passing phase of weakness and anarchy in the Arab world. The movement's feeble transplants, the Frankish states and the Latin empire of Constantinople, soon collapsed. But there were important and permanent results. As we noted, the crusades had embittered still further the division of western from eastern Christendom: the first sackers of Constantinople were crusaders. Secondly, the crusaders had cherished and intensified the sense of unbridgeable ideological separation between Islam and Christianity. Islam was not to infiltrate the West as Christianity and other eastern religions had infiltrated the Hellenistic world of Rome. The crusades both expressed and helped to forge the special temper of western Christianity, giving it a militant tone and an aggressiveness which would make its missionary work especially potent in the future. In it lay the roots of a mentality which, when secularized, would power the world-conquering culture of the modern era. The Spanish, the Reconquest scarcely complete, were by then already looking

559

to the Americas for the battlefield of a new crusade.

Yet Europe was not impervious to Islamic influence. In these struggles she imported and invented new habits and institutions. Wherever contact occurred with Islam, whether in the crusading lands, Sicily or Spain, western Europeans found things to admire. Sometimes they took up luxuries not to be found at home, silk clothes, the use of perfumes and new dishes. One habit acquired by some crusaders was that of taking more frequent baths. This may have been unfortunate, for it added the taint of religious infidelity to a habit already discouraged in Europe by the association of bath-houses with sexual licence. Cleanliness had not yet achieved its later quasi-automatic association with godliness.

One institution which well expressed the militant Christianity of the high Middle Ages was the military order of knighthood. It brought together soldiers who professed vows as members of a religious order, and accepted discipline to fight for the faith. Some of these orders became very rich, owning endowments in many countries. The Knights of St John of Jerusalem are still in existence and were to be for centuries in the forefront of the battle against the Ottomans. The Knights Templar rose to such great power and prosperity that they were destroyed by a French king who feared them, and the Spanish military orders were in the forefront of the Reconquest.

One of these communities operated in the

An unknown knight, stilled in death on his tomb in Dorchester Abbey, yet apparently struggling to draw his sword again for the Faith; we know him to be a Crusader because of the crossed legs of his effigy, the conventional mark of one who had set out for the Holy Land.

north. These were the Teutonic Knights, the spearhead of Germanic penetration of the Slav lands. In this region, too, missionary zeal combined with greed and the stimulus of poverty to change both the European map and the culture of a whole region. The colonizing impulse which failed in the Near East had here a huge success. German expansion to the east was at bottom a huge folk-movement, a centuries-long tide of men and women, clearing forest, planting homesteads and villages, founding towns, building fortresses to protect them and monasteries and churches to serve them. When the crusades were past, and the narrow escape from the Mongols had reminded Europe that it could still be in danger, this movement went steadily on. Out on the Prussian and Polish marches, the soldiers, among whom the Teutonic Knights were outstanding, provided its shield and cutting-edge at the expense of the Slav and Baltic peoples.

This was the beginning of a cultural conflict between Slav and Teuton which persisted down to the twentieth century. The last time that the West threw itself into the struggle for Slav lands was in 1941: many Germans saw Hitler's attack on Russia as another stage in a centuries-old civilizing mission in the East. In the thirteenth century a Russian prince, Alexander Nevsky, grand duke of Novgorod had to beat off the Teutonic Knights (as Russians were carefully reminded by a great film in 1937) at a moment when he also faced the Tatars on another front.

While the great expansion of the German East between 1100 and 1400 made a new economic, cultural and racial map, it also raised yet another barrier to the reunion of the two Christian traditions. Papal supremacy in the West meant that the Catholicism of the late medieval period was more uncompromising than ever to Orthodoxy and also more unacceptable to it. Russia was from the twelfth century onwards more and more separated from western Europe by her own traditions and special historical experience. The Mongol capture of Kiev in 1240 had been a blow to eastern Christianity as grave as the sack of Constantinople in 1204. It also broke the princes of Muscovy. With Byzantium in decline and the Germans and Swedes on their backs, they paid tribute to the Mongols and their Tatar successors of the Golden Horde for two and a half centuries. This long domination by a nomadic people was another historical experience sundering Russia from the West.

Tatar domination had its greatest impact on the southern Russian principalities, the area where the Mongol armies had operated. There appeared, accordingly, a new balance within Russia, Novgorod and Moscow acquiring new importance in the eclipse of Kiev. But both paid tribute to the Tatars in the form of silver, recruits and labour. Their emissaries, like other Russian princes, had to go to the Tatar capital at Sarai on the Volga, and make their separate arrangements with their conquerors. It was the period of greatest dislocation and confusion in the succession patterns of the Russian states. Both Tatar policy and the struggle to survive favoured those Russian states which were most despotic. The future absolutist political tradition of Russia was thus fed by the Tatar period as it had been by the inheritance of imperial ideas from Byzantium. Gradually Moscow

emerged as the focus of a new centralizing trend, and the process can be discerned as early as the reign of Alexander Nevsky's son, who was prince of Muscovy. His successors had the support of the Tatars, who found them efficient tax-gatherers. The Church offered no resistance and the metropolitan archbishopric was transferred from Vladimir to Moscow in the fourteenth century.

Meanwhile, a new challenge had arisen to the West. A half-Slav state, but one which was Roman Catholic, took Kiev for three centuries. This was the big medieval duchy of Lithuania, formed in 1386 in a union by marriage which incorporated the Polish kingdom. Its territory covered much of modern Poland, Prussia, the Ukraine and Moldavia. Fortunately for the Russians the Lithuanians fought the Germans, too, their troops shattering the Teutonic Knights at Tannenberg in 1410. Harassed by the Germans in the north, and the Lithuanians to the west, Moscow somehow survived by exploiting divisions within the Golden Horde.

The fall of Constantinople brought a great change to Russia; from now on it was there, not Byzantium, that eastern Orthodoxy had to find its centre. Russian churchmen soon came to feel that a complex purpose lay in such awful events. Byzantium, they believed, had betrayed its heritage to Catholicism by seeking religious compromise at the Council of Florence. 'Constantinople has fallen', wrote the Metropolitan of Moscow, 'because it has deserted the true Orthodox faith. . . . There exists only one true Church on earth, the Church of Russia.' A few decades later, at the beginning of the sixteenth century, a monk could write to the ruler of Muscovy in a quite new tone: 'Two Romes have fallen, but the third stands, and a fourth will not be. Thou art the only Christian sovereign in the world, the lord of all faithful Christians.' It had been important that the Metropolitan of the Russian Church had established himself in Moscow two centuries earlier.

The end of Byzantium came when other historical changes made Russia's emergence from confusion and Tatar domination possible and

Russian knights in battle; from a fifteenth-century manuscript.

likely. The Golden Horde was rent by dissension in the fifteenth century. At the same time, the Lithuanian state was crumbling apart. These were opportunities and a ruler who was capable of exploiting them came to the throne of Moscow in 1462. Ivan the Great (more precisely, Ivan III) gave Russia something like the definition and reality won by England and France from the twelfth century onwards and some have seen him as first national ruler of Russia. Territorial consolidation was the foundation of his work. When Moscow swallowed the republics of Pskov and Novgorod, Ivan's state stretched at least in theory as far as the Urals. The oligarchies which had ruled them were deported, to be replaced by men who held lands from the Tsar in return for service. The German merchants of the Hansa who had dominated the trade of these republics were expelled, too. The Tatars made another onslaught on Moscow in 1481, but were beaten off, and two invasions of Lithuania gave Ivan much of White Russia and Little Russia in 1503. His successor took Smolensk in 1514.

Ivan the Great was the first Russian ruler to take the title of 'Tsar'. It was a conscious evocation of an imperial past, a claim to the heritage of the Caesars, the word in which it originated. In 1472 Ivan married a niece of the last Greek emperor. He was called 'autocrat by the grace of God' and during his reign the double-headed eagle was adopted which was to remain part of the insignia of Russian rulers until 1917. This Byzantine colouring of Russian monarchy was very important. Because of it, Russian history became still more unlike that of western Europe. By 1500 western Europeans already recognized a distinctive kind of monarchy in Russia; Basil, Ivan's successor, was acknowledged to have a despotic power over his subjects greater than that of any other Christian rulers over theirs.

In eastern Europe, too, therefore, much of the future seems already discernible by the beginning of the sixteenth century. A great process of definition and realization had been going on for centuries. A new phase of western Europe's relations with the rest of the world was about to open. Her land limits were now filled up; in the East further advance was blocked by the consolidation of Christian Russia, in the Balkans by the Ottoman empire of Islam. The first wave of overseas expansion was spent by about 1250, when the crusades came to an end. With the onset of the Ottoman threat in the fifteenth century, Europe was forced on the defensive again in the eastern Mediterranean and Balkans. Those unhappy states with exposed territories in the East, such as Venice, had to look after them as best they could. Meanwhile, Europeans were being pushed towards taking a new look at their oceanic horizons.

In 1400 it had still seemed sensible to see Jerusalem as the centre of the world. Though the Vikings had long ago crossed the Atlantic, men still pictured a world made up of three continents, Europe, Asia and Africa, around the shores of one land-locked sea, the Mediterranean. A huge revolution lay just ahead which for ever swept away such views and the route to it lay across the oceans, because elsewhere advance was blocked. Europe's first direct contacts with the East had been much more dependent on land than on water. The caravan routes of central Asia were their main channel and brought goods then usually shipped from Black Sea or Levant ports. Elsewhere, ships rarely ventured far south of Morocco until the fifteenth century. Then, a mounting wave of maritime enterprise becomes noticeable and it begins the age of true world history.

One explanation of it was the acquisition of new tools and skills. Different ships and new techniques of long-range navigation were needed for oceanic sailing and they became available from the fourteenth century onwards, thus

A model of an English ship of about 1485. This would have been a big ship of about 500 tons; three masts were then still unusual and topsails had not yet come into use. Such a ship can be regarded as the culmination of the medieval style in shipbuilding.

making possible the great effort of exploration which has led to the fifteenth century being called 'the Age of Reconnaissance'. In ship design there were two crucial changes. One was specific, the adoption of the stern-post rudder; though we do not know exactly when this happened, some ships had it by 1300. The other was a more gradual and complex process of improving rigging. This went with a growth in the size of ships. A more complex maritime trade no doubt spurred such developments. By 1500, the tubby medieval 'cog' of northern

Europe, square-rigged with a single sail and mast, had developed into a ship carrying up to three masts, with mixed sails. The main-mast still carried square-rigging, but more than one sail; the mizzen-mast had a big lateen sail borrowed from the Mediterranean tradition; a fore-mast might carry more square-rigged sails, but also newly invented fore-and-aft jib sails attached to a bowsprit. Together with the lateen sail aft, these head-sails made vessels much more manoeuvrable; above all, ships could be sailed much closer to the wind.

Once these innovations were absorbed, the design of ships which resulted was to remain essentially unchanged (though much refined) until the coming of steam propulsion. Though he would have found them small and cramped, Columbus's ships would have been perfectly comprehensible machines to a nineteenth-century clipper captain. Since they carried guns, though tiny ones by comparison with what was to come, they would also have been comprehensible to Nelson.

By 1500 some crucial navigational developments had also taken place. The Vikings had first shown the way in sailing an oceanic course. They had better ships and navigational skill than anything previously available in the West. Using the Pole Star and the sun, whose height above the horizon in northern latitudes at midday was computed in tables by a tenth-century Irish astronomer, they eventually crossed the Atlantic by running along a line of latitude. Then, with the thirteenth century, there is evidence of two great innovations. At that time the compass came to be commonly used in the Mediterranean (it already existed in China, but it is not known if it was transmitted from Asia to the West) and in 1270 there appears the first reference to a chart, one used in a ship engaged on a crusading venture. The next two centuries gave birth to modern geography and exploration. Spurred by the thought of commercial prizes, by missionary zeal and diplomatic possibilities, rulers began to subsidize research. In the fifteenth century they came to employ their own cartographers and hydrographers. Foremost among these princes was the brother of the King of Portugal, Henry, 'the Navigator' as he was later called.

The Portuguese were bound to be seafarers. Their coastline is indented with little harbours and river mouths from which in the fourteenth century there emerged swarms of ships to fish and trade. Together with some Spaniards, Portuguese were soon colonizing the Madeiras and parts of the Canaries in search of free land. Land-locked by Spain, and virtually barred from the Mediterranean trade by the experience and armed force with which the Italians guarded it, they were forced willy-nilly into the Atlantic. They had already familiarized themselves with northern waters when Prince Henry began to launch a series of maritime expeditions. The first provided the data for further exploration down the African coast. Gold and pepper, it was known, came from south of the Sahara; perhaps the Portuguese could find out where from. Perhaps, too, there was a possibility of finding an ally here to take the Turk in the flank. This was the beginning of the age of discovery, and its heart was systematic, government-subsidized research.

The Portuguese pushed steadily south. In 1434 they passed Cape Bojador; ten years later they rounded Cape Verde and established themselves in the Azores. In 1445 they reached Senegal. This first fort was built soon after. In 1473 they crossed the Equator and in 1487 were at the Cape of Good Hope. Ahead lay the Indian Ocean, which now became a geographical reality to Europeans. Arabs had long traded across it and pilots were available. The King of Portugal at this juncture was excited by the thought of tracing the legendary Prester John, but others had other objectives. Across the ocean lay even richer sources of spices. In 1498 Vasco da Gama dropped anchor at last in Indian waters.

By that time, another sailor, the Genoese Columbus, had crossed the Atlantic to look for Asia, confident in the light of Ptolemaic geography that he would soon come to it. He instead discovered the Americas for the Catholic

The first map to show Columbus' discoveries in the New World depicts Cuba, correctly, as an island. Together with the rest of the crew of 1495, the map's draughtsman, Juan de la Cosa, renounced the oath made to Columbus that it was part of the Asian mainland. St Christopher, who appears at the head of the map, was Columbus' patron saint.

Columbus did not cross the Atlantic in an oared galley, but that was how he was imagined at his greeting by Haitians in this woodcut from a Latin translation of his account of his voyage printed at Basle in 1493. It appeared within months of his writing it and is a striking example of the new rapidity in the diffusion of ideas and information (plenty of it false) arising from the invention of the printing press.

Monarchs of Spain. In the name of the 'West Indies' the map commemorates his continuing belief that he had accomplished the discovery of islands off Asia by his astonishing leap in the dark, so different from the cautious, though brave, progress of the Portuguese towards the East round Africa. Unlike them, but unwittingly, he had in fact discovered an entire continent, though even on the much better-equipped second voyage which he made in 1493 he explored only its islands. The Portuguese had reached a known continent by a new route. Soon, though Columbus himself to his dying day refused to admit it, even after further voyages and experience of the mainland, it began to be realized that this was not Asia after all. In 1494 the historic name 'New World' was first applied to his discoveries.

It was by now becoming necessary for the two enterprising Atlantic nations to come to understandings about their respective interests in a world of widening horizons. The first treaty between European nations about trade outside European waters was made by Portugal and Spain in 1479; now they went on to delimit

565

spheres of influence. The pope made a temporary award, based on a division of the world between them along a line a hundred leagues west of the Azores, but this was overtaken by the treaty of Tordesillas in 1494 which gave to Portugal all the lands east of a line of longitude running 370 leagues west of Cape Verde and to Spain those west of it. In 1500 a Portuguese squadron, probably on the way to the Indian Ocean, ran out into the Atlantic to avoid adverse winds and to its surprise struck land which lay east of the treaty line and was not Africa. This was Brazil. Henceforth Portugal had a destiny across the Atlantic as well as in the Orient. But the main Portuguese effort still lay to the east, and it was an Italian in Spanish service, Amerigo Vespucci, who soon afterwards ran far enough to the south to show that not merely islands but a whole new continent lay between Europe and Asia by a western route. Before long it was named after him, America, the first application of the name to the southern continent later being extended to the northern, too.

In 1522, thirty years after Columbus's landfall in the Bahamas, a ship in the Spanish service completed the first voyage round the world. Its commander had been Magellan, a Portuguese, who got as far as the Philippines, where he was killed, having discovered and sailed through the straits named after him. With this voyage and its demonstration that all the great oceans were interconnected, the prologue to the European age can be considered over. Just about a century of discovery and exploration had changed the shape of the world and the course of history. From this time the nations with access to the Atlantic would have opportunities denied to the land-locked powers of central Europe and the Mediterranean. In the first place this meant Spain and Portugal, but they would be joined and surpassed by France, Holland and, above all, England, a collection of harbours incomparably placed at the centre of the newly enlarged hemisphere, all of them easily accessible from their shallow hinterland, and within easy striking distance of all the great European sea routes of the next two hundred years.

A near-contemporary celebration of Magellan's discovery of the straits that bear his name, on the voyage (sponsored by Charles V) on which he met his death. Flanked by the volcanoes of Tierra del Fuego, urged on by the gods of sea and sky, the great navigator is shown sailing through the straits, a new sort of hero, the explorer for exploration's sake.

The enterprise behind these changes had only been possible because of a growing substratum of maritime skill and geographical knowledge. The new and characteristic figure of this movement was the professional explorer and navigator. Many of the earliest among them were, like Columbus himself, Italian. New knowledge, too, underlay not only the conception of these voyages and their successful technical performance, but also allowed Europeans to see their relationship with the world in a new way. To sum the matter up, Jerusalem ceased to be centre of the world; the maps men began to draw, for all their crudity, are maps which show the basic structure of the real globe.

In 1400 a Florentine had brought back from Constantinople a copy of Ptolemy's *Geography*. The view of the world it contained had been forgotten for a thousand years. In the second century AD Ptolemy's world had already included the Canaries, Iceland and Ceylon, all of which found a place on his maps. Translation of his text, misleading as it was, and the multiplication of copies first in manuscript and then in print (after 1477) was a great impulse to better map-making. The atlas – a collection of engraved and printed maps bound in a book – was invented in the sixteenth century; more men than ever could now form a picture of their world. With better projections, navigation was simpler, too. Here the great figure was a Dutchman, Gerhard Kremer, who is remembered as Mercator. He was the first man to print on a map the word 'America' and he invented the projection which is still today the most familiar – a map of the world devised as if it were an unrolled cylinder, with Europe at its centre. This solved the problem of providing a flat surface which would make navigation possible. The Greeks of the fourth century BC had known the world was a globe and the making of terrestrial and celestial globes was another important branch of the geographical revolution (Mercator made his own first globe in 1541) but until the new projection it had not been possible to read necessary navigational data from a flat surface without distortion.

The most striking thing about this progression is its cumulative and systematic nature. European expansion in the next phase of world history would be conscious and directed as it had never been before. Europeans had always wanted land and gold; the greed which lay at the heart of enterprise was not new. Nor was the religious zeal which sometimes inspired them and sometimes cloaked their springs of action even from the actors themselves. What was new was a growing confidence derived from knowledge and success. Europeans stood in 1500 at the beginning of an age in which their energy and confidence would grow seemingly without limit. The world did not come to them, they went out to it and took it.

The full dimensions of such a break with the past were not to be seen at once. In the Mediterranean and Balkans, Europeans still felt threatened and defensive. The sciences of navigation and seamanship still had far to go – not until the eighteenth century, for example, would there be available a time-keeper accurate enough for exact sailing. But the way was

opening to a new relationship between Europe and the rest of the world, and between the parts of Europe itself. Soon, discovery would be followed by conquest. A world revolution was beginning. An equilibrium which had lasted a thousand years was dissolving and its disappearance was to be made manifest in the next two centuries.

The European mind

By 1500 Europe is recognizable as the centre of a new civilization; before long it was to spread to, other lands, too. The heart of this civilization was still religion. The institutional implications and limitations of this have already been touched upon; the Church was a great force of social regulation and government, whatever vicissitudes its central institution had suffered. But it was also the custodian of culture and the teacher of all men.

From the thirteenth century onwards the burden of recording, teaching and study which had been so long borne by the monks was shared by friars and, more important still, by a new institution, in which friars sometimes played a big part, the university. Bologna, Paris and Oxford were the first universities; by 1400 there were fifty-three others. They were new devices both for concentrating and directing intellectual activity and for education. One result soon obvious was the revivifying of the training of the clergy. Already in the middle of the fourteenth century half the English bishops were graduates. But this was not the only reason why universities had been set up. The Emperor Frederick II founded the university of Naples to supply administrators for his south Italian kingdom and when in 1264 an English bishop and royal servant, Walter de Merton, founded the first college at Oxford, among his purposes was that of providing future servants for the crown. One college at Cambridge, King's Hall, was actually founded by the Crown solely with this aim, though it was the only one at either of the ancient English universities of which this was true.

The universities' importance for the future

of Europe was incalculable. Their existence assured that when laymen came to be educated in considerable numbers, they too would be formed by an institution under the control of the Church and suffused with religion. Furthermore, universities would be a great uniting and cosmopolitan force. Their lectures were given in Latin, the language of the Church and the *lingua franca* of educated men until this century. Its former pre-eminence is still commemorated in the vestigial Latin of university ceremonies and the names of degrees.

Law, medicine, theology and philosophy all benefited from the new institution. Philosophy had all but disappeared into theology in the early medieval period. Only one important figure stands out, John Scotus Erigena, an Irish thinker and scholar of the ninth century. Then, three centuries later, European scholars began again to read for themselves works of classical philosophy at first hand. The texts became available from Islamic sources. As the works of Aristotle and Hippocrates were turned into Latin they were at first regarded with suspicion. This persisted until well into the thirteenth century, but gradually a search for reconciliation between the classical and Christian accounts of the world got under way and it became clear, above all because of the work of two Dominicans, Albertus Magnus and his pupil Thomas Aquinas, that reconciliation and synthesis were indeed possible. So it came about that the classical heritage was captured and christened. Instead of providing a contrasting and critical approach to the theocentric culture of Christendom it was incorporated with it. The classical world began to be seen as the forerunner of the Christian. For centuries man would turn for authority in matters intellectual to religion or to the classics. Of the latter it was Aristotle who enjoyed unique prestige. If it did not make him a saint, the Church at least treated him as a kind of prophet.

The immediate evidence was the remarkable systematic and rationalist achievement of medieval scholasticism, the name given to the intellectual effort to penetrate the meaning of

The fifteenth-century tower of the chapel of Merton College, Oxford, looks down on the oldest quadrangle of the oldest of Oxford colleges, Mob Quad. It served once as a refuge from the irritated burghers of the city for the scholars of the university.

Christian teaching. Its strength lay in its embracing sweep, displayed nowhere more brilliantly than in the *Summa theologica* of Aquinas which has been judged both its crowning achievement and a brittle synthesis. It strove to account for all phenomena. Its weakness lay in its unwillingness to address itself to observation and experiment. Christianity gave the medieval mind a powerful training in logical thinking but, only a few men, isolated and untypical, could dimly see the possibility of breaking through authority to a truly experimental method.

Nevertheless, bound by religion though it still was, it is within the Christian cultural achievement that the first signs of liberation from the enclosed world of the early Middle Ages can be seen. Paradoxically, Christendom owed them to Islam. Most important of the places where the two cultures could meet were Sicily and Spain. There the great work of translation of the twelfth and thirteenth centuries took place. Even the Koran was turned into Latin. The process did not involve many people directly. Easy and tolerant relationships between the Faithful and the Infidel were

The tomb of an early professor of law at Bologna, the first important centre of legal learning in Europe, gives us a glimpse of medieval university life. In the relief at the bottom a professor lectures to a room full of students.

possible only in a few places which facilitated face-to-face encounters. The Emperor Frederick II was regarded with the deepest suspicion because although he persecuted heretics he was known to welcome Jews and Saracens to his court at Palermo. Toledo, the old Visigothic capital was another especially important centre. In such places scribes copied and recopied the Latin texts of what were to be the best-sellers of the next six centuries. Euclid's works began a career of being copied, recopied and then printed which may well have meant that in the end they surpassed the success of any book except the Bible – at least until the twentieth century. Such books were to be the basis of university instruction in western Europe until the nineteenth century. In this way the Hellenistic world began again to irrigate the thought of the West.

Roughly speaking, the Islamic transmission of antiquity began with astrology, astronomy and mathematics, subjects closely linked to one another. Ptolemy's astronomical theories reached the West by this route and were found a satisfactory basis for cosmology and navigation until the sixteenth century. The astrolabe had been a

Greek invention, but its use was spread in the West by Arab writings. When Chaucer wrote his treatise on its use, he took as his model an earlier Arab one. More fundamental was the arrival from Arab sources of a new numeration and the decimal point (both originally of Indian origin). This had enormous importance in simplifying calculation; the matter can still be easily tested by attempting sums in the Roman numerals which were all that was available before the Arabic.

Of the sciences of observation, the most important after astronomy to come to the West from Islam was medicine. Here, two levels may be distinguished. Besides providing access through translation to the medical works of Aristotle, Galen and Hippocrates, Arabic medicine also brought into European practice a huge body of therapeutic, anatomical and pharmacological knowledge built up by its own physicians. The prestige of Arab learning and science then made easier the acceptance of more subtly dangerous and subversive ideas and Arab philosophy and theology, too, began to be studied in the West. In the end, even European art seems to have been affected by the Islamic current, for the invention of perspective, which was to transform painting, is said to have come from thirteenth-century Arab Spain. Europe offered little in exchange except the technology of gunnery.

To no other civilization did Europe owe so much in the Middle Ages as to Islam. For all their dramatic and exotic interest, the travels of a Marco Polo or the missionary wanderings of friars in central Asia did little to change the West. The quantity of goods exchanged with other parts of the world was still tiny, even in 1500. Technically, Europe owed to the Far East only her knowledge of silk-making (which had reached her from the eastern empire) and her knowledge of paper which, though made in China in the second century AD, took until the thirteenth to reach Europe and then did so again by way of Arab Spain. Nor did ideas reach Europe from Asia, unless like Indian mathematics they had undergone refinement in

In an early manuscript of Dante's Divine Comedy *the poet is guided through the Inferno by his great predecessor, the Roman poet Virgil. Satan, shown in the lower circle of hell, gnaws the souls of the most abominable among the wicked, Judas, the betrayer of Christ, understandably enough. His fellow-sufferers are surprising: they are Brutus and Cassius, the murderers of Julius Caesar.*

Erasmus of Rotterdam, painted in 1523 by Holbein the Younger, court-painter to Henry VIII of England.

the Arabic crucible. Given the permeability of Islamic culture, it seems less likely that this was because in some sense Islam insulated Europe from the Orient by imposing a barrier between them, than because the Orient could not make its impact felt across such huge distances. It had hardly done so, after all, in pre-Christian antiquity, when communications had been no more difficult.

The reintegration of classical and Christian, though manifested in work like that of Aquinas, was an answer, ten centuries late, to Tertullian's jibing question about what Athens had to do with Jerusalem. In one of the supreme works of art of the Middle Ages – some would judge

the supreme – the *Divine Comedy* of Dante, the importance of the re-attachment of the world of Christendom to its predecessor is already to be seen. Dante describes his journey through Hell, Purgatory and Paradise, the universe of Christian truth. Yet his guide is not a Christian, but a pagan, the classical poet Virgil. This rôle is much more than decorative; Virgil is an authoritative guide to truth, for before Christ, he foretold Him. The classical poet has become a prophet to stand beside those of the Old Testament. Though the notion of a link with antiquity had never quite disappeared (as attempts by enthusiastic chroniclers to link the Franks or the Britons to the descendants of the Trojans had shown) there is in Dante's attitude something marking an epoch. It is an acceptance of the classical world by Christendom, and this, for all the scholastic clutter of its surroundings, was decisive in making possible a change which has usually been seen as more radical, the great revival of humanistic letters of the fifteenth and sixteenth centuries.

Almost the central figure of that moment of cultural history was Erasmus of Rotterdam, sometime a monk and later, as the foremost exponent of classical studies of his day, the correspondent of most of the great humanists. Yet he still saw his classics as the entrance to the supreme study of scripture and his greatest book was an edition of the Greek New Testament. The effects of printing a good text of the Bible were, indeed, to be revolutionary, but Erasmus had no intention of overthrowing religious order, for all the vigour and wit with which he had mocked and teased puffed-up churchmen, and for all the provocation to independent thought which his books and letters provided. His roots lay in the piety of a fifteenth-century mystical movement in the Low Countries called the *devotio moderna*, not in pagan antiquity.

Some of the men who began to cultivate more closely the study of classical authors, and to invoke explicitly pagan classical ideals, invented the notion of the Middle Ages to emphasize their sense of novelty. They in their turn were spoken of as men of a 're-birth' of a lost tradition, a 'Renaissance' of classical antiquity. Yet they were formed in the culture which the great changes in Christian civilization from the twelfth century onwards had made possible. To speak of Renaissance may be helpful if we keep in mind the limitations of the context in which we use the word, but it is to falsify history if we take it to imply a transformation of culture which showed a radical break with medieval Christian civilization. The Renaissance is and was a myth, one of those useful ideas which help men to master their own bearings and therefore to act more effectively. There is no clear line in European history which separates it – whatever the Renaissance may be – from the Middle Ages – however we like to define them.

What can be noticed almost everywhere, though is a change of emphasis. It shows especially in the relation of the age to the past. Men of the thirteenth century, like those of the sixteenth, portrayed the great men of antiquity in the garb of their own day. Alexander the Great at one time looks like a medieval king; later, Shakespeare's Caesar wears not a toga but doublet and hose. There is, that is to say, no real historical sense in either of these pictures of the past, no awareness of the immense differences between past and present men and things. Instead, history was seen at best as a school of examples. The difference between the two attitudes is that in the medieval view antiquity could also be scrutinized for the signs of a divine plan, evidence of whose existence once more triumphantly vindicated the teachings of the Church. This was St Augustine's legacy and what Dante accepted. But by 1500 something else was also being discerned in the past, equally unhistorical, but, men felt, more helpful to their age and predicament. Some saw a classical inspiration, possibly even pagan, distinct from the Christian, and a new attention to classical writings was one result.

The idea of Renaissance is especially linked to innovation in art. Medieval Europe had seen much of this; it seems more vigorous and creative than any of the other great centres of civilized tradition from the twelfth century onwards. In music, drama and poetry new forms and styles were created which move us still. By the fifteenth century, though, it is already clear that they can in no sense be confined to the service of God. Art is becoming autonomous. The eventual consummation of this change was the major aesthetic expression of the Renaissance, transcending by far its stylistic innovations, revolutionary though these were. It was the clearest sign that the Christian synthesis and the ecclesiastical monopoly of culture are breaking up. The slow divergence of classical and Christian mythology was one expression of it; others were the appearance of the Romance and Provençal love poetry (which owed much to Arabic influence), the deployment of the Gothic style in secular building such as the great guildhalls of the new cities, or the rise of a vernacular literature for educated laymen of which perhaps the supreme example is Chaucer's *Canterbury Tales*.

Primavera – Spring – was painted in about 1480 by Sandro Botticelli for the country house of one of the Medici. It is not only an inspiring work of art but an example of the movement towards a humanistic aesthetic. Christian themes are absent; instead, Venus pensively watches the Graces dance, Mercury and the Zephyrs flank the composition, while Spring herself seems gently preoccupied with her private concerns.

Such changes are not easily dated, because acceptance did not always follow rapidly on innovation. In literature, there was a particularly severe physical restriction on what could be done because of a long-enduring shortage of texts. It was not until well into the sixteenth century that the first edition of Chaucer's complete works was published. By then a revolution in thinking was undoubtedly under way, of which all the tendencies so far touched on form parts, but which was something much more than the sum of them and it owes almost everything to the coming of the printed book. Even a vernacular text such as the *Canterbury Tales* could not reach a wide public until printing made large numbers of copies easily available. When this happened, their impact was vastly magnified. This was true of all classes of book, poetry, history, philosophy, technology and, above all, the Bible itself. The effect was the most profound change in the diffusion of knowledge and ideas since the invention of writing; it was the greatest cultural revolution of these centuries.

The new technique owed nothing to stimulus from China, where it was already practised in a modified form, except very indirectly, through the availability of paper. From the fourteenth century, rags were used in Europe to make paper of good quality and this was one of the elements which contributed to the printing revolution. Others were the principle of printing itself (the impressing of images on textiles had been practised in twelfth-century Italy), the use of cast metal for typefaces instead of wood (already used to provide blocks for playing-cards, calendars and religious images), the availability of oil-based ink, and, above all, the use of movable metal type. It was the last invention which was crucial. Although the details are obscure, and experiments with wood letters were going on at the beginning of the fifteenth century in Haarlem, there seems to be no good reason not to credit it to the man whose name has traditionally been associated with it, Johannes Gutenberg, the diamond polisher of Mainz. In about 1450 he and his colleagues brought the elements of modern printing together for the first time, and in 1455 there appeared what is agreed to be the first true printed book in Europe, the Gutenberg Bible.

Gutenberg's own business career was by then a failure; something prophetic of a new age of commerce appears in the fact that he was probably under-capitalized. The accumulation of equipment and type was an expensive business and a colleague from whom he borrowed money took him to court for his debts. Judgement went against Gutenberg, who lost his press, so that the Bible, when it appeared, was not his property. (Happily, the story does not end there; Gutenberg was in the end ennobled by the Archbishop of Mainz, a suitable recognition of what he had done.) But he had launched a revolution. By 1500, it has been calculated, some thirty-five thousand separate editions of books – *incunabula*, as they were called – had been published. This probably means between fifteen and twenty million copies; there may well have been already at that date fewer copies of books in manuscript in the whole world. In the following century there were between a hundred and fifty and two hundred

The oldest illustration of a European printing-press comes from a book of 1499 whose theme is the common late medieval one of the dance of death. Compositor and printers are shown with the tools of their trade, while a bookseller whose shelves still carry books stacked in the medieval fashion is shown in an adjoining shop.

thousand separate editions and perhaps ten times as many copies printed. Such a quantitative change merges into one which is qualitative; the culture which resulted from the coming of printing with movable type was as different from any earlier one as it is also from one which takes radio and television for granted. The modern age was the age of print.

It is interesting but natural that the first printed European book should have been the Bible, the sacred text at the heart of medieval civilization. Through the printing press, knowledge of it was to be diffused as never before and with incalculable results. The first Bible in German was printed in 1466; Italian and French translations followed before the end of the century, but Englishmen had to wait for a printed New Testament in their language until 1526. Into the diffusion of the sacred texts – and the Bible was only the most important of them – pious laymen and churchmen alike poured great resources for fifty to sixty years; presses were even set up in monastic houses. Meanwhile, grammars, histories, and, above all, the classical authors now edited by the humanists also appeared in increasing numbers. The result was a transformation of the European consciousness;

the age of the printed word's dominance had begun.

Its impact could not be contained. With some prescience the pope suggested to bishops in 1501 that the control of printing might be the key to preserving the purity of the faith. But much more was involved than any threat to doctrine, important as that might be. The book itself began to change character; from being a rare work of art, whose mysterious knowledge was accessible only to a few, it became a tool and artifact for the many. Print was to provide an alternative channel of communication for governments and a new medium for artists (the diffusion of pictorial and architectural style in the sixteenth century was much more rapid and widespread than ever before because of the growing availability of the engraved print) and provide a new impetus to the diffusion of technology. A huge demand for literacy and therefore education would be stimulated by it. Probably no single change marks so clearly the ending of one era and the beginning of another.

It is very difficult to formulate judgements about the way in which such changes affected Europe's rôle in the coming era of world history. By 1500, there was certainly much to give confidence to the few Europeans who were likely to think at all about these things. The roots of their civilization, after all, lay in a religion which taught them they were a people voyaging in time, their eyes on a future made a little more comprehensible and perhaps a little less frightening by contemplation of past perils navigated and awareness of a common goal. As a result Europe was to be the first civilization aware of time not as endless (though perhaps cyclical) pressure, but as continuing change in a certain direction, as progress. The chosen people of the Bible, after all, were *going* somewhere; they were not simply people to whom inexplicable things happened which had to be passively endured. From the simple acceptance of change was before long to spring the will to live in change which was the peculiarity of modern man. Secularized and far away from their origins, such ideas could be very important;

the advance of science soon provided an example. In another sense, too, the Christian heritage was decisive for, after the fall of Byzantium, Europeans believed that they alone possessed it (or in effect alone, for there was little sense among ordinary folk of what Slav, Nestorian or Coptic Christianity might be). It was an encouraging idea for men who stood at the threshold of centuries of unfolding power, discovery and conquest. Even with the Ottomans to face, Europe in 1500 was no longer just the beleaguered fortress of the Dark Ages, but a stronghold from which men were beginning to sally forth in counter-attack. Jerusalem had been abandoned to the infidel, Byzantium had fallen. Where should be the new centre of the world?

The men of the Dark Ages who had somehow persevered in adversity and had erected a Christian world from the debris of the past and the gifts of the barbarians had thus wrought infinitely more than they could have known. Yet such implications required time for their development; in 1500 there was little to show that the future belonged to the Europeans. Such contacts as they had with other peoples by no means demonstrated the clear superiority of their own way. Portuguese in West Africa might manipulate black men to their own ends and relieve them of their gold dust and slaves, but in Persia or India they stood in the presence of great cultures whose spectacle often dazzled them. The men of 1500 were thus and in many other ways not modern men. We cannot without an effort understand them, even when they speak Latin, for their Latin had overtones and associations we are bound to miss; it was not only the *lingua franca* of educated men, but the language of religion.

In the half-light of a dawning modernity the weight of that religion remains the best clue to the reality of Europe's first civilization. Religion was one of the most impressive reinforcements of the stability of a culture which has been considered in this book almost entirely from an important perspective, but one fundamentally anachronistic, that of change. Except in the

The opening of the Book of Proverbs, from Gutenberg's 'forty-two-line' Bible (so-called because of the size of the page). The illumination, which includes a picture of Solomon in the initial letter, was added by hand after printing the text; at this time, the printed book had still to establish its own conventions of appearance and design.

shortest term, change was not what many people would have been most aware of in the fifteenth century. For all men, the deepest determinant of their lives was still the slow but ever-repeated passage of the seasons, a rhythm which set the pattern of work and leisure, poverty and prosperity, of the routines of home, workshop and study. English judges and university teachers still work to a year originally divided by the need to get in the harvest. On this rhythm were imposed those of religion itself. When the harvest was in the Church blessed it and the calendar of the Christian year provided the more detailed timetable to which men lived. Some of it was very old, even pre-Christian; it had been going on for centuries and could hardly be imagined otherwise. It even regulated many people's days, for every three hours the religious were called to worship and prayer in thousands of monasteries and convents by the bell of their house. When it could be heard outside the walls, laymen set the pattern of their day by it, too. Before there were striking clocks, only the bell of the parish church, cathedral or monastery supplemented the sun or the burning of a candle as a record of passing time, and it did so by announcing the hour of another act of worship.

It is only in a very special, long perspective that we can rightly speak of centuries during which this went on and on as ones of 'revolutionary' changes. Even the most obvious of them, the growth of a town, an onset of plague, the displacement of one noble family by another, the building of a cathedral or the collapse of a castle all took place in a remarkably unchanged setting. The shapes of the fields tilled by English peasants in 1500 were often still those visited by the men who wrote them down in Domesday Book, over four hundred years before, and when men went to visit the nuns of Laycock in

order to wind up their house in the 1530s, they found, to their amazement, these aristocratic ladies still speaking among themselves the Norman-French commonly used in noble families three centuries earlier.

Such immense inertia must never be forgotten; it was made all the more impressive and powerful by the fleeting lives of most men and women of the Middle Ages. Only very deep in the humus of this society did there lie a future. Perhaps the key to that future's relationship with the past can be located in the fundamental Christian dualism of this life and the world to come, the earthly and the heavenly. This was to prove an irritant of great value, secularized in the end as a new critical instrument, the contrast of what is and what might be, of ideal and actual. In it, Christianity secreted an essence to be utilized against itself, for in the end it would make possible the independent critical stance, a complete break with the world Aquinas and Erasmus both knew. The idea of autonomous criticism would only be born very gradually, though; it can be traced in many individual adumbrations between 1300 and 1700, but they only go to show that, once again, sharp dividing lines between medieval and modern are matters of expository convenience, not of historical reality.

Book Five · The Making of the European Age

After 1500 or so, there are many signs that a new age of world history is beginning. Some of them have already appeared in these pages; the discoveries in the Americas and the first shoots of European enterprise in Asia are among them. At the outset they provide hints about the dual nature of a new age – that it is increasingly an age of truly world history and that it is one whose story is dominated by the astonishing success of one civilization among many, that of Europe. These are two aspects of the same process: there is a more and more continuous and organic interconnexion between events in all countries, but it is largely to be explained by the efforts of Europeans. They eventually became masters of the globe and they used their mastery – sometimes without knowing it – to make the world one. As a result world history has for the last two or three centuries a growing identity and unity of theme.

In a famous passage, Macaulay once spoke of red men scalping one another on the shores of the Great Lakes so that a European king could rob his neighbour of a province he coveted. This was one striking side of the story we must now embark upon – the gradual entanglement of struggles the world over with one another in greater and greater wars – but politics, empire-building and military expansion were only a tiny part of what was going on. The economic integration of the globe was another part of the process; more important still was the spreading of common assumptions and ideas. The result was to be, in a cant phrase of today, 'One world' – of sorts. The age of independent or nearly independent civilizations has come to a close.

Men and nations are still so different from one another that this may seem at first sight a wildly misleading exaggeration. National, cultural and racial differences have not ceased to produce and inspire appalling conflicts; the history of the centuries since 1500 can be (and often is) written mainly as a series of wars and violent struggles and men in different countries obviously do not feel much more like one another than did their predecessors centuries ago. Yet they are much more alike than their ancestors of, say, the tenth century and show it in hundreds of ways ranging from the superficialities of dress to the forms in which they get their living and organize their societies. The origins, extent and limits of this change make up most of the story which follows. It is the outcome of something still going on in many places which we sometimes call modernization. For centuries it has been grinding away at differences between cultures and it is the deepest and most fundamental expression of the growing integration of world history. Another way of describing the process is to say that the world is Europeanized, for modernization is above all a matter of ideas and techniques which are European in origin. Whether 'modernization' is the same as 'Europeanization', though, can be left for later discussion; perhaps it is only a matter of verbal preferences. What is obvious is that, chronologically, it is with the modernization of Europe that the unification of world history begins. A great change in European civilization was the starting-point of modern history.

1 A new kind of society: early modern Europe

'Modern history' is a familiar enough term, but it has not always meant the same thing. As historians have looked more closely at the past its meaning has changed. There was a time when modern history was what had happened since the 'ancient' history whose subject-matter was the story of the Jews, Greeks and Romans; this is a sense which, for example, is still used to define a course of study at Oxford which includes the Middle Ages. Then it came to be distinguished from 'medieval' history, too. Now a further refinement is often made, for historians have begun to make distinctions within it and now sometimes speak of an 'early modern' period. By this, though, they are really drawing our attention to a process, for they apply it to the era in which the modern Atlantic world emerged from the tradition-dominated, agrarian, superstitious and confined Europe of the Middle Ages and this took place at different times in different countries. In England it happened very rapidly; in eastern Europe it was far from complete by 1800. But the reality of the process is obvious, for all the irregularity with which it expressed itself and it was very important, for it laid the groundwork for a European world hegemony.

Tudor London: England's capital and a cradle of the liberating, commercial spirit which carried European civilization to its greatest triumphs. In the foreground is old London Bridge, dating from the twelfth century and for long the only bridge across the Thames at London.

A useful starting-point for thinking about what was involved is to begin with the simple and obvious truth that for most of human history most people's lives have been deeply and cruelly shaped by the fact that they have had little or no choice about the way in which they could provide themselves and their families with shelter and enough to eat. The possibility that things might be otherwise has only recently become a conceivable one to even a minority of the world's population and it became a reality for any substantial number of people only with changes in the economy of early modern Europe.

We can follow some of these changes as we can follow no earlier ones because for the first time there is reasonably plentiful and continuous quantified data. In one important respect, historical evidence shows a notable qualitative improvement in the last four or five centuries: it becomes much more statistical. Measurement therefore becomes easier. The source of new statistical material was often government. For many reasons, governments wanted to know more and more about the resources or potential resources at their disposal. But private records, especially of business, also give us much more numerical data after 1500. The multiplication of copies as paper and printing became more common meant that the chance of their survival was enormously increased. Commercial techniques appeared which required publication of data in collated forms; the movements of ships, or reports of prices, for example. Moreover, as historians have refined their techniques, they have attacked even poor or fragmentary sources with much greater success than was possible even a few years ago.

All this has provided much knowledge of the size and shape of change in early modern Europe, though we must be careful not to exaggerate either the degree of precision such material permits or what can be learnt from it. For a long time the collection of good statistics was very difficult. Even quite elementary questions, about, for example, who lived in a certain place, were very difficult to answer accurately until recent times. One of the great aims of reforming monarchs in the eighteenth century was merely to carry out accurate listings of land within their states, cadastral surveys, as they were called. It was only in 1801 that the first census was held in the United Kingdom – nearly eight centuries after Domesday Book. France did not have her first official census until 1876 nor the Russian empire her only one until 1897. Such delays are not really surprising. A census or a survey requires a complex and reliable administrative machine. It may arouse strong opposition (when governments seek new information, new taxes often follow). Such difficulties are enormously increased where the population is as illiterate as it was in much of Europe for the greater part of modern history.

Of course, new statistical material can also raise as many historical problems as it solves. It can reveal a bewildering variety of contemporary phenomena which often makes generalization harder; it has become much harder to say anything at all about the French peasantry of the eighteenth century since research revealed the diversity hidden by that simple term and that perhaps there was no such thing as *a* French peasantry, but only several different ones. Finally, too, statistics can illuminate facts while throwing no light at all on causes. Nevertheless after 1500 we are more and more in an age of measurement and the overall effect of this is to make it easier to make accurate statements about what was happening than in earlier times at other places.

Demographic history is the most obvious example. At the end of the fifteenth century

Information for a new age of global commerce: Lloyd's list in the eighteenth century, when it was about to double its frequency of publication and to appear twice weekly. Its original form, at the end of the previous century, had been a simple list of prices chalked up in Lloyd's coffee-house.

European population was poised on the edge of growth which has continued ever since. We may crudely distinguish two phases in what followed 1500. Until about the middle of the eighteenth century the increase of population was (except for notable local and temporary interruptions) relatively slow and steady; this roughly corresponds to 'early modern' history and may be thought to be a characteristic of it. In the second phase the increase accelerated and great changes followed. Only the first phase concerns us here, because it regulated the way in which modern Europe took shape. The general facts and trends within it are clear enough, though they rely heavily on estimates. Such estimates are much better based than in earlier times, in part because there was almost continuous interest in population problems from the early seventeenth century onwards. This contributed to the foundation of the science of statistics (then called 'Political Arithmetic') at the end of the seventeenth century, mainly by Englishmen. They did some remarkable work, though their efforts only provided a tiny island of relatively rigorous method in a sea of guesses and inferences. Nevertheless the broad picture is clear. In 1500 Europe had slightly more than 100 million inhabitants, two centuries later she had slightly less than 150 million and in 1800 slightly less than 200 million. Before 1750 Europe had grown fairly steadily at a rate which maintained her share of the world's population at about one-fifth until 1700 or so, but by 1800 she had nearly a quarter of the world's inhabitants.

Obviously, therefore, for a long time there were no such startling disparities as appeared later between the rate of growth in Europe and that elsewhere. It seems reasonable to conclude that this meant that in other ways, too, European and non-European populations were less different than they were to come to be after 1800. The usual age of death among Europeans, for example, still remained low. Before 1800 they were on the average always much younger than nowadays, because people died earlier. At birth a French peasant of the eighteenth century had a life expectancy of about twenty-two years and only a roughly one in four chance of surviving infancy. His chances were therefore much the same as those of an Indian peasant in 1950 or an Italian under imperial Rome. Comparatively few people would have survived their forties, and, since they were less well fed than we are, they would have looked old to us at that age, and probably rather small in stature and unhealthy-looking. As in the Middle Ages, women tended still to die before men and this meant that many men made a second or even a third marriage, not, as today, because of divorce, but because they were soon widowers.

The average European couple had a fairly short married life. If they were well-off they could afford a fairly large family; the poor had smaller ones and there is strong inferential evidence both that some form of family limitation was already taking place in some places in the seventeenth century and that other methods of achieving it than abortion and infanticide were available and widely known. No doubt economic pressures lie in the background of this mysterious topic, but this remains one of those areas where a largely illiterate society is almost impossible to penetrate historically. We can say very little with confidence about the material facts of early birth control and still less about its implications – if there were any – for the ways in which early modern Europeans thought about themselves and their rights and powers over their own lives.

Overall such demographic facts reflect the continuing economic predominance of agriculture. For a long time it produced only slightly more food than was needed and could only feed a slowly growing population. In 1500 Europe was a rural continent of villages in which people lived at a pretty low level of subsistence. It would have seemed very empty to modern eyes. The English population, heavy in relation to area by comparison with the rest of the continent, was in 1800 only about a seventh of today's and in eastern Europe there were huge empty spaces for which population was eagerly sought by rulers who encouraged immigration in all sorts of ways. Yet the towns and cities managed to grow in number and size, one or two of them spectacularly faster than the population as a whole. Amsterdam reached a total of about 200000 inhabitants in the eighteenth century. Paris probably doubled in size between 1500 and 1700, and rose to slightly less than a half-million. London shot ahead of Paris by going up from about 120000 to nearly 700000 in the same two centuries; in a much smaller English population this, of course, meant a much bigger shift to urban life. A significant new word came into use in English: suburbs. But it is not easy to generalize about medium-sized and smaller towns. Most were quite small, still under 20000 in 1700, but the nine European cities of more than 100000 in 1500 had become at least a dozen two hundred years later. Yet Europe's predominance in urbanization was not so marked in these centuries as it was to become and there were still many great cities in other continents. Mexico, for example, outdid all European cities of the sixteenth century with its population of 300000.

Neither urbanization nor population growth was evenly spread. France remained the largest west European nation in these years; she had about nineteen million inhabitants in 1700, when England had only about six million. But it is not easy to make comparisons because estimates are much less reliable for some areas than others and because boundary changes often make it hard to be sure what we are talking about under the same name at different periods. It is clear that some places underwent checks and possibly setbacks in their population growth in a wave of seventeenth-century disasters. Spain, Italy and Germany all had bad outbreaks of epidemic disease in the 1630s and there were other celebrated attacks such as the Great Plague of London of 1665 which were more localized. Famine was another sporadic and local check; we hear even of cannibalism in the middle seventeenth century in Germany. Poor feeding and the lower resistance it led to quickly produced disaster when coupled to the susceptibility of the economy to disruption by a bad harvest. When accentuated by warfare, of which there was always a great deal in central Europe, the result could be cataclysmic. Famine and the diseases which followed armies about in their baggage-trains could quickly depopulate a small area. This was in part a reflection of the degree to which economic life was still localized, though; the converse was that a particular town might get off unscathed even in a campaigning zone if it escaped siege or sack, while only a few miles away another might be devastated. The situation was always precarious until population growth began to be matched by equally important advances in productivity.

In this, as in so many things, different countries have different histories. A renewed expansion of agriculture seems to have got under way in the middle of the fifteenth century, one of its signs being the resumption of land which had reverted to waste in the depopulation of the fourteenth century. Yet this had made little headway in any but a few places before 1550 or so. It remained confined to them for a long time, though by that date there had already been important improvements in techniques which raised the productivity of land, mainly by the application of labour, that is by intensive cultivation. Where their impact was not felt the medieval past long lingered in the countryside. Even the coming of money was slow in breaking into the near self-sufficiency of some communities. In eastern Europe serfdom was actually extending its range when it was dying out elsewhere. Yet by 1800, taking Europe as a whole and a few leading countries in particular, agriculture was one of the two economic sectors where progress was most marked (commerce was the other). Overall, it had at any rate proved capable of sustaining a continuing rise of population at first very slowly, but at a quickening rate.

This progress increasingly took two main forms: orientation towards the market, and technical innovation. They were interconnected. The presence of towns and concentrated population area had even in the fifteenth century made the inhabitants of the Low Countries experts in the techniques of intensive cultivation. It was in Flanders, too, that better use of drainage opened the way to better pasture and, therefore, to a larger animal population. Another area with relatively large town populations was the Po valley; north Italy was an area where new crops were introduced into Europe from Asia. Rice, for example, an important addition to the European larder, appeared in the Arno and Po valleys in the fifteenth century. A large population near by meant a market and therefore an incentive. On the other hand, it did not always mean instant success. It took about two centuries for the potato, which came to Europe from America, to become established as a normal item of consumption in England, Germany and France, in spite of its obvious nutritional value and much folklore stressing its qualities as an aphrodisiac and value in the treatment of warts.

From the Low Countries agricultural improvements spread in the sixteenth century to eastern England where they were slowly elaborated further. In the seventeenth century London at last became a corn-exporting port and in the next other Europeans came to England to learn how to farm. The eighteenth century also brought improvements in husbandry and animal breeding which were to continue in a direct line to yields on crops and a quality of livestock now taken for granted but until then unimaginable. The appearance of the countryside and its occupants was transformed. Agriculture provided the first demonstration of what might be done by science – by experiment, observation, record, and experiment again – to increase Man's control of his environment more rapidly than the selection imposed by custom. Improvements favoured the reorganization of land in bigger farms, the reduction of the number of smallholders except on land which specially favoured them, the employment of wage-labour, and high capital investment in buildings, drainage and machinery. The speed of change must not be exaggerated. One index of change in England was the pace of 'enclosure', the consolidation for private use of the open fields and common lands of the traditional village. It was only at the end of the eighteenth century and the beginning of the nineteenth that the Acts of Parliament authorizing this became frequent and numerous. The complete integration of agriculture with the market economy and the treatment of land simply as a commodity like any other would have to wait for the nineteenth century, even in England, the leader of world agriculture until the opening of the overseas cornlands. Yet by the eighteenth century the way ahead was beginning to appear.

This overall agricultural change in the end eliminated the recurrent dearths which so long retained their power to destroy demographic advance. Perhaps the last moment when European population seems to have pressed on resources so as to threaten another great calamity like that of the fourteenth century came at the end of the sixteenth century. In the next bad spell, in the middle decades of the following century, England and the Netherlands escaped the worst. Thereafter, famine and dearth become in Europe local and national events, still capable, it is true, of causing famine and demographic damage on a large scale, but gradually succumbing to the increasing availability of imported grain. Bad harvests, it has been said, made France 'one great hospital' in 1708–9, but that was in wartime. Later in the century some Mediterranean countries depended for their flour on the rising corn production of the Baltic lands. True, it would be a long time before import would be a sure resource; often it could not operate quickly enough, especially where land transport was required. Some parts of France and Germany were to suffer dearth even in the nineteenth century and in the eighteenth century the French population grew faster than production so that the standard of living of many Frenchmen then actually fell drastically. For the English rural labourer, though, some of that century was later looked back to as a golden age of plentiful wheaten bread and even meat on the table.

In the late sixteenth century one response to the obscurely felt pressure of an expanding population upon slowly growing resources had been the promoting of emigration. By 1800, Europeans had made a large contribution to the peopling of new lands overseas, though far from so great a one as was to come, and this has to be taken into account in their demographic history. In 1751 an American reckoned that North America contained a million persons of British origin; modern calculations are that about 250000 British emigrants went to the New World in the seventeenth century, one and a half millions in the next. There were also Germans (about 200000) there, and Frenchmen in Canada. By 1800 it seems reasonable to suppose that something like two million Europeans

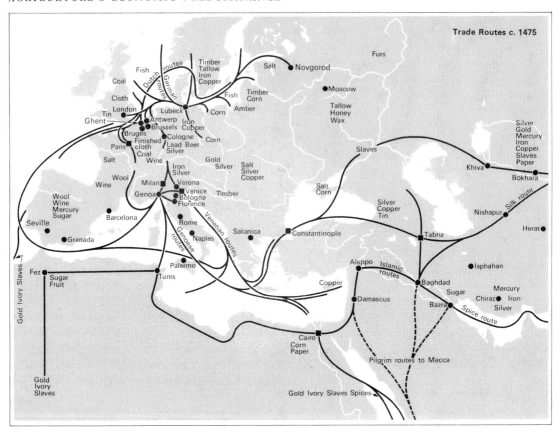

had gone to America north of the Rio Grande. South of it there were about 100 000 Spaniards and Portuguese.

Fears that there was not enough to eat at home helped to initiate these great migrations and reflected the continuing pre-eminence of agriculture in all thinking about economic life. There were important changes in three centuries in the structure and scale of all the main sectors of the European economy, but it was still true in 1800 (as it had been true in 1500) that the agricultural sector predominated even in France and England, the two large western countries where commerce and manufacture had shown most progress. Moreover, nowhere was anything but a tiny part of the population engaged in industry entirely unconnected with agriculture. Brewers, weavers, and dyers all depended on agriculture, while many who grew crops or cultivated land also span, wove or dealt

in commodities for the market. Apart from agriculture, it is only in the commercial sector that we can observe sweeping change. Here there is from the second half of the fifteenth century a visible quickening of tempo. Europe was regaining something like the commercial vigour she had displayed in the thirteenth century. It showed in scale, technique and direction. Again there is a connexion with the growth of towns. They both needed and provided a living for specialists. The great fairs and markets of the Middle Ages still continued. So did medieval laws on usury and the restrictive practices of gilds. Yet a whole new commercial world came into existence before 1800.

It was already discernible in the sixteenth century when there began the long expansion of world commerce which was to last, virtually uninterrupted except by war, until 1930. It carried further the shift of economic gravity from southern to north-western Europe, from the Mediterranean to the Atlantic, which has already been remarked. One contribution to this was made by political troubles and wars such as ruined Italy in the early sixteenth century; others are comprised in tiny, short-lived but crucial pressures like the Portuguese harassment of Jews which led to so many of them going, with their commercial skills, to the Low Countries at about the same time. The great commercial success story of the sixteenth century was Antwerp's, though it collapsed after a few decades in a welter of political and economic disasters. In the seventeenth century Amsterdam and London surpassed it. In each case an important trade based on a well-populated hinterland provided profits for diversification into manufacturing industry, services and banking. The old

Pictures of the Elizabethan baker at work are combined with moral precepts in a manuscript belonging to the Company of Bakers.

banking supremacy of the medieval Italian cities passed first to the Low Countries and the German bankers of the sixteenth century and then, finally, to Holland and London. The Bank of Amsterdam and the Bank of England were already international economic forces in the seventeenth century. About them clustered other banks and merchant houses undertaking operations of credit and finance. Interest rates came down and the bill of exchange, a medieval invention, underwent an enormous extension of use and became the primary financial instrument of international trade.

This was the beginning of the increasing use of paper, instead of metallic currency. In the

585

*From the Middle Ages to the present century,
pogroms of Jews have been endemic in some parts
of Europe. A print of a notorious attack on
the Frankfurt ghetto in 1614.*

*By 1563 the rich Baltic trade already required
for its operation one of the major buildings of
the port of Antwerp, the hall of the Hanse
merchants.*

eighteenth century came the first European
paper currencies and the invention of the cheque.
Joint stock companies generated another form
of negotiable security, their own shares.
Quotation in London coffee-houses in the
seventeenth century was overtaken by the
foundation of the London Stock Exchange. By
1800 such an institution existed in many other
countries. New schemes for the mobilization of
capital and its deployment proliferated in
London, Paris and Amsterdam. Lotteries and
tontines at one time enjoyed a vogue; so
did some spectacularly disastrous investment
schemes, of which the most notorious was the
great South Sea 'Bubble'. But all the time the
world was growing more commercial, more used
to the idea of employing money to make money
and was supplying itself with the apparatus of
modern capitalism.

One effect quickly appeared in the much
greater attention paid to commercial questions
in diplomatic negotiation from the later seventeenth century and in the fact that countries
were prepared to fight over them. The English
and Dutch went to war over trade in 1652 and
this opened a long era during which they, the
French and Spanish, fought again and again
over quarrels in which questions of trade were
important and often paramount.

Governments not only looked after their
merchants by going to war to uphold their
interests, but also intervened in other ways in
the working of the commercial economy. One
advantage they could offer was a grant of
monopoly privileges to a company under a
charter; this made the raising of capital easier
by offering some security for a return. In the
end people came to think that chartered companies might not be the best way of securing
economic advantage and they went into disfavour (enjoying a last brief revival at the end
of the nineteenth century). None the less, such
activities closely involved government and
therefore the concerns of businessmen shaped
both policy and law.

Occasionally the interplay of commercial
development and society seems to throw light
on changes with very deep implications indeed.
One example came when a seventeenth-century
English financier for the first time offered life
insurance to the public. There had already
begun the practice of selling annuities on a
man's life. What was new was the application of
actuarial science and the newly available
statistics of political arithmetic to this business.
A reasonable calculation instead of a bet was
now possible on a matter hitherto of awe-
inspiring uncertainty and irrationality: death.

With increasing refinement men would go on to offer (at a price) protection against a wide range of disaster. This would, incidentally, also provide another and very important device for the mobilization of wealth in large amounts for further investment. But the timing of the discovery of life insurance, at the start of what has sometimes been called the 'Age of Reason', suggests also that the dimensions of economic change are sometimes very far-reaching indeed. It was one tiny source and expression of a coming secularizing of the universe.

The most impressive structural development in European commerce was the sudden new importance to it of overseas trade from the second half of the seventeenth century onwards. This was part of the shift of economic activity from Mediterranean to northern Europe already observable before 1500. By the late seventeenth century, though the closed trade of Spain and Portugal with their transatlantic colonies was important, overseas commerce was dominated by the Dutch, the first great maritime trading nation, and their increasingly successful rivals, the English. Dutch commerce grew out of the supply of salted herrings to European markets and the possession of a particularly suitable bulk-carrying vessel, the 'flute' or 'fly-boat'. With this the Dutch dominated the important Baltic trade from whose mastery they advanced to become the carriers of Europe. In the later seventeenth century they tended to be displaced gradually by the English, though they maintained a wide spread of colonies and trading stations, especially in the Far East. The Atlantic was the basis of English supremacy at sea. Fish was important here, too, The English caught the immensely nutritious and therefore immensely valuable cod on the Newfoundland banks, dried it and salted it ashore, and then sold it in Mediterranean countries, where fish was in great demand because of the practice of fasting on Fridays. *Bacalao*, as it was called, can still be found on the tables of southern Spain, once the tourist coast is left behind. Gradually, both Dutch and English broadened and diversified

The demand for business manuals of all sorts provided a profitable field of publication to printers. They began to appear in large numbers from the seventeenth century; this example, from France, and dedicated to an outstanding finance minister, deals with the complicated science of the exchange of specie, an important part of the banker's skills in an age which still depended heavily for its business on the physical transfer of coin.

their carrying trade and became dealers themselves, too. Nor was France out of the race; her overseas trade doubled in the first half of the seventeenth century.

Rising populations and some assurance of adequate transport (water was always cheaper

European Trading stations and possessions in Africa and Asia c. 1750

ICELAND

FAEROES (Danish)

GREAT BRITAIN

DENMARK and NORWAY

NETHERLANDS

FRANCE

PORTU-GAL SPAIN

St Petersburg

SIBERIA

RUSSIA

JAPAN

MADEIRA (Port.)

CANARIES (Sp.)

GOREE (Fr.)

CAPE COAST CASTLE (Br.)

CAPE VERDE (Port.)

ACCRA (Br.)

Christiansborg (Danish)

FERNANDO PO (Port.)

ST. HELENA (Br.)

ANGOLA

MOZAMBIQUE

CAPE PROVINCE

MADAGASCAR

MAURITIUS (Fr.)

PERSIA

ARABIA

CHINA

PACIFIC OCEAN

Surat (Br.)

Chandernagore (Fr.)

Calcutta (Br.)

Bombay (Br.)

INDIA

Goa (Port.)

Madras (Br.)

Pondicherry (Fr.)

SIAM

Macao (Port.)

PHILIPPINES

CEYLON (DUTCH)

Malacca

BORNEO

SUMATRA

EAST INDIES

CELEBES

NEW GUINEA

JAVA

Batavia

TIMOR (Dutch and Port.)

INDIAN OCEAN

French Territory   Portuguese Territory   Dutch Territory
British Territory   Spanish Territory   Danish - Norwegian Territory

than land carriage) slowly built up an international trade in cereals, while shipbuilding itself promoted the movement of such commodities as pitch, flax or timber, staples first of Baltic trade and later important in the economy of North America. More than European consumption was involved, for all this was taking place in a setting of growing colonial empires and by the eighteenth century we are already in the presence of an oceanic economy, at least in outline. The Portuguese had opened the trade to the Far East and the Dutch, British and French all followed them there. In the Atlantic the Spanish were involved, too. By 1700 an

international trading community had come into being which ran round the globe.

In its business an important and growing part was played by slaves. Most of them were of the black African stocks whose first transplants were shipped across the Atlantic to Brazil, the Caribbean colonies and British settlements on the North American mainland. The demographic, economic and political effects are still with us. African slaves are by no means the only ones to have played an important part in modern history, nor were Europeans the only slavers. None the less, black slavery based on the buying of Africans from other Africans by

Sixteenth-century ship-building: an English drawing.

Englishmen, Dutchmen and Frenchmen, and their sale to other Europeans in the Americas is a phenomenon whose repercussions have carried much further than the enslavement of Europeans by Ottomans or Africans by Arabs. Much of the labour of American colonies came to be supplied by black slaves, though for climatic reasons the slave population was not uniformly spread among them. Always the great majority of slaves worked in agriculture or domestic service: black craftsmen or, later, factory workers were unusual.

The slave trade itself was commercially important. Huge profits were occasionally made – a fact which partly explains the crammed and pestilential holds of the slave-ships in which were confined human cargoes which rarely had a death-rate per voyage of less than 10 per cent and sometimes suffered much more appalling mortality. The supposed value of the trade made it a great and contested prize though the normal return on capital has usually been exaggerated. For two centuries it provoked diplomatic wrangling and even war as nation after nation sought to break into it or mono-polize it for their own colonies. This testified to the trade's importance in the eyes of statesmen, whether it was justified or not.

It was once a popular view that the slave trade's profits did much to provide the capital for European industrialization, though this no longer seems plausible. Industrialization was a slow process. Before 1800, though there were important examples of industrial concentration in several European countries, the growth of both manufacturing and extractive industry was still in the main a matter of the multiplication of small-scale artisan production and its technical elaboration, rather than of new methods and institutions more typical of mature industrial society. Europe had by 1500 an enormous pool of wealth to draw on in her large numbers of skilled craftsmen, already used to investigating new processes and exploring new techniques. Two centuries of gunnery had brought mining and metallurgy to a high pitch. Scientific instruments and mechanical clocks testified to a wide diffusion of skill in the making of precision goods. Such advantages as these shaped the early pattern of the industrial age and soon began to reverse a traditional relationship with Asia. For centuries oriental craftsmen had astounded Europeans by their skill and the quality of their work. Asian textiles and ceramics had a superiority which lives in our everyday language: china, muslin, calico, shan-tung are still familiar words. Then, in the fourteenth and fifteenth centuries, supremacy in some forms of craftsmanship had passed to Europe, notably in mechanical and engineering skills. Asian potentates began to seek Europeans who could teach them how to make effective firearms; they even collected mechanical toys which were the commonplaces of European fairs. Such a reversal of rôles was based on Europe's accumulation of skills in traditional occupations and their extension into new fields. This happened usually in towns; craftsmen often travelled from one to another, following demand. So much it is easy to see. What is harder is to see what it was in the European mind which pressed the European craftsmen forward and also stimulated the interest of his social betters so that a craze for mechanical engineering is as important an aspect of what we call the Renaissance as is the work of its architects and goldsmiths. After all, this did not happen elsewhere.

Early industrial areas grew by accretion, often around the centres of established European industries (such as textiles or brewing) closely related to agriculture. This long continued to be true. These old trades had created concentrations of supporting industry. Antwerp had been the great port of entry to Europe for English cloth; as a result, finishing and dying establishments appeared there to work up further the commodities flowing through the port. In the English countryside, wool merchants shaped the early pattern of industrial growth by putting out to peasant spinners and weavers the raw materials they needed. The presence of minerals was another locating factor; mining and metallurgy were the most important industrial activities independent of agriculture. But industries could stagnate or even, sometimes, collapse. This seems to have happened to Italy. Its medieval industrial pre-eminence disappeared in the sixteenth century while that of the Low Countries and western and southern Germany – the old Carolingian heartland – lasted another century or so until it began to be clear that England, the Dutch Netherlands and Sweden were the new industrial leaders. In the eighteenth century Russia's extractive industries would add her to this list. By that time, too, other factors were beginning to enter the equation of economic development as organized science was being brought to bear on industrial techniques and state policy shaped industry both consciously and unconsciously.

The long-term picture of overall expansion and growth obviously requires much qualification, and dramatic fluctuations could easily occur even in the nineteenth century, when a bad harvest could lead to runs on banks and a contraction of demand for manufactured goods big enough to be called a slump. In a measure this was a reflexion of the growing development and

Morals and economics rarely cohere to everyone's satisfaction: a Flemish engraving condemns the saver whose avarice does the devil's work for him by taking coin out of circulation.

integration of the economy. This could cause new forms of distress. Not long after 1500, for example, it began to be noticed that prices were rising with unprecedented speed. Locally this trend was sometimes very sharp indeed, doubling costs in a year. Though nothing like this rate was anywhere maintained for long the general effect seems to have been a roughly four-fold rise in European prices in a century. Given modern rates of inflation, this does not seem very shocking, but it was quite novel and bound to have great and grave repercussions. Among those who owned some property, some benefited and some suffered. Some landowners reacted by putting up rents and increasing as much as possible the yields from their feudal dues. Some had to sell out. In this sense, inflation accelerated social mobility. Among the poor, the almost universal effects were harsh, for the price of agricultural produce shot up and money wages did not keep pace. Real wages therefore fell. This was sometimes made worse by local factors, too. In England, for example, high wool prices tempted landlords to enclose common land and thus remove it from common use in order to put sheep on it. The wretched peasant grazier starved and, thus, as one famous contemporary comment put it, 'sheep ate men'. Everywhere in the central third of the century there were popular revolts and a running disorder which reveal both the incomprehensibility and the severity of what was going on. Everywhere it was the extremes of society who felt the pinch of inflation most sharply; to the poor it brought starvation while kings were pinched because they had to spend more than anyone else.

Much ink has been spent by historians on explaining this century-long price rise. They no longer feel satisfied with the explanation first put forward by contemporary observers, that the essential cause was a new supply of bullion which followed the opening of the New World mines by the Spanish; inflation was well under way before American bullion began to arrive in any significant quantity, even if gold later aggravated things. Probably the fundamental pressure always came from a population whose numbers were increasing when big advances in productivity still lay in the future. The rise in prices continued until the beginning of the seventeenth century. Then it even began occasionally to show signs of falling until a slower increase was resumed around 1700.

The twentieth century needs no reminders that social change can quickly follow economic change. We have little belief in the immutability of social forms and institutions. Three hundred years ago, many men and women believed them to be virtually God-given and the result was that although social changes took place in the aftermath of inflation (and, it must be said, for many other reasons) they were muffled and masked by the persistence of old forms. Superficially and nominally much of European society remained unchanged between 1500 and 1800 or thereabouts. Yet the economic realities underlying it changed a great deal. Appearances were deceptive.

Rural life had already begun to show this in some countries before 1500. As agriculture became more and more a matter of business (though by no means only because of that), the traditional shape of rural society had to change as well. Forms were usually preserved, and the results were more and more incongruous. Although feudal lordship still existed in France in the 1780s it was by then less a social reality than an economic device. The 'seigneur' might never see his tenants, might not be of noble blood, and might draw nothing from his lordship except sums of money which represented his claims on his tenants' labour, time and produce. Further east, the feudal relationship remained more of a reality. This in part reflected an alliance of rulers and nobles to take advantage of the new market for grain and timber in the growing population of western and southern Europe. They tied peasants to the land and exacted heavier and heavier labour services. In Russia serfdom became the very basis of society.

In England, on the other hand, even the commercialized 'feudalism' which existed in France had gone long before 1800, and though such a thing as noble status existed, it conveyed no legal privilege beyond the rights to be summoned to a parliament and to expect access to the King enjoyed by peers of the realm (their other legal distinction was that like most of the other subjects of King George III, they could not vote in the election of a Member of Parliament). The English nobility was a tiny set; until the end of the eighteenth century the house of lords had less than two hundred hereditary members, whose status could only be transmitted to their one direct heir. There did not therefore exist in England the large class of noble men and women, all of whom enjoyed extensive legal privileges separating them from the rest of the population which existed almost universally elsewhere in Europe. In France there were perhaps a quarter of a million nobles on the eve of the Revolution and all had important legal and formal rights; the corresponding legal order in

England could comfortably have been assembled in the hall of an Oxford college and would have had rights correspondingly less impressive.

On the other hand, the wealth or social influence of the English landowners was immense. Below the peerage stretched the ill-defined class of English gentlemen, linked at the top to the peers' families and disappearing at the other end into the ranks of prosperous farmers and merchants who were eminently respectable but not 'gentlefolk'. This permeability was of enormous value in promoting both cohesion and mobility. Gentlemanly status could be approached by enrichment, by professional distinction, or by personal merit. It was essentially a matter of a shared code of behaviour, still reflecting the aristocratic concept of honour, but one civilized by the purging away of its exclusiveness, its gothicisms and its legal supports. In the seventeenth and eighteenth centuries the idea of the gentleman became one of the formative influences of English history.

It is true that the structures of the ruling hierarchies differed in all countries in some degree. Contrasts could be drawn right across Europe. There would be nothing tidy about the result. None the less, a broad tendency towards social change which implies stress for the old forms is observable in many countries by the eighteenth century. Above all in the most advanced countries it was a change in the meaning of status, in what constituted it and how it was recognized. Though it was not a complete one, we can detect a shift from personal ties to market relationships as a way of defining people's rights and expectations, and a shift from a corporate vision of society to an individualist one. This was most notable in the United Provinces, the republic which emerged in the Dutch Netherlands during this era. It was in effect ruled by merchants, particularly those of Amsterdam, the centre of Holland, its richest province. Here the landed nobility had never counted for as much as the mercantile and urban oligarchs.

Social change had nowhere gone as far in Europe as in Great Britain and the United

The mid-eighteenth-century house of commons, still sitting in the small St Stephen's chapel which was destroyed by fire in 1834, as it appeared to the statesmen of the age in which Great Britain became a world power.

Provinces before 1789. Elsewhere even questioning of traditional status had barely begun. A symptom was the jibe of Figaro, the valet-hero of a notably successful eighteenth-century French comedy, that his aristocratic master had done nothing to deserve his privileges beyond giving himself the trouble to be born. This was recognized at the time as a dangerous and subversive idea, but it need not have caused much alarm. Europe was still soaked in the assumptions of aristocracy (and was to be for a long time even after 1800). Degrees of exclusiveness varied, but the distinction between noble and non-noble remained crucial. Though alarmed aristocrats accused them of doing so, kings would nowhere ally with commoners against them in the last resort. Kings were aristocrats, too; it was their trade, one of them said. Only the coming of a great revolution in France changed things much and then hardly at all outside that country before the end of the century. Men still respected noble blood in most of Europe in 1800. All that had changed was that not quite so many people still automatically thought it was a distinction which ought to be reflected in laws.

Just as men began to feel that to describe society in terms of orders with legally distinct rights and obligations no longer expressed its reality, so also they ceased to feel so sure that religion upheld a particular social hierarchy. It was still for a long time possible to believe that

> The rich man in his castle,
> the poor man at his gate,
> God made them, high and lowly,
> and ordered their estate

as an Ulsterwoman put it in the nineteenth century, but this was not quite the same thing as saying that a fixed unchanging order was the expression of God's will. Even by 1800 a few people were beginning to think God rather liked the rich man to show the wisdom of God's way by making his own place in the world rather than by inheriting his father's place. 'Government is a contrivance of human wisdom for the satisfaction of human wants', said an eighteenth-century Englishman, and he was a conservative, too. A broad utilitarianism was coming to be the basis of judgement of institutions in advanced countries; social institutions would be among them.

The old formal hierarchies were under most pressure where strain was imposed upon them by increasing economic mobility, by the growth of towns, by the rise of a market economy, by the appearance of new commercial opportunities and by the spread of literacy and awareness. Broadly speaking, three situations can be distinguished. In the East, in Russia, and almost to the same extent in Poland or east Prussia and Hungary, agrarian society was still so little disturbed by new developments that the traditional social pattern was not only intact but all but unchallenged at the end of the eighteenth century. In these landlocked countries, safe from the threats to the existing order implicit in the commercial development

of maritime Europe, the traditional ruling classes usually not only retained their position but had often showed that they could actually enlarge their privileges. In a second group of countries, there was enough of a clash between the economic and social worlds which were coming into being and the existing order to provoke demands for change. When political circumstances permitted its resolution, these would demand satisfaction, though they could be contained for a time. France was the outstanding example, but in some of the German states, Belgium and parts of Italy there were signs of the same sort of strain. The third group of countries were those relatively open societies, such as England, the Netherlands and, across the sea, British North America, where the formal distinctions of society already meant little by comparison with wealth or, even talent; legal rights were widely diffused and economic opportunity was felt to be widespread. Even in the sixteenth century, English society seems much more fluid than that of continental countries and, indeed, when the North Americans came to give themselves a new constitution in the eighteenth century they forbad the conferring of hereditary titles. In these countries individualism had a scope almost untrammelled by law, whatever the real restraints of custom and opportunity.

It is only too easy in a general account such as this though, to be over-precise, over-definite. Even the rough tripartite division suggested blurs too much. There were startling contrasts within societies we must misinterpret if we think of them as homogeneous. In the advanced countries there was still much that we should find strange, even antediluvian. The towns of England, France and Germany were for the most part little Barchesters, wrapped in a comfortable provincialism lorded over by a narrow merchant oligarchy, successful guildsmen or a cathedral chapter. Yet Chartres, contentedly rooted in its medieval countryside and medieval ways, its eighteenth-century population still the size of that of five hundred years earlier, was a part of the same country as Nantes or

Bordeaux, thriving, bustling ports which were only two of several which made up the dynamic sector of the French economy. Even the nineteenth century would find its immediate forbears unprogressive; far be it from us, therefore to predicate the existence of a mature and clearly defined individualist and capitalist society wholly conscious of itself as such in any European country. What marked the countries we might call 'advanced' was a tendency to move further and faster in that direction than the great majority of the rest of the world.

Sometimes this already made them appear explicably and admirably revolutionary. Voltaire, even in the early eighteenth century, was greatly struck by the fact that in England a great merchant could be as esteemed and respected as a nobleman. He may have slightly exaggerated and he certainly blurred some important nuances, but it is remarkable – and a part of the story of the rise of Great Britain to world power – that the political class which governed eighteenth-century England was a landed class

The expansion of Bordeaux and its commerce was one of the great success stories of the eighteenth century. It found expression in many handsome new buildings.

and fiercely reflected landed values, yet constantly asserted the commercial interests of the country and accepted the leadership and guidance in this of the collective wisdom of the City of London. Though there was for a long time occasional talk of a political division between the 'moneyed' and the 'landed' interest, and though politics long remained a matter of disputed places and conflicting traditions within the landed class, interests which in other countries would have conflicted with these nevertheless continued to prosper. The explanation must be complex. Some of the elements in it, like the commercialization of British agriculture, go far back into the history of the previous century; some, such as the growth of facilities for private investment in the government and commercial world, were much more recent.

594

The correspondence of the advanced social evolution of the Netherlands and the United Kingdom with their economic, and especially their commercial, success is striking. There was a time when this was largely attributed to their religion: as a result of a great upheaval within Christendom both had ceased to be dominated by the Catholic church. Anti-clericals in the eighteenth century and sociologists in the twentieth both sought to explore this coincidence; Protestantism, it was said, provided an ethic for capitalism. This no longer seems plausible. There were too many Catholic capitalists, for one thing and they were often successful. France and Spain were still important trading countries in the eighteenth century and the first seems to have enjoyed for much of it something like the same rates of growth as the United Kingdom, though she was later to fall behind. They were both countries with Atlantic access, and it was those which had tended to show economic growth ever since the sixteenth century. Yet this is not an explanation which goes very far, either. Scotland – northern, Protestant and Atlantic – long remained backward, poor and feudal. There was more to the differences separating Mediterranean and eastern Europe from the north and west than simple geographical position and more than one factor to the explanation of the varying rate of modernization in Europe. The progress of English and Dutch agriculture, for example, probably owes more to the relative scarcity of land in each country than to anything else.

The European East remained backward and not to be fundamentally changed until the nineteenth century. On its southern flank lay the Balkans and the frontier with Turkey, for most of the centuries a zone of warfare, raiding and banditry. In some areas (Hungary for example) the effects of Turkish rule had been so bad as to depopulate the country. When it was reacquired for Europe, care was taken to tie the peasantry to the land. In the Russia which emerged from Muscovy in this period, too, the serf population grew larger as a proportion of the whole. Harsher laws guaranteed their masters control of the peasants. In other eastern countries, too (Prussia was one), the legal powers of landlords over tenants were strengthened. This was more than just a kingly indulgence of powerful forces which might, if not placated, turn against royal authority. It was also a device for economic development. Not for the first time, nor the last, economic progress went with social injustice; serfdom was a way of making available one of the resources needed if land was to be made productive, just as forced labour was in many other countries at many other times.

One result which is still in some degree visible was a Europe divided roughly along the Elbe. To the west lay countries evolving slowly by 1800 towards more open social forms. To the east lay authoritarian governments presiding over agrarian societies where a minority of landholders enjoyed great powers over a largely tied peasantry. In this area towns did not often prosper as they had done for centuries in the West. They tended to be overtaxed islands in a rural sea, unable to attract from the countryside the labour they needed because of the extent of serfdom. Over great tracts of Poland and Russia even a money economy barely existed. Much of later European history was implicit in this difference between east and west.

It was discernible in informal institutions, too, in the way, for example, in which women were treated, though here another division could be drawn, that between Mediterranean Europe and the north, which was in due course extended to run between Latin and North America. Formally and legally, little changed anywhere in these centuries; the legal status of women remained what it had been and this was only to be questioned right at the end of this period. Nevertheless, the real independence of women and, in particular, of upper-class women, does seem to have been enlarged in the more advanced countries. Even in the fifteenth century it had been remarked by foreigners that Englishwomen enjoyed unusual freedom. This lead does not seem to have diminished, but in the eighteenth century there are signs that in France, at least, a

well-born woman could enjoy considerable real independence.

This was in part because the eighteenth century brought the appearance of a new sort of upper class life, one which had room for other gatherings than those of a royal court, and one increasingly independent of religious and family ritual. At the end of the seventeenth century we hear of men in London gathering in the coffee-houses from which the first clubs were to spring. In the next there appears the *salon,* the social gathering of friends and acquaintances in a lady's drawing-room which was especially the creation of the French; some of them were important intellectual centres and show that it had become proper and even fashionable for a woman to show an interest in things of the mind other than religion. When Mme de Pompadour, the mistress of Louis XV, was painted, she chose to have included in the picture a book – Montesquieu's sociological treatise, *De L'Esprit des Lois.* But even when women did not aspire to blue stockings, the *salon* and the appearance of a society independent of the court presented them with a real, if limited, escape from the confinement of the family, which, together with religious and professional gatherings, had until then been virtually the only structures within which even men might seek social variety and diversion.

By the end of the eighteenth century we have arrived at the age of the female artist and novelist and of acceptance of the fact that spinsterhood need not mean retirement to a cloister. Where such changes came from is not easy to see. In the early years of the century the *Spectator* already thought it worth while to address itself to women readers as well as men, which suggests that we should look a fair way back. Perhaps it helped that the eighteenth century produced such conspicuous examples of women of great political influence – an English queen and four empresses (one Austrian and three Russian) all ruled in their own right and did so with success. But it is not possible to say so with confidence for the prehistory of female emancipation still awaits study.

Finally, none of this touched the life of the overwhelming majority in even the most advanced societies of early modern Europe. There had not yet come into being the mass industrial jobs which would provide the first great force to prise apart the unquestioned certainties of traditional life for most men and women alike. Though they may have weighed most heavily in the primitive villages of Poland in a southern Spain where Moorish influences had intensified the subordination and seclusion of women, those certainties were everywhere still heavy in 1800.

Madame de Pompadour, the famous mistress of Louis XV, did not always choose to be portrayed as a blue-stocking; in this portrait of her in later life she relaxes with her embroidery.

2 Authority and its challengers

In 1800 many Europeans (though, it must be conceded, they lived for the most part in the East) still held ideas about the social and political organization of their countries which would have been comprehensible and appropriate over most of Europe four hundred years earlier. The 'Middle Ages' no more came to a sudden end in this respect than in many others. Ideas about society and government which may reasonably be described as 'medieval' survived as effective forces over a wide area right down to the French Revolution. In some respects they were even strengthened and elaborated. The passage of time had meant that more and more social facts had been fitted into what has been called the 'corporate' organization of society, the grouping of men in bodies with legal privileges which protected their members and defined their status, and this was a medieval idea. Over much of Europe, as we have noted, serfdom had grown more rigid and more widespread. More obviously, there were many direct continuities in political institutions. The Holy Roman Empire still existed in 1800 as it had done in 1500; so did the temporal power of the pope. A descendant of the Capetians was still king of France (though he no longer came from the same branch of the family as in 1500 and, indeed, was in exile). More trivial, but still

The last medieval emperor rides out in defence of Christendom much as he must have thought the great paladins who were his predecessors had done; Charles V, painted by Titian in one of his greatest works.

interesting because it could happen in England as late as 1820, a king's champion rode in full armour into Westminster Hall at the coronation banquet of King George IV, to uphold that monarch's title against all comers. In most countries it was also then taken for granted that the state was a confessional entity, that religion and society were intertwined and that the authority of the Church was established by law. Although such ideas had been much challenged and in some countries had undergone grievous reverses, the weight of history in this as in many matters was still enormous in 1800. It had been even heavier in 1789, the year of the greatest European political revolution and the beginning of the end for much of the past.

Having given these facts their due and considerable acknowledgement, it must then be said that the general tendency of these three centuries was to dissolve the old partnership of kings and landed magnates which was the essence of medieval government. Instead, power and authority tended to flow towards the central concentration provided by the state, and away from 'feudal' arrangements of personal dependence. (The very invention of the 'feudal' idea as a technical term of law was in fact the work of the seventeenth century and it suggests the age's need to define something whose reality was ebbing away.) This tendency had already been observable in the fifteenth century, and it worked both upwards and downwards. The idea of Christendom, for example, though it might be important in emotional, even subconscious ways, effectively lost any political

599

reality in this period. Papal authority had already suffered at the hands of national sentiment in the age of the Schism and that of the Holy Roman emperors had been of small account since the fourteenth century; if it sometimes looked formidable in the hands of an able man, the reality of the emperors' power more and more resembled that of rulers of other states in that it was almost always merely a direct reflexion of the actual resources they could find at any moment in their own hereditary lands.

No new unifying principle emerged to integrate a Europe of states. The test case was the Ottoman threat. Christian princes exposed to the Moslem onslaught might appeal to their fellow-Christians for help, popes might still use the rhetoric of crusade, but the reality, as the Turks well knew, was that Christian states would follow their own interest and ally with the infidel, if necessary. This was the era of *Realpolitik*, of the subordination of principle and honour to intelligent calculation of the interests of the state. It is curious that an age in which Europeans more and more agreed that greater distinctions of culture separated them (to their credit, they were sure) from other civilizations, they should hardly have recognized that there might be an advantage in evolving institutions which acknowledged their essential unity. Between 1500 and 1800 few thinkers advocated the building of institutions which transcended the state. Perhaps, though, it is just in a new awareness of cultural superiority that the explanation lies. Europe was entering an age of triumphant expansion and did not need shared institutions to tell her so.

While restraints on the state from above had all but vanished by 1800, so had many restraints on it from below. Here it is important not to be misled by forms. For all the arguments about who should exercise it, the general trend of these centuries is towards a greater readiness to accept the idea of legislative sovereignty. In other words, Europeans came to feel that, provided the authority of the state were in the right hands, there should be no restriction upon its power to make laws. This idea was rarely grasped very clearly. Frenchmen spent much time in the 1790s writing Declarations of Rights which (they said) might not be infringed and Englishmen vaguely assumed and often talked about the sanctity of property. Nevertheless, in both countries such restraints were often ignored in practice. State power grew within constitutional as well as within absolutist forms. As much as in an eastern autocracy, so in England and France there was no sphere of life in 1800 which was thought to be inaccessible to the law, the articulated will of the sovereign. What still made these countries different from despotisms was that the social groups which mattered sought to ensure that those who made the laws reflected their wishes and assumptions.

The idea of legislative sovereignty was an enormous break with the thinking of the past. To a medieval man the idea that there might not be rights and rules above interference by any man, legal immunities and chartered freedoms inaccessible to change by subsequent lawmakers, fundamental laws which would always be respected, or laws of God which could never be contravened by those of men, would have been social and juridical, as well as theological, blasphemy. English lawyers of the seventeenth century floundered about in disagreement about what the fundamental laws of the land might be, but all thought some must exist and a century later the leading legal minds of France were doing just the same. In the end, nevertheless, there emerged in both countries (as, to a greater or lesser degree, in most others) the acceptance of the idea that a sovereign, legally unrestrained law-making power was the characteristic mark of the state. Yet this took a long time, and for most of the history of early modern Europe it is masked by the fact that the most widely prevalent form of government was monarchy. Struggles about the powers of rulers make up much of European history in these centuries and sometimes it is hard to see exactly what is at stake. The new claims of kings, after all, could be challenged on two quite distinct grounds: there was resistance based on the principle that it would be wrong for *any* government to have powers such as some monarchs claimed (and this might be termed the medieval or conservative defence of freedom) and there was resistance based on the principle that such powers could properly exist, but were being gathered into the wrong hands (and this can be called the modern or liberal defence of freedom). In individual examples in practice, the two claims are often inextricably confused, but the confusion is itself a significant indicator of changing ideas.

Once away from legal principle, the strengthening of the state as a matter of real power first manifests itself in the growing authority of kings and princes. One indicator in the sixteenth and seventeenth centuries was the nearly universal decline in the representative institutions which had emerged in many countries in the later Middle Ages. By 1789, most of Europe was ruled by monarchs little hindered by the existence of effective and continuing representative bodies; the main exception would be in Great Britain. Kings began their ascent to this position in the sixteenth century, when they came to enjoy powers which would have seemed remarkable to medieval barons and burghers. The phenomenon is sometimes described as the rise of absolute monarchy, and provided we do not exaggerate a monarch's chances of getting what he wanted done (for many practical checks might exist to his power which were just as restricting as a representative assembly), the term is acceptable.

The roots of the process lay in a new degree of mastery over the subject. Everywhere, or almost everywhere, the relative strength of the crown improved greatly from the sixteenth century onwards. New financial resources meant that standing armies and artillery could protect kings against great nobles who did not have such advantages. The general economic recovery helped here too. Sometimes the monarchy was able to ally itself with the slow growth of a sense of nationhood. In many countries, too, the late fifteenth century had brought a widespread wish to have done with disorder. People were ready to accept any government if it would guarantee order and peace. There were special reasons in almost every case, but nearly everywhere monarchs raised themselves further above the level of the greatest nobles and buttressed their new pretensions to respect and authority with cannons and taxation. The obligatory sharing of power with their great subjects, whose status entitled them *de facto* and sometimes *de jure* to office, ceased to weigh so heavily upon kings who more and more could choose their own servants. The Tudor Privy Council, for example, was a meritocracy as well as a gathering of magnates.

In the sixteenth and early seventeenth centuries this brought about the apogee of what is sometimes called the 'Renaissance State'. This is a rather grandiose term for what has been called 'at bottom, a great and expanding bureaucracy, a huge system of administrative centralization, staffed by an evergrowing multitude of "courtiers" or "officers"'. This is clear enough if we remember the implied antithesis: the medieval kingdom, whose governmental functions were often in large measure delegated to feudal and personal dependents, or to corporations (of which the Church was the greatest). Of course, neither of these models of political organization can ever be found in history in a pure form. Royal officials had long existed and states still today delegate functions and authority to corporations (such as trade unions). Though the multiplication of royal officials directly dependent upon the Crown and the standardization of administrative procedures are both very obvious in the sixteenth century, there was no sudden transition to the modern 'state': it took centuries. Many obstacles had to be overcome. One was a simple lack of competent officials; no other monarchy hit on the brilliant Tudor device of delegating local government to local squires employed as royal Justices of the Peace. Elsewhere – and in England, too, as Tudor rebellions showed – noblemen had long to be treated with care if they were not to be fatally antagonized. Rebellion was not an exceptional event but a continuing fact of life for the sixteenth-century statesman. Royal troops might prevail in the end, but no monarch wanted to be reduced to reliance on force. The history of the French nobility's turbulence right down to the middle of the seventeenth century, of the effects of antagonizing local interest in England during the same period, of Habsburg attempts to unify their territories at the expense of local magnates all show this. The United Kingdom had its last feudal rebellion in 1745; other countries had theirs still later.

Another limitation was financial. Taxation, because of the danger of rebellion and the inadequacy of machinery, could not be pressed too far, yet officials and armies had to be paid for. One way of ensuring this was to allow officials to charge fees or levy perquisites on those members of the public who needed their services. For obvious reasons, this was not a complete answer. The raising of greater sums by the ruler was therefore necessary. Something might still be done by exploiting royal domains. But all monarchs, sooner or later, were driven back to seek new taxation and it was a problem few could solve.

There were technical problems here which could not be dealt with until the nineteenth century, but great fertility of imagination was to be shown for three centuries in inventing new taxes. Broadly speaking, only consumption (through indirect taxes such as customs and excise or taxes on sales) or real property could be reached by the tax-gatherer. In each case, the effect bore disproportionately upon the poorest who spent a larger part of their small disposable income on necessities than the wealthy, and who could do little to protect themselves against a landowner determined to pass his tax burdens along to the man at the bottom of the property pyramid except by working less hard at obligatory tasks.

Across the path of a possible evolution towards a modern notion of the state and its power and the modern acceptance of legislative sovereignty there lay also the medieval idea of legal immunity, which by no means disappeared completely by 1789. In 1500 it was generally accepted that there were areas, persons and

spheres of action which were specially sacrosanct. They were protected from invasion by the power of the ruler for many reasons. They might be defended by an irrevocable royal grant in past ages such as the judicial privileges of many cities, by contractual agreement such as the English *Magna Carta* was said to be, by immemorial custom, or by divine law. The supreme example was the Church, whose properties were not normally subject to lay taxation, which possessed jurisdiction in its courts of matters thus inaccessible to royal justice, and which controlled important social and economic institutions. But a province, or a town, or a group, or a family might enjoy similar immunities, usually from royal jurisdiction or taxation. Even the French king had to remember that he was only a duke in Brittany and that in some respects his lands were related to one another almost as a collection of little kingdoms. Such facts were the realities from which emerged the 'Renaissance State', and it could do no other than accept their survival. Yet the future lay with the royal bureaucrats and their files.

One episode which greatly facilitated and accelerated the consolidation of state power was the great crisis which shook western Christianity and destroyed forever the old medieval unity of the faith in the early sixteenth century. The heart of the Protestant Reformation was yet another dispute over religious authority, the calling in question of the papal claims whose formal and theoretical structure had successfully survived so many challenges. But the ending of the idea of universal papal authority, important as that was, was not the whole story of the Reformation or even the whole of its political impact. Without anyone expecting it, constitutional and theological quarrel within the Church became a revolution in secular history, too, as the Reformation flowed into the political channels available to it.

There was nothing new about demands for reform. Nor was practical encroachment upon papal authority over local churches unknown, as the concessions made by Rome to princes in the fifteenth century showed. The sense that

The New Testament in Erasmus' edition. This book was printed in 1516 in Basle and the opening verses of St Matthew's gospel are shown. The text is in parallel Greek and Latin versions.

Papacy and Curia did not necessarily serve the interests of Christians was well grounded by 1500. Some critics had already gone on from this to doctrinal dissent. The fifteenth century had been marked by a deep, uneasy devotional swell; there had been a sense of looking for new answers to spiritual questions and of looking for them outside the limits laid down by ecclesiastical authority. Heresy had never been blotted out, it had only been contained. Popular anti-clericalism was an old and widespread phenomenon. There had also appeared in the fifteenth century another current in religious life, perhaps more profoundly subversive than heresy, because, unlike heresy, it contained forces which might in the end cut at the roots of the traditional religious outlook

itself. This was the learned, humanistic, rational, sceptical growth of thought which, for want of a better word, we may call Erasmian after the man who embodied its ideals most clearly in the eyes of contemporaries. Erasmus was profoundly loyal to his faith; he conceived himself as a Christian and that meant, unquestionably, that he remained within the Church. Of that Church he had an ideal which embodied a vision of a possible reformation. He sought a simpler devotion and a purer pastorate. But the authority of the Church, above all, that of the papacy, he did not challenge. In a subtler way, though, he challenged authority in principle, for his textual work had implications which were deeply subversive and so was the tone of the correspondence which he conducted with colleagues the length and breadth of Europe. They learnt from him to disentangle their logic and therefore the teaching of the faith from the Aristotelian mummifications of scholastic philosophy. In his Greek *New Testament* he made available an instrument which provided a firm basis for argument on doctrine at a time when Greek was again becoming widespread. Erasmus, too, was the exposer of the spuriousness of texts on which bizarre dogmatic structures had been raised.

Yet humanism contributed only indirectly to the shattering of Christendom's unity. Erasmus and many others who shared his viewpoint did not attack religious authority outright or in a way which would turn ecclesiastical into universal issues. Humanism, like heresy, discontent with clerical behaviour and the cupidity of princes, was something in the air at the beginning of the sixteenth century, waiting – as many of these things had long waited – for the man and the occasion which would make them into a religious revolution. No other term is adequate to describe what followed the unwitting act of a German monk in 1517 who launched a movement which was to end by fragmenting a Christian unity intact in the West since the disappearance of the Arians.

His name was Martin Luther. Unlike Erasmus, the international man, Luther was all his life except for brief absences the inhabitant of a small German town, almost at the back of beyond at Wittenberg on the Elbe. He was an Augustinian monk, deeply read in theology, somewhat tormented in spirit, who had already come to the conclusion that he must preach the Scriptures in a new light, to present God as a forgiving God, not a punitive one. This need not have made him a revolutionary; the orthodoxy of his views was never in question until he had come into conflict with the papacy. He had been to Rome, and he had not liked what he saw there, for the papal city seemed a worldly place and its ecclesiastical rulers no better than they should be. This did not dispose him to feel warmly towards an itinerant pedlar of indulgences, papal certificates that the possessor, in consideration of payment (which went towards the building of the new and magnificent St Peter's now rising in Rome), would be assured that some of the penalties incurred by him for sin would be remitted. Accounts of the preaching of this man (a Dominican) in the neighbourhood were brought to Luther by peasants who had heard him and bought their indulgences. Research has made it clear that what had been said to them was not only misleading but outrageous; the crudity of the transaction promoted by the preacher displays one of the most unattractive faces of medieval Catholicism. It infuriated Luther, deeply conscious as he was of the overwhelming seriousness of the transformation necessary in a man's life before he could be sure of redemption. Luther formulated his protests against this and certain other practices of the papacy in a set of ninety-five theses setting out his positive views. They were in Latin and, in the tradition of the scholarly disputation he posted them on the door of the castle church in Wittenberg on 31 October 1517. Luther provoked the debate he sought. He had sent the theses to the Archbishop of Mainz, primate of Germany, who sent them to Rome with a request that Luther be forbidden by his order to preach on this theme. By this time the theses had been put into German and technology had transformed the situation: they

Martin Luther painted by Cranach.

were printed and circulated everywhere in Germany. Soon, only the protection of Frederick of Saxony, the ruler of Luther's state, saved him. The elector refused to surrender him. The delay in scotching the chicken of heresy in the egg was fatal. Luther's order abandoned him, but his university supported him and soon the papacy found itself confronted by a national movement of grievance against Rome sustained and inflamed by Luther's own sudden discovery that he was a literary genius of astonishing fluency and productivity, the first to exploit the huge possibilities of the printed pamphlet.

Within two years, Luther was being called a Hussite, but the Reformation had now become entangled in German politics. Even in the Middle Ages would-be reformers had looked to secular rulers to accomplish what they believed the papacy could not or would not. This did not necessarily mean going outside the fold of the faith; the great Spanish churchman Ximenes had sought to bring to bear the authority of the Catholic monarchs on the problems facing the Spanish Church. Often this had encouraged the smouldering embers of heresy to break out again. Kings did not like heretics; their duty was to uphold the true faith. Nevertheless, an appeal to lay authority was likely to open the way to changes which went further than, perhaps, their authors had intended.

This, it seems, was the case with Luther. His arguments had rapidly carried him beyond the desirability and grounds of reform in practice to the questioning of papal authority and the elaboration of his theology. The core of his early protests had not been theological (and early Protestants were usually more interested in other things). Nevertheless, he now rejected transubstantiation (but replaced it with a view of the eucharist which is even more difficult to grasp) and preached that men were justified – that is, set aside for salvation – not by observance of the sacraments only ('works', as it was called), but by faith. This was, clearly, an intensely individualist position and it struck at the root of traditional teaching which saw no salvation possible outside the Church. (Yet, it may be noted, Erasmus, when asked for his view, would not condemn Luther; it was known, moreover, that he thought Luther to have said many valuable things.) In 1520 Luther was excommunicated. Before a wondering audience he burnt the bull of excommunication in the same fire as the books of canon law. He continued to preach and write. Summoned to explain himself before the imperial Diet, he refused to retract his views. Germany seemed on the verge of civil war. After leaving the Diet under a safe-conduct, he disappeared; he had been kidnapped for his own safety. In 1521 Charles V, the emperor, placed him under the Imperial Ban; Luther was now in effect an outlaw.

By then 'Lutheranism' was a German political fact; soon it was to be European. Luther's doctrines, which extended to condemnations of confession and absolution and clerical celibacy, appealed to many Germans. His followers spread them by their preaching and by the dissemination of his German translation of the *New Testament*. Lutheranism soon divided the German princes, who entangled it in their own complicated relations with the emperor and his vague authority over

them. Wars ensued and the word 'Protestant' came into use. By 1548, Germany was irreparably divided into Catholic and Protestant states and this was recognized in agreement at the Diet of Augsburg that the prevailing religion of each state should be that of its ruler. This was to institutionalize religious pluralism, a curious step for an emperor who saw himself as the defender of universal Catholicism, but one necessary if he was to keep the loyalty of Germany's princes. In Catholic and Protestant Germany alike, both religious communities now looked as never before to political authority to uphold their tenets in a world of competing creeds.

By this time, varieties of Protestantism other than Lutheranism had appeared. Sometimes they drew on social unrest. Luther soon had to distinguish his own teaching from the views of peasants who revolted against their masters, invoking his name in justification of what they did. One important and socially radical group were the Anabaptists, whose essential theological distinction was opposition to infant baptism. Their political intractability led to persecution of them by Catholic and Protestant rulers alike. In 1534 Anabaptists seized power in Münster and their leaders' introduction of communism of property and polygamy confirmed their opponents' fears and brought a ferocious suppression upon them.

Lutheranism took root in Germany and, eventually, Scandinavia. Of other forms of continental Protestantism, only one demands notice. In Switzerland, the rejection of Catholicism was briefly led by Zwingli, a more radical theologian than Luther, in Zürich, but it was in Geneva that Calvinism, Switzerland's most important contribution to the Reformation, took shape. It was the creation of a Frenchman who had broken with Catholicism under the influence of Protestant evangelicals. John Calvin was a theologian who soon formulated his essential doctrines: the absolute depravity of man after the Fall of Adam and the impossibility of salvation except for those few, the elect, predestined by God to salvation. If Luther, the

605

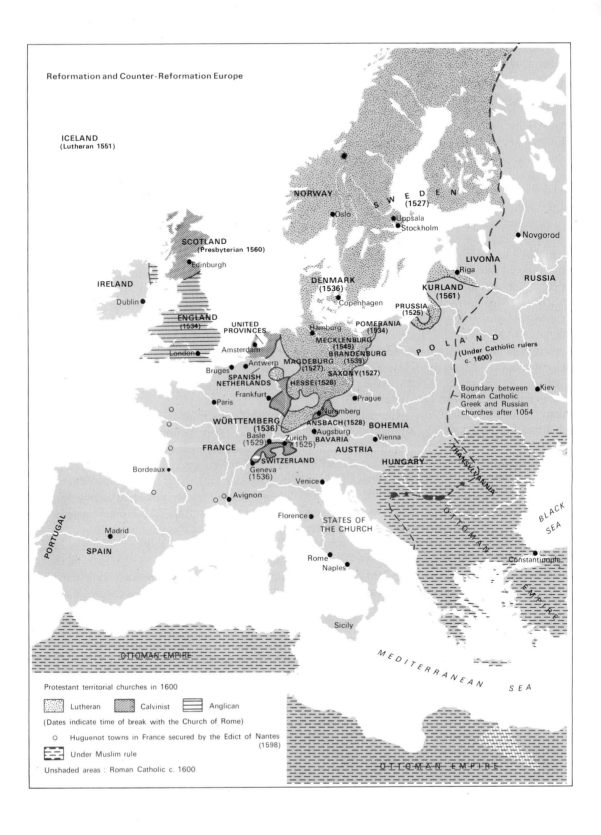

Reformation and Counter-Reformation Europe

ICELAND
(Lutheran 1551)

NORWAY

S W E D E N
(1527)

Oslo

Uppsala
Stockholm

Novgorod

SCOTLAND
(Presbyterian 1560)
Edinburgh

LIVONIA
Riga

RUSSIA

KURLAND
(1561)

IRELAND

DENMARK
(1536)
Copenhagen

Dublin

PRUSSIA
(1525)

P O L A N D

ENGLAND
(1534)

UNITED
PROVINCES

Hamburg

POMERANIA
(1534)

London

Amsterdam

MECKLENBURG
(1549)

Antwerp
BRANDENBURG
(1539)

Bruges

MAGDEBURG
(1527)

SAXONY (1527)

(Under Catholic rulers
c. 1600)

SPANISH
NETHERLANDS

Frankfurt

HESSE (1528)

Kiev

Boundary between
Roman Catholic
Greek and Russian
churches after 1054

Paris

Prague

WÜRTTEMBERG
(1536)

Nuremberg

ANSBACH (1528)

BOHEMIA

FRANCE

Basle
(1529)

Augsburg

Zurich
SWITZERLAND (1525)

BAVARIA

Vienna

Bordeaux

Geneva
(1536)

AUSTRIA

HUNGARY

T
R
A
N
S
Y
L
V
A
N
I
A

Venice

Avignon

BLACK
SEA

PORTUGAL

Florence

STATES OF
THE CHURCH

O
T
T
O
M
A
N

Madrid

SPAIN

Rome
Naples

Constantinople

E
M
P
I
R
E

Sicily

M E D I T E R R A N E A N   S E A

OTTOMAN EMPIRE

Protestant territorial churches in 1600

Lutheran   Calvinist   Anglican

(Dates indicate time of break with the Church of Rome)

o   Huguenot towns in France secured by the Edict of Nantes
(1598)

Under Muslim rule

Unshaded areas : Roman Catholic c. 1600

OTTOMAN EMPIRE

Augustinian monk, spoke with the voice of Paul, Calvin evoked the tones of Augustine. It is not easy to understand the attractiveness of this gloomy creed. But to its efficacy, the history of not only Geneva, but of France, England, Scotland, the Dutch Netherlands, and British North America all witnessed. The crucial step was conviction of membership of the Elect. As the signs of this were outward adherence to the commandments of God and participation in the sacraments, it was less difficult to achieve such conviction than might be imagined.

At Geneva, Calvin drew up the constitution of a theocratic state which provided the framework for a remarkable exercise in communal self-government. Geneva was not a place for the easy-going. The punishment imposed for heresy, blasphemy or witchcraft was death; of course, this would not have struck contemporaries as surprising. But though adultery was a crime in most European countries and one punished by ecclesiastical courts, Calvin's Geneva took this offence much more seriously in prescribing the death penalty for those guilty of it. A distinction of sex was respected: guilty women were

drowned, men beheaded. (This appears to have been a reversal of the normal penal practice of a male-dominated European society; women, considered weaker vessels morally and intellectually, were usually indulged with milder punishments than men.) The most severe punishments, though, were reserved for those guilty of heresy.

From Geneva, where its pastors were trained, the new sect took root in France, where it won converts among the nobility and had more than 2000 congregations by 1561. In the Netherlands, England and Scotland it also enjoyed great success. Finally, Calvinism also spread to Germany, where it challenged Lutheranism, and from there to Poland, Bohemia and Hungary. Thus in its first century it showed a remarkable vigour, surpassing that of Lutheranism which, except in Scandinavia, never spread strongly beyond the German lands which first adopted it.

Curiously, neither Lutheranism nor Calvinism provoked the separation from Rome of the first nation-state to reject papal authority. In England a unique religious change arose almost by accident. A new dynasty originating in Wales, the Tudors, had established itself at the end of the fifteenth century and the second king of this line, Henry VIII, became entangled with the papacy over his wish to dissolve one of his six marriages in order to remarry and get an heir, a considerable and understandable preoccupation. The quarrel provoked one of the most remarkable assertions of lay authority in the whole sixteenth century and one fraught with significance for England's future constitutional history. With the support of his parliament, which obediently passed the required legislation, Henry VIII proclaimed himself Head of the Church in England. Doctrinally, he conceived

The confident romanizing style of the Counter-Reformation in central Europe was well expressed in St Michael's, Munich, built by the ruler of a state which was to maintain the intense catholicism of Loyola's era long after its fervour had ebbed elsewhere.

607

no break with the past; he was, after all, entitled Defender of the Faith by the pope because of a refutation of Luther from the royal pen (his successor still bears the title). But the assertion of the Royal Supremacy opened the way to the development of an English Church separate from Rome. A vested interest in it was provided by a dissolution of monasteries and some other ecclesiastical foundations and the sale of the property they had owned to buyers mainly drawn from among the aristocracy and gentry. Churchmen sympathetic to new doctrines sought to move the doctrine of the Church in England significantly towards continental Protestant ideas in the next reign. Popular reactions were mixed. Some saw this as the satisfaction of old national traditions of dissent from Rome; some resented such innovations as a service-book in English and new ceremonies. From a confused debate emerged one literary masterpiece, *The Book of Common Prayer*, and some martyrs both Catholic and Protestant. The latter were the first to suffer, for there was a reversion to papal authority (and the burning of Protestant heretics) under the fourth Tudor, the unfairly named and unhappy Bloody Mary, perhaps England's most tragic queen. By this time the question of religion was thoroughly entangled with national interest and foreign policy, for the states of Europe drew apart more and more on religious grounds.

This was not all that was notable about the English Reformation which, like the German, was a landmark in the history of a national consciousness. It had been carried out by Act of Parliament and a constitutional question was implicit in the religious settlement: were there any limits to legislative authority? With the accession of Mary's half-sister, Elizabeth I, the pendulum swung back, though for a long time it was unclear how far. Yet Elizabeth insisted, and had Parliament legislate, that she retained the essentials of her father's position; the English Church, or Church of England, as it may henceforth be called, claimed to be Catholic in doctrine but rested on the Royal Supremacy. More important still, because that

Supremacy was recognized by Act of Parliament, England was soon to be at war with a Catholic king of Spain who was well known for his determination to root out heresy in the lands he subjugated and the national cause was identified with the Protestant.

Religious change had another important consequence. The Reformation was one of the factors which helped the English parliament to survive when other medieval representative bodies were going under before the new power of kings. Of course it was far from the whole story, whose origins went back a very long way. A kingdom united since Anglo-Saxon times without provincial assemblies or 'estates' which might rival it made it much easier for parliament to focus national politics than any similar body abroad. The circumstances of the English Reformation helped, too; Henry VIII had squandered a great opportunity to achieve a sound basis for absolute monarchy when he rapidly liquidated the mass of property – about a fifth of the land of the whole kingdom – which he held briefly as a result of the dissolutions. Nor did it damage parliament that he abandoned Thomas Cromwell, a servant who might have been the architect of a true Tudor despotism. Nevertheless, all such imponderables duly weighed, the fact that Henry chose to seek endorsement of his will from the national representative body in creating a national church still seems one of the most crucial decisions in parliament's history.

There were Catholic martyrs under Elizabeth – though they died because they were traitors, not because they were heretics – but England was far less divided by religion than Germany and France. Sixteenth-century France was tormented and torn by Catholic and Calvinist interests. Each was in essence a group of noble clans, who fought for power in the Wars of Religion, of which nine have been distinguished between 1562 and 1598. At times their struggles brought the French monarchy very low in power; the nobility of France came the nearest of any to winning the battle against the centralizing state. Yet, in the end, their divisions benefited a crown which could use one faction against another. For over thirty years the distinction between war and peace hardly seems discernible. The wretched population of France had to bear the brunt of disorder and devastation for most of this time until a group of Frenchmen known as the *politiques* turned to advocate a measure of toleration as the only way out. With their support there came to the throne (after the murder of his predecessor) a member of a junior branch of the royal family, Henry, king of the little state of Navarre. As Henry IV of France, he inaugurated the Bourbon line whose descendants still claim the French throne. He had been a Protestant, but accepted Catholicism as the condition of his succession, recognizing that for all the violence and deeply entrenched nature of French Calvinism, Catholicism was the religion most Frenchmen would cling to. The Protestants were assured special guarantees by a great charter, the Edict of Nantes, which left them a state within a state,

the possessors of fortified towns where the king's writ did not run; this very old-fashioned sort of solution assured protection for their religion and ended civil strife by creating new immunities. Henry and his successors could then turn to the business of re-establishing the authority of a throne badly shaken by assassination and intrigue. But the French nobility were still far from tamed.

Long before this religious struggles had been further enflamed by the movement of internal reassessment and innovation within the Roman Church which is called the Counter-Reformation. Its centre was a great papal enterprise, the summoning in 1545 of a general council, the Council of Trent, which met in three sessions over the next eighteen years. Bishops of the Italian and Spanish churches predominated at it, an important fact, for the Reformers challenged Catholicism little in those countries. The result was somewhat to accentuate the intransigence of its decisions which not only became the touchstone of Catholic orthodoxy in doctrine until the nineteenth century and provided a standard to which Catholic rulers could rally, but also initiated important institutional change. Like the Reformation itself, however, the Counter-Reformation went beyond forms. It also expressed and gave direction to a new devotional intensity and rejuvenated the fervour of laity and clergy alike. Significantly, it made attendance at mass each week obligatory.

Papal authority was not the only source of the desire to put the Catholic house in order; Catholic reform was not merely a response to the Reformation, but in many ways had anticipated it. The spirituality and spontaneous fervour

Nowhere was the vigour and self-confidence of Counter-Reformation Europe expressed so vividly as in its art. Rubens, one of its master-painters, enthusiastically poured out his gifts in a flood of canvases of religious subjects (as in this picture of a miracle attributed to St Ignatius Loyola) as well as in classical and pagan subjects. Catholicism remained a religion of visual imagery while Protestantism turned to the word.

already shown in the fifteenth century among the faithful lay behind it. One of the most potent instruments of the Counter-Reformation and expressions of its spirituality was the invention of a Spaniard, the soldier Ignatius Loyola. By a curious irony he had been a student at the same Paris college as Calvin in the early 1530s, but it is not recorded that they ever met. In 1534 he and a few companions took vows; their aim was missionary work and as they trained for it Loyola devised a rule for a new religious order. In 1540 it was recognized by the pope and named the Society of Jesus. The Jesuits, as they soon came to be called, were to have an importance in the history of the Church akin to that of the early Benedictines or the Franciscans of the thirteenth century. They were the militia of the Church, as their warrior-founder liked to think of them, utterly disciplined and completely subordinate to papal authority through their general, who lived in Rome. They transformed Catholic education. They were in the forefront of a renewed missionary effort which carried their members to every part of the world. In Europe their intellectual eminence and political skill raised them to high places in the courts of kings.

Yet in spite of the new instruments which it brought to the support of papal authority, the Counter-Reformation had the paradoxical effect, like the Reformation, of increasing the authority of the states where it was most successful. The new dependence of religion upon political authority – that is to say upon organized force – extended further the grip of the political apparatus. This was most obvious in the Spanish kingdoms. Here two forces ran together to create an unimpeachably Catholic monarchy long before the Council of Trent. The Reconquest so recently completed had been a crusade; the title of the Catholic Monarchs itself proclaimed the identification of a political process with an ideological struggle. In the second place, the Spanish monarchy had the problem of absorbing suddenly great numbers of non-Christian subjects, both Moslem and Jew. They presented a potential threat

A Jesuit missionary at the Chinese court in the seventeenth century. He is shown with the astronomical instruments he took with him to China and which so impressed the sages of a culture that attached special importance to the accurate management of the calendar.

to security in a multi-racial society. The instrument deployed against them was a new one: an Inquisition not, like the medieval Inquisition, under clerical control, but under that of the Crown. Established by papal bull in 1478, the Spanish Inquisition began to operate in Castile in 1480. The pope soon had misgivings; in Catalonia lay and ecclesiastical authority alike resisted, but to no avail. By 1516, when Charles I, the first ruler to hold both the thrones of Aragon and Castile, became king, the Inquisition was the only institution in the Spanish domains which, from a royal council, exercised authority in all of them, in the Americas, Sicily and Sardinia, as much as in Castile and Aragon. The most striking effects had already been by then the expulsion from them of the Jews and the severe regulation of the Moriscoes, or converted Moors.

This gave Spain a religious unity unbreakable by a few sympathizers with Lutheranism, with whom the Inquisition found it easy to deal. The cost to Spain need not be considered here. What emerges is that already under Charles, himself a fervent Catholic, Spain was in religion as in her secular life, a new kind of centralized, absolutist monarchy, the Renaissance State *par excellence*, in fact. The residues of formal constitutionalism within the peninsula did not affect this. The model for the Counter-Reformation state elsewhere was available in Spain and thanks to Spanish power was to be imposed upon much of Europe by force or example in the century after 1558, when Charles died after a retirement spent largely in his devotions in a palace specially built next to a remote monastery in Estremadura.

Of all European monarchs who identified himself with the cause of the counter-reformation and saw himself as the extirpator of heresy, none was more determined – and bigoted – than his son and successor, Philip II of Spain, widower of Mary Tudor. To him had come half Charles's empire: Spain, the Indies, Sicily and the Spanish Netherlands. (In 1581 he acquired Portugal, too, and it remained Spanish until 1640.) The results of his policies of religious purification in Spain have been variously interpreted. What is not open to dispute is the effect in the Spanish Netherlands, where they provoked the emergence of the first state in the world to break away from the old domination of monarchy and landed nobility and thus helped to inaugurate a new era of European history.

This certainly justifies the importance which has long been attributed by historians to what some call the 'Revolt of the Netherlands' and the Dutch the 'Eighty Years' War'. Yet it was not always understood. Like many other events at the roots of nations, the Revolt provoked myth-making, much of it conscious, but even this has probably done less to obscure its nature

than the assumption that because in the end a very modern sort of society emerged, it was a very 'modern' sort of revolt dominated from the start by a passionate struggle for religious toleration and national independence. Nothing was less true. The troubles of the Netherlands were deeply rooted in a very medieval setting, the old Burgundian inheritance of the lands of the richest state in northern Europe, the duchy which had passed to the Habsburgs by marriage. The Spanish Netherlands were part of this, seventeen provinces of very different sorts. The southern provinces, where many of the inhabitants spoke French, included the most urbanized part of Europe and the great Flemish commercial centre of Antwerp. It had long been a troublesome area. In the late fifteenth century, at the end of Burgundy's life, the Flemish towns at one moment seemed to be trying to turn themselves into independent city-states.

The northern provinces were agricultural and maritime. The inhabitants showed a peculiarly tenacious feeling for their land which may be connected with the fact that since the twelfth century they had actually been recovering it from the sea and making polders. North and south were to be the later Netherlands and Belgium, but this was inconceivable in 1554. Nor could a religious division between the two be then envisaged. Though there was a preponderance of Catholics in the south (which was to grow somewhat as many Protestants emigrated northwards) the two sets were mixed up on both sides of a future boundary. Early sixteenth-century Europe was much more tolerant of religious divisions than after the Counter-Reformation got to work.

Philip's determination to enforce the decrees of the Council of Trent explains something of what followed but the origins of trouble lay in quarrels going back to the days when the Netherlands were part of the duchy of Burgundy. Essentially the Spaniards strove to modernize the relations of central government and local communities as had done the Burgundians but did so with more up-to-date methods and perhaps less tact. Spanish royal envoys came into

611

conflict first with the nobility of the southern provinces, a prickly, touchy crew, as sensitive as other nobilities of the age in defence of the symbolic 'liberties' – that is, privileges and immunities – of their provinces when threatened by a monarch more remote but more assertive than the great Charles who, they felt, had understood them (he spoke their language). The Spanish commander, the Duke of Alva, they argued, was further violating local privilege by interfering with local jurisdictions in the pursuit of heretics. Catholic though they were, they had a stake in the prosperity of the Flemish cities where protestantism had taken root. They were, too, as uneasy as other noblemen of the times about the pressures of inflation. Their opposition began the Revolt.

Resistance to Spanish government therefore began in thoroughly medieval forms, in the Estates of Brabant, and for a few years the brutality of the Spanish army and the leadership of one of their number, William of Orange united the nobles against their lawful ruler. Like his contemporary, Elizabeth Tudor, William (nicknamed the 'Silent' because of his reputed refusal to allow unguarded anger to escape him when he learnt of his ruler's determination to bring his heretic subjects to heel), was one of the first modern and national statesmen; he consciously orchestrated specific grievances into a national programme. But there was always a potential rift between noblemen and Calvinist townsmen who had more at stake. Better political tactics by Spanish governors and the victories of the Spanish armies were in the end enough to force it open and the nobles fell back into line. Thus, without knowing it, the Spanish armies defined modern Belgium. The struggle from this time continued only in the northern provinces, though still under the political direction of William the Silent until his death in 1584 at the hands of an assassin.

The Dutch (as we may now call them) had much at stake and were not encumbered as their southern co-religionists had been with the ambiguous dissatisfactions of the nobility. But they had grave disadvantages to overcome. They were divided among themselves; the provinces could rarely come easily to agreement. But they could use the cry of religious freedom and a broad toleration to disguise their own divisions and also had some factors working in their favour. In the first place, the Spanish army was formidable on land, but could not easily deal with an enemy which retired behind its town walls and surrounded them with water by opening the dykes and flooding the countryside. The Dutch, almost by accident, transferred their main effort to the sea; Zeeland in particular welcomed the prospect of profitable privateering and this meant that Dutch resources were deployed where they could do a great deal of damage to the Spanish on more equal terms. Secondly, Spanish communications with the Netherlands were stretched. The northern sea route was harried by the rebels. It was expensive to maintain a big army in Belgium by the long road up from Italy and even more expensive when other enemies had to be beaten off. This was the third factor telling in favour of the Dutch. The Counter-Reformation had infected international politics with a new ideological element. Together with the interest of the English in maintaining a balance of power on the continent and preventing the complete success of the Spanish, this led to a diplomatic struggle against Spain which eventually became military and naval and brought the Dutch allies. Finally, the Dutch benefited from a great migration of Flemish capital and talent.

The Dutch evolved a remarkable society, a loose federation of seven little republics with a weak central government. Soon, its citizens discovered a forgotten national past (much as decolonized Africans have done in this century) and celebrated the virtues of Germanic tribesmen who provided origins dimly discernible in Roman accounts of rebellion; relics of their enthusiasm remain in the paintings commissioned by Amsterdam magnates depicting attacks upon Roman camps (this was in the era posterity associates with the work of Rembrandt). Now the distinctiveness of the nation thus consciously created rather than inherited is more

Elizabeth I, greatest of the Tudors; she brought to her office a style and glamour which surpassed even that of her father, Henry VIII, and in sagacity and caution she rivalled her grandfather, Henry VII. After her death, she became a folk memory against which were tested the acts of the Stuarts – who were usually found wanting.

interesting than this historical propaganda. Once a period of danger when their survival was at stake was past, this was also a polity which was characterized by religious tolerance and great civic freedom; the Dutch did not allow Calvinism the upper hand in government. The only other important state where this happened, though less markedly, was England, yet there it was accompanied by a great strengthening of the legislative authority of the state, one which carried so far, indeed, the limitation of privilege that at the end of the seventeenth century it was

regarded with amazement by other Europeans.

For a long time this cannot have seemed a likely outcome. Under Elizabeth the English monarchy was secure again it is true. She was an incomparable producer of the royal spectacle and when the myths of beauty and youth faded she acquired the majesty of those who outlive their first counsellors. Elizabeth again demonstrated the Tudor instinct for welding the dynasty's interest to patriotism; unhappily she had no child. In 1603 she had been queen for forty-five years, the centre of a national cult fed by poets of genius, by mundane devices such as the frequent travel (which kept down expenses, since she stayed with her nobility) which made her visible to her people, and by her astonishing skill with her parliaments. Under her successors the accession day of Good Queen Bess, a truly national idol, became an expression of patriotic opposition to them.

What happened in the seventeenth century was not just that a great virtuoso of monarchy passed from the stage. Even Elizabeth had been troubled by loyal members of the House of Commons who worried about religion. Worse, she left an encumbered estate, for her foreign policy was expensive and, like all other rulers of her day, she never had a big enough income. This did not help the first king of the Scottish house of Stuart, who succeeded her, James I. The shortcomings of the males of that dynasty are still difficult to write about with moderation; the Stuarts gave England four bad kings in a row. Still, James was neither as foolish as his son nor as unprincipled as his grandsons and it was probably his lack of tact rather than more serious defects that did most to embitter politics in his reign. If his ambitions, or those of his son Charles, tended to political change at all, it was change towards enhanced monarchical power, as in continental states. Yet foreign experience showed that such enhanced power nowhere went unchallenged. This boded ill in England for a foreign king, short of money.

In the seventeenth century there was a roughly simultaneous crisis of authority in several countries. It is curiously parallel to an economic crisis which was Europe-wide, and some historians have argued that the two were inseparably connected. This may be so, but it is not easy to be sure what the nature of the connexion was. It is also interesting, though equally difficult to interpret the fact, that these civil struggles coincided with the ending of a period of wars which had been opened by the Counter-Reformation and in which religion had been a dominant concern. It is simplest surely to acknowledge a contemporaneous breakdown of normal political life in a number of countries, notably England, France and Spain, in the sense that existing arrangements were called in question and men were prepared once more to rebel in arms against their rulers.

In England the crisis came to a head in civil war, regicide and the establishment of the only republic in English history. Historians still argue about where lay the heart of the quarrel between King and Parliament. The background was growing friction between the two under James I. At that time, three interconnected issues caused trouble. The Crown was poor and required money. Proposals for taxation were ill-received by Parliament. It voiced criticisms not only of fiscal policy but of religious policy – the king was believed to be unduly sympathetic to Roman Catholics – and of foreign policy. An anti-Spanish and pro-Protestant stance in foreign affairs was important to English nationalism in the early seventeenth century.

Religion and foreign affairs opened deep constitutional divisions. It was arguable with whom decisions in these matters lay but the flow of money to support policy was controlled by parliament. After some unhappy experiences in the first years of his reign, Charles I, the second Stuart king, took the advice of those who counselled him to do without parliaments altogether. It was just possible, at the cost of accepting that there could be no activity abroad and that a degree of antagonism would be created at home by attempts to resurrect obsolete sources of revenue or impose new ones which were enforceable.

The trial of Charles I. In January 1649 a high court of justice specially set up for the purpose, tried Charles and condemned him to death. He was beheaded on 30 January before the Banqueting House, Whitehall, and buried in St George's Chapel, Windsor.

The result was called the 'Eleven Years' Tyranny'. England began to look as if it was on the road to absolutism on the continental model and the loss of ground won by her parliament under the Tudors. This did not happen because a foreign war – with Scotland – made the calling of parliament necessary in 1639. Without new taxation, the country could not be defended. Parliament assembled full of grievances, convinced that there had been an attempt to subvert the liberties of Englishmen and suspicious also that there was a royal scheme to overturn the Church by law established from within and reintroduce the power of Rome.

From this point the quarrel between king and parliament was rapidly embittered. Parlia-

At Dunbar in 1650 Cromwell overthrew the Scottish army supporting Charles II. Another victory at Worcester a year later to the day confirmed the triumph, marking the real end of the Civil War; soon, Scotland was united to England and the Commonwealth was safe – until its supporters fell out among themselves.

ment harried the king's servants and sent the two most conspicuous of those who had upheld the Eleven Years' Tyranny to the block (it was another Stuart shortcoming that good servants were sacrificed by bad kings). In 1641 Charles decided that force was the only way out and the Civil War began. In it he was defeated. Parliament was uneasy, as were all men, for if you stepped outside the ancient constitution of King, Lords and Commons, where would things end? But Charles threw away his advantage by seeking a foreign invasion in his support (the Scots were to fight for him, this time). Parliament, or those who dominated it, had had enough and Charles was tried and executed. His son tried unsuccessfully to claim

his inheritance and went into exile with many of his father's supporters. There followed in England an interregnum during which the dominant figure until his death in 1659 was one of the most remarkable of all Englishmen, Oliver Cromwell, a country gentleman who had risen in the parliamentary side's councils by his genius as a soldier. This gave him great power, for provided his army stood by him he could dispense with the politicians, but also imposed limitations on him, for he could not sacrifice the army's support. The result was an English republic which was astonishingly fertile not only in new constitutional schemes, as Oliver cast about to find a way of governing through parliament without delivering England to an intolerant Protestantism such as parliament would embody, but also in political, social and economic debate. This was the Commonwealth.

The greatest single stimulus to this creativity was Puritanism. It was an ill-defined but growing force in English life since Elizabeth's reign. Its spokesmen had originally sought only a particularly close and austere interpretation of religious doctrine and ceremony. There were Puritans inside the Anglican Church as well as among its Protestant critics, but it was to the second that the name was more and more applied. By the seventeenth century it also betokened, besides rigid doctrine and disapproval of ritual, the reform of manners in a strongly Calvinistic sense. Many of the founders of the first English settlements in America were Puritans of this stamp. By the time of the republic, many who had been on the parliament's side in the Civil War seemed to wish to use its victory to impose Puritanism, both doctrinal and moral, by law not only on conservative and royalist Anglicans, but on dissenting religious minorities – Congregationalists, Baptists, Unitarians – which had found their voice under the Commonwealth. There was nothing politically or religiously democratic about Puritanism. Those who were of the Elect might freely choose their own elders and act as a self-governing community, but from outside the self-designated circle of the saved they looked (and were) an oligarchy claiming to know God's will for others, and therefore all the more unacceptable. It was a few, untypical minorities not the dominant Protestant establishment which threw up the democratic and levelling ideas which contributed so much to the great debate which went on for years. The publication of more than 20 000 books and pamphlets on political and religious issues made the Civil War and Commonwealth years a great epoch in English political education and a seedbed of ideas with a great future.

Unfortunately, once Oliver had died, the institutional bankruptcy of the republic was clear. Englishmen could not agree in sufficient numbers to uphold any of its constitutional devices. But most of them would accept the old device of monarchy and so the story of the Commonwealth ended with the restoration of the Stuarts in 1660. This might suggest that nothing important had happened, but this conclusion would be wrong. England had in fact restored her king on unspoken conditions: in the last resort, he came back because parliament said so, and believed he would defend the Church of England. Counter-Reformation Catholicism frightened Englishmen as much as did revolutionary Puritanism. Although the struggle of king and parliament was not over, there would be no absolute monarchy in England: henceforth the Crown was on the defensive. The 'Renaissance State' had failed in England.

Most historians have discerned much more than this in this great episode of English history. Indeed, it is difficult to decide just what the so-called 'English Revolution' expressed. Clearly, religion played a big part in it and extreme Protestantism was given the chance to have an influence on the national life it was never again to have; this earned it the deep dislike of the Church of England. It was not without cause that the best English historian of the struggle has spoken of the 'Puritan Revolution'. But religion no more exhausts the meaning of these years than does the constitutional quarrel. Others have sought a class struggle in the Civil War. Certainly evidence can be found

for the interested nature of men's participation, but there is almost too much of it; it does not fit any clear pattern. Still others have seen a struggle between a swollen 'Court', a governmental nexus of bureaucrats, courtiers and politicians, all linked to the system by financial dependence upon it, and 'Country', the local notables who paid for this. But localities often divided: it was one of the tragedies of the Civil War that even families could be split by it. It remains easier to be clear about the results of the English Revolution than about its origins or meaning.

The troubles of most countries were less fundamental and dramatic than England's (continentals were appalled by the trial and execution of Charles I) but also had important consequences and were no less bloody at times. In France they followed a period of conscious assertion of royal power. Cardinal Richelieu not only reduced the privileges of the Huguenots (as French Calvinists had come to be called) but he had instituted a system of appointing royal officials to reside in the provinces as the direct representatives of royal power; these were the *intendants*. Administrative reform is thus part of the explanation of the almost continuous suffering of the French people in the 1630s and 1640s. There was something of a fiscal revolution in Richelieu's measures and in a simple, still overwhelmingly agricultural economy it was bound to hurt the poor most. Taxes on the peasant doubled and sometimes trebled in a few years. An eruption of popular rebellion, mercilessly repressed, was the result. Some parts of France, moreover, were devastated by the campaigns of the last phase of the Thirty Years War, the phase in which it became a Bourbon–Habsburg conflict. Lorraine, Burgundy and much of the east were reduced to ruins, the population of some areas declining by a quarter or a third.

It was a claim that the French monarchy sought to impose new and, some said, unconstitutional taxation which detonated the crisis of the *Frondes*. The nearest approach in France to a national representative body was

The propaganda of the engraved print at the service of Richelieu. Here the cardinal is depicted as the protector of the monarchy from rebellion and heresy – he has cut away the thistles and now removes the caterpillar which threatened the lilies of France, while the German Eagle of the Empire and the Lion of Spain look on unable to interfere.

the Estates-General, last summoned in 1614. The rôle of defender of the constitution was taken up therefore by special interests, notably the *Parlement* of Paris, the corporation of lawyers who sat in and could plead before the first lawcourt of the kingdom. In 1648 they led an insurrection in Paris where they expressed the wishes of the town notables. Among the things they asked for was the suppression of the *intendants*. A compromise settlement was arrived at but was followed after an uneasy interval by a much more dangerous movement on the part of great noblemen. Though the *Parlement* of Paris did not long maintain a united front with them, these men had the support of the anti-centralist feelings of the provincial nobility, as regional rebellions showed. Yet the Crown survived because the continuation of disorder had alienated from the nobles the popular and urban support they needed. The absolute monarchy of France was still essentially intact in 1660.

In Spain, too, taxation provoked troubles. An attempt by a minister to overcome the provincial-

ism which still persisted in the formally federal structure of the Spanish state led to revolt in Portugal (which had been absorbed into Spain with promises of respect for her liberties from Philip II), among the Basques and in Catalonia. The last was to take twelve years to suppress. There was also a revolt in 1647 in the Spanish kingdom of Naples.

Clearly, in all these instances of civic turbulence, demands for money were fundamental in provoking resistance. In the financial sense, then, the Renaissance State was ceasing to be successful. War was a great devourer of taxes. Yet the burdens of taxation laid on Frenchmen seem far greater than those laid on Englishmen: why, then, did the French monarchy appear to suffer less from the 'crisis'? England, on the other hand, had civil war but not the devastation which went with war abroad. Nor were her occasional riots over high prices to be compared with the appalling bloodshed of the peasant risings of seventeenth-century France. In England, too, there was a specific challenge to authority from religious forces. In Spain this was non-existent and in France it had been contained long before. The Huguenots, indeed, were a vested interest which saw its protector in the monarchy and therefore rallied to it in the *Frondes*. Regionalism was important in Spain, to a smaller extent in France where it provided a foothold for conservative interests threatened by governmental innovation, but seems to have played very little part in England.

Perhaps the outcome of the crisis is more interesting than the search for origins. Although its forms were so different in England and the continental countries, the essence of what happened was that the state continued to gather to itself power and respect. Monarchical absolutism somehow survived in Spain and France and if it failed in England, why, there too the power of the state continued to grow in a different way.

1660, when the young Louis XIV assumed full powers in France and Charles II returned to England, was, in fact, something of a turning-point. In England there was never again, in spite of further constitutional troubles which resulted in the deposition of another king, a struggle such as that of the Civil War. The last English rebellion, a matter of an inadequate pretender and a few thousand deluded yokels in 1685, in no sense revived the dangers with which Tudor rebellions had menaced the state. After 1660 there was an English standing army, after all. As for France, not until 1789 was she to prove ungovernable again. This makes it all the more striking, in retrospect, that men were unwilling to admit the political work in which they were engaged. Englishmen solemnly legislated a series of defences of individual liberty in the Bill of Rights, yet even in 1689 it was hard to agree that what one king in parliament had done, another could not undo. In France everyone agreed the king's power was absolute, yet lawyers went on saying that there were things he could not legally do.

Perhaps the actual success of old institutions in the seventeenth-century crisis made it difficult to recognize the principle of legislative sovereignty. Obviously, it would be in periods of disorder that it would seem most attractive. The greatest of English political philosophers, Thomas Hobbes, expressed this sense in his books, notably in the *Leviathan* of 1651. Hobbes argued that the uncertainties of not agreeing that someone should have the last word in deciding what was law were disadvantages which clearly outweighed the danger that such power might be tyrannically employed. The troubles of his times deeply impressed him with the need to establish certainty about the location of authority. Even when they were not continuous, disorders were always liable to break out: as Hobbes put it (roughly), you do not have to live all the time under a torrential downpour to say that the weather is rainy. The recognition that legislative power – sovereignty – rested, limitless, in the state and not elsewhere, and that it could not be restricted by appeals to immunities, customs, divine law or anything else without the danger of falling into anarchy, was Hobbes' contribution to political theory, though he got small thanks for it and had to

Evocations of power, secular and spiritual, surround the frontispiece of Leviathan, the 'mortal God' whom Thomas Hobbes saw as the only guarantor of the conditions necessary to civilized life.

wait until the nineteenth century for his due recognition. People often acted as though they accepted his views, but he was almost universally condemned. Yet one of the first states to operate on Hobbes' principles was constitutional England. By the early eighteenth century, its rulers accepted in principle and sometimes admitted in practice, that there could be no limits except practical ones to the potential scope of law.

This conclusion was explicitly challenged in England even as late as Victorian times, but was implicit when in 1688 England at last rejected the direct descent of the Stuart male line, pushed James II off the throne and put his daughter and her consort on it on conditions. With the creation of a contractual monarchy England at last broke with her *ancien régime* and began to function as a constitutional state. Effectively, the centralized power was shared; its major component lay with a House of Commons which represented the dominant social interest, the landowning classes. The king still kept important powers of his own but his advisers, it soon became clear, must possess the confidence of the House of Commons. The legislative sovereign, the Crown in Parliament, could do anything by statute. No such immunity as still protected privilege in continental countries existed. The English answer to the danger posed by such a concentration of authority was to secure, by revolution if necessary, that the authority should only act in accordance with the wishes of the most important elements in society.

The year 1688 also brought the ascent to the English throne of a foreigner, William III, to whom the major importance of the 'Glorious Revolution' was not that England became assuredly a constitutional monarchy, but that her power could now be brought into the scale against France, a land-power as threatening to the independence of the United Provinces from which William came as had been the Spain of Philip II. There were too many complicated interests at work for it to be sensible to try to interpret the Anglo-French wars which followed in merely constitutional or ideological terms. Moreover, the presence of the Holy Roman Empire, Spain and various German princes in various anti-French coalitions would certainly make nonsense of any neat contrast of political principle between the two sides. Nevertheless, it rightly struck some contemporaries that there was an ideological element buried somewhere in the struggle. England and Holland were more open societies than the France of Louis XIV. Their constitutions embodied legal protection for the exercise of different religions, even if what the law gave could be by the law taken away. They did not censor the press but left it to be regulated by the laws which protected persons and the state against defamation. They were governed by oligarchies representing a wide spread of the effective possessors of social and economic power. France was at the opposite pole.

Under Louis XIV, absolute government reached its apogee in France and became a model for all European princes. Politics was reduced effectively to administration; the royal councils, together with the royal agents in the provinces, the *intendants* and military commanders, had to take account of such social facts as the existence of the nobility and local immunities, but the reign played havoc with the real independence of the political forces so powerful hitherto in France. This was the era of the establishment of effective government throughout the country and some later saw it as a revolutionary one; it was in the second half of the century that the frame Richelieu knocked together was at last filled up by administrative reality. Louis XIV tamed his nobility by offering them the most glamorous court in Europe; his own sense of social hierarchy made him happy to caress them with honours and pensions, but he always remembered the *Frondes* and controlled them as firmly as had Richelieu. Louis' relatives were excluded from his council, which contained non-noble ministers on whom he could safely rely. The *Parlements* were restricted to their judicial rôle; the French Church's independence of Roman authority was asserted, but only to bring it the more securely under the wing of the monarchy. As for the Huguenots, Louis was determined, whatever the cost, not to be a ruler of heretics and the Edict of Nantes was revoked; those who were not exiled were submitted to a harsh persecution to bring them to conversion.

The coincidence – and interdependence – of one of the greatest ages of French cultural achievement with it seems to make it hard for Frenchmen to recognize the harsh face of the reign of Louis XIV. Yet it was the triumph of hierarchical, corporate, theocratic society which, even if up-to-date in methods, looked to the past for its goals. Louis even hoped to become

Holy Roman Emperor. He refused to allow Descartes, the defender of religion, to be given religious burial in France because of the dangers of his ideas. Yet for a long time his kind of government seems to have been what Frenchmen wanted and, indeed, many of them long continued to want it, preferring the sense of national prestige abroad to liberalism at home. The process of effective government could be brutal, as Huguenots who were coerced into

Louis XIV, unrivalled among European monarchs, in his own and his subjects' eyes, diffuses his glory beneficently over mankind. 1674 was in fact the year in which a formidable coalition of European powers was marshalled against France and in which the unhappy inhabitants of the Palatinate, devastated by a French army, must have felt that they at least could very well do without such rays from the 'sun king' as fell on them.

620

conversion by having soldiers billeted on them, or peasants reluctant to pay taxes who were visited by a troop of calvary for a month or so both knew. Yet it may have been better for some peasants than life a few decades previously. There is evidence that in spite of some exceptionally hard years – and so long a reign could hardly avoid a few – the reign was the end of an era of hardships, not the start of one. France was largely free from invasion and there was a drop in the return to be expected from investment in land which lasted well into the eighteenth century. These were solid realities to underpin the glittering façade of an age later called the *Grand Siècle*.

Louis' European position was won in large measure by success in war (and by the end of the reign, he had undergone bad setbacks), but it was not only his armies and diplomacy which mattered. He carried French prestige to a peak at which it was long to remain because of the model of monarchy he presented; he was the perfect absolute monarch. The physical setting of the Ludovican monarchy was the huge new palace of Versailles. Few buildings or the lives lived in them can have been so successful as models. In the eighteenth century Europe was to be studded with miniature reproductions of the French court, painfully created at the expense of their subjects by would-be *grands monarques* in the decades of stability and continuity which almost everywhere succeeded the upheavals caused by Louis' power.

There were between 1715 and 1740 no important international tensions capable of producing internal change in states, nor were there great ideological divisions such as those of the seventeenth century, nor rapid economic and social development with their consequential strain. In consequence, governments changed little and everywhere society seemed to have settled down after a turbulent century or so. All states for a while seemed well suited by what they had got. Outside England and the United Provinces, the cantons of Switzerland and the fossil republics of Italy, absolute monarchy was the dominant state form, and

was to remain so for most of the eighteenth century, though some of its expressions took the qualified form of it which was soon called 'enlightened despotism' a slippery term, which neither has nor ever had a chance of being confined to a specific reference any more than terms like 'Right' or 'Left' can be confined today. What can be seen is that from about 1750 the wish to carry out practical reforms in some states sometimes led to innovations bearing the stamp of the influence of the advanced thought of the day. Such innovations, when effective, were imposed by the machinery of absolute monarchical powers. It must be stressed that although humanitarian, of course, the policies of 'enlightened despots' were not necessarily politically liberal. They were, on the other hand, often essentially modern; they tended to undermine traditional social and religious authority, they often cut across accepted notions of social hierarchy or legal rights, and they helped to concentrate law-making power in the state and assert its unchallenged authority over its subjects, who were treated increasingly as an aggregate of individuals rather than members of a hierarchy of corporations.

Unfortunately, it is almost impossible to find an example which in practice perfectly fulfils this general description, just as it is impossible to find a definition of a 'democratic' state today, or a 'fascist' state in the 1930s which fits all examples. Among Mediterranean and southern countries, for example, Naples, Spain, Portugal and some other Italian states (even the papal states showed the trend) are conspicuous for reforming ministers who interested themselves in economic reform and encroachment on the powers of the Church. Almost all the courts concerned were part of the Bourbon family connexion and from the involvement of one of the smallest of them, Parma, in a quarrel with the papacy stemmed a general attack in all of these countries on the right arm of the Counter-Reformation Papacy, the Society of Jesus. In 1773 the pope was driven by diplomatic pressure and the harassment of the governments concerned into conceding defeat and the Society was dissolved. This was a great symbolic victory, as important for its demonstration of the strength of advanced anti-clerical principles even in Catholic Europe as for its practical effects.

With the exception of Spain, none of these states had any pretension to great power status. Of the eastern monarchies which may be thought of as enlightened despotisms, on the other hand, three out of four certainly had. The odd man out was Poland, the sprawling ramshackle kingdom where reform on 'enlightened' lines came to grief on constitutional rocks; the enlightenment was there all right, but not the despotism to make it effective. More successfully, Prussia, the Habsburg dominions and Russia, all managed to sustain a façade of enlightenment while strengthening the state. Once more, the clue to change can be found in war, which cost far more than building even the most lavish replica of Versailles. The practical means adopted to levy taxation might still be coloured by or actually embody 'enlightened' aims, but there was no essential connexion with them. In Russia's case there was a process of modernization of the state which went back to the earliest years of the century, when Peter the Great sought to guarantee her future as a great power by means of technical and institutional change. In the second half of the century, the empress Catherine II reaped many of the benefits of this and in addition gave the régime a thin veneer of up-to-the-minute ideas by advertising widely her patronage of letters and humanitarianism. This was all very superficial; the traditional ordering of Russian society was unchanged. It was a conservative despotism whose politics were a matter largely of the struggles of noble factions and families. Nor did 'enlightened despotism' much change things in Prussia, where there was a well-established tradition of efficient, centralized, economical administration embodying much of what reformers sought elsewhere. Prussia enjoyed religious toleration, too, and was without the institutions of theocratic monarchy which tended to accumulate in

the Counter-Reformation lands. Yet Prussia rested on a fundamentally traditional society which was to remain virtually unchanged in the eighteenth century except by the absorption of new non-German subjects. The Prussian king did not have to entangle himself with representative or corporate institutions but he was obliged to recognize – and willingly did so – that his power rested on the acquiescence of his nobles and he carefully preserved their legal and social privilege so as to ensure this. Frederick II remained convinced that only noblemen should be given commissioned rank in his army and at the end of his reign there were more serfs in Prussian territory than there had been at the beginning.

Competition with Prussia was the decisive stimulus in initiating reform in the Habsburg dominions. The Habsburg rulers had to overcome great obstacles. Their territories were very diverse, in nationality, language, institutions; the emperor was King of Hungary, Duke of Milan, Archduke of Austria, to name only a few of his many titles. Centralization and administrative uniformity were essential if this variegated empire was to exercise its due weight in European affairs. Another problem was that, like the Bourbon states, but unlike Russia or Prussia, the Habsburg empire was overwhelmingly Roman Catholic. Everywhere the power of the Church was deeply entrenched; the Habsburg lands included most of those outside Spain where the Counter-Reformation had been most successful. The Church also owned huge properties; legally, it was everywhere protected by tradition, canon law and papal policy, and it had a monopoly of education. Finally, the Habsburgs provided almost without interruption during these centuries the successive occupants of the throne of the Holy Roman Empire. In consequence they had special responsibilities in Germany.

Such a background must have given any modernization in the Habsburg dominions an 'enlightened' colour. Everywhere practical reform seemed to conflict with entrenched social power or the Church. The Empress Maria

Theresia was herself by no means sympathetic to reform which had these implications, but her advisers were able to present a persuasive case for it when, after the 1740s, it became clear that the Habsburg monarchy was engaged in a struggle for supremacy with Prussia. Once the road to fiscal and consequently administrative reform had been entered upon, it was in the end bound to lead to interference with the traditional structures of Church and State. This came to a climax in the reign of Maria Theresia's son and successor, Joseph II, a man who did not share the pieties of his mother and who flaunted his own taste for advanced views. The result was that in his reign reform became especially associated with measures of secularization. Monasteries lost their property, religious appointments were interfered with, the right of sanctuary was removed and education was taken out of the hands of the clergy. This created great opposition, but mattered less than the fact that by 1790 Joseph had antagonized to the point of open defiance the nobles of Brabant, Hungary and Bohemia. As there existed in these lands powerful local institutions – estates and diets – through which they could make their objections to his policies effective, the government of the Habsburg dominions was paralysed over large areas at the end of his reign.

Differences in the circumstances in which they were applied, in the preconceptions which governed them, in the success they achieved and in the degree to which they did or did not embody 'enlightened' ideas, all show how misleading is the idea that there was, anywhere, a 'typical' enlightened despotism to serve as a model. France, whose government was clearly touched by reforming policies and aspirations, provides another confirmation of this. Obstacles to change had, paradoxically, grown stronger in that country after the death of Louis XIV because the monarchy tended to lose power. Under his successor (whose reign began with a minority under a Regent), the real influence of the nobility had grown and increasingly there grew up in the *Parlements* a tendency to use the power of registering new laws as an opportunity for criticism of those which infringed special interest and historic privilege. There was a new and growing resistance to the idea that there rested in the Crown any right of unrestricted legislative sovereignty. As the century wore on, France's international rôle imposed heavier and heavier burdens on her finances and the issue of reform tended to crystallize in the issue of finding new sources of tax revenue – an exercise that was bound to bring on conflicts with the privileged. Onto this rock ran most of the proposals for reform within the French monarchy.

Paradoxically France was by 1789 the country most associated with the articulation and diffusion of critical and advanced ideas, yet also one of those where it seemed most difficult to put them into practice. But this was an issue which was Europe-wide in the traditional monarchies of the end of the eighteenth century. Wherever reform and modernization had been embarked upon, there were present in greater or lesser degree and there had to be navigated with more or less success the hazards of vested historical interest and traditional social structure. In the last resort, it was unlikely that absolutism could have solved this problem in any country. It was too much tied to the past. In the end it could not question historical authority too closely for this was what it rested upon itself. The wholehearted acceptance of the view that legislative sovereignty was unrestricted seemed still in the eighteenth century to call too much in question. If historic rights were infringed, could not property be? This was a fair point. Where those who put it failed in imagination was in not considering how it was that the most successful ruling class in Europe, the English, had succeeded in accepting the theoretical principle that nothing was outside the sphere of legislative competence, nothing beyond the scope of reform, without at any point needing to fear that such a revolutionary engine was likely to be used in a revolutionary way.

With this important qualification, enlightened despotism, too, embodies the theme already

set out. At the heart of this complex story of political evolution in many countries over a period of three centuries, there lies an identifiable unifying theme in the growth of the power of the state. Though there were frequent reactions from aristocrats who tried to put the clock back, their occasional successes almost always proved temporary. In real and in moral or legal terms, a remarkable strengthening of state power is observable and it was something achieved nowhere outside Europe before the nineteenth century.

Yet it is important to see this in its true proportion. Even the most determined enlightened despot had to take account of social forces which could not be ignored. The ablest statesmen had to work with a machinery of state which would to any modern bureaucrat seem woefully inadequate for the tasks it sought to encompass. Though the eighteenth-century state might mobilize resources much greater than had done its predecessors it had to do so with no revolutionary innovations of technique. Communications in 1800 depended just as they had done in 1500 on wind and muscle. Armies could move only slightly faster than three centuries earlier, and if their weapons were improved, they were not improved out of recognition. No police force such as exists today existed in any country; income tax still lay in the future. The change in the power of the state came about because of changes in ideas and because of the development to greater efficiency of well-known institutions, rather than because of technology. In no major state before 1789 could it even be assumed that all its subjects would understand the language of government, while none, except perhaps the United Kingdom, succeeded in so identifying itself with its subjects as to leave its government more concerned to protect them against foreigners than itself against them.

The courageous and attractive empress of Austria, Maria Theresia, in her later years.

3 The new world of great powers

Among the institutions which took their basic shape in the fifteenth and sixteenth centuries and are still with us today are those of formal diplomacy. Rulers had always sent messages to one another and negotiated, but there were many ways of doing this and of understanding what was going on. The Chinese, for example, used the fiction that their emperor was ruler of the world and that all embassies to him were therefore of the nature of petitions or tributes by subjects. Medieval kings had sent heralds, about whom a special ceremonial had grown up and whom special rules protected, or

On 3 June 1666 the Dutch and English fleets fought one of the greatest sea-battles of the century about fourteen miles off Lowestoft. The noise of the guns could just be heard in London and men laid aside their work and walked into the parks or down the river in order to listen, the poet Dryden tells us. It was a great victory for the Royal Navy, though there was to be a return match the following year when the Dutch sailed up the Medway and burnt the ships there, and the Trained Bands of the City of London were called out to prepare to defend the capital. Lowestoft and the other engagements of the Anglo-Dutch wars opened a new era of naval history; for a century and a half the backbone of sea-power was to be provided by ships capable of taking their place in line of battle, mastering their enemy with the power of their guns while absorbing heavy punishment themselves. Nelson or Villeneuve would already have felt at home in a seventeenth-century fleet.

occasional missions of ambassadors to one another. After 1500, it was increasingly the practice to use in peacetime the standard device we still employ, the ambassador permanently resident in a foreign country, through whom all ordinary business is at least initially transacted and who has the task of keeping his own rulers informed about the country to which he is accredited.

The Venetian ambassadors were the first notable examples. It is not surprising that a republic so dependent on trade and the maintenance of regular relationships should have provided the first examples of the professional diplomat. More changes followed. Gradually, the hazards of the life of earlier emissaries were forgotten as diplomats were given special status and were guaranteed by privileges and immunities. The nature of treaties and other diplomatic forms also became more precise and regularized. Procedure became more standardized. All these changes came about slowly, when they were believed to be useful. For the most part, it is true, the professional diplomat in the modern sense had not yet appeared; ambassadors were usually noblemen who had the resources necessary to sustain a representative rôle, not paid civil servants. None the less, the professionalization of diplomacy was beginning. It is one sign that after 1500 a new world of relationships between sovereign powers is replacing that of feudal ties between persons and the vague supremacies of Pope and Emperor.

The most striking characteristic of this new system has remained to this day. This is the assumption that the world is divided into sovereign states. This idea was by no means wholly clear in the sixteenth century. Europe was certainly not then conceived to be completely divided into independent areas, each governed by a ruler of its own, belonging to it alone and to whom alone it belonged. Still less were these units thought to have as their essential any sort of unity which might be called 'national'. That this was so was not only because of the survival of such museums of past practice as the Holy Roman Empire. It was also because the dominating principle of early modern Europe's diplomacy was dynasticism.

Dynasticism meant that the political units of Europe were less states than landed estates. They were accumulations of property put together over long or short periods by aggressiveness, marriage and inheritance – by the same processes and forces, that is to say by which any private family's estate might be built up. The results were to be seen on maps whose boundaries continually changed as this or that portion of an inheritance passed from one ruler to another. The inhabitants had no more say in the matter than might the peasants living on a farm which changed hands. Dynasticism accounts for the monotonous preoccupation of negotiations and treaty-making with the possible consequences of marriages and the careful establishment and scrutiny of lines of succession.

No historical principle, of course, operates in complete purity. Besides their dynastic interests, rulers argued and fought about religion, and, increasingly, trade or wealth. As some of them acquired overseas possessions, this, too, became a complicating factor. Occasionally, the old principles of feudal superiority might still be invoked. There were also always map-making forces at work which fell outside the operation of these principles, such as settlement of new land or a rising national sentiment. Nevertheless, broadly speaking, most rulers in the sixteenth and seventeenth centuries saw themselves as the custodians of inherited rights and interests which they had to pass on. In this they behaved as was expected; they mirrored the attitudes of

Venetian commerce outlived the Byzantine empire which had cradled it in the Near East. A picture by Bellini of a Venetian embassy arriving in Cairo in the early sixteenth century.

other men and other families in their societies. It was not only the Middle Ages which were fascinated by lineage and the sixteenth and seventeenth centuries were the great age of genealogy.

In 1500 the dynastic map of Europe stood at the eve of a major transformation. For some two centuries, two great families were to dispute much of Europe as they were already disputing Italy. These were the house of Habsburg and the ruling house of France, first Valois, then after the accession of Henry IV in 1589, Bourbon. The one would come to be predominantly Austrian and the other's centre would always be France, but both would export rulers and consorts of rulers to much of the rest of Europe. In particular, Spain, Italy and the Low Countries would be disputed between them, though the heart of their quarrel when the sixteenth century began was the Burgundian inheritance. At that time, each of them was far from playing a European rôle. Indeed, there was not a great deal to distinguish them at that date in power – though much in antiquity – from other dynasties, the Welsh Tudors, for example, whose first ruler, Henry VII, had ascended the throne of England in 1485.

Only in England, France and Spain could there be discerned any real national cohesion and sentiment to sustain political unity. England, a relatively unimportant power, was a well-developed example. Insular, secluded from invasion and rid, after 1492, of continental appendages, her government was remarkably centralized and the Tudors, anxious to assert the unity of the kingdom after the long period of civil strife labelled the 'Wars of the Roses', consciously associated national interest with that of the dynasty. Shakespeare quite naturally uses the language of patriotism (and, it may be remarked, says little about religious differences). France, too, had already come far along the road to national cohesion. The house of Valois-Bourbon had greater problems than the Tudors, though, in the continued survival of immunities and privileged enclaves within its territories over which its monarchs did not exercise full sovereignty as kings of France. Some of their subjects did not even speak French. Nevertheless, France was clearly a national state. So was Spain, though to a lesser degree, its two crowns only becoming united when the grandson of the Catholic Monarchs, Charles of Habsburg, became co-ruler with his insane mother in 1516 as Charles I. He had still carefully to distinguish the rights of Castile from those of Aragon, but Spanish nationality was made more self-conscious during his reign because, although at first popular, Charles obscured the national identity of Spain in a larger Habsburg empire and, indeed, sacrificed its national interest to other dynastic aims.

The great diplomatic event of the first half of the century was his election as Charles V, Holy Roman Emperor, in 1519. It was a great dynastic triumph. Charles succeeded his grandfather, who had sought his election, and careful marriages in the past made him, when he was elected, the ruler of the furthest-flung territorial empire the world had ever seen and one to which the title of Holy Roman Emperor only supplied a fitting crown. From his mother he inherited the Spanish kingdoms, the newly discovered Americas and Sicily. From his father, Maximilian's son, came the Netherlands which had been part of the duchy of Burgundy,

and from his grandfather the Habsburg lands of Austria and the Tyrol, with Franche-Comté, Alsace and a bundle of claims in Italy. This was the greatest dynastic accumulation of the age (and it may be remarked here that the crowns of Bohemia and Hungary were held by Charles's brother, Ferdinand, who was to succeed him as Emperor). Habsburg pre-eminence was the central fact of European politics for the first half of the sixteenth century. Its real and unreal pretensions are well shown in the list of Charles's titles when he ascended the imperial throne: 'King of the Romans; Emperor-elect; semper Augustus; King of Spain, Sicily, Jerusalem, the Balearic Islands, the Canary Islands, the Indies and the mainland on the far side of the Atlantic; Archduke of Austria; Duke of Burgundy, Brabant, Styria, Carinthia, Carniola, Luxemburg, Limburg, Athens and Patras; Count of Habsburg, Flanders and Tyrol; Count Palatine of Burgundy, Hainault, Pfirt, Roussillon; Landgrave of Alsace; Count of Swabia; Lord of Asia and Africa'.

Whatever this conglomeration was, it was not national. Within it we may distinguish two main blocks: the Spanish inheritance, rich through the possession of the Netherlands and irrigated by a growing flow of bullion from the Americas, and the old Habsburg lands, demanding an active rôle in Germany to maintain the family's pre-eminence there. Charles, though, saw from his imperial throne much more than this. Revealingly, he liked to call himself 'God's standard-bearer' and campaigned like a Christian paladin of old against the Turk in Africa and up and down the Mediterranean. In his own eyes he was still the medieval emperor who was much more than one ruler among many; he was leader of Christendom and responsible only to God for his charge. Certainly he had a far better claim to be called 'Defender of the Faith' than his rival Henry Tudor; in a measure, Germany, Spain and Habsburg dynastic interest were all sacrificed to Charles's vision of his rôle. Yet what he sought was impossible. The dream of making a reality of universal empire was beyond the powers of any man given the strains imposed by the Reformation and the inadequate apparatus of sixteenth-century communication and administration. Charles, moreover, wished to rule as a personal monarch, travelling ceaselessly in pursuit of this futile aim and thereby, perhaps, he ensured also that no part of his empire (unless it was the Netherlands) felt identified with his house. His aspiration reveals the way in which the medieval world still lived on, but also his anachronism.

The Holy Roman Empire as a formal structure was, of course, distinct from the Habsburg family possessions. It, too, embodied the medieval past, but at its most worm-eaten and unreal. Germany, where most of it lay, was a chaos supposedly united under the emperor and his tenants-in-chief, the imperial Diet. Since the Golden Bull the seven electors were virtually sovereign in their territories. There were also a hundred princes and more than fifty imperial cities, all independent. Another three hundred or so minor statelets and imperial vassals completed the patchwork which was what was left of the early medieval empire. As the sixteenth century began, an attempt to re-form this confusion and give Germany some measure of national unity failed; this suited the lesser princes and the cities. All that emerged were some new administrative institutions. Charles' election as emperor in 1519 was by no means a foregone conclusion; rightly, the danger of a neglect of German interests in the huge Habsburg dominions was feared. Heavy bribery of the electors was needed before he prevailed over the King of France (the only other serious candidate, for nobody believed that the King of England, at first a runner, would be able to pay enough). Habsburg interest was thereafter the only unifying principle at work in the Holy Roman Empire until its abolition in 1806.

Italy, one of the most striking geographical unities of Europe, was also still fragmented into independent states, most of them ruled by princely despots, and some dependencies of external powers. The pope ruled the states of the Church. A King of Naples of the house of

Claims under pressure: Pope (Clement VII) and Emperor (Charles V) are painted as co-equal rulers of a Christendom at a moment when the medieval unity expressed in that idea was about to disintegrate.

Aragon ruled that country (but Sicily belonged to his Spanish relatives). Venice, Genoa and Lucca were republics. Milan was a large duchy of the Po valley ruled by the Sforza family. Florence was theoretically a republic but from 1509 really a monarchy in the hands of the Medici, a former banking house. In north Italy the dukes of Savoy ruled Piedmont, on the other side of the Alps from their own ancestral lands. The divisions of the peninsula made it an attractive prey. Already in the fifteenth century a tangle of family relationships gave plausibility to French and Spanish intervention in Italian affairs. For the first half of the sixteenth century the main theme of European diplomatic history is provided by the rivalry of Habsburg and Bourbon, and its main theatre and its prizes lay first (and in a measure always) in Italy.

A series of Habsburg–Valois wars in Italy which lasted until 1559 and constitute a distinct period in the evolution of the European states system began in 1494 with a French invasion still reminiscent of medieval adventures and raids; after the accession of Charles V and the defeat of Francis in the imperial election, the lines of the dynastic struggle emerged more clearly. There were altogether six wars, more important than might at once appear. To Charles, they brought a fatal distraction from the Reformation problem. To the French, they meant impoverishment, invasion and, in the end, overall defeat, for Spain was left the dominant power in Italy. To Italy they brought disaster; an imperial army sacked Rome in 1527 for the first time since the barbarian invasions and the great days of the city republics were ended for ever by Spanish hegemony and the emigration of skilled craftsmen. Venice was left to face the Turk virtually alone and the hollowness of Christendom's unity was revealed by a French alliance with the Sultan. At one time French and Turkish ships together raided the coasts of Italy. These were good years only for the Ottomans and an enduring and wearying drain on Spanish power. Expeditions by Charles V and his son Philip were defeated and in 1574 the Turks occupied Tunis; their defeat at sea at Lepanto three years before had been only a momentary setback.

Thanks to the flow of silver from America, the Habsburg cause had been well sustained, but to the point at which Charles V, too, was crippled by debt. He abdicated in 1555, the year of the first settlement at Augsburg of the religious disputes of Germany, and was succeeded as emperor by his brother, who took the Austrian inheritance, and as ruler of Spain by his son, Philip II. Charles had been born in the Netherlands and formally abdicated there, in the Hall of the Golden Fleece; he was moved to tears as he left the assembly, leaning on the shoulder of a young nobleman, William of Orange. Charles had needed to learn Spanish; Philip was a Spaniard born and bred. This division of the Habsburg empire marks the watershed of European affairs in the 1550s.

What followed was the blackest period of Europe's history for centuries. With a brief lull in the early seventeenth century, European rulers and their people indulged for a hundred years in an orgy of hatred, bigotry, massacre, torture and brutality which has no parallel until the twentieth century. The dominating facts of this period were the military pre-eminence of Spain, the ideological conflict opened by the Counter-Reformation, the paralysis of France and Germany by internal religious quarrels, the emergence of new centres of power in England, the Dutch Netherlands and Sweden, and the first adumbrations of the overseas conflicts of the next two centuries. Only with the end of this period did it appear that the power of Spain had dwindled and that France had inherited her continental ascendancy.

The best starting-point is the Dutch Revolt. Like the Spanish Civil War of 1936–9 it mixed up the relations of many powers in a confusion of ideological, political, strategic and economic issues. France could not be easy while Spanish armies might invade her from Spain, Italy and Flanders. England's involvement arose in other ways. Though she was Protestant, England was only just Protestant, and Philip tried to avoid an outright break with Elizabeth I. He was for a long time unwilling to sacrifice the chance of a new assertion of his English interests, perhaps even a second marriage to an English queen. Moreover he was long distracted by expensive campaigns against the Ottomans. But national and religious feeling were inflamed in England by the Spanish response to English piracy at the expense of the Spanish empire; Anglo-Spanish relations decayed rapidly in the 1570s and 1580s. Elizabeth overtly and covertly helped the Dutch rebels, whom she did not want to see go under, but did so without enthusiasm; being a monarch, she did not like rebels. In the end, armed with papal approval for the deposition of Elizabeth, the heretic queen, a great Spanish invasion effort was mounted in 1588. 'God blew and they were scattered' said the inscription on an English commemorative medal; bad weather completed the work of Spanish planning and English seamanship and gunnery (though not a ship on either side was sunk by gunfire) to bring the Armada to disaster. War with Spain went on long after its shattered remnants had limped back to Spanish harbours but a great danger was over. Also, almost incidentally, an English naval tradition of enormous importance had been born.

James I strove sensibly to avoid a renewal of the conflict once peace had been made and succeeded, for all the anti-Spanish prejudices of his subjects. England was not sucked into the continental conflict when the revolt of the Netherlands, reignited after a Twelve Years' Truce, was merged into a much greater struggle, the Thirty Years' War. Its heart was a Habsburg attempt to rebuild the imperial authority in Germany by linking it with the triumph of the Counter-Reformation. This called in question the Peace of Augsburg and its principle of a religiously pluralistic Germany. Once again, cross-currents made nonsense of simple ideological conflict. As Habsburg and Valois had disputed Italy in the sixteenth century, Habsburg and Bourbon disputed Germany in the next. Dynastic interest brought Catholic France into the field against the Catholic Habsburgs. Under the leadership of a cardinal, the 'eldest daughter of the Church', as France was known, allied with the Calvinistic Dutch and Swedish Lutherans to assure the rights of German

'God blew, and they were scattered' runs the inscription of an Armada medal. 'It is hard to kick against the pricks' runs another depicting the church and the princes of Europe blindfolded and seated uncomfortably around a bed of nails.

princes. Meanwhile the unhappy inhabitants of much of central Europe had often to endure what was in effect the substitution for ordinary law and order of the whims and capacities of quasi-independent warlords. Cardinal Richelieu has a better claim than any other man to be the creator of a foreign policy of stirring up trouble beyond the Rhine which was to serve France well for over a century. If anyone still doubted it, with him the age of *Realpolitik* and *raison d'état*, of simple, unprincipled assertion of the interest of the sovereign state, had clearly arrived.

Yet though the Peace of Westphalia which ended the Thirty Years' War in 1648 was in several ways a registration of great changes, it also showed traces still of the fading past. This makes it a good vantage-point. It was the end of the era of religious wars in Europe; this was the last time European statesmen would have as one of their main concerns in a general settlement the religious future of their peoples. It also ended Spanish military supremacy on land and the dream of reconstituting the empire of

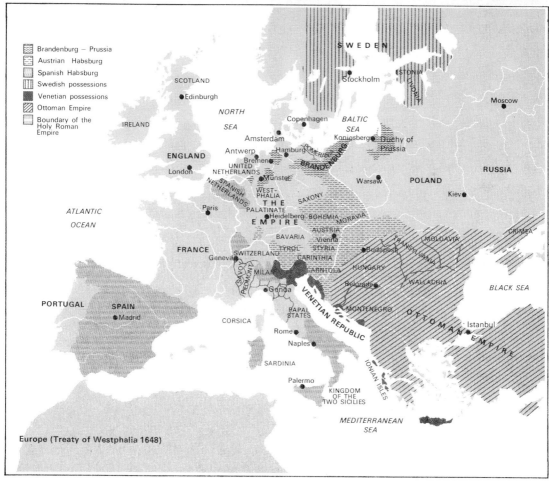

Europe (Treaty of Westphalia 1648)

a Charles V. It closed, too, an era of Habsburg history. From this time, the dynasty's future was an Austrian one, however much its rulers sought to revive their power in Germany. There, a new force had appeared in the Electorate of Brandenburg, with which later Habsburgs would contend, but the frustration of Habsburg power in Germany had been the work of outsiders, Sweden and France. Here was the real sign of the future in Westphalia. A period of French ascendancy was beginning in Europe west of the Elbe.

There are also some negative points to be made about Westphalia. A century and a half after Columbus, when Spain, Portugal, England, France and Holland all already had important overseas empires, these were apparently of no interest to the negotiators of the peace. England was not even present at either of the centres of negotiation and, indeed, had hardly been concerned in the questions at issue once the first phase of the war was over. Preoccupied by internal quarrels and troubled by her Scots neighbours, her foreign policy was inevitably directed still towards ends more extra-European than European – though England was also soon to fight the Dutch (1652–4). Although Cromwell quickly restored peace with the Protestant Republic, telling the Dutch there was room in the world for the trade of both of them, English and Dutch diplomacy were already showing more clearly than that of other nations the influence of commercial and colonial interest.

The French ascendancy was founded on solid natural advantages. France was the most populous state of western Europe and on this simple fact French military strength rested until the nineteenth century; it would always require the assembling of great international forces to contain it. France, though its inhabitants would seem miserably poor to modern eyes, also possessed great economic resources, and was able to sustain a huge efflorescence of French power and prestige under Louis XIV. His reign began formally in 1643, but actually in 1661 when, at the age of twenty-two, he announced his intention of managing his own affairs. This assumption of supreme power was a great fact in international history as well as that of France; Louis was the most consummate exponent of the trade of kingship who has ever lived and it is in a sense only for convenience that his foreign policy may be distinguished from other aspects of his rôle. The building of Versailles, for example, had its justification not only in the gratification of a personal taste, but in buttressing the prestige which was as important to his diplomacy as was the strength of his armies. Similarly, though they may be separated, the principles of his foreign and domestic policy were closely entwined. Louis might wish to improve the strategical shape of France's north-western frontier, but involved in the same question were the facts that (though he might buy millions of tulip bulbs a year from them for Versailles) he despised the Dutch as merchants, disapproved of them as republicans, and detested them as Protestants. Nor did such considerations exhaust the matter; Louis was a legalistic man – kings should be – and he felt that there existed legal claims good enough to give respectability to what he was doing. In one way or another, he found convincing grounds for a foreign policy of expansion, which, though in the end it cost his country dearly, carried France to a pre-eminence from which she was to free-wheel through half the eighteenth century, and created a legend to which Frenchmen still look back with nostalgia.

Louis' first aim was an improved frontier. This meant conflict with Spain, still in possession of the Spanish Netherlands and the Franche-Comté. The defeat of Spain opened the way to war with the Dutch. The Dutch held their own, but the war ended in 1678 with a peace which has usually been seen as the peak of Louis' achievement in foreign affairs. He now turned to Germany. Besides territorial conquest, he sought the imperial crown and to obtain it was willing to ally with the Turk. The turning-point of the international history of his reign came in 1688, when William of Orange, the *Stadtholder* of Holland, took his wife Mary Stuart to England to replace her father on the

'Dutch William', consort of Queen Mary, the daughter of the last Stuart king of England, James II; as William III, he was a monarch disliked by many of his subjects, but accepted by most of them as a disagreeable necessity and for his wife's sake.

English throne. From this time Louis had a new and persistent enemy across the Channel, instead of the complaisant Stuart kings. William could now bring into play on the continent the resources of the leading Protestant power of Europe. For the first time since the days of Cromwell, England was again a land power. William inspired a league of European states (even the pope joined it secretly) against Louis; in King William's war (or the war of the League of Augsburg), Spain, Austria and the Protestant states of Europe were joined together to contain the overweening ambition of the French king and the peace which ended it was the first in which he had to make concessions.

In 1700 the King of Spain died. It was an event Europe had long awaited (for Charles II was a sickly fellow, as well as feeble-minded). Enormous diplomatic preparations had been made because of the great danger and opportunity which this event must present. Charles was childless. A huge dynastic inheritance was therefore at stake and a tangle of claims arising from marriage alliances in the past meant that the Habsburg emperor and Louis XIV (who had passed his rights in the matter on to his grandson) were the two candidates who would have to dispute the matter. But everyone was interested. The English wanted to know what would happen to the trade of Spanish America, the Dutch the fate of the Spanish Netherlands which stood between them and France. Everyone viewed with alarm the prospect of an undivided inheritance going either to Bourbon or Habsburg. The ghost of Charles V's empire walked again. Partition treaties had therefore been made. Unhappily, when it was known that Charles II's will left the whole Spanish inheritance to the Duke of Anjou, Louis's grandson, Louis accepted it and set aside the agreements into which he had entered. He had also offended the English by recognizing the exiled Stuart Pretender as James III of England. A Grand Alliance of Emperor, United Provinces and England was soon formed, and there began the War of the Spanish Succession in which, after twelve years' fighting, France was eventually driven to terms. The crowns of Spain and France were declared for ever incapable of being united on the same head. The first Bourbon king of Spain took his place on the Spanish throne. With Spain he got the Indies, but not the Netherlands, which went to the emperor as compensation and to provide an automatic defence for the Dutch against further French aggression. Austria also profited in Italy. France made concessions overseas to the United Kingdom (as it was after the union of England with Scotland in 1707). The Stuart Pretender was expelled from France and the Protestant succession in England was recognized by Louis.

These are details, but important ones. They express the stabilization of western continental Europe until the French Revolution seventy-five years later. Not everyone liked it (the

635

emperor refused to admit the end of his claim to the throne of Spain) but to a remarkable degree the major definitions of western Europe north of the Alps have remained what they were in 1715. Belgium, of course, did not exist, but the Austrian Netherlands occupied much of the same area as that country, and the United Provinces corresponds to the modern Netherlands. France would keep Franche-Comté and, except for the years from 1871 to 1918, the Alsace and Lorraine which Louis XIV had won for her. Spain and Portugal would after 1715 remain separate within their present boundaries; they still had large colonial empires but were never again to be able to deploy their potential strength so as to lift them out of the second rank of powers. The United Kingdom, the new great power in the west, was complete since 1707; England no longer had to bother about the old northern threat, though once more attached by a personal connexion to the continent because after 1714 its rulers were also Electors of Hanover. South of the Alps, the dust took longer to settle. A still disunited Italy underwent another thirty-odd years of upheaval, minor representatives of European royal houses shuffling around it from one state to another in attempts to tie up the loose ends and seize the left-overs of the age of dynastic rivalry. After 1748 there was only one native dynasty left in the peninsula, that of Savoy, which ruled Piedmont on the south side of the Alps and the island of Sardinia. The papal states, it is true, could be regarded as an Italian monarchy since the fifteenth century, though only occasionally a dynastic one, and the decaying republics of Venice, Genoa and Lucca also upheld the tattered standard of Italian independence. Foreign rulers were installed in the other states.

Western political geography was thus set in a form much of which was to prove remarkably durable. Immediately, this undoubtedly owed much to the need felt by all statesmen to avoid for as long as possible another conflict such as that which had just closed. For the first time a treaty of 1713 declared the aim of the signatories to be the security of peace through a balance of power. So practical an aim was an important innovation in political thinking. There were good grounds for such realism; wars were more expensive than ever and even Great Britain and France, the only countries in the eighteenth century capable of sustaining war against other great powers without foreign subsidy, had been strained. But the end of the War of the Spanish succession also brought the effective settlements of real problems. A new age was opening, foreshadowed by the wars against Louis XIV, in their imperial scope the first true world wars of modern times. With the exception of Italy, most of the political map of the twentieth century was already visible in western Europe. This meant, among other things that dynasticism was already being relegated to the second rank as a principle of foreign policy. The age of national politics had begun, when some kings, at least, could no longer separate the interests of their house from those of their nation.

East of the Rhine and still more east of the Elbe none of this was true. Great changes had already occurred there and many more were to come before 1800. But their origins have to be traced back a long way, as far as the beginning of the sixteenth century. At that time Europe's eastern frontiers were guarded by Habsburg Austria and a vast Polish–Lithuanian kingdom ruled by the Jagellions which had been formed by marriage in the fourteenth century. They shared with the maritime empire of Venice the burden of resistance to Ottoman power, the supreme fact of east European politics at that moment. The Turks won victories and made conquests as late as the eighteenth century, though by then their last great effort was spent. For more than two centuries after the capture of Constantinople, nevertheless, they set the terms of eastern European diplomacy and strategy. The phrase 'Eastern Question' had not then been invented; if it had been, down to 1700 men would have meant by it the problem of defending Europe against Islam.

The capture of Constantinople was followed by a century of naval warfare and Turkish

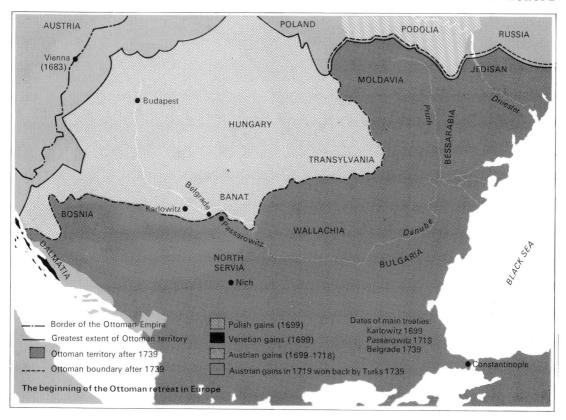

Border of the Ottoman Empire
Greatest extent of Ottoman territory
Ottoman territory after 1739
Ottoman boundary after 1739

Polish gains (1699)
Venetian gains (1699)
Austrian gains (1699-1718)
Austrian gains in 1719 won back by Turks 1739

Dates of main treaties:
Karlowitz 1699
Passarowitz 1718
Belgrade 1739

The beginning of the Ottoman retreat in Europe

expansion to the west from which the main sufferer was Venice. In 1479 the Ionian islands were conquered, in 1571 Cyprus. Turkish success was interrupted in the early seventeenth century but then resumed; in 1669 the Venetians had to recognize that they had lost Crete. Meanwhile, Hungary was invaded in 1664 in what was to be the last Turkish conquest of a European kingdom. Soon the Ukrainians acknowledged Turkish suzerainty and the Poles had to give up Podolia (though the Russians forced them back in the Ukraine within a few years). In 1683 the Turks opened a siege of Vienna and Europe seemed in its greatest danger for over two centuries. In fact it was not. This was to be the last time Vienna was besieged, for the great days of Ottoman power were over. The effort which began with the conquest of Hungary was the last heave.

Difficulties had long troubled the Ottoman empire. The army was no longer abreast of the latest military technology: it lacked the field artillery which had become the decisive weapon of the seventeenth-century battlefield. At sea, the Turks clung to the old galley tactics of ramming and boarding and were less and less successful against the Atlantic nations' technique of using the ship as a floating artillery battery (unfortunately for themselves, the Venetians were conservative too). Turkish power was in any case badly overstretched. It was always engaged in Asia (where the conquest of Iraq from Persia in 1639 brought almost the whole Arab-Islamic world under Ottoman rule) as well as in Europe and Africa, and the strain was too much for a structure allowed to relax by inadequate or incompetent rulers. A great vizier had pulled things together in the middle of the century to make the last offensives possible. But there were weaknesses of structure which he could not correct, for they were inherent in the nature of the empire itself.

637

More a military occupation than a political unity, the Ottoman empire was dangerously dependent on subjects whose loyalty it could not enlist. The Ottomans usually respected the customs and institutions of non-Moslem communities, which were ruled under the *millet* system, through their own authorities. The Greek Orthodox, Armenians and Jews were the most important and each had their own arrangements, the Greek Christians having to pay a special poll-tax, for example, and being ruled, ultimately, by their own patriarch in Constantinople. At lower levels, such arrangements as seemed best were made with leaders of local communities for the support of the military machine which was the heart of the Ottoman structure. In the end this bred over-mighty subjects as pashas feathered their own nests amid incoherence and inefficiency. It gave the subjects of the sultan no sense of identification with his rule. In the background, meanwhile, there deepened an impoverishment of the Ottoman lands in Europe.

The year 1683, therefore, although a good symbolic date as the last time that Europe stood upon the defensive in her old bastion against Islam before going over to the attack, was a less dangerous moment than it looked. Afterwards the tide of Turkish power was to ebb almost without interruption until in 1918 it was once more confined to the immediate hinterland of Constantinople and the old heartland of the Ottomans, Anatolia. The relief of Vienna by the King of Poland, John Sobieski, was followed by the liberation of Hungary. The dethronement of an unsuccessful sultan in 1687 and his incarceration in a cage proved an inadequate remedy for Turkish weakness. In 1699 Hungary became part of the Habsburg dominions again, devastated though it was. In the following century Transylvania, the Bukovina, and most of the Black Sea coasts would follow it out of Ottoman control. By 1800, the Russians had asserted a special protection over the Christian subjects of the Ottomans and had already tried promoting rebellion among them. In the eighteenth century, too, Ottoman rule was to ebb in Africa and

A Polish medal commemorates peace between the Polish state and Muscovy in 1686. One side shows John Sobieski, king of Poland, the other allegorical and appropriately dressed figures of Poland and Muscovy linked in triumph over the Turkish crescent.

Asia; by the end of it, though forms might be preserved, the Ottoman caliphate was somewhat like that of the Abassids in their declining days. Morocco, Algeria, Tunis, Egypt, Syria, Mesopotamia and Arabia were all in varying degrees independent or semi-independent by then.

It was not the traditional guardians of eastern Europe, the once-great Polish–Lithuanian commonwealth and the Habsburgs, who were the legatees of the Ottoman heritage, nor did they inflict the most punishing blows as the Ottoman empire crumbled. The Poles instead were nearing the end of their own history as an independent nation. The personal union of Lithuania and Poland had been turned into a real union of the two countries too late. In 1572, when the last king of the Jagellion line died without an heir, the throne had become not only theoretically but actually elective. His successor was a Frenchman and for the next century Polish magnates and foreign kings disputed this prize at each election, though while they did so their country was under grave and continuing pressure from Turks, Russians and Swedes. Poland prospered against these enemies only when they were embarrassed elsewhere. The Swedes descended on her northern territories during the Thirty Years' War and the last of the Polish coast was given up to them in 1660. Internal divisions had worsened, too; the Counter-Reformation brought religious persecution to the Polish protestants and there were risings of Cossacks in the Ukraine and continuing serf revolts.

The heroic John Sobieski was the last Polish king of Polish blood and his election the last in which a compromise was not imposed by foreign rulers. He had won important victories and managed to preside over Poland's curious and highly decentralized constitutional arrangements. The elected kings had very little legal power to balance that of the landed proprietors. They had no standing army and could rely only on their own personal troops when factions among the gentry or magnates fell back on the practice of armed rebellion ('Confederation') to obtain their wishes. In the Diet, the central parliamentary body of the kingdom, a rule of unanimity stood in the way of any reform. Yet reform was badly needed, if a geographically ill-defined, religiously divided Poland, ruled by a narrowly selfish rural gentry, was to survive. Poland was a medieval community in a modernizing world.

John Sobieski could do nothing to change this situation. There underlay it a social structure strongly resistant to reform. The nobility or gentry were effectively the clients of a few great families of extraordinary wealth. One clan, the Radziwills, owned estates half the size of Ireland and held a court which outshone that of Warsaw; the Potocki estates covered 6500 square miles (roughly half the area of the Dutch Republic). The smaller landowners could not stand up to such grandees. Their estates made up less than a tenth of Poland in 1700. The million or so gentry who were the Polish 'nation' were for the most part poor, and therefore dominated by great magnates reluctant to surrender their power to arrange a confederation or manipulate a Diet. At the bottom of the pile were the peasants, some of the most miserable in Europe, engaged in unending battle with their landlords over feudal dues, over whom landlords still had in 1700 rights of life and death. The towns were powerless. Their total population was only half as big as the gentry and they had been devastated by the seventeenth century wars. Yet Prussia and Russia also rested on backward agrarian and feudal infrastructures and survived. Poland was the only one of the three eastern states to go under completely. The principle of election blocked the emergence of a dynasty which could identify its own instincts of self-aggrandizement with those of the nation, Polish Tudors or Bourbons. Against this background it is hardly surprising that Poland entered the eighteenth century under a foreign king, the Elector of Saxony, who was chosen to succeed John Sobieski in 1697. Within a few years he had been deposed by the Swedes and then put back again on his throne by the Russians.

It was Russia which was to be the future great power in eastern Europe. In the closing years of the seventeenth century this was only beginning to be apparent to western statesmen, though the Poles and Swedes were already alive to the fact.

Used as we are to the idea of Russia as a world power, it now requires an effort to realize how rapid and astonishing was her appearance as a major force. Russia, whose national identity had barely been a reality in 1500, would in the twentieth century be one of the two most powerful states in the world. At the beginning of the European age, when only the ground-plan of the Russian future had been laid out by Ivan the Great, such a future was inconceivable, and so it long remained. The first man formally to bear the title of 'Tsar of all the Russias' was his grandson Ivan IV, crowned in 1547. In spite of a ferocious vigour which earned him his nickname 'the Terrible', he still could not play a significant rôle in European affairs. So little was Russia known even in the seventeenth century that a French king could then write to a Tsar, not knowing that the prince whom he addressed had been dead for ten years. During these centuries the shape of a future Russia was slowly determined, but almost unnoticed in the West. Even after Ivan the Great, Russia had remained territorially ill-defined and exposed. The Turks had pushed into south-west Europe. Between them and Muscovy there were the lands of the Cossacks, the Ukraine, the home of peoples who fiercely protected their independence. So long as they had no powerful neighbours, they found it easy to do so. To the east of Russia, the Urals provided a theoretical though hardly a realistic frontier. Russia's rulers have always found it easy to feel isolated in the middle of hostile space. Almost instinctively, they have sought natural frontiers at its edges or a protective glacis of clients.

The first steps had to be the consolidation of the gains of Ivan the Great which constituted the Russian heartland and then penetration of the wilderness of the north. When Ivan the Terrible came to the throne, Russia had a small Baltic coast and a vast territory stretching up to the White Sea, thinly inhabited by scattered and primitive peoples, but providing a route to the west. The English were reaching Russia by it in the 1550s; in 1584 Archangel was founded. Ivan could do little on the Baltic front but

Russian expansion 1500–1800

turned on the Tatars after they burned Moscow yet again in 1571. He drove them from Kazan and Afghanistan and won control of the whole length of the Volga, carrying Muscovite power to the Caspian.

The other great thrust which began in his reign was across the Urals, into Siberia, and was less one of conquest than of settlement. Most of Russia is Asian. Its possession makes her a world as well as a European power, with a stake in the Far East and Pacific affairs. The first steps towards this outcome, which was inconceivable at the time, were an ironic anticipation of what was to be a great theme of the Siberian frontier: the first Russian settlers across the Urals seem to have been political refugees from Novgorod. Among those who followed were others fleeing from serfdom (there were no serfs in Siberia) and aggrieved Cossacks. Others had less pressing motives and by 1600 there were Russian settlements as much as six hundred miles beyond the Urals. They were closely supervised by a competent bureaucracy out to assure the state tribute in furs.

The rivers were the keys to Siberia, more important even than those of the American frontier. Within fifty years a man and his goods could travel by river with only three portages from Tobolsk, three hundred miles east of the Urals, to the port of Okhotsk, three thousand miles away. There he would be only four hundred miles by sea from Sakhalin, the northernmost of the major islands of the chain which make up Japan – a sea-passage about as long as that from Land's End to Antwerp. By 1700 there were 200000 settlers east of the Urals: it had by then been necessary already to make a treaty with the Chinese to regulate settlement on the Amur, and some Russians, we are told, talked of the conquest of China. The misgivings of the advisers of K'ang-hsi seem justified.

The movement eastward was not much affected by the upheavals and dangers of the 'Time of Troubles' which followed Ivan's death, though in the west there were moments when the outlet to the Baltic was lost and even when Moscow and Novgorod were occupied by Lithuanians or Poles. Russia was still not a serious European power in the early seventeenth century. The then rising strength of Sweden was thrown against her and it was not until the great war of 1654–67 that the Tsars finally regained Smolensk and Little Russia, not to be lost again until 1812, and then only briefly. Maps and treaties now began to define Russia in the west in a way which had some correspondence with reality. By 1700, though she still had no Black Sea coast, her south-western frontier ran on the western side of the Dnieper for most of its length, embracing the great historic city of Kiev and the Cossacks who lived on the east

bank. They had appealed to the Tsar for protection from the Poles and were granted special, semi-autonomous governmental arrangements which survived until Soviet times. Most Russian gains had been at the expense of Poland, long preoccupied with defence and offence against the Turk and Swede. Russian armies joined the Poles in alliance against the Ottomans in 1687; this was an historic moment, too, for it was the beginning of what was later known as the Eastern Question which was to preoccupy European statesmen until 1918, when they found that the problem at the heart of it (what limit, if any, should be placed upon Russian encroachment on the Ottoman empire?) had at last disappeared with the protagonists themselves.

The making of Russia was overwhelmingly a political act. The monarchy was its centre and motor; the country had no obvious racial unity to preordain its existence and precious little geographical definition to impose a shape. It was united by Orthodoxy, but other Slavs were Orthodox, too. The growth of the personal domain of the Tsars and the growth of their power were the keys to the building of the nation. Ivan the Terrible was an administrative reformer. Under him appeared the beginnings of a nobility owing military service in return for their estates, a development of a system employed by the princes of Muscovy to obtain levies to fight the Tatars. It made possible the raising of an army which led the King of Poland to warn the English queen, Elizabeth I, that if they got hold of western technical skills the Russians would be unbeatable; the danger was remote, but this was prescient.

From time to time there were setbacks, though the survival of the state does not seem in retrospect to have been at stake. The last Tsar of the house of Rurik died in 1598. Usurpation and the disputing of the throne between noble families and Polish interventionists went on until 1613, when the first Tsar of a new house, the noble family of Romanov, emerged. This was Michael, and though he was a weak ruler who lived in the shadow of his dominating father, he founded a dynasty which was to rule Russia for three hundred years, until the Tsarist state itself collapsed. His immediate successors fought off the depredations of rival nobles and humbled the great ones among them, the boyars, who had attempted to revive a power curbed by Ivan the Terrible. Beyond their ranks the only potential internal rival was the Church. In the seventeenth century it was first weakened by schism and then a great step in Russian history was taken when the patriarch was deprived in 1667 after a quarrel with the Tsar. There was to be no Investiture Contest in Russia. After this time the Russian Church was structurally and legally subordinated to a lay official. Among believers there would emerge plenty of spontaneous doctrinal and moral opposition to current Orthodoxy, and there began the long-lived and culturally very important movement of underground religious dissent called the *raskol* which would eventually feed political opposition, but Russia was never to know the conflict of Church and State which was so creative a force in western Europe any more than she was to know the stimulus of the Reformation.

The result of these processes was the final evolution of the characteristic Russian governmental form, Tsarist autocracy. It was characterized by the personification in the ruler of a semi-sacrosanct authority unlimited by clear legal checks, by an emphasis on the service owed to the state by all subjects, by the linking of landholding to this idea, by the idea that all institutions within the state except the Church derived from it and had no independent standing of their own, by the lack of a distinction of powers and the development of a huge bureaucracy, and by the paramountcy of military needs. These qualities, as the scholar who listed them points out, were not all present at the start, nor were all of them equally operative and obvious at all times. But they mark Tsardom off from monarchy in western Christendom where, far back in the Middle Ages, towns, estates of the realm, guilds and many other bodies had established the privileges and

liberties on which later constitutionalism was to be built. Louis XIV might believe in Divine Right and aspire to a great concentration of power, but it was always a power explicitly restricted by rights, by religion, by divinely ordained law. Though his subjects knew he was an absolute monarch, they were sure he was not a despot. In England an even more startlingly different monarchy was developing, one under the control of parliament. Yet divergent from one another though English and French monarchical practice might be, they both accepted practical and theoretical limitations inconceivable to Tsardom; they bore the stamp of a western tradition Russia had never known. For the whole of its existence the Russian autocracy was to be in the west a byword for despotism.

Yet it suited Russia. Moreover, the attitudes which underlay it seem in some measure to suit Russia still. Eighteenth-century sociologists used to suggest that big, flat countries favoured despotism. This was over-simple, but there were always latent centrifugal tendencies in a country so big as Russia, embracing so many natural regions and so many different peoples. The Tsars' title, significantly, was 'Tsar of *all* the Russias' and the federal structure of the modern USSR, too, reflects this diversity. Russia had always to be held together by a strong pull towards the centre if the divergences within it were not to be exploited by the enemies on the borders.

The reduction of great families was the inevitable concomitant of the growth of royal authority, but though the humbling of the boyars left the ruling family isolated in its eminence, it was isolated in a sea of nobility. The Russian nobility was increasingly brought to depend on the state until a reverse tendency set in in the middle of the eighteenth century. The theory of this dependence was that nobility derived from service, which was often rewarded in the seventeenth century with land and later with the grant of serfs. All land, indeed, was held on the condition of service to the autocracy and the degrees of service were defined in a

Table of Ranks set out in 1722. This effectively amalgamated all categories of nobility into a single class. The obligations laid on nobles by it were very large, often extending to a man's lifetime, though in the eighteenth century they were progressively diminished until removed altogether. Nevertheless, service still continued to be the route to an automatic ennoblement, and the nobles never acquired quite such independence of their monarch as in other countries. New privileges were conferred upon them later in the century, but no closed caste emerged. Instead, the Russian nobility grew hugely by new accessions and by natural increase. Some of its members were very poor, because there was neither primogeniture nor entail in Russia and property could be much subdivided in three or four generations. Towards the end of the eighteenth century most nobles had less than a hundred serfs.

Of all imperial Russia's rulers the one who made the most memorable use of the autocracy and most deeply shaped its character was Peter the Great. He came to the throne as a ten-year-old child and when he died something had been done to Russia which could never be quite eradicated. In one way he resembled twentieth-century strong men who have striven ruthlessly to drag traditional societies into modernity, but he was very much a monarch of his own day, his attention focussed on victory in war – Russia was only at peace for one year in his entire reign – and he accepted that the road to that goal ran through westernizing and modernizing. His ambition to win a Russian Baltic coast supplied the driving force behind the reforms which would open the way to it. That he should be sympathetic to such a course may owe something to his childhood, growing up as he did in the 'German' quarter of Moscow where the foreign merchants and their retinues lived. A celebrated pilgrimage he made to western Europe showed that his interest in technology was real. Probably in his own mind he did not distinguish the urge to modernize his countrymen from the urge to free them forever from the fear of their neighbour. Whatever the exact balance of his motives, his reforms have ever since served as something of an ideological touch-stone; generation after generation of Russians were to look back with awe and ponder what he had done and its meaning for Russia. As one of them wrote in the nineteenth century, 'Peter the Great found only a blank page . . . he wrote on it the words Europe and Occident'.

His territorial achievement is the easiest to assess. Though he sent expeditions off to Kamchatka and the oases of Bokhara, he had a driving ambition to reach the sea to the west. For a while he had a Black Sea fleet and annexed Azov, but had to abandon it later, because of distractions elsewhere, from the Poles and, above all, the Swedes. The wars with Sweden for the Baltic outlet were a struggle to the death. The Great Northern War, as contemporaries termed the last of them, began in

While travelling in western Europe in 1698, the Tsar Peter heard suddenly that there was a revolt among the streltsy, *the half-military, half-police, but always undisciplined and inefficient force which was the core of Muscovite power. He hurried home and exacted a ferocious vengeance; twelve hundred of the rebels were executed, some after torture and mutilation (it was believed by some foreigners that Peter the Great had taken a hand with the hanging himself). This was the end of any danger that he might face a* coup d'état *from a force which had threatened the monarchy in the past.*

643

1700 and lasted until 1721. The world recognized that something decisive had happened when in 1709 the Swedish king's army, the best in the world, was destroyed at Poltava, in the middle of the Ukraine where its leader had sought to find allies among the Cossacks. The rest of Peter's reign only drove home the point and at the peace Russia was established firmly on the Baltic coast, in Livonia, Estonia and the Karelian isthmus. Sweden's days as a great power were over and she had been the first victim of a new one.

A few years before this, the French *Almanach Royale* for the first time listed the Romanovs as one of the reigning families of Europe. Victory had opened the way to further contact with the West, and Peter had already anticipated the peace by beginning in 1703 to build, on territory captured from the Swedes, St Petersburg, the beautiful new city which was to be for two centuries the capital of Russia. The political and cultural centre of gravity thus passed from the isolation of Muscovy to the edge of Russia nearest the developed societies of the West. Now the westernizing of Russia could go ahead more easily; it was a deliberate break with the past.

Even Muscovy, of course, had never been completely isolated from Europe. A pope had helped to arrange Ivan the Great's marriage, hoping he would turn to the western Church. There was always intercourse with the neighbours, the Roman Catholic Poles, and the English merchants had made their way to Moscow under Elizabeth I, where to this day they are commemorated in the Kremlin by the presence there of one of the most magnificent collections in the world of the work of English silversmiths. Trade continued after this and there also came to Russia the occasional foreign expert from the West. In the seventeenth century the first permanent embassies from European monarchs were established. But there was always a tentative and suspicious response among Russians; as in later times, attempts were made to segregate foreign residents.

Peter threw this tradition aside. He wanted

Poltava, Peter the Great's greatest triumph, commemorated in a Russian engraving.

experts – shipwrights, gun-founders, teachers, clerks, soldiers – and he gave them privileges accordingly. In administration he correspondingly broke with the old traditions of inherited family office and tried to institute a bureaucracy selected on grounds of capacity. He set up schools to teach technical skills and founded an Academy of Sciences, thus introducing the idea of science to Russia, where all learning was hitherto clerical. Like many other great reformers he also put much energy into what might be thought superficialities. Courtiers were ordered to wear European clothes; the old long beards were cut back and women were told to appear in public in German fashions. Such psychological shocks were indispensable in so backward a country. Peter was virtually without allies in what he was trying to do and in the end such things as he achieved had to be driven through by force. They rested on his autocratic power and little else. The old *Duma* of the boyars was abolished and a new senate of appointed men took its place. Those who resisted were ruthlessly broken, but it was less easy for Peter to dispose of the deep conservative force of habit; he had at his disposal

The 'bronze horseman': a drawing of the monument to Peter the Great in St Petersburg.

only an administrative machine and communications that would seem inconceivably inadequate to any modern government.

The most striking index of successful modernization was Russia's new military power. More complicated tests are harder to come by. The extent of cultural westernization, for example, must be assessed very differently according to which part of society is considered. The vast majority of Russians were untouched by Peter's educational reforms, which only obviously affected technicians and a few among the upper class. The result was a fairly westernized higher nobility, focussed at St Petersburg; by 1800 its members were largely French-speaking and in touch with the currents of thought which arose in western Europe. But they were often resented by the provincial gentry and formed a cultural island in a backward nation. The mass of the nobility did not benefit from the new schools and academies. Further down the social scale, the great majority of Russians remained illiterate; those who learnt to read did so for the most part at the rudimentary level offered by the teaching of the village priest, often only one generation removed from

illiteracy himself. A literate Russia would not emerge until the twentieth century.

Her social structure tended more and more to mark off Russia, rather than assimilate itself to the west. Russia was the last country in Europe to abolish serfdom; she did not do so until 1861; among Christian countries only the United States kept bonded labour for longer. While the eighteenth century saw the institution weakening almost everywhere, in Russia it spread and was strengthened. This was largely because labour was always scarcer than land; significantly, the value of a Russian estate was usually assessed in the number of 'souls' – that is, serfs – tied to it, not its size in acres. The number of serfs had begun to go up in the seventeenth century, when the Tsars found it prudent to gratify nobles by giving them land, some of which already had free peasants settled on it. Debt tied them to their landlords and many of them entered into bondage to the estate to work it off. Meanwhile, the law imposed more and more restrictions on the serf and locked the structure of the state more and more into that of the economy. Legal powers to recapture and restrain serfs were steadily increased and landlords had been given a special interest in using such powers when Peter had made them responsible for the collection of the poll-tax and for military conscription. In this way, economy and administration were more completely united than in any western country. Russia's aristocrats were intended to become essentially hereditary civil servants, carrying out tasks for the Tsar.

In return their economic privilege was buttressed by the state. Formally, by the end of the eighteenth century, there was little that a lord could not do to his serfs short of inflicting death on them. If they were not obliged to carry out heavy labour services, money dues were levied upon them almost arbitrarily. There was a high rate of desertion, serfs making for Siberia or even volunteering for the galleys. About a half of the Russian people were in bondage to private lords in 1800, a large number of the rest owing almost the same

645

services to the Crown and always in danger of being granted away to nobles by it. As new lands were annexed, their populations, too, passed into serfdom even if they had not known it before. The result was a great rigidifying of society. By the end of the century, Russia's greatest problem for the next hundred years was already in existence; what to do with so huge a population when both economic and political demands made serfdom increasingly intolerable, but when its scale presented colossal problems of reform. It was like the man riding an elephant; it is all right so long as he keeps going but there are problems when he wants to get off.

Servile labour was the backbone of the Russian economy. Except in the famous Black Earth zone, only beginning to be opened up in the eighteenth century, Russian soil is by no means rich and even on the best land, farming methods were poor. It seems unlikely that production ever kept pace with population until the twentieth century and periodic famine and epidemics were the natural restoratives of balance. Population much more than doubled in the eighteenth century, about seven million of the thirty-six million or so at which it stood at the end having been acquired with new territories, the rest having accumulated by natural increase. This was a faster rate of growth than any other European country. Of this population, only about one in twenty-five at most were townsmen.

The economy based on this growing population made striking progress during the century and was unique in utilizing serfdom to industrialize. Here, it may be thought, was an unequivocal success for Peter's policy of modernization, for though there had been beginnings under the first two Romanovs, it was he who launched Russian industrialization as a guided movement. Yet it was not so simple as that. In the first place, the achievement was only comparative; not only was Russia's starting level very low, but the economies of most European countries were at that time still capable of only very slow growth rates. Though grain production went up and the export of Russian cereals (later a staple of Russian overseas trade) began in the eighteenth century, it was done only by bringing more land under cultivation and perhaps by the more successful extraction of the surplus by the landlord and tax-collector, so that the consumption of the peasant declined. This was to be the story throughout most of the imperial era and sometimes the load was crushing: it has been estimated that taxes took 60 per cent of the peasant's crop under Peter the Great. The techniques were not there to increase productivity and the growing rigidity of the system held it down more and more firmly. Even in the second half of the nineteenth century in Russia the Middle Ages could be seen still going strong, as the peasant wasted what little time was left to him after work for his lord by trudging around the collection of scattered strips which was his holding. In many places his equipment did not even include the plough, and crops had to be raised from the shallow scratching of the soil which was all that was possible.

None the less, this agricultural base somehow supported not only the military effort needed to make Russia a great power, but also the first phase of her industrialization. By 1800 Russia produced more pig-iron and exported more iron ore than any other country in the world. Peter, more than any other man, was responsible for this. He grasped the importance of Russia's mineral resources and built the administrative apparatus to grapple with them. He initiated surveys and imported the miners to exploit them. By way of incentive, the death penalty was prescribed for landlords who concealed mineral deposits on their estates or tried to prevent their use. Communications were developed to allow access to these resources so that during the century the centre of Russian industry shifted towards the Urals. The rivers were crucial. Only a few years after Peter's death the Baltic was already linked by water to the Caspian.

Manufacturing grew up around this core of extractive industry which, together with her forests, ensured Russia a favourable balance of trade for the whole century. Less than a hundred factories in Peter's reign became more than 3000 by 1800. After 1754, when internal customs barriers were abolished, Russia was the largest free-trade area in the world. In this, as in the granting of serf labour or of monopolies, the state continued to shape the Russian economy; Russian industry did not emerge from free enterprise, but from regulation, and this was the only way, for it ran directly against the grain of Russian social fact. There might be no internal customs barriers, but nor was there any important internal trade. Most Russians lived in 1800 as they had done in 1700, within self-sufficient local communities depending on their artisans for their small supply of manufactures and hardly emerging into a money economy. Such 'factories' as there were seem often to have been little more than agglomerations of artisans. Over huge areas, labour service, not rent, was the basis of tenure. Foreign trade was still mainly in the hands of foreign merchants. Moreover, though State grants to exploit their resources and allocations of serfs encouraged mineowners, the need of such encouragement shows that stimuli producing growth elsewhere were lacking in Russia. That eighteenth-century Russia was brought up to the level of economic development of most of the rest of continental Europe by the beginning of the industrial age was a great relative achievement, but does not mean so much in absolute terms.

The monarchy's contribution to this did not end with Peter, but there was a notable flagging of its energy after him. The impetus could not be maintained; there were not enough educated men to allow the bureaucracy to keep up the pressure once his driving power had gone. Peter had not named a successor (he had his own son tortured to death) and the rulers who followed him faced without his force of character and the terror he had inspired a renewed threat of hostility from the great noble families. The direct line was broken in 1730 when Peter's grandson died, to be replaced by one of his nieces. Yet factional quarrels could be exploited by monarchs and this was something of a recovery for the Crown; Anna was put on the throne by the nobles who had dominated her predecessor, but she quickly broke their power. Symbolically, the court returned to St Petersburg from Moscow, to which it had gone after Peter's death (to the delight of the conservatives). Anna turned to foreign-born ministers for help and this worked well enough until her death in 1749. Her infant son was within a year set aside (to be kept in prison until murdered more than twenty years later) in favour of Elizabeth, daughter of Peter the Great, who relied on the support of the Guards regiments and Russians irritated by foreigners. She was succeeded in 1762 by a nephew who reigned barely six months before he was forced to abdicate. The lover of the overmighty subject who subsequently murdered the deposed Tsar was the new Tsarina and widow of the deposed victim, a German princess who became Catherine II.

The glitter with which she subsequently surrounded herself masked a great deal and it was often effective in taking in her contemporaries. Among the things it almost hid was the bloody and dubious route by which she came to the throne. It is probably true, though, that she rather than her husband might have been the victim if she had not struck first. In any case, the circumstances of her accession and of those of her predecessors showed the weakening the autocracy had undergone since Peter. The first part of her reign was a ticklish business; powerful interests existed to exploit her mistakes and for all her identification with her new country (she had renounced her Lutheran religion to become Orthodox) she was a foreigner. 'I shall perish or reign', she once said; in the end she reigned, and to great effect.

Catherine's reign was even more spectacular than that of Peter the Great, though its innovatory force was less. She, too, founded schools and patronized the arts and sciences. The difference was that Peter was concerned with practical effect, Catherine rather to associate the prestige of enlightened thinkers with her court

and legislation. The forms were often forward-looking while the reality was reactionary. Close observers were not taken in by legislative language: the reality was shown by the exile of the young Radischev, who had dared to criticize the régime. Such liberal impulses as she showed perceptibly weakened as the reign went on and foreign considerations distracted her.

The best evidence of Catherine's essential caution was her refusal to tamper with the powers and privileges of the gentry. She was the Tsarina of the landlords, giving them greater power over the local administration of justice and strengthening their control over their serfs, who lost the right to petition against their masters. Only twenty times in the whole of Catherine's reign did the government act to restrain landlords abusing their powers over their serfs. Most significant of all, the obligation to service was abolished in 1762 and a charter of rights was later given to the nobility which sealed a half-century of retreat from Peter's policies towards them. The gentry were exempted from personal taxation, corporal punishment and billeting, could be tried (and be deprived of their rank) only by their peers, and were given the exclusive right to set up factories and mines. The landowner was in a sense taken into partnership by the autocracy.

In the long run this was pernicious. Under Catherine, Russia began to wrap herself more and more tightly in the carapace of her social structure at a time when other countries were beginning to loosen theirs. This would increasingly unfit Russia to meet the challenges and changes of the next half-century. One sign of trouble was the scale of serf revolt. This had begun in the seventeenth century, but the most frightening and dangerous crisis came in 1773, the rebellion of Pugachev, the worst of the

Catherine II, Empress of Russia, who came to the throne, she said, as a poor German girl and who rewarded her adopted country by making greater additions to its territory than any ruler since Peter the Great. This portrait, by an Italian, was painted towards the end of her life.

great regional movements which studded Russian agrarian history before the nineteenth century. Later, better policing would mean that revolt was always local and containable, but it continued through almost the whole of the imperial era. That revolt should occur was hardly surprising. The load of labour services piled on the peasant rose sharply in the Black Earth zone during Catherine's reign. Soon critics would appear among the literate class and the condition of the peasant would be one of their favourite themes, thus providing an early demonstration of a paradox evident in many developing countries in the next two centuries. It was becoming clear that modernization was more than a matter of technology; if you borrowed western ideas, they could not be confined in their effect. The first critics of Orthodoxy and autocracy were beginning to appear. Eventually the need to preserve an ossifying social system would virtually bring to a halt the changes which Russia needed to retain the place that courageous and unscrupulous leadership and seemingly inexhaustible military manpower had given her.

By 1796, when Catherine died, this place was indeed impressive. The most solid ground of her prestige was her armies and diplomacy. She had given Russia seven million new subjects. She said she had been well treated by Russia, to which she had come 'a poor girl with three or four dresses', but that she had paid her debts to it with Azov, the Crimea and the Ukraine. This was in the line of her predecessors. The momentum of Peter's reign carried the foreign policy of Russia forward even when the monarchy was weak and did so still along two traditional lines of thrust, into Poland and towards Turkey. Russia had been favoured by the difficulties under which likely opponents laboured in the eighteenth century. Once Sweden was out of the running only Prussia or the Habsburg empire could provide a counterweight to the new power and since these two were at loggerheads for most of the eighteenth century, Russia could have her own way both over an ailing Poland and a crumbling Ottoman empire.

649

In 1701 the Elector of Brandenburg, with the consent of the emperor, became a king; the kingdom of Prussia was to last until 1918. Prussia had been a duchy united to Brandenburg in the sixteenth century after a Polish king had ended the rule of the Teutonic knights and secularized it. The Hohenzollern dynasty had provided a continuous line of electors since 1415, steadily adding to their ancestral domains. Religious toleration had been the rule in them after an elector was converted to Calvinism in 1613 while his subjects remained Lutheran. One problem facing the Hohenzollerns was the increasingly disparate and dispersed nature of their lands, which stretched from east Prussia to the west bank of the Rhine. The Swedes provided most of the infilling of this scatter of territories in the second half of the seventeenth century, though there were setbacks even for the 'Great Elector', Frederick William, the creator of the Prussian standing army and winner of the victories against the Swedes which were the basis of the finest military tradition in modern European history. Arms and diplomacy continued to carry forward Frederick William's successor to the kingly crown he coveted and to participation in the Grand Alliance against Louis XIV. Prussia was by that fact alone clearly a great power. This imposed a heavy cost but careful house-keeping had again built up the best army and one of the best-filled treasuries in Europe by 1740, when Frederick II came to the throne.

He was to be known as the 'Great' because of the use he made of them, largely at the expense of the Habsburgs and the kingdom of Poland, though also at the expense of his own people whom he subjected to heavy taxation and exposed to foreign invasion. It is difficult to decide whether he was more or less attractive than his brutal father (whom he hated), for he was malicious, vindictive and completely without scruple. But he was highly intelligent and much more cultivated, playing and composing for the flute, and enjoying the conversation of clever men. He was also utterly devoted to the interests of his dynasty, which he saw as the extension of its territories and the magnification of its prestige.

Frederick gave up some possessions too remote to be truly incorporated in the state, but added to Prussia more valuable territories. The opportunity for his first conquest, that of Silesia, came when the Emperor died in 1740 leaving a daughter, whose succession he had sought to assure but whose prospects were uncertain. This was Maria Theresia, who remained Frederick's most unforgiving opponent until her death in 1780. Her intense personal dislike of him was reciprocated. A general European war 'of the Austrian Succession' left Prussia holding Silesia. It was not to be lost in later wars and in the last year of his reign Frederick formed a League of German Princes to thwart the attempt of Maria Theresia's son and successor, Joseph II, to negotiate the acquisition of Bavaria.

There is more significance to this story for European history as a whole than might be thought to lie in competition for a province, however rich, and for the leadership of the princes of Germany. On the one hand, it is a reminder of how alive still in the eighteenth century were the dynastic preoccupations of the past, and on the other it is the opening of a theme with a century of life to it, and consequences great for Europe as a whole. Frederick launched the struggle between Habsburg and Hohenzollern for the mastery of Germany which was only to be settled in 1866. That is further ahead than may be usefully considered at present but it is this context which makes the Hohenzollern appeal to German patriotric sentiment against the emperor, many of whose essential interests were non-German, important. There would be periods of good relations, but in the long struggle which began in 1740 Austria's great handicap would always be that she was both more and less than a German state.

The disadvantages of the spread of her interests were made very obvious in other theatres during the reign of Maria Theresia. The Austrian Netherlands were an administrative nuisance rather than a strategic advantage, but it was in the east that the worst distractions

King Frederick II of Prussia reviewing his troops. Frederick the Great, as he was later called, showed immense military skill in his campaigns against Austria and her Russian allies, and it is as a soldier that he is chiefly remembered.

from German problems arose, and they became increasingly pressing as the second half of the century brought more and more clearly into view the likelihood of a long and continuing confrontation with Russia over the fate of the Ottoman empire.

For thirty years or so Russo-Turkish relations had been allowed to slumber with only occasional minor eruptions over the building of a fort or the raids of the Crimean Tatars, one of the peoples originating in a fragment of the Golden Horde and under Turkish suzerainty.

Even in the seventeenth century, Russian Tsars still paid them tribute; this ended only with Peter the Great. Then, between 1768 and 1774, Catherine fought her most successful war against Turkey and in an obscure Bulgarian village called Kutchuk Kainardji a peace was signed which was one of the most important of the whole century. The Turks gave up their suzerainty over the Crimean Tatars (an important loss both materially, because of their military manpower and morally, because this was the first Islamic people over which the Ottoman empire ceded control), Russia took the territory between the Bug and Dnieper, together with an indemnity, the right of free navigation on the Black Sea and through the straits and, in some ways most pregnant with future opportunity of all the terms, a right to take up with the Turks the interests of 'the church to be built in Constantinople and those who serve it'. This was to say that the Russian government was recognized as the guarantor and protector of new rights granted to the Greek – that is, Christian – subjects of the Sultan. In the following century it was to prove a blank cheque for Russian interference in Turkish affairs.

Almost at once it became clear that this was a beginning, not an end. In 1783 the Crimea was annexed by Russia, and after another war with the Turks Catherine's armies carried her frontier up to the line of the Dniester. The next obvious boundary ahead was the Pruth, which meets the Danube a hundred miles or so from the Black Sea. The possibility of Russia's installation at the mouth of the Danube was to remain an Austrian nightmare, but the danger which appeared in the east before this was that Russia would swallow Poland. With the eclipse of Sweden, Russia had effectively had her own way at Warsaw, happy to leave her interests to be secured through a compliant Polish king. The factions of the magnates and their quarrels blocked the road to reform and without reform Polish independence would be a fiction because effective resistance to Russia was impossible. When there seemed to be for a moment a slight chance of reforms these were checkmated by skilful Russian exploitation of religious divisions to produce confederations which speedily reduced Poland to civil war.

The last phase of Poland's independent history

The first Partition of Poland: an allegorical print shows the east European monarchs at work dividing the spoils.

opened when the Turks declared war on Russia in 1768, with the excuse that they wished to defend Polish liberties. To avoid the danger that the Austrians would declare war on Russia in order to keep their end up when the Russians beat the Turks, Frederick the Great proposed that everyone should have a prize. Thus came about the first 'Partition' of Poland in 1772, in which Russia, Prussia and Austria shared between them about one-third of Poland's territory and one-half of her inhabitants. The old international system which had somewhat artificially preserved Poland had now disappeared. After two more partitions Russia had done best in terms of territorial extent, absorbing something like 180 000 square miles of territory (though in the next century it would be clear that the population of dissident Poles which went with it was by no means an unambiguous gain) but Prussia also did well, emerging from the division of booty to find she had more Slav than German subjects. Nevertheless, so huge a prize set the seal on Russian success; the transformation of eastern Europe since 1500 was complete and the stage was set for the nineteenth century, when there would be no booty left to divert Austria and Russia from the Ottoman succession problem. Meanwhile, independent Poland disappeared from the map for a century and a quarter.

Catherine rightly claimed to have done much for Russia, but she had only deployed a strength already apparent. Even in the 1730s, a Russian army had been as far west as the Neckar; in 1760 another marched into Berlin. In the 1770s there was a Russian fleet in the Mediterranean. A few years later a Russian army was campaigning in Switzerland and, after twenty years, another occupied Paris. The paradox at the heart of such evidences of strength was less obvious; Russian military power was based on a backward social and economic structure which would, in the end, cramp and cripple her and need to be rebuilt. Perhaps this was inherent in what Peter had done. The Russian state rested on a society with which it was fundamentally incompatible and later Russian critics would make much of this theme. Of course, this would not mean that the clock could be put back. The Ottoman empire was for ever gone as a serious competitor for power while Prussia's emergence announced a new age as much as did Russia's. The future international importance of the United Provinces and Sweden had been unimaginable in 1500, but it, too, had waned by 1800; they were still important nations, but of the second rank. France was still a front-rank power in an age of national states as she had been in the days of sixteenth-century dynastic rivalry; indeed, her power was relatively greater and the peak of her dominance in western Europe was still to come. But she faced a new challenger, too, and one which had already defeated her. From the little English kingdom of 1500, cooped up in an island off the coast of Europe under an upstart dynasty, had emerged the world power of Great Britain.

This had happened almost as surprisingly and suddenly as had Russia's own transformation into a major actor on the international stage, and it transformed and transcended the old categories of European diplomacy quite as dramatically. It was another reason why, in three hundred years, the major zones of European conflict and dispute had migrated from the old battlegrounds of Italy, the Rhine and the Netherlands, moving from them to central and eastern Germany, the Danube valley, Poland and Carpathia, the Baltic and, a greater change than any, across the oceans. A new age had opened, foreshadowed in the wars of Louis XIV, the first world wars of the modern era, imperial in their scope.

4 Europe's assault on the world

The change in world history after 1500 is quite without precedent. Never before had one culture spread over the whole globe. From the earliest observable stage of prehistory, the tendency had always been towards differentiation. Now the cultural tide was turning. The essentials of what was happening were evident even by the end of the eighteenth century. Including Russia, European nations by then already laid claim to more than half the world's land surface and, in varying degree, actually controlled about a third of it. To the western hemisphere they had by then already transplanted settler populations large enough to constitute new centres of civilization; a new nation had emerged from former British territory in North America, and to the south the Spaniards had destroyed two mature civilizations to implant their own. To the east, the story was different, but equally impressive. Once past the Cape of Good Hope (where something like 20 000 Dutch lived), an Englishman travelling on an East Indiaman in 1800 would not touch at European colonial communities like those of the Americas unless he wandered as far off course as Australia, just beginning to receive its settlers. But in East Africa, Persia, India, Indonesia he would everywhere find Europeans come to do business and then, in the long or short run, planning to return home to enjoy the profits. They could even be found in Canton, or, in very small numbers, in

The Portuguese arriving in Japan, closely observed by a Japanese artist, even down to the crucifixes carried by two of them.

the closed island kingdom of Japan. Only the interior Africa, protected still by disease and climate, seemed impenetrable.

The remarkable transformation thus begun (and to go much further) was almost entirely a one-way process. Europeans went out to the world, it did not come to them. Few non-Europeans other than Turks entered Europe except as exotic imports or slaves. The Arabs and Chinese were by no means unskilful sailors. They had made oceanic voyages and knew about the compass, while the simple island peoples of the Pacific made long sea crossings on their mysterious errands, but the ships which came round the Horn or the tip of Africa to Atlantic ports were European ships homeward bound, not Asiatic ones.

Under this great transformation of world relationships lay layer upon layer of exploration, enterprise, technical advantage and governmental patronage. The trend seemed irreversible by the end of the eighteenth century and, in a sense, so it was to prove, even if direct European rule was to dissolve more quickly than it was built up. No civilization had been more rapidly and dramatically successful, untroubled in its expansion by any but temporary and occasional setbacks. This was because of its great initial advantages.

One of these lay in the possession by Europeans of powerful motives to succeed. The great thrust behind the Age of Reconnaissance had been the European wish to get into easier and more direct contact with the Far East, the source of the things badly wanted in Europe.

The Far East wanted virtually nothing from Europe. When Vasco da Gama showed what he brought to give to a king, the inhabitants of Calicut laughed at him; he had nothing to offer which could compare with what Arab traders already brought to India from other parts of Asia. It was indeed just the known superiority of so much of the civilization of the Orient that spurred Europeans on to try to reach it on some more regular and assured basis than the occasional trip of a Marco Polo. Coincidentally, China, India and Japan were at something like a cultural peak in the sixteenth and seventeenth centuries. The land blockade of Europe by the Turk made them even more attractive to Europeans than they had been before. There were huge profits to be made and great efforts could be justified.

If the expectation of reward is a good recipe for high morale, so is the expectation of success. By 1500 enough had been done for the business of exploration and new enterprise to be attacked confidently; there was a cumulative factor at work, as each successful voyage added both to knowledge and to the certainty that more could be done. As time went by, it would also add profits for the financing of future expansion. Then there was the psychological asset of Christianity. Soon after the establishment of settlement this found a vent in missionary enterprises, but it was always present as a cultural fact, assuring the European of his superiority both to the peoples with which he began to come into touch for the first time and to those he encountered again. This was, of course, to have disastrous effects in the next centuries for the peoples invaded. Confident in the possession of the true religion, Europeans were impatient and contemptuous of the values and achievements of the civilizations they disturbed. The result was always uncomfortable and often brutal. It is also true that religious zeal could blur easily into less avowable motives. As the greatest Spanish historian of the American conquests put it when describing why he and his colleagues had gone to the Indies, they thought 'to serve God and his Majesty, to give light to

Vasco da Gama, the Portuguese explorer whose achievements were rewarded by wealth and honours, including, in the end, the vice-royalty of Portuguese India, where he died.

those who sat in darkness and to grow rich as all men desire to do'.

Greed quickly led to the abuse of power, to domination and exploitation by force. In the end this led to great crimes – though often unconscious ones – to the destruction of whole societies and a huge traffic in black slaves, but this was only the worst aspect of a theme of dominance present from the beginning in European enterprise. The adventurers who first reached the coasts of India were soon boarding Asian merchantmen, torturing and slaughtering their crews and passengers, looting their cargoes and burning the ravaged hulks. Europeans could usually exact what they wanted in the end because of a technical superiority which exaggerated the power of their tiny numbers and for

A European looks at the East: a Cornishman, Peter Mundy, drew these sketches of Asian vessels during a voyage to Macao in 1637.

a few centuries turned the balance against the great historic agglomerations of population.

The next Portuguese captain after da Gama to go there provided a fitting symbol of this by bombarding Calicut. A little later, when in 1517 the Portuguese reached Canton, they fired a salute as a gesture of friendship and respect, but the noise of their guns horrified the Chinese (who at first called them *folangki* – a remote corruption of the word 'Franks'). These weapons were much more powerful than anything China had. There had long been guns in Asia, and the Chinese had known about gunpowder centuries before Europe, but the technology of artillery had stood still there. European craftsmanship and metallurgy had in the fifteenth century made great strides, producing weapons superior to any available elsewhere in the world. There

were still more dramatic improvements to come, so that the comparative advantage of Europeans was to increase, right down to the twentieth century. This progress had been and was to be, again, paralleled in other fields, notably by the developments in shipbuilding and handling which have already been touched upon. When combined, such advances produced the remarkable weapon with which Europe opened up the world, the sailing-ship which was a gun-carrier. Again, evolution was far from complete in 1517, but already the Portuguese had been able to fight off the fleets organized by the Turks to keep them out of the Indian Ocean. (The Turks had more success in keeping control of the Red Sea, because in those narrower waters the oar-propelled galley which closed with its enemies to grapple and board retained more of its usefulness. Even there, though, the Portuguese were able to penetrate as far as the Suez isthmus.) The Chinese war-junk would do no better than the rowed galley. The abandonment of the oar for propulsion and the mounting, broadside, of large numbers of guns, enormously multiplied the value of Europe's scanty manpower.

This advantage was clear to contemporaries. The Dutch in the seventeenth century were very anxious to keep to themselves the secrets of gun-founding and not to allow them to pass into the hands of Asiatics. Yet pass they did. There had been Turkish gunners in India in the fifteenth century and before they reached China the Portuguese were supplying the Persians with cannon and teaching them how to cast more in order to embarrass the Turks. In the seventeenth century their knowledge of gun-founding and gunnery was one of the attractions which kept the Jesuit Fathers in favour with the Chinese authorities.

Yet although, as the Dutch feared, the knowledge of up-to-date gun-founding penetrated oriental societies it did not offset the European advantage. Chinese artillery remained inferior in spite of the Jesuits' training. There was more to the technological disparity of Europe and the world than mere know-how. One of the assets Europe enjoyed at the beginning of her era was

657

not only knowledge, but an attitude to knowledge different from that of other cultures. There was a readiness to bring it to bear upon practical problems, a technological instinct for the useful. In it lay the roots of another psychological characteristic of Europeans, their growing confidence in the power to change things. Here, perhaps, was the most fundamental difference of all between them and the rest of the world. Europe was open to the future and its possibilities in a way that other cultures were not. On this confidence would long rest a psychological advantage of the greatest importance. Even in 1500 some Europeans had seen the future – and it worked.

Africa and Asia were the first targets against which these advantages were deployed and may be conveniently considered first. In these continents, the Portuguese led for a century and more. They figured so largely and were so successful in the opening of routes to the East that their king took the title (confirmed by the pope) 'Lord of the conquest, navigation and commerce of India, Ethiopia, Arabia and

In the seventeenth century Englishmen, Portuguese, Dutchmen and Swedes all contended for advantage in West Africa. This print shows the Dutch castle at Elmina in the 1660s.

Another view of the Europeans: a ship stands at the top of this Benin ivory salt-cellar of the seventeenth century and Portuguese soldiers cluster menacingly about its base.

Persia', which sufficiently indicates both the scope and the eastern bias of Portuguese enterprise, but is slightly misleading in its reference to Ethiopia, with which Portuguese contacts were small. Any penetration of Africa was impossible on more than a tiny and hazardous basis. The Portuguese suggested that God had especially set a barrier about the African interior in its mysterious and noxious diseases (which were to hold Europeans at bay until the end of the nineteenth century). Even the coastal stations of West Africa were unhealthy and could only be tolerated because of their importance in the slave trade and the substructure of long-range commerce. The East African stations were less unhealthy, but they, too, were of interest only because they were part of a commercial network already created by Arabs, whom the Portuguese deliberately harried so as to send up the cost of the spices purveyed by way of the Red Sea and the Middle East to the Venetian merchants of the eastern Mediterranean. The successors of the Portuguese were to leave the interior of Africa alone as they had done, and the history of that continent was still to move largely to its own rhythms in the obscure fastnesses of its forests and savannahs for another two centuries, except where its inhabitants came into corrosive and stimulating contact with Europeans at its fringes. It is also true, though, that the opening of the European age in Asia showed that none of the powers concerned was in the first place interested in the subjugation or settlement of large areas. The whole of the period down to the middle of the eighteenth century was marked by the multiplication of trading posts, concessions in port facilities, protective forts and bases on the coast, for these by themselves would assure the only thing early imperialism sought in Asia, secure and profitable trade.

The story of this trade in the sixteenth century is one of Portuguese supremacy; their firepower enabled the Portuguese to sweep all before them and they rapidly built up a chain of bases and trading posts. Twelve years after Vasco da Gama arrived at Calicut the Portuguese established their main Indian Ocean trading station some three hundred miles further up the western Indian coast, at Goa. It was to become a missionary centre, as well as a commercial one; once established, the Portuguese empire strongly supported the propagation of the faith, and the Franciscans played a large part in this. In 1513 the first Portuguese ships reached the Moluccas, the legendary spice islands, and the incorporation of Indonesia, south-east Asia, and islands as far south as Timor within the European horizon began. Four years later the first Portuguese ships reached China and opened direct European trade with that empire. Ten years later they were allowed to use Macao; in 1557 they obtained a permanent settlement there and it remains in Portuguese hands to this day. When Charles V gave up to the Portuguese the rights which Spain had claimed as a result of exploration in the Moluccas, keeping only the Philippines in the Far East, and renouncing any interest in the Indian Ocean area, the Portuguese were in possession of a monopoly of eastern empire which was to endure for the next half-century.

It was a trading monopoly, and not only one of trade with Europe; there was much business to be done as carriers between Asian countries; Persian carpets went to India, cloves from the Moluccas to China, copper and silver from Japan to China, Indian cloth to Siam. Both the Portuguese and their successors found this a profitable source of income to offset some of the costs of Europe's unfavourable balance of trade with Asia. For a long time Asia wanted little from Europe except silver. The only serious competitors at sea were the Arabs and they were controlled effectively by Portuguese squadrons operating from the East African bases, from Socotra, at the mouth of the Red Sea, where they had established themselves in 1507, from Ormuz, on the Muscat coast at the entrance to the Persian Gulf, and from Goa. From these places the Portuguese expanded their commerce further and eventually pushed into the Red Sea as far as Massawa and up to the head of the Persian Gulf, where they established a factory at Basra. They had also secured trading privileges in Burma and Siam and in the 1540s were the first Europeans to land in Japan. This network of stations and privileges was supported by a diplomacy of agreements with local rulers and the superiority of Portuguese firepower at sea. Even if they had wished to do so, they could not have developed this power on land, so that a commercial empire was not only economic sense but was all that could be created with the means available.

Portugal's supremacy disguised fundamental weakness: a lack of manpower and a shaky financial base. It lasted until the end of the century and was then replaced by that of the Dutch, who carried the technique and institutions of commercial empire to their furthest development. The Dutch were the trading imperialists *par excellence*, though in the end they also carried out some settlement in Indonesia. Their opportunity arose when Portugal was united with Spain in 1580. This change provided a stimulus to Dutch seamen now excluded from the profitable re-export trade of oriental goods from Lisbon to northern Europe which had been mainly in their hands. The background of the Eighty Years' War with Spain was an additional incentive for the Dutch to enter areas where they might make profits at the expense of the Spanish. With less than two million people, their survival depended on a narrow base; commercial wealth was therefore vitally important to them. They had large advantages in the pool of naval manpower, ships, wealth and experience built up by their ascendancy in fishing and carrying in northern waters and com-

The Asian looks at the mysteriously powerful ships of the Europeans: Portuguese are seen on this painted screen unloading goods for trade in a Japanese port in the sixteenth century.

mercial expertise at home made it easy to mobilize resources for new enterprises. The Dutch were assisted, too, by the simultaneous recovery of the Arabs, who took back the East African stations north of Zanzibar as Portuguese power wavered in the aftermath of the Spanish union.

The first decades of the seventeenth century brought the collapse of much of the Portuguese empire in the east and its replacement by the Dutch. The main objective of the Dutch was the Moluccas. A brief period of individual voyages (sixty-five in seven years, some round the Straits of Magellan, some round Africa) ended when in 1602, at the initiative of the States General, the government of the United Provinces, there was set up the Dutch United East India Company, the organization which was to prove the decisive instrument of Dutch commercial supremacy in the East. Like the Portuguese before them, the company's servants worked through diplomacy with native rulers to exclude competitors, and through a system of trading-stations. How unpleasant the Dutch could be to rivals was shown in 1623, when ten Englishmen were executed at Amboyna; this ended any English attempt to intervene directly in the spice trade. Amboyna had been one of the first Portuguese bases to be seized in a rapid sweeping-up of Portuguese interests, but it was not until 1609, when a resident governor-general was sent to the East, that the reduction of the major Portuguese forts could begin. The centre of these operations was the establishment of the Dutch headquarters at Jakarta, renamed Batavia, in Java, where it was to remain until the end of Dutch colonial rule. It became the centre of an area of settlement, where Dutch planters could rely upon the company to back them up in a ruthless control of their labour force. The early history of the Dutch colonies is a grim one of insurrection, deportation, enslavement and extermination. The trade of local shippers – and of the Chinese junks – was deliberately destroyed in order to concentrate all sources of profit in the hands of the Dutch.

The spice trade to Europe was the centre of Dutch attention and was a huge prize. It accounted during most of the century for over two-thirds of the values of the cargoes sent back to Amsterdam. But the Dutch also set about replacing the Portuguese in the valuable East Asian trade. They could not expel the Portuguese from Macao, though they sent expeditions

An eighteenth-century Japanese painting of the Dutch settlement in Nagasaki bay from which the Dutch traded with the mainland.

against it, but succeeded in setting themselves up in Formosa, from which they built up an indirect trade with the mainland of China. In 1638 the Portuguese were expelled from Japan and the Dutch succeeded them there. In the next two decades, the Portuguese were replaced by the Dutch in Ceylon, too. Their successful negotiation of a monopoly of trade to Siam, on the other hand, was overtaken by another power, France. This country's connexion with the area was opened by accident in 1660 when circumstance took three French missionaries to the Siamese capital. Thanks to their establishment of a mission centre and the presence of a Greek adviser at the Siamese court there followed a French diplomatic and military mission in 1685. But these promising beginnings ended in civil war and failure and Siam moved again out of the sphere of European influence for another two centuries.

In the early eighteenth century there thus existed a Dutch supremacy in the Indian Ocean and Indonesia, and an important Dutch interest in the China seas, which to a remarkable degree reproduced the earlier Portuguese one, although there survived Portuguese stations within it, such as Goa and Macao. Its heart was the Malacca Strait, from which Dutch power radiated through Malaysia and Indonesia, to

Dr Johnson takes tea with the Boswells. The great lexicographer's passion for this drink was only an exaggerated form of a habit already well established among his countrymen.

Formosa and the trading links with China and Japan, and down to the south-east to the crucial Moluccas. This area was by now enjoying an internal trade so considerable that it was beginning to be self-financing, bullion from Japan and China providing its flow of currency rather than bullion from Europe as in the early days. Further west, the Dutch were also established at Calicut, in Ceylon and at the Cape of Good Hope and had set up factories in Persia. Although Batavia was a big town and the Dutch were running plantations to grow the goods they needed, this was still a littoral or insular commercial empire, not one of internal dominion over the mainland. In the last resort it rested on naval power and it was to succumb, though not to disappear, as Dutch naval power was surpassed.

This was clearly beginning to happen in the last decades of the seventeenth century. The unlikely challenger for Indian Ocean supremacy was England. At an early date the English had sought to enter the spice trade. There had been an East Indian Company under James I, but its factors had got bloody noses for their pains, both when they tried to cooperate with the Dutch and when they fought them. The upshot of this was that by 1700 the English had in effect

drawn a line under their accounts east of the Malacca Strait. Like the Dutch in 1580, they were faced with a need to change course and did so. The upshot was the most momentous event in British history between the Protestant Reformation and the onset of industrialization, the acquisition of supremacy in India.

In India the main rivals of the English were not the Dutch or Portuguese, but the French. What was at stake between them did not emerge for a long time. The rise of British power in India was very gradual and after the establishment of Fort St George at Madras and the acquisition of Bombay from the Portuguese as a part of the dowry of Charles II's queen, there was no further English penetration of India until the end of the century. From their early footholds (Bombay was the only territory they held in full sovereignty) Englishmen conducted a trade in coffee and textiles less glamorous than the Dutch spice trade, but one which grew in value and importance. It also changed their national habits, and therefore society, as the establishment of coffee-houses in London showed. Soon, ships began to be sent from India to China for tea; by 1700 Englishmen had found their national beverage and a poet would soon commemorate what he termed 'cups that cheer but not inebriate'.

As a defeat of the East India Company's forces in 1689 showed, military domination in India was unlikely to prove easy. Yet it was not necessary to prosperity and the company did not wish to fight if it could avoid it. Though at the end of the century a momentous acquisition was made when the company was allowed to occupy Fort William, which it had built at Calcutta, the directors in 1700 rejected the idea of acquiring fresh territory or planting colonies in India as quite unrealistic. Yet all preconceptions were to be changed by the collapse of the Moghul empire after the death of Aurungzebe in 1707. The consequences emerged slowly, but their total effect was that India was dissolved into a collection of autonomous states with no paramount power.

The Moghul empire had already before 1707

been troubled by the Marathas. The centrifugal tendencies of the empire had always favoured the *nawabs*, or provincial governors, too, and power was divided between them and the Marathas with increasing obviousness. The Sikhs provided a third focus of power. Originally appearing as a Hindu sect in the sixteenth century, they had turned against the Moghuls but had also drawn away from orthodox Hinduism to become virtually a third religion with it and Islam. The Sikhs formed a military brotherhood, had no castes, and were well able to look after their own interests in a period of disunion. Eventually a Sikh empire appeared in northwest India which was to endure until 1849. Meanwhile, there were signs in the eighteenth century of an increasing polarity between Hindu and Moslem. The Hindus withdrew more into their own communities, hardening the ritual practices which publicly distinguished them. The Moslems reciprocated. On this growing dislocation, presided over by a Moghul military and civil administration which was conservative and unprogressive, there fell also a Persian invasion in the 1730s and consequent losses of territory.

There were great temptations to foreign intervention in this situation. In retrospect it seems remarkable that both British and French took so long to take advantage of it; even in the 1740s the British East India Company was still less wealthy and powerful than the Dutch. This delay is a testimony to the importance still attached to trade as their main purpose. When they did begin to intervene, largely moved by hostility to the French and fear of what they might do, the British had several important advantages. The possession of a station at Calcutta placed them at the door to the part of India which was potentially the richest prize, Bengal and the lower Ganges valley. They had assured sea communications with Europe, thanks to British naval power, and governments listened to the East India merchants in London as they did not listen to French merchants at Versailles. The French were the most dangerous potential competitors but their government was

always likely to be distracted by its European continental commitments. Finally, the British lacked missionary zeal; this was true in the narrow sense that Protestant interest in missions in Asia quickened later than Catholic, and also, more generally, in that they had no wish to interfere with native custom or institution but only – somewhat like the Moghuls – to provide a neutral structure of power within which Indians could carry on their lives as they wished while the commerce from which the company profited prospered in peace.

The way into an imperial future was intervention in Indian politics by providing support for Indian princes. As there were rivalries between princes, this provided the first, indirect, form of conflict between French and British. In 1744 this led for the first time to armed struggle between British and French forces in the Carnatic. India had been irresistibly sucked into the world-wide conflict between British and French power. The Seven Years' War (1756–63) was decisive. Before its outbreak, there had in fact been no remission of fighting in India, even while France and Great Britain were officially at peace after 1748. The French cause had prospered under a brilliant French governor in the Carnatic, Dupleix, who caused great alarm to the British by his extension of French power among native princes by force and diplomacy. But he was recalled to France and the French Indian company was not to enjoy the wholehearted support of the metropolitan government which it needed to emerge as the new paramount power. When war broke out again, in 1756, the *nawab* of Bengal attacked and captured Calcutta. His treatment of his English prisoners, many of whom were suffocated in the soon legendary 'Black Hole', gave additional offence. The East India Company's army, commanded by a young employee, the Scotchman Robert Clive, retook the city from him, seized the French station at Chandernagore and then on 22 June 1757 won a battle over the *nawab*'s much larger armies at Plassey, about a hundred miles up the Hooghly from Calcutta. It was not very bloody (the *nawab*'s army was

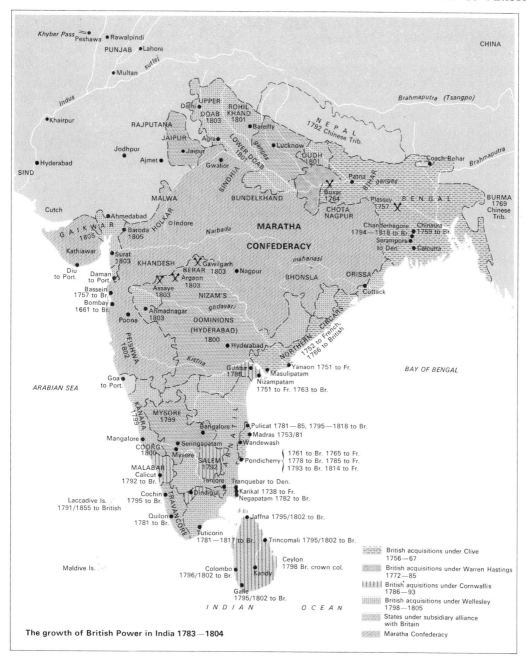

The growth of British Power in India 1783—1804

suborned) but it was one of the decisive battles of world history. It opened to the British the road to the control of Bengal and its revenues. On these was based the destruction of French power in the Carnatic; that opened the way to further acquisitions which led, inexorably to a future British monopoly of India. Nobody planned this. The British government, it is true, had begun to grasp what was immediately at stake in terms of a threat to trade and sent out a battalion of regular troops to help the company; the gesture is doubly revealing, both

665

because it recognized that a national interest was involved, but also because of the tiny scale of military effort which was involved. A very small number of European troops with European field artillery could be decisive. The fate of India turned on the diplomacy of the company's agents and the handful of European and European-trained soldiers in its employ. Upon this narrow base and the necessities of government in a disintegrated India was built the British Raj.

In 1764 the East India Company became the formal ruler of Bengal. This had by no means been the intention of the company's directors who sought not to govern but to trade. However, if Bengal could pay for its own government, then the burden could be undertaken. There were now only a few scattered French bases; the peace of 1763 left five trading posts on condition that they were not fortified. In 1769 the French *Compagnie des Indes* was dissolved. Soon after, the British took Ceylon from the Dutch and the stage was cleared for a unique example of imperialism.

The road would be a long one and for a long time reluctantly followed, but the East India Company was gradually drawn on by its revenue problems and by the disorder of native administrations in contiguous territories to extend its own governmental aegis. The obscuring of the company's primary commercial rôle was not good for business. It also gave its employees even greater opportunities to feather their own nests. This drew the interest of British politicians. The first fruit was a Regulating Act of 1774, which cut into the powers of the directors of the company and provided for government in India by a governor-general and council, and then ten years later came a second Act, this time putting the company firmly under the control of the Crown and setting up a system of 'dual control' in India which was to last until 1858. In the same Act were provisions against further interference in native affairs; the British government hoped as fervently as the company to avoid being dragged any further into the rôle of imperial power in India. But this was what

happened in the next half-century, as many more acquisitions followed. The road was open which was to lead eventually to the enlightened despotism of the nineteenth-century Raj. India was quite unlike any other dependency so far acquired by a European state in that hundreds of millions of subjects were to be added to the empire without any conversion or assimilation of them being envisaged. The character of the British imperial structure would be profoundly transformed by this, as would, eventually, British strategy, diplomacy, external trade patterns and, even, ideology.

Apart from India and Dutch Indonesia, there were no territorial acquisitions in the East in these centuries which could be compared to the vast territorial acquisitions of Europeans in the Americas. The landing of Columbus had been followed by a fairly rapid and complete exploration of the major West Indian islands and some considerable settlement, particularly in Hispaniola and Cuba. The Spanish settlers looked for land, as agriculturalists, and gold, as speculators. At that moment they had no competitors in this zone and, indeed, with the exception of Brazil, the story of the opening up of Central and South America remains Spanish until the end of the sixteenth century. The Spaniards who ranched and looked for gold in the islands were often Castilian gentry, poor, tough and ambitious. When they went to the mainland they were out for booty, though they spoke as well of the message of the Cross and the greater glory of the crown of Castile.

The first penetration of the mainland had come in Venezuela in 1499. Then, in 1513, Balboa crossed the isthmus of Panama and Europeans for the first time saw the Pacific. His expedition built houses and sowed crops; the age of the *conquistadores* had begun, for this was an announcement that the Spaniards were on the mainland to stay. The one among them whose adventures captured and retained the imagination of posterity was Hernán Cortés. In 1519 he left Cuba with an expedition of a few hundreds. He was deliberately flouting the authority of its governor and subsequently justified his acts by the spoils he brought to the Crown. On landing on the coast of Vera Cruz, he burnt the ships he and his men had come in to ensure that they could not go back and then began the march to the high central plateau of Mexico which has become one of the most

A clay figure of a Danish businessman, made in Canton in 1731.

dramatic stories of the whole history of imperialism. When they reached the city of Mexico itself, they were astounded by the civilization they found there. Besides its wealth of gold and precious stones, it was situated in a land suitable for the kind of estate cultivation which was familiar to Castilians at home.

Though the numbers of Cortés' followers were small and their conquest of the Aztec empire which dominated the central plateau has appeared heroic, they had great advantages on their side. The people upon whom they advanced were technologically primitive, easily impressed by the gunpowder, steel and horses the *conquistadores* brought with them. Aztec resistance was hampered by an uneasy feeling that Cortés might be an incarnation of their god, whose return to them they one day expected. The Aztecs were very susceptible to imported diseases, too. Furthermore, they were themselves an exploiting race and a cruel one; the other Indians they ruled were happy to welcome the new conquerors as liberators or at least as a change of masters. Circumstances favoured the Spaniards, therefore. Nevertheless, in the end their own toughness, courage and ruthlessness were the decisive factors.

In 1531 Pizarro set out upon a similar conquest of Peru. This was an even more remarkable achievement than the conquest of Mexico and, if possible, displayed even more vividly the rapacity and ruthlessness of the *conquistadores*. Settlement of the new empire began in the 1540s and almost at once there was made one of the most important mineral discoveries of historical times, that of a mountain of silver at Potosi, which was to be the main source of bullion for Europe for the next three centuries.

By 1700, the Spanish empire in the Americas formally covered a huge area from the modern New Mexico to the River Plate. By way of Panama and Acapulco it was linked by sea to the Spanish in the Philippines. Yet this huge extent on the map was misleading. The Californian, Texan and New Mexican lands north of the Rio Grande were very thinly inhabited; for the most part occupancy meant a few forts and

667

trading posts and a large number of missions. Nor, to the south, was Chile well settled. The most important and most densely populated regions were three: New Spain (as Mexico was called), which was the most civilized part of Spanish America, Peru, which was important for its mines and intensively occupied, and some of the larger and long-settled Caribbean islands. Areas unsuitable for settlement by Spaniards were long neglected by the administration.

The Indies were governed by viceroys at Mexico and Lima as sister kingdoms of Castile and Aragon, dependent upon the Crown of Castile. They had a royal council of their own through which the king exercised direct authority. This imposed a high degree of centralization in theory; in practice, geography and topography made nonsense of such a pretence. It was impossible to control New Spain or Peru closely from Spain with the communications available. The viceroys and captains-general under them enjoyed an important and real independence in their day-to-day business. But the colonies could be run by Madrid for fiscal advantage and, indeed, the Spaniards and Portuguese were the only powers colonizing in the western hemisphere for over a century which managed to make their American posse-sions not only pay for themselves but return a net profit for the metropolis. This was largely because of the flow of precious metals. After 1540 silver flooded across the Atlantic, to be dissipated, unfortunately for Spain, in the wars of Charles V and Philip II. By 1650, 16 000 tons of silver had come to Europe, to say nothing of 180 tons of gold objects.

Whether Spain got other economic benefits is harder to say. She shared with other colonizing powers of the age the belief that there was only a limited amount of trade to go round; it followed that trade with her colonies should be reserved to her by regulation and force of arms. Furthermore, she endorsed the other common-place of early colonial economic theory, the view that colonies should not be allowed to develop industries which might reduce the

An Indian manuscript of the era of the conquistadores *shows Cortés making use of his native mistress as his interpreter.*

opportunities available to the home country in their markets. Unfortunately, Spain was less successful than other countries in drawing advantage from this. Though they successfully prevented the development of any but extractive or handicraft industry in America, the Spanish authorities were increasingly unable to keep out foreign traders, interlopers as they came to be called, from their territories. Spanish planters wanted what metropolitan Spain could not supply – slaves, especially. Apart from mining, the economy of the islands and New Spain rested on agriculture. The islands soon came to depend on black slavery; in the mainland colonies, a Spanish government unwilling to countenance the enslavement of the conquered populations evolved other devices to assure the supply of labour. The first, started in the islands and extended to Mexico, was a kind of feudal lordship: a Spaniard would be given an *enco-mienda*, a group of villages over which he extended protection in return for a share of their labour. The general effect was not always easily distinguishable from serfdom, or even from slavery. It was strongly attacked by churchmen, among them one of the first great humani-

the Spanish and Portuguese to the idea of living in a multi-racial society. They did not show the concern for the purity of their blood which was shown by the English and French and there soon emerged in Latin America a large popula-

chalchicueyca

The native view of the conquistadores' *use of the American population for labour and service: from an Indian codex.*

tarian critics of settler society. This was the Dominican Bartolomé de las Casas, who not only urged the duty of Church and royal government to protect the Indian subjects of the Crown of Castile but was one of the few churchmen who denounced all forms of slavery. He was not without success in influencing legislation but could not much protect the Indians against royal officials on the spot when a fall of population was creating a grave shortage of labour. Smallpox came to the Caribbean with the Spaniards and to the mainland with Cortés; it was one source of a catastrophic decline in population in the first century of Spanish empire in America.

The presence of large pre-colonial native populations to provide labour did as much as the nature of the occupying power to differentiate the colonial experience of Central and South America from that of the north. Centuries of Moorish occupation had accustomed

tion of mixed blood. In Brazil, which the Portuguese finally secured from the Dutch after thirty years' fighting, there was also much interbreeding with the growing Negro population whose origins lay in imported slaves. (In Africa, too, the Portuguese showed no concern at racial interbreeding and its lack of a colour bar was always a redeeming feature of Portuguese imperialism.)

None the less, though the establishment of racially mixed societies over huge areas was one of the enduring legacies of the Spanish and Portuguese empires, these societies were stratified in ways that still in some measure ran along racial lines. The governing classes were the Iberian-born and the *creoles*, persons of European blood born in the colonies. As time passed, the latter came to feel that the former, called *peninsulares*, excluded them from key posts and were antagonistic towards them. From the *creoles* there led downwards a blurred incline of increasing gradations of blood to the poorest and most oppressed, and these were always the pure Indians. Though their languages survived,

669

the dominant languages of the continent became, of course, those of the conquerors. This was the greatest single formative influence making for the cultural unification of the continent.

For the future, another legacy of enormous import was the effective domination of a whole continent by Roman Catholicism. The Church played an enormous part in the opening of Spanish (and Portuguese) America. For three centuries churchmen worked away at the civilization of native Americans. They took Indians from their tribes and villages, taught them Christianity, Spanish and Latin, put them in trousers and sent them back to spread the light among their compatriots. The mission stations of the frontier determined the map of countries which would only come into existence centuries later.

For good or ill the Church saw itself as the protector of the Indian subjects of the Crown. The eventual effect of this would only be felt after centuries had brought important changes in the demographic centre of gravity within the Roman communion, but it had many implications visible much earlier than this. It was, for example, virtually the only means of access to European culture for the peasant, who found some features of Catholicism, in particular the cult of the Virgin, sympathetic and comprehensible. The Catholic monopoly also meant a large measure of identification of the Church with the administrative and political structure; it was an important means of social control for a thinly spread administrative apparatus and it was not only crusading zeal which made the Spanish enthusiastic proselytizers. This had important consequences much later when, although some priests were to play important parts in the revolutionary and independence movements of South America, the Church as a whole could not easily adopt a progressive stance. The Inquisition was soon set up in New Spain and it was the Church of the Counter-Reformation which shaped American Catholicism south of the Rio Grande. In the long run, this meant that clericalism would become an issue in

The gift of the Indies: chocolate, which Neptune is to make known to the world.

the politics of independent Latin America where liberalism took on the associations of anti-clericalism it was to have in Catholic Europe. This was all in marked contrast to the religiously pluralistic society which appeared contemporaneously in British North America.

For all the spectacular inflow of bullion from the mainland colonies, the New World was probably of the greatest economic importance to Europe throughout most of the early modern period because of the Caribbean islands. This importance rested on their agricultural produce, above all, on sugar. Both the Caribbean and Brazil were transformed economically by this crop. Medieval man had sweetened his food with honey; by 1700 sugar, though still expensive, was a European necessity. Tobacco, hardwood and coffee were other important products of the islands. Together, they gave the planters great importance in the affairs of the respective metropolitan countries.

The story of Caribbean agriculture began with the Spanish settlers, who quickly started growing fruit (which they had brought from Europe) and raising cattle. They soon introduced rice and sugar, too, but production of these was for a long time held back by a shortage

An eighteenth-century engraving of a West Indian sugar refinery, showing all the stages of a complex industrial process and its dependence on slave labour.

their first two colonies to be successful in the West Indies, on St Christopher, in the Leeward Isles, and Barbados. Both prospered; by 1630 St Christopher had about 3000 inhabitants and Barbados about 2000. This success was based on tobacco, the drug which, with the cheap automobile, was to be the New World's revenge for its disruption by the old. These tobacco colonies rapidly became of great importance to Britain not only because of the customs revenue they supplied, but also because the growth of population in the Caribbean stimulated demand for exports and provided fresh opportunities for interloping in the trade of the Spanish empire. Soon the English were joined by the French in this lucrative business, the French occupying the Windward Isles, the English the rest of the Leewards. In the 1640s there were about 7000 French in the West Indies, and over 50 000 English.

After this time the tide of English emigration to the New World was diverted to North America and the West Indies were not again to reach such high figures of white settlement. This was partly because sugar came to join tobacco as a staple crop. Tobacco can be produced in small as well as large plantations; it had therefore suited the multiplication of small-holdings and the building up of a large immigrant population of whites. Sugar was only economic if cultivated in large units; it suited the big plantation, worked by large numbers of slaves. The Dutch supplied the slaves and aspired to the sort of general commercial monopoly in the western hemisphere which they were winning in the Far East, working out of a base at the mouth of the Hudson river, New Amsterdam. This was the beginning of a great demographic change in the Caribbean. In 1643 Barbados had 37 000 white inhabitants and over 6000 Negro slaves; by 1660 there were over 50 000 of the latter.

of labour. The native populations of the islands succumbed with alarming swiftness to European ill-treatment and disease. The next economic phase was the establishment by later arrivals of parasitic industries: piracy and smuggling. The Spanish occupation of the larger Caribbean islands – the Greater Antilles – still left hundreds of unoccupied smaller islands, most of them on the Atlantic fringe. These attracted the attention of English, French and Dutch captains who found them useful as bases from which to prey on Spanish ships going home from New Spain, and also for contraband trade with the Spanish colonists who wanted their goods. Some European settlements appeared, too, on the Venezuelan coast where there was salt to be had for preserving meat. Where individuals led, governmental enterprises in the form of English royal concessions and the Dutch West India Company followed in the seventeenth century.

By then, the English had for decades been looking for suitable places for plantations – that is, settler colonies – in the New World. They made lodgements on the North American mainland first. Then, in the 1620s they established

With the appearance of sugar, the French colonies of Guadeloupe and Martinique took on a new importance and they, too, wanted slaves. A complex process of growth was under way. The huge and growing market in the Caribbean for slaves and imported European goods was added to that offered by a Spanish empire increasingly unable to defend its economic monopoly. This set the rôle of the West Indies in the relationships of the powers for the next century. They were long a prey to disorder, the Caribbean an area where colonial frontiers met and policing was poor and there were great prizes to be won (in one year a Dutch captain took the great *flota* bearing home the year's treasure from the Indies to Spain). Not surprisingly, they became the classical and, indeed, legendary hunting ground of pirates, whose heyday was the last quarter of the seventeenth century. Gradually, the great powers fought out their disputes until they arrived at acceptable agreements, but this was to take a long time. Meanwhile, through the eighteenth century the West Indies provided the great market for slaves and sustained most

A contemporary map of Drake's route to the Caribbean on his voyage of 1584–6, a ferocious raid which may be seen as the last straw breaking the patience of Philip of Spain and provoking the launching of the Armada. It was once thought that this voyage led to the introduction of both tobacco and the potato to Europe; this remains at best a plausible tale.

of that trade and also became involved in another economy besides those of Europe, Africa and New Spain: that of British North America.

For a long time, by all the standards of classical colonial theory, North American settlement was a poor second in attractiveness to what was going on in the Caribbean or Latin America. Precious metals were not discovered and though there were furs in the north, there seemed to be little else that Europe wanted from them. Yet there was nowhere else to go, given the Spanish monopoly to the south, and a great many nations tried it. The Spanish expansion north of the Rio Grande need not concern us, for it was hardly an occupation, but rather a missionary exercise, while Spanish Florida's importance was strategical, for it gave some protection to Spanish communications with Europe by the northern outlet from the Caribbean. It was the settlement of the Atlantic coast which drew other Europeans. There was even briefly a New Sweden, taking its place beside New Netherland, New England and New France.

The motives for settling North America were for the most part those which operated elsewhere. For most of the sixteenth century the Englishmen who were the most frequent explorers of North American possibilities thought there might be mines there to rival those of the Spanish Indies. There were some who thought that population pressure made emigration desirable. Increasing knowledge revealed ample land in temperate climates with, unlike Mexico, very few native inhabitants. There was also a constant pull in the lure of finding a north-west passage to Asia.

By 1600, these impulses had produced much exploration, but only one (unsuccessful) settlement north of Florida, that at Roanoke, Virginia. The English were too weak, the French too distracted, to achieve more. With the seventeenth century there came more strenuous, better-organized and better-financed efforts, the discovery of the possibility of growing some important staples on the mainland, a set of political changes in England which favoured emigration and the emergence of England as a great naval power. Between them these facts brought about a revolutionary transformation of the Atlantic littoral. The wilderness of 1600, inhabited by a few Indians, was a hundred years later an important centre of civilization. In many places settlers went as far inland as the mountain barrier of the Alleghenies. Meanwhile the French had established a line of posts along the valley of the St Lawrence and the Great

C. Smith taketh the King of Pamavnkee prisoner · 1608

Almost the first author to exploit what was to become a well-established public taste for tales from the Americas was Captain John Smith whose adventures were published in an illustrated book in 1608.

Lakes. In this huge right angle of settlement lived about a half-million white people, mainly of British and French stock.

Legally, Spain claimed North America, but this had long been contested by the English on the ground that 'prescription without possession availeth nothing'. The Elizabethan adventurers had explored much of the coast and gave the name 'Virginia', in honour of their queen, to all the territory north of thirty degrees of latitude. In 1606 James I granted a charter to a Virginia company to establish colonies. This was only formally the beginning; the company's affairs

673

soon required revision of its structure and there were unprofitable initiatives in plenty, but in 1607 there was already established the first English settlement in America which was to survive, at Jamestown, in modern Virginia. It only just came through its early trials but by 1620 its 'starving time' was far behind it and it prospered. In 1608, the year after Jamestown's foundation, the French explorer Samuel de Champlain built a small fort at Quebec. For the immediate future the French colony was so insecure that its food had to be brought from France, but it was the beginning of settlement in Canada. A curious anticipation of the future soon occurred; the French established good relations with the Huron Indians while the settlers at Jamestown were allying with the Iroquois who were the hereditary foes of the Huron. When the two areas of settlement impinged on one another, and the two European nations began to conflict later in the century, their Indian allies would gladly join in the struggle. Finally, also in 1609, the Dutch had sent an English explorer, Henry Hudson, to find a north-east passage to Asia. When he was unsuccessful he turned completely round and sailed across the Atlantic to look for a north-western one. Instead, he discovered the river that bears his name and established a preliminary Dutch claim by doing so. Within a few years there were Dutch settlements along the river, on Manhattan and Long Island.

The English were in the lead in settlement and remained so. They prospered because of two new facts. One was the technique of which they were the first and most successful exponents, of transporting whole communities, men, women and children. These set up agricultural colonies which worked the land with their own labour and were soon independent of the mother country for their livelihood. The second was the discovery of tobacco which became a staple first for Virginia and then for Maryland, a colony whose settlement began in 1634. Further north, the availability of land which could be cultivated on European lines assured the survival of the colonies; although interest in the area had

Eighteenth-century downtown Manhattan; the Dutch Reformed Church, built in the 1730s in what is now New York's financial centre.

originally been awoken by the prospects of fur-trading and fishery there was soon a small surplus of grain for export. This was an attractive prospect for the land-hungry Englishman in a country widely believed in the early seventeenth century to be overpopulated. Something like 20000 went to New England in the 1630s.

The distinctive feature of the New England colonies was not only economic but ideological and cultural, their association with religious dissent and Calvinistic Protestantism. Although the usual economic motives were at work in the settlements, the leadership among immigrants to Massachusetts in the 1630s of men associated with the Puritan wing of English Protestantism resulted in the evolution of a group of colonies whose constitutions varied from theocratic oligarchy to democracy. Though often the result of initiatives from within the English gentry and led by its members, they shed more rapidly than the southern colonies their inhibitions about radical departures from English social and political practice, and their religious non-conformity was as decisive as the conditions in which they had to survive in bringing this about. At some moments during the English constitutional troubles of the mid-century it even seemed that the colonies of New England might escape from the control of the Crown altogether, but as yet this did not happen.

After the Dutch settlements of what was subsequently New York State had been swallowed up by the British in a victorious peace in 1667, the North American littoral in 1700 from Florida north to the Kennebec river was organized as twelve colonies (a thirteenth, Georgia, appeared in 1732). Further north lay still disputed territory and then lands that were indisputably French. In the English colonies lived some 400000 whites and perhaps a tenth of this number of Negro slaves.

French North Americans were much thinner on the ground. They numbered perhaps 15000 in all and had benefited from no such large migrations of communities as had the English colonies. Many of them were hunters and trappers, missionaries and explorers, strung out over the length of the St Lawrence and dotted about in the Great Lakes region and even beyond. New France was a huge area on the map but outside the St Lawrence valley and Quebec its reality was a scatter of strategically and commercially important forts and trading posts. Nor was density of settlement the only difference between the French and English colonial zones. New France was closely supervised from home; after 1663 a company structure had been abandoned in favour of direct royal rule and Canada was governed by a French governor with the advice of the *intendant* much as a French province was governed at home. There was no religious liberty; the Church in Canada was monopolistic and missionary. Its history is full of glorious examples of bravery and martyrdom, and also of bitter intransigence. The farms of the settled area were grouped in *seigneuries*, a device which had

some value in decentralizing administrative responsibility. Social forms therefore reproduced those of the Old World much more rigidly than in the English settlements, even to the extent of throwing up a nobility with Canadian titles.

The colonies from which were to appear the future United States of America were very different. They represented in their origins a wide range of motives and methods of foundation. They were soon racially diverse, for after 1688 Scots-Irish, German, Huguenot and Swiss emigrants had begun to arrive in appreciable numbers, though for a very long time the predominance of the English language and the relatively small numbers of non-English-speaking immigrants would maintain a culture overwhelmingly Anglo-Saxon. Strung out as they were over almost the whole Atlantic seaboard, the colonies embodied great differences of climate, economy and terrain. In most of them there was by 1700 a large measure of effective religious toleration, though some had a close association with specific religious denominations. There existed already the diversity of a religiously pluralistic society before the colonies had begun to think of themselves as one society at all. They long had no local centre in America; the Crown and the home country were the foci of the colonies' collective life, as its culture was still their background. None the less, it was already obvious that the American colonies offered opportunities for advancement to individuals which were not available either in the more strictly and closely regulated society of Canada or at home in Europe.

By 1700, some colonies had already shown a tendency to grasp whatever independence of royal control was available to them. It is tempting to look back a long way for evidence of the spirit of independence which was later to play so big a part in popular tradition. In fact, it would be a misconception to read the prehistory of the United States in these terms. The Pilgrim Fathers were not rediscovered or inserted in their prominent place in the national mythology until the end of the eighteenth cen-

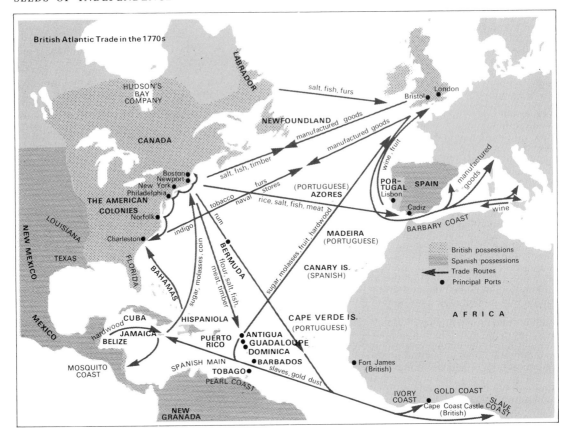

British Atlantic Trade in the 1770s

tury. What can be seen much earlier than the idea of independence is the emergence of facts which would in the future make it easier to think in terms of independence and unity. One was the strengthening of the representative tradition in the first century of settlement. For all their initial diversity in the early eighteenth century each colony had settled down to work through some sort of representative assembly which spoke for its inhabitants to a royal governor appointed in London. Some of the settlements had also needed to cooperate with one another against the Indians at an early date, and in the French wars this had become even more important. The French threat helped to create a sense of common interest which at least at times transcended that of individual colonies. From economic diversity, too, a measure of economic interrelatedness was emerging. The middle and southern colonies produced the plantation crops

of rice, tobacco, indigo and timber; New England built ships, refined and distilled molasses and grain spirits, grew corn and fished. There was a growing and apparent logic in thinking that the Americans might perhaps be able to run their affairs in their own interest – including that of the West Indian colonies – better than in that of the mother country. Economic growth changed the attitudes of some Englishmen, too. The northern mainland colonies of New England were on the whole underprized and even disliked in the United Kingdom. They competed with the English in shipbuilding and, though illegally, in the Caribbean trade; unlike plantation colonies, they produced nothing that the mother country wanted. Besides, they were dissenters.

In the eighteenth century British America made great progress in wealth and civilization. By 1763, Philadelphia could rival many Euro-

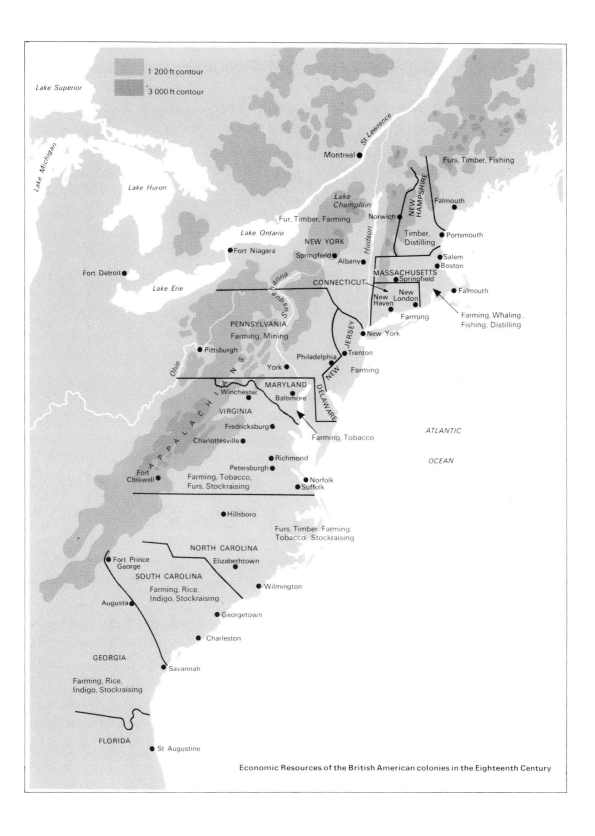

Lake Superior

1 200 ft contour
3 000 ft contour

Lake Michigan

Lake Huron

Lake Ontario

Lake Erie

Fort Detroit

Fort Niagara

Montreal

St Lawrence

Lake
Champlain

NEW
HAMPSHIRE

Furs, Timber, Fishing

Falmouth

Fur, Timber, Farming

Norwich

Portsmouth

Timber,
Distilling

NEW YORK

Springfield

Albany

Salem
Boston

MASSACHUSETTS

Springfield

CONNECTICUT

New
Haven

New
London

Falmouth

Hudson

Farming

Farming, Whaling,
Fishing, Distilling

PENNSYLVANIA

Farming, Mining

Pittsburgh

NEW
JERSEY

New York

Ohio

York

Philadelphia

Trenton

Farming

DELAWARE

Susquehanna

Winchester

MARYLAND

Baltimore

VIRGINIA

Fredricksburg

Farming, Tobacco

Charlottesville

ATLANTIC

OCEAN

Richmond

Petersburgh

Fort
Chiswell

Farming, Tobacco,
Furs, Stockraising

Norfolk
Suffolk

APPALACHIANS

Hillsboro

Furs, Timber, Farming,
Tobacco, Stockraising

NORTH CAROLINA

Fort Prince
George

Elizabethtown

SOUTH CAROLINA

Farming, Rice,
Indigo, Stockraising

Wilmington

Augusta

Georgetown

Charleston

GEORGIA

Savannah

Farming, Rice,
Indigo, Stockraising

FLORIDA

St Augustine

Economic Resources of the British American colonies in the Eighteenth Century pean cities. The population had continued to grow and was well over a million by halfway through the century. As was being pointed out in the 1760s, the mainland colonies were going to be worth much more to Great Britain than the West Indies had been. By 1763, too, a great uncertainty had been removed, for Canada had been conquered and was to remain British. This quite changed the outlook of many Americans both towards the value of the protection afforded by the imperial government and towards the question of further expansion to the west. As farming settlers tended to fill up the coastal plain they came to press against the mountain barrier by way of the river valleys in particular in the region of the Ohio valley and the north-west. The danger of conflict with the French provoked by this pressure was now removed, but this was not the only consideration which faced the British government in handling this movement after 1763. There were the rights

Like the citizens of other major cities in Europe and America, the Philadelphians were attracted by new and fashionable diversions such as the physically exciting exploration of the new science of electricity.

and the likely reactions of the Indians to take into account. To antagonize them would be to court danger, but if Indian wars were to be avoided by holding the colonists back, then the frontier would have to be policed by English troops for that purpose, too. The result was the decision of Great Britain to impose a western land policy which would limit expansion, to raise taxes in the colonies to pay for the costs of defending forces, and to tighten up the commercial system and cease to wink at infringements in its working. It was unfortunate that all this was coming to a head in the last decade in which the old assumptions about the economics of colonial dependencies and their relationship

678

A contemporary presentation of the capture of Quebec in the annus mirabilis *of British victory, 1759.*

to the mother country were accepted without demur by the makers of colonial policy.

By then about two and a half centuries had gone by since European settlement in the New World began. The overall effect of expansion in the Americas upon European history had been immense, but is far from easy to define. Eventually, it is clear, all the colonial powers had, by the eighteenth century, been able to extract some economic profit from their colonies, though they did so in different ways. The flow of silver to Spain was the most obvious expression, but this had, of course, implications for the European economy as a whole and even for Asia. The appearance of large populations in the colonies had also helped to stimulate European exports and manufactures. In this respect the English colonies were of the greatest importance, pointing the way to a growing flow of European emigration which was to produce the last major folk-migrations in the nineteenth century. To the growth of colonies, too, must be linked the enormous growth of European shipping and shipbuilding. Whether engaged in slaving, contraband trading, legal import and export between metropolis and colony or fishing to supply new consumer markets, shipbuilders, shipowners and captains benefited. There was an incremental and incalculable effect at work. It is thus very hard to sum up the total effect of the possession of American colonies in the first age of imperialism.

Of the political and cultural importance of the fact it is easier to speak with confidence. Overall, the fate of the western hemisphere was to be culturally European and that meant, politically, that from Tierra del Fuego to Hudson's Bay it would eventually be organized

679

in a series of sovereign states based on European legal and administrative principles where it did not remain directly dependent on a colonial power. It would also be Christian; when Hinduism or Islam came to the western hemisphere it would be as the possession of small minorities, not as rivals to a basically Christian culture.

More specifically, the greatest political importance of the era lay in the basic forms already given to the evolution of British North America. Here lay much of the world's future as well as that of the Americas. Two great transforming factors had still to operate before that future was fixed in its main lines: the differing environments revealed as the continent filled up by movement to the west and a much greater flow of non-Anglo-Saxon immigration. But these forces would flow into and around moulds set by the English inheritance. This inheritance was as decisive in shaping the future of one of the coming world powers as had Byzantium been in shaping that of Russia. Nations do not shake off their origins, they only learn to see them in different ways. Sometimes outsiders can see this best and it was a great German statesman who remarked towards the end of the nineteenth century that its most important international fact had been that Great Britain and the United States spoke the same language.

5 World history's new shape

At the end of the eighteenth century there began in America a series of colonial revolts which were to take several decades to work themselves out. Besides marking an epoch in American history these upheavals also provide a convenient vantage from which to consider the first phase of European hegemony as a whole. In other parts of the world, too, something of a change of rhythm was marked by such facts as the elimination of serious French competition to the British in India, and the opening of Australasia, the last discovered and habitable continent, to settlement.

Down to this time outright imperial expansion was the main form of European hegemony. It both provided wealth Europe could use to increase still further its relative superiority over other civilizations and set up a political structure which diffused other forms of European influence. This political structure was the work of a handful of states which were the first world powers in the geographical range of their interests, even if not in their strength; the Atlantic nations to which the age of discoveries had given opportunities and historical destinies distinct from those of other European states.

The first to seize these opportunities had been, Spain and Portugal, the only great colonial powers of the sixteenth century. They had long

Amid the pomp of Moghul India, then in its last age of decline, an official of the East India Company is escorted in state about his business.

passed their zenith by the time the Peace of Paris which ended the Seven Years' War was signed in 1763. This treaty is a convenient marker of a new world order replacing that which they had overshadowed. It registered the ascendancy of Great Britain in the rivalry with France overseas which had preoccupied her for nearly three-quarters of a century. The duel was not over, and Frenchmen could still be hopeful that they would recover lost ground. Great Britain, none the less, was the great imperial power of the future. These two nations had eclipsed the Dutch, whose empire had been built, like theirs, in the seventeenth century, in the era of declining Portuguese and Spanish power. But Spain, Portugal and the United Provinces all still held important colonial territories and had left enduring marks on the world map.

These five nations had by the eighteenth century been differentiated by their imperial history from the landlocked states of central Europe or the Mediterranean states so important in earlier centuries. Their colonial and overseas interests had given Europe's courts and chanceries new causes and places over which to quarrel. Of course, some states (Venice for example) had long defended commercial interests by diplomacy; even the English had taken care of their cloth exports to Flanders by treaties. But most states were slow to recognize how essential were their overseas interests. Spain fought grimly for European supremacy in the Thirty Years' War and wasted the treasure of the Indies in the process. In their long duel with Great Britain the French were always liable to be worsted because of the diversion of their energies and resources to continental ends. This was a major fact in helping the British to take and hold their lead. Yet essentially European questions, whether dynastic, religious, or national, became entangled with the regulation of trade to Spanish colonies or the treaties agreed to by Asian princes. The entanglement was inevitable because of the early theory of imperialism, shared by all nations: the interests of the metropolitan power were always seen as paramount. Those interests were financial and commercial; settlement colonies should produce, either by exploitation of their mineral and natural resources, or by their balance of trade with the mother country, a net advantage to the latter and, if possible, economic self-sufficiency, while the trading bases gave her the domination of areas of an international traffic which had finite limits. There was only so much to go round and one country could only gain at the expense of another.

In the early sixteenth century this entanglement of extra-European issues in diplomacy had barely existed. Once the Spanish and Portuguese had demarcated their interests satisfactorily there was little to be done about it by other European nations beyond contesting the vague claims of Spain in North America. The fate of a French Huguenot settlement in Florida or the English flouting of the Spanish claims which was implicit in the Roanoke voyages hardly crossed the minds of European diplomats, let alone shaped their negotiations. This situation began to change when English pirates and adventurers countenanced by Elizabeth I began to inflict real damage on the Spanish fleets and colonies. They were soon joined by the Dutch and from this time one of the great themes of the diplomacy of the next century was apparent; as a French minister wrote under Louis XIV, 'Trade is the cause of a perpetual combat in war and in peace between the nations of Europe.' So much had things changed even by 1700.

The first question on which this became apparent was that of the preservation or in-fringement of the Spanish claim to a monopoly of trade with their empire. It was also clear by 1600 that the answer to this question would be settled by sea-power, and since the defeat of the Armada Spanish sea-power no longer commanded the respect it had done. Essentially, Philip was caught in a dilemma to puzzle later continental rulers; the dispersal of his effort and interest between Europe – where the struggle with the Valois and Elizabeth, the Dutch Revolt, and the Counter-Reformation all claimed his resources – and the Indies, where safety could only have lain in sea-power and the organization of effective Spanish supply of the colonists' needs. The choice was to try to keep the empire, but to use it to pay for European policies. This was to underrate the difficulties of controlling so huge an empire within the possibilities of sixteenth-century bureaucracy and communications. Nevertheless a huge and complicated system of regular sailings in convoy, the concentration of colonial trade in a few authorized ports, and policing by coastguard squadrons was created in an attempt to keep the wealth of the Indies for Spain alone.

It was the Dutch who first made it clear that they were prepared to fight for a share of such prizes and therefore first forced diplomats to turn their attention and skills to regulating matters outside Europe. For them, predominance in trade overrode other considerations. What they would do for it was made clear from the start of the seventeenth century, in the East Indies, the Caribbean, and Brazil where they engaged great fleets against the Spanish-Portuguese defence of the world's chief producer of sugar. It was their only serious setback, for in 1654 the Portuguese were able to evict the Dutch garrisons and resume control without subsequent challenge.

This quest for commercial wealth cut across the wishes of the most Protestant of English seventeenth-century governments; England had been an ally of the Dutch rebels in the previous century and Cromwell would have liked nothing better than the leadership of a Protestant alliance against Catholic Spain. Instead he

Samuel Pepys, an outstanding civil servant, guardian of the interests of the Royal Navy of Charles II and celebrated diarist. Here he holds a song of his own composition; he was a keen amateur musician.

found himself fighting the first of three Anglo-Dutch wars. The first (1652–4) was essentially a trade war. What was at issue was the English decision to restrict imports to England to goods travelling in English ships or those of the country producing the goods. This was a deliberate attempt to encourage English shipping and put it in a position to catch up with the Dutch. It struck at the heart of Dutch prosperity, its European carrying trade and, in particular, that in Baltic goods. The Commonwealth had a good navy and won. The second round came in 1665, after the Dutch had been given the additional provocation of the English seizure of New Amsterdam. In this war the Dutch had the French and Danes as allies and also had the best of it at sea. At the peace they were therefore able to obtain an easing of the English restrictions on imports though they left New Amsterdam to the British in exchange for an

offshoot of Barbados at Surinam. This was decided by the Treaty of Breda (1667), the first multilateral European peace settlement to say as much about the regulation of extra-European affairs as European. By it France surrendered West Indian islands to England and received in return recognition of her possession of the uninhabited and uninviting but strategically important territory of Acadia. The English had done well; the new Caribbean acquisitions followed in a tradition established under the Commonwealth, when Jamaica had been taken from Spain to be added to the existing plantation colonies.

Cromwell's policies seem in retrospect a decision at the junction of the ways for England, the decisive turn towards conscious imperial policy. The returned Stuarts kept intact most of the 'Navigation' system for the protection of shipping and colonial trade, as well as hanging on to Jamaica and continuing to recognize the new importance of the West Indies. Charles II gave a charter to a new company, named after Hudson's Bay, to contest with the French the fur trade of the north and west. He and his in other ways inadequate successor, James II, at least maintained (even if with some setbacks) English naval strength so that it was available to William III in his wars with Louis XIV.

It would be tedious to trace the consequences in the detailed changes of the next century during which the new imperial emphasis first of English and then of British diplomacy came to maturity. A brief third Anglo-Dutch war (it had virtually no important consequences) does not really belong to this epoch which is dominated by the long rivalry of England and France. The War of the League of Augsburg, or King William's War, as it was called in America, brought a great deal of colonial fighting, but no great changes. The War of the Spanish Succession was very different in its results. It was a world war about the fate of the Spanish empire as well as about French power. At its close, the British not only won Acadia (henceforth Nova Scotia) and other acquisitions in the western hemisphere from the French, but also the right to supply slaves to the Spanish colonies and to send one ship with merchandise a year to trade with them.

Overseas matters loomed larger and larger in British foreign policy after this and were not subordinated to European considerations. British policy was hardly affected in its pursuit of extra-European goals by the change of dynasty in 1714, when the Elector of Hanover became the first king of the United Kingdom. Though there were some embarrassing moments, British policy still remained remarkably consistent, always swinging back to the goals of promoting, sustaining and extending British commerce. Often this was best managed by maintaining general peace, sometimes by diplomatic pressure (as when the Habsburgs were persuaded to withdraw a scheme for an Ostend company to trade with Asia), sometimes by fighting to maintain privileges or strategical advantage.

The importance of war became clearer and clearer. The first time that two European powers ever went to war on a purely non-European issue came in 1739 when the British government began hostilities with Spain over, in essence, the Spanish right of search in the Caribbean – or, as the Spanish might have put it, over the steps they properly took to secure their empire against abuse of the trading privileges granted in 1714. This war was to be remembered as the 'War of Jenkins' Ear' – the organ produced in pickle by its owner to inflame the sensitive patriotism of the House of Commons, which was outraged to hear of alleged mutilation by a Spanish coastguard. The conflict was soon caught up with the War of the Austrian Succession, and therefore became an Anglo-French struggle. The peace of 1748 did not much change the respective territorial position of the two rivals, nor did it end fighting in North America, where the French appeared to be about to cut off the colonial settlements for ever from the American west by a chain of forts. The British government sent its first regular contingents to America to meet this danger, but unsuccessfully, and it was not until the Seven Years War that a British minister

The 'Great Commoner', William Pitt, first Earl of Chatham and national leader in the Seven Years War.

grasped that the chance of a final decision in the long duel existed because of France's commitment to her ally Austria in Europe. Once British resources were allocated in accordance with this, sweeping victories in North America and India were followed by others in the Caribbean, some at the expense of Spain. A British force even seized the Philippines. It was a true world war.

The Peace of 1763 did not in fact go so far in crippling France and Spain as imperial powers as many Englishmen had wanted. But it virtually eliminated French competition in North America and India. The primacy of commerce was even marked in this because when it was a question of retaining Canada or Guadeloupe, a sugar-producing island, one consideration in favour of keeping Canada was that competition from increased sugar production within the empire was feared by the other Caribbean growers already under the British flag. Mysteriously, British society, though governed by landowners, continued to sustain in its foreign affairs a posture determined by the interests of commerce and less and less was heard of the opposition of land and 'moneyed' men which had been apparent in the late seventeenth century.

The effect of this was to build by 1763 a huge British empire. The whole of eastern North

From contemporary plans of an Elizabethan ship, the Jonas, *this model was constructed for a modern museum.*

America and the Gulf Coast as far west as the mouth of the Mississippi was then British. The elimination of French Canada had blown away the threat – or, from the French point of view, the hope – of a French empire of the Mississippi valley, stretching from the St Lawrence to New Orleans, which had been created by the great French explorers of the seventeenth century. Off the continental coast the Bahamas were the northern link of an island chain that ran down through the lesser Antilles to Tobago, and all but enclosed the Caribbean. Within it, Jamaica, Honduras and the Belize coast were British. Since 1713, the British had enjoyed a limited legal right to trade in slaves with the Spanish empire which they had exacted by victory and quickly pressed far beyond its intended limits. In Africa there were only a few British posts on the Gold Coast but these were the bases of the huge African slave trade. In Asia the direct government of Bengal was about to provide a start to the territorial phase of British expansion in India.

This imperial supremacy was based on sea-power. Its ultimate origins could be sought in the ships built by Henry VIII, among the greatest warships of the age (the *Harry Grâce à Dieu* carried 186 guns), but this early start was neglected under his successors until the reign of Elizabeth I. Her captains, with little financing available either from Crown or commercial investors, built both a fighting tradition and better ships from the profits made from operations against the Spanish. Again, there was an ebbing of interest and effort under the early Stuart kings. The royal administration could not afford ships (and paying for new ones was, indeed, one of the causes of the taxes Parliament raged over when recalled after the Eleven Years' Tyranny). It was only under the Commonwealth, ironically, that the serious and continuing interest in naval power which sustained the Royal Navy of the future began. By that time, the connexion between Dutch superiority in merchant shipping and their naval strength had been taken to heart and the upshot was the Navigation Law which provoked the first Anglo-Dutch war. A strong merchant marine provided a nursery of seamen for fighting vessels and the flow of trade whose taxation by customs dues would finance the upkeep of specialized warships. A strong merchant marine could only be built in the end upon carrying the goods of other nations: hence the importance of competing, if necessary by gunfire, and of breaking into such reserved areas as the Spanish American trade.

The machines which were evolved to do the fighting in this competition underwent steady improvement and specialization, but no revolutionary change, between the fifteenth and nineteenth centuries. Once square-rigging and broadside firing had been adopted, the essential shape of vessels was determined, though individual design could still do much to give sailing superiority and the French usually built better ships than Great Britain during the eighteenth-century duel between the two countries. In the sixteenth century, under English influence, ships grew longer in proportion to their beam. The relative height of the forecastle and poop above the deck gradually came down, too, over the whole period. Bronze guns reached a high level of development even in the early seventeenth century; thereafter gunnery changed by improvement in design, accuracy and weight of shot. There were two significant eighteenth-

687

century innovations, the short-range but large-calibre and heavy-shotted iron carronade, which greatly increased the power of even small vessels, and a firing mechanism incorporating a flintlock which made possible more precise control of the guns.

Specialization of function and design between warships and merchant vessels was accepted by the middle of the seventeenth century, though the line was still somewhat blurred by the existence of older vessels and the practice of privateering. This was a way of obtaining naval power on the cheap. In time of war, governments authorized individual private captains or their employers to prey upon enemy shipping, taking profits from the prizes they made. It was a form of regularized piracy and English, Dutch and French privateers all operated at various times with great success against one another's traders. The first great privateering war was that fought unsuccessfully against the English and Dutch under King William by the French.

Other seventeenth-century innovations were tactical and administrative. Signalling became formalized and the first Fighting Instructions were issued to the Royal Navy. Recruitment became more important; the press-gang appeared in England, naval conscription in the maritime provinces of France. In this way large fleets were manned and it became very clear that, given equality of skill and the limited damage which could be done even by heavy guns, it was numbers which were in the end always likely to be decisive.

From the seminal period of development in the seventeenth century there emerged a naval supremacy which was to last over two centuries and underpin a world-wide *pax Britannica*. Dutch competition dropped away as the Republic bent under the strain of defending its independence on land against the French. The important maritime rival of the English was France and here it is possible to see that a decisive point had been passed by the end of King William's reign. By then, the dilemma of being great on land or sea had been decided by the French in favour of the land. From that time,

the promise of a French naval supremacy was never to be revived, though French shipbuilders and captains would still win victories by their skill and courage. The English were not so distracted from oceanic power; they had only to keep their continental allies in the field, not to keep up great armies themselves. But there was a little more to it than a simple concentration of resources. British maritime strategy also evolved in a way very different from that of other sea-powers. Here, the French loss of interest in the navy of Louis XIV is in point, for it came after the English had inflicted a resounding defeat in a fleet action in 1692 which discredited the French admirals. It was the beginning of a great series of such victories which demonstrated an appreciation of the strategical reality that sea-power was in the end a matter of commanding the surface of the sea so that friendly ships could move on it in safety while those of the enemy could not. The key to this desirable end was the neutralization of the enemy's fleet. So long as it was there, a danger existed. The early defeat of the enemy's fleet in battle therefore became the supreme aim of British naval commanders for a century during which it gave the Royal Navy almost uninterrupted command of the seas and a formidable offensive tradition.

Naval strategy fed imperial enterprise indirectly as well as directly because it made more and more necessary the acquisition of bases from which squadrons could operate. This aspect of territorial acquisition was particularly important in the history of the British empire. In the late eighteenth century, too, that empire was about to undergo the loss of much of its settled territory and this would bring further into relief the way in which European hegemony was, outside the New World, still in 1800 a matter of trading stations, island plantations and bases, and the control of carrying trade, rather than of occupation of large areas.

Less than three centuries of even this limited form of imperialism revolutionized the world economy. Before 1500, the world consisted of hundreds of more or less self-supporting and self-contained economies, some of them linked by trade. The Americas and Africa were almost, Australasia entirely, unknown to Europe, communication within them was tiny in proportion to their huge extent, and there was a thin flow of luxury trade from Asia to Europe. By 1800, a world-wide network of exchange was in existence. Even Japan was involved in it and central Africa, though still mysterious and unknown, was linked to it through slaving and the Arabs. Its first two striking adumbrations had been the diversion of Asian trade with Europe to the sea routes dominated by the Portuguese and the flow of bullion from America to Europe. Without this, indeed, there could hardly have been a trade with Asia for there was almost nothing produced in Europe that Asia wanted and this may have been the main importance of the bullion flow, which reached its peak at the end of the sixteenth century and in the early decades of the next.

Although a new abundance of precious metals was the first and most dramatically obvious of the economic effects of Europe's new interplay with Asia and America, it was soon less important than the general growth of trade, of which slaves from Africa to the Caribbean and Brazil formed a part. The ships engaged in this usually made their voyage back to Europe from the Americas loaded with the colonial produce which more and more became a necessity to Europe. In Europe, first Amsterdam and then London surpassed Antwerp as international ports in large measure because of the huge growth of the re-export trade in colonial goods which were carried by Dutch and English ships. Around these central flows of trade there proliferated branches and sub-branches which led to further specializations and ramifications. Shipbuilding, textiles and, later, financial services such as insurance all prospered together, sharing in the consequences of a huge expansion in sheer volume. Eastern trade in the second half of the eighteenth century made up a quarter of the whole of Dutch external commerce and during that century the number of ships sent out by the East India Company from London went up

threefold. These ships, moreover, thanks to improvements in design, carried more and were worked by fewer men than those of earlier times.

The material consequences of Europe's new involvement with the world are much easier to measure than some of the others. European diet remains one of the most varied in the world and this came about in the early modern age. The coming of tobacco, coffee, tea and sugar alone brought about a revolution in taste, habit and housekeeping. The potato was to change the lives of many countries by sustaining much larger populations than its predecessors. Scores of drugs were added to the European pharmacopoeia, mainly from Asia.

Beyond such material effects it is harder to proceed. The interplay of new knowledge of the world with European mentality is especially hard to pin down. Men's minds were changing as the great increase in the numbers of books about discoveries and voyages in both East and West showed as early as the sixteenth century. Oriental studies may be said to have been founded as a science in the seventeenth century, though Europeans only begin to show the impact of knowledge of the anthropologies of other people towards its close. Such developments were intensified in the unrolling of their effects by the fact that they took place in an age of printing, too, and this makes the novelty of interest in the world outside Europe hard to evaluate. By the early eighteenth century, though, there were signs of an important intellectual impact at a deep level. The idyllic descriptions of savages who lived moral lives without the help of Christianity provoked reflexion; an English philosopher, John Locke, used the evidence of other continents to show that men did not share any God-given innate ideas. In particular, China furnished examples for speculation on the relativity of social institutions, while the penetration of Chinese literature (much aided by the studies of the Jesuits) revealed a chronology whose length made nonsense of traditional calculations of the date of the Flood described in the Bible as the second beginning of all men.

As its products became more easily available, China also provoked in European eighteenth-century craze for oriental styles in furniture, porcelain and dress. As an artistic and intellectual influence this has remained more obvious than the deeper perspective given to the observation of European life by an awareness of different civilizations with different standards elsewhere. But while such comparisons may have had some disquieting aspects, revealing that Europe had, perhaps, less to be proud of in its attitude to other religions than China, there were still others suggested by exploits such as those of the *conquistadores* which fed Europeans' notions of their superiority.

The impact of Europe on the world is no easier to encapsulate in a few simple formulae than that of the world upon Europe, but it is, in some of its manifestations at least, sometimes more dramatically obvious. It is an appalling fact that almost nowhere in the world can the inhabitants of non-European countries be shown to have benefited materially from the first phase of Europe's expansion and that often they suffered terribly. It must be recognized that this was not always something for which blame attaches to the Europeans – unless they should be blamed for being there at all. In an age with no knowledge of infectious disease beyond the most elementary, the devastating impact of smallpox or other diseases brought from Europe to the Americas could not have been anticipated. But it was disastrous. It has been calculated that the population of Mexico fell by three-quarters in the sixteenth century; that of some Caribbean islands was wiped out altogether.

Such facts as the ruthless exploitation of those who survived, on the other hand, whose labour was so much more valuable after this demographic collapse, are a different matter. Here is expressed that *leitmotiv* of subjection and domination which runs well-nigh through every instance of Europe's impact on the rest of the world. Different colonial environments and different European traditions resulted, inevitably, in gradations of oppression and exploita-

Chinoiserie: in the eighteenth century England and France were swept by a craze for Chinese porcelain and furniture exemplified by this Chinese room in Claydon House, Buckinghamshire.

tion. Not all colonial societies were based on the same extremes of brutality and horror. But all were tainted with it. The wealth of the United Provinces and its magnificent seventeenth-century civilization were fed, among other things, by roots which, in the Spice Islands and Indonesia, lay in bloody ground. Long before expansion in North America went west of the Alleghenies, the brief good relations of the first English settlers of Virginia with the Red Indian had soured and extermination and eviction had begun. The populations of Spanish America had been in some measure protected by the state from the worst abuses of the *encomienda* system, but this had not prevented their reduction to peonage and the destruction of their culture. Nor did the assumption of responsibility for its Indian subjects by the crown mean that they did not have great burdens of compulsory labour laid upon them. In South Africa the fate of the Hottentot and in Australia that of the Aborigine would repeat the lesson that European culture could devastate those whom it touched, unless they had the protection of old and advanced civilizations such as those of India or China. Even in them, great damage would be done, nor would they be able to resist the European once he decided to bring sufficient force to bear. But it was the settled colonies that showed most clearly the pattern of domination.

Their prosperity long depended on one of the most striking examples of Europe's successful aggressiveness, the African slave trade whose economic importance has already been touched upon. It has long obsessed men who have seen in it the most brutal example of the inhumanity of man to man, whether that of white to black, of European to non-European, or of capitalist to labourer. It has properly dominated much of the historiography of Europe's expansion and American civilization, for it was a major fact in both. Less properly, it has diverted attention from other forms of slavery at other times – or even alternative fates to slavery, such as the extermination, intentional or unintentional, which overtook other peoples.

This is understandable. Though African slaves are not the only ones to have played an important part in history, nor Europeans the only slavers, black slavery based on the buying of Africans from other Africans by Europeans, and their sale to other Europeans in the Americas is something with wider and more obvious repercussions than, say, the enslavement of Europeans by Ottomans or Africans by Arabs.

The story begins after slavery had all but withered away in Europe, but while Europeans were still being enslaved by other peoples, in 1434. The Portuguese then brought the first consignment of African slaves to Lisbon. Their enslavement was the work of other Africans; they were members of tribes from the interior sold to the Portuguese by their captors, peoples of the West African coast. Before long the probable importance of this trade dawned on the Portuguese who, as they moved further down the African coast, set up a base there in 1448 to serve as slaving centre. One estimate suggests that about 800 blacks a year were being brought to Europe as slaves in the middle of the fifteenth century, but for a long time there was no great growth in the trade. Until the

middle of the sixteenth century, Europe, together with the Portuguese and Spanish settlements in Madeira, the Canaries and Cape Verde islands, took almost all the slaves West Africa produced. It was only when the European transatlantic colonies entered the market that the trade began a long period of dramatic growth.

The transatlantic outlets were to dominate the direction of the slave trade until its abolition in the nineteenth century. Their importance first appeared with the settlement in the Caribbean of colonies where indigenous labour was scarce. Later came the exploitation of the southern Caribbean shores and the mainland of North America. When this happened others joined the Portuguese who had hitherto dominated the trade. Elizabeth I's 'sea-dogs' were among the earliest. Meanwhile, Portuguese captains began to import slaves direct to Brazil as the sixteenth century went on. The Dutch early in the seventeenth century founded a company to ensure a regular supply of slaves to the West Indies. By 1700 their strong position had been overtaken by French and English slavers who had established their own posts on the 'slave coast' of Africa.

The consequences were enormous. Between nine and ten millions of black slaves were sent to the western hemisphere altogether, 80 per cent of them after 1700. The eighteenth century brought the greatest prosperity to the trades and some six million slaves were shipped during it. European ports like Bristol and Nantes founded a new prosperity on slaving. New lands were opened as black slave labour made it possible to work them. The production on a much greater scale of new crops brought, in turn, great changes in European demand, manufacturing and trading patterns. Racially, too, we still live with the results.

What has disappeared and can now never be measured is the human misery involved not merely in physical hardship (a black might live only a few years on a West Indian plantation even if he survived the horrible conditions of the voyage) but in the psychological and emotional

Africa in the Early Modern Era

tragedies of this huge migration. Historians still debate whether slavery 'civilized' blacks in the Americas by bringing them into contact, willy-nilly, with higher civilizations, or whether it retarded them in quasi-infantile dependence. The question seems as insoluble as the degree of cruelty involved is incalculable; on the one hand is the evidence of the fetters and the whipping-block, on the other the reflexion that these were commonplaces of European life too, and that, *a priori*, self-interest should have prompted the planters to care for their investment. Yet that it did not always do so, slave rebellions showed. Such resistance, though, was infrequent, a fact

which also bears reflexion. It is unlikely that the debate will end.

Estimates of the almost unrecorded damage done in Africa are even harder to arrive at, for the evidence is even more subject to conjecture. The obvious demographic loss may have been offset (some have hazarded) by the introduction to Africa of new foodstuffs from America. Conceivably, such by-products of a European contact determined by the hunt for slaves actually led to population growth, but the hypothesis can hardly be weighed against the equally immeasurable effects of imported disease.

The arguments with which Christians resisted

692

The prices of slaves in an eighteenth-century inventory show some of the reality of plantation life: a carpenter is valued at £330, while the 'indifferent fellow with bad legs' rates only sixpence.

The gravestone of a slave in an English church-yard.

the restriction of this traffic still retain a certain gruesome fascination. Feelings of responsibility and guilt began to emerge widely only in the eighteenth century and mainly in France and England. One expression of it was the British acquisition of another dependency in 1787, Sierra Leone, soon adopted by philanthropists as a refuge for Negro slaves freed in England. Once combined with a favourable political and economic conjuncture the current of public feeling educated by humanitarian thought would destroy the slave trade and, in the European world, slavery. But this is part of a different story. In the unfolding of European world power slavery was a huge social and economic fact. It was to become a great mythical one, symbolizing at its harshest the triumph of force and cupidity over humanity, but it was also only the outstanding expression of a general dominance by force of advanced societies over weaker ones.

Some Europeans recognized this but none the less believed that any evil was outweighed by what they offered to the rest of the world, above all, by the bringing of Christianity. It was a bull of Paul III, the pope who summoned the Council of Trent, which proclaimed that 'the Indians are truly men and . . . are not only capable of understanding the Catholic faith, but according to our information, they desire exceedingly to receive it.' Such optimism was not merely an expression of the Counter-Reformation Spirit, for the missionary impulse had been there almost from the start in the Spanish and Portuguese possessions. Jesuit missionary work began in Goa in 1542 and radiated from there all over the Indian Ocean, south-east Asia and even reached Japan. Like the other Catholic powers, the French, too, emphasized missionary work, even in areas where France was not herself economically or politically involved. A new vigour was none the less given to missionary enterprise in the sixteenth and seventeenth centuries and may be acknowledged as one invigorating effect of the Counter-Reformation. Others were to come; in the Portuguese and Spanish possessions the Inquisition and persecution followed the

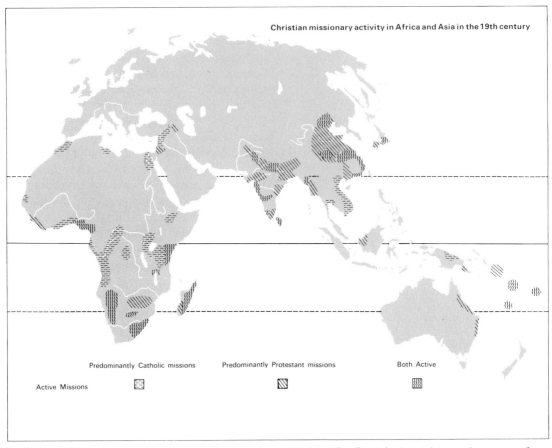

Christian missionary activity in Africa and Asia in the 19th century

Active Missions

Predominantly Catholic missions

Predominantly Protestant missions

Both Active

A plan of a British slave ship used as part of
the propaganda of the anti-slavery campaigners.

missions. Formally, at least, Roman Christianity took in more converts and greater tracts of territory in the sixteenth century than any earlier one. The real impact of this is harder to assess, but if must be allowed that although often unable to achieve much in practice, the Church provided such protection as the native had against his Spanish conquerors and kept alive, however dimly at times, the only notion of trusteeship towards subject peoples which existed in early imperial theory. Protestantism lagged behind. The Dutch hardly did anything and the American colonists were better at enslaving Red Indians than converting them (the Quaker colony of Pennsylvania was a laudable exception). The origins of the great English overseas missionary movement are not to be detected until the end of the seventeenth century. Furthermore, even in the gift of the Gospel to the world when it came there lay a tragic ambiguity. It, too, was a European export of enormously corrosive potential, challenging and undermining traditional structures and ideas, threatening social authority, legal and moral institutions, family and marriage patterns. The missionaries, often in spite of themselves, became instruments of the process of domination and subjugation which run through the story of Europe's intercourse with the rest of the globe.

Perhaps there was nothing Europeans brought with them which would not in the end turn out to be a threat, or at least double-edged. The food plants which the Portuguese took from America to Africa in the sixteenth century – cassava, sweet potatoes, maize – may have improved African diet, but (it has been argued) may also have provoked a growth in population which caused social disruption and upheaval. Plants taken to the Americas, on the other hand, founded new industries which then created a demand for slaves; coffee and sugar were commodities of this sort. Further north, the introduction of wheat by British settlers did not require slavery for its cultivation, but intensified the demand for land and therefore added to the pressures driving the colonists into the ancestral hunting-grounds of the Indians, whom they ruthlessly pushed out of the way.

The lives of generations unborn when such transplants were first made were to be shaped by them, and a longer perspective than one confined by 1800 is helpful here. Wheat was,

Soon after his death William Penn, founder of Pennsylvania, came to be celebrated for the respect he showed to the Indians of the colony. An eighteenth-century painting depicts the almost legendary treaty he made with them and subsequently kept.

after all, ultimately to make the western hemisphere the granary of European cities; in our own century even Russia and Asian countries have drawn on it. A wine industry which still flourishes was implanted by the Spanish in the Madeiras and America as early as the sixteenth century. When bananas were established in Jamaica, coffee in Java and tea in Ceylon, the groundwork was laid of future politics. All such changes, moreover, were in the nineteenth century complicated by varations in demand, as industrialization increased the demand for old staples such as cotton (in 1760 England imported two and a half million pounds of raw cotton – in 1837 the figure was three hundred and sixty million) and sometimes created new ones; it was a consequence of this that rubber was successfully transplanted from South America to Malaya, a change fraught with great strategic significance.

The scope of such implications for the future in the early centuries of European hegemony will appear sufficiently in what follows. Here it is only important to note one more, often-repeated, characteristic of this pattern, its

A Dutch engraving of seventeenth-century Canton.

unplanned, casual nature. It was the amalgam of many individual decisions by comparatively few men. Even their most innocent innovations could have explosive consequences. Ecologically, it is worth recalling that it was the importation of a couple of dozen rabbits which led to the devastation of much of rural Australia by millions of them within a few decades. Similarly,

Captain Cook's crew improve their acquaintance with a threatened species.

but on a smaller scale, Bermuda was to be plagued with English toads.

Conscious animal importations, though, were the most important (the Australians responded to the rabbit scourge by sending for English stoats and weasels). Almost the entire menagerie of European domesticated animals was settled in the Americas by 1800. The most important were cattle and horses. Between them they would revolutionize the life of the Plains Indians; later, after the coming of refrigerated ships, they were to make South America a great meat exporter just as Australasia was to be made one by the introduction of sheep the English had themselves imported originally from Spain. And, of course, the Europeans brought human bloodstock, too. Like the British in America, the Dutch for a long time did not encourage the mixing of races. Yet in Latin America, Goa and Portuguese Africa the effects were profound. So, in an entirely different and negative way were they in British North America, where racial intermarriage was not significant and the near-exact coincidence of colour and legally servile status bequeathed an enormous legacy of political, economic, social and cultural problems to the future.

The creation of large colonial populations shaped the future map, but also presented a problem to the metropolitan powers which they had no theory to solve. The British colonies nearly always had some form of representative institution which reflected parliamentary tradition and practice while France, Portugal and Spain all followed a straightforward authoritarian and monarchical institutional system. None of them envisaged any sort of independence for their colonists, nor any need to safeguard their interests against those of the mother country, whether these were conceived as paramount or complementary. This would in the end cause trouble and there were signs at least in the British North American colonies that this might be on lines reminiscent of seventeenth-century England's struggles between Crown and Parliament. And in their struggles with other nations, even when their governments were not formally at war with them, the colonists always showed a lively sense of their own interests. Even when Dutch and English were formerly allied against France their sailors and traders would fight one another 'beyond the line'.

This was not a problem which would arise except where large populations of European stock existed. In this sense, as in others, it is striking to reflect how much the first phase of settlement imperialism was dominated by the western hemisphere. Elsewhere in the world in 1800, even in India, trade still mattered more than possession. It was evident, too, that important areas had still to feel the full impact of Europe. As late as 1789 the East India Company was sending only twenty-one ships in the year to Canton; the Dutch were allowed two a year to Japan. Central Asia was at that date still only approachable by the long land routes which were used in the days of Chinghis Khan and the Russians were still far from exercising effective influence over the hinterland. Africa was protected by climate and disease. There, as in the Pacific, discovery and exploration had to complete the world map before European hegemony could become a reality. But this was already happening in the South Seas, where Dampier's voyage of 1699 had opened a century of exploration which added Australasia, the last unknown continent, to the map. The voyages of Bougainville and Cook, in the 1760s and 1770s, added Tahiti, Samoa, eastern Australia, Hawaii and New Zealand to the last New World to be opened. Cook even penetrated the Antarctic Circle. In 1788 the first cargo of convicts, 717 of them, was landed with its guards in New South Wales. British judges were calling into existence a new penal world to redress the balance of the old, where, since the American colonies were no longer available for dumping English undesirables, problems of disposal had arisen. In 1797 the first missionaries arrived in Tahiti. With them the blessings of European civilization may be reckoned to have appeared, at least in embryonic form, in every part of the habitable world before the eighteenth century was over.

RA CAMERAM STELLATAM.

6 Ideas old and new

The essence of the civilization Europe was exporting to the rest of the globe lay in ideas. The limits they imposed and the possibilities they offered shaped the way in which that civilization operated. What is more, although the twentieth century has done great damage to them, the leading ideas adumbrated by Europeans between 1500 and 1800 still provide most of the guide-posts by which we still make our way. European culture was then given a secular foundation; it was then, too, that there took hold a progressive notion of historical development as movement towards an apex at which Europeans felt themselves to stand. Finally it was then that there grew up a confidence that scientific knowledge used in accordance with utilitarian criteria would make possible limitless progress. In short, the civilization of the Middle Ages then came to an end in the minds of thinking men.

For all that, things rarely happen cleanly and neatly in history, and only a few Europeans would have been aware of this change by 1800. The traditional institutions of monarchy, hereditary status society and religion still held sway over most of Europe in that year. Only a hundred years before there had been no civil marriage anywhere in Europe and there was still none over most of it. Barely twenty years before

The Royal Observatory was built at Greenwich in 1675 and its primacy is commemorated in the phrase 'Greenwich Mean Time'. A portrait of Charles II, its royal patron looks down from the wall of the room shown in this engraving.

1800 the last heretic had been burned in Poland and even in England an eighteenth-century monarch had, like medieval kings, touched for the King's Evil. The seventeenth century, indeed, had in one or two respects even brought about regression. In both Europe and North America it saw an epidemic of witch-hunting far more widespread than anything in the Middle Ages (Charlemagne had condemned witch-burners to death and canon law had forbidden belief in the night flights and other pranks of witches as pagan). Nor was this the end of superstition. The last English wizard was harried to his death by his neighbours well after 1700 and a Protestant Swiss was legally executed by his countrymen for witchcraft in 1782. The Neapolitan cult of St Januarius was still of political importance in the era of the French Revolution because the successful or unsuccessful liquefaction of the saint's blood was believed to indicate divine pleasure or displeasure of what the government was doing. Penology was barbarous still; some crimes were thought so atrocious as to merit punishment of exceptional ferocity and it was as parricides that the assassin of Henry IV of France and the attempted assassin of Louis XV suffered their abominable torments. The second died under them in 1757, only a few years before the publication of the most influential advocacy of penal reform that has ever been written. The glitter of modernity in the eighteenth century can easily deceive us; in societies which produced art of exquisite refinement and outstanding examples of chivalry and honour, popular

699

amusements focussed on the cruelties of bear-baiting, cock-fighting or pulling the heads off geese.

The culture of the people is always an aspect of society which shows most obviously the weight of the past but until almost the end of these three centuries much of the formal and institutional apparatus which upheld the past also remained intact, over most of Europe. The most striking example to modern eyes would be the primacy still enjoyed almost everywhere in the eighteenth century by organized religion. In every country, Catholic, Protestant and Orthodox alike, even ecclesiastical reformers took it for granted that religion should be upheld and protected by the law and the coercive apparatus of the state. Only a very few advanced thinkers questioned this. In much of Europe there was still no toleration for views other than those of the established Church. The coronation oath taken by a French king imposed on him the obligation to stamp out heresy and only in 1787 did non-Catholic Frenchmen gain any recognized civic status and therefore the right to legitimize their children by contracting legal marriages. In Catholic countries the censorship, though often far from effective, was still supposed and sometimes strove to prevent the dissemination of writings inimical to Christian belief and the authority of the Church. Although the Counter-Reformation spirit had ebbed and the Jesuits were dissolved, the Index and Inquisition were maintained. The universities everywhere were in clerical hands; even in England, Oxford and Cambridge were closed to nonconformist dissenters and Roman Catholics. Religion also largely determined the content of their teaching and the definition of the studies they pursued.

The institutional fabric of society, it is true, also showed the onset of innovation. One of the reasons why universities lost importance in these centuries was that they no longer monopolized so much of the intellectual life of Europe. From the middle of the seventeenth century there appeared in many countries, and often under the highest patronage, academies

A seventeenth-century engraving of the Vice-Chancellor of the University of Oxford, preceded by the Bedels and University Marshal.

and learned societies such as the English Royal Society which was given a charter in 1662, or the French *Académie des Sciences*, founded four years later. In the eighteenth century such associations greatly multiplied; they were diffused through smaller towns and founded with more limited and special aims, such as the promotion of agriculture. A great movement of voluntary socialization was apparent; though most obvious in England and France, it left few countries in western Europe untouched. Clubs and societies of all sorts were a characteristic of an age no longer satisfied to exhaust its potential in the social institutions of the past and they sometimes attracted the attention of government. Some of them made no pretension to have as their sole end literary, scientific or agricultural activity, but provided gatherings and meeting-places at which general ideas were debated, discussed or merely chatted about. In this way they assisted the circulation of new ideas. Among such associations the most remarkable was the international brotherhood of freemasons. It was introduced from England to continental Europe in the 1720s and within a half-century spread widely; there may have been more than a quarter-million masons by 1789. They were

An English masonic print of the eighteenth century, when English lodges still met usually in taverns – hence the inn-signs displayed behind the freemasons, who wear masonic aprons and carry symbols of the craft.

later to be the object of much calumny; the myth was propagated that they had long had revolutionary and subversive aims. This was not true of the craft as a body, however true it may have been of a few individual masons, but it is easy to believe that so far as masonic lodges, like other gatherings, helped in the publicity and discussions of new ideas, they contributed to the breaking up of the ice of tradition and convention.

The increased circulation of ideas and information did not, of course, rest primarily on such meetings, but on the diffusion of print – on, at first, books, then broadsheets, pamphlets, gazettes, and finally newspapers and intellectual journals. One of the crucial transformations of Europe was that it became more literate; some have summed it up as the change from a culture focussed on the image to one focussed on the word. Reading and writing (and especially the former), though not universally diffused, were nevertheless widespread. They were no longer the privileged and arcane knowledge of a small élite, nor were they any longer mysterious in

being intimately and specially connected with religious rites.

In assessing this change we can emerge a little way from the realm of imponderables and enter that of measurable data which shows that somehow, for all the large pools of illiteracy which still existed in 1800, Europe was by then a literate society as it was not in 1500. That is, of course, not a very helpful statement as it stands. There are many degrees of attainment in both reading and writing. Nevertheless, however we define our terms, Europe and its dependencies in 1800 probably contained most of the literate people in the world and therefore had a higher proportion of literates than other cultures. This was a critical historical change. By then, Europe was well into the age of the predominance of print, which eventually superseded, for most people, the spoken word and images as the primary means of education and direction, and lasted until the twentieth century restored oral and visual supremacy by means of radio, cinema and television.

The sources for assessing literacy are not good until the middle of the nineteenth century – when, it appears, somewhere about half of all Europeans still could neither read nor write – but they all suggest that the improvement from about 1500 was cumulative but uneven. There were important differences between countries, between the same countries at different periods, between town and country, between the sexes, and between occupations. All this is still true, though in diminished degree, and it greatly simplifies the problem of making general statements: none but the vaguest are possible until recent times. But specific facts are suggestive about trends.

The first signs of the educational effort underlying the increase of literacy can be seen before the invention of printing. They appear to be another part of that revival and invigoration of urban life between the twelfth and thirteenth centuries whose importance has already been noted. Some of the earliest evidence of the commissioning of schoolmasters and provision of school places come from the Italian cities which were then the vanguard of European civilization. In them there soon appeared a new appreciation that literacy is an essential qualification for certain kinds of office. We find, for example, provisions that judges should be able to read, a fact with interesting implications for the history of earlier periods.

The early lead of the Italian cities had given way by the seventeenth century to England and the Netherlands (both countries with, for the age, a high level of urbanization). These have been thought to be the European countries with the highest levels of literacy in about 1700; the transfer of leadership to them illustrates the way in which the history of rising literacy is geographically an uneven business. Yet French was to be the international language of eighteenth-century publication and the bedrock of the public which sustained this must surely have been found in France. It would not be surprising if levels of literacy were higher in England and the United Provinces, but the numbers of the literate were larger in France, where the total population was so much bigger.

An outstanding place in the overall trend to literacy must surely be given to the spread of printing. By the seventeenth century there was in existence a corpus of truly popular publishing, represented in fairy-stories, tales of true and unrequited love, almanacs and books of astrology, hagiographies. The existence of such material is evidence of demand. Printing had given a new point to being literate, too, for the consultation of manuscripts had necessarily been difficult and time-consuming, because of their relative inaccessibility. Technical knowledge could now be made available in print very quickly and this meant that it was in the interest of the specialist to read in order to maintain his skill in his craft.

Another force making for literacy was the Protestant Reformation. Almost universally, the reformers themselves stressed the importance of teaching believers how to read; it is no coincidence that Germany and Scandinavia both reached higher levels of literacy than many Catholic countries by the nineteenth century.

The Reformation made it important to read the Bible and it had rapidly become available in print in the vernaculars which were thus strengthened and disciplined by the diffusion and standardization which print brought with it. Bibliolatry, for all its more obviously unfortunate manifestations, was a great force for enlightenment; it was both a stimulus to reading and a focus for intellectual activity. In England and Germany its importance in the making of a common culture can hardly be exaggerated, and in each country it produced a translation of the Bible which was a masterpiece.

As the instance of the reformers shows, authority was often in favour of greater literacy, but this was not confined to the Protestant countries. In particular, the legislators of innovating monarchies in the eighteenth century often strove to promote education – which meant in large measure primary education. Austria and Prussia were notable in this respect. Across the Atlantic the puritan tradition had from the start imposed in the New England communities the obligation to provide schooling. In other countries education was left to the informal and unregulated operation of private enterprise and charity (as in England), or to the Church. From the sixteenth century begins the great age of particular religious orders devoted to teaching (as in France).

An important consequence, promoter and concomitant of increased literacy was the rise of the periodical press. From broadsheets and occasional printed newsletters there evolved by the eighteenth century journals of regular publication. They met various needs. Newspapers began in the seventeenth century, a daily newspaper was published in London in 1702 and by the middle of the century there was an important provincial press and millions of newspapers were being printed each year. Magazines and weekly journals began to appear in the first half of the eighteenth century in England and the most important of them, the *Spectator*, set a model for journalism by its conscious effort to shape taste and behaviour. Here was something new. Only in the United Provinces did journal-

NUMB. XII.

The SPECTATOR.

_____ *Veteres avias tibi de pulmone revello.* Per.

Wednesday, March 14. 1711.

An early issue of the Spectator, *which began to appear in 1711. It was a new form of journalism: newspapers already existed but the combination of amusement and edification offered by the Spectator's essays was the first of many serious and semi-serious vehicles of comment and criticism for a large public.*

ism have such success as in England; probably this was because all other European countries enjoyed censorships of varying degrees of efficacy as well as different levels of literacy. Learned and literary journals appeared in increasing numbers, but political reporting and comment were rarely available. Even in eighteenth-century France it was normal for the authors of works embodying advanced ideas to circulate them only in manuscript; in this stronghold of critical thought there was still a censorship, though one irregular and, as the century wore on, less effective in its operation.

It may have been a growing awareness of the subversive potential of easily accessible journalism which led to a change of wind in official attitudes to education. Until the eighteenth century there was no very widespread feeling that education and literacy might be dangerous and should not be widely extended. Though formal censorship had always been a recognition of the potential dangers brought by literacy, there was a tendency to see this in predominantly religious terms; one duty of the Inquisition was to maintain the effectiveness of the Index of prohibited books. In retrospect it may well seem that the greater opportunity which literacy and printing gave for the criticism and questioning of authority in general was a more important effect than their subversion of religion. Yet this was not their only importance. The diffusion of technical knowledge also accelerated other kinds of social change. Industrialization would hardly have been possible without greater literacy and a part of what has been called a 'scientific revolution' in the seventeenth century must be attributed to the simple cumulative effect of more rapidly and widely circulated information.

The fundamental sources of this 'revolution' none the less lie deeper than this, in changed intellectual attitudes. Their core was a changed view of Man's relation to nature. From a natural world observed with bemused awe as evidence of God's mysterious ways men somehow made the great step to a conscious search for means to achieve its manipulation. Although the work of medieval scientists had been by no means as primitive and uncreative as it was once the fashion to believe, it suffered from two critical limitations. One was that it could provide very little knowledge that was of practical use. This inhibited attention to it. The second was its theoretical weakness; it had to be surpassed at a conceptual as well as a technical level. In spite of the beneficial irrigation of Arab ideas and a healthy emphasis on definition and diagnosis in some of its branches, medieval science rested on assumptions which were untested, in part because the means of testing them could not be grasped, in part because the wish to test them did not exist. The dogmatic assertion of the theory that the four elements, Fire, Air, Earth and Water, were the constituents of all things, for example, went unrefuted by experiment. Although experimental work of a sort went on within the alchemical and hermetic traditions, and with Paracelsus came to be directed towards other ends than a search for gold, it was still directed by mythical, intuitive conceptions.

This remained broadly true until the seventeenth century. The Renaissance had its scientific manifestations but they found expression usually in descriptive studies (an outstanding example was that of Vesalius' human anatomy of 1543) and in the solution of practical problems in the arts (such as those of perspective) and mechanical crafts. One branch of this descriptive and classificatory work was particularly impressive, that addressed to making sense of the new geographical knowledge revealed by the discoverers and cosmographers. In geography, said a French physician of the early sixteenth century, 'and in what pertains to astronomy, Plato, Aristotle, and the old philosophers made progress, and Ptolemy added a great deal more. Yet, were one of them to return today, he would find geography changed past recognition.' Here was one of the stimuli for a new intellectual approach to the world of nature.

It was not a stimulus quick to operate. A tiny minority of educated men, it is true, would already in 1600 not have found it easy to accept the conventional world picture based on the great medieval synthesis of Aristotle and the Bible. Some of them felt an uneasy loss of coherence, a sudden lack of bearings, an alarming uncertainty. But for most men who considered the matter at all, the old picture still held true, the whole universe still centred on the earth, and the life of the earth upon man, its

Francis Bacon, Lord Verulam and Viscount St Albans, Lord Chancellor of England.

only rational inhabitant. The greatest intellectual achievement of the next century was to make it impossible for educated men to think like this. It was so important that it has been seen as the essential change to the modern from the medieval world.

Early in the seventeenth century something new is already apparent in science. The changes which then manifested themselves amounted to the second great critical change in the cultural history of the modern world, for an intellectual barrier was crossed and the nature of civilization was altered for ever. There appeared in Europe a new attitude, deeply utilitarian, encouraging men to invest time, energy and resources to master nature by systematic experiment. When a later age came to look back for its precursors in this attitude they found the outstanding one to have been Francis Bacon, sometime Lord Chancellor of England, fondly supposed by some later admirers to be the author of the plays of Shakespeare, a man of outstanding intellectual energy and many unlikable personal traits. His works seem to have had little or no contemporary effect but they attracted posterity's attention for what seemed a prophetic rejection of the authority of the past. Bacon advocated a study of nature based upon observation and induction and directed towards harnessing it for human purposes. 'The true and

William Harvey, most celebrated for his demonstration in 1628 of the circulation of the blood, was also the author of a treatise on human anatomy from which this illustration is taken.

lawful end of the sciences', he wrote, 'is that human life be enriched by new discoveries and powers.' Through them could be achieved 'a restitution and reinvigorating [in great part] of man to the sovereignty and power . . . which he had in his first state of creation'. This was ambitious indeed – nothing less than the redemption of mankind from the consequences of Adam's Fall – but Bacon was sure it was possible if scientific research was effectively organized; in this, too, he was a prophetic figure, precursor of later scientific societies and institutes.

The modernity of Bacon was later exaggerated and other men – notably his contemporaries Kepler and Galileo – had much more to say

which was of importance in the advance of science. Nor did his successors adhere so closely as he would have wished to a programme of practical discovery of 'new arts, endowments, and commodities for the bettering of man's life' (that is, to a science dominated by technology). Nevertheless, he rightly acquired something of the status of a mythological figure because he went to the heart of the matter in his advocacy of observation and experiment instead of deduction from *a priori* principles. Appropriately, he is said even to have achieved scientific martyrdom, having caught cold while stuffing a fowl with snow one freezing March day, in order to observe the effects of refrigeration upon the flesh. Forty years later, his central ideas were the commonplaces of scientific discourse. 'The management of this great machine of the world', said an English scientist in the 1660s, 'can be explained only by the experimental and mechanical philosophers.' Here were ideas which Bacon would have understood and approved and which are central to the world which we still inhabit. Ever since the seventeenth century it has been a characteristic of the scientist that he answers questions by means of experiment and for a long time it was to lead to new attempts to understand what was revealed by these experiments by constructing systems.

This led at first to concentration on the physical phenomena which could best be observed and measured by the techniques available. Technological innovation had arisen from the slow accretion of skills by European workmen over centuries; these skills could now be directed to the solution of problems which would in turn permit the solution of other, intellectual, problems. The invention of logarithms and calculus was a part of an instrumentation which had among other components the building of better clocks and optical instruments. When the clockmaker's art took a great stride forward with the seventeenth-century introduction of the pendulum as a controlling device it in turn made the measurement of time by precision instruments, and therefore astronomy, much easier. With the telescope came

'The air-pump': a detail from a picture by Joseph Wright of Derby, the first and one of the few English painters to choose subjects from science and technology.

new opportunities to scrutinize the heavens; Harvey discovered the circulation of the blood as the result of a theoretical investigation by experiment, but *how* circulation took place was only made comprehensible when the microscope made it possible to see the tiny vessels through which blood flowed.

What was not achieved for a long time was the line of demarcation between the scientist and philosopher which we now recognize. Yet a new world of scientists had come into being, a true scientific community and an international one, too. Here we come back to printing. The rapid diffusion of new knowledge was very important. The publication of scientific books was not its only form; the *Philosophical Transactions* of the Royal Society were published and so were, increasingly, the memoirs and proceedings of other learned bodies. Scientists moreover kept

up huge private correspondences with one another, and much of the material they recorded in them has provided some of the most valuable evidence for the way in which scientific revolution actually occurred. Some of these correspondences were published; they were more widely intelligible and read then than would be the exchanges of leading scientists today.

One feature of the scientific revolution which is especially striking to the modern eye is that it was something in which laymen played a big part. It has been suggested that one of the most important facts explaining why science progressed in Europe while stagnation overtook even outstanding technical achievement in China, was the association with it in Europe of the social prestige of the amateur and the gentleman. The membership of the learned societies which began to appear more widely at about the mid-century was full of gentlemanly dabblers who could not by any stretch of imagination have been called professional scientists but who lent to these bodies the indefinable but important weight of their standing and respectability even though they often refrained from getting their hands dirty in experimental work.

By 1700 specialization between different branches of science already existed but was by no means as important as it was to become. Nor was science so demanding on time; scientists could still make major contributions to their study while writing books on theology or holding administrative office. This suggests some of the limitations of the seventeenth-century revolution; it could not transcend the limits of the techniques available and while they permitted great advances in some fields, they tended to inhibit attention to others. Chemistry, for example, made relatively small progress while physics and cosmology went ahead rapidly and indeed arrived at something of a plateau of consolidation which resulted in less spectacular but steady advance well into the nineteenth century, when new theoretical approaches reinvigorated them.

Altogether, the seventeenth-century scientific achievement was a huge one. First and foremost,

*The title-page of the great work on human
anatomy by the Flemish teacher of surgery at
Padua, Andreas Vesalius. In the same year as
its publication the word 'physiology' was coined.*

The title-page of Kepler's work Tabuliae
Rudolphinae *of 1627. The columns of the
temple of the sciences bear the names of
Copernicus, Brahe and Aristotle.*

it replaced a theory of the universe which saw
phenomena as the direct and often unpredictable
operation of divine power by a conception of it
as a mechanism, in which change proceeded
regularly from the uniform and universal
working of laws of motion. This was still quite
compatible with belief in God. His majesty
was not perhaps shown in daily direct intervention but in His creation of a great machine;
in the most celebrated analogy God was the
great watch-maker. The scientific world view
of the seventeenth century was therefore
neither anti-religious, nor anti-theocentric.
Though it was indubitably important that new
views on astronomy, by displacing man from
the centre of the universe, implicitly challenged
his uniqueness (it was in 1686 that a book
appeared arguing that there might be more
than one inhabited world), this was not what

preoccupied the men who made the cosmological revolution. For them it was only an accident
that the authority of the Church became entangled with the proposition that the sun went
round the earth. The new views they put
forward merely emphasized the greatness and
mysteriousness of God's ways. They took
for granted the possibility of christening the new
knowledge as Aristotle had been christened by
the Middle Ages.

The great roll of the cosmological revolution
has always been headed by the name of Copernicus, a Polish cleric whose book *On the Revolutions of the Celestial Orbs* was published in
1543. This was the same year as Vesalius' great
work on anatomy (and, curiously, of the first
edition of the works of Archimedes); Copernicus was a Renaissance humanist rather than a
scientist – not unreasonably, considering when

he lived. In part for philosophic and aesthetic reasons he hit upon the idea of a universe of planets moving round the sun, explaining their notion as a system of cycles and epicycles. It was (so to speak) a brilliant guess, for he had no means of testing the hypothesis and most commonsense evidence told against it.

The first true scientific data in support of heliocentricity was in fact provided by a man who did not accept it, the Dane Tycho Brahe. Besides possessing the somewhat striking distinction of an artificial nose, Brahe began recording the movements of planets, first with rudimentary instruments and then, thanks to a munificent king, from the best-equipped observatory of his age. The result was the first systematic collection of astronomical data to be made within the orbit of the western tradition since the great Alexandrian era. Kepler, the first great Protestant scientist, who was invited by Brahe to assist him, went on to make even more careful observations of his own and provided a second great constructive theoretical step forward. He showed that the movements of planets could be explained as regular if their courses followed ellipses at irregular speeds. This broke at last with the Ptolemaic framework within which cosmology had been more and more cramped and provided the basis of planetary explanation until the twentieth century. Then came Galileo Galilei, who eagerly seized upon the telescope, an instrument seemingly discovered about 1600, possibly by chance. Galileo was an academic, professor at Padua of two subjects characteristically linked in early science: physics and military engineering. His use of the telescope finally shattered the Aristotelian scheme; Copernican astronomy was made visible and the next two centuries were to apply to the stars what was known of the nature of the planets.

Galileo's major work, nevertheless, was not in observation but theory. He first described the physics which made a Copernican universe possible by providing a mathematical treatment of the movement of bodies. What is more, Galileo formulated it as a result of systematic

Newton's own reflecting telescope.

experiment. On this rested what Galileo called 'two new sciences', statics and dynamics. The published result was the book in which has been seen the first statement of the revolution in scientific thought, Galileo's *Dialogue on the Two Great Systems of the World* (that of Ptolemy and that of Copernicus) of 1632. Less remarkable than its contents, but still interesting, are the facts that it was written not in Latin but the vernacular Italian, and dedicated to the pope; Galileo was undoubtedly a good Catholic. Yet the book provoked an uproar, rightly, for it meant the end of the Christian-Aristotelian world view which was the great cultural triumph of the medieval Church. Galileo's trial followed. He was condemned and recanted, but this did not diminish the effect of his work. Copernican views henceforth dominated scientific thinking.

In the year that Galileo died, Newton was born. It was his achievement to provide the physical explanation of the Copernican universe; he showed that the same mechanical laws explained both what Kepler and what Galileo had said. He employed a new mathematics, the 'method of fluxions' or, in later terminology, the infinitesimal calculus. Newton did not invent this; he applied it to physical phenomena. It provided a way of calculating the positions of bodies in motion. His conclusions were embodied in a discussion of the movements of the planets contained in a book which was the most important and influential scientific work since that of Euclid. The *Principia*, as it is called for short (or, Anglicized, *The Mathematical Principles of Natural Philosophy*), demonstrated how gravity sustained the physical universe. The general cultural consequences of this discovery were comparable with those within science. We have no proper standard of measurement, but perhaps they were even greater. That a single law, discovered by observation and calculation, could explain so much was an astonishing revelation of what the new scientific thinking could achieve. Pope has been quoted to excess, but his epigram still best summarizes the impact of Newton's work on educated men:

Nature and Nature's laws lay hid in night:
God said, 'Let Newton be!' and all was light.

Newton thus in due time became, with Bacon, the second of the canonized saints of a New Learning. There was little exaggeration in this in Newton's case. He was a man of almost universal scientific interests and, as the phrase has it, touched little that he did not adorn. Yet the significance of much of what Newton did is bound to elude the non-scientist. Manifestly, he completed the revolution begun with Copernicus. A dynamic conception of the universe had replaced a static one. In a specialized way the achievement was great enough to provide the physics of the next two centuries and to underpin all the other sciences with a new cosmology. What was not anticipated by Newton and his predecessors was that this might presage an insoluble conflict of science and religion. Newton, indeed, seems even to have been pleased to observe that the law of gravity did not adequately sustain the view that the universe was a self-regulated system, self-contained once created. He welcomed the logical gap which he could fill by postulating divine intervention, for he was a passionate Protestant apologist.

Churchmen, especially Catholic, nevertheless did not find it easy to come to terms with the new science. In the Middle Ages clerics had made important contributions to science, but from the seventeenth to the mid-nineteenth century, very little first-rank scientific work was done by churchmen. This was truer, certainly, of the countries where the Counter-Reformation had triumphed than those where it had not. In the seventeenth century there opened that split between organized religion and science which has haunted European intellectual history ever since, whatever efforts have from time to time been made to patch it up. The symbolic crisis was that of the Neapolitan Bruno. He was not a scientist but a speculator, formerly a Dominican monk who broke with his order and wandered about Europe publishing controversial works, dabbling in a magical 'secret science' supposedly derived from ancient Egypt. In the end the Inquisition took him and after eight years in its hands he was burned at Rome for heresy. His execution became one of the foundations of the later historical mythology of the development of 'free thought', of the struggle between progress and religion as it was to come to be seen.

In the seventeenth century such an antithesis was not much felt by scientists and philosophers. Newton, who wrote copiously on biblical and theological topics and believed his work on the prophetical books to be as flawless as the *Principia*, seems to have held that Moses knew about the heliocentric theory and recommended his readers to 'beware of Philosophy and vain deceit and oppositions of science falsely so called' and to have recourse to the Old Testament. Napier, the inventor of logarithms, was delighted to have in them a new tool to deploy in deciphering the mysterious references in the Book of Revelation to the Number of the Beast. The French philosopher Descartes formulated what he found to be satisfactory philosophical defences of religious belief and Christian truth coherent with his technically sceptical approach to his subject. This did not prevent him (or the philosophical movement which took its name from him, Cartesianism) from attracting the hostility of the Church. The traditional defenders of religious belief correctly recognized that what was at stake was not only the conclusions people arrived at, but the way that they arrived at them. A rationally argued acceptance of religious belief which started from principles of doubt and demonstrated they could satisfactorily be overcome was a poor ally for a Church which taught that truth was declared by Authority. The Church was quite right in setting aside as irrelevant Descartes' own devotion and Christianity and correctly (from its own point of view) put all his works on the Index.

The argument from authority was taken up by a French Protestant clergyman of the later seventeenth century, Pierre Bayle, who pointed out that it had an unsatisfactory open-endedness. What authority prescribed the authority? In the end it seemed to be a matter of opinion. Every dogma of traditional Christianity, he suggested, might be refuted if not in accordance with natural reason. With such ideas a new phase in the history of European thought announced itself; it has been called the Enlightenment.

This word and similar ones were used in the eighteenth century in most European languages to characterize the thinking which men felt distinguished their own age and cut it off from what had gone before. The key image is of the letting in of light upon what was dark, but when the German philosopher Kant asked the question 'what is enlightenment?' in a famous essay he gave a different answer: liberation from self-imposed tutelage. At its heart lay a questioning of authority. The great heritage to be left behind by the Enlightenment was the generalizing of the critical attitude. From this time, everything was exposed to scrutiny. Some felt – and it came in the very long run to be true – that nothing was sacred, but this is somewhat misleading. Enlightenment had its own authority and dogmas; the critical stance itself long went unexamined. This is one reason why it is very difficult either to analyse or outline it. Furthermore, Enlightenment was as much a bundle of attitudes as a collection of ideas and here lies another difficulty in coming to terms with it. Many streams flowed into this result but by no means did they all follow the same course. The

An illustration of the working of the nervous system as Descartes described it in his book De Homine *(first written in French, though published in Latin). He believed he had actually established the physical location of the soul, whose possession, he believed, distinguished man from animals.*

roots of Enlightenment are as confused as its development which always resembled a continuing debate – sometimes a civil war – much more than the advance of a united army of the enlightened.

Descartes had taught men that systematic doubt was the beginning of firm knowledge. Fifty years later, the English philosopher John Locke provided an account of the psychology of knowledge which reduced its primary constituents to the impressions conveyed by the senses to the mind; there were not, he argued against Descartes, ideas innate in man's nature. The mind contained only sense-data and the

John Locke, the parent of the English empiricist philosophical tradition.

connexions it made between them. This was, of course, to imply that mankind had no fixed ideas of right and wrong; moral values, Locke taught, arose as the mind experienced pain and pleasure. There was to be an enormous future for the development of such ideas; from them would flow ideas about education, about society's duty to regulate material conditions and about many other derivations from environmentalism. There was also a huge past behind them: the dualism which Descartes and Locke both expressed in their distinctions of body and mind, physical and moral, have their roots in Plato and Christian metaphysics. Yet what is perhaps most striking at this point is that his ideas could still be associated by Locke with the traditional framework of Christian belief.

Such incoherences were always to run through the Enlightenment, but its general trend is clear. The new prestige of science, too, seemed to promise that the observations of the senses were, indeed, the way forward to knowledge, and knowledge whose value was proved by its utilitarian efficacy. It could make possible the improvement of the world in which men lived. Its techniques could unlock the mysteries of nature and reveal their logical, rational foundations in the laws of physics and chemistry.

All this was long an optimistic creed. The world was getting better and would continue to do so. In 1600 things had been very different. Then, the Renaissance worship of the classical past had combined with the upheavals of war and the always latent feeling of religious men that the end of the world could not long be delayed to produce a pessimistic mood and a sense of decline from a great past. In a great literary debate over whether the achievements of the ancients excelled those of modern times the writers of the late seventeenth century crystallized the idea of progress which emerged from the Enlightenment. It was also a non-specialists' creed. In the eighteenth century it was still possible for an educated man to tie together in a manner satisfactory at least for himself the logic and implications of many different studies. Voltaire was famous as a poet and playwright, but wrote at length on history (he was for a time the French historiographer royal) and expounded Newtonian physics to his countrymen. Adam Smith was renowned as a moral philosopher before he dazzled the world with his *Wealth of Nations*, a book which may reasonably be considered to have founded the modern science of economics.

In such eclecticism religion, too, found a place, yet is also true that in 'enlightened' thought there seemed to be small room for the divine and the theological. It was not just that men no longer felt hell gaping about them and that the world became less mysterious; it also promised to be less tragic. More and more troubles seemed not inseparable from being, but man-made. Awkward problems, it was true, might still be presented by appalling natural disasters such as earthquakes, but if the relief of most ills was possible, if, as one thinker put it, 'Man's proper business is to seek happiness and avoid misery', what was the relevance of the dogmas of Salvation and Damnation? God could still be included in a perfunctory way in the philosopher's account of the universe, as the First Cause had started the whole thing going and the Great Mechanic who prescribed the rules on which it ran, but was there any place for His subsequent intervention in its working, either directly by incarnation or indirectly through His Church and the sacraments it conveyed? Inevitably, the Enlightenment brought revolt against the Church, the supreme claimant to intellectual and moral authority.

Here was a fundamental conflict. The rejection of authority by thinking men in the seventeenth and eighteenth centuries was only rarely complete, in the sense that new authority was sought and discovered in what were believed to be the teachings of science and reason. Yet emphatically the authority of the past was rejected. As the literary argument over ancient and modern culture advanced the destruction of the authority of classical teaching, so had the Protestant Reformation exploded the authority of the Catholic Church, the other pillar of traditional European culture. When the Protestant reformers had replaced old priest by new presbyter (or by the Old Testament) they could not undo the work of undermining religious authority which they had begun and which the men of the Enlightenment were to carry much further.

Such implications took some time to emerge, whatever the quickly formulated and justified misgivings of churchmen. The characteristics of advanced thought in the eighteenth century tended to express themselves in fairly practical and everyday recommendations which in a measure masked their tendency. They are probably best summarized in terms of the fundamental beliefs which underlay them and of which they were consequences. At the basis of all others was a new confidence in the power of mind; this was one reason why the Enlightened

so much admired Bacon, who shared this with them, yet even the creative giants of the Renaissance did not do so much to give European man a conviction of intellectual power as did the eighteenth century. On this rested the assurance that almost indefinite improvement was possible. Most thinkers of the age were optimists who saw it as the apex of history. Confidently they looked forward to the improvement of the lot of mankind by the manipulation of nature and the unfolding to man of the truths which reason had written in his heart. Innate ideas bundled out by the front door crept in again by the back stairs. Optimism was qualified only by the realization that there were grave obstacles to be overcome. The first of these was simply ignorance. Perhaps a knowledge of Final Causes was impossible (and certainly science seemed to suggest this as it revealed more and more complexity in nature) but this was not the sort of ignorance which worried the Enlightened. They had a more everyday level of experience in mind and the combination of reason and knowledge gave confidence that ignorance could be dispersed. The greatest literary embodiment of Enlightenment had precisely this aim. The great *Encyclopédie* of Diderot and D'Alembert was a huge compilation of information and propaganda in twenty-one volumes published between 1751 and 1765. As some of its articles made clear, another great obstacle to enlightenment was intolerance – especially when it interfered with freedom of publication and debate. Parochialism was another barrier to happiness. The values of the Enlightenment, it was assumed, were those of all civilized men. They were universal. Never, except perhaps in the Middle Ages, has the European intellectual élite been more cosmopolitan or shared more of a common language. Its cosmopolitanism was increased by knowledge of other societies, for which the Enlightenment showed an extraordinary appetite. In part this was because of genuine curiosity; travel and discovery brought to men's notice new ideas and institutions and thus made them more aware of social and ethical relativity and provided new grounds for criticism.

A caricature of the historian Edward Gibbon – said to have been called a 'luminous' author by the playwright Sheridan when he meant to speak of the 'voluminous' author of The Decline and Fall of the Roman Empire.

Above all, China captured the imagination of eighteenth-century Europeans, a fact which perhaps suggests how superficial was their acquaintance with its realities.

Once ignorance, intolerance and parochialism were removed, it was assumed that the un-impeded operation of the laws of nature, un-covered by reason, would promote the reform of society in everyone's interest except that of those wedded to the past by their blindness or their enjoyment of indefensible privilege. The *Lettres persanes* of the French author Montes-quieu began the tradition of suggesting that the institutions of existing societies – in his case the laws of France – could be improved by com-parison with the laws of nature. In articulating such a programme, the men of the Enlighten-ment were appointing themselves as the priest-hood of a new social order. In their vision of their rôle as critics and reformers there emerged for the first time a social ideal which has been with us ever since, that of the intellectual. Moralists, philosophers, scholars, scientists al-ready existed; their defining characteristic was specialized competence. What the Enlighten-ment invented was the ideal of the generalized critical intellect. Autonomous, rational, con-tinuous and universal criticism was institu-tionalized as never before and the modern intel-lectual is the outcome.

The eighteenth century did not use this term. It had the type, but called its exemplars simply 'philosophers'. This was an interesting adapta-tion and broadening of a word already familiar; it came to connote not the specialized mental pursuit of philosophical studies but the accep-tance of a common outlook and critical stance. It was a term with moral and evaluative tones, used familiarly by enemies as well as friends to indicate also a zeal to propagate the truths revealed by critical insight to a large and lay public. The archetypes were a group of French writers soon lumped together in spite of their differences and referred to as the *philosophes*. Their numbers and celebrity correctly suggest the preponderance of France in the central period of Enlightenment thought. Other countries neither produced so many and such conspicuous figures within this tradition, nor did they usually confer such prestige and eminence on those they had. Yet the presiding deities of the early Enlighten-ment were the English Newton and Locke; it could be reasonably claimed too that the philosopher who expressed the most extreme development of Enlightenment ideals and me-thods was Bentham, and that its greatest his-toriographical monument is Gibbon's work. Further north, Scotland had a great eighteenth-century cultural efflorescence and produced in Hume one of the most engaging as well as the most acute of the Enlightenment's technical philosophers, who combined extreme intellec-tual scepticism with good nature and social conservatism, and in Adam Smith the author of one of the great creative books of modern times. Among Latin countries, Italy was, outside France, most prolific in its contribution to Enlightenment in spite of the predominance there of the Roman Church. The Italian En-lightenment would be assured of a remembrance even if it had thrown up only Beccaria, the author of a book which founded penal reform and the criticism of penology and gave currency to one of the great slogans of history, 'the greatest happiness of the greatest number'. The German Enlightenment was slower to unroll and less productive of figures who won universal acclaim (possibly for linguistic reasons) but produced in Kant a thinker who, if he consciously sought to go beyond the Enlightenment, nevertheless embodied in his moral recommendations much of what it stood for. Only Spain seemed to lag conspicuously. It was not an unfair impression even allowing for the work of one or two enlightened statesmen; Spanish universities in the eighteenth century were still rejecting Newton to study Aristotle.

Important though the work of other nations was for the history of civilization, that of the French struck contemporaries the most forcefully. There were many reasons: a simple one is that men are always fascinated by power and France under Louis XIV had acquired a prestige long to endure. Another reason is the magnificent instrument for the diffusion of French culture which lay to hand in the French language. It was the *lingua franca* of Europe's intellectuals and its people of fashion alike in the eighteenth century; Maria Theresia and her children exchanged their family correspondence in it and Frederick II wrote (bad) verses in it. A European audience was assured for any book written in French and it seems likely that the success of that language actually held back cultural advance in the German tongue.

A common language made possible propaganda discussion and critical comment, but what would actually be achieved by way of practical reform in the short term was bound to depend on political circumstance. Some statesmen attempted to put 'enlightened' ideas into practice, because there were coincidences between the interests of states and the aims of philosophers. This was especially apparent when 'enlightened despotisms' found themselves running into opposition from vested interest and conservatism. Such conflicts were obvious

in the enforcement of educational reform at the expense of the Church inside the Habsburg dominions, or in Voltaire's attacks, written to the brief of a royal minister, on the *parlement* of Paris when it stood in the way of fiscal innovation. Some rulers, like Catherine the Great of Russia, ostentatiously paraded the influence of Enlightenment ideas on their legislation. Perhaps the most important and influential impact of ideas, apart from those of utilitarian reform which were deployed against the Church, was always in educational and economic matters. In France, at least, the economic recommendations of enlightened thinkers made their mark on administration.

Religious questions drew the attention of the *philosophes* with unique power. The Church and the effects of its teaching were, of course, still inseparable from every side of Europe's life still. It was not just that the Church claimed authority in so much, but also its physical and human presence as a great corporate interest, both social and economic; it was involved in some measure in every aspect of society to which the attention of reformers might be drawn. Whether it was because the abuse of sanctuary or clerical privilege stood in the way of judicial reform, or mortmain impeded economic improvement, or a clerical monopoly of education encumbered the training of administrators, or dogma prevented the equal treatment of loyal and valued subjects, the Church seemed to find itself always opposing improvement. But this was not all that drew the fire of the *philosophes*. Religion could also lead, they thought, to crime. One of the last great scandals of the era of religious persecution was the execution of a Protestant at Toulouse in 1762 on the charge of converting Catholics to heresy. For this he was tortured, tried, convicted and executed. Voltaire made this a *cause célèbre*. They did not change the law, but it is impossible not to believe that, for all the violence of feeling which still divided Catholic and Protestant in southern France, his attacks made it impossible for such a judicial murder ever to be repeated. Yet France did not give even a

The patriarch of the Enlightenment, Voltaire, gets up, dictating to a secretary while he dresses.

limited legal toleration to Protestants until 1787 and then did not extend it to Jews. By that time Joseph II had already introduced religious toleration into his Catholic territories.

This suggests an important limit to the practical success of Enlightenment. For all its revolutionary power, it had to operate within the still very restrictive institutional and moral framework of the *ancien régime*. The relationship between it and despotism was ambiguous: it might struggle against the imposition of censorship or the practice of religious intolerance in a theocratic monarchy, but could also depend on despotic power to carry out reform. Nor, it must be remembered, were enlightened ideas the only source of reform. The institutions Voltaire admired in England did not stem from Enlightenment and such improvements as the eighteenth century brought to that country owed more to religion than to 'philosophy'.

The greatest political importance of the Enlightenment lay in its legacies to the future. It clarified and formulated many of the key demands of liberalism, though here, too, its legacy is ambiguous, for the men of the Enlightenment sought not freedom for its own sake but freedom for the consequences it would bring. Apart from this, their clearest contribution to the future European liberal tradition was specific and negative: the Enlightenment created classical anti-clericalism. Criticism of what the Church had done led to support for attacks by the state upon ecclesiastical organizations and authority. The struggles of Church and State had many roots other than philosophical, but could always be presented as a part of a continuing war of Enlightenment and rationality against superstition and bigotry. In particular, the Papacy attracted criticism – or contempt; Voltaire seems to have once believed that it would in fact disappear before the end of the century. The greatest success of the *philosophes* in the eyes of their enemies and of many of their supporters was the papal dissolution of the Jesuits.

A few *philosophes* carried their attacks on the Church beyond institutions to an attack on religion itself. Out and out atheism (together with deterministic materialism) was given its first serious expression in the eighteenth century. But such views were unusual. Most men during the Enlightenment era who thought about these things were probably sceptical about the dogmas of the Church, but kept up a vague theism. Certainly, too, they believed in the importance of religion as a social force. As Voltaire said, 'one must have religion for the sake of the people'. He, in any case, continued throughout his life to assert, with Newton, the existence of God and died formally at peace with the Church.

Here was a recognition of something that was always in danger of being lost to sight in the Enlightenment, the importance of the non-intellectual and non-rational. The most prophetic figure of the century and one who quarrelled bitterly with many of the leading figures of the Enlightenment was the Genevan Rousseau. His importance in the history of thought lies in his impassioned pleas that due weight be given to the feelings and the moral sense, both in danger of eclipse by rationality. Because of this, he thought, the men of his day were stunted

creatures, partial and corrupt beings, deformed by the influence of a society which encouraged this eclipse.

European culture owes an enormous amount to Rousseau's vision, much of it to prove pernicious in its effect. There can be found in his writings a new attitude to religion (which was to revivify it), a new psychological obsession with the individual which was to flood into art and literature, the invention of the sentimental approach to nature and natural beauty, the origins of the modern doctrine of nationalism, a new child-centredness in educational theory and much else besides. He is, in short, the key figure in the making of what has been called romanticism. In much of this he was an innovator, and one of genius. In much of it he expressed views shared by other men. His distaste for the Enlightenment erosion of community, of the sense that men were brothers and members of a common moral whole was shared, for example, and expressed just as eloquently by the Irish author Edmund Burke, who drew from this very different conclusions. Rousseau was in some measure voicing views beginning to be held by others as the age of Enlightenment passed its zenith. Yet of Rousseau's central and special importance to romanticism, there can be no doubt.

Romanticism is a much used and much misused term. It can be properly applied to things which seem diametrically opposed. Soon after 1800, for example, some men would deny any value to the past and seek to overthrow its legacies just as violently as men of the Enlightenment had done while others sought to uphold historic institutions equally tenaciously at the same time. Both sets of men can be called romantics, because in each of them moral passion counted for more than intellectual analysis. The clearest link between such antitheses lay in the new emphasis of romantic Europe on feeling, intuition, and, above all, the natural. Romanticism, whose expressions were to be so manifold, started almost always from some objection to enlightened thought, whether to the belief that science could provide an answer to all questions, or from a revulsion against rational self-interest. But its positive roots lay deeper than this, in the Reformation's displacement of so many traditional values by the one supreme value of sincerity; it was not entirely wrong to see romanticism as some Catholic critics saw it, as a secularized Protestantism, for above all it sought authenticity, self-realization, honesty, moral exaltation. Unhappily it did so all too often without regard to cost. The great effects were to reverberate through the nineteenth century, usually with painful results, and in the twentieth century would affect many other parts of the world as one of the last manifestations of the vigour of European culture.

Jean-Jacques Rousseau, self-appointed advocate of the pure heart and uncorrupted feeling.

Book Six

The Great Acceleration

In the middle of the eighteenth century most people in the world (and perhaps most Europeans, too) could still believe that the world would go on much as it seemed always to have done. The weight of the past was everywhere enormous and often it was immovable; some of the European efforts to shake it off have been touched upon but nowhere outside Europe was even the possibility of doing so grasped. Though in many parts of the world a few people's lives had begun to be revolutionized by contact with Europeans, most of it was unaffected and much of it was untouched by such contamination of traditional ways.

In the next century and a half change was to come thick and fast almost everywhere and to ignore the fact was to be much harder if not impossible. By 1900 it was obvious that in Europe and the European world of settlement it had irreversibly cut off much of the traditional past. Just as important, impulses from northern Europe and the Atlantic world had also radiated outwards to transform both Europe's relations with the rest of the world and the very foundations of their lives for many of its peoples, however much some of them regretted and resisted it. By the end of the nineteenth century (and this is only an approximate and convenient marker) a world once regulated by tradition was on a new course. Its destiny was now to be continuing and accelerating

transformation and the second adjective was as important as the first. A man born in 1800 who lived out the psalmist's span of three-score years and ten could have seen the world more changed in his lifetime than it had been in the previous thousand years.

The consolidation of the European world hegemony was central to these changes and one of the great motors propelling them. By 1900 European civilization had shown itself to be the most successful which had ever existed. Men might not always agree on what was most important about it but no one could deny that it had produced wealth on an unprecedented scale and that it dominated the rest of the globe by power and influence as no previous civilization had ever done. Europeans (or their descendants) ran the world. Much of their domination was political, a matter of direct rule. Large areas of the world had been peopled by European stocks. As for the non-European countries still formally and politically independent of Europe, most of them had in practice to defer to European wishes and accept European interference in their affairs. Few indigenous peoples could resist, and if they were to do so Europe often won its subtlest victory of all, for successful resistance required the adoption of European practices and, therefore, Europeanization in another form.

IN CONGRESS, JULY 4, 1776

The unanimous Declaration of the thirteen united States of America.

When in the Course of human events, it becomes necessary for one people to dissolve the political bands which have connected them with another, and to assume among the powers of the earth, the separate and equal station to which the Laws of Nature and of Nature's God entitle them, a decent respect to the opinions of mankind requires that they should declare the causes which impel them to the separation.

We hold these truths to be self-evident, that all men are created equal, that they are endowed by their Creator with certain unalienable Rights, that among these are Life, Liberty and the pursuit of Happiness.—That to secure these rights, Governments are instituted among Men, deriving their just powers from the consent of the governed,—That whenever any Form of Government becomes destructive of these ends, it is the Right of the People to alter or to abolish it, and to institute new Government, laying its foundation on such principles and organizing its powers in such form, as to them shall seem most likely to effect their Safety and Happiness. Prudence, indeed, will dictate that Governments long established should not be changed for light and transient causes; and accordingly all experience hath shewn, that mankind are more disposed to suffer, while evils are sufferable, than to right themselves by abolishing the forms to which they are accustomed. But when a long train of abuses and usurpations, pursuing invariably the same Object evinces a design to reduce them under absolute Despotism, it is their right, it is their duty, to throw off such Government, and to provide new Guards for their future security.—Such has been the patient sufferance of these Colonies; and such is now the necessity which constrains them to alter their former Systems of Government. The history of the present King of Great Britain is a history of repeated injuries and usurpations, all having in direct object the establishment of an absolute Tyranny over these States. To prove this, let Facts be submitted to a candid world.

He has refused his Assent to Laws, the most wholesome and necessary for the public good.

He has forbidden his Governors to pass Laws of immediate and pressing importance, unless suspended in their operation till his Assent should be obtained; and when so suspended, he has utterly neglected to attend to them.

He has refused to pass other Laws for the accommodation of large districts of people, unless those people would relinquish the right of Representation in the Legislature, a right inestimable to them and formidable to tyrants only.

He has called together legislative bodies at places unusual, uncomfortable, and distant from the depository of their public Records, for the sole purpose of fatiguing them into compliance with his measures.

He has dissolved Representative Houses repeatedly, for opposing with manly firmness his invasions on the rights of the people.

He has refused for a long time, after such dissolutions, to cause others to be elected; whereby the Legislative powers, incapable of Annihilation, have returned to the People at large for their exercise; the State remaining in the mean time exposed to all the dangers of invasion from without, and convulsions within.

He has endeavoured to prevent the population of these States; for that purpose obstructing the Laws for Naturalization of Foreigners; refusing to pass others to encourage their migrations hither, and raising the conditions of new Appropriations of Lands.

He has obstructed the Administration of Justice, by refusing his Assent to Laws for establishing Judiciary powers.

He has made Judges dependent on his Will alone, for the tenure of their offices, and the amount and payment of their salaries.

He has erected a multitude of New Offices, and sent hither swarms of Officers to harrass our people, and eat out their substance.

He has kept among us, in times of peace, Standing Armies without the Consent of our legislatures.

He has affected to render the Military independent of and superior to the Civil power.

He has combined with others to subject us to a jurisdiction foreign to our constitution, and unacknowledged by our laws; giving his Assent to their Acts of pretended Legislation:

For quartering large bodies of armed troops among us:

For protecting them, by a mock Trial, from punishment for any Murders which they should commit on the Inhabitants of these States:

For cutting off our Trade with all parts of the world:

For imposing Taxes on us without our Consent:

For depriving us in many cases, of the benefits of Trial by jury:

For transporting us beyond Seas to be tried for pretended offences:

For abolishing the free System of English Laws in a neighbouring Province, establishing therein an Arbitrary government, and enlarging its Boundaries so as to render it at once an example and fit instrument for introducing the same absolute rule into these Colonies:

For taking away our Charters, abolishing our most valuable Laws, and altering fundamentally the Forms of our Governments:

For suspending our own Legislatures, and declaring themselves invested with power to legislate for us in all cases whatsoever.

He has abdicated Government here, by declaring us out of his Protection and waging War against us.

He has plundered our seas, ravaged our Coasts, burnt our towns, and destroyed the lives of our people.

He is at this time transporting large Armies of foreign Mercenaries to compleat the works of death, desolation and tyranny, already begun with circumstances of Cruelty & perfidy scarcely paralleled in the most barbarous ages, and totally unworthy the Head of a civilized nation.

He has constrained our fellow Citizens taken Captive on the high Seas to bear Arms against their Country, to become the executioners of their friends and Brethren, or to fall themselves by their Hands.

He has excited domestic insurrections amongst us, and has endeavoured to bring on the inhabitants of our frontiers, the merciless Indian Savages, whose known rule of warfare, is an undistinguished destruction of all ages, sexes and conditions.

In every stage of these Oppressions We have Petitioned for Redress in the most humble terms: Our repeated Petitions have been answered only by repeated injury. A Prince, whose character is thus marked by every act which may define a Tyrant, is unfit to be the ruler of a free people.

Nor have We been wanting in attentions to our British brethren. We have warned them from time to time of attempts by their legislature to extend an unwarrantable jurisdiction over us. We have reminded them of the circumstances of our emigration and settlement here. We have appealed to their native justice and magnanimity, and we have conjured them by the ties of our common kindred to disavow these usurpations, which, would inevitably interrupt our connections and correspondence. They too have been deaf to the voice of justice and of consanguinity. We must, therefore, acquiesce in the necessity, which denounces our Separation, and hold them, as we hold the rest of mankind, Enemies in War, in Peace Friends.

We, therefore, the Representatives of the united States of America, in General Congress, Assembled, appealing to the Supreme Judge of the world for the rectitude of our intentions, do, in the Name, and by Authority of the good People of these Colonies, solemnly publish and declare, That these United Colonies are, and of Right ought to be Free and Independent States; that they are Absolved from all Allegiance to the British Crown, and that all political connection between them and the State of Great Britain, is and ought to be totally dissolved; and that as Free and Independent States, they have full Power to levy War, conclude Peace, contract Alliances, establish Commerce, and to do all other Acts and Things which Independent States may of right do.—And for the support of this Declaration, with a firm reliance on the protection of divine Providence, we mutually pledge to each other our Lives, our Fortunes and our sacred Honor.

John Hancock

Button Gwinnett
Lyman Hall
Geo Walton.

Wm Hooper
Joseph Hewes,
John Penn

Edward Rutledge.
Thos Heyward Junr.
Thomas Lynch Junr.
Arthur Middleton

Samuel Chase
Wm Paca
Thos Stone
Charles Carroll of Carrollton
George Wythe
Richard Henry Lee
Th Jefferson
Benja Harrison
Thos Nelson jr.
Francis Lightfoot Lee
Carter Braxton

Robt Morris
Benjamin Rush
Benja Franklin
John Morton
Geo Clymer
Jas Smith.
Geo Taylor
James Wilson
Geo. Ross
Caesar Rodney
Geo Read
Tho M:Kean

Wm Floyd
Phil. Livingston
Frans Lewis
Lewis Morris
Richd Stockton
Jno Witherspoon
Fras Hopkinson
John Hart
Abra Clark

Josiah Bartlett
Wm Whipple
Saml Adams
John Adams
Robt Treat Paine
Elbridge Gerry
Step Hopkins
William Ellery
Roger Sherman
Samel Huntington
Wm Williams
Oliver Wolcott
Matthew Thornton

1 Long-term change

In 1798 Thomas Malthus, an English clergyman, published an *Essay on Population* which was to prove the most influential book ever written on the subject. He described what appeared to be the laws of population growth but his book's importance transcended this apparently limited scientific task. Its impact on, for example, economic theory and biological science was to be just as important as the contribution it made to demographic studies. Here, though, such important consequences matter less than the book's status as a symptom of a change in thinking about population. Roughly speaking, for two centuries or so European statesmen and economists had agreed that rising population was a sign of prosperity. Kings should seek to increase the number of their subjects, it was thought, not

The Declaration of Independence, the central document of the American Revolution, has never ceased to be a source of inspiration and renewal in the public life of the United States. Perhaps that is because the man who drafted it, Thomas Jefferson, resolutely set out to write a profoundly conservative document: it looked back to accepted truths rather than strove to startle or excite men with new discoveries. 'It was', he said, 'intended to be an expression of the American mind.' His purpose was 'not to find out new principles, or new arguments never before thought of, not merely to say things which had never been said before, but to place before mankind the common sense of the subject'. Therein, no doubt, lies the genius of the noble prose which was the result.

merely because this would provide more tax-payers and soldiers but because a bigger population both quickened economic life and was an indication that it had done so. Obviously, larger numbers showed that the economy was providing a living for more people. This view was in its essentials endorsed by no less an authority than the great Adam Smith himself, whose *Wealth of Nations*, a book of huge influence, had agreed as recently as 1776 that an increase in population was a good rough test of economic prosperity.

Malthus doused this view with very cold water. Whatever the consequences for society as a whole might be judged to be, he concluded that a rising population sooner or later spelt disaster and suffering for most of its members, the poor. In a famous demonstration he argued that the produce of the earth had finite limits, set by the amount of land available to grow food. This in turn set a limit to population. Yet population always tended to grow in the short run. As it grew, it would press increasingly upon a narrowing margin of subsistence. When this margin was exhausted, famine must follow. The population would then fall until it could be maintained with the food available. This mechanism could only be kept from operating if men abstained from having children (and prudence, as they regarded the consequences, might help them by encouraging late marriage) or by other horrors, such as the natural check imposed by disease or war.

Much more could be said about the complexity and refinement of this gloomy thesis. It aroused huge argument and counter-argument, and whether true or false, a theory attracting such attention must tell us much about the age. Somehow, the growth of population had begun to worry people so that even prose so unattractive as that of Malthus had great success. People had become aware of rapid population growth as they had not been aware of it before at a moment when it was to become faster than ever. In the nineteenth century, in spite of what Malthus had said, the numbers of some divisions of the human race were to grow with a rapidity and to levels hitherto inconceivable.

A long view is best for measuring such a change; there is nothing to be gained and much to be lost by worrying about precise dates and the overall trends can be traced well into the twentieth century. If we include Russia (whose population has until very recent times to be estimated from very poor statistics) then a European population of about 190 million in 1800 rose to about 420 million a century later. As the rest of the world seems to have grown rather more slowly, this represented a change in Europe's share of the total population of the world from about one-fifth to one-quarter; for a little while, her disadvantage in numbers by comparison with the great Asiatic centres of population was reduced (while she continued to enjoy her technical and psychological superiority). Moreover, at the same time, Europe was sustaining a huge emigration of her stocks. In the 1830s European emigration overseas first passed the figure of 100 000 a year; in 1913 it was over a million and a half. Taking an even longer view, perhaps fifty million people left Europe to go overseas between 1840 and 1930, most of them to the western hemisphere. All these people *and their descendants* ought to be added to the totals in order to grasp how much European population growth accelerated in these years.

This growth was not shared evenly within Europe and this made important differences to the standing of great powers. Their strength was usually reckoned in terms of military manpower and it was a crucial change that Germany replaced France as the largest mass of popula-tion under one government west of Russia in the second half of the nineteenth century. A dramatic increase had been shown earlier in the United Kingdom, whose population grew from about eight million when Malthus wrote to 22 million by mid-century. It was to reach 36 million by 1914. Another way of looking at such changes would be to compare the respective shares of Europe's population enjoyed by the major military powers at different dates. Between 1800 and 1900, for example, that of Russia grew from 21 to 24 per cent of the total, Germany's from 13 to 14, while France's fell from 15 to 10 per cent, and that of Austria slightly less from 15 to 12.

Yet everywhere population grew, though at different rates at different times. The poorest agrarian regions of eastern Europe, for example, experienced their highest growth rates only in the 1920s and 1930s. This is because the basic mechanism of population increase in this period, underlying change everywhere, was a fall in mortality. Never in history has there been so spectacular a fall in death-rates as in the last hundred years, and it showed first in the advanced countries of Europe in the nineteenth century. Roughly speaking, before 1850 most European countries had birth-rates which slightly exceeded death-rates and both were about the same in all countries. They reflected, that is to say, how little impact had been made by that date upon the fundamental determinants of men's life in a still overwhelmingly rural society. After 1880 this changed rapidly. The death-rate in advanced European countries fell pretty steadily, from about 35 per thousand inhabitants per year to about 28 by 1900, 18 by 1950. Less advanced countries still maintained rates of 38 per thousand between 1850 and 1900, and 32 down to 1950. This produced a striking inequality between two Europes. In the richer, expectation of life was much higher. Since, in large measure, advanced European countries lay in the west, this was (in spite of Spain, a poor country with high mortality) a fresh intensification of older divisions between east and west, a new accentuation of the

The problems of paternity: a Mr Quiverful grapples with the problems of the new census return in an English cartoon of the early nineteenth century.

Population control by one of Malthus's natural checks is grimly evidenced by the message of this poster.

imaginary line from the Baltic to the Adriatic.

Other factors besides lower mortality helped. Earlier marriage and a rising birth-rate had showed themselves in the first phase of expansion, as economic opportunity increased, but now they mattered much more, since the children of earlier marriages were much more likely to survive from the nineteenth century onwards, thanks to greater humanitarian con-

cern and medical and engineering progress. The great killing diseases with which doctors first came to grips – mainly from about 1870 onwards – were the child-killers: diphtheria, scarlet fever, whooping-cough, typhoid. Infant mortality was thus dramatically reduced and expectation of life at birth greatly increased. Even earlier than this, social reformers and engineers had already done much to reduce the incidence of these and other diseases (though not their fatality) by building better drains and devising better cleaning arrangements for the growing cities. Cholera was eliminated in industrial countries by 1900, though it had devastated London and Paris in the 1830s and 1840s. No western European country had an important plague outbreak after 1899. As such changes affected more and more countries, their general tendency was everywhere to raise the average of death with, in the long run, dramatic results. By the second quarter of the twentieth

723

century, men and women in North America, the United Kingdom, Scandinavia and industrial Europe could expect to live two or three times as long as their medieval ancestors. Immense consequences flowed from this.

Just as accelerated population increase first announced itself in those countries which were economically the most advanced, so did the slowing down of growth which was the next discernible demographic trend. This was produced by a declining number of births, though it was for a long time masked because the fall in the death-rate was even faster. In every society this showed itself first among the better-off; to this day, it remains a good rough working rule that fecundity varies inversely with income (celebrated exceptions among wealthy American political dynasties notwithstanding). In some societies this was because marriage tended to be put off longer than hitherto so that women were married for a smaller part of their fertile lives: in some it was because couples chose to have fewer children – and could now do so with confidence, thanks to effective contraceptive techniques. Possibly there is a long history of some knowledge of such techniques in some European countries; it is at least certain that the nineteenth century brought both improvements in them (some made possible by scientific and technical advance in manufacturing the necessary devices) and propaganda which spread knowledge of them. Once more, a social change touches upon a huge ramification of influences, because it is difficult not to connect such spreading knowledge with, for example, greater literacy, and with rising expectations. Although people were beginning to be wealthier than their ancestors, they were all the time adjusting their notion of what was a tolerable life – and therefore a tolerable size of family. Whether they followed the calculation by putting off the date of marriage (as French and Irish peasants did) or by adopting contraceptive techniques (as the English and French middle classes seem to have done) was shaped by other cultural factors.

Changes in the way men died and in the way they lived in their families transformed the structures of society. On the one hand, the western countries in the nineteenth and twentieth centuries had absolutely more young people about and, for a time, also had them about in a greater proportion than ever before. It is difficult not to think that the expansiveness, buoyancy and vigour of nineteenth-century Europe owed much to this. On the other hand, advanced societies gradually found a much higher percentage of their members surviving into old age than ever before. This increasingly strained the social mechanism which had in earlier centuries maintained the old and incapable of work; the problem grew worse as competition for industrial employment became more intense. By 1914, there was no country in Europe or North America where much thought had not gone into the problems of poverty and dependence, however great the differences in scale and success of efforts to cope with them.

Such trends would not begin to manifest themselves in eastern Europe until after 1918, when their general pattern was already well established in the advanced western countries. Death-rates long continued to fall more sharply than did the birth-rate, even in advanced countries, so that absolute population growth has continued in the European world as a whole. It is one of the most important themes in the history of the era, linked to almost every other. Its material consequences can be seen in unprecedented urbanization and the rise of huge consumer markets for large-scale manufacturing industry. Its social consequences range from strife and unrest to the adoption of institutions to grapple with it. There were international consequences as statesmen took into account population figures in deciding what risks they could (and which they had to) take, or as people became more and more alarmed about the consequences of overcrowding. Worries in the nineteenth-century United Kingdom over the prospect of too many poor and unemployed led to the encouragement of emigration which, in its turn, shaped people's thinking and feelings about empire. Later, the Germans discouraged

THE DISTRIBUTION

Once destitution was identified as a responsibility for society as a whole, the first relief measures sought to improve, rationalize and enlarge the traditional devices of charity. The soup-kitchen of the Victorian slum replaced the monastery's distribution of its broken meats in the Middle Ages.

emigration because they feared the loss of military potential, while the French and Belgians pioneered the award of children's allowances for the same reason.

Some of these measures suggest, correctly, that the gloomy prophecies of Malthus tended to be forgotten as the years went by and the disasters he feared did not take place. The nineteenth century brought demographic calamities to Europe; Ireland and Russia had spectacular famines and near-famine conditions occurred in many places. But such things grew rarer. A food-producing revolution eliminated famine from advanced countries and helped to make disease a less damaging force in demographic terms. Meanwhile Europe enjoyed two long periods of virtually undisturbed peace from 1815 to 1848 and from 1871 to 1900; war, another of Malthus' checks also seemed to be

less of a scourge. Finally, his diagnosis actually seemed to be disproved when a rise in population was accompanied by higher standards of living – as rising expectations of life seemed to show. Pessimists could only reply (reasonably) that Malthus had not been answered; all that had happened was that there had turned out to be much more food available than had been feared. It did not follow that it was limitless.

In fact, there was occurring one of the few great changes of history which have decisively transformed the basic conditions of human life, a change reasonably described as a food-producing revolution. Its beginnings have already been traced. In the eighteenth century European agriculture was already capable of obtaining about two and a half times the yield on its seed normal in the Middle Ages. Now the culmination of agricultural improvement was at hand. Yields would go up to still more spectacular levels. From about 1800, it has been calculated, Europe's agricultural productivity grew at a rate of about one per cent a year, dwarfing all previous improvement. More important still as time passed European industry and commerce would make it possible to tap huge larders in other parts of the world. Both of these changes

725

were aspects of a single process, the accelerating investment in productive capacity which made Europe and North America by 1870 clearly the greatest concentration of wealth on the face of the globe, and agriculture was fundamental to it. People have spoken of an 'agricultural revolution' and provided this is not thought of as implying rapid change, it is an acceptable term; nothing much less strong will describe the huge increase in output achieved between 1750 and 1870 and later surpassed. But it was a process of great complexity, not a simple matter of a few innovations, drawing on many different sources and linked to the other sectors of the economy in indispensable ways. Nor was it a self-contained process, but only one aspect of a whole economy's change involving in the end not merely continental Europe, but the Americas and Australasia as well.

These important qualifications once made, it is possible to particularize. By 1750 English agriculture was the best in the world. The most advanced techniques were practised and the integration of agriculture with a commercial market economy had gone furthest in England, whose lead was to be maintained for another century or so. European farmers came to England to observe methods, buy stock and machinery, seek advice. Meanwhile, the English farmer, benefiting from peace at home (that there were no large-scale and continuous military operations on British soil after 1650 was literally of incalculable benefit to the economy) and a rising population to buy his produce, generated the profits which provided capital for further improvement. His willingness to invest them in this way was, in the short run, an optimistic response to the likely commercial outlook, but also says something deeper about the nature of English society. The benefits of better farming went in England to individuals who owned their own land or held it securely as lease-holding tenants on terms shaped by market realities. English agriculture was a part of a capitalist market economy in which land was even in the eighteenth century treated almost as a commodity like any other. Restraints on its use

familiar in European countries had disappeared faster and faster from the time of Henry VIII's sequestration of monastic property onwards. After 1750, the last great stage of this came with the spate of Enclosure Acts at the turn of the century (significantly coincident with high prices for grain) which mobilized for private profit the English peasant's traditional rights to pasture, fuel or other economic benefits. One of the most striking contrasts between English agriculture in the early nineteenth century and European was that the traditional peasant all but disappeared in England. England had wage labourers and smallholders, but the huge European rural populations of individuals with some, if minuscule, legal rights linking them to the soil through communal usages and a mass of tiny holdings, did not exist.

Inside the framework provided by prosperity and English social institutions, technical progress was continuous. For a long time, much of this was hit-and-miss. Early breeders of better animals succeeded not because of a knowledge of chemistry, which was in its infancy, or of genetics, which did not exist, but because they backed hunches. Even so, the results were remarkable. The appearance of the livestock inhabiting the landscape changed; the scraggy medieval sheep whose backs resembled, in section, the Gothic arches of the monasteries which bred them, gave way to the fat, square, well-covered animal familiar today. 'Symmetry, well-covered' was an eighteenth-century country farmer's toast. The appearance of farms changed as draining and hedging progressed and big, open medieval fields with their narrow strips, each cultivated by a different peasant, gave way to enclosed fields worked in rotation and made a huge patchwork of the English countryside. In some of these fields machinery could be seen at work even by 1750. Much thought was given to its use and improvement in the eighteenth century, but it does not seem that it really made much of a contribution to productivity until after 1800, when more and more large fields became available, and it became more productive in relation to cost. It was not

Millet, the French artist who made this etching, was almost the first painter of the countryside to depict peasants realistically, after their idyllic appearances in eighteenth-century pictures.

long before steam engines were driving threshers and with their appearance in English fields, the way was open which would lead eventually to an almost complete replacement of muscular by machine power on the twentieth-century farm.

Such improvements and changes spread, *mutatis mutandis* and with a lag in time, to continental Europe. There, they did not transform agricultural society so completely. Preliminary changes were needed in social institutions which went much further than anything experienced in England. The French formally abolished serfdom in 1789; this probably did not mean much, for there were few serfs in France at that date, but the abolition of the 'feudal system' in the same year was a much more important matter. What was meant by this vague term was,

the destruction of the whole mass of traditional and legal usages and rights which stood in the way of the exploitation of land by individuals as an investment like any other. Almost at once, it began to appear that many of the peasants who had thought they wanted this discovered that they did not altogether like it in practice; they discriminated. They were happy to abolish the customary dues paid to the lord of the manor, but did not welcome the loss of customary rights to common land. The whole change was made more confusing and difficult to measure still by the fact that there took place at the same time a big redistribution of property. Much land previously belonging to the Church was sold within a few years to private individuals. The consequent increase in the number of people owning land outright and growth in the average size of properties should, on the English analogy, have led to a period of great agricultural advance for France, but it did not. There was very slow progress and little consolidation of properties on the English pattern.

This suggests, rightly, that generalizations about the pace and uniformity of what was happening should be cautious and qualified. For all the enthusiasm Germans were showing for travelling exhibitions of agricultural machinery in the 1840s, theirs was a huge country and one of those (France was the other) of which a great economic historian commented that 'broadly speaking, no general and thoroughgoing improvement can be registered in peasant life before the railway age'. Yet the dismantling of medieval institutions standing in the way of agricultural improvement did go on steadily before that and prepared the way for it. It was accelerated in some places by the arrival of French armies and occupation during the Napoleonic period which introduced French law, and after this by other forces, so that by 1850 peasants tied to the soil and obligatory labour had disappeared from most of Europe. This did not mean, of course, that attitudes from the *ancien régime* did not linger after its institutions had disappeared. Prussian and Polish landlords seem, for good and ill, to have main-

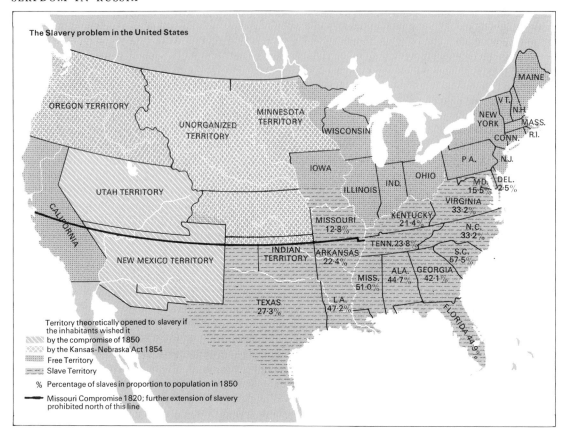

The Slavery problem in the United States

MAINE

OREGON TERRITORY

V.T.
N.H
NEW YORK
MASS.
R.I.
CONN.

MINNESOTA TERRITORY

WISCONSIN

UNORGANIZED TERRITORY

P.A.
N.J.

IOWA

OHIO
MD. 15·5%
DEL. 2·5%

INDIANA

ILLINOIS

VIRGINIA 33·2%

UTAH TERRITORY

CALIFORNIA

MISSOURI 12·8%

KENTUCKY 21·4%

N.C. 33·2%

TENN. 23·8%

INDIAN TERRITORY

ARKANSAS 22·4%

S.C. 57·5%

NEW MEXICO TERRITORY

ALA. 44·7%
GEORGIA 42·1%

MISS. 51·0%

TEXAS 27·3%

LA. 47·2%

FLORIDA 44·9%

Territory theoretically opened to slavery if the inhabitants wished it
by the compromise of 1850
by the Kansas-Nebraska Act 1854
Free Territory
Slave Territory
% Percentage of slaves in proportion to population in 1850
Missouri Compromise 1820; further extension of slavery prohibited north of this line

tained much of their more or less patriarchal authority in the manor even after its legal supports had vanished, and did so as late as 1914. This was important in assuring a continuity of conservative aristocratic values in a much more intense and concentrated way in these areas than in western Europe. The Junker accepted the implications of the market in planning his own estate management, but not in his relations with his tenants.

The longest resistance to change in traditional legal forms in agriculture came in Russia. There, serfdom itself persisted until abolished in 1861. This act did not at once bring Russian agriculture entirely under the operation of individualist and market economy principles, but with it an era of European history had closed. From the Urals to Corunna there no longer survived in law any substantial working land on the basis of obligatory labour services, nor were

peasants any longer bound to landlords whom they could not leave. It was the end of a system which had been passed from antiquity to western Christendom in the era of the barbarian invasions and had seen the basis of European civilization for centuries. Instead, after 1861, the rural proletariat everywhere worked for wages or keep; the pattern which had begun to spread in England and France with the fourteenth-century agricultural crisis had become universal.

Formally, the medieval usage of bond labour lasted longest in some of the American countries forming part of the European world. Obligatory labour in its most unqualified form, slavery, was legal in some of the United States, the most important of these countries, until the end of a great civil war in 1865. At that moment the abolition of slavery promulgated by the victorious government two years before became

New European cities across the seas began simply enough. Sydney in this early sketch appears as a scatter of buildings still interspersed with farms, but striving to preserve the styles familiar in the Old Europe.

effective throughout the whole territory of the republic. The great war which had made this possible had been in some measure a distraction from the already rapid agricultural development of the country, now to be resumed and to become of vital significance to Europe. Yet even before the war the very agricultural operation which had been the centre of debates over slavery, cotton-growing, had already indicated one way in which the New World was to supplement European agriculture on such a scale as to become almost indispensable. After the war the way was open for the supply to Europe not merely of products such as cotton, which she could not easily grow, but also of foods which she could herself provide in only slowly growing quantities.

The United States – and Canada, Australia and New Zealand, the Argentine and Uruguay – were soon to show they could provide food at much cheaper prices than Europe herself. Two things made this possible. One was the immense

729

In the nineteenth century the demands of American farming led to great advances in the production of agricultural machinery. One of the most spectacular was the mechanical reaper, which had evolved by the end of the century into the giant machines which made possible the farming of the vast cornlands of the prairies.

natural resources of these new lands. The American plains, the huge stretches of pasture in the South American pampas and the temperate regions of Australasia provided vast areas for the growing of grain and the raising of livestock. The second was a revolution in transport which made them exploitable for the first time. Steam-driven railways and ships came into service in increasing numbers from the 1860s. These quickly

Faster transport made the diffusion of perishable foodstuffs much easier.

brought down transport costs and did so all the faster as lower prices bred growing demand. Thus further profits were generated to be put into more capital investment on the ranges and prairies of the New World. On a smaller scale the same phenomenon was at work inside. Europe, too. From the 1870s the eastern European and German farmers began to see that they had a competitor in Russian grain, able to reach the growing cities much more cheaply when railways were built in Poland and western Russia and steamships could bring it from Black Sea ports.

Even in this elementary sketch the story of agricultural expansion bursts its banks; after first creating civilization and then setting a limit to its advance for thousands of years,

agriculture suddenly became its propellant; within a century or so it suddenly demonstrated that it could feed many more people than ever before. The demand of the growing cities, the coming of railways, the availability of capital, all point to its inseparable interconnexion with other sides of a growing trans-oceanic economy between 1750 and 1870. For all its chronological primacy and its huge importance as a generator of investment capital, the story of

Huge quantities of cargo – in this case, baled cotton – were carried by the Mississippi stern-wheelers. This example was built in 1884, when the commerce of the river-valley still depended heavily on its thousands of miles of navigable water.

The great London markets – Billingsgate, Smithfield and Covent Garden (shown here in a print of 1810) – had grown large enough to supply the needs of a city which in the early nineteenth century nevertheless still harboured thousands of cattle for its provisioning and relied upon large numbers of itinerant food-sellers. As the century progressed new markets were built as specialized buildings to handle a much larger volume of trade in conditions which reflected rising standards of hygiene.

agriculture in this period can only for convenience be separated from that of overall growth registered in the most obvious and spectacular way by the appearance of a whole new society, one based on the phenomenon of large-scale industrialization.

This is a colossal subject. It is not easy to see even just how big it is. It produced the most striking change in European history since the barbarian invasions, but it has been seen as even more important, as the biggest change in human history since the coming of agriculture, iron or the wheel. Within a fairly short time – a century and a half or so – it turned societies of peasants and craftsmen into societies of machine-tenders and book-keepers. Ironically, it ended the ancient primacy of agriculture from which it had sprung. It was one of the major facts turning human experience back from the differentiation produced by millennia of cultural evolution to common experiences which would tend once more to cultural convergence.

Even to define it is by no means easy, though the processes which lie at its heart are obvious around us. One of these is the replacement of human or animal labour by machines driven by power from mineral sources. Another is the organization of production in much larger units. Another is the increasing specialization of productive work. But all these things have implications and ramifications which quickly take us far beyond them. Although it embodied conscious decision, or, rather, countless conscious decisions by countless *entrepreneurs* and customers, industrialization was also a blind force sweeping across social life with transforming power, one of the 'senseless agencies' a philosopher once detected as half the story of revolutionary historical change. Industrialization meant new kinds of urbanization, new educational requirements, new patterns of social relationships.

Coalbrookdale, Shropshire, in 1758. Fifty years after the first smelting of iron with coke instead of charcoal, the appearance of this early industrial centre was still remarkably rural.

The origins of so complex a change are very deep. They go back, as so much in Europe does, well beyond the early modern period. The creation of capital for investment was made possible by agricultural and commercial changes occurring slowly over centuries. Even the technical changes which sometimes seem so dramatic have roots deep in the past. The men of the 'Industrial Revolution' (as a Frenchman of the early nineteenth century named the phenomenon which identified his epoch) stood on the shoulders of innumerable craftsmen and artificers of pre-industrial times who had built up the skills and experience on which later development rested. As early as the fourteenth century, for example, Rhinelanders learnt to make cast iron; by 1600 the gradual spread of blast furnaces had begun to remove the limits hitherto set to the use of iron by its high cost and in the eighteenth century came the inventions making it possible to use coal instead of wood as fuel for some things. Once cheap iron was available, even in what were by later standards small quantities, new ways of using it would be more freely experimented with and further changes would then follow. Growing demand for it gave new importance to areas where

ore was easily to be found. With the development of techniques of smelting which permitted the use of mineral rather than vegetable fuel, the location of supplies of both coal and iron then became a major factor in determining the later industrial geography of Europe and North America. In the northern hemisphere lies much of the discovered coal supply of the world, in a great belt running from the basin of the Don, through Silesia, the Ruhr, Lorraine, the north of England and Wales to Pennsylvania and West Virginia.

Better metal and richer fuel made their decisive contribution to early industrialization with the invention of a new source of energy, the steam engine. Again, the roots are very deep. That the power of steam could be used to produce movement was known in Hellenistic Alexandria. What was lacking was the technology to develop this knowledge and the economy to make it worth while to strain to do so. The eighteenth century brought a series of refine-

733

The Great Eastern, *with a displacement of 32,000 tons, was launched in 1858. Driven by both paddle-wheels and screw propellers, she was later used to lay the Atlantic telegraph cable.*

Travel to work was eased by the coming of railways. This picture of workmen about to leave for Enfield was taken at Liverpool Street station in 1884. It shows how quickly the camera added to the documentation of social history.

ments so important that they really deserve to be considered as fundamental changes. The result was a source of power rapidly recognized as a revolutionary force. The new steam-engines were not only the product of coal and iron, they also consumed them, directly both as fuel and as materials used in their own construction. Indirectly they stimulated production by making possible other processes which led to increased demand for them. The most obvious and spectacular was railway-building. It required huge quantities of first iron and then steel for rails and

rolling-stock. But it also made possible the movement of objects at much lower cost. What the new trains moved might well again be coal, or ore, thus allowing them to be used cheaply away from the areas in which they were easily found and dug. New industrial areas followed the lines, from which the railway could carry away goods to distant markets.

The railway was not the only means by which steam changed transport and communications. The first steamship to make a sea voyage did so in 1809. By 1870, though there were still many sailing-ships at sea and navies were still building battleships with a full spread of sail, regular ocean sailings by steamers were commonplace. The shrinking of space which they and, even more, the railways produced overturned men's ideas of the possible. Since the domestication of

Makers of the new age; the greatest of Victorian engineers, Isambard Kingdom Brunel, cigar in mouth, views his new ship, the Great Eastern. *A Portsmouth boy (educated for a time at a famous Parisian school, the* Lycée Henri IV*) he made his reputation as a bridge-builder and railway engineer and the English landscape is still studded with his achievements. He died when only 53, a few days after the* Great Eastern's *trial voyage began.*

An optimistic advertising artist of the 1880s indulged his imagination with this vision of the possibilities of global commerce.

COLUMBUS BUGGY CO.
STANDARD.
WORLD OVER.
COLUMBUS, OHIO, U.S.A.

735

[Jacquard Weaving Shed.—Akroyd's Worsted Factory.]

A new scale of industrial organization: the big iron looms of an English textile mill in the 1840s, centrally powered from one engine-house.

More and more rapidly a new industrial landscape spread across Europe in the nineteenth century. In spite of the cattle watering themselves in the foreground, this print of Silesian factories in the 1840s is already an age away from the Coalbrookdale of the 1750s.

the horse and the invention of the wheel, Man had been able to convey himself and his goods at speeds which certainly varied greatly according to the local roads available, but probably did so always within limits of one and five miles per hour over any considerable distance. Faster travel was possible on water and this had perhaps increased somewhat over the millennia in which ships underwent quite considerable modification. But all such change and improvement was dwarfed when in a man's lifetime he could witness the difference between travel on horseback and in a train capable of forty or even fifty miles an hour for long periods.

We have now lost one of the most pleasant of industrial sights, the long, streaming plume of steam from the funnel of a locomotive at speed, hanging for a few seconds behind it against a green landscape before it disappears. It greatly struck those who first saw it and so, less agreeably, did other visual aspects of the industrial transformation. One of the most terrifying was the industrial town, dominated by a factory with smoking chimneys, as the pre-industrial town had been by the spire of church or cathedral. So dramatic and novel was the factory, indeed, that it has often gone unremarked that it was an unusual expression of the early stages of industrialization, not a typical one. Even in the middle

of the nineteenth century the majority of English industrial workers were employed in manufacturing enterprises of less than fifty. For a long time it was only in textiles that great agglomerations of labour were to be found and the huge Lancashire cotton mills which first gave that area a visual and urban character distinct from earlier manufacturing towns were startling because unique. Yet by 1850 it was apparent that in more and more manufacturing processes the trend was towards the centralization under one roof made attractive by economies of transport, specialization of function, the use of more powerful machinery and the imposition of effective work discipline.

In the middle of the nineteenth century the changes of which these were the most striking had only created a mature industrial society in one country, Great Britain. Long and unconscious preparation lay behind this. Domestic peace and less rapacious government than on the continent had bred confidence for investment. Agriculture had provided its new surpluses first in England. Mineral supplies were plentiful for the new technological apparatus which began to be available after two or three generations of

736

remarkable invention in the eighteenth century. An expanding overseas commerce generated profits for investment and the basic machinery of finance and banking was already in being before industrialization needed to call on it. Finally, an increasing population provided both labour and a rising demand for manufactured goods. All these forces flowed together in a society receptive as were few others to innovation and change and the result was unprecedented industrial growth, first apparent as something totally new and irreversible in the second quarter of the nineteenth century. By 1870 Germany, France, Switzerland, Belgium and the United States had joined Great Britain in showing the capacity for self-sustained economic growth but she was still first among them both in the scale of her industrial plant and in her historic primacy. The inhabitants of 'the workshop of the world', as they liked to term Great Britain, were fond of running over the figures which showed how big a transformation of British wealth and power had already followed upon industrialization. In 1850, for example, the United Kingdom owned half the world's ocean-going ships and contained half the world's railway mileage. On those railways trains ran with a precision and regularity and even a speed not much improved upon for a hundred years after. They were regulated by 'time-tables' which were the first examples of their kind (and occasioned the first use of the word) and their operation relied on the electric telegraph. They were ridden in by men and women who had a few years before ridden in stage-coaches. In 1851, a year when a great international exhibition at London advertised her supremacy, Great Britain smelted two and a half million tons of iron. It does not sound much, but it was five times as much as the United States of America and ten times as much as Germany. At that moment, British steam engines could produce more than 1·2 million horsepower, more than half that of all Europe together.

By 1870 a change had started to appear in relative positions. Great Britain was still then in most ways in the lead, but less decisively. She

An ominous Prussian contribution by Messrs Krupp to the Paris exhibition of 1867.

still had more steam horsepower than any other European country, but the United States (which had already had more in 1850) was ahead of her and Germany was coming up fast. In the 1850s both Germany and France had made the important transition already made in Great Britain from smelting most of its iron by charcoal to smelting with mineral fuels. British superiority in manufacturing iron was still there and her pig-iron output had gone on rising, but now it was only three and a half times that of the United States and four times that of Germany. These were still huge superiorities, none the less, and the age of British industrial dominance had not yet begun to close.

The industrial countries of which Great Britain was the first were puny creatures in comparison with what they were to become. Among them only Great Britain and Belgium had a large majority of their population living in urban districts in the middle of the nineteenth century and the census of 1851 showed that agriculture was still the biggest single employer of labour among British industries (and was rivalled only by domestic service). But in these countries the growing numbers engaged in manufacturing industries, the rise of new concentrations of economic wealth and a new scale of urbanization all made very visible the process of change which was going forward.

The Second Empire in France showed justifiable pride in carrying out a vast reconstruction of the sewers and water supply of Paris, as a precaution against diseases which had ravaged past generations. So celebrated did the sewers become, that frequent visits were paid to them by tourists.

The Aldgate pump in 1874. Much less than a century ago, such pumps provided the only source of water for large areas of London.

This was especially true of the towns which grew at a spectacular rate in the nineteenth century, particularly in its second half, when the appearance of big centres that would be the nuclei of what a later age would call 'conurbations' was especially marked. There are difficulties in reckoning other indices of urbanization, largely because in different countries urban areas were defined in different ways, but this does not conceal the main lines of what was happening. London, Paris and Berlin in 1800 had, respectively, about 900 000, 600 000 and 170 000 inhabitants. In 1900 the corresponding figures were 4·7 million, 3·6 million and 2·7 million. In that year, too, Glasgow, Moscow, St Petersburg and Vienna also had more than a million inhabitants each. These were the giants; just behind them were sixteen more European cities with over 500 000, a figure only passed by London and Paris in 1800. These great cities and the smaller ones which were still immeasurably bigger than the old ones they overshadowed were recruited mainly by immigration from the countryside, though this went fastest and furthest in Great Britain and Germany. This reflected the tendency for urbanization to be most marked in the relatively few countries where industrialization first made headway, because it was the wealth and employment generated by industry which above all drew men to them. Of the twenty-three cities of more than 500 000, thirteen in all were in four countries, the United Kingdom (6), Germany (3), France (3) and Belgium (1).

Opinion about cities has undergone many changes. As the eighteenth century ended, something like a sentimental discovery of rural life was in full swing. This coincided with the first phase of industrialization and the nineteenth century opened with the tide of aesthetic and moral comment on the turn against a city life which was indeed about to reveal a new and often unpleasant face. That urbanization was seen as an unwelcome, even unhealthy, change by many people, was a tribute to the revolutionary force of what was going on.

A Russian working-class family at home in the corner which they rented in a large room in St Petersburg.

Conservatives distrusted and feared cities. Long after European governments had demonstrated the ease with which they could control urban unrest, the cities were regarded suspiciously as likely nests of revolution. This is hardly surprising; conditions in many of the new metropolitan centres were indeed often harsh and terrible for the poor. The East End of London could present appalling evidence of poverty, filth, disease and deprivation to anyone who chose to penetrate its slums. A young German businessman, Frederick Engels, wrote in 1844 one of the most influential books of the century in his study of *The Condition of the English Working-Class* which revealed the appalling conditions in which lived the poor of Manchester, but many other English writers were drawn to similar themes. In France the phenomenon of the 'dangerous classes', as the Parisian poor were called, preoccupied governments for the first half of the century, and poverty fired a succession of revolutionary outbreaks between 1789 and 1871. Clearly, it was not unreasonable to suppose that the conditions to be found in growing cities could breed resentment and hatred of the rulers of society and those who were its beneficiaries, and that this was a potentially revolutionary force.

It was also reasonable to predicate that the city made for ideological subversion. It was the great destroyer of traditional patterns of behaviour in nineteenth-century Europe and a crucible of new social forms and ideas, a huge and anonymous thicket in which men and women easily escaped the scrutiny of priest, squire and neighbours which had been the regulators of rural communities. In it (and this was especially true as literacy slowly spread downwards) new ideas were brought to bear upon long-unchallenged assumptions. The nineteenth century was particularly struck by what it believed to be the tendency of city life to atheism and irreligion. More was at stake in this, it was felt, than merely sound doctrine. Religion was the great sustainer of morals and the support of the established social order. A revolutionary writer sneered that religion was 'the opium of the people'; the possessing classes would hardly have put it in the same terms, but they acknowledged the importance of religion as social cement. One result was a long-continued series of attempts both in Catholic and Protestant countries to find a way of recapturing the towns for Christianity. The effort was misconceived in so far as it presumed that the Churches had ever had any footing in new urban areas which had long since swamped the traditional parish structures and religious institutions of the old towns and villages at their hearts. But it had a variety of expressions, from the building of new churches in industrial suburbs to the creation of missions combining evangelism and social service which taught churchmen the facts of modern city life. By the end of the century the religious-minded were at least well aware of the challenge they faced, even if their predecessors had not been. One great English evangelist used in the title of one of his books words precisely calculated to emphasize the parallel with missionary work in pagan lands overseas: *Darkest England*. His answer was to found a quite new instrument of religious propaganda, designed to appeal specifically to a new kind of population and to combat specifically the ills of urban society, the Salvation Army.

Here once more the revolution brought by industrialization has an impact far beyond material life. It is an immensely complicated problem to distinguish how modern civilization, the first of which we have knowledge which does not have some formal structure of religious belief at its heart, came into being. Perhaps we cannot separate the rôle of the city in breaking down traditional religious observance from, say, that of science and philosophy in corrupting the beliefs of the educated. Yet a new future was visible already in the English industrial population of 1870, in a large measure literate, alienated from traditional authority, secular-minded and beginning to be conscious of itself as an entity. This was a different basis for civilization from anything yet seen.

This is to anticipate, but legitimately, for it suggests once again how rapid and deep was the impact of industrialization on every side of life. Even the rhythm of life changed. For the whole of earlier history, most men's economic behaviour had been regulated fundamentally by the rhythms of nature. In an agricultural or pastoral economy they imposed a pattern on the year which dictated both the kind of work which had to be undertaken and the kind which could be. Operating within the framework set by the seasons were the subordinate divisions of light and darkness, fair weather and foul. Men lived in great intimacy with their tools, their animals and the fields in which they won their bread. Even the relatively few townsmen lived, in large measure, lives shaped by these pacemakers; in Great Britain and France a bad harvest could still blight the whole economy even after 1850. Yet by then many people were living lives whose rhythms were dictated by quite different pacemakers. Above all they were set by the means of production and their demands – by the need to keep machines economically employed, by the cheapness or dearness of investment capital, by the availability of labour. The symbol of this was the factory whose machinery set a pattern of work in which accurate time-keeping was essential. Men began to think in a quite new way about time as a consequence of their industrial work.

At the same time as imposing new rhythms, industrialism also related the labourer to his work in new ways. It is difficult, but important,

to avoid sentimentalizing the past in assessing this. At first sight the disenchantment of the factory worker with his monotonous routine, with its exclusion of personal involvement and its background of the sense of working for another's profit justifies the rhetoric it has inspired, whether this takes the form of regret for a craftsman's world that has vanished or analysis of what has been identified as the alienation of the worker from his product. But the life of the medieval peasant was monotonous, too, and much of it was spent working for another's profit. Nor is an iron routine necessarily less painful because it is set by sunset and sunrise instead of an employer. Yet the new disciplines involved a revolutionary transformation of the ways men won their livelihood, however we may evaluate the results by comparison with what had gone before.

A clear example can be found in what soon became notorious as one of the persistent evils of early industrialism, its abuse of child labour. A generation of Englishmen braced morally by the abolition of slavery and by the exaltation that accompanied it was also one which was intensely aware of the importance of religious training – and therefore of anything which might stand between it and the young – and one disposed to be sentimental about children in a way earlier generations had not been. All this helped to create an awareness of this problem which perhaps distracted attention from the fact that the brutal exploitation of children in factories was only one part of a total transformation of patterns of employment. About the use of children's labour in itself there was nothing new. Children had for centuries provided swineherds, birdscarers, gleaners, maids-of-all-work, crossing-sweepers, prostitutes and casual drudges in Europe (and still do in most non-European societies). The terrible picture of the lot of unprotected children in Hugo's great novel *Les Misérables* (1862) is a picture of their life in a *pre*-industrial society. The difference made by industrialism was that their exploitation was regularized and given a quite new harshness by the institutional forms of the

As in the Europe they and their parents had left, children were exploited for their cheap labour in the rapidly growing industrial economy of the United States. Nevertheless, to judge by photographs such as this one of youngsters employed sorting coal, they were better fed and clad than their European counterparts.

factory. Whereas the work of children in an agricultural society had perforce been clearly differentiated from that of adults by their inferior strength, there existed in the tending of machines a whole range of activity in which children's labour competed directly with that of adults. In a labour market normally over-supplied, this meant that there were irresistible pressures upon the parent to send the child into the factory to earn a contribution to the family income as soon as possible, sometimes at the age of five or six. The consequences were not only often terrible for the victims, but also revolutionary in that the relation of child to society and the structure of the family were trans-

formed. This was one of the 'senseless agencies' of history at its most dreadful.

The problems created by such forces were too pressing to remain without attention and men quickly made a start in taming the most obvious evils of industrialism. By 1850, the law of England had already begun to intervene to protect, for example, women and children in mines and factories; in all the millennia of the history of agriculturally based economies, it had still been impossible by that date to eradicate slavery in the Atlantic world. Given the unprecedented scale and speed with which social transformation was upon them, the men of early industrial Europe need not be blamed without qualification for not acting more quickly to remedy ills whose outlines they could only dimly grasp. Even in the early stage of English industrialism, when, perhaps, the social cost was most heavy, it was difficult for men to cast off their belief that the liberation of the economy from legal interference was the

741

Before and after: one of the first agencies to use photography for systematic social record was the Victorian charity founded by Dr Barnardo, a philanthropist who devoted himself to the rescue and education of abandoned, orphaned and destitute children. Children were photographed at admission and at the completion of their education or apprenticeship.

main explanation of the enormous generation of new wealth they saw about them.

True, it is almost impossible to find economic theorists and publicists of the early industrial period who advocated absolute non-interference with the economy. Yet there was a broad, sustaining current which favoured the view that much good would result if the market economy was left to operate without the help or hindrance of politicians and civil servants. One force working this way was the teaching often summed up in a phrase made famous by a group of Frenchmen: *laissez-faire*. Broadly speaking, economists after Adam Smith had said with growing consensus that the production

of wealth would be accelerated, and therefore the general well-being would increase, if the use of economic resources followed the 'natural' demands of the market. Another reinforcing trend was individualism, embodied in both the assumption that individuals knew their own business best and the increasing organization of society around the rights and interests of individuals.

These were the sources of the long-enduring association between industrialism and liberalism; they were deplored by conservatives who regretted a hierarchical, agricultural order of mutual obligations and duties, settled ideas, and religious values. Yet liberals who welcomed the new age were by no means taking their stand on a simply negative and selfish base. The creed of 'Manchester', as it was called because of the symbolic importance of cotton-spinning in English industrial and commercial development, was for its leaders much more than a matter of mere self-enrichment. A great political battle which for years preoccupied Englishmen in the early nineteenth century made this clear. Its focus was a campaign for the repeal of what were called the 'Corn Laws', a tariff system originally imposed to provide protection for the British farmer from imports of cheaper foreign grain. The 'repealers', whose ideological and political leader was a businessman, Richard Cobden, argued that much was at stake. To begin with, retention of the duties on grain demonstrated the grip upon the legislative machinery of the agricultural interest, the traditional ruling class, who ought not to be allowed a monopoly of power. Opposed to it were the dynamic forces of the future which sought to liberate the national economy from such distortions in the interest of particular groups. Back came the reply of the anti-repealers: the manufacturers were themselves a particular interest who only wanted cheap food imports in order to be able to pay lower wages; if they wanted to help the poor, what about some regulation of the conditions under which they employed women and children in factories? There, the inhumanity of the produc-

743

tion process showed a callous disregard for the obligations of privilege which would never have been tolerated in rural England. To this, the repealers responded that cheap food would mean cheaper goods for export. And in this, for

From the inside of 'the Free-Trade hat', a graphic representation of the creed of Free Trade which for some Victorians came to be revered almost as much as the teachings of Holy Scripture themselves.

744

someone like Cobden, much more than profit was involved. Only a worldwide expansion of Free Trade untrammelled by the interference of mercantilist governments would lead to international progress both material and spiritual, he thought; trade brought peoples together, exchanged and multiplied the blessings of civilization and increased the power in each country of its progressive forces. On one occasion he even committed himself to the view that Free Trade was the expression of the Divine Will.

There was much more to the Free Trade issue (of which the Corn Law debate was the focus) than a brief summary can resume. The more it is expounded, the more it becomes clear that industrialism involved a creative, positive ideology which implied intellectual, social and political challenge to the past. This is why it should not be the subject of simple moral judgements, though both conservatives and liberals thought it could be at the time. The same man might resist legislation to protect the workman against long hours while proving himself a model employer, actively supporting educational and political reform and fighting the corruption of public interest by privileged birth. His opponent might struggle to protect children working in factories and act as a model squire, a benevolent patriarch to his tenants, while bitterly resisting the extension of the franchise to those not members of the established Church or any reduction of the political influence of landlords. It was all very muddled. In the specific issue of the Corn Laws the outcome was paradoxical, too, for a conservative Prime Minister was in the end convinced by the arguments of the repealers. When he had the opportunity to do so without too obvious an inconsistency he persuaded parliament to make the change in 1846. His party contained men who never forgave him and this great climax of Sir Robert Peel's political career, for which he was to be honoured by his liberal opponents, came shortly before he was dismissed from power by his own followers.

Only in England was the issue fought out so explicitly and to so clear-cut a conclusion. In other countries, paradoxically, the protectionists soon turned out to have the best of it. Only in the middle of the century, a period of expansion and prosperity, especially for the British economy, did Free Trade ideas get much support outside the United Kingdom, whose prosperity was regarded by believers as evidence of the correctness of Free Trade views and even mollified their opponents; Free Trade became a British political dogma, untouchable until well into the twentieth century. The prestige of British economic leadership helped to give it a brief popularity elsewhere, too. The prosperity of the era owed as much to other influences as to this ideological triumph, but the belief added to the optimism of economic liberals. Their creed was the culmination of the progressive view of Man's potential as an individual whose roots lay in Enlightenment ideas.

The solid grounds for this optimism can nowadays be too easily overlooked. In assessing the impact of industrialism we labour under the handicap of not having before us the squalor of the past it left behind. For all the poverty and the slums (and the worst was over by then), the people who lived in the great cities of 1900 consumed more and lived longer than their ancestors. This did not, of course, mean they were either tolerably off, by later standards, or contented. But they were often, and probably for the most part, materially better off than their predecessors or most of their contemporaries in the non-European world. Amazing as it may seem, they were part of the privileged minority of mankind. Their longer lives were the best evidence of it.

2 Political change in an age of revolution

In the eighteenth century the word 'revolution' came to have a new meaning. Traditionally it meant only a change in the composition of government and not necessarily a violent one (though one reason why the English 'Glorious Revolution' of 1688 was thought glorious was that it had been non-violent, Englishmen learnt to believe). Men could speak of a 'revolution' occurring at a particular court when one minister replaced another. After 1789 this changed. Men came to see that year as the beginning of a new sort of revolution, characterized by violence, by limitless possibilities for fundamental change, social, political and economic, and began to think, too, that this new phenomenon might transcend national boun-

Violence, above all, was what the French Revolution came to mean to those who feared it. At first sight this is odd; there was no lack of violence before 1789 and it was a familiar fact of life. But the French Revolution gave a new shape and menace to the old fear of the mob, now channelled by men for socially transforming ends. Many revolutionaries endorsed this emphasis on violence. The great 'days' – journées – of the Revolution were celebrated in popular rhetoric and images like this picture. It purports to show the attack on the royal palace of the Tuileries on 10 August 1792 which was the turning point of the Revolution. The king was immediately suspended from the exercise of his functions by a frightened legislature; soon afterwards France was declared a Republic.

daries and have something universal and general about it. Men who disagreed very much about the desirability of such a revolution could none the less agree that this new sort of revolution existed and that it was fundamental to the politics of their age.

It would be misleading to seek to group all the political changes of this period under the rubric of 'revolution' conceived in such terms as these. But it remains a useful characterization of the period for two reasons. One is that there were indeed within a century or so many more changes which could be called revolutions in this extreme sense than hitherto, even though many of them failed and others brought results far different from those they had led people to expect. In the second place, if we give the term a little more elasticity, and allow it to cover examples of greatly accelerated and fundamental political change which certainly go beyond the replacement of one set of governors by another, then there are many less dramatic political changes in these years which are distinctly revolutionary. The first and most obvious was the dissolution of the first British empire, whose central episode later became known as the American Revolution.

In 1763 British imperial power in North America was at its height. Canada had been taken from the French; the old fear of a Mississippi valley cordon of French forts enclosing the thirteen colonies had been blown away. This might seem to dispose of any grounds for future misgiving, yet some prophets had already suggested, even before the French defeat, that their

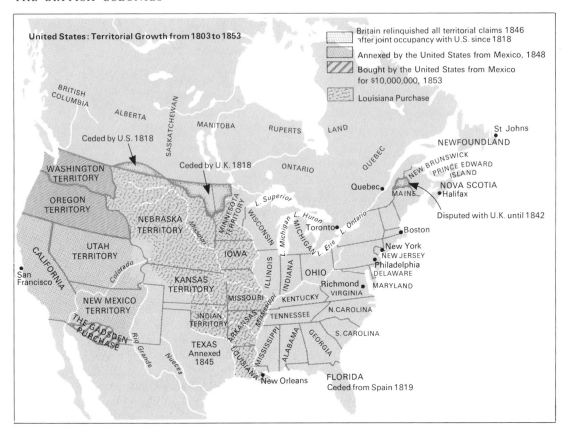

United States: Territorial Growth from 1803 to 1853

Britain relinquished all territorial claims 1846
after joint occupancy with U.S. since 1818

Annexed by the United States from Mexico, 1848

Bought by the United States from Mexico
for $10,000,000, 1853

Louisiana Purchase

removal might not strengthen but weaken the British grasp in North America. In the British colonies, after all, there were already colonists in larger numbers than the population of many sovereign states of Europe. Many were not of English descent or native English-speakers. They had economic interests not necessarily congruent with those of the imperial power, yet the grip of the British government on them was bound to be slack, simply because of the huge distances which separated London from the colonies. Once the threat from the French (and from the Indians whom the French had egged on) was gone, the ties of empire might have to be allowed to grow slacker still.

Difficulties appeared almost at once in the wake of the French expulsion. How was the West to be organized? What relation was it to have to the existing colonies? How were the new Canadian subjects of the Crown to be treated?

American colonists in the middle of the eighteenth century were already politically highly conscious; their political education went on apace under the impact of radical propaganda which sometimes took curious forms.

748

These problems were given urgency by 'Pontiac's rebellion', an Indian revolt in the Ohio valley in 1763 in response to pressure by the colonists who saw the West as their proper domain for settlement and trade. The imperial government immediately proclaimed the area west of the Alleghenies closed to settlement. This, as a start, offended many colonials who had looked forward to the exploitation of these regions, and it was followed by still more irritation as British administrators negotiated treaties with Indians and worked out arrangements for a garrisoned frontier to protect the colonists and Indians from one another.

This was the beginning of ten years during which the dormant potential for American independence matured and came to a head. Grumbles about grievances turned first into resistance, then rebellion. Time after time, provocative British legislation was used by colonial politicians to radicalize American politics by making the colonists believe that the practical liberty they already enjoyed was in danger. The pace throughout was set by British initiatives. Paradoxically, Great Britain was ruled at this time by a succession of ministers anxious to carry out reforms in colonial affairs; their excellent intentions helped to destroy a *status quo* which had previously proved workable. They thus provide one of the first examples of what was to be a frequent phenomenon of the next few decades, the goading of vested interests into rebellion by well-meant but politically ill-judged reform.

One principle firmly grasped in London was that the Americans ought to pay a proper share of the taxes which contributed to their defence and the common good of the empire. There were two distinct attempts to assure this. The first, in 1764–5, took the form of imposing duties on sugar imported to the colonies and a Stamp Act which was to raise money from revenue stamps to be put on various classes of legal documents. The important thing about these was not the amounts they proposed to raise, nor even the novelty of taxing the internal transactions of the colonies (which was much

discussed) but rather that these were, as both English politicians and American taxpayers clearly saw, unilateral acts of legislation by the imperial parliament. The usual way in which colonial affairs were handled and revenue raised hitherto had been by haggling with their own assemblies. What was now brought into question was something so far hardly even formulated as a question: whether the undoubted legislative sovereignty of the parliament of the United Kingdom also extended to its colonies. Riots, non-importation agreements and angry protest followed. The unhappy officials who held the stamps were given a bad time. Ominously, representatives of nine colonies attended a Stamp Act Congress to protest. The Stamp Act was withdrawn.

The London government then took a different tack in its second fiscal initiative. It turned to external duties on paint, paper, glass and tea. As there were not internal taxes and the imperial government had always regulated trade, they seemed more promising. But it proved an illusion. Americans were by now being told by their radical politicians that no taxation at all should be levied on them by a legislature in which they were not represented. As George III clearly saw, it was not the Crown but parliament whose power was under attack. There were more riots and boycotts and one of the first of those influential scuffles which make up so much of the history of decolonization, when the death of possibly five rioters in 1770 was mythologized into a 'Boston Massacre'.

Once more, the British government retreated. Three of the duties were withdrawn: that on tea remained. Unfortunately, the issue was by now out of hand; it transcended taxation, as the British government saw, and had become one of whether or not the imperial parliament could make laws enforceable in the colonies. As George III put it a little later: 'We must either master them, or totally leave them to themselves.' The issue was focussed in one place, though it manifested itself throughout the colonies. By 1773, after the destruction of a cargo of tea by radicals (the 'Boston Tea Party'), the crucial question for the British government was: could Massachusetts be governed?

There were to be no more retreats: George III, his ministers and the majority of the House of Commons were agreed on this. A number of coercive acts were passed to bring Boston to heel. The New England radicals were heard all the more sympathetically in the other colonies at this juncture because a measure of 1774, providing for the future of Canada, the Quebec Act, stirred up wide feeling. Some disliked the privileged position it gave to Roman Catholicism (it was a sensible, humane measure, intended to leave French Canadians as undisturbed as possible in their ways by their change of rulers), while others saw its extension of Canadian boundaries south to the Ohio as another block to expansion in the west. In September the same year there met a Continental Congress of delegates from the colonies at Philadelphia. It severed commercial relations with the United Kingdom and demanded the repeal of much existing legislation, including the Quebec Act. By this time the recourse to force was probably inevitable. The radical colonial politicians had brought out into the open the practical sense of independence already felt by many Americans. But it was inconceivable that any eighteenth-century imperial government could have grasped this. The British government was in fact remarkably reluctant to act on its convictions by relying simply on force until disorder and intimidation of the law-abiding and moderate colonials had already gone very far. At the same time, they made it clear that they would not willingly bend on the principles of sovereignty.

Arms were gathered in Massachusetts. In April 1775 a detachment of British soldiers sent to Lexington to seize some of them fought the first action of the American Revolution. It was not quite the end of the beginning. It took a year more for the feelings of the colonists' leaders to harden into the conviction that only complete independence from Great Britain would rally an effective resistance. The result was the Declaration of Independence of July 1776 and the debate was transferred to the battlefield.

The famous Boston Massacre, a godsend to radical propagandists though the soldiers who were subsequently tried by a local court were acquitted of the charge of murder.

The British lost the war which followed because of the difficulties imposed by geography, because American generalship succeeded in avoiding superior forces long enough to preserve an army which could impose its will on the British at Saratoga in 1777, because the French entered the war soon afterwards to win a return match for the defeat of 1763, and because the Spanish followed them and thus tipped the balance of naval power against Great Britain. The British had a further handicap; they dared not fight the kind of war which might win military victory, by terrorizing the American population and thus encouraging those who wished to remain under the British flag to cut the supplies and freedom of movement which General Washington's army enjoyed. They could not do this because their overriding aim had to be to keep open the way to a conciliatory peace with colonists willing again to accept British rule. In these circumstances, the Bourbon coalition was fatal. The military decision came in 1781, when a British army found itself

France enters the war: an allegorical print shows Louis XVI offering to the Americans a charter entitled 'Libertas', at his feet lies the yoke of oppression and the manacles of slavery.

trapped at Yorktown between the Americans on land and a French squadron at sea. Only seven thousand or so men were involved, but their surrender was the worst humiliation yet undergone by British arms and the end of an era of imperial rule. Peace negotiations soon began and two years later, at Paris, a treaty was signed in which Great Britain recognized the independence of the United States of America, whose territory the British negotiators had already conceded should run to the Mississippi. This was a crucial decision in the shaping of a new nation; the French, who had envisaged making a recovery in the Mississippi valley were disappointed. The northern continent was to be shared by the rebels only with Spain and Great Britain, it appeared.

For all the loose ends which would need to be tied up in boundary disputes for decades to come, the appearance of a new state of great potential resources in the western hemisphere was by any standard certainly a revolutionary change. If it was at first often seen as something

less than this by foreign observers, that was because the weaknesses of the new nation were at the time more apparent than its potential. Indeed, it was far from clear that it was a nation at all; the colonies were weak and divided and many expected them to fall to quarrelling and disunion. Their great and inestimable advantage was their remoteness. They could work out their problems virtually untroubled by foreign intervention, a blessing crucial to much that was to follow.

Victory in war was followed by a half-dozen critical years during which a handful of American politicians took decisions shaping much of the future history of the world. As in all civil wars and wars of independence, deep divisions had been created which accentuated political weakness. Among these, those which divided loyalist from rebels were, for all their bitterness, perhaps the least important. That problem had been solved, brutally, by emigration of the defeated; something like 80 000 loyalists left the rebel colonies, for a variety of motives running from dislike of intimidation and terror to simple loyalty to the Crown. Other divisions were likely to cause more trouble in the future. Class and economic interests separated farmers, merchants and plantation-owners. There were differences between the former colonies as units and between regions or sections of the country; one of these, that imposed by the economic importance of black slavery to the southern states, was to take decades to work out. On the other hand, the Americans also had great advantages as they began the process of nation-building. They faced the future without the terrible incubus of a huge illiterate and backward peasant population such as stood in the way of evolving a democratic system in many other countries. They had ample territory and great economic resources even in their existing areas of occupation (though the extent of these could not yet be known). Finally, they had European civilization to draw upon, subject only to the modifications its legacies might undergo in transplantation to a virgin – or near-virgin – continent.

The war against the British had imposed a certain discipline. Articles of Confederation had been agreed between the former colonies and came into force in 1781. In them appeared the name of the new nation, the United States of America. The peace brought a growing sense that these arrangements were unsatisfactory. There were two areas of particular concern. One was disturbance arising fundamentally from disagreement about what the Revolution ought to have meant in domestic affairs. The central government came to many Americans to appear to be far too weak to deal with disaffection and disorder. The other arose from a post-war economic depression, particularly affecting external trade and linked to currency problems arising from the independence of individual states (as the former colonies had come to call themselves). To deal with these, too, the central government seemed ill-equipped. It was accused of neglecting American economic interests in its conduct of relations with other countries. Whether true or not, this was widely believed. The outcome was a meeting of delegates from the states in a constitutional convention at Philadelphia in 1787. After four months' work they signed a draft constitution which was then submitted to the individual states for ratification. When nine states had ratified it the constitution came into effect in the summer of 1788. In April 1789 George Washington, the former commander of the American forces in the war against the British, took the oath of office as the first president of the new republic, thus inaugurating a series of presidencies which has continued unbroken to this day.

Much was said about the need for simple institutions and principles clear in their intention, yet the new constitution was still to be revealing its potential for development a hundred and fifty years later. For all the determination of its drafters to provide a document which would unambiguously resist reinterpretation, they were (fortunately) unsuccessful. The United States constitution was to prove capable of spanning a historical epoch which separated a scatter of largely agricultural societies from a

The American commander, George Washington, in 1777. In him, his countrymen found an outstanding leader for the opening years of the war when defeat seemed very near. Later they found in him a father-figure for a young nation.

giant and industrial world power. In part this was because of the provision for conscious amendment, but in larger measure it was due to the evolving interpretation of the doctrines it embodied. But also much remained unchanged; though often formal, these features of the constitution are very important. Besides them, too, there were fundamental principles which were to endure, even if there was much argument about what they might mean.

To begin with its most obvious feature: the constitution was republican. This was by no means normal in the eighteenth century and should not be taken for granted. Some Americans felt that republicanism was so important and so insecure that they even disapproved of the constitution because they thought it (and particularly its installation of a president as the head of the executive) 'squinted towards monarchy', as one of them put it. The ancient republics were as familiar to classically educated Europeans for their tendency to decay and faction as for their legendarily admirable morals. The history of the Italian republics was unpromising, too, and much more unedifying than that of Athens and Rome. Republics in eighteenth-century Europe were few and apparently unflourishing. They seemed to persist only in small states, though it was conceded that the remoteness of the United States might protect republican forms which would elsewhere ensure the collapse of a large state. Still, observers were not sanguine about the new nation. The later success of the United States was therefore to be of incalculable importance in reversing opinion about republicanism. Very soon, its capacity to survive, its cheapness and a liberalism wrongly thought to be inseparable from it focussed the attention of critics of traditional governments all over the civilized world. European advocates of political change soon began to look to America for inspiration; soon, too, the influence of republican example was to spread from the northern to the southern American continent.

The second characteristic of the new constitution which was of fundamental importance was that its roots lay largely in British political experience. Besides the law of England, whose Common Law principles passed into the jurisprudence of the new state, this was true also of the actual arrangement of government. The founding fathers had all grown up in the British colonial system in which elected assemblies had debated the public interest with monarchical governors. They instituted a bicameral legislature (although they excluded any hereditary element in its composition) on the English model, to offset a president. They thus followed English constitutional theory in putting a monarch, albeit an elected one, at the head of the executive machinery of government. This was not how the British constitution of the eighteenth century actually worked, but it was a good approximation to its theory. What they did, in fact, was to take the best constitution they knew, purge it of its corruptions (as they saw them) and add to it the modifications appropriate to

American political and social circumstance. What they did not do was to emulate the alternative principle of government available in contemporary Europe, monarchical absolutism, even in its enlightened form. The Americans wrote a constitution for free men because they believed that the British already lived under one. They thought it had failed only in so far as it had been improperly employed to deprive Americans of the rights they too ought to have possessed under it. Because of this, the same principles of government (albeit in much evolved forms) would one day be propagated and patronized in areas which shared none of the cultural assumptions of the Anglo-Saxon world on which they rested.

One way in which the United States differed radically from most other existing states and diverged consciously from the British constitutional model was in adherence to the principle of federalism. This was indeed fundamental to it, since only large concessions to the independence of individual states made it possible for the new union to come into existence at all. The former colonies had no wish to set up a new central government which would bully them as they believed the government of King George had done. The federal structure provided an answer to the problem of diversity – *e pluribus unum*. It also dictated much of the form and content of American politics for the next eighty years. Question after question whose substance was economic or social or ideological would find itself pressed into the channels of a continuing debate about what were the proper relations of the central government and the individual states. It was a debate which would in the end come within an ace of destroying the Union. Federalism would also promote a major readjustment within the constitution, the rise of the Supreme Court as an instrument of judicial review. Outside the Union, the nineteenth century would reveal the appeal of federalism to many other countries, impressed by what it appeared to have achieved within it. It was to be seen by European liberals as a crucial device for reconciling unity with freedom and British governments found it a great standby in their handling of colonial problems.

Finally, in any summary however brief of the historic significance of the constitution of the United States, attention must be given to its opening words: 'We the People' (even though they seem to have been included almost casually). The actual political arrangements in several of the states of 1789 were by no means democratic, but the principle of popular sovereignty was enunciated clearly from the start. In whatever form the mythology of a particular historical epoch might cloak it, the popular will was to remain the ultimate court of appeal in politics for Americans. Here was a fundamental departure from British constitutional practice, and it owed something to the way in which seventeenth-century colonists had sometimes given themselves constitutions. Yet this had been within the overall framework of kingship. British constitutionalism was prescriptive; the sovereignty of king in parliament was not there because the people had once decided it should be, but because it was there and was unquestioned. As Maitland, the great English constitutional historian once put it, Englishmen had taken the authority of the Crown as a substitute for the theory of the state. The new constitution broke with this and with every other prescriptive theory (though this was not quite a clean break with British political thinking, for Locke had said in the 1680s that governments held their powers on trust and that the people could upset governments which abused that trust and on this ground, among others, some Englishmen had justified the Glorious Revolution).

The American adoption of a democratic theory that all governments derive their just powers from the consent of the governed, as it had been put as early as the Declaration of Independence, was epoch-marking. But it by no means solved the problems of political authority at a stroke. Many Americans feared what a democracy might do and sought to restrict the popular element in the political system right from the start. Another problem was suggested by the fundamental rights set out in the first ten

amendments to the constitution at the end of 1789. These were presumably as much subject to reamendment at the hands of popular sovereignty as any other part of the constitution. Here was an important source of disagreement for the future: Americans have always found it easy to be somewhat confused (especially in the affairs of other countries but even in their own at times) about whether democratic principles consist in following the wishes of the majority, or in upholding certain fundamental rights. Nevertheless, the adoption of the democratic principle in 1787 was immensely important and justifies the consideration of the constitution as a landmark in world history. For generations to come the new United States would become the focus of the aspirations of men longing to be free the world over – 'the world's last, best hope', as one American said. Even today, when America has become a great conservative power, the democratic ideal of which for so long it was the custodian and exemplar retains its power in many countries, and the institutions it fertilized are still working.

Paris was the centre of social and political discussion in Europe. To it returned some of the French soldiers who had helped to bring to birth the young American Republic. It is hardly surprising, then, that although most European nations in some measure responded to the transatlantic revolution, Frenchmen were especially aware of it. American example, and the hopes it raised, were a contribution, though a subsidiary one, to the huge release of forces which is still, in spite of later upheavals, called *the* French Revolution. Unfortunately, this all too familiar and simple term puts obstacles in the way of understanding. Politicians and scholars have offered many different interpretations of what the essence of the Revolution was, have disagreed about how long it went on and what were its results, and even about when it began. They agree about little except that it was very important. In fact, it changed the whole concept of revolution, though there was much in it that looked to the past rather than the future. In the great boiling-over of the pot of French society which occurred at the end of the eighteenth century there was the same sort of jumbled mixture of conservative and innovating elements which there had been in the 1640s in England, and much the same mixture of consciousness and unconsciousness of direction and purposes, too.

This confusion was the symptom of big dislocations and maladjustments in the material life and government of France. She was the greatest of European powers and her rulers neither could nor wished to relinquish her international rôle. The first way in which the American Revolution had affected her was by providing an opportunity for revenge; Yorktown was the retaliation for defeat at the hands of the British in the Seven Years' War, and to deprive them of the Thirteen Colonies was some compensation for the French loss of India and Canada. Yet the successful effort was costly. The second great consequence was that for no considerable gain beyond the humiliation of a rival, France added yet another layer to the huge and accumulating debt piled up by her efforts since the 1630s to build and maintain her European supremacy.

Attempts to liquidate this debt and cut the monarchy free from the cramping burden it imposed (and it was becoming clear after 1783 that France's real independence in foreign affairs was narrowing sharply because of it) were made by a succession of ministers under Louis XVI, the young, somewhat stupid, but high-principled and well-meaning king who came to the throne in 1774. None of them succeeded in even arresting the growth of the debt, let alone in reducing it. There were complicated reasons for this, but their essential characteristic was that the whole social and political structure of France stood in the way of tapping the wealth of the better-off, the only sure way of emerging from the financial *impasse*. Ever since the days of Louis XIV himself, it had proved impossible to levy a due weight of taxation on the wealthy without resorting to force, for the whole legal and social structure of France, its privileges, special immunities and prescriptive rights, blocked the way ahead. The paradox of eight-eenth-century government could be seen at its most evident in France; a theoretically absolute monarchy could not infringe the mass of liberties and rights which made up the essentially medieval constitution of the country without threatening its own foundations. Monarchy itself rested on prescription.

To more and more Frenchmen it appeared that France needed a transformation of her governmental and constitutional structure if she was to emerge from her difficulties. But some went further. They saw in the inability of government to share fiscal burdens equitably between classes the extreme example of a whole range of abuses which needed reform. The issue was more and more exaggerated in terms of polarities: of reason and superstition, of freedom and slavery, of humanitarianism and greed. Above all, it tended to concentrate on the symbolic question of legal privilege. The class which focussed the anger this aroused was the nobility, an immensely diverse and very large body (there seem to have been between 200 000 and 250 000 noble males in France in 1789) about which cultural, economic or social generalization is impossible, but whose members all shared the common characteristic of a legal status which in some degree conferred privilege at law.

While the logic of their financial extremity pushed the governments of France more and more towards conflict with the privileged, there was a natural unwillingness on the part of many of the royal advisers, themselves usually noblemen, and of the king himself to proceed except by agreement. When in 1788 a series of failures nerved the government to accept that conflict was inevitable, it still sought to confine the conflict to legal channels, by summoning the nearest thing to a national representative body that France had ever possessed, the Estates General. This body of representatives of nobles, clergy and commoners, had not met since 1614. It was hoped that it would provide sufficient moral authority to squeeze agreement from the fiscally privileged for the payment of higher taxes. It was an unimpeachably consti-

The ancient Estates General of France meets under the presidency of its king in May 1789 at Versailles.

tutional step, but had as a solution the disadvantage that great expectations were aroused while what the Estates General could legally do was obscure. More than one answer was given and some of them said that it could legislate for the nation, even if historic and undoubted legal privileges were at issue.

This very complicated political crisis was coming to a head at the end of a period in which France was also under other strains. Underlying everything was an increasing population. Since the second quarter of the century this had risen at what a later age would think a slow rate, but still fast enough to outstrip growth in the production of food. This sustained a long-run inflation of food prices which bore most painfully upon the poor, the vast majority of Frenchmen who were peasants with little or no land. Given the coincidence of the fiscal demands of governments – which for a long time staved off the financial crisis by putting up the direct and

indirect taxes which fell most heavily on the poor – and the efforts of landlords to protect themselves in inflationary times by holding down wages and putting up rents and dues, the life of the poor Frenchman was growing harsher and more miserable for nearly all the century. To this general impoverishment should be added the special troubles which from time to time afflicted particular regions or classes, but which, coincidentally, underwent something of an intensification in the second half of the 1780s. Bad harvests, cattle disease and a recession which badly affected the areas where peasants' families produced textiles as a supplement to their income all sapped the precarious health of the economy in the 1780s. The sum effect was that the elections to the Estates General in 1789 took place in a very excited and embittered atmosphere. Millions of Frenchmen were desperately seeking some way out of their troubles, were eager to seek and blame scapegoats, and had quite unrealistic and inflated notions of what the good king, whom they trusted, could do for them.

Thus a complex interplay of governmental impotence, social injustice, economic hardship and reforming aspiration brought about the French Revolution. But before this complexity is lost to sight in the subsequent political battles and the simplifying slogans they generated, it is important to emphasize that almost no one either anticipated this result or desired it. There was much social injustice in France, but no more than many other eighteenth-century states found it easy to live with. There was a welter of expectant and hopeful advocates of particular reforms ranging from the abolition of the censorship to the prohibition of immoral and irreligious literature, but no one doubted that such changes could easily be carried out by the king, once he was informed of his people's wishes and needs. What did not exist was a party of revolution clearly confronting a party of reaction.

These only came into existence when the Estates General had met. This is one reason why the day on which they did so, 5 May 1789 (a week after George Washington's inauguration), is a date in world history, because it opened an era in which to be for or against the Revolution became the central political question in most continental countries, and even tainted the very different politics of Great Britain and the United States. What happened in France was bound to matter elsewhere. At the simplest level the internal affairs of the greatest European power affected her international conduct; the Estates General would either paralyse her (as many foreign diplomats hoped) or liberate her from her difficulties to play again a forceful rôle. Beyond this, France was also the cultural leader of Europe. What her writers and politicians said and did was immediately accessible to people elsewhere because of the universality of the French language, and it was bound to be given respectful attention because people were in the habit of looking to Paris for intellectual guidance.

In the summer of 1789 the Estates General turned itself into a national assembly claiming sovereignty. Breaking with the assumption that

The fourteenth of July remains the most important of French national holidays; on that day in 1789 the Paris mob, reinforced by discontented soldiers, attacked the Bastille, and forced its surrender. Symbolically it marked the end of the authority of the old absolute monarchy. A year later the holiday was celebrated for the first time.

it represented the great medieval divisions of society, the majority of its members now claimed to represent all Frenchmen without distinction. It was able to take this revolutionary step because the turbulence of France both frightened the government and those deputies to the assembly who opposed such a change. Rural revolt and Parisian riot alarmed ministers no longer sure that they could rely upon the army. This led first to the monarchy's abandonment of the privileged classes, and then its concession, unwillingly and uneasily, of many other things asked for by the politicians who led the new National Assembly. At the same time these concessions created a fairly clear-cut division between those who were for the Revolution and

757

those who were against it; in language to go round the world they were soon called Left and Right (because of the places in which they sat in the assembly).

The main task which the National Assembly set itself was the writing of a constitution, but in the process it transformed the whole institutional structure of France. Before 1791, when it dispersed, it had nationalized the lands of the Church, abolished what it termed 'the feudal system', ended censorship, created a system of centralized representative government, obliterated the old provincial and local divisions and replaced them with the 'departments' under which Frenchmen still live, instituted equality before the law, and separated the executive from the legislative power. These were only the most remarkable things done by one of the most remarkable bodies the world has ever seen. Its failures tend to mask this huge achievement; they should not be allowed to do so. Broadly speaking, they removed the main legal and institutional checks on the modernization of France. Popular sovereignty, administrative centralization, and individual legal equality were from this time poles towards which her institutional life always returned.

Many Frenchmen did not like all this; some liked none of it. By 1791 the king had given clear evidence of his own misgivings, the goodwill which had supported him in the early Revolution was gone and he was suspected as an anti-Revolutionary. Some noblemen had already disliked enough of what was going on to emigrate; they were led by two of the king's brothers, which did not improve the outlook for royalty. But most important of all, many Frenchmen felt bound to turn against the Revolution when, because of papal policy, the National Assembly's settlement of Church affairs was called in question. Much in it had appealed deeply to many Frenchmen, churchmen among them, but the pope rejected it and this raised the ultimate question of authority. French Catholics had to decide whether the authority of the pope or that of the French constitution was supreme for them. The result was the most important division which came to embitter revolutionary politics.

In 1792 a great crisis occurred. France went to war with Austria at the beginning of the year and Prussia soon after. The issue was complicated but many Frenchmen believed that foreign powers wished to intervene to bring the Revolution to an end and put the clock back to 1788. By the summer, as things went badly and shortages and suspicion mounted at home, the king was discredited. A Parisian insurrection overthrew the monarchy and led to the summoning of a new assembly to draw up a new and republican constitution. This body, called the Convention, was the centre of French government until 1796. Through civil and foreign war and economic and ideological crisis it achieved the survival of the Revolution. Most of its members were politically not much more advanced in their views than their predecessors. They believed in the individual, the sanctity of property (they prescribed the death penalty for anyone proposing a law to introduce agrarian communism) and that the poor are always with us, though they allowed some of them a small say in affairs by supporting direct universal adult male suffrage. But they were willing to go rather further to meet emergencies than earlier French assemblies (especially when frightened by the possibility of defeat) and they sat in a capital city which was for a long time manipulated by more extreme politicians to push them into somewhat democratic measures and very democratic language. Consequently, they frightened Europe much more than their predecessors had done.

Their symbolic break with the past came when the Convention voted for the execution of the king in January 1793. The judicial murder of kings had hitherto been believed to be an English aberration; now the English were as shocked as the rest of Europe. They, too, now went to war with France, because they feared the strategical and commercial result of French success against the Austrians in the Netherlands. But the war looked more and more like an ideological struggle and to win it the French

When, in 1792, the monarchy was abolished the
the statue of Louis XIV was removed from the
Place des Victoires in Paris: an example of the
passionate attention to symbolism the Revolution
displayed.

government appeared increasingly bloodthirsty
at home. A new instrument for humane execution, the guillotine (a characteristic product of
pre-revolutionary enlightenment, combining as
it did technical efficiency and benevolence in the
swift, sure death it afforded its victims), became
the symbol of the Terror, the name soon given
to a period during which the Convention strove
by intimidation of its enemies at home to assure
survival to the Revolution. There was much that
was misleading in this symbolism. Some of the
Terror was only rhetoric, the hot air of politicians trying to keep their own spirits up and
frighten their opponents. In practice it often
reflected a jumble of patriotism, practical
necessity, muddled idealism, self-interest and
petty vengefulness as old scores were settled in
the name of the republic. Many people died,
of course – something over 35 000, perhaps –
and many emigrated to avoid danger, yet the
guillotine only killed a minority of the victims,
most of whom died in the provinces often in
conditions of civil war and sometimes with arms
in their hands. In eighteen months or so the

Frenchmen whom contemporaries regarded as
monsters killed about as many of their countrymen as died in ten days of street-fighting and
firing-squads in Paris in 1871. To take a different
but equally revealing measure, the numbers of
those who died in this year and a half are
roughly twice those of the British soldiers who
died on the first day of the battle of the Somme
in 1916. Such bloodshed drove divisions
even deeper between Frenchmen, but their
extent should not be exaggerated. All noblemen, perhaps, had lost something in the Revolution, but only a minority of them found it
necessary to emigrate. Probably the clergy
suffered more, man for man, than the nobility
and many priests fled abroad. Yet there were
fewer emigrants from France during the Revolution than from the American colonies after
1783. A much larger proportion of Americans
felt too intimidated or disgusted with their
Revolution to live in the United States after
independence than the proportion of Frenchmen
who could not live in France after the Terror.

The Convention won victories and put down
insurrection at home. By 1797, only Great
Britain had not made peace with France, the
Terror had been left behind, and the republic
was ruled by something much more like a parliamentary régime under a constitution whose
adoption closed the Convention era in 1796.

The Revolution was safer than ever. But it did not seem so. Abroad, the royalists strove to get allies with whom to return and also intrigued with malcontents inside France. The return of the old order was a prospect which few Frenchmen would welcome, though. On the other hand, there were those who argued that the logic of democracy should be pressed further, that there were still great divisions between rich and poor which were as offensive as had been the old distinctions of legally privileged and unprivileged, and that the Parisian radicals should have a greater say in affairs. This was almost as alarming as fears of a restoration to those who had benefited from the Revolution or simply wanted to avoid further bloodshed. Thus pressed from Right and Left, the Directory (as the new régime was called) was in a measure in a good position, though it made enemies who found the (somewhat zigzag) *via media* it followed unacceptable. In the end it was destroyed from within when a group of politicians intrigued with soldiers to bring about a *coup d'état* which instituted a new régime in 1799.

At that moment, ten years after the meeting of the Estates General, it was at least clear to most observers that France had for ever broken with the medieval past. In law this happened very rapidly. Nearly all the great reforms underlying it were legislated at least in principle in 1789. The formal abolition of feudalism, legal privilege and theocratic absolutism and the organization of society on individualist and secular foundations were the heart of the 'principles of '89' then distilled in the Declaration of the Rights of Man and the Citizen which prefaced the constitution of 1791. Legal equality and the legal protection of individual rights, the separation of Church and State and religious toleration were their expressions. The derivation of authority from popular sovereignty acting through a unified National Assembly, before whose legislation no privilege of locality or group could stand, was the basis of the jurisprudence which underlay them. Other Europeans watched aghast or at least amazed as this powerful legislative engine was employed to

The mythology of the Revolution: two English cartoons embody views of it which were to dominate most Europeans' thinking for decades – on the one hand a carnival of cruelty and animality, on the other a liberation of man by reasoned virtue from the fetters of a barbarous past.

overturn and rebuild institutions at every level of French life. Legislative sovereignty was a great instrument of reform, as the enlightened despots had known. Judicial torture came to an end, and so did titular nobility, juridical inequality and the old corporate guilds of French workmen. Incipient trades unionism was scotched in the egg by legislation forbidding association by workers or employers for collective economic ends. In retrospect, the signposts to market society seem pretty plain. Even the old currency based on units in the ratios of 1:20:12 (*livres*, *sous*, and *deniers*) gave way to a decimal system of *francs* and *centimes*, just as the chaos of old-fashioned weights and measures was (in theory) replaced by the metric system later to become almost universal.

Such great changes were bound to be divisive, the more so because men's minds change more slowly than their laws. Peasants who eagerly welcomed the abolition of feudal dues were much less happy about the disappearance of the communal usages from which they benefited which were also part of the 'feudal' order. Such conservatism was especially hard to interpret in religious affairs, yet was very important. The holy vessel kept at Rheims from which the kings of France had been anointed since the Middle Ages was publicly destroyed by the authorities during the Terror, an altar to Reason replaced the Christian one in the cathedral of Notre Dame and many priests underwent fierce personal persecution. Clearly, the France which did this was no longer Christian in the traditional sense, and the theocratic monarchy went unmourned by most Frenchmen. Yet the treatment of the Church aroused popular opposition to the Revolution as nothing else had done, the cults of quasi-divinities such as Reason and the Supreme Being which some revolutionaries promoted were a flop, and many Frenchmen (and perhaps most Frenchwomen) would happily welcome the restoration of the Catholic Church to French life when it eventually came.

The divisions aroused by revolutionary change in France could no more be confined within its borders than could the example of the principles of '89. These at once commanded much admiration and, at first, not much explicit condemnation or distrust in other countries, though this soon changed, in particular when French governments began to export their principles by propaganda and war. Change in France soon generated debate about what was practicable or desirable in other countries. Such debate was bound to reflect the terminology and circumstances in which it arose. In this way France gave her politics to Europe and this is the second great fact about the revolutionary decade. During it, modern politics began, for the terms Right and Left have been with us ever since. Liberals and conservatives (though it was to be a decade or so before the terms were used) came into political existence when the French Revolution provided what appeared to be a comprehensive way of classifying political standpoints. On one side were republicanism, a wide suffrage, individual rights, free speech and free publication; on the other were order, discipline, and emphasis on duties rather than rights, the recognition of the function of hierarchy and a wish to temper market forces by morality.

Some Frenchmen had always stressed that the French Revolution had universal significance. In the language of enlightened thought they advocated the acceptance by other nations of the recipes they employed for the settlement of French problems. This was not entirely arrogant. Societies in pre-industrial and traditional Europe still had many features in common; all could learn something from France. In this way the forces making for French influence were reinforced by conscious propaganda and missionary effort. So events in France entered universal history.

Arguments formulated to meet the unprecedented challenge of the Revolution were one expression of this. It crystallized the political thinking of conservatism, of which many of the constituent elements were lying about in such phenomena as irritation over the reforming measures of enlightened despotism, clerical resentment of the prestige and effect of 'advanced' ideas, and the emotional reaction from the fashionable and consciously rational which is the centre of romanticism. Such forces were especially prevalent in Germany, but it was in England that there appeared the first and in many ways the greatest statement of the conservative, anti-revolutionary argument. This was the *Reflections on the Revolution in France* which were published in 1790 by Edmund Burke. As might easily be inferred from his former rôle as defender of the rights of the American colonists, this book was far from a mindless defence of privilege. In it a conservative stance shook itself clear of the legalistic defence of institutions and expressed itself in a theory of society as the creation of more than will and reason.

The new polarization which the Revolution brought to Europe's politics promoted also the new idea of revolution itself, and it was one which was to have great consequences. The old idea that a political revolution was merely a circumstantial break in an essential continuity was replaced by one which took it as radical, comprehensive upheaval, leaving untouched no institution and limitless in principle, tending, perhaps, even to the subversion of such basic institutions as the family and property. According to whether people felt heartened or dismayed by this prospect, they sympathized with or deplored revolution wherever it occurred as a manifestation of a universal phenomenon. In the nineteenth century they came even to speak of the Revolution as a universally, eternally present force. This idea was the extreme expression of an ideological form of politics which is by no means yet dead. There are still people who, broadly speaking, feel that insurrectionary and subversive movements in all countries should, in principle, be approved of or condemned without regard to the particular circumstances of cases. This mythology has produced much misery, but first Europe and then the world which Europe transformed have had to live with those who respond emotionally to it, just as earlier generations had to live with the follies of religious divisions. Its survival, unhappily, is testimony still of the impact of the French

'*I want to be painted calm on a fiery horse*' *was Napoleon's command to the painter David. In this portrait he crosses the St Bernard Pass in 1800. In 1802 a plebiscite confirmed his position as first consul for life and in 1804 another granted him the title of Emperor of France.*

Revolution on European history and, through it, on that of the world.

Many dates can be chosen as the 'beginning' of the French Revolution; a specific date to 'end' it would be meaningless. The year 1799 none the less was an important punctuation mark in its course. The *coup d'état* which then swept the Directory away brought to power a man who quickly inaugurated a dictatorship which was to last until 1814 and turn international relations upside-down. This was Napoleon Bonaparte, formerly general of the republic, now First Consul of the new régime and soon to be the first Emperor of France. Like most of the leading figures of his age, he was still a young man. He had already shown exceptional brilliance and ruthlessness as a soldier. His victories combined with a shrewd political sense and a readiness to act in an insubordinate manner to win him a glamorous reputation; in many ways he now seems the greatest example of the eighteenth-century type of 'the adventurer'. In 1799 he had a great personal prestige and popularity. No one except the defeated politicians much regretted it when he shouldered them aside and assumed power. Immediately he justified himself by defeating the Austrians (who had joined again in a war against France) and making a victorious peace for France (as he had done once already). This removed the threat to the Revolution; no one doubted Bonaparte's own commitment to its principles. His consolidation of them was his most positive achievement.

Although Napoleon (as he was called officially after 1804, when he proclaimed his empire) reinstituted monarchy in France, it was in no sense a restoration. Indeed, he took care so to affront the exiled Bourbon family that any reconciliation with it was inconceivable. He sought popular approval for the empire in a plebiscite and got it. This was a monarchy Frenchmen had voted for; it rested on popular sovereignty, that is the Revolution. It assumed the consolidation of the Revolution which the Consulate had already begun. All the great institutional reforms of the 1790s were confirmed or at least left intact; there was no disturbance of the land sales which had followed the confiscation of Church property, no resurrection of the old corporations, no questioning of the principle of equality before the law. Some measures were even taken further, notably when each department was given an administrative head, the prefect, who was in his powers something like one of the emergency emissaries of the Terror (many former revolutionaries served Napoleon as prefects). Such further centralization of the administrative structure would, of course, have been approved also by the enlightened despots. In the actual working of government, it is true, the principles of the Revolution were often infringed in practice. Like all his predecessors in power since 1793, Napoleon controlled the press by a punitive censorship, locked up people without trial and in general gave short shrift to the Rights of Man so far as

civil liberties were concerned. Representative bodies existed under consulate and empire, but not much attention was paid to them. Yet it seems that this was what Frenchmen wanted, as they had wanted Napoleon's greatest creative act of statesmanship, a Concordat with the pope which reconciled Catholics to the régime.

All in all, this amounted to a great consolidation of the Revolution and one guaranteed at home by firm government and by military and diplomatic strength abroad. Both were eventually to be eroded by Napoleon's huge military efforts. These for a time gave France the dominance of Europe; her armies fought their way to Moscow in the east and Portugal in the west and garrisoned the Atlantic and northern coast from Corunna to Stettin. Nevertheless, the cost of this was too great; France could not sustain it indefinitely against the coalition of all the other European countries which Napoleon's arrogant assertion of his power aroused. When, after his invasion of that country in 1812, Russia entered the field against him, and the greatest army he ever led crumbled into ruins in the snows of the winter, he was doomed to defeat unless his enemies should fall out with one another. This time they did not. Napoleon himself blamed the British, who had been at war with him and, before him, with the Revolution with only one short break since 1792. There is something in this; the Anglo-French struggle was the last and most important round in a century of rivalry as well as a war of constitutional monarchy against military dictatorship. It was the sea-power brought to bear at Aboukir in 1798 and Trafalgar in 1805 which confined Napoleon to Europe, British money which financed her allies when they were ready to come forward, and a British army in the Iberian peninsula which kept alive there from 1809 onwards a front which drained French resources and gave hope to other Europeans.

By the beginning of 1814, Napoleon could defend only France and although he did so at his most brilliant, the resources were not available to fight off Russian, Prussian and Austrian armies in the east, and a British invasion in the south-west. At last his generals and ministers were able to set him aside and make peace without a popular outcry, even though this meant the return of the Bourbons. But it could not by then mean the return of anything else of significance from the years before 1789. The Concordat remained, the departmental system remained, equality before the law remained, a representative system remained; the Revolution, in fact, had become part of the established order in France. Napoleon had provided the time, the social peace and the institutions for that to happen. Nothing survived of the Revolution except what he had confirmed.

This makes him very different from a monarch of the traditional stamp, even the most modernizing – and, in fact, he was often very conservative in his policies, distrusting innovation. In the end he was a democratic despot, whose authority came from the people, both in the formal sense of the plebiscites, and in the more general one that he had needed (and won) their goodwill to keep his armies in the field. He is thus nearer to twentieth-century rulers than to Louis XIV in style. Yet he shares with that monarch the credit for carrying French international power to an unprecedented height and both of them have because of this retained the admiration of their countrymen, who like to have a good conceit of themselves. But again there is an important, and twofold, difference: Napoleon not only dominated Europe as Louis XIV never did, but because the Revolution had taken place his hegemony represented more than mere national supremacy, though this fact should not be sentimentalized. The Napoleon who was supposed to be a great European was the creation of later legend. The most obvious impact he had on Europe between 1800 and 1814 was the bloodshed and upheaval he brought to every corner of it. There can be little doubt that this was often the consequence of megalomania and personal vanity. But there were also important side-effects, some intentional, some not. They all added up to the further spread and effectiveness of the principles of the French Revolution.

Their most obvious expression was on the map. The patchwork quilt of the European state system of 1789 had undergone some revision already before Napoleon took power, when French armies in Italy, Switzerland and the United Provinces had created new satellite republics. But these had proved incapable of survival once French support was withdrawn and it was not until after French hegemony was re-established under the Consulate that there appeared a new organization which would have enduring consequences in some parts of Europe. The most important of these was west Germany. Here, the political structure was revolutionized and its medieval foundations swept away. German territories on the left bank of the Rhine were annexed to France for the whole of the period from 1801 to 1814, and this began a period of destroying historic German polities. Beyond the river, France provided the plan of a reorganization which secularized the ecclesiastical states, abolished nearly all the Free Cities, gave extra territory to Prussia, Hanover, Bavaria and Baden to compensate them for losses elsewhere, and abolished the old independent imperial nobility. The practical effect was to diminish the Catholic and Habsburg influence in Germany while strengthening the influence of its larger princely states (especially Prussia). The constitution of the Holy Roman empire was revised, too, to take account of these changes. In its new form it lasted only until 1806, when another defeat of the Austrians led to more changes in Germany and its abolition. So came to an end the institutional structure which, however inadequately, had given Germany such political unity as it had possessed since Ottonian times. A Confederation of the Rhine was now set up which provided a third force balancing that of Prussia and Austria. Thus were triumphantly asserted the national interests of France in a great work of destruction. Richelieu and Louis XIV would have enjoyed the contemplation of a French frontier on the Rhine with, beyond it, a Germany divided into interests likely to hold one another in check. But there was another side to it; the old structure, after all, had been a hindrance to German consolidation. No future rearrangement would ever contemplate the resurrection of the old structures. When, finally, the allies came to settle post-Napoleonic Europe, they too provided for a German Confederation, different from Napoleon's not least in that Prussia and Austria were members of it in so far as their territories were German, the Napoleonic consolidations remained. A complicated structure of over three hundred political units with different principles of organization in 1789 was reduced to thirty-eight states in 1815.

Consolidation was less dramatic in Italy and its substantive effects less revolutionary. The Napoleonic system provided in the north and south of the peninsula two large units which were nominally independent, while a large part of it (including the papal states) was formally incorporated in France and organized in departments. None of this structure survived in 1815, but neither was there a complete restoration of the old régime. In particular, the ancient republics of Genoa and Venice were left in the tombs to which the armies of the Directory had first consigned them. They were absorbed by bigger states, Genoa by Sardinia, Venice by Austria. Elsewhere in Europe, at the height of Napoleonic power, France had annexed and governed directly a huge block of territory whose coasts ran from the Pyrenees to Denmark in the north and from Catalonia almost without interruption to the boundary between Rome and Naples in the south. Lying detached from it was a large piece of modern Yugoslavia. Satellite states and vassals of varying degrees of real independence, some of them ruled over by members of Napoleon's own family, divided between them the rest of Italy, Switzerland and Germany west of the Elbe. Isolated in the east was another satellite, the 'grand duchy' of Warsaw which had been created from former Russian territory.

In most of these countries common administrative practice and institutions provided a large measure of shared experience. That experience, of course, was experience of institutions and ideas which embodied the principles of the Revolution. These forces hardly reached beyond

The shattered French army masses before the bridges across the Beresina during the 1812 retreat from Russia. Ambulances have been abandoned in the foreground and some of the soldiers have plunged into the freezing water of the river in order to get across.

the Elbe except in the brief Polish experiment and thus the French Revolution, too, came to be another of those great shaping influences which again and again have worked to differentiate eastern and western Europe. Within the French empire, Germans, Italians, Illyrians, Belgians and Dutch were all governed by the Napoleonic legal codes; the bringing of these to fruition was the result of Napoleon's own initiative and insistence, but the work was essentially that of revolutionary legislators who had never been able in the troubled 1790s to draw up the new codes so many Frenchmen had hoped for in 1789. With the codes went concepts of family, property, the individual, public power and others which were thus generally spread through Europe. They sometimes replaced and sometimes supplemented a chaos of local, customary, Roman and ecclesiastical law. Similarly, the departmental system of the empire imposed a common administrative practice, service in the French armies imposed a common discipline and military regulation and French weights and measures and the decimal system replaced scores of local scales. Such innovations exercised an influence beyond the actual limits of French rule, providing models and inspiration to modernizers in other countries. The models were all the more easily assimilated because French officials and technicians worked in many of the satellites while many nationalities other than French were represented in the Napoleonic service.

Such changes took time to produce their full effect but it was a deep one and was revolutionary. A more subtle revolution also deriving from the Napoleonic impact lay in the reaction and resistance it provoked. In spreading revolutionary principles the French were often putting a rod in pickle for their own backs. Popular sovereignty lay at the heart of the Revolution and it is an idea closely linked to that of nationalism. French principles said that peoples ought to govern themselves and that the proper unit in which they should do so was the nation: the revolutionaries had proclaimed their own republic 'one and indivisible' for this reason. Many of their foreign admirers applied this principle to their own countries; manifestly, Italians and Germans did not live in national states, and perhaps they should. But this was only one side of the coin. French Europe was run for the benefit of France, and it thus denied the national rights of other Europeans. They saw their agriculture and commerce sacrificed to French economic policy, found they had to serve in the French armies, or had to receive at the hands of Napoleon a French king. When even those who had welcomed the principles of the Revolution felt such things as grievances, it is hardly surprising that those

who had never welcomed them at all should begin to think in terms of national resistance, too. European nationalism was given an immense fillip by the Napoleonic era, even if governments distrusted it and felt uneasy about employing it. Germans began to think of themselves as more than Westphalians and Bavarians, and Italians began to believe they were more than Romans or Milanese because they discerned a common interest against France. In Spain and Russia the identification of patriotic resistance with resistance to the Revolution was virtually complete. Though the dynasty Napoleon hoped to found and the empire he set up both proved fragile, his work was of great importance because of the processes which it allowed to mature. Napoleon unlocked huge reserves of energy in other countries just as the Revolution had unlocked them in France, and afterwards they could never be quite shut up again. He ensured the legacy of the Revolution its maximum effect.

His unconditional abdication in 1814 was not quite the end of the story. Just under a year later the emperor returned to France from Elba where he had lived in a pensioned exile, and the restored Bourbon régime crumbled at a touch. The allies none the less determined to overthrow him, for he had frightened them too much in the past. Napoleon's attempt to anticipate the gathering of overwhelming forces against him came to an end at Waterloo, on 18 June 1815, when the threat of a revived French empire was destroyed by the Anglo-Belgian and Prussian armies. This time the victors sent him to St Helena, thousands of miles away in the South Atlantic, where he died in 1821. The final alarm that he had given them strengthened their determination to make a peace that would avoid any danger of a repetition of the twenty years of almost continuous war which Europe had undergone in the wake of the Revolution. Thus Napoleon still shaped the map of Europe, not only by the changes he had made in it, but also by the fear France had inspired under his leadership.

3 Political change: a new Europe

In spite of the hopes of conservative statesmen in 1815, the era of political upheaval in Europe had only just begun. By 1871, a year in which a newly united Germany took its place among the great powers, most of Europe west of a line drawn from Trieste to Stettin was organized in states based on the principle of nationality, even if some minorities still loudly denied it. Before 1914 the triumph of nationalism went further still and most of the Balkans and the Americas were organized as nation-states, too. Within the political framework thus established, other new principles were also making headway. Terms like democracy and liberalism do not help very much in defining them, though they must be used in default of better ones. In most countries there was a general trend towards associating

European government was changed much more during the nineteenth century by such blind forces as those of population growth, urbanization, railways and mass literacy than by revolution. Yet the idea of revolution continued to fascinate and terrify men even when it achieved little in practice. France, understandably, was the supreme example of a country where the myth of revolution bemused politicians and artists alike. Delacroix's celebrated painting of Liberty leading the people across the barricades, symbolic Phrygian cap on her head and tricolour in her hand, is still one of the most moving evocations of the idealization of what a priest once called la sainte canaille – *the mob whose brutality is seen as purged of evil in its commitment to the cause of freedom for all men.*

more and more subjects of the state with its operation through the representative institutions asked for by liberals and democrats. More and more, too, the individual became the basis of political and social organization. The nation increasingly seemed to be the only group enjoying the respect of legislators and bureaucrats as a focus of rights and duties. In progressive countries the individual's membership of communal, religious, occupational and family units was steadily given less importance than his individual rights. This meant in some ways greater theoretical and practical freedom, in some ways much less. The state was actually much more powerful in relation to its subjects in the nineteenth century than ever before.

In part this was because of the French Revolution, whose greatest influence outside France came in the years from 1815 to 1870. Its lessons were then worked out in other countries and old institutions were in many of them swept away as they had been swept away already in France. Other forces were also at work to change the economy and society and their effect wove in and out of the unrolling patterns of political change. They shaped a revolutionary tradition which was at its height in these years. That tradition expressed itself mainly in three ways: in the belief that Europe was, for good or ill, in a state of potential revolution along lines which were essentially those laid down in France after 1789, in the operation of the doctrine of nationalism, and in what, for want of a better word, must be called liberalism, an attitude which strove at different times for many different goals, but

769

Europe in 1815

——— Boundary of German Confederation

which always promoted the liberation of the individual from restraints laid upon him by traditional society or political authority. Liberalism was the political creed of a market society.

These principles had powerful success. By and large, they dominated the history of Europe down to about 1870 and provided the dynamic of its politics. But they did not achieve all that was hoped, their realization in practice had many qualifications, and they had many competitors. Yet they provide guiding threads in the rich and turbulent history of nineteenth-century Europe, already a political laboratory whose discoveries where changing the rest of the world.

They operated in international life as well as within particular societies. This could be seen in the foundation deed of the nineteenth-century international order, the Treaty of Vienna of

1815, which closed the era of the French wars. Its central aim was to prevent their repetition. The peace-makers sought the containment of France and the avoidance of revolution, using as their materials the principle of legitimacy which was the ideological core of conservative Europe and practical territorial arrangements against future French aggression. Thus Prussia was given large acquisitions on the Rhine, a new northern state appeared under a Dutch king ruling both Belgium and the Netherlands, the kingdom of Sardinia was given Genoa, and Austria not only recovered her former Italian possessions, but kept Venice and was allowed a virtually free hand in keeping the other Italian states in order. In most of these cases legitimacy bowed to expediency; those despoiled in the revolutionary and Napoleonic eras did not ob-

Europe in 1914

tain restoration. But the powers still talked legitimacy and (once the arrangements were complete) did so with some success. For nearly forty years the Vienna settlement provided a framework within which disputes were settled without war. Most of the régimes installed in 1815 were still there, though some somewhat shaken, forty years later.

This owed much to the salutary fear of revolution. In all the major continental states the restoration era (as the years after 1815 have been termed) was a great period for policemen and plotters alike. But there was no subversive threat that could not be handled easily enough. Austrian troops dealt with attempted *coups* in Piedmont and Naples, French soldiers restored the power of a reactionary Spanish king hampered by a liberal constitution, the Russian

empire survived a military conspiracy and a Polish revolt. The Austrian predominance in Germany was not threatened at all and it is difficult in retrospect to discern any very real danger to any part of the Habsburg monarchy before 1848. Russian and Austrian power, the first in reserve, the second the predominant force in central Europe and Italy during the years 1815–48, were the two rocks on which the Vienna system rested.

Mistakenly, liberalism and nationalism were usually supposed to be inseparable; this was to prove terribly untrue in later times, but in so far as a few people did seek to change Europe by revolution before 1848, it is broadly true that they wanted to do so by advancing both the political principles of the French Revolution – representative government, popular sovereignty,

771

freedom of the individual and the press – and those of nationality. Many of them confused the two; the most famous and admired of those who did so was Mazzini, a young Italian. By advocating an Italian unity most of his country-men did not want and conspiring unsuccessfully to bring it about, he became an inspiration and model for other nationalists and democrats in every continent for over a century and one of the first idols of radical *chic*. The age of the ideas he represented, none the less, had not yet come.

To the west of the Rhine, where the writ of the Holy Alliance (as the three conservative powers, Russia, Austria and Prussia, were called) did not run, the story was different; there, legitimism was only briefly secure, during the immediately post-Waterloo years. The very restoration of the Bourbon dynasty in 1814 had itself been a compromise with the principle of legitimacy. Louis XVIII was supposed to have reigned like any other king of France since the death of his predecessor, Louis XVII, in prison in Paris in 1795. In fact, as everyone knew but

'Papa, look after my piece for me', says Napoleon's little son, the 'King of Rome', in this satirical print of the emperor's intervention in the peace-making of greedy monarchs in 1815. In fact, there was to be no consultation of Napoleon and the sword with which he is here shown defending his heritage was broken at Waterloo.

legitimists tried to conceal, he came back in the baggage trains of the Allied armies which had defeated Napoleon and he only did so on terms acceptable to the French political and military élites of the Napoleonic period and to the mass of Frenchmen. The restored monarchy was regulated by a charter which created a constitu-tional monarchy, albeit with a limited suffrage. The rights of individuals were guaranteed and the land settlement resulting from revolutionary confiscations and sales was unquestioned; there was no return to 1789. Nevertheless, there was some uncertainty about the future; battle be-tween right and left began with arguments about the charter itself – was it a contract

Giuseppe Mazzini, for forty years the advocate of Italian unification and revolution and one of the purest embodiments of the faith in nationalism. Yet he died in exile from his newly united country, deeply embittered by the form in which its unification had come about.

between king and people, or a simple emanation of the royal benevolence which might therefore be withdrawn as easily as it had been granted? – and went on over a whole range of issues which raised questions of principle (or were thought to do so) about ground won for liberty and the possessing classes in the Revolution. The uncertainty persisted until 1830, but then perished at the hands of the last king of the direct Bourbon line, Charles X. He foolishly attempted to break out of the constitutional limitations which bound him by what was virtually a *coup d'état*. Paris rose against him, liberal politicians hastily put themselves at its head, and, to the chagrin of republicans, ensured that a new king replaced Charles on the throne.

Louis Philippe was head of the junior branch of the French royal house, the Orléans family, but to many conservative eyes he was the Revolution incarnate. His father had voted for the execution of Louis XVI (and went to the scaffold himself soon after) while the new king had fought as an officer in the republican armies and had even been a member of the reputedly infamous Jacobin club, widely believed to have been the conspiracy at the heart of the Revolution and certainly a forcing-house which produced some of its most prominent leaders. To liberals he was attractive for much the same reasons; he reconciled the Revolution with the stability provided by monarchy. To people on the left wing this was a disappointment. The régime over which he presided for eighteen years proved remarkably conservative, but it was also unimpeachably constitutional, fostering the interests and upholding the ideals of the well-to-do. It suppressed urban disorder (of which poverty produced plenty in the 1830s) and preserved the essential freedoms which enabled its voters to take the advice of a prominent politician and enrich themselves (*enrichissez-vous*) – a recommendation much ridiculed and misunderstood. Its author was trying to tell Frenchmen that the way to obtain the vote was to obtain the qualification which wealth conferred. This is an indicator of the narrowness of the régime; in 1830 only about a third as many Frenchmen as Englishmen had a vote for their national representatives while the population of France was about twice that of England.

Nevertheless, the theory of the July Monarchy was that the state rested once more on popular sovereignty. In the 1830s there was sharply evident a division between a Europe of constitutional states – England, France, Spain and Portugal – and that of the legitimist, dynastic states of the East, with their Italian and German satellites. The conservative states were alarmed when the Belgians rebelled against their Dutch king in 1830, but could not support him because the British and French favoured the Belgians and Russia had a Polish rebellion on her hands. It took until 1839 to secure the establishment of an independent Belgium, the only important change in the state system created by the Vienna settlement before 1848. Elsewhere, a revolution of 'Greeks' (that is, Orthodox Christian subjects of the sultan) against their Turkish rulers in 1821, had led to the successful emergence of a new kingdom of Greece in 1832. Russian national interests in this case favoured the rebels and cut across conservative principles; religion and the old pull of Russian imperialist expansion to the south-east made it impossible for the Holy Alliance to support the sultan as it supported rulers against their subjects elsewhere. Indeed, the Russians went to war with the Turks. Thus the Greek revolt announced that the nineteenth-century eastern question was going to be additionally complicated by nationalism, for the new kingdom was bound to give ideas to other peoples in the Balkans.

In 1848 it briefly seemed that the whole 1815 settlement was in jeopardy. Social strain coincided with political exasperation to produce a potential for outbreak in many countries at the same time. Once revolution was detonated in one place, the example was contagious and weakened the ability of the general security system to deal with further outbreaks. By the middle of the year, government in every major European capital except London and St Petersburg and in scores of other cities appeared to be in retreat. Then the revolutionary movements began to show their own weaknesses and divisions and by the end of 1849 the formal structure of Europe was again much what it had been in 1847, though there had been important changes within some countries.

The 1840s had been years of economic hardship, food shortages and distress in many places. They were particularly felt in Ireland in 1846, where there was a great famine, and then in central Europe and France in 1847, where a commercial slump starved the cities. Unemployment was widespread and this was the background to violence in 1848 which gave new edge to radical movements everywhere. When, in February 1848, Louis Philippe realized that he would not be supported in his resistance to a broader suffrage by the middle classes on whom

he had hitherto relied, he abdicated. This was the February Revolution. There emerged a republic in France and with its installation every revolutionary in Europe took heart. The dreams of thirty years' conspiracies and the plans of countless exiles now seemed realizable. The *Grande Nation* was great again and the armies of the Great Revolution might march once more to uphold its principles in other countries.

Reality was very different. In the end the Second Republic made a diplomatic genuflexion in the direction of martyred Poland, the classical focus of the nationalists sympathies, and the only military operations it undertook were in defence

In 1848 monarchs everywhere trembled. In this Punch *cartoon, the uncrowned figure in the boat is Louis-Philippe, already turned off the French throne when it was published.*

of the pope, an unimpeachably conservative cause. But there were complicated reasons for this, not the least being the very divergent and confusing paths which were followed by the revolutionaries in 1848.

They had been provoked by very different situations and had many different aims. In most of Italy and central Europe there were revolutions against governments which were thought of as oppressive because they were illiberal; the great symbolic demand there was for constitutions which would guarantee essential freedoms. When such a revolution occurred in Vienna itself, Metternich, the embodiment of the conservative order, was driven into exile. But successful revolution at Vienna meant the paralysis

Errichtung und Vertheidigung einer Barrikade an der Rheinbrücke zu Mannheim am 26. April.

Extemporized street barricades were a universal sign of rebellion in 1848. This print presents a somewhat romantic view of one across a bridge at Mannheim.

and therefore the dislocation of the whole of central Europe because Austria dominated it. The German states were now free to have their revolutions without fear of Austrian intervention. So were other nationalities within the Austrian dominions; Italians turned on the Austrian armies in Lombardy and Venetia, Hungarians revolted at Budapest, and Czechs at Prague. This much complicated things. Many of these revolutionaries wanted national independence rather than constitutionalism, though constitutionalism seemed for a time the way to independence because it attacked the principles of dynastic autocracy.

If the liberals were successful in getting constitutional governments installed in all the capitals of central Europe and Italy, then it followed there would actually come into existence nations hitherto without a state structure of their own, or at least without one for a very long time. If Slavs achieved their own national liberation it had to follow that states previously thought of as German would be shorn of huge tracts of their territory, notably in Poland and Bohemia. It took some time for this to sink in. The German liberals suddenly fell over this problem in 1848 and quickly drew their conclusions; they chose nationalism for themselves. The Italians were still coming to terms with their own version of the dilemma a hundred years later. The German revolutions of 1848 failed, essentially, because the German liberals decided that they could not do without a strong Prussia and must accept its terms for the future of Germany, since German nationalism required the preservation of German lands in the east. There were other signs,

775

too, that the tide had turned before the end of 1848. The Austrian army had mastered the Italians. In Paris a Parisian rising to take the Revolution further in the direction of democracy was crushed with great bloodshed in June and it was evident that the republic was, after all, to be a conservative one. In 1849 came the end. The Austrians overthrew the Sardinian army which was the only shield of the Italian revolutions and monarchs all over the peninsula began to withdraw the constitutional concessions they had made while Austrian power was in abeyance. German rulers did the same, led by Prussia. The pressure was kept up on the Habsburgs by the Croats and Hungarians, but then the Russian army came to its ally's help.

Liberals saw in 1848 a 'springtime of the nations'. If it was one, the shoots had not lived long before they withered. Nationalism had certainly been very important in 1848, but it had also demonstrated that it was neither strong enough to sustain governments nor necessarily an enlightened force. Its failure in 1848 shows that the charge that the statesmen of 1815 'neglected' to give it due attention is false; no new nation emerged from 1848 for none was ready to do so. The basic reason for this was that although nationalities might exist, over most of Europe nationalism was an abstraction; only relatively few and well-educated or at least half-educated people much cared about it. Where national differences also embodied social issues there was sometimes effective action by national groups, but it did not lead to the setting up of new nations; the Ruthene peasants of Galicia in 1847 had happily murdered their Polish landlords when the Habsburg administration allowed them to do so, thus satisfying themselves and in consequence remaining loyal to the Habsburgs in 1848.

There were some genuinely popular revolutions in 1848, but they had many and diverse ends. In Italy they were usually revolts of townsmen rather than peasants; the Lombard peasants, indeed, cheered the Austrian army when it returned, because they saw no good for them in a revolution led by the aristocrats who were their landlords. In parts of Germany over much of which the traditional structures of landed rural society remained intact, the peasants went on as they had done in France in 1789, burning their landlords' houses, not merely through personal animus but in order to destroy the hated and feared records of rents, dues and labour services. Such outbreaks frightened urban liberals as much as the Parisian outbreak of despair and unemployment in the June Days frightened the middle classes in France. There, because the peasant was since 1789 (speaking broadly) a conservative, the government was assured the support of the provinces in crushing the Parisian poor who had given radicalism its brief success. Almost always the social weaknesses of liberalism were brought into the open in 1848 by popular revolution.

Altogether, the social importance of 1848 is as complex and escapes easy generalization as much as its political content. But it was probably in the countryside of eastern and central Europe that most was, in fact, achieved by the revolutions. Here, liberal principles and the fear of popular revolt went hand in hand to impose change on the landlords. It is fair to say that wherever outside Russia obligatory peasant labour and bondage to the soil survived, it was abolished as a result of 1848. That year carried the rural social revolution launched with the abolition of feudalism in France to its conclusion in central and most of eastern Europe. The way was now open for the reconstruction of agricultural life in Germany and the Danube valley on individualist and market lines. Though many of its practices and habits of mind were still to linger, feudal society had in effect now come to an end all over Europe. The political components of French revolutionary principles, though, would have to wait longer for their expression.

In the case of nationalism this was not very long. A dispute over Russian influence in the Near East, where Turkish power was visibly declining, led in 1854 to the first war between great powers since 1815. The Crimean War, in which the French and British fought as allies of the Turks against the Russians was in many

The actual appearance of the battlefield began to be photographed in the Crimean War. A Russian battery after its capture by the French.

Industrial technology goes to war. This ingenious portable drying-cupboard was sent to the main British hospital at Scutari during the Crimean war.

Newly-Invented Drying-Closet, for the Hospital at Scutari.

ways a notable struggle. Fighting took place in the Baltic, in southern Russia, and in the Crimea, the last theatre attracting most attention. There, the allies had set themselves to capture Sebastopol, the naval base which was the key to Russian power in the Black Sea. Some of the results were surprising. The British army fought gallantly, as did its opponents and allies, but was especially distinguished by the inadequacy of its administrative arrangements; the scandal these caused launched an important wave of radical reform at home. Incidentally the war also helped to found the prestige of a new profession for women, that of nursing, for the collapse of British medical services had been particularly striking. Florence Nightingale's work launched the first major extension of the occupational opportunities available to respectable women since the creation of female religious communities in the Dark Ages. The conduct of the war is also noteworthy in another way as an index of modernity: it was the first between

777

major powers in which steamships and a railway were employed.

Yet these things, however portentous, mattered less in the short run than the war's effect on international relations. Russia was defeated and her long enjoyment of a power to intimidate Turkey was bridled for a time. A step was taken towards the establishment of another new Christian nation, Romania, which was finally brought about in 1862. Once more, nationality triumphed in former Turkish lands. But the crucial effect of the war was that the Holy Alliance had disappeared. The old rivalry of the eighteenth century between Austria and Russia over what would happen to the Turkish inheritance in the Balkans had broken out again when Austria warned Russia not to occupy the Danube principalities (as the future Romania was termed) during the war and then occupied them herself. This was five years after Russia had intervened to restore Habsburg power by crushing the Hungarian revolution. It was the end of friendship between the two powers. The next time Austria faced a revolutionary threat she would have to do so without the Russian policeman of conservative Europe at her side.

In 1856, when peace was made, few people can have anticipated how quickly that time would come. Within ten years Austria lost in two short, sharp wars her hegemony both in Italy and in Germany, and those countries were united in new national states. Nationalism had indeed triumphed, and at the cost of the Habsburgs, as had been prophesied by enthusiasts in 1848, but in a totally unexpected way. Not revolution, but the ambitions of two traditionally expansive monarchical states, Sardinia and Prussia, had led each to set about improving its position at the expense of Austria, whose isolation was at that moment complete. Not only had she sacrificed the Russian alliance, but after 1852 France was ruled by an emperor who again bore the name Napoleon and was the nephew of the first to do so. He had been elected president of the Second Republic, whose constitution he then set aside by *coup d'état*. The name Napoleon was itself a programme of inter-national reconstruction – or revolution. Napoleon III (the second was a legal fiction, a son of Napoleon I who had never ruled) stood for the destruction of the anti-French settlement of 1815 and therefore of the Austrian predominance which propped it up in Italy and Germany. He talked the language of nationalism with less inhibition than most rulers and seems to have believed in it. With arms and diplomacy he forwarded the work of two great diplomatic technicians, Cavour, Prime Minister of Sardinia, and Bismarck, Prime Minister of Prussia.

In 1859 Sardinia and France fought Austria; after a brief war the Austrians were left with only Venetia in Italy. Cavour now set to work to incorporate other Italian states into Sardinia, a part of the price being that Sardinian Savoy had to be given to France. Cavour died in 1861, and debate still continues over what was the extent of his real aims, but by 1871 his successors had produced a united Italy under the former King of Sardinia, who was thus recompensed for the loss of Savoy the ancestral duchy of his house. In that year Germany was united, too. Bismarck had begun by rallying German liberal sentiment in a nasty little war against Denmark in 1864. Two years later Prussia defeated Austria in a lightning campaign in Bohemia, thus at last ending the Hohenzollern–Habsburg duel for supremacy in Germany begun in 1740 by Frederick II. The war in which he did this was rather a registration of an accomplished fact than its achievement, for Austria since 1848 was much weakened in German affairs. The German liberals had then offered a German crown, not to the emperor, but to the King of Prussia. Nevertheless, some states had still looked to Vienna for leadership and patronage, and they were now left alone to meet Prussian bullying. The Habsburg empire now became purely Danubian, its foreign policy preoccupied with south-east Europe and the Balkans. It had retired from the Netherlands in 1815, Venetia had been exacted by the Prussians for the Italians in 1866, and now it left Germany to its own devices, too. Immediately after the peace the Hungarians seized the opportunity to inflict

The new emperor drives home with three other German kings as his footmen – a French cartoonist's comment on the way Bismarck really saw the German unity under Prussia which he had engineered.

a further defeat on the humiliated monarchy by obtaining a virtual autonomy for the half of the Habsburg monarchy made up of the lands of the Hungarian crown. The empire thus became, in 1867, the Dual or Austro-Hungarian monarchy, divided rather untidily into two halves linked by little more than the dynasty itself and the conduct of a common foreign policy.

German unification required one further step. It had gradually dawned in France that the assertion of Prussian power beyond the Rhine was not in the French interest; instead of a disputed Germany, she now faced one dominated by one important military power. The Richelieu era had crumbled away unnoticed. Bismarck used this new awareness, together with Napoleon III's weaknesses at home and international isolation to provoke France into a foolish declaration of war in 1870. Victory in this war set

the coping-stone on the new edifice of German nationality, for Prussia had taken the lead in 'defending' Germany against France – and there were still Germans alive who could remember what French armies had done in Germany under an earlier Napoleon. The Prussian army destroyed the Second Empire in France (it was to be the last monarchical régime in that country) and created the German empire, the Second Reich, as it was called, to distinguish it from the medieval empire. In practice, it was a Prussian domination cloaked in federal forms, but as a German national state it satisfied many German liberals. It was dramatically and appropriately founded when the king of Prussia accepted the crown of united Germany (which his predecessor had refused to take from German liberals in 1848) from his fellow-princes in 1871 in the palace of Louis XIV at Versailles.

There had thus been in fifty years a revolution in international affairs. Germany had replaced France as the dominant land-power in Europe as France had replaced Spain in the seventeenth century. This fact dominated Europe's international relations until they ceased to be determined by forces originating within her. The outcome owed just a little to revolutionary politics in the narrow and strict sense. Yet the conscious revolutionaries of the nineteenth century had achieved nothing comparable with the work of Cavour, Bismarck and, half in spite of himself, Napoleon III. This is very odd, given the hopes entertained of revolution in this period, and the fears felt for it. Revolution had achieved little except at the fringes of Europe and had even begun to show signs of flagging. Down to 1848 there had been plenty of revolutions, to say nothing of plots, conspiracies and *pronunciamientos* which did not justify the name. After 1848 there were very few. Another Polish revolution took place in 1863, and this was the only outbreak of note in the lands of the great powers until 1871.

An ebbing of revolutionary effort is understandable. Revolutions seemed by 1850 to have achieved little outside France and had there brought disappointments. Some of their goals, too, were being achieved in other ways. Cavour and his followers had after all created a united Italy, greatly to the chagrin of Mazzini, since it was not one of which that revolutionary could approve, and Bismarck had done what many of the German liberals of 1848 had hoped for by providing a Germany which was indisputably a great power. Other ends were being achieved by economic progress; for all the horror of the poverty which it contained, nineteenth-century Europe was getting richer and was giving more and more of its peoples a larger share of its wealth. Even quite short-term factors helped here. The year 1848 was soon followed by the great gold discoveries of California which provided a flow of bullion to stimulate the world economy in the 1850s and 1860s; confidence grew and unemployment fell in these decades and this was good for social peace.

A more fundamental reason why revolutions grew rarer was, perhaps, that they became more difficult to carry out. Governments were finding it steadily more easy to grapple with them, largely for technical reasons. The nineteenth century created modern police forces. Better communications by rail and telegraph gave new power to central government in dealing with distant revolt. Above all, armies had a growing technical superiority to rebellion. As early as 1795 a French government showed that once it had control of the regular armed forces, and was prepared to use them, it could master Paris. During the long peace from 1815 to 1848 many European armies in fact became much more instruments of security, directed potentially against their own populations, than means of international competition, directed against foreign enemies. It was only the defection of important sections of the armed forces which permitted successful revolution in Paris in 1830 and 1848; once such forces were available to the government, battles like that of the June Days of 1848 (which one observer called the greatest slave-war in history) could only end with the defeat of the rebels. From that year, indeed, no popular revolution was ever to succeed in a major European country against a government whose control of its armed forces was unshaken by defeat in war or by subversion, and which was determined to use its power.

This was vividly and bloodily demonstrated in 1871, when a rebellious Paris was once again crushed by a French government in a little more than a week with a toll of dead as great as that exacted by the Terror of 1793–4. A popular régime which drew to itself a wide range of radicals and reformers set itself up in the capital as the 'Commune' of Paris, a name evocative of traditions of municipal independence going back to the Middle Ages and, more important, to 1793, when the Commune (or city council) of Paris had been the centre of revolutionary fervour. The Commune of 1871 was able to take power because of the government's powerlessness in the aftermath of defeat by the Germans to disarm the capital of the weapons with which it had successfully withstood a siege, and because the same defeat had inflamed many Parisians against the government they believed to have let them down. During its brief life (there were a few weeks of quiet while the government prepared its riposte) the Commune did very little, but it produced a lot of left-wing rhetoric and was soon seen as the embodiment of social revolution. This gave additional bitterness to the efforts to suppress it. They came when the government had reassembled its forces from returning prisoners of war to reconquer Paris, which became the scene of brief but bloody street-fighting. Once again, regularly constituted armed forces overcame workmen and shopkeepers manning hastily improvised barricades.

If anything could do so, the ghastly failure of the Paris Commune should have killed the revolutionary myth, both in its power to terrify and its power to inspire. Yet it did not. If anything, it strengthened it. Conservatives found it a great standby to have the Commune example to hand in evoking the dangers lurking always ready to burst out from under the surface of society. Revolutionaries had a new episode of heroism and martyrdom to add to an apostolic succession of revolutionaries running already from 1789 to 1848. But the Commune also revivi-

As in the great revolution eighty years before, during the Commune's short rule some Parisians turned upon the symbols of the past. A huge operation was mounted to pull down the column crowned with a statue of Napoleon I in the Place Vendôme. Later it was to be replaced.

fied the revolutionary mythology because of a new factor whose importance had already struck both left and right. This was socialism.

This word (like its relative 'socialist') has come to cover a great many different things, and did so almost from the start. Both words were first commonly used in France around about 1830 to describe theories and men opposed to a society run on market principles and an economy operated on *laissez-faire* lines, of which the main beneficiaries (they thought) were the wealthy. Economic and social egalitarianism is fundamental to the socialist idea. Most socialists have been able to agree up to that point. They have usually believed that in a good society there would be no classes oppressing one another through the advantages given to one by the ownership of wealth. They welcomed the thought that one day no advantage of wealth would give a man power to command the lives of others. All socialists, too, could agree that there was nothing sacred about property, whose rights buttressed injustice; some sought its complete abolition and were called communists. 'Property is theft' was one very successful slogan.

Such ideas might be frightening, but were not very novel. Egalitarian ideas have fascinated men throughout history and the Christian rulers of Europe had managed without difficulty to reconcile social arrangements resting on sharp contrasts of wealth with the practice of a religion one of whose greatest hymns praised God for filling the hungry with good things and sending the rich empty away. What happened in the early nineteenth century was that such ideas seemed to become at once more dangerous and more popular. There was also a need for new terms because of other developments. One was that the success of liberal political reform revealed that legal equality was not enough, if it was deprived of content by dependence on other men's economic power or denatured by poverty and attendant ignorance. Another was that already in the eighteenth century a few thinkers had seen big discrepancies of wealth as irrationalities in a world which should be regulated to produce the greatest good of the greatest number. In the upheavals of the French Revolution this already resulted in the emergence of some thinkers and agitators who pressed forward demands in which later generations would see socialist ideas. Egalitarian ideas none the less only became socialism in a modern sense when they began to grapple with the problems of the new epoch of economic and social change, above all with those presented by industrialization.

This often required a great perspicacity, for these changes were very slow in making their impact outside Great Britain and Belgium, the first continental country to be industrialized in the same degree. Yet perhaps because the contrast they presented with traditional society was so stark, even the small beginnings of concentration in capitalist finance and manufacturing were remarked. One of the first men to grasp their implications for social organization was a French nobleman, Claude Saint-Simon. His seminal contribution to socialist thought was to consider the impact on society of the new facts of technological and scientific advance. Saint-Simon thought that they not only made planned organization of the economy imperative, but implied great changes in society, demanding the replacement of the traditional ruling classes, aristocratic and rural in their outlook, by élites representing new economic and intellectual forces. Such ideas influenced many thinkers (most of them French) who in the 1830s advocated greater egalitarianism; they seemed to show that rational grounds as well as ethical ones made such change desirable. Their doctrines made enough impact and were enough talked about to terrify the French possessing classes in 1848, who thought they saw in the June Days a 'socialist' revolution. Socialists willingly identified themselves for the most part with the tradition of the French Revolution, picturing the realization of their ideals as its next phase.

In 1848, at this juncture, there appeared a pamphlet which is perhaps the finest of the century and certainly the most important document in the history of socialism. This was *The Communist Manifesto*. It was largely the work of a young German Jew, Karl Marx, and with it the point is reached at which the prehistory of socialism can be separated from its history. Marx proclaimed a complete break with what he called the 'utopian socialism' of his predecessors. Nothing, according to him, could be hoped for from arguments to persuade people that change was morally desirable. Everything depended on the actual and inevitable creation of a new working class by industrial society, the rootless wage-earners of the new industrial cities which he termed the industrial proletariat. This class was bound, according to him, to act in a revolutionary way. History was working upon them so as to generate revolutionary capacity and mentality. It would present them with conditions to which revolution was the only logical outcome and that revolution was, by those conditions, guaranteed success. Utopian socialists attacked industrial capitalism because they thought it was unjust; Marx claimed that this was beside the point. What mattered was not that capitalism was morally wrong, but that it was already out of date and therefore historically doomed. In his view a particular society had a particular system of property rights and class relationships,

Karl Marx and his wife.

and these accordingly shaped its particular political arrangements. Politics were bound to express economic forces. They would change as the particular organization of society changed under the influence of economic developments, and therefore, sooner or later (and Marx seems to have thought sooner), the revolution would sweep away capitalist society and its forms as capitalist society had already swept away feudal.

There was much more to Marx than this, but the confidence that history was on their side expressed in *The Communist Manifesto* was a great tonic to revolutionaries. They learnt with gratitude that the cause to which they were impelled anyway by motives ranging from a sense of injustice to the promptings of envy was predestined to triumph. This was essentially a religious faith. For all the intellectual possibilities of the doctrine in competent hands as an analytical instrument, Marxism came to be above all a popular mythology, resting on a view of history which said that men are bound by necessity because their institutions would be determined by the evolving methods of production, and on a faith that the working class were the Chosen People whose pilgrimage through a wicked world would end in the triumphal establishment of a just society where necessity's iron law would cease to operate. Social revolutionaries could thus feel confident of scientifically irrefutable arguments for irresistible progress towards the socialist millennium while clinging to a revolutionary creed it seemed to make unnecessary. Marx himself seems to have followed his teaching more cautiously, applying it only to the broad, sweeping changes in history which individuals are powerless to resist and not to its detailed unfolding. Perhaps it is not surprising that, like many masters, he did not recognize all his pupils: he came later to protest that he was not a Marxist.

This new religion was an inspiration to working-class organization. Trades unions and cooperatives already existed; the first international organization of working men appeared in 1863. Though it included many who did not subscribe to Marx's views, his influence was paramount within it (he was its secretary). Its name soon had power to frighten conservatives, some of whom blamed the Paris Commune on it. Whatever their justification, their instincts were right. What happened in the years after 1848 was that socialism captured the revolutionary tradition from the liberals, and the future ideology of an industrial working class still barely visible outside England (let alone predominant in most countries) would be tacked on to the liberal tradition which held that, broadly speaking, revolution could not be wrong. The forms of thinking about politics evolved in the French Revolution were thus transferred to societies to which they would prove increasingly inappropriate. How easy and also how successful such a transition could be was shown by the way Marx snapped up the Paris Commune for socialism. In a powerful

tract he annexed it to his own theories, though it was, in fact, the product of many complicated and differing forces and expressed very little in the way of egalitarianism, let alone 'scientific' socialism. It emerged, moreover, in a city which, though huge, was not one of the great manufacturing centres in which he predicted proletarian revolution would mature. They remained, instead, stubbornly quiescent. The Commune was, in fact, the last and greatest example of revolutionary and traditional Parisian radicalism. It was a great failure (and socialism suffered from it, too, because of the repressive measures it provoked), yet Marx made it an important episode in socialist mythology. The ultimate effects of this must be recognized to transcend both its own failure and the incoherence of the arguments with which Marx justified this view of it.

In one way or another, the revolutionary tradition deeply affected many European countries by 1870. Only Russia seemed, except in her Polish lands, immune to it. The French Revolution turned out to be another of those experiences which, like feudalism, Renaissance or Reformation, decisively shaped western Europe and passed Russia by. Although Alexander I, the tsar under whom Russia met the 1812 invasion, had indulged himself with liberal ideas and had even thought of a constitution, nothing seemed to come of this. The formal liberalization of Russian institutions did not begin until the 1860s and then its source was not revolutionary contagion. It is true that liberalism and revolutionary ideologies did not quite leave Russia untouched before this; Alexander's reign had seen something of an opening of Pandora's box, so far as ideas were concerned and it had thrown up a small class of critics of the régime who found their models in the West. West European experience prompted some of the Russian officers who went there with the armies which pursued Napoleon to Paris to make unfavourable comparisons with their homeland and this was the beginning of Russian political opposition. In an autocracy this was bound to be conspiratorial. Some of them took part in the organization of secret societies which attempted a *coup* amid the uncertainty caused by the death of Alexander in 1825, the 'Decembrist' movement. It collapsed but only after giving a fright to Nicholas I, a tsar who decisively and negatively affected Russia's historical destiny at a crucial moment by ruthlessly harrying political liberalism.

In part because of the immobility which he imposed upon 'Russia, Nicholas's reign was more formative than that of any other tsar since Peter the Great. A dedicated believer in autocracy, he confirmed the Russian tradition of authoritarian bureaucracy, the management of cultural life, and the rule of the secret police just when the other great powers were, however unwillingly, beginning to move in precisely the opposite direction. There was, of course, much to build on already in the historical legacies which differentiated Russian autocracy from western European monarchy. But there were also great challenges to be met and Nicholas' reign was a response to these as well as a simple inheritance of despotic means by a man determined to use them. The ethnic, linguistic and geographical diversity of the empire, for example, had by then posed problems far out-running the capacity of Muscovite tradition to deal with them. The population of the empire itself more than doubled in the forty years after 1770. This ever-diversifying society none the less remained overwhelmingly backward; its few cities were hardly a part of the vast rural expanses in which they stood and they themselves often seemed insubstantial and impermanent, more like temporary though huge encampments than settled centres of civilization. The greatest expansion had been to the south and south-east; here new élites had to be incorporated in the imperial structure and to stress the religious ties between the Orthodox was one of the easiest ways to do this. As the conflict with Napoleon had compromised the old prestige of things French, a new emphasis on religion was important in the evolution of a new ideological basis for the Russian empire, 'Official Nationality' as it was called, which was propagated under Nicholas I.

Slavophile and religious in doctrine, bureaucratic in form, it gave Russia an ideological unity it had lost since outgrowing its historic centre in Muscovy.

The importance of official ideology was to be from this time one of the great differences between Russia and western Europe. Russian government has never since lost its belief in ideology as a unifying force. Yet this did not mean that daily life either for the civilized classes or the mass of a backward population was in the middle of the century much different in its reality from that of other parts of eastern and central Europe. Argument went on, too, among Russian intellectuals about whether Russia was or was not predominantly a European country. Nevertheless, a decisive turn was taken under Nicholas; from the beginning of the reign possibilities of change which were at least being felt in other dynastic states in the first half of the nineteenth century were simply not allowed to operate in Russia. In the long run this was bound to exclude also certain possibilities of modernization (though other obstacles rooted in Russian society seem equally important), but in the short run it was highly successful. Russia passed through the whole nineteenth century without revolution; revolts in Russian Poland in 1830–1 and 1863–4 were ruthlessly suppressed, the more easily because Poles and Russians cherished traditions of mutual dislike.

The other side of the coin was the almost continuous rural violence and disorder of a savage and primitive society and a mounting and more and more violent tradition of conspiracy which perhaps incapacitated Russian society even further for normal politics, which depend upon a measure of shared assumptions. Unfriendly critics variously described Nicholas's reign as an ice age, a plague zone and a prison, but not for the last time in Russian history the preservation of a harsh and unyielding despotism at home was not incompatible with a strong international rôle. This rested upon Russia's huge military superiority at a time when armies contended with muzzle-loaders and no important technological differences distinguished one from another. In these conditions numbers were decisive. On Russian military strength rested the anti-revolutionary security system, as 1849 showed. But Russian foreign policy had other successes, too. Pressure was consistently kept up on the central Asian khanates and China. The left bank of the Amur became Russian and in 1860 Vladivostok was founded. Great concessions were exacted from Persia and during the nineteenth century Russia obtained Georgia and a part of Armenia. For a time there was even a determined effort to pursue Russian expansion in North America where there were forts in Alaska and settlements in northern California until the 1840s.

The major effort of Russian foreign policy, nevertheless, was directed to the south-west, towards Turkish Europe. War in 1806–12 and 1828 carried the Russian frontier across Bessarabia to the mouth of the Danube. It was by now clear that the eastern question of the nineteenth century would be about the partition of Turkey as that of the previous century had been about the partition of Poland, but there was an important difference: the interests of more powers were involved this time and the complicating factor of national sentiment among the subject peoples of the Ottoman empire would make an agreed outcome much more difficult. As a result, Turkey survived far longer than might have been expected and the eastern question is still bothering statesmen, though its focus is now the Aegean and Levantine legacy of the Ottoman empire, rather than the European.

Some of these complicating factors led to the Crimean War which was much more important in Russia's internal affairs than in those of any other country. It revealed that the military colossus of the 1815 restorations now no longer enjoyed an unquestioned superiority. She was defeated on her own territory and obliged to accept a peace which involved the renunciation for the foreseeable future of her traditional goals in the Black Sea area. Fortunately, in the middle of the war Nicholas I had died and this simplified the problems of his successor; defeat made it clear that change had to come. It was bound to require some degree of modernization of Russian institutions if Russia was again to generate a national power commensurate with her vast potential, which had become unrealizable within the framework of her institutions. When the Crimean War broke out there was still no Russian railway south of Moscow. Russia's once important contribution to European industrial production had hardly grown since 1800 and was now far outstripped by the western countries. Her agriculture remained one of the most unproductive in the world and yet her population steadily rose, pressing harder upon its resources. It was in these circumstances that Russia, too, at last underwent radical change. Though less dramatic than many upheavals in the rest of Europe it was in fact more of a revolution than much that went by that name elsewhere, for what was at last disturbed was the institution which lay at the very roots of Russian life, serfdom.

Its rise had been the leading characteristic of Russian social history since the seventeenth century. Even Nicholas had agreed that it was the central evil of Russian society. His reign had been marked by increasingly frequent serf insurrections, attacks on landlords, crop-burning and cattle-maiming. The refusal of dues was almost the least alarming form of popular resistance to it. Yet it was appallingly difficult for the rider to get off the elephant. The vast majority of Russians were serfs. They could not be transformed overnight by mere legislation into wage labourers or smallholders, nor could the state accept the administrative burden which would suddenly be thrown upon it if the services discharged by the manorial system should be withdrawn and nothing put in their place. Nicholas had not dared to proceed. Alexander III did. After years of study of the evidence and possible advantages and disadvantages of different forms of abolition, the Tsar issued in 1861 the edict which marked an epoch in Russian history and won him the title of the 'Tsar Liberator'. The one card Russian government could play was the unquestioned authority of the autocrat and it was now put to good use.

785

Main Asian railway

Russian Border 1914

Territory acquired after 1850

Russian zone of influence in Persia agreed in 1907

Imperial Russia in Asia 1850 - 1915

The edict gave the serfs personal freedom and ended bond labour. It also gave them allotments of land. But these were to be paid for by redemption charges whose purpose was to make the change acceptable to the landowners. To secure the repayments and offset the dangers of suddenly introducing a free labour market, the peasant remained to a considerable degree subject to the authority of his village community, which was given the charge of distributing the land allotments on a family basis.

It would not be long before a great deal would be heard about the shortcomings of this settlement. Yet there is much to be said for it and in retrospect it seems a massive achievement. A few years later the United States would emancipate its Negro slaves. There were far fewer of them than there were Russian peasants and they lived in a country of much greater economic opportunity, yet the effect of throwing them on the labour market, exposed to the pure theory of *laissez-faire* economic liberalism, was to exacerbate a colour problem with whose ultimate consequences the United States is still grappling. In Russia the largest measure of social engineering in recorded history down to this time was carried out without social and economic dislocation and it opened the way to modernization for what was potentially one of the strongest powers on earth. It was the indispensable first step towards making the peasant look beyond the estate for available industrial employment.

More immediately liberation opened an era of reform; there followed a series of measures which by 1870 gave Russia a representative system of local government and a reformed judiciary. When, in 1871, the Russians took advantage of the Franco-Prussian War to denounce some of the restrictions placed on their freedom in the Black Sea in 1856, there was almost a symbolic warning to Europe in what they did. After tackling her greatest problem and beginning to modernize her institutions Russia was again announcing that she would after all be master in her own house. The resumption of the most consistently and long-pursued policies of expansion in modern history was only a matter of time.

WAITING FOR AN ANSWER.

4 Political change: the Anglo-Saxon powers

No European nation so successfully seeded the globe with its own stocks as did the United Kingdom. As a result, in the nineteenth century there was an Anglo-Saxon world which was an identifiable sub-unit within the ambit of European civilization, with a historical destiny diverging from that of the European continent. Its components included growing British communities in Canada, Australia, New Zealand and South Africa (the first and last containing other important national components, too). At the heart of this world were the two great Atlantic nations, one the greatest world power of the nineteenth century, one that of the next.

They were at first sight so different – and so many people found it profitable to keep on pointing it out – that it is easy to overlook how much the United Kingdom and the United States of America had in common for much of the nineteenth century. For one thing, though one was a monarchy and the other a republic, their politics were in a similar way unlike those of continental Europe. Both countries escaped first the absolutist and then the revolutionary traditions. Anglo-Saxon politics, of course, changed quite as radically as those of any other

COLUMBIA'S FIX.

COLUMBIA. "WHICH ANSWER SHALL I SEND?"

On 7 November 1861 a British steamer homeward bound from Havana was stopped by a United States sloop, boarded and forced to surrender two diplomatic passengers, representatives of the rebellious Confederate government of the South. The result was the last crisis in which there seemed a real danger of war between the two Anglo-Saxon powers. During the weeks of uncertainty Punch *published these two cartoons. In the end, the United States government released its prisoners. There was never again to be so great a danger of collision, for popular feeling had been greatly excited on both sides of the Atlantic. It was already true, though, that by that date no British government could contemplate a war with the United States with anything but dismay.*

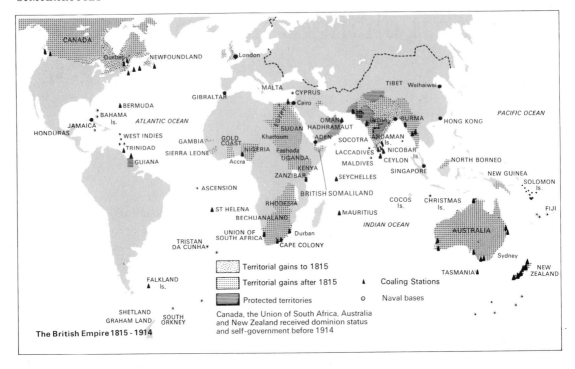

Territorial gains to 1815
Territorial gains after 1815 ▲ Coaling Stations
Protected territories ○ Naval bases

Canada, the Union of South Africa, Australia
and New Zealand received dominion status
and self-government before 1914

The British Empire 1815 - 1914

country in the nineteenth century. But they were not transformed by the same political forces as those of continental states nor in the same way.

Their similarity arose in part because the two countries shared more than they usually admitted, and one aspect of their curious relations was that the United States could still without a sense of paradox call England the mother country. The heritage of English culture and language was for a long time paramount in the United States; immigration from other European countries only became overwhelming in the second half of the nineteenth century. Though by the middle of the century many Americans – perhaps most – already had the blood of other European nations in their veins, the tone of society was long set by those of British stock. It was not until 1837 that there was a president who did not have an English, Scots, or Irish surname (the next would not be until 1901, and there have been only four such down to the present day).

Post-colonial problems made, as they did in far later times, for emotional, sometimes violent, always complex relations between the United States and the United Kingdom. But they were also much more than this. They were, for example, shot through with strong economic connexions. Far from dwindling (as had been feared) after independence, commerce between the two countries had gone on from strength to strength. English capitalists found the United States an attractive place for investment even after repeated and unhappy experiences with the bonds of defaulting states. British money was heavily invested in American railroads, banking, and insurance. Meanwhile the ruling élites of the two countries were at once fascinated and repelled by each other. Englishmen commented acidly on the vulgarity and rawness of American life but warmed as if by instinct to its energy, optimism and opportunity; Americans found it hard to come to terms with monarchy and hereditary titles but sought to penetrate the fascinating mysteries of English culture and society no less eagerly for that.

More striking than the huge differences

790

between them was what the United Kingdom and the United States had in common when considered from the standpoint of continental Europe. Above all, both were able to combine liberal and democratic politics with spectacular advances in wealth and power. They did this in very different circumstances, but at least one was common to both, the fact of isolation: Great Britain had the Channel between herself and Europe, the United States had the Atlantic Ocean. This physical remoteness long masked from Europeans the international potential of the young republic and the huge opportunities facing its citizens in the West. At the peace of 1783 the British had defended its frontier interests in such a way that there inevitably lay ahead a period of American expansion; what was not clear at that time was how far it might carry nor with what other powers it might entangle her. This was in part a matter of geographical ignorance. No one knew for certain what the western half of the continent might contain. For decades the huge spaces just across the eastern mountain ranges would provide a big enough field of expansion. In 1800 the United States was still psychologically and actually very much a matter of the Atlantic seaboard and the Ohio valley.

Its political frontiers were then ill-defined, but imposed relations with France, Spain and the United Kingdom. None the less, if frontier questions could be settled, then a practical isolation might be attained, for the only other interests which might involve Americans in the affairs of other countries were, on the one hand, trade and the protection of her nationals, and, on the other, foreign intervention in the affairs of the United States. The French Revolution appeared briefly to pose the chance of the latter, and caused a quarrel, but for the most part it was frontiers and trade which preoccupied American diplomacy under the young republic. Both were, of course, issues which aroused powerful and often divisive or potentially divisive forces in domestic politics.

The American aspiration to non-involvement with the outside world was already clear in 1793, when the troubles of the French revolutionary war led to a Neutrality Proclamation, rendering American citizens liable to prosecution in American courts if they took any part in the Anglo-French war. The bias of American policy already expressed in this received its classical formulation in 1796. In the course of Washington's Farewell Address to his 'Friends and Fellow-Citizens' as his second term as president drew to a close, he chose to comment on the objectives and methods which a successful republican foreign policy should embody, in language to be deeply influential for later American statesmen and upon the national psychology. In retrospect, what is now especially striking about Washington's thoughts is their predominantly negative and passive tone. 'The great rule of conduct for us', he began, 'in regard to foreign nations is, in extending our commercial relations, to have with them as little political connection as possible.' 'Europe has a set of primary interests', he continued, 'which to us have none, or a very remote relation . . . Our detached and distant situation invites and enables us to pursue a different course . . . It is our true policy to steer clear of permanent alliances with any portion of the foreign world.' Moreover, Washington also warned his countrymen against assumptions of permanent or special hostility or friendship with any other nation. In all this there was no hint of America's future destiny as a world power (Washington did not even consider other than European relations; America's future Pacific and Asian rôle was inconceivable in 1796).

By and large, a pragmatic approach, case by case, to the foreign relations of the young republic was indeed the policy pursued by Washington's successors in the presidency. There was only one war with another great power, that between the United States and Great Britain in 1812. Besides contributing to the growth of nationalist feeling in the young republic (it was during this war that Uncle Sam made his appearance as the caricature embodiment of the nation and the 'Star-spangled Banner' was composed) it marked an important

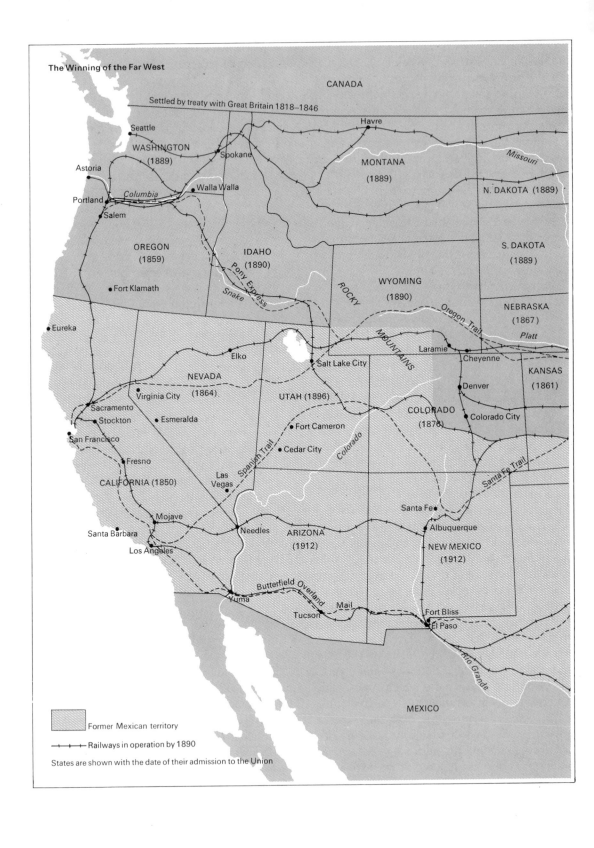

The Winning of the Far West

Settled by treaty with Great Britain 1818–1846

CANADA

Seattle

WASHINGTON (1889)

Astoria

Portland

Salem

Columbia

Walla Walla

Spokane

Havre

MONTANA (1889)

Missouri

N. DAKOTA (1889)

OREGON (1859)

IDAHO (1890)

Pony Express

Snake

ROCKY

WYOMING (1890)

S. DAKOTA (1889)

Fort Klamath

Oregon Trail

NEBRASKA (1867)

Platt

Eureka

Elko

Salt Lake City

MOUNTAINS

Laramie

Cheyenne

KANSAS (1861)

NEVADA (1864)

Virginia City

UTAH (1896)

COLORADO (1876)

Denver

Sacramento

Stockton

Esmeralda

Fort Cameron

Colorado City

San Francisco

Fresno

Cedar City

Colorado

Spanish Trail

Santa Fe Trail

CALIFORNIA (1850)

Las Vegas

Santa Fe

Santa Barbara

Mojave

Needles

ARIZONA (1912)

Albuquerque

Los Angeles

NEW MEXICO (1912)

Butterfield Overland

Yuma

Tucson

Mail

Fort Bliss

El Paso

Rio Grande

MEXICO

Former Mexican territory

Railways in operation by 1890

States are shown with the date of their admission to the Union stage in the evolving relations of two countries. Officially, British interference with trade during the struggle with the Napoleonic blockade had caused the American declaration of war, but more important had been the hopes of some Americans that the conquest of Canada would follow. It did not; the failure of military expansion did much to determine that the future negotiation of the boundary problems with the British should be by peaceful negotiation. Though anglophobia had been aroused again in the United States by the war, the fighting (which had its humiliations for both sides) cleared the air. In future boundary disputes it was tacitly understood that neither American nor British governments were willing to consider war except under extreme provocation. In this setting the northern boundary of the United States was soon agreed as far west as the 'Stony Mountains' (as the Rockies were then called); in 1845 it was carried further west to the sea and by then the disputed Maine boundary, too, had been agreed.

The greatest change in American territorial definition was brought about by the Louisiana Purchase. Roughly speaking, 'Louisiana' was the area between the Mississippi and the Rockies. In 1803 it was theoretically in French possession, the Spanish having ceded it to them in 1800. This change had provoked American interest; if Napoleonic France envisaged a revival of French American empire, New Orleans, which controlled the mouth of the river down which so much American commerce already passed, was of vital importance. It was to buy freedom of navigation on the Mississippi that the United States entered a negotiation which ended with the purchase of an area larger than the then total area of the republic. On the modern map it includes Louisiana, Arkansas, Iowa, Nebraska, both the Dakotas, Minnesota west of the Mississippi, most of Kansas, Oklahoma, Montana, Wyoming and a big piece of Colorado. The price was $11 250 000.

This was the largest sale of land of all time and its consequences were appropriately huge. It changed American domestic history by opening the way to the trans-Mississippi West: the social result would be a shift in demographic and political balance of revolutionary import for the politics of the young republic. This shift was already showing itself in the second decade of the century when the population living west of the Alleghenies more than doubled. When completed with the acquisition of the Floridas from Spain the United States had by 1819 legal sovereignty over territory bounded by the Atlantic and Gulf coasts from Maine to the Sabine river, the Red and Arkansas rivers, the Continental Divide and the line of the 49th Parallel agreed with the British.

The United States was thus already incontrovertibly the most important state in the Americas. Though there were still some European colonial possessions there, a major effort would be required to contest this fact, as the British had discovered in war. None the less, alarm about a possible European intervention in Latin America, together with Russian activity in the Pacific north-west led to a clear American statement of the republic's determination to rule the roost in the western hemisphere. This was the 'Monroe doctrine', enunciated in 1823, which said that no future European colonization in the hemisphere could be considered and that intervention by European powers in its affairs would be seen as unfriendly to the United States. As this suited British interests, the Monroe doctrine was easily maintained because it had the tacit underwriting of the Royal Navy; no European power could conceivably mount an American operation if British sea-power was used against it.

The Monroe doctrine remains the bedrock of American hemisphere diplomacy to this day. One of its consequences was that other American nations would not be able to draw upon European support in defending their own independence against the United States. The main sufferer before 1860 was Mexico. American settlers within its borders rebelled and set up an independent Texan republic which was subsequently annexed by the United States. In the war that followed Mexico did very badly. The

The American army enters Mexico City in 1847 at the climax of a war which added more territory to the United States than any acquisitions since the Louisiana Purchase.

peace of 1848 stripped her, in consequence, of what would one day become Utah, Nevada, California and most of Arizona, an acquisition of territory which left only a small purchase of other Mexican land to be made to round off the central mass of territory of the United States in its modern form by 1853.

In seventy years since the Peace of Paris the republic had expanded to fill half a continent. Nearly four million people in 1790 had become nearly twenty-four million by 1850. Most of these still lived east of the Mississippi, it was true, and the only cities with more than 100000 inhabitants were the three great Atlantic ports of Boston, New York and Philadelphia: none the less, the centre of gravity of the nation was moving westward. For a long time the political, commercial and cultural élites of the eastern seaboard would continue to dominate American society. But from the moment that the Ohio valley had been settled a western interest had been in existence and Washington's Farewell Address had already recognized its importance. The West was an increasingly decisive contributor to the politics of the next seventy years, when there came to a head the greatest crisis in the history of the United States and one which settled her destiny as a world power.

Expansion was not only territorial but economic and both shaped American history as profoundly as the democratic bias of her political institutions. Its influence on those institutions, too, was very great and sometimes glaring; often there was a transformation of their operation and significance. The most notable example of this was provided by slavery. When Washington began his presidency there were a little under 700000 Negro slaves within the territories of the Union. This was a large number, but the framers of the constitution paid no special attention to them, except in so far as questions of political balance between the different states which were involved. In the end it had been decided that a slave should count as three-fifths of a free man in deciding how many representatives each state should have.

Within the next half-century three things revolutionized this state of affairs. The first was an enormous extension of slavery, whose support was a rapid increase in the world's consumption of cotton (above all of its consumption by the mills of England). This led to a doubling of the crop in the 1820s and then its doubling again in the 1830s: by 1860, cotton provided two-thirds of the value of the total exports of the United States. This huge increase was obtained largely by cropping new land and new plantations meant more labour. By 1820 there were already a million and half Negro slaves, by 1860 about four million. In the southern states slavery had become the foundation of the economic system. Because of this, southern society became even more distinctive; it had always been aware of the ways it differed from the more mercantile and urban northern states, but now its 'peculiar institution', as slavery was called, came to be regarded as the essential core of a particular civilization. By 1860 many citizens of the southern states thought of themselves as a nation with a way of life they idealized and believed to be threatened by tyrannous interference from the outside. The expression and symbol of this interference was the growing hostility of Congress to slavery.

The growing political importance of slavery was the second development changing its rôle in American life and was part of a general evolution in American politics evident also in other ways. The early politics of the republic had reflected what were to be later called 'sectional' interests and the Farewell Address itself had drawn attention to them. Roughly speaking, this produced political parties reflecting, on the one hand, mercantile and business interests which tended to look for strong federal government and protectionist legislation, and, on the other, agrarian and consumer interests which tended to assert the rights of individual states and cheap

An early (1804) example of anti-slavery propaganda.

money policies. At this stage slavery was hardly the stuff of politics; most political leaders seem to have thought of it as an evil which must succumb (though no one quite knew how) with the passage of time.

This political world gradually gave way to a more modern one, partly as a result of the inherent tendencies of American institutions, partly because of social change. Judicial interpretation gave a strongly national and federal emphasis to the constitution. At the same time as congressional legislation was thus given new potential force, the law-makers were becoming more representative of American democracy; the presidency of Andrew Jackson has traditionally been seen as especially important in this. The growing democratization of politics reflected other changes; the United States was not to be troubled by a proletariat of townsmen driven off the land because in the West the possibility long existed of realizing the dream of independence; the social ideals of the independent smallholder could remain central to the American tradition. The opening up of the western hinterland by the Louisiana Purchase was as important in revolutionizing the wealth and population distributions which shaped American politics as was the commercial and industrial growth of the North.

This was above all true in relation to slavery. The opening of the West inevitably brought slavery into politics, for there was great scope for dispute about the terms on which new territories should be joined to the Union, a question raised as the organization first of the Louisiana Purchase and then territory taken from Mexico had to be set in train.

Finally, this political evolution was affected also by the rise of a fierce anti-slavery movement in the North. This dragged the slavery issue to the forefront of American politics and kept it there until it overshadowed every other question. Its campaign for the abolition of the slave trade and the eventual emancipation of the Negro stemmed from much the same forces which produced such demands in other countries towards the end of the eighteenth century. But the American movement was importantly different, too. In the first place it was confronted with a *growth* of slavery at a time when it was disappearing elsewhere in the European world, so that the universal trend seemed to be at least checked, if not reversed, in the United States. Secondly, it involved a tangle of constitutional questions because of argument about the extent to which private property could be interfered with in individual states where local laws upheld it, or even in territories that were not yet states. Moreover the abolitionists, as they were called, brought forward a question which lay at the heart of the constitution, and, indeed, of the political life of every European country, too: who was to have the last word? The people were sovereign, that was clear: but was the 'people' the majority of its representatives in

Congress, or the populations of individual states acting through their state legislatures and asserting the indefeasibility of their rights even against Congress? Thus slavery was by mid-century entangled with almost every side of American politics.

These great issues were contained so long as the balance of power between the southern and northern states remained roughly the same. Although the North had a slight preponderance of numbers, the crucial equality in the Senate was maintained. Down to 1819, new states were admitted to the Union on an alternating system, one slave, one free; there were then eleven of each. Then came the first crisis, over the admission of the state of Missouri. In the days before the Louisiana Purchase French and Spanish law permitted slavery there and its settlers expected this to continue. They were indignant, and so were representatives of the southern states when a northern congressman proposed restrictions upon slavery in the new state's constitution. There was great public stir and debate about sectional advantage; there was even talk of secession from the Union, so strongly did some southerners feel. Yet the moral issue was muted. It was still possible to reach a political answer to a political question by the 'Missouri Compromise' which admitted Missouri as a slave state, but balanced her by admitting Maine at the same time, and prohibiting any further extension of slavery in United States territory north of a line of latitude 36° 30'. This confirmed the doctrine that Congress had the right to keep slavery out of new territories if it chose to exercise it, but there was no reason to believe that the question would again arise for a long time. Indeed, so it proved until a generation had passed. But already some had seen the future it contained: Thomas Jefferson, a former president and the man who drafted the Declaration of Independence, wrote that he 'considered it at once as the knell of the Union', and another (future) president wrote in his diary that the Missouri question was 'a mere preamble – a title-page to a great, tragic volume'.

Yet the tragedy did not come to its climax for

forty years. In part this was because Americans had much else to think about – territorial expansion above all – and in part because no question arose of incorporating territories suitable for cotton-growing, and therefore requiring slave labour, until the 1840s. But there were soon forces at work to agitate public opinion and they would be effective when the public was ready to listen. It was in 1831 that a newspaper was established in Boston to advocate the unconditional emancipation of Negro slaves. This was the beginning of the 'abolitionist' campaign of increasingly embittered propaganda, electoral pressure upon politicians in the North, assistance to runaway slaves and opposition to their return after recapture to their owners, even when the law courts said they must be sent back. Against the background abolitionists provided, a struggle raged in the 1840s over the terms on which territory won from Mexico should be admitted. It ended in 1850 in a new Compromise, but one not to last long. From this time, politics were strained by increasing feelings of persecution and victimization among the southern leaders and a growing arrogance on their part in the defence of their states' way of life. National party allegiances were already affected by the slavery issue; the Democrats took their stand on the finality of the 1850 settlement.

The 1850s brought the descent to disaster. The need to organize Kansas blew up the truce which rested on the 1850 Compromise and brought about the first bloodshed as abolitionists strove to bully pro-slavery Kansans into accepting their views. There emerged a Republican party in protest against the proposal that popular sovereignty in the territory should decide whether Kansas should be slave or free: Kansas was north of the 36° 30′ line. The anger of abolitionists now mounted, too, whenever the law supported the slave-owner, as it did in a notable Supreme Court decision in 1857 which returned a Negro to his master. In the South, on the other hand, such outcries were seen as incitements to disaffection among the blacks and a determination to use the electoral system

against southern liberties – a view which was, of course, justified, because the abolitionists, at least, were not men who would compromise, though they could not get the Republican party to support them. The Republican presidential candidate in the election of 1860 campaigned on a programme which in so far as it concerned slavery envisaged only the exclusion of slavery from all territories to be brought into the Union in the future.

This was already too much for some southerners. Although the Democrats were divided, the country voted on strictly sectional grounds in 1860; the Republican candidate Abraham Lincoln, who was to prove the greatest of American presidents, was elected by northern states, together with the two Pacific coast ones. This was the end of the line for many southerners. South Carolina formally seceded from the Union as a protest against the election. In February 1861 she was joined by six other states and the Confederate States of America which they set up had its provisional government and president installed a month before President Lincoln was inaugurated in Washington.

Both sides accused one another of revolutionary designs and behaviour. It is very difficult not to agree. The heart of the northern position, as Lincoln saw, was that democracy should prevail, a claim of potentially limitless revolutionary implication. In the end, what the North achieved, too, was a social revolution in the South. On the other side, what the South was asserting in 1861 (and three more states joined the Confederacy after the first shots were fired) was that it had the same right to organize its life as had, say, revolutionary Poles or Italians in Europe. It is unfortunate, but generally true, that the coincidence of nationalist claims with liberal institutions is rarely exact, or even close. At the same time, though these great issues of principle were certainly at stake, they presented themselves in concrete, personal and local terms which make it very difficult to state clearly the actual lines along which the Republic divided for the great crisis of its history and

797

LIBERTY, EQUALITY, FRATERNITY.

DEDICATED TO THE SMARTEST NATION IN ALL CREATION.

identity. They ran through families, towns and villages, religions, and sometimes ran round groups of different colours. It is the tragedy of civil wars to be like that.

War also has a revolutionary potential of its own. Much of the particular impact of what one side called the Rebellion and the other side the War between the States grew out of the necessities of the struggle. It took four years for the Union forces to beat the Confederacy and in that time an important change had occurred in Lincoln's aims. At the beginning of the war he had spoken only of restoring the proper order

A comment on the democracy which tolerated slavery from Punch, *1848.*

New shapes of war. The first duel between totally ironclad ships was between the northern Monitor, *a strange vessel which was little but a floating turret, and the southern* Virginia *adapted from the hulk of a captured frigate, the* Merrimac. *The result was a stalemate. Neither ship could inflict real damage on the other.*

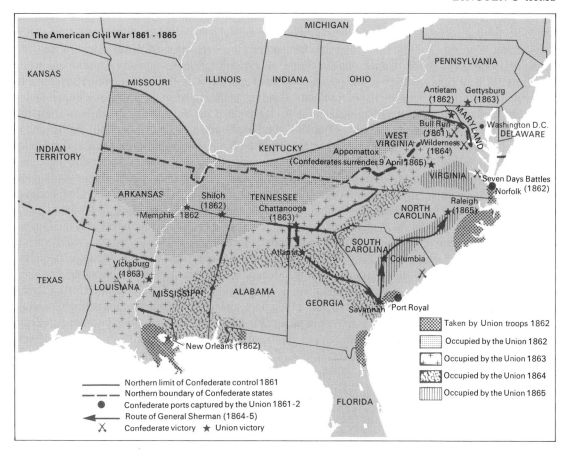

The American Civil War 1861 - 1865

KANSAS

MISSOURI

ILLINOIS

INDIANA

OHIO

MICHIGAN

PENNSYLVANIA

Antietam (1862)

Gettysburg (1863)

INDIAN TERRITORY

KENTUCKY

WEST VIRGINIA

Bull Run (1861)

Washington D.C.

DELAWARE

Wilderness (1864)

Appomattox
(Confederates surrender 9 April 1865)

VIRGINIA

Seven Days Battles

Norfolk (1862)

ARKANSAS

Shiloh (1862)

TENNESSEE

Chattanooga (1863)

Memphis 1862

NORTH CAROLINA

Raleigh (1865)

Atlanta

SOUTH CAROLINA

Columbia

TEXAS

Vicksburg (1863)

LOUISIANA

MISSISSIPPI

ALABAMA

GEORGIA

Savannah

Port Royal

New Orleans (1862)

Taken by Union troops 1862

Occupied by the Union 1862

Occupied by the Union 1863

Occupied by the Union 1864

Occupied by the Union 1865

FLORIDA

————— Northern limit of Confederate control 1861
— — — Northern boundary of Confederate states
● Confederate ports captured by the Union 1861-2
◄——— Route of General Sherman (1864-5)
X Confederate victory ★ Union victory

of affairs: there were things happening in the southern states, he told the people, 'too powerful to be suppressed by the ordinary course of judicial proceedings' and they would require military operations. This view broadened into a consistent reiteration that the war was fundamentally about preserving the Union; Lincoln's aim in fighting was to reunite the states which composed it. For a long time this meant that he failed to satisfy those who sought from the war the abolition of slavery. But in the end he came round to it. In 1862 he could still say in a public letter that

If I could save the Union without freeing any slave, I would do it; and if I could save it by freeing all the slaves I would do it; and if I could save it by freeing some and leaving others alone, I would also do that,

but he did so at a moment when he had already decided that he must proclaim the emancipation of slaves in the rebel states. It became effective on New Year's Day 1863; thus the nightmare of Southern politicians was reality at last, though only because of the war they had courted. It transformed the nature of the struggle, though not very obviously. In 1865 the final step was taken in an amendment to the constitution which prohibited slavery anywhere in the United States. By that time the Confederacy was defeated, Lincoln was dead and the cause which he had imperishably summed up as 'government of the people, by the people, for the people' was safe.

In the aftermath of its military victory that cause could hardly appear as an unequivocally noble or righteous one to all Americans, but its triumph was pregnant with importance not only for America but for mankind. It was the only

799

political event of the century whose implications were as far-reaching as, say, the Industrial Revolution. The war settled the future of the continent; one great power would continue to dominate the Americas and exploit the resources of the richest untapped domain yet open to man. That fact in due course settled the outcome of two world wars and therefore the history of the world. The Union armies also decided that the system which would prevail in American politics would be the democratic one; this was not, perhaps, always true in the sense of Lincoln's words but the political institutions which in principle provided for the rule of the majority were henceforth secure from direct challenge. This was to have the incidental effect of linking democracy and material well-being closely in the minds of Americans; industrial capitalism in the United States would have a great pool of ideological commitment to draw upon when it faced its later critics.

There were other domestic consequences, too. The most obvious was the creation of a new colour problem. In a sense there had been no colour problem while slavery existed. Servile status was the barrier separating the overwhelming majority of blacks (there had always been a few free among them) from whites and legal sanctions upheld it. Emancipation swept away the framework of legal inferiority and replaced this with the framework, or myth, of democratic equality when very few Americans were ready to give this social reality. Millions of Negroes in the South were suddenly free. They were also for the most part uneducated, largely untrained except for field labour, and virtually without leadership of their own race. For a little while in the southern states they leant for support on the occupying armies of the Union; when this prop was removed blacks disappeared from the legislatures and public offices of the southern states to which they had briefly aspired. In some areas they disappeared from the polling-booths, too. Legal disabilities were replaced by a social and physical coercion which was sometimes harsher than had been the old régime of slavery. The slave at least had the value to his master of

being an investment of capital; he was protected like other property and was usually ensured a minimum security and maintenance. Competition in a free labour market at a moment when the economy of large areas of the South was in ruins, with impoverished whites struggling for subsistence, was disastrous for the black. By the end of the century he had been driven by a poor white population bitterly resentful of defeat and emancipation into social subordination and economic deprivation. From this was to stem emigration to the North in the twentieth century and the racial problems of our own day.

As another consequence of the war the United States retained a two-party system. Between them, Republicans and Democrats have, continued to divide the presidency to this day, though sometimes threatened by third parties. There was nothing to make this probable before 1861. Many parties had come and gone, reflecting different movements in American society. But the war was to rivet upon the Democratic party a commitment to the Southern cause which at first was a grave handicap because it carried the stigma of disloyalty (no Democrat was president until 1885). Correspondingly, it won for the Republicans the loyalty of northern states and the hopes of radicals who saw in them the saviours of the Union and democracy, and the liberators of the slave. Before the inadequacy of these stereotypes was clear, the parties were so deeply rooted in certain states that their predominance in them, let alone survival, was unchallengeable. Twentieth-century American politics would proceed by internal transformation of the two great parties which long reflected their primitive origins.

For the moment the Republicans of 1865 had it all their own way. Perhaps they would have found a way to reconcile the South if Lincoln had not been murdered. As it was, the impact of their policies upon a South both defeated and devastated made the 'Reconstruction' years bitter ones. Many Republicans strove honestly to use the power they had to ensure democratic rights for the blacks in the South; thus they ensured the future hegemony there of the

Those over whom the war was fought: Negro field hands on a Tennessee plantation after the War between the States.

Democrats. But they did not do too badly. Soon, too, the economic tide was with them as the great expansion interrupted briefly by the war was resumed.

It had been going on for seventy years and was already prodigious. Its most striking mani-festation had been territorial; it was about to become economic. The phase of America's advance to the point at which her citizens would have the highest *per capita* income in the world was just opening in the 1870s. In the euphoria of this huge blossoming of confidence and expectation, all political problems seemed for a while to have been solved. Under Republican administrations America turned, not for the last time, to the assurance that the business of

801

*Main street, Rufus, Oregon, in 1880 or so. For
fifty years the westward trails carried pioneers to
such little towns, whose appearance registered
the 'winning of the West'.*

America was not political debate but economic
advance. The South remained largely untouched by the new prosperity and slipped even
further behind the North; it had no political
leverage until an issue capable of bringing support to the Democrats in other sections turned
up.

Meanwhile, the North and West could look
back with confidence that the astonishing
changes of the previous seventy years promised
even better times ahead. Foreigners could feel
this, too; that is why they were coming to the
United States in growing numbers – two and a
half million in the 1850s alone. They fed a
population which had grown from just over five
and a quarter millions in 1800 to nearly forty
millions in 1870. About half of them by then
lived west of the Alleghenies and the vast
majority of them in rural areas. The building of
railroads was opening the Great Plains to settlement and exploitation which had not yet really
begun. In 1869 the golden spike was driven
which marked the completion of the first trans-
continental railroad link. In the new West the

United States would find its greatest agricultural expansion yet; already, thanks to the
shortage of labour experienced in the war years,
machines were being used in numbers which
pointed to a quite new scale of farming, the way
to a new phase of the world's agricultural revolution which would make North America the
granary of Europe. There were a quarter of a
million mechanical reapers alone at work by the
end of the war. Industrially, too, great years lay
ahead; the United States was not yet an industrial power to compare with Great Britain (in
1870 there were still less than two million
Americans employed in manufacturing), but the
groundwork was done. With a large, increasingly
well-off domestic market the prospects for
American industry were bright.

Poised on the brink of their most confident
and successful era, Americans were not being
hypocritical in forgetting the losers. They
understandably found it easy to do so in the
general sense that the American system worked
well. The blacks and the poor whites of the
South had now joined the Indian, who had
been a loser steadily for two centuries and a half,
as the forgotten failures. The new poor of the
growing northern cities should probably not be
regarded, comparatively, as losers; they were at
least as well off, and probably better, than the

poor of Manchester or Naples. Their willingness to come to the United States showed that she was already a magnet of great power. Nor was that power only material. Besides the 'wretched refuse', there were the 'huddled masses yearning to breathe free'. The United States was in 1870 still a political inspiration to political radicals elsewhere, though perhaps her political practice and forms had more impact in Great Britain – where people linked (both approvingly and disapprovingly) democracy with the 'Americanization' of British politics – than in continental Europe.

Such transatlantic influences and connexions were aspects of the curious, fitful, but tenacious relations between the two Anglo-Saxon countries. They both underwent similar revolutionary change and here, perhaps, the achievement of Great Britain in the early nineteenth century is even more remarkable than the transformation of the United States. At a time of unprecedented and potentially dislocating social upheaval, which turned her into the first industrialized and urbanized society of modern times within a man's lifetime, Great Britain managed to maintain an astonishing continuity in her constitutional and political forms. At the same time, too, she was acting as a world and European power as the United States never had to, and ruled a great empire. In this setting she began the democratization of her institutions while retaining most of her buttresses of individual liberty.

Socially the United Kingdom was far less democratic than the United States in 1870 (if the blacks are set aside as a special case). Social hierarchy (conferred by birth and land if possible, but if not, money would do) stratified the United Kingdom; every observer was struck by the assured confidence of the English ruling classes that they were meant to rule. There was no American West to offset the deep swell of deference with the breeze of frontier democracy; Canada and Australia attracted restless emigrants, but in so doing removed the possibility of their changing the tone of English society. Political democracy developed faster

than social, on the other hand, even if the universal male suffrage already long-established in the United States would not be introduced until 1918; by 1870, the democratization of English politics was already past the point of reversibility.

This great change had come about within a few decades. Though it had deeply liberal institutions – equality at law, personal liberty, a representative system – the English constitution of 1800 had not rested on democratic principles. Its basis was the representation of individual and historic rights and the sovereignty of the Crown in parliament. As late as 1832, the accidents of the past produced from these elements an electorate large by contemporary European standards, but the word 'democratic' was a pejorative one and few thought it indicated a desirable goal. To most Englishmen, democracy meant the French Revolution and military despotism. Yet the most important step in the English political history of the century towards democracy was taken in 1832. This was the passing of a Reform Act which carried out a great revision of the representative system, removing anomalies (such as the tiny constituencies which had been effectively controlled by patrons), to provide a constituency system which better reflected the needs of a country of growing industrial cities, and above all to change and make more orderly the franchise. It had been based on a jumble of different principles in different places; now, the main categories of persons given the vote were freeholders in the rural areas, and househoulders who owned or paid rent for their house at a middle-class level in the towns. The model elector was the man with a stake in the country, although dispute about the precise terms of the franchise still left some oddities. The immediate result was an electorate of about 650000 and a house of commons which did not look very different from its predecessor. None the less, dominated by the landed gentry as it still was, it marked the beginning of nearly a century during which British politics were to be completely democratized, because once the consti-

In England's overwhelmingly conservative countryside the grip of the landlord was still very strong in the 1870s. These labourers and their families are standing outside the cottage from which they have just been evicted for membership of a trades union.

tution had been changed in this way, then it could be changed again and the house of commons more and more claimed the right to say what should be done. In 1867, another Act produced an electorate of about two millions and in 1872 the decision that voting should take place by secret ballot also followed: a great step.

This process would not be completed before the twentieth century, but it soon brought other changes in the nature of British politics. Slowly, and somewhat grudgingly, the traditional political class began to take account of the need to organize parties which were something more than family connexions or personal cliques of members of parliament. This was much more obvious after the emergence of a really big electorate in 1867. But the implication – that there was a public opinion to be courted which was more than that of the old landed class – was grasped sooner than this. All the greatest of English parliamentary leaders in the nineteenth century were men whose success rested on their ability to catch not only the ear of the house of commons, but that of important sections of society outside it. The first and possibly most significant example was Sir Robert Peel, who

created English conservatism. By accepting the verdicts of public opinion he gave conservatism a pliability which always saved it from the intransigence into which the right was tempted in so many European countries.

The great political crisis of Corn Law Repeal demonstrated this. It was not only about economic policy but about who should govern the country, and was in some ways a complementary struggle to that for parliamentary reform before 1832. By the middle of the 1830s the conservatives had been brought by Peel to accept the consequences of 1832 and in 1846 he was just able to make them do the same over the Corn Laws, whose disappearance showed that landed society no longer had the last word. Vengefully, his party, the stronghold of the country gentlemen who considered the agricultural interest the embodiment of England and themselves the champions of the agricultural interest, soon afterwards turned on Peel and rejected him. They were right in sensing that the whole tendency of his policy had been directed to the triumph of the Free Trade principles which they associated with the middle-class manufacturers. Their decision divided their party and condemned it to paralysis for twenty years, but Peel had in fact rid them of an incubus. He left it free when reunited to compete for the electorate's goodwill untrammelled by commitment to the defence of only one among several economic interests.

The redirection of England's tariff and fiscal policies towards Free Trade was one side, though in some ways the most spectacular, of a general alignment of British politics towards reform and liberalization in the central third of the century. During this time a beginning was made with local government reform (significantly, in the towns, not in the countryside where the landed interest was still the master), a new Poor Law was introduced, factory and mining legislation was passed and began to be effectively policed by inspection, the judicial system was reconstructed, disabilities on protestant nonconformists, Roman Catholics and Jews were removed, a postal system was set up

This engraving symbolized the claim of some of the political reformers to represent a true national as opposed to a sectional interest.

THE BRITISH LION IN 1850;

OR, THE EFFECTS OF FREE TRADE.

A certain complacency appears in British public life during the prosperous mid-century.

which became the model on which all others were based, and a beginning was even made with tackling the scandal of neglect in public education. All this was accompanied by unprecedented growth in wealth, whose confident symbol was the holding in 1851 of a Great Exhibition of the world's wares in London under the patronage of the queen herself and the direction of her consort. If Englishmen were inclined to bumptiousness, as they seem to have been in the central decades of Victoria's reign, then it may be said that they had grounds.

Not everyone was pleased. Some noticed only their loss of economic privilege: in fact it remained considerable enough for England to demonstrate extremes of wealth and poverty as great as any other country's. There was some-

what more substance to the fear of creeping centralization. Parliamentary legislative sovereignty led to bureaucracy invading more and more areas which had previously been immune to government intervention in practice. England in the nineteenth century was very far from concentrating power in her state apparatus to the degree which has now become usual in all countries, but some people felt worried that she might be going the way of France, a country whose highly centralized administration was taken to be sufficient explanation of the failure to achieve liberty which had accompanied the French success in establishing equality. In offsetting such a tendency, the Victorian reforms of local government, some of which came only in the last two decades of the century, were crucial.

Some foreigners admired. Most wondered how, in spite of the appalling conditions of her factory towns, England had somehow navigated the shoals of popular demands which had proved fatal to orderly government in other states. She had deliberately undertaken huge reconstructions of her institutions at a time when the dangers of revolution were clearly apparent elsewhere, and had emerged unscathed, her power and wealth enhanced and the principles of liberalism even more apparent in her politics. She did not have the advantage of geographical remoteness and almost limitless land which was enjoyed by the United States – and even the United States had fought one of the bloodiest wars in human history to contain a revolution. How, then, had Great Britain done it?

This was a leading question, though one historians still sometimes ask without thinking about its implications that there exist certain conditions which make revolution likely and that Great Britain seems to have fulfilled them. It may be, rather, that no such propositions need be conceded. Perhaps there never was a potentially revolutionary threat in this rapidly changing society. Many of the basic changes which the French Revolution brought to Europe had already existed in Great Britain for centuries, after all. The fundamental institutions offered large possibilities. Even in unreformed days, the English House of Commons and House of Lords were not the closed corporate institutions which were all that was available in many European states. Already before 1832, they had shown their capacity to meet new needs, even if slowly and belatedly; the first Factory Act (not, admittedly, a very helpful one) had been passed as early as 1801. Once 1832 was behind, then there were good grounds for thinking that if parliament were only pressed hard enough from the outside, it would carry out any reforms that were required. There was no legal restraint on its power to do so. Even the oppressed and angry seem to have seen this. There were many outbreaks of desperate violence and many revolutionaries about in the 1830s and 1840s (which were especially hard times for the poor) but it is striking that the most important popular movement of the day, the great spectrum of protest gathered together in what was called 'Chartism', asked in the

Inside the Crystal Palace: one of the mechanical sections of the Great Exhibition of 1851.

People's Charter which was its programme for measures which would make parliament more democratic and responsive to popular needs, not for its abolition.

Yet it is not likely that the capacity of parliament to provide reform would have been called upon unless other factors had operated. Here it is perhaps significant that the great reforms of Victorian England were all ones which interested the middle classes as much as the masses, with the possible exception of factory legislation. The English middle class came to an early share in political power as its continental counterparts had not and could therefore use it to obtain change; it was not tempted to ally with revolution, the recourse of desperate men to whom other avenues were closed. But in any case it does not seem that the English masses were themselves very revolutionary. At any rate, their failure to act in a revolutionary way has caused much distress to later left-wing historians. Whether this is because their sufferings were too great, not great enough or whether simply there were too many differences between different sections of the working class has been much disputed. But it is at least worth noticing, as did contemporary visitors that in England traditional patterns of behaviour died hard; it was long to remain a country with habits of deference to social superiors which much struck foreigners – especially Americans. Moreover, there were working-class organizations which provided alternatives to revolution. They were often 'Victorian' in their admirable emphasis on self-help, caution, prudence, sobriety. Of the elements making up the great English Labour movement, only the political party which bears that name was not in existence already before 1840; the others were mature by the 1860s. The 'friendly societies' for insurance against misfortune, cooperative associations and, above all, trades unions all provided effective channels for personal participation in the improvement of working-class life, even if at first only to a few and slowly. This early maturity was to underlly the paradox of English socialism, its later dependence on a very conservative and unrevolutionary trade-union movement, the largest and best organized in the world.

Once the 1840s were over, economic trends may have helped to allay discontent. At any rate working-class leaders often said so, almost regretfully; they, at least, thought that betterment told against a revolutionary danger in England. As the international economy picked up in the 1850s good times came to the industrial cities of an England which was the workshop of the world and its merchant, banker, and insurer, too. As employment and wages rose, the support which the Chartists had mustered crumbled away and they were soon only a reminiscence.

The symbols of the unchanging form which contained so much change were the central institutions of the kingdom, parliament and the

The Six Points
OF THE
PEOPLE'S
CHARTER.

1. A VOTE for every man twenty-one years of age, of sound mind, and not undergoing punishment for crime.

2. THE BALLOT.—To protect the elector in the exercise of his vote.

3. No PROPERTY QUALIFICATION for Members of Parliament —thus enabling the constituencies to return the man of their choice, be he rich or poor.

4. PAYMENT OF MEMBERS, thus enabling an honest tradesman, working man, or other person, to serve a constituency, when taken from his business to attend to the interests of the country.

5. EQUAL CONSTITUENCIES, securing the same amount of representation for the same number of electors, instead of allowing small constituencies to swamp the votes of large ones.

6. ANNUAL PARLIAMENTS, thus presenting the most effectual check to bribery and intimidation, since though a constituency might be bought once in seven years (even with the ballot), no purse could buy a constituency (under a system of universal suffrage) in each ensuing twelvemonth; and since members, when elected for a year only, would not be able to defy and betray their constituents as now.

Subjoined are the names of the gentlemen who embodied these principles into the document called the "People's Charter," at an influential meeting held at the British Coffee House, London, on the 7th of June, 1837:—

Daniel O'Connell, Esq., M.P.,
John Arthur Roebuck, Esq., M.P.
John Temple Leader, Esq., M.P.
Charles Hindley, Esq. M.P.
Thomas Perronet Thompson, Esq., M.P.
William Sharman Crawford, Esq., M.P.

Mr. Henry Hetherington.
Mr. John Cleave.
Mr. James Watson.
Mr. Richard Moore.
Mr. William Lovett.
Mr. Henry Vincent.

W. COLLINS, PRINTER, "WEEKLY TIMES" OFFICE, DUDLEY.

The claims of the Chartists. All except the last have been enacted.

Crown. When the Palace of Westminster was burned down and a new one was built, a mock-medieval design was chosen to emphasize the antiquity of the Mother of Parliaments. In such ways the violent changes of the most revolutionary era of English history were masked by the robes of custom and tradition. Above all, the monarchy continued. Already when Victoria ascended the throne, it was second only to the Papacy in antiquity among the political institutions of Europe yet it was no less changed in reality, for all that. It had been brought very low in public esteem by George III's successor,

NORTH FRONT OF THE SPEAKERS RESIDENCE AND FRONT TOWARDS NEW PALACE YAR

A detail of the design with which Sir Charles Barry won the competition to build the new Houses of Parliament replacing those burned down in 1834.

the worst of English kings, and not much improved by his heir. Victoria and her husband were to make it again unquestioned. In part this was against the grain for the queen herself; she did not pretend to enjoy the political neutrality appropriate to a constitutional monarch when the Crown had withdrawn above the political battle. None the less, it was in her reign that this withdrawal was seen to be made. She also domesticated the monarchy; for the first time since the days of the young George III the phrase 'the Royal Family' was a reality and could be seen to be such. It was one of many ways in which her German husband, Prince Albert, helped her, though he got little thanks for it from an ungrateful English public.

There was only one sphere in which the capacity for imaginative change seemed always to fail the British people. This was in their dealings with Ireland, the one place where England faced a real revolutionary danger and had had to put down a rebellion in 1798. In the 1850s and 1860s things were quiet. But the

reason was in large measure an appalling disaster which overtook Ireland in the middle of the 1840s when the failure of the potato crop was followed by famine, disease and thus, brutally, a Malthusian solution of Ireland's over-population. There were other problems in Ireland which would emerge later. For the moment, the demand for the repeal of the Act of Union which had joined her to Great Britain in 1801 was muted, the dislike of her predominantly Catholic population for an alien and established Protestant Church was in abeyance and there was no serious disturbance among a peasant population feeling no loyalty to absentee English landlords. The problems none the less remained and the Liberal government which took office in 1868 addressed itself above all else to them. All that emerged was a new Irish nationalist movement, demanding 'Home Rule'. This demand was to haunt British politics and overturn their combinations and settlements for the rest of the century. Through its capacity to wreck British Liberalism, Ireland again became of importance in world history after over a thousand years. She made another important and indirect impact upon it at about the same time, with the Irish emigration to the United States.

808

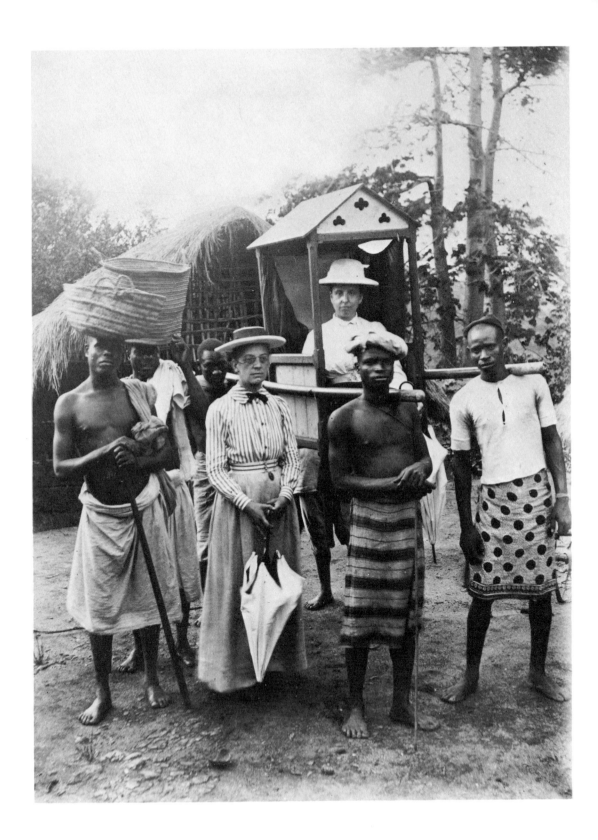

5 The European world hegemony

In 1900 European nations and nations of European stock overseas dominated the globe. This was not always to the disadvantage of non-Europeans, but they were almost always the underdogs. If they were not ruled directly by European governments, they were either helplessly involved in European commerce or gave individual Europeans a big share in the direction of their affairs. Sometimes (perhaps most important of all as a demonstration of inferiority) they succumbed to the attractive force of European ideals or, most diabolical of all European exports, to a new set of expectations. Such things make it reasonable to talk about the hegemony of European civilization. Some have preferred the term 'western', because the United States played a big part in it, at some times and in some places. This is acceptable but unnecessarily finicky; the rest of the world hardly distinguished American from European and the Americas belong to the European tradition of civilization. Given the current use of the phrase 'western world', it is easier, clearer and more accurate to speak here in terms of Europe, making other distinctions when it is necessary to do so.

European hegemony in about 1900 can be pictured as a succession of concentric circles. The innermost was old Europe itself, which

At the beginning of this century Christian missionaries were still the pioneers and spearhead of European influence in many parts of the world. These indomitable ladies were about to set off when photographed on a West African journey.

had grown in wealth and population for three centuries thanks to an increasing mastery of its own and the world's resources. Europeans distinguished themselves more and more from other men by taking and consuming a growing share of the world's goods and by the energy and skill they showed in manipulating their environment. Their civilization was already rich and was all the time getting richer. Industrialization had confirmed its self-feeding capacity to open up and create new resources; furthermore, the power generated by new wealth made possible the appropriation of the wealth of other parts of the world. The profits of Congo rubber, Burmese teak or Persian oil would not for a long time be reinvested in those countries. The poor European and American benefited from low prices for raw materials, and mortality rates tell the story of an industrial civilization finding it possible to give its peoples a richer life. Even the European peasant could buy cheap manufactured clothes and tools while his contemporaries in Africa and India still lived in the Stone Age.

This wealth was shared by the second circle of European hegemony, that of the European cultures transplanted overseas. The United States is the greatest example; Canada, Australia, New Zealand, South Africa and the countries of South America make up the list. They did not all stand on the same footing towards the Old World, but together with Europe proper they make up what is sometimes called the 'western world', an unhelpful expression, since they are scattered all round the globe, but one which expresses the important fact of the similarity of the ideas and institutions of the Europeans who first settled in them and laid their foundations. Of course, this was not all that shaped them. They all had their frontiers, they all had to face special environmental challenges and historical circumstances. But what they had in common were ways of dealing with these challenges, institutions which different frontiers would re-shape in different ways. They were all formally Christian – no one ever settled new lands in the name of atheism until the twentieth century – all regulated their affairs by European systems of law, and all had access to the great cultures of Europe with which they shared their languages.

In 1900 this world was sometimes called the 'civilized world'. It was called that just because it was a world of shared standards; the confident people who used the phrase could not easily see that there was much else deserving of the name of civilization in the world. When they looked for it, they tended to see only heathen, back-ward, benighted peoples. Such an attitude was itself part of the story of European success which fed it; what were taken to be demonstra-tions of the inherent superiority of European ideas and values nerved men to fresh assaults on the world and inspired fresh incomprehension of it. The progressive values of the eighteenth century provided new arguments for superiority and Europeans had by the end of it lost almost all of their humility towards the achievements of other civilizations. Their own social practice seemed obviously superior to the unintelligible barbarities found elsewhere and the advocacy of individual rights, a free press, universal suffrage, the protection of women, children (and even animals) from exploitation, have been ideals pursued right down to our own day in other lands by Europeans and Americans, often wholly unconscious that they might be in-appropriate. Philanthropists and progressives long continued to be confident that the values of European civilization should be universalized as were its medicine and sanitation, even when de-ploring other assertions of European superiority. Science, too, has often seemed to point in the

Samuel Ajayi Crowther, who had been rescued as a child from a slave ship and became the first black bishop of the Church of England.

same direction, to the destruction of supersti-tion and the bringing of the blessings of a rational exploitation of resources, the provision of for-mal education and the suppression of backward social customs. There was a well-nigh universal assumption that the values of European civiliza-tion were better than indigenous ones and a large obliviousness to any disruptive effects they might have.

Fortunately, it was thought, for the peoples of some of the lands over which 'thick darkness' (as the Victorian hymn put it) brooded, they were in many instances ruled directly by Euro-peans or European stocks: subject peoples formed the third concentric circle of European civilization. In many colonies enlightened ad-ministrators toiled to bring the blessings of rail-

This European magnate in his chauffeur-driven car was carved in the Belgian Congo in the early years of this century.

ways, western education, hospitals, law and order to peoples whose own institutions had clearly failed (the evidence of their inadequacy was that they had failed to stand up to the challenge and competition of a superior civilization). Even when native institutions were protected and preserved, it was from a position which assumed the superiority of the culture of the colonial power.

That conscious superiority is no longer admired or admissible. In one respect, nevertheless, it achieved an end which the most scrupulous critics of colonialism still accept as a good one, even when suspecting the motives which brought it about. This was the abolition of slavery in the European world in all its senses and the deployment of force and diplomacy to damage it even in countries Europeans did not control. The crucial steps were taken in 1807 and 1834, when the British parliament abolished first the trade in slaves and then slavery itself in the British empire. This action by the major naval, imperial and commercial power was decisive; similar measures were soon enforced by other European nations and slavery finished in the United States in 1865. The end of the process may be reckoned to be the

emancipation of slaves in Brazil in 1888, at which date colonial governments and the Royal Navy were pressing hard on the operations of Arab slave-traders in the African continent and the Indian Ocean. Many forces, intellectual, religious, economic and political, contributed to and explain this great achievement, and debate about their precise individual significance continues. It is perhaps worth pointing out here only that, however abolition came about, and though it was after three hundred years and more of large-scale slave-trading, no civilization once dependent on slavery has ever been able to eradicate it except the European. Furthermore, though in the present century slavery in effect returned to Europe, it cannot now be sustained except by force. It cannot be much consolation to their unhappy occupants, but the forced-labour camps of our own day are run by men who have to pay a tribute of hypocrisy to virtue by disguising their slaves as the subjects of re-education or judicial punishment.

Beyond this outermost circle of directly ruled territories lay the rest of the world. Its peoples were shaped by Europe, too. Sometimes their values and institutions were corroded by contact with it – as was the case in the Chinese and Ottoman empires – and this might lead to indirect European political interference as well as the weakening of traditional authority. Sometimes they were stimulated by such contacts and exploited them: Japan is the only example of an important nation doing this with success. What was almost impossible was to remain untouched by Europe. The busy, bustling energy of the European trader would alone have seen to that.

Thus in many ways the areas which were not directly ruled by Europeans make the point of European supremacy most forcibly of all. European values were transferred on the powerful wings of encouragement and envy. Geographical remoteness was almost the only security and even Tibet was invaded by the British in 1907. Ethiopia is virtually the solitary example of successful independence; it survived British and Italian invasion in the nineteenth

813

century, but, of course, had the important moral advantage of claiming to have been a Christian country in the first place, albeit not a western one and only intermittently, for some fourteen centuries.

Whoever opened the door, a whole civilization was likely to try to follow them through it, but one of the most important agencies bringing European civilization to the rest of the world has always been Christianity, because of its especially close and intimate interest in so much of human behaviour. The territorial spread of the organized churches and the growth in their numbers of official adherents in the nineteenth century made it the greatest century of Christian expansion since apostolic times. Much of this was the result of a renewed wave of missionary activity; new orders were set up by Catholics, new societies for the support of overseas missions appeared in Protestant countries. Yet the paradoxical effect was the intensifying of the European flavour of what was supposedly a creed for all sorts and conditions of men. In most of the receiving countries, Christianity was long seen as just one more aspect of European civilization, rather than as a spiritual message which might use a local idiom. An interesting if trivial example was the concern missionaries often showed over dress. Whereas the Jesuits in seventeenth-century China had discreetly adopted the costume of their hosts, their nineteenth-century successors set to work with zeal to put Bantus and Solomon Islanders into European garments which were often of almost freakish unsuitability. This was one way in which Christian missionaries diffused more than a religious message. Often, too, they brought important material and technical benefits: food in time of famine, agricultural techniques, hospitals and schools, some of which could be disruptive of the societies which received them. Through them filtered the assumptions of a progressive civilization.

The ideological confidence of Europeans, missionaries and non-missionaries alike, rested in the last resort on the knowledge that they could not be kept away even from countries which were not colonized; Europeans had force on their side. There appeared to be no part of the world where Europeans could not, if they wished, impose themselves by armed strength. The development of weapons in the nineteenth century gave Europeans an even greater relative advantage than they had enjoyed when the first Portuguese broadside was fired at Calicut. Even when advanced devices were available to other peoples, they could rarely deploy them effectively. At the battle of Omdurman, in the Sudan in 1898 a British regiment opened fire on its opponents at 2000 yards' range with the ordinary magazine rifle of the British army of the day. Soon afterwards, shrapnel shell and machine-guns were shredding to pieces the masses of the Dervish army, who never reached the British line. By the end of the battle 10000 of them had been killed for a loss of 48 British and Egyptian soldiers. It was not, as an Englishman put it soon afterwards, simply the case that

> Whatever happens, we have got
> The Maxim gun, and they have not,

for the Mahdi had machine-guns in his armoury at Omdurman, too. He also had telegraph apparatus to communicate with his forces and electric mines to blow up the British gunboats on the Nile. But none of these things was properly employed; not only a technical, but a mental transformation was required before non-European cultures could use the instrumentation of the Europeans to defeat them.

In one other sense, more benevolent and less disagreeable, European civilization rested upon force. This was because it could prosper and mature in the *Pax Britannica* which throughout the whole nineteenth century stood in the way of European nations fighting each other for mastery of the non-European world. There was no repeat performance of the colonial wars of the seventeenth and eighteenth centuries, though the greatest extension of direct colonial rule in modern times was going on. Traders of all nations could move without let or hindrance on the surface of the seas and they were often the

A demonstration of the water-cooled Maxim gun, the first successful fully automatic, self-loading weapon and the basis of the machine-guns used by most European armies down to the Great War.

key figures in the spread of European influence. British naval supremacy was a precondition of the informal expansion of European civilization.

It guaranteed, above all, the international framework of trade. By 1900, the centre of this was Europe. In spite of temporary disruptions, a world economy existed which transcended the economies of particular continents. The old peripheral exchanges by a few merchants which had linked them had, from the seventeenth century onwards, been replaced gradually by integrated relationships of interdependence whose outstanding feature was a broad distinction of rôle between industrial and non-indus-

trial countries; the second tended to be primary producers meeting the needs of the increasingly urbanized populations of the first. But this crude distinction needs much qualification and individual countries often do not fit it; the United States, for example, was both a great primary producer and the world's leading manufacturing power in 1914, with an output as great as those of Great Britain, France and Germany together. Nor was this distinction one which ran exactly between nations of European and non-European culture. Japan and Russia were both industrializing faster than China or India in 1914, but Russia, though European, Christian and imperialist, could certainly not be regarded as a developed nation, and most Japanese (like most Russians) were still peasants. Nor could a developed economy be found in Balkan Europe. All that can be asserted is that in 1914 a nucleus of advanced countries existed

*A fanciful deployment of the glamour of
exploration, pride in technological advance and
conviction of Europe's cultural superiority in an
advertisement of the 1890s.*

with social and economic structures quite
different from those of traditional society, and
that these were the core of an Atlantic group of
nations which was increasingly the world's main
producer and consumer.

The world economy came to a sharp focus in
London, where the financial services which sustained the flow of world trade were centered.
A huge amount of the world's business was
transacted by means of the sterling bill of
exchange; it rested in turn upon the international gold standard which sustained con-

fidence by ensuring that the main currencies
remained in fairly steady relationships with one
another. All major countries had gold currencies
and world travel was possible with a bag of gold
sovereigns, five-dollar pieces, gold francs or any
other major medium of exchange without any
doubts about their acceptability.

London was also in another sense the centre
of the world economy because although the
United Kingdom's gross output was by 1914
overtaken in important respects by that of the
United States and Germany, she was the greatest of trading nations. The bulk of the world's
shipping and carrying trade was in British
hands. She was the main importing and
exporting nation and the only one which sent
more of its manufactures to non-European

nations than to European. Great Britain was also the biggest exporter of capital and drew a huge income from her overseas investments, notably those in the United States and South America. Her special rôle imposed a roughly triangular system of international exchange. The British bought goods, manufactured and otherwise, from Europe and paid for them with their own manufactures, cash and overseas produce. To the rest of the world they exported manufactures, capital and services, taking in return food and raw materials and cash. This complex system illustrates how little the European relationship with the rest of the world was a simple one of exchanging manufactures for raw materials. And there was, of course, always the unique instance of the United States, little involved in export, but gradually commanding a greater and greater share of its own domestic market for manufactured goods, and still a capital importer.

Most British economists believed in 1914 that the prosperity which this system enjoyed and the increasing wealth which it made possible showed the truth of Free Trade doctrine. Their own country's prosperity had grown most rapidly in the heyday of such ideas. Adam Smith had predicted that prosperity would continue if a closed imperial system reserving trade to the mother country were abandoned and so, in the case of America, it had soon proved, for a big expansion had come to the Anglo-American trade within a few years of the peace of 1783. By 1800 a majority of British exports were already going outside Europe and there then still lay ahead the greatest period of expansion of trade in India and East Asia. Understandably, British imperial policy was directed not to the potentially embarrassing acquisition of new colonies, but to the opening of areas closed to trade, for that was where prosperity was deemed to lie. The outstanding example was the Opium Wars of 1840 and 1841 which opened five Chinese ports to trade and gave Great Britain Hong Kong as a base for its commercial activities.

In the middle of the nineteenth century there had been for a couple of decades a high tide of Free Trade ideas when more governments seemed willing to act upon them than ever before or after. In this phase, tariff barriers were demolished and the comparative advantage of the British, first among trading and manufacturing nations, had continued. But this era passed in the 1870s and 1880s. The onset of a world-wide recession of economic activity and falling prices meant that by 1900 Great Britain was again the only major nation without tariffs for protection and even in that country questioning of the old Free Trade dogmas was beginning to be heard as competition from Germany grew fiercer and more alarming.

Nevertheless, by comparison with that of today the economic world of 1914 must still seem to be one of astonishing economic freedom and confidence. A long European peace provided the soil in which trading connexions could mature. Stable currencies assured great flexibility to a world price system; exchange control existed nowhere in the world and Russia and China were as completely integrated into this market as other countries. Freight and insurance rates had grown cheaper and cheaper, food prices had shown a long-term decline and wages had shown a long-term rise. Interest rates and taxation were low. It seemed as if a capitalist paradise might be achievable.

As this system had grown to incorporate Asia and Africa, it, too, came to be instrumental in a diffusion of ideas and techniques originally European, but soon acclimatized in other lands. Joint stock companies, banks, commodity and stock exchanges spread round the world; they began to displace traditional structures of commerce. The building of docks and railways, the infrastructures of world trade, together with the beginnings of industrial employment, began in some places to turn peasants into an industrial proletariat. Sometimes the effects on local economies could be bad; the cultivation of indigo in India, for example, more or less collapsed when synthetic dyes became available in Germany and Great Britain. Isolation first disturbed by explorers, missionaries and soldiers was destroyed by the arrival of the telegraph and the railway; in the twentieth century the motor-car which had already appeared in Europe and the United States would take this further. Deeper relationships were being transformed, too; the canal opened at Suez in 1869 not only shaped British commerce and strategy, but once again gave the Mediterranean new importance, not this time as a centre of a special civilization, but as a route.

Economic integration and institutional change were inseparable from cultural diffusion. The formal instruments of missionary religion, educational institutions and government policy are only a tiny part of this story. The European languages which were used officially, for example, took with them European concepts and opened to educated élites in non-European countries the heritage not only of Christian civilization, but of secular and 'enlightened' European culture, too. Missionaries spread more than dogma or medical and educational services; they also provoked the criticism of existing and traditional society and, in some colonies criticism of the colonial régime itself, because of the gap between its performance and the pretension of the culture it imposed.

In the perspectives of the twentieth century, much of what is most durable and important in the impact of Europe on the world can be traced to such unintended, ambiguous effects as these. Above all, there was the simple urge to imitate, whether expressed ludicrously in the adoption of European dress or much more importantly, in the conclusion drawn by many who sought to resist European hegemony that to do so it was necessary to adopt European ways. Almost everywhere, radicals and reformers advocated Europeanization and this survived both the passing of colonial empires and the fragmentation of the world economy. The ideas of 1789 and 1848 are still at work in Asia and Africa and the world still debates its future in European terms.

This extraordinary outcome is too often overlooked. In its unravelling, 1900 is only a vantage point, not the end of the story. The Japanese are a gifted people who have inherited exquisite

It was a minor cultural tragedy that European prestige and influence were at their peak when European women's dress was perhaps uglier than it had ever been. In consequence ladies the world round, were, like this Japanese, persuaded by fashion to discard their own graceful and becoming costume for the horrors of bonnet, shawl and heavy, voluminous skirts.

artistic traditions, yet they have adopted not only western industrialism (which is understandable enough) but western art forms, western dress and even western drink in preference to their own. Though the Japanese find whisky and claret fashionable, *sake* has never swept Europe or the United States. The Chinese nowadays revere Marx, a German philosopher who articulated a system of thought rooted in nineteenth-century German idealism and English social and economic facts. This suggests another curious fact: the balance-sheet of cultural influence is overwhelmingly one-sided. The world gave back to Europe occasional fashions, but no idea or institution of comparable effect to those Europe gave to the world. The teaching of Marx is a force throughout Asia today; the last non-European whose words had any comparable authority in Europe was Jesus Christ. For centuries, thousands of European

The badge of civilization in South Africa in the 1890s: two Kaffir girls in European dress.

European migrants crossing the Atlantic to the United States in about 1890.

ships sailed to Calicut, Nagasaki, Canton. During those same centuries not one Indian, Japanese or Chinese ship ever docked at Tilbury, Genoa or Amsterdam. Not until 1867 did a Japanese steamer sail to the west coast of America. Yet by then the age of the Marco Polos and other isolated, exotic travellers beyond Europe had long since given way to that of steady, regular commercial enterprise, supported by a great network of communications and services across thousands of miles of sea.

These communications also made possible the movement of Europeans who wished to emigrate to the European communities in other continents.

Outside the United States, the two most important groups of these were (as they still are) in South America and the former British colonies of white settlement which, though formally subject to London's direct rule for much of the nineteenth century, were in fact long oddly hybrid, not quite independent nations, but not really colonies either. Both groups were fed during the nineteenth century, like the United States, by the great diaspora of Europeans whose numbers justify one name which has been

given to this era of European demography: the Great Resettlement. Before 1800, there was little European emigration on a large scale except from the British Isles. Since then, something like sixty million Europeans have gone overseas, and this tide began to flow strongly for the first time in the 1830s. In the nineteenth century most of it went to North America, and then to Latin America (especially Argentina and Brazil), to Australia and South Africa. At the same time a concealed European emigration was also occurring across land inside Russia, a country which occupies one-sixth of the world's land surface and which had vast spaces to draw migrants in Siberia. The peak of European emigration overseas actually came on the eve of the First World War, in 1913, when over a million and a half left Europe; over a third of these were Italians, nearly 400000 were British and 200000 were Spanish. Fifty years earlier, Italians figured only to a minor degree, Germans and Scandinavians loomed much larger. All the time, the British Isles contributed a steady flow; between 1880 and 1910 8·5 million Britons went overseas (the Italian figure for this period was just over 6 million).

Chinese on the Canadian Pacific Railway.
European entrepreneurs employed cheap Asiatic
labour in many parts of the world.

The greatest number of British emigrants went to the United States (about 65 per cent of them between 1815 and 1900), but large numbers went also to the self-governing colonies; this ratio changed after 1900 and by 1914 a majority of British emigrants was going to the latter. Italians and Spaniards also went to South America in large numbers, though Italians preferred the United States. That country remained the greatest of the receivers for all other nationalities, and the greatest overall: between 1820 and 1950 the United States benefited by the arrival of over 33 million Europeans.

The explanation of this striking demographic evolution is not far to seek. Rising populations in Europe always pressed upon economic possibilities as the discovery of the phenomenon of 'unemployment', a word invented in the nineteenth century, shows. In the last decades of the nineteenth century, when emigration was rising

fastest, European farmers were especially pressed by overseas competition. For the first time in human history there were obvious opportunities in other lands, where labour was needed and there were also easy and cheap means of getting there. The steamship and railroad greatly changed demographic history and they both began to produce their greatest effect after 1880. They permitted much greater local mobility, too, so that temporary migrations of labour, and movements within continents became much easier. Great Britain exported large numbers of Irish peasants, Welsh miners and steelworkers and English farmers; she took in at the end of the nineteenth century an influx of Jewish communities from eastern Europe which remained a distinguishable element in British society. To the seasonal migration of labour which had always characterized such border districts as southern France were now added longer-term movements as Poles came to France to work in coal-mines and Italian waiters and ice-cream men became part of British folklore. When, for political reasons, the North African

Buenos Aires, a major European city of the Americas, in the 1820s.

A well-off Brazilian family goes to mass in the 1830s.

shore became accessible, it, too, was changed by short-range migration from Europe; Italians, Spaniards and Frenchmen were drawn there to settle or trade in the coastal cities and thus created a new society with interests distinct from those of the societies from which the migrants had come.

Easier travel did not only provoke European emigration. Chinese and Japanese migration to the Pacific coasts of North America was already important by 1900. The British empire provided a huge framework within which Indian communities spread round the world. Chinese migrants moved down into south-east Asia, Japanese to Latin America; the spectacle frightened Australians, who sought to preserve a 'White Australia' by limiting immigration by racial criteria. But these movements, though important, were subordinate to the major phenomenon of the nineteenth century, the last great *Völkerwanderung* of the European peoples, and one as decisive for the future as the Barbarian invasions had been.

In 'Latin America' (the term was invented in the middle of the nineteenth century), which attracted in the main Italians and Spaniards, southern Europeans could find much that was familiar. There was the framework to cultural and social life provided by Catholicism, there were Latin languages and social customs. The political and legal framework also reflected the imperial past, some of whose institutions had persisted through an era of political upheaval at the beginning of the nineteenth century which virtually ended Spanish and Portuguese colonial rule on the mainland. This happened because events in Europe had led to a crisis in which weaknesses in the old empires proved fatal.

This was not for want of effort, at least on the part of the Spanish. In contrast to the British in the north, the metropolitan government had carried out sweeping reforms in the eighteenth century. When the Bourbons replaced the last Habsburg on the Spanish throne in 1701 a new era of Spanish imperial development had begun, though it took some decades to become apparent. When changes came they led first to reorganization and then to 'enlightened' reform. The two viceroyalties of 1700 became four, new ones appearing in New Granada (Panama and the area covered by Ecuador, Colombia and Venezuela), and La Plata, which ran from the mouth of the river across the continent to the border of Peru. This structural rationalization was followed by relaxations of the closed commercial system, at first unwillingly conceded and then consciously promoted as a means to prosperity. These stimulated the economy both of the colonies and of those parts of Spain (notably the Mediterranean littoral) which benefited from the ending of the monopoly of colonial trade hitherto confined to the port of Seville.

None the less, these healthy tendencies were offset by grave weaknesses which they did not touch. A series of insurrections revealed deep-seated ills. In Paraguay (1721–35), Colombia (1781) and, above all, Peru in 1780 there were real threats to colonial government which could only be contained by great military efforts. Among others, these required levies of colonial militia, a double-edged expedient, for it provided the *creoles* with military training which they might turn against Spain.

The deepest division in Spanish colonial society was between the Indians and the colonists of Spanish descent, but that between the *creoles* and *peninsulares* was to have more immediate political importance. It had widened with the passage of time. Resentful of their exclusion from high office, the *creoles* noted with attention the success of the British colonists of North America in shaking off imperial rule. At first, too, the French Revolution suggested possibilities rather than dangers.

As these events unrolled, the Spanish government grew more embarrassed in other ways. In 1790 a quarrel with Great Britain led at last to surrender of the remnants of the old Spanish claim to sovereignty throughout the Americas, when it conceded that the right to prohibit trade or settlement in North America only extended within an area of thirty miles around a Spanish settlement. Then came wars, first with France,

AÑO · DE · 1834

A Mexican political allegory of 1834: father Miguel Hidalgo y Costilla had led a successful rising against the viceregal government in 1810. He was later captured and shot. Here he is shown crowning Mexico with victory as the chains that bind her are struck off.

then with Great Britain (twice), and finally in fact (though not in law) with France again, during the Napoleonic invasion. These wars not only cost Spain Santo Domingo, Trinidad and Louisiana, but also its dynasty, which was forced to abdicate by Napoleon in 1808. The end of Spanish sea-power had already come at

Trafalgar. In this state of disorder and weakness, when, finally, Spain itself was engulfed by French invasion, the *creoles* decided to break loose and in 1810 the Wars of Independence began with risings in New Granada, La Plata and New Spain.

The *creoles* were not at first successful and in Mexico they found that they had a racial war on their hands when the Indians took the opportunity to turn on all whites. But the Spanish government was not able to win them over nor to muster sufficient strength to crush further waves of rebellion. British sea-power guaranteed that no other conservative European power could

823

PANAMA (1903)

VENEZUELA
1830

BRITISH
DUTCH
FRENCH

COLOMBIA
1831
(name taken in 1861)

GUIANA

ECUADOR
1830

Amazon

BRAZIL
1822
(Empire until 1889)

PERU
1821

BOLIVIA
1825

PARAGUAY
1811

ARGENTINA
1810
(Argentine
Confederation
until 1853)

CHILE
1818

URUGUAY
1828

Main blocks of territory disputed
and changing hands during the
wars of the nineteenth century

European possessions

PERU and BOLIVIA were confederated 1836-39

FALKLAND ISLANDS
(1820-1833 to Argentina, then to Great Britain)

South America after Independence

step in to help the Spanish and thus practically fulfilled the Monroe doctrine. So, there emerged from the fragments of the former Spanish empire a collection of republics, most of them ruled by soldiers.

In Portuguese Brazil the story had gone differently, for though a French invasion of Portugal had in 1807 provoked a new departure, it was different from that of the Spanish empire. The Prince Regent of Portugal had himself removed from Lisbon to Rio de Janeiro which thus became the effective capital of the Portuguese empire. Though he went back to Portugal as king in 1820 he left behind his son, who took the lead in resisting an attempt by the Portuguese government to reassert its control of Brazil and, with relatively little fighting, became the emperor of an independent Brazil in 1822.

A glance at the map of contemporary South America reveals the most obvious of many great differences between the revolution of 1776 and those of 1810 onwards. No United States of South America was to emerge from the Wars of Independence. Although the great hero and leader of independence, Bolivar, hoped for much from a Congress of the new states at Panama in 1826, nothing came of it. It is not difficult to understand why. For all the variety of the thirteen British colonies and difficulties facing them, they had after their victory relatively easy intercommunications by sea and few insurmountable obstacles of terrain. They also had some experience of cooperation and a measure of direction of their own affairs even while under imperial rule. With these advantages, their divisions still remained important enough to impose a constitution which gave very limited powers to the national government. It is hardly surprising that the southern republics could not achieve continental unity for all the advantages of the common background of Spanish rule which most of them shared.

The absence of unifying factors may not have been disadvantageous, for the Latin Americans of the early nineteenth century faced no danger or opportunity which made unity desirable. Against the outside world they were protected

by Great Britain and the United States. At home the problems of post-colonial evolution were far greater than had been anticipated and were unlikely to be tackled more successfully by the creation of an artificial unity. Indeed, as in Africa a century and a half later, the removal of colonial rule revealed that geography and community did not always make for political units which corresponded to the old administrative divisions. The huge, thinly populated states which emerged from the Wars of Independence were constantly threatened by the danger of falling apart into small units as the urban minorities who had guided the independence movement found it impossible to control their followers. Some did break up. There were racial problems, too; the social inequalities they gave rise to were not removed by independence. Not every country experienced them in the same way. In Argentina, for example, there were few Indians. The country was celebrated by the end of the nineteenth century for the extent to which it resembled Europe. At the other extreme, Brazil had a population the majority of which was black and, at the time of independence, much of it still in slavery (which was not abolished there until 1888). To deal with such problems the new states could not draw upon any tradition of self-government, for the colonial administrations had been absolutist and had not thrown up representative institutions. For the political principles they sought to apply, the leaders of the republics looked in the main to the French Revolution, but these were advanced ideas for states whose tiny élites did not even share among themselves agreement about accepted practice; they could hardly produce a framework of mutual tolerance. Worse still, revolutionary principles quickly brought the Church into politics, a development which was perhaps in the long run inevitable, given its huge power as a landowner and popular influence, but unfortunate in adding anti-clericalism to the woes of the continent. In these circumstances, it was hardly surprising that during most of the century each republic found that its affairs tended to drift into the hands of *caudillos*,

825

military adventurers and their cliques who controlled armed forces sufficient to give them power until more powerful rivals came along.

The cross-currents of civil war and wars between the new states – some very bloody – led by 1900 to a map which is substantially still that of today. Mexico, the most northern of the former Spanish colonies, had lost land in the north to the United States. Four mainland central American republics had appeared and two island states, the Dominican Republic and Haiti. Cuba was on the point of achieving independence. To the south were the ten states of South America. All of these countries were republican; Brazil had given up its monarchy in 1889. Though all had been through grave civic disorders, they represented very different degrees of stability and constitutional propriety. In Mexico, an Indian had indeed become president, to great effect, in the 1850s, but everywhere there remained the social divisions between Indians and the *mestizos* (those of mixed blood) on the one hand, and those of European blood (much reinforced in numbers when immigration became more rapid after 1870) on the other. The Latin American countries had contained about 19 million people in 1800; a century later they had 63 million.

This argues a certain increase in wealth. Most of the Latin American countries had important natural resources in one form or another and usually these became more valuable as Europe and the United States became more industrialized. Argentina had space and some of the finest pasture in the world: the invention of refrigerator ships in the 1880s made it England's butcher and later grain grower as well. Chile had nitrates and Venezuela had oil; both grew more important with the twentieth century. Brazil had coffee and Mexico oil, too. The list could be continued but would confirm that the growing wealth of Latin America came above all from primary produce. The capital to exploit this came from Europe and the United States and this produced new ties between these European nations overseas and Europe itself.

This increase in wealth nevertheless was connected with two related drawbacks. One was that it did little to reduce the disparities of wealth to be found in these countries; indeed, they may have increased. In consequence, social, like racial, tensions remained largely unresolved. An apparently Europeanized urban élite lived lives wholly unlike those of the Indian and *mestizo* masses. This was accentuated by the dependence of Latin America on foreign capital. Not unreasonably, foreign investors sought security. They by no means always got it, but it tended to divert some of their resources to the support of the existing social and political authorities, who thus enhanced still further their own wealth. It would take only a few years of the twentieth century for conditions resulting from this sort of thing to produce social revolution in Mexico.

The irritation and disappointment of foreign investors who could not collect the debts due to them led sometimes to diplomatic conflicts and even armed intervention. The collection of debt was, after all, not seen as a revival of colonialism and European governments sent stiff messages and backed them up with force on several occasions during the century. When in 1902 Great Britain, Germany and Italy together instituted a naval blockade of Venezuela in order to collect debts due to their subjects who had suffered in revolutionary troubles) this provoked the United States to go further than the Monroe doctrine.

From the days of the Texan republic onwards, the relations of the United States with its neighbours had never been easy: nor are they today. Too many complicating factors were at work. The Monroe doctrine expressed the basic interest of the United States in keeping the hemisphere uninvolved with Europe and the first Pan-American Congress was another step in this direction when the United States organized it in 1889. But this could no more prevent the growth of economic links with Europe than could the revolution sever those of the United States with Great Britain (and North Americans were among the investors in South American countries and soon had their special pleas to make to their government). Moreover, as the century came to an end, it was clear that the strategic situation which was the background to the Monroe doctrine had changed. Steamships and the rise of American interest in the Far East and the Pacific were the main causes of change. This made the United States much more sensitive, in particular, to developments in central America and the Caribbean, where an isthmian canal was more and more likely to be built.

The outcome was greater heavy-handedness and even arrogance in United States policy towards its neighbours in the early twentieth century. When, after a brief war with Spain, the United States won Cuba its independence, special restraints were incorporated in the new Cuban constitution to ensure she would remain a satellite. The territory of the Panama Canal was obtained by intervention in the affairs of Colombia. The Venezuelan debt affair was followed by an even more remarkable assertion of American strength – a 'corollary' to the Monroe doctrine. This was the announcement (almost at once given practical expression in the Dominican Republic) that the United States would exercise a right of intervention in the affairs of any state in the western hemisphere whose internal affairs were in such disorder that they might tempt European intervention. Later, one American president sent marines to Nicaragua in 1912 on this ground and another occupied the Mexican port of Vera Cruz in 1914 as a way of coercing a Mexican government.

This was not the end of an unhappy era of relations between the United States and her neighbours, though far enough to take it for the moment. Their importance here, in any case, is only symptomatic of the ambiguous standing of the Latin American states in relation to Europe. Rooted in its culture, tied to it by economics, they none the less were constrained politically to avoid entanglement with it. This did not, of course, mean that they did not stand, so far as Europeans were concerned, on the white man's side of the great distinction more and more drawn between those within the pale of European civilization and those outside it. When the European thought of 'Latin Americans' he thought of those of European descent, the urban, literate, privileged minority, not the Indian and black masses.

The crumbling of the Spanish empire so soon after the defection of the thirteen colonies long led many people to expect that the other settlements of the British empire would soon throw off the rule of London, too. In a way, this happened, but hardly as had been anticipated. At the end of the nineteenth century, the British magazine *Punch* printed a patriotic cartoon in which the British Lion looked approvingly at rows of little lion-cubs, armed and uniformed, who represented the colonies overseas. They were appropriately dressed as soldiers, for the volunteer contingents sent from other parts of the empire to fight for the British in the war they were then engaged upon in South Africa were of great value and importance. A century earlier, no one could have anticipated that a single colonial soldier would be available to the mother country. The year 1783 had burnt deep into the consciousness of British statesmen. Colonies, they thought they had learnt, were tricky things, costing money, conferring few benefits, engaging the metropolitan country in fruitless strife with other powers and native peoples and in the end usually turning round to bite the hand that fed them. The distrust of colonial entanglements which such views engendered helped to swing British imperial interest towards the East, to the possibilities of Asian trade and the absence of complications caused by European settlers with the confidence that in eastern seas no need for expensive force would be required which could not easily be met by the Royal Navy.

Broadly speaking, this attitude was maintained in British official circles during the whole nineteenth century. It led them to tackle the complicated affairs of each colony in ways which sought, above all else, economy and the avoidance of trouble. In the huge spaces of Canada and Australia this led, stormily, to the eventual uniting of the individual colonies in federal structures with responsibility for their own government. It was in 1867 that the Dominion of Canada came into existence, and in 1901 there followed the Commonwealth of

Australia. In each case, union had been preceded by the granting of responsible government to the original colonies and in each case there had been special difficulties. In Canada the outstanding one was the existence of a French Canadian community in the province of Quebec, in Australia the clashes of interest between settlers and convicts – of whom the last consignment was delivered in 1867. Each, too, was a huge, thinly populated country which could only gradually be pulled together by communications to generate a sense of nationality. In each case the process was slow: it was not until 1885 that the last spike was driven on the transcontinental line of the Canadian Pacific Railway and transcontinental railways in Australia were delayed for a long time by the adoption of different gauges in different states. In the end, nationalism was assisted by the growth of awareness of potential external threats – United States economic strength and Asian immigration – and, of course, by bickering with the British.

New Zealand also achieved responsible government, but a unified one, as befitting a country of much smaller size. This was a colony acquired reluctantly. Europeans had arrived there from the 1790s onwards and they found a native people, the Maori, with an advanced and complex culture, whom the visitors set about corrupting. Missionaries followed, and did their best to keep out settlers and traders. But they arrived just the same. When it seemed that a French *entrepreneur* was likely to establish a French interest, the British government at last gave way to the pressure brought upon it by missionaries and some of the settlers and proclaimed British sovereignty in 1840. In 1856 the colony was given responsible government and only wars with the Maoris delayed the withdrawal of British soldiers until 1870. In the later years of the century, New Zealand governments showed remarkable independence of mind in the pursuit of advanced social policies and achieved Dominion status, that is, full self-government, in 1907.

That was the year after a Colonial Conference in London had decided that the name 'Dominion' should in future be used of all the self-governing dependencies, which meant, in effect, the colonies of white settlement. One more remained to be given this status before 1914, the Union of South Africa, which came into existence in 1910. This was the end of a long and unhappy chapter – the unhappiest in the history of the British empire and one which closed only to open another which now looks almost as bleak.

No British colonists had settled in South Africa until after 1814, when Great Britain for strategical reasons retained the former Dutch colony at the Cape of Good Hope. This was called 'Cape Colony' and there soon arrived some thousands of British settlers who, though outnumbered by the Dutch, had the backing of the British government in introducing British assumptions and law. This opened a period of whittling away of the privileges of the Boers, as the Dutch farmers were called. In particular, they were excited and irked by limitation of their freedom to deal with the native African as they wished. Their especial indignation was aroused when, as a result of the general abolition of slavery in British territory, some 35000 of their blacks were freed with, it was said, inadequate compensation. Convinced that the British would not abandon a policy unduly favourable to the native African – and, indeed, given the pressures upon British governments, this was a reasonable view – a great exodus of Boers took place in 1835. This Great Trek north across the Orange river was of radical importance in making the Afrikaaner consciousness. It was the beginning of a long period during which Anglo-Saxon and Boer struggled in Africa to live sometimes apart, sometimes together, but always uncomfortably, their decisions as they did so dragging in their train others about the fate of the black African.

A Boer republic in Natal was soon made a British colony, in order to protect the African from exploitation, and prevent the establishment of a Dutch port which might some day be used by a hostile power to threaten British communications with the Far East. Another exodus of Boers followed the annexation, this time north of the Vaal river. This was the first extension of British territory in South Africa but set a pattern which was to be repeated. Besides humanitarianism, the British government and the British colonists on the spot were stirred by the need to establish good relations with African peoples which would otherwise (as the Zulus had already shown against the Boers) present a continuing security problem (not unlike that posed by Red Indians in the American northwest in the previous century). By mid-century, there existed two Boer republics in the north (the Orange Free State and the Transvaal), while Cape Colony and Natal were under the British flag, with elected assemblies for which black men who met the required economic tests could vote. There were also native states under British protection. In one of these, Basutoland, this actually placed Boers under black jurisdiction, an especially galling subjection for them.

Happy relations were unlikely in these circumstances and, in any case, British governments were often in disagreement with the colonists at the Cape, who, after 1872, had, responsible government of their own. New facts arose, too. The discovery of diamonds led to the British annexation of another piece of territory which, since it lay north of the Orange, angered the Boers. British support for the Basutos, whom the Boers had defeated, was another irritant. Finally, the governor of Cape Colony committed an act of folly by annexing the Transvaal Republic. After a successful Boer rising and a nasty defeat of a British force, the British government had the sense not to persist and restored independence to the republic in 1881, but from this moment Boer distrust of British policy in South Africa was probably insurmountable.

Within twenty years this led to war. This occurred because of two further unanticipated changes. One was a small-scale industrial revolution in the Transvaal republic, where gold was found in 1886. The result was a huge influx of miners and speculators, the involve-

The Gold Fields of South Africa,
LIMITED.
(Incorporated under the Companies' Acts of 1862 to 1886.)

CAPITAL
£250,000 in 230,000 Shares of £1 each.
And 200 Founders' Shares of £100 each.

First issue 126,000 Shares (26,000 being reserved for issue in South Africa) leaving 100,000 Shares for issue in this country, of which 70,000 Shares have been already applied for, the balance of 80,000 Shares being now offered for subscription, 5/ per Share payable on application, and 5/ on allotment, the balance as required at intervals of not less than 3 months.

Directors.
WILLIAM M. FARMER, Esq., of Messrs. Wm. Anderson & Co., Cape Town, 14, Rosary Gardens, South Kensington.

J. J. HAMILTON, Esq., of Messrs. Sinclair, Hamilton & Co., 17, St. Helen's Place, London, E.C.

LEIGH HOSKYNS, Esq., (late Crown Prosecutor, Cape Colony,) Abingdon, Berks.

Sir RICHARD POLLOCK, K.C.S.I., Director of the Southern Mahratta Railway.

THOMAS RUDD, Esq., of Messrs. Rudd & Co., 63, Queen Victoria Street, E.C.

Managing Directors.
*C. D. RUDD, Esq., M.L.A., of Kimberley. | Directors of the De Beers
*Honble C. J. RHODES, M.L.A., of Kimberley. | Mining Company.
*These gentlemen will join the Board after allotment of the Shares

Bankers.
The ALLIANCE BANK, Limited, Bartholomew Lane, E.C.
STANDARD BANK OF SOUTH AFRICA, Limited, Clement's Lane, Lombard St., E.C.

Solicitors.
Messrs. MARKBY, STEWART & Co., 57, Coleman Street, London, E.C.

Brokers.
Messrs. WHITEHEADS & COLES, 39, Throgmorton Street, London, E.C.

Prospectus of a mining company 1887. The exploitation of minerals was the foundation of industrial capitalism in South Africa.

ment of outside financial interests in the affairs of South Africa, and the possibility that the Afrikaaner State might have the financial resources to escape from the British suzerainty it unwillingly accepted. The index of what had happened was Johannesburg, which grew in a few years to a city of 100000 – the only one in Africa south of the Zambezi. The second change was that other parts of Africa were being swallowed in the 1880s and 1890s by other European powers and the British government was reacting by stiffening in its determination that nothing must shake the British presence at the Cape, essential to its control of sea-routes to the East and increasingly dependent on traffic to and from the Transvaal for its revenues. The general effect was to make British governments view with concern any possibility of the Transvaal obtaining independent access to the Indian Ocean. This concern made them vulnerable to the pressure of an oddly assorted crew of

The coach running between Johannesburg and Pretoria, 1895.

idealistic imperialists, Cape politicians, English demagogues and shady financiers who provoked a confrontation with the Boers in 1899 which ended in an ultimatum from the Transvaal's president, Paul Kruger, and the outbreak of the Boer War. Kruger had a deep dislike of the British; as a boy he had gone north on the Great Trek.

The highest traditions of the British army of Victorian times were amply sustained in the last war of the reign, both in the level of ineptness and incompetence shown by some of its higher commanders and the administrative services and in the gallantry shown by regimental officers and their men in the face of a brave and well-armed enemy whom their training did not prepare them to defeat. But of the outcome there could be no doubt; as the Queen herself remarked, with better strategical judgement than some of her subjects, the possibilities of defeat did not exist. South Africa was a theatre

isolated by British sea-power; no other European nation could help the Boers and it was only a matter of time before greatly superior numbers and resources were brought to bear upon them. This cost a great deal – over a quarter of a million soldiers were sent to South Africa – and aroused great bitterness in British domestic politics; further, it did not present a very favourable picture to the outside world. The Boers were regarded as an oppressed nationality; so they were, but the nineteenth-century liberal obsession with nationality in this case as in others blinded observers to some of the shadows it cast. Fortunately, British statesmanship recovered itself sufficiently to make a generous treaty to end the war in 1902 when the Boers had been beaten in the field. This was the end of the Boer republics. But concession rapidly followed; by 1906 the Transvaal had a responsible government of its own which in spite of the large non-Boer population brought there by mining, the Boers controlled after an electoral victory the following year. Almost at once they began to legislate against Asian immigrants, mainly

The Chicago Irish contingent raised to fight for the Boers, 1899. Anti-British sentiment among Irish-Americans has remained a persistent factor in American politics.

Indian. (One young Indian lawyer, Mohandas Gandhi, now entered politics as the champion of his community.) When, in 1909, a draft constitution for a South African Union was agreed, it was on terms of equality for the Dutch and English languages and, all-important, it provided for government by an elected assembly to be formed according to the electoral regulations decided in each province. In the Boer provinces the franchise was confined to white men.

At the time, there was much to be said for the settlement. When people spoke of a 'racial problem' in South Africa at that moment, they meant the problem of relations between the British and Dutch whose conciliation seemed the most urgent need. The defects of the settlement would take some time to appear. When they did it would be not only because the historical sense of the Afrikaaner proved to be tougher

Freedom fighters of 1899: three generations of Boer farmers in dress typical of that in which most Boers took the field against the British.

The dispossessed: a Maori chief in his hut. The photograph was taken shortly before 1880.

than people had hoped, but also because the transformation of South African society which had begun by the industrialization of the Rand could not be halted and would give irresistible momentum to the issue of the black Africans.

In this respect, South Africa's future had been just as decisively influenced as had those of all the other British white dominions by being caught up in the trends of the whole world economy which Europe dominated. Canada, like the United States, became with the coming of the railroad to her plains one of the great granaries of Europe. Australia and New Zealand first exploited their huge pastures to produce the wool for which European factories were increasingly in the market; then, with the invention of refrigeration, they used them for meat and, in the case of New Zealand, dairy produce. In this way these new nations found staples able to sustain economies much greater than those permitted by the tobacco and indigo of the seventeenth-century plantations. The case of South Africa was to be different in that she was to reveal herself only gradually (as much later would Australia) as a producer of minerals. The

beginning of this was the diamond industry, but the great step forward was the Rand gold discovery of the 1880s. The exploitation of this sucked in capital and expertise to make possible the eventual exploitation of other minerals. The return which South Africa provided was not merely in the profits of European companies and shareholders, but also an augmentation of the world's gold supply which stimulated European commerce much as had done the California discoveries of 1849.

Because of the growth of humanitarian and missionary sentiment in England and because of the well-founded Colonial Office tradition of distrust of settler demands, it was not so easy to forget the native populations of the white dominions as it had been for Americans to sweep aside the Red Indian. In all these nations, nineteenth-century society made its impact not upon ancient civilizations but on primitive societies, some of which were at a very low stage of achievement indeed, Neolithic if not Palaeolithic. The Canadian Indians and Eskimos were a smaller problem than the American Red Indian, because they were fewer and presented no such important obstacle to the exploitation of the west and north-west as had done the Plains Indians' struggle to keep their hunting-grounds. The story in Australia was far bloodier. The hunting and gathering society of the aborigine was disrupted by settlement, tribes were antagonized and provoked into violence by the uncomprehending brutality of the white Australians, and new diseases cut fast into their numbers. The early decades of each Australian colony are stained by the blood of massacred aborigines and there is perhaps no other population inside former British territory which underwent a fate so like that of the American Indian. In New Zealand, the arrival of the first white men brought guns to the Maori, who employed them first on one another, with disruptive effects upon their societies. Later came the wars with the government, whose essential origin lay in the settlers' displacement of the Maori from their lands. At their conclusion, the government took steps to safeguard

In 1816 the governor of Tasmania used pictures in this proclamation asserting the juridical equality of aboriginal and white Tasmanians. None the less, the aborigine population disappeared within the next sixty years.

these tribal lands from further expropriation, but the introduction of English notions of individual ownership led to the disintegration of the tribal holdings and the virtual loss of their lands by the end of the century. The Maoris, too, declined in numbers, but not so violently or irreversibly as did the Australian aborigines.

As for South Africa, the story is a mixed one. British protection enabled some of its native peoples to survive into the twentieth century on their ancestral lands living lives which changed only slowly. Others were driven off or exterminated. In all cases, though, the crux of the situation was that in South Africa as elsewhere, the fate of the native inhabitants was never in their own hands. They depended for their survival upon the local balance of governmental interest and benevolence, settler needs and traditions, economic opportunities and exigencies. Al-

though in the short run they could sometimes present formidable military problems (as did the Zulus of Cetewayo, or the guerrilla warfare of the Maoris) they could not in the end generate from their own resources the means of effective resistance any more than had the Aztecs been able successfully to resist Cortés. For non-European peoples to do that, they would have to Europeanize. The price of establishing the new European nations beyond the seas always turned out to be paid by the native inhabitant, often to the limit of his ability.

Yet this should not be quite the last word. There remains the problem of self-justification: Europeans witnessed these things happening and did not stop them. It is too simple to explain this by saying they were all bad, greedy men and, in any case, the work of humanitarians makes the blackest judgement untenable. The answer must lie somewhere in mentality. Many Europeans who could recognize that something was happening to the native populations even when the white contact with them was benevolent in intention could not be expected to understand the corrosive effect of their culture on established structures. This requires an anthropological knowledge and insight Europe had still to achieve. It was all the more difficult when, clearly, a lot of native culture was simple savagery and the European's missionary confidence was strong. He *knew* he was on the side of Progress and Improvement, and might well still see himself as on the side of the Cross, too. This was a confidence which ran through every side of European expansion, the white settler colonies, possessions directly ruled or the arrangements made with dependent societies. The confidence in belonging to a higher civilization was not only a licence for predatory habits as Christianity had earlier been, but the nerve of a confidence akin, in many cases, to that of crusaders. It was their sureness that they brought something better that blinded men all too often to the actual and material results of substituting individual freehold for tribal rights, of turning the hunters and gatherers, whose possessions were what they could carry, into wage-earners.

6 European imperialism and imperial rule

The ruling of alien peoples and other lands by Europeans was the most striking demonstration of the European hegemony. In spite of enormous argument about what imperialism was and is, it seems helpful to confine the notion of it to such direct and formal overlordship, blurred though the boundaries with other types of power over the non-European world may be. This does not raise or answer questions about causes or motives, on which much time, ink and thought have been spent. It is probably best to recognize from the outset that different and changing causes were at work, and that not all the motives involved were unavowable or self-deceiving. In this sense, too, imperialism was not the manifestation of only one age, for it has been observable all through history, nor was it peculiar to Europe's relations with non-Europeans overseas, for imperial rule has advanced overland as well as across the seas and some Europeans have ruled others and some non-Europeans Europeans. None the less, in the nineteenth and twentieth centuries the word came to be associated with European expansion in particular because the direct domination of Europeans over the rest of the world had by then become much more obvious than ever before.

In 1800 or so, recent events in North America suggested that the European empire built up

The Queen-Empress. Victoria, R.I., ruler of an empire larger in extent and more numerous than any in history, looks out over the maidan of Calcutta, long the capital of British India.

over the preceding three centuries was now in decline. This seemed confirmed soon after by events in Latin America. Surprisingly, this trend was soon reversed even more dramatically. In the nineteenth century European imperialism was carried further and became more effective than ever before. This happened in two distinguishable phases, and one running down to about 1870 can conveniently be considered first. During this, some of the old imperial powers continued to enlarge their empires impressively; such were Russia, France and Great Britain. Others stood still or found theirs reduced; this group included the Dutch, Spanish and Portuguese.

The Russian expansion has at first sight something in common both with the American experience of filling up the North American continent and dominating its weaker neighbours, and something with that of the British in India, but was in fact a very special case. In one direction – the west – Russia faced matured, established European states where there was little successful hope of expansion. The same was only slightly less true of Russian expansion into the Turkish territories of the Danubian regions, for here the interests of other powers were likely always to come into play against her in the end. Her main freedom of action lay southwards and eastwards; in both directions the first three-quarters of the nineteenth century brought Russia great acquisitions. A successful war against Persia (1826–8) led to the establishment of Russian naval power on the Caspian as well as gains of territory in Armenia. In central

Asia an almost continuous advance into Turkestan and towards the central oases of Bokhara and Khiva culminated in the annexation of the whole of Transcaspia in 1881. In Siberia, aggressive expansion was followed by the exaction of the left bank of the Amur from China and the founding in 1860 of Vladivostok, the Far Eastern capital. Soon after, Russia liquidated her commitments in America by selling Alaska to the United States, thus appearing to indicate she would be an Asian and Pacific, but probably not an American, power.

The other two expanding powers of this era, France and Great Britain, had to expand overseas. Many of Great Britain's gains were made at the expense of France in the Revolutionary and Napoleonic Wars, which were in this respect the final round of the great colonial Anglo-French contest of the eighteenth century. As in 1714 and 1763, many of Great Britain's acquisitions at a victorious peace in 1815 were intended to reinforce her maritime strength. There was a general prejudice in official circles against acquiring new dependencies, but naval supremacy and the commercial prosperity it protected rested on good bases and communications. In 1815 Malta, St Lucia, the Ionian islands, the

Gibraltar was one of the most important links in the chain of British naval supremacy. A Highland regiment is here photographed posting sentries on one of the batteries, in the 1860s.

Cape of Good Hope, Mauritius and Trincomalee were all kept for this reason. With the coming of steam later, the location of desirable bases was sometimes significantly different from earlier ones and considerations of the convenience of coaling began to be taken into account; this could lead to further acquisitions. In 1839, an internal upheaval in the Ottoman empire, to which Arabia belonged, gave the British the opportunity to take Aden, a base of strategic importance on the route to India, and others were to follow. No power could successfully challenge such acquisitions after Trafalgar. It was not that resources did not exist elsewhere which, had they been assembled, could have wrested naval supremacy from Great Britain. But to do so would have demanded a huge effort. No other nation operated either the number of ships nor possessed the bases which could make it worth while to challenge this thalassocracy, and there were even advantages to other nations in having the world's greatest commercial power undertake a policing of the seas from which all traders could benefit. Naval supremacy guarded the trade which gave the British colonies participation in the fastest-growing commercial system of the age. Already before the American Revolution British policy had been more liberal in its encouragement of commercial enterprise than the Spanish or French. Thus the old colonists themselves had grown in wealth and prosperity and the later Dominions were to benefit from it. But settlement colonies were out of fashion in London after the American Revolution; they were seen mainly as sources of trouble and expense. Nevertheless, they grew in population and importance in the nineteenth century – when Great Britain was the only European country founding new colonies of settlement – and they, too, sometimes drew the mother country into yet further extensions of territory by annexation and conquest and therefore to further rule over alien lands.

In some of these acquisitions (notably in South Africa) there can be seen at work a new imperial concern about communication with Asia. This is a complicated business. No doubt American independence and the Monroe doctrine diminished the attractiveness of the western hemisphere as a region of imperial expansion, but the origins of a shift of interest to the East can be seen before 1783, in the opening up of the South Pacific and in a growing Asian trade. War with the Netherlands when it was a French satellite subsequently led to new British enterprise in Malaya and Indonesia. Above all, there was the steadily deepening British involvement in India. By 1800 the importance of the Indian trade was already a central, unquestioned axiom of British commercial and colonial thinking. By 1850, it has been urged, much of the rest of the empire had only been acquired because of the strategical and commercial needs of India. By then, too, the extension of British control inside the subcontinent itself was virtually complete. It was and remained the centrepiece of British imperialism.

This had hardly been expected. In 1784 the

The old régime in British India. An officer of the East India Company relaxes in the oriental indulgence of the hookah in this late eighteenth-century Indian painting.

British government had again moved a step nearer to assuming a direct responsibility for the affairs of the East India Company by the institution of 'Dual Control' and had also taken steps to resist the further acquisition of Indian territory; the American experience had reinforced the view that new commitments were to be avoided. Yet there was a continuing problem, in that through its management of revenue the company's affairs inevitably became entangled in Indian administration and native politics. This made it more important still to prevent excesses by its individual officers such as had been tolerable in the early days of private trading; slowly, agreement emerged that the government of India was not only of interest to Parliament because it might be a great source of patronage, but also because the government in London had a responsibility for the good government of Indians. There began to emerge, thus, a notion of trusteeship.

Government controlled the terms on which

British India 1858-1947

Map legend:
- British Territory in 1858
- Acquisitions since 1858
- Protected and dependent native states

Map labels: AFGHANISTAN, Kabul, Peshawar, NORTH WEST FRONTIER PROVINCES, KASHMIR, BALUCHISTAN, PUNJAB, UNITED PROVINCES, Delhi, NEPAL, BHUTAN, ASSAM, UPPER BURMA (1886), RAJPUTANA, SIND, Karachi, Indus, KUTCH, CENTRAL INDIA, Lucknow, Ganges, BENGAL, Calcutta, BURMA, Mandalay, ARABIAN SEA, CENTRAL PROVINCES, Nagpur, EASTERN STATES, ARAKAN, Bombay, Poona, HYDERABAD, Hyderabad, BAY OF BENGAL, PEGU, SIAM, Rangoon, Goa (Portuguese), MADRAS, MYSORE, Madras, Mysore, Pondicherry (French), TRAVANCORE, CEYLON

the Company's charter was periodically renewed. In 1813 the renewal made London's control tighter and also abolished the company's monopoly of trade with India. The wars with France had already led to the gradual extension of British power over south India through annexation and the negotiation of treaties with native rulers which secured control of their foreign policy. By 1833, when the charter was again renewed, the only important block of territory not ruled directly or indirectly by the company was in the north-west. The annexation of the Punjab and Sind followed in

the 1840s and with British paramountcy established in Kashmir, British imperialism had filled up virtually the whole geographical unity of the subcontinent.

The company had in fact ceased to be a commercial organization and had become a government. The 1833 charter took away its trading functions (not only those with India but those with China); in sympathy with current thinking, the Asian trade was henceforth to be conducted on a free trade basis, and the Company confined to an administrative rôle. The way was open to the consummation of many real and symbolic breaks with India's past and the final incorporation of the subcontinent in a modernizing world. Symbolically, the name of the Moghul emperor was removed from the coinage, but it was more than a symbol that Persian ceased to be the legal language of record and justice. This step not only marked the advance of English as the official language (and therefore of English education), but also disturbed the balance of forces between Indian communities. Anglicized Hindus would do better than less enterprising Moslems. In a subcontinent so divided in so many ways, the adoption of English as the language of administration was complemented by the important decision to provide primary education through instruction given in English.

At the same time an enlightened despotism exercised by successive governors-general began to impose material and institutional improvement. Evangelical Christian concern supported them as strongly as utilitarianism. Roads and canals were built and the first railway followed in 1853. Legal codes were introduced. English officials for the Company's service began to be trained specially in a college established for this purpose. The first three universities in India were founded in 1857 and were based on institutions already founded well before this. There were other educational structures, too; as far back as 1791 a Scotchman had founded a Sanskrit college at Benares, the Lourdes of Hinduism. Much of the transformation which India was gradually undergoing arose not from the direct work of government but from the increasing freedom with which other agencies were allowed to operate. Missionaries were at work from 1813 onwards, and their arrival gradually built up another constituency in England with a stake in what happened in India.

The coming of the steamship brought India nearer to England. More Englishmen began to live in India and make their careers there. This gradually transformed the nature of the British presence. The comparatively few officers of the eighteenth-century Company had been content to live the lives of exiles, seeking rewards in their commercial opportunities and relaxation in a social life closely integrated with that of the Indians. They often lived much in the style of Indian gentlemen, some of them taking to Indian dress and food, some to Indian wives and concubines. Reform-minded officials, intent on the eradication of the backward and barbaric in native practice – and in such practices as female infanticide and suttee they had good cause for concern – missionaries with a creed to preach which was corrosive of the whole structure of Hindu or Moslem society and, above all, the Englishwomen who arrived to make homes in India for two and three years at a time while their husbands worked there all radically changed the temper of the British community.

The essence of this change was that the British in India lived more and more apart from the natives, more and more convinced of their superiority and that it sanctioned the ruling of Indians who were culturally and morally inferior. One of them spoke approvingly of his countrymen as representatives of a 'belligerent civilization' and defined their task as 'the introduction of the essential parts of European civilization into a country densely peopled, grossly ignorant, steeped in idolatrous superstition, unenergetic, fatalistic, indifferent to most of what we regard as the evils of life and preferring the repose of submitting to them to the trouble of encountering and trying to remove them'. This robust creed was far from that of the Englishmen of the previous century who had innocently sought to do no more in India than make money, and while the legislation it inspired was antagonizing powerful native interests, those who held it had less and less social contact with Indians; more and more they confined the educated Indian to the lower ranks of the administration and withdrew into an enclosed, but conspicuously privileged, life of their own. They grew consciously more alien from those they ruled. Earlier conquerors had been absorbed by Indian society in greater or lesser measure; the Victorian Englishman and Englishwoman, thanks to a modern technology which constantly renewed their contacts with the homeland and their complete confidence in their

The British view of the Mutiny: Major Skene blows out his brains over the lifeless bodies of his wife and child rather than risk capture.

intellectual and religious superiority, remained immune, increasingly aloof, as no earlier conqueror had been. They could not be quite untouched by India, as many legacies to the English language and the English breakfast- and dinner-table still testify, but they created a civilization that was not Indian, even if it was not wholly English; 'Anglo-Indian' in the nineteenth century was a word applied not to a person of mixed blood, but to an Englishman who made his career in India, and it indicated a cultural and social distinctiveness.

The separateness of Anglo-Indian society from India was made virtually absolute by the appalling damage done to British confidence by the rebellions of 1857 called the Indian Mutiny. Essentially, this was a chain reaction of outbreaks, initiated by a mutiny of Hindu soldiers who feared the polluting effect of using a new type of cartridge, greased with animal fat. This detail is significant. Much of the rebellion was the spontaneous and reactionary response of traditional society to innovation and modernization. By way of reinforcement there were the irritations of native rulers, both Moslem and Hindu, who regretted the loss of their privileges and thought that the chance might have come to recover their independence; the British were after all very few. The response of those few was prompt and ruthless. With the help of loyal

Indian soldiers the rebellions were crushed, though not before there had been some massacres of British captives and the most important force of British in rebel territory had held out at Lucknow under siege for some months.

The Mutiny and its suppression were disasters for British India, though not quite unmitigated. It did not much matter that the Moghul empire was at last formally brought to an end by the British (the Delhi mutineers had proclaimed the last emperor their leader). Nor was there, as later Indian nationalists were to suggest, a crushing of a national liberation movement whose end was a tragedy for India. Like many episodes important in the making of nations, the Mutiny was to be important as a myth and an inspiration; what it was later believed to have been was more important than what it actually was, a jumble of essentially reactionary protests. The really disastrous and important effect it had lay in the wound it gave to British goodwill and confidence. Whatever the expressed intentions of British policy from this time, the consciousness of the British in India was suffused by the memory that Indians had once proved almost fatally untrustworthy. Among Anglo-Indians as well as Indians the mythical importance of the Mutiny grew with time. The atrocities actually committed were bad enough, but unspeakable ones which had never occurred were from this time alleged as grounds for a policy of repression and social exclusiveness. Immediately and institutionally, the Mutiny marked an epoch because it ended the government of the company. The governor-general now became the queen's viceroy, responsible to a British cabinet minister. This structure provided the framework of the British Raj for the whole of its life.

The Mutiny changed Indian history only by thrusting it more firmly in a direction to which it already tended. Another fact which was equally revolutionary for India was much more gradual in its effects. This was the nineteenth-century flowering of the economic connexion with Great Britain. Commerce was the root of the British presence in the subcontinent and it continued to shape its destiny. The first major

Though they had themselves been only recently forced to accept British rule, Sikh soldiers remained loyal during the Mutiny.

During the nineteenth century, the Suez canal was only one of the most spectacular additions to the network of communications which sustained world commerce. Others were provided by the trans-continental railway-builders.

development came when India became the essential base for the China trade. Its greatest expansion came in the 1830s and 1840s when, for a number of reasons, access to China became much easier. It was at about the same time that there took place the first rapid rise in British exports to India, notably of textiles, so that, by the time of the Mutiny, a big Indian commercial interest existed which involved many more Englishmen and English commercial houses than the old company had ever done.

The story of Anglo-Indian trade was now locked into that of the general expansion of British manufacturing supremacy and world commerce. The Suez Canal brought down the costs of shipping goods to Asia by a huge factor. By the end of the century the volume of British trade with India had more than quadrupled. The effects were felt in both countries, but were decisive in India, where a check was imposed on an industrialization which might have gone ahead more rapidly without British competition. Paradoxically, the growth of trade thus delayed India's modernization and alienation from its own past. But there were other forces at work, too. By the end of the century the framework provided by the Raj and the stimulus of the cultural influences it permitted had already made impossible the survival of wholly unmodernized India.

No other nation in the early nineteenth century so extended its imperial possessions as Great Britain, but the French, too, had made substantial additions to the empire with which they had been left in 1815. They did not lose to sight in the next half-century France's interests elsewhere (in West Africa and the South Pacific for example) but the major expression of a reviving French imperialism came in Algeria. The whole of North Africa was at that time open to imperial expansion by European powers because of the decay of the formal overlordship of the Ottoman sultan. Right round the southern and eastern Mediterranean coasts the issue was posed of a possible Turkish partition. French interest in the area was natural; it went back to a great extension of the country's Levant trade in the eighteenth century and an expedition to Egypt under Bonaparte in 1798.

Algeria's conquest began uncertainly in 1830. A series of wars not only with its native inhabitants but with the sultan of Morocco followed until, by 1870, most of the country had been subdued. This was, in fact, to open a new phase of expansion, for the French then turned their attention to Tunis, which accepted a French protectorate in 1881. To both their sometime Ottoman dependencies there now began a steady

841

flow of European immigration, not only from France, but from Italy and, later, Spain. This built up substantial settler populations in a few cities which were to complicate the story of French rule. The day was past when the African Algerian might have been exterminated or all but exterminated, like the Aztec, Red Indian or Australian aborigine. His society, in any case, was more resistant, formed in the crucible of an Islamic civilization which had contested European civilization successfully. None the less, he suffered, notably from the introduction of land law which broke up his traditional usages and impoverished the peasant by exposing him to the full blast of market economics.

At the eastern end of the African littoral a national awakening in Egypt had led to the emergence there of the first great modernizing nationalist leader outside the European world, Mehemet Ali, pasha of Egypt. Admiring Europe, he sought to borrow its ideas and techniques while asserting his independence of the sultan. When he was later called upon for help by the sultan against the Greek revolution, Mehemet Ali went on to attempt to seize Syria as his reward. This threat to the Ottoman empire provoked an international crisis in the 1830s in which the French took his side. They were not successful, but thereafter French policy continued to interest itself in the Levant and Syria, too, an interest which was eventually to bear fruit in the brief establishment in the twentieth century of a French presence in the area.

The feeling that Great Britain and France had made good use of their opportunities in the early part of the nineteenth century was no doubt one of the sentiments inspiring other powers to try to follow them from 1870 onwards. But envious emulation does not go far as an explanation of the extraordinary suddenness and vigour of what has sometimes been called the 'imperialist wave' of the late nineteenth century. Outside Antarctica and the Arctic, there remained by 1914 less than a fifth of the world's land surface which was not under a European flag or that of a country of European settlement; and of this small fraction only

Japan, Ethiopia and Siam enjoyed real autonomy.

The explanation of this has been much debated. Clearly one part of the story is one of the sheer momentum of accumulated forces. The European hegemony became more and more irresistible as it built upon its own strength. The theory and ideology of imperialism were up to a point mere rationalizations of the huge power the European world suddenly found itself to possess. Practically, for example, as medicine began to master tropical infection and steam provided quicker transport, it became easier to establish permanent bases in Africa and to penetrate its interior; the Dark Continent had long been of interest but its exploitation began to be feasible for the first time in the 1870s. Such technical developments made possible and attractive an extension of European rule which could promote and protect trade and investment. The hopes such possibilities aroused were often ill-founded and usually disappointed. Whatever the appeal of 'undeveloped estates' in Africa (as one British statesman liked to put it), or the supposedly vast market for consumer goods constituted by the penniless millions of China, industrial countries still found other industrial countries their best customers and trading partners and it was former or existing colonies rather than new ones which attracted most overseas capital investment. By far the greatest part of British money invested abroad went to the United States and South America; French investors preferred Russia to Africa, and German money went to Turkey.

On the other hand, economic expectation excited many individuals. Because of them, imperial expansion always had a random factor in it which makes it hard to generalize about it. Explorers, traders and adventurers on many occasions took steps which led governments, willingly or not, to new acquisitions of territory. They were often popular heroes, for this most active phase of European imperialism coincided with a great growth of popular participation in public affairs. By buying newspapers, voting or cheering in the streets the masses were more and more involved in politics which (among other things) emphasized imperial competition as a form of national rivalry. The new cheap press often pandered to this by dramatizing exploration and colonial warfare. Some thought, too, that social dissatisfactions might be soothed by the contemplation of the extension of the rule of the national flag over new areas even when the experts knew that nothing was likely to be forthcoming except expense.

But cynicism is no more the whole story than is the profit motive. The idealism which inspired some imperialists certainly salved the conscience of many more. Men who believed that they possessed true civilization were bound to see the ruling of others for their good as a duty. Kipling's famous poem did not urge Americans to take up the White Man's Booty, but his Burden, for the gift of civilization was seen as a precious one justifying self-sacrificial labour.

All these elements were tangled together in more complicated patterns than ever after 1870, because they all had to find a place in a context of changing international relationships which imposed its own logic on colonial affairs. When Bismarck, for example, wanted to show the British the value of his goodwill in Europe, he bullied them on a colonial issue, South-West Africa. This was subsidiary to his real purposes and, essentially, only a gesture, but in fact led to the extension of German rule in this singularly uninviting area. In turn, this gave angry British imperialists leverage against their own government, supposedly careless of imperial interests.

The story of international relations and their entanglement with imperialism after 1870 need not be explained in detail, but two continuing themes which stood out in it may none the less be remarked as usually important. One is that because she was the only truly world-wide imperial power, Great Britain had more quarrels with more states over colonies than anyone else. She had possessions everywhere. The centre of her concerns was more than ever India; the acquisition of African territory to safeguard the Cape route and the new one via Suez, and fre-

quent alarms over dangers to the lands which were India's glacis both showed this. Between 1856 and 1914 the only crises over non-European issues which made war between Great Britain and another great power seem possible arose over Russian influence in Afghanistan and a French attempt to establish themselves on the Upper Nile, though there were also lesser frictions troubling these three states. British officials were also much concerned about French penetration of West Africa and Indo-China, and Russian influence in Persia.

These facts indicate the second continuing theme and it is a negative one. Though European nations quarrelled about what happened overseas for forty years or so, and though the United States went to war with one of them (Spain), the partition of the non-European world was achieved with amazing ease. When a Great War at last broke out in 1914, Great Britain, Russia and France, the three nations which had quarrelled most over imperial difficulties, would be on the same side; it was not overseas colonial rivalry which caused the conflict. Only once since 1900, in Morocco, had a real danger of war occasioned by a quarrel over non-European lands arisen between two European great powers and here the issue was not really one of colonial rivalry, but of whether Germany could bully France without fear of her being supported by others. Quarrels over non-European affairs before 1914 seem in fact to have been a positive distraction from the more dangerous rivalries of Europe itself; they may even have helped to preserve European peace.

Imperial rivalry had its own momentum. When one power got a concession or a colony, it almost always spurred on others to go one better. The imperialist wave was in this way both nourished from many sources and self-feeding. By 1914 the most striking results were to be seen in Africa. Here the activities of explorers, missionaries, and the campaigners against slavery early in the nineteenth century had prepared a public to accept that the extension of European rule there was a matter of spreading enlightenment and humanitarianism – the

Africa in 1880

Legend:
- British possessions
- French possessions
- Portuguese possessions
- Spanish possessions
- Turkish possessions

Map labels: CANARY ISLANDS, FEZ, ALGERIA, TUNIS (Turk. Suzerainty), TRIPOLI, SAHARA DESERT, Cairo, EGYPT (Turk Suzerainty), RED SEA, Nile, SENEGAL, Senegal, Niger, Timbuktu, GAMBIA, SUDANESE EMPIRES, LAKE CHAD, Fashoda, ABYSSINIA, HARAT, SIERRA LEONE, PORTUGUESE GUINEA, LAGOS, LIBERIA, GOLD COAST, RIO MUNI, UGANDA, ATLANTIC OCEAN, SÃO TOMÉ (Portuguese), GABON, Congo, LAKE VICTORIA, INDIAN OCEAN, Mombasa, ZANZIBAR, LAKE TANGANYIKA, BANTU KINGDOMS, ANGOLA, LAKE NYASA, Zambesi, MOZAMBIQUE, MADAGASCAR, KALAHARI DESERT, WALVIS BAY, TRANSVAAL, BECHUANALAND, NATAL, ORANGE FREE STATE, BASUTOLAND, CAPE COLONY, Cape Town

blessings of civilization, in fact. On the African coasts, the experience of centuries of trade showed that desirable products were available in the interior. White communities at the Cape had already shown a disposition to push further inland, often under the stimulus of Boer resentment of British rule. This explosive mixture was set off when a British force was sent to Egypt in 1881 to secure that country's government against a nationalist revolution whose success (it was feared) might threaten the safety of the Suez Canal. The corrosive power of European culture – for this was the source of the ideas of the Egyptian nationalists – thus both touched off another stage in the decline of the Ottoman empire of which Egypt was still formally a part and launched what was called the 'Scramble for Africa'.

The British had hoped soon to withdraw their soldiers from Egypt, yet in 1914 they were still there. British officials were virtually running the administration of the country while to the south, Anglo-Egyptian rule had been pushed deep into the Sudan. Meanwhile, Turkey's western provinces in Libya and Tripolitania had been taken by the Italians (who felt unjustly

844

Partitioned Africa: Frontiers in 1914 (after the establishment of the British Protectorate over Egypt)

**Map labels:**

SPANISH MOROCCO · Algiers · MOROCCO (Fr. Protectorate) · ALGERIA · Tunis · TUNISIA · CANARY ISLANDS · Morocco · Tripoli · Cairo · SUEZ CANAL · RIO DE ORO · LIBYA (Tripoli and Cyrenaica) · EGYPT · MAURITANIA · FRENCH WEST AFRICA · NIGER · CHAD · Khartoum · ERITREA · FRENCH SOMALILAND · Dakar · Gambia · DAHOMEY · ANGLO-EGYPTIAN SUDAN · BRITISH SOMALILAND · PORTUGUESE GUINEA · FRENCH GUINEA · NIGERIA · Addis Ababa · SIERRA LEONE · IVORY COAST · Fashoda · ABYSSINIA · ITALIAN SOMALILAND · LIBERIA · Lagos · GOLD COAST · TOGOLAND · CAMEROONS · FRENCH EQUATORIAL AFRICA · SPANISH GUINEA · UGANDA · BRITISH EAST AFRICA · BELGIAN CONGO · Mombasa · ZANZIBAR (Br. Protectorate) · Leopoldville · GERMAN EAST AFRICA · NYASALAND · ANGOLA · MOZAMBIQUE · Mozambique · NORTHERN RHODESIA · GERMAN SOUTH-WEST AFRICA · BECHUANALAND · SOUTHERN RHODESIA · MADAGASCAR · Walvis Bay (U. of S. Africa) · Pretoria · SWAZILAND · Johannesburg · ORANGE FREE STATE · UNION OF SOUTH AFRICA · BASUTOLAND · Cape Town

Legend:

British Dominions, Colonies and Protectorates
French Territories and Protectorates
German possessions
Italian possessions
Portuguese possessions
Spanish possessions

squeezed out of Tunisia by the French protectorate there), Algeria was French, and the French enjoyed a fairly free hand in Morocco, except where the Spanish were installed. Southwards from Morocco to the Cape of Good Hope, the coastline was entirely divided between the British, French, Germans, Spanish, Portuguese and Belgians with the exception of the isolated black republic of Liberia. The empty wastes of the Sahara were French; so was the basin of the Senegal and much of the northern side of that of the Congo. The Belgians were installed in the rest of it on what was soon to prove some of the richest mineral-bearing land in Africa. Further east, British territories ran from the Cape up to Rhodesia and the Congo border. On the east coast they were cut off from the sea by Tanganyika (which was German) and Portuguese East Africa. From Mombasa, Kenya's port, a belt of British territory stretched through Uganda to the borders of the Sudan and the headwaters of the Nile. Somalia and Eritrea (in British, Italian and French hands) isolated Ethiopia, the only African country other than Liberia still independent of European rule. The ruler of this ancient but Christian

845

polity was the only non-European ruler of the nineteenth century to remove the threat of colonization by military success.

This was a colossal extension of European power, for the most part achieved after 1881, and it transformed African history. The bargains of European negotiators, the accidents of discovery and the convenience of colonial administrations in the end determined the channels and the influences through which modernization came to Africa. Different colonial régimes operated with different cultural and economic impact. Long after the colonialists had gone, there would be big distinctions between countries where, say, French administration or British judicial practice had taken root. All over the continent, too, Africans found their patterns of employment changed, learnt something of European ways through European schools or service in colonial regiments, saw things to admire and things to hate in the white man's ways which now came to regulate their lives. They did not have the power to resist successfully, as the French suppression of Algerian revolt in 1871, or the British destruction of the Zulu and Matabele, or, worst of all, the German massacre of the Herrero of South-West Africa, all showed. Even when, as in some British possessions, great emphasis was placed on rule through traditional native institutions, these had to work in a new context. Tribal and local unities would still reassert themselves in the twentieth century, but often only against the grain of new structures created by colonialism and left as a legacy to independent Africa.

The imperial age had other less obvious results as well as these. The suppression of inter-tribal warfare and the introduction of even elementary medical services allowed the population to grow in some areas. As in America centuries earlier, the introduction of new crops had made it possible to sustain greater populations. In the end, this was also to affect the balance of races in the areas of white settlement.

Europe was hardly changed by the African adventure and though it has been given so much attention, it is easy to overestimate the

Opening up the Dark Continent: German railway-building in East Africa.

A West African's carving of Queen Victoria.

difference it briefly made to European history. Clearly, it was important that Europeans could lay their hands on yet more easily exploitable wealth, yet probably only Belgium drew from Africa resources which made a real difference to its national future. Sometimes, too, the exploiting of Africa aroused political opposition in European countries; there was more than a touch of the *conquistadores* about some of the late nineteenth-century adventurers. The Congo administered by the Belgian King Leopold or forced labour in Portuguese Africa were notorious examples, but there were other places where Africa's natural resources – human and material – were ruthlessly exploited or despoiled in the interests of profit by Europeans with the connivance of imperial authorities, and this soon created an anti-colonial movement. Some nations recruited African soldiers, though not for service in Europe, where only the French hoped to employ them to offset the weight of German numbers. Some countries hoped for outlets for emigration which would ease social problems, but the possibilities presented by Africa for European residence were very mixed. The two large blocks of settlement were in the south, where the British would later extend their area of settlement into Kenya and Rhodesia where there were lands suitable for white farmers. Apart from this, there were the cities of French North Africa, and also a growing community of Portuguese in Angola. The hopes entertained of Africa as an outlet for Italians, on the other hand, were disappointed, and German emigration was tiny and almost entirely temporary. Some European countries – Russia, Austria, Hungary and the Scandinavian nations – sent virtually no settlers to Africa at all.

Of course, there was much more than Africa to the story of nineteenth-century imperialism. The Pacific was partitioned in a less conspicuous way, but in the end no independent political unit survived among its island peoples. There was also a big expansion of British, French and Russian territory in Asia. The French established themselves in Indo-China, the British in Malaya and Burma, which they took to safe-

guard the approaches to India. Siam retained her independence because it suited both powers to have a buffer between them. The British also asserted their superiority by an expedition to Tibet, with the same considerations of Indian security in mind. Most of these areas, like much of the zone of Russian overland expansion, were formally under Chinese suzerainty. Their story is part of that of the crumbling Chinese empire, a story which paralleled that of the corrosion of other empires, such as the Ottoman, Moroccan and Persian, by European influence, though it has even greater importance for world history. At one moment it looked as if a Scramble for China might follow the partition of Africa. This story is better considered elsewhere. Here it is convenient to notice that the imperialist wave in the Chinese sphere as in the Pacific was in one other way importantly different from that in Africa. This was because the United States of America took part.

Americans had always been uneasy and distrustful over imperial ventures outside the continent they long regarded as God-given to them. Even at its most arrogant, imperialism had to be muffled and muted in the republic in a way unnecessary in Europe. The very creation of the United States had been by successful rebellion against an imperialist power. The constitution contained no provision for the ruling of colonial possessions and it was always very difficult to see what could be the position under it of territories which could not be envisaged as eventually moving towards full statehood, let alone that of non-Americans who stayed under American rule. On the other hand, there was much that was barely distinguishable from imperialism in the nineteenth-century territorial expansion of the United States, though Americans might not recognize it when it was packaged as a 'Manifest Destiny'. The most blatant examples were the war of 1812 against the British and the treatment of Mexico in the middle of the century. But there was also the dispossession of the Red Indian to consider and the dominating implications of the Monroe doctrine.

In the 1890s the overland expansion of the

'On the road to Mandalay' – a Burmese position overrun by British forces in the 1885 campaign.

United States was complete and it was announced that the continuous frontier of domestic settlement no longer existed. At this moment, economic growth gave great importance to the influence of business interests in American government. It was sometimes expressed in terms of an economic nationalism, for example in the imposition of high tariff protection. Some of these interests directed the attention of American public opinion abroad, notably to Asia. The United States was sometimes believed to be in danger of exclusion from trade there by the European powers. There was an old connexion at stake (the first American Far Eastern squadron had been sent out in the 1820s) as a new era of Pacific awareness dawned with California's rapid growth in population. A half-century's talk of a canal across Central America

also came to a head at the end of the century; it stimulated interest in the doctrines of strategic planners who suggested that the United States might need an oceanic glacis in the Pacific to maintain the Monroe doctrine.

All these currents flowed into a burst of expansion which has remained to this day a unique example of American overseas imperialism because, for a time, it set aside traditional restraint on the acquisition of new territory overseas. The beginnings must be tracked back to the increased opening of China and Japan to American commerce as to European in the 1850s and 1860s and to participation with the British and the Germans in the administration of Samoa (where a naval base obtained in

848

LAUNCHED 1890, BLOWN UP IN HAVANA HARBOR AT 9.40 P.M.
DESTRUCTION OF THE U.S. BATTLESHIP MAINE
IN HAVANA HARBOR FEB'Y 15TH 1898.

The explosion of the Maine *which detonated war between the United States and Spain in 1898.*

1878 has remained a United States possession). This was followed by two decades of growing intervention in the affairs of the kingdom of Hawaii, to which the protection of the United States had been extended since the 1840s. American traders and missionaries had established themselves there in large numbers. Benevolent patronage of the Hawaiians decayed under the efforts of these Americans to achieve annexation to the United States in the 1890s. Washington already had the use of Pearl Harbour as a naval base but was led to land marines in Hawaii when a revolution occurred there. In the end, the government had to give way to the forces set in motion by the settlers and a short-lived Hawaiian Republic

was annexed as a United States Territory in 1898.

In that year, a mysterious explosion destroyed an American cruiser, the USS *Maine*, in Havana harbour. This led to a war with Spain. In the background was both the long Spanish failure to master revolt in Cuba, where American business interests were prominent and American sentiment was aroused, and the growing awareness of the importance of the Caribbean approaches to a future canal across the isthmus. In Asia, American help was given to another rebel movement against the Spaniards in the Philippines. When American rule replaced Spanish in Manila, the rebels turned against their former allies and a guerrilla war began. This was the first phase of a long and difficult process of disentangling the United States from

A United States battleship passes through the Panama Canal soon after it was opened.

her first Asian colony. At that moment, given the likelihood of the collapse of the Chinese empire, it seemed best in Washington not to withdraw. In the Caribbean, the long history of Spanish empire in the Americas at last came to an end. Puerto Rico passed to the United States and Cuba obtained its independence on terms which guaranteed its domination by the United States. American forces were back to occupy the island under these terms from 1906 to 1909, and again in 1917.

This was the prelude to the last major development in this wave of American imperialism. The building of an isthmian canal had been canvassed since the middle of the nineteenth century and the completion of Suez gave it new plausibility. American diplomacy negotiated a way round the obstacle of possible British participation; all seemed plain sailing but a snag arose in 1903 when a treaty providing for the

acquisition of a canal zone from Colombia was rejected by the Colombians. A revolution was engineered in Panama, where the canal was to run. The United States prevented its suppression by the Colombian government and a new Panamanian republic emerged which gratefully bestowed upon the United States the necessary territory, jurisdiction within it, and the right to intervene in its affairs in order to maintain order. The work could now begin and the canal was opened in 1914. The possibility of rapidly transferring ships from one ocean to another made a great difference to American naval strategy. It was also the background to the 'corollary' to the Monroe doctrine proposed by President Theodore Roosevelt; when the Canal Zone became the key to the naval defence of the hemisphere, it was more important than ever to assure its protection by stable government and United States predominance in the Caribbean states. A new vigour in American intervention in them was soon evident.

Though its motives and techniques were different – for one thing, there was virtually no permanent American settlement in the new possessions – the actions of the United States were part of the last great seizure of territories carried out by the European world. Almost all of its nations had taken part except the South Americans; even the Australians had pushed forward in New Guinea. By 1914 a third of the world's surface was under the flags of two of them, the United Kingdom and Russia (though how much Russian territory should be regarded as colonial is, of course, debatable). To take a measure which excludes Russia, in 1914 the United Kingdom ruled 400 million people outside its own borders, France over 50 million and Germany and Italy about 14 million each; this was an unprecedented aggregation of formal authority.

At that date, there were already signs that imperialism overseas had run out of steam, if for no other reasons than because China had proved a disappointment and there was little left to divide, though Germany and Great Britain discussed the possibility of partitioning the Portuguese empire, which seemed to be about to follow the Spanish. On the whole, it seemed as if the most likely area for further European imperialism was the decaying Ottoman empire, whose dissolution seemed at last to be imminent when the Italians seized Tripoli in 1912 and a Balkan coalition formed against Turkey took away almost all that was left of her European territories in the following year. Such a prospect did not seem likely to be so free from conflict between great powers as had been the partition of Africa; much more crucial issues would be at stake in it for them.

7 Asia's response to a Europeanizing world

A perceptive Chinese observer might have found something revealing in the disgrace which in the end overtook the Jesuits at K'ang-hsi's court. For more than a century these able men had judiciously and discreetly sought to ingratiate themselves with their hosts. To begin with they had not even spoken of religion, but had contented themselves with studying the language and customs of China. They had even worn Chinese dress, which, we are told, created a very good impression. Great successes had followed. Yet the effectiveness of their mission was suddenly paralysed; their acceptance of Chinese rites and beliefs and their sinicizing of Christian teaching led to the sending of two papal emissaries to China to check such improper flexibility. This was striking: evidently Europeans, unlike all other conquerors of China, would not easily succumb to its cultural pull. There was a message for all Asia in this revelation of the intransigence of European culture.

Pu-Yi, last emperor of China. In 1912, a year after this picture was taken, he abdicated and twenty-five centuries of imperial rule came to an end. Pu-Yi was once more restored to the Chinese throne for a few days in 1917 and then again reigned – nominally – as a puppet emperor of Manchukuo on behalf of the Japanese from 1934 to 1945. Five years in Russian hands were then followed by political 're-education' by the Chinese communists, from which the former emperor emerged to take a job as an archivist in 1959. In 1967 he died aged sixty-one.

It was more important to what was going to happen in Asia – and was already under way there – than even the technology of the new-comers. It was certainly more decisive than any temporary or special weaknesses of the eastern empires as China's own history was to show. Under the immediate successors of K'ang-hsi, the Manchu empire was already past its peak; its slow and eventually fatal decline would not have in itself been surprising given the cyclical pattern of dynastic rise and fall in the past. What made the fate of the Ch'ing dynasty different from that of its predecessors was that it survived long enough to preside over the country while it faced a quite new threat, one from a culture stronger than that of traditional China. For the first time in nearly two thousand years, Chinese society would have to change, not the imported culture of a new wave of barbarian conquerors. The Chinese Revolution was about to begin.

In the eighteenth century, no Chinese official could have been expected to discern this. When Lord Macartney arrived in 1793 to ask for equality of diplomatic representation and free trade the confidence of centuries was intact. The first western advances and encroachments had been successfully rebuffed or contained. The representative of George III could only take back messages which refused his applications to what the Chinese emperor was pleased to call 'the lonely remoteness of your island, cut off from the world by intervening wastes of sea'. It can hardly have improved matters that George III was patted on the back for his 'submissive

853

The encounter of British diplomacy and Manchu empire: Lord Macartney's mission as seen, somewhat imaginatively, by an English cartoonist. The cartoon reveals more of European attitudes than of Chinese.

loyalty in sending this tribute mission' and encouraged to 'show even greater devotion and loyalty in future'.

Such language shows more than mere pomposity and arrogance. The assumption of cultural and moral superiority was then as unquestioned a part of the mental world of the educated Chinese as it was a century later of that of the European and American missionaries and philanthropists who unconsciously patronized the people they came to serve. Such language embodied the Chinese world view, in which all nations paid tribute to the emperor, possessed of the Mandate of Heaven, and in which China already had all the materials and skills for the highest civilization and would only waste her time and energy in indulging relations with Europe going beyond the limited trade tolerated at Canton (where by 1800 there were perhaps a thousand Europeans). Nor was this nonsense. Nearly three centuries of trade with China had failed to reveal any manufactured goods from Europe which the Chinese wanted except the mechanical toys and clocks which they found amusing. European trade with China rested on the export to her of silver or other Asian products. As a British merchant concisely put it in the middle of the eighteenth century, the 'East India trade . . . exports our bullion, spends little of our product or manufactures and brings in commodities perfectly manufactured which hinder the consumption of our own'.

At that time, as much confidence was still felt in China about her internal régime as about her cultural superiority. True, signs of future difficulties can be seen in retrospect. The secret societies and cults which kept alive a smouldering national resentment against a foreign dynasty and the central power, still survived and

Greatest extent of Manchu possessions, tributary territories and suzerainty
The British Empire
Russian Conquests
Original country of the Manchus
Border of Chinese possessions and claims to suzerainty in 1912

RUSSIAN EMPIRE

Manchuria

Ussuri

MANCHU

OUTER MONGOLIA (1697)

INNER MONGOLIA (1635)

KOREA

Peking
Weihaiwei (British)

LAKE BALKHASH

CASPIAN SEA

The Great Wall of China

Kiaochow (German)

TURKESTAN
Tashkent

Sinkiang

KANSU
Shensi

Shanghai

Acquisitions of territory by China or impositions of her suzerainty:

KOREA 1627
INNER MONGOLIA 1635
SHENSI 1644
FUKIEN 1646
MIAO c. 1650 (NOMINAL)
ANNAM 1666
SZECHWAN 1678
YUNNAN 1681
TAIWAN 1683
OUTER MONGOLIA 1697
TIBET 1720
SINKIANG 1724
BURMA 1769
NEPAL 1792

Samarkand

Kabul

TIBET

SZECHWAN
MIAO

Fukien

TAIWAN

Delhi

NEPAL

Kwang Chowwan (French)

Hong Kong (British)

YUNNAN

Macao (Portuguese)

China 1644—1912

BENGAL

BURMA

Annam

even prospered. They found fresh support as the surge of population became uncontainable; in the century before 1850 numbers seem to have more than doubled to reach about 430 million by 1850. Pressure on cultivated land became much more acute because the area worked could only be increased by a tiny margin; times grew steadily harder and the lot of the peasantry more and more miserable. There had been warning signs in the 1770s and 1780s when a century's internal peace was broken by great revolts, so often the sign of dynastic decline. Early in the next century they became still more frequent and destructive. To make matters worse, they were accompanied by another economic deterioration, inflation in the price of the silver in which taxes had to be paid. Most daily transactions (including the payment of wages) were carried out in copper and this added to the crushing burdens already suffered by the poor. Yet none of this seemed likely to be fatal, except, possibly, to the dynasty. It could all be fitted into the traditional

pattern of the historic cycle. All that was required was that the service gentry should remain loyal for even the dynasty's survival to be possible. If they did not, then, though a collapse of government might follow, there was no reason to believe that in due course another dynasty would not emerge to preserve the formal framework of an unchanging China.

It was not, in the end, to turn out like this because of the drive and power of the nineteenth-century barbarian challenge. The inflation itself was a result of a change of China's relations with the outside world which within a few decades made nonsense of the reception given to Macartney. Before 1800 the West could offer China little that she wanted except silver, but within the next three decades of the nineteenth century this ceased to be so, largely because British traders at last found a commodity the Chinese wanted: opium. Naval expeditions forced the Chinese to open their country to sale (albeit at first under certain restrictions) of this drug, produced in India, but the 'Opium Wars'

855

of the 1840s were only registering the completion of a change in China's economic relations with the West. The Canton monopoly and the tributary status of the foreigner came to an end together. Once they had kicked it ajar, the British were to struggle to open still further the door to western trade. Others were to follow them through it.

Unwittingly, the government of Queen Victoria thus launched the Chinese Revolution. It can now be seen that the 1840s were the beginning of a period of upheaval which took over a century to come to completion. The revolution would slowly reveal itself as a double repudiation, both of the foreigner and of much of the formal Chinese tradition. The first would increasingly express itself in the nationalist modes and idioms of the progressive European world. Because such ideological forces could not be contained within the traditional framework, they would in the end prove fatal to it, when the Chinese sought to remove the obstacles to modernization and national power. More than a century after the Opium Wars the Chinese Revolution at last finally shattered a social system which had been the source of Chinese life for thousands of years. By that time it would also appear that China's troubles had only been part of a much wider upheaval, a Hundred Years War of Asia and the West whose turning-point came in the early twentieth century.

These implications matured only slowly. In the beginning, western encroachments in China usually produced only a simple, xenophobic hostility and even this was not universal. After all, for a long time very few Chinese were directly or obviously much concerned with the coming of the foreigners. A few (notably Canton merchants involved in the foreign trade) even sought accommodation with them. Hostility was a matter of anti-British mobs in the towns after the Opium Wars and of the rural gentry. The officials at first saw the problem as a precise one: that of the addiction of the subjects of the empire to a dangerous drug. They were humiliated, in particular, by the weaknesses

which this revealed in their own people and administration; there was much connivance and corruption involved in the opium trade. They do not at first seem to have seen the deeper issue of the future, that of the questioning of an entire order. They did not sense a cultural threat; China had suffered defeats in the past and its culture had survived unscathed.

The first portent of a deeper danger came when, in the 1840s, the imperial government had to concede that missionary activity was legal. Though still limited, this was a real corrosive of tradition. Officials in the Confucian mould who felt its danger stirred up popular feeling against missionaries – whose efforts made them easy targets – and there were scores of riots in the 1850s and 1860s. Such demonstrations only accelerated decay. Sometimes foreign consuls would be drawn in; exceptionally a gunboat would be sent. The Chinese government's prestige would suffer in the ensuing exchange of apologies and punishment of culprits. Meanwhile, the activity of the missionaries was steadily undermining the traditional society in more direct and didactic ways by preaching an individualism and egalitarianism alien to it and by acting as a magnet to converts to whom it offered economic and social advantages.

The process of undermining China also went forward directly in the decades after the Opium Wars by military and naval means; there were further impositions of concessions by force. But there was a growing ambiguity in the Chinese response. The authorities did not always resist the arrival of the foreigners. First the gentry of the areas immediately concerned and then the Peking government came round to feeling that foreign soldiers might not be without their value for the régime. Social disorder was growing. It could not be canalized solely against the foreigners and was threatening the establishment; China was beginning to undergo a cycle of peasant revolts which were to be the greatest in the whole of human history. In the middle decades of the century the familiar symptoms multiplied: banditry, secret societies. In the

The last argument of a great commercial power; a British gun-boat fires on war junks, 1841.

1850s the 'Red Turbans' were only suppressed at great cost. Such troubles frightened the establishment, and threw it on to the defensive, leaving it with little spare capacity to resist the steady gnawing of the West. These great rebellions were fundamentally caused by hunger for land and the most important and distinctive of them was the Taiping rebellion or, as it may more appropriately be called, revolution, which lasted from 1850 to 1864.

The heart of this great convulsion, which cost the lives of more people than died the world over in the First World War, was a traditional peasant revolt. Hard times and a succession of natural disasters had helped to provoke it. It drew on a compound of land hunger, hatred of tax-gatherers, social envy and national resentment against the Manchus (though it is hard to see exactly what this meant in practice, for the bulk of the officials who actually administered

the empire were, of course, themselves Chinese). It was also at least in essence a regional outbreak, originating in the south and even there promoted by an isolated minority of settlers from the north. The new feature behind the revolt and one which made it ambiguous in the eyes of both Chinese and Europeans was that its leader, Hung Hsiu-ch'uan, had a superficial but impressive acquaintance with the Christian religion in the form of American protestantism and this led him to denounce the worship of other gods, destroy idols – which included the Confucian ancestor tablets – and to talk of establishing the kingdom of God on earth. He had been rejected by his own culture, for he had been an unsuccessful candidate in the examinations which conferred status on lowly-born Chinese. Within the familiar framework of one of the periodic peasant upheavals of old China, that is to say, a new ideology was at work and showing itself subversive of the traditional culture and state. Some of its opponents at once grasped this and saw the Taiping movement as an ideological as well as a social challenge. Thus

857

Soldiers of the 'ever-victorious army' raised and trained to resist the Taipings by a British general, Gordon, on behalf of the Chinese government. He was later to meet what many of his countrymen regarded as a martyr's death at Khartoum, in the Sudan (1885).

the revolution can be seen as an epoch in the western disruption of China.

The Taiping army at first had a series of spectacular successes. By 1853 they had captured Nanking and established there the court of Hung Hsiu-ch'uan, now proclaimed the 'Heavenly King'. In spite of alarm further north, this was as far as they went. After 1856 the revolution was on the defensive. Nevertheless, it announced important social changes (which made it a source of inspiration for later Chinese reformers) and although it is by no means clear how widely these were effective or even appealing, their disruptive ideological effect was considerable. The basis of Taiping society was communism: there was no private property but communal provision for general needs. The land was in theory distributed for working in plots graded by quality to provide just shares. Even more revolutionary was the extension of social and educational equality to women. The traditional binding of their feet was forbidden and an important degree of sexual austerity marked the movement's aspirations (though not the conduct of the 'Heavenly King' himself). These things reflected the mixture of religious and social elements which lay at the root of the Taiping cult and the danger it presented to the traditional order.

The movement benefited at first by the demoralization brought about in the Manchu forces by their defeats at the hands of the Europeans and by the usual weaknesses shown by central government in China in a relatively

圖之領占城津天

CAPTURE OF
TIEN-TSIN
(JAPAN CHINA WAR)

A Japanese print celebrates the capture of Tien-tsin in the Sino-Japanese war of 1894.

distant and distinct region. As time passed and the Manchu forces were given abler (sometimes European) commanders the bows and spears of the Taiping were proved insufficient. The foreigners, too, came to see the movement as a threat but kept up their pressure while the imperial government grappled with the Taipings. Treaties with France and the United States which followed that with Great Britain guaranteed the toleration of Christian missionaries and began the process of reserving jurisdiction over foreigners to consular and mixed courts. The danger presented by the Taiping revolution brought yet more concessions: new fighting resulted in the opening of more Chinese ports to foreign trade, the taking over of Chinese customs administration by foreigners, the legalization of the sale of opium and the cession to

the Russians of the province in which Vladivostok was to be built. It is hardly surprising that in 1861 the Chinese decided for the first time to set up a new department to deal with foreign affairs. The old myth that all the world recognized the mandate of heaven and owed tribute to the imperial court was dead.

In the end, the foreigners joined in against the Taipings (a response by no means illogical, given that the revolution was strongly against opium). Whether their help was needed to end it may never be known; certainly there is evidence that the Taiping movement was already failing. In 1864 Hung died and shortly afterwards Nanking fell to the Manchu. This was a victory for traditional China: the rule of the bureaucratic gentry had survived one more threat from below. None the less, an important turning-point had been reached. A rebellion had offered a revolutionary programme announcing a new danger, that the old challenge of peasant rebellion might be reinforced by an ideology from outside deeply corrosive to Confucian China. Nor did the end of the Taiping rebellion mean internal peace; from the middle of the 1850s until well into the 1870s there were great Moslem risings in the north-west and south-west as well as other rebellions.

Immediately, China showed even greater weakness in the face of the West. Large areas had been devastated in the fighting; in many of them the soldiers were powerful and threatened the control of the bureaucracy. If the enormous loss of life did something to reduce pressure on land, this was probably balanced by a decline in the prestige and authority of the dynasty. Concessions had already had to be made to the western powers under and because of these disadvantaged conditions; there would be more. The methods which had drawn the sting of nomadic invaders were not likely to be efficacious with the confident Europeans whose ideological assurance and increasing technical superiority protected them from the seduction of Chinese civilization, and the spate of treaty concessions to the foreigner went on to admit trade in more 'treaty ports', to the establishment of resident diplomatic representation at Peking, and to the removal of restraints on the travel of Europeans. When Roman Catholic missionaries were given the right to buy land and put up buildings Christianity was linked to economic penetration; soon the wish to protect converts meant involvement in the internal affairs of public order and police. It was impossible to contain the slow but continuous erosion of Chinese sovereignty. Never formally a colony, China was beginning none the less to undergo a measure of colonialization.

Then there were territorial losses as the century wore on. In the 1870s the Russians seized the Ili valley (though they later handed much of it back) and in the next decade the French established a protectorate in Annam. Loosely asserted but ancient Chinese suzerainty was being swept away; the French began to absorb Indo-China and the British annexed Burma in 1886. The worst blow was from another Asiatic state; in the war of 1894–5 the Japanese took Formosa and the Pescadores, while China had to recognize the independence of Korea, from which they had received tribute since the seventeenth century. Following the Japanese success came further encroachments by other powers; provoked by the Russians, who established themselves in Port Arthur, England, France and Germany all extracted long leases of ports at the end of the century. Before this, the Portuguese, who had been in China longer than any other Europeans, converted their tenure of Macao into outright ownership. Even the Italians were in the market, though they did not actually get anything. And long before these acquisitions were made concessions, loans and agreements had been exacted by western powers to protect and foster their own economic and financial interests. It is hardly surprising that when a British Prime Minister spoke at the end of the century of two classes of nation, the 'living and the dying'; China was regarded as an outstanding example of the second class and statesmen began to envisage her partition.

Before the end of the nineteenth century it was evident to many Chinese intellectuals and civil servants that the traditional order could not generate the energy necessary to resist the new barbarians. Attempts to work along the old lines had failed. New tendencies began to appear. A 'society for the study of self-strengthening' was founded to consider western ideas and inventions which might be helpful. Its leaders cited the achievements of Peter the Great and, more significantly, those of contemporary reformers in Japan, an example all the more telling because of the superiority shown by the Japanese over China in war in 1895. Yet the would-be reformers still hoped that they would be able to root change in the Confucian tradition, albeit one purified and invigorated. They were members of the gentry and by 1898 they succeeded in obtaining the ear of the emperor; they were thus working within the traditional framework and machinery of power to obtain administrative and techno-

Soldiers of the modernized and westernized Chinese regular army of 1900, under inspection by officers each wearing his pigtail in regulation style, the end stowed in his pocket.

logical reform without compromising the fundamentals of Chinese culture and ideology.

Unfortunately this meant that the Hundred Days of Reform of 1898 (as it came to be known) was almost at once tangled up in the court politics of the rivalry between the emperor and the dowager empress, to say nothing of Chinese–Manchu antagonism. Though a stream of reform edicts was published, they were swiftly overtaken by a *coup d'état* by the empress who locked up the emperor. The basic cause of the reformers' failure was the provocation offered by their inept political behaviour. Yet although the movement had failed, it was important that it had existed at all. It was to be a great stimulus to wider and deeper thinking about China's future.

For the moment, China seemed to have turned back to older methods of confronting the threat from outside, as a dramatic episode, the 'Boxer movement', showed. Exploited by

Europeans depicted in flight from the Boxers in a cartoon from a Shanghai newspaper of 1900.

the empress, this was essentially a backward-looking and xenophobic upheaval which was given official encouragement. Missionaries and converts were murdered, a German minister killed and the foreign legations at Peking besieged, but the Boxers were unable to stand up to western fighting-power. They once more revealed the hatred of foreigners which was waiting

861

THE SAME OLD BEAR.

Russian Bear (to British Lion). "YOU'VE GOT SO MUCH TO DO ELSEWHERE, I'LL TACKLE THIS OBSTREPEROUS PARTY."
British Lion. "OH, THANKS! BUT I WOULDN'T LEAVE YOU ALONE WITH HIM FOR WORLDS!"

Every intervention by a foreign power in China had implications for other powers who might find the balance of their own interests threatened. The anti-Boxer campaign attracted wide support for just this reason, as Punch *noted.*

Yuan Shih-k'ai at his inauguration as president in 1912.

to be tapped, but also showed how little could be hoped for from the old structure, for its most conservative forces had dominated the movement, not the few reformers who became involved in it. It was suppressed by a military intervention which provides the only example in history of the armed forces of all the great powers operating under the same commander (a German, as it happened). The sequel was yet another diplomatic humiliation for China; an enormous indemnity was settled on customs henceforth under foreign direction.

The ending of the Boxer movement rendered the internal situation still more unstable. Reform had failed in 1898; so now had reaction. Perhaps only revolution lay ahead. Officers in the parts of the army which had undergone reorganization and training on western lines began to think about it. Students in exile had already begun to meet and discuss their country's future, above all in Tokyo. The Japanese were happy to encourage subversive movements which might weaken their neighbour; in 1898 they had set up an 'East Asian Cultural Union' from which emerged the slogan 'Asia for the Asians'. The Japanese had great prestige in the eyes of the young Chinese radicals as Asians

who were escaping from the trap of traditional backwardness which had been fatal to India and seemed to be about to engulf China. Japan could confront the West on terms of equality. Other students looked elsewhere for support, some to the long-enduring secret societies. One of them was a young man called Sun Yat-Sen. His achievement has often been exaggerated, but, nevertheless, he attempted revolution ten times altogether. In the 1890s, he and others were asking only for a constitutional monarchy, but it was a very radical demand at that time.

Discontented exiles drew on support from Chinese businessmen abroad, of whom there were many, for the Chinese had always been great traders. They helped Sun Yat-Sen in 1905 to form in Japan a revolutionary alliance which sought the expulsion of the Manchus and the initiation of Chinese rule, a republican constitution, land reform. It sought to conciliate the foreigners, at this stage a wise tactical move, and the new programme showed the influence of western thinkers (notably that of the English radical John Stuart Mill and the American economic reformer Henry George); once again the West provided the stimulus and some of the ideological baggage of a Chinese reform movement. This was the beginning of the party eventually to emerge as the dominant clique in the Chinese Republic.

862

Its formation, though, may well be thought less significant than another event of the same year, the abolition of the traditional examination system. Of a series of constitutional and administrative reforms carried out after 1901, this was possibly the one of the greatest importance. More than any other institution, the examination system had still continued to hold Chinese civilization together by providing the bureaucracy it recruited with its internal homogeneity and cohesion. These would not quickly wane. Moreover, it removed the distinction between the mass of Chinese subjects and the privileged ruling class. Meanwhile, returning students from abroad, dissatisfied with what they found and no longer under the necessity of accommodating themselves to it by going through the examination procedure if they wished to enter government service, exercised a profoundly disturbing influence. They much increased the rate at which Chinese society began to be irradiated by western ideas. Together with the soldiers in a modernized army, more and more of them looked to revolution for a way ahead.

There were a number of rebellions (some directed by Sun Yat-Sen from Indo-China with French connivance) before the empress and her puppet emperor died on successive days in 1908. The event raised new hopes but the Manchu government continued to drag its feet over reform. On the one hand it made important concessions of principle and promoted the flow of students abroad; on the other it showed that it could not achieve a decisive break with the past or surrender any of the imperial privileges of the Manchus. Perhaps more could not have been asked for. By 1911, the situation had deteriorated badly. The gentry class showed signs of losing its cohesion: it was no longer to back the dynasty in the face of subversion as it had done in the past. Governmentally, there existed a near-stalemate of internal power, the dynasty effectively controlling only a part of China. In October a revolutionary headquarters was discovered at Hankow. There had already been revolts which had been more or less contained earlier in the year. This precipitated one which

at last turned into a successful revolution. Sun Yat-Sen, whose name was used by the early rebels, was taken by surprise: he was in the United States at the time.

The course of the revolution was largely set by the defection from the régime of its military commanders. The most important of these was Yüan Shih-k'ai; when he turned on the Manchus, the dynasty was lost. The Mandate of Heaven had been withdrawn and on 12 February 1912 the last, six-year-old, Manchu emperor abdicated. A republic had already been proclaimed, with Sun Yat-Sen its president, and a new nationalist party soon appeared behind him. In March he resigned the presidency to Yüan Shih-k'ai, thus acknowledging where power really lay in the new Republic and inaugurating a new phase of Chinese government, in which an effective constitutional régime at Peking disputed the practical government of China by warlords. This alone meant that China had still a long way to travel before she would be a modern nation-state. None the less, she had begun the march which would take a half-century to regain the reality of an independence lost in the nineteenth century to foreigners.

By this time, Japan had shown a very different response to the challenge of the western barbarians. At the beginning of the nineteenth century, there was little to show a superficial observer that she might have greater powers of adaptability than China. Japan was then, like any other pre-industrial society, deeply conservative. Yet much had already changed since the establishment of the shogunate and there were signs that the changes would cut deeper and faster as the years went by. One paradox is that this is in part attributable to the success of the Tokuwaga era itself. It had brought peace and one obvious result of that was that Japan's military system became old-fashioned and inefficient. The *samurai* themselves were evidently a parasitic class; warriors, there was nothing for them to do except to cluster in the castle-towns of their lords, consumers without employment, a social and economic problem.

They were not the only problem caused by prolonged peace. It also led to a money economy, the beginnings of a quasi-capitalist structure in agriculture which eroded the old feudal relationships, and the growth of towns. Osaka, the greatest mercantile centre, had between three and four hundred thousand inhabitants in the last years of the shogunate; Yedo may have had a million. These great centres of consumption were sustained by financial and mercantile arrangements which had grown enormously in scale and complication since the seventeenth century. They made a mockery of the old nation of the inferiority of the merchant order. Even their techniques of salesmanship were modern; the eighteenth-century shops of the house of Mitsui (still today one of the great pillars of Japanese capitalism) gave free umbrellas marked with their trademark to customers caught in their shops by the rain.

Many of these changes registered the creation of new wealth from which the shogunate had not itself benefited, largely because it was unable to tap it at a rate which kept pace with its own growing needs. The main revenue was the rice tax which flowed through the lords. It did not take away the new wealth arising from better cultivation and land reclamation and because this remained in the hands of the better-off peasants and village leaders, this led to sharpening contrasts in the countryside. The poorer peasantry were often driven to the towns at a time when others prospered. This was another sign of disintegration in the feudal society. In the towns, which suffered from an inflation made worse by the shogunate's debasement of the coinage, only the merchants seemed to prosper. A last effort of economic reform failed in the 1840s. The lords grew poorer and their retainers lost confidence; before the end of the Tokugawa, some *samurai* were beginning to dabble in trade. Their share of their lord's tax yield was often still only that of their seventeenth-century predecessors. Regional differences existed, but everywhere could be found impoverished, politically discontented swordsmen – and some aggrieved families of great

Commodore Perry, the American naval officer who forced Japan to open her ports to foreigners. A photograph and a Japanese impression.

The Japanese were passionately interested in the details of the dress and accoutrements of the first American officers to land in Japan, as these sketches show.

lords who recalled the days when their race had stood on equal terms with the Tokugawa.

The obvious danger of this potential instability was all the greater because insulation against western ideas had long since ceased to be complete. A few learned men had interested themselves in books which entered Japan through the narrow aperture of the Dutch trade. In one important respect Japan was very different from China, its technical receptivity. 'The Japanese are sharp-witted and quickly learn anything they see', said a sixteenth-century Dutchman. They had soon grasped and exploited as the Chinese never did the advantages of European firearms and began to make them in quantity. They copied the European clocks which the Chinese treated as toys. They were eager to learn from Europeans, as unhampered by their traditions as the Chinese seemed bogged down in theirs. On the great fiefs there were notable schools or research centres of 'Dutch studies'. The shogunate itself had authorized the translation of foreign books, an important step in so

literate a society, for education in Tokugawa Japan had been almost too successful: there was a high degree of literacy and even young *samurai* were beginning to enquire about western ideas. The islands were relatively small and communications good, so that new ideas got about easily. Thus, the situation in which Japan had, suddenly, to face a new and unprecedented challenge from the West, though not one entirely unannounced, was by no means the same as that of China.

The first period of western contact with Japan had ended in the seventeenth century with persecution and exclusion of all but a few Dutchmen who were allowed to conduct trade from an island at Nagasaki. Europe had not then been able to challenge this outcome. That the situation had changed was shown in the 1840s by what happened to China, whose fate some of Japan's rulers observed with increasing alarm. The Europeans (to whom might at any moment be joined the North Americans) had, it was clear, both a new interest in breaking into Asian trade and new and irresistible strength to do it. The King of the Netherlands warned the *shogun* in the 1840s that exclusion was no longer a realistic policy. But there was no agreement among Japan's rulers about whether resistance or con-

865

A very European-looking station has been built to handle traffic on the Japanese railway shown here; the first line in Japan, it ran from Tokyo to Yokohama.

cession was better. Finally, in 1851, the President of the United States commissioned a naval officer, Commodore Perry, to open relations with Japan. Under him, the first foreign squadron to sail into Japanese waters entered Edo Bay in 1853. In the following year it returned and the first of a series of treaties with foreign powers was made by the shogunate.

Perry's arrival could be seen in Confucian terms as an omen or sign that the end of the shogunate was near. No doubt some Japanese saw it in that way. Yet it did not at once follow and there were a few years of somewhat muddled response to the barbarian threat. Japan's rulers did not straightway come round to a wholehearted policy of concession (there was one further attempt to expel foreigners by force) and Japan's future course was not decided until well into the 1860s.

Within a few years the success of the West was already embodied in and symbolized by a series of so-called 'unequal treaties'. Commercial privileges, extra-territoriality for western

residents, the presence of diplomatic representatives and restrictions on the Japanese export of opium were the main concessions won by the United States, Great Britain, France, Russia and the Netherlands. Soon afterwards the shogunate came to an end; its inability to resist the foreigner was one contributing factor and another was the threat from two great aggregations of feudal power which had already begun to adopt western military techniques in order to replace the Tokugawa by a more effective and centralized system under their control. There was fighting between the Tokugawa and their opponents, but it was followed not by a relapse into disorder and anarchy but by a resumption of power by the imperial court and administration in 1868 in the so-called 'Meiji Restoration'.

It cannot be doubted that the re-emergence of the emperor and the widespread acceptance of the revolutionary renewal which followed was attributable above all to the passionate desire of most literate Japanese to escape from a 'shameful inferiority' to the West which might have ended in their sharing the fate of the Chinese and Indians. In the 1860s both the *bakufu* and some individual clans had already sent several missions to Europe. Anti-foreign agitation was dropped in order to learn from the West the secrets of its strength. There was a paradox in this, for, as in some European countries, a nationalism rooted in a conservative view of society was to dissolve much of the tradition in whose name it was developed.

The transference of the court to Yedo, the modern Tokyo, was the symbolic opening of the Meiji restoration and the regeneration of Japan; its indispensable first stage was the abolition of feudalism. What might have been a difficult and bloody business was made simple by the voluntary surrender to the emperor of their lands by the four greatest clans, who set out their motives in a memorial they addressed to the emperor. They were returning to the emperor what had originally been his, they said, 'so that a uniform rule may prevail throughout the empire. Thus the country will be able to rank equally with the other nations of the world'. This was a concise expression of the patriotic ethic which was to inspire Japan's leaders for the next half-century and was widely spread in a country with a large degree of literacy where local leaders could make possible the acceptance of national goals to a degree impossible elsewhere. True, such expressions were not uncommon in other countries. What was peculiar to Japan was the urgency which observation of the fate of China lent to the programme, the emotional support given to the idea by Japanese social and moral tradition, and the fact that in the imperial throne there was available within the established structure a source of moral authority not committed merely to maintaining the past. These conditions made possible a Japanese 1688: a conservative revolution opening the way to radical change.

Rapidly, Japan adopted the institutions of western government and some of those of western society. A prefectoral system of administration, posts, a daily newspaper, a ministry of education, military conscription, the first railway, religious toleration and the Gregorian calendar all arrived within the first five years. A representative system of local government was inaugurated in 1879 and ten years later a new constitution set up a bicameral Parliament (a peerage had already been created in preparation for the organization of the upper house). In fact, this was a somewhat less revolutionary innovation than might appear, given the strong authoritarian strain in the document. At about the same time, too, the innovatory passion was beginning to show signs of flagging; the period when things western were a craze was over; no such enthusiasm was to be seen again until the second half of the twentieth century. In 1890 an imperial Rescript on Education, subsequently to be read on great days to generations of Japanese schoolchildren, enjoined the observation of the traditional Confucian duties of filial piety and obedience and the sacrifice of self to the state if need be.

Much – perhaps the most important part – of old Japan was to survive the Meiji revolution and was to do so very obviously; this is in part the secret of the fascination of the story of modern Japan. But much, too, had gone. Feudalism could never be restored, generously compensated with government stock though the lords might be. Another striking expression of the new direction was the abolition of the old ordered class system. Care was shown in removing the privileges of the *samurai*; some of them could find compensation by the opportunities offered to them in the new bureaucracy, in business – no longer to be a demeaning activity – and in the modernized army and navy. For these foreign instruction was sought, because the Japanese sought proven excellence. Gradually they dropped their French military advisers and took to employing Germans after the Franco-Prussian War; the British provided instructors for the navy. Young Japanese were sent abroad to learn at first hand other secrets of the wonderful and threatening puissance of the West. It is still hard not to be moved by the ardour of many of these young men and of their elders and impossible not to be impressed by their achievement, which went far beyond Japan and their own time. The *shishi* (as some of the most passionate and dedicated activists of reform were called), later inspired national leaders right across Asia, from India to China. Their spirit was still at work in the young officers of the 1930s who were to launch the last and most destructive wave of Japanese imperialism.

The crudest indexes of the success of the reformers are the economic, but they are very striking. Remote from the Restoration though the successes of the twentieth-century economy were to be, they were prepared for by the work of the nineteenth century which released in Japan a current of growth achieved by no other non-western state. It was an advantage that the country was already well-supplied with entrepreneurs who took for granted the profit motive and was undoubtedly richer than, say China. Much of the explanation of the great leap forward by Japan lay in the overcoming of inflation and the liquidation of feudal restraints which made it hard to tap Japan's full potential. The first sign of change was a great increase in agricultural production, little though the peasants who made up four-fifths of the population in 1868 benefited from it. Japan managed in the nineteenth century to feed a growing population by bringing more land under cultivation for rice and by cultivating existing fields more intensively. Though the dependence on the land tax lessened as a bigger portion of the revenue could be found from other sources, it was still upon the peasant that the cost of the new Japan fell most heavily. Right down to 1941, Japanese peasants benefited little from modernization. There were few non-agricultural resources. It was the increasingly productive tax on land which paid for investment. Consumption remained low, though there was not the suffering of, say, the later industrialization process of Stalin's Russia. A high rate of saving (12 per cent in 1900) spared Japan dependence on foreign loans but, again, restricted consumption. This was the other side of the balance sheet of expansion whose credit entries were clear enough: the infrastructure of a modern state, an indigenous arms industry, a usually high credit rating in the eyes of foreign investors and a huge expansion of cotton-spinning and other textiles by 1914.

Eventually, it was to become clear that a heavy spiritual cost had been paid for these successes. Even while seeking to learn from the West, Japan turned inward. The 'foreign' religious influences of Confucianism and even, at first, Buddhism, were attacked by the upholders of the state Shintoist cult. Even under the shogunate this had begun to stress and enhance the rôle of the emperor as the embodiment of the divine. The demands of loyalty to the emperor as the focus of the nation came to override the principles embodied in the new constitution which might have been developed in liberal directions in a different cultural setting. The quality of the régime did not express itself in such institutions, but in the repressive actions of the imperial police. Yet it is difficult to see how an authoritarian emphasis could, in fact, have been avoided given the two great tasks facing the statesmen of the Meiji Restoration. The modernization of the economy meant not planning in the modern sense but a strong governmental initiative and harsh fiscal policies. The other problem was order. The imperial power had once before gone into eclipse because of its failure to meet the threat on this front and now there were new dangers, because not all conservatives could be reconciled to the new model Japan. Discontented *ronin* – rootless *samurai* without masters – were one source of trouble. Another was peasant misery; there were scores of agrarian revolts in the first decade of the Meiji era. In the Satsuma rebellion of 1877 the government's new conscript forces showed that they could handle conservative resistance. This was the last of several rebellions against the Restoration and its last great challenge from conservatism.

The energies of the discontented *samurai* were gradually to be siphoned off into the service

A parliament house of basically European design was built for the new Japanese parliament, here being opened in 1891 by the emperor, seated at the right. Not only have the members been made to look very Europeanized in this print, but the ladies in the gallery, too, wear European dress.

Japanese expansion 1895—1942

▨	Japanese Empire before 1928
⣿	Occupied by Japan 1928-1936
▥	Occupied by Japan 1937-40
▤	Occupied by Japan 1941-43
▦	Extent of Japanese conquest 1942

of the new state, but this did not mean that the implications for Japan were all beneficial. They intensified in certain key sectors of the national life an assertive nationalism which was to lead eventually to aggression abroad. Immediately, this was likely to find expression not only in resentment of the West but also in expansion on the nearby Asian mainland. Modernization at home and adventure abroad were often in tension in Japan after the Meiji Restoration, but their long-term tendency was to pull in the same direction. The popular and democratic movements especially felt the tug of imperialism.

China was the predestined victim and was to be served as harshly by her fellow-Asians as by any of the western states. At first, however, she was threatened only indirectly. Just as China had her supremacy over the dependencies on her borders challenged in Tibet, Indo-China and Manchuria by Europeans, so the Japanese threatened it in the ancient empire of Korea, long a tributary of Peking. Japanese interest there went back a long way. In part this was strategic; the Tsushima straits were the place where the mainland was nearest to her. In 1876 an overt move was made; under the threat of military and naval action which was very much like that used on China by the Europeans – and on Japan by Perry – the Koreans agreed to open three of their ports to the Japanese and to exchange diplomatic representation. Some Japanese already wanted more. They remembered earlier Japanese invasions and successful piracy on the Korean coast and pointed to the mineral and natural wealth of Korea. The statesmen of the Restoration did not at once give way to such pressure, but in a sense they were only making haste slowly. In the 1890s another step forward was taken which led Japan into her first major war since the Restoration, and it was against China. It was sweepingly successful but was followed by an appalling national humiliation, when in 1895 a group of western powers forced Japan to accept a peace treaty much less advantageous than the one she had imposed on the Chinese (which had included a declaration of Korea's independence).

Korea (with some unwillingness on the part of her rulers) underwent measures of modernization at the hands of the Japanese. One measure of 1895 prescribed the removal of the pigtail in the cause of progress, a symbolic demand which has parallels in many reforming countries.

At this point resentment of the West fused with enthusiasm for expansion in Asia. Popular resentment of the 'unequal treaties' had been running high and the 1895 disappointment brought it to a head. The Japanese government had its own interests in backing Chinese revolutionary movements and now it had the new slogan to offer them: 'Asia for the Asians'. It was becoming clear, too, to the western powers that dealing with Japan was a very different matter from bullying China. Japan was increasingly recognized to be a 'civilized' state, not to be treated like other non-European nations. The great symbol of the change was their relinquishing in 1899 of extra-territoriality in Japan; throughout the world it was one of the most humiliating signs of European predominance. Then came the greatest of all marks of Japan's acceptance as an equal by the West, an Anglo-Japanese alliance in 1902. Japan, it was said, had joined Europe.

The greatest of European Far Eastern powers was Russia. Her rôle had been important in 1895 and her advance since then made it clear that the longed-for prize of Korea might elude the Japanese if they delayed much longer. The building of railways, the development of Vladivostok, and the activities of Russian businessmen in Korea all looked alarming. Korean politics were virtually a matter of the rivalry between pro-Japanese and pro-Russian factions. Most serious of all was a Russian lease of the naval base of Port Arthur from the enfeebled Chinese. In 1904 the Japanese struck at the Russians in Manchuria. The result, after a year of war, was a humiliating defeat for the Russians. For the first time since the Middle Ages non-Europeans defeated a European power in a major war. They had done it with European arms and training and the implications were colossal. The immediate consequences, too, were far-reaching, for it was the end of Tsarist pretensions in Korea and South Manchuria, where Japanese influence was henceforth dominant and other territories passed into Japanese possession to remain there until 1945. In 1910 Korea was at last annexed.

With this event, with the Chinese Revolution of 1911 and the end of the Manchu dynasty, the first discernible phase of Asia's response to the West can be given a boundary. It had been marked by importantly different reactions in the two states which were to be the great Asian powers of the second half of the twentieth century. One of them had been able to inoculate herself against the threat of modernization by accepting the virus; the other had not. In each case, the West provided both direct and indirect stimulus to upheaval, though in one case it was successfully contained and in the other it was not. In each case, too, the fate of the Asian power was decided not only by the response it could itself generate, but by the relations of the western powers among themselves. The rivalries of western powers in China generated the scramble there which so alarmed and tempted the Japanese, and it was the Anglo-Japanese alliance that gave them the assurance that they could strike at their great enemy Russia and find her unsupported. A few years more and Japan and China would both be participants as (formally) equals with other powers in the First World War. Meanwhile, Japan's example and, above all, its victory over Russia, was an inspiration to other Asians, the greatest single reason for them to ponder whether European hegemony was bound to be their lot. What Japan had done, they might do. But Japan had turned Europe's skills against her; the disturbance brought by the aggressive civilization had provoked imitation.

In other Asian countries European agencies had themselves launched changes which contributed in the end to the crumbling of Europe's political hegemony. They had brought assumptions about nationalism and humanitarianism, the Christian missionary's dislocation of local society and belief, and the experience of an exploitation not sanctioned by tradition; all of which often set in train important economic and social change. Primitive, almost blind, responses like the Indian Mutiny or Boxer rebellion were the first and obvious consequences of the European impact, but there were others which had a much more important future ahead. In particular, this was true in India, the biggest and most important of all colonial territories.

In 1877 Parliament had bestowed the title of 'Empress of India' upon Queen Victoria; some Englishmen laughed and a few disapproved, but it does not seem that there were many who did either. Most took the British supremacy there to be permanent or near-permanent and were not much concerned about names. They would have agreed with their compatriot who said 'we are not in India to be pleasant' and held that only a severe and firm government could be sure to prevent another Mutiny. Others would also have agreed with the British viceroy who declared as the twentieth century began that 'As long as we rule India, we are the greatest power in the world. If we lose it, we shall drop straightaway to a third-rate power.' Two important truths underlay this assertion. One was

A railway station showing remarkable fidelity to English models in Baluchistan, at the periphery of a railway system which was one of the finest in the world and the source of justifiable pride to British India.

that the Indian tax-payer paid for the defence of much or most of the British empire; Indian troops had been used to sustain it from Malta to China and in the subcontinent there was always a strategical reserve. The second was that Indian tariff policy was subordinated to British commercial and industrial realities.

These were harsh facts, whose weight was harder and harder to ignore. Yet they were not the whole story of the Raj. There was more to it than just fear, greed, cynicism or the love of power. Human beings do not find it easy to pursue collective purposes without some sort of myth to justify them and this was true of the British in India. Some of them saw themselves as the successors of the Romans whom a classical education taught them to admire, stoically bearing the burden of a lonely life in an alien land to bring peace to the warring and law to peoples without it. Others saw in Christianity a precious gift with which they must destroy idols and cleanse evil custom. Some never formulated such clear views but were simply convinced that what they brought was better than what they

found and therefore what they were doing was good. At the basis of all these views there was a conviction of superiority and there was nothing surprising about this; it had always animated some imperialists. But in the later nineteenth century it was especially reinforced by fashionable racialist ideas and a muddled reflexion of what was being said by current biological science about the survival of the fittest. Such ideas provided a rationale for the much greater social separation of the British in India from native Indians after the shock of the Mutiny. Although there was a modest intake of nominated Indian landlords and native rulers into the legislative branch of government it was not until the very end of the century that these were joined by elected Indians. Moreover, though Indians could compete to enter the civil service, there were important practical obstacles in the way of their entry to the ranks of the decision-makers. In the army, too, Indians were kept out of the senior commissioned ranks.

The largest single part of the British army was always stationed in India, where its reliability and monopoly of artillery combined with the officering of the Indian regiments by Europeans to ensure that there would be no repetition of the Mutiny. The coming of railways, telegraphs and more advanced weapons in any case told

*With the modernization of India's commercial
structure there appeared in many Indian cities
curious buildings, neither of East nor West, but
the work of architects of astonishing self-confidence.
One was the Victoria railway terminus, Bombay.*

*Universities, colleges and special schools were
the main channel through which European ideas
and standards reached Indians. By the beginning
of this century, Indian orderlies and assistants
were available in increasing numbers, as this
picture of the operating theatre of a Bombay
medical college shows. Most spectacular is the
Indian – or Anglo-Indian – girl in nurse's
uniform; an early example of the liberation of
women in India from traditional rules.*

in favour of government in India as much as in
any European country. But armed force was not
the explanation of the self-assuredness of British
rule, any more than a conviction of racial superiority. The Census Report of 1901 recorded
that there were just under 300 million Indians.
These were governed by about 900 white civil
servants. Usually there was about one British
soldier for every 400 Indians. As an Englishman once put it, picturesquely, had all the
Indians chosen to spit at the same moment, his
countrymen would have been drowned.

The Raj rested also on carefully administered
policies. One assumption underlying them after
the Mutiny was that Indian society should be
interfered with as little as possible. Female
infanticide might be forbidden, but there was
to be no attempt to prohibit polygamy or child
marriage (though after 1891 it was not legal for
a marriage to be consummated until the wife
was twelve years old). The line of the law was
to run outside what was sanctioned by Hindu
religion. This conservatism was reflected in a

new attitude towards the native Indian rulers.
The Mutiny had shown that they were usually
loyal; it was believed that those who turned
against the government had been provoked by
resentment against British annexation of their
lands. Their rights were therefore scrupulously
respected after the Mutiny; the princes ruled
their own states independently and virtually
irresponsibly, checked only by their awe of the
British political officers resident at their courts.
The native states included over a fifth of the
population. Elsewhere, the British cultivated
the native aristocracy and the landlords. This
was part of a search for support from key groups
of Indians, but often led the British to lean on
those whose own leadership powers were already being undermined by social change. Enlightened despotism at their expense, but in

873

Indian India: a young prince and his advisers. The government stationed a British political officer at each Indian court representing the sovereign power in the native states, whose internal administration was in their own hands – unless it became so intolerably inadequate as to present danger or embarrassment to the Raj itself.

the interests of the peasantry (such as had been shown earlier in the century) none the less now disappeared. These were all some of the unhappy consequences of the Mutiny.

Yet no more than any other imperial government was the Raj able permanently to ensure itself against change. Its very success told against it. The suppression of warfare favoured the growth of population – and one consequence was more frequent famine. But the provision of ways of earning a living other than by agriculture (which was a possible outlet from the problem of an over-populated countryside) was made very difficult by the obstacles in the way of

Indian industrialization. These arose in large measure from a tariff policy in the interest of British manufactures. A slowly emerging Indian class of industrialists did not, therefore, feel warmly towards government, but were antagonized by it. Their ranks also included many of the growing number of Indians who had received an education along English lines and had subsequently been irritated to compare its precepts with the practice of the British community in India. Some who had gone to England to study at Oxford, Cambridge or the Inns of Court found the contrast especially galling: in England there were even Indian members of parliament in the nineteenth century, while an Indian graduate in India might be slighted by a British private soldier, and there was an outcry from British residents when, in the 1880s, a viceroy wished to remove the 'invidious distinction' which prevented a European from being brought before an Indian magistrate. Some, too, had pondered what they read in their

Indian India: victims of the 1898 famine.

studies; John Stuart Mill and Mazzini were thus to have a huge influence in India, and, through its leaders, in the rest of Asia.

Resentment was especially felt among the Hindus of Bengal, the historic centre of British power: Calcutta was the capital of India. In 1905 this province was divided in two. This partition was an important landmark, for it for the first time brought the Raj into serious conflict with something not existing in 1857, the Indian nationalist movement.

At every stage this movement had been fed and stimulated by non-Indian forces. British orientalists, at the beginning of the nineteenth century, had begun the rediscovery of classical Indian culture which was essential both to the self-respect of Hindu nationalism and the overcoming of the subcontinent's huge divisions. Indian scholars began to rediscover, under European guidance, the culture and religion em-

bedded in the neglected Sanskrit scriptures; through these they could formulate a conception of a Hinduism far removed from the rich and fantastic, but also superstitious, accretions of its popular form. By the end of the nineteenth century this recovery of the Aryan and Vedic past – Islamic India was virtually disregarded – had gone far enough for Hindus to meet with confidence the reproaches of Christian missionaries and offer a cultural counter-attack; a Hindu emissary to a 'Parliament of Religions' in Chicago in 1893 not only awoke great personal esteem and obtained serious attention for his assertion that Hinduism was a great religion capable of revivifying the spiritual life of other cultures, but actually made converts.

The Hindu national consciousness, like the political activity it was to reinforce, was for a long time confined to a few. The proposal that Hindi should be India's language seemed wildly unrealistic when the hundreds of languages and dialects which fragmented Indian society were considered but could only appeal to an élite seeking to strengthen its links across a subcontinent. The definition of its membership was education rather than wealth: its backbone was provided by those Hindus, often Bengali, who felt especially disappointed at the failure of their educational attainments to win them an appropriate share in the running of India. The Raj seemed determined to maintain the racial predominance of Europeans and to rely upon such conservative interests as the princes and landlords, to the exclusion and, possibly even more important, the humiliation of the *babu*, the educated, middle-class, urban Hindu.

A new cultural self-respect and a growing sense of grievance over rewards and slights were the background to the formation of the Indian National Congress. The immediate prelude was a flurry of excitement over government proposals, subsequently modified because of the outcry of European residents, to equalize the treatment of Indians and Europeans in the courts. Disappointment caused an Englishman, a former civil servant, to take the steps which led

875

British India: the members of a hunt pose for a group photograph at Poona early in this century. The ladies' sun helmets and hats are virtually the only concession made to the climate.

to the first conference of the Indian National Congress in Bombay in December 1885. Vice-regal initiatives, too, had played a part in this, and Europeans were long to be prominent in the administration of Congress. Even longer would they patronize it with protection and advice in London. It was an appropriate symbol of the complexity of the European impact on India that some Indian delegates attended in European dress, improbably attired in morning-suits and top-hats of comical unsuitability to the climate of their country, but the formal attire of its rulers.

Congress was soon committed by its declaration of principles to national unity and regenera-tion: as in Japan already and China and many other countries later, this was the classical product of the impact of European ideas. But it did not at first aspire to self-government. Congress sought, rather, to provide a means of communicating Indian views to the viceroy and proclaimed its 'unswerving loyalty' to the British Crown. Only after twenty years, in which much more extreme nationalist views had won adherents among Hindus, did it begin to discuss the possibility of independence. During this time its attitude had been soured and stiffened by the vilification it received from British residents who declared it unrepresentative, and the unresponsiveness of an administration which endorsed this view and preferred to work through more traditional and conservative social forces. Extremists became more insistent. In 1904 came the inspiriting victories of Japan over Russia. The issue for a clash was

Major religions of Asia in the early 20th century

Tokyo

Peking

Shanghai

Kabul

Amritsar

Karachi

Benares

Canton

Bombay

Calcutta

Manila

Rangoon

Bangkok

Islam

Hinduism

Christianity

Confucianism in China, Shintoism in Japan

Southern Buddhism (Hinayana)

Northern Buddhism (Mahayana)

Sikhs

Singapore

provided in 1905 by the administrative division of Bengal.

The purpose of the partition was twofold: it was administratively convenient and it would possibly weaken Bengal's nationalism. It produced a West Bengal where there was a Hindu majority, and an East Bengal with a Moslem majority. This detonated a mass of explosive materials long accumulating. Immediately, there was a struggle for power in Congress. At first a split was avoided by agreement on the aim of *swaraj*, which in practice might mean independent self-government such as that enjoyed by the white dominions: their example was suggestive. The extremists were heartened by anti-partition riots. A new weapon was deployed against the British, a boycott of goods, which, it was hoped, might be extended to other forms of passive resistance such as non-payment of taxes and the refusal of soldiers to obey orders. By 1908 the extremists were excluded from Congress. By this time, a second consequence

The review at the Delhi Durbar, 1911, possibly the most spectacular manifestation of British imperial power ever to take place. In this picture, the royal carriage containing George V and Queen Mary, both wearing their robes of state, follows a Sovereign's Escort of the Life Guards through the ranks of British and Indian soldiers.

was apparent: extremism was producing terrorism. Again, foreign models were important. Russian revolutionary terrorism now joined the works of Mazzini and the biography of Garibaldi, the guerrilla leader hero of Italian independence, as formative influences on an emerging India. The extremists argued that political murder was not ordinary murder. Assassination and bombing were met with special repressive measures.

The third consequence of partition was perhaps the most momentous. It brought out into the open the division of Moslem and Hindu.

For reasons which went back to the percolation of Moslem India before the Mutiny by an Islamic reform movement, the Arabian Wahhabi sect, Indian Moslems had for a century felt themselves more and more distinct from Hindus. Distrusted by the British because of attempts to revivify the Moghul empire in 1857 they had little success in winning posts in government or on the judicial bench. Hindus had responded more eagerly than Moslems to the educational opportunities offered by the Raj; they were of more commercial weight and had more influence on government. But Moslems had found their British helpers, too, who had launched the education of Moslems at a new, Islamic college, providing the English

878

education they needed to compete with Hindus, and had helped to set up Moslem political organizations. Some English civil servants began to grasp the potential for balancing Hindu pressure which this could give the Raj. Intensification of Hindu ritual practice such as a cow protection movement were not likely to do anything but increase the separation of the two communities.

Nevertheless, it was only in 1905 that the split became, as it remained, one of the fundamentals of the subcontinent's politics. The anti-partitionists campaigned with a strident display of Hindu symbols and slogans. The British governor of eastern Bengal favoured Moslems against Hindus and strove to give them a vested interest in the new province. He was dismissed, but his inoculation had taken: Bengal Moslems deplored his removal. An Anglo-Moslem *entente* was in the making. This further inflamed Hindu terrorists. To make things worse, all this was taking place during five years (from 1906 to 1910) in which prices rose faster than at any time since the Mutiny.

An important set of political reforms conceded in 1909 did not do more than change somewhat the forms with which to operate the political forces which were henceforth to dominate the history of India until the Raj came to an end nearly forty years later. Indians were for the first time appointed to the council which advised the British minister responsible for India and, more important, further elected places were provided for Indians in the legislative councils. But the elections were to be made by electorates which had a communal basis; the division of Hindu and Moslem India, that is to say, was institutionalized.

In 1911, for the first and only time, a reigning British monarch visited India. A great imperial durbar was held at Delhi, the old centre of Moghul rule to which the capital of British India was now transferred from Calcutta. The princes of India came to do homage; Congress did not question its duty to the throne. The accession to the throne of George V that year had been marked by the conferring of real and symbolic benefits, of which the most notable and politically significant was the reuniting of Bengal. If there was a moment at which the Raj was at its apogee, this was it.

Yet India was far from settled. Terrorism and seditious crime continued. The policy of favouring the Moslems had made Hindus more resentful while Moslems now felt that the government was going back on its understandings with them in withdrawing the partition of Bengal. They feared the resumption of a Hindu ascendancy in the province. Hindus, on the other hand, took the concession as evidence that resistance had paid and began to press for the abolition of the communal electoral arrangements which the Moslems prized. The British had therefore done much to alienate Moslem support when a further strain appeared. The Indian Moslem élites which had favoured cooperation with the British were increasingly under pressure from more middle-class Moslems susceptible to the violent appeal of a pan-Islamic movement. The pan-Islamists could point to the fact that the British had let the Moslems down in Bengal, but also noted that in Tripoli (which the Italians attacked in 1911) and the Balkans in 1912 and 1913, Christian powers were attacking Turkey, the seat of the Caliphate, the institutional embodiment of the spiritual leadership of Islam, and Great Britain was, indisputably, a Christian power. The intense susceptibilities of lower-class Indian Moslems were excited to the point at which even the involvement of a mosque in the replanning of a street could be presented as a part of a deliberate plot to harry Islam. When Turkey decided in 1914 to go to war with Great Britain, though the Moslem League remained loyal, some Indian Moslems accepted the logical consequence of the Caliphate's supremacy, and began to prepare revolution against the Raj. They were few. What was more important for the future was that by that year not two but three forces were making the running in Indian politics, the British, Hindu and Moslem. Here was the origin of the future partition of the only complete political unity the subcontinent had ever known,

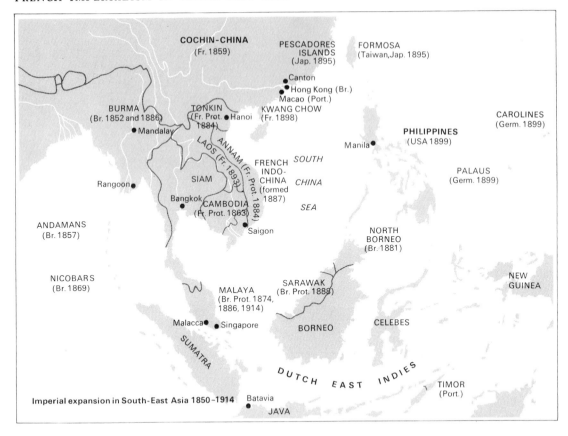

Imperial expansion in South-East Asia 1850–1914

and, like that unity, it was as much the result of the play of non-Indian as of Indian forces.

India was the largest single mass of non-European population and territory under European rule in Asia, but to the south-east and in Indonesia, both part of the Indian cultural sphere, lay further imperial possessions. Few generalizations are possible about so huge an area and so many peoples and religions. One negative fact was observable: in no other European possession in Asia was there such transformation before 1914 as in India, though in all of them modernization had begun the corrosion of local tradition. The forces which produced this were those which have already been noted at work elsewhere: European aggression, the example of Japan, and the diffusion of European culture. But the first and last of these forces operated in the region for a shorter time before 1914 than in China and

India. In 1880 most of mainland South-East Asia was still ruled by native princes who were independent rulers though they had usually had to make concessions already in 'unequal treaties' to European power. In the following decade this was rapidly changed by the British annexation of Burma and continuing French expansion in Indo-China. The sultans of Malaya acquired British residents at their courts who directed policy through the native administration. By 1900 only Siam was still independent among the kingdoms of this region.

Most of them had been shaped by cultural influences which were Indian in origin. The only one which was culturally more closely linked to China was Vietnam, that part of Indo-China known in the early stages of French Asian expansion as Annam. Vietnam had the longest tradition of national identity and a history of national revolt long before the European imperial era. It is not therefore surprising to find that it was in this part of the French *Union Indo-chinoise* that resistance to Europeanization was most marked.

French interest in the area went back to the seventeenth century and had been a missionary one in its origins. In the 1850s the persecution of Christianity led the French to intervene again in south Vietnam. This of course brought about diplomatic conflict with China, which claimed sovereignty over the country. A war between the two imperial powers (1883–5) established the French there and they set about the creation of a structure which disguised a centralized régime behind a system of protectorates. Though this meant the preservation of native rulers (the emperor of Vietnam and the kings of Cambodia and Laos), the aim of French colonial policy was always assimilation. French culture was to be brought to new French subjects whose élites were to be gallicized because this was believed to be the best way to modernization and civilization.

The centralizing tendencies of French administration soon made it clear that the formal structure of native government was a sham. Unwittingly, the French thus sapped local institutions without replacing them with others enjoying the loyalty of the people. This was a dangerous course. There were also other important by-products of the French presence. It brought with it, for example, French tariff policy, which was to slow down industrialization. This eventually led Indo-Chinese businessmen, like their Indian equivalents, to wonder in whose interests their country was run. Moreover, the conception of an Indo-China which was integrally a part of France, whose inhabitants should be turned into Frenchmen, also brought problems. The French administration had to grapple with the paradox that access to French education could lead to reflexion on the inspiring motto to be found on official buildings and documents of the Third Republic: it read, 'liberty, equality and fraternity'. Finally, French law and notions of property broke down the structure of village landholding and threw power into the hands of money-lenders and landlords. With a growing population in the rice-growing areas, this was to build up a revolutionary potential for the future.

Japan and China provided catalysts for Indo-Chinese grievances embodied in these facts and the legacy of traditional Vietnamese nationalism soon made itself felt. The Japanese victory over Russia led several young Vietnamese to go to Tokyo, where they met Sun Yat-Sen and the Japanese sponsors of 'Asia for the Asians'. After the Chinese Revolution of 1911, one of them organized a society for a Vietnamese Republic. None of this much troubled the French who were well able to contain such opposition before 1914, but it curiously paralleled conservative opposition to them among the Vietnamese Confucian scholar class. Though they opened a university in 1907, the French had to close it almost at once and it remained closed until 1918 because of fears of unrest among the intellectuals. This important section of Vietnamese opinion was already deeply alienated by French rule within a couple of decades of its establishment.

Further south, too, French history had already had an indirect impact in Indonesia. By the end of the nineteenth century there were some sixty million Indonesians; population pressure had not yet produced there the strains that were to come, but it was the largest group of non-Europeans ruled by a European state outside India. Their ancestors had nearly two centuries of sometimes bitter experience of Dutch rule before the French Revolution led to the invasion of the United Provinces, the setting up of a new revolutionary Republic there in 1795 and the dissolving of the Dutch East India Company. Equally important, there soon followed a British occupation of Java. The British troubled the waters by important changes in the revenue system, but there were also other influences now at work to stir up Indonesia. Though originally an outcropping of the Hindu civilization of India, it was also part of the Islamic world, with large numbers of Moslems among its peoples, and commercial ties with Arabia. In

881

At the outset of the war with Japan, Russian confidence was high – and Russian antagonism towards other Pacific and Far Eastern powers was strong, as this cartoon suggests.

the early years of the nineteenth century this had new importance. Indonesian pilgrims, some of them of birth and rank, went to Mecca and then sometimes went on to Egypt and Turkey. There they found themselves directly in touch with reforming ideas from further west.

The instability of the situation was revealed when the Dutch returned and had, in 1825, to fight a 'Java War' against a dissident prince which lasted five years. It damaged the island's finances so that the Dutch were constrained to introduce further changes. The result was an agricultural system which enforced the cultivation of crops for the government. The workings of this system led to grave exploitation of the peasant which began in the second half of the nineteenth century to awaken among Dutchmen an uneasiness about the conduct of

their colonial government. This culminated in a great change of attitude; in 1901 a new 'Ethical Policy' was announced which was expressed in decentralization and a campaign to achieve improvement through village administration. But this programme often proved so paternalistic and interventionist in action that it, too, sometimes stimulated hostility. This was utilized by the first Indonesian nationalists. Some of them were inspired by Indians and in 1908 they formed an organization to promote national education. Three years later an Islamic association appeared whose early activities were directed as much against Chinese traders as against the Dutch. By 1916 it had gone so far as to ask for self-government while remaining in union with the Netherlands. Before this, however, a true independence party had been founded in 1912. It opposed Dutch authority in the name of native-born Indonesians, of any race; a Dutchman was among its three founders and others followed him. In 1916 the Dutch took the first step towards meeting the demands of these groups, by authorizing a parliament with limited powers for Indonesia.

Though European ideas of nationalism were by the early years of the twentieth century at work in almost all Asian countries, they took their different expressions from different possibilities presented by history. Not all colonial régimes behaved in the same way. The British encouraged nationalism in Burma, while the United States doggedly pursued a benevolent paternalism in the Philippines, where the Americans inherited an insurrection originally directed against the Spanish (they had the additional peculiarity of operating in the only Christian country of Asia, thanks to their predecessor, though French missionary work produced important Christian communities in Vietnam). But history did not only operate through different colonial traditions: it shaped the futures of these societies also because of the different legacies these colonial régimes played upon. Above all, the forces of historical possibilities and historical inertia showed themselves in Japan and China, where the fact of direct European influence had effects just as dramatic as in India or Vietnam. But in every instance, the context in which it operated was decisive in shaping the future; at the end of a discussion of Asia in revolution, it must be remembered how much remained intact. A huge residue of customary thought and practice remained undisturbed. Too much history was present for European expansion alone to explain twentieth-century Asia. The catalytic and liberating power of that expansion, none the less, was what brought Asia into the modern era.

Book Seven

The end of the Europeans' World

In 1900 Europeans could look back on two, per-haps three, centuries of astonishing growth. Most of them would have said that it was growth for the better – that is, progress. Their history since the Middle Ages looked very much like a continuing advance to goals evidently worth while which few questioned. Whether the criteria were intellectual and scientific, or material and economic (even if they were moral and aesthetic, some said, so persuasive was the gospel of progress), a look at their own past assured Europeans that they were set on a progressive course – which meant that the world was set on a progressive course, for their civilization was spread world-wide. What was more, limitless advance seemed to lie ahead. Europeans showed in 1900 much the same confi-dence in the continuing success of their culture as the Chinese had shown in theirs a century earlier. The past, they were sure, proved them right.

Even so, a few did not feel so confident. They felt that the evidence could equally well imply a pessimistic conclusion. Though there were far fewer pessimists than optimists, they numbered in their ranks men of acknowledged standing and powerful minds. Some of them argued that the civilization in which they lived had yet to reveal its full self-destructive potential and sensed that the time when it would do so might not be far away. Some of them saw a civilization more and more obviously drifting away from its moorings in religion and absolute morality, carried along by the tides of materialism and barbarity probably to complete disaster.

As it turned out, neither optimists nor pessimists were wholly right, perhaps because their eyes were glued too firmly to what they thought

were the characteristics of European civilization. They looked to its own inherent powers, tendencies, or weaknesses for guidance about the future; very few of them paid any attention to the way Europe was changing the world in which her own ascen-dancy had been built and was thus to alter once again the balance between the major centres of civilization. Few looked further than Europe and Europe beyond the seas except the unbalanced cranks who fussed about the 'Yellow Peril', though Napoleon had a century earlier warned that China was a sleeping giant best left undisturbed.

It is tempting to say in retrospect that the pessi-mists have had the best of the argument and it may be true. But hindsight is sometimes a disadvantage to the historian; in this instance it makes it difficult to see how the optimists could once have felt so sure of themselves. Yet we should try to do so. For one thing, there were men of vision and insight among them; for another, optimism was for so long an obstacle to the solution of certain problems in this century that it deserves to be understood as a historical force in its own right. And much of what the pessimists said was wrong too. Appalling though the disasters of the twentieth century have been, they fell on societies more resilient than those shattered by lesser troubles in earlier times, and they have not always been those feared seventy-five years ago. Optimists and pessi-mists alike in 1900 had to work with data which could be read in more than one way and it is not reprehensible, merely tragic, that they found it so hard to judge exactly what lay ahead. We are not so successful in shorter-term prediction with better information that we are in a position to condemn them.

1 Strains in the system

One historical trend very obvious as the twentieth century opened was the continuing increase of population in the European world. In 1900 Europe had about 400 million inhabitants – a quarter of them Russians – the United States about 76 million and the British overseas Dominions about 15 million between them. This kept the dominant civilization's share of world population high. On the other hand, this growth was already beginning in some countries to slow down in the first decade of this century. This was most obvious in the advanced countries which were the heart of western Europe, where growth depended more and more on falling death-rates. In them there was evidence that conscious restriction of the family's size was now spreading downwards through society. Traditional contraceptive knowledge of a sort had long been available, but the nineteenth century had brought to the better-off more effective techniques. When these were taken up more widely (and there were soon signs that they were), their impact on population structure would be very great.

In eastern and Mediterranean Europe, on the other hand, such effects were far away. There, rapid growth was only just beginning to produce grave strains. The growing availability of outlets in emigration in the nineteenth century had made it possible to surmount these; there might

A German magazine faces a new century with symbols which suggest hopefulness. 1900 was, of course, the last year of the nineteenth century, not the first of the twentieth.

be trouble to come if these outlets ceased to be so easily available. Further afield, even more pessimistic reflexions might be prompted by considering what would happen when the agencies at work to reduce the death-rate in Europe came to spread to Asia and Africa. In the world civilization the nineteenth century had created, this could not be prevented. In that case, Europe's success in imposing itself would have guaranteed the eventual loss of the demographic advantage recently added to her technical superiority. Worse still, the Malthusian crisis once feared but lost to sight as the nineteenth-century economic miracle removed the fear of over-population might at last become a reality.

It had been possible to set aside Malthus' warnings because the nineteenth century brought about the greatest expansion of wealth the world had ever known. Its sources lay in the industrialization of Europe and the techniques for assuring the continuance of this growth were by no means exhausted or compromised in 1900. There had not only been a vast and accelerating flow of commodities available only in (relatively) tiny quantities a century before, but whole new ranges of goods had come into existence. Oil and electricity had joined coal, wood, wind and water as sources of energy. A chemical industry existed which could not have been envisaged in 1800. Growing power and wealth had been used to tap seemingly inexhaustible natural resources, both agricultural and mineral. Railways, electric trams, steamships, motor cars and bicycles gave millions of men a new control over their environ-

English elegance on display; the start of a balloon race at Ranelagh, 1907.

The other face of English society: children from the East End of London waiting for food during a dock strike, 1912.

ment; they accelerated travel from place to place and eased transport for the first time since animals had been harnessed to carts thousands of years before. The overall result of such changes had been that in many countries a growing population had been easily carried on an even faster growing production of wealth; between 1870 and 1900, for example, Germany's output of pig-iron increased sixfold, but her population rose only by about a third. In terms of consumption, or of the services to which they had access, or in the enjoyment of better health, even the mass of the population in developed countries were much better off in 1900 than their predecessors a hundred years before. This still left out people like the Russian or Andalusian peasants (though the comparison is by no means easy to make nor the result a foregone conclusion). But, none the less, the way ahead looked promising even for them, inasmuch as a key to prosperity had been found which could be made available in all countries.

In spite of this cheerful picture, doubts could break in. Even if what might happen in the future were ignored, contemplation of the cost of the new wealth and doubts about the social justice of its distribution were troubling. Most people were still terribly poor, whether or not they lived in rich countries where the illogi-

cality of this was particularly more striking than in earlier times. Poverty was all the more afflicting when society showed such obvious power to create new wealth. Here was the beginning of a change of revolutionary import in expectations. Another change in the way men thought about their condition arose over their power to get a livelihood at all. It was not new that men should be without work. What was new was that situations should suddenly arise in which the operation of blind forces of boom and slump produced millions of men without work concentrated in great towns. This was 'unemployment', the new phenomenon for which a new word had been needed. Some economists thought that it might be an inevitable concomitant of capitalism. Nor were the cities themselves yet rid of all the evils which had so struck the first observers of industrial society. By 1900 the majority of western Europeans were town-dwellers and they lived in more than 140 cities of over a 100000 inhabitants in 1914. In some of them, millions of people were cramped, ill-housed, under-provided with schools and fresh air, let alone amusement other than that of the streets, and this often in sight of the wealth their society helped to produce. 'Slums' was another word invented by

Probably the worst European poverty at the beginning of this century was to be found in eastern Europe and Russia. This photograph was taken in Nizhni Novgorod, but has something almost Asiatic about it.

The 1905 revolution in Russia achieved much, but far from what many Russian revolutionaries had hoped. Here, members of the Workers' Council of St Petersburg pose after their exile to Siberia. Marked with a cross stands the young Trotsky, who was exiled again (this time to Kazakhstan and by a successful revolutionary régime) twenty-three years later.

the nineteenth century. Two converging conclusions were often drawn from contemplating them. One was that of fear; many sober statesmen at the end of the nineteenth century distrusted the cities still as centres of revolutionary danger, crime and wickedness. The other was hopeful: the condition of the cities gave grounds for assurance that revolution against the injustice of the social and economic order was inevitable. (What both these responses neglected, of course, was the accumulating evidence of experience that revolution in western Europe was in fact less and less likely.)

The fear of revolution drew also on real evidence of social strain, even if that evidence was misinterpreted and exaggerated. In Russia, a country which was clearly a part of Europe if it is contrasted with the rest of the world, but one which had not moved forward rapidly along the lines of economic and social progress, reform had not modified autocracy sufficiently and there was a continuing revolutionary movement. It broke out in terrorism – one of the victims of which was a Tsar – and was supplemented by continuing and spontaneous agrarian unrest. Peasant attacks on landlords and their bailiffs reached a peak in the early years of the century. When they were followed by defeat in war at the hands of the Japanese and the momentary shaking of the régime's confidence, the result was a revolution in 1905. Russia might be, and no doubt was, a special case, but Italy, too, had something that some observers thought of as barely contained revolution in 1898 and 1914, while one of the great cities of Spain, Barcelona, exploded into bloody street-fighting in 1909. Strikes and demonstrations could become violent in industrialized countries without revolutionary traditions as the United States amply showed in the 1890s; even in Great Britain before 1914 there were examples of death resulting from them. This was the sort of data which, when combined with the sporadic activities of anarchists, kept policemen and respectable citizens on their toes. The anarchists especially succeeded in pressing themselves on the public imagination during the 1890s when a series of acts of terrorism and assassinations received wide publicity; there was by then a value in such acts which transcended their immediate object because the growth of the press had meant that great publicity value could be extracted from a bomb or a dagger-stroke. In using such methods, not all anarchists shared the same aims, but they were children of their epoch: they protested not only against the state in its governmental aspect, but also against a whole society which they judged unjust.

Socialists contributed most to the rhetoric which sustained the fear of revolution. By 1900 socialism almost everywhere meant Marxism. An important alternative tradition and mythology existed only in England, where the early growth of a numerous trade-union movement and the possibility of working through one of the major established political parties produced a non-revolutionary radicalism. The supremacy of Marxism among continental socialists, by contrast, was formally expressed in 1896, when the 'Second International', an international working-class movement set up seven years before to coordinate socialist action in all countries, expelled the anarchists who had until then belonged to it. There was a well-established tradition of hostility between anarchism and the Marxism which increasingly dominated socialist organizations. Four years later, the International opened a permanent administrative centre in Brussels. Within this movement, numbers, wealth and theoretical contributions gave practical preponderance to the German Social Democratic Party. This party had prospered in spite of police persecution thanks to Germany's rapid industrialization, and by 1900 was an established fact of German politics, their first truly mass organization. Its numbers and wealth alone would have made it likely that Marxism, the official creed of the German party, would be that of the international socialist movement, even had Marxism not had its own intellectual and emotional appeal. This appeal lay above all in its assurance that the world was going the way socialists hoped, and the emotional satisfaction it provided of participating in a struggle of classes, which, Marxists insisted, must end in violent revolution.

Avanti! *(Forward!) The cover of an issue of the Italian socialist newspaper (whose editor in 1912 was the young Mussolini). Much early socialist iconography and propaganda stressed the appeal of the healthiness, virility and youth of the movements' aspirations, as opposed to the supposed effeteness and decadence of capitalist society.*

Though such a mythology confirmed the fears of the established order, some intelligent Marxists had noticed that after 1880 or so the facts by no means obviously supported it. Manifestly, great numbers of people had been able to obtain a higher standard of living within the capitalist system. The unfolding of that system in all its complexity was not simplifying and sharpening class conflict in the way Marx had predicted. Moreover, capitalist political institutions had been able to serve the working class. This was very important; in Germany, above all, but also in England, important advantages had been won by socialists using the

A new Estate of the realm: Trade Union banners at a strike rally at Tower Hill.

opportunities provided by parliaments. The vote was available as a weapon and they were not disposed to ignore it while waiting for the revolution. This led some socialists to attempt to restate official Marxism so as to take account of such trends; they were called 'Revisionists' and, broadly speaking, they advocated a peaceful advance towards the transformation of society by socialism. If people liked to call that transformation, when it came, a revolution, then only a definition was involved. Inside this theoretical position and the conflict it provoked was a practical issue which came to a head at the end of the century: whether socialists should or should not sit as ministers in capitalist governments.

The debate which this aroused took years to settle. What emerged in the end was explicit condemnation of revisionism by the Second International while national parties, notably the

Germans, continued to act on it in practice, doing deals with the existing system as suited them. Their rhetoric continued to be about revolution. Many socialists even hoped that this might become a reality by refusing to fight as conscripts if their governments tried to make them go to war. One socialist group, the majority in the Russian party, continued vigorously to denounce revisionism and advocate violence; no doubt this recognized the peculiarity of the Russian situation, where there was little opportunity for effective parliamentary activity and a deep tradition of revolution and terrorism. This group was called Bolshevik, from the Russian word signifying a majority, and more was to be heard of it.

Socialists claimed to speak for the masses. Whether they did or did not, by 1900 many conservatives worried that the advances gained by liberalism and democracy in the nineteenth century might well prove irresistible except by force. A few of them were still living in a mental world which was pre-nineteenth rather than pre-twentieth century. In much of eastern Europe quasi-patriarchal relationships and the traditional authority of the landowner over his estates were still intact. Such societies could still produce aristocratic conservatives who were opposed in spirit not merely to encroachments upon their material privilege, but also to the values and assumptions of what was to be called 'market society'. But this line was more and more blurred and, for the most part, conservative thinking tended to fall back upon the defence of capital, a position which, of course, would in many places half a century earlier have been regarded as radically liberal, because individualist. The new form of capitalist, industrial conservatism opposed itself more and more vigorously to the state's interference with its wealth, an interference which had grown steadily with the state's acceptance of a larger and larger rôle in the regulation of society. There was a crisis in England on the issue which led to a revolutionary transformation of what was left of the 1688 constitution in 1911 by the crippling of the power of the house of lords to restrain an elected house of commons. In the background were many issues, among them higher taxation of the rich to pay for social services. Even France had by 1914 accepted the principle of an income tax.

Such changes registered the logic of the democratizing of politics in advanced societies. By 1914, universal adult male suffrage existed in France, Germany and several smaller European countries; Great Britain and Italy had electorates big enough to come near to meeting this criterion. This brought forward another disruptive question: if men had, should not women have the vote in national politics? This was already causing uproar in English politics. But only Finland and Norway had women in their parliamentary electorates by 1914 and this issue was to be open in many countries for another thirty years.

Political rights were only one side of the whole question of women's rights in a society whose overall bias, like that of every other great civilization which had preceded it, was towards the interests and values of men. Yet discussion of women's rôle in society had begun in the eighteenth century and it was not long before cracks appeared in the structure of assumptions which had so long enclosed it. Women's right to education, to employment, to control of their own property, to moral independence, even to wear more comfortable clothes, had increasingly been in debate in the nineteenth century. Ibsen's play *A Doll's House* was interpreted as a trumpet-call for the liberation of women instead of, as the author intended, a plea for the individual. The bringing forward of such issues, implied a real revolution. The claims of women in Europe and North America threatened assumptions and attitudes which had not merely centuries, but even millennia, of institutionalization behind them. They awoke complex emotions, for they were linked to deepseated notions about the family and sexuality. In these ways, they troubled some people – men and women alike – more deeply than the threat of social revolution or political democracy. People were right to see the question in this dimension.

International Women's Day 1914; a German poster demanding the vote for women.

In the early European feminist movement was the seed of something whose explosive content would be even greater when transferred (as it soon was) to other cultures and civilizations assaulted by western values.

The politicization of women and political attacks on the legal and institutional structures which were felt by them to be oppressive probably did less for women than other changes which undermined tradition. Three of these were of slowly growing but, eventually, gigantic importance. The first was the development of the advanced capitalist economy. By 1914 this already meant that great numbers of jobs – as typists, secretaries, telephone operators, factory hands, department store assistants and teachers – existed for women in some countries. Almost none of these had existed a century earlier. This meant a huge practical accession of

THOU SHALT NOT COVET.

Household machines were the humble instruments of the liberation of women from age-old drudgery. This poster of a mangle-cum-washing-machine was commissioned as an advertisement in about 1900. Mass advertising was to prove a major educational force, just because it could play so powerfully on simple emotions – such as envy.

for example, for education and professional training.

The second great transforming force was even further from showing its full potential to change women's lives by 1914. This was contraception. It had already decisively affected demography. What lay ahead was a revolution in power and status as more women absorbed the idea that they might control the demands of childbearing and rearing which hitherto had throughout history dominated most women's lives; beyond that lay an even deeper change, only beginning to be discerned in 1914, as women came to see that they could pursue sexual satisfaction without necessarily entering the obligations of lifelong marriage.

To the third great tendency moving women imperceptibly but irresistibly towards liberation from ancient ways and assumptions it is much harder to give an identifying single name, but if it has a governing principle, it is technology. It was a process made up of a vast number of innovations, some of them slowly accumulating already for decades before 1900 and all tending to cut into the iron time-tables of domestic routine and drudgery, however marginally at first. The coming of piped water, or of gas for heating and lighting, are among the first examples; electricity's cleanliness and flexibility was later to have even more obvious effects. Better shops were the front line of big changes in retail distribution which not only gave a notion of luxury to someone other than the rich, but also made it easier to meet household needs. Imported food, with its better processing and preserving, slowly changed habits of family catering once based – as they are still often based in India or Africa – on daily or twice-daily visits to the market. The world of detergents and easily cleaned artificial fibres still lay in the future in 1900, but already soap and washing soda were far more easily and cheaply available than a century before, while the first domestic machines – gas cookers, vacuum cleaners, washing machines – began to make their appearance at least in the homes of the rich early in this century.

economic power to women: if they could earn their own living, they were at the beginning of a road which would eventually transform family structures. Soon, too, the demands of warfare in the industrial societies would accelerate this advance as the need for labour opened an even wider range of occupations to women. Meanwhile, for growing numbers of them even by 1900, a job in industry or commerce at once meant a chance of liberation from parental regulation and the trap of married drudgery. Most women did not by 1914 so benefit, but an accelerating process was at work, because such developments would stimulate other demands,

893

Historians who would recognize at once the importance of the introduction of the stirrup or the lathe in earlier times have none the less strangely neglected the cumulative force of such humble commodities and instruments as these. Yet they implied a revolution for half the world. It is more understandable that their long-term implications interested fewer people at the beginning of this century than the antics of the 'suffragettes'. This was the name by which the women who sought the vote in England were called. The immediate stimulus to their activity was the evident liberalization and democratization of political institutions in the case of men. This was the background which their campaign presupposed. Logically, there were grounds for pursuing democracy across the boundaries of sex even if this meant doubling the size of electorates.

But the formal and legal structure of politics was not the whole story of their tendency to show more and more of a 'mass' quality. The masses had to be organized. By 1900 there had appeared to meet this need the modern mass political party, with its simplifications of issues in order to present them as clear choices, its apparatus for the spread of political awareness, and its cultivation of special interests. From Europe and the United States it spread round the world. Old-fashioned politicians deplored the new model of party and by no means always did so insincerely, because it was another sign of the coming of mass society and the need for traditional élites to adapt their politics to the ways of the man in the street.

The importance of public opinion had begun to be noticed in England early in the nineteenth century. It had been thought decisive in the struggles over the Corn Laws. By 1870, the French emperor felt he could not resist the popular clamour for a war he feared and which he was to lose. Bismarck, the quintessence of conservative statesmen, felt he must give way to public opinion and promote Germany's colonial interests. The manipulation of public opinion, too, seemed to have become possible (or so, at least, many newspaper owners and

The campaign for women's political rights in the United Kingdom provoked extraordinary out-bursts of feeling on both sides – perhaps because the contenders were not themselves conscious of the depth and complexity of the emotions awoken by feminist demands. This lady attempted to chain herself to the railings of Buckingham Palace in 1914.

statesmen believed). Growing literacy had two sides to it. It had been believed on the one hand that investment in mass education was necessary in order to civilize the masses for the proper use of the vote. What seemed to be the consequence of rising literacy, however, was that a market was created for a new cheap press which often pandered to emotionalism and sensationalism, and for the sellers and devisers of advertising campaigns, another invention of the nineteenth century.

The political principle which undoubtedly still had the most mass appeal was nationalism. Moreover, it kept its revolutionary potential. This was clear in a number of places. In Turkish Europe from the Crimean War onwards the successes of nationalists in fighting the Ottoman

Ottoman decline and the emergence of modern Turkey 1683—1923

empire and creating new nations had never flagged. Serbia, Greece and Romania were solidly established by 1870. By the end of the century they had been joined by Bulgaria and Montenegro. In 1913, in the last wars of the Balkan states against Turkey before a European conflict swallowed the Turkish question, there appeared Albania, and by then an autonomous Crete already had a Greek governor. These nationalist movements had at several times dragged greater states into their affairs and always presented a potential danger to peace. This was not so true of those within the Russian

empire, where Poles, Jews, Ukrainians and Lithuanians felt themselves oppressed by the Russians, but seemed an increasingly likely outcome of strains in the Austro-Hungarian empire, where nationalism presented a real revolutionary danger in the lands within the Hungarian half of the monarchy. Slav majorities there looked across the border to Serbia for help against Magyar oppressors. Elsewhere in the monarchy – in Bohemia and Slovakia, for example – feeling was less high, but nationalism was no less the dominant question. Great Britain faced no such dangers as these, but even

895

she had a nationalist problem, in Ireland. Indeed, she had two. That of the Catholic Irish was for most of the nineteenth century the more obvious. Important reforms and concessions had been granted to it, though they fell short of the autonomous state of 'Home Rule' to which the British liberal party was committed. By 1900, however, agricultural reform and better economic conditions had done much to draw the venom from the Irish question. It was reinserted by the appearance of another Irish nationalism, that of the protestant majority of the province of Ulster, which was excited to threaten revolution if the government in London gave Home Rule to the Roman Catholic Irish nationalists. This was much more than merely embarrassing. When the machinery of English democracy did finally deliver Home Rule legislation in 1914, some foreign observers were misled into thinking that British policy would be fatally inhibited from intervention in European affairs by revolution at home.

All such expressions of nationalism with greater or less justification believed themselves to be on behalf of the oppressed. But the nationalism of the great powers was also a disruptive force. France and Germany were psychologically deeply sundered by the former's loss of two provinces, Alsace and Lorraine, to Germany in 1871. French politicians whom it suited to do so assiduously cultivated the theme of *revanche*. Nationalism in France gave especial bitterness to political quarrels because they seemed to raise questions of loyalty to great national institutions. Even the supposedly sober British from time to time grew excited about national symbols. There was a brief but deep enthusiasm for imperialism and always great sensitivity over the preservation of British naval supremacy. More and more this appeared to be threatened by Germany, a power whose obvious economic dynamism also caused alarm by the danger it presented to British supremacy in world commerce. It did not matter that the two countries were one another's best customers; what was more important was that they appeared to have interests

'*One empire, one people, one God.*' Germany under Wilhelm II, less than fifty years united.

opposed in many specific ways. Additional colour was given to this by the stridency of German nationalism under the reign of the Emperor Wilhelm II. Conscious of Germany's potential, he sought to give it not only real but symbolic expression. One effect was his enthusiasm for building a great navy; this especially annoyed the British who could not see that it could be intended for use against anyone but them. But there was a generally growing impression in Europe, far from unjustified, that the Germans were prone to throw their weight about unreasonably in international affairs. National stereotypes cannot be summarized in a phrase, but because they helped to impose terrible simplifications upon public reactions they are part of the story of the disruptive power of nationalist feeling at the beginning of this century.

Those who felt confident could point to the diminution of international violence in the nineteenth century; there had been no war between European great powers since 1876 (when Russia and Turkey had come to blows) and, unhappily, European soldiers and statesmen failed to understand the portents of the American civil war, the first in which one commander could control over a million men, thanks to railway and telegraph, and the first to show the power of modern mass-produced weapons to inflict huge casualties. While such facts were overlooked, the summoning of congresses in

1899 and 1907 to halt competition in armaments could be viewed optimistically, though they failed in their aim. Certainly acceptance of the practice of international arbitration had grown and some restrictions on the earlier brutality of warfare were visible. A significant phrase was used by the German emperor when he sent off his contingent to the international force fielded against the Chinese Boxers. Stirred to anger by reports of atrocities against Europeans by Chinese, he urged his soldiers to behave 'like Huns'. The phrase stuck in people's memories. Though thought to be excessive at the time, its real interest lies in the fact that he should have believed such a recommendation was needed. Nobody would have had to tell a seventeenth-century army to behave like Huns, because it was in large measure then taken for granted that they would. By 1900, European troops were not expected to behave in this way and had therefore to be told to do so. So far had the humanizing of war come. 'Civilized warfare' was a nineteenth-century concept and far from a contradiction in terms. In 1899 it had been agreed to forbid, albeit for a limited period, the use of poison gas, dum-dum bullets and even the dropping of bombs from the air.

The restraint exercised on kings and states by the consciousness of any unity other than that of a common resistance to revolution had, of course, long since collapsed together with the idea of Christendom. Nineteenth-century religion was only a palliative or mitigation of international conflict, a minor and indirect force, trickling through to a humanitarianism and pacifism fed from other sources. Christianity had proved as feeble a check to violence as would the hopes of socialists that the workers of the world would refuse to fight one another in the interests of their masters. Whether this was a result of a general loss of power by organized religion is not clear. Certainly much misgiving was felt by 1900 about its declining force as an agent regulating behaviour. This was not because a new religion of traditional form challenged the old Christian Churches. There had been, rather, a continuing development of

trends observable in the eighteenth century and much more marked since the French Revolution. Almost all the Christian communions seemed more and more touched by the blight of one or other of the characteristic intellectual and social advances of the age.

Though they all felt it, the Roman Catholic Church was the most obvious victim, the Papacy having especially and specifically suffered both in its prestige and power. It had openly proclaimed its hostility to progress, rationality and liberalism in statements which became part of the dogmas of the Church. Politically, Rome had begun to suffer from the whittling away of the Temporal Power in the 1790s, when the French revolutionary armies brought revolutionary principles and territorial change to Italy. Often, later infringements of the Papacy's rights were to be justified in terms of the master ideas of the age: democracy, liberalism, nationalism. Finally, in 1870, the last territory of the old papal states still outside the Vatican itself was taken by the new kingdom of Italy and the Papacy became almost entirely a purely spiritual and ecclesiastical authority. This was the end of an era of temporal authority stretching back to Merovingian times and some felt it to be an inglorious end for an institution long the centre of European civilization and history.

In fact, it was in some ways to prove advantageous. Nevertheless, at the time the spoliation confirmed both the hostility to the forces of the century which the Papacy had already expressed and the derision in which it was held by many progressive thinkers. Feeling on both sides reached new heights when in 1870 it became a part of the dogma of the Church that the pope, when he spoke *ex cathedra* on faith and morals, did so with infallible authority. There followed two decades in which anti-clericalism and priest-baiting were more important in the politics of Germany, France, Italy and Spain than ever before. Governments took advantage of anti-papal prejudice to advance their own legal powers over the Church. Persecution bred intransigence. In conflict, it emerged that whatever view might be taken on the abstract status of the teachings of the Roman Church, it could still draw on vast reservoirs of loyalty among believers. Moreover, these were still being recruited in the mission field overseas by conversion and would soon be added to in still greater numbers by demographic trends. Though the Church might not make much progress among the new city-dwellers of Europe, untouched by an inadequate ecclesiastical machine and paganized by the slow stain of the secular culture in which they were immersed, it was far from dying, let alone dead, as a political and social force. Indeed, the liberation of the papacy from its temporal rôle made it easier for Roman Catholics to feel uncompromised loyalty towards it.

The Roman Catholic Church had been the most demanding of the Christian churches and was in the forefront of the battle of religion with the age, but the claims of revelation and the authority of priest and clergyman were everywhere questioned. This was one of the most striking features of the nineteenth century, all the more so because so many Europeans and Americans still retained simple and literal beliefs in the dogmas of their Churches and the story contained in the Bible. They felt great anxiety when such beliefs were threatened, yet this was happening increasingly and in all countries. Traditional religious belief was at first threatened only among an intellectual élite, often consciously holding ideas drawn from Enlightenment sources: 'Voltairean' was a favourite nineteenth-century adjective to indicate anti-religious and sceptical views. As the nineteenth century proceeded, such ideas were reinforced by two other intellectual currents, both also at first a concern of élites, but increasingly with a wider effect in an age of growing mass literacy and cheap printing.

The first of these influential groups of ideas came from biblical scholars, the most important of them German, who from the 1840s onwards not only demolished many assumptions about the value of the Bible as historical evidence, but also, and perhaps more fundamentally, brought about something of a psychological change in the whole attitude to the scriptural text. In essence this change made it possible henceforth simply to regard the Bible as a historic text like any other, to be approached critically. An immensely successful (and scandal-provoking) *Life of Jesus*, published in 1863 by a French scholar, brought such an attitude before a wider public than ever before. The book which had been the central text of European civilization since its emergence in the Dark Ages would never recover its position.

The second source of ideas damaging to traditional Christian faith – and therefore to the morality, politics, and economics for so long anchored in Christian assumptions – was to be found in science. Enlightenment attacks on internal and logical inconsistency in the teaching of the Church became much more alarming when science began to produce empirical evidence that things said in the Bible (and therefore based on the same authority as everything else in it) plainly did not fit observable fact. The starting-point was geology; ideas which had been about since the end of the eighteenth century were given a much wider public in the 1830s by the publication of *Principles of Geology* by an English scientist, Charles Lyell. This book explained landscape and geological structure in terms of forces still at work, that is, not as the result of a single act of creation, but of wind, rain and so on. Moreover, Lyell pointed out that if this were correct, then the presence of fossils of different forms of life in different geological strata implied that the creation of new animals had been repeated in each geological age. If this were so, the biblical account of creation was clearly in difficulties. That biblical chronology was simply untrue in relation to man was increasingly suggested by discoveries of stone tools in British caves along with the fossilized bones of extinct animals. The argument that man was much older than the biblical account allowed may perhaps be regarded as officially conceded when, in 1859, British learned societies heard and published papers establishing 'that in a period of antiquity remote beyond any of which we have hitherto found traces' men had lived in Palaeolithic societies in the Somme valley.

It is an over-simplification, but not grossly distorting, to say that the same year brought many of these questions to a head by an approach along a different line, the biological, when Charles Darwin published one of the seminal books of modern civilization, the book called, for short, *The Origin of Species*. Much in it he owed without acknowledgement to others. Its publication also came at a moment and in a country where it was especially likely to cause a stir; the issue of the rightfulness of the traditional dominance of religion (for example, in education) was in the air in England. The word 'evolution' with which Darwin's name came especially to be connected was by then already familiar (and he tried to avoid using it). Nevertheless, though this explains some of the interest shown in what he said, his book was the greatest single statement of the evolutionary hypothesis – namely, that living things were what they were because their forms had undergone long evolution from simpler ones. This, of course, included man, as he made explicit in another book, the *Descent of Man*, of 1871. Different views were held about how this evolution had occurred. Darwin, impressed by Malthus' vision of the murderous competition of mankind for food, took the view that the qualities which made success likely in hostile environments ensured the 'natural selection' of those creatures embodying them: this was a view to be vulgarized (and terribly misrepresented) by the use as a slogan of the phrase 'survival of the fittest'. But important though many aspects of his work were to be in inspiring fresh thought, here it is important rather to see that Darwin dealt a blow against the biblical account of creation (as well as against the assumption of the unique status of Man) which had wider publicity than any earlier one. In combination with biblical criticism and geology, his book made it impossible for any conscientious and thoughtful man to accept – as he had still been able to do in 1800 – the Bible as literally true.

The undermining of the authority of scripture remains probably the most obvious single way in which science affected formulated beliefs. Yet just as important, if not more so, was a new, vague but growing prestige which science was coming to have among a public more broadly based than ever before. This was because of its new status as the supreme instrument for the manipulation of nature, which was seen as increasingly powerless to resist it. Here was the beginning of what was to grow into a mythology of science. Its essence lay in the fact that while the great achievements of seventeenth-century science had not often resulted in changes in the lives of ordinary men and women, those of the nineteenth century increasingly did. Men who understood not a word of what might be written by Joseph Lister, who established the need and technique of using antiseptics in surgery, or by Michael Faraday, who more than any other man made possible the generation of electricity, knew none the less that the medicine of 1900 was different from that of their grandfathers. Some of them saw electricity about them in their work and homes. By 1914, radio messages could be sent across the Atlantic, flying-machines which did not rely upon support by bags of gas of lower density than air were common, aspirins were easily available and an American manufacturer was offering the first cheap mass-produced automobile. The objective achievements of science were by no means adequately represented by such facts, but material advance of this sort impressed the average man and led him to worship at a new shrine.

His awareness of science came through technology because for a long time this was almost the only way in which science had a positive impact on the lives of most people. Respect for it therefore usually grew in proportion to spectacular results in engineering or manufacture and even now, though science makes its impact in other ways, it still makes it very obviously through industrial processes. But though deeply entwined in this way with the dominant world civilization and so interwoven with society, the growth of science was also a much greater change than one of sheer power. In the years down to 1914 the foundations were laid for what would be evident in the second half of the twentieth century, a science which was as much as anything the mainspring of the dominant world culture. So rapid has been the advance to

The idea of evolution by natural selection was the most influential scientific idea of the nineteenth century. Although at least one other scientist arrived at the idea independently of him, and although he himself attributed crucial importance to the influence of Malthus it is associated with Darwin's name above all.

this state of affairs that science has already affected every part of human life while people are still trying to grapple with some of its most elementary philosophical implications.

The easiest observations of this change which can be made (and the easiest to take as a starting-point) are those which display the status of science as a social and material phenomenon in its own right. From the moment when the first great advances in physics were made, in the seventeenth century, science was already a social fact. Institutions were then created in which men came together to study nature in a way which a later age could recognize as scientific, and scientists even then were sometimes employed by rulers to bring to bear their expertise on specific problems. It was noticeable, too, that in the useful arts – and they were more usually called arts than sciences – such as navigation or agriculture, experiment by those who were not themselves practising technicians could make valuable contributions. But a terminological point helps to set this age in perspective and establish its remoteness from the nineteenth century and after: at this time scientists were still called 'natural philosophers'. The word 'scientist' was not invented until about a third of the way through the nineteenth century, when men felt that there was need to distinguish a rigorous experimental and observational investigation of nature from speculation on it by unchecked reason. Even then, though, there was little distinction in most men's minds between the man who carried out such an investigation and the applied scientist or technologist who was the much more conspicuous representative of science in an age of engineering, mining and manufacturing on an unprecedented scale.

The nineteenth century was none the less the first in which science was taken for granted by educated men as a specialized field of study, whose investigators had professional standing. Its new status was marked by the much larger place given to science in education, both by the creation of new departments at existing universities, and by the setting up in some countries, notably France and Germany, of special scien-

tific and technical institutions. Professional studies, too, incorporated larger scientific components. Such developments accelerated as the effects of science on social and economic life became increasingly obvious. The sum effect was to carry much further an already long-established trend. Since about 1700 there has been a steady and exponential increase in the world population of scientists: their numbers have doubled roughly every fifteen years (which explains the striking fact that ever since then there have always been, at any moment, more scientists alive than dead). In the nineteenth century, other measurements of the growth of science became available (the establishment of astronomical observatories, for example) and these, too, provide exponential curves of growth.

This social phenomenon underlay the growing control of his environment and the improvement of his life which were so easily grasped by the layman. This was what made the nineteenth century the first in which science truly became an object of religion – perhaps of idolatory. By 1914, educated Europeans and Americans took for granted the presence of the motorcar, the steam turbine, harder and specialized steels, the aeroplane, the telephone, the wireless and many more marvels which had not existed a century previously; their effects were already very great. Perhaps the most widely apparent were those stemming from the availability of cheap electrical power; it was already shaping cities by making electric trams and trains available to suburban householders, work in factories through electric motors, and domestic life through the electric light. Even animal populations were affected: the 36 000 horses pulling trams in Great Britain in 1900 had only 900 successors in 1914. Of course, the practical application of science was by no means new. There has never been a time since the seventeenth century when there has not been some obvious technological fall-out from scientific activity though, to begin with, it was largely confined to ballistics, navigation and map-making, agriculture and a few elementary industrial processes. Only in the nineteenth century did science really begin to play an important rôle in sustaining and changing society which went beyond a few obviously striking and spectacular accomplishments. The chemistry of dyeing, for example, was a vast field in which nineteenth-century research led to sweeping innovations which flooded through the manufacture of drugs, explosives, antiseptics – to mention only a few. These had human and social, as well as economic, repercussions. The new fast dyes themselves affected millions of people; the unhappy Indian grower of indigo found that his market dried up on him, and the industrial working classes of the West found they could buy marginally less drab clothes and thus began to move slowly forward along the road at the end of which mass-production methods and man-made fibres all but obliterated visible difference between the clothes of different classes.

This already takes us across the boundary between sustaining life and changing it. Fundamental science was to go on changing society, though some of what was done before 1914 – in physics, for example – is better left for discussion at a later point. One area in which effects are easier to measure was medicine. By 1914, advances had been made which were huge by comparison with the state of medicine a century earlier. A skill had become a science. Great bridgeheads had been driven into the theory and control of infection; antiseptics, having been introduced by Lister only in the 1860s, were taken for granted a couple of decades later, and he and his friend Louis Pasteur, the most famous and greatest of French chemists, laid the foundations of bacteriology. Queen Victoria herself had been a pioneer in the publicizing of new medical methods; the use of anaesthetics during the birth of a prince or princess was important in giving quick social acceptance to techniques only in their infancy in the 1840s. Fewer people, perhaps, would have been aware of the importance of such achievements as the discovery in 1909 of Salvarsan, a landmark in the development of selective treatment of infection, or the identification of the carrier of malaria, or the

discovery of 'X-rays'. Yet all these advances, though of great importance, were to be far surpassed in the next fifty years.

Enough impact was made by science even before 1914 to justify the conclusion that it generated its own mythology. In this context, 'mythology' implies no connotations of fiction or falsity. It is simply a convenient way of calling attention to the fact that science, the vast bulk of its conclusions no doubt validated by experiment and therefore 'true', has also come to act as an influence shaping the way men look at the world, just as great religions have done in the past. It has, that is to say, come to be important as more than a method for exploring and manipulating nature. It has been thought also to provide guidance about metaphysical questions, the aims men ought to pursue, the standards they should employ to regulate behaviour. Above all it has been a pervasive influence in shaping popular attitudes. All this, of course, has no intrinsic or necessary connexion with science as the pursuit of scientists. But the upshot in the end was a civilization whose élites had, except vestigially, no dominant religious belief or transcendent ideals. It is a civilization whose core, whether or not this is often articulated, lies in belief in the promise of what can be done by manipulating nature. In principle, it believes that there is no problem which need be regarded as insoluble, given sufficient resources of intellect and money; it has room for the obscure, but not for the essentially mysterious. Many scientists have drawn back from this conclusion. The implications of it are still far from being grasped. But it is the assumption on which a dominant world view now rests and it was already formed in essentials before 1914.

Confidence in science in its crudest form has been called scientism, but probably very few people held it with complete explicitness and lack of qualification, even in the late nineteenth century, its heyday. Equally good evidence of the prestige of the scientific method, though, is provided by the wish shown by intellectuals to extend it beyond the area of the natural sciences. One of the earliest examples was to be found in the wish to found 'social sciences' which can be seen in the utilitarian followers of the English reformer and intellectual Jeremy Bentham, who wished to base the management of society upon calculated use of the principles that men responded to pleasure and pain, and that pleasure should be maximized and pain minimized, it being understood that what was to be taken into account were the sensations of the greatest number and their intensity. Later in the nineteenth century, Marx (who was greatly impressed by the work of Darwin) also exemplified the wish to found a science of society. A name for one was provided by the French philosopher Auguste Comte – sociology. These (and many other) attempts to emulate the natural sciences proceeded on a basis of a search for general quasi-mechanical laws; that the natural sciences were at that moment abandoning the search for such laws does not signify here, for the search itself still testified to the prestige of the scientific model.

Paradoxically, science too was thus obviously contributing by 1914 to an ill-defined sense of strain in European civilization. This showed most obviously in the problems posed to traditional religion, without doubt, but it also operated in a more subtle way; in determinisms such as those many men drew from thinking about Darwin, or from the relativism suggested by anthropology or the study of the human mind, science itself sapped the confidence in the values of objectivity and rationality which had been so important to it since the eighteenth century. By 1914 there were signs that liberal, rational, enlightened Europe was under strain just as much as traditional, religious and conservative Europe.

Doubt must not loom too large. The most obvious fact about early twentieth-century Europe is that although many Europeans might be sceptical or fearful about its future, it was almost never suggested that it would not continue to be the centre of the world's affairs, the greatest concentration of political power in the globe and the real maker of the world's destinies. Diplomatically and politically, European statesmen could ignore the rest of the world for all important matters, except in the western hemisphere, where another nation of European origins, the United States, was paramount, and the Far East, where Japan was increasingly important and the Americans had interests which they might require others to respect. It was on their relationships with one another, nevertheless, that the attention of European statesmen was directed in 1900; for most of them there was nothing so important to worry about at this time.

2 The era of the First World War

Against the one clear favourable fact that great wars had been successfully averted by European states ever since 1870, could be set some political evidence that the international situation was none the less growing dangerously unstable by 1900. Some major states had grave internal problems, for example, which might imply external repercussions. For all the huge difference between them, United Germany and United Italy were new states; they had not existed forty years earlier and this made their rulers especially sensitive to internal divisive forces and consequently willing to court chauvinistic feeling. Some of Italy's leaders went in for disastrous colonial ventures, keeping alive suspicion and unfriendliness towards Austria-Hungary (formally Italy's ally, but the ruler of territories still regarded by Italians as 'unredeemed') and the country finally plunged into war with Turkey in 1911. Germany had the advantages of huge industrial and economic success to help her, yet after the cautious Bismarck had been sent into retirement, her foreign policy was conducted more and more with an eye to winning the impalpable and slippery prizes of respect and prestige – a 'place in the sun', as some Germans summed it up. Germany had also to face the consequences

Twentieth-century warfare's new face: the British Grand Fleet of 1914 represented the apex of marine and armaments technology. Above is one of the first fragile naval aircraft – a tiny portent of the evolution which would make the battleship obsolete by mid-century.

of industrialization. The new economic and social forces it spawned were increasingly difficult to reconcile with the conservative character of her constitution which gave so much weight in imperial government to a semi-feudal, agrarian aristocracy.

Nor was internal tension the monopoly of new states. The two great dynastic empires of Russia and Austria-Hungary each faced grave internal problems; more perfectly than any other states they still fitted the assumption of the Holy Alliance era that governments were the natural opponents of their subjects. Yet both had undergone great change in spite of apparent continuity. The Habsburg monarchy in its new, hyphenated form was itself the creation of a successful nationalism, that of the Magyars. In the early years of the twentieth century there were signs that it was going to be more and more difficult to keep the two halves of the monarchy together without provoking other nations inside it beyond endurance. Moreover, here, too, industrialization (in Bohemia and Austria) was beginning to add new tensions to the old. Russia, as has been indicated, actually exploded in political revolution in 1905, and was also changing slowly but deeply. Autocracy and terrorism between them destroyed the liberal promise of the reforms of Alexander II; they did not prevent the start of faster industrial growth by the end of the century. This was the beginning of an economic revolution to which the great emancipation had been the essential preliminary. Policies designed to exact grain from the peasant provided a commodity for export to pay for the service of foreign loans. With the twentieth century, Russia began to show at last a formidable rate of economic advance. The quantities were still small – in 1910 Russia produced less than a third as much pig-iron as the United Kingdom and only about a quarter as much steel as Germany. But these quantities had been achieved at a very high rate of growth. Probably more important, there were signs that by 1914 Russian agriculture might at last have turned the corner and be capable of producing a grain harvest which would grow faster than population. A determined effort was made by a minister to provide Russia with a class of prosperous, independent farmers whose self-interest was linked to raising productivity by removing the last of the restraints on individualism imposed by the terms of serfdom's abolition. Yet there was still much backwardness to overcome. Even in 1914 less than 10 per cent of Russians lived in towns and only about three million out of a total population of more than 150 million worked in industry. The debit side still loomed large in foreign estimates of Russia's progress. She might be a potential giant, but was one still entangled with grievous handicaps. The autocracy governed badly, reformed unwillingly and opposed all change (though it was to make constitutional concessions in 1905). The general level of culture was low and unpromising; industrialization would demand better education and that would cause new strains. Liberal traditions were weak; terrorist and autocratic traditions were strong. Russia was still dependent on foreign suppliers for the capital she needed, too.

Most of this came from her ally, France. With the United Kingdom and Italy, the Third Republic represented liberal and constitutional principles among Europe's great powers. Socially conservative, France was in spite of her intellectual vitality uneasy and conscious of weakness. In part, a superficial instability was a matter of bitter exchanges between politicians; in part it was because of the efforts of some who strove to keep alive the revolutionary tradition and rhetoric. Yet the working-class movement was weak. France moved only slowly towards industrialization and, in fact, the Republic was probably as stable as any other régime in Europe, but slow industrial development indicated another handicap of which Frenchmen were very aware, their military inferiority. The year 1870 had shown that the French could not on their own beat the German army. Since then, the disparity of the two country's positions had grown even greater. In manpower, France had fallen further still behind and in economic development, too, she had been dwarfed by her neighbour. Just before 1914, France was raising about one-sixth as much coal as Germany, made less than a third as much pig-iron and a quarter as much steel. If there was ever to be a return match for 1870, Frenchmen knew they needed allies.

An ally was not, in 1900, to be looked for in Great Britain. This was mainly because of colonial issues; France (like Russia) came into irritating conflict with Great Britain at a great many places around the globe where British interests lay. For a long time, the United Kingdom found it possible to remain clear of European entanglements; this was an advantage, but she, too, had troubles at home. The first industrial nation was also one of the most troubled by working-class agitation and, increasingly, by uncertainty about her relative strength. By 1900 some British businessmen were clear that Germany was a major rival and there were plenty of signs that in technology and method German industry was greatly superior to British. The old certainties began to give way; Free Trade itself was called in question. There were even signs, in the violence of Ulstermen and suffragettes and the embittered struggles over social legislation with a house of lords determined to safeguard the interests of wealth, that parliamentarianism itself might be threatened. There was no longer a sense of the sustaining consensus of mid-Victorian politics. Yet there was also a huge solidity about British institutions and political habits. Parliamentary monarchy had proved able to carry through vast changes since 1832 and there was little reason for fundamental doubt that it could continue to do so.

Only a perspective which Englishmen of the day found hard to recognize reveals the fundamental change in the position of the United Kingdom within half a century or so. This is provided by a view from Japan or the United States, the two great extra-European powers. The Japanese portent was the more easily discerned of the two, perhaps, because of the military victory over Russia, yet there were signs for those who could interpret them that the United States would shortly emerge as a power capable of dwarfing Europe and as the most powerful nation in the world.

The great nineteenth-century expansion of the United States came to a climax with the establishment of her supremacy on an unquestionable footing of power in her hemisphere. The war with Spain and the building of the Panama canal rounded off the process. American domestic, social and economic circumstances were such that the political system proved easily able to handle the problems it faced once the great mid-century crisis was surmounted. Amongst these, some of the gravest resulted from industrialization. The confidence that all would go well if the economically strongest were simply allowed to drive all others to the wall first began to be questioned towards the end of the nineteenth century. But this was after an industrial machine of immense scale had already matured. It would be the bedrock of future American power. By 1914 American production of pig-iron and steel was more than twice that of Great Britain and Germany together; the United States mined almost enough coal to outpace them, too. At the same time the standard of living of her citizens continued to act as a magnet to immigration; in her natural resources and a stream of cheap, highly motivated labour lay two of the sources of America's economic might. The other was foreign capital. She was the greatest of debtor nations.

Though her political constitution was older in 1914 than that of any major European state except Great Britain or Russia, the arrival of new Americans long helped to give the United States the characteristics and pyschology of a new nation. A need to integrate her new citizens often led to the expressions of strong nationalist feeling. But because of geography, the tradition of rejecting Europe, and the continuing domination of American government and business by élites formed in the Anglo-Saxon tradition, this did not take violent forms outside the western hemisphere. The United States in 1914 was still a young giant waiting in the wings of history, whose full importance would only become manifest when Europe needed to involve America in its quarrels.

In that year a war began as a result of those quarrels. Though it was not the bloodiest nor most prolonged war in history, nor strictly, as it was later termed, the 'first' World War, it was the most intensely fought struggle and the greatest in geographical extent to have occurred down to that time. Nations in every continent took part. It was also costlier than any earlier war and made unprecedented demands upon resources. Whole societies were mobilized to fight it, in part because it was also the first war in which machines played an overwhelmingly important part; war was for the first time transformed by science. The best name to give it remains the simple one used by those who fought in it: the *Great* War. This is justified by its unprecedented pyschological effect.

It was also the first of two wars whose central issue was the control of German power. The damage they did ended Europe's political, economic and military supremacy. Each of these conflicts began in essentially European issues and the war always had a predominantly European flavour; like the next great struggle detonated by Germany though, it sucked into it other conflicts and jumbled together a whole anthology of issues. But Europe was the heart of the matter and self-inflicted damage in the end deprived her of world hegemony. This did not happen by 1918, when the Great War ended (though irreparable damage had already been done, even by then) but it was obvious in 1945, at the end of a 'Second World War'.

That left behind a continent whose pre-1914 structure had vanished. This has led some historians to speak of the whole era from 1914 to 1945 as an entity, as a European 'civil war'. It is not a bad metaphor, provided it is borne in mind that it is a metaphor. Europe had never been free from wars for long and the containment of internal disorder is the fundamental presupposition of a state: Europe had never been united and could not therefore have a true civil war. But it was the source and seat of a civilization which was a unity and Europeans saw themselves as having more in common with other Europeans than with black, brown or yellow men. Furthermore, it was a system of power which in 1914 was an economic unity and had just experienced its longest period of internal peace. These facts, all of which were to vanish by 1945, make the metaphor of civil war vivid and acceptable; it signifies the self-destructive madness of a civilization.

A European balance had kept the peace between great states for over forty years. By 1914 this was dangerously disturbed. Too many people had come to feel that the chances of war might offer them more than a continued peace. This was especially so in Germany, Austria-Hungary and Russia, among those who were in a position to take the major decisions. By the time that they had come to feel this, there existed a complicated set of ties, obligations and interests between states which so involved them with one another that it was unlikely that a conflict could be limited to two, or even to a few of them. Another force making for instability was the existence of small countries enjoying special relations with larger ones; confident of their protector's power, some of them were in a position to take the effective power to make decisions from the hands of those who would have to fight a major war.

This delicate situation was made all the more dangerous by the psychological atmosphere in which statesmen had to work by 1914. It was an age when mass emotions were easily aroused, in particular by nationalist and patriotic stimuli. There was widespread ignorance of the dangers

Every major country rapidly underwent the far-reaching changes imposed by the new scale of war after 1914. In England women were swept into manufacturing industry in unprecedented numbers – with all that it implied for Trade Unions, social services and psychological attitudes.

of war, because nobody except a tiny minority foresaw a war which would be different from that of 1870; they remembered the France of that year, and forgot Virginia and Tennessee only a few years earlier, where modern war had first shown its face in prolonged slaughter and huge costs. Everyone knew that wars could be destructive and violent, certainly, but also believed that in the twentieth century they would be swiftly over. The very cost of armaments made it inconceivable that civilized states could sustain a prolonged struggle such as that with Napoleonic France; the complex world economy and the taxpayer, it was said, could not survive one. This perhaps diminished misgivings about courting danger. There are even signs, too, that many Europeans were bored by their lives in 1914 and saw in war an emotional release purging away a sense of decadence and sterility. Revolutionaries, of course, welcomed international conflict because of the opportunities they thought it might bring. Finally, it is worth remembering that the long success of diplomats in negotiating grave crises without war was itself a danger. Their machinery had worked so many times, that when it was presented with facts more than ordinarily recalcitrant in July 1914, their significance for a time seemed to escape many of those who had to deal with them. On the very eve of conflict, statesmen were still finding it difficult to see why another conference of ambassadors or even a European congress should not extricate them from their problems.

One of the conflicts which came to a head in 1914 went back a very long way. This was the old rivalry of Austria-Hungary and Russia in south-eastern Europe. Its roots lay deep in the eighteenth century, but its last phase was dominated by the accelerated collapse of the Ottoman empire in Europe from the Crimean War onwards. For this reason the First World War is from one point of view well described as the war of the Ottoman succession. After the Congress of Berlin in 1878 had pulled Europe through one dangerous moment, Habsburg and Romanoff policy had settled down to a sort of understanding by the 1890s. This lasted until Russian interest in the Danube valley revived after the checking of Russian imperial ambition in the Far East by the Japanese. At that moment, events outside the Habsburg and Turkish empires were giving a new aggressiveness to Austro-Hungarian policy, too.

At the root of this was revolutionary nationalism. A reform movement looked for a while as if it might put the Ottoman empire together again and this provoked the Balkan nations to try to undo the *status quo* established by the great powers and the Austrians to look to their own interests in a situation once again fluid. They offended the Russians by a mismanaged annexation of the Turkish province of Bosnia in 1909; the Russians had not been given a corre-

sponding and compensating gain. Another consequence of Bosnia's annexation was that the Dual Monarchy acquired more Slav subjects. There was already discontent among the monarchy's subject peoples, in particular, the Slavs who lived under Magyar rule. More and more under the pressure of Magyar interests, the government in Vienna had shown itself hostile to Serbia, a nation to which these Slav subjects might look for support. Some of them saw Serbia as the nucleus of a future state embracing all South Slavs and its rulers seemed unable (and perhaps unwilling) to restrain South Slav revolutionaries who used Belgrade as a base for terrorism and subversion in Bosnia. Lessons from history are often unfortunate; the Vienna government was only too ready to conclude that Serbia might play in the Danube valley the rôle that Sardinia had played in uniting Italy. Unless the serpent were scotched in the egg, another loss of Habsburg territory would then follow. Having been excluded from Germany by Prussia and from Italy by Sardinia, she was now threatened with exclusion from the lower Danube valley by a potential Yugoslavia. This would mean the end of her as a great power and of Magyar supremacy in Hungary, for fairer treatment of Slavs who remained in Hungarian territory would be insisted upon by south Slavdom. The continuing subsidence of the Ottoman empire could then only benefit Russia, the power which stood behind Serbia, determined there should not be another 1909.

Into this complicated situation, the other powers were pulled by interest, choice, sentiment and formal diplomacy. Of these, the last was perhaps less important than was once thought. Bismarck's efforts in the 1870s and 1880s to ensure the isolation of France and the supremacy of Germany had spawned a system of alliances unique in peacetime. Their common characteristic was that they defined conditions on which countries would go to war to support one another, and this seemed to cramp diplomacy. But in the end they did not operate as planned. This does not mean that they did not contribute to the coming of war, only that formal arrangements can only be effective if people want them to be, and other factors decided this in 1914.

At the root of the whole business was the German seizure of Alsace and Lorraine and the consequent French restlessness for revenge. Bismarck guarded against this first by drawing together Germany, Russia and Austria-Hungary on the common ground of dynastic resistance to revolutionary and subversive dangers which France, the only republic among the major states was still supposed to represent; after all, there were still alive in 1871 people born before 1789 and many others who could remember the comments of those who had lived through the years of the great Revolution. The conservative alliance nonetheless lapsed in the 1880s, essentially because Bismarck felt he must in the last resort back Austria-Hungary if a conflict between her and Russia proved unavoidable. To Germany and the Dual Monarchy was then added Italy; thus was formed in 1882 the Triple Alliance. But Bismarck still kept a separate 'Reinsurance' treaty with Russia, though he seems to have felt uneasy about the prospect of keeping Russia and Austria-Hungary at peace in this way.

Yet a conflict between them did not again look likely until after 1909. By then, Bismarck's successors had allowed his Reinsurance treaty to lapse and Russia had become in 1892 an ally of France. From that date the road led away from Bismarck's Europe, where everyone else had been kept in equilibrium by Germany's central rôle, to a Europe divided into two camps. This was made worse by German policy. In a series of crises, she showed that she wanted to frighten other nations with her displeasure and make herself esteemed. In particular, in 1905 and 1911, her irritation was directed against France, and commercial and colonial issues were used as excuses to show by displays of force that France had not won the right to disregard German wishes by making an ally of Russia. German military planning had already by 1900 accepted the need to fight a two-front war if necessary, and made preparations to do so by a quick overthrow of France while the resources of Russia were slowly mobilized.

As the twentieth century opened, it had therefore become highly probable that if an Austro-Russian war broke out, Germany and France would join in. Moreover, Germans had within a few years made this more likely by patronizing the Turks. This was much more alarming to the Russians than it would have been earlier, because a growing export trade in grain from Russia's Black Sea ports had to pass through the Straits. The Russians began to improve their fighting-power. One essential step in this was the completion of a railway network which would make possible the mobilization and delivery to the battlefields of eastern Europe of her vast armies.

In all this, there was no obvious need for Great Britain to be concerned, had not German policy perversely antagonized her. At the end of the nineteenth century Great Britain's quarrels were above all with France and Russia. They arose where imperial ambitions clashed, in Africa and central and south-eastern Asia. Anglo-German relations were more easily managed, if occasionally prickly. As Great Britain entered the new century she was still preoccupied with imperial issues, not with Europe. Her first peacetime alliance was with Japan, to safeguard her interests in the Far East. Then came a settlement of long outstanding disputes with France in 1904; this was in essence an agreement about Africa, where France was to be given a free hand in Morocco in return for Great Britain having one in Egypt – a way of settling another bit of the Ottoman succession – but it rounded up other colonial quarrels the world over, some going back as far as the peace of Utrecht. A few years later, Great Britain made a similar (though less successful) agreement with Russia about spheres of interest in Persia. But the Anglo-French settlement grew into much more than a clearing away of grounds for dispute. It became what was called an *entente*, or special relationship.

This was Germany's doing. Irritated by the Anglo-French agreement, the German government decided to show France that it would have to have its say in Morocco's affairs at an international conference. They got it, but bullying France solidified the *entente*; the British began to realize that they would have to concern themselves for the first time in decades with the continental balance of power. If they did not, Germany would dominate it. This was a road whose end was their acceptance of a rôle as a great military power on land, a change of the assumptions which British strategy had followed since the days of Louis XIV and Marlborough, the last age in which the country had put its major weight into an effort on the Continent. Secret military talks with the French explored what might be done to help their army against a German invasion through Belgium. This was not going far, but Germany then threw away the chance to reassure British public opinion, by pressing forward with plans to build a great navy. It was inconceivable that such a step could be directed against any power except Great Britain. The result was a naval race which most British were determined to win (if they could not end it) and therefore the further inflammation of popular feeling. In 1911, when the gap between the two countries' fleets was narrowest and most felt in Great Britain, German diplomacy provoked another crisis over Morocco. This time, a British minister said publicly something that sounded very much like an assertion that Great Britain would go to war to protect France.

Yet when war came, it was in the South Slav lands. Serbia did well in the Balkan Wars of 1912–13, in which the young Balkan nations first despoiled Turkey of most that was left of her European territory and then fell out over the spoils. But Serbia might have got more had the Austrians not objected. Behind Serbia stood Russia, launched on the programme of rebuilding and expanding her forces which would take three or four years to bring to fruition. If South Slavs were to be shown that the Dual Monarchy could humiliate Serbia so that they could not hope for her support, then the sooner the better. Given that Germany was the Dual

Monarch's ally, she was unlikely to seek to avoid fighting Russia while there was still time to be sure of winning.

The crisis came when an Austrian archduke was assassinated by a Bosnian terrorist at Sarajevo in June 1914. The Austrians decided that the moment had come to teach Serbia her lesson and for ever kill the pan-Slav agitation. The Germans supported them. The Austrians declared war on Serbia on 28 July. A week later all the great powers were at war though, ironically, the Austro-Hungarians and Russians were still at peace with one another; it was only on 6 August that the Dual Monarchy at last declared war on its old rival. Before that date German military planning had dictated the timetable of events. The key decision to attack France before Russia had been made years before; German planning required such an attack to be made through Belgium, whose neutrality the British among others had guaranteed. Thereafter the sequence of events fell almost automatically into place. When Russia mobilized to bring pressure on Austria-Hungary for Serbia's protection, the Germans declared war on Russia. Having done that, they had to attack the French and declared war on them. Thus, the Franco-Russian alliance never actually operated. By Germany's violation of Belgian neutrality, the British government, uneasy about a German attack on France, but not seeing clearly on what grounds they could justify intervention to prevent it, was given an issue to unite the country and take it into war against Germany on 4 August.

Just as the duration and intensity of the war were to outrun all expectations, so did its geographical spread. Japan and the Ottoman empire joined in soon after the outbreak; the former on the side of the Allies (as France, Great Britain and Russia were called) and Turkey on that of the Central Powers (Germany and Austria-Hungary). Italy joined the Allies in 1915, in return for promises of Austrian territory. Other efforts were made to pick up new supporters by offering cheques to be cashed after a victorious peace; Bulgaria joined the Central

The trenches, the scene of the appalling experiences which came to symbolize the Great War. The one in the photograph was in reasonably good order when visited on a quiet day, though the sentry in the background maintained a close watch through the periscope.

Powers in September 1915 and Romania the Allies in the following year. Greece became another Allied state in 1917. Portugal's government had tried to enter the war in 1914, but though unable to do so because of internal troubles was finally faced with a German declaration of war in 1916. Thus, by the end of that year, the original issues of Franco-German and Austro-Russian rivalry had been thoroughly confused by other struggles. The Balkan states were fighting a third Balkan war (the war of the Ottoman succession in its European theatre), the British a war against German naval and commercial power, the Italians the last war of the *Risorgimento*, while outside Europe the British, Russian and Arabs had begun a war of Ottoman partition in Asia and the Japanese were pursuing another highly profitable and cheap episode in the assertion of their hegemony in the Far East.

One reason why there was a search for allies in 1915 and 1916 was that the war then showed every sign of bogging down in a stalemate no one had expected. The nature of the fighting had surprised almost everyone. It had opened with a German sweep into northern France. This did not achieve the lightning victory which was its aim but gave the Germans possession of all but a tiny scrap of Belgium and much French territory, too. In the east, Russian offensives had been stopped by the Germans and Austrians. Thereafter, though more noticeably in the west than the east, the battlefields settled down to siege warfare on an unprecedented scale. This was because of two things. One was the huge killing-power of modern weapons. Magazine rifles, machine-guns and barbed wire could stop any infantry attack not preceded by pulverizing bombardment. Demonstrations of this truth were provided by the huge casualty lists. By the end of 1915 the French army alone had lost 300000 dead; that was bad enough but in 1916 one seven-month battle before Verdun added another 315000 to this total. In the same battle 280000 Germans died. While it was going on, another struggle further north, on the Somme, cost the British 420000 casualties and the Germans about the same. The first day of that battle, 1 July, remains the blackest in the history of the British army, when it suffered 60000 casualties, of whom more than a third died.

Such figures made nonsense of the confident predictions that the cost of modern war would be bound to make the struggle a short one. This was a reflexion of the second surprise, the revelation of the enormous war-making power of industrial societies. Plenty of people were weary by the end of 1916, but by then the warring states had already amply demonstrated a capacity greater than had been imagined to conscript and organize their peoples as never before in history to produce unprecedented quantities of material and furnish the recruits for new armies. Whole societies were engaged against one another; the international solidarity of the working class might never have been thought of for all the resistance it imposed to this, nor the international interests of ruling classes against subversion.

Inability to batter one another into submission on the battlefields accelerated the strategic and technical expansion of the struggle. This was why diplomats had sought new allies and generals new fronts. The Allies in 1915 mounted an attack on Turkey at the Dardanelles in the hope, not to be realized, of knocking her out of the war and opening up communication with Russia through the Black Sea. The same search for a way round the French deadlock later produced a new Balkan front at Salonika; it replaced the one which had collapsed when Serbia was overrun. Colonial possessions, too, had ensured from the first that there would be fighting all round the globe, even if on a small scale. The German colonies could be picked up

France, 1916. A British battalion moves to the rear with its wounded while a supply column goes forward to the front.

fairly easily, thanks to the British command of the seas, though the African ones provoked some lengthy campaigning. The most important and considerable extra-European operations, though, were in the eastern and southern parts of the Turkish empire. A British and Indian army entered Mesopotamia. Another force advanced from the Suez canal towards Palestine. In the Arabian desert, an Arab revolt against the Turks provided some of the few romantic episodes relieving the brutal squalor of industrial war.

The technical expansion of the war was most noticeable in its industrial effects and in the degeneration of standards of behaviour. The American civil war a half-century before had prefigured the first of these, too, in revealing the economic demands of mass war in a democratic age. The mills, factories, mines and furnaces of

The new dimension of war. Bombing from the air became a serious matter during the Great War. British aeroplanes in action against a railway junction in Palestine, as painted by a war-artist.

Near Persepolis, 1916, officers and men of an Indian cavalry regiment pose before the relief of Shapur, conqueror of Valerian, who is shown abasing himself before the great Sassanid, at Naqsh-i Rustam, where a series of fine reliefs commemorate the Sassanid kings. Persia was of great importance to British strategy because of Turkey's entry to the war.

Europe now worked as never before. So did those of the United States and Japan, the former accessible to the Allies but not to the Central Powers because of the British naval supremacy. The maintenance of millions of men in the field required not only arms and ammunition, but food, clothing, medical equipment, and machines in huge quantities. Though a war in which millions of animals were still needed, it was also the first war of the internal-combustion engine; trucks and tractors swallowed petrol as avidly as horses and mules ate their fodder. Many statistics illustrate the new scale of war but one must suffice; in 1914 the whole British empire had 18 000 hospital beds and four years later it had 630 000.

The repercussions of this vast increase in

The 'tank', as it was named by the British to conceal the nature of their invention, was the answer to machine-guns and barbed wire; essentially it was a self-propelled fortress which could cross all but very large obstacles. Specialized tanks were soon developed. This French example was a light, two-man machine, and fairly fast.

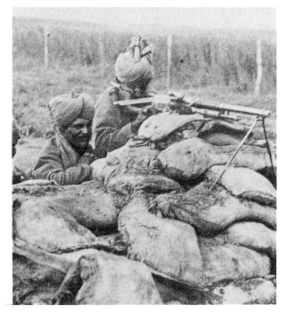

Indian soldiers were for a time deployed by the British in France in the Great War though, mainly for climatic reasons, they were later withdrawn from this theatre.

demand rolled outwards through society, leading in all countries in varying measure to the governments' control of the economy, conscription of labour, the revolutionizing of women's employment, the introduction of new health and welfare services. They also rolled overseas. The United States ceased to be a debtor nation; the Allies liquidated their investments there to pay for what they needed and became debtors in their turn. Indian industry received the fillip it had long required. Boom days came to the ranchers and farmers of the Argentine and the British white Dominions. The latter also shared the military burden, sending soldiers to Europe and fighting the Germans in their colonies.

915

This technical expansion also made the war more frightful. This was not only because machine-guns and high explosive made possible such terrible slaughter. It was not even because of new weapons such as poison gas, flame-throwers or tanks, all of which made their appearance as soldiers strove to find a way out of the deadlock of the battlefield. It was also because the fact that whole societies were engaged in warfare brought with it the realization that whole societies could be targets for war-like operations. Attacks on the morale, health and efficiency of civilian workers and voters became desirable. When such attacks were denounced, the denunciations were themselves blows in another sort of campaign, that of propaganda. The possibilities of mass literacy and the recently created cinema industry supplemented and overtook such old standbys as pulpit and school in this kind of warfare. To British charges that the Germans who carried out primitive bombing raids on London by airship were 'baby-killers', Germans retorted that the same could be said of the sailors who sustained the British blockade. The rising figures of German infant mortality bore them out.

In part because of the slow but apparently irresistible success of the British blockade and because of its unwillingness to risk the fleet whose building had done so much to poison pre-war feeling between the two countries, the German High Command devised a new use for a weapon whose power had been underrated in 1914, the submarine. It was launched at Allied shipping and the ships of neutrals who were supplying the Allies, attacks often being made without warning and on unarmed vessels. This was first done early in 1915, though few submarines were then available and they did not do much damage. There was an outcry when a great British liner was torpedoed that year, with the loss of 1200 lives, many of them Americans, and the unrestricted sinking of shipping was called off by the Germans. It was resumed at the beginning of 1917. By then it was clear that if Germany did not starve Great Britain first, she herself would be choked by British blockade.

During that winter there was famine in Balkan countries and people were starving in the suburbs of Vienna. The French had by then suffered 3 350 000 casualties and the British over a million, the Germans had lost nearly two and a half million and were still fighting a war on two fronts. Food riots and strikes were becoming more frequent; infant mortality was rising towards a level 50 per cent higher than that of 1915. There was no reason to suppose that the German army, divided between east and west, would be any more likely to achieve a knockout than had been the British and French and it was in any case more favourably placed to fight on the defensive. In these circumstances the German general staff chose to resume unrestricted submarine warfare, the decision which brought about the first great transformation of the war in 1917, the entry to it of the United States. The Germans knew this would happen, but gambled on bringing Great Britain to her knees – and thus France – before American weight could be decisive.

American opinion, by no means favourable to one side or the other in 1914, had since then come a long way. Allied propaganda and purchases had helped; so had the first German submarine campaign. When the Allied governments began to talk about war aims which included the reconstruction of Europe on the basis of safeguarding the interests of nationalities it had an appeal to 'hyphenated' Americans. The resumption of unrestricted submarine warfare was decisive; it was a direct threat to American interests and the safety of her citizens. When it was also revealed to the American government that Germany hoped to negotiate an alliance with Mexico and Japan against the United States, the hostility aroused by the submarines was confirmed. Soon, an American ship was sunk without warning and the United States declared war shortly afterwards.

The impossibility of breaking the European deadlock by means short of total war had thus sucked the new world into the quarrels of the old, almost against its will. The Allies were

May Day 1919; Lenin in Red Square, Moscow, with perhaps just a hint of the cult of personality in the background.

delighted; victory was now assured. Immediately, though, they faced a gloomy year. The year 1917 was even blacker for Great Britain and France than 1916. Not only did the submarine take months to master but a terrible series of battles in France (usually lumped under one name, Passchendaele), inflicted an ineffaceable scar upon the British national consciousness and cost another 400000 men to gain five miles of mud. The French army underwent a series of mutinies, worn out by its heroic efforts in 1916. Worst of all for the Allies, the Russian empire collapsed and Russia ceased, by the end of the year, to be a great power for the foreseeable future.

The Russian state was destroyed by the war and this was the beginning of the revolutionary transformation of central and eastern Europe, too. The makers of what was called a revolution in Russia in February 1917 were the German armies which had in the end broken the hearts of even the long-enduring Russian soldiers. Defeated Russian armies had behind them cities starving because of the breakdown of the transport system, and a government of incompetent and corrupt men who feared constitutionalism and liberalism as much as defeat. At the beginning of 1917 the security forces themselves could no longer be depended upon. Food-riots were followed by mutiny and the autocracy was suddenly seen to be powerless. A provisional government of liberals and socialists was formed and the tsar abdicated. The new government then itself failed, in the main because it attempted the impossible, the continuation of the war; the Russians wanted peace and bread, as Lenin, the leader of the Bolsheviks, saw. His determination to take power from the moderate provisional government was the second reason for their failure. Presiding over a disintegrating country, administration and army, still facing the unsolved problems of privation in the cities, the provisional government was itself swept away in a second change, the *coup* called the October Revolution which, together with the American entry to the war, marks 1917 as a break between two eras of European history. Previously, Europe had settled its own affairs; now the United States would be bound to have a large say in its future and there had come into being a state which was committed by the beliefs of its founders to the destruction of the whole pre-war European order, a truly and consciously revolutionary centre for world politics.

The immediate and obvious consequences of the establishment of the Soviet state, as Russia was called, after the workers' and soldiers' councils which were her basic political institution after the revolution, was a new strategic situation. The Bolsheviks consolidated their *coup d'état* by dissolving the only freely elected representative body based on universal suffrage Russia has ever had (since they did not control it) and by trying to secure the peasants' loyalties by the assurance of land and peace. This was essential if they were to survive; the backbone of the party which now strove to assert its authority over Russia was the very small industrial working class of a few cities. Only peace could provide a safer and broader foundation. At first the terms demanded by the Germans were thought so objectionable that the Russians stopped negotiation; they then had to accept a much more punitive peace, the Treaty of Brest-Litovsk, in March 1918. It imposed severe losses of territory, but gave the new order the peace and time it desperately needed to tackle its internal troubles.

The Allies were furious. They saw the Bolsheviks' action as a treacherous defection. Nor was their attitude towards the new régime softened by the intransigent revolutionary propaganda it directed against their citizens. The Russian leaders expected a revolution of the working class in all the advanced capitalist countries. This gave an extra dimension to a series of military interventions in the affairs of Russia by the Allies. Their original purpose was strategic, in that they hoped to stop the Germans exploiting the advantage of being able to close down their eastern front but they were quickly interpreted by many people in the capitalist countries and by all Bolsheviks as anti-communist crusades. Worse still, they became entangled in a civil war which seemed likely to destroy the new régime. Even without the doctrinal filter of Marxist theory through which Lenin and his colleagues saw the world, these episodes would have been likely to sour relations between Russia and the capitalist countries for a long time; once translated into Marxist terms they seemed a confirmation of an essential and ineradicable hostility. Their recollection has dogged Russian attitudes ever since. They also helped to justify the Russian revolution's turn downwards into authoritarian government. Fear of the invader as a restorer of the old order and patron of landlords combined with Russian traditions of autocracy and police terrorism to stifle any liberalization of the régime.

Russian Empire in 1914

Central powers and their allies

Allies of the Entente

Neutral

Soviet Russia 1918

Occupied by the central powers 1918

Frontier line at the cease-fire in 1917

Russia in 1918

The Russian communists' conviction that revolution was about to occur in central and western Europe was in one sense correct, yet crucially wrong. In its last year, war's revolutionary potential indeed became plain, but in

The homecoming German army of 1918 soon came to regard itself not as a defeated army, but a betrayed one.

Appeals for private assistance were one response in aid of demobilized soldiers: this poster sought to persuade Germans to contribute to a fund for the disabled.

national, not class, forms The Allies were provoked (in part by the Bolsheviks) to a revolution strategy of their own. The military situation looked bleak for them at the end of 1917. It was obvious that they would face a German attack in France in the spring without the advantage of a Russian army to draw off their enemies and

that it would be a long time before American troops arrived in large numbers to help them in France. But they could adopt a revolutionary weapon. They could appeal to the nationalities of the Austro-Hungarian empire. This had the additional advantage of emphasizing in American eyes the ideological purity of the Allied cause now that it was no longer tied to tsardom. Accordingly, in 1918, subversive propaganda was directed to the Austro-Hungarian armies and encouragement was given to Czechs and South Slavs in exile. Before Germany gave in, the Dual Monarchy was already dissolving under the combined effects of this and a Balkan campaign which at last began to provide victories. This was the second great blow to old Europe. The political structure of the whole area bounded by the Urals, the Baltic and the Danube valley was now in question as it had not been for centuries. There was even a Polish army again in existence. It was patronized by the Germans as a weapon against Russia while the American president announced that an independent Poland was an essential of Allied peacemaking. All the certainties of the past century seemed to be in the melting-pot.

The crucial battles were fought against this increasingly revolutionary background. By the summer, the Allies had managed to halt the last great German offensive. It had made huge gains, but not enough. When the Allied armies began to move forward victoriously in their turn, the German leaders sought an end: they, too, thought they saw signs of revolutionary collapse at home. When the emperor abdicated the third of the dynastic empires had fallen; the Habsburgs had already gone, so that the Hohenzollerns just outlasted their old rivals. A new German government requested an armistice and the fighting came to an end.

The cost of this huge conflict has never been adequately computed. One figure which is approximate indicates its scale: about ten million men had died as a result of direct military action. Yet typhus probably killed another million in the Balkans alone. Even such horrible figures as these do not indicate the physical cost in maiming, blinding, the loss to families of fathers and husbands, the spiritual havoc in the destruction of ideals, confidence and goodwill. Europeans looked at their huge cemeteries and were appalled at what they had done. The economic damage was immense, too. Over much of Europe people starved. A year after the war manufacturing output was still nearly a quarter below that of 1914; Russia's was only 20 per cent of what it had then been. Transport was in some countries almost impossible to procure. Moreover all the complicated, fragile machinery of international exchange was smashed and some of it could never be replaced. At the centre of this chaos lay, exhausted, a Germany which had been the economic dynamo of central Europe. 'We are at the dead season of our fortunes', wrote a young British economist at the peace conference, J. M. Keynes. 'Our power

The horrific carnage of the Great War was not the only price that Europe paid. This one street of the sacked town of Termonde shows the enormity of the task of material re-building. To do this economic reconstruction, without the help of a dynamic Germany on which Europe had so heavily relied, became a prime objective.

of feeling or caring beyond the immediate questions of our own material wellbeing is temporarily eclipsed . . . We have been moved beyond endurance, and need rest. Never in the lifetime of men now living has the universal element in the soul of man burnt so dimly.'

Delegates to a peace conference began to assemble at the end of 1918. It was once the fashion to emphasize their failures, but perspective and the recognition of the magnitude of their tasks imposes a certain respect for what they did. It was the greatest settlement since 1815 and its authors had to reconcile great expectations with stubborn facts. The power to make the crucial decisions was remarkably concentrated: the British and French prime ministers and the American president Woodrow Wilson dominated the negotiations. These took place between the victors; the defeated Germans were subsequently presented with their terms. In the diverging interests of France, aware above all of the appalling danger of any third repetition of German aggression, and of the Anglo-Saxon nations, conscious of standing in no such peril, lay the central problem of European security, but many others surrounded and obscured it. The peace settlement had to be a world settlement. It not only dealt with territories outside Europe – as earlier great settlements had done – but many non-European voices were heard in its making. Of twenty-seven states whose representatives signed the main treaty, a majority, seventeen, lay in other continents. The United States was the greatest of these; with Japan, Great Britain, France and Italy she formed the group described as the 'principal' victorious powers. For a world settlement, nevertheless, it was ominous that no representative attended from Russia, the only great power with both European and Asian frontiers.

Technically, the peace settlement consisted of a group of distinct treaties made not only with Germany, but Bulgaria, Turkey and the 'succession states' which claimed the divided Dual Monarchy. Of these, a resurrected Poland, an enlarged Serbia called Yugoslavia and an entirely new Czechoslovakia were present at the conference as allies, while a much reduced Hungary and the Germanic heart of old Austria were treated as defeated enemies with whom peace had to be made. All of this posed difficult problems. But the main concern of the Peace Conference was the settlement with Germany embodied in the Treaty of Versailles signed in June 1919.

This was a punitive settlement and explicitly stated that the Germans were responsible for the outbreak of war. But most of the harshest terms arose not from this moral guilt but from the French wish, if possible, so to tie Germany down that any third German war was inconceivable. This was the purpose of economic reparations, which were the most unsatisfactory part of the settlement. They angered Germans and made acceptance of defeat even harder. Moreover they were economic nonsense. Nor was the penalizing of Germany supported by arrangements to ensure that Germany might not one day try to reverse the decision by force of arms and this angered the French. Germany's territorial losses, it went without saying, included Alsace and Lorraine, but were otherwise greatest in the east, to Poland. In the west the French did not get much more reassurance than an undertaking that the German bank of the Rhine should be 'demilitarized'.

The second leading characteristic of the peace was its attempt where possible to follow the principles of self-determination and nationality. In many places this merely meant recognizing existing facts; Poland and Czechoslavakia were already in existence as states before the peace conference met, and Yugoslavia was built round the core of the former Serbia. Already by the end of 1918, therefore, these principles had already triumphed over much of the area occupied by the old Dual Monarchy (and were soon to do so also in the former Baltic provinces of Russia). After outlasting even the Holy Roman Empire, the Habsburgs were gone at last and in their place appeared states which, though not uninterruptedly, have all survived to this day. The principle of self-determination was also followed in providing that certain frontier zones should have their destiny settled by plebiscite.

Unfortunately, the principle of nationality could not always be applied. Geographical, historical, cultural and economic realities cut across it. When it prevailed over them – as in the destruction of the Danube's economic unity – the results could be bad; when it did not they could be just as bad because of the aggrieved feelings left behind. Eastern and central Europe was studded with national minorities embedded resentfully in nations to which they felt no allegiance. A third of Poland's population did not speak Polish; a third of Czechoslovakia's consisted of minorities of Poles, Russians, Magyars and Ruthenes; an enlarged Romania now contained over a million Magyars. In some places, the infringement of the principle was felt with especial acuteness as an injustice. Germans resented the existence of a 'corridor' connecting Poland with the sea across German lands, Italy was disappointed of Adriatic spoils held out to her by her allies when they had needed her help and the Irish had still not got Home Rule after all.

The most obvious non-European question concerned the disposition of the German colonies. Here there was an important innovation. Old-fashioned colonial greed was not acceptable to the United States; instead, tutelage for non-European peoples formerly under German or Turkish rule was provided by the device of trusteeship. 'Mandates' were given to the victorious powers (though the United States declined any) by the League of Nations to administer these territories while they were prepared for self-government; it was the most imaginative idea to emerge from the settlement.

The League of Nations owed much to the enthusiasm of Woodrow Wilson. He secured its creation and gave its Covenant – its constitution – pride of place as the first part of the Peace Treaty. It was the one instance in which the settlement transcended the idea of nationalism (even the British Empire had been represented as individual units, one of which was India). It also transcended that of Europe; it is another sign of the new era that twenty-six of the original forty-two members of the League were countries outside Europe. Unfortunately, because of domestic politics Wilson had not taken into account, the United States was not among them. This was the most fatal of several grave weaknesses which made it impossible for the League to satisfy the expectations it had aroused. Perhaps these were all unrealizable in principle given the actual state of world political forces. None the less, the League was to have

The appalling bloodshed of the Great War led some to think that Europe's main handicap in setting her house in order after 1918 was the absence of a generation slaughtered on the battlefields. Some statesmen, certainly, for all their goodwill and ability, still leave an impression of wrestling with issues born in a world they did not understand and perhaps this was more marked in the great democracies than elsewhere. Two British prime ministers of these years, Stanley Baldwin and Ramsay MacDonald, at a meeting of the League of Nations.

its successes in usefully handling matters which might without its intervention have proved dangerous. If exaggerated hopes had been entertained that it might do more, it does not mean it was not a practical as well as great and imaginative idea.

Russia was absent from the League just as she was from the peace conference. Probably the latter was the more important. The political arrangements to shape the next stage of European history were entered into without consulting her, though in eastern Europe this meant the drawing of boundaries in which any Russian government was bound to be vitally interested. It was true that the Bolshevik leaders did all they could to provide excuses for excluding them. They envenomed relations with the major powers by revolutionary propaganda, and were convinced that the capitalist countries were determined to overthrow their state. The British prime minister, Lloyd George, and Wilson were in fact more flexible – even sympathetic – than many of their colleagues and electors in dealing with Russia. Their French colleague, Clemenceau, on the other hand, was passionately anti-Bolshevik and had the support of many French ex-soldiers and investors in being so; Versailles was the first great European peace to be made by powers all the time aware of the dangers of disappointing democratic electorates. But however the responsibility is allocated, the outcome was that Russia, the European power which had, potentially, the greatest weight of all in the affairs of the Continent, was not consulted in the making of a new Europe. Though for the time being virtually out of action, she was bound eventually to join the ranks of those who wished to revise the settlement or overthrow it. It only made it worse that her rulers detested the social system it was meant to protect.

Huge hopes had been entertained of this settlement. They were often unrealistic, yet in spite of its manifest failures, the peace has been over-condemned, for it had many good points. When it failed, it was for reasons which were for the most part beyond the control of the men who made it. In the first place, the days of a European world hegemony in the narrow political sense were over. The peace treaties of 1919 could do little to secure the future beyond Europe. The old imperial policemen were now too weakened to do their job inside Europe, let alone outside; some had disappeared altogether. In the end the United States had been needed to ensure Germany's defeat and now she plunged into a period of artificial isolation from Europe. Nor did Russia wish to be involved in the Continent's stabilizing. The isolationism of the one power and the sterilization of the other by ideological preconceptions left Europe to its own inadequate

devices. When no revolution broke out in Europe, the Russians turned in on themselves; when Americans were given the chance by Wilson to be involved in Europe's peace-keeping, they refused it. Both decisions are comprehensible, but their combined effect was to preserve an appearance of European autonomy which was no longer a reality and could no longer be an adequate framework for handling its problems. Finally, the settlement's gravest immediate weakness lay in the economic fragility of the new structures it presupposed. Here its terms were more in question: self-determination often made nonsense of economics. But it is difficult to see on what grounds self-determination could have been set aside. Ireland's problems are still with us more than a half-century after an independent Irish Free State appeared in 1922.

The situation was all the more likely to prove unstable because many illusions persisted in Europe and many new ones arose. Allied victory and the rhetoric of peace-making made many think that there had been a great triumph of liberalism and democracy. Four autocratic anti-national illiberal empires had collapsed, after all, and to this day the peace settlement retains the distinction of being the only one in history made by great powers all of whom were democracies. Liberal optimism also drew strength from the ostentatious stance taken by Wilson during the war; he had done all he could to make it clear that he saw the participation of the United States as essentially different in kind from that of the other Allies, being governed (he reiterated) by high-minded ideals and a belief that the world could be made safe for democracy if other nations would give up their bad old ways. Some thought that he had been shown to be right; the new states, above all the new Germany, adopted liberal, parliamentary constitutions and often republican ones, too. Finally, there was the illusion of the League; the dream of a new international authority which was not an empire seemed at last a reality.

Yet all this was rooted in fallacy and false premise. Since the peace-makers had been obliged to do much more than enthrone liberal principles – they had also to pay debts, protect vested interests, and take account of intractable facts – those principles had been much muddied in practice. Above all, they had left much unsatisfied nationalism about and had created new and fierce nationalist resentments in Germany. Perhaps this could not be helped, but it was a soil in which other things than liberalism could grow. Further, the democratic institutions of the new states – and the old ones, too, for that matter – were being launched on a world at peace, but one badly damaged economically. Everywhere, poverty, hardship and unemployment exacerbated political struggle and in many places they were made worse by the special dislocations produced by respect for national sovereignty. The crumbling of old economic patterns of exchange in the war made it much more difficult to deal with problems like peasant poverty and unemployment, too; Russia, once the granary of much of western Europe, was now inaccessible economically. This was a background which revolutionaries could exploit. The communists were happy and ready to do this, for they believed that history had cast them for this rôle, and soon their efforts were reinforced by another radical political phenomenon, fascism.

Communism threatened the new Europe in two ways. Internally, each country soon had a revolutionary communist party. They effected little that was positive, but caused great alarm. They also did much to prevent the emergence of strong progressive parties. This was because of the circumstances of their birth. A 'Comintern', or Third International, was devised by the Russians in March 1919 to provide leadership for the international socialist movement which might otherwise, they feared, rally again to the old leaders whose lack of revolutionary zeal they blamed for a failure to exploit the opportunities of the war. The test of socialist movements for Lenin was adherence to the Comintern, whose principles were deliberately rigid, disciplined and uncompromising, in accordance with his view of the needs of an effective revolutionary

party. In almost every country this divided socialists into two camps, those who adhered to the Comintern and took the name communist, and those who, though sometimes claiming still to be Marxist, remained in the rump national parties and movements. The two movements were now in competition for working-class support and fought one another bitterly.

The new revolutionary threat on the left which was presented by communism was all the more alarming to many Europeans because there were indeed revolutionary disturbances which the communists sought to exploit. The most conspicuous led to the installation of a Bolshevik government in Hungary, but more startling, perhaps, were attempted communist coups in Germany, some briefly successful. The German situation was especially ironical, for the government of the new republic which emerged there in the aftermath of defeat was dominated by socialists who were forced back to reliance upon conservative forces – notably the professional soldiers of the old army – in order to prevent revolution. This happened even before the founding of the Comintern and it gave a special bitterness to the divisions of the Left in Germany. But everywhere, communist policy made united resistance to conservatism more difficult while at the same time alarming other sections of the population with revolutionary rhetoric and conspiracy.

Above all in eastern Europe, this was because the social threat was seen also as a Russian threat. The Comintern was manipulated as an instrument of Russian foreign policy by the Russian leaders; this was justifiable, given their assumption that the future of world revolution depended upon the preservation of the first socialist state as a citadel of the international working class. In the early years of civil war and slow consolidation of Bolshevik power in Russia this led to the deliberate incitement of disaffection abroad in order to preoccupy capitalist governments. But in eastern and central Europe there was more to it than this, because the actual territorial settlement of that area was in doubt long after the Versailles treaty. The First

Part of the bitter aftermath of war, revolution and civil war, the famine of 1921 brought immeasurable suffering to millions of Russians.

World War did not end there until in March 1921 a peace treaty between Russia and the new Polish Republic provided frontiers lasting until 1939. Poland was the most anti-Russian by tradition, the most anti-Bolshevik by religion as well as the largest and the most ambitious of the new nations. But all of them felt threatened by a recovery of Russian power, and were now especially troubled because it was tied up with the threat of social revolution. This connexion has much to do with the tendency of so many of these states to turn before 1939 to dictatorial or military governments which would at least guarantee a strong anti-communist line.

Fear of communist revolution in eastern and central Europe was most evident in the immediate post-war years, when economic collapse and uncertainty about the outcome of the Polish–Russian war (which, at one time, appeared to threaten Warsaw itself) provided the background. In 1921, with peace at last and, symbolically, the establishment of orderly official relations between Russia and Great Britain, there was a noticeable relaxation. This con-

nected with the Russian government's own sense of emerging from a period of acute danger in the civil war. It did not produce much in the way of better diplomatic manners, because it was all the time cut across by revolutionary propaganda and denunciation of capitalist countries, but from the Russian point of view they at last had time to engineer the recovery of their own shattered land. In 1921 Russian pig-iron production was about one-fifth of its 1913 level, that of coal a tiny 3 per cent or so, while the railways had less than half as many locomotives in service as at the start of the war. Livestock had declined by over a quarter and cereal deliveries were less than two-fifths of those of 1916. On to this impoverished economy there fell in 1921 a drought in south Russia and more than two million died in the subsequent famine. Even cannibalism was reported.

Liberalization of the economy brought about a turnround. By 1927 both industrial and agricultural production were nearly back to pre-war levels. The régime in these years was undergoing great uncertainty in its leadership. This had already been apparent before Lenin died in 1924, but the removal of a man whose acknowledged ascendancy had kept forces within it in balance opened a period of evolution and debate in the leadership of the communist party. This was not about the centralized, autocratic nature of the régime which had emerged from the 1917 Revolution, for none of the protagonists considered that political liberation was conceivable or that the use of secret police and party oversight could be dispensed with in a world of hostile capitalist states. But they could disagree about economic policy and tactics and personal rivalry sometimes gave extra edge to this.

Broadly speaking, two viewpoints emerged. One emphasized that the revolution depended on the goodwill of the mass of Russians, the peasants; they had first been allowed to take the land, then antagonized by attempts to feed the cities at their expense, then conciliated again by the liberalization of the economy and what was known as 'NEP', the New Economic Policy

In a propaganda poster proclaiming the successful completion of the first five-year plan in four years, Stalin looks with amusement at the rag-bag of opposition – church, capital, social democrats, Mensheviks.

which Lenin had approved as an expedient. Under it, the peasants had been able to make profits for themselves and accordingly had begun to grow more food and to sell it to the cities. The other viewpoint looked at the same facts in a longer perspective. To conciliate the peasants would slow down industrialization, which Russia needed to survive in a hostile world. The party's proper course, argued those who took this view, was to rely upon the revolutionary militants of the cities and to exploit the still non-Bolshevized peasants in their interest while pressing on with industrialization and the promotion of revolution abroad. The communist leader Trotsky took this view.

What happened was roughly that he was shouldered aside, but his view prevailed. From the intricate politics of the party there emerged eventually the ascendancy of a member of its bureaucracy, Joseph Stalin, a man far less attractive intellectually than either Lenin or Trotsky and equally ruthless, but of greater historical importance. Gradually arming himself with a

power which he used against former colleagues and old Bolsheviks as willingly as against his enemies, he carried out the real Russian revolution to which the Bolshevik seizure of power had opened the way and created a new élite on which a new Russia was to be based. For him the industrialization of Russia was paramount. The road to it lay through finding a way of forcing the peasant to pay for it by supplying the grain he would rather have eaten if not offered a good profit. Two Five Year Plans carried out an industrialization programme from 1928 onwards, and their roots lay in the collectivization of agriculture. The party now for the first time conquered the countryside. In a new civil war millions of peasants were killed or transported and grain levies brought back famine. But the towns were fed, though the police apparatus kept consumption down to the minimum. There was a fall in real wages. But by 1937 80 per cent of Russian industrial output came from plant built since 1928. Russia was again a great power and the effects of this would alone assure Stalin a place in history.

The price in suffering was enormous. The enforcement of collectivization was only made possible by brutality on a scale far greater than anything seen under the Tsars and it made Russia a totalitarian state far more effective than the old autocracy had been. Stalin in this light, none the less, looks a fully Russian figure, a despot whose ruthless use of power is anticipated by an Ivan the Terrible or a Peter the Great. He was also a somewhat paradoxical claimant to Marxist orthodoxy, which taught that the economic structure of society determined its politics; Stalin precisely inverted this and demonstrated that if the will to use political power was there, the economic substructure could be revolutionized by force.

Critics of liberal capitalist society in other countries often pointed to Soviet Russia, of which they held a very rosy picture, as an example of the way in which a society might achieve progress and a revitalization of its cultural and ethical life. But this was not the only model available to those who found the civilization of the West disappointing. In the 1920s in Italy a movement appeared called fascism. It was to lend its name to a number of other and only loosely related radical movements in other countries which had in common some degree of rejection of liberalism and a strong anti-Marxism. The Great War had badly strained constitutional Italy. She was poorer than other countries regarded in 1914 as great powers, her share of fighting had been very heavy and often unsuccessful and much of it had taken place on Italian territory. Inequalities had accentuated social divisions as the war went on. With peace came even faster inflation, too. The owners of property, whether agricultural or industrial, and those who could ask higher wages because of a labour shortage, were more insulated against it than the middle classes and those who lived on

investment or fixed incomes. This was on the whole the class which before 1914 supplied the most convinced supporters of the unification completed in 1870. They had sustained a constitutional and liberal state while conservative Roman Catholics and revolutionary socialists had long opposed it. They had seen the war begin in 1915 as an extension of the *Risorgimento*, as a crusade to remove Austria from the last soil she ruled which was inhabited by those of Italian blood or speech. Like all nationalism, this was a muddled, unscientific notion, but it was powerful. With the peace settlement came deep disillusion; many nationalist dreams were left unrealized. Moreover, as the immediate post-war economic crisis deepened, the socialists grew stronger in parliament and seemed more alarming. They had now in the background the new encouragement that a socialist revolutionary state existed in Russia. Disappointed and frightened, tired of anti-nationalism, many Italians began to cast loose from liberal parliamentarianism and to look for a way out of Italy's disappointments. They became sympathetic to intransigent nationalism abroad (which found expression in wide sympathy for an adventurer who seized the Adriatic port of Fiume which the Peace Conference had failed to give to Italy) and violent anti-Marxism at home. The second was bound to be attractive in a Roman Catholic country, but it was not only from the traditionally conservative Church that the new leadership against Marxists came.

In 1919 a journalist and ex-serviceman who had before the war been an extreme socialist, Benito Mussolini, formed a movement called the *fascio di combattimento*, which can be roughly translated as 'union for struggle'. It sought power by any means, among them violence by groups of young thugs, directed at first against socialists and working-class organizations, then against elected authorities. The movement prospered. Italy's constitutional politicians could neither control it nor tame it by cooperation. Soon the fascists (as they came to be called) often enjoyed official or quasi-official patronage and protection from local officials and police. Gangsterism was semi-institutionalized. By 1922 they had not only achieved important electoral success but had virtually made orderly government impossible in some places by terrorizing their political enemies, especially if they were communist or socialist. In that year, other politicians having failed to master the fascist challenge, the king called Mussolini to form a government; he did so, on a coalition basis, and the violence came to an end. This was what was called in later fascist mythology the 'March on Rome', but was not quite the end of constitutional Italy. Mussolini only slowly turned his position into a dictatorship. In 1926 government by decree began; elections were suspended. There was little opposition.

The new régime had terrorism in plenty at its roots, and it explicitly denounced liberal ideals, yet Mussolini's rule was far short of totalitarian and was much less brutal than the Russian (of which he sometimes spoke admiringly). He undoubtedly had aspirations to revolutionary change, and many of his followers much stronger ones, but this turned out in practice to be largely a propaganda claim; Mussolini's own temperamental impatience with an established society from which he felt excluded lay behind it, as much as real radical pressure in his movement. Italian fascism in practice and theory rarely achieved coherence; instead, it reflected more and more the power of established Italy. Its greatest domestic step was a diplomatic agreement with the Papacy which in return for substantial concessions to the authority of the Church in Italian life (which persist to this day) recognized the Italian state officially. For all fascism's revolutionary rhetoric, the Lateran treaties of 1929 which embodied this agreement were a concession to the greatest conservative force in Italy. 'We have given back God to Italy and Italy to God', said the pope. Just as unrevolutionary were the results of fascist criticism of free enterprise. The subordination of individual interest to the state boiled down to depriving trades unions of their power to protect their members' interests. Few checks were placed on the freedom of employers and fascist

economic planning was a mockery. Only agricultural production notably improved.

The same divergence between style and aspiration on the one hand and achievement on the other was also to be marked in movements elsewhere which have been called fascist. Though indeed reflecting something new and post-liberal – they were inconceivable except as expressions of mass society – such movements in almost all countries in practice made compromising concessions to conservative influences. This makes it difficult to speak of the phenomenon 'fascism' at all precisely; in many countries régimes appeared which were authoritarian – even totalitarian in aspiration – intensely nationalist, and anti-Marxist. But fascism was not the only possible source of such ideas. Such governments as those which emerged in Portugal and Spain, for example, drew upon traditional and conservative forces rather than upon those which arose from the new phenomenon of mass politics. In them, true radicals who were fascists often felt discontented at concessions made to the existing social order. Only in Germany, in the end, did a movement some termed 'fascist' succeed in a revolution which mastered historical conservatism. For such reasons, the label of fascism sometimes confuses as much as it clarifies.

Perhaps it is best merely to distinguish two separable phenomena of the twenty years after 1918. One is the appearance (even in stable democracies such as Great Britain and France) of ideologists and activists who spoke the language of a new, radical politics, emphasized idealism, will-power and sacrifice, and looked forward to rebuilding society and the state on new lines without respect to vested interests or concessions to materialism. This was a phenomenon which could be found in many places, but only triumphed in two major states, Italy and Germany. In each of these, economic distress, outraged nationalism and anti-Marxism were the sources of success, though that in Germany did not come until 1933. If one word is wanted for this, let it be fascism. In other countries, usually under-

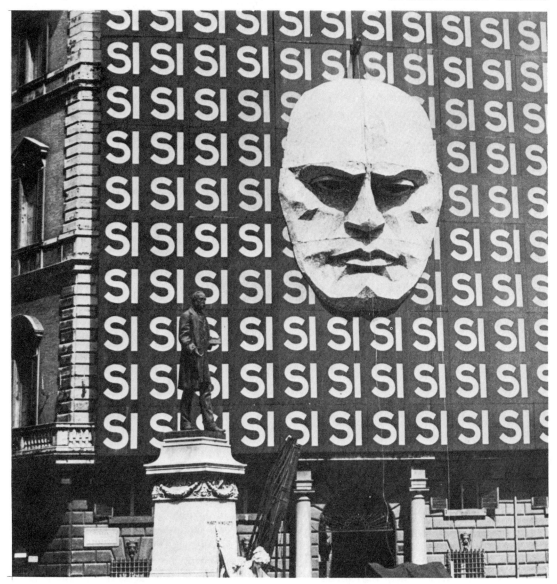

The simple message of Fascism: 'Si' – 'vote yes' – for Mussolini, whose effigy stares down.

developed economically, it might be better to speak of authoritarian, rather than fascist, régimes, especially in eastern Europe. There, large agricultural populations presented problems aggravated by the peace settlement. Sometimes alien national minorities appeared to threaten the state. Liberal institutions were only superficially implanted in many of the new countries and traditional conservative social and religious forces were strong. As in Latin America, where similar economic conditions could be

found, their apparent constitutionalism tended to give way sooner or later to the rule of strong men and soldiers. This proved the case before 1939 in the new Baltic states, Poland and all the successor states of the Dual Monarchy except Czechoslovakia, the one effective democracy in central Europe or the Balkans. The need of these states to fall back on such régimes demonstrated

929

both the unreality of the hopes entertained of their political maturity in 1918 and the new fear of Marxist communism, especially acute on Russia's borders. Such pressures operated also – though less acutely – in Spain and Portugal, where the influence of traditional conservatism was even stronger and Catholic social thinking counted for more than fascism.

The failures of democracy between the wars did not proceed at an even pace; in the 1920s it was still possible to hope for the liberal futures of the new states. Their bad economic start was followed by a gradual recovery of prosperity in which most of Europe outside Russia shared and the years from 1925 to 1929 were on the whole good ones. Currencies emerged from appalling inflation in the first half of the decade and were once more stable; the resumption by many countries of the gold standard was a sign of confidence that the old pre-1914 days were returned. In 1925 the production of food and raw materials in Europe for the first time passed the 1913 figure and a recovery of manufacturing was also under way. With the help of a world-wide recovery of trade and huge investment from the United States, now an exporter of capital, Europe reached in 1929 a level of trade not to be touched again until 1954. Yet collapse followed. Economic recovery had been built on insecure foundations; in spite of appearances, the pre-war economic order was not resumed. When faced with a sudden crisis, the new prosperity crumbled rapidly and there followed not merely a European but a world economic crisis which was the single most important event between two world wars.

The complex but remarkably efficient economic system of 1914 was irreparably damaged. International exchange was hampered by a huge increase of restrictions immediately after the war as new nations strove to protect their infant economies with tariffs and exchange control, and bigger and older nations tried to repair their enfeebled ones. The Versailles treaty made things worse by saddling Germany, the most important of all the European industrial states,

with an indefinite burden of reparation in kind and in cash which not only distorted her economy and delayed its recovery for years, but also took away much of the incentive to make it work. To the east, Germany's greatest potential market, Russia, was almost entirely cut off behind an economic frontier which little trade could penetrate; the Danube valley and the Balkans, another great area of German enterprise, was divided and impoverished. Temporarily, these difficulties were gradually overcome by the availability of American money, which Americans were willing to supply (though they would not take European goods and retired behind their tariff walls). But this brought about a dangerous dependence on the continued prosperity of the United States.

In the 1920s the United States produced nearly 40 per cent of the world's coal and over half the world's manufactures. This abundance, enhanced by the demands of war, had transformed the life of many Americans, the first people in the world to be able to take for granted the possession of family automobiles. Unfortunately, American domestic prosperity carried the world. On it depended the confidence which provided American capital for export. Because of this, a swing in the business cycle turned into a world economic disaster. In 1928 short-term money began to be harder to get in the United States. There were also signs that the end of the long boom might be approaching. These two factors led to the calling back of American loans from Europe. Soon some European borrowers were in difficulties. Meanwhile, demand was slackening in the United States as people began to think a severe slump might be on the way. Almost accidentally, this detonated a particularly sudden and spectacular stock market collapse in October 1929. It did not matter that there was thereafter a temporary rally and that great bankers bought to restore confidence. It was the end of American business confidence and of overseas investment. After a last brief rally in 1930 American money for investment abroad dried up. The world slump began.

Economic growth came to an end because of the collapse of investment, but another factor was soon operating to accelerate disaster. As the debtor nations tried to put their accounts in order, they cut imports. This caused a drop in world prices, so that countries producing primary goods could not afford to buy abroad. Meanwhile, at the centre of things, both the United States and Europe went into a financial crisis; as countries struggled, unsuccessfully, to keep the value of their currencies steady in relation to gold (an internationally acceptable means of exchange – hence the expression 'gold standard') they adopted deflationary policies to balance their books which again cut demand. By 1933 all the major currencies, except the French, were off gold. This was the symbolic expression of the tragedy, the dethronement of one old idol of liberal economics. Its reality was a level of unemployment which may have reached 30000000 in the industrial countries. In 1932 (the worst year for industrial countries) the index of industrial production for the United States and Germany was in each case only just above half of what it had been in 1929.

The effects of economic depression rolled outwards with a ghastly and irresistible logic. The social gains of the 1920s, when many people's standard of living had improved, were wiped out. No country had a solution to unemployment and though it was at its worst in the United States and Germany it existed in a concealed form all round the world in the villages and farmlands of the primary producers. The national income of the United States fell by 38 per cent between 1929 and 1932; this was exactly the figure by which the prices of manufactured goods fell, but at the same time raw material prices fell by 56 per cent and foodstuffs by 48 per cent respectively. Everywhere, therefore, the poorer nations and the poorer sectors of the mature economies suffered disproportionately. They may not always have seemed to do so, because they had less far to fall; an eastern European or an Argentinian peasant may not have been absolutely much worse off for he was always badly off, while an unemployed German clerk or factory hand certainly was and knew it.

There was to be no world recovery before another great war. Nations cut themselves off more and more behind tariffs and strove in some cases to achieve economic self-sufficiency by an increasing state control of their economic life. The disaster was a promising setting for the communists and fascists who expected or advocated the collapse of liberal civilization and now began to flap expectantly about the presumably dying carcass. The end of the gold standard and the belief in non-interference with the economy mark the collapse of liberal civilization in its economic dimension as strikingly as the rise of totalitarian régimes and the rise of nationalism to its destructive climax mark it in its political. Liberal civilization, frighteningly, had lost its power to control events. Many Europeans still found it hard to see this, though, and they continued to dream of the restoration of an age when that civilization enjoyed unquestioned supremacy. They forgot that its values had rested on a political and economic hegemony which, for a time, had worked but was already visibly in decay all round the world.

3 A new Asia in the making

Europe's troubles could not be confined to one continent. They were bound soon to cramp her ability to dominate affairs elsewhere and the earliest signs of this came in Asia. Unchallengeable and unchallenged European colonial power in Asia was, in the perspective of world history, very short-lived. By 1914 one European power, Great Britain, had decided to make an ally of Japan in order to safeguard her interests in the Far East, rather than rely on her own resources. Another, Russia, had been beaten by Japan in war and had turned back towards Europe after twenty years of pressure towards the Yellow Sea. Even the bullying of China which seemed likely to prove fatal at the time of the Boxer rebellion was relaxed; she lost no more territory to European imperialist powers after that. As tensions in Europe mounted and the difficulty of indefinitely frustrating Japanese ambitions became clear, European statesmen realized that the time for acquiring new ports or dreaming of partitions of the Sick Man of the Far East was over. It would suit everyone better to turn to what was always, in effect, British policy, that of an Open Door through which all countries might seek their own commercial advantage. That advantage, too, showed signs of being much less spectacular than had been thought in the sanguine days of the 1890s and here was

Japanese infantry celebrate their victory after storming the North Station, Shanghai, during the conquest of the city, China's major port, in November 1937.

another reason to tread more softly in the Far East.

The peak of the European onslaught on Asia and the moment of its greatest success was therefore past by 1914. The internal revolutionizing of Asia which stemmed from colonialism and western cultural and economic influences had already produced defensive reflexes which had to be taken seriously. They had gone furthest in Japan and it was their indirect operation as catalysts of modernization, channelled through this local and Asian force which set the pace of the next phase of the Hundred Years War of East and West. Japanese dynamism dominates Asian history in the first forty years of this century; China's revolution had no similar impact until after 1945 when, together with new change-making forces from outside, that country again surpassed Japan in importance as a shaper of Asian affairs and closed the Western Age in Asia.

Japan's dynamism showed itself both in economic growth and territorial aggressiveness. For a long time the first was more obvious. It was part and parcel of an overall process of 'westernizing' Japan which could in the 1920s still sustain a mood of liberal hopefulness about Japanese society and politics. It therefore helped to mask Japanese imperialism. In 1925 universal suffrage was introduced and in spite of much available evidence from the West that this had no necessary connexion with liberalism or moderation, it seemed to confirm once again a pattern of steady constitutional progress begun in the nineteenth century.

933

This confidence, shared both by foreigners and by Japanese, did not go long untroubled by the results of industrial growth, but was for a time helped by it, notably in the mood of expansive optimism awoken by the Great War, which gave Japan great opportunities: markets (especially in Asia) in which she had been faced by heavy western competition were abandoned to her when their former exploiters found they could not meet the demands of the war in their own countries; the Allied governments ordered great quantities of munitions from Japanese factories; a world shipping shortage gave her new shipyards the work they needed. Though the boom collapsed in 1920, expansion was resumed later in the decade and in 1929 the Japanese had an industrial base which (though it still engaged less than one in five of the population) had in twenty years seen its steel production rise almost tenfold, its textile production tripled, and its coal output doubled. Her manufacturing sector was beginning to influence other Asian countries, too; she imported iron ore from China and Malaya, coal from Manchuria. Still small though her manufacturing industry was by comparison with that of the western powers, and though it coexisted with an enduring small-scale and artisan sector, Japan's new industrial strength was beginning to shape both domestic politics and foreign relations in the 1920s. In particular, it affected her relations with mainland Asia.

A contrast to the pre-eminent and dynamic rôle of Japan was provided there by the continuing eclipse of China, potentially the greatest of Asian and world powers. The 1911 revolution had been of enormous importance, but did not by itself end this eclipse. In principle, it marked an epoch far more fundamentally than the French or Russian revolutions: it was the end of more than two thousand years of history during which the Confucian state had held China together and Confucian ideals had dominated Chinese culture and society. Inseparably intertwined, Confucianism and the legal order fell together. The 1911 revolution proclaimed the shattering of the standards by which tradi-

Japanese labour was cheap; low wages paid for much of the industrialization and modernization of the new world power. In the early years of this century, little girls like these looked after babies both of whose parents were factory workers.

The penetration of Japan by Western ideas about the rôles of the sexes remains very much qualified. One aspect of change was caught in 1936 by a Japanese artist where girls are shown handling modern scientific equipment.

Asia contemplates the instruments of recovery from Western domination; Chinese officers examine some of the first products of the new Nanking arsenal, built at the end of the nineteenth century. In spite of such innovations, the imperial régime could not sufficiently liberate itself from the past to use China's resources adequately. Its successors were to have greater success – perhaps because they found better opportunities in the disarray of the old great powers among themselves.

China in 1927, as the warlord era moves to its close. The executioners of a Kuomintang 'Pacification Commissioner' carry out their duties.

tional China lived. On the other hand, the revolution was limited, in two ways especially. In the first place, it was destructive rather than constructive. The monarchy had held together a vast country, virtually a continent, of widely different regions. Its collapse meant that the centrifugal regionalism which so often expressed itself in Chinese history could again have full rein. Many of the revolutionaries were animated by a bitter envy and distrust of Peking. Local concentrations of power, secret societies, the gentry and military commanders were ready and willing to take a grip of affairs in their own regions. These tendencies were somewhat masked while Yuan Shih-k'ai remained at the head of affairs (until 1916), but then burst out. The revolutionaries were split between a group round Sun Yat-sen called the Chinese National People's Party, or *Kuomintang* (KMT), and those who upheld the central government based on the parliamentary structure at Peking. Sun's support was drawn mainly from Canton businessmen and certain soldiers in the south. Against this background warlords thrived. They were soldiers who happened to have control of substantial forces and arms at a time when the central government was continuously weak. Between 1912 and 1928 there were some 1300 of them; some at times controlled important areas and Yuan Shih-k'ai himself can be regarded as the greatest of them. Some of them carried out reforms. Some were simply bandits. Some had considerable status as plausible pretenders to governmental power. It was a little like the end of the Roman empire, though less drawn out. Nothing took the place of the old scholar-bureaucrats and the soldiers stepped forward to fill the void.

This reflected the second limitation of the revolution of 1911: it provided no basis of agreement for further progress. Sun Yat-sen had said that the solution of the national question would have to precede that of the social. But even about the shape of a nationalist future there was much disagreement and the removal of the dynasty took away the common enemy that had delayed its emergence. Although eventually creative, the intellectual confusion marked among the revolutionaries in the first decade of the Chinese Revolution was deeply divisive and symptomatic of the huge task awaiting China's would-be renovators.

From 1916 a group of cultural reformers began to gather particularly at the university of Peking. The year before, one of them, Ch'en Tu-hsin, had founded a journal called *New Youth* which was the focus of the debate they ignited. Ch'en preached to Chinese youth, in whose hands he believed the revolution's destiny to lie, a total rejection of the old Chinese cultural tradition. Like other intellectuals who talked of Huxley and Dewey and introduced to their bemused compatriots the works of Ibsen, Ch'en still thought the key lay in the West; in its Darwinistic sense of struggle, its individualism and utilitarianism, it still seemed to offer a way ahead. But important though such leadership was and however enthusiastic its disciples might be, an emphasis on a western re-education for China was a handicap. Not only were many educated and patriotic Chinese sincerely attached to the traditional culture, but western ideas were only sure of a ready welcome among the most untypical elements of Chinese society, the seaboard city-dwelling merchants and their student offspring, often educated abroad. The mass of Chinese could hardly be touched by such ideas and appeals, and the demand of other reformers for a vernacular literature was one evidence of this fact.

Insofar as they were touched by nationalist feeling the Chinese were likely to turn against the West and against the western-inspired capitalism which, for many of them, meant one more kind of exploitation and was the most obvious constituent of the civilization some modernizers urged them to adopt. But for the most part they were peasants and seemed after 1911 relapsed in passivity, apparently unmoved by events and unaware of the agitation of angry and westernized young men. They grew more miserable throughout the whole first half of this century. As the population steadily increased, nothing was done to meet the peasants' hunger for land; instead, the number of the endebted and landless grew, their wretched lives frequently made even more intolerable by war, whether directly, or through its concomitants, famine and disease. The Chinese Revolution would only be assured success when it could activate these people, and the cultural emphasis of the reformers sometimes masked an unwillingness to envisage the practical political steps necessary for this.

China's weakness remained Japan's opportunity. A world war was the occasion to push forward again her nineteenth-century policies; it was not only extreme nationalists who urged that the Europeans' quarrels with one another should be exploited. Japan's allies could hardly object to her seizure of the German ports in China; even if they had done, they could do nothing about it while they needed Japanese ships and manufactures. There was always the hope, too, that the Japanese might send their own army to Europe to fight, though nothing like this happened. Instead, the Japanese finessed by arousing fears that they might make a separate peace with the Germans and pressed ahead in China.

At the beginning of 1915 the Japanese government presented to China a list of twenty-one demands, following them up with an ultimatum. In their entirety they amounted to a proposal for a Japanese protectorate over China. The United Kingdom and United States did what diplomacy could do to have them reduced but, in the end, the Japanese got much of what they asked for. It included further confirmation of their special commercial and leasehold rights in Manchuria. Chinese patriots were enraged, but there was nothing they could do at a moment when their internal politics were in disorder. They were so confused, indeed, that Sun Yat-sen was himself at this moment seeking Japanese support.

The next intervention came in 1916, when Japanese pressure was brought to bear on the British to dissuade them from approving Yuan Shih-k'ai's attempt to restore stability by making himself emperor. In the following year came another treaty, this time extending the recognition of Japan's special interests as far as Inner Mongolia. In August 1917 the Chinese government went to war with Germany, partly in the hope of winning goodwill and support which would ensure her an independent voice at the peace, but only a few months later the United States formally recognized the special interests of Japan in China in return for endorsement of the principle of the 'Open Door' and a promise to maintain Chinese integrity and independence. All that the Chinese had got from the Allies was the ending of German and Austrian extra-territoriality and the concession that payment of Boxer indemnities to the Allies should be delayed. The Japanese, moreover, secured more concessions from China in secret agreements in 1917 and 1918.

Yet, when the peace came, it deeply disappointed both the great Asian powers of the future. Japan was now indisputably a world power; she had in 1918 the third largest navy in the world. It was true, too, that she won solid gains at the peace: she retained the former German rights in Shantung (promised to her by the British and French in 1917), was granted a mandate over many of the former German Pacific islands and was given a permanent seat on the Council of the League of Nations. But the gain in 'face' implied in such recognition was offset in Japanese eyes by a failure to have a declaration in favour of racial equality written into the Covenant of the League. The Chinese had much more to feel aggrieved about, for in spite of widespread sympathy over the Twenty-One Demands (notably in the United States) they were unable to obtain a reversal of the Shantung decision. Disappointed of American diplomatic support and crippled by the divisions within their own delegation between the representatives of the Peking government and those of the Kuomintang at Canton, the Chinese refused to sign the treaty.

An almost immediate consequence was a movement in China to which some commentators have given an importance as great as that of the 1911 revolution itself. This was the 'May 4th Movement' of 1919. It stemmed from a student demonstration in Peking against the peace, which had been planned for 7 May, the anniversary of China's acceptance of the 1915 demands, but was brought forward to anticipate action by the authorities. It escalated, though at first only into a small riot and the resignation of the head of the university. This then led to a nation-wide student movement (one of the first political reflexions of the widely spread establishment in China of new colleges and universities after 1911). This in turn spread to embrace others than students and to manifest itself in strikes and a boycott of Japanese goods. A movement which had begun with intellectuals and their pupils spread to include other city-dwellers, notably industrial workers and the new Chinese capitalists who had benefited from the war. It was the most important evidence yet seen of the mounting rejection of Europe by Asia.

For the first time, an industrial China entered the scene. China, like Japan, had an economic boom during the war. Though a decline in European imports to China had been partly offset by increased Japanese and American sales, Chinese entrepreneurs in the ports had found it profitable to invest in production for the home market. The first important industrial areas outside Manchuria began to appear. They belonged to progressive capitalists who sympathized with revolutionary ideas all the more when the return of peace brought renewed western competition and evidence that China had not earned her liberation from tutelage to the foreigner. The workers, too, felt this resentment: their jobs were threatened. Many of them were first-generation town-dwellers, drawn into the new industrial areas from the countryside by the promise of employment. An uprooting from the tenacious soil of peasant tradition was even more important in China than in Europe a century before. Family and village ties were especially strong in China. The migrant to the town broke with patriarchal authority and the reciprocal obligations of the independent producing unit, the household: this was a further great weakening of the age-old structure which had survived the revolution and still tied China to the past. New material was thus made available for new ideological deployments.

The May 4th Movement first showed what could be made of such forces as these by creating the first broadly based Chinese revolutionary coalition. Progressive western liberalism had not been enough and there was implicit in the movement's success the disappointment of the hopes of many of the cultural reformers. Capitalist western democracy had been shown up by the Chinese government's helplessness in the face of Japan. Now, that government had another humiliation from its own subjects: the boycott and demonstration forced it to release the arrested students and dismiss its pro-Japanese ministers. But this was not the only important consequence of the May 4th Movement. For all their limited political influence, reformers had for the first time, thanks to the students, broken through into the world of social action. This aroused enormous optimism and greater popular political awareness than ever before. This is the case for saying that contemporary Chinese history begins positively in 1919 rather than 1911.

Yet ultimately the explosion had come because of an Asian force, Japanese ambition. That force, not in itself a new one in China's affairs, was by 1919 operating on a China whose cultural tradition was dissolving fast. The ending of the examination system, the return of the westernized exiles and the great literacy and cultural debate of the war years had all pushed things too far for any return to the old stable state. With no effective heir to the imperial government, the era of the warlords provided no new authority to identify and sustain orthodoxy. And now even the great rival of the Confucian past, western liberalism, was under attack because of its association with the exploiting foreigner. Western liberalism had never had mass appeal; now its charm for intellectuals was threatened just as another rival ideological force had appeared on the scene. The Bolshevik revolution gave Marxism a homeland to which its adherents abroad could look for inspiration,

guidance, leadership and, sometimes, material support. This was a great new factor now introduced the world over into an already dissolving historical epoch, and bound to accelerate its end.

Both the February 1917 revolution and the Bolshevik victory had been warmly welcomed by one of the contributors to *New Youth*, Li Ta-chao, who was from 1918 librarian at Peking University. Soon he saw in Marxism the motive force of world revolution and the means to vitalize the Chinese peasantry. At that moment of disillusion with the West, Russia was very popular among Chinese students. It seemed that the successors of the Tsar had driven out the old imperialist Adam, for one of the first acts of the Soviet government had been a formal renunciation of all extra-territorial rights and jurisdictions enjoyed by the Tsarist state. In the eyes of the nationalists, Russia therefore, had, clean hands. Moreover, her revolution – a revolution in a great peasant society – claimed to be built upon a doctrine whose applicability to China seemed especially plausible in the wake of the industrialization provoked by the war. In 1918 there had begun to meet at Peking University a Marxist study society; one of its members was an assistant in the university library, Mao Tse-tung, and others were prominent in the May 4th Movement. By 1920 there was an outlet for Marxist ideas in one of the student magazines which expressed the aspirations of that movement and the first attempts had been successfully made to deploy Marxist and Leninist principles by organizing strikes in support of it.

Yet Marxism opened divisions between the reformers. Ch'en Tu-hsin himself turned to it as a solution for China's problems in 1920. He threw his energies into helping to organize the emerging Chinese Left around Marxism. The liberals were beginning to be left behind. The Comintern observed its opportunities and had sent its first man to China in 1919 to help Ch'en and Li Ta-chao. The effects were not entirely happy; there were quarrels. Nevertheless, in circumstances still obscure – we know precisely neither names nor dates – a Chinese

Communist party was formed by delegates from different parts of China in Shanghai in 1921 (Mao Tse-tung was among them).

So began the last stage of the Chinese Revolution and the latest twist of that curious dialectic which has run through the relations of Europe with Asia. Once more an alien western idea, Marxism, born and shaped in a society totally unlike the traditional societies of the East, embodying a background of assumptions whose origins were rooted in Judaeo-Christian culture, was taken up by an Asian people and put to their use. It was to be deployed not merely against the traditional sources of inertia in China, in the name of the western goals of modernization, efficiency and universal human dignity and equality, but against the source from which it, too, came – the European world.

Communism benefited enormously in China from the fact that capitalism could reasonably be seen as the unifying, connecting principle behind foreign exploitation and aggression. In the 1920s, China's divisions were thought to justify treating her as of little account in international affairs, though nine powers with Asiatic interests were got to guarantee her territorial integrity and Japan agreed to hand back former German territories in China which she had taken in the Great War. This was part of a complicated set of agreements made at Washington whose core was the international limitation on naval strength (there was great uneasiness about the cost of armaments); these in the end left Japan relatively stronger. The four major powers guaranteed one another's possessions, too, and this provided a decent burial for the Anglo-Japanese alliance, whose ending had long been sought by the Americans. But the guarantee to China, everyone knew, was worth no more than the preparedness of the Americans to fight to support it; the British had been obliged by the treaties *not* to build a naval base at Hong Kong. Meanwhile, foreigners continued to administer the customs and tax revenues on which the Peking government of an 'independent' China depended and foreign agents and businessmen dealt directly with the warlords when it suited

them. Though American policy had further weakened the European position in Asia, this was not apparent in China.

This is one reason why Marxism's appeal to intellectuals went far beyond the boundaries of the formal structure of the Chinese communist party. Sun Yat-sen stressed his doctrinal disagreement with it but adopted views which helped to carry the KMT away from conventional liberalism and in the direction of Marxism. In his view of the world, Russia, Germany and Asia had a common interest as exploited powers against their oppressors and enemies, the four imperialist powers (Germany was well regarded after she had undertaken in 1921 to place her relations with China on a completely equal footing). He coined a new expression, 'hypo-colony', for the state of affairs in which China was exploited without formal subordination as a dependency. His conclusion was collectivist: 'On no account must we give more liberty to the individual', he wrote; 'let us secure liberty instead for the nation.' This was to give new endorsement to the rejection of the ideal of individual liberty which had always been present in the classical Chinese outlook and tradition. The claims of family, clan and state on the individual had always been paramount and Sun Yat-sen envisaged a period of one-party rule in order to make possible mass indoctrination to reconfirm an attitude which had been in danger of corruption by western ideas.

There was apparent, then, no grave obstacle to the cooperation of the Chinese communist party (CCP) and KMT. The behaviour of the western powers and of the warlords provided common enemies and the Russian government helped to bring them together. Cooperation with the anti-imperialist power with which China had her longest land frontier seemed at least prudent and potentially very advantageous. The policy of the Comintern, for its part, favoured cooperation with the KMT in the interests of safeguarding Russian interests in Mongolia and constituting some kind of barrier to Japan. Russia had been left out of the

SOVIET UNION

REPUBLIC OF MONGOLIA
(1921)

INNER MONGOLIA
(1947)

MANCHUKUO
(1932)

MANCHURIA

JEHOL
(1933)

• Mukden

• Peking

SIN KIANG
(1955)

SHANSI

TIBET

Nanking

• Shanghai

Yiangtze Kiang

Chung
King

HUNAN

FUKIEN

KWANGSI

KUANTUNG

• Canton

• Hong Kong (British)

TAIWAN
(Nationalist China 1949)

KOREA

HAI NAN

Main areas of communist support before 1934

Areas occupied by Japanese 1937–1942

Area annexed and occupied by Japanese 1931–33

- - - - - Area of main Kuomintang strength 1927–37

——— The Long March of Mao Tse-Tung

Area of communist regrouping after 1932

– – – Territory occupied by Communists 1947–1949

China 1918—1949

Washington conferences, though no power had greater territorial interests in the Far East. For her, cooperation with the likely winners in China was an obvious course even if Marxist doctrine had not also fitted such a policy. From 1924 onwards the CCP was working with the KMT under Russian patronage, in spite of some doubts among Chinese communists. As individuals, though not as a party, they could belong to the KMT. Sun Yat-sen's able young soldier, Chiang K'ai-shek, was sent to Moscow for training and a military academy was founded in China to provide ideological as well as military instruction.

In 1925 Sun Yat-sen died; he had made communist cooperation with his followers easier, but the united front still endured. Sun Yat-sen's will (which Chinese schoolchildren learnt by heart) had said that the revolution was not yet complete and while the communists in certain provinces made important advances in winning peasant support for the revolution, the new revolutionary army led by idealistic young officers made headway against the warlords. By 1927 something of a semblance of unity had been restored to the country under the leadership of the KMT. Anti-imperialist feeling resulted in a successful boycott of British goods, which led the British government, alarmed by the evidence of growing Russian influence in China, to surrender its concessions at Hankow and Kiukiang. It had already promised to return Wei-hai-wei to China (1922) and the United States had renounced its share of the Boxer indemnity. Such successes added to signs that China was on the move at last.

One important aspect of this revolution long went unremarked. Theoretical Marxism stressed the indispensable revolutionary rôle of the industrial proletariat. The Chinese communists were proud of the progress they had made in politicizing the new urban workers, but the mass of Chinese were peasants. Still trapped in the Malthusian vice of rising numbers and land shortage, their centuries of suffering were, if anything, intensified by the breakdown of central authority in the warlord years. Some

A Chinese river police patrol at Canton, 1925, during the period of violent anti-British rioting.

Chinese communists saw in the peasants a revolutionary potential which, if not easy to reconcile with contemporary Marxist orthodoxy (as retailed by the Moscow theorists), none the less embodied Chinese reality. One of them was Mao Tse-tung. He and those who agreed with him turned their attention away from the cities to the countryside in the early 1920s and began an unprecedented effort to win over the rural masses to Communism. Paradoxically, Mao seems to have continued to cooperate with the Kuomintang longer than other Chinese Communists just because it was more sympathetic to the organization of the peasants than was his own party.

A great success followed. It was especially marked in Honan, but altogether some ten million or so peasants and their families were by 1927 organized by the communists. 'In a few months', wrote Mao, 'the peasants have accomplished what Dr Sun Yat-sen wanted, but failed, to accomplish in the forty years he devoted to the national revolution'. Organization made possible the removal of many of the ills which beset the peasants. Landlords were not dispossessed, but their rents were often reduced. Usurious rates of interest were brought down to reasonable levels. Rural revolution had eluded all previous progressive movements in China and was stigmatized by Mao as the failure of the 1911 revolution; the communist success in reaching this goal was based on the discovery that it could be brought about by using the revolutionary potential of the peasants themselves. This had enormous significance for the future, for it implied new possibilities of historical development throughout Asia. Mao grasped this and revalued urban revolution accordingly. 'If we allot ten points to the democratic revolution', he wrote, 'then the achievements of the urban dwellers and the military units rate only three points, while the remaining seven points should go to the peasants in their rural revolution.' In an image twice-repeated in a report on the Honan movement he compared the peasants to an elemental force; 'the attack is just like a tempest or hurricane; those who submit to it survive, those who resist perish'. Even the image is significant; here was something rooted deeply in Chinese tradition and the long struggle against landlords and bandits. If the communists tried hard to set tradition aside by eradicating superstition and breaking family authority, they nevertheless drew upon it, too.

Communism's rural lodgement was the key to its survival in the crisis which overtook its relations with the KMT after Sun Yat-sen's death. Sun's removal permitted a rift to open in the KMT between a 'left' and a 'right' wing. The young Chiang, who had been seen as a progressive, now emerged as the military representative of the 'right', which reflected mainly the interests of capitalists and, indirectly, landlords. Differences within the KMT over strategy were resolved when Chiang, confident of his control of his troops, committed them to destroying the left factions and the communist party's organization in the cities. This was accomplished with much bloodshed in Shanghai and Nanking in 1927, under the eyes of contingents of European and American soldiers who had been sent to

The strong man of a new China, as Chiang K'ai-shek appeared in the 1920s.

China to protect the concessions. The CCP was proscribed, but this was not quite the end of its cooperation with the KMT, which continued in a few areas for some months, largely because of Russian unwillingness to break with Chiang. Russian direction had already helped towards the destruction of the city communists; the Comintern in China, as elsewhere, myopically pursued what were believed to be Russian interests refracted through the mirror of dogmatic Marxism. These interests were for Stalin in the first place domestic; in external affairs, he wanted someone in China who could stand up to the British, the greatest imperialist power, and the KMT seemed the best bet for that. Theory fitted these choices; the bourgeois revolution had to precede the proletarian, according to Marxist orthodoxy. Only after the triumph of the KMT was clear did the Russians withdraw their advisers from the CCP, which gave up open politics to become a subversive, underground organization. Chinese nationalism had in fact done well out of Russian help even if the CCP had not.

Nevertheless, the KMT was left with grave problems and a civil war on its hands at a time when the revolution needed to satisfy mass demands if it was to survive. The split within the revolution was in fact a setback, making it impossible to dispose finally of the warlord

Chinese Nationalist soldiers setting out on an
expedition against Communist forces in the 1930s.

problem and, more serious, weakening the anti-foreign front – above all against Japan whose pressure had continued in the 1920s after the temporary setback of handing back Kiao-chou. Its domestic background was changing in an important way. When the wartime economic boom finally ended in 1920 hard times and growing social strains followed. At the end of the decade came the onset of the world economic depression. By 1931, half Japan's factories were idle; a shattering effect on the Japanese economy had been produced by the collapse of European colonial markets. Exports of manufactures went down by two-thirds and the importance of Japan's outlets on the Asian

mainland was now crucial. Anything that seemed to threaten them provoked intense irritation. Above all, the position of the Japanese peasant deteriorated, millions being ruined or selling their daughters into prostitution in order to survive. Grave political consequences were soon manifest though (unlike the European response) less in the intensification of class conflict than in the provocation of nationalist extremism. The forces which were to pour into this had for a long time been absorbed in the struggle against the 'unequal treaties'. With those out of the way, a new outlet was needed, though anti-western feeling continued (and the harsh operation of industrial capitalism in times of depression provided it with fresh fuel).

There was a traditional and obvious one in

943

Asian expansion. The circumstances seemed propitious. The western colonial powers were clearly on the defensive, if not in full retreat. The Dutch faced rebellions in Java and Sumatra in the 1920s, the French a Vietnamese revolt in 1930; in both places there was the sinister novelty of communist help to nationalist rebels. The British were not in quite such difficulties in India. Yet though some Englishmen were not yet reconciled to the idea that India must move towards self-government, it was the proclaimed aim of British policy. In China the British had already shown in the 1920s that they wanted only a quiet accommodation with a nationalist movement they found hard to assess and not too grave a loss of face. Their Far Eastern policies looked even feebler after economic collapse which also knocked the stuffing out of American opposition to Japan. Finally, Russian power, too, seemed in eclipse after its attempt to influence events in China. Chinese nationalism, on the contrary, had won notable successes, showed no sign of retreat and was considered to be

A British comment on Japanese respect for the League of Nations just after the seizure of Manchuria. Later in the year Japan withdrew from the League after an adverse report on the Manchuria affair by League commissioners; many Japanese felt that their case had not been considered fairly at Geneva.

beginning to threaten the long-established Japanese presence in Manchuria. All these factors were present in the calculations made by Japanese statesmen as the depression deepened.

Manchuria was the crucial theatre. The Japanese presence there went back to 1905. Heavy investment had followed. At first the Chinese acquiesced, but in the 1920s began to question it, with support from the Russians who foresaw danger from the Japanese pushing their influence towards Inner Mongolia. In 1929 the Chinese in fact came into conflict with the Russians over control of the railway which ran across Manchuria and was the most direct route to Vladivostok, but this can only have impressed

China 1932. Under the gaze of the languid sirens of Westernized film posters, Japanese sailors and marines man a strongpoint. Identification markers are laid out on the ground for the benefit of the Japanese air force.

the Japanese with the new vigour of Chinese power; the nationalist KMT was reasserting itself in the territories of the old empire. There had been armed conflict in 1928 when the Japanese had tried to prevent KMT soldiers from operating against warlords in north China whom they found it convenient to patronize. Finally, the Japanese government was by no means unambiguously in control on the spot. Effective power rested in Manchuria with the commanders of the Japanese forces there and when in 1931 they organized an incident near Mukden which they used as an excuse for taking over the whole province, those in Tokyo who wished to restrain them could not do so.

There followed the setting up of a new puppet state, Manchukuo (ruled by the last Manchu emperor), an outcry at the League of Nations against Japanese aggression, assassinations in Tokyo, the establishment there of a government much more under military influence, and the expansion of the quarrel with China. In 1932 the Japanese replied to a Chinese boycott of their goods by landing at Shanghai; in the following year they invaded Jehol, crossing the Great Wall to impose a peace which left Japan dominating a part of historic China itself and trying unsuccessfully to organize a secessionist north China. There matters stood until 1937 when there opened the 'China incident' and with it the first campaigns of the Second World War.

The KMT government thus proved unable, after all, to resist imperialist aggression. Yet from its new capital, Nanking, it appeared to control successfully all save a few border areas. It continued to whittle away at the treaties of inferiority and was helped by the fact that as the western powers saw in it a means of opposing communism in Asia, they began to show themselves somewhat more accommodating. These achievements, considerable though they were, none the less masked important weaknesses which compromised the KMT's domestic success. The crux was that though the political revolution might have continued, the social revolution had come to a stop. Intellectuals withdrew their moral support from a régime which had not provided reforms of which a need to do something about land was the most pressing. The peasants had never given the KMT their allegiance as some of them had given it to the communists. Unfortunately for the régime, Chiang fell back more and more at this juncture upon direct government through his officers and showed himself more and more conservative at a time when the traditional culture had decayed beyond repair. The régime was tainted with corruption in the public finances, often at the highest level. The foundations of the new China were therefore insecure. And there was once more a rival waiting in the wings.

The central leadership of the CCP for some time continued to hope for urban insurrection; in the provinces, none the less, individual communist leaders continued to work along the lines indicated by Mao in Honan. They dispossessed absentee landlords and organized local soviets, a shrewd appreciation of the value of the traditional peasant hostility to central government. By 1930 they had done better than this, by organizing an army in Kiangsi, where a Chinese Soviet Republic ruled fifty million people, or claimed to. In 1932 the CCP leadership abandoned Shanghai to join Mao in this sanctuary. KMT efforts were directed towards destroying this army, but always without success. This meant fighting on a second front at a time when Japanese pressure was strongest. The last great KMT effort had a partial success, it is true, for it forced the communists out of their sanctuary, thus forcing on them the 'Long March' to Shenshi which began in 1934, the epic of the Chinese Revolution and the inspiration of Mao's followers ever since. Once there they were safe; the demands of resistance to the Japanese prevented the KMT from doing more.

Consciousness of the external danger explains why there were tentative essays in cooperation between the CCP and KMT again in the later 1930s. They owed something, too, to another change in the policies of the Comintern; it was an era of 'Popular Fronts' elsewhere which allied communists with other parties. The KMT was also obliged to mute its anti-western line and this won it a certain amount of easy sympathy in England and, above all, the United States. But neither the cooperation of communists nor the sympathies of western liberals could prevent the nationalist régime from being forced on the defensive when the Japanese launched their attack in 1937.

This was the opening of eight years' fighting which did enormous social and physical damage to China. At the end of 1937 the government removed itself for safety's sake to Chungking in the far west. There it watched the Japanese occupy all the important northern and coastal areas. League condemnation of Japan and Russian deliveries of aircraft seemed equally unable to stem the onslaught. The only bonus in the first black years was an unprecedented degree of patriotic unity in China; communists and nationalists alike saw that the national revolution was at stake. This was the view of the Japanese, too; significantly, in the area they occupied, they encouraged the re-establishment of Confucianism. Meanwhile, the western powers felt deplorably unable to intervene. Their protests, even on behalf of their own citizens, were brushed aside by the Japanese who by 1939 made it clear that they were prepared to blockade the foreign settlements if recognition of the Japanese new order in Asia was not forthcoming. For British and French weakness there was an obvious explanation: they had troubles enough elsewhere. American ineffectiveness had deeper roots; it went back to a long-established fact that however the United States might talk about mainland Asia, Americans would not fight for it, perhaps wisely. When the Japanese bombed and sank an American gunboat near Nanking the State Department

*A Kuomintang propaganda poster of 1938
encouraging civilians to assist the armed forces
in their resistance to the Japanese.*

huffed and puffed but eventually swallowed
Japanese 'explanations'. It was all very different
from what had happened to the USS *Maine* in
Havana harbour forty years before, though the
Americans did send supplies to Chiang Kai-
shek.

By 1941, China was all but cut off from the
outside world. At the end of that year her
struggle would at last be merged with a world
war, but by then much damage had been done
to her. In the long duel between the potential
Asian rivals, Japan was so far clearly the
winner. On the debit side of Japan's account
had to be placed the economic cost of the
struggle to her and the increasing difficulty
experienced by her occupying forces in China.
On the other hand, her international position
had never seemed stronger; she showed it by
humiliating western residents in China and by
forcing the British in 1940 to close the Burma
Road by which supplies reached China, and the
French to admit an occupying army to Indo-
China. Here was a temptation to further adven-

ture, and it was not likely to be resisted while the
prestige of the military and their power in
government remained as high as it had been
since the mid-1930s.

Yet there was also a negative side to this.
Aggression made it more and more imperative
to seize the economic resources of south-east
Asia and Indonesia. Yet it also slowly prepared
the Americans psychologically for armed defence
of their interest. It was clear by 1941 that the
United States would, before long, have to
decide whether it was to be an Asian power at
all and what that might mean. In the background
of all this, too, lay one of the most important
effects of all. For all her aggression against
China, it was with the window-dressing slogan
of 'Asia for the Asians' that Japan advanced on
the crumbling western position in Asia. Just as
the defeat of the Tsar in 1905 marked an epoch
in the psychological relations of Europe and
Asia, so did the independence and power which
Japan showed in 1938–41. When followed by
conquest of the European empires, as it was to
be, it would signal the beginning of the era of
decolonialization; this was to be fittingly inaugurated by the one Asian power at that time
successful in its 'westernization'.

4 The Ottoman heritage and the western Islamic lands

During the nineteenth century the Ottoman empire all but disappeared in Europe and Africa. The basic causes were the same in each place; the disintegrating effect of nationalism and the predatory interest of European powers. The Serbian revolt of 1804 and Mehemet Ali's establishment of himself as the governor of Egypt in 1805 together opened the final though drawn-out era of Turkish decline. In Europe the next step was the Greek revolt; from that time the story of the Ottoman empire in Europe can be told in the dates of the establishment of new nations, until in 1914, Turkey was left with only eastern Thrace.

In Islamic Africa the decline of Ottoman power had by then gone even further, but, since much of North Africa was virtually independent of the Porte early in the nineteenth century, nationalism was usually directed more against Europeans than against the Ottomans. It was also a culturally revolutionary force. Islam had not been so stimulated by new ideas and forms since the seventh century, and the

In 1906 – nearly twenty-five years after a British force had arrived in Egypt for what was believed to be a temporary occupation – men of the Lancashire Fusiliers were photographed on an outing to Giza. The British presence in Egypt was one of the curiosities of modern imperialism, for there was no attempt to make Egypt a colony. Yet the presence of the Suez Canal made British governments determined not to withdraw before they had to.

story again begins with Mehemet Ali. Though he himself never went further west than his birthplace, Kavalla, he admired European civilization and thought Egypt could learn from it. He imported technical instructors, employed foreign consuls in the direction of health and sanitation measures, printed translations of European books and papers on technical subjects, and sent boys to study in France and England. Yet he was working against the grain. His practical achievements disappointed him though he opened Egypt to European influence as never before. Most of this influence was French and flowed through educational and technical institutions. This in part reflected an old French interest in the trade and affairs of the Ottoman empire which was also marked linguistically; French was the second language of educated Egyptians. Soon, there grew up a large French community in Alexandria, one of the great cosmopolitan cities of the Mediterranean.

Few modernizing statesmen in the non-European world have been able to confine their borrowings from the West to technical knowledge. Some young Egyptians began to pick up political ideas; there were plenty of them available in French, too. A compost was forming which would in the end help to transform Europe's relations with Egypt. Egyptians would draw the same lesson as Indians, Japanese and Chinese: the European disease had to be caught in order to generate the necessary antibodies against it. Modernization and nationalism became inextricably intertwined. Here lay the

The Post-Ottoman Middle East

Constantinople
Ankara
TURKEY
(Republic 1923)
CYPRUS
(Br. Prot. 1878,
annexed 1914)
SYRIA
(Fr. Mandate 1920)
LEBANON
Beirut (Fr. Mandate 1920)
Damascus
Baghdad
PALESTINE
(Br. Mandate 1920)
IRAQ
(Br. Mandate 1920)
Tel-Aviv
Jerusalem
KUWAIT
(Br. prot. 1899)
TRANS-JORDAN
(Br. Mandate 1920)
Cairo
Aqaba
Bahrain
MEDITERRANEAN SEA
EGYPT
(Br. Prot. 1914
Kingdom 1922)
OMAN
(Br. Prot. 1891)
Medina
KINGDOM OF HEJAZ AND NEJAL (1926),
later Saudi Arabia (1932)
RED SEA
Mecca
ASIR (1926)
ANGLO-EGYPTIAN
SUDAN
YEMEN
(Kingdom 1919)
HADHRAMAUT
(Br. Prot. 1888)
ADEN
(Br. 1839)
Ottoman Empire until 1918
Turkey after Treaty of Lausanne (1923)
ABYSSINIA

origin of a curious weakness in Middle Eastern nationalism. It was long to be the creed of an advanced élite cut off from a society whose masses lived in an Islamic culture still largely uncorroded by western ideas. Paradoxically, the nationalists were usually the most European-ized members of Egyptian, Syrian and Lebanese societies and this was true until well into the twentieth century.

Another landmark was the opening of the Suez Canal in 1869. This did more (though in-

directly) than any other single fact to doom Egypt to intervention and therefore increasing irritation by the foreigner. Yet the Canal was not the immediate cause of the first intervention of Europeans in Egypt's government since 1798. It came about because of the actions of Ismail, the first ruler of Egypt to obtain from the sultan the title of khedive. He had been educated in France, liked Frenchmen and up-to-date ideas, and travelled much in Europe. He was very extravagant. Fortunately, when he became ruler, in 1863, the price of cotton, Egypt's main export, was high because of the American Civil War. Ismail's financial prospects therefore looked good. Unhappily, his financial management was less than orthodox. The results were to be seen in the rise in the Egyptian national debt; £7 000 000 at Ismail's accession, it stood at nearly £100 000 000 thirteen years later. The interest charges amounted to £5 000 000 a year in an age when such sums still mattered. In 1876 the Egyptian government was bankrupt and ceased to pay its debts.

The outcome was the management of Egypt by foreigners; two controllers, one British, one French, were installed to make sure that Egypt was governed by Ismail's son with the priority of keeping up revenue and paying off the debt. They were soon blamed by nationalists for the huge burdens of taxation laid upon the Egyptian poor in order to provide the revenue to pay interest on Ismail's loans. They were also (correctly) blamed for economies, such as the reduction of the army and reducing salaries of officials. The European financial officials who worked in the name of the khedive were, in the nationalists' eyes, the agents of foreign imperialism. There was growing resentment of the privileged legal position of the many foreigners in Egypt and their special courts.

These grievances led to the formation of nationalist political groups and eventually to revolution. As well as the westernizing xenophobes there were a few who began to urge the reform of Islam, the unity of the Moslem world and a pan-Islamic movement adapted to modern life. Some took a more local view, antagonized by the preponderance of Turks in the khedive's entourage. But such divisions mattered less than British intervention in frustrating a revolution in 1882. That intervention took place not for financial reasons, but because British policy, even under a Liberal prime minister who favoured nationalism in other parts of the Ottoman empire, could not accept the danger that the security of the Canal route to India might be jeopardized by an unfriendly government at Cairo. It was unthinkable at the time, but British soldiers were to remain in the Canal Zone until 1955.

After 1882 the British became the prime targets of nationalist hatred in Egypt. They were soon bogged down there, too. Though they asserted that they wanted to withdraw as soon as a dependable government was available, they could not do so for none acceptable to them was conceivable. Instead, British administrators took more and more of a share in the government of Egypt. This was not wholly regrettable inasmuch as they reduced the debt, carried out irrigation schemes which made it possible to feed a growing population (it doubled to about twelve million between 1880 and 1914), but they antagonized Egyptians by keeping them out of government service, by maintaining high taxes and by being in their country at all. After 1900 there was growing unrest and violence. The British and the puppet Egyptian government proceeded firmly against agitation, but also sought a way out through reform. At first administrative, this led in 1913 to a new constitution providing for much more representative elections to a more powerful legislative assembly. Unfortunately, the assembly could only meet for a few months before it was suspended at the outbreak of war. The Egyptian government was pushed into war with Turkey, a khedive suspected of anti-British plotting was replaced, and at the end of the year the British proclaimed a protectorate. The khedive now took the title of sultan.

By then, the Ottoman government had also lost Tripolitania to the Italians, who attacked that dependency in 1911 partly because of another manifestation of reforming nationalism, in Turkey itself. In 1907 a successful rebellion had been started there by the Young Turk movement, which had a complicated history, but a simple purpose. As one of the Young Turks once put it: 'we follow the path traced by Europe . . . even in our refusal to accept foreign intervention'. The first part of this meant that they sought constitutional and liberal government. They wished to end the despotic rule of Abdul Hamid and restore a liberal constitution granted in 1876 and subsequently withdrawn. But they wanted this less for its own sake than because they thought it would revive and reform the empire, making possible the modernization which would arrest the process of decay. Both this programme and the Young Turks' methods of conspiracy owed much to Europe; they used, for example, masonic lodges as cover and organized secret societies such as those which had flourished among European liberals in the days of the Holy Alliance. But they much resented the increasing interference in the internal affairs of the empire by Europeans, notably in the management of finance, for, as in Egypt, the securing of interest on money lent for internal development had been followed by loss of independence. European bullying had also resulted (they felt) in the Ottoman government's long and humiliating retreat in the Danube valley and the Balkans.

After a series of mutinies and revolts, the sultan gave way in 1908 over the constitution. Liberals abroad smiled on constitutional Turkey; it seemed that misrule was at last to end. But an attempted counter-revolution led to a Young Turk *coup* which deposed Abdul Hamid and installed a virtual dictatorship. From 1909 to 1914 the revolutionaries ruled with increasingly dictatorial means from behind the façade of constitutional monarchy.

When we look back at them, the Young Turks seem more comprehensible than they were at the time. Essentially, they faced problems faced later by many modernizers in non-European countries and their violent methods have been emulated by many since from necessity or imagined necessity. They threw themselves into reform of every branch of government (importing many European advisers). But they took power in the middle of a shattering succession of humiliations in foreign affairs which weakened their appeal and led them to rely on force. After the annexation of Bosnia, the ruler of Bulgaria won an acknowledgement of Bulgarian independence, and the Cretans announced their union with Greece. After a brief pause there came the Italian attack on Tripoli, then the Balkan Wars.

Under such strain, it soon became apparent that the unity among the peoples of a reformed empire on which liberalism had relied was a chimera. Religion, language, social custom, nationality still fragmented even what was left of the empire. The Young Turks were driven back more and more upon the assertion of one nationalism among many, that of the Ottomans. This, of course, led to resentment among other peoples. The result was renewed massacre, tyranny and assassination, the time-honoured instruments of rule at the Porte; from 1913 they were deployed by a triumvirate of Young Turks who ruled as a collective dictatorship until the outbreak of the war.

Though they had disappointed many of their admirers, these men had the future on their side. They represented the ideas which would one day remake the Ottoman heritage: nationalism and modernization. They had even – willy-nilly – done something towards this by losing most of the little that was left of the Ottoman empire in Europe, thus releasing themselves from a burden. But their heritage was still too encumbering in 1914. Before them lay no better alternative as a vehicle for reform than nationalism. How little pan-Islamic ideas would mean was to be shown by what happened after 1914 in the largest remaining block of Ottoman territory, the largely Moslem provinces of Asia.

In 1914 these covered a large and strategically very important area. From the Caucasus the frontiers with Persia ran down to the Gulf near Basra, at the mouth of the Tigris. On the southern shore of the Gulf Turkish rule ran round Kuwait and then back to the coast as far south as Qatar. From here the coasts of Arabia right round to the entrance of the Red Sea were in one way or another under British influence, but the whole interior and Red Sea coast were Ottoman. Under British pressure the Sinai desert had been surrendered to Egypt a few years before, but the ancient lands of Palestine, Syria and Mesopotamia were still all Turkish. This was the heartland of historical Islam, and the sultan was still caliph, its spiritual leader. Yet this heritage, too, was to crumble as the strategy and politics of world war played upon it bringing about in the end a revolutionary disruption as complete as that which had destroyed the Ottoman Europe.

In some of these lands, too, there had been signs before 1914 that nationalist forces were at work. In part, this was a matter of the old-established European cultural influences which operated in Syria and the Lebanon much more strongly than in Egypt. French influence was predominant, but it had been joined by American missionary efforts which led to the foundation of schools and colleges to which there came Arab boys, both Moslem and Christian, from all over the Arab world. The Levant was culturally advanced and there was wide literacy. On the eve of the world war over a hundred Arabic newspapers were published in the Ottoman empire outside Egypt.

An important crystallization of Arab nationalism occurred with the triumph of the Young Turks and their Ottomanizing tendencies. Secret societies and open groups of dissidents were formed among Arab exiles, notably in Paris and Cairo. In the background was another uncertain factor: the rulers of the Arabian peninsula whose allegiance to the sultan was shaky. The most important of them was Hussein, Sherif of Mecca, in whom by 1914 the Turkish government had no confidence. There had also been the ominous sign of a meeting of Arabs in 1913 in Persia to consider the independence of Iraq. Against this, the Turks could really only hope for benefit from the divisiveness of the different interests represented among the Arabs.

Finally, although it was in no sense an immediate danger, the latest converts to the religion of nationalism were the Jews. Their history had taken a new turn when, in 1897, there appeared a Zionist Congress whose aim was the securing of a national home in Palestine. Thus, in the long history of Jewry, assimilation, barely achieved in many European countries, was now replaced as an ideal by territorial nationalism. Jewish immigration to Palestine had begun, though still on a small scale. The unrolling of the war was to change its significance.

Curious parallels exist between the Ottoman and Habsburg empires in 1914. Both sought war, seeing it, in part, as a solution to their problems. Yet both were likely to suffer from war, because too many people inside and outside their borders saw in it an opportunity to score at their expense. In the end, too, both were destroyed by it. Perhaps at the outset only Russia was obviously presented with an opportunity by Turkey's entry to the war. For her, there appeared the chance of at last gaining the great prize of Constantinople; the long opposition of the British and French to this evaporated. The French, in any case, had their own fish to fry in the Middle Eastern pan. Though their irritation over the British presence in Egypt had subsided somewhat with the making of the *entente* and a free hand for France in Morocco, there was a tradition of a special French presence in the Levant. The evocations of St Louis and the Crusaders with which some French Middle Eastern enthusiasts made play did not have to be taken seriously, but it was undeniable that the French had for a hundred years exercised a special protection of Catholicism in the Ottoman empire – and this was important in Syria, to which a French army had gone in the 1860s. There was also the cultural predominance evinced by the wide use of the French language by educated men in the Levant, and much French capital invested there. These were not forces which could be overlooked.

Nevertheless, in 1914 the main antagonists of Turkey outside Europe were likely to be Russia, in the Caucasus, and Great Britain, at Suez. The defence of the Canal was still the foundation of British strategic thinking in the area. In the event, it soon became clear that no great danger from the Turk threatened it. Early in 1915 when an attempt to force the Dardanelles by combined naval and land operations began, policy towards Turkey could take into account other possibilities. Two events had by then taken place which announced the appearance of the new factors which would in the end turn the Middle and Near East upside-down. At the end of 1914 an Indian-British army landed at Basra to safeguard oil supplies from Persia. This was the beginning of the interplay of oil and politics in the historical destiny of this area, though it was not to show itself very prominently until well after the Ottoman empire had ceased to exist. An approach which the British governor of Egypt made to Hussein of Mecca in October 1914, on the other hand, bore fruit very quickly. This was the start of the use of the weapon of Arab nationalism beyond Egypt.

The attraction of striking a blow against Germany's ally became all the greater as fighting went on bloodily but indecisively in Europe (this was one of the reasons for the Dardanelles expedition). Thus Europe's civil war once more set in train forces one day to be turned against her. But there was a limit to what could be offered for Arab allies. Terms were not agreed with Hussein until the beginning of 1916. He had demanded independence for all the Arab lands south of a line running along the 37th degree of latitude – this was about eighty miles north of a line from Aleppo to Mosul and included, in effect, the whole of the Ottoman empire outside the borders of Kurdistan. It was much more than the British could take at the gallop. The French had to be consulted, too, because of their special interest in Syria. When an agreement was made between the British and French on spheres of influence in a partitioned Ottoman empire it left many questions still unsettled for the future, including the status of Iraq.

The future of such undertakings was soon in doubt. The Arab revolt began in June 1916 with an attack on the Turkish garrison of Medina. The rising was never to be more than a distraction but it became a legend and prospered. Soon the British felt they must take the Arabs more seriously; Hussein was recognized as king of the Hejaz. Their own troops pressed forwards in 1917 into Palestine, taking Jerusalem. In 1918 they were to enter Damascus together with the Arabs. Before this, though, two other events had further complicated the situation. One was the American entry to the war; President Wilson favoured 'an absolute unmolested opportunity of development' for the non-Turks of the Ottoman empire in a statement of American war aims. The other was the Bolshevik publication of their predecessors' secret diplomacy; this revealed Anglo-French proposals for spheres of influence in the Middle East. One part of this agreement had been that Palestine should be administered internationally and a further irritant was added when British policy was declared to be in favour of the establishment of a national home in Palestine for the Jewish people. The 'Balfour Declaration' which said this can be accounted the greatest success of Zionism down to this time. It was not necessarily incompatible with what had been said to the Arabs, and President Wilson had joined in the good work by introducing to it qualifications to protect those who were not Jews, but it is almost inconceivable that it could have operated unchallenged even had not yet further British and French expressions of goodwill towards Arab aspirations followed in 1918. The result was a thoroughly confused situation on the morrow of Turkish defeat.

Hussein was at that moment recognized as King of the Arab peoples by Great Britain, but this did little for him. It was outside forces – primarily British and French, but soon the League of Nations, too, which, rather than Arab nationalism, were to lay out the main lines of the map of the modern Arab world, and it was not until the 1930s that they were complete. There was a confused decade in which the British and French became embroiled with the Arabs whom they had themselves conjured on to the stage of world politics, while the Arab leaders quarrelled among themselves. Islamic unity had now once more disappeared but, mercifully, so had the Russian threat (even if only briefly), so only two great powers were involved in the Middle East. The British and French distrusted one another, but could agree, roughly on the basis that if the British had their way in Iraq, the French could have theirs in Syria. This was legitimized subsequently by the League of Nations awarding three mandates to

*Three makers of the post-Ottoman Middle East:
General Allenby, the former British commander
in the Palestine campaign, King Feisal and
the British Prime Minister, Lloyd George,
photographed in London in 1919.*

them for Arab lands. Palestine, Transjordan and
Iraq went to the British and Syria to the French,
who governed high-handedly from the start,
having to instal themselves by force after a
national congress had asked for independence or
a British or American mandate. They evicted
the king the Arabs had chosen, Hussein's son.
Subsequently they had to face a full-scale insurrection. The French were still holding their own
by force in the 1930s, though there were by then
signs that they would concede some power to
the nationalists. Unfortunately, the Syrian
situation soon also showed the dangers of
nationalism in the Near East, when the Kurdish
people of north Syria revolted against the prospect of submergence in an Arab state.

The Arabian peninsula was meanwhile
racked by a struggle between Hussein and yet
another king with whom the British had negotiated a treaty. (His followers, to make things
more difficult still, were Wahabi Moslems;

members of a puritanical sect who added religious to dynastic and tribal conflict). Hussein
was displaced and the new kingdom of Saudi
Arabia emerged in 1932 in the place of the
Hejaz. From this flowed other problems, for sons
of Hussein were by this time kings of Iraq and
Transjordan. After heavy fighting had shown
the difficulties ahead, the British had moved as
fast as they dared towards the ending of the
Mandate over Iraq, seeking only to secure
British strategic interests. This was done by
preserving a military and air force presence. In
1932, accordingly, Iraq entered the League as
an independent and fully sovereign state.
Earlier, Transjordan had been recognized as
independent by the British in 1928, again with
some retention of military and financial powers.

Palestine was the most difficult problem.
From 1921 onwards, when there were anti-
Jewish riots by Arabs alarmed over Jewish
immigration and Jewish acquisition of Arab
land, that unhappy country was never to be long
at peace. More was at stake than merely religious
or national feeling. Jewish immigration was
bound to mean the irruption of a new westernizing and modernizing force, its operation changing economic relationships and imposing new
demands on a traditional society. The British
mandatory power was caught between the outcry of Arabs if it did not restrict Jewish immigration, and the outcry of Jews if it did. Furthermore, Arab governments now had to be taken
into account, and they occupied lands economically and strategically important to British
security. World opinion was becoming involved,
too. The question became more inflamed than
ever when there came to power in Germany in
1933 a régime which persecuted the Jews and
began to take away the legal and social gains they
had been making since the French Revolution.
By 1937 there were pitched battles between
Jews and Arabs in Palestine and a British army
was engaged in containing an Arab insurrection.

The collapse of the paramount power in the
Arab lands had at many times in the past been
followed by a period of disorder. What was
unclear this time was whether this would be

955

followed – as earlier periods of anarchy had eventually been – by the establishment of a new imperial hegemony. The British at least did not want that rôle; after a brief spell of imperial intoxication in the aftermath of victory, they desired only to secure their own fundamental interests in the area, the protection of the Suez Canal and the swelling flow of oil from Iraq and Iran. Between 1918 and 1934 a great pipeline had been built from northern Iraq across Transjordania and Palestine to Haifa, this giving yet another new twist to the future of these territories. The consumption of oil in Europe was not yet so large that there was any general dependence on this supply at this time, nor had the great discoveries been made which would again change the political position in the 1950s. But a new factor was making itself felt; the

One minor but real operational success achieved by British imperial power between the two great wars was the cheap and humane policing of large areas of the Arab Middle East by air-power and motor cars. Much of Iraq, Transjordan and Palestine (where this picture was taken) was controlled by relatively small numbers of men of the Royal Air Force, who operated armoured car patrols as well as aircraft.

Royal Navy had turned over to oil for its ships.

The British believed Suez to be secured best by a force in Egypt, but this caused increasing trouble. The war had brought a great growth of national feeling. Armies of occupation are never popular; when wartime sent up prices the foreigner was blamed. Some of the Egyptian nationalist leaders had attempted in 1919 to put their case to the Paris Peace Conference but were prevented from doing so; there followed a rising against the British which was quickly put down. But the British were on the retreat in Egypt, too. The protectorate was ended in 1922 in the hope of getting ahead of nationalist feeling. Yet the new kingdom of Egypt had an electoral system which returned nationalist majority after nationalist majority, thus making it impossible for an Egyptian government to come to terms which any British government would find acceptable. The result was a prolonged constitutional crisis and intermittent disorder until in 1936 the British finally agreed to be content with a right to garrison the Canal Zone for a limited number of years. An end was also announced to the jurisdictional privileges of foreigners.

The British concession was part of a general imperial withdrawal which can be detected elsewhere after 1918; it was also a reflexion of an overstretching of power and resources, as British foreign policy began to be preoccupied by other challenges. Such changes in the world relationships of individual powers were important external influences on post-Ottoman developments in Islamic lands. Another novel but less important one was communism. During the whole of the years between the wars, Russian radio broadcasting to the Arab countries supported the work of the first Arab communists. But for all the worry this caused, communism showed no sign of being able to displace the strongest revolutionary influence of the area, that of Arab nationalism, whose focus came by 1938 to be Palestine. In that year a great congress was held in Syria to support the Arab case there. Arab resentment of the brutality of the French in Syria was beginning to be evident, too, as well as an Arab response to the outcry of the Egyptian nationalists against the British. In pan-Arab feeling lay a force which might override in the end the divisions of the Hashemite Kingdoms.

Allied agreements during the war also complicated the history of the Ottoman homeland. The British, French, Greeks and Italians had all

The first oil well operating in Iraq on the day of its inauguration, 14 October 1927, an event as symbolic of a new historical era for the Middle East as the collapse of the Ottoman empire.

agreed on their shares of the booty in Turkey; the only simplification brought by the war had been the elimination of the Russian claim to Constantinople and the Straits. Faced with Greek and Italian invasion, the sultan signed a ludicrously humiliating peace. Greece was given large concessions, Armenia was to be an independent state while what was left of Turkey was divided into British, French and Italian spheres of influence. This was the most blatant imperialism. As if to make the point European financial control was re-established together with the humiliating capitulations.

The result was a resistance movement and thereafter the first successful revision of any part of the peace settlement. It was largely the work of one man, a former Young Turk and an outstanding soldier, Mustafa Kemal, who drove out French and Greeks in turn after frightening away the Italians. With Bolshevik help he crushed the Armenians. The British decided to negotiate and so a second treaty was made in 1923. It was a triumph of nationalism over the decisions at Paris, and it was the only part of the peace settlement which was negotiated between equals and not imposed on the defeated. It was also the only one in which Russian negotiators took part and lasted better than any of the other peace treaties. The capitulations and financial control disappeared. Turkey gave up her claims to the Arab lands and the islands of the Aegean, Cyprus, Rhodes and the Dodecanese. A big exchange of Greek and Turkish populations followed and the hatred of these peoples for one another received fresh reinforcement. So the Ottoman empire outside Turkey was wound up after six centuries, and a new republic began its existence in 1923 as a national state under a dictator who proved rapidly to be one of the most effective of modernizers. Appropriately, the caliphate followed the empire, being abolished in 1924. In one obvious way, this was the end of the Ottoman story. In another it was not. By 1918 the Anatolian Turks were for the first time in five or six centuries the majority people of the empire and what began in 1923 was another chapter of the story of that people, now turned away from Islam and towards the goal of national modernization by a modernizing autocracy.

Kemal, as he tended to call himself (the name meant 'Perfection') was something of an enlightened despot, something of a Peter the Great (though not interested in expansion after the successful revision of the dictated peace). The law was secularized (on the model of the Napoleonic code), the Moslem calendar abandoned, and in 1928 the constitution was amended to remove the statement that Turkey was an Islamic state. Polygamy was forbidden.

The latinization of the Turkish script was one of the innovations of Kemal Ataturk who is shown here undertaking a model lesson to publicize the reform programme.

In 1935 the weekly day of rest, formerly Friday, the Islamic holy day, became Sunday and a new word entered the language: *vikend*, the period from 1 p.m. Saturday to midnight Sunday. Schools ceased to give religious instruction. The fez was forbidden; although it had actually come from Europe it was considered Moslem. Such symbols were important; Kemal was conscious of the radical nature of the modernization he wished to achieve. They were signs, but signs of something very important, the replacement of traditional Islamic society by a European one. The alphabet was latinized and this had great importance for education, henceforth obligatory at the primary level. A national past was rewritten in the books and in the schools; it was popularly said that Adam was a Turk.

Kemal – on whom the National Assembly

The father of modern Iran, Reza Khan, the soldier who became Shah in 1925. His son, the present Shah, is seated on his knee in this picture.

conferred the name of Ataturk, or 'Father of the Turks' – is an immensely significant figure. He is what Mehemet Ali perhaps wanted to be, the first transformer of an Islamic state by modernization. He remains strikingly interesting; until his death in 1938 he seemed determined not to let his revolution congeal. The result was the creation of a state then in some ways among the most advanced in the world. A much greater break with the past was involved in Turkey in giving a new rôle to women than in Europe, but in 1934 Turkish women received the vote and they were encouraged to enter the professions.

The most important Islamic country which had not been under direct imperial rule either by Europeans or Ottomans before 1914 was Persia. The British and Russians had interfered in her affairs after agreeing over spheres of influence in 1907, but Russian power had lapsed with the Bolshevik Revolution, though British forces had operated on Persian territory during the war to ensure that this remained true. Resentment against the British was excited when a Persian delegation, too, was not allowed to state its case to the Peace Conference. There was a confused period during which the British struggled to find means of maintaining resistance to the Bolsheviks after their withdrawal of their forces. There could be no question of retaining Persia by force, given the overtaxing of British strength. Almost by accident, a British general discovered the man who was to do this, though hardly in the way anticipated.

This was an officer, Reza Khan, who carried out a *coup d'état* in 1921 and at once used the Bolshevik fear of the British to get a treaty which conceded all Russian rights and property in Persia and the withdrawal of Russian forces. Reza Khan then went on to defeat separatists who had British support. In 1925 he was given dictatorial powers by the national assembly and a few months later was proclaimed Shah of Shahs. He was to rule until 1941 (when the Russians and British together turned him off the throne) and revealed himself an Iranian Kemal. The abolition of the veil and religious schools showed his secularist aims, though they were not pressed so far as in Turkey. In 1928 an important symbolic step was taken, when the capitulations were abolished; meanwhile industrialization and the improvement of communications was pressed forward. A close association with Turkey was cultivated. Finally, the Persian strong man won in 1933 the first notable success in a new art, the diplomacy of oil, when the concession held by the Anglo-Persian Oil Company was cancelled. When the British government took the question to the League of Nations another was eventually negotiated, but on terms much more favourable to Persia. It was Reza Shah's greatest victory and the best evidence of the independence of Persia. A new era had opened in the Gulf, fittingly marked in 1935 by the official change of name of the state from Persia to Iran.

959

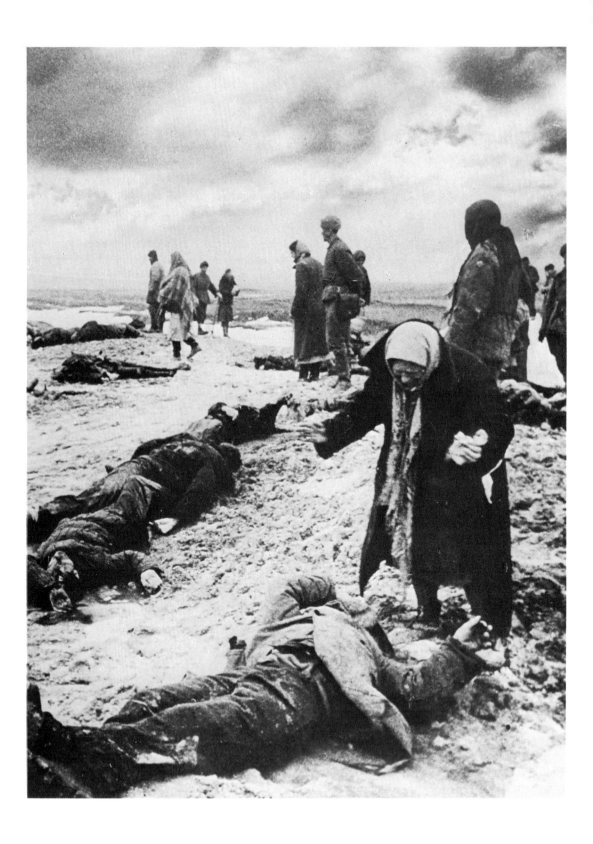

5 The Second World War

The demonstration that the European age was at last over was made in another world war. It began in 1939 like its predecessor, as a European struggle, and like it became a combination of wars. Like it, too, but to a far greater degree, it made unprecedented demands; this time they were on a scale which left nothing untouched, unmobilized, undisturbed. It was realistically termed 'total' war.

By 1939, there were already many signs for those with eyes to see that a historical era was ending. Though 1919 had brought a few last extensions of territorial control by colonial powers, the behaviour of the greatest of them, Great Britain, showed that imperialism was on the defensive, if not already in retreat. The vigour of Japan meant that Europe was no longer the only focus of the international power system; a prescient South African statesman said as early as 1921 that 'the scene has shifted away from Europe to the Far East and to the Pacific'. His prediction now seems more than ever justified and it was made when the likelihood that China might soon again exercise her due weight was far from obvious. Ten years after he spoke, the economic foundations of western preponderance had been shaken even more plainly than the political; the United States, greatest of industrial powers, had still in 1939 ten million unemployed. Though none of the European industrial states was by then in

Kerch, 1944. Survivors of a village discover the bodies of those murdered by the retreating German army.

quite such straits, the confidence which took the health of the basic foundations of the economic system for granted had evaporated for ever. Industry might be picking up in some countries – largely because rearmament was stimulating it – but attempts to find recovery by international cooperation came to an end when a World Economic Conference broke down in 1933. After that, each nation had gone its own way; even the United Kingdom at last abandoned Free Trade. *Laisser-faire* was dead, even if people still talked about it. Governments were by 1939 deliberately interfering with the economy as they had not done since the heyday of mercantilism.

If the political and economic assumptions of the nineteenth century had gone, so had many others. It is more difficult to speak of intellectual and spiritual trends than of political and economic, but though many people still clung to old shibboleths, for the élite which led thought and opinion the old foundations were no longer firm. Many people still attended religious services – though only a minority, even in Roman Catholic countries – but the masses of the industrial cities lived in a post-Christian world in which the physical removal of the institutions and symbols of religion would have made little difference to their daily lives. So did intellectuals; they perhaps faced an even greater problem, too, because many of the liberal ideas which had helped to displace Christianity from the eighteenth century were by now being displaced in their turn. In the 1920s and 1930s, the liberal certainties of the autonomy of the indi-

961

vidual, objective moral criteria, rationality, the authority of parents, and an explicable mechanical universe all seemed to be going under along with the belief in Free Trade.

This was clearest in the arts. For three or four hundred years, since the age of humanism, it had been presumed that the arts expressed aspirations, insights and pleasures accessible in principle to ordinary men, even though they might be raised to an exceptional degree of fineness in execution, or be especially concentrated in form so that not all individual men would always enjoy them. At any rate, it was possible for the whole of that time to retain the notion of the cultivated man who, given time and study, could discriminate with taste among the arts of his time because they were expressions of a shared culture with shared standards. This idea was first weakened when the nineteenth century, in the wake of the romantic movement, came to idealize the artist as genius – Beethoven was one of the first examples – and formulated the notion of the *avant-garde*. By the first

decade of the twentieth century, further developments had occurred which made it very difficult for trained eyes and ears to recognize art in much of what was done by contemporary artists. The best symbol of this was the dislocation of the image in painting. Here, the flight from the representational still kept a tenuous link with tradition as late as Cubism, but by then it had long ceased to be apparent to the average 'cultivated man' – if he still existed. Artists retired into a less and less accessible chaos of private visions, whose centre was reached in the world of Dada and Surrealism. The years after 1918 are of the greatest interest as something of a culmination of disintegration; in Surrealism even the notion of the objective disappeared, let alone its representation. As one Surrealist put it, the movement meant 'thought dictated in the absence of all control exerted by reason, and outside all aesthetic or moral preoccupations'. Through

The Paris Dadaists painted by one of their number, Max Ernst, in 1922.

chance, symbolism, shock, suggestion and violence the Surrealists sought to go beyond consciousness itself. In so doing, they were only doing what writers and musicians were trying to do, too.

Such phenomena provide evidence in widely different forms of the decay of liberal culture which was the final outcome of the high civilization of the European age. It is significant that such disintegratory movements were often prompted by a sense that the traditional culture was too limited because of its exclusion of the resources of emotion and experience in the unconscious. Probably few of the artists who would have agreed with this would have read the work of the man who, more than any other, gave the twentieth century a language in which

A congress of psychoanalysts at Weimar in 1911 brought together many of the founders of this school of psychological medicine, among them Freud and Jung (on his left, with large bow tie) standing next to one another in the middle of the first row of those standing.

to explore this area and the confidence that it was there that the secrets of life lay.

This was Sigmund Freud, the founder of psychoanalysis and a man who deserves in the history of culture a place beside Newton or Darwin, for he changed the way educated men thought of themselves. He introduced several new ideas into ordinary discourse: the special meaning we now give to the words 'complex', 'unconscious' and 'obsession', and the appearance of the familiar terms 'Freudian slip' and 'libido' are monuments to the power of his teaching. His influence quickly spread into literature, personal relations, education, politics. Like that of many prophets, his message was often distorted. What he was believed to have said was much more important than the specific clinical studies which were his contribution to science. Again like Newton and Darwin, Freud's importance beyond science – where his influence was mose profound – lay in providing a new mythology. It was to prove highly corrosive.

The message men took from Freud suggested that the unconscious was the true source of most significant behaviour, that moral values and attitudes were projections of the influences which had moulded this unconscious, that, therefore, the idea of responsibility was at best a myth and probably a dangerous one, and that perhaps rationality itself was an illusion. It did not matter much that Freud's own assertions would have been nonsense had this been true or that this left out the subtlety and science of his work. This was what many people believed he had proved – and still believe. Such a bundle of ideas called in question the very foundation of liberal civilization itself, the idea of the rational, responsible, consciously motivated individual, and this was its general importance.

Freud's teaching was not the only intellectual force contributing to the loss of certainty and the sense that men had little firm ground beneath their feet. But it was the most apparent in the intellectual life of the interwar period. From grappling with the insights he brought, or with the chaos of the arts, or with the incomprehensibility of a world of science which seemed suddenly to have abandoned Laplace and Newton, men plunged worriedly into the search for new mythologies and standards to give them bearings. Politically, this led to fascism, Marxism, and the more irrational of the old certainties, extreme nationalism, for example. People did not feel inspired or excited by tolerance, democracy, and the old individual freedoms.

Such influences made it all the more difficult to deal with the deepening uncertainty and foreboding clouding international relations in the 1930s. The heart of this was the German problem which threatened a greater upheaval than could Japan. Germany had not been destroyed in 1918; it was a logical consequence, therefore, that she would one day again exercise her due weight. Geography, population and industrial power all meant that in one way or another a united Germany must dominate central Europe and overshadow France. What was at issue at bottom was whether this could be faced without war; only a few cranks thought it might be disposed of by dividing again the Germany united in 1871.

Germans soon began to demand the revision of the settlement of Versailles. This demand eventually became unmanageable, though in the 1920s it was tackled in a hopeful spirit. The real burden of reparations was gradually whittled away and the Treaty of Locarno was seen as a great landmark because by it Germany gave her consent to the Versailles territorial settlement in the west. But it left open the question of revision in the east and behind this loomed the larger question: how could a country potentially so powerful as Germany be related to its neighbours in a balanced, peaceful way, given the particular historical and cultural experience of the Germans?

Most people hoped this had been settled by the creation of a democratic German republic whose institutions would gently and benevolently reconstruct German society and civilization. It was true that the constitution of the Weimar Republic (as it was called from the place where its constituent assembly met) was very liberal, but too many Germans were out of sympathy with it from the start. That Weimar had solved the German problem was revealed as an illusion when economic depression shattered the narrow base on which the German Republic rested and set loose the destructive nationalist and social forces it had masked.

When this happened, the containment of Germany again became an international problem. But for a number of reasons, the 1930s were a very unpromising decade for containment to be easy. To begin with, some of the worst effects of the world economic crisis were felt in the relatively weak and agricultural economies of the new eastern European countries. France had always looked for allies against a German revival there, but such allies were now gravely weakened. Furthermore, their very existence made it doubly difficult to involve Russia, again an indisputable (if mysterious) great power, in the containment of Germany. Her ideological distinction presented barriers enough to cooperation with the United Kingdom and France, but there was also her strategic remoteness. No Russian force could reach central Europe without crossing one or more of the east European states whose short lives were haunted by fear of Russia and communism: Romania, Poland and the Baltic states, after all, were built from, among other things, former Russian lands.

Nor were the Americans of any help. The whole trend of American policy since Wilson's failure to get his countrymen to join the League had been back towards a self-absorbed isolation which was suited to traditional ideas. Americans who had gone to Europe as soldiers did not want to repeat the experience. Justified apparently by boom in the 1920s, isolation was paraxodically confirmed by slump in the 1930s. When Americans did not confusedly blame Europe for their troubles – the question of debts from the war years had great psychological impact because it was believed to be tied up with international financial problems (as indeed it was, though not quite as Americans thought) – they felt distrustful of further entanglement. Anyway, the depression gave them enough on their plate. With the election of a Democratic president in 1932 they were, in fact, at the beginning of an era of important change which would in

the end sweep away this mood, too, but this could not be seen.

The next phase of American history was to be presided over by Democrats for five successive presidential terms, the first four of them after elections won by the same man, Franklin Roosevelt. To stand four successive times as presidential candidate was almost unprecedented (only the unsuccessful socialist, Eugene Debs, also did so); to win, astonishing. To do so with (on each occasion) an absolute majority of the popular vote was something like a revolution. No earlier Democratic candidate since the Civil War had ever had one at all, and no other was to have one until 1964. Moreover, Roosevelt was a rich, patrician figure. It is all the more surprising, therefore, that he should have emerged as one of the greatest popular leaders of the early twentieth century. He did so in an electoral contest which was basically one of hope versus despair. He offered confidence and the promise of action to shake off the blight of economic depression. A political transformation followed his victory, the building of a Democratic hegemony on a coalition of neglected constituencies – the South, the poor, the farmer, the Negro – which then attracted further support as it seemed to deliver results.

There was some degree of illusion in this. The 'New Deal' on which the Roosevelt administration embarked was still not grappling satisfactorily with the economy by 1939. None the less it changed the emphasis of the working of American capitalism and its relations with government. A huge programme of unemployment relief with insurance was launched, millions were poured into public works, new regulation of finance was introduced and a great experiment in public ownership was launched in a hydro-electric scheme in the Tennessee

Franklin D. Roosevelt, a cripple of magnetic personal quality whose greatest gift when he became President in the depths of the economic slump may have been the contagion of his jaunty confidence that America's problems were manageable if only tackled with courage.

valley. This in the end gave capitalism a new lease of life, in a new governmental setting. The New Deal brought the most important extension of the power of the Federal authorities over American society and the states that had ever occured in peacetime and it has proved irreversible. Thus American society reflected the same pressures towards collectivism which affected other countries in the twentieth century. In this sense, too, the Roosevelt era was historically decisive. It changed the course of American constitutional and political history as nothing had done since the Civil War and incidentally offered to the world a democratic alternative to fascism and communism by providing a liberal version of large-scale governmental intervention in the economy. This achievement is all the more impressive in that it rested almost entirely on the interested choices of politicians committed to the democratic process and not on the arguments of economists, some of the more farsighted of whom were already advocating greater central management of the economy in capitalist nations. It was a remarkable demonstration of the ability of the

Agricultural depression in the United States produced thousands of migrant seekers after work; they were fewer than the unemployed of the great industrial cities, but they seemed to strike the imagination of the public more forcibly. In the end a government agency, the Farm Security Administration, helped to alleviate the distress of some of them by building them shacks like the one shown.

American political system to deliver what people felt they wanted.

The same machinery, of course, could also only deliver what most Americans would tolerate as a foreign policy. Roosevelt was much more aware than the majority of his fellow-citizens of the dangers of persistent American isolation from Europe's problems. But he could reveal his own views only slowly. With Russia and the United States unavailable, only the western European great powers remained to confront Germany if she revived. Great Britain and France were badly placed to do this. They had memories of their difficulties in dealing with Germany even when Russia had been at their side. Furthermore, they had been much at odds with one another since 1918. They were also militarily weak. France, conscious of her inferiority in manpower should Germany ever re-arm, had invested in a programme of strategic defence which looked impressive but effectively deprived her of the power to act offensively. The Royal Navy was no longer without a rival, nor, as in 1914, safe in concentrating its resources in European waters. British governments long pursued the reduction of expenditure on armaments at a time when world-wide commitments were a growing strain on her forces. Economic depression reinforced this tendency. Many Englishmen, too, believed that Germany's grievances were just. They were disposed to make concessions in the name of German nationalism and self-determination, even by handing back German colonies. Both Great Britain and France were also troubled by a joker in the European pack, Italy. Under Mussolini, hopes entertained of her as a force against Germany had disappeared by 1938.

This arose from a belated attempt by Italy to participate in the Scramble for Africa when, in 1935, her forces invaded Ethiopia. Such action posed the question of what should be done by the League of Nations; it was clearly a breach of its Covenant that one of its members should attack another. France and Great Britain were in an awkward position. As great powers, Mediterranean powers and African colonial powers, they were bound to take the lead against Italy at the League. But they did so feebly and half-heartedly, for they did not want to alienate an Italy they would like to have with them against Germany. The result was the worst possible one. The League failed to check aggression and Italy was alienated after all. Ethiopia lost its independence, though, it later proved, only for six years.

This was one of several moments at which it later looked as if a fatal error was committed. But it is impossible to say in retrospect at what stage the situation which developed from these facts became unmanageable. Certainly the emergence of a much more radical and ferociously opportunist régime in Germany was the

major turning-point. But the depression preceded this and made it possible. Economic collapse also had another important effect. It made plausible an ideological interpretation of events in the 1930s and thus further embittered them. Because of the intensification of class conflict which economic collapse brought with it, interested politicians sometimes interpreted the development of international relations in terms of fascism versus communism, and even of Right versus Left or Democracy versus Dictatorship. This was easier after Mussolini, angered by British and French reactions to his invasion of Ethiopia in 1935, came to ally himself to Hitler and talk of an anti-communist crusade. But this was misleading, too. All ideological interpretations of international affairs in the 1930s tended to obscure the central nature of the German problem – and, therefore, to make it harder to tackle.

Here Russian propaganda was important, too. During the 1930s her internal situation was precarious. The industrialization programme was imposing grave strains and sacrifices. These were mastered – though perhaps also exaggerated – by a savage intensification of dictatorship which expressed itself not only in the collectivization struggle against the peasants, but in the turning of terror against the cadres of the régime itself from 1934 onwards. In five years millions of Russians were executed imprisoned or exiled, often to forced labour. The world looked on amazed as batches of defendants grovelled with grotesque 'confessions' before Soviet courts. Nine out of ten generals in the army went, and it has been estimated, half the officer corps. A new communist élite replaced the old one in these years; by 1939 over half the delegates who had attended the Party Congress of 1934 had been arrested. It was very difficult for outsiders to be sure what was happening, but it was clear to them that Russia was by no means either a civilized, liberal state nor necessarily a very strong potential ally.

More directly, this affected the international situation because of the propaganda which accompanied it. Much of this, no doubt, arose from the deliberate provocation inside Russia of a siege mentality; far from being relaxed, the habit of thinking of the world in terms of Us versus Them which had been born in Marxist dogma and the interventions was encouraged in the 1930s. As this notion took hold, so, outside, did the preaching of the doctrine of international class-struggle by the Comintern. The reciprocal effect was predictable. The fears of conservatives everywhere were intensified. It became easy to think of any concession to left-wing or even mildly progressive forces as a victory for the Bolsheviks. As attitudes thus hardened on the Right, so communists were given new evidence for the thesis of inevitable class-conflict and revolution.

Yet there was not one successful left-wing revolution. The revolutionary danger had subsided rapidly after the immediate post-war years. Labour governments peacefully and undramatically ruled England for part of the 1920s. The second ended in financial collapse in 1931, to be replaced by conservative régimes which had overwhelming electoral support and proceeded to govern with remarkable fidelity to the tradition of progressive and piecemeal social and administrative reform which had marked Great Britain's advance into the 'Welfare State'. This direction had been followed even further in the Scandinavian countries, often held up for admiration for their combination of political democracy and practical socialism, and as a contrast to communism. Even in France, where there was a large and active communist party, there was no sign that its aims were acceptable to the bulk of the electorate even after the depression. In Germany the communist party before 1933 had been able to get more votes, but it was never able to displace the Social Democrats in control of the working-class movement. In less advanced countries than these, communism's revolutionary success was even smaller. In Spain it had to compete with socialists and anarchists; Spanish conservatives certainly feared it and may have been right to fear also the tendency to slide towards social revolution felt under the republic which was established in

1931, but they had better grounds for seeing elsewhere than in Spanish communism the real danger facing them.

Yet the ideological interpretation had great appeal, even to many who were not communists. It was much strengthened by the accession to power in 1933 of a new ruler in Germany, Adolf Hitler, whose success makes it very difficult to deny him political genius. In the early 1920s he was only a disappointed nationalist agitator, who had failed in an attempt to overthrow a government (the Bavarian) and who poured out his obsessive nationalism and anti-semitism not only in hypnotically effective speeches but in a long, shapeless, semi-autobiographical book which few people read. In 1933, the National Socialist German Workers Party which he led ('Nazi' for short) was strong enough for him to be appointed Chancellor of the German republic by the president. Politically, this may have been the most momentous single decision of the century, for it meant the revolutionizing of Germany, its redirection upon a course of aggression which ended by destroying the old Europe and Germany too, and a new world.

Though Hitler's messages were simple, his appeal was complex. He preached that Germany's troubles had identifiable sources. The Treaty of Versailles was one. The international capitalists were another. The anti-national activities of German Marxists and Jews were others. He also said that the righting of Germany's political wrongs must be combined with the renovation of German society and culture, and that this was a matter of purifying the biological stock of the German people, by excising its non-Aryan components.

In 1922 such a message could get very little way. In 1930 it won Hitler 107 seats in the German Parliament – more than the communists (who had 77). The Nazis were already the beneficiaries of economic collapse, and it was to grow worse. There are several reasons why the Nazis benefited, but one of the most important was that the communists spent as much energy fighting the socialists as their other opponents.

President Hindenburg with his new Chancellor, Adolf Hitler, 1 May 1933, a former socialist holiday renamed 'National Labour Day'.

This had fatally handicapped the Left in Germany all through the 1920s. Another reason was that under the democratic Republic anti-Semitic feeling had grown because of the much more prominent part played in the state by Jews than in imperial times. It was exacerbated by economic collapse, too. Anti-semitism, like nationalism, was an appeal which cut across classes as an explanation of Germany's troubles, unlike the equally simple Marxist explanation in terms of class war which, naturally, antagonized some as well as (it was hoped) attracting others.

By 1930 the Nazis showed they were a power in the land. They attracted more support, and won backers both from those who saw in their street-fighting gangs an anti-communist insurance, from nationalists who sought rearma-

ment and revision and from conservative politicians who thought that Hitler was a party leader like any other who might now be valuable in their own game. The manoeuvres were complicated, but in 1932 the Nazis became the biggest party in the German parliament, though without a majority. In January 1933 Hitler was called to office legally and constitutionally by the head of the republic. There followed new elections, in which the régime's monopoly of the radio and use of intimidation still did not secure the Nazis a majority; none the less, they had one when supported by some right-wing members of Parliament who joined them in voting special enabling powers to the government; the most important was that of governing by emergency decree. This was the end of parliament. Armed with these powers, the Nazis proceeded to carry out a revolutionary destruction of democratic institutions. By 1939, there was virtually no sector of German society not controlled or intimidated by them. The conservatives, too, had lost, for they found that Nazi interference with the independence of traditional authorities went very far.

This system, like that of Stalin's Russia, rested in large measure on terror used mercilessly against enemies of the régime. It was also unleashed against the Jews and an astonished Europe found itself witnessing revivals in one of its most advanced societies of the pogroms of medieval Europe or tsarist Russia. This was indeed so amazing that many people outside Germany found it difficult to believe that it was happening. Confusion over the nature of the régime made it even more difficult to deal with it. Some saw Hitler simply as a nationalist leader bent, like an Ataturk, upon the regeneration of his country and the assertion of its rightful claims. Others saw him as a crusader against Bolshevism. Even when people only thought he might be a useful barrier against it, that increased the likelihood that men of the Left would see him as a tool of capitalism. But no simple formula will contain Hitler or his aims – and there is still great disagreement about what these were – and probably a reasonable approximation to the truth is simply to recognize that he expressed the resentments and exasperations of German society in their most negative and destructive forms and embodied them to a monstrous degree. When his personality was given scope by economic disaster, political cynicism and a favourable arrangement of international forces, he could release these negative qualities at the expense of all Europeans, in the long run, his own countrymen included.

The path by which Germany came to be at war again in 1939 is complicated and there is still much argument about when, if ever, there was a chance of avoiding the final outcome. One important moment, clearly, was when Mussolini, formerly wary of German ambitions in central Europe, became Hitler's ally. After he had been alienated by British and French policy over his Ethiopian adventure, a civil war broke out in Spain when a group of generals mutin-

ied against the left-wing republic. Hitler and Mussolini both sent contingents to support the man who emerged as the rebel leader, general Franco. This, more than any other single fact, gave an ideological colour to Europe's divisions; Hitler, Mussolini and Franco were all now identified as 'fascist' and Russian foreign policy began to coordinate support for Spain within western countries by letting local communists abandon their attacks on other left-wing parties and encouraging 'Popular Fronts'. Thus Spain came to be seen as a conflict between Right and Left in its purest form; this was a distortion, but it had much effect in accustoming people to think of Europe as divided into two camps.

British and French governments were by this time well aware of the difficulties of dealing with Germany. Hitler had already in 1935 announced that her rearmament (forbidden at Versailles) had begun. Until their own rearmament was completed, they remained very weak. The first consequence of this was shown when German troops re-entered the 'demilitarized' zone on the eastern bank of the Rhine in which their presence had been forbidden by the Treaty of Versailles. No attempt was made to resist this move. After the civil war in Spain had thrown opinion in Great Britain and France into further disarray, Hitler seized Austria. The provisions of Versailles which had forbidden the fusion of Germany and Austria seemed hard to uphold; to the French and British electorates this could be presented as a matter of legitimately aggrieved nationalism. The Austrian republic had also long had internal troubles. The *Anschluss* (as union with Germany was called) took place in 1938. In the autumn came the next German aggression, the seizure of part of Czechoslovakia. Again, this was justified by the specious claims of self-determination; the areas involved were so important that their loss crippled the prospect of future Czechoslovak self-defence, but they were areas with many German inhabitants. Memel would follow, on the same grounds, the next year. Hitler was gradually fulfilling the old dream which had been lost when Prussia beat

*A republican poster of the Spanish civil war
satirizing the grouping of forces on which the
nationalist cause was based – clergy, army,
German credit, colonial troops and the gibbet.*

Austria – the dream of a Great Germany, defined as the lands containing those of German blood.

The dismemberment of Czechoslovakia was something of a turning-point. It was achieved by a series of agreements at Munich in September 1938 in which Great Britain and Germany took the main parts. This was the last great initiative of British foreign policy to try to satisfy Hitler. The British prime minister was still too unsure of rearmament to resist, but hoped also that the transference of the last substantial group of Germans from alien rule to that of their homeland might deprive Hitler of the motive for further revision of Versailles – a settlement which was now somewhat tattered in any case.

He was wrong, because Hitler went on to inaugurate a programme of expansion into Slav lands. The first step was the absorption of what was left of Czechoslovakia, in March 1939. This brought forward the question of the Polish settlement of 1919. Hitler resented the 'Polish Corridor' which separated East Prussia from Germany and contained Danzig, an old German city given an internationalized status in 1919. At this point the British government, though hesitatingly, changed tack and offered a guarantee to Poland and other east European countries against aggression. It also began a wary negotiation with Russia.

Russian policy remains hard to interpret. It seems that Stalin kept the Spanish civil war going with support to the republic as long as it seemed likely to tie up German attention, but then looked for other ways of buying time against the attack from the west which he always feared. To him, it seemed likely that a German attack on Rusisa might be encouraged by Great Britain and France who would see with relief the trouble they had so long faced turning eastwards. No doubt they would have done. There was little possibility of working with the British or French to oppose Hitler, however, even if they were willing to do so, because no Russian army could reach Germany except through Poland – and this the Poles would never permit. Accordingly, as a Russian diplomat remarked to a French colleague on hearing of the Munich decisions, there was now nothing for it but a fourth partition of Poland. This was arranged in the summer of 1939. After all the propaganda each had directed against Bolshevik-Slav barbarism and fascist-capitalist exploitation, Germany and Russia made an agreement in August which provided for the division of Poland between them; authoritarian states enjoy great flexibility in the conduct of diplomacy. Armed with this, Hitler went on to attack Poland. He thus began the Second World War on 1 September 1939. Two days later the British and French honoured their guarantee to Poland and declared war on Germany.

Their governments were not very keen on doing so, for it was obvious that they could not help Poland. That unhappy nation disappeared

The Great War 1914—1918

- - - - - Limit of Allied advance
——— Limit of advance of Central Powers

Central Powers in August 1914

Neutral States which later joined the Central Powers (with dates of joining)

The Allies in August 1914

Neutral States which later joined the Allies (with dates of joining)

States neutral throughout the War

once more, divided by Russian and German forces about a month after the outbreak of war. But not to have intervened would have meant acquiescing in the German domination of Europe, for no other nation would have thought British or French support worth having. So, uneasily and without the enthusiasm of 1914, the only two constitutional great powers of Europe found themselves facing a totalitarian régime. Neither their peoples nor governments had much enthusiasm for this rôle, and the decline of liberal and democratic forces since 1918 put them in a position much inferior to that of 1914, but exasperation with Hitler's long series of aggressions and broken promises made it hard to see what sort of peace could be made which would reassure them. The basic cause of the war was, as in 1914, German nationalism. But whereas then Germany had gone to war because *she* felt threatened, now Great Britain and France were responding to the danger presented by her expansion. *They* felt threatened this time.

To the surprise of many observers, the first six months of the war were almost uneventful once the short Polish campaign was over. It was quickly plain that mechanized forces and air-power were to play a much more important part than between 1914 and 1918. The memory of the slaughter of the Somme and Verdun was too vivid for the British and French to plan anything but an economic offensive; the weapon of blockade, they hoped, would be effective against Germany. Hitler was unwilling to disturb them, because he was anxious to make peace. This deadlock was only broken when the British wished to intensify the blockade in Scandinavian waters. This coincided, remarkably, with a German offensive to secure ore supplies which conquered Norway and Denmark. Its launching on 9 April 1940 opened an astonishing period of fighting. Only a month later there began a brilliant German invasion first of the Low Countries and then of France. A powerful armoured attack through the Ardennes opened the way to the division of the Allied armies and the capture

Germany and its allies (1942)

Areas under German and Italian control Oct. 1942

Areas under Allied control Oct. 1942

Neutral countries 1942

Unoccupied France 1940—42

Allied invasion of Normandy begins 6/6/1944

Front lines, May 1944

Front lines, Dec. 1944

Limit of German occupation until Nov. 1942

Europe during the war of 1939—45

of Paris. On 22 June France signed an armistice with the Germans. By the end of the month, the whole European coast from the Pyrenees to the North Cape was in German hands and Italy had joined in on the German side. A new French government at Vichy broke off relations with Great Britain after the British had seized or destroyed French warships they felt might fall into German hands. The Third Republic effectively came to an end with the installation of a French marshal, a hero of the First World War, as Head of State. With no ally left on the continent, Great Britain faced a worse strategical situation by far than that in which she had struggled against Napoleon.

This was a huge change in the nature of the war. It was not exactly true that Great Britain was alone. There were the Dominions, all of which had entered the war on her side, and a number of governments in exile from the over-run continent. Some of these commanded forces of their own and Norwegians, Danes, Dutchmen, Belgians and Poles were to fight gallantly, often with decisive effect, in the years ahead. The most important exiled contingents were those of the French, but they represented a faction within France, not its legal government. A general who had left France before the armistice and was condemned to death *in absentia* was their leader: de Gaulle. He was recognized by the British as 'leader of the Free French'; he saw himself as the custodian of France's interests and honour

973

and soon began to show an independence which was in the end to make him the greatest servant of France since Clemenceau.

De Gaulle's position was important because of uncertainties about what might happen to parts of the French empire where he hoped to find sympathizers who wished to join him to continue the fight. This was one way in which the war was now extended geographically. Another resulted from Italy's entry to the war, since her African possessions and the Mediterranean sea-lanes then became operational areas. Finally, the availability of Atlantic and Scandinavian ports meant that what was later called the 'Battle of the Atlantic', the German struggle to sever British sea communications by submarine, surface, and air attack was now bound to become much fiercer.

Immediately, the British Isles faced direct attack. The hour had already found the man to brace the nation against such a challenge. Winston Churchill, after a long and chequered political career, had become Prime Minister when the Norwegian campaign collapsed, because no other man commanded support in all parties in the house of commons. To the coalition government which he immediately formed he gave vigorous leadership, something hitherto felt to be lacking. More important than this, he called forth in his people, whom he addressed frequently by radio, qualities they had forgotten they possessed. It was soon clear that only defeat after direct assault was going to get the British out of the war.

This was even more certain after a great air battle over southern England in August and September had been won by British science and the Royal Air Force. For a moment, Englishmen knew the pride and relief of the Greeks after Marathon. It was true, as Churchill said in a much quoted speech, that 'never in the field of human conflict was so much owed by so many to so few'. This victory made a German seaborne invasion impossible (though a successful one was always unlikely). It also established that Great Britain could not be defeated by air bombardment alone. The islands had a bleak

outlook ahead, but this victory changed the direction of the war, for it was the beginning of a period in which a variety of influences turned German attention in another direction. In December 1940 planning began for a German invasion of Russia.

By that winter, Russia had made further gains to her west, apparently with an eye to securing a glacis against a future German attack. A war against Finland gave her important strategic areas. The Baltic states were swallowed in 1940. Bessarabia, which Romania had taken from Russia in 1918, was now taken back, together with the northern Bukovina. In the last case, Stalin was going beyond tsarist boundaries. The German decision to attack Russia in part arose because of some disagreements about the future direction of Russian expansion: Germany sought to keep Russia away from the Balkans and the Straits. It was also aimed at demonstrating, by a quick overthrow of Russia, that further British war-making was pointless. But there was also a deep personal element in the decision. Hitler had always sincerely and fanatically detested Bolshevism and maintained that the Slavs, a racially inferior group, should provide Germans with living-space and raw materials in the east. This was a last, perverted vision of the old struggle of Teuton to impose western civilization on the Slav east and many Germans responded to such a theme. It was to justify more appalling atrocities than any earlier crusading myth.

In a brief spring campaign, which provided an overture to the holocaust ahead, the Germans overran Yugoslavia and Greece, with which Italian forces had been unhappily engaged since October 1940. Once again British arms were driven from the mainland of Europe. Crete, too, was taken by a spectacular airborne assault. Now all was ready for 'Barbarossa,' as the great onslaught on Russia was named, after a crusading German emperor of the Middle Ages.

The attack was launched on 22 June 1941 and had huge early successes. Vast numbers of prisoners were taken and the Russian armies fell back hundreds of miles. The German advance guard came within a narrow margin of entering Moscow. But that margin was not quite eliminated and by Christmas the first successful Russian counter-attacks had announced that in fact Germany was pinned down. German strategy had lost the initiative. If the British and Russians could hold on and if they could keep in alliance with one another then, failing a radical technical modification of the war by the discovery of new weapons of great power, their access to American production would inexorably increase their strength. This did not, of course, mean that they would inevitably defeat Germany, only that they might bring her to negotiate terms.

The American president was clear that Great Britain had to be supported up to the limits permitted by his own public and the law of neutrality. In fact, he went well beyond both at times. By the summer of 1941, Hitler knew that to all intents and purposes the United States was an undeclared enemy. A crucial step had been the American Lend-Lease Act of March that year which provided production and services to the Allies without payment. Soon afterwards, the American government extended naval patrols and the protection of its shipping further eastward into the Atlantic. After the invasion of Russia came a meeting between Churchill and Roosevelt which resulted in a statement of shared principles – the Atlantic Charter – in which a nation at war and another formally at peace spoke of the needs of a post-war world 'after the final destruction of the Nazi tyranny'. This was a long way from isolationism and was the background to Hitler's second fateful but foolish decision of 1941, a declaration of war on the United States on 11 December after a Japanese attack on British and American territories four days earlier. Hitler had earlier promised the Japanese to do this. The war thus became global. The British and American declarations of war on Japan might have left two separate wars to rage, with only Great Britain engaged in both; Hitler's action threw away the chance that American power might have been kept out of Europe and deployed only in the Pacific. Few single acts have so marked the end of an epoch, for this announced the eclipse of European affairs. Europe's future would now be settled not by her own efforts but by the two great powers on her flanks, the United States and Soviet Russia.

The Japanese decision was also a rash one, though the logic of Japanese policy had long pointed towards conflict with the United States. Japan's ties with Germany and Italy, though they had some propaganda value for both sides, did not amount to much in practice. What mattered in the timing of Japanese policy was the resolution of debates in Tokyo about the danger, or lack of it, of a challenge to the United States which must involve war. The crux of the matter was that Japan's needs for a successful conclusion of the war in China included oil which she could only obtain with the tacit consent of the United States that Japan was to destroy China. This no American government could have given. Instead, in October 1941 the American government imposed an embargo on all trade by United States citizens with Japan.

There followed the last stages of a process which had its origins in the ascendancy established in Japan by reactionary and militant forces in the 1930s. The question had by this time become for the Japanese military planners purely a strategic and technical one; since they would have to take the resources in South-East Asia which they needed by force, all that had to be settled was the nature of the war against the United States and its timing. Such a decision was fundamentally irrational, for the chances of ultimate success were very small; once arguments of national honour had won at this point, though, the final calculations about the best point and moment of attack were carefully made. The choice was made to strike as hard a blow as possible against American sea power at the outset in order to gain the maximum freedom of movement in the Pacific and South China Sea. The result was the onslaught of 7 December, whose centrepiece was an air attack on the American fleet at Pearl Harbour which was one of the most brilliantly conceived and executed

Pearl Harbour, 7 December 1941; an American battleship listing after the Japanese attack.

operations in the history of warfare. By mischance it fell just short of complete success, for it did not destroy American naval air power, though it gave the Japanese for months the strategical freedom they sought. This failure was enough; after it the Japanese faced a prolonged war they were bound to lose in the end. Pearl Harbour united Americans as little else could have done. Isolationism could virtually be considered dead on 8 December; Roosevelt had a nation behind him as Wilson never had.

When a few Japanese bombs fell on the American mainland, it was obvious that this was much more truly a world war than the first had been. The German operations in the Balkans had by the time of Pearl Harbour left Europe with only four neutral countries – Spain, Portugal, Sweden and Switzerland. The war in North Africa raged back and forth between Libya and Egypt. It was extended to Syria by the arrival there of a German mission and to Iraq when a nationalist government supported

by German aircraft was removed by a British force. Iran had been occupied by the British and Russians in 1941. In Africa, Ethiopia was liberated and the Italian colonial empire destroyed.

With the opening of the Far Eastern war the Japanese wrought destruction on the colonial empires there, too. Within a few months they took Indonesia, Indo-China, Malaya, the Philippines. They pressed through Burma towards the Indian border and were soon bombing the north Australian port of Darwin from New Guinea. Meanwhile, the naval war was fought by German submarine forces, aircraft and surface raiders all over the Atlantic, Arctic, Mediterranean and Indian Ocean. Only a tiny minority of countries were still outside this struggle. Its demands were colossal and carried much further the mobilization of whole societies than had the First World War. The rôle of the United States was decisive. Her huge manufacturing power made the material preponderance of the 'United Nations' (as the coalition of states fighting the Germans, Italians and Japanese was called from the beginning of 1942) incontestable.

None the less, the way ahead was still a hard one. The first part of 1942 was still very bleak for the United Nations. Then came the turning-point, in four great and very different battles. In June a Japanese fleet attacking Midway Island was broken in a battle fought largely by air-craft. Japanese losses in carriers and crews were such that she never regained the strategical initiative and the long American counter-attack in the Pacific now began to unroll. At the beginning of November the British army in Egypt decisively defeated the Germans and Italians and began a march west which was to end with the eviction of the enemy from all North Africa the following May. The battle of El Alamein had coincided with landings by Anglo-American forces in French North Africa which had subsequently moved westwards. At the end of the year, the Russians had bottled up at Stalingrad on the Volga a German army rashly exposed by Hitler. The remnants surrendered in February in the most demoralizing defeat yet suffered in Russia, and yet one which was only part of three splendid months of winter advance which marked the turning-point of the war in Russia.

The other great Allied victory has no specific date, but was as important as any of these. This was the Battle of the Atlantic. Its peak came in the early months of 1942. In March nearly 850000 tons of shipping were lost and six U-boats were sunk; six months later, the figures were 560000 tons and eleven U-boats. The tide had turned, though there was still hard fighting ahead. At the end of the year nearly eight million tons of shipping had been lost for eighty-seven U-boats sunk. In 1943 the figures were three and a quarter million tons and 237 U-boats. This was the most crucial battle of all for the Allies, for on it depended their ability to draw on American production.

Command of the sea also made possible re-

Burma, 1944. Indian soldiers armed with American weapons fight other Asians on a battlefield dominated by the temples of Burmese Buddhism – which are themselves built from that most characteristic product of European industrialism, corrugated iron.

entry to Europe. Roosevelt had agreed to give priority to the defeat of Germany but the mounting of an invasion of France to take the strain off the Russian armies could not in the end be managed before 1944, and this angered the Russians. When it came, the Anglo-American invasion of northern France in June 1944 was the greatest seaborne expedition in history. Mussolini had by then been overthrown by Italians and Italy had already been invaded from the south; now Germany was fighting on three fronts. Soon after the landings in Normandy, the Russians entered Poland. Going faster than their allies, it still took them until next April to reach Berlin. In the west, Allied forces had broken out of Italy into central

977

A South Lancashire battalion lands in Normandy, on 6 June 1944, after the successful first assault of the greatest amphibious operation in history.

Europe and from the Low Countries into northern Germany. Almost incidentally, terrible destruction had been inflicted on the German cities by a great air offensive which, until the last few months of the war, exercised no decisive strategic effect. When, on 30 April, the man who had ignited this conflagration killed himself in a bunker in the ruins of Berlin, historic Europe was literally as well as figuratively in ruins.

The war in the Far East took a little longer. At the beginning of August 1945 the Japanese government knew it must be defeated. Many of Japan's former conquests had been retrieved, her cities were devastated by American bombing and her sea-power, on which communications and safety from invasion rested, was in ruins. At this moment two nuclear weapons of a destructive power hitherto unapproached were dropped with terrible effect on two Japanese

cities by the Americans. Between the explosions, the Russians declared war on Japan. On 2 September the Japanese government abandoned its plans of a suicidal last-ditch stand and signed an instrument of surrender. The Second World War had come to an end.

In its immediate aftermath it was difficult to measure the colossal extent of what happened. Only one clear and unambiguous good was at once visible, the overthrow of the Nazi régime. As the allied armies advanced into Europe, the deepest evils of a system of terror and torture were revealed by the opening of the huge prison camps and the revelations of what went on in them. It was suddenly apparent that Churchill had spoken no more than the bare truth when he told his countrymen that 'if we fail, then the whole world, including the United States, including all that we have known and cared for, will sink into the abyss of a new Dark Age made more sinister, and perhaps more protracted, by the lights of perverted science'. The reality of this threat could be seen in Belsen and Buchenwald. Distinctions could hardly be meaningful between degrees of atrocity inflicted on political prisoners, slave labourers from other countries or some prisoners of war. But the world's imagination was most struck by the systematic attempt which had been made to wipe out European Jewry, the so-called 'Final Solution' sought by Germans, an attempt which was carried far enough to change the demographic map: the Polish Jews were almost obliterated, and Dutch Jews, too, suffered heavily in proportion to their numbers. Overall, though complete figures may never be available, it is probable that between five and six million Jews were killed, whether in the gas-chambers and crematoria of the extermination camps, by shootings and extermination on the spot in east and south-east Europe, or by overwork and hunger.

Few people and no nations had engaged in the war because they saw it as a struggle against such wickedness, though no doubt many of them were heartened as it proceeded by the sense that the conflict had a moral dimension. Propaganda contributed to this. Even while England was the only nation on her feet and fighting for her survival, a democratic society had sought to see in the struggle positive ends which went beyond survival and beyond the destruction of Nazism. Hopes of a new world of cooperation between great powers and social and economic reconstruction were embodied in the Atlantic Charter and United Nations. They were encouraged by sentimental goodwill towards allies which terribly blurred differences of interest and social ideals only too quickly to re-emerge. Much of wartime rhetoric boomeranged badly as disillusionment followed inspection of the world after the guns were silent. Yet for all this, the war of 1939–45 in Europe

The reward of the heroic endurance of the Red Army: the Russian flag over occupied Berlin May 1945.

remains a moral struggle in a way, perhaps, in which no other has ever been. It is important to emphasize this because so much has been heard of the regrettable consequences of Allied victory. What was indisputably achieved was the overthrow of the worst challenge to liberal civilization which has ever arisen.

Some far-sighted men could see a deep irony in this. Germany had been one of the most progressive countries in Europe; the embodiment of many of the most central features of its civilization. That Germany should fall prey to collective derangement on this scale suggested that something had been wrong at the root of that civilization itself. The crimes of Nazism had been carried out not in a fit of barbaric intoxication with conquest, but in a systematic,

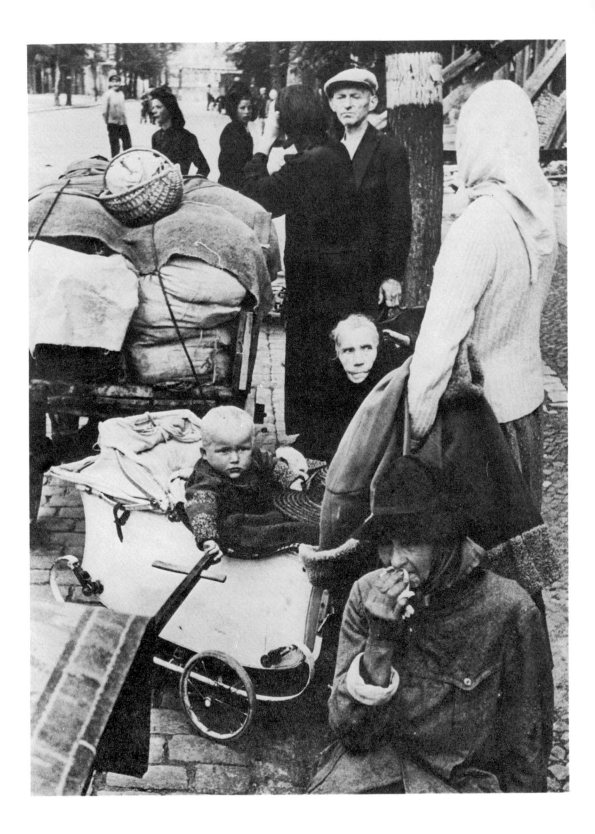

scientific, controlled, bureaucratic way about which there was little that was irrational except the appalling end which it sought. In this respect the Asian war was importantly different. Japanese imperialism replaced the old western imperialisms for a time, but often the subject peoples did not much regret the change. Propaganda during the war attempted to give currency to the notion of a 'fascist' Japan, but this was a distortion of so traditional a society's character. No such appalling consequences as faced European nations under German rule would have followed from a Japanese victory.

The second obvious result of the war which showed itself at once was its unparalleled destructiveness. It was most visible in the devastated cities of Germany and Japan, where aerial bombing, one of the major innovations of the Second World War, proved much more destructive of life and buildings than had been the bombing of Spanish cities in the Spanish civil war. Yet even the primitive and limited incursions of those days into this new form of warfare had then convinced many observers that bombing alone could bring a country to its knees. In fact, although often invaluable in combination with other forms of fighting, the huge strategic bombing offensive against Germany built up by the British Royal Air Force from 1941 onwards and steadily supplemented by the United States Air Force up to the point at which the combined bomber forces could provide a target with continuous day and night bombing, achieved very little until the last few months of the war. Nor was the destruction of the Japanese cities strategically so important as the elimination of her sea-power.

Not only cities had been shattered by bombing. The communications of central Europe had also been grievously stricken. In 1945, millions of refugees were wandering about in it, trying

Wandering about amid the debris of bombed towns and battlefields were millions of Europeans like this family from the East which had made its way to Berlin.

to get home. There was grave danger of famine and epidemic because of the difficulty of supplying food. The tremendous problems of 1918 were upon Europe again, and this time confronted nations demoralized by defeat and occupation; only the neutrals and Great Britain had escaped them. After fighting all over the continent, there were abundant arms in private hands, and a revolutionary threat could be feared. These conditions could also be found in Asia, but there the physical destruction was less severe and prospects of recovery better.

In Europe, too, the revolutionary political impact of the war was obvious in 1945. The power structure which had been a reality until 1914 and had an illusory prolongation of life between the two world wars was doomed in 1941. Two great peripheral powers dominated Europe politically and were established militarily in its heart. Once again, important new differences would separate the paths followed by the continent's eastern and western halves. Once again a Trieste–Baltic line became a reality. To the east of it in 1945 were revived states, all of which had communist governments or governments in which communists shared power with others. All of them had been overrun by the Russian army which proved itself a far better instrument for the extension of international communism than revolution had ever been.

Above all, Germany, the centre of the old power structure, had effectively ceased to exist. A phase of European history which she had dominated as had others before her was at an end and Bismarck's creation was partitioned into zones occupied by the Russians, Americans, British and French. The other major political units of western Europe had reconstituted themselves after occupation and defeat, but were feeble; Italy, which had changed sides after Mussolini had been overthrown, had, like France, a much strengthened and enlarged communist party which, it could not be forgotten, was still committed to the revolutionary overthrow of capitalism. Only Great Britain retained her stature of 1939 in the world's eyes, and it was certainly enhanced morally by her solitary stand in 1940 and 1941. She remained for a while the recognized equal of Russia and the United States. (Formally, this was true of France and China, too, but less attention was paid to them). Yet Great Britain's moment was past. By a huge effort of mobilizing her re-

On 17 July 1945, at Potsdam, the heart of the Prussian military tradition, the allied war leaders met for the first time after the defeat of Germany. President Truman had taken up his office automatically on the death of Roosevelt; Winston Churchill was soon afterwards to lose his after defeat in a general election. Only Stalin straddled war and peace.

sources and social life to a degree unseen outside Stalin's Russia, she had been able to retain her standing. But she had been let out of a strategic impasse only by the German attack on Russia, and kept afloat only by the American Lend-Lease which made available resources she could otherwise not have called upon. And this aid had not been without its costs: the Americans had insisted on the sale of British overseas assets to meet the bills of the United Kingdom before it was forthcoming. Moreover, the sterling area was dislocated, too; American capital was now to move into the old dominions on a large scale. Those dominions had learnt new lessons both from their new wartime strength and, paradoxically, from their weakness in so far as they had relied upon the mother country for their defence. From 1945, they more and more acted with full as well as formal independence.

It only took a few years for this huge change in the position of the greatest of the old imperial powers to become clear. Symbolically, when Great Britain made her last great military effort in Europe, in 1944, the expedition was commanded by an American general and though British forces in Europe for a few months afterwards matched the Americans, they were by the end of the war outnumbered. In the Far East, too, though the British reconquered Burma, the defeat of Japan was the achievement of American naval and air power. For all his close relationship and sympathy with Churchill, Roosevelt was by the end of the war negotiating over his head with Stalin, proposing *inter alia* the dismantling of the British Empire. Great Britain for all her huge efforts and the moral prestige she gained by standing alone in 1940 had not escaped the shattering impact of the war on Europe's political structure. Indeed, she was in some ways the power which, with Germany, illustrated it best.

Thus was registered in Europe the passing of the European supremacy evident also at its periphery. British forces secured Dutch and French territories in time to hand them back to their former owners and prevent the seizure of power by anti-colonial régimes. But fighting almost immediately began and it was clear that the imperial powers would have difficulties ahead. The year 1945 is therefore not a good place at which to pause; reality was still in some degree masked by appearance and some people could still not see that, at least in political and economic terms, the European age was for the visible future over.

6 The shaping of a new world

During the war many decisions had been taken about the post-war world. One of the most important had been that there should be an international organization with the aim of maintaining international peace. The fact that the great powers saw such an organization in different ways, the Americans as a beginning to the regulation of international life by law and the Russians as a means of keeping the Grand Alliance in being, did not prevent them pressing forward so that the United Nations Organization could come into being at San Francisco in 1945.

Much thought, naturally, had been given to the lessons of the League of Nations, which had not come up to expectations. One great defect of the League was remedied in 1945: the United States and Russia were members of the new organization from the start. Apart from this, the basic structure of the United Nations reproduced that of the League in outline, in consisting of two essential organs, a small Council and a large Assembly. Permanent representatives of all member states were to sit in the General Assembly. The Security Council had at first eleven members, of whom five were permanent; these were the representatives of the United States, Russia, Great Britain, France (at the insistence of Winston Churchill) and China. The Security Council was given greater power than the old League Council and this was largely the doing of the Russians. They saw that there was a strong likelihood that they

The United Nations Building, New York.

would always be outvoted in the General Assembly – where, at first, fifty-one nations were represented – because the United States could rely not only on the votes of its allies, but also on those of its Latin American satellites. Naturally, not all the smaller powers liked this strengthening of the body which would have the last word and in which the great powers would carry the main weight. Nevertheless, the structure the great powers wanted was adopted, as, indeed, it had to be if any organization was to work at all.

They agreed less easily with one another about the other main issue which caused grave constitutional dispute, the giving of a veto power to the permanent members of the Security Council. But this was a necessary feature if the great powers were to accept the organization and in the end the veto was restricted somewhat, in that a permanent member could not prevent investigation and discussion of matters which affected it especially unless they were likely to lead to action inimical to its interests.

In theory the Security Council possessed very great powers, but, of course, their operation was bound to reflect political reality. In the end, the greatest importance of the United Nations was to prove to lie not in its power to act, but in the forum it provided for discussion. For the first time, a world public linked as never before by radio and film – and later, by television – would have to be presented with a case made at the General Assembly for what sovereign states did. This was something quite new. The United Nations gave a new dimension to international politics rather than a new instrumentation for dealing with its problems. Sometimes, this produced feelings of sterility, as increasingly bitter and unyielding views were set out in debates which persuaded no one to change their mind. But even in these, an educational force was at work and it was especially important that it was soon decided that the permanent seat of the General Assembly should be in New York, since this drew American attention to it and helped to offset the historic pull of isolationism.

The first meeting of the United Nations General Assembly was held in London in 1946. Bitter debates began at once; attention was drawn to the Russian failure to withdraw its soldiers from the Iranian territory of Azerbaijan, occupied during the war, and the Russians at once replied by attacking Great Britain for keeping her forces in Greece. Within a few days, the first veto was cast, by the Russians. There were to be many more. The instrument which the Americans and British had regarded and continued to use as an extraordinary measure for the protection of special interests became a normal piece of Russian diplomatic technique. Already in 1946 the United Nations was an arena. In it, Russia contended with a still inchoate western bloc which her policies were to do much to solidify.

Though it has become fashionable to trace the origins of conflict between the United States and Russia back a very long way, the impression of the British in the later years of the war was that the Americans made too many concessions to Russia and were over-friendly. Of course, there was always a fundamental ideological division; if the Russians had not always had a deep preconception about the roots of behaviour of capitalist societies, they would certainly have behaved differently after 1945 towards their wartime ally. It is also true that evidence could be found that some Americans always deeply distrusted Russia and saw in it a revolutionary threat to their own society, though this is not the same thing as saying that they had significant impact in the making of American policy. But in 1945, when the war ended, American distrust of Russian intentions was much less than it later became. Of the two states the more suspicious and wary was Russia.

At that moment, Russia and the United States were the only great powers left. For all the legal fictions expressed in the composition of the Security Council, Great Britain was gravely overstrained, France barely risen from the living death of occupation. She was also plagued by internal divisions and a large communist party which threatened her stability. Italy had discovered that new divisions had been added to old ones which still troubled her. Japan was occupied and militarily powerless while China had never yet been a great power in modern times. The Americans and Russians therefore enjoyed an immense superiority over all possible rivals. Moreover, they were the only real victors. They alone had made positive gains from the war. All the other victorious states had, at the most, won survival or resurrection. To the United States and Russia, the war brought huge new empires.

Though Russia's had been won at huge cost, she now had greater strength than she had ever known under the tsars. Russian armies dominated a huge European glacis, much of which was formally Russian territory; the rest was organized in states which were by 1948 in every sense satellites. This area included Germany's second greatest industrial region. Beyond it lay Yugoslavia, the only communist state, which made itself without the help of Russian occupation, to emerge since the war; in 1945 she seemed an assured ally of Moscow. Russia's advantageous position owed most to the fighting of the Red Army, but also something to decisions taken both by western governments and by their commander in Europe during the closing stages of the war, General Eisenhower, who had resisted pressure to get to Prague and Berlin before the Russians. The resulting Russian strategical preponderance in central Europe was all the more menacing because no conceivable land-power existed as a counterweight. The old traditional barriers to Russian power provided by a Habsburg empire and a strong Prussia had gone. An exhausted Great Britain and slowly reviving France could not be expected to stand up to the Red Army.

Russian armies also stood in 1945 on the borders of Turkey and Greece – where a communist rising was under way – and still occupied northern Persia. In the Far East they had held much of Sinkiang, Mongolia, northern Korea and the naval base of Port Arthur as well as liberating the rest of Manchuria, though the only territory they actually took from Japan was the southern half of the island of Sakhalin and the Kuriles. The rest of these gains were effectively at China's expense. Yet in China there was already visible at the end of the war the possibility of a new communist state. Stalin might have backed the wrong horse there in the past, but the Chinese communists could not hope for moral and material help from anyone else and it seemed that in Asia, too, a new Russian satellite might be in the making.

The new scale of the United States' world power rested much less on occupation of territory, though she, too, had at the end of the war a garrison in the heart of Europe and naval and air bases round much of the Eurasian land mass. Though Russia was a far greater Asian power than ever before, the elimination of Japanese naval power together with the acquisition of island airfields and technological changes which made huge fleet trains possible had turned the Pacific Ocean into an American lake. Finally, Hiroshima and Nagasaki had demonstrated the power of the new weapon which the United States alone possessed, the atomic bomb.

The deepest roots of American empire nevertheless lay elsewhere, above all in her economic strength. Apart from the land-power of the Red Army, the decisive material factor behind the Allied victory had been the overwhelming industrial power of the United States. She had equipped not only her own huge forces but those of her allies. Moreover, victory had cost her little, by comparison with them. American casualties were relatively fewer than theirs; even

those of the United Kingdom were heavier in relation to population and those of Russia colossally so. The home base of the United States had been immune to enemy attack in any but a derisory sense and was undamaged; her fixed capital was intact, her resources little depleted. She was a great creditor country, with capital to invest abroad in a world where no one else could supply it. Her citizens had actually seen their standard of living rise during the war; the armament programme ended a depression which had not been mastered by the New Deal. Finally, America's old commercial and political rivals were soon staggering under the troubles of recovery. Their economies drifted into the ambit of the American because of their own lack of resources. The result was a world-wide surge of indirect American power, its beginnings visible even before the war ended.

Something of the future implicit in the great power polarization could already be seen dimly before the fighting stopped in Europe. It was made clear, for example, that the Russians would not be allowed to participate in the occupation of Italy or the dismantling of her colonial empire, and that the British and Americans were powerless to obtain a Polish settlement other than the one wanted by Stalin. Yet the Americans were not happy about explicit spheres of influence, for all their assertion of the principle in Latin America and the Caribbean; the Russians were more ready to take it as a working basis. There is no need to read back into such divergences assumptions which became current a few years after the war, when conflict between the two powers was presumed to have been sought from the start by one or other of them. Appearances can be deceptive. For all the power possessed by the United States in 1945, there was little political will to use it; the first concern of American military policy after victory was to achieve as rapid a demobilization as possible. Electors made sure of that. The cutting off of the Lend-Lease arrangements simply weakened allies the United States needed; they were faced with grave enough problems of recovery without having to shoulder those of providing a new security system to replace American strength. Nor could the use of the atomic bomb be envisaged except in the last resort: it was too powerful.

It is much harder to be sure of what was going on in Russia, but it is at least obvious that she had suffered appallingly from the war, more, possibly, even than Germany had done. No one has yet been able to do more than provide rough estimates, but it seems likely that over twenty million Russians may have died. Stalin may well have been much less conscious of his strength than his weakness when the war ended. True, Russian governmental methods relieved him of any need, such as faced western countries, to demobilize the huge land forces which gave him supremacy on the spot in Europe. But Russia had no atomic bomb nor a significant strategic bomber force. Stalin's decision to develop nuclear weapons put a further grave strain on the Russian economy at a time when general economic reconstruction was desperately needed. Some students have judged that the years immediately after the war were as grim for Russians as had been those of the industrialization race of the 1930s. Yet in 1949 an atomic explosion took place in Russia and in the following March it was officially announced that she had an atomic weapon. By then much had changed. Piecemeal, relations between the United States and Russia had deteriorated very badly and this happened mainly because of Europe, the area most in need of imaginative and coordinated reconstruction in 1945.

Europe's destruction has never been accurately measured in the places where it was worst, Germany and Russia. Leaving out the Russians, about fourteen and a quarter million Europeans were dead; if they were included, the total might rise as high as forty million. Those who survived lived amid shattered factories and communications. One estimate is that about seven and a half million dwellings were destroyed in Germany and Russia. There was nothing with which to pay for the imports Europe needed and currencies were in ruins;

Victory, like defeat, allowed the venting of many old passions and the wiping out of many old scores. A Breton accused of collaborating with the Germans faces his accusers.

allied occupation forces found that cigarettes and bully-beef were better than money. Civilized society had collapsed not only under the horrors of Nazi warfare, but also because occupation had transformed lying, swindling, cheating and stealing into acts of virtue; they were not only necessary to survival, but they could be glorified as acts of 'resistance'. The struggles against German occupying forces had bred new divisions; as countries were liberated by the advancing Allied armies, the firing squads got to work in their wake and old scores were wiped out. It is said that in France more perished in the 'purification' of liberation than in the great terror of 1793.

Above all, more finally even than in 1918, the economic structure of Europe had disintegrated. European economic life had long had the unity of a machine whose fly-wheel was industrial Germany. But even if the communications and the productive capacity to restore the machine had been there, the Allies were at first bent on holding down German industrial production to prevent her recovery. Furthermore, Germany was divided. From the start the Russians had been carrying off capital equipment as 'reparations' to repair their own ravaged lands – as well they might; the Germans had destroyed 39 000 miles of railway track alone in their retreat in Russia and Russia may have lost a quarter of her gross capital equipment.

A political division between eastern and western Europe was also coming to be evident before the end of the war and it would have economic implications. The British, in particular, had been alarmed by the handling of Poland's future because it seemed to show that Russia would only tolerate governments in eastern Europe which were subservient. This was hardly what the Americans had envisaged as freedom for nations in eastern Europe to choose their own rulers, but until the war was over neither government nor public opinion in the United States was much concerned or doubted the possibility of coming to reasonable agreement with the Russians. Broadly speaking, Roosevelt was sure that his country could get on with the Russians given the common ground of fears of a revival of German power and shared support of anti-colonialism. Neither he nor the American public sensed the historic tendencies of Russian policy in south-eastern Europe. They disapproved strongly of British intervention in Greece against the communist guerrillas who sought to overthrow the monarchy after the German withdrawal. (Stalin, on the other hand, did not object: he agreed with Churchill that Great Britain should have a virtually free hand in Greece in return for Russia having one in Romania.)

President Truman (who succeeded Roosevelt on his death in April 1945) and his advisers came to change their views about Russia largely as a result of their experience in Germany. The early omens had been good; the Russians had been punctilious in carrying out their agreement to admit British and American (and later French) armed forces to Berlin and share the administration of the city. There is every indication that they wished Germany to be governed

as a unit as envisaged by the victors at the Potsdam Conference in 1945. They had a powerful incentive in that this would give them a hand in controlling the Ruhr, potentially a treasure-house of reparations. Yet the German economy soon bred friction between West and East. Russian efforts to ensure security against German recovery led to the increasing separation in practice of her zone of occupation from that of the three other occupying powers. Probably this was at first intended to provide a solid and reliable (i.e. communist) core for a united Germany, but it led in the end to a solution by partition to the German problem which no one had envisaged. First, the western zones of occupation were for economic reasons integrated, without the eastern zone. Meanwhile Russian occupation policy aroused increasing distrust the more it was considered. Its methods of ensuring communist superiority in its zone of Germany seemed to repeat a pattern seen in other eastern European countries. Though there were in 1945 communist majorities only in Bulgaria and Yugoslavia, and elsewhere the communists shared power in coalition governments, it increasingly appeared to outsiders that eastern European governments could, in fact, do little more than behave as Russian puppets. Something like a bloc was appearing in eastern Europe in 1946.

It is rash to dogmatize about Russian motives at that moment. Stalin obviously feared any reunification of Germany except under a government he could control; Russia had too much historical experience of attack from the west to trust a united Germany. It would always have a potential for aggression which a satellite could not have and this would have been true whatever the ideological character of the Russian régime; it only made it worse that a united Germany might be capitalist. Elsewhere, though, more flexibility was shown by the Russians. While they were anxiously organizing eastern Germany on the Russian side of a line slowly appearing across Europe, they were still in China officially supporting the KMT. In Iran, on the other hand, Anglo-American concern was aroused by the reluctance of Russia to withdraw her forces as had been agreed and even when they went they left behind a satellite communist republic in Azerbaijan – later to be obliterated by the Iranians. By 1947 the Americans were giving Iran military aid. In the Security Council the Russian veto was more and more employed to frustrate her former allies and it was clear that the communist parties of western Europe were manipulated in Russian interests. Stalin's calculations at this moment must remain in doubt, though it seems likely that he was expecting and relying upon economic collapse in the capitalist world.

There was still much goodwill for Russia among her former allies. When Winston Churchill drew attention to the increasing division of Europe by an 'Iron Curtain' he by no means spoke either for all his countrymen or for his American audience. Yet though the British Labour government elected in 1945 was at first hopeful that 'Left could speak to Left' it soon came to be more sceptical. British and American policy began to converge during 1946, as it became clear that the British intervention in Greece had in fact made possible free elections and as American officials had more experience of the tendency of Russian policy. Nor did President Truman have the disadvantage of having to shed his predecessor's prejudices in favour of Russia. The British, moreover, were by now clearly embarked upon a deliberate policy of leaving India, and that counted much with American official opinion.

These were the circumstances in which Mr Truman took a momentous decision in February 1947. The occasion was a communication from the British government which, perhaps more than any other, embodied the long-resisted admission that Great Britain was no longer a world power. The British economy had been gravely damaged by the huge efforts made during the war. There was urgent need for investment at home. The first stages of decolonialization, too, were expensive. One result was that it became clear in 1947 that the British balance of payments could only be maintained if

forces were withdrawn from Greece. President Truman at once decided that the United States must fill the gap by giving financial aid to Greece and Turkey, so as to enable them to survive the pressure they were under from Russia. He deliberately drew attention to the implication; much more than propping up two countries was involved. Although only Turkey and Greece were to receive aid, he deliberately offered 'the free peoples' of the world American leadership to resist, by efforts which would have American support, 'attempted subjugation by armed minorities or by outside pressures'. This was a reversal of the apparent return to independence of Europe which the United States had seemed to wish to pursue in 1945 and a greater break than any earlier one with the tradition imposed by history and geography upon American foreign policy. The decision to 'contain' Russian power, as it was called, was possibly the most important in American diplomacy since the Louisiana Purchase. Ultimately, it was to lead to unrealistic assessments of the effective limits of American power, but this could not be seen at the time. It was provoked by Russian behaviour and the growing fears Stalin's policy had aroused over the previous eighteen months as well as by British weakness.

A few months later, the 'Truman Doctrine' was completed by another much more pondered step, an offer of American economic aid to European nations which would come together to plan jointly their economic recovery. This was the Marshall Plan, named after the American Secretary of State who announced it in a public speech. Its aim was a non-military, unaggressive form of containment. It surprised everyone. The British Foreign Secretary, Ernest Bevin, was the first foreign statesman who revealed a grasp of its implications and, with the French, pressed for the acceptance of the offer by western Europe. It was made, of course, to all Europe. But the Russians would not participate nor did they allow their satellites to do so. More, they bitterly attacked the plan. When, with obvious regret, the Czechoslovakian coalition government also declined to adhere,

Like Fascism and Nazism before it in Italy and Germany, Communism came to power in Czechoslovakia by management from above; the armed police and militia, the keys to power, march past the new government after the coup.

that country, the only one in eastern Europe still without a fully communist government and not regarded as a Russian satellite, was obviously having to toe the line, too. Any residual hope of Czechoslovakia's independence was removed by a communist coup in February 1948. Another sign of Russian intransigence was an old pre-war propaganda device, the Comintern, revived as the Cominform in September 1947. It at once began the denunciation of what it termed a 'frankly predatory and expansionist course . . . to establish the world supremacy of American imperialism'. Finally, when western Europe set up an Organization for European Economic Cooperation to handle the Marshall Plan the Russians replied by organizing their own half of Europe in Comecon, a Council for Mutual Economic Assistance which was for a long time largely window-dressing.

The Cold War had begun and the first phase of Europe's post-war history was over. The next phase was one in global history, too, and was to continue well into the 1960s. In it, two groups of states, one led by the United States and one by Soviet Russia, strove throughout a succession of crises to achieve their own security by all means short of war between the principal contenders. Much of what was said was put into ideological terms, and the Cold War therefore in some western countries also appeared as civil war or near-war, and as moral debate about values such as freedom, social justice and individualism. Some of it was fought in marginal theatres by propaganda and subversion or by guerrilla movements sponsored by the two

991

great states. Fortunately, they always stopped short of the point at which they would have to fight with the nuclear weapons whose increasing power made the notion of a successful outcome more and more unrealistic. The Cold War was also an economic competition by example and by offers of aid to satellites and uncommitted nations. Inevitably, much opportunism was mixed up in the process with doctrinaire rigidity. In retrospect, for all the simple brutalities of the language it generated, the Cold War now begins to look somewhat like the complex struggles of religion in sixteenth- and seventeenth-century Europe, when ideology could provoke violent emotion, but could never wholly contain the complexities and cross-currents of the day. Above all, it could not contain those introduced by national interest. Like the religious struggles of the past, too, though somewhat more rapidly, there was soon every sign that although the Cold War might die down and disaster be avoided, the rhetoric and mythology of the struggle would go rolling on long after it ceased to reflect reality.

The most important complication cutting across the Cold War and continuously influencing it was the existence of a growing number of states which did not feel committed to one side or the other. Many new nations came into existence within a few years after 1945 as a result of decolonization, which caused just as great an upheaval in international relations as the Cold War. The United Nations General Assembly was more important as a platform for anti-colonial than for Cold War propaganda.

There were many differences of circumstance and timing but by and large the Asian nationalist movements were guaranteed eventual success when the war exploded the card castle of European imperialism. This was first obvious in South-East Asia and Indonesia, but its repercussions were great even in areas (such as the Indian subcontinent) where the imperial power was not displaced by the Japanese. The surrender of 60 000 British, Indian and Dominions troops at Singapore in 1942 was the signal that empire in Asia was doomed. No efforts could

retrieve a loss of face far worse than Yorktown for it compromised the confidence and prestige of every European in the Far East. It did not matter that the Japanese often behaved badly to their new conquests. Parachuting arms to formerly subject peoples to resist the Japanese only strengthened the likelihood that they would be used in due course against their former rulers in London, Paris or The Hague. Furthermore, though life went on in most Asian villages undisturbed by comparison with the upheavals caused by bombing, fighting, labour conscription, starvation and disease in Europe, there had been notable side-effects. There was a big potential for change when the Japanese were defeated. In the end, imperial possessions in the Far East were all but swept away within a few years of 1945. Yet this was not all that was at stake. Though Russian and American spheres of influence in Europe were (with the possible exception of Berlin) clearly enough demarcated in 1948 to remain unchanged for a quarter of a century, the settlement of spheres of interest in the Far East was to be in doubt for much longer. In part this was because two new great powers would appear on the scene: a communist China and a revived Japan.

Some thought India might become a great power too, but this did not happen although the subcontinent's history took a new turn. Even before 1939 it was plain that what was at issue there was no longer the survival of imperial rule, but the timetable and form of its replacement. Englishmen who favoured Indian independence hoped to keep it linked to the British Commonwealth of Nations, the name usually given to the empire since the Imperial Conference of 1926. That conference had produced the first official definition of 'Dominion Status' as independent association to the Commonwealth in allegiance to the Crown, with complete control of internal and external affairs. This set a conceivable goal for India, though it was not one which British governments could see as an immediate aim before 1940. Yet though unevenly, some progress was made before this, and this is a part of the explanation of the absence in India of so complete a revulsion of anti-western feeling as had occurred in China.

Indian politicians had been deeply disappointed by their treatment after the First World War. They had for the most part then rallied loyally to the Crown; India had made big contributions of men and money to the imperial war effort, and Gandhi had been one of those who had worked for it in the belief that this would bring a due reward. In 1917, the British government had indeed announced that it favoured a policy of steady progress towards responsible government for India within the empire – Home Rule, as it were – though this was short of the Dominion status some Indians were beginning to ask for. Reforms announced in 1918 were very disappointing, but satisfied some moderates. Unfortunately, even this limited success was soon dissipated. Moreover, those Indian soldiers who had served abroad had sometimes seen their masters defeated and their respect and loyalty was no longer unquestioning.

One of the factors influencing the situation was the continuing isolation of the British community in India. Convinced that Indian nationalism was a matter of a few ambitious intellectuals, its members pressed merely for strong measures against conspiracy, a course which recommended itself to administrators now confronted with the consequences of the Bolshevik revolution (though the Indian communist party was not founded until 1923). The result was legislation against the wishes of all the Indian members of the legislative council which suspended normal legal safeguards in order to deal with conspiracy. This provoked Gandhi's first campaign of strikes and pacifist civil disobedience. In spite of his efforts to avoid violence there were riots and when some Englishmen were killed and others were attacked at Amritsar in 1919, a foolish general decided to disperse a crowd by force. When the firing stopped, nearly four hundred Indians had been killed and over a thousand wounded. A bad blow to British prestige was then made worse by the very vocal approval by British residents

in India and some members of parliament for what this man had done.

A period of boycott and civil disturbance followed in which Gandhi's programme was adopted by Congress, which became a mass party; although he himself emphasized that his campaign was non-violent there was nevertheless much disorder and Gandhi was arrested and imprisoned for the first time in 1922. He was soon released because of the danger that he might die in prison, but this was the end of significant agitation in India for the next few years and in 1927 British policy began to move slowly forward again. A commission was sent to India to look into the working of the last series of constitutional changes, though it caused more trouble because no Indians had been included in it. On the other hand, much of the enthusiasm which had sustained unity among the nationalists had by now evaporated and there was a danger of a rift bridged by Gandhi's efforts and prestige between those who stuck to the demand for complete independence and those who wanted to work for dominion status. Congress was, in any case, a less solid structure than its rhetoric suggested. It was less a political party with deep roots in the masses than a coalition of local bigwigs and interests. Finally, a more serious division still was the now deepening one between Hindu and Moslem. The leaders of the two communities had watched the relations between their followers deteriorate rapidly in the 1920s. Every year there was communal rioting and bloodshed. By 1930 the president of the Moslem political league was proposing that the future constitutional development of India should include the establishment of a separate Moslem state in the north-west.

That year was a violent one. The British viceroy had announced that a conference was to take place with the aim of achieving dominion status, but this undertaking was made meaningless by opposition in Great Britain. The result was that Gandhi would not take part. Civil disobedience was resumed after a second conference foundered on the question of minorities' representation and was made as distress deepened with the world economic depression. But the wheels of the India Office were beginning to turn as they absorbed the lessons of the discussions and the 1927 commission.

A real devolution of power and patronage came in 1935, when a Government of India Act was passed which took still further the establishment of representative and responsible government, leaving in the viceroy's sole control only such matters as defence and foreign affairs. This was the culmination of legislation by the British which effectively called national politics into being by making it increasingly clear that at all levels the decisive struggles between Indians would have to be fought out within the Congress party. The Act once more affirmed the principle of separate communal representation and almost immediately its working provoked further hostility between Hindu and Moslem. Congress was by now to all intents and purposes a Hindu organization, though it refused to concede that the Moslem League should therefore be the sole representative of Moslems. But Congress had its internal problems, too, divided as it was between those who still wished to press forwards to independence and those – some of them beginning to be alarmed by Japanese aggressiveness – who were willing to work the new institutions in cooperation with the imperial government. The evidence that the British were in fact devolving power was bound to be a divisive force as different interests sought to protect themselves against an uncertain future.

Under the surface, the tide was running fast by 1941. Nearly two decades of the working of representative institutions in local government and the progressive Indianization of the higher civil service had already produced a country which could not be governed except by the substantial consent of its élites. Though the approach of war made the British increasingly aware of their need of the Indian army, they had already abandoned the notion of making India pay for it. By 1941 the British were bearing the cost of its modernization. Then the Japanese attack forced the hand of the British

Calcutta, 1940; the dispersing of an anti-British riot. In spite of the extra strains imposed by war, the Raj was never near losing its grip on public order in the sub-continent and could rely upon the support of Indian civil servants, police and soldiers until the very end in 1947.

The end of the Raj: The Somerset Light Infantry dips the colours in salute in the last British parade held in India.

The cremation of Gandhi's body after his murder by a Hindu fanatic.

government, but too late; it offered the nationalists autonomy after the war and a right of secession from the Commonwealth, but they now demanded immediate independence. Their leaders were arrested and India continued to be ruled by Great Britain. A rebellion in 1942 was crushed much more rapidly than had been the Mutiny nearly a century earlier, but the sands were running out if the British wanted to go peacefully. One new factor was pressure from the United States. President Roosevelt discussed confidentially with Stalin the need to prepare for Indian independence (as well as that of other parts of Asia, and the need for trusteeship for French Indo-China); the involvement of the United States implied revolutionary change in other people's wars just as it had, done in 1917.

In the end it also mattered that in 1945 the Labour party, which had long had the independence of India and Burma as part of its programme, came to power at Westminster. On 14 March 1946, while India was torn with Hindu–Moslem rioting and its politicians were squabbling over the future, the British government offered full independence. Nearly a year later, it put a pistol to the head of the Indians by announcing that it would hand over power not later than June 1948. Thus the tangle of communal rivalries was cut and the partition of the subcontinent followed. The only unity it had ever enjoyed as a whole was ended and two new Dominions appeared within it, Pakistan and India. The first was Moslem and divided into two slabs of land at the extremities of northern India. The cost of such a partition was enormous. The psychic wound to many nationalists was symbolized by the murder of Gandhi by a Hindu fanatic for his part in it. Huge massacres occurred in areas where there were minorities. Something like two million people fled to where their coreligionists were in control. Almost the only clear political gain on the morrow of independence was the solution, a bloody one, of the communal problem for the foreseeable future. Apart from this, the only assets of the new states were the goodwill (arising from very mixed motives) shown to them by great powers, the inheritance of a civil service already largely native before independence and an important infrastructure of institutions and services. These inheritances were, however, not equally shared, India tending to enjoy more of them than Pakistan.

Such advantages could not do much to deal with the grave problems of the subcontinent's economic and social backwardness. The worst problem was that of demographic growth. A steady rise in population had begun under British rule. Sometimes it was briefly mitigated by Malthusian disasters like the great influenza epidemic at the end of the First World War which struck down five million Indians or a famine in Bengal during the Second World War which carried off other millions. But in 1951 there was famine again in India and in 1953 in Pakistan. The spectre of it was still there in 1975.

The subcontinent's industrialization, which had made important strides in the twentieth century (notably in the Second World War) did not offset this danger. It could not provide new jobs and earnings at a rate equal to that at which the population grew. Though the new India had most of what industry there was, her problems were graver in this respect than those of Pakistan. Though there were huge Indian cities, where conditions worsened rapidly in the quarter-century after independence, most Indians were landless peasants, living in villages where, for all the egalitarian aspirations of some of the leaders of the new republic, inequality remained as great as ever. The landlords who provided the funds for the ruling Congress party and dominated its councils stood in the way of any land reform which could have dealt with this.

India has seemed more resistant to change than any other developing nation, and this was part of the legacy of traditional Hindu society. The past lay heavy on a state proclaiming ideals and aims essentially western – democracy, secularism, material progress – and it tangled the path of reform every inch of the way. After the outlawing of 'untouchability' in the last days of the Raj little has been done to tackle the enormous obstacles to change presented by Hindu social practice. India has remained a country where marriage outside one's caste is still im-

probable (in 1947 it was virtually unthinkable) and where auspicious days can still determine the calendar of a businessman or even a public servant.

China, of course, had for a long time seemed as resistant to change as India, but she had also been engaged longer in fighting off a different sort of imperialism. The completion of this long revolution was made possible by the Second World War. The political phase of this transformation began in 1941 when the Sino-Japanese War merged in a world conflict. This gave China powerful allies and a new international standing. Significantly, the last vestiges of the 'unequal treaties' with Great Britain, France and the United States were then swept away. This was more important than the military help the Allies could give; for a long time they were too busy extricating themselves from the disasters of early 1942 to do much for China. A Chinese army, indeed, came instead to help to defend Burma from the Japanese. Still hemmed in to the west, though supported by American aircraft, the Chinese had for a long time to hold out as best they could, in touch with their allies only by air or the Burma Road. None the less a decisive change had begun.

China had at first responded to Japanese attacks with a sense of national unity long desired but never hitherto forthcoming except, perhaps, in the May 4th Movement. There had been friction between the communists and the nationalists, sometimes breaking out into open conflict, but on the whole this unity survived until 1941. Then, the new fact that the United States was now Japan's major enemy, and would eventually destroy her, subtly began to transform the attitude of the nationalist government. It came to feel that as ultimate victory was certain, there was no point in using up men and resources in fighting the Japanese when they might be husbanded for the struggle against the communists after the peace. Some of its members went further. Soon the KMT was fighting the communists again.

Two Chinas appeared. Nationalist China increasingly displayed the lethargy, self-seeking

A brief harmony. Mao and Chiang K'ai-shek in Chungking 1946.

and corruption which had from the early 1930s tainted the KMT because of the nature of the support on which it drew. The régime was repressive and stifled criticism. It alienated the intellectuals. Its soldiers, sometimes badly officered and undisciplined, terrorized the peasant as much as did the Japanese. Communist China was different. In large areas controlled by the communists (often behind the Japanese lines) a deliberate attempt was being made to ensure the support of as wide a spectrum of interests as possible by moderate but unambiguous reform and disciplined behaviour. Outright attacks on landlords were usually avoided, but peasant goodwill was cultivated by enforcing lower rents and abolishing usury. Meanwhile, Mao published a series of theoretical writings designed to prepare the new communist cadres for the task that lay ahead. There was a need for political education as the party and the army grew steadily in numbers; when the Japanese

collapsed in 1945 there were about a million Chinese communist soldiers.

The suddenness of victory was the second factor which shaped the last stage of the Chinese Revolution. Huge areas of China had suddenly to be reoccupied and reincorporated in the Chinese state. But many of them were already effectively under communist control before 1945 and others could not possibly be reached by nationalist forces before the communists dug themselves in there. The Americans did what they could by sending soldiers to hold some of the ports until the nationalists could take them over. In some places the Japanese were told to hold on until the Chinese government could re-establish its authority. But when the final and military phase of the revolution opened, the communists held more territory than they had ever done before and held it in the main with the support of the population who found that communist rule was by no means as bad as they had heard.

All unwittingly, the Japanese, by launching

997

*31 January 1949: the entry of the victorious
Communist soldiers to Peking.*

their attack on the KMT régime, had in the end
brought about the very triumph of the Chinese
revolution they had long striven to avoid. It is
at least possible that if the nationalists had been
undistracted by foreign invasion and had not
suffered the crippling damage it inflicted, they
might have been able to master Chinese communism in the short run. In 1937 the KMT
could still draw heavily on patriotic goodwill;
many Chinese believed that it was the authentic
carrier of the revolution. The war destroyed the
chance of exploiting this, if it existed, but also
enabled China to resume for the last time her
long march towards world power from which
she had been deflected first by Europeans and
then by fellow-Asians. The long frustration of
Chinese nationalism was about to end, and the
beneficiary would be communism.

The defeat of the KMT took three years.
Although the Japanese usually sought to surrender to the KMT or Americans, the communists had acquired authority in new areas and
often large stocks of arms when they gave in.
The Russians, who had invaded Manchuria,
in the last days before the Japanese surrender,
helped the communists and gave them access to
the Japanese arms there. Against this background Mao made deliberately moderate policy

pronouncements and continued to push forward
with land reform. This conferred a further great
advantage on the communists in the civil war
which continued until 1949; victory in that war
was essentially a victory of the countryside over
a city-based régime.

American policy was increasingly disillusioned by the revealed inadequacy and corruption of the Chiang Kai-shek régime. In 1947
American forces were withdrawn from China
and the United States abandoned the efforts it
had hitherto made to mediate between the two
Chinas. In the following year, with most of the
north in communist hands, the Americans
began to cut down the amount of financial and
military aid given to the KMT. From this time,
the nationalist government ran militarily and
politically downhill; it became obvious, and
more and more employees of government and
local authorities sought to make terms with the
communists while they might still do so. The
conviction spread that a new era was dawning.
By the beginning of December, no important
nationalist military force remained intact on the
mainland and Chiang withdrew to Formosa
(Taiwan). The Americans cut off their aid while

998

this withdrawal was under way and publicly blamed the inadequacies of the nationalist régime for the débâcle. Meanwhile, on 1 October 1949, the People's Republic of China was officially inaugurated at Peking and the largest communist state in the world had come into existence. Once again, the mandate of Heaven had passed.

In South-East Asia and Indonesia the Second World War was as decisive as elsewhere in ending colonial rule though the pace was faster in Dutch and French colonies than British. The grant of genuine representative institutions by the Dutch in Indonesia had not checked the growth of a nationalist party before 1939, and a flourishing communist movement had appeared by then, too. Some nationalist leaders, among them one Achmed Sukarno, collaborated with the Japanese when they occupied the islands in 1942. They were in a favourable position to seize power when the Japanese surrendered, and did so by proclaiming an independent Indonesian republic before the Dutch could return. Fighting and negotiation followed for nearly two years until agreement was reached for an Indonesian republic still linked to Holland under the Dutch Crown; this did not work. Fighting went on again, the Dutch pressing forwards vainly with their 'police operations' in one of the first campaigns by a former colonial power to attract the full blast of communist and anti-colonial stricture at the United Nations. Both India and Australia (which had concluded that she would be wise to conciliate the independent Indonesia which must eventually emerge) took the matter to the Security Council. Finally the Dutch gave in. The story begun by the East India Company of Amsterdam three and a half centuries before thus came to an end in 1949 with the creation of the United States of Indonesia, a mixture of more than 100 million people scattered over hundreds of islands, of scores of races and religions. A vague union with the Netherlands under the Dutch Crown survived, but was dissolved five years later.

For a time the French in Indo-China seemed

A Japanese officer takes a salute from a French guard of honour in Vietnam, 1940. The French authorities continued to administer the colony after the Japanese occupied it for their own strategic and economic purposes.

to be holding on better than the Dutch. That area's wartime history had been somewhat different from that of Malaysia or Indonesia because although the Japanese had exercised complete military control there since 1941 French sovereignty was not formally displaced until early 1945. The Japanese had amalgamated Annam, Cochin-China and Tongking to form a new state of Vietnam under the Emperor of Annam and as soon as the Japanese surrendered, the chief of the local communist party, the Viet Minh, installed himself in the government palace at Hanoi and proclaimed the Vietnam republic. This was Ho Chi Minh, a man with long experience in the communist party and also in Europe. The revolutionary movement quickly spread. It was soon evident that if the French wished to re-establish themselves it would not be easy. A large expeditionary force was sent to Indo-China and a concession was made in that the French recognized the republic of Vietnam as an autonomous state within the French Union. But now there arose the question of giving Cochin-China separate status and on this all attempts to agree broke down. Meanwhile, French soldiers were sniped at and their convoys were attacked. At the end of 1946 there was an attack on residents in Hanoi and many deaths. Hanoi was relieved by French troops and Ho Chi Minh fled.

Thus began a war in which the communists were to struggle essentially for the nationalist aim of a united country, while the French tried to retain a diminished Vietnam which, with the other Indo-Chinese states, would remain inside the French Union. By 1949 they had come round to including Cochin-China in Vietnam and recognizing Cambodia and Laos as 'associate states'. But new outsiders were now becoming interested. The government of Ho Chi Minh was recognized in Moscow and Peking, that of the Annamese emperor whom the French had set up by the British and Americans.

In Asia the processes of decolonialization had thus quickly escaped from the simple forms in which they had been envisaged by Roosevelt. The British began to liquidate their recovered heritage, too. Burma and Ceylon had become independent in 1947. In the following year, communist-supported guerrilla war began in Malaya; though it was to be unsuccessful and not to impede steady progress towards independence in 1957, it was one of the first post-colonial phenomena to present American policy with a problem which was to dog it. The development of antagonism with the communist world soon cut across the simplicities of American anti-colonialism. Only in the Middle East was the outlook still relatively uncomplicated for the United States in 1948.

In May that year, there came into being in Palestine a new state, Israel. This marked the end of an era lasting since 1918 in which the Middle East's fundamental stability had rested on the fact that only two great powers had to agree in order to dominate the area. France and Great Britain had not found this too difficult, but as in other parts of the world, the war had greatly changed things. In 1939 the French still held mandates in Syria and the Lebanon (their original mandate had been divided into two), and the British retained theirs in Palestine, but elsewhere in the Islamic lands they exercised varying degrees of influence or power according to terms negotiated with individual states. The most important areas were Iraq, where a small British force, mainly of air force units, was maintained, and Egypt, where there was a substantial garrison to protect the Suez Canal. This had become a more and more important matter in the 1930s as Italy showed increasing hostility to Great Britain. After Italy's entry to the war, when Egypt suddenly found herself with a war on her western border, it became one of the most vital areas of British strategy. Egypt remained neutral almost to the end, but was in effect a British base and little else. The war also made it far more vital to assure the supply of oil from the Gulf and this increased the importance attached to Iraq. This led to intervention when Iraq threatened to move in a pro-German direction after yet another nationalist coup in 1941. A British and Free French invasion of Syria to keep it, too, out of German hands led in 1941 to an independent Syria. Soon afterwards the Lebanon proclaimed its independence. The French tried to re-establish their authority at the end of the war, but unsuccessfully, and during 1946 these two countries saw the last foreign garrisons leave. The French also had difficulties further west, where fighting broke out in 1945 in Algeria. There, nationalists were at that moment asking only for autonomy in federation with France and the French went some way in this direction in 1947, but this was far from the end of the movement.

Where British influence was paramount, anti-British sentiment was still a good rallying-cry for agitators and in both Egypt and Iraq there was much hostility to British occupation forces in the post-war years. In 1946 the British announced that they were prepared to withdraw from Egypt but negotiations on the basis of a new treaty broke down so badly that Egypt referred the matter (unsuccessfully) to the United Nations. By this time the whole question of the future of the Islamic lands had been overtaken by a decision which has dogged the politics of the area ever since, that of the Jews to establish a national state in Palestine by force.

The catalyst in the Palestine question was the Nazi revolution in Germany. At the time of the Balfour Declaration there had been 600 000 Arabs in Palestine and 80 000 Jews – a number already felt by Arabs to be threateningly large. In some years after this, though, Jewish emigration actually exceeded immigration and there was ground for hope that the problem of reconciling the promise of a 'national home' for Jews with respect for 'the civil and religious rights of the existing non-Jewish communities in Palestine' (as the Declaration had put it) might be resolved. Hitler changed this.

From the beginning of the Nazi persecution the numbers of those who wished to come to Palestine rose and as the extermination policies began to unroll in the war years, they made nonsense of British attempts to restrict immigration which were the side of British policy unacceptable to Jews (the other side – the partitioning of Palestine – was rejected by the Arabs). The issue was dramatized as soon as the war was over by the World Zionist Congress demanding that a million Jews should be admitted to Palestine at once. Other new factors now began to operate. The British, in 1945, had looked benevolently on the formation of an 'Arab League' of Egypt, Syria, Lebanon, Iraq, Saudi Arabia, the Yemen and Transjordan. There had always been in British policy a strand of hopefulness that Pan-Arabism might prove the way in which the Middle East could be persuaded to settle down and that the coordination of the policies of Arab states would open the way to the solution of many problems. In fact the League was soon preoccupied with Palestine to the virtual exclusion of anything else.

The other novelty was Russian and American interest in the Middle East. In the immediate post-war era, Stalin seems to have been impressed still with the pre-war communist view that Great Britain was the main imperialist power and prop of the international capitalist system. Attacks on her position and influence

therefore followed and in the Middle East this, of course, coincided with traditional Russian interests. This was a revival: Russia had shown little interest in the area between 1919 and 1939. It was also a complement to the pressure being brought to bear at the same time on Turkey at the Straits. Accordingly, Russian policy was deployed continuously to support Zionism, the most disruptive element in the situation. It did not need extraordinary political insight to recognize the implications of a resumption of Russian interest in the area of the Ottoman legacy. At just the same time, American policy became anti-British, or, rather, pro-Zionist. This could hardly have been avoided. In 1946 mid-term congressional elections were held and as they approached the votes of American sympathizers with Zionism became important. Since the Roosevelt revolution in domestic politics, a Democratic president could hardly envisage an anti-Zionist position.

Thus beset, the British sought to disentangle themselves from the Holy Land. From 1945 they faced both Jewish and Arab terrorism and guerrilla warfare in Palestine. Unhappy Arab, Jewish and British policemen struggled to hold the ring while the British government once more strove to find a way acceptable to both sides of bringing the mandate to an end. On one occasion it even enlisted American help, but to no avail; Truman wanted a pro-Zionist solution. In the end the British took the matter to the United Nations. It, too, recommended partition, still a non-starter for the Arabs. Warfare between the two communities grew fiercer and the British decided to withdraw without more ado. On the day that they did so, the state of Israel was proclaimed and was immediately recognized both by the United States and Russia; they were to agree about little else in the Middle East for the next quarter-century.

Israel was also attacked almost at once by the forces of the Arab League. These she fought off and a truce, supervised by the United Nations, followed, during which a Zionist terrorist assassinated the United Nations mediator. In 1949 the Israeli government moved to Jeru-

Proposed UN partition 1947

Israel 1948-1967

Israel 1967-1975

salem, a Jewish national capital again for the first time since the days of imperial Rome. Half of the city was still occupied by Jordanian forces, but this was almost the least of the problems left to be solved. Through American and Russian diplomatic support and American private money, Jewish energy and initiative had successfully established a new national state where no basis for one had existed twenty-five years before, but at enormous cost. The disappointment and humiliation of the Arab states assured their continuing hostility and therefore opportunities for great power intervention in the future; here was the fruit of the unhappy and tangled policies followed by Great Britain in the Middle East since 1914. Moreover, the deliberate terrorism of some Zionist extremists and the far from conciliatory behaviour of Israeli forces in 1948-9 led to an exodus of Arab refugees. Soon there were 750 000 of them in camps in Egypt and Jordan, a social and economic problem, a burden on the world's conscience, and a potential military and diplomatic weapon in Arab hands. It would hardly be surprising were it true (as some students believe) that the first president of Israel quickly

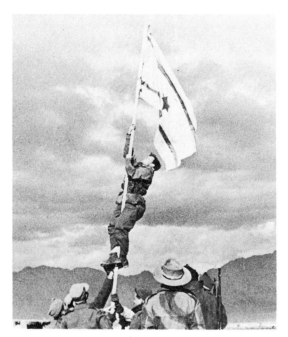

The flag of the new state of Israel raised at the port of Elath, on the gulf of Aqaba, during the 1948 war.

The Egyptian government's confidence that the new Jewish state would be overthrown was expressed in a commemorative postage stamp which proved ill-judged.

began to encourage his country's scientists to begin work on a nuclear energy programme.

Thus many currents flowed together in a curious and ironical way to swirl in confusion in an area always a focus of world history. Victims for centuries, the Jews were in their turn now seen by Arabs as persecutors. The problems with which the peoples of the area had to grapple were poisoned by forces flowing from the dissolution of centuries of Ottoman power, from the rivalries of successor imperialisms, from the rise of two new world powers which dwarfed these in their turn, from the interplay of nineteenth-century European nationalism and ancient religion, from the strategical needs of European states and the first effects of the revolution implied in the growing twentieth-century dependence of developed nations on oil. There are few moments in the twentieth century so soaked in history as the establishment of Israel and it is a good point at which to pause before turning to the last part of this book, the story of the contemporary world.

Book Eight   The Post-European Age

For most of the time since 1945, great powers have at least been able to avoid fighting one another openly, unlikely though this has sometimes seemed. On the other hand, for all the hopes and rhetoric swirling about the infant United Nations Organization, nations belonging to it have gone to war with one another many times. There has been no return to what from this distance seems the Augustan peace of the late nineteenth century. We have frequent enough reminders of persistent divisions within mankind and enough reports of new ones to take it for granted that the world has never been so fragmented. Nationality, ideology and economic interest still cut across it with irresistible force as debates at the United Nations show. Yet this is a view from a particular perspective and there are others.

It is also true – and has already been argued here – that in many ways there has never been a time when world civilization has been more of a reality. Mankind is now tied together by some common experience as it has not been tied together since it was liberated from the simplest and most crushing restraints of environment. From that moment many paths led for many thousands of years to human diversity. They began to move back together once again when a pattern of life first evolved in Europe was gradually spread world-wide from that geographical base in the process called 'modernization' or 'westernization'.

Of course, it is just as important not to exaggerate the completeness of this change as it is not to underestimate it. The disparities of experience between rich and poor are greater than ever. Furthermore, some traditions have shown great tenacity in resisting disruption by European civilization. The East Asian sphere of civilization whose roots lie in the diffusion of Chinese culture has been especially impervious to fundamental change and the Islamic lands and India have in varying degree rejected the individualism of western civilization. Yet it remains true that as a consequence of the European political supremacy of the eighteenth and nineteenth centuries and of advances in communication in our own, experience and assumptions are shared more widely than ever.

The Second World War released many currents which put new force behind the urge to modernize, and this complicated force seems to lie at the heart of the latest era. It is difficult to seize, not only because of its vastness (though that makes it hard enough to distinguish major trends from accidental details), but also because our perspective in the last quarter-century changes almost day by day. The war in the Middle East in 1973 was from one point of view merely one more of many indecisive conflicts which have followed the collapse of Ottoman empire, but in another perspective, it was the first to reveal a reversal of the relations of some great industrial societies to the Islamic world because of dependence on its oil. No doubt yet other perspectives will refresh and transform our view of this period in another ten or even five years' time. Nevertheless, we have to try to understand such changes historically: this is almost a definition of the responsibility of the historian. If we can discern the general tendencies in the background to the events, their shape may sometimes make the overwhelming rush of those events just a little more comprehensible.

Albert Einstein
Old Grove Rd.
Nassau Point
Peconic, Long Island

August 2nd, 1939

F.D. Roosevelt,
President of the United States,
White House
Washington, D.C.

Sir:

Some recent work by E.Fermi and L. Szilard, which has been com-
municated to me in manuscript, leads me to expect that the element uranium may be turned into a new and important source of energy in the immediate future. Certain aspects of the situation which has arisen seem
to call for watchfulness and, if necessary, quick action on the part
of the Administration. I believe therefore that it is my duty to bring
to your attention the following facts and recommendations:

In the course of the last four months it has been made probable -
through the work of Joliot in France as well as Fermi and Szilard in
America - that it may become possible to set up a nuclear chain reaction
in a large mass of uranium,by which vast amounts of power and large quantities of new radium-like elements would be generated. Now it appears
almost certain that this could be achieved in the immediate future.

This new phenomenon would also lead to the construction of bombs,
and it is conceivable - though much less certain - that extremely powerful bombs of a new type may thus be constructed. A single bomb of this
type, carried by boat and exploded in a port, might very well destroy
the whole port together with some of the surrounding territory. However,
such bombs might very well prove to be too heavy for transportation by
air.

1 A world civilization

Anything that happens anywhere in the world nowadays can produce effects very rapidly elsewhere. Affairs of all parts of the world are increasingly tangled up in one large process. It is less obvious, equally important and much more remarkable that so many people recognize this. At first sight, after all, it is surprising that Indians should demonstrate against nuclear weapons tests in the South Pacific or that the Chinese government should interest itself in an Arab–Israeli war. Some of the reasons for this new sense of world-wide interconnexion lie in factors such as ideology and the more rapid communication of information, but something more fundamental is involved, too. This is the generalization of an idea once confined to cultures of European origin, the notion that human life and the condition of the world may be indefinitely improved for the better.

This is a very new idea in most parts of the globe. It is still true, too, that few people could formulate it clearly or consciously. Nonetheless it now affects the behaviour of human beings all

The post-war era has been dominated by the awareness that quite unprecedented dangers face mankind in the destructive power of nuclear weapons. The technology of these was created with amazing swiftness. This letter, drafted by a Hungarian scientist, Leo Szilard, and signed by Einstein, was sent to President Roosevelt less than a month before war began in Europe. Six years and four days later, the first atomic bomb to be used was dropped at Hiroshima.

over the world. It has not been diffused so much by conscious preaching as by the simple pressure of material changes on an enormous scale. One of the most important aspects of all the many material changes which have affected more and more people in this century is the fact that they happened at all; they broke up the cake of custom. This has had a great psychological impact, simply by bringing to many parts of the world the idea that change is in fact possible, that things need not always be what they have been. Though a huge gulf still separates, say, the European factory worker from the Asian peasant (and it is one wider than that between their ancestors a thousand years ago), to implant the assumption that change is possible, inevitable, perhaps desirable is the last and most important conquest to be made by European culture.

Such an effect can be seen, paradoxically, in the response to one of the changes wholly unwilled and, seemingly, uncontrollable by man, the huge and accelerating rise in world population which is now going on. Accuracy is still a highly relative business in computing populations – we can only estimate to within one or two hundred millions how many people are now alive – but the degree of error in our estimates is not such that the general bearing of what has happened is not clear. In round numbers, a world population of about 730 million in 1750 more than doubled by 1900, when it stood at about 1600 million. Thus about 850 million had been added to it in about a century and a half, but it took only fifty years to add the next 850 million and more; by 1950 the population of the world stood at about 2500 million. Even more striking, the next 850 million had been added by the middle of the 1960s – in, say, fifteen years – and now the total is just over 4000 million, that magic figure having probably been passed on the last Sunday in March, 1975. Though it had taken at least 50000 years for *homo sapiens* to increase to 1000 million (a figure reached in the mid-nineteenth century) the last 1000 million of his species took only 15 years to be added to a total growing more and more rapidly.

Fortunately, as Malthus himself observed, 'no estimate of future population or depopulation, formed from any existing rate of increase or decrease, can be depended upon'. We cannot be sure what may change or modify such an acceleration. Nonetheless it is understandable that much alarm has been generated by such figures. The spectre of Malthusian disaster has been revived. Efforts have been made to ensure some control of population increase. In 1974 the first world conference on population ever to be held met in Romania – uneasiness about its future for the first time compelled the human race to unite to consider the problem. Uncontrolled change had already led many societies in the preceding twenty years to accept for the first time the possibility that conscious control of their shape and size is feasible. In one sense, of course, this is not a new idea; infanticide and abortion have long played a part in controlling demands upon scarce resources in some countries. Babies were exposed to die in medieval Japan and female infanticide was widespread in India a century and a half ago. What is now new is that in some countries simpler and more humane means of population control are now being provided with the authority of governments behind them. Their aim is positive economic improvement instead of merely the avoidance of family and personal disaster.

Such efforts are not made in all poor countries and are all but unknown in rich ones. This is one of the most obvious aspects of the complex truth that population growth, though a worldwide fact, neither everywhere takes the same form nor can be expected to produce the same

effects. It is only approximately true to say that a trend first visible in Europe has now spread to the rest of the world and certainly we cannot now expect a pattern shown there to be simply repeated elsewhere. Though most non-European countries have followed nineteenth-century Europe in first showing a fall in death-rates without a corresponding fall in reproduction rates, it would be rash to prophesy either that the next phase of population history in developed countries will now be repeated elsewhere, or that it will not. The dynamics of population growth or decline are exceedingly complex and reflect not only the limits set by man's control of nature, but also social and personal attitudes, a very tricky area for interpretation.

There is, indeed, plenty of scope in many countries for the further development of trends already seen. They may mean, at the very least, that some poor countries will not achieve population stability for a long time. The European world only began to reduce its natality as growing prosperity made it more attractive to individuals to have smaller families; few countries with fast-growing populations today are anywhere near this point. Further progress may in fact make things much worse. Medicine – whose own advances have been colossal since the nineteenth century and which has made especially huge strides in the last thirty years – still has to cut into mortality in some of them as dramatically as it did in Europe between 1800 and 1900. When it does so, a great new acceleration will be given to the rise in humanity's numbers.

One of the best rough indicators of the potential for further growth is infant mortality. In the century before 1970 this fell from an average of about 225 per thousand live births to under 20 in developed countries; in 1967 the comparative figures for Mexico, the United States and Great Britain were 63·1, 22·1 and 18·8. Such discrepancies exist – sometimes they are much greater – between many of the poor and rich countries. There are comparable differences in life expectancy, too. In developed countries, life expectancy at birth rose from rather more than 40 in 1870 to slightly over 70 a hundred

years later and now shows a remarkable even-
ness. Life expectancy at birth in the United
States, Great Britain and Russia in 1967, for
example, was 70·5, 71·6 and 70 years respectively. In India it was 41·8 and in Haiti 32·6 in
that year; the last figure is rather better than
either India's at the beginning of this century
or that of France in 1789. The possibility of
reducing such discrepancies makes it unlikely
that the steam will go out of the curve of population growth for some time yet, because there
are good prospects that the worst rates can be
brought much lower.

For the present and immediate future, important economic and political divergences are
all likely to follow from population growth.
They will greatly offset the world-wide technical and cultural pressures towards uniformity,
for population changes do not take place in a
vacuum. For most of human history, for
example, all societies have resembled pyramids,
with very large numbers of young people and a
few old; they were alike one another in this
respect. Now, developed societies are beginning
to look like slowly tapering columns for they
have a larger proportion of older people than in
the past. This has further consequences and
implications which are too complicated for discussion here, but emphasizes the fact that overall
population growth is a somewhat unreal notion.
Although the world's population grows mightily,
it does so in ways which have different historical
origins and produce different historical effects.

Big changes in population balance are among
them. In 1968, world population was calculated
to be distributed roughly as follows:*

Europe	693 *million*	20·6%
Asia	1883	56·0%
Africa	290	8·6%
Latin America	258	7·7%
North America	223	6·6%
Australasia and Oceania	16	0·5%

*M. Reinhard, *et al.*, *Histoire générale de la population
mondiale* (Paris, 1968), pp. 680–81. This table divides a
Russian population of perhaps 215 million between Europe
and Asia; probably it is reasonable to count about 75 million
as the population of European Russia.

The fall in Europe's share of world population
since the nineteenth century is striking; until the
1920s, moreover, Europe had been an exporter
of manpower to other continents, notably the
Americas. This emigration was cut by restrictions on entry to the United States in the 1920s
and dwindled even more during the world
depression. It has never recovered its importance, though some countries still send out
many emigrants (more Britons still leave their
country each year than are needed to balance
an inflow from abroad). Instead, industrialized
Europe now attracts North Africans, Turks,
Asians and West Indians who seek employment
lacking at home. Nor is the present pattern of
world population likely to be unchanged for
long. Asia now contains over half mankind and
one country, China, one fifth of it, but huge as
the rates of growth have been which have
produced these totals, they are not so fast as
those of South America. World population
increase averages out at about 2 per cent
per annum while that of Brazil, for example,
was running at about 3·5 per cent in the early
1960s. In some Latin American countries, too,
where standards of living and life expectancy are
not very much removed from the European
levels in the first quarter of this century, high
growth has continued in spite of this, births
continuing at a high level even when mortality
fell. These are all countries in which the Roman
Catholic Church exercised great influence and
where there has long been resistance to contraception; in all of them, too, abortion is illegal.
But religion is far from the whole story. The
attitudes of Latin American males have very
complex historical sources and explain many of
the social disciplines which impose large
families on Latin American women – who are,
because of these same disciplines, often unquestioningly compliant. It matters, too, that
South American countries are very big; both
Argentina and Brazil, for example, have population policies – but ones based on the assumption that they need many more people if they
are to exploit their potential.

Such cultural and political differences add to

the difficulties of guessing what will be the effect of any conscious attempts to stem population growth. For a long time, the communist states did not warm to the ideas of population stabilization or reduction, but now they have begun to do so; with very different historical backgrounds, both China and Russia have now accepted the view that population growth should be controlled by encouraging people to delay marriage and have smaller families. For a time it was widely held that propaganda for the western answer to over-population, contraception, was the best way to proceed in poor countries with high natality, but it has now become clear that there was no universal correlation between the resources put into this and the results achieved. In India large sums have been spent, but with negligible effect. Once again the weight of history can be felt.

India was neither revolutionized by industrialization (as was Japan), nor by a political attack on its traditional institutions (as was China). It remained an agrarian society in which numerous children provided an insurance against starvation in old age and British administrators after the Mutiny and Indian governments after independence have been for different reasons equally respectful of social tradition where it was not grossly objectionable. The upshot has been the survival of a whole complex of ideas and institutions making population control almost inconceivable. One example is the continuance, outside a tiny minority among India's ruling and economic élites, of a vast and traditional inequality in the status and employment prospects of men and women. Were attitudes towards women's independence which are taken for granted in Europe or North America (and frequently denounced there as inadequate) even partially introduced to India, it would be likely to have a dramatic effect in raising the average age of women at marriage, and therefore in reducing the number of children in the average family. But to bring about this change would imply a much more fundamental revolution in Indian life, in the provision of new opportunities of employment

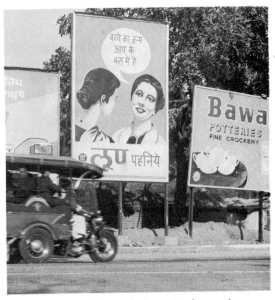

Modern advertising techniques in the service of government. An Indian poster of 1967 shows a woman doctor advising a young mother to adopt the loop as a contraceptive device.

and in the redistribution of authority inside the family and village. It would be a much more radical break with the Indian past than the achievement of independence in 1947. No country should be expected to shake off its past easily and no great tradition of civilization can be got rid of painlessly. Where countries have achieved real breaks with their past, they appear usually to be coupled with economic growth.

This causes upsets always painful for the losers and sometimes for conservatives, whether achieved within a free market or a socialist system, but perhaps it suggests that we need not be too gloomy and Malthusian. A solution to population growth may after all be found along the lines of western experience. Even in Latin America, economic growth has been followed by at least the beginning of a decline in natality in the teeth of hostility from tradition and authority. There is still a huge revolutionary power in the expanding, developing civilization of the European tradition; whether it comes packaged as capitalism or communism, it is the most powerful solvent of traditional structures in all history. A population structure changed in one way or another seems as unavoidable a concomitant of it as the weakening of religious culture, the building of factories or the liberation of women – and the list can be hugely extended.

Meanwhile, differences of population mean differences of power. There cannot be a quite simple translation of one term to the other, for culture and resources also come into the matter, and power for one purpose is not always power for another. But China, once again part of a world which she shunned for thousands of years, is bound to be a great power on grounds of population alone, for in a sense she is militarily unbeatable. Her social revolution may have begun to increase her wealth, whereas the most obviously distorting influence preventing many other highly populated countries from being very powerful is their poverty. This is sometimes absolute, in the sense that natural resources are poor, and sometimes relative, in that they are swallowed by population growth which is too fast. In many countries the cashing of the cheque of aid from abroad and the reaping of the reward of improved technology and planned investment, have been held up because population has grown so rapidly that it has at once consumed any new wealth which has resulted.

It is not easy, though, to generalize about this complicated subject. India, for example, was in the early 1970s thought to be about to enter a period of self-sufficiency in food. Her agricultural output doubled between 1948 and 1973, while even her huge population had not done that. It seems, then, that there ought to have been more food available per head, that the country grew richer. And the fact of overall world population increase is in itself a telling clue: the gross output of world food must have risen dramatically, for though many have starved many others have lived. Even if millions have died in local famines, there has been (so far) no disaster on a world-wide scale. Undeniably, the world has proved able to feed a growing population; if it had not, that population would be smaller. Whether this can continue is another matter. Some experts have concluded that a phase of agricultural plenty is drawing to a close. Ominously, in the middle of the 1970s these fears coincide with other economic and political trends which threaten to disrupt world trade and throw markets into disarray. If this is so, it could be that a reversion to an earlier and tragic pattern of history would occur, with one of those appalling collapses through famine and disease such as punctuated the growth of all pre-industrial societies, when population pressed too closely upon the margins of production.

There is one hopeful sign here. For millennia increased agricultural production was obtained by clearing and breaking in new land rather than by technical improvement. There is still a lot of land left which, with proper investment, could raise crops (and much has been done in the last twenty-five years to use such land, even in a crowded country like India). Yet it is not by such means that world output has recently risen so dramatically. The explanation is a continuation of the innovatory era in agriculture which began in early modern Europe. Down to the 1930s wheat crops were still being successfully introduced to lands in which, for climatic reasons, they had not been grown hitherto, one of the first of the twentieth-century scientific contributions to agriculture comparable in effect to the 'Improvement' of earlier times. It was mainly the work of plant geneticists who evolved new strains of cereals. Such work continues to be important; there is only a finite amount of land in the world and the more that can grow food the better. Still greater contributions to world food supplies have come from increasing the production of existing grain-growing areas, and this is a consequence of improvement in the chemistry of fertilizers as well as of the engineering of new strains. An unprecedented rate of replacement of nitrogen in the soil is the basic explanation of the huge yields which have now become commonplace in countries with advanced agriculture and these methods are beginning to be extended to other areas. Of course, they have their costs, too. A

Social and economic obstacles to increased agricultural productivity can sometimes be outflanked by chemical and biological innovation. A high-yielding rice being tested at an Indian research station.

Insecticides are an important weapon in the struggle to increase agricultural production. Here they are employed by Ethiopian farmers growing cotton.

huge energy input is now needed to raise the huge crops and herds of advanced American agriculture, for example.

This is part of a change which, even more than the transformations of earlier times has the right to be called an 'agricultural revolution'. Fertilizers are only one theme in a story of radical innovation in agricultural chemistry. Effective herbicides and insecticides began to be available commercially in the 1940s and 1950s. At the same time the use of machinery in agriculture in the developed countries enormously increased. England had the most mechanized farming in the world in terms of horsepower per acre cultivated in 1939, but English farmers then still did much of their work with horses, while combine harvesters (already common in the United States) were rare. Now working horses are preserved as interesting curiosities by rich farmers – though there are grounds for thinking that there may be some reintroduction of them for certain types of work where the rising cost of petrol would not justify

the use of a tractor as a prime mover. But the fields are not the only part of the farm to be mechanized. The coming of electricity has brought automatic milking, grain-drying, threshing, the heating of animal sheds in winter and many other changes which have pushed up agricultural productivity. They have also made advanced agriculture less dependent on labour; the agricultural workforce has continued to fall while production per acre has risen.

One social result is that subsistence farming is on the retreat. There are probably more subsistence farmers in the world today than in 1900, but only because there are more people. Their relative share of cultivated land and of the value of what is produced has fallen. In Europe the peasant is fast disappearing, as he disappeared in Great Britain two hundred and more years ago. But this change is unevenly spread and easily disrupted by special factors. In one of the great traditional agricultural economies – Russia – there was a famine in 1947 so severe as once more to provoke cannibalism in some areas, according to Khruschev. Such

Agriculture still provides the most vivid examples of the contrasts thrown up by uneven development. In Ecuador the wooden plough is still in use (as it is in much of Asia) centuries after its replacement by the iron ploughshare in Europe.

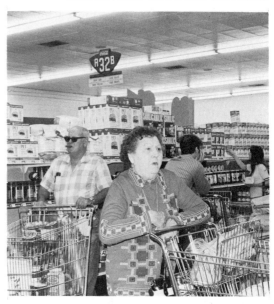

An abundance of daily food has come to be taken for granted for the first time in history by millions of people in developed countries in this century.

local disasters are even more likely in countries with large and rapidly growing populations in which subsistence agriculture is the norm and productivity remains low. Just before the First World War, the British yield of wheat per acre was already more than two and a half times that of India; by 1968 it was roughly five times. Over the same period the Americans raised their rice yields from 4·25 to nearly 12 tons an acre, while that of Burma, sometimes called the 'rice bowl of Asia', rose from 3·8 to 4·2. Another way of looking at these facts is to consider how many families can be provided for by one agricultural worker in different countries. In 1968 the answer for Egypt was slightly more than one, while for New Zealand the figure was over forty.

Such divisions have origins more complicated than a simple presence or absence of technique and they are too complicated to go into here. Usually, though, advanced agriculture is found in countries advanced in other ways. This has helped to penalize countries where there is most

need to increase agricultural productivity because unless they have a special mineral resource like oil, or a particular tropical agricultural speciality, they have found it very difficult to produce more cheaply something which the industrial countries need than can those countries themselves. Ironic paradoxes result, the Russians, Indians and Chinese, big grain and rice producers, have found themselves buying American and Canadian wheat. The consequence has been growing disparities between developed and undeveloped countries and the most striking index of this has been their relative consumption of the world's resources. Roughly half the world's population consumes about six-sevenths of the world's production and the other half consumes the other seventh. Moreover, even among the wealthy nations there are wide disparities. There are about six Americans in every hundred human beings; in 1970 they used about forty out of every hundred barrels of oil produced in the world. *Per capita*, they consume about a quarter-ton of paper products a year; the corresponding figure for China is about twenty pounds. The electrical energy used by China in a year would (it has been said) just sustain the supply of power to the United States' air conditioners.

These are extreme instances of the difference between rich and poor societies. It is so much more marked today than ever before that at first sight it seems to make nonsense of the thesis that world history is a unity. A rough division can be drawn in all parts of the world between rich and poor nations in which the disparity since 1945 has grown more and more marked. This is not because the poor have grown poorer, but because the rich have grown much richer. The usual measurements of this are the growth of the Gross National Product or the *per capita* income. Even spectacular accelerations of production (Asian countries, for example, augmented their agricultural production between 1952 and 1970 more than Europe and much more than North America) have rarely succeeded in improving the position of poor countries in relation to that of the rich. On the one hand the poor countries have been beset by the problems of rising population and, on the other, advanced countries began at a higher level. As a result, though their ranking in relation to one another has changed, more or less the same dozen or so countries which enjoyed the highest standards of living in 1950 still enjoy them today, and their lead over poorer countries has increased.

Roughly speaking, the rich are the industrialized countries. In 1970 three of the great industrial agglomerations of the world were still, as in 1939, the United States, Europe and Russia; the only important Asian industrial society of 1939, Japan, has now joined these. No single European country alone can any longer match the two giants. The American recovery from the depression began with the approach of war and the beginnings of rearmament, and the war and the subsequent continuing federal expenditure provided a firm undertone for expansion to continue. The outcome is an industrial economy which is the greatest in the world, though its rate of growth seems to have been nowhere near as rapid as that of Soviet Russia where, if we are to believe the official figures, central planning succeeded in pushing up industrial production at more than 12 per cent a year after 1945.

The major industrial economies no longer much resemble their nineteenth-century predecessors. Although the old heavy and manufacturing industries still provide the backbone of economic strength, there have been changes of emphasis. Modern industry is much more than a simple extrapolation in technology and structure from the past. Much of the economic growth of rich countries has been in industries – electronics and plastics are examples – which barely existed even in 1945. Coal, which replaced wood in the nineteenth century as the major source of energy, has long since been joined by hydro-electricity, oil and natural gas; very recently, power generated by nuclear fission has been added to these and may yet lead to more revolutionary changes still in the comparative standing of industrial countries. What has not changed is the steady accretion in all of them of wealth which has been more and more widely spread in the form of cheaper and more numerous commodities. Advances in the basic industries have helped to raise standards of living at a fundamental level, by providing cheaper power and materials. By improving transport they have further lowered the cost of goods indirectly. But industrial growth in advanced countries has now for a century or so been characterized by an enormous growth in the production of goods directly for the use and pleasure of the consumer.

Many illustrations could be given of this, but one must suffice. In 1885 there appeared the first machine propelled by an internal-combustion engine – one, that is to say, in which the energy produced by heat was used directly inside the cylinder of an engine driving a piston instead of being transmitted from an external flame through the making of steam. Nine years later came a four-wheeled vehicle which is a recognizable ancestor of the modern car. It was

THE MOTOR CAR: SYMBOL OF LUXURY

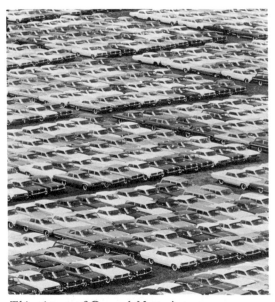

This picture of General Motors' storage acreage in New Jersey is not only symbolic of the huge productive power of industrial capitalism but also of the crippling problems of pollution and traffic management to come.

the French Panhard, and France and Germany for some time kept a lead in producing cars in the next decade or so; they were few, and rich men's toys. This was automobile prehistory. Its history began in the United States when Henry Ford in 1907 set up a production line for his Model T. The price of the first was $950, an unprecedentedly low one: Ford was deliberately planning for a mass market. By 1926 his price had fallen to less than $300. An enormous success was under way. Demand rose so rapidly that by 1915 Ford was producing a million cars a year. This was the beginning of mass consumption of something previously regarded as a luxury. There are now more cars than households in the United States.

Ford's achievement was thus not only technical and commercial, but cultural. He changed the world by allowing people of modest incomes to enjoy a mobility unavailable to millionaires fifty years earlier. This is a huge increase in amenity; subsequently it gradually penetrated all parts of the world. Ford also

changed history by stimulating a new and rising demand for oil – though transport is not its only major consumer. Finally, he carried through in his factories a social and technical revolution by showing what could be done with mass-production. Like many great revolutionaries he brought together other men's ideas as well as providing his own, but the result was the assembly line, the characteristic modern form of the manufacture of consumer goods. By it, the article under manufacture was moved steadily from worker to worker, each one of them carrying out in the minimum necessary time the precisely delimited and, if possible, small task in which he was skilled. The very real costs of mass-production in the psychological effect on the worker were soon apparent, but the technique was fundamental to a wider sharing of the wealth of the industrial economy. Ford saw that such work would be very boring and paid high wages to compensate for it, thereby contributing to another revolutionary economic change, the fuelling of economic prosperity by increasing purchasing power and, therefore, demand.

An expanding market, falling unit costs and improvement in the technique of their mass-production all helped to cheapen a huge range of goods. As they became more accessible, the idea has steadily spread that articles once thought luxuries are now to be taken for granted. Furthermore, there seems to be no reason why the further cheapening and availability of luxury goods should not be limitless. In the second half of this century, rising expectations became normal for the majority of those who live in the developed countries. For many people the flow of consumer goods shattered the last links that held them to the idea that they lived in a world of stable expectations and the effect has begun to spread. The spectacle of the new wealth of industrial societies is most striking in the undeveloped nations, where cheap consumer goods – transistor radios, for example – often bring in their train important social changes. Such goods are often important signs of status and provide an incentive for men and women to seek work where they can get higher wages to buy them; this often involves leaving the villages in which a majority of mankind lives even today and severing ties with an ordered, stable society.

The always-hastening onrush of a modernity rolling outwards from industrialized societies has strained such ties in many ways. Aeroplanes are now the normal form of long-distance travel, but the first flight by a man-carrying, powered, heavier-than-air machine was only made in 1903, within the lifetime of many men still alive today. Flight offers a mobility to the individual which was hardly imaginable during their boyhood. Some of those men may well have grown to maturity even before Marconi exploited electro-magnetic theory to make possible the sending of the first 'wireless' messages. The first to cross the Atlantic did so, appropriately, in 1901, the first year of a century whose communications were revolutionized by the invention. A large-scale radio broadcasting service existed by 1930; a few years earlier the first demonstration had been made of the technical devices on which television was based. In 1936 the BBC opened the first regular television broadcasting service; twenty years later the medium was commonplace in the leading industrial countries.

Technical progress of this rapidity has had an incalculable impact. Its ramifications cannot be traced here but it has usually acted as a solvent of inherited ways. Sometimes it has affected mentality very directly and obviously; it is too soon to measure its extent, but it is difficult not to feel that radio and television imply a qualitative change in the history of culture which transcends even the coming of print. Technical progress has also affected mentality in less direct ways, too. One way in which this has happened is through its tendency to emphasize the seemingly magical power of science to transform life by way of technology. For a long time, this was almost the only way in which science had a positive impact on the lives of most people. In some industrial processes the science is very obvious to the eye: the use of nuclear fission to generate energy, or of computers to control a factory will serve as recent examples. In others – and the production of plastics materials for almost every conceivable requirement is one of the most common – the basic science still lies concealed from the layman in processes fairly remote from manufacture. Industry was by the last quarter of the twentieth century dependent on science as never before, whether directly or indirectly, whether obviously or not, and the transformation of fundamental science into an end product has now become very fast indeed. The accumulation of technological and scientific skill has steadily reduced the time between scientific discovery and its practical application. The gap between the first use of penicillin and its large-scale manufacture was about three years; the generalization of the use of the motor-car after the principle of the internal-combustion engine was grasped took more like half a century.

One reason for this is structural and economic, the gradual spread of the idea of purposive research and of a willingness to put money into it. Most practical results of nineteenth-century science were by-products of scientific curiosity and sometimes accidental. By 1900 a change was under way; a few scientists were beginning to see that consciously directed and concentrated research was sensible. Twenty years later, large industrial companies were beginning to accept the idea that research was a proper call on their investment, albeit a small one. The research departments of some industrial concerns were in the end to grow into enormous establishments in their own right as petrochemicals, plastics, electronics and biochemical medicine made their appearance later in the century. Nowadays, the ordinary citizen of a developed country would find great trouble in leading a life which does not rest on a foundation of applied science. This pervasiveness of science, coupled with its impressiveness in its most spectacular achievements, was one of the great reasons for the ever-growing recognition given to it. Money is one yardstick. The Cavendish Laboratory at Cambridge, for

One of the most important new instruments extending human control of the natural world by its acceleration of the handling of information has been the computer. This, the first electro-mechanical computer was installed at Harvard University in 1944. Its relation to modern computers is something like that of piston-engined biplanes to the modern Jumbo Jet, cumbersome and limited in capacity as it was. For all this, it seems impressive enough to the layman.

example, in which some of the fundamental experiments of nuclear physics were carried out before 1914, had then a grant from the university of about £300 – roughly $1500 a year at rates then current. When, during the war of 1939–45 the British and Americans decided that a major effort must be mounted to produce nuclear weapons, the resulting 'Manhattan Project' (as it was called) is estimated to have cost as much as all the scientific research previously conducted by mankind from the beginnings of recorded time.

Such huge sums – and there were to be much larger bills to meet once scientists began to take up the investigation of space – mark another social fact about science, its increasing importance to government. Science became a political fact in the twentieth century. Only governments can provide resources on the scale needed for some of the things done since 1945. Unfortunately, the usual benefit they sought was better weapons, and this undoubtedly explains much of the huge scientific investment of the United States and Russia, which are of comparable

magnitude, while the whole of western Europe's research expenditure is less than a third of the Russian. The mobilization of science in two world wars showed its importance to war-making power. The increasing interest and participation of governments has not, on the other hand, meant that science has grown more nationalistic; indeed, the reverse is true. Science is bound to be international for theoretical and technical reasons, to say nothing of the tradition of international communication among scientists, which is one of their most splendid inheritances from the first great age of science in the seventeenth century.

The general psychological effect of the growth of science has been to create a much wider acceptance of its omnipresence and importance than ever before. There are more scientists about than ever, more attention than ever is given to science in education, there is more widely diffused and readily comprehensible scientific information. Most of this has only come about since 1918; a significant break in scale becomes observable about then. Paradoxically, this has perhaps led to some diminution of the wonder felt in earlier times at what science could do. Success provides diminishing returns in awe. When more and more things prove possible, there is nothing very surprising about the latest marvel. There is even irrational disappointment and irritation when some problems prove recalcitrant. Meanwhile, the master idea of our civilization, the notion that purposive change can be imposed upon Nature if sufficient resources are made available, has undoubtedly grown stronger. This stems from European civilization; the science now carried on around the globe is all based on the European experimental tradition.

In the twentieth century science continued to throw up ideas and implications disruptive of traditional, theocentric views of life. This was the high phase of the long process of dethroning the idea of the supernatural. Newtonian physics had provided a satisfying philosophical framework for a century and a half. It was not until the nineteenth century that James Clark Maxwell, the first professor of experimental physics at Cambridge, did the work in electromagnetism and thermodynamics which broke effectively into fields and problems left untouched by the seventeenth century. Maxwell's theoretical work and its experimental investigation profoundly affected the post-Newtonian view that the universe obeyed natural, regular and discoverable laws of a somewhat mechanical kind and that it essentially consisted of lumps of indestructible matter in various combinations and arrangements. To this picture had now to be fitted a new component, the electro-magnetic fields whose technological possibilities quickly fascinated laymen and scientists alike.

It was on this basis that the crucial work which founded modern physical theory was done between 1895 and 1914, by Röntgen who discovered X-rays, Becquerel who discovered radioactivity, Thomson who identified the electron, the Curies who isolated radium and Rutherford who carried out the investigation of the atom's structure. As a result of what they did, it became possible to see the physical world in a new way. Instead of lumps of matter, the universe began to look more like an aggregate of atoms which were tiny solar systems of particles in particular arrangements. These particles seemed to behave in a way which blurred the established distinction between lumps of matter and electro-magnetic fields. Moreover, such arrangements of particles were not fixed, for in nature one arrangement might give way to another and thus elements could change into other elements. Rutherford's work was decisive

in establishing that atoms could be 'split' because of their structure as a system of particles and thus that matter, even at this fundamental level, could be manipulated (though as late as 1935 he said that nuclear physics would have no practical implications – and no one rushed to contradict him). Two such particles were soon identified, the proton and the electron; others not until after 1932, when Chadwick discovered the neutron. But Rutherford, together with Bohr, provided the scientific world with an experimentally validated picture of the atom's structure as a system of particles.

What this radically important experimental work did not do was supply a new theoretical framework to replace the Newtonian one which it had damaged beyond repair. This was only achieved by a long revolution in theory, beginning in the last years of the nineteenth century and coming to its culmination in the 1920s. It was focussed on two different sets of problems which gave rise to the work designated by the terms relativity and quantum theory.

The pioneering work was done by Max Planck and Albert Einstein who provided experimental and mathematical demonstration by 1905 that the Newtonian laws of motion were an inadequate framework for explanation of a fact which could no longer be contested. This was that energy transactions in the material world took place not in an even flow but in discrete jumps – *quanta*, as they came to be termed. Planck showed that radiant heat from, for example, the sun was not, as Newtonian physics required, emitted continuously; he argued that this was true of all energy transactions. Einstein argued that light was propagated not continuously but in particles. Though much important work was to be done in the next twenty or so years, Planck's contribution had the most profound effect and it was once more unsettling. Newton's views had been found wanting, but there was nothing to put in their place.

Meanwhile, after his work on quanta, Einstein had published in 1905 the work for which he was to be most celebrated, the state-

Einstein and Niels Bohr photographed in Brussels in 1933.

ment of the theory of relativity. This was essentially a demonstration that the traditional distinctions of space and time, and mass and energy, could not be consistently maintained. Instead of Newton's three-dimensional physics, he directed men's attention to a 'space–time continuum' in which the interplay of space, time and motion could be understood. This was soon to be corroborated by astronomical observation of facts for which Newtonian cosmology could not properly account, but which could find a place in Einstein's theory. One strange and unanticipated consequence of the work on which relativity theory was based was Einstein's demonstration of the relations of mass and energy which he formulated as $E = mc^2$, where E is energy, m is mass, and c is the constant speed of light. The importance and accuracy of this theoretical formulation was not to be clear until much more nuclear physics had been done; it would then be apparent that the relationships observed when mass energy was

converted into heat energy in the breaking up of nuclei also corresponded to this formula.

While these advances were absorbed, attempts continued to rewrite nuclear physics in the light of Planck's work. These did not get far until a major theoretical breakthrough in 1926 finally provided a mathematical framework for what Planck had observed and, indeed, for nuclear physics. So sweeping was the achievement of Schrödinger and Heisenberg, the two mathematicians mainly responsible, that it seemed for a time as if quantum mechanics might be of virtually limitless explanatory power in the sciences. The behaviour of particles in the atom observed by Rutherford and Bohr could now be accounted for. Further development of their work led to predictions of the existence of new nuclear particles, notably the positron, which was duly identified in the 1930s. Quantum mechanics seemed to have inaugurated a new age of physics.

By mid-century much more had disappeared in science than just a once – accepted set of general laws now proved inadequate (and in any case it remained true that, for most everyday purposes, Newtonian physics was still all that was needed). In physics, from which it had spread to other sciences, the whole notion of a general law was being replaced by the concept of statistical probability as the best that could be hoped for. The concept, as well as the content, of science was changing. Furthermore, the boundaries between sciences collapsed under the onrush of new knowledge made accessible by new theories and instrumentation. Any one of the great traditional divisions of science was soon beyond the grasp of any single man. The conflation involved in importing physical theory into neurology or mathematics into biology put a further barrier in the way of attaining that synthesis of knowledge which had been the dream of the nineteenth century.

It would be implausible to suggest that much of this filtered through to laymen. Most of humanity rested undisturbed in its traditional pieties, whether Christian, Hindu, Marxist or anything else. Yet we need to try to achieve at least a tentative idea of the role of science in changing generally accepted views if we are to have a balanced view of the history of our culture. One distinction which makes for difficulty is that between the effects of ideas on intellectual élites (who are, of course, disproportionately prominent in histories of thought and culture which stress their major documents) and that which is exercised by ideas, even if in nonsensically distorted forms, on masses of men who respond to the climate of opinion in which they live. The second effect is perhaps more important in recent history than at earlier times because rising literacy and increasing rapidity of communication have made mass culture more responsive to new ideas than ever before. Unfortunately, the impact of scientific ideas on élites is much easier to trace. Newtonian cosmology had been able to settle down in the eighteenth century into coexistence with Christian religion (and other theocentric modes of thought) and managed to leave untroubled the wide range of social and moral beliefs which were tied to them. As time passed, though, science seemed increasingly hard to reconcile with any fixed belief at all. It appeared to stress relativism and the pressure of circumstance to the exclusion of any unchallengeable assumption or viewpoint. This was especially easy to see in some attempts to investigate human behaviour scientifically. The most important of these were made by the practitioners of the new branch of study, psychology, which had evolved from the traditional study of mental philosophy.

Psychology tended to take one of two paths after 1900. On the one hand was that which was eventually followed by, among others, Freud, the social impact of whose work has already been touched upon. Here, certainly, is a clear example of something which a layman – though not all scientists – would call science having an important and widespread effect. In the first place, Freud undermined the confidence of an élite in traditional assumptions, with the result that his ideas were then diffused further through advanced societies in derivative forms, such as a new attitude to sexuality, or to responsibility and

therefore to punishment. In the second place his teaching and writing led to a body of work which, whatever its exact status and method, was based on the belief that therapy could be pursued and relevant material assembled by interrogating subjects about their wishes, feelings and thoughts, and interpreting this data in accordance with an appropriate body of theory. This was the foundation of the activities which may conveniently be grouped under the name applied to Freud's own work, psychoanalysis.

The other twentieth-century approach to psychology was much more mechanistic, but generated a body of experimental data certainly as impressive (if not more so) as the successes claimed by psychoanalysis. The outstanding name associated with this branch of psychological study is that of the Russian, I. P. Pavlov. In a series of celebrated experiments with dogs he established generalizations which, with appropriate modification, proved to be applicable to human beings. His most important single discovery was the 'conditioned reflex'. Essentially this was the manipulation of one of a pair of variables in an experiment in order to produce a predicted piece of behaviour by a 'conditioned stimulus'. The classical experiment provided for a bell to be sounded before food was given to dogs. After a time, the sounding of the bell produced salivation in the dog which had earlier been produced by the production of food. Subsequently, many refinements and developments of such procedures were explored. This remarkable work has not only been the source of a great deal of insight into human psychology but has also been exploited to provide instrumentation for a number of purposes. One of the most depressing features of our age, perhaps, is that it has been put to work by torturers (though not with a success which demonstrates conclusively their superiority to earlier practitioners). Scientifically, this school of psychology (which may be called 'Behaviourist') made great advances many of which were put to beneficient use, notably in the treatment of mental illness and teaching techniques. But if an attempt is to be made to grasp so shapeless a

Paul VI, here shown driving through the streets of Bombay, was the first pope to visit the great Catholic populations of South America, Asia and Africa. His tours in the later 1960s revealed for the first time to many of his European flock the extent to which the Church had ceased to be their private possession.

subject, the diffused effect of Behaviourism, though confined consciously to relatively few, seems curiously parallel to that of Freudianism, in that its bias is towards the demolition of the sense of responsibility and individualism which is the heart of European and Christian moral tradition.

It is indeed difficult to believe that such studies, like those of other sciences, have not contributed importantly to a decline of religious belief. But this fact, often alleged to be characteristic of the contemporary era, needs very careful qualification. When people talk about the waning power of religion, they often mean only the formal and organized authority of

Christian churches. They may also mean that there are changes in widely held assumptions in advanced societies, and that these have a tendency which goes beyond inimical effects on formal Christianity. They point, for example, to the fact that India is now a republic which is non-confessional and secular in its constitution; confessional states and religious establishments are now unusual. But they do not usually mean that the real power of Islam or Hinduism over their adherents has declined, or that there have not appeared new religions in other parts of the world which are important, or that it is not true that probably more people than ever in history give serious attention to what is said by the pope. They tend, nevertheless, to believe that in this matter as in others, western society has indicated a path which other societies will follow. It may be so, but it may not be, and the interplay of religion and society is so complex that it is best to be cautious.

It is obvious, for example, that Islam has

survived corruption by the technology and materialism of the European tradition, that it appears also to have been able to resist that tradition's latest ideological expressions, atheistic communism, that it is still an expanding and missionary faith and even that the notion of Islamic unity is not dead in the Arab lands. In the last respect it shows that religion can still nerve men to political action and should remind us that this is not true only of Islam; this sometimes destructive aspect of religion can be seen in many places still and is by no means confined to the Middle East or the non-Christian world.

United with strong social forces, religion has produced terrifying massacres in the Indian subcontinent, both during the months of partition in 1947 and since, in the struggles which led to the breaking away of East Bengal from Pakistan and the establishment of the new state of Bangladesh. In Ulster, Irishmen still bitterly dispute the future of their country in terms of the religious wars of the seventeenth century. Though the hierarchies and leaders of different religions find it appropriate to exchange public courtesies and provide a gaping world with the bizarre spectacle of Tibetan lamas hobnobbing with Anglican bishops, it cannot be said that religion has ceased to be a divisive force. Whether, on the other hand, that means that the supernatural content of religion is or is not losing its hold and that it is not, rather, important today merely as a badge of group membership, is debatable.

What is less debatable is that within the world whose origins are Christian, the decline of sectarian strife has been a concomitant of a general decline of religious belief and a loss of nerve. Ecumenism, the Christian movement whose most considerable achievement to date has been the setting up of the World Council of Churches in 1948, has been easier because all Christians have had a growing sense of living in a hostile environment. The only unequivocal sign of the advance of Christianity has been the extension of the Roman Catholic Church overseas (largely a matter of natural increase) to which attention was drawn by papal visits to South America and

Asia in the 1960s, the first which had been made by the Supreme Pontiff. As for the Papacy's position within the church, that appeared to be undergoing some weakening, of which an ecumenical council held at the Vatican in the 1960s provided some symptoms. But it is hazardous to project trends in the history of an institution whose fortunes have shown such fluctuations in the past (up with Hildebrandine reform, down with Schism and conciliarism; up with Trent, down with the Enlightenment; up with the first Vatican council . . .) and safest simply to recognize that a new issue – contraceptive practice – may face it for the first time with a real threat to its unquestioned authority in the eyes of millions of Catholic believers.

Like the notion of a fixed, unchanging moral law often closely associated with it, religion has been until now always among the most impressive of mankind's achievements in social regulation. They have both much weakened recently, but the other great historic agent of social order, the state, has kept its end up much better. If anything, it has emerged with enhanced powers from the dangers of an era of revolutionary change which were once thought to threaten it. The world contains more states than ever before and more people look to their governments than ever before as the ultimate source of their well-being. In many countries, politics has apparently replaced religion or liberal economics as the focus of a faith that can move mountains and the source of expectations of a new heaven and earth. This is partly because the state has everywhere for the greater part of a century been asked to do more and more and has been given more power for this purpose. Great wars and even the international tensions of peacetime have helped; they threw unprecedented powers into the hands of government because of the huge mobilizations of resources they were thought to require. To such effects have been added those arising from demands that governments promote the welfare of their subjects directly and undertake the provision of services left in earlier times to individuals or such 'natural' social units as the family or village.

William of Orange, victor of the Battle of the Boyne in 1690 which ended the hopes of a Catholic Ireland loyal to the House of Stuart, is still evoked as a symbol of sectarianism on the walls of a house in the Protestant district of Londonderry. Irishmen, Catholic and Protestant alike, often tend to see their present concerns in the lurid light thrown by legends of events long ago.

Finally, there has been the urge to modernize; few countries outside Europe achieved this without direction from above and even Europe had despots among its modernizers in the past. The twentieth century here provided outstanding examples in Russia and China, two great agrarian societies which undertook their modernization by using the power of the state to impose it.

The success of the state – if we may so put it – has not gone unquestioned but it has thus proved very difficult to resist. Even in settled states where there is a tradition of distrusting governmental power and institutions exist to check it, there is a sense that it is much stronger and less resistible than even a few years ago. The strongest checks on the abuse of power remain those of habit and assumption; so long as electorates in liberal states can assume that governments will not quickly fall back on the use of force, they do not feel very alarmed. But there are now many more dictators, and many more illiberal political régimes in the world than in 1939. The cause of democracy looks much less hopeful than in 1918. Like the collapse of liberal economics and the undermining of liberal intellectual assumptions, this is a measure of the narrowing base of what was once thought the ideology of the future, but was only that of a few advanced societies of the nineteenth century. This does not mean that the forms of its politics have not survived. They have, indeed, prospered in one sense, for the rhetoric of democracy and constitutionalism has never been more widely employed and nationalism is stronger than ever. Yet the freedoms once associated with these ideas are more conspicuously in danger and the lack of connexion between nationalism and liberalism is more obvious than ever.

One reason for this is that they have been exported to contexts inimical to them. It is unhistorical to deplore what has followed; as Burke pointed out long ago, political principles take their colour from circumstances. It has in many instances in the last twenty-five years been shown that representative institutions and democratic forms cannot work properly in societies lacking solid foundations in habits which are coherent with them, or where there are powerful divisive influences. In such circumstances, the imposition of an authoritarian

Lenin's tomb in Red Square, Moscow, is the centrepiece for huge demonstrations whose careful orchestration provides, it is hoped, visual evidence of mass support for the régime. Increasingly, such support has been felt to be needed to legitimize state authority in this century.

style of government has often been the best way of resisting the fragmentation of a nation once the discipline imposed by a colonial power is withdrawn. Only too obviously, this has not meant greater freedom in all post-colonial countries, though whether greater happiness has not followed may be more debatable.

The rôle of the urge to modernize in strengthening the state – something prefigured long ago outside Europe in such figures as Mehemet Ali or Kemal – was an indication of new sources from which the state increasingly drew its moral authority. Instead of resting as it once had done on personal loyalty to a dynasty or on supernatural sanction, it rested increasingly on the democratic argument that it was able to satisfy collective desires. Usually these were for material improvement, but sometimes not. If one value more than any other validates state authority still today it is that of nationalism, still the motive force of much of world politics. It has proved astonishingly tenacious, as the experience of communist Europe has shown, and has been successful in mobilizing allegiance as no other force has been able to do. Against it, ideologies have not proved effective; the forces telling against it and helping to make the whole world one political system have been economics, communications and technology, not a comparably powerful moral idea or mythology.

Finally, of course, the state has continued to benefit from its virtual monopoly of the main instruments of physical control. Even a hundred years ago, the police and armed forces of governments unshaken by war or revolution gave it virtual assurance of survival. Improved technology has only increased this near-certainty. New repressive techniques and weapons, moreover, are now only a small part of the story of state power. State intervention in the economy, through its power as consumer, investor or planner, and the improvement of mass communications in a form which leaves access to them highly centralized are also political facts of great importance. They did not appear suddenly in 1945. The welfare state was a reality in Great Britain before 1914, Hitler and Roosevelt made great use of radio (though for very different ends) and the regulation of economic life is as old as government itself. They were, however, all only slight prefigurings of an increase in state power whose results we have witnessed since 1945 and which is in its intense form still very new. When a British foreign secretary said in the late 1940s that he wished to see a state of affairs in which a man could set off for a foreign country with no need to worry about anything except buying a ticket, without passport, visa or other officially imposed documentation, he was virtually asking for the return of conditions taken for granted eighty years earlier.

2 The politics of a new world

Cold War

A revolution in both the economic and political organization of the world has been going on ever since the end of the Second World War. The result is a world still in movement whose structure is already very different from what might have been expected twenty or even ten years ago. Some of it derives from forces which have been detected at work long before the 1940s. They can, for example, be related to the energy needs of industrial societies which have grown steadily for a century or more, or to the triumph of ideas first announced in the French Revolution. But they are far from the whole story. Other great changes seem to have more of accident, circumstance or personality about them. They are not easy to explain, for both the evidence and the perspective needed to understand many of them are unavailable. Tracing the steps by which one sort of world turned into another is none the less the first step towards historical judgement.

One fact which is indisputable is that world history was long dominated by a prolonged and bitter Soviet–American antagonism, the 'Cold War' as it was called. This brought into the forefront of world affairs a rupture in the diplomatic history of the modern era which had

The Anglo-American 'airlift' of supplies into a blockaded Berlin was the first victory for the West in the Cold War and a revelation of potential strength which caused surprise on both sides of the Iron Curtain.

opened in 1917. A state then made its appearance which, for the first time in more than a century and far more vigorously than any predecessor, approached international society with radically new assumptions. Soviet Russia was an ideological state which regarded diplomacy not as a civilized way of doing business but as a weapon for the advance of ideology, however qualified at times by circumstances. Moreover, the Bolshevik aims were specifically stated to include the overthrow of the social institutions of non-communist societies. After 1945 other states came into existence which took the same view. The result was a world which looked as if it were divided into two camps, one led by Russia, one by the United States.

The opening of the Marshall Aid programme was almost at once followed by what was to prove to be the first battle of the Cold War and the decisive one for Europe, over the fate of Berlin. It established the point at which, in Europe, the United States was prepared to fight. It does not seem that this outcome was anticipated by the Russians, who provoked it. Their basic concern was to avoid the re-emergence of a reunited and economically powerful Germany which was not under their influence. The western powers had a different interest, to reanimate the economy of western Germany at least. They sought to get on with this before the future political shape of Germany was settled, holding that it was essential to the recovery of western Europe as a whole. Among other things they introduced a new currency reform in their sectors without Russian agreement. Following on Marshall Aid, which of course extended to the western-occupied zones but not to the Russians, this decision cut Germany in two, because it meant that the recovery of the eastern half would not proceed as a unit integrated with western Europe, but that a strong western Germany might emerge by itself. That the western powers should get on with the business of putting German industry on its feet was undoubtedly economic sense but the decision put eastern Germany decisively on the other side of the Iron Curtain. Moreover, the introduction of the currency reform in western Berlin divided that city, too, and thereby prejudiced Russian chances of a political *putsch* there.

The Russians duly responded by interference with communications between the western zones of Germany and Berlin. Whatever their motives at this stage, the dispute over this escalated. Some western officials had already had it in mind that a severing of western Berlin from western Germany might be attempted before this crisis and the word 'blockade' had been used. Now the Russians' steps were interpreted in this sense. To keep up communication with West Berlin, the British and Americans organized an airlift to supply the city. When this happened, a trial of strength was under way. The western powers, in spite of the enormous cost of maintaining such a supply of food, fuel and medicine as would just keep West Berlin going, announced they were prepared to keep it up indefinitely. The implication was that the Russians could stop them only by force. For the first time since the war American strategic bombers moved back to bases in England. The Russians, on the other hand, wanted to demonstrate to the West Berliners that the western powers could not stay there if the Russians did not want them to; they hoped thus to remove the obstacle which the presence of elected non-Communist municipal authorities presented to Soviet control of Berlin as a prelude to the reuniting of Germany. The blockade lasted over a year and the Russians lost. They were neither able to prevent Allied

Contrasted shading distinguishes the allied German occupation zones of 1945. The three western zones constitute the Present Federal Republic, the Russian zone is the territory of the (East) German Democratic Republic. Berlin remains under four-power occupation.

Post-war Germany and Central Europe

supply nor to intimidate the West Berliners. The Russians made the best of this by deliberately splitting the city and refusing the mayor access to his office. Meanwhile the western powers got on with the organization of West Germany and had signed a treaty setting up a new alliance for Atlantic security, the North Atlantic Treaty Organization. The blockade ended in May 1949.

Remarkable though it was as a technical achievement (there was only one airfield and it handled over a thousand aircraft a day for most of the time, with an average daily delivery of 5000 tons of coal alone) the real significance of the crisis had been political. It had been shown

American bombers attacking a chemical works in North Korea. For the whole decade of the 1950s, American air-power was the first-line deterrent to what many people in the West regarded as an aggressive and expanding Communism; no comparable offsetting force existed in the East until the coming of the intercontinental ballistic missile.

that neither side wanted to fight, but also that all hope of cooperation on the basis of the war-time agreement to create a centralized German administration was dead. Henceforth, there were to be two Germanies as well as two Europes.

It was also beginning to appear that there might be two worlds. NATO was the first Cold War creation to transcend Europe. The United States and Canada were members as well as the western European states. Only Sweden, Switzerland and Spain did not belong to it. It was explicitly a defensive alliance, providing for the mutual defence of any member attacked. This was another break with the now almost vanished isolationist traditions of American foreign policy.

It can be argued that NATO and the Berlin crisis ended the dangerous phase of Cold War in Europe, but it soon re-erupted in Asia. In 1945 Korea had been divided, its industrial north and agricultural south being occupied respectively by Russian and American forces. The problem of reunification was eventually referred to the United Nations which, after efforts to obtain elections for the whole country under its supervision, recognized a government set up in South Korea as the only lawful government of the Republic of Korea. Meanwhile, the Russian zone had also produced a government claiming sovereignty over the whole country. When Russian and American forces had both been withdrawn, North Korean forces invaded the south in June 1950. Within

two days President Truman intervened by sending American forces to fight them, acting in the name of the United Nations which had voted to resist aggression. A procedural accident had prevented the Russians from using their power on the Security Council to veto United Nations action.

The Americans always provided the bulk of the United Nations forces in Korea, but other nations sent contingents. Within a few months it seemed likely that the North Koreans would be overthrown. United Nations forces were operating well north of the 38th parallel which had divided the country and were soon nearing the Manchurian border. At this point Chinese communist forces intervened and drove them back. There was now a danger of a much bigger conflict. China was the second largest communist state in the world, and the largest in terms of population. Behind it stood Russia; a man could walk from Erfurt to Shanghai without once leaving communist territory. The question arose of direct action, possibly with nuclear weapons, by the United States against China.

1029

This did not occur, though Truman's insistence that the United States must not become involved in a major war on the Asian mainland could only in the end be maintained by dismissing the United Nations commander-in-chief, MacArthur. It began to seem likely that although the Chinese might be able to keep the North Koreans in the field so long as the war was not extended to their territory, they could not overturn South Korea against American wishes. Armistice talks began. The new American administration which came into office in 1953 was Republican and unequivocally anti-communist, but knew its predecessor had demonstrated its will and capacity to uphold an independent South Korean state and felt that the real centre of the Cold War was in Europe rather than in Asia. The armistice was signed in July 1953. All subsequent efforts to turn this into a formal peace failed. Yet in Korea as in Berlin, Americans could see that they had halted the expansion of communism into non-communist areas. They had won the first battles of the Cold War.

Shortly before the armistice, Stalin had died. It was very difficult for observers outside Russia to interpret what this might mean. In due course, it appeared that this was something of a break in the continuity of Russian development and policy, but that was not clear at the time and President Eisenhower was as distrustful of Russian intentions as ever. In the middle of the 1950s, the Cold War was at its most intense. It was not improved by the new Russian government's revelation that they too had the improved type of nuclear weapon known as the hydrogen bomb. This was shortly after Stalin's death and was something of a memorial to his achievement in assuring Russia her proper status in the postwar world. What is not clear is that this status could only have been achieved or was worth achieving at such cost. Russia was now a great industrial power, showing the trends in urbanization and population growth which had marked other industrializing nations, but her peoples had been rewarded with precious little but the knowledge of their international strength. Domestic consumption was still kept down in post-war

Russia and both the propaganda to which they were subjected and the brutalities of the police system seemed, if anything, to have been intensified after some relaxation during the war. But in such things Stalin had only carried to their logical conclusion the repressive policies of Lenin; his greater historical stature derives from his own contribution to Russia's new role in world history.

Outside Russia, Stalin's monument was a divided Europe, of which the western half was by 1953 substantially rebuilt thanks to American financial support. Germany was split down the middle; from 1949 the Federal Republic in the west and the German Democratic Republic in the east had moved further and further apart. On two successive days in March 1954 the Russians announced that the eastern republic now possessed full sovereignty and the West German president signed the constitutional amendment permitting the rearmament of his country. In 1955 West Germany entered NATO and the Russian riposte was to set up its own reply to NATO in the Warsaw Pact. Berlin's future was still in doubt, but it was clear that the NATO powers would fight to resist changes in its status except by agreement. In the east, the new German state had agreed to settle with old enemies: the line of the Oder-Neisse would be the frontier with Poland. Hitler's dream of realizing the greater Germany of the nineteenth-century nationalists had ended only by destroying Bismarckian Germany and delivering historic Prussia helpless to rule by a revolutionary communist régime. The new West Germany was federal in structure, non-militarist in tradition and dominated by Catholic and Social Democratic politicians whom Bismarck would have seen as enemies of the state. So ended the problem of containing the German power which had twice devastated Europe by war.

We cannot, of course, attribute to Stalin or any one person another division world-wide after the establishment of communism in China, that between what we may call capitalist and socialist economic systems. Yet Stalin's policies contributed importantly to its deepen-

In China, 1949, the year of the establishment of the Communist People's Republic, a great French photographer caught the atmosphere as the long-drawn-out struggle of traditional and revolutionary China came to a climax. The result was this picture of an old gentleman against a background provided by a column of new recruits to the army.

ing. Trade between Soviet Russia and other countries had from the start been encumbered by political obstacles. There had also been a great disruption of patterns of world trade after 1931 by the collapse of capitalist economies. After 1945, none the less, the divisions of the world market were transcended by a great new one; two methods of organizing the distribution of scarce resources increasingly divided the world between them and intercourse between them was henceforth limited. The essential determinant of one system, the capitalist, was the market – though a market very different from that envisaged by the old liberal Free Trade ideology and in many ways a very imperfect one; in the communist-controlled group of

nations political authority was the decisive economic factor.

Neither economic system remained unchanged and contacts between them multiplied as the years passed. None the less, they competed as models of economic growth for nations seeking to achieve it. This competition had been negligible before 1945 but was both inflamed by the political struggles of the Cold War and actually helped to spread its antagonisms. This was not a static situation, it must be said. In due course, the one system would come to be less completely dominated by the United States and the other less completely dominated by Russia than in 1950. Both shared in the continuing growth which dominated world economic history in the 1950s and (a little less markedly) in the 1960s. None the less the distinction between two economic systems remains fundamental to an understanding of the pattern of world economic development since 1945, for it shut off some possibilities and suggested others.

The entry of China to the socialist economic systems was of course of great importance but somewhat masked other significant implications of what had happened. It tended to be seen almost purely in Cold War terms. In fact, by the time of Stalin's death there were already other signs that the prophecy made by the South African statesman Smuts more than a quarter-century before that 'the scene had shifted away from Europe to the Far East and the Pacific' was, in fact, realized. Although the German problem persisted as the focus of the Cold War, Korea was only the most striking event already revealing that the centre of gravity of world history was again on the move, this time from Europe to the Orient.

Asian revolution

The collapse of imperial power in Asia was bound to be followed by further changes as the new states which emerged there came to be aware of their interests and power (or lack of it). In some instances their shape and unity had been given them by imperial rule and was not long to outlast it; the subcontinent of India lost its unity at the moment of decolonialization and Malaysia and Indo-China were to undergo important changes. They were not always welcome ones. There were internal strains in some of these new nations, too. Singapore and Indonesia, for example, had large numbers of Chinese inhabitants who often had a disproportionate share of economic power. Another shared characteristic which was almost certain to produce tension and therefore pressure for change was that nearly all these countries had fast-growing populations and were economically backward. Taken all round, it is hardly surprising that the end of European domination now hardly seems so much of a turning-point as once it seemed.

In part, what has happened since has revealed how limited the impact of Europe had been in some ways. Europeans had swayed the fate of millions of Asians, but had often barely touched their hearts and minds. This was largely because European civilization had contended with much deeper-rooted and more powerful traditions in Asia than in any other part of the world. Asian culture could not be swept aside as easily as that of pre-Columbian America. As in the Arab Islamic world, both the direct efforts of Europeans and the indirect diffusion of European culture through self-imposed modernization met formidable obstacles. The deepest layers of thought and behaviour often remained undisturbed even in those who believed themselves most emancipated from their country's past; nativities are still cast in educated Hindu families when children are born and marriages are contracted, and the Chinese Marxist draws on an unassailable sense of moral superiority grounded in age-old Chinese attitudes to the non-Chinese world.

Very roughly, Asia can be divided into two zones for the purpose of understanding her recent rôle in world history. There is a western sphere whose boundaries are set by the mountain ranges of northern India, the Burmese and Siamese highlands and the huge archipelago of which Indonesia is the major component. The centre of this sphere is the Indian Ocean and in

its history the major cultural influences have been three: the Hindu civilization spreading from India to the south-east, Islam (which also spread eastward across it), and the European impact, which worked through long periods not only of commercial and religious activity, but of direct political domination.

The other sphere is East Asian. It is dominated by China, in large measure by the simple geographical fact of that country's huge mass, but also indirectly through the migration of her people and, more remotely, by the fundamental cultural influence she has exercised on its peripheral nations. The most important of these are Japan, Korea, and Indo-China. In this area, direct European political domination had been short-lived and does not compare with the extent and duration of that in the Indian Ocean zone.

It has been easy to lose sight of the important differences between these two Asias since 1945 because each of them showed much in common in the first stages of decolonization. Both, for example, provided examples of angry rejections of the West and expressed them in western forms, notably in a touchy nationalism and appeals to world opinion. India showed her truculence, for example, by absorbing within a few years of independence both the princely states which had survived during the Raj and the remaining enclaves of French and Portuguese territory. But India's relationships with Asian countries also quickly turned out to be more difficult than expected. In particular, she quarrelled with her neighbour Pakistan. This was mainly because of Kashmir, a princely state containing a majority of Moslems under a Hindu prince. In 1947 fighting broke out there when the Moslems tried to bring about union with Pakistan: the Maharajah asked for Indian help and acceded to the Indian Republic. By way of complication, the Moslem spokesmen of Kashmir were themselves divided. India refused to hold a plebiscite recommended by the Security Council and the question has remained a running sore in Indo–Pakistan relations while some two-thirds of Kashmir are in Indian

Without much justification, the Russian leaders Bulganin and Khruschev (in particular) acquired a certain superficial popularity abroad and encouraged by their demeanour the hope that Russian policy might become somewhat milder. The contrast with Stalin may have been enough by itself to explain the phenomenon, but it was also encouraged by a certain willingness on their part not to stand on their dignity too unyieldingly on state occasions such as the visit to India during which this photograph was taken.

hands. Fighting went on until 1949; it then broke out again in 1965–6 and in 1969–70. The issue was further complicated by disputes about boundary demarcation which involved minorities on the wrong side of the border and about the fair use of the Indus waters. Finally in 1972 came a new eruption when East Pakistan broke away to form a new state on its own, Bangladesh, under Indian patronage but with economic problems possibly even graver than those of the other two republics of the subcontinent. In 1975, a violent change of government there seemed to show not only that its problems were unsolved, but that Indian patronage, too, was attracting resentment.

In these troubled passages, India has shown great ambitions (perhaps going so far as a wish to reunite the subcontinent) and a blatant disregard of the interests of other peoples (such as the Nagas). The hostility aroused by Indian aspirations was moreover further complicated by the behaviour of outside powers. The Indian

Republic soon asserted its determination to remain independent of either side in the Cold War. In the 1950s, this meant in practice the cultivation of warmer relations with Russia and communist China than with the United States; indeed, India's prime minister, Nehru, appeared to relish opportunities of criticizing American action. They fitted comfortably alongside the adoption of mildly socialist programmes in domestic affairs to maintain an image of a progressive, peaceful, non-aligned India. It came as all the more of a shock, therefore, to the Indian public to learn in 1959 that fighting had been going on with Chinese forces on the northern borders for about three years before the government admitted it. At the end of 1962, large-scale warfare began. Nehru took the improbable step of asking the Americans for military aid and, even more improbably, of receiving it at the same time as he took it from Russia.

Logically, Pakistan had not courted the same friends as India. The young Pakistan was much weaker than her neighbour. She had only a tiny trained civil service (Hindus had joined the old Indian Civil Service in much larger numbers than Moslems), was divided geographically in two, and almost at once had lost her ablest leader, Jinnah. Even under the Raj Moslem leaders had always (and perhaps realistically) shown less confidence in democratic forms than Congress, and after a turbulent period a general took power in 1958. Pakistan now turned to the path of 'guided democracy'. This signified a somewhat authoritarian régime seeking to ensure military survival against India and economic development, including land reform. India, meanwhile, preserved parliamentary forms, though restrictions on opposition and press in 1975 revealed that she, too, had come to the end of the road of constitutional government. This displeased some of India's former admirers in the West who had never grasped how shallow the roots of liberal politics were bound to be in Asia (let alone Africa).

The two states were further divided by the fact that Pakistan was Islamic, while the Indian republic was constitutionally non-confessional and secular, but the religious question hardly affected Pakistan's foreign policy. In the context of a world apparently increasingly divided in the early 1950s into two camps by the Cold War she leaned towards the non-communist West. But as the decade went on, a new grouping also made its appearance which for a time confused the patterns of diplomacy in Asia and the relations of India and Pakistan among them. An association of professedly neutralist powers known by the vague and sometimes misleading name of the 'Third World' resulted from a meeting of representatives of twenty-nine African and Asian states at Bandung in 1955. The conference included China and the group later took in Yugoslavia, a country long excommunicated from western communist orthodoxy. Most of the other 'Third World' nations were ex-colonial territories, poor and needy, more suspicious of the United States than Russia and more attracted to China than to either, but the term is unsatisfactory because their vague similarities masked important differences between them.

Thus, not very surprisingly, the coherence of 'Third World' politics was not to prove very enduring. Nevertheless, this was the first demonstration in the post-war world that the weak had power if they chose to use it, and that greater states in search of allies would have to take them into account. In the 1950s there were signs already in China's relations with the Bandung states that there was a divergence of interest between that country and Russia in that both wished to claim the leadership of the underdeveloped and uncommitted world. At first this emerged obliquely and in the disguise of differing attitudes to the Yugoslavs; it was in the end to be a world-wide contest. One early result was the paradox of Pakistan drawing closer to China (in spite of a treaty with the United States) and Russia closer to India as the 1950s wore on. Pakistan's own border disputes with China were settled amicably and after the United States declined to supply arms during her 1965 war with India, Pakistan turned to China. She got

much less than had been hoped for, but this was an early example of a new fluidity which began to mark international affairs in the 1960s.

No more than the communist states were the Americans able to ignore this. Indeed, the Cold War quickly produced an ironical change in the rôle of the United States in Asia; from being the patron of anti-colonialism of 1945, which had done so much to dismantle its allies' empires, it began in some areas almost to appear as their supplanter. This was less true in the Indian Ocean sphere than in the Far East. Nor did the change in United States' policy for a long time appear unambiguous to its allies who were former colonial powers. Long and unrewarded American efforts to placate India still pointed the other way. Perhaps the clearest example, though, of the difficulties posed to great powers by the new Asia was provided by Indonesia.

The most obvious of the formidable problems confronting the new Indonesia was posed by the variety of communities and the wide divergence of political interests in its vast sprawl of territories. The basic culture of the Sumatrans and Javanese was Hindu; Indonesia had long been a part of the Indian cultural zone. But there were also large numbers of Moslems; Islam had been brought to Indonesia centuries before by Arab traders. As if this were not enough, the Chinese immigration was also long-established and had tended to produce a preponderance of Chinese in administrative and commercial positions. The colonial régime's removal released some of the communal tensions from the discipline imposed by a common ruler. This happened, moreover, while the usual post-colonial problems of over-population, under-development and inflation began to make their impact. In the 1950s central government was increasingly resented and by 1957 it was only in control of Java. Attempts to use the time-honoured device of distracting opposition by a nationalist campaign against the continued Dutch presence in West New Guinea were not successful in rebuilding popular support.

Under Sukarno, Indonesian government

moved rapidly away from the liberal forms which had been adopted at the birth of the new state towards another version of 'guided democracy'. This meant leaning more heavily on Russian support and, in 1960, the dismissal of parliament. In 1963, Sukarno was named president for life. Yet American support had long been forthcoming because of fears that he might turn to China for help. It made possible the absorption of the independent state which had emerged from West New Guinea, to the irritation of the Dutch. Sukarno then turned to a confrontation with the new federation of Malaysia, set up in 1957 from the fragments of British empire in South-East Asia. Indonesian attacks on Borneo and Sarawak and eventually on the Malayan mainland were mastered with British help. Although he still enjoyed American patronage (the brother of President Kennedy appeared in London to advocate a settlement favourable to Indonesia) this failure seems to have been the turning-point for Sukarno. The distraction of foreign adventure had just enabled him to ride the storm at home when food shortages and inflation went out of control. The details of what followed are obscure but it seems that an attempt by Sukarno to forestall his opponents by killing several army officers antagonized the armed forces. The people's agitation over economic crisis was exploited by those who feared Sukarno's dependence on the (mainly Chinese) communists; significantly, the traditional shadow plays which are one of the distinctive forms of Indonesian art were for months presenting the old Hindu epics which were their staple material with political allusions and overtones of coming change. Finally the storm broke. The army stood back ostentatiously while popular massacres of communists took place which removed possible support on which Sukarno might have relied. He was set aside by a military régime in 1966.

American sympathy for him reflected the belief that the best opponents of communism were strong and prosperous national states. It appears from the history of Far Eastern Asia in the last quarter-century or so that there was

indeed much to be said for this, but its expression in American policy cannot be said to have been an unqualified success. There is a big gap between appreciating the principle and drawing the right practical conclusion from it. Even more than in the Indian Ocean sphere, the dominant fact of post-war history to the east of Singapore was the revival of Chinese power. Though régimes appeared in both South Korea and Japan which successfully resisted communism, they too benefited in growing independence of the West from the Chinese revolution. The East Asians had always defended themselves more successfully against the Europeans than the Indian Ocean countries and since 1947 they have shown increasing ability to assert their independence in both communist and non-communist forms. It is difficult not to see in this the effects of the continuing operation of fundamental attitudes in societies drawing so much upon Chinese example. In their discipline, capacity for constructive social effort, disregard for the individual, respect for authority and hierarchy and deep self-awareness as members of civilizations proudly distinct from the West, the East Asians drew on something much deeper than the Chinese Revolution – and, indeed, that revolution is only comprehensible against the background dominated by that something.

We may nevertheless begin with the development of that revolution after its installation in power. In retrospect, it may be thought notable that Peking was again chosen as capital of the new China. It seemed to indicate that China might again be more aware of pressure from her land frontiers in the north than of the threat she had faced for a century from the sea. However this may be, Russia had been the first state to recognize the new China, closely followed by the British, Indian and Burmese governments.

Given Cold War preoccupations elsewhere and the circumstances of the nationalist collapse, the new China did not in fact face any real threat from the outside to distract her rulers from the long overdue task of modernization;

the nationalists, cooped up in Taiwan, could be disregarded, even though they might for the time being be irremovable. When a major threat did materialize, as the United Nations forces approached the Yalu river frontier of Manchuria and Korea in 1950, the Chinese reaction was strong and immediate: they sent a large army to Korea. But the main preoccupation of the first years of communist China was the internal state of the country, which presented problems formidable enough. Material and physical construction and reconstruction was overdue, population pressure on land loomed as seriously as ever, and the moral and ideological void presented by the collapse of the *ancien régime* over the preceding century had to be filled.

The peasants were the starting-point. Here the establishment of communism is not a very significant date, for it only punctuated and extended a process of land reform which had been going on since the 1920s. It was largely carried out by the peasants themselves, under party leadership; though by 1956 China's farms were collectivized this was coupled with a social transformation of the villages which gave control of the new units to their inhabitants. The essential change was the overthrow of the local village leaders and landlords; it was by no means non-violent and such persons must have made up a large number of the 800000 Chinese who were reported later by Mao to have been liquidated in the first five years of the People's Republic. Meanwhile a programme of industrialization was also pressed forward. This depended largely upon Russian help, the only source from which China could draw. By 1956 it had produced an increase in the Chinese net domestic product proportionately greater than the increase in the production of food.

By then China was already acting as a major influence abroad, though her independence was long masked by the superficial unity of the communist bloc and her continued exclusion from UNO at the insistence of the United States. A Sino-Russian treaty in 1950 was the first landmark. It was interpreted abroad – especially in the United States – as evidence that China was entering the Cold War on the Russian side. Certainly, the régime was communist and talked revolution and anti-colonialism. Moreover, its choices were bound to be confined by the parameters of the Cold War. Yet in a longer perspective traditional concerns now seem to have had important weight in Chinese communist policy from the start. At a very early point, there emerged a concern to re-establish Chinese power within the area it had always tended to fill up.

The securing of Manchuria is by itself enough to explain Chinese military intervention in Korea, for example; the peninsula too had long been an area of dispute between imperial China and Japan. An occupation of Tibet in 1951 was another incursion into an area which had for centuries been under Chinese suzerainty; it called into question, inevitably, borders with India established by British force. But from the start the most vociferous demand made for regaining control of the Chinese periphery was for the eviction of the nationalist government from Taiwan, which had been taken from the Chinese in 1895 by the Japanese and only restored in 1945 to control by the mainland. By 1955, a United States government was so deeply committed to the support of the nationalist régime there that the president announced that the United States would protect not merely the island itself but the smaller islands near the Chinese coast which were thought essential to its defence. About this issue and against a background provided by a sense of inexplicable rebuff by a China long patronized by American philanthropy and missionary effort, the interest of the United States in Chinese affairs tended to crystallize for over a decade. It did so so obsessively that at times it seemed that the Chinese nationalist tail was wagging the American dog. Conversely, during the 1950s, both the Indian government and the Russian supported Peking over Taiwan, insisting that the matter was one of Chinese internal affairs. It was therefore all the more sensational when the next decade brought about actual armed conflict between China and these two powers.

The quarrel with India grew out of the Chinese occupation of Tibet and its reordering as an autonomous region. Indian policy still seemed basically sympathetic to China when in 1959 the Chinese further tightened their grasp on Tibet; India then discountenanced an attempt by Tibetan exiles to set up a government on her soil. But by then the Chinese advance had already provoked the territorial disputes about which the public had not been told and they led to clashes even in 1959. In the course of discussing them in the following year the Chinese announced that they did not consider that their border with India ran along the lines drawn by a British–Tibetan negotiation in 1914 which had never been formally accepted by any Chinese government. Forty-odd years' usage was hardly significant against the background provided by China's historical continuity.

This resulted in much heavier fighting in the autumn of 1962 when Nehru demanded a Chinese withdrawal from Indian territory. The Indians did badly and received defence help not only from the United States but from Russia, notably by the supply of aeroplane engines. Suddenly, early in 1963, a startled world heard Russia bitterly denounced by the Chinese communist party for, on the one hand, helping India and on the other for stopping economic and military aid to China three years before.

The second charge indicated complicated origins to this quarrel, but by no means went to the root of the matter. Some Chinese communists (Mao among them) could, after all, remember the consequences of the subordination of the Chinese revolution to the international interest of communism, as interpreted by the Russians, as far back as the 1920s. Since that time there had always been a division in the leadership of the Chinese party between Russian and native forces. Mao represented the sinicizing of Marxism. He envisaged a society different from Soviet Russian as well as from

capitalist. Unfortunately, such subtleties were difficult to disentangle because Chinese resentment of Russian policy had to be presented to the rest of the world in Marxist jargon. Since the new leadership in Russia was engaged in the dismantling of the Stalin myth, this almost accidentally led the Chinese in consequence to become more Stalinist than Stalin in their public pronouncements even when they were pursuing radically non-Stalinist policies.

Finally there is an even more remote past than this to recall. Well before the foundation of the CCP the Chinese revolution had been a movement of national regeneration, one of whose primary aims was the recovery of China's control over her own destiny from the foreigners. Among these foreigners were the Russians. The long history of their encroachment upon the Chinese sphere went back to Peter the Great and it had continued in the Soviet era. A protectorate over Tannu Tuva was established in 1914 by the tsars; the area was annexed by the Soviets in 1944. In 1945 Russian armies entered Manchuria and north China and reconstituted the tsarist Far East; they remained in Sinkiang until 1949, in Port Arthur until 1955. In Mongolia their withdrawal left behind a satellite Mongolian People's Republic set up in 1946. Even after 1955 the Russians and Chinese shared something like 4500 miles of frontier (if Mongolia is included) and there was great potential for dispute along its huge length.

Finally, we should take into account the personal views of Mao Tse-tung. Although his later intellectual formation had been Marxist and although he found its categories helpful in explaining his country's predicament, he appears always to have combined with them a certain pragmatism. He escaped the Marxist dogma of the Bolshevik period because of a firm attachment to lessons of experience. Mao's attitude to knowledge and ideas was predominantly utilitarian and moralistic; in this it is very much in the Chinese tradition. The whole complex of phenomena presenting itself to him at any time was classified by him into contending forces on which there can play human will—

The official Chinese caption on this picture of an incident on the Ussuri river frontier with the Soviet Union reads 'Chinese frontier guards reason with the Soviet revisionist frontier troops who intrude into China's Chenpao Island area, in a tit-for-tat struggle. Having a guilty conscience and an unjust cause, the Soviet revisionist frontier troops have to put their armoured cars in reverse. However, a little big shot of the Soviet revisionist frontier troops (5th from left) keeps arguing.'

power to bring about morally valuable and creative change.

Mao's relationship with the CCP had not always been smooth. His great opportunity had come when his policy towards the peasantry provided a way ahead after disaster had overtaken urban communism. After a temporary setback in the early 1930s he had a virtually undisputed supremacy within the party from about 1935. Rural influences within the party were on top at last. The way was also open for Mao later to have an enormous international influence; the notion of a protracted revolutionary war waged from the countryside and carried into the towns had huge potential in parts of the world for which the orthodox Marxist belief that industrial development was needed to create a revolutionary proletariat was not attractive.

The Sino–Russian conflict continued fiercely after 1963 until it involved the whole communist world. It was accentuated by Russian tactlessness. Not content with alarming the Chinese by signs of doctrinal deviation, the Russians seem to have been as careless as any western imperialists of relations with Asiatic allies: Khruschev later made the revealing remark that when touring in China, he and other Russians 'used to laugh at their primitive forms of organization'. The worst affront had been the withdrawal of Russian economic and technical help in 1960 just when natural disasters such as floods – said by official Chinese sources to have affected 150 million acres of agricultural land – had followed the collapse of a great economic offensive launched in 1958 by Mao, the 'Great Leap Forward'. What happened is obscure; the aim appears to have been to decentralize the economy into 'Communes', of which there were some 25 000, thus setting aside centralized planning on the Russian model with its bureaucratic dangers, and also calling directly upon the participation of local forces from which the régime had previously benefited. Clearly, it failed. Mao's own standing appears to have suffered until the later 1960s.

By then, his rivals had managed to put the economy back on the road to modernization again. The most striking evidence, perhaps, was the explosion of a Chinese nuclear weapon in 1964, an expensive admission card to a very exclusive club. Even more important was the fact that the régime managed to avoid crippling famine and to keep the loyalty of the people. Though more slowly than in the early nineteenth century, the Chinese population has continued to rise, and to rise to colossal totals. 545 million has been thought a reasonable estimate for 1950, 685 million ten years later, and 750 million in the middle of the 1960s; this is about one-fifth of the population of the world. Demographically, China was stronger by the beginning of the 1960s than ever in her history. China's leaders talked as if they were unmoved by the possibility of nuclear war; their enormous population made it likely that Chinese would survive in greater numbers than the peoples of other countries. More positively, there were signs that Russia was alarmed by the presence of so great a power on the border of her most thinly populated regions. China is, after all, not only one of the most highly, but also one of the most densely, populated countries in the world.

Meanwhile, the revolution seemed not to have lost any of its dynamic and the party strove to keep it going. Much turned on the evidence of what had happened in the USSR. There was fear that something similar might happen in China. This fear lay behind the 'cultural revolution' of 1966-9, a consequence also of the re-establishment of Mao's supremacy with the aid of the army. It was a huge upheaval sweeping through party and administration in an attempt to offset the danger that a new ruling class would emerge. One way in which it expressed itself was the closing of universities and enforcement of practical work on all citizens; this had as its object a changing of traditional attitudes to intellectuals. The emphasis of the cultural revolution was upon self-sacrifice and subordination to the thought of Mao Tse-tung. By 1968 the country had been turned upside-down by 'Red Guards' fighting entrenched officialdom and in the end there were signs that Mao himself believed things had gone too far. After the army re-established order and instituted new cadres a party congress reconfirmed Mao's leadership.

The obvious moral preoccupation of this still mysterious episode is very striking. Mao clearly felt a danger that the revolution might congeal and lose the moral *élan* which had carried it so far. In seeking to protect it, old ideas – the traditional honour paid to the intellectual in China, for example – had to go. This should not seem surprising. Of the great revolutions of world history, the Chinese has been unquestionably one of the most far-reaching because it had to be. Society, government and economy were enmeshed and integrated with one another into a whole system in China as nowhere else. The 'demotion' of intellectuals was a necessary consequence of the desire to make a new China, for their prestige embodied the old order just as

The cultural revolution showed great touchiness about symbols of reaction; Red Guards are shown here pulling down the sign (said to be tinged with colonialism) over a clock and watch shop.

had the examination system whose abolition more than fifty years earlier had been one of the announcements that a real revolution and not just a change of régime was under way in the most unchanging society on earth. It is in this perspective that Chinese communism's achievement and direction stands out from the mystifying welter of events which bemuse the foreign reader of the newspapers. The deliberate attack on the family as an authority is not merely an attempt by an insecure régime to encourage informers and delation, but an attack on the most fundamental of all Chinese social institutions. The deliberate advancement of women and propaganda to discourage early marriage have a dimension going beyond 'progressive' feminist ideas or population control; they are

The herdsmen of the High Pamirs wave the little red books containing the thoughts of Chairman Mao to an approving patrol of Chinese frontier guards. In the background can be seen a tent of the kind used by Central Asian nomads even before the days of the Mongol empire.

an assault on the past such as no other revolution has ever made, for in China the past meant a rôle for women far inferior to anything to be found in pre-revolutionary America, France or Russia. The attacks on party leaders which accuse them of flirtation with Confucian ideas are more than the jibes which comparable attacks would be in western countries; indeed, they could not occur in them, for no vision of a past to be rejected which was so total could exist in the West, which has known cultural pluralism for hundreds of years.

Yet rejection is not the whole story. The more than two thousand years of China's essential continuity, stretching back to the Ch'in and perhaps further, must be taken into account if we are to penetrate the meaning of the Chinese revolution. The clue is the rôle of authority in it. For all its cost and cruelty, the revolution is a heroic endeavour; in scale it is matched only by such gigantic social efforts as the coming of Islam, or Europe's assault on the world in early modern times. The difference is that this move-

ment is at least in intention centrally controlled and directed by the state. Here is the paradox of the Chinese revolution: it rests on popular fervour, but is unimaginable without conscious direction from a state inheriting all the mysterious prestige of the traditional bearers of the Mandate of Heaven. Chinese tradition respects authority and gives it a moral endorsement long hard to find in the West. No more than any other great state can communist China shake off its history.

This history sometimes gives communist China a paradoxically conservative appearance. No large society had for so long driven home to its peoples the assumptions that the individual mattered less than the collective whole, that authority could rightfully command the services of millions at any cost to themselves in order to carry out great works for the good of the state, that the government's authority is unquestioned so long as it is exercised for the common good. The notion of opposition is distasteful to the Chinese because it suggests a disruption of society. What such ideas imply, of course, is the rejection of the kind of revolution involved in the adaptation of western individualism. Mao himself fits well into the Chinese popular tradition of the ruler-sage. He is presented as much as a teacher as a politician; western commentators have been amused by the status given to his thoughts by the omnipresence of the Little Red Book (though there have been areas of the West since the Protestant Reformation where similar attention has been given to the Bible), but the utterances of great teachers have always commanded respect in China. He is the spokesman of a moral doctrine which is as much the core of society as Confucianism ever was. There is also something traditional in Mao's artistic interests; he is admired by the people as a poet and his poems command the respect of qualified judges. The régime over which he presides benefits from the Chinese past as well as destroying it, because Mao is easily comprehensible within its idea of authority. Traditionally, power has been sanctioned in China by the notion that the ruler did good

Immense efforts were made to enhance the prestige of Mao Tse-tung during the 1950s and 1960s. Huge posters such as this one, showing him against a background provided by hundreds of red banners (and with a cigarette casually in his hand) were commonplace. No other Chinese leader was the object of so deliberate an attempt to elevate him above the status of ordinary mortal. It was somewhat reminiscent of the adulation given in Russia to Stalin.

A humiliation for France psychologically comparable to the loss of Singapore by the British thirteen years earlier: French prisoners being marched away from Dien Bien Phu, 1954.

things for his people. This has sometimes presented certain obstacles to the communists' effort to get things done by the people themselves, but it has also helped to make easy the acceptance of action by the authorities for the collective good.

The weight of the past is also obvious in the suggestive continuities of Chinese foreign policies. The new régime came to patronize revolutions all over the world, but its main concern was with the Far East and, in particular, with Indo-China, where Russian and Chinese policy seems often to have diverged. After the Korean War the Chinese began to supply arms to the communist guerrilla forces in South Vietnam. In 1953 the French had to give up both Cambodia and Laos. In 1954 they lost a battle at a base called Dien Bien Phu which was decisive both for French prestige and the will to fight of the French electorate. After this, it was impossible for the French to maintain themselves in the Red River delta and a conference at Geneva agreed to partition Vietnam between the French and the Viet Minh, pending elections which might reunite the country. The elections never took place. What happened instead was that there soon opened in Indo-China the fiercest phase since 1945 of the Asian war begun in 1941 against the West.

The western contenders were no longer the former colonial powers, but the Americans: on the other side were a mixture of Indo-Chinese communists, nationalists and reformers supported by the Chinese and Russians. American anti-colonialism and the belief that the United States should support indigenous governments led it to back the South Vietnamese government as it backed South Koreans and Filipinos. Unfortunately in neither Laos nor South Vietnam, nor, eventually, in Cambodia, did régimes appear of unquestioned legitimacy in the eyes of all their subjects. One unfortunate effect of American patronage was that it often identified such clients with the western enemy disliked almost universally in east Asia. Another weakness was the knowledge that they could depend on American support often removed the incentive to carry out essential reforms which would have united people behind these régimes. This was especially true in Vietnam, where the *de facto* partition did not produce good or stable government in the south. While Buddhists and Roman Catholics quarrelled bitterly and the peasants were more and more alienated from the régime by the failure of land reform, an apparently corrupt ruling class seemed able to survive government after government. This benefited the communists. They sought reunification on their own terms and maintained from the north support for the communist underground movement in the south, the Viet Cong.

By 1960 the Viet Cong had won control of much of the south. This was the background to a momentous decision taken by President Kennedy in 1962, when he authorized the despatch not only of financial and material help but also of 4000 American 'advisers' to help the South Vietnam government put its military house in order. This was the beginning of a road which led in a few years to the situation Truman had been determined to avoid, the involvement of the United States in a major war on the mainland of Asia and, in the end, to the loss of 50000 American lives.

Washington's response to Cold War in Asia

had also led to efforts to safeguard as long as possible the special position arising from the American occupation of Japan, which was virtually a monopoly, with only token participation by British Commonwealth forces. This had been possible because of the Russian delay in declaring war on Japan and the speed of Japan's surrender, which had taken Stalin by surprise. The Americans firmly rejected Russian requests for a share in an occupation they had done nothing to bring about. The results of this were startling, for the Japanese once more demonstrated their astonishing gift for learning from others only what they wished to learn while safeguarding their own society against fundamental change.

When the war ended in defeat the Japanese faced deep and troubling problems. These went far beyond the questions of physical reconstruction; they concerned the national identity and purpose. The westernization of the Meiji era had eventually produced the dream of 'Asia for the Asians'. In its Japanese version, this idea was now blown away by defeat. It had really meant a kind of Japanese Monroe doctrine underpinned by the anti-western sentiment so widespread in the Far East. The slogan was realized in a different sense after 1945 by the rolling back of colonialism; this did not leave Japan with an obvious Asian rôle. In any case, at that moment she seemed unlikely for a long time to have the power to act in one. Moreover, the war had shown Japan's vulnerability and it had been a great shock; like the United Kingdom she had depended on shipping and loss of control of the surface of the sea had doomed her. Then there were the other results of defeat; the loss of domestic territory to Russia on Sakhalin and the occupation by the Americans. Finally, there was huge physical and human destruction to repair.

On the credit side, the Japanese in 1945 still had the unshaken central institution of the monarchy, whose prestige was undimmed and, indeed, had made possible the surrender. The American commander in the Pacific, General MacArthur, believed in the importance of main-

Campaigning in two languages, a right-wing candidate struggles vigorously for election to the Japanese parliament. The Cold War and establishment of the Chinese Communist régime made such appeals very persuasive to many Japanese in the 1950s and 1960s.

taining it as an instrument of a peaceful occupation and took care to have a new Japanese constitution adopted before republican enthusiasts in the United States could interfere. There was also a great resource in Japanese social cohesiveness and discipline, though for a time it seemed that the American occupation might undermine this by the determination with which it pressed democratic institutions upon the Japanese. By 1951 this democratic education seemed to have been successful enough for a peace treaty to be made between Japan and most of her former opponents except the Russians and nationalist Chinese; terms with them followed within a few years. The peace treaties restored to Japan her full sovereignty including a right to arms for defensive purposes. On the other hand, the Japanese gave up virtually all their former overseas possessions. Thus Japan emerged from the post-war era into one in which she again had control of her own affairs (although an agree-ment with the United States provided for the maintenance of American forces on her soil), but was confined to her own islands and faced a China stronger and better consolidated than for a century. In less than twenty years this much reduced status was to be transformed again by foreign affairs and economic growth.

They could be seen at work even before 1951. The Cold War quite changed the implications of the American occupation. Japanese territory was separated from that of Russia and China by respectively 10 and 500 miles of water; it was significant, too, that Japan was only 150 miles from Korea, her old area of expansion and soon a battleground. The spread of the Cold War to Asia guaranteed to Japan even better treatment from the Americans, now anxious to see Japan working convincingly as an example of democracy and capitalism, and also gave Japan the protection of the United States nuclear umbrella. The Korean war gave Japan a new importance as a base, and galvanized the Japanese economy. The index of industrial production quickly went back up to the level of the 1930s. The United States promoted Japanese interests abroad and used her diplomatic resources to do so. Finally, these benefits were unaccompanied by the burden of defence costs, since Japan was until 1951 forbidden to have any armed forces.

Japan's close connexion with the United States, proximity to the communist world, and her advanced and stable economy and society, all made it natural that she should take her place in the security system built up after 1945 by the United States in Asia and the Pacific. Its foundations were treaties with Australia, New Zealand and the Philippines (given their independence in 1946). Others followed with Pakistan and Thailand; these were the Americans' only Asian allies other than Taiwan. Indonesia and (much more important) India remained aloof. These alliances reflected, in part, the new conditions of Pacific and Asian international relations after the British withdrawal from India. For a little longer there would still be British forces east of Suez, but the Dominions of Australia and New Zealand had discovered during the war that the United Kingdom could not defend them and the United States could. The fall of Singapore in 1942 had been decisive. Though British forces still supported the Malaysians against the Indonesians in the 1950s and 1960s, their important colony at Hong Kong survived, they knew, only because it suited the Chinese that it should. On the other hand, there was no question of sorting out the complexities of the new Pacific by simply lining up states in the teams of the Cold War. The peace treaty with Japan itself caused great difficulty because United States policy saw Japan as a potential anti-communist force while others – notably Australia and New Zealand – remembered 1941 and feared a revival of Japanese power.

Thus more was already influencing American policy than ideology. None the less, it was unduly affected by what was believed to be the disaster of the communist success in China. The people who pointed to Chinese patronage of revolutionaries as far away as Africa and South America were misled. There had certainly been a transformation in China's international position and it would go further, but its primary significance did not lie in ideology but in China's re-emergence as a power in her own right. This in the end did not reinforce the dualist, Cold War system but made nonsense of it. Though at first within the former Chinese sphere only, it was bound to bring about a big change in relative power relationships; the first indication of this was seen in Korea, where United States land power was stopped and it became necessary to consider whether air power would be used against China. But the rise of China was also of the most acute importance to Russia which, from one pole of a bipolarized system became the corner of a triangle, as well as losing its unchallenged pre-eminence in the world revolutionary movement. And it was in relation to Russia, perhaps, that the wider significance of the Chinese revolution most readily appeared. Overwhelmingly the most important example of it though it might be, the Chinese revolution was only the outstanding fact of a rejection of western domination which

The buildings erected in 1964 for the Tokyo Olympic Games carefully evoked traditional Japanese forms.

An oil refinery on the Persian Gulf – the face of revolution in the Arab world. With more than two-thirds of the world's known oil reserves, the Middle East produced by 1970 more than a third of the world's total output of oil.

was Asia-wide and which had begun in 1941 – or perhaps 1904. Paradoxically, of course, that rejection in all Asian countries was most obviously expressed in forms borrowed from the West itself, whether they were industrial capitalism, nationalism or Marxism.

The inheritors of empire in Africa and the Middle East

The establishment of Israel in 1948 was the first of three big upheavals in the politics of the Arab world; the others were the coming of the Cold War and a huge rise in the world's consumption of oil. Israel focussed Arab nationalism as even Great Britain had not done. On the injustice of the seizure of what were regarded as Arab lands, the need for the Palestine refugees to return and the obligations of the great powers and the United Nations to act on their behalf, all the Arab states were able to agree. After their defeat in 1948–9, they were not for some time disposed again to commit their own forces openly, though there were continuing border incidents in the early 1950s. More reliance was placed upon raids from Egyptian and Syrian territory upon Israel by bands of young guerrilla soldiers recruited from the refugee Arabs of the camps.

Meanwhile, emigration, hard work and foreign money consolidated the new Israel. A series of armistices established *de facto* borders with Jordan, Syria and Egypt which lasted until 1967 (though the formal state of war was to last, too). A sense of siege helped to stabilize Israeli politics; the prestige of the party which had brought about the very existence of the new state was scarcely troubled. Helped by a flow of official and unofficial aid from abroad – above all from the United States – the Jews transformed their new country. Within a few years they could show massive progress in bringing barren land under cultivation and establishing industries. The gap between Israel's *per capita* income and that of the Arab states steadily widened.

This gap was another irritant for the Arabs. Although Arab countries received foreign aid,

it did not produce anything like the dramatic change in their condition that followed in Israel. This was largely because Egypt, the most important of the Arab states, faced grave problems posed by a high rate of population growth. This social strain gave fuel to continuing agitation against the foreigner, but this was often in itself a distraction from badly needed social reform. Most of the Arab countries were ruled by small, wealthy, nationalist and westernized élites, little interested in the Islamic substrata of poverty-stricken peasants and slum-dwellers who were their countrymen. In the case of the Egyptians, the British, who still had a garrison in Egypt and were now blamed for their part in allowing the establishment of Israel, were a good scapegoat for domestic injustice. The British government, for its part, did its best to cooperate with the Arab states and prevent revolution in them because of its fears of Russian influence in the area.

Pan-Arabism's inability to transcend its own divisions had always been a weakness, but began to show some signs of being overcome. The Hashemite kingdoms, the Arabian sheikdoms, and the Europeanized urban states of North Africa and the Levant had, of course, both divergent interests and very different historical traditions. Islam was a cultural tie, but seemed not much more; few Moslems saw it any longer as a militant, aggressive faith. This gave added importance to the Israeli issue, which provided a common enemy, and to a revolution in Egypt from which emerged a leader who for a time seemed to be able to unite much of the Arab world and to open the way to social change. This was a young soldier, Gamal Abdel Nasser. In 1954 he became the leader of a military junta which had overthrown the monarchy two years previously.

At that time strong anti-western currents were appearing elsewhere in the Arab world. In 1951 the King of Jordan had been assassinated; his successor would have to make it clear that he had severed the old special tie with Great Britain if he was to survive. At the other end of the Mediterranean, the French had been forced to recognize the complete independence of Morocco and Tunisia soon after the war, and in 1954 an Algerian national rebellion began. This was to become a full-scale war, because the French government was not disposed to abandon a country where there were over a million settlers of French blood and where oil had just been discovered in the Sahara.

In these circumstances Nasser's programme of social reform and nationalism looked like a model for wide acceptance among emerging and revolutionary Arab nations. His anti-Israeli feelings were not in doubt. One of his first successes was the negotiation at last of a treaty with Great Britain which provided for the evacuation of the Suez base within twenty months. The Americans, increasingly aware of Russian menace in the Middle East since the Republican administration had taken over in 1953, looked on him for a while with favour as a spotless anti-colonialist and potential client.

Nasser's independence soon led to the waning of his attractiveness to them. The guerrilla raids from Egyptian territory (the 'Gaza Strip', where the most important Palestinian refugee camps lay) on Israel provoked retaliation. The British, French and Americans had in 1950 already said they would supply no arms to anyone in the area and so Nasser turned to the communists. This brought the Cold War seriously to the Middle East and opened much more promising prospects for communism there. An Egyptian arms deal with Czechoslovakia on the security of the cotton crop and the Egyptian recognition of communist China prompted second thoughts in the United States about Nasser.

By way of indicating displeasure, an American and British offer to finance a cherished project of internal development, a high dam on the Nile, was withdrawn. As a riposte, Nasser seized the assets of the private Suez Canal Company, saying its profits should finance the dam; this touched an old nerve of British imperial sensibility. Instincts only half-disciplined by imperial withdrawal seemed for once to be coherent first with anti-communism and then

with friendship towards more traditional Arab states whose rulers looked askance at Nasser. Ironically, the loss of India had not made Suez seem less important to Great Britain, for a new problem had arisen, that of the security of the oil supplies brought through the Canal from the Gulf.

The British and French protested over the seizure of the Canal; the latter felt they had additional grievance in Nasser's support for the Algerian insurrection. Then, in October 1956, the Israelis suddenly invaded Egypt to destroy, they said, the bases from which guerrillas harassed their settlements. The British and French now urged that the freedom of transit through the Canal was in danger and called for a ceasefire; when Nasser rejected this they launched first an air attack and then a seaborne invasion of Egypt (appropriately, on Guy Fawkes' Day). Collusion with the Israeli government was denied but the denial has remained incredible. By this time, the Americans were thoroughly alarmed; they saw a danger of Russian profit in this resurrection of imperialism. Financial pressure by them forced a British acceptance of a ceasefire negotiated by the United Nations.

The Suez affair was disastrous for western interests in the Middle East in the short run, but in the long run had little importance. It had badly distracted the West from events in eastern Europe at that moment, where a revolution in Hungary against its Soviet satellite government was crushed by the Russian army while the western powers were quarrelling. It confirmed Arab hatred of Israel and the suspicion that she was indissolubly linked to the West; it therefore made them yet more receptive to approaches from the East. But the essentials of Middle East history continued more or less as before. One was the continuing excitement of Arab nationalism, for Suez had raised Nasser's prestige among Arabs even higher.

One mark of this was an attempt to unite Syria and Egypt in a United Arab Republic in 1958. The hitherto pro-western government of the Lebanon was overthrown in the following

The last attempt by a British government to impose its will abroad by force took place in 1956, when the ill-omened Suez expedition was mounted with the French. Though militarily successful, its end was failure and humiliation.

year, when monarchy in Iraq was swept aside by revolution and a general took power. But soon differences between Arab countries again asserted themselves. The world watched the curious spectacle of American forces being summoned to the Lebanon and British to Jordan for brief periods to help maintain their governments. Inside Syria and Iraq, pro-Nasser forces were continually troubled by local groups who sought to reassert their interests. Meanwhile, fighting went on sporadically on the Syrian–Israeli border, though guerrillas were for a time held in check.

Until 1967 the most important event in the Islamic Arab world after Suez was the final success of the Algerian revolution. The intransigence of the French settlers and the bitterness of many soldiers who felt they were asked to do an impossible job there nearly brought about a revolution in France itself. The government of General de Gaulle nevertheless opened secret negotiations with the Algerian provisional government in Cairo in June 1960. In July 1962, after a referendum, France formally granted independence to Algeria.

Libya had become independent under United Nations trusteeship at the end of the war, so that the entire North African coast was now clear of European supremacy. Suez had only been a

flash in the pan. Yet external influences still bedevilled the history of the Arab lands as they had done ever since the Ottoman conquests centuries before. They were now being exercised indirectly, through aid and diplomacy, as the United States and Russia sought to buy friends among the Arab states. The United States laboured under the disadvantage that its governments could not abandon Israel because of the importance of Jewish sympathy for Israel among American voters. Also, in spite of Suez, Arab policy had more and more alienated the United States since 1946. Russia, on the other hand, had reversed its early support of Israel as soon as that had ceased to be a useful weapon with which to embarrass the British. It was replaced by a steady pro-Arab line and the fanning of Arab resentment of the survivals of British imperialism still to be found at Aden and in the Gulf. Marginally, too, by the treatment of their own Jews in the later 1960s the Russians earned a certain bonus of Arab approval very cheaply.

The other factor slowly changing the terms of the Middle Eastern problem was oil. In the 1950s two important developments occurred. One was a much greater rate of discovery of oil than hitherto, particularly on the southern shores of the Persian Gulf, in the small sheikdoms then still under British influence and in Saudi Arabia. The second was that there began to be noticeable the great acceleration of energy consumption in western countries, especially in the United States, which has gone on ever since. The prime beneficiaries of this were Saudi Arabia, Libya, Kuwait and then, some way behind, Iran. This had two important consequences. The great powers which were dependent upon Middle Eastern oil – the United States, Great Britain, Germany and, soon, Japan – had to take this into account in their diplomacy in the area. It also meant big changes in the relative standing of Arab states. None of the three leading oil producers was either heavily populated or traditionally very important, unless Saudi Arabia is thought to be.

The full impact of oil was still not apparent

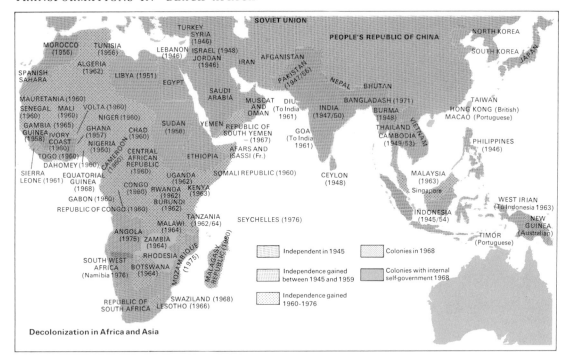

Decolonization in Africa and Asia

in the last Middle East crisis of the 1960s, which began when a much more extreme government took power in Syria and presented an obvious challenge to Nasser for the leadership of the Arab world. The King of Jordan was threatened if he did not act in support of the Palestinian guerrillas (organized since 1964 as the Palestine Liberation Organization). Egyptian and Jordanian forces therefore began to group themselves for an attack on Israel. But the Israelis struck first. In a brilliant campaign they destroyed the Egyptian air force and the army in Sinai and hurled back the Jordanians, winning in six days' fighting new frontiers on the Suez Canal, the Golan Heights, and the Jordan. For defence, these were far superior to the previous boundaries of Israel and the Jews announced that they would keep them.

Outright colonialism had less striking expressions north of the Sahara than in Black Africa; this was where the 'Scramble for Africa' had occurred, while, with the exception of Algeria and the Italian colonies, direct European rule had always been less obvious in the Islamic lands

of Atlantic and Mediterranean Africa. This helps to produce an impression of much more radical changes on the map of equatorial and sub-equatorial Africa after 1945. Yet though the legal status of most of Africa's surface was transformed in the 1950s and 1960s, this was for a long time surprisingly peaceful. Only in the Algerian War did the making of a new Africa of national, post-colonial states provoke much bloodshed, though there was plenty to come in the post-colonial era. With the exception of Portugal (which only gave in after a domestic revolution in 1973), the major colonial powers in Africa ceded their powers peacefully, concentrating their attention on trying to retain some sort of influence by showing ostentatiously benevolent interest in their former subjects.

The new Black Africa had its basic shape determined by decisions taken by European statesmen at the end of the nineteenth century, for the new African nations were usually defined by the boundaries of former colonies. These boundaries often brought together peoples of many languages, stocks and customs,

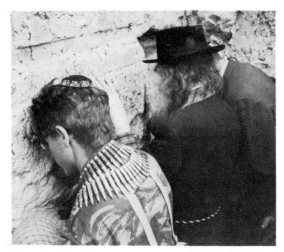

In 1967 Israel won full control of the hitherto partitioned city of Jerusalem. Thousands of Jews, this young soldier among them, flocked to pray at the Wailing Wall, until then outside the Jewish sector.

Kwame Nkrumah, pictured on a supporter's dress, was prime minister, then president of Ghana which became independent in 1957. Arrogating to himself the title of 'Redeemer', he centralized power in his own hands.

over which colonial administrations had hardly ever ruled long enough to provide anything more than a formal unity. Nor was there in Africa the offsetting and unifying influence of great indigenous civilizations to counteract the colonial division of the continent, as there had been in Asia. At independence the result was to be seen in a Balkanization of Africa. The doctrine of nationalism which appealed to westernized African élites confirmed the fragmentation on the continent, sometimes ignoring important realities which the theory and practice of colonialism had been able to contain or manipulate. One of the most important of them was the persistence of old social and ethnic divisions within the new states and one obvious response to the dangers of such centrifugal factors was the strident nationalism of the new rulers. West Africans combed the historical record – such as it was – of ancient Mali and Ghana, while east Africans brooded over the past which might be hidden in relics such as the ruins of Zimbabwe in order to forge national mythologies like those of earlier nation-makers in Europe.

Nor were internal divisions the only or worst problems facing the new Africa. In spite of the continent's great economic potential, the economic and social foundations for a prosperous future were shaky. The colonial régimes had left behind feebler cultural and economic infrastructures than in Asia. Rates of literacy were low and Africa's important economic resources, especially mineral, required for their exploitation skills, capital and marketing facilities which could only come from the world outside – and white South Africa counted as 'outside' to many Black politicians. This would long continue to be so. In these circumstances, it is not surprising that discontent and disillusion sometimes followed decolonialization.

In 1945 the only completely independent countries in Africa other than Egypt had been Ethiopia and Liberia, though the Union of South Africa was a self-governing Dominion of the British Commonwealth and is therefore excluded from this category only in a formal sense, while a slightly vaguer status cloaked also

1049

the virtual independence of the British Crown colony of Southern Rhodesia. By 1961, when South Africa was a fully independent Republic, twenty-three other new African states had come into existence and more were to follow. Ten years later, Portugal was the only former colonial power to retain her Black African possessions and by the end of 1975 they had gone, too; fittingly, the Iberians who may justly claim to have launched Europe on her adventure of overseas dominion were almost the last to abandon it.

As Africa shook off colonialism, the dangers facing the new states quickly became apparent in their politics. There were two especially bad outbreaks of strife. In the former Belgian Congo an attempt by the mineral-rich region of Katanga to break away provoked a civil war in which rival Russian and American influences quickly became entangled and the United Nations strove to restore peace. Then, at the end of the 1960s, came a distressing civil war in Nigeria, hitherto one of the most stable and promising of the new African states. This, too, drew non-Africans to dabble in the bloodbath. One reason for this was that Nigeria had joined the ranks of the oil producers. In other countries, there were less bloody but still fierce struggles between factions, regions and tribes which distracted the small westernized élites of politicians and quickly led them to abandon the democratic and liberal principles so many had talked in the heady days when a colonial system was in retreat.

In almost all the new nations, the need, real or imaginary, to prevent disintegration, suppress open dissent and strengthen central authority had led by the 1970s to one-party, authoritarian government or to the exercise of political authority by soldiers. It was not unlike the history of South America after the Wars of Liberation. Nor did an older independent Africa escape. Impatience with an *ancien régime* seemingly incapable of providing peaceful political and social change led in 1974 to revolution in Ethiopia and the setting aside of the 'Lion of Judah'; it was almost incidentally the end of the

oldest Christian monarchy in the world and of a line of kings supposed to run back to the son of Solomon and the Queen of Sheba in the most picturesque version of the story. A year later, the military régime which had taken power seemed just as discredited as it predecessors. From such changes there sometimes emerged tyrant-like political leaders who reminded Europeans of early dictators, but this comparison may be misleading. Africanists suggest that many of the 'strong men' of the new nations are more understandable as the inheritors of the mantle of precolonial African kingship, than in western terms. Some, too, are simply bandits.

Such troubles, and the violent nationalism they stimulated, did nothing to diminish the frequent irritation with which Africans reacted to the outside world. Some of the roots of this may lie very deep, in (for example) the mythological drama built on the old European slave trade as a supreme example of racial exploitation, or in the sense of political inferiority which lay near the surface in a continent of little states whose total population was less than that of some of the nations of Asia (Nigeria, with some fifty million inhabitants, contained about a quarter of the whole population of Africa in 1970). In political and military terms, a disunited Africa could not expect to have much weight in international affairs. Attempts were therefore made to overcome the weakness which arose from division and an abortive attempt in 1958 to found a United States of Africa opened an era of alliances, partial unions, and essays in federation which culminated in the emergence in 1963 of the Organization for African Unity. This came about in large measure thanks to the stimulus provided by the Ethiopian emperor, Haile Selassie, who was to lose power eleven years later.

In political terms, the Organization's success has been limited by the need to preserve agreement between régimes of widely differing outlooks facing widely differing problems. In economic affairs, though, it has been thought a success, bringing to a conclusion in 1975 a successful negotiation with Europe in defence of African producers. The very disappointment of much of the early political history of independent Africa directed the attention of thoughtful politicians towards the possibilities of an economic development which implied cooperation with one another, above all in relation to Europe whose former colonial powers remain Africa's most important market and most important source of capital, skill and counsel.

This has not necessarily meant overtly better relations with former colonial states. Independence has bred its own new resentments. Yet, with one exception, the completeness and rapidity of decolonialization in Africa and its geographical remoteness, to say nothing of the lack of real power of the new states, tended to focus such resentments less on the former imperial rulers than on the racial division of black and white in Africa itself. This was flagrant in the most powerful of African states, the Boer-dominated Union of South Africa.

Here resentments which went back as far as the Great Trek and had been intensified by defeat in the Boer War had led to the progressive destruction of ties with the British Commonwealth after the First World War. South Africa had, it is true, entered the second and supplied important forces to fight in it on the British side, but even then intransigent Boers (or 'Afrikaaners', as they increasingly called themselves) had supported a movement favouring cooperation with the Nazis (its leader became Prime Minister in 1948). As the Afrikaners steadily engrossed power to themselves inside the Union, and built up their economic position in the industrial and financial sectors, the prospect of imposing a policy towards the Black African which diverged from their deep prejudices was soon inconceivable. The eventual result was the construction of a system of separation of the races – *apartheid* – which systematically embodied and reinforced the reduction of the Black African to an inferior status justified by Boer ideology.

This system sometimes appealed – on even less excusable grounds than the primitive super-

stitions or supposed economic necessities of the Afrikaners – to white people elsewhere in Africa. The only country where a similar balance of black and white population and a similar concentration of wealth existed was Southern Rhodesia which, to the great embarrassment of the British government, seceded from the Commonwealth in 1965. The aim of the secessionists, it was feared, was to begin a slow evolution towards a society which seemed likely to become more and more like the Republic of South Africa. The British government dithered and missed its chance. There was then nothing that the African states could immediately do about Rhodesia, and not much that the United Nations could do either, though 'sanctions' were invoked in the form of an embargo on trade with the former colony whose enforcement was left to individual countries. Meanwhile, Great Britain's stock sank in the eyes of Africans who, understandably, did not see why a British government could not intervene militarily to suppress what was, formally speaking, a colonial rebellion as flagrant as that of 1776. Of course some British reflected that it was precisely that precedent which made the outlook for intervention by a remote and military weak imperial sovereign look so discouraging.

Though South Africa, the richest and strongest state in the area, seemed secure, she was, together with Rhodesia and the Portuguese colonies, the object of growing black African anger as the 1970s began. By then something like an Arab-Israeli confrontation was in the making south of the Zambesi. The drawing of the racial battle-lines was hardly offset by such minor concessions as South Africa made to her own blacks and the importance of her economic ties with some black states. There was a growing danger, too, that outside powers might soon be involved; after the Portuguese withdrawal, a Marxist régime which took power in Angola did so with the support of foreign communist soldiers and equipment.

The South African government soon showed it was having second thoughts, and sought to detach itself from the embarrassment of association with an unyielding Rhodesia (whose prospects had sharply worsened with the end of Portuguese rule in Mozambique and the beginning of a guerrilla war against her). The end came when the American government assessed the dangers of a Rhodesian collapse at the hands of black nationalists owing their success to communist support. American pressure was applied to the South Africans, who applied it to the Rhodesians. On 24 September 1976, the end came, when the Rhodesian prime minister told his countrymen – sadly, but not without dignity – that the last attempt to found a white-dominated country in Africa had failed and that Rhodesia would soon be ruled by a black majority.

Latin America

By the end of the nineteenth century, many Latin American states had settled down to stability and prosperity. Their upper classes were highly Europeanized; to the original colonial implantation of culture had been added the influence of nineteenth-century France to which the Latin American élites had been drawn in the post-colonial period. Although manufacturing industry was inconsiderable – almost all of these states were primary producers – they were relatively highly urbanized, but this did not seem to present them with the problems of nineteenth-century Europe. The only important revolution in a Latin American state before 1914 (as opposed to mere changes of personnel), the one which overthrew the Mexican dictator Porfirio Diaz in 1911, was essentially one in which the primary rôle was played by a middle class which felt excluded from the benefits of the régime, not by an industrial proletariat. Indeed, it was noticeable that Latin American countries did not appear to share the class conflict which had appeared in industrialized Europe although there had been large-scale European immigration in the nineteenth century.

These promising-looking societies survived

An allegorical mural of Mexican history by Diego Rivera is dominated by Juarez, the Indian president of the Mexican republic who overthrew the last attempt by a European power (France) to impose a monarch on an American state. In his hands he holds a copy of the constitution.

the First World War prosperously but not without important changes in their relations with other continents. Before 1914, though she was the predominant political influence in the lives of the Caribbean countries, the United States did not yet exercise her later weight in South America's affairs. In 1914 she supplied only seventeen per cent of all foreign investment south of the Rio Grande; Great Britain was overwhelmingly ahead of her. The liquidation of British holdings in the Great War changed this; by 1929 the United States was the largest investing power in South America, providing about forty per cent of the continent's capital from abroad. Then came the world economic crisis; 1929 was for the Latin American states the doorway to a new and unpleasant era, the beginning of their twentieth century. Many of them defaulted on their payments to foreign investors and it became almost impossible to borrow further capital abroad. The collapse of prosperity led to growing nationalist assertiveness, sometimes against other Latin American states, sometimes against the North Americans and Europeans; foreign oil companies were expropriated in both Mexico and Bolivia. The traditional Europeanized oligarchies were compromised by their failure to meet the problems posed by falling national incomes. From 1930 onwards there were military coups in every country except Mexico.

1939 began a period of improvement as commodity prices again rose because of demand caused by war (in 1950 the Korean war prolonged this trend). By and large, the American republics were sympathetic to the cause of the allies, who courted them; most joined the United Nations side before the war ended, and one, Brazil, sent a small expeditionary force to Europe, a striking symbol of a changed relationship. The more important effects of the war, though, were economic and they brought changes. One of great significance was that the dependence of Latin America on the United States and Europe for manufactured goods now became apparent in shortages; there was not enough to go round. In consequence, there gathered speed an intensive drive to industrialize. On the urban work forces which industrialization built up was founded a new kind of political power which entered the lists as a competitor with the military and the traditional élites in the post-war era. These were the authoritarian but popular mass movements which brought to power a new kind of strong man. Perón in Argentina in 1955 was the most famous, but Colombia in 1957 and Venezuela in 1959 threw up similar régimes. It was striking that communism had no such conspicuous success among the masses.

A significant change also came about (though not as a result of war) in another continuing feature of the continent's life, the exercise of the preponderant power of the United States. In the first twenty years of the century American armed forces had intervened directly no fewer than twenty times in the affairs of neighbouring republics. They even went so far as to establish protectorates over Haiti and the Dominican Republic. After 1920, there were only two such interventions before the Second World War, in Honduras in 1924 and Nicaragua two years later. Indirect pressure also declined. In large measure this was a sensible recognition of changed circumstances. There was nothing to be got by direct intervention in the 1930s and President Roosevelt made a virtue of this by proclaiming a 'Good Neighbour' policy which stressed non-intervention by all American states in one another's affairs. Yet after 1950, there was again to be a change of direction. While American policy was dominated by European concerns in the early phase of the Cold War, it began slowly to look southwards again after Korea. Washington had not been unduly alarmed by the earlier manifestations of Latin American nationalism – which always tended to find a scapegoat in American policy – but became increasingly concerned lest the hemisphere provide a lodgement for Russian influence. This led to covert operations, for example, to overthrow in 1954 a government in Guatemala which had communist support.

At the same time United States policy was anxious that the footholds provided for communism by poverty and discontent should be removed. It made available much more economic aid (Latin America had only a tiny fraction of what went to Europe and Asia in the 1950s but much more in the next decade) and interested itself in governments which proclaimed they sought social reform. Unfortunately, whenever the programmes of such governments moved towards the eradication of American control of capital, by nationalization, American policy tended to veer into opposition, demanding compensation on such a scale as to make reform very difficult. On the whole, therefore, while it might deplore the excesses of an individual régime, such as that in Cuba before 1958, the American government tended to find itself, as in Asia, supporting conservative interests opposed to social reform. This was not invariably so; some governments did act effectively and a notable example was a land reform

Legend:

- Communist territory
- Colonies
- Capital Aid (in Millions of US dollars) 1961—1964
- Central American Defence Council 1962
- ★ Revolutionary opposition movements
- ▲ Sites of Russian missiles spotted by US Air Reconnaisance

482 MEXICO
BELIZE
50
29
76 40
53 70
Panama Canal

Havana
CUBA
JAMAICA (1962)
DOMINICAN REPUBLIC (Puerto Rico)
HAITI
170

TOBAGO (1962)
TRINIDAD (1962)
Caracas
VENEZUELA
188
Georgetown
GUYANA
SURINAM
CAYENNE

COLOMBIA
Bogotá
368
Quito
ECUADOR
120

218
PERU
Lima

194
La Paz
BOLIVIA

B R A Z I L
960
Brasilia

37
PARAGUAY

Rio de Janeiro

560

38
URUGUAY
Santiago
CHILE
271
Buenos Aires
Montevideo

ARGENTINA

Cities with more than
■ 1,000,000
□ 500,000
• 100,000 inhabitants

Population of Latin America (In Millions)

132 — 1945
189 — 1955
233 — 1965
303 — 1975

Post-War Latin America

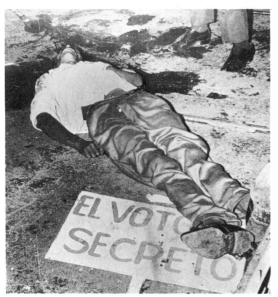

The body of a demonstrator shot by the Nicaraguan police in the 1950s while campaigning for a secret ballot in elections.

Amid enthusiastic applause, Fidel Castro ends his days as a guerilla in the hills and enters Havana in triumph.

in Bolivia in 1952. But it was generally true that the worst-off Latin Americans were the Indian peasants and these had virtually no hearing from any régime whether populist or conservative, in that both listened only to the towns.

Yet in spite of American nervousness the revolutionary potential for change in Latin America remained low. This was one of the lessons of the one successful revolution, that carried out with momentous consequences in Cuba. That country was in a number of respects a very exceptional case. One was geographical; its island position in the Caribbean, within a relatively short distance of the United States, gave it special strategic significance. The whole area of the approaches to the Canal Zone had even more importance in American thinking than Suez in the British; this had often been shown in earlier times. In the second place, Cuba had been especially badly hit in the depression; it was virtually dependent on one crop, sugar, and that crop had only one outlet, the United States. This economic tie, moreover, was only one of several which gave Cuba a closer 'special relationship' with the United States than any other Latin American state. There were historic connexions in the background to independence before 1898. Until 1934 the Cuban constitution had included special provisions restricting Cuba's diplomatic freedom and the Americans still had a naval base on the island. There was heavy American investment in urban property and utilities and Cuba's poverty and low prices made it an attractive holiday resort for Americans. All in all, there was no shortage of reasons for Cuba to produce, as it did, a nationalist movement which was strongly anti-American.

Inevitably, the United States was seen as the real power behind the conservative post-war Cuban régime. Under the dictator Batista who came to power in 1952 this in fact ceased to be so; the State Department disapproved of him and cut off help to him. By the time this happened, in 1957, a young nationalist doctor, Fidel Castro, had already begun a guerrilla campaign against the régime. In two years he was successful and incidentally something of a hero in the United States. In 1959 he became Prime Minister of a revolutionary Cuba, describing his régime as 'humanistic' and, specifically, not communist.

Castro's original views are still not known. Perhaps he was himself not clear what he thought. From the start he worked with a wide spectrum of people from liberals to Marxists who wanted to overthrow Batista. This helped to reassure the United States which patronized him as a Caribbean Sukarno; American public opinion idolized him as a romantic figure. This relationship quickly soured. Not surprisingly Castro turned to interference with American business interests, starting with agrarian reform which required the nationalization of sugar concerns. He also held up for public denunciation Americanized elements in Cuban society which had supported the old régime. Anti-Americanism was a logical means – perhaps the only one – open to Castro for uniting his people behind the revolution. Soon, the United States broke off diplomatic relations with Cuba and began to bring to bear other kinds of pressure. Before long, the American government was convinced that Cuba was likely to fall into the hands of the communists upon whom Castro increasingly relied. It did not help when Khruschev warned the United States of the danger of retaliation from Soviet rockets if it acted militarily against Cuba and declared the Monroe Doctrine dead; the State Department quickly announced that it was alive. Finally, after Castro had declared himself a Marxist, the American government decided to promote his overthrow by force.

The plans which were made for this were to be carried out by Cuban exiles. All was under way when the presidency changed hands in 1961 and John Kennedy thus inherited a policy which he had not initiated but which he was neither cautious nor thoughtful enough to impede. This was a grave failure because there was much else in the new president's attitude to Latin America, where it had been obvious for some time that the United States needed to cultivate goodwill, which promised well. As it was, the possibilities of a more positive approach were blown to pieces by the fiasco known as the Bay of Pigs operation, when an expedition of Cuban exiles supported by American money and arms came to a miserable end in April 1961. Cuban policy now turned in earnest towards Russia. At the end of the year Castro declared himself a Marxist–Leninist.

Thus the Cold War was, at last, truly extended to the western hemisphere, and it had started badly for the United States, which incurred disapproval everywhere for its attempt to overthrow a genuinely popular and solidly based régime. From this time, Cuba was a revolutionary magnet in Latin America. Meanwhile, Castro's government pressed forwards with policies which, together with American pressure, badly damaged the economy, but also showed that the régime was unequivocally egalitarian and bent to achieve real social reform, even if through an equality of poverty. It was almost as a by-product of the Cuban revolution that there took place the events which gave it a place in world history, providing the most serious confrontation of the whole Cold War and perhaps its turning-point.

It cannot yet be known how the decision came to be taken that the Russians should install in Cuba missiles capable of reaching anywhere in the United States and thus roughly double the number of bases or cities which were potential targets. Nor is it known where the initiative came from, though it seems likeliest that it was Russian. But whatever the circumstances, photographic reconnaissance confirmed in October 1962 that the Russians were building missile sites in Cuba. President Kennedy waited until this could be shown to be incontrovertible and then announced that the United States Navy would stop any ship delivering further missiles to Cuba and that those already in Cuba would have to be withdrawn. One Lebanese ship was boarded and searched in the days that followed; Russian ships were only observed. The American nuclear striking force was prepared for war. After a few days and some exchanges of personal letters between Kennedy and Khruschev, the latter agreed that the missiles should be removed.

This was a crisis which had by far transcended the history of the hemisphere. Its repercussions for the rest of the world are best discussed elsewhere, but it revealed that although the United States was prepared to promise to refrain from invading Cuba, that state was being used as a pawn by the Russians in their own game of international chess.

The United States continued to try to isolate Cuba as much as possible from the rest of the hemisphere, though this was ultimately a sterile hope. But though the appeal of Cuba's revolution seemed for a while to gain ground among the young in other countries, this did not make other Latin American governments more sympathetic towards Castro. This was increasingly true as he began to make claims that Cuba should be a revolutionary centre for the rest of Latin America. In the event, as an unsuccessful attempt in Bolivia showed, this was not likely to prove easy. Cuban circumstances had been very untypical. The hopes entertained of mounting a peasant movement – to start a Vietnam in South America as one revolutionary put it – proved illusory. The official communists, indeed, appear to have deplored this campaign. While there were plenty of materials about for revolution in some places they turned out to be urban rather than rural and it was urban guerrilla movements in Latin America which, within a few years, were taking the headlines. Though spectacular and dangerous, it is not clear that they enjoyed wide popular support. Yet anti-Americanism continued to run high. Kennedy's hopes for a new American initiative, based on social reform, an 'Alliance for Progress' as he termed it, made no headway against the animosity aroused by American treatment of Cuba. Kennedy's successor, President Johnson, did no better, perhaps because he was less interested in Latin American than in domestic reform and tended to leave hemisphere policy to fellow-Texans who were interested in it. The initiative was never recaptured after the initial flagging of

the Alliance. Worse still, it was overtaken in 1965 by fresh evidence of the old Adam of intervention. This occurred in the Dominican Republic, where, four years before, American help had been forthcoming to assist the overthrow and assassination of a corrupt and tyrannical dictator and his replacement by a reforming democratic régime. When this was pushed aside by soldiers acting in defence of the privileged who felt threatened by reform, the Americans cut off aid; it looked as if, after all, the Alliance for Progress might be used discriminatingly. But aid was restored – as it was to other right-wing régimes – when Johnson came to power. A revolution against this military régime in 1965 resulted in the arrival of 20 000 American troops who put down the rebellion.

By the end of the decade the Alliance had virtually been forgotten, in part because of the persistent fears of communism which led American policy to put its weight behind Latin American conservatives, in part because the United States had lost interest in Latin America, having plenty of problems elsewhere. One result was a new wave of attacks on American property by governments which did not have to fear the loss of American support while the communist threat seemed to endure. Chile nationalized the largest American copper company, the Bolivians took over oil concerns and the Peruvians plantations owned by Americans. In 1969 there was a historic meeting of Latin American governments at which no United States representative was present and much *Yanqui* behaviour explicitly and implicitly condemned. A tour undertaken by a representative of the president of the United States that year led to protests, riots, the blowing up of American property and requests that he should not visit some countries. It was quite like the end of the previous decade when Eisenhower's vice-president had been mobbed and spat upon by crowds during a goodwill tour. All in all, it looked as if at the end of the 1960s the nationalism of Latin America was entering a new and vigorous period. If Cuba-inspired guerrillas had ever presented a danger, they appeared

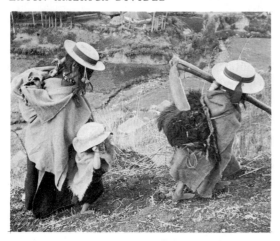

The peasants of the Andean regions pose grave problems of poverty, illiteracy and malnutrition; in the late 1960s, the villages to which such peasants as these Ecuadorians belong became the target of special efforts for development launched by international agencies.

to do so no longer, and with the spur of an internal fear removed there was little reason for the governments of the Latin American countries not to try to capitalize on anti-American feeling since, in a period when American policy was obviously regretting earlier positive initiatives, they need fear no reprisals.

What could not be seen was that the real problems of Latin America were yet being met. For all the achievements of an industrialization which had gone very far, very rapidly, the continent was threatened by an appallingly fast growth of population. In 1961 it was expected to double in twenty-five years. This was a faster rate of growth than anywhere else in the world and it began to be obvious just as the difficulties of the Latin American economies were again beginning to display their intractability. The aid programme of the Alliance for Progress patently failed to cope with them and failure spawned quarrels over the use of American funds. Moreover, the divisions of society still remained. There were great discrepancies of wealth and education even in the most advanced Latin American countries. Their strength was

clearly shown when Chile, a country with a more continuous history of constitutional democracy than other Latin American states, acquiesced in a military coup which overthrew in 1973 a government many believed to be under the control of communists. The counter-revolutionary movement was tainted by evidence of United States approval and possibly support, but many Chileans were willing to accept it because they had been frightened by the revolutionary tendencies of the elected régime. What followed, the installation of a very authoritarian régime which seemed unable to extract the country from economic disaster, seemed to many observers to have destroyed even this limited consensus by 1976.

Altogether, Latin America remains an explosive, disturbed continent full of nations increasingly unlike one another, for all their shared roots. Even culture is still a divisive force. To the layers laid down by Indian, slave, colonial and post-colonial experiences, all of which were reflected strongly in differences of economic level, have now been added the differences brought by the arrival in the 1950s of the American high technology culture of consumption, available to the better-off but not to the poor who observe them. Just as in Asia, though perhaps less markedly, the strains of the impact of modern civilization on a historically deep-rooted society are now more obvious than ever before, even though Latin America has been undergoing some of them since the sixteenth century.

The end of bipolarity?

When the series of Congresses which followed the treaty of Vienna at last came to an end the British foreign secretary, Canning, is said to have been delighted. Things were getting back to normal in diplomacy, he thought, a state which he summed up as 'each for himself and God for us all'. Many people might have echoed him and perhaps his sentiments as they contemplated the unrolling of international events in the 1960s. What was happening, essentially, was that the rigid simplicities of the Cold War era were beginning to crumble. This happened in many ways, but the result was always to diminish the freedom of action of the two giants who had dominated the world since 1945. A world system of two more or less disciplined blocs in a sea of small fry trying to escape being swallowed by them, was replaced by one in which the blocs showed signs of strain and even disintegration, new quarrels between new states cut across the old ideological divisions, and new competitors for the rôle of superpower began to emerge. The two old superpowers did not suffer equally. In the middle of the 1970s it was evident that the United States had lost its former preponderance over Russia and that it was at least uncertain that another Cuban crisis would result in Russian withdrawal. But it also seemed to some observers less likely that another Cuban crisis would occur. There were still only two superpowers and some discerned a tendency for them to cooperate more and for their behaviour to grow more alike. By the middle of the 1970s the vague word *détente* was the fashionable diplomatic cant term for what had happened.

There is nothing magical about the beginning of a decade and to speak of so great a change as a process of the 1960s only means it came to a head then. But many of the factors behind it were at work before 1960, though they began to register their effect in a new fluidity of international relations only after 1962.

The death of Stalin had produced no obvious immediate change in Russian policy, but even more difficulty in interpreting it. The changes of personnel in Russian government which followed resulted after nearly two years in the emergence in directing rôles of Bulganin and Khruschev. The first was later to drop into the background and this still did not at once produce noticeable changes in policy. But in both 1955 and 1956 the Russian government announced it was reducing its armed forces because international tensions had lessened. In the latter year, too, Molotov, Stalin's old henchman and veteran of Cold War diplomacy,

The Berlin Wall. Its building seemed to symbolize, as did almost no other single act of the Cold War, an unbridgeable division across Europe and the World. Yet it may have made things easier by increasing the security of the most vulnerable of the satellite régimes of Communist Europe, the German Democratic Republic.

resigned his post as foreign minister. Above all, there arrived in the West news of a sensational speech made by Khruschev at a secret session of the twentieth congress of the Soviet communist party in which he denounced the misdeeds of the Stalin era and declared 'coexistence' the goal of Russian foreign policy.

All in all, 1956 seemed promising. Suddenly, the atmosphere was fouled by the Suez invasion and a revolution in Hungary. The first at once led to Russian threats to Great Britain and France; the Russians were not going to jeopardize Arab goodwill by failing to support Egypt openly. The second event operated in a somewhat more complicated way.

Ever since 1948, Russian policy had been almost morbidly sensitive to signs of deviation or dissatisfaction among its satellites. In that year Russia recalled its advisers from Yugoslavia, whose communist ruler, Marshal Tito, had been showing too much independence. Yugoslavia was expelled from the Cominform,

Post-war Europe

her treaties with Russia and other communist states were denounced by them and there followed five years of vitriolic attacks on 'Titoism' by orthodox communists. In the end, the Russians climbed down and asked to reopen diplomatic relations. In 1955 Khruschev went to Belgrade to apologize for what had happened; a return visit to Moscow by Tito soon followed.

Yugoslavia's survival had been damaging and embarrassing for Russia and made Russian policy sensitive to weakness in the eastern camp. There had been trouble and anti-Soviet riots, too, in East Berlin in 1953 and Poland in the summer of 1956. Nationalism, obviously, was still stronger than communism. It was against this background that riots in Budapest in October grew into a nation-wide movement which led to the withdrawal of Russian forces from Budapest and a promise from a new government of free elections and the end of one-party rule. Unfortunately, it soon went further, denouncing the Warsaw Pact and asking the United Nations to take up the Hungarian

question. At this, the Russian army returned (with those of other Warsaw Pact countries) and crushed the Hungarian revolution. The United Nations General Assembly recorded – twice – its condemnation of Russia's action.

This episode hardened attitudes considerably on both sides. The Russians were once more made aware of how little they had reconciled the peoples of eastern Europe and therefore became even more distrustful of western talk of 'liberating' them. Western Europe, on the other hand, was once again reminded of the real face of Russian power, and sought to consolidate itself further.

Attention was thus drawn back to Europe where the Russians, much impressed with the potential danger of a rearmed West Germany, sought to strengthen their own satellite, the German Democratic Republic, to which the continued existence of West Berlin inside its territory was a grave weakness. The city's frontiers were open and easily crossed and its prosperity and freedom drew more and more

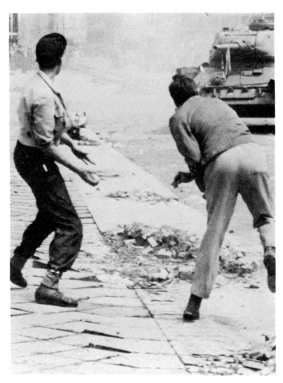

In 1953, East Berliners took to the streets armed with little but cobble-stones against the Russian tanks upholding their government, when it was announced that work norms were to be raised by ten per cent.

In the briefly successful Hungarian revolution of 1956 the frustration and bitterness of years exploded, often with brutal results for members of the régime's former security police, many of whom were lynched.

East Germans – especially skilled workers – to defect to the West. This led the Russians to denounce the arrangements under which Berlin had been run since 1948; they said they would hand over their sector to the East Germans if better ones could not be found. This was in 1958 and there opened some two years of long-drawn-out diplomacy which by 1961 seemed only to have brought Russia and the United States into a new confrontation. In August of that year the East Germans suddenly erected a wall to cut off the Russian sector of Berlin from the western. They felt driven to do this by a huge increase in the outflow of refugees which had occurred as the atmosphere of crisis over Berlin deepened. 140000 crossed in 1959, 200000 in 1960 and more than 100000 in the first six months of 1961. The wall raised the temperature in the short run, but in the long run probably helped to lower it. It met the essential concern of the East German state to stop emigration and Khruschev was not disposed to maintain his more extreme demands when it was clear that the United States was not prepared to yield a change in the legal status of Berlin even at the risk of war.

Substantially, this rhythm was repeated the following year in the Caribbean, although the risk was then far greater. The allies of the United States were not directly involved in the Cuba crisis as they had been over a possible change in the German settlement, nor did the Russians give any sign of paying any attention to Cuba's interests. It was much more of a 'pure' confrontation of superpowers and the Russians were unambiguously forced to give way. While studiously avoiding action or language which might have been provocatively dangerous because wounding, and while leaving a simple route of retreat open to the Russians by confining his demands to the essential, President Kennedy none the less made no concessions and struck no bargains (such as, for example, would have been implied in acceptance of the Russian demand for a balancing withdrawal of American bombers from Turkey).

The importance to modern military intelligence of photographic and television observation from aircraft and satellites was dramatically illustrated when the United States government produced its photographs (of which this is one) of missile sites under construction in Cuba in 1962.

It is difficult, even in ignorance of Russian thinking, not to believe that this was a major turning-point. The prospect of nuclear war as the ultimate price of Cold War had been faced and found unacceptable. The Russians' withdrawal thereby registered a new era. It was symbolized in one way by the inauguration of direct telephone communication between the heads of the two states – the 'hot line'. This was a recognition that the danger of conflict through misunderstanding made necessary some more intimate connexion than that provided by the channels of ordinary diplomacy. It was also clear that in spite of Russian boasting to the contrary, American preponderance in weapons still remained as great as ever. The new weapon which mattered for purposes of direct conflict between the two superpowers was the inter-continental rocket missile; at the end of 1962 the Americans had a superiority in this weapon of more than six to one over the Russians. In the next few years the Russians set to work to reduce this disparity but for the moment it probably helped to achieve the conclusion of the first agreement between Great Britain, the United States and Russia on the restriction of nuclear weapons' testing in space, the atmos-

phere or underwater. Disarmament had been pursued without success for many years; this was the first positive achievement of any negotiations about nuclear weapons.

Cuba was a humiliation for the Russian leadership. We do not know how much it contributed to the change, but in 1964, Khruschev was removed from office. It was clear that the Soviet Union had not yet mastered the techniques of orderly political change, for he was set aside by colleagues whom he had offended and alarmed, with the connivance of the army. But he was not killed, sent to prison or appointed to run a power-station in Mongolia. The contrast with earlier transfers of power was striking and the nature of the régime such that people accounted this progress.

Undoubtedly Russian society had undergone some relaxation after Stalin's death. The speech at the Twentieth Congress was itself bound to have effects; it could not be unsaid, even if much of it was aimed at diverting criticism from those who (like Khruschev himself) had been participants in the crimes of which Stalin was accused. Symbolically, the body of Stalin was removed from Lenin's tomb, the national shrine. In the next few years there was what was sometimes called a 'thaw' in that marginally greater freedom of expression was allowed to writers and artists, while the régime appeared briefly to be a little more concerned about its appearance in the eyes of the world over such matters as its treatment of Jews. The evidence for this is fragmentary and hard to interpret; overall, the authoritarian nature of Russian government seems unchanged in principle – which is what might be expected. The immediate motives of Russian rulers remain as obscure as ever and have to be inferred from their behaviour.

It seems that after Stalin's death and particularly during the era of Khruschev's ascendancy, the party re-emerged as a much more independent factor in Russian life. The dominance exercised by the police was reduced and the party undertook much more real scrutiny of policy and administration. It also seems likely that Khruschev's own contribution to Russian development was to provide a great shaking up of Russian policy on every front. He had a huge failure over agriculture, a great impact in changing the emphasis of the Russian armed services towards the strategic rocket services which became their élite arm, and undertook many initiatives in foreign policy besides his disastrous one over Cuba. Meanwhile, there were also proceeding long-term changes in Russian society which had their roots in the Stalinist era.

In an exaggerated and extravagant way, the argument has been put forward that these developments have led to the United States and Soviet Russia growing more and more alike, and that this has played an important part in making Russian leaders less intransigent. This gives a distorted emphasis to the undoubted truth that they have become the two leading industrial powers of the world. But that general statement must be glossed in terms of differences between them which go beyond politics and ideology. Russian industrial growth, though very great, is overwhelmingly still a matter of heavy manufacture. The private consumer is still much less well supplied with manufactured goods in Russia than the United States, even though since 1953 there has been a very large relative change of emphasis as the government has sought to improve both quantities and qualities of goods available. Another important difference is that Russia has had nothing like the success of the United States in developing its agriculture; paradoxically, it has found itself buying American grain.

Yet Russia is regarded – rightly – by many undeveloped countries as a developed one and a rich one. This is an important qualification of the obvious disparity between the United States and Russia as consumer societies; to the poor they both look alike. Two more should perhaps be made. One is that the comparison present in the minds of Russians is not with the modern United States but with an infinitely more impoverished past which is not very remote. The second is that there are sectors in

A Moscow school, 1954. Soviet education has huge successes to its credit in the virtually complete eradication of illiteracy and the provision of technical and scientific manpower on an unprecedented scale. This success has for the most part been achieved by methods considered outmoded by educational theorists in countries where less agreement about the purpose of schooling exists.

which the comparison of the two industrial systems is by no means as unfavourable as in that of manufactured consumer goods. Russian investment in education, for example, has been so considerable and successful that it has actually achieved a literacy rate very slightly higher than the American one. Health services, too, while not commanding investment on the scale of American, nevertheless provide a very large majority of Soviet citizens with provision better than that available to many poor Americans.

But such comparisons, which fall easily over the line from quantitative to qualitative judgement, do not alter the basic fact that the *per capita* national income of the Russian still remains substantially behind that of the American. There has been a long legacy of backwardness and disruption to eliminate; it was not until 1952 that real wages in Russia even got back to the 1928 level. What has been possible, none the less, has been the creation of a scientific and industrial base which matches that of the United States at its best.

The obvious example of this, and one of the great sources of patriotic pride to the Soviet citizen, is the exploration of space. There is now so much ironmongery in orbit that it is difficult to recapture the impression made in 1957 when the first satellites were launched by the Russians. Although American successes speedily followed, some of them, indeed spectacular, the Russians' space achievements remained of the first rank. It was militarily significant that Russia relied on rockets of very large size; there were implications here for their offensive power. But there was also something in space exploration to feed the Russian imagination and reward Russian patience with other aspects of daily life. It is not too much to say that for some Russians, Russian space technology justified the revolution; Russia was shown by it to be able to do anything another nation could do, and much that only one other could do. Russia was modernized at last.

Whether this meant that she was in some sense becoming a satisfied nation, less prone to disturb the international scene, with leaders more confident and less suspicious of the outside world is an entirely different matter. About it only speculation is possible. Certainly Russian responses to the rise of China are not encouraging. Any speculations moreover would have at least to take into account the appearance in the Soviet Union of signs of strain such as those shown by other societies. Dissent and criticism, particularly of restraints upon intellectual freedom, became much more obvious at the end of the 1960s. So did symptoms of anti-social behaviour, such as hooliganism, corruption and alcoholism. But these probably held as little potential for significant change as in other countries. Less spectacular facts may turn out to be more important in the long run; it may be that later perspectives will reveal that one of the most important watersheds of Russian history was passed in the 1970s, when Russians for the first time became a minority in the Soviet Union.

For obvious reasons, changes in the United States since 1945 have been more easily ob-served than those in the Soviet Union, but this has not always made it easier to discern what is fundamental. Some are obvious. Of the growth of American power there can be no doubt, nor of its importance to the world. In 1968 the American population passed the 200 million mark, only one in twenty of whom were not native-born; the United States had ceased to be a nation of immigrants. This growth followed an unexpected increase in births at a time when death rates continued to drop; the United States was unique among developed countries in accelerating growth in this way. More of these Americans than ever lived in cities or the suburbs of cities.

In the middle of the 1950s the United States contained about 6 per cent of the world's population – a figure which has remained roughly the same – and produced more than half the world's manufactured goods. Her immensely successful industrial structure was increasingly dominated by very large corporations, many of them possessing resources and wealth greater than those of some small states. Attention was more and more drawn to the difficulties of securing attention to the public interest and the consumer's needs in such a structure. But no doubts could be expressed about its ability to create wealth and power. As in Russia, the most dramatic evidence of it was space exploration, whose climax came when a man-carrying vehicle landed on the surface of the moon on 21 July 1969 and was seen to do so by millions of people watching their television sets. Though it was to be shown that the immense power which had brought this about could not do everything that might be asked of it, nevertheless it was the great constant of the post-war world. It sustained the huge military establishment upon which the conduct of American foreign policy rested, notably in its provision of a great armoury of nuclear weapons.

Not surprisingly, American economic success deeply affected American politics, not least by the generation of mythologies. President Truman's second administration and those of

President Eisenhower were marked by noisy symbolic struggles and debate about the danger of interference with free enterprise and the threat of socialism. In so far as this crystallized in legislative proposals, attempts were made under Truman by his opponents to demolish the agencies and legislation of the New Deal and under Eisenhower to rid the federal government of some of its powers in economic matters. Yet there was a lot of shadow-boxing about all this. In the first place, government has since 1945 continued to hold and indeed increase its importance as the first of the customers of the American economy. Government spending has been the primary stimulant of the economy and hopes of balanced budgets and economical, business-like administration such as bemused the Republicans of the 1950s always ran aground upon this fact. A second fact was that the United States was a democracy; whatever the doctrinaire objections to it, and however much rhetoric might be devoted to attacking it, the Welfare State had come to stay because electorates wanted it. These facts made the old ideal of free enterprise unchecked and uninvaded by the influence of government more unrealistic than ever. They also helped to prolong the Democratic coalition. Republican presidents were elected in 1952 and 1968, but on each occasion they benefited from war-weariness and neither was able to persuade Americans that they should also elect Republican congresses. On the other hand, signs of strain were already apparent in the Democratic bloc before 1960 – Eisenhower appealed to some southern voters – and by 1970 something a little more like a national conservative party had appeared under the Republican banner because southerners had been offended by Democratic legislation on behalf of the Negro.

What was open to different administrations was the possibility of changing emphasis. The Eisenhower years leave an impression that little happened in the domestic history of the United States during them; it was not part of that president's vision of his office that he should provide a strong policy lead at home. By itself Kennedy's election by a narrow margin of the popular vote in 1960 – the arrival of a new man (and a young one, too) – helped to produce a sense of striking change. Too much was made at the time of the more superficial aspects of this, but in retrospect it can be seen that both in foreign and domestic affairs, the eight years of renewed Democratic rule from 1961 brought great change to the United States. Unhappily, this did not happen in the way in which Kennedy or his vice-president, Lyndon Johnson, can have hoped when they took office.

One issue which had already begun to emerge was the Negro question. A century after emancipation, the American Negro was poorer, more likely to be on relief, less well housed, more often unemployed and less healthy than the white American. This suddenly began to appear so intolerable that it became a great political question. This was due to three facts. One was the transformation of a local southern question into a national problem by Negro migration. Between 1940 and 1960 the Negro population of northern states almost trebled. New York became the state with the biggest black population of the Union. This brought the Negro into view in a new sense; it also revealed that the problem facing him was not only one of legal rights, but a complex one involving economic and cultural deprivation, too. The second factor pushing the question forward onto the national stage was the growing importance of the goodwill of other nations, many of which were themselves formed of coloured peoples. It was an embarrassment – of which communist propaganda had always made good use – for the United States to have at home so flagrant a contravention of the ideals she espoused abroad as was provided by the restraints under which the Negro laboured. Finally, the question was changed by the Negroes themselves; their own action under their own leaders, and above all that part of it which was inspired by Gandhian principles of passive resistance to oppression, did much to alter white attitudes. In the end, the position of the black American had been radically altered, though not to the extent that some had hoped. It was also obvious that bitter-

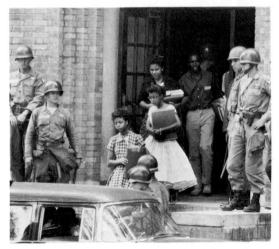

Central High School, Little Rock, Arkansas, September 1957. When a federal court ordered the school authorities to accept the enrolment of nine Negro children at this hitherto all-white school and the state authorities claimed to be unable to control the local mob's reactions, President Eisenhower ordered the army to secure enforcement of the law of the land. Under the protection of the federal power, the original Supreme Court decision of 1954 on desegregation was thus given substance and a turning-point was reached for the public school system in the South.

ness and resentment had not been eliminated but had in some places actually increased.

The first and most successful phase of the campaign for equal status for the Negro was a struggle to ensure him Civil Rights, of which the most important was the unhindered exercise of the franchise (always formally available but actually not in some southern communities) and new rights to equality of treatment in other ways which began to be granted to him by decisions of the Supreme Court in 1954 and 1955. The process began, that is to say, not with legislation but with judicial interpretation. These important first decisions provided that the segregation of different races within the public-school system was unconstitutional and should be brought to an end where it existed within a reasonable time. This was to challenge the social system in many southern states. It

was to take until 1963 to arrive at a point at which Negroes were attending public schools together with white children in every state of the Union.

Before this, the first legislation on Civil Rights had set up a Civil Rights Commission to oversee this subject. But legislative action to help the Negro was not really important until after 1961. Kennedy then initiated a programme of important measures which were brought to maturity by his successor and went beyond the securing of voting rights to attack segregation and deprivation of many kinds. This was after the inauguration of a successful campaign of 'sit-ins' by Negro leaders which itself achieved many important local victories. Yet when all this had been done, there still remained a hard core of poverty and resentment arising from it which legislation seemed powerless to touch.

This provoked ugly manifestations in riot and arson in what came to be called 'ghetto' areas of great American cities. More was involved than just the Negro's position. Poverty, poor housing, bad schools in run-down urban areas were symptoms of deep dislocations inside American society. Its inequalities had been made more irksome by the increasing affluence in which they were set. The Kennedy administration had been aware of these problems and its appeal to Americans to see the removal of these evils as one of the calls of the 'New Frontier' was followed by the even greater emphasis given to legislation to remove them by Lyndon Johnson, potentially one of America's great reforming presidents.

Unhappily, he was to prove a tragically unsuccessful president in spite of great achievements and all his experience and skill. His own southern and poor background made him a convinced and convincing exponent of the 'Great Society' in which he discerned America's future. But his great constructive and reforming work was soon forgotten when his presidency came to be overshadowed by an Asian war which became terrifying enough before it ended to be called America's Sicilian Expedition.

Under President Eisenhower American policy

The Korean War
June–November 1950

CHINA

Nanam
Hyesanjin
Yalu
Hungnam
Wonsan
NORTH
Pyongyang
KOREA
Seoul
Inchon
SOUTH
KOREA
Kunsan
Taegu
Pusan
Area held by U.N.
throughout the war

Area reconquered
Held by U.N. late October
to early November
U.N. front line early October
U.N. front line late November
North Korean attack
U.N. counter attack
Area conquered by North Korea

The Korean War
November 1950
November 1951

CHINA

Nanam
Hyesanjin
Yalu
Hungnam
NORTH
Pyongyang KOREA Wonsan
Seoul
Inchon
SOUTH
KOREA Yongdok
Kunsan Taegu
Pusan

Chinese gains
U.N. counter attack
Chinese advance
Final Armistice line
Furthest Chinese advance

had come to rest on the dogma that Indo-China was essential to security in South-East Asia. The elections stipulated in 1954 as the prelude to reuniting the country had never been held and the United States had therefore become the backer of the conservative government of South Vietnam. The view had come to be held that this country had to be kept in the western camp if all the other states of the area – perhaps as far away as India and Australia – were not to be subverted. Though disposed to be optimistic when he took office, President Kennedy had not questioned this view and began the process of backing up American military aid with 'advisers'. At the time of his murder in November 1963 there were 23000 of them in South Vietnam. His successor, President Johnson, also took the same view on the importance of Vietnam and felt that pledges to other countries had to be shown to be sound currency by what the United States did in Vietnam. But the governments which succeeded one another in South

Vietnam were obviously inadequate and when at the beginning of 1965 Johnson was advised that they might collapse without additional American help, he chose to provide it. Soon afterward, air attacks were made on targets in North Vietnam and the first American combat units arrived. From this moment the American participation soared out of control. In 1968 there were over 500000 American personnel in Vietnam and by Christmas that year a heavier tonnage of bombs had been released on North Vietnam than fell on Germany and Japan together in the entire Second World War.

This was disastrous. It was almost the least of Johnson's worries that the American balance of payments was damaged by the huge costs which were eventually to be borne. The expense also took money from the badly-needed reform projects at home. Worse was the bitter distaste for the policy which arose at home as the weight of effort and the casualties mounted and attempts to negotiate seemed to get nowhere. It

1067

THE VIETNAM WAR

French Indo-China in 1939

CHINA
BURMA
Hanoi
Haiphong
GULF OF TONKIN
Vinh
LAOS
THAILAND
Mekong
Dividing line of North and South 1954
Khe Sanh
Hué
Phubal
Danang
Tamky
Chulai
Quangugai
Bangkok
Vietcong supply route
Pleiku
Ankhe
Quinhon
CAMBODIA
Nhatrang
Pnompenh
Datat
Camranh Bay
Phanrang
Saigon
Bienhoa
Tan Son Nhut
Cantho
Vungtan
Soctran
Caman

South Vietnam (overrun by communist forces 1975)
North Vietnam
Areas of Vietcong activity
Principle U.S. bases by 1968

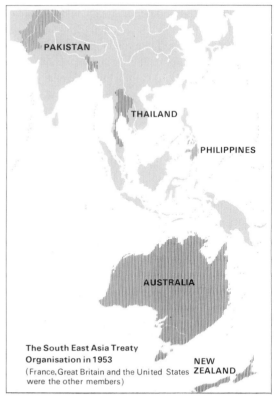

PAKISTAN
THAILAND
PHILIPPINES
AUSTRALIA
NEW ZEALAND

The South East Asia Treaty Organisation in 1953
(France, Great Britain and the United States were the other members)

was small consolation that Russia's costs as she supplied arms to North Vietnam were also heavy.

For all the immediate bitterness which Vietnam caused in the United States, it can now be seen that more was involved than the agitation of young people rioting in protest and distrust of their government or the anger of conservatives who found their ideals outraged by ritual desecrations of the symbols of patriotism and refusals to carry out military service. Vietnam revealed at last a great transformation in the American way of looking at the outside world. It was in South-East Asia that the powerlessness of the United States to obtain any results she wanted at any reasonable cost was at last borne in on many of her citizens. The late 1960s were a sunset era, though the sunset was not of American power but of what has been called the illusion of American omnipotence. Americans had approached the post-war world with this illusion intact. It was quite

plausible to say that it was American power which had decided two world wars. Before them there stretched back a century and a half of virtually unchecked and unhindered continental expansion, of immunity from European intervention, of the growth of a hegemony in the hemisphere which was all but limitless. It had been easy and natural for this to breed a careless assumption of limitless possibility which was carried over all too easily from domestic to foreign concerns. It was understandable that Americans should forget the special conditions of continental isolation and the supremacy of British sea-power on which their long success had been founded. The reckoning began to be drawn up in the 1950s, when many Americans had to be content with a lesser victory in Korea than they had hoped for and there began twenty years of frustrating negotiations with nations enjoying not a tenth of the power of the United States but apparently able to thwart her. Then came the Vietnam disaster in which both the full cost of power and its limits were at last revealed.

It soon affected American politics. When in March 1968 the strength of domestic opposition was shown clearly in the primary elections, Johnson had already drawn the conclusion that the United States could not win, had restricted bombing and asked the North to open negotiations again. Dramatically, he also announced that he would not stand for re-election in 1968. Just as the casualties of the Korean War won Eisenhower election in 1952, so the casualties of Vietnam, on the battlefield and at home, helped to elect another Republican president in 1968, only four years after a huge Democratic majority for Johnson. Vietnam was not the only factor, but it was one of the most important in dislocating the old Democratic coalition.

The new president began to withdraw American ground forces from Vietnam soon after his inauguration. This was one element in a peace-making which took three years. In 1970 secret negotiations began between North Vietnam and the United States, accompanied by further withdrawals of ground forces but also by renewed and intensified bombing of the north by the Americans. The negotiations were tortuous and difficult. The United States could not admit it was abandoning its ally, though it had to do so in fact, nor would the North Vietnamese accept terms which would not give them through their sympathizers in the south some power to harass the southern régime. In the end, amid considerable public outcry in the United States, bombing was briefly resumed at the end of 1972 but for the last time. Soon afterwards, on 27 January 1973, a cease-fire was signed in Paris. The war had cost the United States vast sums in money and 56000 dead. But this was not the largest item in the account. The war had also done grave damage to American prestige and diplomatic freedom, had ravaged the country's domestic politics and frustrated reform at home. What had been achieved was the brief preservation of a shaky South Vietnam, still saddled with internal problems which made its survival uncertain, and the infliction of

Main Street USA, 1968. The meeting of the Democratic Convention in Chicago that year occasioned such violent clashes between opponents of the Vietnam war and the police that the National Guard were called out to patrol the streets and maintain order.

terrible destruction on the peoples and economies of North and South Vietnam alike. Perhaps the abandonment of the illusion of American omnipotence offsets these costs.

What is undoubtedly true is that it was at least a success in domestic politics to disentangle the United States from this morass and the still-mysterious man who succeeded Johnson, President Nixon, reaped the benefit of this. The liquidation of the venture had followed other changes which showed more and more how much the world had already changed since Cuba. The most striking of these was a new American policy of establishing normal and direct relations with China which came to a climax with a visit of the president to China in February 1972 which was not only an attempt to start to bridge what he described as '16000 miles and twenty-two years of hostility' (he might have added 'and 2500 years of history'), but the first visit ever paid by any American president to Asia. Diplomatic relations with the United States at the highest level were paralleled by another great gain for China, her entry to the

United Nations Organization and assumption in it of a seat on the Security Council.

When the American president visited Moscow in May 1972, and this was followed by an agreement on arms limitation, it was obvious that an important change had come about in post-war diplomacy. The polarized simplicities of the Cold War were clearly gone, however doubtful might be what came next. The Vietnam settlement followed and can hardly have been unrelated to it; Moscow had to be squared as well as Peking, if there was to be a cease-fire. China's attitude to the Vietnamese struggle was, we may guess, by no means simple; it was complicated by the nationalism of the Viet Cong, by the potential danger from Russian policy and by interest in the United States' use of its power elsewhere in Asia, notably in Taiwan and Japan.

Meanwhile, though they might have had the support of China, it was by no means clear that the Indo-Chinese communists (who had great successes to their credit by the end of 1974) would be her satellites at the end of the day. Vietnamese nationalism had a history of struggle against Chinese as well as French imperialism behind it. In the immediate aftermath of the American withdrawal, too, the nature of the struggle going on was more and more clearly revealed as a civil war in both Vietnam and Cambodia.

In the first, the North Vietnamese had not waited long before resuming operations. For a time the United States government had to pretend not to see this; there was too much relief at home over the liquidation of the Asian commitment for scruples over the actual observation of the peace terms which had made withdrawal possible. Then came a huge political scandal which forced the American president's resignation and left his successor facing a Congress much more suspicious of the administration and determined to thwart what it saw as dangerous foreign adventures than any since the 1930s. It was against this background that American Asian policy had now to be made and this meant that there was going to be no

attempt to maintain the peace terms of 1972 in so far as these guaranteed the South Vietnamese régime against overthrow. By the spring of 1975 all American aid had come to an end and a government in Saigon which had lost virtually all the remainder of its territory to the North was reduced to a backs-to-the-wall attempt to hold the capital city and lower Mekong itself with a demoralized and defeated army. At the same time, communist forces were destroying a régime formerly supported by the United States in Cambodia; here, too, Congress prevented the sending of further military and financial help. A pattern in American diplomacy which had first been shown in China in 1947 was now being repeated; the United States had eventually to cut its losses at the expense of others who could not survive without its help. Such an outcome was doubly ironical. In the first place it seemed to demonstrate the truth of what the hardliners on Asian policy had said all along – that only the knowledge that the United States was in the last resort prepared to fight for them would guarantee the post-colonial régimes' survival against communism. Secondly, the swing back to isolationism in the United States was accentuated, not muffled, by defeat and disaster as those who reflected on the American dead and missing and the huge cost of Indo-China now saw the whole sacrifice as only a pointless and unjustifiable waste on behalf of peoples who would not fight to defend themselves.

Communism was not the only source of revolutionary change in Asia; Japan's recovery of world status was the most dramatic but not the only demonstration of the continuing revolutionary potential of capitalism. The rapidity of change it brought about had obvious implications for that old country's place both in the Asian and the world balance of power. By 1970 the Japanese had the second highest GNP in the non-communist world. They had renewed their country's heavy industrial base and had moved with great success into new areas of manufacture such as electronics and motor-cars, of which Japan made more than any country

The Japanese economic miracle has been most visible in a flood of high-quality consumer goods which pour out of her factories; this plant, at Osaka, is the largest electronics assembly works in Japan.

except the United States. This even caused resentment among American manufacturers, the supreme compliment. The debit side of this account was provided by a fast-growing population which held in check *per capita* national income and by the ample evidence of the cost of economic growth in the destruction of the Japanese environment and the wear and tear of urban life.

Japan was long favoured by circumstances (Vietnam was an advantage as Korea had been). Yet there have to be men to take advantage of favourable circumstances, and Japanese attitudes helped. Post-war Japan could deploy intense pride and an unrivalled willingness for collective effort among her people; both sprang from the deep cohesiveness and capacity for subordinating the individual to collective purposes which had always marked Japanese society. Strangely, such attitudes seemed to survive the introduction of democratic institutions. The Americans had entertained great

hopes of these, but it may be too early to judge how deeply they are rooted. They have, after all, been tried in Japan before. The way in which they worked after 1951 was to produce something like one-party rule, though irritation with this apparently unshakable predominance expressed itself soon in the emergence of more extreme groupings, some anti-liberal. There were signs that such extremism appealed increasingly to youth.

There were also Japanese to whom the pace of social change began in the 1960s to appear to be too fast. There was mounting uneasiness over what was happening to traditional values and institutions. The costs of economic growth were to be seen not only in huge conurbations and pollution, but also in the emergence of social problems which strained even Japanese custom. Great firms still operated with success on the basis of group loyalties which were buttressed by traditional attitudes and institutions. None the less, at a different level the Japanese family seemed to be undergoing just the same strains which had so weakened it in other industrialized societies.

Economic progress also helped to change the context of foreign policy which, in any case, moved away in the 1960s from the simplicities of the preceding decade. Economic strength meant that the yen became an important trading currency; Japan was therefore drawn into the monetary diplomacy of Europe. Moreover, Japanese prosperity involved her in the affairs of many parts of the world. In the Pacific basin, she became a consumer of raw material from Australia and New Zealand. In the Middle East she became a large buyer of oil. In Europe, though the aggregate share of Japan was not large, her investment was thought alarming by some, while her exports of manufactured goods threatened European equivalents. Even Japan's food supplies for her large population involved disputes with other nations; in the 1960s Japan drew 90 per cent of her requirements for protein from fishing and this led to growing international concern that the Japanese might be overfishing important grounds.

Such questions changed the atmosphere and content of foreign relations as much as did the behaviour of other powers, especially in the Pacific area. Japan assumed there in the 1960s a position in relation to other Pacific countries not unlike that of Germany to central and eastern Europe before 1914. New Zealand and Australia, in particular, found their economies increasingly and profitably tied in to Japanese consumption rather than the old British market. Both of them supplied meat and Australia minerals, too, notably coal and iron ore. On the Asian mainland the Russians and the South Koreans complained about Japanese fishing and in the second case this added a new complication to an old story of economic involvement there. Korea was Japan's second largest market (the United States was the biggest) and the Japanese started to invest there again after 1951. This revived a traditional distrust; it was ominous to find that South Korean nationalism had so anti-Japanese a tone that in 1959 the president of South Korea could urge his countrymen to unite 'as one man' against not their northern neighbour, but Japan.

Greater strength also meant greater responsibilities. The withdrawal of American direction was logically rounded off twenty years later when Okinawa (one of the first of her overseas possessions to be re-acquired) was returned to Japan. There remained the question of the Kuriles, still in Russian hands, and of Taiwan, in the possession of the Chinese nationalists and claimed by the Chinese communists but Japanese attitudes on all these matters remains – no doubt prudently – obscure. There was also the possibility that the question of Sakhalin might be reopened.

All of these questions began to look much more susceptible to investigation in the 1960s because of the great changes brought to the Asian scene by Chinese and Japanese revival. With the Chinese–Russian quarrel, Japan clearly had much greater freedom for manoeuvre, both towards the United States, her erstwhile patron, and China and Russia. The embarrassment which too close a tie with the Americans might bring was to be shown as the United States became more deeply involved in the Vietnam War and political opposition to this grew in Japan. Japan's freedom was limited, in the sense that all three of the other great powers of the area were equipped with nuclear weapons by 1970 (and she of all nations had most reason to know their effect), but there was little doubt of Japan's capacity to produce them within a relatively brief time if she required them. Altogether, the Japanese stance was potentially one which might develop in various different directions; clearly, for example, there was concern in Tokyo about the possibility of better Sino–American relations after the presidential visit to Peking. In a world situation more fluid than it had been since 1941, prediction was hazardous. What was indisputable was that Japan was becoming once more a world power to reckon with.

Another ambiguous prospect was presented by the Middle East. Time and oil were on the side of the Arabs, but not much else was clear by 1970. The Six-Day War of 1967 solved nothing. It merely exacerbated Arab feeling – there were even new waves of refugees – and gave Israel good strategic frontiers for the next round. When the Israelis embarked upon the establishment of settlements in their new-won territories, Arab resentment grew even stronger. It could obtain expression in the United Nations, where a 'Group of 77' supposedly non-aligned countries achieved the suspension of Israel (like South Africa) from certain international organizations. More important, perhaps, was a unanimous resolution of 1967 condemning the Israeli annexation of Jerusalem and another calling for Israeli withdrawal from Arab lands in exchange for recognition by her neighbours. So far as Israeli policy was concerned, this was seed falling on stony ground. It was clear that it would only be a matter of years before there was another war. In that case, the danger presented itself that, because of the identification of American and Russian interests with opposing sides, a world war might suddenly blow up out of a local conflict, as in 1914.

At the same time, there were a few signs that the decreasing importance of a bipolar structure might bring hopeful changes even here. For one thing, the British strove to mend their bridges with the Arabs. This was made a little easier by the British withdrawal from Aden and was given urgency by the British need, as the country which more than any other depended on Middle Eastern oil, to improve relations with the Gulf states. The British had taken the lead in drafting the United Nations resolution on Israeli withdrawal from occupied territories in return for recognition. But little could be done by a former imperial power now clearly in decline through economic weakness.

It was into this situation that an attack by Egypt and Syria on Israel erupted in the autumn of 1973. It was supported by all the other Arab states except Jordan. In the fighting which followed heavy casualties were inflicted on the Israelis, who for the first time faced the prospect of military defeat by the greatly improved and Russian-armed forces of their opponents. This did not happen, but the Russians were reported to have sent nuclear weapons to Egypt and the Americans put their forces on the alert round the world.

This grim background, like the possibility that the Israelis themselves might have nuclear weapons they would be prepared to use in extremity, was not fully discernible to the public at the time. Then, possibly greater grounds for concern were given to the peoples of supposedly 'uninvolved' nations by the Arab oil states' part in the quarrel. By announcing restrictions on oil supply to Europe, Japan and the United States they suddenly revealed that the fundamental diplomatic support on which Israel had always been able to rely might not be available to her for ever: the Jews might not always be able to count the effect produced on Western diplomacy by guilt about what had happened to Jews in Germany, sympathy and admiration for a civilized and liberal state in a backward region, and the pressure of Jewish voters in the United States. Nor was this all. The immediate impact of the new 'oil diplo-macy' was also immediately felt in higher prices for oil. Overnight, the economic problems of industrial states (which had gone grumbling along but tolerated in the 1960s as the pressures of international monetary difficulties grew) now became acute. Dependence on oil imports played havoc with balance-of-payment problems. Even the United States was badly shaken, but Japan and Europe were soon showing even more serious signs of economic recession and people were soon speaking of a new world depression like that of the 1930s.

Eastern Europe was somewhat insulated from this as from other trends. There had long before 1970 been signs that new problems faced the Russian bloc after the Sino–Soviet quarrel. This could be seen in the violence with which Albania, the tiniest of Europe's communist countries, condemned Russia and applauded Peking. But Albania had no frontier with the Warsaw Pact countries and was thus not likely to have to take account of the Russian army. Nevertheless, even in countries within the pact the currents of national independence first seen in the 1950s soon showed they were still alive in the next decade.

This first became clear when Romania successfully contested the direction of her economy by Comecon, asserting a national right to develop it in her own interest. She went further than this by taking up a vaguely neutralist position on questions of foreign policy – though remaining loyal to the Warsaw Pact. Poland showed parallel tendencies, which were summed up by an Italian communist as 'polycentrism'. But that there were limits to the dislocation of the old monolithic unity of communism was shown in 1968. Romania had no land frontier with a NATO country, an eight-hundred-mile one with Russia, and had Chinese backing for her independent line. Her skittishness could therefore be tolerated. None of these conditions held in Czechoslovakia where, in 1968, a communist government was both deliberately liberalizing its internal structure and developing trade relations with West Germany. After a series of attempts to bring her to heel Czechoslovakia

A dramatic confrontation in Prague during the Russian invasion of 1968.

was invaded in May by Warsaw Pact forces. To avoid a repetition of what had happened in Hungary in 1956, the Czech government did not resist and the brief attempt to provide an example of 'socialism with a human face', as a Czech statesman had put it, was obliterated.

With the Sino–Soviet quarrel, tremblings within the eastern bloc and the United States no longer so sure of her interests and policies in Latin America, it could plausibly be said by 1970 that the world as a whole had abandoned bipolarity for polycentrism. The process of disintegration of the Cold War simplicities had been rapid and surprising. Yet perhaps the most striking example of all of the improbabilities of history was to be found in western Europe, the place where the evolution of a world history had actually begun; by 1970 it provided some of the first if feeble signs of the breaking of nationalism's grip on the human potential for organization.

Western Europe was shaped from legacies of common experience going back to the Carolingians, but the decisive agents in the last quarter-century have been the war and Russian policy; between them they have ended the German problem. This removed the old fears of France and the possibility of another great civil war in the West. Soviet policy then went on to give the western countries many new reasons to cooperate more closely. The Marshall Plan and NATO turned out to be only the first two important steps; in 1950 came a French proposal for a Coal and Steel Community to regulate the industrial heartland of western Europe which was the first positive step towards the integration of western Germany into a new international structure.

By then much had already changed in the

West. The internal political weaknesses caused to France and Italy by the existence of large communist parties in those countries had been overcome by a variety of forces of which economic recovery was the most important. They had in each case ended communist participation in governments as early as 1947 and with that the dangers of a fate such as Czechoslovakia's had disappeared. In both countries (as in West Germany) anti-communist opinion had then coalesced about right-wing parties whose essence was Roman Catholicism, an integrating force. Broadly speaking, governments of the Right in continental western Europe pursued similar aims of economic recovery and increasing realization of Welfare State principles from that time onwards. One effect was more and more governmental intervention in the economy in France, Italy and the 'Benelux' countries (Belgium, the Netherlands and Luxemburg), though less so in western Germany.

The trend to supra-national organization in Europe also continued. In 1952 the Coal and Steel Community was set up which provided for the international organization of these industries in France, Germany and the Low Countries. The most important functional organizations for Europe appeared in 1957: the European Economic Community (or 'Common Market') and Euratom. In the first it faintly appeared that earlier attempts to unite Europe politically might at last be within sight of success. Whether this were true or not, moreover, it was certain that the statesmen who made these arrangements had abandoned the assumption that war could ever again be an acceptable alternative to cooperation and negotiation between their countries. The era of European civil war, which went back centuries to the beginnings of the national state system, was over. Tragically, though accepting that fact, the rulers of Great Britain had not seized the chance to join in giving it institutional expression.

Yet for a long time the most determined opposition to an evolution from economic arrangements towards further political integra-

tion came from France. They were expressed most strongly by General de Gaulle, who returned to politics at a moment of crisis in 1958 to become president. France was threatened with civil war because of its divisions over Algeria. His first task was to negotiate these rapids, then, after carrying through important constitutional reforms, de Gaulle performed a service to his country as great as had been his wartime rôle by liquidating France's Algerian commitment in 1961. The act freed both him and her for a more vigorous international rôle but a very negative one. De Gaulle's view of European consolidation was limited to cooperation between independent nation-states: his thinking remained firmly nationalist and he saw the EEC as essentially a device for the protection of French economic interests. He was quite prepared to strain the new organization badly to get his way. Further, in effect, he twice vetoed British application to join it.

Wartime experience had left de Gaulle with a deep distrust of the 'Anglo-Saxons'. In 1964 he annoyed the United States by exchanging diplomatic representatives with communist China. He insisted, too, that France go ahead with her own nuclear weapons programme, declining to be dependent on American patronage. Finally, after causing it much trouble, he withdrew from NATO. This looked like the coming of 'polycentrism' to the western bloc, too. None the less, when de Gaulle resigned after an unfavourable result to a referendum on constitutional change in 1969, a major political force making for uncertainty and disarray in western Europe disappeared. His successors were less intransigent and circumstances, rather than political opposition, have since been the main obstacle to further European consolidation.

Although French policy still opposed the evolution of the Common Market in the direction of a more complete cohesion, Great Britain finally joined in 1972, a recognition, at last, of the facts of twentieth-century history by the most conservative of nations. It complemented the withdrawal from empire and acknowledged that the British frontier lay no longer (as was believed still between the wars) on the Rhine, but on the Elbe. It was the climax of an era of uncertainty which had lasted almost since 1945 (though not quite the end of it). For a quarter-century all British governments had failed to combine sustained economic growth, increased social service provision and a high level of employment. The second depended ultimately on the first, but when difficulty arose, the first had always been sacrificed to the last. The vulnerability of the traditional British economy's commitment to international trade was a handicap here. True, the poor British economic performance was relative. The United Kingdom still grew richer, but did so more slowly than other developed countries – and too slowly for many of its citizens. Yet the British had to their credit some achievements which tended to be overlooked. The two outstanding ones were negative, the acceptance of a decline in international power and the achievement of a rapid decolonialization without the violence and domestic bitterness visible elsewhere. Among the positive achievements were the creation of the first comprehensive national system of social services and rights to medical treatment in a capitalist economy and a liberal state which was a great power, the maintenance of a level of orderliness and social cooperation which as late as 1970 still made the country attractive to foreigners, and the preservation of traditional constitutional liberties.

By 1976 it was much harder to be sure that these achievements could be sustained. In particular, the threat posed to order and civilization by the Protestant and Catholic hooligans of Ulster, who seemed bent on destroying that province rather than cooperate with their rivals inside it, was not mastered. The old threat of lunatic nationalism was as alive there as ever and cost the lives of hundreds of British soldiers, policemen and civilians. Fortunately it did not disrupt British politics as Irish questions had done in the past. The British electorate was preoccupied, rather, by its own material concern, above all with inflation, running at un-

'Lo, all our pomp of yesterday,' wrote Kipling when Queen Victoria celebrated her Diamond Jubilee, 'Is one with Nineveh and Tyre . . .'. A young citizen of the new state of Guyana scrutinizes an overturned statue of the great queen, shortly after independence came to the former British Guiana in the reign of her great-great-granddaughter.

precedented rates and giving new fierceness to industrial troubles in the 1970s, while many leaders and interpreters of opinion seemed obsessed with the themes of social division. Even the question whether the United Kingdom should remain in the EEC, which was submitted to the revolutionary device of a referendum in June 1975, was often put in these terms. It was therefore all the more surprising to many politicians when the outcome of the referendum was unambiguously favourable to continued membership. It was the first sign for a decade or so that the views of the country at large were not normally well represented by those who

" I wonder why children never want Grandma to depart through the front door but always long to kick her down the back stairs ?"

The abandonment of empire did not much embitter British politics, but neither was it an occasion for rejoicing (except to a minority on the Left). Perhaps a puzzled and sometimes regretful acquiescence was the response of most Englishmen. Something of that mood was caught by this cartoon by David Low.

A detachment of British soldiers faces a stone-throwing mob in Belfast.

were considered their spokesmen; it was also possible that it was a decision which would in the end prove a turning-point in the history of a once great nation, by closing off one sequence of choices which would have flowed ineluctably from a reassertion of insularity.

None the less, bad times (economically speaking) lay immediately ahead: inflation was at last identified in 1975 by government as the major threat, and it was by then at last dawning that the era of unquestioned growth in consumption was over. It was unfortunate that the United Kingdom had joined Europe on the eve of this bad economic setback, which owed something also to the international crisis over oil and the recession which followed it in every industrial country. For a time the energy problems seemed likely to prise the Common Market apart and gave new bitterness to bickerings on relative advantage within it. It detonated a currency problem which soon created further divisiveness. As the economic climate grew worse everywhere and the good times which had underpinned earlier cooperation evaporated, it was vividly apparent that for all her potential, Europe's fate lay less in her own hands than those of others. Clearly, even to those who had not already seen it, the European age was over – or was it? In 1973 it became certain that huge oilfields lay around Europe itself, although beneath the sea-bed.

Such troubles helped to remind Europeans of the limited extent to which the world had progressed beyond bipolarity. Though many of them realistically saw that greater European unity, a growing prosperity and a habit of cooperation were essential prerequisites of greater independence of both American and Russian policy, there was a sense in which such independence was still wholly unrealistic unless Europe could turn herself, too, into a superpower. For all the dramatic changes across the whole world since the Cuban crisis, the Soviet Union and the United States were still in 1975 the only two states whose might gave them unquestioned status as (to use an official Russian definition) 'the greatest world powers, without whose participation not a single international problem can be solved'. Allowing for the implicit nature of this participation in some instances, this definition reflects continuing reality, even in the era of a resurgent Far East and oil blackmail.

This was not to say, though, that the relationship between these two powers was what it had been in 1962, let alone what it had been earlier. First, that relationship had changed because its world context had changed. Then there was the change which some had taken to mean that the Soviet Union and the United States were growing more alike. This, were it true, need not necessarily mean a decline in hostility between them; European states of the *ancien régime* which enjoyed very similar ideological and social systems had never been able to dispense with going to war with one another. But it did suggest a possible moderating development as it became clear that both had much to lose in the event of war.

This change was more notable, possibly, in the instance of the Soviet Union. Though it was hard to observe, there were signs by the early 1970s that the Russians were finding it hard to resist a truism that Marxism itself proclaimed, that consciousness evolves in accordance with material conditions. Among other results of the obvious success of Soviet society in providing more wealth for its citizens were two: an apparent dissidence which suggested a demand for greater spiritual freedom such as that which had earlier accompanied the transition to a society of plenty in the West and a less explicit, but real, groundswell of opinion that further material gains should be forthcoming. These could hardly be provided at the same time as the Soviet Union spent colossal sums on armaments unless a huge introduction of western technology, management technique and, possibly, western capital were accepted. What

changes they would bring in their train was debatable, but that there would be some was certain.

Another tie between the United States and the Soviet Union was, none the less, even more compelling. After 1962 a huge Soviet effort of armament placed the Soviet Union in a position in which it was superior in offensive power to the United States. But superiority in these matters is a rather limited affair. The Americans, with their gift for the arresting slogan, have concisely expressed the situation as MAD; that is to say, both countries have the capacity to produce 'Mutually Assured Destruction'. More precisely, this is the name of a situation in which each of the two potential combatants has enough striking power to ensure that even after a surprise attack by its opponent deprived it of the cream of its weapons, what remained would be sufficient to ensure a reply so appalling as to leave its opponent's great cities a smoking wilderness and its armed forces capable of little but attempting to control the terrorized survivors.

This bizarre possibility is a great conservative force. Dr Johnson's observation that the knowledge you are to be hanged wonderfully clears the mind requires extension in the case of collectivities threatened with disaster on this scale: even the knowledge that you *may* be hanged if you make a blundering move is a great stimulus to prudence. In this fact may well lie the most fundamental explanation of a new degree of cooperation – expressed in many bilateral agreements – shown since 1970 by the United States and the Soviet Union and in the exchange of visits between their leaders, culminating in the Helsinki agreement of 1975. For all the macabre attraction which the MAD situation seems to offer, though, it is not true that it implies any equivalence of power between the United States and the Soviet Union. The most striking change in bipolarity since 1962 lies exactly here: the balance was not more then than now even, but its terms are reversed.

In 1962 the United States was top dog. She enjoyed superior military power, allies, clients

and satellites which were (with the exception of France) reliable, and a public will which sustained a world diplomatic and military effort until well into the second half of the decade. By 1976 the situation was very different. The Soviet Union had achieved a level of military parity which was not only expressed in the ghastly algebra of MAD, but in an ability to provide a naval presence rivalling that of the United States and established in the Indian Ocean, the only great maritime region in which confrontation had yet to occur. But this was not all. In the Middle East, the traditional tsarist concern for a proper Russian influence in the area was at last brought to fruition in the patronage of Arab states.

Though this patronage, like other aspects of Soviet policy, did not always seem to bring the rewards which must have been hoped for, it could also be said to suit the Russians that almost everywhere United States policy overseas seemed in the middle of the decade to be in dissarray. The American wish not to offend the Arabs seemed to bring into question even that hitherto unyielding dogma of Middle Eastern affairs, unflinching American support for Israel; American voters showed signs of reacting violently against the expense of new war abroad and the discomfort of a possible Arab oil boycott. Nor was this all in the Middle East. A Greek revolution and a consequent outbreak of hostility between Turks and Greeks in Cyprus led to a situation in which the Americans offended both NATO allies, Greece and Turkey. And at the other end of Europe, Portugal underwent a revolution in 1974 and that country, too, seemed in danger of a period of government by men unsympathetic to the United States and, possibly, even withdrawal from NATO – an act which would have grave consequences for

Polaris, a missile capable of being launched from submarines and therefore independent of fixed bases, was added to the western powers' armoury in the late 1960s. Such innovations threatened the delicate balance of terror established between the nuclear powers.

Atlantic strategy. Finally, as 1976 wore on, communist success in Italian elections raised the spectre of communist participation in government in that country, too, before long.

These events would in themselves have shaken the confidence of other allies of the United States and unequivocally benefited the Soviet Union. But in the background were yet more Indo-China disasters and a setback in Africa. The Vietnam war had destroyed President Johnson. His successor's presidency was built on that and it was the political fact which underlay American withdrawal and the 1973 settlement. It was soon clear how little that settlement was worth, but unhappily, it became clear only when a domestic scandal had destroyed – perhaps temporarily – American confidence in the traditional leadership of the president in foreign affairs. President Ford faced a Congress unwilling to countenance even further economic aid to American allies in Indo-China, let alone military. As Cambodia collapsed and South Vietnam closely followed, questions were heard about the lengths to which a world-wide retreat of American power might go. Clearly the United States would not fight over Indo-China, though it had once done so. Would it, then, fight over Siam? More alarmingly still, would Americans fight over Israel – or even Berlin? There were good reasons (it must also be said) to think the American mood of resignation and dismay would not last, but while it lasted, her allies were bound to feel uneasy and look about them. One thing was certain: the United States was no longer the top dog she had been even ten years before. But then, a richer and more prudent Soviet Union could not be top dog in that sense, either. Perhaps no one could any more.

3 The world of the 1970s

Deliberately, there are no neat lines dividing periods of history in this book, and now there is to be no neat ending either. Logically, of course, history cannot have an end; unless we extinguish the human race someone will always be able to think about its past. History is always unrolling – as this is being written and while it will in due course be read – and a history of the world cannot be pinned down to a finish on a clean chronological boundary.

Nor can it be pinned down in a neat pattern of 'significant' topics; what is historically significant is what one age thinks worth noting about another and the significances of our age will only appear when people in the future start to wonder about what made *their* world. This is another difficulty about ending a book like this and it has been apparent in the last two or three chapters. It is the old problem of perspective – a good image, which we too easily take for granted, forgetting its pictorial and visual origins. It means getting things in their right relationship to one another on the same scale. It is all too obvious today that events alter perspective with startling rapidity. In the aftermath of yet another war there, the Middle East of 1976 looks very different from that of 1967, after the great Israeli victories. To take another example, the early 1970s showed that even the short span of an American presidential term can bring startling changes in people's view of the

The first steps of men on the moon, seen by approximately five hundred million people, thanks to television.

office and **its** incumbent and that this may have momentous consequences for trends and policies hitherto taken for granted. In non-political history, too (or at least history which is not at first sight political though it may have important political dimensions), the Japanese economic miracle of the 1960s now requires qualification in the light of restrictions imposed on world oil supplies by the Arabs.

Faced with such difficulties, it is best not to try to do too much and to be content with having a last word at all. This book will not be published until we are well into the second half of the 1970s and by then no doubt the world will have changed still more and thrown up new surprises to make very recent history look different. Above all, prophecy must be avoided; it is not the historian's business, even if he disguises it as extrapolation from past trends. To indulge in it may have a temporary and didactic usefulness in clarifying thought, but often only because the exercise demonstrates that the trend logically *cannot* continue. The number of scientists in the world, for instance, like annual expenditure on science, cannot continue to increase at the rate of the last couple of centuries; if it did the population of the world would within a finite time consist of nothing but scientists. Not dissimilar considerations appear if thought is given to the consumption of energy resources by industrial nations, though in that case recent events have provided empirical evidence against basing arguments on extrapolation from past trends.

The only permissible subject for the historian

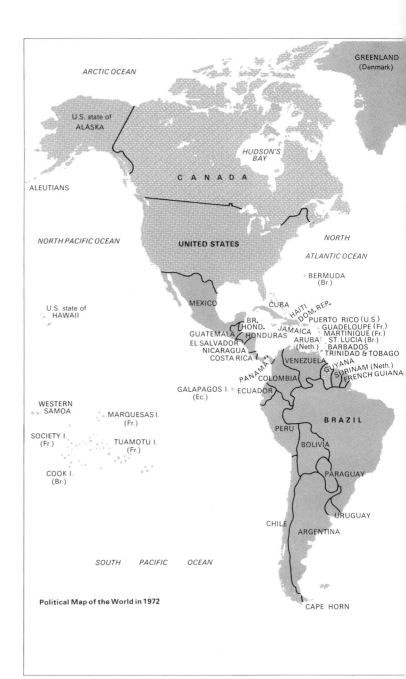

GREENLAND
(Denmark)

ARCTIC OCEAN

U.S. state of
ALASKA

HUDSON'S
BAY

C A N A D A

ALEUTIANS

NORTH PACIFIC OCEAN

UNITED STATES

NORTH

ATLANTIC OCEAN

BERMUDA
(Br.)

U.S. state of
HAWAII

MEXICO

CUBA

HAITI

DOM. REP.

PUERTO RICO (U.S.)
GUADELOUPE (Fr.)
MARTINIQUE (Fr.)
ST. LUCIA (Br.)
BARBADOS
TRINIDAD & TOBAGO

BR.
HOND.
HONDURAS
GUATEMALA
EL SALVADOR
NICARAGUA
COSTA RICA

JAMAICA

ARUBA
(Neth.)

VENEZUELA
GUYANA
SURINAM (Neth.)
FRENCH GUIANA

PANAMA
COLOMBIA

GALAPAGOS I.
(Ec.)
ECUADOR

WESTERN
SAMOA

MARQUESAS I.
(Fr.)

PERU

BRAZIL

SOCIETY I.
(Fr.)

TUAMOTU I.
(Fr.)

BOLIVIA

COOK I.
(Br.)

PARAGUAY

URUGUAY

CHILE
ARGENTINA

SOUTH   PACIFIC   OCEAN

Political Map of the World in 1972

CAPE HORN

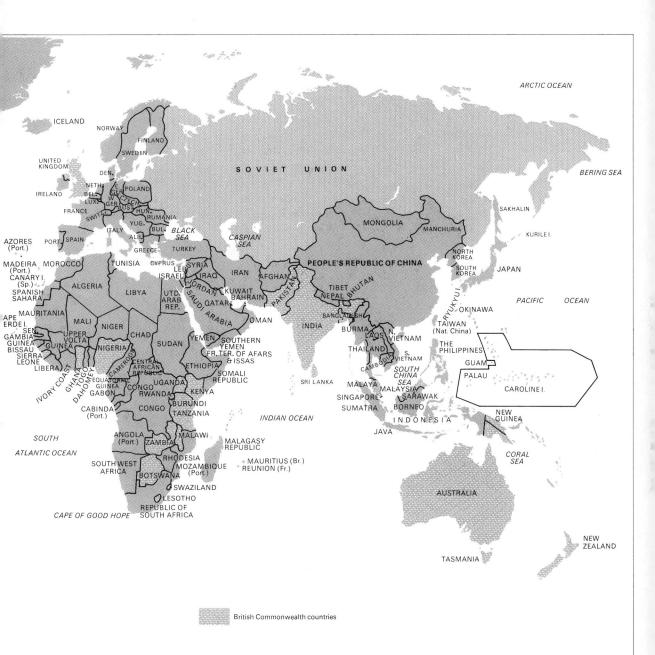

ARCTIC OCEAN

ICELAND

NORWAY

FINLAND

SWEDEN

BERING SEA

UNITED
KINGDOM

DEN.

SOVIET UNION

IRELAND

NETH.

E.
GER.

POLAND

SAKHALIN

FRANCE

BEL.
LUX.

W.
GER.

CZECH.

AUST.

HUN.

RUMANIA

KURILE I.

MONGOLIA

MANCHURIA

SWITZ.

YUG.

AZORES
(Port.)

PORT.

SPAIN

ITALY

ALB.

BUL.

BLACK
SEA

CASPIAN
SEA

NORTH
KOREA

GREECE

TURKEY

PEOPLE'S REPUBLIC OF CHINA

SOUTH
KOREA

JAPAN

MADEIRA
(Port.)

MOROCCO

TUNISIA

CYPRUS

LEB.

SYRIA
IRAQ

IRAN

AFGHAN.

PACIFIC   OCEAN

CANARY I.
(Sp.)

ISRAEL

JORDAN

RYUKYU I.

OKINAWA

SPANISH
SAHARA

ALGERIA

LIBYA

UTD.
ARAB
REP.

SAUDI ARABIA

KUWAIT
BAHRAIN
QATAR

TIBET

NEPAL BHUTAN

PAKISTAN

TAIWAN
(Nat. China)

MAURITANIA

MALI

NIGER

OMAN

BANGLADESH

BURMA

LAOS
N.
VIETNAM

THE PHILIPPINES

GUAM

APE
ERDE I.

CHAD

SUDAN

YEMEN

INDIA

PALAU

SEN.
GAMBIA
GUINEA
BISSAU

UPPER
VOLTA

NIGERIA

SOUTHERN
YEMEN

THAILAND

S.
VIETNAM

CAROLINE I.

GUINEA

FR. TER. OF AFARS
& ISSAS

CAMBODIA

SOUTH
CHINA
SEA

SIERRA
LEONE

CENTRAL
REPUBLIC

ETHIOPIA

SOMALI
REPUBLIC

SRI LANKA

MALAYA

LIBERIA

CAMEROUN

SINGAPORE

MALAYSIA

SARAWAK

NEW
GUINEA

IVORY COAST
GHANA
TOGO
DAHOMEY

EQUATORIAL
GUINEA

GABON

CONGO

UGANDA

RWANDA

KENYA

SUMATRA

BORNEO

INDONESIA

CABINDA
(Port.)

CONGO

BURUNDI

TANZANIA

INDIAN OCEAN

JAVA

CORAL
SEA

SOUTH

ANGOLA
(Port.)

ZAMBIA

MALAWI

MALAGASY
REPUBLIC

ATLANTIC OCEAN

RHODESIA

MOZAMBIQUE
(Port.)

MAURITIUS (Br.)
REUNION (Fr.)

SOUTH WEST
AFRICA

BOTSWANA

SWAZILAND

AUSTRALIA

CAPE OF GOOD HOPE

LESOTHO

REPUBLIC OF
SOUTH AFRICA

NEW
ZEALAND

TASMANIA

British Commonwealth countries

is the past and it is reasonable for him to try to see consistency or inconsistency, continuity or discontinuity, in the relationship of recent events to what has gone before. Here we are back with the difficulties posed by the mass of facts which crowds in on us. The very confusion they present suggests a much more revolutionary period than any preceding it and all that has been said so far about the continuing acceleration of change confirms this. This does not, on the other hand, imply that these more violent and sweeping changes are not consistent with what has gone before.

If there is any general trend at all in earlier history, this book has argued, it is twofold, in the direction of a growing unity of human experience and of a growing human capacity to control the environment. It is at least arguable that recent history can be read so as to confirm that these trends are still observable in it.

So much misuse has been made of the slogan 'one world' that it is now little more than a cant term. In so far as the people who first used it hoped to ease the way to common political action too, it seems exploded. There is just too much conflict and quarrelling about. In 1931 the Japanese opened the Manchurian campaign and in the forty-odd years since then there has hardly been a space of more than a few weeks in which someone was not fighting someone else somewhere in the world. Moreover, some political divisions, even when they do not break out in overt violence, still produce quarrels which are expensive and dangerous: the Cold War is an example. This line of thought can be summed up in the reflexion that although there emerged from victory in 1945 an international institution which took the name of the *United* Nations, it is still based on the theory that the whole surface of the globe is divided into territories belonging to sovereign states and it now has nearly 150 members. None of this can be denied and much, much more could be said along the same lines.

Yet it does not quite meet the thesis already set out. The point could be made by thinking about a more remote period. Nobody would dream of denying, for example, that the world of Islam during the European Middle Ages was the scene of struggles between different Islamic rulers and displays plenty of evidence of strife. Yet Islam was, none the less, a unity. It was a civilization and all over the Islamic world institutions and behaviour expressed this by uniformities which were not observable between or in, say, Inca Peru and Christian Europe. One argument of this book is that, for all the conflicts of the modern world, they resemble more and more – though still far from completely – civil wars between contestants sharing a common background than conflicts of civilizations. At this level, though, the argument can hardly be put without it being overstated. More humdrum matters may make the point more exactly.

Curiously enough, it is most obvious at the level of personal experience, though this is usually the level at which men feel most acutely the distinctions between them. In the days when men of neighbouring villages all over the world spoke significantly different dialects even if they shared a common language, when their movement in the whole of their lives would only exceptionally take them ten miles from their homes, when even their clothes and tools might provide in their workmanship evidence of big differences of technology, style and custom, then the human experience of the world was in important ways more highly differentiated than it is now. Nor are such cases the extreme ones. The great physical, racial and linguistic divisions of the past were much less easily overcome than their equivalents today. It is easy to trace the course of this in improved communication, mass education, mass production of commonly required artifacts and so on; much has already been said about such things in these pages. But the results are less noted, though they are obvious to a traveller in any part of the modern world.

Clothes strike him by their exotic or unfamiliar appearance, but this is really an illusion; more people now dress in a manner more generally widespread than ever before. It is

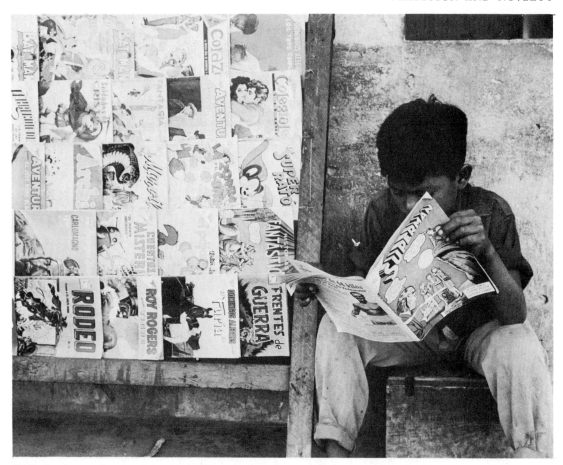

Global culture. A scene from Venezuela.

only rural districts or consciously nationalist régimes which now cling to traditional local costume instead of the near universal shirt-and-trousers. Kilts, kaftans, kimonos are becoming tourist souvenirs, or the carefully preserved relics of a sentimentalized past; less picturesque but truly traditional clothes, meanwhile, are more and more the sign of poverty and backwardness. The conduct of self-consciously conservative and nationalist régimes does not affect the general argument here; it even bears it out. When Rousseau sought in the eighteenth century to encourage the Poles on their way to national regeneration, he urged them to do so by zealously guarding their national pastimes and amusements and rejecting foreign fashion. He has his disciples today. When Uganda legislates against the mini-skirt or Zaire encourages traditional dancing, it is because the common experience pouring in from the world outside is corrosive of tradition. Conversely, Ataturk forbad Turks to wear the fez and veil and Peter the Great dressed his courtiers in western European clothes because they sought to destroy tradition. These statesmen thus recognized that more was involved in such a change than fashion. What was at stake was orientation towards a new range of experience and this is unwelcome in many societies, however much they yearn for economic or technical modernization.

A wider basis of shared experience than ever before is now available to many human beings if they live in modernizing societies. They are increasingly liberated from differences of climate by electricity, air-conditioning and medicine.

All over the world millions of them live in cities with electric street-lighting and traffic signals, policemen on point duty, banks, shops and bus-stops. In the shops there is a growing likelihood that the same goods will be available as in other countries; toothpaste can be bought worldwide though it was only invented a short time ago. Men not understanding one another's language can drive and service the same machines and derive the same or very similar advantages and disadvantages from their use. Everywhere in the world the motor-car has imposed in greater or lesser degree the same demands on urban living and everywhere threatens it with the same level of intolerability. Again, the

In Zaire (formerly part of the Belgian Congo) an advertisement for an all-but-universal product exemplifies the impact of such commodities, whether native or not, on local patterns of consumption.

countryside still escapes many of these blessings, but the shared experience is clearly to be seen in the cities.

The point can be made by an effort of historical imagination. A traveller who went from imperial Rome to imperial Peking would have wondered at everything he saw; not only would clothes have been cut differently and made of different materials, but food would have been different, the animals in the streets would have

Mexicans still eat traditional foods, in spite of the availability of standard packaged goods. The photograph was taken in 1963; surrounded by mass-produced pots, pans and pails, the housewife still prepares the tortilla *in traditional fashion, using the top of an old oil drum as a baking tin.*

been of different breeds, the weapons of the soldiers and their armour would have been shaped differently. Even the wheelbarrow would have had a different design. A modern American would now find much less to surprise him – and China is perhaps still one of the cultures most resistant to external trends. Even if Chinese cuisine retains its distinctiveness, a Chinese airliner looks like any other.

It may well be argued that such shared experience is peripheral to the lives of the great mass of mankind. Most people, after all, still live in villages and struggle to get a living from the soil, often with traditional tools and ideas. It is also true that the most startling divergence of human experience now visible in the world far transcends any difference which existed in the past. This is that between rich and poor nations. A thousand years ago all societies were by modern standards poor and consequently

The river was the easiest place in which to dispose of the body of this child drowned in the cyclone which struck East Pakistan in 1970. It revealed to a world dominated by the vision of the power of technology the vulnerability in which its poorer societies still lived.

closer to one another in their experience than they are today. The difficulty of winning one's daily bread and the fragility of man's life before the mysterious, implacable forces which cut him down like grass were the things all men had in common, whatever language they spoke or creed they followed. Such shared experience has gone from a world where a large minority of people live in countries with an average *per capita* annual income of over $3000 and millions of others in countries where the corresponding figure is about one-thirtieth of this sum. There are even colossal distinctions among the poor to be taken into account, for people have begun to talk of a 'Fourth World' separated from the 'Third', as countries enjoying great revenues from their exploitation of scarce natural resources such as oil have stood out more and more as countries with a potential for self-sustained development virtually inconceivable in the truly poor.

This is a respectable point of view, often powerfully argued. Yet the importance of the contrasts it points out can be exaggerated. They are, in the first place, the product of a relatively recent and brief historical era; we may no more assume they will endure for centuries than we may assume they will simply disappear. Moreover, the leading classes and élites even in the poorest countries almost always look to some version of the European package of modernization as a way out of their troubles. Their societies, that is to say, wherever they display vitality and an urge to change, provide evidence of the pervasiveness of the style of civilization which has proved so triumphant elsewhere.

This cannot be ignored by saying that modernization is only a matter of technology and that more fundamental matters of belief, institutions and attitudes are the real determinants of social behaviour. Such a comment in any case side-steps the question of the bearing of such material experience on culture, but there is not space to discuss that here. It is easier to reply by pointing to the evidence that ideas and institutions, too, have in fact become more generally spread among mankind, even if not with the same obviousness as material artifacts.

Not a great deal of practical respect is given to such documents as the United Nations Declaration of Human Rights but great interest has been shown in drawing them up and signing them; why? Although many of the signatory nations have little intention of respecting them, a decent regard for the opinion of mankind – to borrow a phrase – compels them to pay lip-service to common principles. Such principles usually turn out to be derived from the European tradition of civilization (as, indeed, the notion of a 'Declaration of Rights' suggests) and this is only a recent example of the tendency of the last three centuries for that civilization to extend its influence around the whole world. Its heartland is still Europe and North America and its strongest expressions in political domination have now passed, but the reasonable grounds for calling it the first world civilization have already been argued. It is not culturally arrogant to point out that Aztec and Inca civilization could not stand up to the Spanish. Such things are true or untrue: they are neither admirable nor repugnant. Whether we regard the European tradition as greedy, aggressive, brutal and exploitative, or as objectively improving, beneficent and humane is neither here nor there. It was either the master-source of the modern world or it was not and that is all our concern here.

Not too much should be expected to flow from this. The point is not that European ideas and institutions have everywhere replaced traditional ones, for they have not, as this book has argued at perhaps excessive length. Men still live in worlds shaped by deeply different traditions of culture. Women are not treated in the same way – again, whether for good or ill is irrelevant – in Islamic and Christian societies. Indians still take into account astrology in fixing the day of a wedding while English people may find the state of public transport more significant. The philosophy (or what is taken to be the philosophy) of ancient Asia has a cult attractiveness for a minority of modern

Americans but the roots of American behaviour are still to be found, if in any ideological source, in the confidence of the Enlightenment and the conviction felt by so many early puritan settlers that they were a people set apart, a city builded on a hill. One could go on and on with such contrasts. Differing traditions even make the use of shared technology and ideas different. Japanese capitalism is not the same thing in its working as British, and the explanation lies deep in the different historical traditions of two societies. What remains true in spite of this is that no other tradition has shown the same vigour and attractiveness in alien settings as the European: it has no competitors as a world shaper.

This can be seen in one of its grossest manifestations, its material greed and rapacity. Societies rooted in changeless acceptance of things as they are have taken up the belief that limitless improvement in material well-being is a proper goal for them and so assume much of the mental heritage of an expanding Europe. The very idea that willed change is possible is itself deeply subversive. Many other such European ideas have imposed on top of social institutions of great antiquity and toughness a layer of assumptions and myths drawn from the experience of European liberalism; republics are common the world round and everyone speaks the language of democracy and the rights of man. There is an effort, too, to bring to bear the rationalizing and utilitarian tradition in government and administration and to repeat models of institutions which have been found successful in countries in the European tradition. One reason why many black men clamour vociferously against the white societies they live in is that they in fact wish to realize the ideals of human rights and dignity evolved by European civilization. Meanwhile, their black cousins in new nations wish to participate in the benefits of the rising wealth made possible by industrialization and hope to realize the values it generates even when preaching the merits of 'negritude'.

It is very striking that so few cultures have been able altogether to resist this vigorous tradition: even China bows to Marx and science. Some have been more successful at resistance than others, but almost everywhere the individuality of the great traditions of civilization has been sapped. When modernizers have sought to take some things but not others from the dominant mode, they have not found it easy to do so. It is difficult (though possible, at a certain cost) to obtain selective modernity; it usually comes in a package, some of whose other contents may be unwelcome.

The emancipation of women provides an obvious instance. The impact of this movement on family structure and authority, on economic life and culture, and through them upon the emotions and attitudes of individuals, would be bound to prove revolutionary in many parts of the world, even were it carried only so far as to produce the state of affairs in advanced western countries often decried as inadequate by many feminists. Few non-European countries and cultures have made any but partial concessions to the principle; in some Arab countries girls now go to universities in considerable numbers but they emerge from them to take their places in an Islamic world ruled by tradition so far as the relations of the sexes are concerned. As for uneducated women – above all the millions of peasant women who make up most of the female population of Africa and Asia – they remain untouched even by such changes, though they may well have benefited occasionally from the practical improvement of their lot brought by the arrival of pumped water or the digging of a well.

Clearly, not all such disparities are the result of conscious selection from the European tradition. Organic change is something that can only come about slowly in any social tradition. Liberation has taken a long time to come as far as it has done in western countries. Christianity had from the start a fundamental (even if at first slight) bias towards the improvement of the lot of women because it took for granted that they, like men, had souls of infinite value in the eyes of God. On this was to be built the modern freedom of women in societies in the Christian tradition. However theologians might chip away at the idea in the interests of male prejudice, they could not in the end gainsay the principle. Yet it still took some seventeen centuries to produce the first advocates of feminism and another two to arrive at the substantial legal equality of men and women in the west today. It needed, too, the reinforcement provided by industrialization, with its practically liberating effects upon women before this could be achieved.

Conscious rejection of some elements in the package, the sheer inertia of well-established cultural patterns and the relative accessibility of the material as opposed to the moral products of the European tradition, sufficiently explain the impression of superficiality which modernizing change presents in some countries. It is a little like Hellenization in the Near East in the centuries after Alexander. Borrowed institutions, ideas and styles often show something of the same lack of real spirit and inspiration as the borrowings of Greek ideas by the East. There is the same prevalence of the signs and symbols of material achievement – dams, universities, steelworks, airlines, instead of baths, theatres, temples – the same standard forms of government and administration, the same literary and artistic fashion and even the same aesthetic. English has even become the *lingua franca* of business and intellectual life as Greek once was. Yet the results often fail to ring true; successfully transplanted to other traditions though such things seem to have been they are somehow not the same.

What this means is not that the experience of civilization now so widely diffused is unreal, but that it is inevitably selective, though hardly ever in the way hoped for. This does not invalidate the claim that for the first time in human history the variety of human experience is converging instead of diverging. The most obvious sign of this is what all parts of the world have found most seductive and compelling about European culture, its promise of material success. The outstanding success of European civilization came when it began to convince people in other cultures that through it lay the only road to success for themselves. Thus the Europeanization of a country was to be synonymous with its modernization. What were then seized upon were not only techniques and institutions, not merely such superficialities as clothes, but goals and patterns of behaviour, and these sometimes produced incongruous and unanticipated results in the societies where this happened. The idea of progress as unlimited material advance, of the right of the individual to assert himself, of nationalism as the proper determinant of political organization, would all produce consequences going far beyond what was expected by the Europeans who so confidently passed on to others the recipes which they believed to underlie their own success. Similarly, the introduction of new machines, the building of railways and mines, could transform social life in ways no one had willed or envisaged. The process, once begun, was irreversible. Once European methods and goals were accepted (as they were, eventually and in a measure, by élites in all countries), then an uncontrollable evolution had begun. Even in the most tightly controlled examples, modernization was bound to create new needs and demands.

The prestige and attractiveness of this model of civilization rested at bottom on the power of its techniques and tools to bring about rapid and progressive change, above all in the production of greater material well-being. It was this which underlay a real revolution in the minds of men which has been going on with increasing vigour for over a century – the acceptance of the idea that continuous material improvement is possible. This was the climax of centuries of experience of growing manipulation of the environment. Ironically, the idea took root over all the world almost at the moment when widespread misgivings were beginning to be felt about it in its birthplace. Of course, there have always been misgivings about man's interference with the environment and his attempts to control it, but until recently

Old and new in twentieth-century India.

they have seemed to rest on non-rational grounds, such as the fear of provoking divine anger or of nemesis. But for most of human history such uneasiness was steadily eroded by the palpable advantages and improvements which such interference brought about. The most obvious form of this was the creation of new wealth; it is undeniable that today more people live longer and at a higher standard of living than most of their predecessors.

Some doubts which have recently arisen about our civilization agree that it is supremely good at creating material improvement, but note that wealth in itself does not remove all man's dissatisfactions and may actually irritate some of them more acutely. Pollution, the oppressive anonymity of crowded cities and the nervous stress and strain of modern work conditions do much to erase satisfaction with a mere increase of material goods. Things have come to a pretty pass in one of the most beautiful cities in the world when, as we now discover, the noise level in the *Place de l'Opéra* is greater than that at the Niagara Falls, and the Seine is found to carry more sewer water than its natural flow. Scale has become a problem in its own right, too, as well as creating others. Problems made bigger in modern cities may even have grown to the point at which they are insoluble. Still greater misgivings are felt about the threat of over-population and the reality of increasing pressure on diminishing energy resources – with the result, perhaps, that competition for them must grow more intense and the world in consequence more politically unstable. In any case, energy and material resources are now so wastefully and inequitably employed that a new version of the Malthusian peril seems likely. Whereas we have by no means reached the end (or anything like it) of our capacity to produce food, it is far more likely that other

The problem of numbers is not only one of sharing basic necessities, but of sharing pleasures and scarce recreational resources, too: Coney Island, the favoured bathing beach of New Yorkers, on a sunny day.

things will run out before food does so, whatever may be the hardships experienced from time to time in specific places. Certainly there would at once be an impossible situation if every nation in the world sought to consume goods other than foods at the level of the developed countries today. There is a limit to the food which can be consumed by any one human being. There is virtually no limit to the goods he or she can consume in terms of a better environment, medicine, social services and the like and these rest in the end on energy and material resources which are not limitless. It can no longer seem reasonable that natural resources should be consumed at the rate at which we have been consuming them for the last two or three decades. But the social and political changes which must follow from this fact have not yet begun to be grasped.

In this connexion we may return to the greatly accelerated population growth of the last century or so. One of the difficulties posed by it is that there exists to deal with it nothing like the knowledge or technique which is available, for example, to put a man on the moon. Many different methods of restricting population exist but there is no assured outcome because societies are very complicated things. While population growth has been slowed down in some societies, it is not known whether the conditions which produce this are transferable to different societies and it is unlikely, if they are, that the outcome will be the same. The impact of sterilization and contraceptive propaganda in India, for example, seems in spite of great efforts to be insignificant.

This has led to some pessimism. To say whether pessimism or optimism about the future is justified is not (it must be repeated) the historian's job. But he can say whether some historical facts have been or have not been taken into account in making a judgement about the present. Substantially, it is now often urged that man's undoubted success in manipulating the bio-system is in danger of disappearing because of two interconnected tendencies. One is for the creation of new problems to follow rapidly upon success and perhaps too rapidly for an answer to be found before irreversible damage is done. Thus we face the problems of depleted natural resources, disturbance of existing ecologies, the creation of new stresses and dangers such as those involved in gathering people into great industrial cities. The second tendency is that the achievements of science outrun our capacities for the social control of its techniques. Examples are the dangers inherent in the proliferation of nuclear weapons, the reduction in death-rate through medical advance which leads to rapid population growth, the provision of mass communication before cultural preparation enables it to be dealt with critically. If these observations are correct, then the present age indeed seems to represent a break in historical continuity. It would imply that the progressive power to control environment which marked the whole of earlier history and all known prehistory was at an end.

This would certainly be a prospect not to be lightly regarded, but there are no reasons to believe that the process of discovering techniques to meet problems in the past cannot again be brought to bear successfully to solve the problems of the future. There are no grounds either logical or empirical for thinking that the steady accretion of control over nature which has marked all history until now will not continue. The factor that has changed, simply, is that scale and acceleration have grown. But this applies to solutions as well as problems.

The depressing effect of such considerations is bound to be diminished if we reflect that we know of nothing in the nature of the problems now facing the human race which in principle renders them incapable of solution. They may be more urgent and potentially more damaging, but this is only to say that their solution may require more urgent and radical methods, more drastic political and social change, not that they are not soluble at all. We may have to decide to live in a different way but we need not assume mankind will be extinguished. There is no reason to conclude that this series of tests will prove fatal to man when earlier ones which he

faced with infinitely less resources, both mental and technological – the onset of the Ice Ages, for example – did not. We have plenty of evidence of human adaptability in the past. The only clear warning which does stand out is that, whatever we do, we are likely to be gravely misled about the future if we simply extrapolate present trends. We must prepare for discontinuity as well as continuity.

The most spectacular achievement of the last few years suggests that the capacity of our culture to meet unprecedented challenges is as great as ever. It also, almost incidentally, marks a break in historical continuity as important as the European discovery of the Americas, or the Industrial Revolution. This was the opening of the exploration of space, the greatest of Man's material triumphs to date. If a symbolic date for a breach in the continuity of history were needed, then there is much to be said for 20 July 1969, the day when men first arrived on the surface of the moon, and, therefore, when there began the latest and greatest extension by Man of his environment, truly a new phase of history, the beginning of the history of Man on other celestial bodies.

The technical story has deep roots in the imaginations and aspirations of scientists for decades and in the development of high-powered rockets before and during the Second World War, but the moment when the space age began for most people came in October 1957, when an unmanned Russian satellite was launched by rocket. This was Sputnik I, which orbited the earth emitting radio signals. It was of great political importance because it shattered any illusion that Russian technology lagged far behind American. But what was much more important was that it ended the era when the principle of space travel was still in doubt. The future had begun.

This was shown by a further rapid burst of

The landscape of the mature industrial economy; Düsseldorf chimneys exemplify the problems and threats posed to the environment by modern processes.

satellite activity. The United States had begun its own satellite programme in 1955, though with much more modest hardware than the Russian. The first American satellite weighed only three pounds. When an attempt was made to launch it at the end of December with great attendant publicity the rocket caught fire instead of taking off and a sad little bleeping from the sands near the launching site was all that resulted. There was soon a much more impressive and successful American launch, but already within a month of Sputnik I the Russians had put up Sputnik II, an astonishingly successful machine, weighing half a ton and carrying the first passenger in space, a black and white mongrel called Laika. For nearly six months Sputnik II orbited the earth, visible to the whole inhabited world.

The Russian and American space programmes had already diverged. The Russian strength lay and was to continue to lie in the power and size of the rockets employed, which could lift big loads. This had military implications more obvious than the equally profound but less spectacular ones which flowed from American concentration on the science of data-gathering and on instrumentation. A competition for prestige was soon under way, but although people soon spoke of a 'space race' the contestants were really running towards different goals, and with one great exception (the wish to put a man in space) were probably not much influenced by one another's performance. The contrast was clear enough when Vanguard, the American satellite which failed in December 1957, was successfully launched in the following March. In spite of its tiny size, it went much deeper into space than any predecessor and has provided more valuable scientific information in proportion to its size than any other satellite. It is likely to be going around for another couple of centuries or so.

New achievements now followed so quickly that only the main ones need be noted. At the end of 1958 the first satellite for communications purposes was launched successfully. It was American. Information and experience were now making progress faster and faster. In 1960 the Americans scored another 'first' – the recovery of a capsule after re-entry. The Russians soon followed this by orbiting and retrieving Sputnik V, a four-and-a-half-ton satellite, carrying two dogs, who therefore became the first living creatures to have explored space and returned to earth. In the spring of the following year, on 12 April, a Russian rocket took off carrying the first man to travel in space, Yuri Gagarin. After making one orbit around the earth he landed 108 minutes later. The age of man in space had begun, four years after Sputnik I.

Possibly spurred by a wish to offset the unfortunate failure of the Bay of Pigs, President Kennedy proposed in May 1961 that the United States should try to land a man on the moon and return him safely to earth before the end of the decade. His reasons for recommending this were interestingly different from the aims which had led the rulers of fifteenth-century Portugal and Spain to back the Magellans and Da Gamas. One was that such a project provided a good national goal, the next that it would be prestigious – 'impressive to mankind' were the president's words – the third was that it was of great importance for the exploration of space, and the fourth was (somewhat oddly) that it was of unparalleled difficulty and expense. Nothing was said of the advancement of science, or commercial or military advantage. Surprisingly, the project met virtually no opposition and soon the first money was allocated towards the most expensive technological exercise in history.

During the early 1960s the Russians continued to make spectacular progress in manned flight in space, but were clearly overtaken by the American programme at some time in 1966–7. The Russians had by then done some remarkable things. The world was perhaps more struck by the sending of a woman into space in 1963, but their technical competence continued to be best shown by the size of their vehicles – a three-man machine was launched in 1964 – and in the achievement the following year of the first 'space walk', when one of the crew emerged from his vehicle and moved about outside while in orbit (though reassuringly attached to it by a lifeline). The Russians were to go on to important advances in arranging rendezvous for vehicles in space and in engineering their docking, but after 1967 the glamour passed to the Americans. It was in that year, too, that the first death through space travel occurred when a Russian was killed during re-entry. In 1968, the American programme achieved a sensational success by sending a three-man vehicle around the moon in orbit and transmitting television pictures of its surface. It was by now clear that 'Apollo', as the moon-landing project was named, was going to succeed.

In May 1969 Apollo X, a vehicle put into orbit with the tenth rocket of the project, approached to within six miles of the moon's surface to assess the techniques of the final stage of landing. A few weeks later a three-man crew were sent into space on 16 July. Their lunar module landed on 20 July on the moon's surface. On the following morning, the first human being to set foot on the moon was Neil Armstrong, the commander of the mission. President Kennedy's goal had been achieved with time in hand. Other landings were to follow.

The cost had been so great that this wonderful achievement has been decried by some. Though there is plenty of fall-out in scientific and technological knowledge applicable in other fields, and some kind of economic stimulus in such expenditure, it was felt that such a huge mobilization of resources as the programme needed was not justifiable because it was irrelevant to the real problems of the earth. To some, the technology of space travel has seemed to be our civilization's equivalent of the Pyramids, a huge investment in the wrong things in a world crying for the allocation of resources to education, malnutrition and mental health – to name only a few pressing needs. It is difficult not to feel some sympathy for such a view at first sight, but more difficult to maintain it.

In the first place, much of the scientific and economic effect is hardly quantifiable and may be very far-reaching; the use of knowledge of miniaturization needed to make control systems, for example, rapidly spills over into other fields. It cannot be said that this knowledge would necessarily have been available had not the investment in space come first. Nor, indeed, can we be confident that the resources made available for space would have been made available for any other great scientific or social goals, had they not been used in this way. Our social machinery does not operate like that. But there are also some striking positive characteristics about the space programmes of the powers engaged in space exploration, among whom, by 1970, were numbered also the British and French.

In estimating these the mythical importance of what was happening must not be neglected. Developed societies today – even communist ones – have shown signs of being unable to generate much interest and enthusiasm among their members for collective purposes except in war. The imagination is not much spoken to by the prospect of adding marginally to the GNP or introducing one more refinement to a system of social services, however intrinsically desirable these things may be. Life in Sweden does not seem very appealing. Kennedy's identification of a national goal was shrewd; in the troubled 1960s, the United States had much else to trouble and divide it, but no one turned up to disrupt the launching of satellites. There is something inspiring in the achievement of a difficult objective even at the sacrifice of present goods of other kinds.

This dimension of the space programme goes beyond the participating countries. Landing on the moon was the most complete and dazzling affirmation to that date of the belief that Man lives in a universe he can manage. The instruments for doing so were once magic and prayer; they are now science and technology. But there is a continuity in the growing confidence of Man through history that he can manage the natural world.

About the more practical implications of

Saturn V, whose design was chosen for the landing on the moon.

space travel for the enlargement of our environment it is still very difficult to say much. It cannot be said that landing on the moon is more or less important than, say, the mastery of fire, the invention of agriculture or the discovery of nuclear power in adding to man's power to enlarge and dominate it. But it is emphatically an event of that order. It is tempting to compare

Old myths still have great power and civilized man has not had so very long in which to invent new ones. The legend of the Flood and the story of the Ark go back to Sumer; they are still evocative and can easily be restated in the mythologies of an age obsessed by the power of science.

FANTASTIC

OCTOBER STORIES OF IMAGINATION

35¢

DELUGE II
By Robert F. Young

THE MOTHER
By David H. Keller, M.D.

LAST DRUID
By Joseph E. Kelleam

it with the last great age of discovery. The time-scales are interestingly different. Something like about eighty years of exploration were required to take the Portuguese round Africa to India; there were eight between the launching of the first man into space and the arrival of men on the moon. The target set in 1961 was achieved with about six months to spare. Exploration in space is safer, too. It long had no fatalities; in terms of deaths per passenger-mile travelled it is still the safest form of transport known to man, while fifteenth-century seafaring was a perilous business at best. If you did not die of shipwreck there was a good chance that tropical disease, scurvy or irritated natives might take you off. Actuarially, the risk of travelling in the *Santa Maria* – or even the *Mayflower* – must have been much greater than that faced by the crew of Apollo II.

This is not a frivolous point. It indicates something important about the nature of the moon achievement. This is its predictable and cumulative quality, in which it aptly summarizes the whole trend of our scientific society. Apollo was launched from a very wide base, nothing less than the whole aggregate of the scientific knowledge of mankind. The distance to the moon was already known; so were the conditions which would greet men arriving there, most of the hazards they might encounter, the quantities of power, supplies and the nature of the other support systems they would need to return, the stresses their bodies would undergo. In part this diminished the tremendous impact of the event. Though things might have gone wrong, there was a widespread feeling that they would not. Since 1969, even more impressive technical operations have been carried out nearer to earth; men have lived in space for weeks on end, and after the Russians had carried out an astonishingly complex programme of establishing space stations where work can be undertaken, a remarkable experiment was successfully carried out some hundred and fifty miles above the earth when, in July 1975, Russian and American machines connected themselves so that their crews could move from one to the other. Meanwhile, the visual exploration of further space was carried beyond Jupiter by unmanned satellite and a little more than a year after the rendezvous of July 1975 came the first landing of an unmanned exploration vehicle on the surface of the planet Mars. These achievements are tremendous, yet they have become almost normal, so jaded are our imaginations. This is not entirely because of the new familiarity with the idea of space travel which has grown up; it is also because of the confidence that science can in the end always produce the predicted result.

Another interesting feature of the space exploration effort has been its collective nature. It is true that before the 1970s there was little cooperation between the two greatest nations concerned, the United States and Russia, and that this undoubtedly led to wasteful duplication of effort and inefficiencies. Yet the space programmes have been the apotheosis of the collective nature of modern science. Thousands of people in hundreds of laboratories, test-stations and factories made the landing of Man on the moon possible. The relative anonymity of the space explorers themselves reflects this. Though their courage and professional skill cannot be doubted, men like Gagarin, Armstrong and their colleagues are remembered because they were the first to do certain things, not for enterprise in carrying through their own programmes of investigation and discovery. For them to have done that would, of course, have been impossible. They were the spearhead of a huge process, only in small degree something more than human projectiles whose trajectory was controlled from the ground. There is no name which emerges from a decade of colossal additions to human knowledge and experience of space which will be remembered with the same sense that it sums up an era as those of Columbus, Magellan or Da Gama.

It was interesting, too, that in the first instance space exploration seemed no more than the great discoveries of the fifteenth and sixteenth centuries to require changes of outlook or ideology. Perhaps some will appear in due course, but besides the symbols of American nationality left on the moon, of which the flag was the most obvious, an American astronaut read aloud from the Bible during the orbiting of his mission about the moon. Ten years earlier, the Russians had dropped a Lenin pennant on it, thus providing its surface with the symbols of an alternative mythology. This might seem ominous; nationalism might provoke a scramble for space. There was a basic fact of national rivalry in the 'space race' itself. Fortunately, the worst dangers of competition were avoided and it was soon agreed that celestial objects were not subject to appropriation by any one state.

Space exploration is the latest and greatest step in an increasing mastery of nature, most of which has been achieved in the last seven or eight millennia. It has to be set against the hundreds of thousands of years during which prehistoric technology inched forwards from the discovery that a cutting edge could be put on a stone chopper and that fire could be mastered. In that era, the weight of genetic programming and environmental pressure still loomed much larger than conscious control and this must have been true until well into civilized times. The dawning of consciousness that more than this was possible was the major step in man's evolution after his physical structure had settled into more or less what it is today. The control and use of experience became possible with it, and then experiment and analysis. There is no need to conclude that they will not still provide mankind with the tool-kit he needs to survive in a world which he has made so different from that of even his recent ancestors.

But neither, of course, must we conclude that such a tool-kit will be found, or, if found, properly and usefully employed. Two particular dangers seem immediately threatening and could be fatal to the world we know. One, though manifested in many ways, boils down to the simple possibility that the acceleration of change of all sorts will outpace the capacity of the human race to produce answers to its problems. It may even appear in due course that the generation of new difficulties of all sorts is already faster than our ability to transcend them. The other danger arises from the disturbance of the international balance since the early 1960s. One superpower appears to have begun to accept that it cannot be sure in a future confrontation that it will be able to impose its will on the other by the threat of war and new temptations must be presented to the rulers of the Soviet Union by this. This has happened, too, in a world further destabilized by the proliferation of new states in the last twenty years, by the increasing unreality of the United Nations Organization as a reflexion of the interests of great powers, and by the spread of nuclear capability. At the same time a huge shift in economic and financial power has taken place away from the developed world to a group of countries of the underdeveloped world, the oil states. This has placed continued economic growth in jeopardy and that poses further dangers to international order.

It may seem disappointing to some readers of a history of the world, but there are no grounds for unequivocal assertions one way or the other about what the outcome of such uncertainties may be. If they feel such disappointment, it arises because they expect too much. At the end of the day, the only advantage of being a historian in considering this sort of problem, is that one may be a little less surprised by the outcome, whatever it is. Only two general truths emerge from the study of history. One is that things tend to change much more, and more quickly, than one might think. The other is that they tend to change much less, and much more slowly, than one might think. Both truths tend to be exemplified by any specific historical situation and so, for good and ill, we shall always find what happens somewhat surprising.

Index

Page references to illustration captions are in italics

Acknowledgements

For permission to reproduce illustrations we are grateful to the following (numbers refer to pages where illustrations occur):

Albert Einstein Trustees, 1019
Alinari, 252, 262, 293, 351
André Held, 97, 98, 101, 246, 269
Anglo-Chinese Educational Institute, 172 (top left), 492, 499, 1038, 1039, 1040
Antikensammlung, Munich, 199
Antonello Perisinotto, 317
Archaeological Survey of India, 138, 144, 149
Archiv, 338 (bottom)
Archives Photographiques, George Rainbird, 738 (left), 821 (top and bottom)
Arthur Lockwood, 578 (Brompton Studio), 592, 614, 669, 672, 696 (bottom)
Ashmolean Museum, 56, 657
Associated Press, 965
ATA, 448
'Au Rendez-vous des Amis' by Max Ernst, © S.P.A.D.E.M. 1976, photo Wallraf-Richartz Museum, Cologne, 962
Avery Brundage Collection, 161, 163
Axel Poignant, 38
Barnabys Picture Library, 86, 95, 105, 288, 510, 942
Bayerisches Nationalmuseum, Munich, 551
Bernisches Historisches Museum, 286
Bettmann Archive, 802, 819, 850, 864 (bottom)
Bibliothèque Municipale, Dijon, photo R. Rémy, 527 (right)
Bibliothèque Nationale, 210, 391, 439, 441 (right), 487, 522, 533, 542, 570 (left), 971
Bildarchiv Foto Marburg, 458, 541
Bildarchiv Preussischer Kulturbesitz, 919 (top)
Bodleian Library, Oxford, 376, 657
Bollingen Foundation and Princeton University Press, 297
Bord Fáilte, 336
British Library, 432, 451 (top), 454, 543, 547, 549, 562, 573, 574

British Museum, 22, 37 (left), 61, 75, 80, 94, 106, 125, 128, 134, 136, 159, 167, 172 (bottom left), 181, 206, 223, 232, 235 (top right), 259 (right), 277 (right), 338 (top), 430, 489, 495, 506, 514, 516, 517, 518, 520, 585, 656, 703 (Mansell collection), 833
British Museum (Natural History), 20, 26, 27
British Petroleum, 957
Buchholz, 759
Bundesarchiv, 969
Caisse Nationale des Monuments Historiques, 37 (right), 39 (right), 41
Calico Museum, Ahmedabad, photo Christina Gascoigne, 479
Camera Press, 8, 462, 1015, 1021, 1023, 1049 (bottom), 1059, 1077 (bottom), 1088, 1094, 1097
Capitoline Museum, 266
Central Library, Leeds, 736 (left)
Central Office of Information, 1080
Ceylon Tea Centre, 663
Chicago Historical Society, 849
Collection Doris Wiener Gallery, New York, 480
Colonial Williamsburg Foundation, Williamsburg, Virginia, 748
F. H. Crossley and Cannon M. H. Ridgway, 560
Culver Pictures, 801
David Low by arrangement with the Trustees and the London Evening Standard, 944, 1077 (top)
Department of Archaeology, Government of Pakistan, 141
Department of the Environment, 283 (top)
C. M. Dixon, 115, 174
Dr Barnado's Photo Library, 742, 743
Dudley Library, 723 (bottom)
Du-magazine, 963
Dumbarton Oaks Collections, 180
Earl Hines, George Eastman Collection, 741

Editions Arthaud photo G. Franceschi, 176
Editions d'Art Albert Skira, 415
Egyptian Museum, Cairo, 92, 93, 100
Ekdotike Athenon S.A., 245
Elsevier Archives, Amsterdam, 565 (right)
FAO, 1010, 1012, 1013 (left), 1058, 1089 (top)
A. G. Formetti, 179 (bottom), 519
Franklin D. Roosevelt Library, 1006
Gabinetto Fotografico Nazionale, Rome, 204
Giraudon, 325, 339, 359, 387, 746, 757
Glyptothek, Munich, 241
Goro Sakamoto, 70
Government of India Tourist Office, 469
Hans Steiner, 437
Dr Harald Busch, 459
Hirmer Fotoarchiv, 104, 313, 323, 386, 393, 397, 443
Holle Bildarchiv, 340, 470, 471
IBM United Kingdom Ltd, 1017
Ikon, 603, 654, 656, 658 (right), 660, 661, 668, 670, 674, 693 (top and bottom), 710, 725, 734 (top), 777 (bottom), 816, 823, 864 (top), 865, 866
Illustrated Newspapers Ltd, 737, 948
Imperial War Museum, 914 (bottom), 915 (top), 978
Indian Office Library, 846 (top), 848, 872, 873, 874, 875, 876
Institute of History and Philology, Academia Sinica, Taipei, 165
Instytut Sztuki, PAN, 408
Inter Nationes, 1061 (top)
Iran Bastan Museum, 58, 251, 259, 358
Iraq Museum Library, Baghdad, 72, 78
Israel Defence Department, 1003
Israel Government Tourist Office, 377
Israel Museum, 300
Italian State Tourist Office, 342, 343
J. Allan Cash, 143, 278
James Mellaart, 50, 51

ACKNOWLEDGEMENTS

Japan Information Centre, London, 507 (left), 1044 (top)
Jean Roubier, 438, 529, 531 (right)
Jericho Excavation Fund, 44, 48
John Donat, 396
John Freeman, 277 (left), 354, 566, 672, 722, 760, 772, 798, 805 (right), 854, 926, 960
John Hillelson Agency Ltd, 777 (Ikon) (top), 830, 832, 836, 858, 922 (photo Erich Salomon), 995 (photo Henri Cartier-Bresson), 1031 (photo Henri Cartier-Bresson), 1044 (photo Raymond Depardon/ Gamma), 1049 (top) (photo Cornel Capa), 1063 (photo Henri Cartier-Bresson), 1069 (photo Charles Harbutt), 1074, 1087 (photo Thomas Hopker)
Kelsey Museum, University of Michigan, 309
A. F. Kersting, 382, 450, 531 (left), 559 (right)
Mrs Kitako Ohta, photo Sakai Shashin, 934 (bottom)
Kodansha Ltd, Tokyo, 934 (top)
Kremsünster Convent, 441 (left)
Kunsthistorisches Museum, Vienna, 281, 341, 349
Kupferstichkabinett, Berlin (West), photo Jörg P. Anders, 556
Lahore Museum, 151
Library Company of Philadelphia, 678
Library of Congress, 731, 801, 966
Louvre, 73, 74, 79, 82, 89, 90, 192 (bottom), 209, 275, 553 (left), 570 (right)
Mansell Collection, 235 (left and bottom right), 243, 265 (top), 283 (bottom), 298, 306, 572, 578, 580, 586 (right and left), 587, 590, 594, 596, 598, 604, 607, 609, 610, 617, 618, 620, 624, 628, 630, 632, 633, 643, 648, 651, 652, 671, 673, 685, 686, 695, 696 (top), 700, 701, 703, 705, 707 (right and left), 713, 715, 716, 720, 744, 751, 756, 760 (bottom) 762, 773, 774, 775, 782, 805 (left), 852, 861, 862 (left), 900
Mary Evans Picture Library, 723 (top) (Dudley Library), 736, 806
Mas, 331, 370, 379, 390, 455
Master and Fellows of Corpus Christi College, Cambridge, 535
Metropolitan Museum of Art, New York, 131, 366, 375, 421, 530, 538, 553 (right), 750
Michael Holford, 68, 107, 682

Miguel Mujica Gallo Collection, 521
Ministry of Information and Tourism, Tehran, 959
Mittet Foto, 447
Musée des Antiquities Nationales, Saint-Germain-en-Laye, 39 (left)
Musée d'Aquitaine, Bordeaux, 32
Musée des Arts Décoratifs, 893
Musée Gréco-Romain, Alexandria, 255
Museo Civico, Bologna, 265 (bottom)
Museo Civico Medievale di Bologna, photo Fotofast, 534, 569
Museo Civico Luigi Bailo, Salce Collection, 890
Museum of Archaeology and Ethnology, Cambridge, 30
Museum of English Rural Life, University of Reading, 735 (top), 804
Museum of Far Eastern Antiquities, Stockholm, 157
Museum of Fine Arts, Boston, 140, 213, 228
NASA, 1082, 1100
National Army Museum, 815
Trustees, National Gallery, London, 425
National Maritime Museum, 626, 679, 694, 857
National Monuments Record of the Royal Commission on Historical Monuments, 451 (bottom), 690
National Museum of India, New Delhi, 153
National Palace Museum, Taipei, Taiwan, 410, 496, 500, 501
National Portrait Gallery, 613, 615, 635, 704, 711
National Tourist Organisation of Greece, 196, 233, 244
Naturhistorisches Museum, Vienna, 182
New York Historical Society, 735 (bottom left)
New York Public Library, Map Room, 565 (left)
Niedersächsische Staats- und Universitätsbibliothek, Göttingen, 457
Northern Archives, 820
Novosti, 250, 404, 638, 639, 644, 739, 889, 917, 960, 979
Office of the Press Counsellor, Turkish Embassy, London, 958
Oriental Institute, Leningrad/Islamic Museum, Berlin, 413
Oriental Institute, University of Chicago, 64, 102, 110
Osterreichischer National Bibliograthek 658 (right)

Palazzo Vecchio, Florence, 310
Paolino Museum, 280
Paris Match, 1055 (top)
Paul Elek Ltd, photo Wim Swaan, 527 (left)
Pennsylvania University Museum, Philadelphia, 185
Peter Clayton, 334
Phaidon Press Ltd, photo Percy Hennell, 540
Picturepoint, 794, 882, 886, 914 (top)
Pontificia Commissione di Archeologia Sacra, 304
Popperfoto, 834, 861 (top), 894, 908, 913, 915 (bottom), 920, 945, 956, 976, 977, 982, 994 (bottom), 997, 1033, 1041, 1047, 1062
Press Association, 891, 955
Princetown University Library, 795
Public Records Office, 808
Punch, photo Godfrey New, 788, 789
Radio Times Hulton Picture Library, 645, 729, 732, 733, 781, 831 (bottom), 840, 841, 862 (right), 868, 876, 888 (right and left), 912, 935 (top), 941, 980, 991, 1061 (bottom)
Regents of the University of California and the University of California Press, photo R. I. M. Campbell, 16
Reverenda Fabbrica della Basilica di San Pietro, 308
Rheinisches Landesmuseum, Bonn, 537
Robert Harding Associates, 422
Robert Harding Associates/Times Newspapers Ltd, 482, 494
Robert Hunt Library, 1029
Roger-Viollet, 76, 254, 925, 943
Roger Wood, 108, 186, 190, 192 (top), 289, 315, 357
Roloff Beny, 202, 220
Ronald Sheridan, 117, 119, 120, 256, 299
Royal Ontario Museum, 497
Sakamoto Photo Research Laboratory, 503, 504
Scala, 320, 332, 526, 532
Science Museum, 563, 589, 687, 698, 708, 730 (top and bottom right) (New York Historical Society)
Service de Documentation Photographique, 768
Smithsonian Institute, Freer Gallery of Art, Washington DC, 171, 352, 429
Snark International, 896
Staatliche Antikensammlung, Munich, 268
Staatliche Museen, Berlin, 226, 227, 242, 374

Staatsbibliothek Preussischer
Kulturbesitz, 419
Staatsgalerie Stuttgart, 919 (bottom)
State Museum of Oriental Art, Moscow,
photo Christina Gascoigne, 476
Stern, 1093
Tadeusz Biniewski, 318
Tate Gallery, 706
Thomas Head, 568
Time Life Picture Agency © Time
Inc. 1976, 988 (photo Bob Landre),
1026 (photo Walter Sanders),
1055 (bottom) (photo Grey Villet),
1066 (photo George Silk), 1089
(bottom) (photo Larry Burrows)
Tom Hanley, 152

Topix, 1076
Topkapi Saray Museum, 420, 427, 431
Transworld Feature Syndicate, 766
Ullstein Bilderdienst, 555, 932
Ulster Museum, 831
United Nations, 984
United Press International, 935 (bottom)
USPG, 810, 812, 819, 846 (bottom)
Vatican Library and Weidenfeld and
Nicolson Archives, 392, 395
Vautier Decool, 179 (top), 1013 (right),
1043, 1052, 1071
Victor Kennett, 407
Victoria and Albert Museum, 333, 378,
467, 507 (right), 559 (left), 859, 870
Wadsworth Atheneum, 219

Wellcome Historical Medical Museum,
738 (right)
Werner Forman Archive, 225, 321,
361, 512, 658 (left), 662, 667, 813,
818, 837
William Rockhill Nelson Gallery of
Art, Kansas City, 162, 172 (right),
486
Württembergische Landesbibliothek,
Stuttgart, 440
Yigael Yadin and Weidenfeld and
Nicolson Archives, 294
Ziff-Davis Publishing Co. Inc./
Ultimate Publishing Co. Inc.,
1101
Zodiaque, 183